THE RIGHT TO FAIR HOUSING

ASPEN COURSEBOOK SERIES

THE RIGHT TO FAIR HOUSING

Cases, Statutes, and Context

FLORENCE WAGMAN ROISMAN
William F. Harvey Professor of Law and Chancellor's Professor
Indiana University Robert H. McKinney School of Law

STACY E. SEICSHNAYDRE
William K. Christovich Professor of Law
Robert A. Ainsworth Professor of the Courts and Federal System
Tulane University Law School

RIGEL C. OLIVERI
Isabelle Wade and Paul C. Lyda Professor of Law
University of Missouri School of Law

Cover image: musicalryo/Shutterstock.com

To contact Customer Service, e-mail customer.service@aspenpublishing.com, call 1-800-950-5259, or mail correspondence to:

Aspen Publishing
Attn: Order Department
1 Wall Street
Burlington, MA 01803

Printed in the United States of America.

1 2 3 4 5 6 7 8 9 0

ISBN 979-8-8890-6123-6

Library of Congress Cataloging-in-Publication Data

Names: Roisman, Florence Wagman, author. | Seicshnaydre, Stacy E., author. | Oliveri, Rigel C., author.
Title: The right to fair housing: cases, statutes, and context / Florence Wagman Roisman, William F. Harvey Professor of Law and Chancellor's Professor, Indiana University Robert H. McKinney School of Law; Stacy E. Seicshnaydre, William K. Christovich Professor of Law, Robert A. Ainsworth Professor of the Courts and Federal System, Tulane University Law School; Rigel C. Oliveri, Isabelle Wade and Paul C. Lyda Professor of Law, University of Missouri School of Law.
Description: First edition. | Burlington: Aspen Publishing, 2025. | Series: Aspen coursebook series | Includes bibliographical references and index. | Summary: "Casebook addressing the right to fair housing across all transactions, all protected groups, and all dwelling types"— Provided by publisher.
Identifiers: LCCN 2024048379 | ISBN 9798889061236 (paperback) | ISBN 9798889061243 (ebook)
Subjects: LCSH: Right to housing—United States. | Discrimination in housing—Law and legislation—United States. | Housing policy—United States. | LCGFT: Textbooks.
Classification: LCC KF5740.R67 2025 | DDC 344.73/063635—dc23/eng/20241017
LC record available at https://lccn.loc.gov/2024048379

About Aspen Publishing

Aspen Publishing is a leading provider of legal educational content and digital learning solutions in the U.S. and around the world. Aspen provides best-in-class solutions through authoritative textbooks, written by renowned authors, and breakthrough products such as Connected eBooks, Connected Quizzing, PracticePerfect, and JD-Next.

The Aspen Casebook Series (famously known among law faculty and students as the "red and black" casebooks) encompasses hundreds of highly regarded textbooks in more than eighty disciplines, from large enrollment courses, such as Torts and Contracts, to emerging electives, like Sustainability and the Law of Policing. Study aids such as *Examples & Explanations* help law students master complex subject matter. Aspen's Paralegal, Criminal Justice, and Business Law series bring our hallmark publishing standards to undergraduate students. JD-Next is an innovative online law school prep course and admissions test that offers a realistic preview of law school, teaches underlying skills for academic success, and assesses applicants' academic readiness for law school.

Aspen Publishing is proud to be a UWorld company

Since 2003, UWorld has been a global leader in developing high-quality learning tools for students preparing for high-stakes exams. With a commitment to excellence, UWorld has helped millions of students in undergraduate, graduate, and professional programs in fields such as medicine, nursing, finance, and law achieve their academic and career goals.

Founded by Chandra S. Pemmasani, M.D., during his medical residency, UWorld began focusing on medical education and has since expanded into various academic fields, including law. In 2020, UWorld launched its Legal vertical, starting with its comprehensive Multistate Bar Exam (MBE®) Question Bank, followed by the acquisition of Themis Bar Review, which integrated resources to provide a complete bar exam preparation experience. In 2024, UWorld expanded its offerings by acquiring Aspen Publishing, enhancing its suite of legal education products.

Today, UWorld offers an unparalleled range of study materials that blend active learning methods with expert content, ensuring students and educators can access the most effective resources. From bar preparation to law school success, UWorld is committed to supporting the next generation of legal professionals. Learn more at uworld.com.

It is customary for the authors of casebooks to offer dedications separately to specific individuals who are important in their lives. We deviate from that practice. The three of us believe that a book such as this, which focuses on the long, painful, and often violent struggle for fair housing, belongs to those who have helped move our society closer to that goal.

Thus, we dedicate this book to the activists, plaintiffs, advocates, scholars, judges, lawmakers, and administrators who have worked (sometimes at great personal risk) to achieve justice and equality in housing. We stand on the shoulders of many brave, principled, far-seeing, and creative people; we offer this book as an homage to them all.

SUMMARY OF CONTENTS

CONTENTS

PREFACE

Housing is a fundamental resource and a human right. Many of today's persistent social inequities and domestic policy challenges can be traced back to the fact that different groups in our society have been denied equal access to housing. This denial has been perpetrated by governments at every level, by housing professionals, and by countless private individuals. This denial takes many forms, from mundane zoning decisions to biased property appraisals to outright violence. And this denial is deeply embedded in the very infrastructure of our nation: our neighborhoods, which in turn affect virtually every aspect of life.

As longstanding, pervasive, and destructive as housing discrimination has been in the United States, there has been an equally persistent and stubborn resistance to it. Activists, advocates, policymakers, researchers, and everyday people have fought to expose and correct these injustices. The path has been difficult, and the gains often incremental, but the commitment to the cause remains. Thus, we chose to title this book *The Right to Fair Housing*, to emphasize the goal of the struggle — the aspirational direction toward which, in the words of Dr. King and Rev. Theodore Parker, the arc of the moral universe is bending.

We, the authors, have devoted much of our professional lives to practicing, studying, and teaching fair housing law. We know the stakes in this area could not be higher. And yet we have also observed a dearth of teaching materials on the subject for students at the law school level. This book arose from our collective belief that such a text is badly needed to educate new generations of students who will become the activists, advocates, and leaders of their time.

The right to fair housing touches all of us. We all are renters or homeowners, residents of neighborhoods, and members of communities. We understand that home is life and that place matters. And so, we believe, this book matters. We hope you will agree.

ACKNOWLEDGMENTS

From all three of us:

- The Aspen staff, who have been responsive, supportive, and unrelenting.
- Bob Schwemm. It is impossible to overstate the role he has played in the field of fair housing law. His seminal treatise, referred to by most just as "Schwemm" or "the Red Book," sits on the desks of all of us. This book, and his many articles, have informed generations of practitioners and scholars about virtually every aspect of fair housing law. Indeed, he is cited extensively throughout this text. He is also a generous and gracious colleague, quick to offer feedback, provide opportunities for junior scholars, and give advice and mentorship.
- Colleagues who read and commented on portions of this book and supplied information, advice, and material for the book: Heather Abraham, Michael Allen, Gideon Anders, Laura Beshara, Hilary Botein, Jade Craig, Stephen Dane, Michael M. Daniel, Andrew Darcy, Nadiyah Humber, Betsy Julian, Allison Martin, Michael Pitts, Alex Polikoff, Stuart Rossman, Phil Tegeler, staff at the National Housing Law Project, and anonymous reviewers.
- One another, who have made working on this book a true intellectual and personal pleasure.

From Florence:

I am deeply grateful to:

- The people who first taught me about the significance of race: Tony Henry of the American Friends Service Committee, and Elizabeth (Betsy) K. Julian and Michael M. Daniel.
- Many legendary "housers" and advocates and scholars of race who no longer are with us: David B. Bryson, Gordon Cavanaugh, Cushing Nils Dolbeare, George Grier, Chester Hartman, Arnold Hirsch, David Madway, Marilyn Melkonian, J.L. Jay Pottenger, Bill Powers, Yale Rabin, Shirley Adelson Siegel, Marty Sloane, Arnold Sternberg, and Bill and Harriet Taylor.
- The Robert H. McKinney School of Law for providing a nurturing and stimulating professional home for almost three decades and for a series of summer research grants and sabbaticals and a research leave.

- The John S. Grimes Faculty Grants and Fellowships Endowment for Faculty Fellowships in 2017 and 2019, for work on this casebook, and for a Faculty Grant in 2016.
- The Ruth M. Lilly Library staff, notably Ryan Scott Overdorf and Ben Keele.
- Many student research assistants, including Michael Seidel, Simarjit Kaur, Jerrick T. Adams, George Sorrells, TaNay Porshonda Morris, and Graciela Macias, Esq.
- Extraordinarily helpful faculty assistants, including Mary Deer, Danny Perdue, and Jenn Watson.
- My family by birth and choice, who inspire me: Abram, Rachel, B.J., Jason, Cassie, Madeline, Martha, Karen, Deborah, Sarah, Grace, Michael, Henry, Margaret Rachel, G.K., and J., my BFF.

From Stacy:

I would like to acknowledge first and foremost my clients, who taught me everything, especially J.K., S.J., and B.J.; Jane Johnson, my forever mentor, sage, friend, colleague, and role model who inspired generations of lawyers to be the best versions of themselves; Bill Quigley who, with Jane, introduced me to my first fair housing case as a student attorney and opened the door to a lifelong vocation; the Lawyers' Committee civil rights lions who took a chance on a bayou neophyte; the civil rights lawyers I met while practicing in D.C. and then serving on ICP's board, who became enduring sources of counsel and support in all the years since; Kathy Fletcher, the People's Institute, and all those who helped launch GNOFHAC and keep it accountable; the NFHA brain trust; Keith Werhan, the Tulane Vice Dean who steered the creation of my first fair housing course; my Tulane colleagues who commented on articles and patiently listened to fair housing stories; Tulane Law School, for its generous research and institutional support; years of research assistants including Sanjay Das, Haley Gentry, Drusilla Hebert, Heather Heintz, Laura Lehrfeld, Malcolm Lloyd, Lily McHale, Riley McKay, Andrew Meaders, Samuel Montanari, Demi Moore, Lauren Perry, Tom Polites, Kate Reissig, and Henry Solotaroff-Webber; my fair housing students who provided feedback on various iterations of the course, some of whom have made incredible impact in this field; my clinic students who kept me going by displaying just the right amount of outrage at just the right moments; all of my family, including my shining lights Annelise and Josef, who never questioned and always cheered on my fair housing pursuits; and, especially, Greg, who is the universe's best partner, ever.

From Rigel:

I am deeply grateful to:

- My former colleagues at the DOJ's Civil Rights Division, Housing and Civil Enforcement Section. Working with them was one of the great privileges of my life. I am particularly indebted to Tim Moran, who patiently taught me how to be a fair housing lawyer and modeled the very best of thoughtful, tenacious, and committed advocacy.

- The University of Missouri School of Law and its leadership for providing support, encouragement, and research leave; The University of Missouri Law School Foundation for a number of generous summer research grants.
- My Fair Housing Law students for their embrace of this subject matter, their insights, and their enthusiasm for making the world a better place.
- Research assistants Harry Bell, Allison Cichocki, Aubrey Manculich, and the entire MU library staff, especially Cindy Shearrer.
- Mr. Mann, Mr. Rhodenhauser, and Mr. Patterson, my Civics, History, and Government teachers at Western Albemarle High School in Crozet, Virginia. They inspired a 15-year-old Rigel to become a civil rights lawyer, which set the trajectory for my life.
- Finally, Griffin and Shennie, for their patience during all the time their mom spent working on "The Book"; and Michael, who always knew I would write this book one day, but did not live to see it. It finally happened, sweetie!

The authors would like to acknowledge the following sources of material which appear in the book:

Associated Press. Aerial view of Levittown showing its $30,000,000 development of over 10,000 new homes on Long Island, 25 miles from New York, on February 25, 1950. Copyright © 1950 AP. All rights reserved.

Associated Press/The Tyler Morning Telegraph. Photograph of Judge William Wayne Justice. Copyright © 2009 AP/The Tyler Morning Telegraph. All rights reserved.

Austin, Jay Sterling. Photograph of New Orleans Shotgun House. Reprinted with permission via Creative Commons license CC BY 4.0.

Hughes, Langston. "Harlem," from The Collected Poems of Langston Hughes, Copyright © 1994. Reprinted with permission of Harold Ober Associates and International Literary Properties LLC.

Kleina, Bernard. Photograph of street protest, Chicago Freedom Movement. bernardkleina.com.

Wilson, Bradley. Photograph of Walter Mondale. Reprinted with permission via Created Commons license, 2.0.

NOTE TO THE READER

Language: As civil rights scholars, we are aware that there is not universal agreement on the appropriate words to describe the diverse populations in the United States or even on whether or not particular descriptors should be capitalized. We intend in all cases to be respectful and inclusive, rather than exclusive, and in no case to diminish the significance of the viewpoint of any person or to injure a person or group through our terminology.

For purposes of this book, we have used the following language: Black, Latino or Hispanic, Asian American, and white. We choose to capitalize Black, but not white. We refer to "neighborhoods of color" or specify the predominant race(s) of a neighborhood, rather than use the term "minority." We also employ the term "disability," rather than "handicap" (the term in the Fair Housing Act). We do retain older, less preferred terminology when it appears in cases or other sources; we also retain the way some racial terms are capitalized in those materials.

Some cases involve racial, ethnic, sexual, and other slurs. We are aware that these terms are extraordinarily offensive and may be difficult to encounter. We have chosen to retain most of these because their offensive and discriminatory nature are central to the cases, and we believe it is important for students to confront the reality of such language within the cases. Some cases contain profanity, which we also retain. There is one slur, however, which we will refer to only as n—.

To save space (and make room for more content), we have edited—in text and in cases—by using FHA for Fair Housing Act, FHAA for Fair Housing Amendments Act, CRA for various civil rights acts, state abbreviations, HUD for the Department of Housing and Urban Development, and DOJ for Department of Justice. (There are places where we discuss the Federal Housing Administration, but we try to make clear by context that this FHA is not the Fair Housing Act.) We usually refer to the Fair Housing Act as the FHA; where particular aspects of the 1988 Amendments are under discussion, some courts refer to the Act as the Fair Housing Amendments Act, or FHAA.

Case Editing: We have edited the cases in this book in a manner that seeks to preserve important language, doctrine, and factual information, while eliminating material that is redundant or less relevant to the discussion at hand. For the sake of readability, at times we eliminate paragraphs and sentences without using ellipses. We also eliminate string citations when they distract from, rather than enhance, the propositions they follow.

Within the cases, we have abbreviated commonly used terms such as the National Association for the Advancement of Colored People (NAACP). We have made other minor editorial adjustments in some cases, such as eliminating errant apostrophes and hyphens for terms so that they appear consistent throughout the book. At times, we have fixed minor typographical errors that appear in the cases.

Citations: The original Fair Housing Act's sections were numbered 801-819 and 901. When the Act was codified as part of 42 U.S.C., these section numbers became 3601-3619 and 3631. We cite the Act using the "3601-" numbering system. For consistency and to minimize reader confusion, we have converted case references using the "801-" numbering into the "3601-" numbering.

Throughout this book we cite a magisterial treatise, *Housing Discrimination: Law and Litigation*, by Professor Robert G. Schwemm. We reference it so frequently that we have chosen to use a shortened form: Schwemm, HDLL. For other sources we generally adhere to Bluebook citation conventions, with some modifications.

Imperfection: This book covers a wealth of material. We have tried to eliminate errors, but we know that nothing human is perfect. We welcome feedback and encourage you to contact us with any corrections or suggestions. We will attempt to address them in the Teacher's Manual and in any future updates or editions. We can be reached at froisman@iu.edu, sseicshn@tulane.edu, and oliverir@missouri.edu.

PART I

HISTORICAL FOUNDATION: HOUSING DISCRIMINATION AND SEGREGATION FROM 1865 TO 1968 AND THE CIVIL RIGHTS ACT OF 1866

W hat is past is indeed prologue. To understand the challenges of fair housing in the 21st century, one must comprehend how pervasive racial discrimination and segregation came to characterize living patterns in the United States. In this part, we address the period from the end of the Civil War through Reconstruction, "Redemption," the New Deal, World War II, and the Civil Rights Movement, leading to the enactment of the Fair Housing Act in 1968. Chapter 1 reviews this history and points to other texts that address the history in greater depth. Chapter 2 discusses the fair housing law of the Reconstruction era, a portion of the 1866 Civil Rights Act codified as 42 U.S.C. §1982, to which the Supreme Court gave new life in its 1968 decision, *Jones v. Mayer.*

The inscription on the base of the statue representing "Future" at the National Archives building reminds us that "What Is Past Is Prologue."

(National Archives, photo by Rania Hassan)

CHAPTER 1

DISCRIMINATION AND SEGREGATION IN HOUSING IN THE UNITED STATES: 1865 TO 1968

Beginning in 1968, against a backdrop of powerful social movements for change, historically marginalized groups of people gained rights under federal law to access housing in neighborhoods of their choice with the Supreme Court's reinterpretation of the 1866 Civil Rights Act in *Jones v. Mayer* (see Chapter 2) and Congress's enactment of the Civil Rights Act of 1968, known as the federal Fair Housing Act or Title VIII (see Chapter 3 and following). Most of this casebook addresses post-1968 actions and analyses. The pre-1968 history is essential, however, to understand how and why the systemic injustices of housing discrimination and segregation arose and some of the tools used to address them. This chapter addresses that history. We first provide a narrative introduction and then, in individual sections, present some cases and text that illuminate the history. We focus on race, but much of this material is relevant also to color, national origin, and religion, which were the only other protected characteristics in the original version of the Fair Housing Act. The protected categories added later—sex, disability, and familial status—are discussed in later chapters.

The colonial and pre–Civil War eras in the United States were marked by massive and violent assertions of power by people largely of Western European ancestry over the living places and conditions of other groups of people. These eras saw the conquest and dispossession of indigenous people, enslavement of Black people, and restrictions on the property interests of women, immigrants, and other people of color. With the Civil War (1860-1865) and Reconstruction (1865-1877), especially the Reconstruction Amendments and the Civil Rights Acts of 1866 and 1870, came some efforts to extend property rights at least to some people. These ended with the period of Redemption and Jim Crow—1877 until at least the 1950s—that saw restrictions on the rights of Black people, other people of color, and immigrants that evoked comparisons to the centuries of slavery.[1] As W.E.B. Du Bois wrote: "The slave went free; stood a brief moment in the sun; then moved back again toward slavery."[2]

Despite these assertions of domination, until the late 19th century, there was considerably less residential racial segregation between Black and white people and between white people and other people of color than there is today.[3] Indeed, "Blacks and whites were much more likely to be housed in the same neighborhood in the nineteenth century than they are in the twenty-first century."[4] There also was less economic segregation—tradespeople and craftspeople and their employees often lived and worked in close proximity to one another.[5]

Beginning in the late 19th century, private and public actors undertook an "intentional and inter-related" set of actions that severely limited the housing options of Black people and other people of color.[6] This started with explicit racial zoning, racial covenants, and then use zoning (now often called Euclidean zoning). During the New Deal (1933-1945), redlining by the Home Owners Loan Corporation (HOLC) and the de jure segregated public housing and Federal Housing Administration (FHA) home ownership programs followed. World War II's end brought the GI Bill's Veterans Administration (VA) homeownership program, urban renewal, and federal-aid interstate highways. The single-family homeownership that was promoted by the FHA

---

1. *See, e.g.*, C. Vann Woodward, THE STRANGE CAREER OF JIM CROW (Oxford U. Press 1955); Eric Foner, THE SECOND FOUNDING: HOW THE CIVIL WAR AND RECONSTRUCTION REMADE THE CONSTITUTION (Norton 2019); Michael Klarman, FROM JIM CROW TO CIVIL RIGHTS (Oxford U. Press 2006); David M. Oshinsky, "WORSE THAN SLAVERY": PARCHMAN FARM AND THE ORDEAL OF JIM CROW JUSTICE (Free Press 1996); Douglas A. Blackmon, SLAVERY BY ANOTHER NAME: THE RE-ENSLAVEMENT OF BLACK AMERICANS FROM THE CIVIL WAR TO WORLD WAR II (Doubleday 2008); David M.P. Freund, COLORED PROPERTY: STATE POLICY & WHITE RACIAL POLITICS IN SUBURBAN AMERICA 14 (U. Chicago Press 2007) ("Whites' preoccupation with residential exclusion arose in northern cities at the turn of the century and solidified during and after World War I").

2. W.E.B. DuBois, BLACK RECONSTRUCTION IN AMERICA 30 (Atheneum 1992).

3. Douglas S. Massey & Nancy A. Denton, AMERICAN APARTHEID: SEGREGATION AND THE MAKINGS OF THE UNDERCLASS 19-22 (Harvard U. Press 1993); Jeannine Bell, HATE THY NEIGHBOR: MOVE-IN VIOLENCE AND THE PERSISTENCE OF RACIAL SEGREGATION IN AMERICAN HOUSING 11-13 (NYU Press 2013).

4. Bell, *supra* note 3, at 11.

5. Massey & Denton, *supra* note 3, at 19.

6. For additional historical treatment of the role of government in creating and perpetuating residential racial segregation, see Richard Rothstein, THE COLOR OF LAW: A FORGOTTEN HISTORY OF HOW OUR GOVERNMENT SEGREGATED AMERICA (Liveright 2017). For "intentional and inter-related," we are indebted to Elizabeth K. Julian, Esq., formerly Assistant Secretary for Fair Housing and Equal Opportunity at the U.S. Department of Housing and Urban Development. The discussion in this chapter is by no means exhaustive, as many oppressive practices are not addressed here. *See, e.g.*, Thomas W. Mitchell, HISTORIC PARTITION LAW REFORM: A GAME CHANGER FOR HEIRS' PROPERTY OWNERS 65 (Cassandra J. Gaither et al. eds. 2019), available at https://scholarship.law.tamu.edu/facscholar/1327 (stating that many African Americans "have experienced substantial involuntary land loss, most likely totaling in the millions of acres over . . . the past 100 years[,]" due to "violence, discrimination . . . and forced transfers[, including] foreclosure, eminent domain, adverse possession, tax sales, and partition sales").

and VA programs was federally subsidized also by tax advantages and the interstate highways. During all these decades, predatory real estate practices and white supremacist violence were pervasive.

This chapter discusses each of these elements and early efforts to address residential racial discrimination and segregation, including state and local fair housing laws, fair housing organizations, President Kennedy's Executive Order of 1962, and Title VI of the Civil Rights Act of 1964. Later chapters address whether and to what extent the right to fair housing has been successful in disestablishing federally sanctioned segregation.

A. INTRODUCTION AND HISTORICAL OVERVIEW

1. The Beginnings: Explicit Racial Zoning, Racial Covenants, and Use or Euclidean Zoning

Both explicit racial zoning and racial covenants began in the 19th century. Racial zoning began on the West Coast, directed against people of Asian descent; in 1910 it was used against Black people in Baltimore, and its imposition spread widely from there. In 1917, in *Buchanan v. Warley* (below), the Supreme Court held racial zoning unconstitutional.

Meanwhile, also beginning in the 19th century, real estate entrepreneurs used private agreements—restrictive racial covenants or deed restrictions—to keep people of color out of neighborhoods deemed "white" by those with other interests in those neighborhoods. These "real covenants" were powerful because they "ran with the land"; that is, they bound future property owners even if those owners had not agreed to the covenants.[7] Also, other property owners could seek judicial enforcement of the covenants to preserve the all-white character of the neighborhood, which often meant seeking evictions of Black owners from homes they had purchased.

The use of explicit racial covenants spread rapidly among city planners, real estate developers, and municipal officials; indeed, the same people often migrated among such positions.[8] Covenants against sale to or occupancy by Black people became "standard," and such restrictions were extended to other groups of people considered "undesirable," including Asians, Mexicans, and Jews.[9] "Realtors often treated religion, national origin, and

---

7. William B. Stoebuck & Dale A. Whitman, THE LAW OF PROPERTY 470 (West Group 3d ed. 1992).

8. Paige Glotzer, HOW THE SUBURBS WERE SEGREGATED: DEVELOPERS AND THE BUSINESS OF EXCLUSIONARY HOUSING, 1890-1960, at 95-98 (Columbia U. Press 2020); Beryl Satter, FAMILY PROPERTIES: RACE, REAL ESTATE, AND THE EXPLOITATION OF BLACK URBAN AMERICA 40-41 (Henry Holt 2009) (stating that "By the 1940s, . . . [r]acial deed restrictions covered approximately half of the city's [Chicago's] residential neighborhoods").

9. Glotzer, *supra* note 8, at 97; William S. Worley, J.C. NICHOLS AND THE SHAPING OF KANSAS CITY 149-51 (U. Missouri Press 1990).

race as interchangeable for the purposes of establishing a racial hierarchy."[10] Although cities continued to enact and enforce racial zoning laws despite the Supreme Court's rulings in *Buchanan* and two subsequent cases, covenants became increasingly popular as instruments of exclusion (by themselves or in connection with other de jure segregated housing programs). Their use also was accelerated by the substantial migration of Black people from the South to other parts of the country.

Despite frequent challenges to racial covenants by the National Association for the Advancement of Colored People (NAACP) and others, the Supreme Court upheld their validity as purely private agreements.[11] Finally, in 1948, the Supreme Court held that judicial enforcement of racial covenants by state courts violated the Equal Protection Clause of the Fourteenth Amendment and that federal courts also could not lawfully enforce racial covenants. The cases that so held—*Shelley v. Kraemer* and *Hurd v. Hodge*—are presented and discussed below.

As explicit racial zoning became problematic, "officials, planners, and businesspeople" created comprehensive use zoning ordinances that "protect[ed] single-family residences from factories, stores, and apartments" and also "restrict[ed] . . . populations viewed as racially suspect . . ."[12] Although these ordinances did not use racial language, this use "zoning had from the outset, a racialist foundation and a racial intent . . . that . . . enabled postwar suburbanites to employ municipal ordinances as instruments of racial exclusion."[13] Just as covenants dictated single-family uses, minimum building widths, setback space, free yard space, status of outbuildings, minimum cost of construction, architectural controls, and similar matters,[14] use zoning ordinances established comparable standards. Professor David M.P. Freund describes the ways in which:

> zoning and racial covenants shared an intellectual, cultural, and even legal provenance. . . . Early zoning politics was heavily influenced by the theory that certain kinds of development (industrial, high-density residential) and certain populations (renters, racially suspect groups) posed a calculable threat to private homeowners. . . . Both racially restrictive covenants and restrictive zoning

---

10. Glotzer, *supra* note 8, at 131; *id.* at 126-28 (re: Jews); *id.* at 131 (re: Italians); *see also* Freund, *supra* note 1, at 94 (discussing covenants barring "Indians," "Asiatics," "Mongolians," "Jews," "Japanese," "members of the Balkan races," "South Europeans," and "Armenians"). The 1924 revised code of ethics of the National Association of Realtors (then the National Association of Real Estate Boards) prohibited a member from "introducing into a neighborhood a character of property or occupancy, members of any race or nationality, or any individual whose presence will clearly be detrimental to property values in that neighborhood." Glotzer, *supra* note 8, at 140.

11. Corrigan v. Buckley, 271 U.S. 323 (1926).

12. Freund, *supra* note 1, at 60, 63.

13. *Id.* at 46; Glotzer, *supra* note 8, at 110.

14. Freund, *supra* note 1, at 59; Worley, *supra* note 9, at 132 (describing deed restrictions used by J.C. Nichols starting in 1922); 135; 148 (stating that the earliest written racial restrictions were in 1908 and 1909, but the possibility of Black owners purchasing in these areas was "probably unimaginable" before then).

laws were legally grounded upon the assumption that certain land uses and certain populations categorically threatened the value of private property and the "health and welfare" of white property owners.[15]

Marc Weiss posits that covenants "served as both the physical and political model for zoning laws and subdivision regulations."[16]

Use zoning was given a substantial boost with the federal "Standard State Zoning Enabling Act," first circulated in 1922.[17] This "set of federally sanctioned standards for restrictive zoning . . . facilitated and often accelerated passage of numerous state enabling acts."[18] With the Act, the U.S. "Department of Commerce helped set the stage for decades of exclusionary zoning theory and practice by providing federal sanction to an emerging land-use science that would view black occupancy as a threat to white people."[19] "The 1920s [saw] an explosion of zoning laws and restrictive covenants. It was also when developers would turn their informal networks into a coordinated national project to standardize exclusion."[20]

When, in *Buchanan v. Warley*, the Supreme Court ruled against the use of explicit "racial zoning ordinances, restrictive covenants and land-use zoning filled the vacuum. With the latter based on restrictive covenants and with developers joining zoning commissions, the line between municipal law and development practice was blurred."[21]

The Supreme Court upheld use zoning in Village of Euclid, Ohio v. Ambler Realty Co., 272 U.S. 365 (1926). It overruled the district court's invalidation, which had been based in part on the Supreme Court's decision in *Buchanan v. Warley*, thus paving the way for a century of facially neutral zoning laws that could be used to achieve the same result as those with explicit racial restrictions.

2. New Deal Programs: The Home Owners Loan Corporation, Public Housing, and the Federal Housing Administration

The "New Deal-era and postwar housing programs—most famously the programs of the Public Housing Administration (PHA), the Urban Renewal Administration (URA), and the Federal Housing Administration (FHA)—accepted and codified white racial prejudices, in turn facilitating urban and suburban development patterns that systematically segregated populations by race while denying most racial minorities access to home-ownership and better quality accommodations."[22] The New Deal programs

---

15. Freund, *supra* note 1, at 92-93; *see also id.* at 93-98.
16. Marc Weiss, THE RISE OF THE COMMUNITY BUILDERS: THE AMERICAN REAL ESTATE INDUSTRY AND URBAN LAND PLANNING 3-4 (Columbia U. Press 1989).
17. Freund, *supra* note 1, at 77.
18. *Id.* at 79-80.
19. *Id.* at 80.
20. Glotzer, *supra* note 8, at 114.
21. *Id.*
22. Freund, *supra* note 1, at 5-6.

had two tiers—the lower was public housing and the top tier comprised federal provision of "low-cost capital to producers and consumers of market-produced housing."[23] This included the HOLC and the 1934 FHA homeownership program, which later was supplemented by the very similar homeownership program of the VA (now the Department of Veterans Affairs). The tiers "held racial significance; the upper tier nourished a growing, virtually all-white constituency while public housing struggled to support primarily a fragment of the minority community with which it became identified."[24]

The HOLC was created in 1933, in the heart of the Great Depression, when millions of Americans had lost their homes to foreclosure. As part of Franklin Delano Roosevelt's New Deal, its role was to refinance mortgages in danger of foreclosure. In Kenneth Jackson's classic description:

> The HOLC . . . introduced, perfected, and proved in practice the feasibility of the long-term, self-amortizing mortgage with uniform payments spread over the whole life of the debt. [It] systematized appraisal methods [and] devised a rating system that undervalued neighborhoods that were dense, mixed, or aging.[25]

The ratings were color-coded, with the First, highest quality (A), labeled green and the Fourth, lowest quality (D), labeled red. The First were "new, homogeneous, and 'in demand as residential locations in good times and bad.' Homogenous meant 'American business and professional men,'" which did not include Jews or people of color. "[B]lack neighborhoods were invariably rated as Fourth grade. . . ."[26] "[E]ven . . . neighborhoods with small proportions of black inhabitants were usually rated Fourth grade or 'hazardous.'"[27] The HOLC institutionalized preexisting "notions of ethnic and racial worth in real-estate appraising on an unprecedented scale."[28] This was the origin of "redlining" to designate neighborhoods unworthy of investment.

Another major federal innovation was the federally financed, low-rent public housing program, which began in 1933 as part of the Public Works Administration but then was codified in the U.S. Housing Act (USHA) of 1937.[29] The USHA provided limited federal financing for capital expenses only—not operating costs—primarily for multifamily rental developments designed, sited, and controlled by local decisionmakers; the local control

23. Gail Radford, MODERN HOUSING FOR AMERICA: POLICY STRUGGLES IN THE NEW DEAL ERA 197-98 (U. Chicago Press 1996).

24. Arnold R. Hirsch, *Choosing Segregation: Federal Housing Policy Between* Shelley *and* Brown, *in* FROM TENEMENTS TO THE TAYLOR HOMES: IN SEARCH OF AN URBAN HOUSING POLICY IN TWENTIETH-CENTURY AMERICA 206, 210 (John F. Bauman et al. eds., Penn State U. Press 2000).

25. Kenneth T. Jackson, CRABGRASS FRONTIER: THE SUBURBANIZATION OF THE UNITED STATES 196-97 (Oxford U. Press 1985).

26. *Id.* at 197-98.

27. *Id.* at 201.

28. *Id.* at 109.

29. *Id.* at 221, 223-24; Radford, *supra* note 23, at 85-109.

meant that the developments often created and otherwise "invariably reinforced racial segregation."[30]

In contrast, the FHA homeownership program assured private lenders and
developers that if they adhered to standards set by FHA the agency would
reimburse any defaults the homebuyers might cause.[31] The FHA standards
revolutionized home mortgage finance and made homeownership accessible
to millions of middle-class and working-class people by introducing long-
term, fully amortized, low-downpayment, low-interest home mortgage loans
and applying those standards across the industry.

These significant and unprecedented resources were not available to all,
however: The FHA required that the developments it protected be racially
homogenous, and almost all of them were exclusively white. The FHA
Underwriting Manual prohibited the introduction of "inharmonious" racial
groups, and FHA promoted racial covenants until 1950. As Professor Jackson
observed, the "FHA exhorted segregation and enshrined it as public policy,"[32]
with enduring effects on private mortgage lending standards, home appraisals, and access to wealth-building homeownership.

3. Post–World War II Programs: The Veterans Administration Program, the 1949 Housing Act, Urban Renewal, and Interstate Highways

After World War II, there was an enormous housing shortage in the United
States. The GI Bill's homeownership program, administered by the VA, combined with the FHA program, on which it was modeled. The two programs
together went far to meet the housing needs of white veterans.[33] The VA, like
the FHA, insisted on racial homogeneity, encouraged racial covenants, and
made most of its resources available only to white people. The two homeownership programs "introduced equity into the estates of over 35 million families between 1933 and 1978."[34] "Between 1945 and 1960, less than 2 percent of
all homes constructed with FHA assistance and 3 percent of VA-guaranteed
properties were occupied by nonwhites."[35] In addition to direct housing benefits, homeowners received substantial tax advantages starting in the 1940s,[36]
and the highways developed in the 1950s helped to make the suburban subdivisions attractive for white homeowners.

---

30. Jackson, *supra* note 25, at 225; *see also* Gail Radford, *The Federal Government and Housing During the Great Depression, in* FROM TENEMENTS TO THE TAYLOR HOMES, *supra* note 24, at 102, 118 (describing public housing as "stingy, physically alienating, and means tested").

31. The FHA insured the loans; the VA guaranteed their repayment.

32. Jackson, *supra* note 25, at 213.

33. Elaine Tyler May, HOMEWARD BOUND: AMERICAN FAMILIES IN THE COLD WAR ERA 151 (Basic Books 1999) ("Housing starts went from 114,000 in 1944 to an all-time high of 1,692,000 in 1950").

34. Jackson, *supra* note 25, at 216.

35. Freund, *supra* note 1, at 449 n.18.

36. May, *supra* note 33, at 151.

The 1949 Housing Act had some elements that appeared favorable to housing reformers, but overall it probably did more harm than good. It did declare a race-neutral "national housing goal": "the realization as soon as feasible of the goal of a decent home and a suitable living environment for every American family."[37] On the other hand, Congress rejected the Bricker-Cain amendment, which would have banned racial segregation in public housing. Republican Senators Bricker and Cain had introduced the amendment in the hope that it would destroy the underlying legislation. To avoid that result, "liberal" Senators voted against the amendment, and housing officials used the defeat of the amendment as the basis for arguing that they had no authority to prevent racial segregation in federal housing programs.[38]

The 1949 Act introduced the urban renewal program. State and local governments long had used the power of eminent domain to condemn and take over property owned by Black people and other people of color.[39] This system was federalized with the urban renewal program of the 1949 and 1954 Housing Acts. As Arnold Hirsch observed, "[t]he implementation of slum clearance and urban renewal, as authorized by the new laws, racially segmented the metropolitan United States in unparalleled fashion."[40] Under these programs, federal money went to municipal and private interests to allow them to take land where, for the most part, Black people lived, raze the improvements, and resell the land at reduced prices to private developers who would build as the white, monied interests preferred. Urban renewal made no meaningful provision for relocation of the people who were displaced, and the program came to be known as "Negro removal."[41]

This chapter includes the Supreme Court's 1954 decision in *Berman v. Parker*, validating the urban renewal program, in an opinion that ignored the interests of the Black residents of the area (who comprised 99.5 percent of the total) and the likely impact of the urban renewal program on efforts to achieve the public school desegregation that the Court had held only months earlier was constitutionally required. To introduce that decision, we also discuss New York's Stuyvesant Town, "the first project of slum clearance and

---

37. Housing Act of 1949, Pub. L. No 81-171, §2, 63 Stat. 413 (codified as 42 U.S.C. §1441 (2000)); reaffirmed in the Housing & Urban Development Act of 1968, Pub. L. No. 90-448, §2, 82 Stat. 476 (1968) (codified as 42 U.S.C. §1441a).

38. Hirsch, *supra* note 24, at 214-15.

39. Historically, for example, parks had been created to displace "undesirable communities," with New York City's Central Park providing a classic illustration of this. *See* Roy Rosenzweig & Elizabeth Blackmar, The Park and the People: A History of Central Park (Henry Holt 1992).

40. Hirsch, *supra* note 24, at 208; *see also* Report of the [Douglas] National Commission on Urban Problems, Building the American City 152 (1968) (The Housing Act of 1954 changed to "urban renewal" what had been called "urban redevelopment" and "slum clearance.").

41. Mark I. Gelfand, A Nation of Cities: The Federal Government and Urban America, 1933-1965, at 212 (Oxford U. Press 1973). This expression, which came to be common, may first have been used by James Baldwin in a televised interview on June 24, 1963, https://american archive.org/catalog/cpb-aacip_15-0v89g5gf5r. Our thanks to Jerrick Adams for locating this source.

redevelopment attempted by private enterprise with public assistance," which "established a pattern for this country's multibillion dollar urban renewal program after the war."[42]

The damage wrought by the urban renewal program was compounded by the federally financed interstate highway program of 1956, which provided $100 billion to pay for more than 41,000 miles of highway.[43] The highways helped to make the new homes in the suburbs feasible. With local people in control of siting, highways slashed through Black business and residential neighborhoods and effective relocation was not provided. The *Triangle Improvement Council* case below illustrates this. As Professor Deborah Archer notes:

> In almost every region of the country, the new interstate highway sys-
> tem uprooted, displaced, and isolated hundreds of thousands of people.
> The United States Department of Transportation estimates that more than
> 475,000 households and more than a million people were displaced nation-
> wide as a direct result of federal highway building. Millions of additional
> people were left living in "hollowed-out communities" after the bulldoz-
> ers left. The neighborhoods destroyed and families displaced were over-
> whelmingly Black and poor. This was by design. Transportation policy in
> the 1950s and 1960s was crafted to reinforce racial and class inequalities
> and divisions.[44]

4. The Constants: Predatory Real Estate Practices and Racial Violence

Throughout these decades, two forces persevered in maintaining the color line: predatory land transactions and violence.

Federal policy and private exploitation, extraction, and land theft built wealth for white people while destroying or restricting the wealth of Black people and other people of color.[45] Black people and other people of color were unable to secure standard mortgage financing; they could achieve home-ownership only by using financing instruments like installment land sales contracts, which imposed predatory rates and terms causing the borrower to lose all money invested if there were a single late payment. We present below a case involving Chicago's Contract Buyers League to illustrate community organizing and legal challenges against this form of exploitation of and profi-teering from segregation.

---

42. Arthur Simon, STUYVESANT TOWN USA: PATTERN FOR TWO AMERICAS 4 (NYU Press 1970).

43. May, *supra* note 33, at 151.

44. Deborah Archer, *"White Men's Roads Through Black Men's Homes": Advancing Racial Equity Through Highway Reconstruction,* 73 VAND. L. REV. 1259, 1274 (2020).

45. *See, e.g.,* Vann R. Newkirk II, *The Great Land Robbery: The Shameful Story of How 1 Million Black Families Have Been Ripped from Their Farms,* THE ATLANTIC (September 2019) ("The dispossession of black agricultural land resulted in the loss of hundreds of billions of dollars of black wealth."). https://www.theatlantic.com/magazine/archive/2019/09/this-land-was-our-land/594742/.

White violence against Black people was frequent after the Civil War. The Equal Justice Institute has reported that between Reconstruction and World War II, some 4,480 people were lynched.[46] Particularly dramatic instances of white supremacist oppression were frequent; massive, white-on-Black massacres destroyed Black neighborhoods and forced survivors to leave permanently. Some details are provided below.

5. The Resistance Gathers Steam: Fair Housing Organizations, State and Local Fair Housing Laws, the 1962 Executive Order, the Referendum Cases, and Title VI of the 1964 Civil Rights Act

While traditional civil rights organizations like the NAACP and the Congress of Racial Equality (CORE) long had been fighting discrimination and segregation in housing, a fair housing movement arose in the 1940s, beginning with Chicago's Hyde Park-Kenwood Community Conference.[47] In 1948, the New York State Committee on Discrimination in Housing grew out of the effort to fight Stuyvesant Town's ban on occupancy by Black people (discussed below); in 1950, this became the National Committee Against Discrimination in Housing.[48] The American Friends Service Committee (AFSC) was active in promoting residential racial integration from the 1940s.[49] A widespread fair housing group, National Neighbors, evolved from many local groups in 1969 and endured until 1989.[50] The National Fair Housing Alliance was founded in 1988.[51] It boasts a membership of "more than 200 private, nonprofit fair

---

46. Equal Justice Institute, LYNCHING IN AMERICA: CONFRONTING THE LEGACY OF RACIAL TERROR (3d ed. 2005), https://eji.org/wp-content/uploads/2005/11/lynching-in-america-3d-ed-110121.pdf; *see also* Sherrilyn A. Ifill, ON THE COURTHOUSE LAWN: CONFRONTING THE LEGACY OF LYNCHING IN THE TWENTY-FIRST CENTURY (Beacon Press 2007).

47. Juliet Saltman, A FRAGILE MOVEMENT: THE STRUGGLE FOR NEIGHBORHOOD STABILIZATION 22 (Greenwood Press 1990); *see also* Charles Abrams, FORBIDDEN NEIGHBORS: A STUDY OF PREJUDICE IN HOUSING 337 (Harper & Bros. 1955) (praising the work also of the ACLU, American Jewish Congress, National Urban League, Anti-Defamation League, and American Jewish Committee). As to CORE, see August Meier & Elliott Rudwick, CORE: A STUDY IN THE CIVIL RIGHTS MOVEMENT (U. Ill. Press 1975).

48. Simon, *supra* note 42, at 5, 85; Robert A. Caro, THE POWER BROKER: ROBERT MOSES AND THE FALL OF NEW YORK 961 (Alfred A. Knopf 1974); Abrams, *supra* note 47, at 337; Kenneth Coleman & Charles Johnson, National Committee Against Discrimination in Housing, Amistad Research Center at Tulane University, https://amistad-finding-aids.tulane.edu/agents/corporate_entities/41 (last visited June 27, 2023).

49. Bell, *supra* note 3, at 38-40; James Wolfinger, *"The American Dream—For All Americans": Race, Politics, and the Campaign to Desegregate Levittown,* 38 J. URBAN HIST. 430 (2012); Tracy E. K'Meyer, TO LIVE PEACEABLY TOGETHER: THE AMERICAN FRIENDS SERVICE COMMITTEE'S CAMPAIGN FOR OPEN HOUSING (U. Chicago Press 2022).

50. Saltman, *supra* note 47, at 22, 313-68 (describing the formation of National Neighbors from local organizations in Chicago; Cincinnati; Denver; Indianapolis; Los Angeles; New Rochelle, New York; Oklahoma City; Philadelphia; Shaker Heights, Ohio; University City, Missouri; and Washington, DC); Bell, *supra* note 3, at 48-49 (re: Neighbors Inc. in the 1950s in Washington, DC).

51. Our Members, National Fair Housing Alliance, https://nationalfairhousing.org/ (last visited Sept. 7, 2024).

housing organizations and state and local civil rights agencies from throughout the United States."[52]

Also beginning in the 1940s, some cities and states enacted fair housing
laws. Usually, such laws applied only to public or publicly assisted housing.
The New Jersey state law involved in the Levitt case below is an example of
such a state law that prohibited discrimination in publicly assisted housing.
The first such law to apply to private housing was enacted by New York City
in 1944.[53] In 1950, New York State banned racial discrimination in publicly
assisted housing projects.[54]

Gunnar Myrdal's landmark 1944 study, An American Dilemma, urged
planning to meet the great need for housing anticipated after World War II
and admonished decisionmakers

> not to overlook segregation and the abominable housing conditions for
> Negroes. Gross inequality in this field is not only a matter for democratic
> American conscience, but it is also expensive in the end.[55]

In 1947, President Truman's Committee on Civil Rights issued its important
report, To Secure These Rights. It recommended, among other things, the
"[p]rohibition of discrimination and segregation . . . in all public or publicly
supported . . . housing projects."[56]

Housing discrimination and segregation, especially in public and publicly
assisted housing, became an issue in the election of 1960. On November 20,
1962, President Kennedy issued Executive Order 11063, which directed federal agencies to avoid discrimination in housing owned, operated, or financed
by the federal government.[57] The executive order, however, provided no
means of enforcement.

In 1965, the National Committee Against Discrimination in Housing
reported that there were more than 1,000 fair housing groups in the United
States and that 17 states and 28 cities had enacted fair housing laws.[58]
Opponents used referenda to oppose such legislation. In 1964, a California
referendum invalidated that state's fair housing law; in Reitman v. Mulkey,
387 U.S. 369 (1967), the U.S. Supreme Court held, 5-4, that the referendum

---

52. Member Directory, National Fair Housing Alliance, https://nationalfairhousing.org
/member-directory/ (last visited June 27, 2023).

53. Simon, *supra* note 42, at 46 ("Because of Stuyvesant Town, the City Council initiated
early in 1944 the nation's first legislation in fair housing that aimed sanctions against private
property owners"); *cf.* Saltman, *supra* note 47, at 15 (stating that in 1957, "New York City became
the first city to pass a law banning racial discrimination in housing").

54. Simon, *supra* note 42, at 86.

55. Gunnar Myrdal, An American Dilemma: The Negro Problem and Modern
Democracy 627 (Harper & Bros. 1944).

56. To Secure These Rights: The Report of the President's Committee on Civil Rights
171 (Simon & Schuster 1947).

57. 27 Fed. Reg. 11,527 (1962), reprinted in notes to 42 U.S.C.A. §1982 (2012). President
Carter amended EO 11063 in EO 12259, 46 Fed. Reg. 1253 (1980).

58. Wendell E. Pritchett, Robert Clifton Weaver and the American City: The Life and
Times of an Urban Reformer 287 (U. Chicago Press 2018).

violated the Equal Protection Clause of the Fourteenth Amendment. In Hunter v. Erickson, 393 U.S. 385 (1969), the Court rejected another effort by voters to nullify a fair housing law, but in James v. Valtierra, 402 U.S. 137 (1971), the Court upheld against an Equal Protection challenge a referendum requirement for subsidized housing developments. After the 1968 decision in *Jones v. Mayer* (Chapter 2) and the enactment of the federal Fair Housing Act, the significance of these state developments was greatly reduced.[59]

In 1964, Congress passed one of the most pivotal pieces of legislation of the 20th century, the Civil Rights Act of 1964.[60] Title VII of that Act, dealing with equal employment opportunity, is of great significance with respect to housing because the federal Fair Housing Act of 1968 is in many ways modeled on it. The public accommodations, education, and other titles of the 1964 Act also are highly pertinent to civil rights generally. With respect to housing, the most important provision is Title VI, which prohibits discrimination on the basis of race, color, or national origin in federal programs and programs that receive federal financial assistance, which certainly include public housing and some other forms of federal housing assistance. In Chapter 12, we present *Gautreaux v. Romney* and *Young v. Pierce*, both of which address liability under Title VI.

B. RACIAL ZONING, RACIAL COVENANTS, AND THE BEGINNINGS OF "USE" OR EUCLIDEAN ZONING

1. Explicit Racial Zoning

Explicit racial zoning began on the West Coast, directed at people of Chinese descent. This may be the first, and certainly is the classic, case.

In re Lee Sing
43 F. 359 (N.D. Cal. 1890)

SAWYER, J:

The petitioners are under arrest for the violation of order No. 2190, commonly called the "Bingham Ordinance," requiring all Chinese inhabitants to remove from the portion of the city heretofore occupied by them, outside the city and county, or to another designated part of the city and county.

Article 14, Sec. 1, of the constitution of the United States reads as follows:

Section 1. All persons born or naturalized in the United States, and subject to the jurisdiction thereof, are citizens of the United States, and of the state wherein they reside. No state shall make or enforce any law which shall

---

59. *See* Schwemm, HDLL §3.5.

60. *See* Todd S. Purdum, AN IDEA WHOSE TIME HAS COME: TWO PRESIDENTS, TWO PARTIES, AND THE BATTLE FOR THE CIVIL RIGHTS ACT OF 1964 (Henry Holt 2014); Clay Risen, THE BILL OF THE CENTURY: THE EPIC BATTLE FOR THE CIVIL RIGHTS ACT (Bloomsbury 2014).

abridge the privileges or immunities of citizens of the United States; nor shall any state deprive any person of life, liberty, or property, without due process of law, nor deny to any person within its jurisdiction, the equal protection of the laws.

Article 6 of the Burlingame treaty with China, provides, that

Chinese subjects, visiting or residing in the United States, shall enjoy the same privileges, immunities and exemptions, in respect to travel or residence, as may there be enjoyed by the citizens or subjects of the most favored nation.

Section 1977 of the Revised Statutes of the United States [42 U.S.C. §1981(a)] provides:

All persons within the jurisdiction of the United States shall have the same right in every state and territory to make and enforce contracts, to sue, be parties, give evidence, and to the full and equal benefit of all laws and proceedings for the security of persons and property as is enjoyed by white citizens, and shall be subject to like punishment, pains, penalties, taxes, licenses, and exactions of every kind, and to no other.

And article 6, subd. 2, of the national constitution provides, that, "this constitution, and the laws of the United States which shall be made in pursuance thereof, and all treaties made, or which shall be made, under the authority of the United States, shall be the supreme law of the land; and the judges in every state shall be bound thereby, anything in the constitution or laws of any state to the contrary notwithstanding."

The discrimination against Chinese, and the gross inequality of the operation of this ordinance upon Chinese, as compared with others, in violation of the constitutional, treaty, and statutory provisions cited, are so manifest upon its face, that I am unable to comprehend how this discrimination and inequality of operation, and the consequent violation of the express provisions of the constitution, treaties and statutes of the United States, can fail to be apparent to the mind of every intelligent person, be he lawyer or layman.

The ordinance is not aimed at any particular vice, or any particular unwholesome or immoral occupation, or practice, but it declares it "to be unlawful for any Chinese to locate, reside or carry on business within the limits of the city and county of San Francisco, except in that district of said city and county hereinafter provided for their location."

It further provides that "within sixty days after the passage of this ordinance all Chinese now located, residing or carrying on business within the limits of said city and county of San Francisco, shall either remove without the limits of said city and county of San Francisco, or remove and locate within the district of the city and county of San Francisco, herein provided for their location." And again, section 4 provides that "any Chinese residing, locating, or carrying on business within the limits of the city and county, contrary to the provisions of this order, shall be deemed guilty of a misdemeanor, and upon conviction thereof, shall be punished by imprisonment in the county jail for a term not exceeding six months." Upon what other people are these requirements, disabilities and punishments imposed? Upon none.

The obvious purpose of this order, is, [to] forcibly drive out a whole community of twenty-odd thousand people, old and young, male and female, citizens of the United States, born on the soil, and foreigners of the Chinese race, moral and immoral, good, bad, and indifferent, and without respect to circumstances or conditions, from a whole section of the city which they have inhabited, and in which they have carried on all kinds of business appropriate to a city, mercantile, manufacturing, and otherwise, for more than 40 years. Many of them were born there, in their own houses, and are citizens of the United States, entitled to all the rights, and privileges under the constitution and laws of the United States, that are lawfully enjoyed by any other citizen of the United States. They all, without distinction or exception, are to leave their homes and property, occupied for nearly half a century, and go, either out of the city and county, or to a section with prescribed limits, within the city and county, not owned by them, or by the city. This, besides being discrimination, against the Chinese, and unequal in its operation as between them and all others, is simply an arbitrary confiscation of their homes and property, a depriving them of it, without due process or any process of law. And what little there would be left after abandoning their homes, and various places of business would again be confiscated in compulsorily buying lands in the only place assigned to them, and which they do not own, upon such exorbitant terms as the present owners with the advantage given them would certainly impose. It must be that or nothing. There would be no room for freedom of action, in buying again. They would be compelled to take any lands, upon any terms, arbitrarily imposed, or get outside the city and county of San Francisco.

That this ordinance is a direct violation, of, not only, the express provisions of the constitution of the United States, in several particulars, but also of the express provisions of our several treaties with China, and of the statutes of the United States, is so obvious, that I shall not waste more time, or words in discussing the matter. To any reasonably intelligent and well-balanced mind, discussion or argument would be wholly unnecessary and superfluous. To those minds, which are so constituted, that the invalidity of this ordinance is not apparent upon inspection, and comparison with the provisions of the constitution, treaties and laws cited, discussion or argument would be useless. The authority to pass this order is not within any legitimate police power of the state.

Let the order be adjudged to be void, as being in direct conflict with the constitution, treaties, and statutes, of the United States, and let the petitioners be discharged.

NOTES AND QUESTIONS

1. *In re Lee Sing* **in Context.** During the 19th century, significant numbers of people of Asian descent immigrated to the United States, particularly to the West Coast, and there was substantial hostility toward them. The federal, state, and local governments enacted many types of laws to prevent these people from living as and where "white" people did. Federal law made all "non-white" persons ineligible for naturalized citizenship from 1790 to 1952.[61] The Bingham Ordinance, at issue in *In re Lee Sing*, was authorized by the 1879 California constitution and an 1880 state law.

The area designated for Chinese people in San Francisco "had by previous legislation been set aside for slaughter houses, tallow factories, hog factories and other businesses thought to be prejudicial to the public health or comfort."[62]

Professor McClain writes that the city's written defense of the ordinance:

> represents undoubtedly one of the more appalling statements of racial bigotry in Western legal history. Among its allegations: that the Chinese were as a race criminal, vicious, and immoral; that they were all incorrigible perjurers; that they abandoned their sick in the street to die; that their occupation of property anywhere decreased the value of surrounding property; that their presence in any number anywhere was offensive to the senses and dangerous to the morals of other races. . . ."[63]

2. **The Aftermath of** *In re Lee Sing*: **Racial Zoning Against Black People in Baltimore.** Although in *In re Lee Sing* the federal district court invalidated the ordinance, stating that it "is not within any legitimate police power of the state," states and cities continued to impose such expulsive and explicit racial zoning.[64] In California, where Japanese immigration followed the Chinese,[65] the legislature attempted to discourage the sizable number of Japanese farmers by enacting a 1913 law that prohibited ownership of agricultural land and leases longer than three years by aliens ineligible for citizenship:[66] "[t]he

---

61. Ian F. Haney López, WHITE BY LAW: THE LEGAL CONSTRUCTION OF RACE 28 (NYU Press 10th ed. 2006).

62. Charles J. McClain, IN SEARCH OF EQUALITY: THE CHINESE STRUGGLE AGAINST DISCRIMINATION IN NINETEENTH-CENTURY AMERICA 224 (U. Cal. Press 1994).

63. *Id.* at 229.

64. *See, e.g.,* Christopher Silver, *The Racial Origins of Zoning in American Cities, in* URBAN PLANNING AND THE AFRICAN AMERICAN COMMUNITY: IN THE SHADOWS 21 (June Manning Thomas & Marsha Ritzdorf eds., Sage 1996).

65. McClain, *supra* note 62, at 282; *see also* Klarman, *supra* note 1, at 63.

66. McClain, *supra* note 62, at 283; Roger Daniels, THE POLITICS OF PREJUDICE: THE ANTI-JAPANESE MOVEMENT IN CALIFORNIA AND THE STRUGGLE FOR JAPANESE EXCLUSION 49 (U. Cal. Press 1962); *see also* Ann Firor Scott ed., PAULI MURRAY & CAROLINE WARE: FORTY YEARS OF LETTERS IN BLACK AND WHITE 34 (UNC Press 2006) (in a September 16, 1944 letter to Ware about Carey McWilliams's article, A Lawyer's View of Segregation, Murray writes: "He . . . points out the anti-oriental laws here on the West Coast did not come about as a result of crystallization of public opinion but that public opinion was manufactured by certain interest groups who wished

phrase designated solely persons of Asian parentage and was obviously aimed against Japanese."[67]

Baltimore was the first jurisdiction to direct such ordinances at Black people. In 1910, a Black lawyer named William Ashbie Hawkins purchased a home in a Baltimore neighborhood otherwise occupied by whites; he rented the house to his law partner, George W.F. McMechen, who also was Black.[68] After violence failed to force the McMechens to move, the neighbors secured "the passage of the country's first comprehensive municipal residential segregation ordinance."[69] The Maryland courts repeatedly invalidated the Baltimore ordinances, but racial zoning against Black people was adopted in other jurisdictions. Although state courts usually invalidated these laws, governments continued to produce them.[70] The Supreme Court invalidated explicit racial zoning a few years later.

Buchanan v. Warley
245 U.S. 60 (1917)

Before Chief Justice White and Justices McKenna, Holmes, Day, Van Devanter, Pitney, McReynolds, Brandeis, and Clarke.

Mr. Justice DAY delivered the opinion of the Court.

Buchanan brought an action for the specific performance of a contract for the sale of certain real estate situated in the City of Louisville. The offer in writing to purchase the property contained a proviso:

> It is understood that I am purchasing the above property for the purpose of having erected thereon a house which I propose to make my residence, and it is a distinct part of this agreement that I shall not be required to accept a deed to the above property or to pay for said property unless I have the right under the laws of the State of Kentucky and the City of Louisville to occupy said property as a residence.

---

to profit by it—unfortunately one of them was the growing labor movement on West Coast being manipulated by politicians").

67. Alexander Saxton, THE INDISPENSABLE ENEMY: LABOR AND THE ANTI-CHINESE MOVEMENT IN CALIFORNIA 257 (U. Cal. Press 1971).

68. Garrett Power, *Apartheid Baltimore Style: The Residential Segregation Ordinances of 1910-13*, 42 MD. L. REV. 289, 298 (1983); Glotzer, *supra* note 8, at 83. Mr. Hawkins's legal education is worthy of note. He enrolled in the University of Maryland law school in 1890, but was "forced out . . . during his first year as a result of an 'anti-black petition signed by a majority of the student body.' It would take a lawsuit filed fifty-five years later by Charles Hamilton Houston and Thurgood Marshall to force the University of Maryland to again open its doors to blacks." J. Clay Smith, Jr., EMANCIPATION: THE MAKING OF THE BLACK LAWYER 1844-1944, at 38 (U. Pa. Press 1993).

69. Glotzer, *supra* note 8, at 83.

70. *See, e.g.*, Jade A. Craig, *"Pigs in the Parlor": The Legacy of Racial Zoning and the Challenge of Affirmatively Furthering Fair Housing in the South*, 40 MISS. C. L. REV. 5, 24 (2022) (discussing the Virginia legislature's authorizing cities to enact racial zoning laws, a statute invalidated by the state supreme court).

This offer was accepted by the plaintiff.

[T]he defendant by way of answer set up the condition above set forth, that he is a colored person, and that on the block of which the lot in controversy is a part there are ten residences, eight of which at the time of the making of the contract were occupied by white people, and only two (those nearest the lot in question) were occupied by colored people, and that under and by virtue of the ordinance of the city of Louisville, approved May 11, 1914, he would not be allowed to occupy the lot as a place of residence.

In reply the plaintiff set up that the ordinance was in conflict with the Fourteenth Amendment to the Constitution of the United States, and hence no defense. The Court of Appeals of Kentucky held the ordinance valid and of itself a complete defense to the action.

The title of the ordinance is:

> An ordinance to prevent conflict and ill-feeling between the white and colored races in the City of Louisville, and to preserve the public peace and promote the general welfare by making reasonable provisions requiring, as far as practicable, the use of separate blocks for residences, places of abode and places of assembly by white and colored people respectively.

The objection is made that this writ of error should be dismissed because the alleged denial of constitutional rights involves only the rights of colored persons, and the plaintiff in error is a white person. This court has frequently held that while an unconstitutional act is no law, attacks upon the validity of laws can only be entertained when made by those whose rights are directly affected by the law or ordinance in question. Only such persons, it has been settled, can be heard to attack the constitutionality of the law or ordinance. But this case does not run counter to that principle.

The right of the plaintiff in error [a white man] to sell his property was directly involved and necessarily impaired [by the ordinance] because it was held in effect that he could not sell the lot to a person of color who was willing and ready to acquire the property, and had obligated himself to take it.

We pass then to a consideration of the case upon its merits. This ordinance prevents the occupancy of a lot in the City of Louisville by a person of color in a block where the greater number of residences are occupied by white persons; where such a majority exists colored persons are excluded. This interdiction is based wholly upon color; simply that and nothing more. In effect, premises situated as are those in question in the so-called white block are effectively debarred from sale to persons of color, because if sold they cannot be occupied by the purchaser nor by him sold to another of the same color. [Eds.—The ordinance imposed a reciprocal racial restriction on the entry of whites into a majority Black block and created an exception for existing owners or lessors, as well as "white or colored servants or employees" of housing occupants.]

This drastic measure is sought to be justified under the authority of the State in the exercise of the police power. It is said such legislation tends to promote the public peace by preventing racial conflicts; that it tends to maintain racial purity; that it prevents the deterioration of property owned and occupied by white people, which deterioration, it is contended, is sure to follow the occupancy of adjacent premises by persons of color.

The authority of the State to pass laws in the exercise of the police power, having for their object the promotion of the public health, safety and welfare is very broad as has been affirmed in numerous and recent decisions of this court. Furthermore, the exercise of this power, embracing nearly all legislation of a local character, is not to be interfered with by the courts where it is within the scope of legislative authority and the means adopted reasonably tend to accomplish a lawful purpose. But it is equally well established that the police power, broad as it is, cannot justify the passage of a law or ordinance which runs counter to the limitations of the Federal Constitution.

The Federal Constitution and laws passed within its authority are by the express terms of that instrument made the supreme law of the land. The Fourteenth Amendment protects life, liberty, and property from invasion by the States without due process of law. Property is more than the mere thing which a person owns. It is elementary that it includes the right to acquire, use, and dispose of it. The Constitution protects these essential attributes of property. Property consists of the free use, enjoyment, and disposal of a person's acquisitions without control or diminution save by the law of the land.

True it is that dominion over property springing from ownership is not absolute and unqualified. The disposition and use of property may be controlled in the exercise of the police power in the interest of the public health, convenience, or welfare. Harmful occupations may be controlled and regulated. Legitimate business may also be regulated in the interest of the public. Certain uses of property may be confined to portions of the municipality other than the resident district, such as livery stables, brickyards and the like, because of the impairment of the health and comfort of the occupants of neighboring property. Many illustrations might be given from the decisions of this court, and other courts, of this principle, but these cases do not touch the one at bar.

The concrete question here is: May the occupancy, and, necessarily, the purchase and sale of property of which occupancy is an incident, be inhibited by the States, or by one of its municipalities, solely because of the color of the proposed occupant of the premises? That one may dispose of his property, subject only to the control of lawful enactments curtailing that right in the public interest, must be conceded. The question now presented makes it pertinent to enquire into the constitutional right of the white man to sell his property to a colored man, having in view the legal status of the purchaser and occupant.

Following the Civil War certain amendments to the Federal Constitution were adopted, which have become an integral part of that instrument, equally binding upon all the States and fixing certain fundamental rights which all are bound to respect. The Thirteenth Amendment abolished slavery in the United States and in all places subject to their jurisdiction, and gave Congress power to enforce the Amendment by appropriate legislation. The Fourteenth Amendment made all persons born or naturalized in the United States citizens of the United States and of the States in which they reside, and provided that no State shall make or enforce any law which shall abridge the privileges or immunities of citizens of the United States, and that no State shall deprive any person of life, liberty, or property without due process of law, nor deny to any person the equal protection of the laws.

The effect of these Amendments was first dealt with by this court in The Slaughter House Cases. While a principal purpose of the [Fourteenth] Amendment was to protect persons of color, the broad language used was deemed sufficient to protect all persons, white or black, against discriminatory legislation by the States. This is now the settled law. In many of the cases since arising the question of color has not been involved and the cases have been decided upon alleged violations of civil or property rights irrespective of the race or color of the complainant. In The Slaughter House Cases it was recognized that the chief inducement to the passage of the Amendment was the desire to extend federal protection to the recently emancipated race from unfriendly and discriminating legislation by the States.

In giving legislative aid to these constitutional provisions Congress enacted in 1866 that:

> All citizens of the United States shall have the same right in every State and Territory, as is enjoyed by white citizens thereof to inherit, purchase, lease, sell, hold, and convey real and personal property.

And in 1870:

> All persons within the jurisdiction of the United States shall have the same right in every State and Territory to make and enforce contracts, to sue, be parties, give evidence, and to the full and equal benefit of all laws and proceedings for the security of persons and property as is enjoyed by white citizens, and shall be subject to like punishment, pains, penalties, taxes, licenses and exactions of every kind, and no other.

In the face of these constitutional and statutory provisions, can a white man be denied, consistently with due process of law, the right to dispose of his property to a purchaser by prohibiting the occupation of it for the sole reason that the purchaser is a person of color intending to occupy the premises as a place of residence?

The statute of 1866, originally passed under sanction of the Thirteenth Amendment and practically reenacted after the adoption of the Fourteenth Amendment, expressly provided that all citizens of the United States in any State shall have the same right to purchase property as is enjoyed by white citizens. Colored persons are citizens of the United States and have the right to purchase property and enjoy and use the same without laws discriminating against them solely on account of color. These enactments did not deal with the social rights of men, but with those fundamental rights in property which it was intended to secure upon the same terms to citizens of every race and color. *Civil Rights Cases*. The Fourteenth Amendment and these statutes enacted in furtherance of its purpose operate to qualify and entitle a colored man to acquire property without state legislation discriminating against him solely because of color.

The defendant in error insists that *Plessy v. Ferguson* is controlling in principle in favor of the judgment of the court below. In that case this court held that a provision of a statute of Louisiana requiring railway companies carrying passengers to provide in their coaches equal but separate accommodations for the white and colored races did not run counter to the provisions of the Fourteenth Amendment. It is to be observed that in that case there was no attempt to deprive persons of color of transportation in the coaches of the public carrier, and the express requirements were for equal though separate accommodations for the white and colored races. In *Plessy v. Ferguson*, classification of accommodation was permitted upon the basis of equality for both races.

In *Carey v. City of Atlanta*, the Supreme Court of Georgia [held] an ordinance, similar in principle to the one herein involved, to be invalid.

That there exists a serious and difficult problem arising from a feeling of race hostility which the law is powerless to control, and to which it must give a measure of consideration, may be freely admitted. But its solution cannot be promoted by depriving citizens of their constitutional rights and privileges.

As we have seen, this court has held laws valid which separated the races on the basis of equal accommodations in public conveyances, and courts of high authority have held enactments lawful which provide for separation in the public schools of white and colored pupils where equal privileges are given. But in view of the rights secured by the Fourteenth Amendment to the Federal Constitution such legislation must have its limitations, and cannot be sustained where the exercise of authority exceeds the restraints of the Constitution. We think these limitations are exceeded in laws and ordinances of the character now before us.

It is the purpose of such enactments, and, it is frankly avowed it will be their ultimate effect, to require by law, at least in residential districts, the compulsory separation of the races on account of color. Such action is said to be essential to the maintenance of the purity of the races, although it is to be noted in the ordinance under consideration that the employment of colored servants in white families is permitted, and nearby residences of colored persons not coming within the blocks, as defined in the ordinance, are not prohibited.

The case presented does not deal with an attempt to prohibit the amalgamation of the races. The right which the ordinance annulled was the civil right of a white man to dispose of his property if he saw fit to do so to a person of color and of a colored person to make such disposition to a white person.

It is urged that this proposed segregation will promote the public peace by preventing race conflicts. Desirable as this is, and important as is the preservation of the public peace, this aim cannot be accomplished by laws or ordinances which deny rights created or protected by the Federal Constitution.

It is said that such acquisitions by colored persons depreciate property owned in the neighborhood by white persons. But property may be acquired by undesirable white neighbors or put to disagreeable though lawful uses with like results.

We think this attempt to prevent the alienation of the property in question to a person of color was not a legitimate exercise of the police power of the State, and is in direct violation of the fundamental law enacted in the Fourteenth Amendment of the Constitution preventing state interference with property rights except by due process of law. That being the case, the ordinance cannot stand.

NOTES AND QUESTIONS

1. **What Was the Basis for the Supreme Court's Decision?** On whose rights does the Court focus? Is this case about property rights or civil rights? Does that matter?

2. **What Were the Bases for the Louisville Ordinance?** Is there a difference between what the city said were the purposes and what we think the purposes really were? How does the Court view these purposes?

3. **The Importance of the Law of Nuisance.** Note that racial zoning laws relied on the law of nuisance, a malleable concept in tort and property law that supports challenges to land use and other conduct that "unreasonably" interferes with the property or other interests of the complainant. As nuisance law stigmatized undesirable land uses, racial zoning laws targeted people who were considered undesirable.[71] Do you see ways in which nuisance law is reflected in contemporary land use and other doctrines related to fair housing?

4. **How Much, if Any, Deference Does the Court Give to the City Council?** Compare the treatment of the City Council's justifications in this case with the degree of deference accorded in *Euclid v. Ambler* (below) ("If the validity of the legislative classification for zoning purposes be fairly debatable, the legislative judgment must be allowed to control"[72]) and in *Berman v. Parker* (below) ("Subject to specific constitutional limitations, when the legislature has spoken, the public interest has been declared in terms well-nigh

---

71. Glotzer, *supra* note 8, at 52. On other attempts to use nuisance law against Black people, see Rachel D. Godsil, *Race Nuisance: The Politics of Law in the Jim Crow Era*, 105 Mich. L. Rev. 505 (2008); Taja-Nia Y. Henderson & Jamila Jefferson-Jones, *#LivingWhileBlack: Blackness as Nuisance*, 69 Am. U. L. Rev. 863 (2020).

72. Euclid v. Ambler, 272 U.S. 365, 388 (1926).

conclusive. . . . The role of the judiciary in determining whether that power is being exercised for a public purpose is an extremely narrow one.").[73]

Observe that one purpose of the ordinance—to prevent racial conflict—is virtually identical to the purported purpose of the law restricting train passengers in *Plessy v. Ferguson*. How does the Court distinguish *Plessy* (which it does not overrule)?

5. **Comparing Ordinances and Opinions.** The district court in *Lee Sing* had little difficulty determining that the San Francisco ordinance violated the Constitution and could not stand. More than 25 years later, the Supreme Court devoted considerably more ink to striking down the Louisville ordinance in *Buchanan*. In what ways were the two measures different? Why did the Louisville ordinance require more analysis?

6. **The Story of *Buchanan v. Warley*.** *Buchanan v. Warley* was a carefully contrived test case in which Buchanan, a white real estate broker, sold a lot to William Warley, a Black man who was president of the Louisville chapter of the NAACP, which had been organized to challenge the ordinance.[74] The case was argued twice in the U.S. Supreme Court—first on April 10 and 11, 1916, and again on April 27, 1917.[75] Apparently, Justice Holmes's view after the first argument was that the case should be dismissed because it was a collusive lawsuit.[76] As evidence that no good deed goes unpunished, Mr. Warley was fired from his job because of his involvement in this case.[77] The case against the ordinance was argued by Moorfield Storey, one of the most distinguished lawyers in the United States at the time, the first president of the NAACP, and counsel for the NAACP in five of its first cases before the U.S. Supreme Court.[78] (Storey was white.[79]) Among the several amicus briefs was one by Mr. W. Ashbie Hawkins on behalf of the Baltimore Branch of the NAACP.

---

73. Berman v. Parker, 348 U.S. 26, 32 (1954).

74. Susan D. Carle, *From* Buchanan *to* Button: *Legal Ethics and the NAACP (Part II)*, 8 U. CHI. L. SCH. ROUNDTABLE 281, 283 (2001) (to create the right circumstances for this test case, a national staff lawyer organized a new Louisville NAACP chapter, spoke at public meetings to raise money and recruit litigants, and drafted test language for a real estate contract).

75. Benno C. Schmidt Jr., *Principle and Prejudice: The Supreme Court and Race in the Progressive Era. Part I: The Heyday of Jim Crow*, 82 COLUM. L. REV. 444, 498-99 (1982).

76. Carle, *supra* note 74, at 284.

77. Susan D. Carle, *Race, Class, and Legal Ethics in the Early NAACP (1910-1920)*, 20 LAW & HIST. REV. 97, 127-28 (2002); *id.* at 133 n.132 (describing William Warley's act of courage in agreeing to serve as defendant, an act that cost Warley his employment at the local post office); *see also* Carle, *supra* note 74, at 283-84; Susan D. Carle, DEFINING THE STRUGGLE: NATIONAL ORGANIZING FOR RACIAL JUSTICE, 1880-1915, at 279, 286, 289 (Oxford U. Press 2013).

78. Storey, heir to the Conscience Whigs of Massachusetts, was Secretary to Senator Charles Sumner during Reconstruction. William B. Hixon, Jr., MOORFIELD STOREY AND THE ABOLITIONIST TRADITION 8-11 (1972); Richard Kluger, SIMPLE JUSTICE: THE HISTORY OF *BROWN v. BOARD OF EDUCATION* AND BLACK AMERICA'S STRUGGLE FOR EQUALITY 164 (Alfred A. Knopf 1975); *see also* Kluger at 119, 122, 129, 135, 141-42, 147, 152, 155; B. Joyce Ross, J.E. SPINGARN AND THE RISE OF THE NAACP 57-58 (1972).

79. On the shift to Black lawyers as counsel in civil rights cases, see Kenneth W. Mack, REPRESENTING THE RACE: THE CREATION OF THE CIVIL RIGHTS LAWYER (Harvard U. Press 2012).

7. *Buchanan v. Warley's* **Impact.** Despite the decision in *Buchanan v. Warley*, states and cities continued to enact racial zoning ordinances, even though the Supreme Court invalidated racial zoning again in 1927 and 1930.[80] Professor Klarman writes:

> *Buchanan* notwithstanding, urban housing became vastly more segregated. In the deep south, legal regulation was plainly unnecessary to maintain residential segregation. Blacks in cities such as Birmingham, Alabama, knew better than to enter white neighborhoods uninvited. As one southern newspaper put it, "there may be no written law saying where a negro shall live and where a white man shall live, but in a white man's town there need be no law, because the negroes cannot mix with the whites."[81]

As late as 1950, a racial zoning ordinance in Birmingham, Alabama, was the subject of a divided federal appellate decision,[82] and as late as 2005 there were press reports of laypersons' understandings that certain areas were "zoned 'for whites only.'"[83] Why do you think the impact of explicit racial zoning lasted for so long?

8. **"Use" or Euclidean Zoning.** Municipalities can employ their zoning power to regulate the uses to which land can be put. This power allows a city to limit minority groups' access to housing in various indirect ways, most commonly by prohibiting or restricting multifamily, clustered, or small lot housing that might be more affordable than large-lot, single-family homes. The seminal case upholding use zoning was *Euclid v. Ambler Realty* in 1926. The Supreme Court's reasoning focused on the advantages of "excluding from residential districts apartment houses, business houses, retail stores and shops, and other like establishments." Relying on the law of nuisance, the Court gave the legislature great deference, stating: "A nuisance may be merely a right thing in the wrong place, like a pig in the parlor instead of the barnyard. If the validity of the legislative classification for zoning purposes be fairly debatable, the legislative judgment must be allowed to control." The Court said that "the village, though physically a suburb of Cleveland, is politically a separate municipality, with powers of its own and authority to govern itself as it sees fit, within the limits of the organic law of its creation and the state and federal Constitutions."

The district court in Ambler Realty Co. v. Village of Euclid, 297 F. 307, 312-13 (N.D. Ohio 1924), had invalidated the zoning ordinance, in part on the basis that it was inconsistent with *Buchanan v. Warley*:

> It seems to me that no candid mind can deny that more and stronger reasons exist, having a real and substantial relation to the public peace, supporting such

---

80. Harmon v. Tyler, 273 U.S. 668 (1927); City of Richmond v. Deans, 281 U.S. 704 (1930).

81. Klarman, *supra* note 1, at 90.

82. City of Birmingham v. Monk, 185 F.2d 859 (5th Cir. 1950), *cert. denied*, 341 U.S. 940 (1951); *see* J. Mills Thornton III, DIVIDING LINES: MUNICIPAL POLITICS AND THE STRUGGLE FOR CIVIL RIGHTS IN MONTGOMERY, BIRMINGHAM, AND SELMA 158-64 (U. Ala. Press 2002).

83. Motoko Rich, *Restrictive Covenants Stubbornly Stay on the Books*, NY TIMES, Apr. 20, 2005, at D1.

an ordinance than can be urged under any aspect of the police power to support the present ordinance as applied to plaintiff's property. And no gift of second sight is required to foresee that if this Kentucky statute had been sustained, its provisions would have spread from city to city throughout the length and breadth of the land. And it is equally apparent that the next step in the exercise of this police power would be to apply similar restrictions for the purpose of segregating in like manner various groups of newly arrived immigrants. The blighting of property values and the congesting of population, whenever the colored or certain foreign races invade a residential section, are so well known as to be within the judicial cognizance.

But the Supreme Court in *Euclid v. Ambler* upheld the zoning ordinance and did not mention *Buchanan v. Warley*, thus enabling jurisdictions to employ use zoning to create and perpetuate racially segregated communities.

C. RACIAL COVENANTS

Those who sought the segregative results of racial zoning developed alternatives to it. Racial covenants existed before *Buchanan v. Warley*, but they certainly became more popular after the decision in *Buchanan*. Moreover, to a considerable extent, Euclidean, or use, zoning proliferated because explicit racial zoning was being invalidated and use zoning could accomplish the same purposes without directly referencing race.[84]

In *Gandolfo v. Hartman* (1892), a California federal court invalidated a racial restriction against Chinese renters on grounds of the Fourteenth Amendment and a treaty between the United States and China.[85] In that same year, 1892, when developers in the Baltimore suburbs first tried to ban Black people from purchasing or living in the homes the developers were producing, Maryland legal experts said that such restraints would be unlawful, so the developers used restrictions that made the homes more expensive, which would indirectly exclude many Black people.[86] In 1907, a developer in Kansas City used deed restrictions that explicitly forbade home sales to Black people; in 1908, bans on sales or occupancy by Black people were imposed by the influential developer J.C. Nichols.[87] By 1913, without legal objection, the Maryland developers used explicit racial covenants to accomplish that result directly.[88] Like racial zoning, racial covenants were rooted in nuisance law.[89]

The next two cases are canonical decisions about racial covenants.

---

84. Freund, *supra* note 1, at 47-49.
85. Gandolfo v. Hartman, 49 F. 181 (S.D. Cal. 1892).
86. Glotzer, *supra* note 8, at 52-54.
87. Worley, *supra* note 9, at 129-33 (discussing use of the "standard" restriction against sale to or occupancy by Black people).
88. Glotzer, *supra* note 8, at 85, 88-89, 93-95.
89. Nayan Shah, Contagious Divides: Epidemics and Race in San Francisco's Chinatown 73 (U. Cal. Press 2001) (stating that "the rationale of nuisance law underwrote the cultural logic of residential covenants").

Shelley v. Kraemer
334 U.S. 1 (1948)

Before Chief Justice Vinson and Justices Black, Frankfurter, Douglas, Murphy, and Burton; Justices Reed, Jackson, and Rutledge took no part in the consideration or decision of this case.[90]

Mr. Chief Justice VINSON delivered the opinion of the Court.

These cases present for our consideration questions relating to the validity of court enforcement of private agreements, generally described as restrictive covenants, which have as their purpose the exclusion of persons of designated race or color from the ownership or occupancy of real property.

The first of these cases comes [from] Missouri. On February 16, 1911, thirty out of a total of thirty-nine owners of property fronting both sides of Labadie Avenue between Taylor Avenue and Cora Avenue in St. Louis, signed an agreement, which was subsequently recorded, providing in part:

> . . . the said property is hereby restricted to the use and occupancy for the term of Fifty (50) years from this date, so that it shall be a condition all the time and whether recited and referred to as [sic] not in subsequent conveyances and shall attach to the land, as a condition precedent to the sale of the same, that hereafter no part of said property or any portion thereof shall be, for said term of Fifty-years, occupied by any person not of the Caucasian race. . . .

The entire district described in the agreement included fifty-seven parcels of land. The thirty owners who signed the agreement held title to forty-seven parcels, including the particular parcel involved in this case. At the time the agreement was signed, five of the parcels in the district were owned by Negroes. One of those had been occupied by Negro families since 1882, nearly thirty years before the restrictive agreement was executed. The trial court found that owners of seven out of nine homes on the south side of Labadie Avenue, within the restricted district and "in the immediate vicinity" of the premises in question, had failed to sign the restrictive agreement in 1911. At the time this action was brought, four of the premises were occupied by Negroes, and had been so occupied for periods ranging from twenty-three to sixty-three years. A fifth parcel had been occupied by Negroes until a year before this suit was instituted.

On August 11, 1945, pursuant to a contract of sale, petitioners Shelley, who are Negroes, for valuable consideration received from one Fitzgerald a warranty deed to the parcel in question. The trial court found that

---

90. [EDS.—Justices Reed, Jackson, and Rutledge did not participate, "reportedly because each of them owned property which was covered by a restrictive covenant." C. Herman Pritchett, CIVIL LIBERTIES AND THE VINSON COURT 142 (U. Chicago Press 1954); *see also* Clement E. Vose, CAUCASIANS ONLY: THE SUPREME COURT, THE NAACP, AND THE RESTRICTIVE COVENANT CASES 9-10 (U. Cal. Press 1959).]

petitioners had no actual knowledge of the restrictive agreement at the time of the purchase.

On October 9, 1945, respondents, as owners of other property subject to the terms of the restrictive covenant, brought suit . . . praying that petitioners Shelley be restrained from taking possession of the property and that judgment be entered divesting title out of petitioners Shelley and revesting title in the immediate grantor or in such other person as the court should direct. The trial court denied the requested relief. . . .

[T]he Supreme Court of Missouri sitting en banc reversed and directed the trial court to grant the relief for which respondents had prayed. [The discussion of the companion Michigan case is omitted.]

I.

Whether the equal protection clause of the Fourteenth Amendment inhibits judicial enforcement by state courts of restrictive covenants based on race or color is a question which this Court has not heretofore been called upon to consider. Only two cases have been decided by this Court which in any way have involved the enforcement of such agreements. The first of these was the case of Corrigan v. Buckley, 271 U.S. 323 (1926). There, suit was brought in the District of Columbia to enjoin a threatened violation of certain restrictive covenants. Relief was granted, and the case was brought here on appeal. It is apparent that that case, which had originated in the federal courts and involved the enforcement of covenants on land located in the District of Columbia, could present no issues under the Fourteenth Amendment; for that Amendment by its terms applies only to the States. Nor was the question of the validity of court enforcement of the restrictive covenants under the Fifth Amendment properly before the Court, as the opinion of this Court specifically recognizes. The only constitutional issue which the appellants had raised in the lower courts, and hence the only constitutional issue before this Court on appeal, was the validity of the covenant agreements as such. This Court concluded that since the inhibitions of the constitutional provisions invoked apply only to governmental action, as contrasted to action of private individuals, there was no showing that the covenants, which were simply agreements between private property owners, were invalid. Accordingly, the appeal was dismissed for want of a substantial question. Nothing in the opinion of this Court, therefore, may properly be regarded as an adjudication on the merits of the constitutional issues presented by these cases, which raise the question of the validity, not of the private agreements as such, but of the judicial enforcement of those agreements.

The second of the cases involving racial restrictive covenants was Hansberry v. Lee, 311 U.S. 32 (1940). In that case, petitioners, white property owners, were enjoined by the state courts from violating the terms of a restrictive agreement. The state Supreme Court had held petitioners bound by an earlier judicial determination in litigation [deemed a class action but] in which petitioners were not parties, upholding the validity of the restrictive agreement, although, in fact, the agreement had not been signed by the number of owners necessary to make it effective under state law. This Court reversed the judgment of the state Supreme Court upon the ground that petitioners had been denied due process of law in being held estopped to challenge the validity of the agreement. In arriving at its result, this Court did not reach the issues presented by the cases now under consideration.

It is well, at the outset, to scrutinize the terms of the restrictive agreements involved in these cases. In the Missouri case, the covenant declares that no part of the affected property shall be "occupied by any person not of the Caucasian race, it being intended hereby to restrict the use of said property . . . against the occupancy as owners or tenants of any portion of said property for resident or other purpose by people of the Negro or Mongolian Race." Not only does the restriction seek to proscribe use and occupancy of the affected properties by members of the excluded class, but as construed by the Missouri courts, the agreement requires that title of any person who uses his property in violation of the restriction shall be divested. It should be observed that these covenants do not seek to proscribe any particular use of the affected properties. Use of the properties for residential occupancy, as such, is not forbidden. The restrictions of these agreements, rather, are directed toward a designated class of persons and seek to determine who may and who may not own or make use of the properties for residential purposes. The excluded class is defined wholly in terms of race or color, "simply that and nothing more."

It cannot be doubted that among the civil rights intended to be protected from discriminatory state action by the Fourteenth Amendment are the rights to acquire, enjoy, own and dispose of property. Equality in the enjoyment of property rights was regarded by the framers of that Amendment as an essential pre-condition to the realization of other basic civil rights and liberties which the Amendment was intended to guarantee. Thus, §1978 of the Revised Statutes, derived from §1 of the Civil Rights Act of 1866 which was enacted by Congress while the Fourteenth Amendment was also under consideration, provides:

> All citizens of the United States shall have the same right, in every State and Territory, as is enjoyed by white citizens thereof to inherit, purchase, lease, sell, hold, and convey real and personal property.

This Court has given specific recognition to the same principle. *Buchanan v. Warley.*

It is likewise clear that restrictions on the right of occupancy of the sort sought to be created by the private agreements in these cases could not be squared with the requirements of the Fourteenth Amendment if imposed by state statute or local ordinance. We do not understand respondents to urge the contrary. In the case of *Buchanan v. Warley* a unanimous Court declared unconstitutional the provisions of a city ordinance which denied to colored persons the right to occupy houses in blocks in which the greater number of houses were occupied by white persons. . . .

In Harmon v. Tyler, 273 U.S. 668 (1927), a unanimous court, on the authority of *Buchanan v. Warley*, declared invalid an ordinance which forbade any Negro to establish a home on any property in a white community or any white person to establish a home in a Negro community, "except on the written consent of a majority of the persons of the opposite race inhabiting such community or portion of the City to be affected."

The precise question before this Court in both the *Buchanan* and *Harmon* cases involved the rights of white sellers to dispose of their properties free from restrictions as to potential purchasers based on considerations of race or color. But that such legislation is also offensive to the rights of those desiring to acquire and occupy property and barred on grounds of race or color is clear, not only from the language of the opinion in *Buchanan v. Warley*, but from this Court's disposition of the case of Richmond v. Deans, 281 U.S. 704 (1930). There, a Negro, barred from the occupancy of certain property by the terms of an ordinance similar to that in the *Buchanan* case, sought injunctive relief in the federal courts to enjoin the enforcement of the ordinance on the grounds that its provisions violated the terms of the Fourteenth Amendment. Such relief was granted, and this Court affirmed, finding the citation of *Buchanan v. Warley* and *Harmon v. Tyler* sufficient to support its judgment.

But the present cases, unlike those just discussed, do not involve action by state legislatures or city councils. Here the particular patterns of discrimination and the areas in which the restrictions are to operate, are determined, in the first instance, by the terms of agreements among private individuals. Participation of the State consists in the enforcement of the restrictions so defined. The crucial issue with which we are here confronted is whether this distinction removes these cases from the operation of the prohibitory provisions of the Fourteenth Amendment.

Since the decision of this Court in the Civil Rights Cases, 109 U.S. 3 (1883), the principle has become firmly embedded in our constitutional law that the action inhibited by the first section of the Fourteenth Amendment is only such action as may fairly be said to be that of the States. That Amendment erects no shield against merely private conduct, however discriminatory or wrongful.

We conclude, therefore, that the restrictive agreements standing alone cannot be regarded as a violation of any rights guaranteed to petitioners by the Fourteenth Amendment. So long as the purposes of those agreements are effectuated by voluntary adherence to their terms, it would appear clear that there has been no action by the State and the provisions of the Amendment have not been violated.

But here there was more. These are cases in which the purposes of the agreements were secured only by judicial enforcement by state courts of the restrictive terms of the agreements. The respondents urge that judicial enforcement of private agreements does not amount to state action; or, in any event, the participation of the State is so attenuated in character as not to amount to state action within the meaning of the Fourteenth Amendment. Finally, it is suggested, even if the States in these cases may be deemed to have acted in the constitutional sense, their action did not deprive petitioners of rights guaranteed by the Fourteenth Amendment. We move to a consideration of these matters.

II.

That the action of state courts and of judicial officers in their official capacities is to be regarded as action of the State within the meaning of the Fourteenth Amendment, is a proposition which has long been established by decisions of this Court. That principle was given expression in the earliest cases involving the construction of the terms of the Fourteenth Amendment. . . . In the *Civil Rights Cases*, this Court pointed out that the Amendment makes void "State action of every kind" which is inconsistent with the guaranties therein contained, and extends to manifestations of "State authority in the shape of laws, customs, or judicial or executive proceedings."

Similar expressions, giving specific recognition to the fact that judicial action is to be regarded as action of the State for the purposes of the Fourteenth Amendment, are to be found in numerous cases which have been more recently decided. . . .

One of the earliest applications of the prohibitions contained in the Fourteenth Amendment to action of state judicial officials occurred in cases in which Negroes had been excluded from jury service in criminal prosecutions by reason of their race or color. . . . Thus, in Strauder v. West Virginia, 100 U.S. 303 (1880), this Court declared invalid a state statute restricting jury service to white persons as amounting to a denial of the equal protection of the laws to the colored defendant in that case. . . . Ex parte Virginia, [100 U.S. 339 (1880)] held that a similar discrimination imposed by the action of a state judge denied rights protected by the Amendment. . . .

In numerous cases, this Court has reversed criminal convictions in state courts for failure of those courts to provide the essential ingredients of a fair hearing. . . . But the examples of state judicial action which have been held by this Court to violate the Amendment's commands are not restricted to situations in which the judicial proceedings were found in some manner to be procedurally unfair. It has been recognized that the action of state courts in enforcing a substantive common-law rule formulated by those courts may result in the denial of rights guaranteed by the Fourteenth Amendment, even though the judicial proceedings in such cases may have been in complete accord with the most rigorous conceptions of procedural due process.

The short of the matter is that from the time of the adoption of the Fourteenth Amendment until the present, it has been the consistent ruling of this Court that the action of the States to which the Amendment has reference, includes action of state courts and state judicial officials. . . .

III.

Against this background of judicial construction, extending over a period of some three-quarters of a century, we are called upon to consider whether enforcement by state courts of the restrictive agreements in these cases may be deemed to be the acts of those States; and, if so, whether that action has denied these petitioners the equal protection of the laws which the Amendment was intended to insure.

We have no doubt that there has been state action in these cases in the full and complete sense of the phrase. The undisputed facts disclose that petitioners were willing purchasers of properties upon which they desired to establish homes. The owners of the properties were willing sellers; and contracts of sale were accordingly consummated. It is clear that but for the active intervention of the state courts, supported by the full panoply of state power, petitioners would have been free to occupy the properties in question without restraint.

These are not cases, as has been suggested, in which the States have merely abstained from action, leaving private individuals free to impose such discriminations as they see fit. Rather, these are cases in which the States have made available to such individuals the full coercive power of government to deny to petitioners, on the grounds of race or color, the enjoyment of property rights in premises which petitioners are willing and financially able to acquire and which the grantors are willing to sell. The difference between judicial enforcement and nonenforcement of the restrictive covenants is the difference to petitioners between being denied rights of property available to other members of the community and being accorded full enjoyment of those rights on an equal footing.

The enforcement of the restrictive agreements by the state courts in these cases was directed pursuant to the common-law policy of the States as formulated by those courts in earlier decisions. In the Missouri case, enforcement of the covenant was directed in the first instance by the highest court of the State after the trial court had determined the agreement to be invalid for want of the requisite number of signatures. The judicial action in each case bears the clear and unmistakable imprimatur of the State. We have noted that previous decisions of this Court have established the proposition that judicial action is not immunized from the operation of the Fourteenth Amendment simply because it is taken pursuant to the state's common-law policy. Nor is the Amendment ineffective simply because the particular pattern of discrimination, which the State has enforced, was defined initially by the terms of a private agreement. State action, as that phrase is understood for the purposes of the Fourteenth Amendment, refers to exertions of state power in all forms. And when the effect of that action is to deny rights subject to the protection of the Fourteenth Amendment, it is the obligation of this Court to enforce the constitutional commands.

We hold that in granting judicial enforcement of the restrictive agreements in these cases, the States have denied petitioners the equal protection of the laws and that, therefore, the action of the state courts cannot stand. We have noted that freedom from discrimination by the States in the enjoyment of property rights was among the basic objectives sought to be effectuated by the framers of the Fourteenth Amendment. That such discrimination has occurred in these cases is clear. Because of the race or color of these petitioners they have been denied rights of ownership or occupancy enjoyed as a matter of course by other citizens of different race or color. The Fourteenth Amendment declares "that all persons, whether colored or white, shall stand equal before the laws of the States, and, in regard to the colored race, for whose protection the amendment was primarily designed, that no discrimination shall be made against them by law because of their color." *Strauder v. West Virginia.*

Only recently this Court has had occasion to declare that a state law which denied equal enjoyment of property rights to a designated class of citizens of specified race and ancestry, was not a legitimate exercise of the state's police power but violated the guaranty of the equal protection of the laws. *Oyama v. California.* Nor may the discriminations imposed by the state courts in these cases be justified as proper exertions of state police power. Cf. *Buchanan v. Warley.*

Respondents urge, however, that since the state courts stand ready to enforce restrictive covenants excluding white persons from the ownership or occupancy of property covered by such agreements, enforcement of covenants excluding colored persons may not be deemed a denial of equal protection of the laws to the colored persons who are thereby affected. This contention does not bear scrutiny. The parties have directed our attention to no case in which a court, state or federal, has been called upon to enforce a covenant excluding members of the white majority from ownership or occupancy of real property on grounds of race or color. But there are more fundamental considerations. The rights created by the first section of the Fourteenth Amendment are, by its terms, guaranteed to the individual. The rights established are personal rights. It is, therefore, no answer to these petitioners to say that the courts may also be induced to deny white persons rights of ownership and occupancy on grounds of race or color. Equal protection of the laws is not achieved through indiscriminate imposition of inequalities.

Nor do we find merit in the suggestion that property owners who are parties to these agreements are denied equal protection of the laws if denied access to the courts to enforce the terms of restrictive covenants and to assert property rights which the state courts have held to be created by such agreements. The Constitution confers upon no individual the right to demand action by the State which results in the denial of equal protection of the laws to other individuals. And it would appear beyond question that the power of the State to create and enforce property interests must be exercised within the boundaries defined by the Fourteenth Amendment.

The problem of defining the scope of the restrictions which the Federal Constitution imposes upon exertions of power by the States has given rise to many of the most persistent and fundamental issues which this Court has been called upon to consider. That problem was foremost in the minds of the framers of the Constitution, and since that early day, has arisen in a multitude of forms. The task of determining whether the action of a State offends constitutional provisions is one which may not be undertaken lightly. Where, however, it is clear that the action of the State violates the terms of the fundamental charter, it is the obligation of this Court so to declare.

The historical context in which the Fourteenth Amendment became a part of the Constitution should not be forgotten. Whatever else the framers sought to achieve, it is clear that the matter of primary concern was the establishment of equality in the enjoyment of basic civil and political rights and the preservation of those rights from discriminatory action on the part of the States based on considerations of race or color. Seventy-five years ago this Court announced that the provisions of the Amendment are to be construed with this fundamental purpose in mind. Upon full consideration, we have concluded that in these cases the States have acted to deny petitioners the equal protection of the laws guaranteed by the Fourteenth Amendment. Having so decided, we find it unnecessary to consider whether petitioners have also been deprived of property without due process of law or denied privileges and immunities of citizens of the United States.

Hurd v. Hodge
334 U.S. 24 (1948)

Before Chief Justice Vinson and Justices Black, Frankfurter, Douglas, Murphy, and Burton; Justices Reed, Jackson, and Rutledge took no part in the consideration or decision of this case.

Mr. Chief Justice VINSON delivered the opinion of the Court.

These are companion cases to *Shelley v. Kraemer* and *McGhee v. Sipes*.

In 1906, twenty of thirty-one lots in the 100 block of Bryant Street, Northwest, in the City of Washington, were sold subject to the following covenant:

> . . . that said lot shall never be rented, leased, sold, transferred or conveyed unto any Negro or colored person, under a penalty of Two Thousand Dollars ($2,000), which shall be a lien against said property.

Prior to the sales which gave rise to these cases, the twenty lots which are subject to the covenants were at all times owned and occupied by white persons, except for a brief period when three of the houses were occupied by Negroes who were eventually induced to move without legal action. The remaining eleven lots in the same block, however, are not subject to a restrictive agreement and were occupied by Negroes for the twenty years prior to the institution of this litigation.

Whether judicial enforcement of racial restrictive agreements by the federal courts of the District of Columbia violates the Fifth Amendment has never been adjudicated by this Court. In *Corrigan v. Buckley*, 1926, the only constitutional question before this Court related to the validity of the private agreements as such. Nothing in the opinion of this Court in that case, therefore, may properly be regarded as an adjudication of the issue presented in this case which concerns, not the validity of the restrictive agreements standing alone, but the validity of court enforcement of the restrictive covenants under the due process clause of the Fifth Amendment.

This Court has declared invalid municipal ordinances restricting occupancy in designated areas to persons of specified race and color as denying rights of white sellers and Negro purchasers of property, guaranteed by the due process clause of the Fourteenth Amendment. *Buchanan v. Warley; Harmon v. Tyler; City of Richmond v. Deans*. Petitioners urge that judicial enforcement of the restrictive covenants by courts of the District of Columbia should likewise be held to deny rights of white sellers and Negro purchasers of property, guaranteed by the due process clause of the Fifth Amendment.

Upon full consideration, however, we have found it unnecessary to resolve the constitutional issue which petitioners advance; for we have concluded that judicial enforcement of restrictive covenants by the courts of the District of Columbia is improper for other reasons. . . .

Section 1978 of the Revised Statutes, derived from §1 of the Civil Rights Act of 1866, provides:

> All citizens of the United States shall have the same right, in every State and Territory, as is enjoyed by white citizens thereof to inherit, purchase, lease, sell, hold, and convey real and personal property.[91]

All the petitioners in these cases are citizens of the United States. We have no doubt that, for the purposes of this section, the District of Columbia is included within the phrase "every State and Territory." Nor can there be doubt of the constitutional power of Congress to enact such legislation with reference to the District of Columbia.

We may start with the proposition that the statute does not invalidate private restrictive agreements so long as the purposes of those agreements are achieved by the parties through voluntary adherence to the terms. The action toward which the provisions of the statute under consideration is directed is governmental action. . . .

In considering whether judicial enforcement of restrictive covenants is the kind of governmental action which the first section of the Civil Rights Act of 1866 was intended to prohibit, reference must be made to the scope and purposes of the Fourteenth Amendment; for that statute and the Amendment

---

91. [Eds.—This is now 42 U.S.C. §1982.]

were closely related both in inception and in the objectives which Congress sought to achieve.

Both the Civil Rights Act of 1866 and the joint resolution which was later adopted as the Fourteenth Amendment were passed in the first session of the Thirty-Ninth Congress. Frequent references to the Civil Rights Act are to be found in the record of the legislative debates on the adoption of the Amendment. It is clear that in many significant respects the statute and the Amendment were expressions of the same general congressional policy. Indeed, as the legislative debates reveal, one of the primary purposes of many members of Congress in supporting the adoption of the Fourteenth Amendment was to incorporate the guaranties of the Civil Rights Act of 1866 in the organic law of the land. Others supported the adoption of the Amendment in order to eliminate doubt as to the constitutional validity of the Civil Rights Act as applied to the States.

The close relationship between §1 of the Civil Rights Act and the Fourteenth Amendment was given specific recognition by this Court in *Buchanan v. Warley*. There, the Court observed that, not only through the operation of the Fourteenth Amendment, but also by virtue of the "statutes enacted in furtherance of its purpose," including the provisions here considered, a colored man is granted the right to acquire property free from interference by discriminatory state legislation. In *Shelley v. Kraemer*, we have held that the Fourteenth Amendment also forbids such discrimination where imposed by state courts in the enforcement of restrictive covenants. That holding is clearly indicative of the construction to be given to the relevant provisions of the Civil Rights Act in their application to the Courts of the District of Columbia.

Moreover, the explicit language employed by Congress to effectuate its purposes leaves no doubt that judicial enforcement of the restrictive covenants by the courts of the District of Columbia is prohibited by the Civil Rights Act. That statute, by its terms, requires that all citizens of the United States shall have the same right "as is enjoyed by white citizens . . . to inherit, purchase, lease, sell, hold, and convey real and personal property." That the Negro petitioners have been denied that right by virtue of the action of the federal courts of the District is clear. The Negro petitioners entered into contracts of sale with willing sellers for the purchase of properties upon which they desired to establish homes. Solely because of their race and color they are confronted with orders of court divesting their titles in the properties and ordering that the premises be vacated. White sellers, one of whom is a petitioner here, have been enjoined from selling the properties to any Negro or colored person. Under such circumstances, to suggest that the Negro petitioners have been accorded the same rights as white citizens to purchase, hold, and convey real property is to reject the plain meaning of language. We hold that the action of the District Court directed against the Negro purchasers and the white sellers denies rights intended by Congress to be protected by the Civil Rights Act and that, consequently, the action cannot stand.

But even in the absence of the statute, there are other considerations which would indicate that enforcement of restrictive covenants in these cases is judicial action contrary to the public policy of the United States, and as such should be corrected by this Court in the exercise of its supervisory powers over the courts of the District of Columbia. The power of the federal courts to enforce the terms of private agreements is at all times exercised subject to the restrictions and limitations of the public policy of the United States as manifested in the Constitution, treaties, federal statutes, and applicable legal precedents. Where the enforcement of private agreements would be violative of that policy, it is the obligation of courts to refrain from such exertions of judicial power.

We are here concerned with action of federal courts of such a nature that if taken by the courts of a State would violate the prohibitory provisions of the Fourteenth Amendment. *Shelley v. Kraemer.* It is not consistent with the public policy of the United States to permit federal courts in the Nation's capital to exercise general equitable powers to compel action denied the state courts where such state action has been held to be violative of the guaranty of the equal protection of the laws. We cannot presume that the public policy of the United States manifests a lesser concern for the protection of such basic rights against discriminatory action of federal courts than against such action taken by the courts of the States.

NOTES AND QUESTIONS

1. **Companion Cases, Different Bases for Decision.** Why are there two decisions about judicial enforcement of racially restrictive covenants? What are the different bases for the holdings in the two cases? How might the two have been decided on the same basis?

2. **Avoiding a Constitutional Decision in *Hurd v. Hodge*.** The Court avoided deciding *Hurd v. Hodge* on constitutional grounds, but was not able to escape a constitutional ruling about the Fifth Amendment when it addressed *Bolling v. Sharpe*, the District of Columbia companion case to *Brown v. Board*, in 1954. What do you think was the best basis for decision in *Hurd v. Hodge*? Why? If the Court did not decide the case on that basis, why do you think it did not do so?

3. **Covenants in the District of Columbia.** In the two decades before *Hurd v. Hodge* went to the D.C. Circuit, that court heard seven racial covenant cases, more than any other appellate court.[92] Of the 12 judges who heard those cases, two ruled against the covenants: Wiley B. Rutledge (who later ascended to the Supreme Court) and Henry W. Edgerton.[93] Then-Judge Rutledge's

---

92. Vose, *supra* note 90, at 93.
93. *Id.* at 93; *see* John M. Ferren, SALT OF THE EARTH, CONSCIENCE OF THE COURT: THE STORY OF JUSTICE WILEY RUTLEDGE (UNC Press 2004).

disagreement with his colleagues in a 1942 case was diffidently expressed, but Judge Edgerton penned two powerful dissents in *Mays v. Burgess* in 1945 (initially and on rehearing).[94] *Mays v. Burgess* "was something of a *cause célèbre* in Washington during World War II, and Edgerton's forceful dissents stimulated interest in the whole problem of discrimination in housing."[95] Judge Edgerton then was on the panel in *Hurd v. Hodge,* and wrote an even stronger dissent.[96] Judge Edgerton, who had studied at Wisconsin, Cornell, and the University of Paris as well as Harvard Law School, had taught at Cornell Law School; he was extremely influential with the Supreme Court, which "commonly granted certiorari in cases where Edgerton dissented," and reversed in 17 of 23 cases in which he had dissented.[97]

4. **Counsel in the Cases.** The lawyers for the petitioners in *Shelley* and *Hurd* include several names well known in civil rights history, and more that are not but deserve to be. The lawyers who argued *Shelley* itself, from Missouri, were George L. Vaughn and Herman Willer. Vaughn, the son of an enslaved person, was a St. Louis lawyer active in the NAACP.[98] Herman Willer was "an influential white lawyer . . . [who] had joined Vaughn. . . ."[99] The companion case from Michigan had been handled by two Black Michigan lawyers, Willis M. Graves and Francis Morse Dent.[100] They litigated the case through the Michigan Supreme Court, but when the Supreme Court granted certiorari, they ceded control of the case to the national NAACP, with argument to be presented by Thurgood Marshall and Loren Miller.[101] Thurgood Marshall, of course, served as Director-Counsel of the NAACP Legal and Educational Defense Fund (LDF), then on the U.S. Court of Appeals for the Second Circuit, then as the first Black Solicitor General, and then as the first Black justice on the U.S. Supreme Court.[102] Loren Miller was a California

---

94. Mays v. Burgess, 147 F.2d 869 (D.C. Cir. 1945).

95. Vose, *supra* note 90, at 93-94.

96. *Id.* at 95.

97. *Id.* at 99, 157.

98. Mark V. Tushnet, MAKING CIVIL RIGHTS LAW: THURGOOD MARSHALL AND THE SUPREME COURT, 1956-1961, at 90 (Oxford U. Press 1994); Vose, *supra* note 90, at 121. For a discussion of the oral argument, *see id.* at 199-205.

99. Peter Irons, THE COURAGE OF THEIR CONVICTIONS: SIXTEEN AMERICANS WHO FOUGHT THEIR WAY TO THE SUPREME COURT 71 (Penguin 1991); Vose, *supra* note 90, at 160.

100. Graves held an LL.B. from Howard Law School and was active in the NAACP and the National Association of Real Estate Brokers (NAREB). NAREB was founded as a civil rights advocacy organization for Black real estate professionals, consumers, and communities in the United States. (In contrast, the National Organization of Real Estate Boards was all white). Dent had attended Amherst College with Charles Hamilton Houston and then the Detroit College of Law. Both were members of the NAACP National Legal Committee. Vose, *supra* note 90, at 122, 127; Smith, *supra* note 68, at 579.

101. Vose, *supra* note 90, at 158-59.

102. Justice Marshall is the subject of several biographies; *see, e.g.,* Tushnet, *supra* note 98; Mark V. Tushnet, MAKING CONSTITUTIONAL LAW: THURGOOD MARSHALL AND THE SUPREME COURT, 1961-1991 (Oxford U. Press 1997).

lawyer and journalist—"the best civil-rights lawyer on the West Coast"—who battled unrelentingly against racial covenants.[103]

The lawyers who were on the briefs with Marshall and Miller were William H. Hastie, Spottswood W. Robinson, III, Charles Hamilton Houston, William R. Ming, Jr., James M. Nabrit, Jr., Marian Wynn Perry, Ruth Weyand, Andrew Weinberger, and George M. Johnson.[104] William H. Hastie and Spottswood W. Robinson, III became distinguished federal appellate judges.[105] James Madison Nabrit, Jr. was a "pioneer voting rights lawyer in Texas" and Oklahoma and then joined the faculty at Howard Law School, where he introduced the first course in civil rights ever taught in a U.S. law school. He later was lead counsel in *Bolling v. Sharpe*, the Washington, DC, school desegregation case that was a companion to *Brown v. Board*.[106] Charles Hamilton Houston, who also was one of the counsel who argued *Hurd v. Hodge*, was Thurgood Marshall's teacher and mentor and the former Vice Dean of Howard Law School.[107] He was a leading force in developing civil rights law and Howard Law School. William Robert Ming, Jr. taught at Howard Law School (1937-1942) and then the University of Chicago Law School (1947); he also was one of the small first group of Black lawyers sworn in to the Army Judge Advocate General Corps (in 1942). He was "the first black [person] to publish a lead article in the *University of Chicago Law Review*."[108]

---

103. Smith, *supra* note 68, at 487, 489, 501, 519; Amina Hassan, LOREN MILLER: CIVIL RIGHTS ATTORNEY AND JOURNALIST (U. Okla. Press 2014); Kluger, *supra* note 78, at 253 ("the best . . ."). There had been movement against racial covenants in California: Justice Roger Traynor had dissented in Fairchild v. Raines, 24 Cal. 2d 818 (Cal. 1944) and in 1946 the state Attorney General had participated amicus curiae attacking such covenants. Vose, *supra* note 90, at 153-54.

104. Vose, *supra* note 90, at 186.

105. Gilbert Ware, WILLIAM HASTIE: GRACE UNDER PRESSURE (Oxford U. Press 1984). Hastie, who was Charles Hamilton Houston's cousin, earned an A.B. from Amherst College (magna cum laude and Phi Beta Kappa) and an LL.B. and S.J.D. from Harvard (where he was a member of the law review); he was Dean of Howard Law School, the first Black federal judge (appointed to the District Court of the Virgin Islands) and the Governor of the Virgin Islands and later a judge on the U.S. Court of Appeals for the Third Circuit. Robinson graduated from Howard Law School in 1939 and promptly joined the faculty there. Tushnet, *supra*, note 98, at 72. As "the brainiest and most painstaking of the younger Howard law graduates," he also worked on the brief in *Hurd* and many other important cases handled by the NAACP LDF. Kluger, *supra* note 78, at 253. Robinson later was named to the U.S. Court of Appeals for the District of Columbia Circuit.

106. Nabrit earned his law degree at Northwestern, where he was the first Black student elected to the Order of the Coif and an editor of the law review. Smith, *supra* note 68, at 51, 349, 354, 510, 520; Kluger, *supra* note 78, at 518-23.

107. THURGOOD MARSHALL: HIS SPEECHES, WRITINGS, ARGUMENTS, OPINIONS, AND REMINISCENCES 206, 480 (Mark V. Tushnet ed., 2001); *see* Genna Rae McNeil, GROUNDWORK: CHARLES HAMILTON HOUSTON AND THE STRUGGLE FOR CIVIL RIGHTS (U. Penn. Press 1983); Rawn James, Jr., ROOT AND BRANCH: CHARLES HAMILTON HOUSTON, THURGOOD MARSHALL, AND THE STRUGGLE TO END SEGREGATION (Bloomsbury Press 2010).

108. Ming studied at the University of Chicago Law School, where he was a member of the Order of the Coif and the University of Chicago Law Review, in which he published as a student and later as a faculty member. His Note was "Validity of Party Resolution Depriving Negro Rights to Vote in Party Primary" (1933). He may have been "the first black student on law review in the nation to publish an article directly on a black issue." Ming later participated in the NAACP LDF's presentation of a white primary case, *Smith v. Allwright*, to the U.S. Supreme

Marian Wynn Perry, a white woman graduate of Brooklyn Law School (1943), was active in the National Lawyers Guild and then worked for the NAACP LDF (1945-1949) on employment and housing discrimination cases.[109] She later was Deputy Director of the U.S. Civil Rights Commission. Ruth Weyand, also a white woman, was a graduate of the University of Chicago Law School. She participated in several civil rights cases with the NAACP LDF, and then became a distinguished labor lawyer, working at the National Labor Relations Board and the Equal Employment Opportunity Commission.[110]

George M. Johnson was the Dean of Howard Law School and a member of the National Legal Committee of the NAACP.[111] Andrew D. Weinberger had represented Black defendants in a 1947 racial covenant case in New York.[112]

Houston's co-counsel in *Hurd* was Phineas Indritz, a white attorney in the Department of the Interior; a graduate of the University of Chicago and its law school, he was involved in many civil rights cases and had been instrumental in securing the participation of the federal government in the covenant cases.[113] They had some help in the Supreme Court from Spottswood Robinson and in the lower courts from Raphael Urciolo, a white real estate dealer and lawyer.[114]

5. **Amici Curiae.** Note that the United States appeared in these cases as amicus curiae for the petitioners and the Solicitor General himself argued. These were the first private civil rights cases in which the United States participated.[115] Such involvement by the United States signals to the Supreme Court not only the Executive Branch's keen interest in the subject but also the independent, responsible judgment of the Solicitor General, as the "Tenth Justice," one who is an advocate for justice.[116] Cases in which the United States participates are much more likely to be resolved in favor of the side endorsed by the

---

Court. His lead article was *Racial Restrictions and the Fourteenth Amendment: The Restrictive Covenant Cases*, 16 U. CHI. L. REV. 203 (1949). Smith, *supra* note 68, at 52, 71 n.79, 551, 570, 602 n.224 (U. Penn. Press 1993).

109. Tushnet, *supra* note 98, at 35.

110. Bart Barnes, *EEOC Counsel Ruth Weyand Identified as Crash Victim*, WASH. POST, Nov. 20, 1986, available at https://www.washingtonpost.com/archive/local/1986/11/20/eeoc-coun sel-ruth-weyand-identified-as-crash-victim/5c7e1b6d-b25e-42cd-8241-5cace80b1e7d/ (last visited July 13, 2023).

111. Vose, *supra* note 90, at 46, 262 n.82.

112. *Id*. at 155.

113. Tushnet, *supra* note 98 , at 91; Vose, *supra* note 90, at 159; Wolfgang Saxon, *Phineas Indritz, 81, Counsel to Several House Committees*, N.Y. TIMES, Oct. 20, 1997, at 38; Bart Barnes, *Phineas Indritz Dies at 81*, WASH. POST, Oct. 18, 1997.

114. Vose, *supra* note 90, at 159. Urciolo had made a good deal of money selling to Black people homes that were subject to racial covenants and a case involving his sales had been consolidated with the *Hurd* case. *Id*. at 80, 93-94.

115. Mary L. Dudziak, COLD WAR CIVIL RIGHTS: RACE AND THE IMAGE OF AMERICAN DEMOCRACY 91-92 (Princeton U. Press 2000).

116. Lincoln Caplan, THE TENTH JUSTICE (Alfred A. Knopf 1987).

United States.[117] The personal appearance of the Solicitor General underscores the strength of the Executive Branch's interest. It is the Solicitor General, not the Attorney General, who represents the United States before the Court; the addition of the name of the Attorney General to the brief is another signal of the great importance attached to the case.

Participation by the United States was the result of a coordinated campaign by the NAACP, other counsel, and several federal employees.[118] In 1946, President Truman had appointed the President's Committee on Civil Rights, which issued its report, To Secure These Rights, in October 1947.[119] Thanks to advocacy by Phineas Indritz and others, the report urged government intervention in the litigation. Solicitor General Perlman, Attorney General Clark, and President Truman all were involved in the decision that the United States would appear.[120] Uniquely, Generals Perlman and Clark caused the government's brief to be published as a book titled Prejudice and Property.[121]

President Truman had a complicated record when it came to civil rights.[122] He took many actions advancing civil rights, including issuing executive orders to desegregate the U.S. armed forces and federal employment[123] as well as establishing the President's Committee on Civil Rights and then immediately releasing, endorsing, and acting on its principal recommendations. He was the first President to address the NAACP. On the other hand, he was openly critical of some civil rights activists, apparently concerned about their alleged links to communism. Truman's Attorney General, Tom Clark, would later serve on the Supreme Court, where he ruled with the majority in a number of cases overturning segregationist laws; he also sat on the Seventh Circuit in *Gautreaux v. CHA* (below and Chapter 12). When he stepped down from the Supreme Court in 1967, Justice Clark was succeeded by Thurgood Marshall, who had represented the petitioners in *Shelley*.

In addition to that of the United States, 18 briefs amici curiae were filed on behalf of those who challenged the covenants; these were from organizations representing racial, ethnic, and religious groups (Blacks, American Indians, Jews, people of Japanese descent) who suffered from such covenants, large labor organizations, religious bodies, and sympathetic political groups.[124]

---

117. *Id.* at 4.

118. Vose, *supra* note 90, at 168-74.

119. *Id.* at 168-69.

120. Tushnet, *supra* note 98, at 91-92. There is some controversy about the significance of the roles played in this drama by staff of the Solicitor General's office. *See* Randall Kennedy, *A Reply to Philip Elman*, 100 Harv. L. Rev. 1938 (1987).

121. Tom Campbell Clark & Philip Benjamin Perlman, Prejudice and Property: An Historic Brief Against Racial Covenants (Public Affairs Press 1948).

122. Kluger, *supra* note 78, at 249 ("Franklin Roosevelt may have opened the White House door wide to Negroes, but Harry S Truman risked his future tenancy there in their behalf—and because of his own conception of what America was all about").

123. Kluger, *supra* note 78, at 255 (Truman also called on Congress to end lynching, poll taxes, and segregation in interstate transportation, and create a permanent fair employment practices commission and civil rights commission).

124. Vose, *supra* note 90, at 193-97.

Amici curiae briefs supporting the covenants were filed by property owners' associations in several cities and by the National Association of Real Estate Boards.[125]

6. *Hansberry v. Lee.* The *Hansberry v. Lee* case discussed by the Court in *Shelley* involved the family of playwright Lorraine Hansberry. She wrote a famous letter to the editor of the New York Times, published on April 23, 1964, discussing her family's struggle to occupy a home in a neighborhood "defended" by white violence. This experience was the topic of her award-winning play, *A Raisin in the Sun,* the title of which is taken from a well-known poem (*Harlem*) by Langston Hughes:

> What happens to a dream deferred?
> Does it dry up
> Like a raisin in the sun?
> Or fester like a sore—
> And then run?
> Does it stink like rotten meat?
> Or crust and sugar over—
> Like a syrupy sweet?
>
> Maybe it just sags
> Like a heavy load,
>
> *Or does it explode?*[126]

7. **The Sociological Harms of Racial Covenants.** A significant part of the advocacy against racial covenants was sociological and other non-legal writing about the damage done by such covenants. Some of it was independent of the litigation efforts, but much of it was initiated as part of that advocacy and then used in "Brandeis briefs" in some of the lower courts and in several of the principal and amicus briefs in the Supreme Court. Racial covenants had been condemned in Gunnar Myrdal's important study, AN AMERICAN DILEMMA, published in 1947, and in the report of the President's Committee on Civil Rights.[127] Significant work was done by Charles Abrams and by Robert C. Weaver, a Black economist who later became the first Secretary of the Department of Housing and Urban Development (1966-1968) and the first Black member of the President's

---

125. *Id.* at 197-99.

126. Langston Hughes, *Harlem, in* THE COLLECTED POEMS OF LANGSTON HUGHES 426 (Arnold Rampersad & David Roessel eds., Knopf 1994); Lorraine Hansberry, TO BE YOUNG, GIFTED, AND BLACK 20-21 (Vintage 1969); Imani Perry, LOOKING FOR LORRAINE: THE RADIANT AND RADICAL LIFE OF LORRAINE HANSBERRY (Beacon Press 2018); *see also* Jay Tidmarsh, *The Story of* Hansberry: *The Rise of the Modern Class Action, in* CIVIL PROCEDURE STORIES 233 (Kevin M. Clermont ed., 2d ed. Foundation Press 2008).

127. Judge Edgerton's dissent in *Hurd v. Hodge* cited work by Myrdal and Weaver. Vose, *supra* note 90, at 95.

cabinet.[128] He described this work in the preface to his 1948 book, THE NEGRO GHETTO.[129]

8. **FHA Actions After *Shelley* and *Hurd*.** The FHA for years had recommended racial covenants for housing it insured, providing a model racial covenant in its manual.[130] Thurgood Marshall was able to persuade the FHA to remove the suggestion, but not to stop approving insurance for deeds that included racial covenants.[131] The 1947 Report of the President's Committee on Civil Rights "commended" the FHA "on its recent abandonment of 'the policy by which it encourages the placing of racial restrictive covenants on projects supported by government guarantees.'"[132] But even after the decisions in *Shelley* and *Hurd*, the FHA resisted compliance; Charles Abrams in 1949 "charged that 'discrimination is indulged in today as freely as ever on F.H.A.-insured loans.'"[133] Finally, in 1949, Solicitor General Perlman announced that FHA would refuse to insure mortgages on any deeds that included racial restrictions filed of record after February 15, 1950. Those recorded before that date would be honored.[134]

9. **Racial Covenants Still Legal After *Shelley* and *Hurd*.** Note that neither *Shelley* nor *Hurd* held that racially restrictive covenants were illegal, just that they were unenforceable by courts. Thus, private discriminatory agreements and refusals to sell or rent property were still lawful and were quite often used until the passage of the Civil Rights Act of 1968 (the Fair Housing Act).

10. **Other Forms of Restrictive Covenants.** Residential subdivisions, cooperatives, and condominiums have restrictive covenants that do not address the race, ethnicity, or religion of occupants but may nonetheless have fair housing consequences. Most frequently, these are covenants that limit use to single-family occupancy and therefore may be understood to bar group homes for people with disabilities. Also, if such covenants are said to bar transitional or other housing facilities for women who are victims of domestic violence, the covenants may be said to discriminate on the basis of sex. Further, if covenants limit occupancy to a small number of persons "related by blood, marriage, genetics, or adoption," they may discriminate on the basis of familial status. These issues are discussed in the chapters addressing discrimination on the bases of disability, sex, and familial status. Covenants also may limit or bar occupancy by renters or those who use housing vouchers. These may be vulnerable to challenges on the basis of disparate racial impact and intentional discrimination (see Chapters 6 and 7).

---

128. Vose, *supra* note 90, at 161-63 (with respect to Abrams, *see* Ch. VII); *see* Pritchett, *supra* note 58.

129. Robert C. Weaver, THE NEGRO GHETTO (Harcourt Brace & Co. 1948); Vose, *supra* note 90, at 162-63.

130. Jackson, *supra* note 25, at 208; *see also* Rothstein, *supra* note 6, at 81-85 (describing FHA refusals to insure private developers of integrated housing).

131. Tushnet, *supra* note 98, at 87.

132. Vose, *supra* note 90, at 225 (quoting the Report of the President's Committee).

133. Rothstein, *supra* note 6, at 85-91; Vose, *supra* note 90, at 225.

134. Vose, *supra* note 90, at 225-27.

In general, covenants may impose the same kinds of restrictions as are imposed by zoning ordinances, but the legal consequences may be different.

11. **What to Do About Racial Covenants?** Although racial covenants have been illegal at least since 1968, they still exist in millions of deeds and it is difficult to remove them. Some jurisdictions have enacted legislation to facilitate removal or allow renouncement.[135] In several jurisdictions, groups are mapping those covenants so residents will understand where racial lines were drawn.[136] Richard Rothstein recommends adding to such deeds language repudiating the "unenforceable, unlawful, and morally repugnant" provisions.[137] Professor Roisman has suggested marking the homes whose deeds bear such covenants, as European countries have marked the sites where the victims of Nazis were seized.[138] What remedy, if any, do you favor? Why?

D. NEW DEAL PROGRAMS: PUBLIC HOUSING, THE FEDERAL HOUSING ADMINISTRATION, AND THE VETERANS ADMINISTRATION

1. Public Housing

The public housing program—both as part of the Public Works Administration and, after 1937, under the U.S. Housing Act—was operated on a de jure, racially discriminatory and segregated basis.[139] Along with challenges to state and federal discrimination and segregation in public education there were challenges to local, state, and federal discrimination and segregation in public housing. The first major success was in the *Gautreaux* litigation in Chicago. The litigation began in 1966 with suits against the Chicago Housing Authority (CHA) and HUD in which plaintiffs, "black tenants in and applicants for public housing, . . . charg[ed] that CHA had intentionally violated 42 U.S.C.A. §1981 and §1982 in maintaining existing patterns of residential separation of races by its tenant assignment and site selection procedures, contrary to the

---

135. *See, e.g.*, In re That Portion of Lots 1 & 2 v. Spokane Cnty., 199 Wash. 2d 389, 506 P.3d 1230 (Wash. Sup. Ct. 2022).

136. *See, e.g.*, City Roots Community Land Tr. & Yale Envtl. Prot. Clinic, *Confronting Racial Covenants: How They Segregated Monroe County and What to Do About Them* (2020) (identifying cities where restrictive covenants are being mapped); https://www.mappingsegregationdc.org/ (Washington, DC). The cities include Seattle, Minneapolis, South Bend, and Washington, DC. *See also* Yiorgo Topalidis, *Forging an Anti-Racist Praxis: Housing Discrimination Against Ottoman Greek Immigrants in Early-Twentieth-Century Portland and Seattle*, 50 J. Urban Hist. 858, 861 (2024) (discussing mapping racial covenants in Seattle and Portland).

137. *See* Rothstein, *supra* note 6, at 222.

138. Florence Wagman Roisman, *Stumbling Stones at Levittown: What to Do About Racial Covenants in the United States*, 30 ABA J. of Affordable Hous. & Community Dev. L. 461 (2022).

139. Hirsch, *supra* note 24, at 206, 209 (although Harold Ickes required nondiscrimination in PWA employment and one-third of the units were occupied by Black people, "segregation remained the rule. . . . [Under the 1937 Act,] localities assumed the power to select project sites and to determine racial occupancy").

Equal Protection Clause of the Fourteenth Amendment; and that HUD had 'assisted in the carrying on . . . of [a] racially discriminatory public housing system within the City of Chicago' in violation of the Fifth Amendment." Gautreaux v. CHA, 503 F.2d 930, 931 (7th Cir. 1974).

In 1969, the district court held for the plaintiffs in the case against CHA. No appeal ever was taken from that judgment. Here is the Seventh Circuit's later description of the findings with respect to CHA:

> As far back as 1954, the District Court found that CHA had continuously refused to permit black families to reside in four public housing projects built before 1944; and that as far back as 1954 CHA had imposed a black quota on the four projects to the end that at the beginning of 1968 black tenants only occupied between 1 percent to 7 percent of the 1,654 units in the projects. The non-white population of Chicago at that time was 34.4 percent. In 64 public housing sites, having 30,848 units (other than the four above mentioned), the tenants were 99 percent black. All during this period Illinois law required that CHA secure prior approval of new sites for public housing from the City Council of the City of Chicago, but the District Court found that CHA set up a preclearance arrangement under which the alderman in whose ward a site was proposed would receive an informal request from CHA for clearance. The alderman, the Court found, to whom sites in the white neighborhoods were submitted, vetoed the sites and the City Council rejected 99½ percent of the units proposed for white sites while only 10 percent were refused in black areas. Moreover, the Court found that during this period about 90 percent of the waiting list of some 13,000 applicants to CHA for occupancy in its projects were black. These findings were neither challenged nor appealed. Furthermore, as early as July 1, 1969, a judgment order was entered herein, requiring CHA to build 700 new housing units in predominantly white areas and requiring 75 percent of all future units built by CHA to be constructed in such areas. This judgment also ran against the City Council of the City of Chicago (not then a party) on the basis of notice. Finally, CHA was directed by the District Court to "affirmatively administer its public housing system . . . to the end of disestablishing the segregated public housing system which has resulted from CHA's unconstitutional site selection and tenant assignment procedures . . . [and] use its best efforts to increase the supply of Dwelling Units as rapidly as possible . . . ." 304 F. Supp. 736 (1969). No appeal was taken from this judgment.
>
> Meanwhile, in the separate suit against HUD filed simultaneously with the one against CHA . . ., the District Court had dismissed all four counts. On appeal [the Seventh Circuit] held that HUD had violated the due process clause of the Fifth Amendment and reversed with directions to enter a summary judgment for the appellants. [The court of appeals] found that HUD had approved and funded family housing sites chosen by CHA in black areas of Chicago. HUD's explanation was "it was better to fund a segregated housing system" than deny housing altogether. Th[e] Court found that in the sixteen years (1950–1966) HUD spent nearly $350 million on such projects "in a manner which perpetuated a racially discriminatory housing system in Chicago"; that its excuse of community and local government resistance has not been accepted as viable and that th[e] Court was "unable to avoid the conclusion that the Secretary's past actions constituted racial discriminatory conduct in their own right." Gautreaux v. Romney, 448 F.2d 731 (7th Cir. 1971).[140]

---

140. Gautreaux v. CHA, 503 F.2d 930, 932-33 (7th Cir. 1974).

The 1974 decision of the Seventh Circuit further stated: "Indeed, anyone reading the various opinions of the District Court and of this Court quickly discovers a callousness on the part of the appellees towards the rights of the black, underprivileged citizens of Chicago that is beyond comprehension."

NOTES AND QUESTIONS

1. **De Jure Racial Segregation in Public Housing.** What actions did the Chicago Housing Authority, HUD, and the City of Chicago (which later became a defendant in this litigation) take to implement racial discrimination and segregation in the early years of the public housing program? What steps were taken after 1954, when *Brown v. Board* was decided? The racial segregation in public housing throughout the United States, imposed from 1933 through at least 1968, has continued to have profound impacts on the country since then. These are discussed further in Chapter 12.

2. **More About the *Gautreaux* Litigation.** The 1974 decision of the U.S. Court of Appeals for the Seventh Circuit addressing relief was affirmed by the U.S. Supreme Court as *Hills v. Gautreaux*. The earlier decision of the Seventh Circuit, *Gautreaux v. Romney*, held HUD liable for its role in the de jure racial discrimination and segregation. Both decisions are in Chapter 12.[141] That chapter also contains further discussion of the significant impacts this litigation has had on social policy.

2. The FHA and the VA[142]

The public housing program may be contrasted with the FHA and VA homeownership programs, which served almost exclusively white residents in all-white neighborhoods. The FHA became closely identified with various sectors of the real estate industry: "The FHA . . . had a long history of independence. Because its operations were funded through insurance premiums paid by home mortgages, FHA staff came to view themselves as employees of a quasi-private institution. . . . The FHA's clients—the home builders, financial institutions, and realtors . . . were happy with this arrangement. . . ."[143] The following case shows how the FHA functioned.

---

141. *See also* Alexander Polikoff, WAITING FOR GAUTREAUX: A STORY OF SEGREGATION, HOUSING, AND THE BLACK GHETTO (Northwestern U. Press 2006). Polikoff was lead counsel for the plaintiffs from the time it was filed until he retired in 2021. The case still is being litigated. Email from Polikoff to Roisman (July 3, 2024) (on file with Roisman).

142. Although the VA program is a postwar program, it is so similar to the FHA program that we consider them together.

143. Pritchett, *supra* note 58, at 233.

Levitt and Sons, Inc. v. Division Against Discrimination in State Department of Education

31 N.J. 514, 158 A.2d 177 (N.J. 1960), *appeal dismissed,*
363 U.S. 418 (1960)

For affirmance—Justices Burling, Jacobs, Francis, Proctor, Hall and Schettino.
For reversal —None. The opinion of the court was delivered by Burling, J.

BURLING, J.

The plaintiff Levitt and Sons, Inc. . . . . is the developer of a single home housing project called Levittown, located in Levittown Township, Burlington County, New Jersey. The plaintiff Green Fields, Inc. is the developer of a similar project called Green Fields Village located in West Deptford Township, Gloucester County, New Jersey. Defendants Todd and James allegedly were rejected by Levitt as purchasers of houses in Levittown because of their color; both are Negroes. Defendant Gardner, also a Negro, allegedly was rejected by Green Fields as a purchaser of a house in Green Field Village because of his color. All three, Todd, James and Gardner, filed individual complaints with the New Jersey Division Against Discrimination [(DAD)] charging the plaintiffs with refusals to sell to the individual defendants in violation of the New Jersey Law Against Discrimination. . . . Findings of probable cause for the complaints were made by the DAD and attempts at conciliation were unsuccessful. . . .

Levitt and Green Fields instituted independent suits challenging the jurisdiction of the DAD to hear the discrimination complaints and attacking the constitutionality of the New Jersey Law Against Discrimination. . . .

Levitt's single home housing project, Levittown, in which approximately 2,000 houses have been built to the present time, will contain 16,000 houses when completed, according to original plans. Green Fields' project, Green Fields Village, comprises approximately 550 houses. Both projects have been planned and constructed in order that they might qualify for purchase money loans insured by the Federal Housing Administration (FHA), a process which requires attention to the desired end from the very earliest beginnings of the development.

Before construction has begun, a housing project developer who seeks to have FHA insured loans available to purchasers of his houses must contact an FHA office in the region in which the project will be located to obtain FHA approval of the site. Once a site approval is given, the developer will submit detailed subdivision information to the FHA office, on a form prepared by the FHA, together with certain exhibits, such as a topographic map, photographs, detailed development plan and like items; frequently these are amended or completely revised to accord with suggestions made by the FHA. When the subdivision information and exhibits are satisfactory to the FHA, that agency issues a subdivision report, giving FHA requirements concerning street layouts, curb and sidewalk specifications, utilities, drainage, open spaces, lot improvements and similar matters. House plans are submitted to determine if they meet FHA requirements; the FHA architectural section will often recommend changes in these plans. Upon receiving the subdivision report, the developer arranges with an FHA-approved lending institution to submit individual applications for commitments for FHA insurance on any loan which [will] be made by the institutions. These individual applications are reviewed by the architectural, valuation and mortgage credit sections in addition to the Chief Underwriter's office, after which commitments are issued to the approved lending institution covering the individual properties contemplated in the application. These commitments take various forms. One is a conditional commitment, an agreement between the FHA and the approved lending institution that, subject to the conditions stated in the commitment and subject to the approved lending institution's submitting a proposed purchaser whose qualifications are satisfactory to the FHA, a loan made to finance the purchase of the property in question will be insured. Another form of commitment is an "Operative-Builder Firm Commitment," which differs from a conditional commitment primarily in that the former also contemplates loans being made directly to the developer, prior to sale, if requested.

Once the commitment is issued, the developer may commence construction. As construction progresses, the developer or the approved lending institution through which the FHA commitment was made arranges for an FHA inspection. Normally three such inspections are made during the course of construction. In some larger developments, such as Levittown, an FHA inspector is stationed at the project. Often the inspector or other FHA personnel will meet with the developer to discuss problems that have arisen during construction affecting compliance with FHA requirements. As the houses are sold by the developer to purchasers interested in obtaining an FHA insured mortgage loan, an application for approval of the purchaser is submitted to the FHA by the approved lending institution to whom the conditional commitment was made. If the qualifications of the purchaser are satisfactory to the FHA, an individual firm commitment is issued to the approved lending institution in the name of the purchaser. After title is closed, the approved lending institution submits the mortgage bond to the FHA along with copies of the bond, the mortgage and the original commitment. When these are approved, the FHA endorses the bond for insurance, which comprises the contract between the FHA and the lender.

Having received conditional commitments, the developer advertises the availability of FHA financing to purchasers. By using FHA insured loans, a purchaser needs only a 3% downpayment on a principal sum of up to $13,500, 15% on the difference between $13,500 and $16,000, and 30% on the difference between $16,000 and $20,000. The term of the loan may be as long as 30 years. Conventional financing often involves downpayments of 20% to 25% and frequently will be limited to terms of 20 to 25 years. Thus it is apparent that FHA financing is a large factor in stimulating home buying, since the low down payment opens the home market to persons who have accumulated only small savings and the extended term of the loan allows home ownership to be achieved by payments from income by a much larger proportion than would ordinarily be the case. Concerning the importance of FHA approval to the large housing project developer, Robert A. Budd, president of Green Fields, stated on his deposition that such approval "is the basics (sic) on which to go on." William Levitt, president of Levitt, stated before the House Subcommittee on Housing of the Committee on Banking and Currency of the Eighty-Fifth Congress that "We are 100 percent dependent on Government. Whether this is right or wrong it is a fact." Only a very small percentage of the buyers of homes in Levittown and Green Fields Village financed their purchase other than with federally insured loans.

II.

First to be determined is whether the DAD has jurisdiction under the Law Against Discrimination to entertain the complaints brought by the individual defendants against the plaintiffs. The first [question] is whether the plaintiffs' developments are "publicly assisted housing accommodation" as that phrase is used in the Law Against Discrimination.

The statute plainly includes, as publicly assisted housing, housing projects such as those here involved as to which, at the time of the discrimination, an FHA insured loan is committed. And the public assistance demonstrated by the federal insurance of such loans is much the same, under the circumstances of this case, as that demonstrated by an FHA commitment to insure housing loans. Just as ownership of housing and its concomitant benefits attributable to an FHA insured loan is said by the statute to be publicly assisted, by the same reasoning the advantages which accrue to the developers in question from the FHA commitments are plainly the result of public assistance. The very existence of the development can be attributed to the FHA commitment. The mass market opened by FHA and other government insured purchase money housing loans accounts for the prospect of sufficient buyers to purchase the housing in question. Without such a mass market, it is inconceivable that the developments would have been built; the number of prospective purchasers with adequate savings accumulated to make the downpayment required by conventional financing and with sufficient income to meet from their income the payments on a conventionally financed debt would not warrant the mass housing construction in evidence today. Thus the very fact that there are houses with which to discriminate in the development in question is primarily attributable to public assistance. We need not here decide what are the outer limits of the term "publicly assisted housing accommodation." Suffice it to say that the public assistance rendered the housing here in question places it within the definition of that term as used in N.J.S.A. 18:25-4. . . .

NOTES AND QUESTIONS

1. **The Levittowns and Similar Developments.** There were several Levittowns—in New York, Pennsylvania, New Jersey, Maryland, Virginia, and Puerto Rico.[144] Other developers operated in other parts of the country. Developments that used FHA and VA financing often were enormous, as was the Levittown involved in this case; the first Levittown, in New York, had 17,400 houses for 82,000 residents.[145] The developers were called "community builders." The homes in Levittowns and other FHA/VA financed developments were "the deal of the century": It was less expensive to buy such a home than to rent. "Provided they were white, veterans could buy homes in Levittown, with a thirty-year mortgage and no down payment, by spending only $56 a month [when] . . . the average apartment rental in many cities was $93."[146]

Levittown, Long Island, New York, 1950.

2. **Public Financing; Public and Private Discrimination.** Notice that as a matter of federal law, these developers were free to reject applicants, even those who were veterans, because they were Black—and this despite the fact that, as William Levitt had testified, "We are 100 percent dependent on Government." It was only a state law that provided a basis for the lawsuit in New Jersey; the New Jersey law barred discrimination only in "publicly assisted housing." In an earlier New York case, *Dorsey v. Stuyvesant Town* (below), the New York Court of Appeals (the highest court in the state) held 4-3 that a development by the Metropolitan Life Insurance Company that received significant aid from the state and city governments was not state assisted and therefore was not subject to antidiscrimination requirements of the state and federal constitutions; a more specific statute was required to impose liability.

3. **The VA Program.** In 1944, Congress enacted the Servicemen's Readjustment Act, commonly known as the G.I. Bill of Rights, which provided home mortgage guarantees (and educational assistance) to veterans.[147] The initial legislation was not very effective, but by 1950 Congress had created a VA program of homeownership assistance modeled on the

---

144. There were Levittowns in New York, New Jersey (3), Maryland (2), and Virginia, as well as Puerto Rico. *See The Levittowns of the United States*, WORLD ATLAS, https://www.worldatlas.com /articles/the-levittowns-of-the-united-states.html (last visited July 17, 2024).

145. May, *supra* note 33, at 152.

146. *Id.* at 151.

147. Pub. L. No. 78-346, 58 Stat. 284 (1944).

FHA program. Both relied on private lenders, which meant that non-white veterans were subjected to discrimination. There was no rental assistance program for veterans, so those who could not afford homeownership received no aid. It was "an extremely limited measure that was available only to some veterans and provided eligible veterans with restricted aid. . . . The housing provisions excluded some people by design and others by administration and left a legacy of veterans living in unaffordable, over-crowded, or otherwise substandard housing, in shelters and in cars, and literally on the streets."[148] For the first 20 years of the program, almost all the benefits flowed only to whites in all-white neighborhoods, so that "even those non-white veterans who had the financial capacity to utilize the program were precluded from doing so." Moreover, non-white veterans and their families "were disproportionately too poor to use the homeownership programs. . . ."[149]

4. **The Long-Term Impact of the FHA and VA Programs: Continued Segregation and the Racial Wealth Gap.** The all-white Levittowns and other communities that were created by the FHA and VA programs have continued to be almost all white today.[150] What do you think may be the sociological, economic, and political consequences of this reality? Enabling white families to purchase homes under those programs created intergenerational wealth that has financed educational and commercial advantages for the homeowning families and helped to fuel the racial wealth gap.[151] Do you think anyone has an obligation to redress this? If so, how do you think that might be accomplished?

E. POSTWAR PROGRAMS: URBAN RENEWAL AND INTERSTATE HIGHWAYS

The two principal postwar programs fueling racial residential segregation were urban renewal and interstate highways. *Dorsey v. Stuyvesant Town* describes urban redevelopment, the model for the urban renewal program. *Berman v. Parker* is the foundational case validating urban renewal.

---

148. Florence Wagman Roisman, *National Ingratitude: The Egregious Deficiencies of the United States' Housing Programs for Veterans and the "Public Scandal" of Veterans' Homelessness*, 38 IND. L. REV. 103, 111 (2005).

149. *Id.* at 151.

150. *See, e.g.,* Rachelle Bildner, *Long Island Divided*, NEWSDAY (Nov. 17, 2019), available at https://projects.newsday.com/long-island/levittown-demographics-real-estate/ (in 2017, Levittown, New York, was 75 percent white, 14.6 percent Hispanic, 7 percent Asian, 1 percent Black); Levittown, PA, DATAUSA, https://datausa.io/profile/geo/levittown-pa/. (As of 2022, Levittown, Pennsylvania's population was 79.9 percent white and 3.2 percent Black.).

151. *See, e.g.,* Melvin Oliver & Thomas Shapiro, BLACK WEALTH/WHITE WEALTH: A NEW PERSPECTIVE ON RACIAL INEQUALITY (Taylor & Francis 2013); Andre M. Perry, Hannah Stephens, and Manann Donoghoe, BLACK WEALTH IS INCREASING, BUT SO IS THE RACIAL WEALTH GAP (Brookings 2024) ("in 2022, for every $100 in wealth held by white households, Black households held only $15").

1. Urban Renewal

Dorsey v. Stuyvesant Town Corporation
299 N.Y. 512, 87 N.E.2d 541 (N.Y. 1949),
cert. denied, 339 U.S. 981 (1950)

Lewis, Conway and Dye, JJ., concur with Bromley, J.; Fuld, J., dissents in opinion in which Loughran, Ch. J., and Desmond, J., concur.

BROMLEY, J.

[EDS.—Setting the design for the federal urban renewal program of the 1950s, New York created in 1943 a redevelopment scheme that enabled the city to assemble huge swaths of land by exercising the power of eminent domain and transferring that land, at cost, to a private company that would construct housing and other improvements approved by the city, with "lucrative tax exemptions" and other government assistance.[152] The first exercise of this authority was the construction of Stuyvesant Town in Manhattan, which involved the city's acquisition of 18 city blocks, the displacement (without relocation requirements) of some 12,000 low-income residents, and the construction of a walled "suburb in a city" comprising 35 13-story apartment buildings housing 25,000 residents in some 8,759 apartments. The one facility that was not provided within Stuyvesant Town was schools; an official with developer Metropolitan Life Insurance Company explained that "if there were a public school in the project the City would allow some children, including Negroes, to attend from outside the area."[153] Robert Moses, a powerful urban planner and New York City Park Commissioner, reported that 11,000 site residents would have to be relocated elsewhere as their incomes were too low for even the controlled rents at Stuyvesant Town. Stuyvesant Town stretched north from East 14th Street to East 20th Street and East from 1st Avenue to the East River Drive (or Avenue C). Metropolitan Life invested some $90,000,000 in the project and insisted that it control the occupancy, specifically so that it could deny occupancy to Black people.][154]

In the Dorsey suit, plaintiffs are Negro veterans who have applied for apartments. . . . The matter of the exclusion of Negroes from the development arose in connection with the approval by the Governor of the 1943 amendments to the Redevelopment Companies Law and in contract negotiations between Metropolitan and the city. Commissioner Robert Moses, active in

---

152. *See* Abrams, *supra* note 47, at 244 (with respect to redevelopment in general and Stuyvesant Town in particular).

153. Simon, *supra* note 42, at 36.

154. Most of these facts are from the *Dorsey* opinion. Some are from Simon, *supra* note 42, at 19 (12,000 people in 1940); at 26 (8,759 apartments); at 30 (11,000 displacement); at 40 ("a parklike town sealed off from its surroundings, an all-white suburb within the city"); or from A. Scott Henderson, HOUSING & THE DEMOCRATIC IDEAL: THE LIFE AND THOUGHT OF CHARLES ABRAMS, Chapter 7 (Columbia U. Press 2000); *see also id.* at 131 ("approximately 3000 families would be evicted").

the plan, stated publicly to the Governor and the board of estimate that if any requirement was imposed which deprived the landlord of the right to select its tenants, no private venture would go into the business. Certainly the general impression was created—which Metropolitan did nothing to dispel—that Stuyvesant Town would not rent to Negroes. For that reason and others, unsuccessful attacks were made upon the desirability of the project. In the board of estimate at least three votes were cast against approval of the contract on the ground that exclusion on racial grounds would be practiced. The contract was finally approved without any provision regarding discrimination in the selection of tenants.[155] It may be noted in passing that thereafter the New York City Council passed legislation withholding tax exemption from any subsequent redevelopment company unless it gave assurance that no discrimination would be practiced in its rental policies. This provision, however, expressly excluded from its operation any project "hitherto agreed upon or contracted for."

In 1943, respondent Stuyvesant was formed by Metropolitan pursuant to the statute. A contract with the city was approved by the board of estimate of the City of New York in June, 1943. Under the contract the City of New York agreed to condemn and bring under one good title the entire area. Stuyvesant agreed to acquire the area, demolish the old buildings and construct new ones, all without expense to the city. Metropolitan agreed to advance the necessary funds to Stuyvesant, guaranteed performance by the latter, and, with Stuyvesant, assumed all risks of the venture. The city granted tax exemption for twenty-five years only to the extent of the enhanced value to be created by the project. Stuyvesant agreed to convey to the city bordering strips around the periphery of the project in exchange for land in streets which the city agreed to close.[156]

Appellants point to the acknowledged contribution made by government to the project—principally the tax exemption amounting to many millions of dollars, and aggregation of the land through use of the city's power of eminent domain and through exchange of bordering tracts for city streets which had been closed. Moreover, we are urged to consider the size of the project as in reality forming a large community within the city. [Eds.—Despite the substantial government involvement, a majority of the court upheld the plans for an all-white Stuyvesant Town for reasons explained in the dissent.]

---

155. [Eds.—Both The New York Times and The Herald Tribune applauded the decision to allow Metropolitan Life to exclude Black people from Stuyvesant Town. Simon, *supra* note 42, at 34. "The *Amsterdam News* of Harlem . . . [reported that although] nearly two million Negroes are estimated to be holding policies in Metropolitan Life, . . . that company never employed Negroes except possibly as janitors." Roy Wilkins of the NAACP commented: "Not even a janitor." *Id*. at 35.]

156. [Eds.—"For Metropolitan's benefit that profit was also guaranteed in the proposed contract with the city." *Id*. at 23.]

FULD, J. (dissenting).

While the Stuyvesant Town housing project was in blueprint and under construction, the public understood, and rightly, that it was an undertaking on which the State and the City of New York had bestowed the blessings and benefits of governmental powers. Now that the development is a reality, the public is told in effect that, because the Metropolitan Life Insurance Company and Stuyvesant Town Corporation are private companies, they are not subject to the equal protection clause, and may, if they choose, discriminate against Negroes in selecting tenants. That conclusion strikes me as totally at odds with common understanding and not less so with the facts and circumstances disclosed by the record.

In the City of New York as well as in other communities of this State, there are blighted areas whose rehabilitation has been the concern of public bodies for many years. Bent upon "the clearance, replanning, reconstruction and rehabilitation" of such areas, the People in 1938 adopted a new constitutional provision dealing with housing (N.Y. Const., art. XVIII). In aid of those purposes, the Legislature enacted the Redevelopment Companies Law. After announcing the State's concern over the existence of substandard and insanitary conditions which impaired real estate values, jeopardized public revenues, and depressed living standards, the Law declared that "these conditions cannot be remedied by the ordinary operations of private enterprise." Though providing that the actual work was to be done by privately owned redevelopment companies, the statute acknowledged and recognized that there was need for "the cooperation of the state and its subdivisions."

The co-operative activities set forth in the statute demonstrate that the state and city governments were to have a deep interest in, and a close connection with, these redevelopment enterprises. Not only did it fix their maximum rents and profits but it laid down careful limitations with respect to their financing and mortgaging, the selling or disposing of the property and the altering of the structures. To the city governments, the statute gave authority to approve any plan for a proposed development, and power to include, by contract, provisions for the "operation and supervision of the project." In addition, the City was enabled to use certain of its governmental powers to aid the work. It was empowered to condemn property by eminent domain in order to assemble the area to be rehabilitated, and then to convey the property to the redevelopment companies at cost; to close off and transfer public streets; and to grant tax exemption on the improvements for a twenty-five-year period. In sum, the companies and the enterprises were to be governmentally aided and effectuated, as well as supervised and regulated, in numerous ways. Streets in the area are "private" and signs at all entrances give the public notice of that fact.

Unmistakable are the signs that this undertaking was a governmentally conceived, governmentally aided and governmentally regulated project in urban redevelopment. If the City had zoned the site of Stuyvesant Town and closed it to Negroes, no one would doubt that the equal protection clause had been violated. (*Buchanan v. Warley.*) If the City, instead of doing that, had built a similar development and leased it to private operators for occupancy by white tenants only, the discrimination would have been condemned with equal vigor. Here, instead of a zoning ordinance or a city lease, there is a city-approved and city-executed contract, providing for a housing project from which it was realized Negroes would be barred, and a city law ratifying that discrimination. No one claims or even suggests that the City adopted an alternative strategem to effect discrimination, but it may not be gainsaid that the development plan, the contract and the local law brought about precisely the same situation as if the City had zoned or leased a "white" development. We draw distinctions too fine and too subtle when we say that the several cases are different or that they merit different consideration.

NOTES AND QUESTIONS

1. **The Role of Robert Moses.** Robert Moses, who was an overwhelmingly powerful and controversial figure in the development of major infrastructure projects and housing developments in New York City and State and a key actor in the development of Stuyvesant Town, is the subject of Robert A. Caro's book, *The Power Broker,* a classic in the literature of political science and land use. Moses was responsible also for the Parkchester and Peter Cooper Village developments, which similarly excluded Black people from enormous swaths of New York City.[157] The highways and parkways Moses sited throughout New York displaced tens of thousands of people, many of them people of color and most of them people with relatively low incomes.[158]

2. **Counsel in the Case.** Counsel for those advocating for inclusion of Black people at Stuyvesant Town included Thurgood Marshall and Charles Abrams. Marshall is discussed above. Abrams was a distinguished "lawyer, college professor, urban reformer, author, lecturer, government official, and housing consultant."[159] He opposed Robert Moses on many issues. One of his several books was FORBIDDEN NEIGHBORS: A STUDY OF PREJUDICE IN HOUSING (Associated Faculty Press 1955). Among many other public service contributions, Abrams was head of the New York State Commission Against Discrimination and President of the National Committee Against Discrimination in Housing.[160]

3. **The Plaintiffs in *Dorsey.*** Joseph R. Dorsey, a former Captain in the U.S. Army, had a master's degree and a job as a caseworker; Monroe Dowling, who also had been an Army Captain, was a Harvard graduate and a Senior

---

157. *Id.* at 30, 32 (Parkchester's 35,000 tenants all white); *id.* at 41 (Moses says he induced Metropolitan to build Stuyvesant Town and Riverton; the company disagrees).

158. *See, e.g.,* Caro, *supra* note 48, at 520-25, 848-49, 859-61, 879-83, 963-76, 1007-08.

159. Henderson, *supra* note 154, at 1, 139-144, 150, 159.

160. *See id.* at 158, 167.

Employment Manager for the New York State Employment Service. Calvin B. Harper was a disabled veteran.[161]

4. **White Resistance to Exclusion of Black People.** A plaintiff in the *Dorsey* suit was the Town and Village Tenants' Committee to End Discrimination in Stuyvesant Town, a group of residents of Stuyvesant Town and Peter Cooper Village who invited Black people to live in their apartments and took a variety of actions to end the ban on Black residents. One well-known leader of the group was Bill Mauldin, a famous cartoonist.[162] Metropolitan Life threatened to refuse to renew the leases of 35 tenants who had been publicly identified with the resistance.[163]

———————

The next case is significant to the fight for fair housing because it expanded government eminent domain power to demolish properties and displace people, most of whom were Black renters. In this challenge under the Takings Clause, the Supreme Court upheld the validity of a federal urban renewal program under a "broad and inclusive" concept of the public welfare.

Berman v. Parker
348 U.S. 26 (1954)

Before Chief Justice Warren and Justices Black, Reed, Frankfurter, Douglas, Burton, Clark, and Minton.

Mr. Justice Douglas delivered the opinion of the Court.

This is an appeal from a three-judge District Court['s] dismissal of a complaint seeking to enjoin the condemnation of appellants' property under the District of Columbia Redevelopment Act of 1945. The challenge was to the constitutionality of the Act, [which the] District Court sustained. . . .

By §2 of the Act, Congress made a "legislative determination" that "owing to technological and sociological changes, obsolete layout, and other factors, conditions existing in the District of Columbia with respect to substandard housing and blighted areas, including the use of buildings in alleys as dwellings for human habitation, are injurious to the public health, safety, morals, and welfare, and it is hereby declared to be the policy of the United States to protect and promote the welfare of the inhabitants of the seat of the Government by eliminating all such injurious conditions by employing all means necessary and appropriate for the purpose."

———————

161. Simon, *supra* note 42, at 57-58.
162. *Id.* at 73-75.
163. *Id.* at 82.

Section 2 goes on to declare that acquisition of property is necessary to eliminate these housing conditions. Congress further finds in §2 that these ends cannot be attained "by the ordinary operations of private enterprise alone without public participation"; that "the sound replanning and redevelopment of an obsolescent or obsolescing portion" of the District "cannot be accomplished unless it be done in the light of comprehensive and coordinated planning of the whole of the territory of the District of Columbia and its environs"; and that "the acquisition and the assembly of real property and the leasing or sale thereof for redevelopment pursuant to a project area redevelopment plan . . . is hereby declared to be a public use."

Section 4 creates the District of Columbia Redevelopment Land Agency (hereinafter called the Agency), which is granted power to acquire and assemble, by eminent domain and otherwise, real property for "the redevelopment of blighted territory in the District of Columbia and the prevention, reduction, or elimination of blighting factors or causes of blight."

Section 6(a) of the Act directs the National Capital Planning Commission (hereinafter called the Planning Commission) to make and develop "a comprehensive or general plan" of the District, including "a land-use plan" which designates land for use for "housing, business, industry, recreation, education, public buildings, public reservations, and other general categories of public and private uses of the land." Section 6(b) authorizes the Planning Commission to adopt redevelopment plans for specific project areas. These plans are subject to the approval of the District Commissioners after a public hearing. . . . Once the Planning Commission adopts a plan and that plan is approved by the Commissioners, the Planning Commission certifies it to the Agency. At that point, the Agency is authorized to acquire and assemble the real property in the area.

After the real estate has been assembled, the Agency is authorized to transfer to public agencies the land to be devoted to public purposes, and to lease or sell the remainder as an entirety or in parts to a redevelopment company, individual, or partnership. The leases or sales must provide that the lessees or purchasers will carry out the redevelopment plan. Preference is to be given to private enterprise over public agencies in executing the redevelopment plan.

The first project undertaken under the Act relates to Project Area B in Southwest Washington, D.C. In 1950 the Planning Commission prepared and published a comprehensive plan for the District. Surveys revealed that in Area B, 64.3% of the dwellings were beyond repair, 18.4% needed major repairs, only 17.3% were satisfactory; 57.8% of the dwellings had outside toilets, 60.3% had no baths, 29.3% lacked electricity, 82.2% had no wash basins or laundry tubs, 83.8% lacked central heating. In the judgment of the District's Director of Health it was necessary to redevelop Area B in the interests of public health. The population of Area B amounted to 5,012 persons, of whom 97.5% were Negroes.

The plan for Area B specifies the boundaries and allocates the use of the land for various purposes. It makes detailed provisions for types of dwelling units and provides that at least one-third of them are to be low-rent housing.

After a public hearing, the Commissioners approved the plan and the Planning Commission certified it to the Agency for execution. The Agency undertook the preliminary steps for redevelopment of the area when this suit was brought.

Appellants own property in Area B at 712 Fourth Street, S.W. It is not used as a dwelling or place of habitation. A department store is located on it. Appellants object to the appropriation of this property for the purposes of the project. They claim that their property may not be taken constitutionally for this project. It is commercial, not residential property; it is not slum housing; it will be put into the project under the management of a private, not a public, agency and redeveloped for private, not public, use. That is the argument; and the contention is that appellants' private property is being taken contrary to two mandates of the Fifth Amendment—(1) "No person shall be deprived of property, without due process of law"; (2) "nor shall private property be taken for public use, without just compensation." To take for the purpose of ridding the area of slums is one thing; it is quite another, the argument goes, to take a man's property merely to develop a better balanced, more attractive community.

The power of Congress over the District of Columbia includes all the legislative powers which a state may exercise over its affairs. We deal, in other words, with what traditionally has been known as the police power. An attempt to define its reach or trace its outer limits is fruitless, for each case must turn on its own facts. The definition is essentially the product of legislative determinations addressed to the purposes of government, purposes neither abstractly nor historically capable of complete definition. Subject to specific constitutional limitations, when the legislature has spoken, the public interest has been declared in terms well-nigh conclusive. In such cases the legislature, not the judiciary, is the main guardian of the public needs to be served by social legislation, whether it be Congress legislating concerning the District of Columbia or the States legislating concerning local affairs. This principle admits of no exception merely because the power of eminent domain is involved. The role of the judiciary in determining whether that power is being exercised for a public purpose is an extremely narrow one.

Public safety, public health, morality, peace and quiet, law and order—these are some of the more conspicuous examples of the traditional application of the police power to municipal affairs. Yet they merely illustrate the scope of the power and do not delimit it. Miserable and disreputable housing conditions may do more than spread disease and crime and immorality. They may also suffocate the spirit by reducing the people who live there to the status of cattle. They may indeed make living an almost insufferable burden. They may also be an ugly sore, a blight on the community which robs it of charm, which makes it a place from which men turn. The misery of housing may despoil a community as an open sewer may ruin a river.

We do not sit to determine whether a particular housing project is or is not desirable. The concept of the public welfare is broad and inclusive. The values it represents are spiritual as well as physical, aesthetic as well as monetary. It is within the power of the legislature to determine that the community should be beautiful as well as healthy, spacious as well as clean, well-balanced as well as carefully patrolled. In the present case, the Congress and its authorized agencies have made determinations that take into account a wide variety of values. It is not for us to reappraise them. If those who govern the District of Columbia decide that the Nation's Capital should be beautiful as well as sanitary, there is nothing in the Fifth Amendment that stands in the way.

Once the object is within the authority of Congress, the right to realize it through the exercise of eminent domain is clear. For the power of eminent domain is merely the means to the end. Once the object is within the authority of Congress, the means by which it will be attained is also for Congress to determine. Here one of the means chosen is the use of private enterprise for redevelopment of the area. Appellants argue that this makes the project a taking from one businessman for the benefit of another businessman. But the means of executing the project are for Congress and Congress alone to determine, once the public purpose has been established. The public end may be as well or better served through an agency of private enterprise than through a department of government—or so the Congress might conclude. We cannot say that public ownership is the sole method of promoting the public purposes of community redevelopment projects.

In the present case, Congress and its authorized agencies attack the problem of the blighted parts of the community on an area rather than on a structure-by-structure basis. That, too, is opposed by appellants. They maintain that since their building does not imperil health or safety nor contribute to the making of a slum or a blighted area, it cannot be swept into a redevelopment plan by the mere dictum of the Planning Commission or the Commissioners. The particular uses to be made of the land in the project were determined with regard to the needs of the particular community. The experts concluded that if the community were to be healthy, if it were not to revert again to a blighted or slum area, as though possessed of a congenital disease, the area must be planned as a whole. It was not enough, they believed, to remove existing buildings that were insanitary or unsightly. It was important to redesign the whole area so as to eliminate the conditions that cause slums—the overcrowding of dwellings, the lack of parks, the lack of adequate streets and alleys, the absence of recreational areas, the lack of light and air, the presence of outmoded street patterns. It was believed that the piecemeal approach, the removal of individual structures that were offensive, would be only a palliative. The entire area needed redesigning so that a balanced, integrated plan could be developed for the region, including not only new homes but also schools, churches, parks, streets, and shopping centers. In this way it was hoped that the cycle of decay of the area could be controlled and the birth of future slums prevented. Such diversification in future use is plainly relevant to the maintenance of the desired housing standards and therefore within congressional power.

It is not for the courts to oversee the choice of the boundary line nor to sit in review on the size of a particular project area. Once the question of the public purpose has been decided, the amount and character of land to be taken for the project and the need for a particular tract to complete the integrated plan rests in the discretion of the legislative branch.

It is not for the courts to determine whether it is necessary for successful consummation of the project that unsafe, unsightly, or insanitary buildings alone be taken or whether title to the land be included, any more than it is the function of the courts to sort and choose among the various parcels selected for condemnation.

The rights of these property owners are satisfied when they receive that just compensation which the Fifth Amendment exacts as the price of the taking.

The judgment of the District Court, as modified by this opinion, is affirmed.

NOTES AND QUESTIONS

1. **The Significance of *Berman v. Parker*.** *Berman v. Parker* is a seminal case for several reasons, in addition to its upholding the constitutionality of the urban renewal program. Justice Douglas's opinion provides the basis for aesthetic zoning, given its interpretation of the "public welfare" and "police power" as authorizing the "legislature to determine that the community should be beautiful as well as healthy, spacious as well as clean, well-balanced as well as carefully patrolled." It also sets a high standard for deference in land use decisions, stating: "Subject to specific constitutional limitations, when the legislature has spoken, the public interest has been declared in terms well-nigh conclusive." *Berman* lays the foundation for such later decisions as *Kelo v. City of New London*,[164] the effect of which, Justice O'Connor wrote for the four dissenters, was: "Nothing is to prevent the State from replacing any Motel 6 with a Ritz-Carlton, any home with a shopping mall, or any farm with a factory."

2. ***Berman v. Parker* and Race.** Although *Berman v. Parker* was decided only months after *Brown v. Board* and involved the displacement of "5,012 persons, of whom 97.5% were Negroes," the Court made no reference whatever to the difficulties Black people would have in finding replacement housing. The urban renewal program did not have even facially effective relocation provisions until 1968. These issues are discussed in a compelling article by

---

164. 545 U.S. 469, 503 (2005).

Professor Wendell Pritchett.[165] A Note after the next case, *Triangle Improvement Council v. Ritchie*, discusses relocation provisions for the urban renewal and federal aid highway programs.

3. **Counsel in the Case.** In the Supreme Court, the United States was represented by the Solicitor General, Simon Sobeloff, who defended the constitutionality of the urban renewal statute. Sobeloff became a judge on the U.S. Court of Appeals for the Fourth Circuit, and dissented in the next case, *Triangle Improvement Council v. Ritchie*. As Solicitor General, Sobeloff said that his "client's chief business is not to achieve victory, but to establish justice," and he "famously refused to sign the government's brief or argue on the government's behalf in one case about a McCarthy-era loyalty review board's dismissal of a federal government employee, in which he thought that principle had been neglected."[166]

2. Interstate Highways

The next case reveals the delayed enactment of protections for those displaced by the site selection and construction of interstate highways, the resulting effects on neighborhoods as well as people of color, and government resistance to compliance with federal law. In *Triangle Improvement Council*, plaintiffs who had not yet been displaced by an authorized interstate highway filed suit to enforce statutory protections that had become available months earlier. The district court denied relief that would have required a formal state relocation plan designed to identify adequate replacement housing. A panel of the Fourth Circuit in one sentence affirmed per curiam "on the opinion of the district court" even though the federal Department of Transportation had established after the district court's opinion that such a plan was required. The full Fourth Circuit denied a motion for reconsideration en banc. Two judges dissented.

Triangle Improvement Council v. Ritchie
29 F.2d 423 (4th Cir. 1970)

SOBELOFF, Circuit Judge, dissenting from the denial of a rehearing in banc: Winter, Circuit Judge, joins in this opinion:

In light of the cryptic treatment given this appeal by the panel which decided it, I feel constrained briefly to set forth the issue, the panel's rationale, and the reasons for my disagreement.

165. Wendell E. Pritchett, *The "Public Menace" of Blight: Urban Renewal and the Private Uses of Eminent Domain*, 21 YALE L. & POL'Y REV. 1 (2003).

166. Simon E. Sobeloff, *Attorney for the Government: The Work of the Solicitor General's Office*, 41 A.B.A. J. 229, 229 (1955); Maryland Center for History and Culture, Judge Simon Sobeloff—Moderate to the Extreme, https://www.mdhistory.org/simon-sobeloff/ (last visited November 3, 2024).

The appellants are residents of Charleston, West Virginia's black ghetto, known as the Triangle, who will shortly be uprooted from their homes to make way for the construction of an interstate highway. They have now abandoned their futile efforts to halt or divert the road. Their sole objective at this point is to assure that when displaced they will be able to obtain adequate replacement housing, as guaranteed by federal law.

The plaintiffs' concern arises from a critical housing situation in Charleston. According to one study they cite, standard housing is only sparsely available for poor people generally, and hardly at all for poor blacks.[167] The problem of an ever shrinking housing supply has been grossly aggravated by a series of public projects, including highway construction, which have extensively eliminated housing facilities and continue to do so.

Despite informal promises made to them by state and federal officials that adequate housing will be available, the appellants are seriously apprehensive that when the time comes for them to move there will be nowhere to go except to substandard, inferior quarters. It is for this reason that they demand that the state authorities comply fully with the federal requirement to submit a detailed, comprehensive relocation plan. Such a study, they say, will demonstrate that contrary to the representations of defendants, there are gross deficiencies in the housing potentially available to displacees. If the survey does support their claims there will be time before displacement to take steps, in conformity with federal law, to alleviate the problem.

The defendants assert that adequate replacement housing will exist, yet they reject the necessity for an analysis that would definitely test, either to contradict or corroborate, their assertion.[168] The sole issue on this appeal is whether federal law requires submission of a detailed relocation plan as insisted by appellants.

---

167. [Fn.1 in original] Additionally, three memoranda of the federal right-of-way officer support this contention.

168. [Fn.2 in original] In response to this litigation the state authorities prepared a purported "relocation plan." This has not been reviewed by federal officials and there is no contention that it meets the federal standards for a sufficient plan. According to the appellants much of the proposed replacement housing referred to in the plan is either far above the financial eligibility of the displacees, not available to black people, or already occupied. Furthermore, the plan, it is said, gives no consideration to the competing demands of displacees from outside the Triangle area.

Instead of furnishing a comprehensive plan, the defendants now rely on the District Judge's finding that "adequate relocation housing, on an open racial basis, will be available in the Charleston area for an orderly relocation of the displacees from the interstate highway corridor." The plaintiffs dispute the finding and, moreover, point out that it is not up to us, nor was it for the District Court, to weigh the validity of the state's relocation program. Under the 1968 amendments, which the plaintiffs insist are applicable, there is a precise, effective administrative procedure for evaluation of the adequacy of proposed replacement housing.

If the 1968 amendments are indeed applicable, this case would seem, in light of the defendants' conduct during this lawsuit, to be a particularly appropriate one in which to insist upon strict compliance with the letter of the law.

In 1968 Congress recognized the predicament of poor persons whose homes are destroyed to make way for a highway, with no provision of alternative accommodations. Thus the Congress passed extensive amendments to the Federal-Aid Highway Act to provide for the "prompt and equitable relocation and reestablishment of persons" displaced by federal highway programs. Theretofore no duty was owed to displaced persons save to furnish them information. The cold administrative indifference to the plight of those left without roofs over their heads mounted to the level of a national scandal. Under the new provisions, enacted to alleviate the inequity[,] the Secretary may not approve a highway project unless he receives "satisfactory assurances" that, inter alia, prior to displacement, there will be available in adequate number and within the financial means of displaced persons "decent, safe and sanitary dwellings."

What constitutes "satisfactory assurances" has been defined by regulation. They may not be merely vague or general promises. Instead, the statute and the regulations adopted pursuant thereto make mandatory a plan of relocation which describes the methods and procedures to be used and specifies detailed data concerning the replacement housing to be provided. There must also be a report probing relocation problems, analyzing other public programs affecting the availability of housing, furnishing information on concurrent displacement caused by other agencies, estimating the time required to accomplish the plan, and demonstrating that the plan is adequate "to carry out a timely, orderly and humane relocation program." It is this accumulation of proposal and fact that enables federal officials to review the plan to determine whether the State's relocation plan is realistic and is adequate to provide orderly, timely, and efficient relocation of displaced individuals and families to decent, safe, and sanitary housing with minimum hardship on those affected.

Approval by the Secretary is necessary at two junctures of a project; first before right-of-way acquisition and then again before actual construction. Rights-of-way for the projects involved in this case were authorized in 1966 and 1967. However, there has yet to be final approval of the construction phase. Thus it would seem that the above described requirement of a thorough plan must be fulfilled before construction in the Triangle may proceed.

[EDS.—There was a dispute about whether the 1968 amendments should apply to projects that obtained Secretary approval prior to 1968. The district court and the court of appeals adopted the defendant's argument that, per a DOT interpretation, assurances were not required.]

However, subsequent to the opinion of the District Court the federal authorities issued new guidelines. These declarations, a policy directive of the Secretary of Transportation and an implementing memorandum of the Federal Highway Administration, reveal that federal regulations no longer subscribe to the view of limited applicability of the 1968 amendments. Rather, the new policy makes clear that, as interpreted by the Department of Transportation, the amendments pertain to all approvals of construction, even when projects have been previously authorized.

It remains to inquire why this court has not acted on these developments. The initial panel opinion, adopting the reasoning of the District Court, logically cannot serve to answer this question because the new administrative regulations came after the opinion [of the district court] below. The opinionless order denying a rehearing provides no further elucidation. It is therefore necessary to set out the panel's view as I infer it to be. There is, of course, no dispute within the court that the appellants' position on the applicability of the 1968 amendments has now become the law and that comprehensive relocation plans are required before construction can be approved. Rather, my brethren seem to think that the new regulation, expressly recognizing the plaintiffs' rights under the 1968 amendments, has somehow eliminated the need for relief. Their position apparently is that there is no reason to suppose that the new policy will not be applied to the Triangle and, accordingly, appellants' claim is thus mooted, at least for the time being.

I cannot subscribe to this expectation. The question is anything but moot. The defendants have consistently taken the position that the state authorities need not submit and the federal officials need not review a formal relocation plan. They have continued to press this contention on appeal in spite of the policy change of which they were aware. Moreover, they have been less than forthright in the course of this litigation. They resisted, without justification, producing the very memorandum of the Secretary that announced the new position and did not supply it until ordered to do so by the court. Under these circumstances I cannot think that court-ordered relief would be superfluous. On the contrary, the defendants' refusal to accord the plaintiffs their rights cries out for redress.

Nor do I perceive any justification for the cavalier treatment accorded the appeal and the petition for rehearing. Even if injunctive relief is not appropriate this court should not, by its silence, permit any possible implication that the obligations on the defendants have not been altered since the District Court's order. As I understand it, the affirmance is based on confidence that the defendants will perform their duty, not that they have none to fulfill. When the court acknowledges the duty but without explanation does nothing to enforce it, the decision will be read by some as a holding that there is no duty. At the very least the court should have explicated its rationale to underscore the obligation and prevent misreading. Its failure to do so constitutes serious error.

NOTES AND QUESTIONS

1. **Facts and Counsel in the Case.** The basic facts of *Triangle Improvement Council* were paradigmatic: Most highways blazed through neighborhoods occupied primarily by people who were poor and Black, destroying communities and living patterns. The highways displaced families and businesses, owners

and tenants, with almost no relocation assistance or replacement housing.[169] One thing that was unusual in this case was that the displacees were represented by experienced counsel from the NAACP Legal Defense Fund (LDF).

2. **Relocation Requirements for Highways.** Not surprisingly, because highway design and construction is a long-term project, the law governing relocation changed as plans for this highway proceeded. The statutory provisions changed in 1968, when more displacee-friendly provisions were added to the highway act requiring a plan of relocation satisfactory to the Secretary of Transportation. Initially, the defendants in this case took the position that those amendments did not apply to this highway because certain authorizations had already been obtained. However, early in 1970, the Secretary of Transportation and the Federal Highway Administration promulgated memoranda stating that the 1968 amendments did apply to this highway because approval of construction had not yet occurred. (The federal defendants resisted producing the Secretary's memorandum until ordered to do so by a panel of the Fourth Circuit.)

3. **Agency "Regulations."** The court repeatedly referred to the "regulations" of the Department of Transportation although the documents are in fact memoranda, and the court also described these as "guidelines." The latter is the word that would be used exclusively today. In decades past, the courts often were somewhat cavalier in their use of the word "regulations."

In reading the Supreme Court decision in *Triangle Improvement Council*, consider that there was no court-issued stay of construction while the case on compliance with the 1968 relocation plan requirement made its way to the high court. Construction had been authorized in 1969 and indeed proceeded, residents were displaced, and homes were demolished, leaving only nine people remaining in the Triangle at the time of oral argument. Without explanation, the Supreme Court dismissed the writ of certiorari as improvidently granted; four Justices dissented.

Triangle Improvement Council v. Ritchie
402 U.S. 497 (1971)

Before Chief Justice Burger and Associate Justices Black, Douglas, Harlan, Brennan, Stewart, White, Marshall, and Blackmun.

---

169. *See* Archer, *supra* note 44; Raymond Mohl, *Planned Destruction, in* From Tenements to the Taylor Homes, *supra* note 24; Raymond A. Mohl, *Race and Space in the Modern City: Interstate-95 and the Black Community in Miami, in* Urban Policy in Twentieth-Century America 100 (Arnold R. Hirsch & Raymond A. Mohl eds., Rutgers U. Press 1993); Martin Anderson, The Federal Bulldozer; A Critical Analysis of Urban Renewal 1949-1962 (MIT Press 1964).

Opinion: Per Curiam
The writ of certiorari is dismissed as improvidently granted.

Mr. Justice Douglas, with whom Mr. Justice Black, Mr. Justice Brennan, and Mr. Justice Marshall concur, dissenting.

This case involves two federal-aid interstate highway projects in Charleston, West Virginia. . . . Many of the residents of the Triangle district are elderly and almost all have comparatively low incomes. As often happens with interstate highways, the route selected was through the poor area of town, not through the area where the politically powerful people live.

The common urban housing shortage is severe in Charleston, in part, because many homes have been demolished for public projects. The impact of public projects in the Triangle has been exceptionally severe. Land clearance for a proposed expansion of a local water company displaced some 243 persons a few years ago. The planned interstate highway will displace about 300 more. And a proposed urban renewal project (which has been postponed indefinitely because of lack of replacement housing) will displace almost all of the area's 2,000 residents. There were about 300 persons to be dislocated within Triangle.

On August 23, 1968, the 1968 amendments to the Federal-Aid Highway Act relating to relocation benefits for persons displaced by federal-aid highways became effective. By that date the vast majority of persons within the Triangle area, who were to be dislocated by the highway, had not yet been displaced.

Prior to trial only 17 households had been moved and over 280 persons remained to be displaced. Once the construction began however, displacement did occur and the Solicitor General's brief, filed just before oral argument, informs us that only nine persons are left in the Triangle and virtually all the vacant housing has been demolished.

Much is made of the fact that although originally about 300 people were to be displaced in the Triangle, there remain only nine who have not been taken care of or who have not on their own found new shelter. If only one person were involved, the case would, in my view, be no different. For under our regime even one person can call a halt where government acts lawlessly. And this is patently a case where the federal bureaucracy has defied a congressional mandate.

It is notorious that interstate highways have left displaced citizens without homes because no efforts or inadequate efforts have been made for relocation. In 1962 Congress amended the Federal-Aid Highway Act to require assurances of "relocation advisory assistance" and authorized minimal payments for relocation assistance. But, as Judge Sobeloff noted below, the "cold administrative indifference to the plight of those left without roofs over their heads mounted to the level of a national scandal." In 1968

Congress passed certain amendments to the Act to rectify this "national scandal."[170]

The 1968 amendments provide that any person displaced by a federal-aid highway project "may elect to receive actual reasonable expenses in moving." If a property owner, he is entitled to a payment from the State, in addition to the acquisition price of the property taken, of up to $5,000, representing the difference between the acquisition price and the cost of obtaining a comparable dwelling. A tenant may receive up to $1,500 to enable him to rent for a period of two years, or make the down payment on the purchase of a decent, safe, and sanitary dwelling "not . . . less desirable" than his existing one.

The duty of the Secretary of Transportation under the amendments was made explicit. He is to see that the amendments are effective. He is not to approve any project "which will cause the displacement of any person, business, or farm operation unless he receives satisfactory assurances from the State Highway department that" (1) fair and reasonable relocation and other payments will be afforded in accordance with the Act, (2) relocation assistance programs will be afforded in accordance with the Act, and (3) "within a reasonable period of time prior to displacement there will be available, to the extent that can reasonably be accomplished, in areas not generally less desirable in regard to public utilities and public and commercial facilities and at rents or prices within the financial means of the families and individuals displaced, decent, safe, and sanitary dwellings . . . equal in number to the number of and available to such displaced families and individuals and reasonably accessible to their places of employment."

Satisfactory assurances have been strictly defined by regulation. [The program must be "realistic"; the state must show how] the needs of every individual to be displaced will be evaluated and correlated with available decent, safe, and sanitary housing [and the methods] by which the State will . . . inventory . . . currently available comparable housing."

[In 1968, before the amendments became effective,] a federal division engineer stated [that the State's submission] "would not be considered, in our opinion, a complete relocation plan since it did not provide information either factual, estimated or projected as to the availability of replacement housing."

[After the amendments became effective,] the Secretary did not require the State to comply with the requirements. Yet as of the effective date of the 1968 amendments there had been no authorization of construction and at least 280 persons remained in the project area to be dislocated. The State finally did prepare a relocation plan, but only in response to this lawsuit and while the federal officials have obtained a copy of it, we are told they have made no attempt to review it. The plan that was prepared does not consider competing

---

170. [Fn. 1 in original] It is true, of course, that the 1968 amendments were repealed by the Uniform Relocation Assistance and Real Property Acquisition Policies Act of 1970. That Act, however, is so similar to the 1968 amendments that any necessary interpretation of the 1968 amendments would be equally applicable to the 1970 Act.

and simultaneous needs of other displaced persons because competition was not considered relevant. Subsequent to the District Court order dismissing petitioners' complaint construction was authorized.

This petition should not be dismissed as improvidently granted. Our "rule of four" allows any four Justices to vote to grant certiorari and set the case for consideration on the merits. The four who now dissent were the only ones to vote to grant the petition. The rule should not be changed to a "rule of five" by actions of the five Justices who originally opposed certiorari.

NOTES AND QUESTIONS

1. **Denial of the Writ as Improvidently Granted.** What does it mean to grant a writ improvidently? The Court dismissed in one sentence without reasons, but Justice Harlan in a concurring opinion pointed to the "less than 10 persons" who had not yet been displaced and the fact that the 1968 Act under review had been repealed and replaced by a new statute. Under these circumstances, the already displaced residents sought from the Court not merely a formal relocation plan but a review of whether their new locations met statutory standards; Justice Harlan considered this expanded request for relief untenable. Justice Harlan also noted that the statute at issue here had been replaced by the 1970 Uniform Relocation Assistance and Real Property Acquisition Policies Act. With respect to this point, consider the Court's statement in the 1969 decision in *Sullivan v. Little Hunting Park* (Chapter 2): "It would be irresponsible judicial administration to dismiss a suit because of an intervening Act which has no possible application to events long preceding its enactment." (In that case, too, Justice Harlan would have dismissed the writ as improvidently granted.) Consider also the Court's ruling in *Jones v. Mayer* (Chapter 2).

2. **Displacement and Relocation Rights.** Redevelopment, urban renewal, and highway construction all involved displacement of huge numbers of people. Invariably, as Judge Sobeloff said, these projects were sited through the homes, businesses, and communities of people who had relatively little political power—usually people who were poor and non-white. From the beginning, no adequate provision was made to provide relocation assistance or replacement housing for displacees. Stuyvesant Town set the pattern: At the request of the Chair of Metropolitan Life, provisions for tenant relocation were eliminated from the legislation that authorized that project.[171]

The urban renewal and highway statutes also imposed no requirements for effective assistance to displacees or relocation housing; "[n]ot until 1965, when much of the Interstate system had already been built, did the federal government require advance relocation housing for families and businesses displaced...."[172]

---

171. Henderson, *supra* note 154, at 126-27.
172. Mohl, *Race and Space, supra* note 169, at 226, 231.

Moreover, until 1968, people displaced by those programs were held not to have standing to sue about their displacement.[173] As indicated in the *Triangle Improvement Council* opinions, the urban renewal and highway statutes were amended in 1968 to strengthen the relocation provisions, but only rhetorically: The statutes required only that federal officials find that there were "satisfactory assurances" that replacement housing would be available and, as the *Triangle* opinions also show, government officials usually were not diligent about enforcing these requirements.[174] In 1970, these requirements were combined in the Uniform Relocation Assistance and Real Property Acquisition Policies Act, but the language of the act was interpreted very narrowly[175] and, in any event, by 1970, most of the displacement caused by urban renewal and highways had already occurred.

F. THE CONSTANTS: PREDATORY REAL ESTATE PRACTICES AND RACIAL VIOLENCE

1. Predatory Real Estate Practices

There were many forms of predatory real estate practices that wrested land from Native American, Latino, Asian, Black, and other non-white people. A common form in urban areas was the use of installment land sales contracts, which provided much less protection than did mortgage financing but often were the only financing available to people of color. Under an installment sales contract, the land company retained title to the real estate until the entire amount of the deferred balance was satisfied; upon default and repossession, the land companies retained the entire amount paid by the contract purchaser, along with any improvements. In Chicago, there was an organized opposition to this predatory financing.[176] The following case excerpts describe challenges to some of those practices in Chicago and its suburbs.

From Contract Buyers League v. F&F Investment Co., 300 F. Supp. 210 (N.D. Ill. 1969)

The First count of the complaint relates essentially to the allegations, here taken as admitted for purposes of the motions to dismiss, that defendants exploited a system of de facto racial segregation that existed in the City of Chicago, and that by taking advantage of the scarcity of housing for negroes in the City of Chicago, defendants have secured unlawful advantage in the contracts executed by plaintiffs. As described in the complaint, the scheme of exploitation often

---

173. The seminal displacee standing case was Norwalk CORE v. Norwalk Redev. Agency, 395 F.2d 920 (2d Cir. 1968).

174. *See also* Western Addition Community Org. v. Romney, 320 F. Supp. 308 (N.D. Cal. 1969) (upholding a certification that satisfactory assurances had been provided).

175. Alexander v. HUD, 441 U.S. 39 (1979).

176. *See* Satter, *supra* note 8.

included obtaining purchase money mortgages based on false and excessive appraisals of used residential property. The essence of the scheme is alleged to have been the purchase of residential properties from white homeowners and the resale, often in the nature of quick "turn-around" transactions, at greatly inflated prices to negro purchasers, who were disadvantaged by the system of de facto segregation and the resulting shortage of housing for negroes in Chicago. The terms of the contracts, especially the price, are alleged to represent unlawful profit gained through this pattern of exploitation.

The complaint also alleges that some defendants amplified and fostered the de facto segregation on which the contracts depended. The complaint asserts that some of the defendants engaged in what is popularly known as "block-busting," that some of the defendants stimulated and preyed on racial bigotry and fear by initiating and encouraging rumors that negroes were about to move into a given area, that all non-negroes would leave, and that the market values of properties would descend to "panic prices" with residence in the area becoming undesirable and unsafe for non-negroes. The complaint thus charges not only that defendants exploited the existing condition of de facto segregation, but that by prompting and encouraging a stampede of white sellers, some defendants extended and developed the underlying inequity of segregation that was the breeding ground for their discriminatory profit.

In the instant case, the discrimination alleged is the sale of used residential property to negroes at higher prices and on more burdensome terms than similar property is sold to whites.

Defendants present the discredited claim that it is necessarily right for a businessman to secure profit wherever profit is available, arguing specifically with respect to this case that they did not create the system of de facto segregation which was the condition for the alleged discriminatory profit. But the law in the United States has grown to define certain economic bounds and ethical limits of business enterprise. Developed areas of the law such as are invoked under the fraud and antitrust counts of this complaint are characteristic examples. . . . There cannot in this country be markets or profits based on the color of a man's skin.

The claim that defendants sold to negroes at a higher price than similar property would be sold to whites will be subject to proof on trial. Second, and most important, defendants' position elaborated is that if property is sold to a negro above what can be demonstrated to be the usual market price, there can be no discrimination unless the same seller actually sells to whites at a lower price. It should be clear that in law this result would be obnoxious. In logic, it is ridiculous.

From Clark v. Universal Builders, Inc., 501 F.2d 324 (7th Cir. 1974), cert. denied, 419 U.S. 1070 (1974)

Plaintiffs are a class of black citizens who purchased newly constructed houses in Chicago from defendants under land installment contracts during the period from 1958 to 1968. Defendants include the building contractor of the houses and the various land companies through which the houses were sold to plaintiffs.

Plaintiffs' "exploitation" theory of liability [is]: As a result of racial discrimination there existed two housing markets in Chicago, one for whites and another for blacks, with the supply of housing available in the black market far less than the demand. Defendants entered the black market selling homes for prices far in excess of their fair market value and far in excess of prices which whites pay for comparable homes in the white market and on more onerous terms than whites similarly situated would encounter. Plaintiffs contend that by so acting defendants seized upon and took advantage of the opportunity created by racial residential segregation to exploit blacks. . . .

It is defendants' position that they offered the plaintiffs the same terms and prices they would offer whites. Therefore it is asserted that plaintiffs had the same right as white citizens. This argument ignores current realities of racial psychology and economic practicalities. Defendants can find no justification for their actions in a claim that they would have sold on the same terms to those whites who elected to enter the black market and to purchase housing in the ghetto and segregated inner-city neighborhoods at exorbitant prices, far in excess of prices for comparable homes in the white market. It is no answer that defendants would have exploited whites as well as blacks. To accept defendants' contention would be tantamount to perpetuating a subterfuge behind which every slumlord and exploiter of those banished to the ghetto could hide by a simple rubric: The same property would have been sold to whites on the same terms.

Defendants urge that other sellers and not they were the active agents of discrimination. That is, blacks were excluded from the white market by other sellers who refused to sell to plaintiffs and that accordingly plaintiffs' action lies solely against those other owners and real estate operators and not the defendants. We find repugnant to the clear language and spirit of the Civil Rights Act the claim that he who exploits and preys on the discriminatory hardship of a black man occupies a more protected status than he who created the hardship in the first instance. Moreover, defendants' actions prolong and perpetuate a system of racial residential segregation, defeating the assimilation of black citizens into full and equal participation in a heretofore all white society. Through the medium of exorbitant prices and severe, long-term land contract terms blacks are tied to housing in the ghetto and segregated inner-city neighborhoods from which they can only hope to escape someday without severe financial loss. By demanding prices in excess of the fair market value of a house and in excess of what whites pay for comparable housing, defendants extract from blacks resources much needed for other necessities of life, thereby reducing their standard of living and lessening their chances of escaping the vestiges of a system of slavery and oppression.[177] Indeed, defendants'

---

177. [Fn. 5 in original] Charging prices greater than white citizens pay for comparable housing means that blacks are required to dedicate a greater portion of their income to housing than white citizens, leaving less to spend on other necessary items such as education, medical care, food, clothing, home improvements and recreation. As a result, the exploitation of the dual

activity encourages overt discrimination by others since it deflects or fore-
stalls a frontal attack on such discrimination by offering the long-oppressed
black an unattractive yet alternative choice to that of a confrontation for equal
buyers' rights in a white neighborhood.

Defendants in effect contend that this is solely a matter of economics and not
of discrimination. We cannot accept this contention for although the laws of supply and demand may function so as to establish a market level for the buyer in
the black housing areas, it is clear that these laws are affected by a contrived market condition which is grounded in and fed upon by racial discrimination—that
is, the available supply of housing is determined by the buyer's race. In other
contexts the law has prevented sellers from charging whatever the market will
bear when special circumstances have occasioned market shortages or superior
bargaining positions. In such instances sellers were denied the opportunity to
exploit others merely because the opportunity existed.

Contrary to the trial court's stance, the shortage of housing here was
triggered not by an economic phenomenon but by a pattern of discrimination that has no place in our society.[178] Accordingly, neither prices nor
profits—whether derived through well-intentioned, good-faith efforts or
predatory and unethical practices—may reflect or perpetuate discrimination against black citizens. We agree with Judge Will's statement that "there
cannot in this country be markets or profits based on the color of a man's
skin." Price and profit differentials between individual buyers may be justified on a multitude of grounds; for example, the prospective purchaser's
reputation or his financial position and potential earning power. But price
or profit may not turn on whether the prospective buyer has dark or light
pigmentation.

By demanding prices far in excess of a property's fair market value and
far in excess of prices for comparable housing available to white citizens the
seller ventures into the realm of unreasonableness. The statute does not mandate that blacks are to be sold houses at the exact same price and on the exact
same terms as are available to white citizens. Reasonable differentials due to

---

housing market assists in the relegation of blacks to a continuing position of social inequality
and inferiority while those who exploit the dual housing market enjoy the benefits of enormous
wealth exacted from black citizens.

178. [Fn. 6 in original] In analyzing the market shortage confronting plaintiffs the trial judge
stated:

> The same economic forces and the law of supply and demand create and destroy mar-
> kets for building boom towns in time of war and dying ghost towns in time of peace.
> The same thing occurs in other economic phenomena, such as a gold rush, a uranium
> strike, a new highway, a railway or the St. Lawrence Waterway. One area is distressed;
> another is incremented by increased activity.

The "economic phenomena" referred to by the trial judge have nothing to do with the race
of the persons involved; the financial impact upon the citizenry is the same regardless of their
color. The impact of the phenomenon of racial discrimination, however, falls solely on the black
citizenry.

a myriad of permissible factors can be expected and are acceptable. But the statute does not countenance the efforts of those who would exploit a discriminatory situation under the guise of artificial differences.

The practices that have befallen plaintiffs have long besieged other black citizens. In the year 1962 the United States Commission on Civil Rights recognized that:

> Throughout the country large groups of American citizens—mainly Negroes, but other minorities too—are denied an equal opportunity to choose where they will live. Much of the housing market is closed to them for reasons unrelated to their personal worth or ability to pay. New housing, by and large, is available only to whites. And in the restricted market that is open to them, Negroes generally must pay more for equivalent housing than do the favored majority. "The dollar in a dark hand" does not "have the same purchasing power as a dollar in a white hand."[179]

When a seller in the black market demands exorbitant prices and onerous sales terms relative to the terms and prices available to white citizens for comparable housing, it cannot be stated that a dollar in the hands of a black man will purchase the same thing as a dollar in the hands of a white man. Such practices render plaintiffs' dollars less valuable than those of white citizens—a situation that was spawned by a discarded system of slavery and is nurtured by vestiges of that system.

There was sufficient evidence to establish, prima facie, the existence of dual housing markets in the Chicago metropolitan area as a result of racial residential segregation. Dr. Karl E. Taeuber, a professor of sociology, testified as an expert witness about the results of his extensive research on the dispersion of population in the city of Chicago. His statistical analysis indicated that Chicago was a highly segregated city and that there was a very high degree of residential segregation between whites and blacks. Moreover, despite the decrease of white population in the city accompanied by a rapid increase of the black population, the supply of new housing available to whites was much greater than that available to blacks. Also, during the pertinent time period the expanding suburban housing market was limited almost completely to whites. Dr. Taeuber testified that the main obstacle to the movement of blacks into the white areas of Chicago and suburban residential areas was the high degree of discrimination against blacks in the white market. As a result the supply of housing available to whites was far greater in both absolute and relative terms to the supply of new housing available to blacks.

Significantly, defendants seemingly concede the existence of a dual housing market in Chicago. Nor do we think it beyond the strictures of judicial notice to observe that there exists in Chicago and its environs a high degree of racial residential segregation.

---

179. [Fn. 9 in original] U.S. Comm'n on Civil Rights Rep., Part IV, at 1 (1961).

We turn to the second element of the case, whether there was a sufficient prima facie showing of an unreasonable differential in price and sale
terms between the housing sold or offered by defendants to plaintiffs and
comparable housing available to whites. Concerning the testimony of Scott
Tyler and John Hank . . . , both witnesses utilized the market data method
of appraisal in arriving at a fair market value of a sampling of plaintiffs'
homes. The fair market value appraisals were based on sales of comparable
homes in all-white neighborhoods which were located in close geographical proximity to plaintiffs' homes and had similar communal amenities
such as transportation, schools, churches, and quality of neighborhood.
Both witnesses testified that the comparable white housing was sold at
prices substantially below the prices commanded by defendants. Expert
witness Tyler's appraisals demonstrated that on the average the contract
prices charged by defendants exceeded the fair market value of the homes
by $6,508, or 34.5 percent. Expert witness Hank was of the opinion that on
the average defendants' prices exceeded fair market value by $4,209, or
20.6 percent. Plaintiffs adduced additional appraisal testimony from Paul
Underwood who had been an appraiser for a savings and loan association
which had loaned money to one of the defendant land companies for construction of houses sold to plaintiffs. Pursuant to this financing arrangement
Underwood appraised thirty of defendants' houses for which he testified
that the sales price charged by defendants, on the average, exceeded fair
market value by $4,296, or 20.9 percent. Based on the foregoing we think a
jury could reasonably reach the conclusion that defendants' price differential was unreasonably in excess of fair market value and prices available to
white citizens for comparable housing.

Turning to the issue of the reasonableness of the sale terms differential
the evidence at trial indicated that defendants refused to sell other than on
land contract to plaintiffs.[180] There was testimony to the effect that defendants
refused to participate in any sales through a deed and mortgage arrangement
despite the prospective buyer's ability to obtain mortgage financing. The evidence indicates that plaintiffs were of the equivalent economic status as many
whites who routinely obtained mortgages to finance the purchase of houses
and that a competing construction company in the black market sold the vast
majority of its homes on deed and mortgage to blacks similarly situated economically to plaintiffs. Also, the evidence demonstrates that some plaintiffs
made down payments of up to forty-five percent of the contract price—well
above the amount needed to qualify for mortgages—and yet defendants
refused to deal on terms other than contract. On the basis of this evidence it
could reasonably be inferred that defendants utilized the contract method of

---

180. [Fn. 12 in original] The average contract term was 28 years; some terms ranged
upwards to 40 or more years. The contracts prohibited installation of improvements such as
storm windows, fences, patios, and garages, unless prior permission was obtained from the
land company.

sales to facilitate their exorbitant pricing practices[181] and not because of significant differences between plaintiffs' economic status and that of whites similarly situated who were able to utilize mortgage financing.

Furthermore, plaintiffs offered evidence . . . sufficient to establish a prima facie case pursuant to the traditional theory of discrimination. Under that theory there must be a showing of "treating, in similar circumstances, a member or members of one race different from the manner in which members of another race are treated." That is, a black prospective buyer of a dwelling demonstrates discriminatory conduct if he proves that an owner utilizes different pricing policies with respect to blacks and whites similarly situated.

The proffered evidence . . . involved the sales of new houses to white buyers in Deerfield, Illinois and Park Forest South, Illinois, both being suburban residential developments. The sellers of the houses in Deerfield were Universal Construction Company and a joint venture comprised of the Deerfield Home Development Company and Universal Builders, Inc., while the houses in Park Forest South were sold by the P.F.S. Development Company. The plaintiffs contended that these corporations were owned and managed by the same persons that owned and managed defendants and that these persons were engaged in discriminatory conduct through the use of different pricing practices in Deerfield and Park Forest South from those used in pricing defendants' houses.

Plaintiffs' expert witnesses testified that in the housing industry prices are established on the basis of direct costs, consisting generally of the investment in the land and the cost of construction, including materials. Once the direct costs are calculated, an allowance for overhead and profit is added to the direct costs to attain the sales price. The allowance for overhead and profit is the gross profit on sales which plaintiffs' expert witness testimony indicated was generally found in the real estate industry to be from fifteen to nineteen percent of the sales price. Defendants testified to the utilization of this method of pricing in their sales to plaintiffs; however, the statistical evidence presented by plaintiffs tends to refute that assertion.

Viewing the evidence, first in absolute terms, it shows that defendants' pricing policy in Chicago produced an average gross profit substantially in excess of that produced by the Deerfield and Park Forest South operations. In

---

181. [Fn. 14 in original] Mr. Justin Hulman, a former Illinois Commissioner of Savings and Loan Associations, testified for plaintiffs with respect to the direct relationship between fair housing prices and mortgage availability. Mr. Hulman indicated that it was the practice of lending institutions during 1959 to 1969 to make mortgages of up to 90 percent of the appraised value of the property, the difference being the down payment. As the sales price increases relative to the appraisal value of a home the disparity—as reflected in the amount of the down payment—becomes more apparent and the availability of mortgage money lessens. By forcing plaintiffs to purchase on contract the defendants kept plaintiffs ignorant of the appraised value of the properties and the great disparity between fair market value and the sales price. Sales on contract avoided intervention by mortgage lending institutions and the certain disclosure by the institutions of the disparity between sales price and appraised value. To that extent the contract method of sales facilitated defendants' exorbitant pricing practices.

relative percentage terms defendants reaped a gross profit of 27.6 percent of sales, well above the industry figure of 14 to 19 percent and considerably in excess of the gross profit percentages of the Deerfield and Park Forest South operations.[182] Second, analyzing the same data in terms of the mark-up of the sales price over the direct costs, it is clear that the mark-up—as a percentage of direct costs—was much higher in the sales to plaintiffs than in the sales to white buyers in Deerfield and Park Forest South.

The statistical evidence substantiates the claim that defendants priced plaintiffs' houses much higher relative to direct costs than the houses sold in Deerfield and Park Forest South and belies any contention that defendants utilized comparable pricing policies in their sales to plaintiffs. Plaintiffs presented Dr. Richard Freeman, a Professor of Economics, who analyzed the statistical data pertaining to the difference in gross profits between defendants' sales to plaintiffs and the suburban operations. His analysis demonstrated that the difference in pricing practices was due to the race of the buyer and not economic factors.

In summary, it is difficult as a prima facie matter to infer that the substantial disparity between the pricing practices of defendants in the black real estate market and the pricing practices in the white market was attributable to some factor other than the race of the buyers. Whether defendants afforded plaintiffs the "same right" to purchase housing as offered white buyers was, based on the foregoing evidence, an issue to be properly submitted to the jury.

NOTES AND QUESTIONS

1. **The Subsequent History of** *Clark v. Universal Builders.* On remand, the district court after a bench trial held that plaintiffs had failed to meet their burden of proof on either theory of liability, and the Seventh Circuit affirmed a judgment for defendants. Here is an excerpt from that opinion, Clark v. Universal Builders, Inc., 706 F.2d 204 (7th Cir. 1983):

> Plaintiffs have had, through the course of this litigation, two alternative theories of liability. Under a "traditional" theory, plaintiffs claim that defendants violated their civil rights by selling homes to black buyers at higher prices and on less favorable terms than were available to similarly situated white buyers. Plaintiffs have also argued an "exploitation" theory of discrimination. Under this theory, plaintiffs have attempted to prove that as a result of racially-based residential segregation a "dual" housing market existed in Chicago which defendants exploited by demanding prices and terms of black buyers which were unreasonably in excess of the prices and terms available to white buyers of comparable housing.

---

182. [Fn. 18 in original] In Deerfield, Universal Construction realized a gross profit of 17.1% while the gross profit of the Deerfield Home-Universal Builders joint venture was 17.6%. The operations in Park Forest South turned an average gross profit of 15.5% of sales price.

To prove their case under the traditional theory, plaintiffs attempted to show that the defendants had sold homes in the suburban town of Deerfield, Illinois to white home buyers on different terms than they were using to sell "comparable" homes to black buyers on the south side of Chicago. The district court found that the homes in question were not comparable, and this finding is not clearly erroneous. The district court considered the evidence as a whole and concluded that there was "a complete dissimilarity between the Deerfield and south side homes in terms of community environment, lot size, building materials, design, and layout." In the face of such a finding, we must defer to the conclusion of the district court that the homes in question were not comparable.

[With respect to the exploitation theory], [t]he district court took judicial notice of "the fact that during all time periods relevant to this case Chicago residential patterns have been characterized by a high degree of racial segregation," but found that the plaintiffs did not meet "their burden of showing that [these] patterns presented the defendant with the opportunity to charge exorbitant prices."

Extensive evidence was presented concerning the dual market phenomenon. Several sociologists and demographic experts testified as to the widespread racial segregation which was responsible for the exclusion of black home buyers from white neighborhoods. It was shown that disparities in ability to afford housing were not sufficient to explain existing patterns of residential segregation. Several of the plaintiffs also testified as to their personal encounters with racially-motivated housing discrimination. In sum, the plaintiffs succeeded in painting a deplorable picture of the discrimination reflected in Chicago housing patterns during the period in question.

[T]he district court accepted plaintiffs' contention that Chicago suffered from a high degree of racial residential discrimination and that there was a substantial demand for housing among black households, but did not accept plaintiffs' further contention that this phenomenon enabled defendants to exploit the plaintiffs. We find that this conclusion is not clearly erroneous.

Even if we fully accept the proposition that blacks were completely restricted to the particular geographical housing market in which defendants were operating, there has been no evidence presented which shows how defendants could have in fact charged higher prices or demanded more restrictive terms than their competitors in that particular location.

While we agree with plaintiffs' general contention that the Chicago housing market was significantly affected by racial discrimination, we cannot agree that the plaintiffs have met their burden of proving that these market conditions were such that defendants could have exploited them to their advantage.

2. **Nondiscriminatory Exploitation?** What do you make of the differences between the two Seventh Circuit decisions in *Clark*? Does the standard of review explain the substantial deference the Seventh Circuit exercised in reviewing the district court's factual findings after trial? Does the appellate court refer to credibility determinations in its discussion of the evidence? For discussion of FHA challenges to predatory lending practices four decades later, see Chapter 11.

2. Racial Violence

Behind the legal restraints on housing, and the exclusionary and predatory practices described above, lay the constant and very real threat of racial violence. This violence was often perpetrated to prevent Black people from moving into neighborhoods, to drive them out of neighborhoods, or to destroy existing Black communities altogether. A complete history of this violence might never be known, but a number of incidents have been documented. What follows is illustrative, not exhaustive.

From the end of the Civil War, there were numerous major attacks on Black people by white supremacists; these were efforts to prevent Black people from voting, "block . . . access to education, den[y] entrance to trades, . . . prevent . . . land ownership," or impose other penalties. These occurred in the South and the North, in Memphis (1866), New Orleans (1866 and 1868), Eutaw, Alabama (1870), Philadelphia, Pennsylvania (1871), Eufaula, Alabama (1874),[183] Colfax, Louisiana (1873),[184] and Wilmington, North Carolina (1898).[185] In 1899, in Carterville, Illinois, five Black strikebreakers were killed by white miners, and the other Black people living in Carterville were forced to leave.[186] There were white-on-Black riots in New York City (1900),[187] Atlanta (1906),[188] Brownsville, Texas (1906), and Springfield, Illinois (1908). During the Atlanta riot, then 13-year-old Walter White, later Executive Secretary of the NAACP (1929-1955), joined his father in armed protection of their lives and home.

The NAACP was formed in 1910. In its 1912 Second Annual Report, it focused on "an issue that would become increasingly important in future years, the use of violence to enforce de facto housing segregation. . . .In Kansas City in 1912, blacks who purchased homes in previously white neighborhoods had been subjected to at least five incidents of dynamiting."

Of the 1917 E. St. Louis, Illinois riots, an observer said: "'The whites . . . fired the homes of black folk and either did not allow them to leave the burning houses or shot them the moment they dared attempt to escape the flames.'" Also in 1917, there was a white-on-Black riot in Houston, Texas.[189] In 1918, a mob responded when Black people attempted to move into a "white"

---

183. Herbert Shapiro, WHITE VIOLENCE AND BLACK RESPONSE: FROM RECONSTRUCTION TO MONTGOMERY 10-19 (U. Mass. Press 1988).

184. Charles Lane, THE DAY FREEDOM DIED: THE COLFAX MASSACRE, THE SUPREME COURT, AND THE BETRAYAL OF RECONSTRUCTION (Henry Holt 2008).

185. David Zucchino, WILMINGTON'S LIE: THE MURDEROUS COUP OF 1898 AND THE RISE OF WHITE SUPREMACY (Atlantic Monthly Press 2020).

186. Bell, *supra* note 3, at 14 (citing James Loewen, SUNDOWN TOWNS: A HIDDEN DIMENSION OF AMERICAN RACISM 64 (New Press 2018)).

187. Shapiro, *supra* note 183, at 93-96.

188. Gregory Mixon, THE ATLANTA RACE RIOT: RACE, CLASS, AND VIOLENCE IN A NEW SOUTH CITY (U. Press of Fla. 2004).

189. Shapiro, *supra* note 183, at 104-07 (Brownsville, Texas); 103-04 (Springfield, Illinois); 101-02 (Walter White, Atlanta); 143 (NAACP and Kansas City); 115-17 (E. St. Louis, Illinois) 107-11, 196 (Houston, Texas).

neighborhood in Philadelphia, Pennsylvania.[190] In 1919's "Red Summer," Black people were killed and Black homes and businesses destroyed in Chicago, Washington, DC, and some three dozen other places, including Charleston, South Carolina, Knoxville, Tennessee, Omaha, Nebraska, and Elaine, Arkansas.[191]

In 1919 and 1920, in Chicago, "a number" of homes owned by Black people "were bombed . . . clearly to prevent blacks from moving into previously all-white neighborhoods."[192] Between 1917 and 1921, "there were fifty-eight recorded bombings of properties rented or purchased by blacks in white Chicago neighborhoods."[193]

In the Tulsa, Oklahoma (Black Wall Street) race massacre of 1921, white people destroyed the homes, businesses, churches, schools, and other buildings of Black people, more than 35 square blocks of the neighborhood. About 10,000 Black people were left homeless, and many left the city permanently.[194] In 1921, "whites had rampaged through the . . . black section" of Springfield, Ohio; this "was the third riot that had devastated the town in two decades."[195] In 1923, a mob reacted violently when a Black family moved into an Italian neighborhood in Philadelphia.[196] There were at least two instances of housing-related threats and intimidation in New York (in Brooklyn and in Staten Island) in 1921 and 1925.[197]

1925 saw the infamous trials of Ossian Sweet, M.D. and his family, who defended their right to move into a "white" neighborhood in Detroit.[198] Another Black doctor, Alexander Turner, was driven out of the home he purchased in another "white" neighborhood of Detroit.[199] Professor Bell says:

> At this time white hostility was of paramount importance in determining where blacks lived; white animosity—often in the form of violence—restricted blacks' housing choices. . . . Upper-middle-class blacks were frequently the target of resistance despite having similar—and in some cases, higher—class status than those whites already living in the neighborhood."[200]

---

190. Bell, *supra* note 3, at 21.

191. Shapiro, *supra* note 183, at 148-57 (Charleston, South Carolina, Elaine, Arkansas, Omaha, Nebraska, Washington, DC, Knoxville, Tennessee, Chicago).

192. *Id.* at 175.

193. Satter, supra note 8, at 39.

194. Alfred L. Brophy, Reconstructing the Dreamland: The Tulsa Riot of 1921: Race, Reparation, and Reconciliation (Oxford U. Press 2002); *see also* Shapiro, *supra* note 183, at 180-85.

195. Thomas J. Sugrue, Sweet Land of Liberty: The Forgotten Struggle for Civil Rights in the North 11 (Random House 2008).

196. Bell, *supra* note 3, at 21.

197. Stephen Grant Meyer, As Long as They Don't Move Next Door: Segregation and Racial Conflict in American Neighborhoods 33-34 (Rowman & Littlefield 2000).

198. Kevin Boyle, Arc of Justice: A Saga of Race, Civil Rights, and Murder in the Jazz Age (Henry Holt 2004); Phyllis Vine, One Man's Castle: Clarence Darrow in Defense of the American Dream (Amistad Press 2005); Shapiro, *supra* note 183, at 185-94.

199. Bell, *supra* note 3, at 21-22.

200. *Id.* at 21.

In 1927, in Little Rock, Arkansas, the lynching of John Carter was followed by the destruction of a Black business area.

In the following decades, whites "consistently mobilized to exclude minorities from their neighborhoods. They pressured real estate agents, wrote race-restrictive covenants into their deeds, blocked construction of low income and rental housing projects, and . . . resorted to intimidation and assault."[201] In 1935, there was a riot in New York City's Harlem.[202] In 1937, a Black doctor in Atlanta was forced out of the white neighborhood in which he had purchased a home. In Dallas, when several Black people purchased homes on Howell Street, "white . . . resistance . . . resulted in nearly twenty bombings over a fifteen-month period. . . . Black newcomers' houses were stoned and a black physician's house was burned to the ground."[203]

During World War II (1939-1945), "violence against blacks remained a prominent feature of American society," including much violence directed at Black servicemembers.[204] "Especially during the 1940s, whites in Chicago responded to black 'move-ins' by gathering outside the homes of the newly arrived families, harassing and threatening them. Typically, these unreported riots 'involved thousands of participants and continued for days.'"[205] 1942 saw the infamous Sojourner Truth housing controversy in Detroit; when the first Black family moved in, 40 people were injured and 220 arrested.[206] Black people who moved into the Allied Gardens district of Compton in Los Angeles were met with, among other things, "'burning crosses in their front yards.'"[207] In Chicago, between 1943 and 1946, there were 59 documented attacks on Black homes, "including 'twenty-nine arson-bombings, twenty-two stonings, three shootings, three house-breakings, and two stink bombs.'"[208]

Sojourner Truth Housing Project, 1942.

201. Freund, *supra* note 1, at 4.

202. Dominic J. Capeci, Jr., THE HARLEM RIOT OF 1943, at 86 (Temple U. Press 1977); Shapiro, *supra* note 183, at 261-72.

203. Bell, *supra* note 3, at 26; Meyer, *supra* note 197, at 59, 62.

204. Shapiro, *supra* note 183, at 305, 305-10.

205. Amanda I. Seligman, BLOCK BY BLOCK: NEIGHBORHOODS AND PUBLIC POLICY AND CHICAGO'S WEST SIDE 166 (U. Chicago Press 2005) (quoting Arnold R. Hirsch, MAKING THE SECOND GHETTO (Cambridge U. Press 1983)).

206. Dominic J. Capeci, Jr., RACE RELATIONS IN WARTIME DETROIT: THE SOJOURNER TRUTH HOUSING CONTROVERSY OF 1942 (Temple U. Press 1984).

207. Bell, *supra* note 3, at 27 (quoting Eric Avila, POPULAR CULTURE IN THE AGE OF WHITE FLIGHT: FEAR AND FANTASY IN SUBURBAN LOS ANGELES 31 (U. Cal. Press 2004)).

208. Bell, *supra* note 3, at 37 (citing the Chicago Council Against Racial and Religious Discrimination).

In 1943, there were major white-on-Black race riots in Detroit and Harlem. The Detroit riot that began on June 20, 1943, "was the ugly climax to an increasingly bitter racial conflict between whites and blacks in the wartime city over jobs and housing . . .";[209] it followed a wildcat strike in which 25,000 white workers walked out of a plant because three Black workers "had been upgraded to skilled jobs."[210] Because of the "enormity" of the Detroit riot, many efforts were made to attempt to avoid an explosion in New York, including freezing of rents to quiet tensions about high rents.[211] An historian of the 1943 riots notes that while causes of racial disorder often are hard to discern, those that provoked the 1943 Harlem riot are "readily identifiable."[212] "Contemporaries believed that Metropolitan's actions [in excluding people of color from Stuyvesant Town] were one reason for the Harlem riot . . ."; it was the "most disturbing" of the city's plans.[213]

The late 1940s in Chicago "have been compared to 1917-1921, 'when one racially motivated bombing or arson occurred every twenty days.' . . . [I]n Chicago hundreds, if not thousands, of whites aimed violence at individual homeowners moving in. . . . Between . . . 1944 and . . . 1946, forty-six black homes were reported attacked by vandalism, arson, or bombing."[214] In February 1946, the National Guard threatened the Black community; many Black people were arrested and two were killed.[215] "In Atlanta, black expansion into white neighborhoods was first resisted by extremists—the Ku Klux Klan and an Atlanta-based organization of brown-shirted fascists known as the Colombians [, who used] . . . a combination of intimidation and violence," including bombing. In 1947, the West End Cooperative Corporation assumed the role of using intimidation and violence against Black people who moved to white areas. This violence "in Atlanta continued until the early 1960s."[216] In post-World War II Chicago, "hundreds and sometimes thousands of whites

209. Sidney Fine, VIOLENCE IN THE MODEL CITY: THE CAVANAGH ADMINISTRATION, RACE RELATIONS, AND THE DETROIT RIOT OF 1967, at 1 (U. Mich. Press 1989); Shapiro, *supra* note 183, at 311-30 (discussing both Sojourner Truth and the 1943 riot, and emphasizing the importance of housing to the latter); Sugrue, *supra* note 195, at 65-68. For another of the innumerable connections of violence to racial discrimination and segregation in housing, see Vose, *supra* note 90, at 124-25 (discussing the Detroit riots of 1942 (Sojourner Truth) and 1943 in the context of a study stating "that overcrowding in dwellings was . . . one of the most serious causes of these riots").
210. Simon, *supra* note 42, at 43, 45; Robert Shogan & Tom Craig, THE DETROIT RACE RIOT 89 (Clinton Books 1964); Dominic J. Capeci, Jr., & Martha Frances Wilkerson, LAYERED VIOLENCE: THE DETROIT RIOTERS OF 1943 (U. Press of Mississippi 1991).
211. Capeci, *supra* note 202, at 86-87. For a discussion of Metropolitan Life Insurance Company's refusal to allow Black people to live in Stuyvesant Town, see the earlier discussion of *Dorsey v. Stuyvesant Town Corp.*
212. Capeci, *supra* note 202, at 134.
213. Henderson, *supra* note 154, at 278-79 n. 13; Capeci, *supra* note 202, at 13-14, 136, 140-41; *see also* Shapiro, *supra* note 183, at 330-40.
214. Bell, *supra* note 3, at 27.
215. Shapiro, *supra* note 183, at 362-65.
216. Bell, *supra* note 3, at 40-41; Shapiro, *supra* note 183, at 374-75 (pointing out that the violence was directed at Jewish as well as Black people).

rioted against black entry into previously all-white housing areas." Between 1945 and 1950, of 485 racial incidents reported to the Chicago Commission on Human Relations, 357 related to housing."[217] This rioting included efforts in 1946 by a mob of 1,500 to 3,000 to prevent Black veterans from occupying temporary housing at Airport Homes and, in that same year, violence by several thousand people to protest a Black physician's arrival at a home in Park Manor; 1947 riots of 1,500 to 5,000 in Fernwood Park Homes, and 1949 protests by up to 10,000 against the sale of a home in Englewood to a Black family.[218] In 1949, Chicago's "Peoria street riot" saw protests against the rumored sale of a home to a Black family. "For three nights hundreds of people stoned the . . . home, shattering windows and screaming 'Burn the house'" and epithets.[219] Between 1946 and 1965, "there were fifty dynamite attacks directed at African Americans" in Birmingham, Alabama, which was called "Bombingham."[220]

In 1951, Illinois Governor Adlai Stevenson called the National Guard to Cicero, an all-white city into which one Black family had sought to move.[221] "For two days, a mob of between two thousand and five thousand whites attacked the Clarks' apartment building, burning and looting it. Order was restored only when 450 National Guardsmen reported to aid the 200 Cicero and Cook County sheriff's police attempting to quell the disorder."[222] In 1953 there was massive resistance to Black occupancy of the Chicago Housing Authority's Trumbull Park development in Chicago; the introduction of a Black veteran's family led to "nearly a decade of sporadic violence."[223] In the early to mid-1950s in Detroit, white opponents of residential integration used both "collective action" and "individualized threats": "Newcomers suffered . . . broken windows, anonymous threats, firebombings, and other types of vandalism designed to drive them out. . . . In Detroit, between the end of World War II and 1960 there were more than two hundred incidents of harassment, stoning of houses, arson, and physical attacks directed at black [persons] moving to white neighborhoods."[224] In the late 1950s, "Blacks moving to the West Side of Chicago . . . and real estate brokers who sold them houses, received threats and were targeted with violence. In some cases this led to riots, like that occurring near the end of July 1957 in the Italian community of North Lawndale of Chicago's West

217. Shapiro, *supra* note 183, at 376.

218. *Id.* at 376-77.

219. Satter, *supra* note 8, at 25; it might be this incident that is described also by Shapiro, *supra* note 183, at 377.

220. Bell, *supra* note 3, at 41.

221. Saltman, *supra* note 47, at 14.

222. Bell, *supra* note 3, at 35; Shapiro, *supra* note 183, at 419 (reporting a mob estimated at 6,000).

223. Arnold R. Hirsch, *Massive Resistance in the Urban North: Trumbull Park, Chicago, 1953-66*, 82 J. OF AMERICAN HIST. 522, 523, 529 (1995).

224. Bell, *supra* note 3, at 36.

Side."[225] A Black homebuyer in "the white neighborhood of East Garfield Park . . . also [was] targeted with violence."[226] In a famous incident in Louisville, Kentucky, Anne and Carl Braden purchased a home for a Black family, the Wades. The Bradens and the Wades were met with threats against the adults and the children, a cross burning, shots fired, rocks thrown through the windows of the home, and dynamite; the insurance company cancelled the Wades' home insurance and the mortgage company demanded payment in full.[227] In September 1963, hundreds of white people protested what they thought was a Black family's move into Dearborn, Michigan.[228] When a Black man, his white wife, and their child moved to Warren, Michigan in 1967, "residents burned crosses on their lawn, threw rocks through their windows, and shouted obscenities as they passed the family's home."[229] Governor George Romney said he "had to send the state police . . . to protect them. . . ."[230]

This "white vigilantism"[231] "was not especially risky behavior . . . ; [p]olice were reluctant to seek out perpetrators, and even more reluctant to make arrests. Thus, whites rarely faced prosecution for crimes of anti-integrationist violence, and when they did, the charges against them were minor."[232] This review addresses only the years up to 1968, but even after that year, many whites "continued to violently resist African American moves into their neighborhoods."[233]

G. THE 1962 EXECUTIVE ORDER AND TITLE VI OF THE 1964 CIVIL RIGHTS ACT

During the close 1960 Presidential contest between John F. Kennedy and Richard Nixon, Kennedy criticized the Eisenhower administration's civil rights record, especially with respect to housing. "Calling on the president to issue an executive order banning discrimination in federal housing programs, Kennedy stated, 'If he does not do it, a new Democratic Administration will.'"[234] Kennedy repeated this in October, stating "one stroke of the pen would have worked wonders for millions of Negroes who want their children to grow up in decency."[235]

---

225. Bell, *supra* note 3, at 37; *id.* at 1 (quoting Amanda I. Seligman, BLOCK BY BLOCK: NEIGHBORHOODS AND PUBLIC POLICY AND CHICAGO'S WEST SIDE 167 (U. Chicago Press 2005)).
226. Bell, *supra* note 3, at 38.
227. *Id.* at 42-43.
228. Freund, *supra* note 1, at 3-4.
229. Christopher Bonastia, KNOCKING ON THE DOOR: THE FEDERAL GOVERNMENT'S ATTEMPT TO DESEGREGATE THE SUBURBS 105 (Princeton U. Press 2006).
230. *Id.* at 106.
231. Freund, *supra* note 1, at 4-5.
232. Bell, *supra* note 3, at 43.
233. *Id.* at 52 and *passim*.
234. Pritchett, *supra* note 58.
235. *Id.* at 212-13; Carl M. Brauer, JOHN F. KENNEDY AND THE SECOND RECONSTRUCTION 43 (Columbia U. Press 1977) ("the moderate Civil Rights Commission had suggested" this previously).

After the election, Kennedy did take a significant action: He nominated Dr. Robert C. Weaver, an experienced Black housing advocate, to be Administrator of the Housing and Home Finance Agency. Dr. Weaver's background in civil rights generally and as a proponent of integrated housing made this a very controversial nomination; its success made Dr. Weaver the highest ranking Black official in the Kennedy Administration.[236]

Kennedy did not, however, issue the executive order he had promised. Leaders of the National Committee Against Discrimination in Housing (NCDH)—Charles Abrams, Algernon Black, Eleanor Roosevelt, and Roy Wilkins—pressed him; NCDH issued a report citing "massive evidence that the federal Government is actually promoting and strengthening nationwide patterns of residential segregation," especially in urban renewal and public housing.[237] Hearing opposition from Northern as well as Southern political figures, Kennedy delayed the executive order until after the November 1962 elections and then announced it as inconspicuously as possible.[238] (Kennedy had been trying to induce Congress to create a Department of Urban Affairs, which he had said he would appoint Dr. Weaver to head.[239])

Most significantly, Kennedy made the scope of the order as narrow as possible. Executive Order 11063, issued on November 20, 1962, stated: "The granting of federal assistance for . . . housing and related facilities from which Americans are excluded because of their race, color, creed, or national origin is unfair, unjust, and inconsistent with the public policy of the United States as manifested in its Constitution and laws."[240] The order covered all Housing and Home Finance Agency (HHFA, a precursor to HUD) programs, but "did not regulate the financial institutions that funded housing development, and it did not apply retroactively. The order directed agencies to use their 'good offices' (i.e., persuasion) to get existing projects to comply. Exempting the sale of homes by individuals, the order applied solely to commercial builders."[241] The order was so narrow that President Kennedy was concerned that Dr. Weaver might resign in protest.[242] The EO "produced only limited returns,"[243] but it did have one immediate, beneficent impact: "the realtors' industry . . . changed its code of ethics to state for the first time that realtors who sold home[s] to blacks in previously all-white neighborhoods did not violate association rules."[244] In short, while the executive order had symbolic importance, it "had little impact on racial patterns in housing."[245]

---

236. Pritchett, *supra* note 58, at 2, 243.
237. *Id.* at 225.
238. *Id.* at 237-38; Brauer, *supra* note 235, at 52, 206, 208.
239. Pritchett, *supra* note 58, at 228-29.
240. Equal Opportunity in Housing, 27 FED. REG. 11527 (Nov. 24, 1962).
241. Pritchett, *supra* note 58, at 239; Brauer, *supra* note 247, at 207-08.
242. Brauer, *supra* note 235, at 208.
243. Pritchett, *supra* note 58, at 237.
244. *Id.* at 240.
245. Brauer, *supra* note 235, at 210.

A more significant advance was made in the Civil Rights Act of 1964, Title VI of which prohibited racial discrimination in programs that receive federal funding.[246] Title VI provides:

> No person in the United States shall, on the ground of race, color, or national origin, be excluded from participation in, be denied the benefits of, or be subjected to discrimination under any program or activity receiving Federal financial assistance. Each Federal department which is empowered to extend Federal financial assistance to any program or activity, by way of grant, loan, or contract other than a contract of insurance or guaranty, is authorized and directed to effectuate the provisions of . . . this title . . . by issuing rules, regulations, or orders of general applicability which shall be consistent with the achievement of the objectives of the statute authorizing the financial assistance. . . .

Title VI definitely included public housing, although it did not include the FHA programs. Public housing was overseen by HHFA until September 1965, and by HUD after creation of that agency. On January 13, 1966, President Lyndon Johnson announced that he would nominate Robert Weaver to be Secretary of HUD. HHFA and HUD did not make much use of Title VI, but civil rights advocates did. It was a basis for the seminal *Gautreaux* public housing desegregation cases (Chapter 12) and for many other cases that appear throughout this book.

DR. ROBERT CLIFTON WEAVER, THE FIRST SECRETARY OF HUD

Robert Clifton Weaver (1907-1997), appointed in 1966 by President Lyndon Baines Johnson to be the first Secretary of HUD, was the first Black person to hold a U.S. cabinet position. The HUD building in Southwest Washington, DC is named for him. Dr. Weaver held a B.S., an M.A., and a Ph.D. in Economics from Harvard (being the first Black person to earn this last distinction) and wrote several books, including THE NEGRO GHETTO (1948). He was an aide to Interior Secretary Harold Ickes, working with the Public Works Administration, and became part of President Franklin Roosevelt's "Black Cabinet." He had a strong background in civil rights, having been a founder and president of the NCDH and very active with the NAACP, which awarded him its Spingarn Medal. He later became president of Baruch College in New York City. He and his close friend and aide, Frank Horne, tried for decades to reduce the racial discrimination and segregation in the federal housing agencies and their programs.[247]

---

246. Pub. L. 88-352, Title VI, July 2, 1964, 78 Stat. 252, 42 U.S.C. 2000d *et seq.*

247. *See* Pritchett, *supra* note 58; as to Dr. Weaver's close aides, Frank Horne and Corinne Morrow, see Arnold R. Hirsch, *"Containment" on the Home Front: Race and Federal Housing Policy from the New Deal to the Cold War*, 26 J. URBAN HIST. 158 (2000), and Pritchett, *supra* note 58, *passim.*

Chapter Summary

- Key origins of today's residential racial segregation and discrimination are in the late 19th and early 20th century use of nuisance law, covenants, and zoning to bar certain categories of people from favored, resource-rich neighborhoods.
- Although explicit racial zoning was outlawed by the Supreme Court in 1917—and then again in 1927 and 1930—communities continued to enact such laws and to enforce them.
- Although racial covenants were held judicially unenforceable in 1948 and made illegal in 1968, they continue to influence the way neighborhood lines are drawn.
- The early New Deal programs—public housing and FHA homeownership—established a two-tier system of housing assistance that created an unprecedented level of neighborhood segregation: multifamily rental increasingly identified as housing for people of color in dense urban areas and single-family, wealth-building homeownership for whites in suburbs. This was compounded by the postwar VA homeownership program.
- Amidst the dual housing markets created in part by federal policy, the urban renewal and federal-aid highway programs callously and ruthlessly destroyed the homes and businesses of hundreds of thousands of families, mostly of color, without providing relocation housing.
- The decades leading to 1968 were characterized by predatory real estate practices that grossly disadvantaged people of color and violence that drove and kept them from neighborhoods with desirable facilities and services.

CHAPTER 2

THE 1866 CIVIL RIGHTS ACT

Serious federal action against housing discrimination began in 1968 with the Supreme Court's holding in *Jones v. Mayer* interpreting the 1866 Civil Rights Act and Congress's enactment of the federal Fair Housing Act. *Jones v. Mayer* and its implications are considered in this chapter. The federal Fair Housing Act is the subject of most of the rest of this book.

A. THE WATERSHED CASE: *JONES v. MAYER*

Jones v. Alfred H. Mayer Co.
392 U.S. 409 (1968)

Before Chief Justice Warren and Justices Black, Douglas, Harlan, Brennan, Stewart, White, Fortas, and Marshall. Justices Harlan and White dissent.

Mr. Justice STEWART delivered the opinion of the Court.

In this case we are called upon to determine the scope and constitutionality of an Act of Congress, 42 U.S.C. §1982, which provides that:

> All citizens of the United States shall have the same right, in every State and Territory, as is enjoyed by white citizens thereof to inherit, purchase, lease, sell, hold, and convey real and personal property.

[P]etitioners alleged that the respondents had refused to sell them a home in the Paddock Woods community of St. Louis County for the sole reason that petitioner Joseph Lee Jones is a Negro. The District Court dismiss[ed] the complaint, and the Court of Appeals for the Eighth Circuit affirmed, concluding that §1982 applies only to state action and does not reach private refusals to sell. [W]e reverse the judgment of the Court of Appeals. We hold that §1982 bars all racial discrimination, private as well as public, in the sale or rental of property, and that the statute, thus construed, is a valid exercise of the power of Congress to enforce the Thirteenth Amendment.

I.

At the outset, it is important to make clear precisely what this case does not involve. Whatever else it may be, 42 U.S.C. §1982 is not a comprehensive open housing law. In sharp contrast to the FHA, the statute in this case deals only with racial discrimination and does not address itself to discrimination on grounds of religion or national origin. It does not deal specifically with discrimination in the provision of services or facilities in connection with the sale or rental of a dwelling. It does not prohibit advertising or other representations that indicate discriminatory preferences. It does not refer explicitly to discrimination in financing arrangements or in the provision of broker-age services.[1] It does not empower a federal administrative agency to assist aggrieved parties. It makes no provision for intervention by the Attorney General. And, although it can be enforced by injunction, it contains no provision expressly authorizing a federal court to order the payment of damages. [EDS.—This issue is addressed in the next case.]

Thus, although §1982 contains none of the exemptions that Congress included in the [Fair Housing Act], it would be a serious mistake to suppose that §1982 in any way diminishes the significance of the law recently enacted by Congress. Indeed, the Senate Subcommittee on Housing and Urban Affairs was informed in hearings held after the Court of Appeals had rendered its decision in this case that §1982 might well be "a presently valid federal stat-utory ban against discrimination by private persons in the sale or lease of real property." The Subcommittee was told, however, that even if this Court should so construe §1982, the existence of that statute would not "eliminate the need for congressional action" to spell out "responsibility on the part of the federal government to enforce the rights it protects." The point was made that, in light of the many difficulties confronted by private litigants seeking to enforce such rights on their own, "legislation is needed to establish fed-eral machinery for enforcement of the rights guaranteed under §1982 even if the plaintiffs in *Jones v. Alfred H. Mayer Company* should prevail in the United States Supreme Court."

On April 10, 1968, Representative Kelly of New York focused the attention of the House upon the present case and its possible significance. She described the background of this litigation, recited the text of §1982, and then added:

> When the Attorney General was asked in court about the effect of the old law (§1982) as compared with the pending legislation which is being considered on the House floor today, he said that the scope was somewhat different, the remedies and procedures were different, and that the new law was still quite necessary.

---

1. [Fn. 10 in original] Contrast §3606. In noting that 42 U.S.C. §1982 differs from the FHA in not dealing explicitly and exhaustively with such matters, we intimate no view upon the question whether ancillary services or facilities of this sort might in some situations constitute "property" as that term is employed in §1982. Nor do we intimate any view upon the extent to which discrimination in the provision of such services might be barred by 42 U.S.C. §1981.

Later the same day, the House passed the [Fair Housing Act]. Its enactment had no effect upon §1982 and no effect upon this litigation, but it underscored the vast differences between, on the one hand, a general statute applicable only to racial discrimination in the rental and sale of property and enforceable only by private parties acting on their own initiative, and, on the other hand, a detailed housing law, applicable to a broad range of discriminatory practices and enforceable by a complete arsenal of federal authority. Having noted these differences, we turn to a consideration of §1982 itself.

II.

This Court last had occasion to consider the scope of 42 U.S.C. §1982 in 1948, in *Hurd v. Hodge* [Chapter 1]. That case arose when property owners in the District of Columbia sought to enforce racially restrictive covenants against the Negro purchasers of several homes on their block. A federal district court enforced the restrictive agreements by declaring void the deeds of the Negro purchasers. It enjoined further attempts to sell or lease them the properties in question and directed them to "remove themselves and all of their personal belongings" from the premises within 60 days. The Court of Appeals for the District of Columbia Circuit affirmed and this Court granted certiorari.

The agreements in *Hurd* covered only two-thirds of the lots of a single city block, and preventing Negroes from buying or renting homes in that specific area would not have rendered them ineligible to do so elsewhere in the city. Thus, if §1982 had been thought to do no more than grant Negro citizens the legal capacity to buy and rent property free of prohibitions that wholly disabled them because of their race, judicial enforcement of the restrictive covenants at issue would not have violated §1982. But this Court took a broader view of the statute. Although the covenants could have been enforced without denying the general right of Negroes to purchase or lease real estate, the enforcement of those covenants would nonetheless have denied the Negro purchasers "the same right 'as is enjoyed by white citizens . . . to inherit, purchase, lease, sell, hold, and convey real and personal property.'" That result, this Court concluded, was prohibited by §1982. To suggest otherwise, the Court said, "is to reject the plain meaning of language."

Hurd v. Hodge squarely held, therefore, that a Negro citizen who is denied the opportunity to purchase the home he wants "(s)olely because of (his) race and color," has suffered the kind of injury that §1982 was designed to prevent. *Accord, Harmon v. Tyler; City of Richmond v. Deans.* The basic source of the injury in *Hurd* was, of course, the action of private individuals — white citizens who had agreed to exclude Negroes from a residential area. But an arm of the Government — in that case, a federal court — had assisted in the enforcement of that agreement. Thus *Hurd v. Hodge* did not present the question whether *purely* private discrimination, unaided by any action on the part of government, would violate §1982 if its effect were to deny a citizen the right to rent or buy property solely because of his race or color.

It is true that a dictum in *Hurd* said that §1982 was directed only toward "governmental action," but neither *Hurd* nor any other case before or since has presented that precise issue for adjudication in this Court. Today we face that issue for the first time.

III.

We begin with the language of the statute itself. In plain and unambiguous terms, §1982 grants to all citizens, without regard to race or color, "the same right" to purchase and lease property "as is enjoyed by white citizens." As the Court of Appeals in this case evidently recognized, that right can be impaired as effectively by "those who place property on the market" as by the State itself. For, even if the State and its agents lend no support to those who wish to exclude persons from their communities on racial grounds, the fact remains that, whenever property "is placed on the market for whites only, whites have a right denied to Negroes." So long as a Negro citizen who wants to buy or rent a home can be turned away simply because he is not white, he cannot be said to enjoy "the *same* right . . . as is enjoyed by white citizens . . . to . . . purchase (and) lease . . . real and personal property." 42 U.S.C. §1982. (Emphasis added.)

On its face, therefore, §1982 appears to prohibit all discrimination against Negroes in the sale or rental of property—discrimination by private owners as well as discrimination by public authorities. Indeed, even the respondents seem to concede that, if §1982 "means what it says"—to use the words of the respondents' brief—then it must encompass every racially motivated refusal to sell or rent and cannot be confined to officially sanctioned segregation in housing. Stressing what they consider to be the revolutionary implications of so literal a reading of §1982, the respondents argue that Congress cannot possibly have intended any such result. Our examination of the relevant history, however, persuades us that Congress meant exactly what it said.

IV.

In its original form, 42 U.S.C. §1982 was part of §1 of the CRA of 1866. That section was cast in sweeping terms:

> *Be it enacted by the Senate and House of Representatives of the United States of America in Congress assembled,* That all persons born in the United States and not subject to any foreign power, . . . are hereby declared to be citizens of the United States; and such citizens, of every race and color, without regard to any previous condition of slavery or involuntary servitude, . . . shall have the same right, in every State and Territory in the United States, to make and enforce contracts, to sue, be parties, and give evidence, to inherit, purchase, lease, sell, hold, and convey real and personal property, and to full and equal benefit of all laws and proceedings for the security of person and property, as is enjoyed by white citizens, and shall be subject to

like punishment, pains, and penalties, and to none other, any law, statute, ordinance, regulation, or custom, to the contrary notwithstanding.

The crucial language for our purposes was that which guaranteed all citizens "the same right, in every State and Territory in the United States, . . . to inherit, purchase, lease, sell, hold, and convey real and personal property . . . as is enjoyed by white citizens. . . ." To the Congress that passed the CRA of 1866, it was clear that the right to do these things might be infringed not only by "State or local law" but also by "custom, or prejudice."[2] Thus, when Congress provided in §1 of the CRA that the right to purchase and lease property was to be enjoyed equally throughout the United States by Negro and white citizens alike, it plainly meant to secure that right against interference from any source whatever, whether governmental or private.

Indeed, if §1 had been intended to grant nothing more than an immunity from *governmental* interference, then much of §2 would have made no sense at all. For that section, which provided fines and prison terms for certain individuals who deprived others of rights "secured or protected" by §1, was carefully drafted to exempt private violations of §1 from the criminal sanctions it imposed. There would, of course, have been no private violations to exempt if the only "right" granted by §1 had been a right to be free of discrimination by public officials. Hence the structure of the 1866 Act, as well as its language, points to the conclusion urged by the petitioners in this case — that §1 was meant to prohibit *all* racially motivated deprivations of the rights enumerated in the statute, although only those deprivations perpetrated "under color of law" were to be criminally punishable under §2.

In attempting to demonstrate the contrary, the respondents rely heavily upon the fact that the Congress which approved the 1866 statute wished to eradicate the recently enacted Black Codes — laws which had saddled Negroes with "onerous disabilities and burdens, and curtailed their rights . . . to such an extent that their freedom was of little value. . . ." Slaughter-House Cases, 16 Wall. 36, 70, 21 L.Ed. 394 [1873]. The respondents suggest that the only evil Congress sought to eliminate was that of racially discriminatory laws in the former Confederate States. But the Civil Rights Act was drafted to

---

2. [Fn. 30 in original] Several weeks before the House began its debate on the CRA of 1866, Congress had passed a bill (S. 60) to enlarge the powers of the Freedmen's Bureau (created by Act of March 3, 1865) by extending military jurisdiction over certain areas in the South where, "in consequence of any State or local law, . . . custom, or prejudice, any of the civil rights . . . belonging to white persons (including the right . . . to inherit, purchase, lease, sell, hold, and convey real and personal property . . .) are refused or denied to negroes . . . on account of race, color, or any previous condition of slavery or involuntary servitude. . . ." Both Houses had passed S. 60, and although the Senate had failed to override the President's veto the bill was nonetheless significant for its recognition that the "right to purchase" was a right that could be "refused or denied" by "custom or prejudice" as well as by "State or local law." Of course an "abrogation of civil rights made 'in consequence of . . . custom, or prejudice' might as easily be perpetrated by private individuals or by unofficial community activity as by state officers armed with statute or ordinance." J[acobus] tenBroek, EQUAL UNDER LAW 179 (1965 ed.).

apply throughout the country, and its language was far broader than would have been necessary to strike down discriminatory statutes.

That broad language, we are asked to believe, was a mere slip of the legislative pen. We disagree. For the same Congress that wanted to do away with the Black Codes *also* had before it an imposing body of evidence pointing to the mistreatment of Negroes by private individuals and unofficial groups, mistreatment unrelated to any hostile state legislation. "Accounts in newspapers North and South, Freedmen's Bureau and other official documents, private reports and correspondence were all adduced" to show that "private outrage and atrocity" were "daily inflicted on freedmen. . . ." The congressional debates are replete with references to private injustices against Negroes — references to white employers who refused to pay their Negro workers, white planters who agreed among themselves not to hire freed slaves without the permission of their former masters, white citizens who assaulted Negroes or who combined to drive them out of their communities.

Indeed, one of the most comprehensive studies then before Congress stressed the prevalence of private hostility toward Negroes and the need to protect them from the resulting persecution and discrimination. The report noted the existence of laws virtually prohibiting Negroes from owning or renting property in certain towns, but described such laws as "mere isolated cases," representing "the local outcroppings of a spirit . . . found to prevail everywhere" — a spirit expressed, for example, by lawless acts of brutality directed against Negroes who traveled to areas where they were not wanted. The report concluded that, even if anti-Negro legislation were "repealed in all the States lately in rebellion," equal treatment for the Negro would not yet be secured.

In this setting, it would have been strange indeed if Congress had viewed its task as encompassing merely the nullification of racist laws in the former rebel States. That the Congress which assembled in the Nation's capital in December 1865 in fact had a broader vision of the task before it became clear early in the session, when three proposals to invalidate discriminatory state statutes were rejected as "too narrowly conceived." From the outset it seemed clear, at least to Senator Trumbull of Illinois, Chairman of the Judiciary Committee, that stronger legislation might prove necessary. After Senator Wilson of Massachusetts had introduced his bill to strike down all racially discriminatory laws in the South, Senator Trumbull said this:

> I reported from the Judiciary Committee the second section of the [Thirteenth Amendment] for the very purpose of conferring upon Congress authority to see that the first section was carried out in good faith . . . and I hold that under that second section Congress will have the authority, when the constitutional amendment is adopted, *not only to pass the bill of the Senator from Massachusetts, but a bill that will be much more efficient to protect the freedman in his rights.* . . . And, sir, when the constitutional amendment shall have been adopted, if the information from the South be that the men whose liberties are secured by it are deprived of the privilege to go and come when they please, *to buy and sell when they please,* to make contracts and enforce contracts, I give notice that, if

no one else does, I shall introduce a bill and urge its passage through Congress that will secure to those men every one of these rights: they would not be freemen without them. *It is idle to say that a man is free who cannot go and come at pleasure, who cannot buy and sell, who cannot enforce his rights.* . . . (So) when the constitutional amendment is adopted I trust we may pass a bill, if the action of the people in the southern States should make it necessary, that will be *much more sweeping and efficient than the bill under consideration.*

Five days later, on December 18, 1865, the Secretary of State officially certified the ratification of the Thirteenth Amendment. The next day Senator Trumbull again rose to speak. He had decided, he said, that the "more sweeping and efficient" bill of which he had spoken previously ought to be enacted

> at an early day for the purpose of quieting apprehensions in the minds of many friends of freedom lest by local legislation *or a prevailing public sentiment* in some of the States persons of the African race should continue to be oppressed and in fact deprived of their freedom. . . .

On January 5, 1866, Senator Trumbull introduced the bill he had in mind—the bill which later became the CRA of 1866. He described its objectives in terms that belie any attempt to read it narrowly:

> Mr. President, I regard the bill to which the attention of the Senate is now called as the most important measure that has been under its consideration since the adoption of the constitutional amendment abolishing slavery. That amendment declared that all persons in the United States should be free. This measure is intended to give effect to that declaration and secure to all persons within the United States practical freedom. There is very little importance in the general declaration of abstract truths and principles unless they can be carried into effect, unless the persons who are to be affected by them have some means of availing themselves of their benefits.

Of course, Senator Trumbull's bill would, as he pointed out, "destroy all (the) discriminations" embodied in the Black Codes, but it would do more: It would affirmatively secure for all men, whatever their race or color, what the Senator called the "great fundamental rights":

> the right to acquire property, the right to go and come at pleasure, the right to enforce rights in the courts, to make contracts, and to inherit and dispose of property.

As to those basic civil rights, the Senator said, the bill would "break down *all* discrimination between black men and white men."

That the bill would indeed have so sweeping an effect was seen as its great virtue by its friends and as its great danger by its enemies but was disputed by none. Opponents of the bill charged that it would not only regulate state laws but would directly "determine the persons who [would] enjoy . . . property within the States," threatening the ability of white citizens "to determine who [would] be members of [their] communit[ies]. . . ." The bill's advocates did not deny the accuracy of those characterizations. Instead, they defended the propriety of employing federal authority to deal with "the white man . . . [who] would invoke the power of local prejudice" against the Negro. Thus, when the Senate passed the Civil Rights Act on February 2, 1866, it did so fully aware of the breadth of the measure it had approved.

In the House, as in the Senate, much was said about eliminating the infamous Black Codes. But, like the Senate, the House was moved by a larger objective—that of giving real content to the freedom guaranteed by the Thirteenth Amendment. Representative Thayer of Pennsylvania put it this way:

> [W]hen I voted for the amendment to abolish slavery . . . I did not suppose that I was offering . . . a mere paper guarantee. And when I voted for the second section of the amendment, I felt . . . certain that I had . . . given to Congress ability to protect . . . the rights which the first section gave. . . .
>
> The bill which now engages the attention of the House has for its object to carry out and guaranty the reality of that great measure. It is to give to it practical effect and force. It is to prevent that great measure from remaining a dead letter upon the constitutional page of this country. . . . The events of the last four years . . . have changed [a] large class of people . . . from a condition of slavery to that of freedom. *The practical question now to be decided is whether they shall be in fact freemen. It is whether they shall have the benefit of this great charter of liberty* given to them by the American people.

Representative Cook of Illinois thought that, without appropriate federal legislation, any "combination of men in [a] neighborhood [could] prevent [a Negro] from having any chance" to enjoy those benefits. To Congressman Cook and others like him, it seemed evident that, with respect to basic civil rights—including the "right to . . . purchase, lease, sell, hold, and convey . . . property," Congress must provide that "there . . . be no discrimination" on grounds of race or color.

It thus appears that, when the House passed the Civil Rights Act, it did so on the same assumption that had prevailed in the Senate: It too believed that it was approving a comprehensive statute forbidding *all* racial discrimination affecting the basic civil rights enumerated in the Act.

President Andrew Johnson vetoed the Act, and in the brief congressional debate that followed, his supporters characterized its reach in all embracing terms. One stressed the fact that §1 would confer "the right . . . to purchase . . . real estate . . . without any qualification and without any restriction whatever. . . ." Another predicted, as a corollary, that the Act would preclude preferential treatment for white persons in the rental of hotel rooms and in the sale of church pews. Those observations elicited no reply. On April 6 the Senate, and on April 9 the House, overrode the President's veto by the requisite majorities, and the CRA of 1866 became law.

In light of the concerns that led Congress to adopt it and the contents of the debates that preceded its passage, it is clear that the Act was designed to do just what its terms suggest: to prohibit all racial discrimination, whether or not under color of law, with respect to the rights enumerated therein—including the right to purchase or lease property.

Nor was the scope of the 1866 Act altered when it was re-enacted in 1870, some two years after the ratification of the Fourteenth Amendment. It is quite true that some members of Congress supported the Fourteenth Amendment "in order to eliminate doubt as to the constitutional validity of the Civil Rights Act as applied to the States." But it certainly does not follow that the adoption of the Fourteenth Amendment or the subsequent readoption of the CRA were meant somehow to *limit* its application to state action. The legislative history furnishes not the slightest factual basis for any such speculation, and the conditions prevailing in 1870 make it highly implausible. For by that time most, if not all, of the former Confederate States, then under the control of "reconstructed" legislatures, had formally repudiated racial discrimination, and the focus of congressional concern had clearly shifted from hostile statutes to the activities of groups like the Ku Klux Klan, operating wholly outside the law.

Against this background, it would obviously make no sense to assume, without any historical support whatever, that Congress made a silent decision in 1870 to exempt private discrimination from the operation of the CRA of 1866. "The cardinal rule is that repeals by implication are not favored." All Congress said in 1870 was that the 1866 law "is hereby re-enacted." That is all Congress meant.

As we said in a somewhat different setting two Terms ago, "We think that history leaves no doubt that, if we are to give (the law) the scope that its origins dictate, we must accord it a sweep as broad as its language." "We are not at liberty to seek ingenious analytical instruments," to carve from §1982 an exception for private conduct—even though its application to such conduct in the present context is without established precedent. And, as the Attorney General of the United States said at the oral argument of this case, "The fact that the statute lay partially dormant for many years cannot be held to diminish its force today."

V.

The remaining question is whether Congress has power under the Constitution to do what §1982 purports to do: to prohibit all racial discrimination, private and public, in the sale and rental of property. Our starting point is the Thirteenth Amendment, for it was pursuant to that constitutional provision that Congress originally enacted what is now §1982. The Amendment consists of two parts. Section 1 states:

> Neither slavery nor involuntary servitude, except as a punishment for crime whereby the party shall have been duly convicted, shall exist within the United States, or any place subject to their jurisdiction.

Section 2 provides:

> Congress shall have power to enforce this article by appropriate legislation.

As its text reveals, the Thirteenth Amendment "is not a mere prohibition of state laws establishing or upholding slavery, but an absolute declaration that slavery or involuntary servitude shall not exist in any part of the United States." Civil Rights Cases, 109 U.S. 3, 20 [1883]. It has never been doubted, therefore, "that the power vested in Congress to enforce the article by appropriate legislation," includes the power to enact laws "direct and primary, operating upon the acts of individuals, whether sanctioned by state legislation or not." Id. at 23. Thus, the fact that §1982 operates upon the unofficial acts of private individuals, whether or not sanctioned by state law, presents no constitutional problem. If Congress has power under the Thirteenth Amendment to eradicate conditions that prevent Negroes from buying and renting property because of their race or color, then no federal statute calculated to achieve that objective can be thought to exceed the constitutional power of Congress simply because it reaches beyond state action to regulate the conduct of private individuals. The constitutional question in this case, therefore, comes to this: Does the authority of Congress to enforce the Thirteenth Amendment "by appropriate legislation" include the power to eliminate all racial barriers to the acquisition of real and personal property? We think the answer to that question is plainly yes.

"By its own unaided force and effect," the Thirteenth Amendment "abolished slavery, and established universal freedom." *Civil Rights Cases*. Whether or not the Amendment *itself* did any more than that—a question not involved in this case—it is at least clear that the Enabling Clause of that Amendment empowered Congress to do much more. For that clause clothed "Congress with power to pass *all laws necessary and proper for abolishing all badges and incidents of slavery in the United States.*" (Emphasis added.)

Those who opposed passage of the CRA of 1866 argued in effect that the Thirteenth Amendment merely authorized Congress to dissolve the legal bond by which the Negro slave was held to his master. Yet many had earlier opposed the Thirteenth Amendment on the very ground that it would give Congress virtually unlimited power to enact laws for the protection of Negroes in every State. And the majority leaders in Congress—who were, after all, the authors of the Thirteenth Amendment—had no doubt that its Enabling Clause contemplated the sort of positive legislation that was embodied in the 1866 Civil Rights Act. Their chief spokesman, Senator Trumbull of Illinois, the Chairman of the Judiciary Committee, had brought the Thirteenth Amendment to the floor of the Senate in 1864. In defending the constitutionality of the 1866 Act, he argued that, if the narrower construction of the Enabling Clause were correct, then

> the trumpet of freedom that we have been blowing throughout the land has given an "uncertain sound," and the promised freedom is a delusion. Such was not the intention of Congress, which proposed the constitutional amendment, nor is such the fair meaning of the amendment itself. . . . I have no doubt that under this provision . . . we may destroy all these discriminations in civil rights against the black man; and if we cannot, our constitutional amendment amounts to nothing. It was for that purpose that the second clause of that amendment was adopted, which says that Congress shall have authority, by appropriate legislation, to carry into effect the article prohibiting slavery. Who is to decide what that appropriate legislation is to be? The Congress of the United States; and it is for Congress to adopt such appropriate legislation as it may think proper, so that it be a means to accomplish the end.

Surely Senator Trumbull was right. Surely Congress has the power under the Thirteenth Amendment rationally to determine what are the badges and the incidents of slavery, and the authority to translate that determination into effective legislation. Nor can we say that the determination Congress has made is an irrational one. For this Court recognized long ago that, whatever else they may have encompassed, the badges and incidents of slavery—its "burdens and disabilities"—included restraints upon "those fundamental rights which are the essence of civil freedom, namely, the same right . . . to inherit, purchase, lease, sell and convey property, as is enjoyed by white citizens." *Civil Rights Cases*.[3] Just as the Black Codes, enacted after the Civil War to restrict the free exercise of those rights, were substitutes for the slave system, so the exclusion of Negroes from white communities became a substitute for the Black Codes. And when racial discrimination herds men into ghettos and makes their ability to buy property turn on the color of their skin, then it too is a relic of slavery.

Negro citizens, North and South, who saw in the Thirteenth Amendment a promise of freedom—freedom to "go and come at pleasure" and to "buy and sell when they please"—would be left with "a mere paper guarantee" if Congress were powerless to assure that a dollar in the hands of a Negro will purchase the same thing as a dollar in the hands of a white man. At the very least, the freedom that Congress is empowered to secure under the Thirteenth Amendment includes the freedom to buy whatever a white man can buy, the right to live wherever a white man can live. If Congress cannot say that being a free man means at least this much, then the Thirteenth Amendment made a promise the Nation cannot keep.

Representative Wilson of Iowa was the floor manager in the House for the CRA of 1866. In urging that Congress had ample authority to pass the pending bill, he recalled the celebrated words of Chief Justice Marshall in *McCulloch v. State of Maryland*:

> Let the end be legitimate, let it be within the scope of the constitution, and all means which are appropriate, which are plainly adapted to that end, which

---

3. [Fn. 78 in original] The Court did conclude in the *Civil Rights Cases* that "the act of . . . the owner of the inn, the public conveyance or place of amusement, refusing . . . accommodation" cannot be "justly regarded as imposing any badge of slavery or servitude upon the applicant." "It would be running the slavery argument into the ground," the Court thought, "to make it apply to every act of discrimination which a person may see fit to make as to the guests he will entertain, or as to the people he will take into his coach or cab or car, or admit to his concert or theatre, or deal with in other matters of intercourse or business." Mr. Justice Harlan dissented, expressing the view that "such discrimination practised by corporations and individuals in the exercise of their public or quasi-public functions is a badge of servitude the imposition of which congress may prevent under its power, by appropriate legislation, to enforce the thirteenth amendment." Whatever the present validity of the position taken by the majority on that issue—a question rendered largely academic by Title II of the CRA of 1964—we note that the entire Court agreed upon at least one proposition: The Thirteenth Amendment authorizes Congress not only to outlaw all forms of slavery and involuntary servitude but also to eradicate the last vestiges and incidents of a society half slave and half free, by securing to all citizens, of every race and color, "the same right to make and enforce contracts, to sue, be parties, give evidence, and to inherit, purchase, lease, sell and convey property, as is enjoyed by white citizens."

are not prohibited, but consist with the letter and spirit of the constitution, are constitutional.

"The end is legitimate," the Congressman said, "because it is defined by the Constitution itself. The end is the maintenance of freedom. . . . A man who enjoys the civil rights mentioned in this bill cannot be reduced to slavery. . . . This settles the appropriateness of this measure, and that settles its constitutionality."

We agree. The judgment is reversed.

NOTES AND QUESTIONS

1. ***Jones v. Mayer* in Context.** *Jones v. Mayer* is the seminal case interpreting the Civil Rights Act of 1866 and the Thirteenth Amendment. Its construction of the Act governs cases under both §1982 and §1981 (now §1981a), which applies to contract actions and often is used in employment discrimination cases as an analogue to Title VII of the 1964 Civil Rights Act (as §1982 is an analogue to the Fair Housing Act).

2. **The Holdings in *Jones v. Mayer*.** There are two important holdings in *Jones v. Mayer*—one is statutory; the other, constitutional. Be sure you identify each. With respect to the statutory holding, the Court acknowledged in Part II that *Hurd v. Hodge* (Chapter 1) "said that §1982 was directed only toward 'government action.'" But the *Jones* Court concluded that this "dictum" in *Hurd v. Hodge* was not an accurate statement of the law. What do you think of the way in which the *Jones* Court dealt with *Hurd*?

3. **Counsel and Amici in *Jones v. Mayer*.** Counsel for Mr. and Mrs. Jones was Samuel H. Liberman, a staff attorney for the Greater St. Louis Committee for Freedom of Residence.[4] In *Jones v. Mayer*, as in *Shelley v. Kraemer* and *Hurd v. Hodge*, the United States appeared amicus curiae supporting the civil rights claimants; argument was presented by the Attorney General, Ramsey Clark.

4. ***Jones v. Mayer* in the Eighth Circuit.** When the case was before the Eighth Circuit, then-Judge Harry Blackmun was on the panel and wrote the opinion affirming the dismissal of the complaint. Legal analyst Linda Greenhouse has shown us that Judge (eventually Justice) Blackmun "was in the unusual position, for a lower-court judge, of hoping to be reversed. . . ."[5] His opinion, 393 F.2d 33 (8th Cir. 1967), laid out three ways in which

---

4. *See* Tim O'Neil, *A St. Louis Couple Win a Landmark Housing-Rights Case, but They Never Get Their Dream House*, St. Louis Post-Dispatch, June 17, 2068, https://www.stltoday.com/news/archives/june-17-1968-a-st-louis-couple-win-a-landmark-housing-rights-case-but-they/article_08928410-2a54-5da6-b749-243ac259a83f.html (last visited July 3, 2023).

5. Linda Greenhouse, Becoming Justice Blackmun: Harry Blackmun's Supreme Court Journey 29-30 (Times Books 2005).

§1982 might "reach discrimination in private subdivision housing," but he wrote that:

> It is not for our court, as an inferior one, to give full expression to any personal inclination any of us might have and to take the lead in expanding constitutional precepts when we are faced with a limiting Supreme Court decision which, so far as we are told directly, remains good law. . . .
>
> It would not be too surprising if the Supreme Court one day were to hold that a court errs when it dismisses a complaint of this kind. . . .

Judge Blackmun wrote to one colleague on the Eighth Circuit:

> I did my best to serve the issues up on a tray, figuratively, for the Supreme Court to take. I hope they will. This is the kind of situation where one does not mind being reversed. Perhaps I should be more willing to strike out for the frontier and be less influenced by Supreme Court decisions which remain on the books.[6]

And to another:

> I did my best . . . to spell out precisely how the opposite decision could be reached. The implication was that we were bound by existing Supreme Court utterances. I am fairly convinced, personally, that fair housing is an important factor in the elimination of the ghetto.[7]

Do you think Judge Blackmun and his colleagues should have been more willing "to strike out for the frontier?" Where should a judge draw the line between following precedent that the judge thinks will be distinguished or overruled by a higher court and ruling in a way that the judge believes is righteous? Compare, for example, the situation of Judge Frank M. Johnson and his colleagues when, in the wake of the Montgomery Bus Boycott, they invalidated legislation requiring racial segregation in intrastate transportation.[8] *Plessy v. Ferguson* had not been overruled, but *Brown v. Board of Education* had held that "in the field of public education the doctrine of 'separate but equal' has no place. Separate educational facilities are inherently unequal." Brown v. Board of Education, 347 U.S. 483, 495 (1954). Judge Johnson is discussed in Chapter 6.

   5. *Jones v. Mayer* **in Temporal Context.** 1968 was an extraordinary year. Dr. Martin Luther King, Jr. was assassinated in April; his murder was followed by disorders in 138 localities.[9] Later in the year, Robert Kennedy was assassinated in June and police rioted[10] in Chicago at the Democratic National Convention in August.

---

   6. *Id.*

   7. *Id.*

   8. Browder v. Gayle, 142 F. Supp. 707 (M.D. Ala. 1956), *aff'd mem.*, 352 U.S. 903 (1956) (per curiam).

   9. Christopher Bonastia, Knocking on the Door: The Federal Government's Attempt to Desegregate the Suburbs 77 (Princeton U. Press 2006).

   10. *See* Daniel Walker (Chicago Study Team), *Rights in Conflict. Convention Week in Chicago, August 25–29, 1968*, a report to the National Commission on the Causes and Prevention of Violence 1, 10-11 (E.P. Dutton 1968).

Jones v. Mayer landed right in the middle of pivotal events for the cause of fair housing. The case was argued on April 1 and 2, just one month after the Kerner Commission Report issued a call for fair housing legislation, even as a fair housing bill was languishing in the House (Chapter 3). Two days later, on April 4, Dr. Martin Luther King, Jr. was assassinated. The Court met for its first conference on the case on April 5. Unrest broke out in urban areas across the country, including several uprisings in Washington, DC. The District was placed under martial law, and by April 8, army troops surrounded Capitol Hill, where the Supreme Court sat. The fair housing bill was signed into law on April 11. The Supreme Court handed down its opinion in *Jones v. Mayer* just nine weeks later, on June 17, 1968.

6. **The Independence of §1982 from Title VIII.** The Supreme Court makes clear in *Jones v. Mayer* (and in the two cases that follow, *Sullivan* and *Tillman*) that the 1866 Civil Rights Act provides a cause of action wholly independent of the 1968 Fair Housing Act. Thus, properties that are exempt under the 1968 Act may be covered by the 1866 Act; for example, personal property and real property that is not a "dwelling" are covered by the 1866 Act but not by the Fair Housing Act. On the other hand, only "citizens" are protected by §1982, but no such limitation applies to the Fair Housing Act. Also, the 1866 Act applies only to race, although the 1968 Act, as amended in 1988, prohibits discrimination also on the bases of color, sex, disability, familial status, national origin, and religion (the latter two characteristics may be to some extent the same as "race" for purposes of the 1866 Act; see *St. Francis College v. Al-Khazraji* and *Shaare Tefila Congregation v. Cobb*, discussed in Chapter 14). Thus, although both the 1866 and 1968 statutes sometimes apply to the same situation, there are many cases in which only one of the statutes applies. Another important distinction, discussed in Chapters 6 and 7, is that liability under the 1866 Act is established only by a showing of intentional discrimination, although liability under the 1968 Act also may be established by a showing of disparate impact.[11]

7. **Who May Maintain an Action Under §§1981 and 1982?** The Supreme Court has held that white people claiming "reverse discrimination" against them in favor of Black people may recover under the 1866 Act. McDonald v. Santa Fe Trail Transp. Co., 427 U.S. 273 (1976) (interpreting §1981 in an opinion by Justice Thurgood Marshall). (The Court has held that §§1981 and 1982 should be interpreted similarly.[12]) You might read that opinion and

---

11. *See* General Bldg. Contractors Ass'n, Inc. v. Pennsylvania, 458 U.S. 375 (1982) (a §1981 case). The Court also has held that a plaintiff in a case under §1981 must plead and prove "but for" causation. Comcast Corp. v. National Ass'n of African American-Owned Media, 589 U.S. 327 (2020). *See* Chapter 6.

12. CBOCS West, Inc. v. Hedrick G. Humphries, 553 U.S. 442 (2008).

consider whether you agree that a statute that guarantees the same rights as "white citizens" should be used to protect "white citizens" claiming "reverse discrimination."

A white person—Mrs. Jones—was a plaintiff in *Jones v. Mayer*. Her claim, of course, was that she had been denied the right to purchase a home because of the race of her husband. White people also are among the plaintiffs in the next two cases, *Sullivan* and *Tillman*, as well, though their claims are not for "reverse discrimination" or the inability to acquire property. And the plaintiffs in *Al-Khazraji* (Iraqi) and *Shaare Tefila* (Jewish) would be considered "white" today, but the question in those cases is whether they are "white" for purposes of the 1866 Act. (*See* Chapter 14.) For a discussion of the types of plaintiffs able to establish standing under the 1866 Act, see Chapter 4.

8. **What Actions Are Covered by the 1866 Act?** Note that §1982 guarantees the same right "to *inherit*, purchase, lease, sell, *hold*, and convey" property (emphasis added). The meaning of "hold" is discussed in connection with *City of Memphis v. Greene*, below. As to the meaning of "the same right . . . to inherit," see Florence Wagman Roisman, *The Impact of the Civil Rights Act of 1866 on Racially Discriminatory Donative Transfers*, 53 ALA. L. REV. 463 (2002). Under the Fair Housing Act, questions have arisen about the extent to which protections apply after property has been acquired, but §1982 unquestionably applies to postacquisition discrimination.

In Part I of *Jones v. Mayer*, the Court noted that many actions that specifically are covered by Title VIII are not mentioned in the single sentence that is §1982. Some such actions are addressed in the following Supreme Court cases; others, in lower court decisions. Professor Schwemm concludes that §1982 seems to bar most actions that would violate §§3604(a) and (d) of Title VIII; also, *Clark v. Universal Builders*, in Chapter 1, upholds a §1982 claim for discriminatory "terms or conditions," analogous to §3604(b).

9. **Who May Be Held Liable Under §1982?** Courts have held that federal defendants are protected by the doctrine of sovereign immunity from damage claims under §1982 and state defendants are protected by the Eleventh Amendment from any damage claims under the statute, to the extent they are sued in their official capacities. Further, the Supreme Court has held in a §1981 case that respondeat superior may not be used to impose liability on local governments "for the isolated violations of their employees."[13]

---

13. *See* Schwemm, HDLL §27:4 (citing cases).

B. THE IMPLICATIONS OF *JONES v. MAYER: SULLIVAN v. LITTLE HUNTING PARK,* AND *TILLMAN v. WHEATON-HAVEN*

Two cases in the suburbs of the District of Columbia, *Sullivan v. Little Hunting Park* and *Tillman v. Wheaton-Haven,* implemented and expanded the holding in *Jones v. Mayer.* They are presented below.

Sullivan v. Little Hunting Park, Inc.
396 U.S. 229 (1969)

Opinion of the Court by Mr. Justice DOUGLAS, announced by Mr. Justice Black, who joined the opinion with Justices Brennan, Stewart, and Marshall. Justice Harlan, joined by Chief Justice Burger and Justice White, dissented.

[In Part I, the Court explained that the case was before it for the second time. Originally, the Virginia trial court had denied relief, the Supreme Court of Virginia refused review on procedural grounds, and on petition for certiorari the Supreme Court remanded for reconsideration. The Supreme Court of Virginia reinstated its earlier decision and the Supreme Court again granted certiorari.]

I.

Little Hunting Park, Inc., is a Virginia nonstock corporation organized to operate a community park and playground facilities for the benefit of residents in an area of Fairfax County, Virginia. A membership share entitles all persons in the immediate family of the shareholder to use the corporation's recreation facilities. Under the bylaws a person owning a membership share is entitled when he rents his home to assign the share to his tenant, subject to approval of the board of directors. Paul E. Sullivan and his family owned a house in this area and lived in it. Later he bought another house in the area and leased the first one to T. R. Freeman, Jr., an employee of the U.S. Department of Agriculture, and assigned his membership share to Freeman. The board refused to approve the assignment because Freeman was a Negro. Sullivan protested that action and was notified that he would be expelled from the corporation by the board. A hearing was accorded him and he was expelled, the board tendering him cash for his two shares.

Sullivan and Freeman sued under 42 U.S.C. §§1981, 1982 for injunctions and monetary damages. Since Freeman no longer resides in the area served by Little Hunting Park, his claim is limited solely to damages.

The trial court denied relief to each petitioner. We reverse those judgments.

In *Jones v. Alfred H. Mayer Co.*, we reviewed at length the legislative history of 42 U.S.C. §1982. We concluded that it reaches beyond state action and operates upon the unofficial acts of private individuals and that it is authorized by the Enabling Clause of the Thirteenth Amendment.

The Virginia trial court rested on its conclusion that Little Hunting Park was a private social club. But we find nothing of the kind on this record. There was no plan or purpose of exclusiveness. It is open to every white person within the geographic area, there being no selective element other than race. What we have here is a device functionally comparable to a racially restrictive covenant, the judicial enforcement of which was struck down in *Shelley v. Kraemer* by reason of the Fourteenth Amendment.

In *Jones v. Mayer*, the complaint charged a refusal to sell petitioner a home because he was black. In the instant case the interest conveyed was a leasehold of realty coupled with a membership share in a nonprofit company organized to offer recreational facilities to owners and lessees of real property in that residential area. It is not material whether the membership share be considered realty or personal property, as §1982 covers both. Section 1982 covers the right "to inherit, purchase, lease, sell, hold, and convey real and personal property." There is a suggestion that transfer on the books of the corporation of Freeman's share is not covered by any of those verbs. The suggestion is without merit. There has never been any doubt but that Freeman paid part of his $129 monthly rental for the assignment of the membership share in Little Hunting Park. The transaction clearly fell within the "lease." The right to "lease" is protected by §1982 against the actions of third parties, as well as against the actions of the immediate lessor. Respondents' actions in refusing to approve the assignment of the membership share in this case was clearly an interference with Freeman's right to "lease." A narrow construction of the language of §1982 would be quite inconsistent with the broad and sweeping nature of the protection meant to be afforded by §1 of the CRA of 1866, from which §1982 was derived.

We turn to Sullivan's expulsion for the advocacy of Freeman's cause. If that sanction, backed by a state court judgment, can be imposed, then Sullivan is punished for trying to vindicate the rights of minorities protected by §1982. Such a sanction would give impetus to the perpetuation of racial restrictions on property. That is why we said in Barrows v. Jackson, 346 U.S. 249, 259 [1953], that the white owner is at times "the only effective adversary" of the unlawful restrictive covenant. Under the terms of our decision in *Barrows*, there can be no question but that Sullivan has standing to maintain this action.[14]

We noted in *Jones v. Mayer*, that the Fair Housing Title of the Civil Rights Act of 1968 in no way impaired the sanction of §1982. What we said there is adequate to dispose of the suggestion that the public accommodations

---

14. [EDS.— *Barrows v. Jackson* extended *Shelley v. Kraemer* to bar a suit for damages for violation of a racial covenant.]

provision of the Civil Rights Act of 1964 in some way supersedes the provisions of the 1866 Act.

We held in *Jones v. Mayer* that although §1982 is couched in declaratory terms and provides no explicit method of enforcement, a federal court has power to fashion an effective equitable remedy. That federal remedy for the protection of a federal right is available in the state court, if that court is empowered to grant injunctive relief generally, as is the Virginia court.

Finally, as to damages, Congress, by 28 U.S.C. §1343(4), created federal jurisdiction for "damages or . . . equitable or other relief under any Act of Congress providing for the protection of civil rights. . . ." We reserved in *Jones v. Mayer*, the question of what damages, if any, might be appropriately recovered for a violation of §1982.

The existence of a statutory right implies the existence of all necessary and appropriate remedies. [Eds. — This proposition has been abrogated. The Court now looks to the statutory text to determine whether Congress has intended to confer a particular remedy; "a private cause of action will not be created through judicial mandate." Ziblar v. Abbasi, 582 U.S. 120, 131-33 (2017).] Compensatory damages for deprivation of a federal right are governed by federal standards, as provided by Congress in 42 U.S.C. §1988.[15] [We read §1988 to say] that both federal and state rules on damages may be utilized, whichever better serves the policies expressed in the federal statutes. The rule of damages, whether drawn from federal or state sources, is a federal rule responsive to the need whenever a federal right is impaired. We do not explore the problem further, as the issue of damages was not litigated below. It is suggested, not by any party, but by the dissent, that any relief should await proceedings under [the Fair Housing Act]. But petitioners' suits were commenced two years before that Act was passed. It would be irresponsible judicial administration to dismiss a suit because of an intervening Act which has no possible application to events long preceding its enactment.

Reversed.

Mr. Justice HARLAN, with whom The Chief Justice and Mr. Justice White join, dissenting.

Today, the Court goes yet beyond *Jones [v. Mayer]* (1) by implying a private right to damages for violations of 42 U.S.C. §1982; (2) by interpreting §1982 to prohibit a community recreation association from withholding, on the basis of race, approval of an assignment of a membership that was transferred incident to a lease of real property; and (3) by deciding that a white person who is

---

15. [Eds. — 42 U.S.C. §1988 provides, in pertinent part, that civil rights cases shall be adjudicated in conformity with federal law or the law of the state in which the court sits. For example, this has operated to render state tort law on statutes of limitations applicable to cases brought under the Civil Rights Act of 1866.]

expelled from a recreation association "for the advocacy of (a Negro's) cause" has "standing" to maintain an action for relief under §1982.

II.

Because Congress has now provided a comprehensive scheme for dealing with the kinds of discrimination found in this case, I think it very unwise as a matter of policy for the Court to use §1982 as a broad delegation of power to develop a common law of forbidden racial discriminations. I believe that the Court should not decide this case but should instead dismiss the writ of certiorari as improvidently granted. This Court's certiorari jurisdiction should not be exercised simply "for the benefit of the particular litigants," Rice v. Sioux City Memorial Park Cemetery, 349 U.S. 70, 74 (1955) [denying review of cemetery's refusal, because of a racially restrictive covenant, to bury a Native American veteran], but instead for the "settlement of (issues) of importance to the public, as distinguished from . . . the parties."

NOTES AND QUESTIONS

1. **Was Supreme Court Review Warranted?** The dissenters say that the Court should not have granted the petition for certiorari because the "comprehensive" 1968 Fair Housing Act would have resolved the legal questions presented. It could not, of course, provide relief to the plaintiffs in this case, as it was not enacted until after the events at issue had occurred. This seems to be the decision the Supreme Court reached in *Triangle Improvement Council v. Ritchie* (Chapter 1), where the Court dismissed the writ of certiorari as improvidently granted, apparently in part because of the statutory provisions that had been enacted after the plaintiffs were displaced. Do you agree that Supreme Court review should be limited in this way?

2. **What Remedy Is the Court Reading into §1982?** The Court is reading into §1982 a right to sue for damages for violation of that section. What is the basis for the Court's reading and do you agree with it? Why or why not? In the years since *Sullivan,* the Court has become much more restrictive about implying private rights of action into statutes, instead looking for express authorization in the statutory text.

3. **Think About the People Involved.** Dr. T.R. Freeman, to whom Mr. Sullivan leased the house, was an agricultural economist with a Ph.D. degree from the University of Wisconsin; at the time of the events of this suit he was employed by the Foreign Agriculture Division of the United States Department of Agriculture. He also held the rank of Captain in the District of Columbia National Guard. To Paul Sullivan, the rejection of Dr. Freeman and his family because they were Negro "was shocking, and as a matter of his religious teaching and conviction, immoral. . . . Furthermore, as a resident of the neighborhood for many years and as a member of Little Hunting Park, Inc. since its

inception, he could not believe their assertion that the board's action reflected the unanimous view of the members of the corporation."[16] Although omitted from this excerpt, some of Mr. Sullivan's exchanges with the Little Hunting Park board are described by the petitioners; they do not mention that after an early meeting, "Sullivan and Dr. Freeman, who was also his fellow parishioner, sought the advice of their priest, Father Eugene Walsh, who suggested that the board might reconsider its action if the directors had an opportunity to meet with Dr. Freeman and consider his case on its merits. The suggestion that such a meeting be held was rebuffed . . . by the corporation's president. . . . At about the same time, Sullivan spoke with several other shareholders, who, upon learning of the board's action, wrote letters to [the] President . . . in which they expressed their strong disagreement with the board's action in disapproving Dr. Freeman."[17]

4. **What Is the Basis for Recovery by Dr. Freeman? Mr. Sullivan?** Dr. Freeman had no difficulty leasing his house from Mr. Sullivan; what was withheld was the "membership share in a nonprofit company organized to offer recreational facilities to owners and lessees of real property in that residential area." The Court did not make clear whether this was part of the leasehold or a separate item of personal or real property; the Court said that any of those would be encompassed within the statute's protection of the right "to inherit, purchase, lease, sell, hold, and convey real and personal property." Mr. Sullivan, on the other hand, was not being deprived of any property interest. The Court said that he "has standing" to vindicate the rights of Dr. Freeman. Consider the discussion of standing in Chapter 4. Do Mr. Sullivan's claims and injury resemble those of the plaintiffs in *Trafficante* and *Gladstone*, which were decided at roughly the same time?

5. **"Broad and Sweeping Protection."** Note the Court's emphasis that §1982 must be interpreted generously: "A narrow construction of the language of §1982 would be quite inconsistent with the broad and sweeping nature of the protection meant to be afforded by §1 of the CRA of 1866, from which §1982 was derived." This interpretive standard is repeated in later cases. Notice similar language in cases throughout this text describing the broad construction to be afforded the Fair Housing Act.

Tillman v. Wheaton-Haven Recreation Association, Inc.
410 U.S. 431 (1973)

Before Chief Justice Burger and Justices Douglas, Brennan, Stewart, White, Marshall, Blackmun, Powell, and Rehnquist.

---

16. Brief for Petitioners at 9-10, Sullivan v. Little Hunting Park, Inc., 396 U.S. 229 (1969) (No. 33), 1969 WL 120121.

17. *Id.* at 10.

Mr. Justice BLACKMUN delivered the opinion for a unanimous Court.

Wheaton-Haven Recreation Association, Inc., a non-profit Maryland corporation, was organized in 1958 for the purpose of operating a swimming pool. After a membership drive to raise funds, the Association obtained zoning as a "community pool" and constructed its facility near Silver Spring, Maryland. The Association is essentially a single-function recreational club, furnishing only swimming and related amenities.

Membership is by family units, rather than individuals, and is limited to 325 families. This limit has been reached on at least one occasion. Membership is largely keyed to the geographical area within a three-quarter-mile radius of the pool.[18] A resident (whether or not a homeowner) of that area requires no recommendation before he may apply for membership; the resident receives a preferential place on the waiting list if he applies when the membership is full; and the resident-member who is a homeowner and who sells his home and turns in his membership, confers on the purchaser of his property a first option on the vacancy created by his removal and resignation. A person residing outside the three-quarter-mile area may apply for membership only upon the recommendation of a member; he receives no preferential place on the waiting list if the membership is full; and if he becomes a member, he has no way of conferring an option upon the purchaser of his property. Beyond-the-area members may not exceed 30% of the total. Majority approval of those present at a meeting of the board of directors or of the general membership is required before an applicant is admitted as a member.

Only members and their guests are admitted to the pool. No one else may gain admission merely by payment of an entrance fee.

In the spring of 1968 petitioner, Harry C. Press, a Negro who had purchased from a nonmember a home within the geographical preference area, inquired about membership in Wheaton-Haven. At that time the Association had no Negro member. In November 1968 the general membership rejected a resolution that would have opened the way for Negro members. Dr. Press was never given an application form, and respondents concede that he was discouraged from applying because of his race.

In July 1968 petitioners Murray and Rosalind N. Tillman, who were husband and wife and members in good standing, brought petitioner Grace Rosner, a Negro, to the pool as their guest. Although Mrs. Rosner was admitted on that occasion, the guest policy was changed by the board of directors, at a special meeting the following day, to limit guests to relatives of members. Respondents concede that one reason for the adoption of this policy was to prevent members from having Negroes as guests at the pool. Under this new policy Mrs. Rosner thereafter was refused admission when the Tillmans

18. [Fn. 1 in original] The Association's bylaws provide that "[m]embership shall be open to bona fide residents (whether or not homeowners) of the area within a three-quarter mile radius of the pool," and "may be extended" to others "who shall have been recommended . . . by a member."

sought to have her as their guest. In the fall of 1968 the membership, by reso-lution, reaffirmed the policy.

In October 1969 petitioners (Mr. and Mrs. Tillman, Dr. and Mrs. Press, and Mrs. Rosner) instituted this civil action against the Association and individ-uals who were its officers or directors, seeking damages and declaratory and injunctive relief, particularly under the CRA of 1866, now 42 U.S.C. §1982, the CRA of 1870, now 42 U.S.C. 1981, and Title II of the CRA of 1964. The District Court held that Wheaton-Haven was a private club and exempt from the nondiscrimination provisions of the statutes. It granted summary judgment for defendants. The Court of Appeals affirmed, one judge dissenting. It later denied rehearing en banc over two dissents. We granted certiorari to review the case in the light of *Sullivan v. Little Hunting Park, Inc.*

I.

In *Jones v. Alfred H. Mayer Co.*, this Court held that [§1982] reaches beyond state action and is not confined to officially sanctioned segregation. The Court subse-quently applied §1982 in *Sullivan* to private racial discrimination practiced by a nonstock corporation organized to operate a community park and playground facilities, including a swimming pool, for residents of a designated area. The Presses contend that their §1982 claim is controlled by *Sullivan*. We agree.

A. The Court of Appeals held that §1982 would not apply to the Presses because membership rights in Wheaton-Haven could neither be leased nor transferred incident to the acquisition of property. In *Sullivan*, the Court con-cluded that the right to enjoy a membership share in the corporation, assigned by a property owner as part of a leasehold he was granting, constituted a right "to . . . lease . . . property" protected by §1982. The Court of Appeals distin-guished property-linked membership shares in *Sullivan* from property-linked membership preferences in Wheaton-Haven by emphasizing the speculative nature of the benefits available to residents of the area around Wheaton-Haven. We conclude that the Court of Appeals erroneously characterized the property-linked preferences conferred by Wheaton-Haven's bylaws.

Under the bylaws, a resident of the area within three-quarters of a mile from the pool receives the three preferences noted above: he is allowed to apply for membership without seeking a recommendation from a current member; he receives preference over others, except those with first options, when applying for a membership vacancy; and, if he is an owner-member, he is able to pass to his successor-in-title a first option to acquire the membership Wheaton-Haven purchases from him.[19] If the membership is full, the resident

---

19. [Fn. 3 in original] Under the Wheaton-Haven system, a within-the-area member selling his home may either retain his membership or seek to sell it back to the Association. If Wheaton-Haven is willing to purchase, it pays 80% of the initial cost if the membership is not full, and 90% if the membership is full. The purchaser of the member's home then has a first option on the membership so released by the seller. The practical effect of this system is to prefer applicants who purchase from members over other applicants, particularly at a time when the membership is full.

is placed on the waiting list; other applicants, however, are required to reapply after those on the waiting list obtain memberships.

The Court of Appeals concluded, incorrectly it later appeared, that the membership had never been full, and that the option possibility, therefore, was "far too tenuous a thread to support a conclusion that there is a transfer of membership incident to the purchase of property." Since the Presses had not purchased their area home from a member, the court found no transaction by which the Presses could have acquired a membership preference.

We differ from the Court of Appeals in our evaluation of the three rights obtained. The record indicates that the membership was full in the spring of 1968 but dropped, perhaps not unexpectedly in view of the season, in the fall of that year. We cannot be certain, either, that the membership would not have remained full in the absence of racial discrimination,[20] or that the membership will never be full in the future. As was observed in dissent in the Court of Appeals:

> Several years from now it may well be that a white neighbor can sell his home at a considerably higher price than Dr. and Mrs. Press because the white owner will be able to assure his purchaser of an option for membership in Wheaton-Haven. Dr. and Mrs. Press, however, are denied this advantage.

Similarly, the automatic waiting-list preference given to residents of the favored area may have affected the price paid by the Presses when they bought their home. Thus, the purchase price to them, like the rental paid by Freeman in *Sullivan*, may well reflect benefits dependent on residency in the preference area. For them, however, the right to acquire a home in the area is abridged and diluted.

When an organization links membership benefits to residency in a narrow geographical area, that decision infuses those benefits into the bundle of rights for which an individual pays when buying or leasing within the area. The mandate of 42 U.S.C. §1982 then operates to guarantee a nonwhite resident, who purchases, leases, or holds this property, the same rights as are enjoyed by a white resident.

B. Respondents contend that even if 42 U.S.C. §1982 applies, Wheaton-Haven nevertheless is exempt as a private club under §201(e) of the CRA of 1964, 42 U.S.C. §2000a(e),[21] with a consequent implied narrowing effect upon the range and application of the older §1982. In *Sullivan* we found it unnecessary to consider limits on §1982 as applied to a truly private association because we found "no plan or purposes of exclusiveness" in *Little Hunting Park*. But here, as there, membership "is open to every white person within

---

20. [Fn. 5 in original] The record reveals that a number of members withdrew when the present suit was filed. Tr. of Oral Arg. in District Court 15.

21. [Fn. 6 in original] "The provisions of this subchapter shall not apply to a private club or other establishment not in fact open to the public, except to the extent that the facilities of such establishment are made available to the customers or patrons of an establishment within the scope of subsection (b) [covering public accommodations]." 42 U.S.C. §2000a(e).

the geographic area, there being no selective element other than race." The only restrictions are the stated maximum number of memberships and, as in *Sullivan*, the requirement of formal board or membership approval. The structure and practices of Wheaton-Haven thus are indistinguishable from those of Little Hunting Park. We hold, as a consequence, that Wheaton-Haven is not a private club and that it is not necessary in this case to consider the issue of any implied limitation on the sweep of §1982 [imposed by] §2000a(e).

II.

Mrs. Rosner and the Tillmans, relying on 42 U.S.C. §§1981,[22] 1982, and 2000a *et seq.*, contend that Wheaton-Haven could not adopt a racially discriminatory policy toward guests. The District Court granted summary judgment for the respondents on these claims also, holding that Wheaton-Haven was a private club and exempt from all three statutes.

The operative language of both §1981 and §1982 is traceable to the Act of April 9, 1866. In light of the historical interrelationship between §1981 and §1982, we see no reason to construe these sections differently when applied, on these facts, to the claim of Wheaton-Haven that it is a private club. Consequently, our discussion and rejection of Wheaton-Haven's claim that it is exempt from §1982 disposes of the argument that Wheaton-Haven is exempt from §1981.

NOTES AND QUESTIONS

1. **The Private Club Exemption.** The 1866 Act has no exemption for private clubs (or anything else). Title II of the 1964 Civil Rights Act, the public accommodations title, does have an exemption for private clubs, and so does the Fair Housing Act. (*See* Chapter 5.) In both *Sullivan* and *Tillman*, the Supreme Court rejected the argument that the clubs involved were private clubs, so the Court did not need to decide whether an exemption for private clubs should be read into §1982. Professor Schwemm tells us that the "lower courts have not reached a consensus on this issue."[23] For additional background on the movement to desegregate public pools and its aftermath, see Heather McGhee, THE SUM OF US: WHAT RACISM COSTS EVERYONE AND HOW WE CAN PROSPER TOGETHER 17-39 (2021) ("'Beginning in the mid-1950s northern cities generally stopped building large resort pools and let the ones already constructed fall into disrepair.' Over the next decade, millions of white Americans who once swam in public for free began to pay rather than swim for free with black people; desegregation in the mid-fifties coincided

---

22. [EDS.—The Civil Rights Act of 1991 made what had been §1981 into §1981(a).]
23. Schwemm, HDLL §27:6.

with a surge in backyard pools and members-only swim clubs."). *See also* Katherine Graham, Personal History 186 (Knopf 1997) (describing violent reactions to efforts to integrate public pools in DC in 1949).

2. **What Is Dr. Press's Claim?** Dr. Press's claim, like Dr. Freeman's (advanced by him and by Mr. Sullivan) was that his property interests were impaired. Dr. Freeman's right to lease property had been impaired; Dr. Press's right to purchase (and to hold) property had been impaired. As in *Sullivan*, consider the people involved. Dr. Harry C. Press, who had purchased a home in the geographical preference area, was a physician at Howard University Hospital.[24]

3. **What Are the Bases for the Claims by the Tillmans and Mrs. Rosner?** In *Tillman*, as in *Sullivan*, some of the plaintiffs—here, Mr. and Mrs. Tillman—are white. What are their claims? They rely on §1981(a) (contract claims) as well as §1982. (Note that §1981(a) applies to "persons" while §1982 applies to "citizens.") What is the basis for Mrs. Rosner's claim? Many lower courts have held that §1982 protects Black guests and their hosts.[25]

Almost a decade later, the Supreme Court took a more restrictive view of the 1866 Act in City of Memphis v. Greene, 451 U.S. 100 (1981). The case arose after the city of Memphis sought to close a portion of the streets that traversed a small, all-white community called Hein Park. This would effectively create a quiet and exclusive enclave for the residents of Hein Park, while establishing a "barrier" against the predominantly Black community north of Hein Park, making it more difficult for these Black residents to access their homes. Some Black residents sued, alleging that this decision violated §1982 and the Thirteenth Amendment.

The district court denied relief because it concluded that the plaintiffs had not demonstrated a racially discriminatory purpose behind the decision. The court of appeals held that the district court had erred by focusing too narrowly on whether the city had granted the street closing application while denying a comparable benefit to Black persons. Instead, the court of appeals concluded that relief under §1982 was required by the facts: (1) that the closing would benefit a white neighborhood and adversely affect Black people; (2) that a "barrier was to be erected precisely at the point of separation of these neighborhoods and would undoubtedly have the effect of limiting contact between them"; (3) that the closing was not part of a citywide plan but rather was a "unique step to protect one neighborhood from outside influences which the residents considered to be 'undesirable'"; and (4) that there was evidence of "an economic depreciation in the property values in the predominantly black residential area."

---

24. Emma Brown, *Harry C. Press Jr. Led Howard University's Radiology Department*, 78, Wash. Post, July 29, 2010, available at https://groups.google.com/g/alt.obituaries/c/0g5pdA3j wU0?pli=1.

25. Schwemm, HDLL §27:6.

The Supreme Court, with Justice Stevens writing for the majority, disagreed, holding that the harm to property interests that the plaintiffs alleged (which the Court characterized as a "minor inconvenience" to drivers) was not significant enough to fall within the broad ambit of §1982. Justice Stevens distinguished *Sullivan* and *Tillman*, reasoning that:

> Although these cases broadly defined the property rights protected by §1982, our cases, like the statutory language itself, all concerned the right of black persons to hold and acquire property on an equal basis with white persons and the right of blacks not to have property interests impaired because of their race. Therefore, as applied to this case, the threshold inquiry under §1982 must focus on the relationship between the street closing and the property interests of the respondents. . . . The injury to respondents established by the record is the requirement that one public street rather than another must be used for certain trips within the city. We need not assess the magnitude of that injury to conclude that it does not involve any impairment to the kind of property interests that we have identified as being within the reach of §1982.

The Court similarly held that the road closures did not implicate the plaintiffs' constitutional rights under the Thirteenth Amendment. Noting that the record contained no evidence of explicit racial motivation by the city, the Court concluded that:

> The argument that the closing violates the Amendment must therefore rest, not on the actual consequences of the closing, but rather on the symbolic significance of the fact that most of the drivers who will be inconvenienced by the action are black.

> But the inconvenience of the drivers is a function of where they live and where they regularly drive—not a function of their race; the hazards and the inconvenience that the closing is intended to minimize are a function of the number of vehicles involved, not the race of their drivers or of the local residents. Almost any traffic regulation—whether it be a temporary detour during construction, a speed limit, a one-way street, or a no-parking sign—may have a differential impact on residents of adjacent or nearby neighborhoods. Because urban neighborhoods are so frequently characterized by a common ethnic or racial heritage, a regulation's adverse impact on a particular neighborhood will often have a disparate effect on an identifiable ethnic or racial group. To regard an inevitable consequence of that kind as a form of stigma so severe as to violate the Thirteenth Amendment would trivialize the great purpose of that charter of freedom.

Justice Thurgood Marshall (joined by Justices Brennan and Blackmun) authored a vigorous dissent, in which he argued that the street closing would inflict much more than a slight inconvenience on the plaintiffs:

> [T]he problem is less the closing of West Drive in particular than the establishment of racially determined districts which the closing effects. I can only agree with the Court of Appeals, which viewed the city's action as nothing more than "one more of the many humiliations which society has historically visited" on Negro citizens. In my judgment, respondents provided ample evidence that erection of the challenged barrier will harm them in several significant ways. Respondents are being sent a clear, though sophisticated, message that because of their race, they are to stay out of the all-white enclave of Hein

Park and should instead take the long way around in reaching their destinations to the south. Combined with this message are the prospects of increased police harassment and of a decline in their property values.

Noting that "[i]n this picture a group of white citizens has decided to act to keep Negro citizens from traveling through their urban 'utopia,' and the city has placed its seal of approval on the scheme," Justice Marshall concluded that "the carving out of racial enclaves within a city is precisely the kind of injury that [§1982] was enacted to prevent."

NOTES AND QUESTIONS

1. **A Strong Dissent.** Usually, Supreme Court justices who dissent state that they do so "respectfully." Justice Marshall omits that adverb in his dissent in *City of Memphis v. Greene*. It is reasonable to infer that this is because his disagreement with the majority is significant and very important to him. Whose position in this case do you think is more persuasive—that of the majority (and the district court) or that of the dissenters and the court of appeals? Why?

2. **Breadth of §1982.** Although *City of Memphis v. Greene* ruled against the civil rights plaintiffs, the opinion has a strong reading of §1982. The majority stated that it "has broadly construed [the statute's] language to protect not merely the enforceability of property interests acquired by black citizens" but also "the right of black persons to hold and acquire property on an equal basis with white persons and the right of blacks not to have property interests impaired because of their race." Further, the Court recognized that

> [T]he statute would support a challenge to municipal action benefiting white property owners that would be refused to similarly situated black property owners[, and] the statute might be violated by official action that depreciated the value of property owned by black citizens. Finally, the statute might be violated if the street closing severely restricted access to black homes, because blacks would then be hampered in the use of their property.

3. **Distinguishing *Greene* from *Sullivan* and *Tillman*.** The *Greene* majority cites *Sullivan* and *Tillman*, but, unlike those cases, rules against the Black litigants. How does the Court distinguish those cases? How closely related are the benefits at issue in each case to property interests? What role (if any) does the identity of the defendant play? Note that in *Greene* the defendant was a municipality, making decisions that fell under its zoning and land use powers, whereas in *Sullivan* and *Tillman* the defendants were private corporations seeking to enforce private policies. Do you think the passage of a decade or changes in the composition of the Court had any bearing on the differences in result? Similar debates and line drawing have occurred in determining what kinds of municipal services are sufficiently connected to housing rights to come under the Fair Housing Act. *See* Chapter 8.

Chapter Summary

- *Jones v. Mayer*, the authoritative interpretation of the 1866 Civil Rights Act, holds that the statute forbids discrimination by private as well as government actors.
- *Jones v. Mayer* holds also that the application of the 1866 Act to private action is authorized by the Thirteenth Amendment.
- Later precedent clarified that damages are available under §1982.
- Many acts of discrimination specified in the Fair Housing Act and not specified in the 1866 Civil Rights Act are nonetheless covered by the 1866 Act (with the significant exception of discriminatory advertising, notices, and statements).
- The Fair Housing Act differs from the 1866 Act in a variety of ways, including its broad standing to sue, availability of disparate impact claims, more numerous protected characteristics, explicit exemptions, and coverage restricted to residential dwellings.

PART II

FAIR HOUSING ACT FUNDAMENTALS: LEGISLATIVE HISTORY, STATUTORY FRAMEWORK, INTERPRETIVE TOOLS, PROPER PARTIES, AND COVERAGE

This part introduces the Fair Housing Act (FHA)—the nation's seminal legislation protecting the right to fair housing. It begins in Chapter 3 with historical background on the FHA's passage, which is essential for understanding the "broad and inclusive" construction courts have given the FHA from its inception. Chapter 3 also provides a roadmap for understanding the structure, scope, and coverage of the statute; it further summarizes interpretive tools courts have used to apply the statute, including agency action (regulations, adjudication, and guidance) and judicial interpretations of other civil rights laws (primarily Title VII of the 1964 Civil Rights Act). Chapter 4 covers proper parties under the FHA: who may sue and who may be liable. This chapter illustrates the breadth of the statutory text in its granting the right to sue to all "aggrieved persons" while not explicitly limiting categories of covered defendants. Chapter 5 addresses "dwellings," which are the types of properties covered under the FHA, as distinguished from commercial properties and places of public accommodation, which are covered under different civil rights laws. This chapter also discusses the narrowly defined exemptions from the FHA's reach, which include exceptions for certain small-scale property owners and particular religious and private organizations.

CHAPTER 3

OVERVIEW OF THE FAIR HOUSING ACT

The federal Fair Housing Act (FHA) is the most significant piece of legislation guaranteeing the right to fair housing in the United States, and it is the focus of much of the rest of this book.[1] This chapter is an introduction to the statute. First, it provides an account of the fast-moving legislative and historic events that occurred during the bill's journey to becoming law. Next, it outlines the framework, coverage, and provisions of the FHA, which are discussed in detail in subsequent chapters. Finally, it addresses two historically important interpretive tools for the FHA: regulations and guidance issued by the Department of Housing and Urban Development (HUD), and judicial interpretation of Title VII of the Civil Rights Act of 1964 and analogous statutes.

A. LEGISLATIVE HISTORY AND CONTEXT[2]

The decisive push for federal fair housing legislation began on April 28, 1966, when President Lyndon Johnson sent to Congress his proposal for an omnibus civil rights bill. The bill had a number of provisions, the most controversial of which was Title IV, which banned discrimination in the sale and rental of housing.

In May, Representative Emanuel Celler introduced the bill as HR 14765 in the House. The bill quickly drew the opposition of the National Association of Real Estate Boards (NAREB) and its allies in Congress. It soon became clear that without some form of compromise, Title IV would bring down the entire bill. President Johnson dispatched negotiators to meet with the bill's opponents behind the scenes, and he exerted pressure on Congress to act. On June 1

---

1. Housing discrimination may be actionable under a number of constitutional standards (the Thirteenth, Fourteenth, or Fifth Amendments) and under any of several statutes (§§1981 or 1982 of the 1866 Civil Rights Act, Title VI of the 1964 Civil Rights Act, the Rehabilitation Act, the Americans with Disabilities Act, or the Equal Credit Opportunity Act).

2. The historical information in this section appears in Rigel C. Oliveri, *The Legislative Battle for the Fair Housing Act, in* THE FIGHT FOR FAIR HOUSING: CAUSES, CONSEQUENCES, AND FUTURE IMPLICATIONS OF THE 1968 FEDERAL FAIR HOUSING ACT (Gregory D. Squires ed., Routledge 2017).

and 2, the White House convened a Conference on Civil Rights with more than 2,400 participants. The conference ultimately produced a 100-page report that called for legislation to ban racial discrimination in housing.

Meanwhile, the Chicago Open Housing Movement (also known as the Chicago Freedom Movement) was underway. Spearheaded by Dr. Martin Luther King, Jr., the Southern Christian Leadership Conference, and the American Friends Service Committee, the Movement sought to press Chicago to enforce its existing fair housing ordinance and eliminate segregated and slum housing conditions in the city. The choice of location was intentional: Organizers sought to bring home the message that racism and segregation were problems not only in the South, where so many of the earlier civil rights battles had been fought, but all over the United States. In late July, the Movement staged a number of demonstrations and marches in all-white neighborhoods on Chicago's West Side. The hostile and often violent responses from whites—covered by the national media—were so intense that Dr. King remarked that even in the Deep South he had not encountered mobs as antagonistic to civil rights as those in Chicago.

Chicago 1966, Courtesy of Bernie Kleina.

Following negotiations and concessions by the Johnson Administration, the bill emerged in a weakened state, exempting approximately 60 percent of private housing from coverage. Despite misgivings by advocates and continued opposition from NAREB, the bill passed the House on August 9.

On August 12 the bill was reported to the Senate. There it met the fierce opposition of Minority Leader Everett Dirksen of Illinois, whose support was necessary if the bill had any hopes of passing. He was motivated in part by the violence and upheaval that was occurring in his home state in response to attempts at neighborhood integration. Despite the fact that most of the violence was carried out by whites against Blacks, Dirksen still seemed to blame the Black demonstrators for forcing the issue. He questioned Congress's constitutional authority to reach the sales of residential real estate. He also held a view voiced by many of the bill's opponents: The law simply could not—or at least should not—compel people of different races to live together.

For two weeks, opponents in the Senate filibustered attempts to proceed with debate on the bill. On September 19, after the second of two motions for cloture (calling for a vote) failed, Majority Leader Mansfield reluctantly gave up and moved on to other matters. The first attempt at comprehensive, national fair housing legislation had failed.

In March 1967, Senator Walter Mondale of Minnesota introduced a new fair housing bill. Although it was also comprehensive in scope, S.1358 allowed the implementation of fair housing law to proceed in three phases: First, it would apply to all federally assisted housing; second, to all private multifamily housing; and third, to all private, single-family housing.

The summer of 1967 saw crowded, substandard living conditions and excessive policing in heavily segregated neighborhoods of color explode into violence in more than 150 U.S. cities. The upheavals resulted in the deaths of 83 people and tens of millions of dollars in property damage. As the nation reeled, some people blamed civil rights advocates for creating an atmosphere of lawlessness. Opinion polls showed waning public support for any new civil rights legislation.

In the meantime, the House had passed a narrow civil rights bill, HR 2516, which protected civil rights workers from violence and intimidation but contained no housing provisions. The bill was reported to the full Senate in November 1967. Senator Mondale met with Senator Edward Brooke, the first Black person elected to the Senate since Reconstruction, and the two agreed to cosponsor S.1358 as a fair housing amendment to the worker protection bill.

Senate opponents of both parties mounted an expected filibuster. A motion for cloture, although approved by a 55-37 vote, failed to obtain the requisite two-thirds majority necessary to shut off debate. Another motion for cloture was scheduled. The bill's proponents could see that they had significant support and determined that the only way to get over the two-thirds hurdle by the next cloture vote was to negotiate a compromise.

Throughout these debates, as he had in 1966, Senator Dirksen registered his firm resistance to federal fair housing legislation. He had voted against cloture and again voiced concern about how fair housing laws might erode state power. However, shortly thereafter he made the surprising announcement that he would like to see civil rights legislation pass in that session and would be willing to support a more moderate version of the bill. A few days later he voted against cloture but entered into intense negotiations with the bill's supporters.

Publicly, Dirksen stated that the reasons for his change of heart were the growing unrest in the nation's cities and the injustice of the fact that Black veterans of the Vietnam War were returning home to face housing discrimination. (There also is evidence that he may have had more self-interested political motives.[3]) Regardless of his motivations, this change of position

---

3. Senator Dirksen was up for reelection in the fall. His Democratic opponent would be selected by the Cook County Democratic Organization, which was controlled by party boss Richard Daley, the Mayor of Chicago and a friend of President Johnson. Daley had a group of strong potential candidates from whom to choose: the head of the Office of Economic Opportunity (and Kennedy brother-in-law) Sargent Shriver, state Treasurer Adlai Stevenson, or state Senator Paul Simon. All three were dynamic and well known and would be formidable challengers. In the crucial days after the motion for cloture failed, President Johnson reached out to Senator Dirksen and the two scheduled a closed-door meeting. Afterward, Dirksen changed his position and expressed openness to compromise. Then, just a few days later Mayor Daley announced that he had chosen Illinois Attorney General William A. Clark, an obscure party functionary who was unlikely to mount a vigorous campaign, as Dirksen's opponent for the upcoming Senate race. Dirksen ultimately won with 53 percent of the vote.

provided momentum for the efforts of fair housing advocates. The bill's proponents had expected Senator Dirksen to seek the exemption of *all* single-family dwellings from coverage—in essence to drop Mondale's third stage of implementation—a compromise that they apparently were willing to accept. However, the only change in coverage Dirksen proposed was the exemption of single-family dwellings sold by owner-occupiers without the services of a real estate broker (the same fairly modest exemption in the failed 1966 bill). With respect to enforcement, Dirksen proposed eliminating HUD's authority to issue cease-and-desist orders, leaving HUD only with the power to pursue voluntary conciliation.

The so-called Dirksen Compromise took the form of an amendment to the worker protection bill, to be substituted for Mondale's fair housing amendment. On February 28, 1968, Senator Dirksen filed a cloture petition on his substitute amendment. Despite these efforts, the motion failed by just four votes.

The next morning, March 1, 1968, the bipartisan National Advisory Commission on Civil Disorders (commonly known as the Kerner Commission for its chair, former Illinois Governor Otto Kerner) published a report on the mass disorders of the previous summer. It stated in no uncertain terms that systemic racism and segregation were among the greatest threats to the nation. It concluded that "America is moving toward two societies, one black, one white—separate and unequal," and warned:

> To pursue our present course will involve the continuing polarization of the American community and, ultimately, the destruction of basic democratic values. . . .
>
> What white Americans have never fully understood—but what the Negro can never forget—is that white society is deeply implicated in the ghetto. White institutions created it, white institutions maintain it, and white society condones it.[4]

Among the Commission's top recommendations was that Congress enact sweeping fair housing legislation that would cover the sale or rental of all housing, including single-family homes. The bill's supporters recognized that the Kerner Commission Report presented an opportunity for moving the bill forward. The Senate Majority Leader scheduled a fourth vote for cloture on March 4. This time the measure narrowly passed. The bill passed the full Senate on March 11. It was then referred to the House Rules Committee, where supporters feared it would die.

The significant case of *Jones v. Mayer* (discussed in Chapter 2), which presented the question whether the Civil Rights Act of 1866 applied to private acts of housing discrimination, was argued before the Supreme Court on April 1 and 2.

At this point came a catastrophic series of events: On April 4, Dr. Martin Luther King, Jr. was assassinated in Memphis, Tennessee, shocking the nation.

---

4. *Report of the National Advisory Commission on Civil Disorders* 1 (1968).

U.S. Capitol, 1968.

Unrest broke out in urban areas across the country, including several uprisings in Washington, DC, quite close to the Capitol building and the Supreme Court. Washington, DC was placed under martial law, and by April 8, army troops surrounded Capitol Hill. On April 9, a clearly rattled Rules Committee reported the bill to the full House, which passed it overwhelmingly the following day. On April 11, President Johnson signed the Fair Housing Act into law.

Although the passage of the FHA was an undeniable step forward, the true cost of the Dirksen Compromise was clear. Without significant enforcement power, HUD was incapable of doing anything other than attempting to reach a voluntary conciliation between parties. In the decades to follow, the FHA was viewed by many as failing to live up to its promise. In addition, other categories beyond race, color, national origin, and religion were in need of civil rights protections in housing.

Attempts to expand both enforcement and coverage of the FHA began soon after the law took effect. Between 1970 and 1974, legislators made numerous attempts in both the House and Senate to add "sex" to the FHA's list of protected characteristics. These efforts finally succeeded when Congress passed the massive Community Development Act of 1974; an amendment to that bill adding sex to the FHA's list of protected characteristics passed without debate.

In the mid-1970s, efforts to improve the FHA's enforcement mechanisms began to dovetail with the nascent disability rights movement. In 1979, the House considered HR 5200. It would strengthen HUD's enforcement powers by allowing the agency to process administrative complaints, allowing matters to be adjudicated by administrative law judges who were empowered to award "appropriate relief" as well as civil penalties, and allowing HUD to seek temporary and preliminary injunctions. HR 5200 also added "handicap" as a protected class and required housing providers (1) to permit reasonable modifications to allow handicapped people to access housing, and (2) to make reasonable accommodations in policies, services, or facilities to afford handicapped persons equal enjoyment of housing. In 1980, the bill passed the House but was filibustered in the Senate.

Over the next few years, legislators introduced a number of similar bills in the House and Senate. Although these attempts failed, support for adding handicap to the FHA and for strengthening its enforcement mechanism in some way had high-level support that was generally bipartisan in nature. President Ronald Reagan himself proclaimed during his 1983 State of the Union address that effective enforcement of the fair housing laws was essential to ensuring equal opportunity, and Senator Robert Dole, who became Senate Majority Leader in 1985, was a veteran with service-related disabilities and a strong proponent of disability rights.

In February of 1987, HR 1158 was introduced in the House. Like HR 5200, it created an administrative enforcement mechanism within HUD and added handicap as a protected characteristic. An identical companion bill, S.558, was introduced in the Senate. The House bill subsequently was amended to include an "election" procedure, which would allow a HUD complainant or respondent to elect to have the case heard in federal court, with the Department of Justice responsible for filing suit. The handicap provisions were also amended to include affirmative requirements for accessible design and construction of newly built multifamily housing. The legislation also added "familial status" as a protected characteristic, because discrimination based on familial status (defined as having children under the age of 18 in the household) had been recognized in recent years as a serious housing barrier.

Despite the length of time it took for congressional advocates to move a bill to the floor for debate, the Fair Housing Amendments Act was much less controversial than the law it sought to amend. The bill had a bipartisan coalition of sponsors and was endorsed by both the Leadership Conference on Civil Rights and the National Association of Realtors (formerly NAREB). The bill passed the House on June 29, by a significant margin: 376-23. The Senate approved it on August 2, by a vote of 94-3. President Reagan signed the Fair Housing Amendments Act into law on September 13, 1988.

B. STATUTORY FRAMEWORK AND SUBSTANTIVE PROVISIONS

The Fair Housing Act, as amended, is codified at 42 U.S.C. §§3601-3619 and §3631. This section provides a brief overview of its provisions, which are discussed in greater detail in the chapters to follow.

The FHA begins with §3601 and a declaration of purpose: "It is the policy of the United States to provide, within constitutional limitations, for fair housing throughout the United States." This broad language, which courts have said indicates a Congressional intent of expansive application, has been significant in determining the statute's intended reach. Section 3602 defines terms used in the statute, including the properties ("dwellings") and persons it covers. Sections 3603 and 3607 contain statutory exemptions. Covered dwellings and exemptions of the FHA are discussed in Chapter 5.

The FHA's substantive provisions are as follows:

- **§3604(a)** makes it unlawful "to refuse to sell or rent after the making of a bona fide offer, or to refuse to negotiate for the sale or rental of, or otherwise make unavailable or deny, a dwelling to any person" because of protected characteristics.
- **§3604(b)** prohibits "discriminat[ion] against any person in the terms, conditions, or privileges of sale or rental of a dwelling, or in the provision of services or facilities in connection therewith" because of protected characteristics.
- **§3604(c)** makes it illegal "to make, print, or publish, or cause to be made, printed, or published any notice, statement, or advertisement, with respect to the sale or rental of a dwelling that indicates any preference, limitation, or discrimination based on [protected characteristics], or an intention to make any such preference, limitation, or discrimination."
- **§3604(d)** makes it unlawful "to represent to any person because of [protected characteristics] that any dwelling is not available for inspection, sale, or rental when such dwelling is in fact so available."
- **§3604(e)** makes it unlawful "for profit, to induce or attempt to induce any person to sell or rent any dwelling by representations regarding the entry or prospective entry into the neighborhood of a person or persons" with a particular protected characteristic, a practice colloquially referred to as "blockbusting."
- **§3604(f)** addresses disability (or "handicap"). It prohibits the discriminatory conduct described in §§3604(a) and (b), creates affirmative rights for disabled people to reasonable accommodations in housing policies and reasonable modifications of housing units, and sets forth accessibility requirements for the design and construction of certain multifamily dwellings built following a grace period after passage of the Fair Housing Amendments Act.
- **§3605** makes it unlawful "for any person or other entity whose business includes engaging in residential real estate-related transactions to discriminate against any person in making available such a transaction, or in the terms or conditions of such a transaction," because of protected characteristics.
- **§3606** makes it unlawful "to deny any person access to or membership or participation in any multiple-listing service, real estate brokers' organization or other service, organization, or facility relating to the business of selling or renting dwellings, or to discriminate against [that person] in the terms or conditions of such access, membership, or participation," because of protected characteristics.
- **§3617** makes it unlawful "to coerce, intimidate, threaten, or interfere with any person in the exercise or enjoyment of, or on account of his having exercised or enjoyed, or on account of [that person's] having aided or encouraged any other person in the exercise or enjoyment of,

any right granted or protected by section 3603, 3604, 3605, or 3606 of this title."

- **§3631** makes it a crime to use force or threat of force to willfully injure, intimidate, or interfere with persons who are exercising their fair housing rights under the substantive provisions of the statute, or aiding or encouraging others to do so.
- **§3608** sets forth the authority of HUD to administer housing and urban development programs and requires that HUD and all executive departments and agencies administer such programs in a manner that affirmatively furthers fair housing. This is understood to include a positive duty that HUD promote integration.

Sections 3604(a), (b), (d), and (e) are discussed in Chapter 8. Section 3604(c) is covered in Chapter 9. Section 3604(f) is discussed in Chapter 17. Chapter 11 covers §3605. Chapter 10 addresses §§3617 and 3631. Chapter 13 describes HUD's duty to affirmatively further fair housing under §3608.

It is important to note that most of the substantive provisions apply to discrimination only when it is engaged in "because of" certain protected characteristics.[5] The characteristics protected by the statute are:

- Race, color, and national origin (Chapter 14).
- Religion (Chapter 14).
- Sex (including sexual orientation and gender identity) (Chapter 15).
- Familial status (Chapter 16).
- Disability (Chapter 17).

The meaning of "because of" is more complicated than the two simple words might suggest, involving sometimes thorny questions of theory and proof, specifically whether the "intent" (disparate treatment) or "effects" (disparate impact) of actions (or both) must be established and how to make those showings. Chapters 6 and 7 analyze issues and methods of proof for disparate treatment and disparate impact.

The statute's enforcement provisions are contained in §§3610-3614. The FHA has three methods of enforcement, which are briefly summarized here and exemplified throughout the book:

---

5. There are a few exceptions to this. Section 3604(c) prohibits statements, notices, or advertisements, "that indicate[]" a preference or limitation "based on" protected characteristics. As discussed in Chapter 9, this means that the focus is on whether the statement would be interpreted as discriminatory by an ordinary listener or reader, and not on the intent of the defendant in making the statement. Section 3617 prohibits interference, coercion, interference, or threats on account of a person exercising housing rights or assisting another in doing so. As discussed in Chapter 10, this does not require that the plaintiff establish a violation of the underlying right, although it does require that an underlying or predicate right be identified. In addition, certain parts of §3604(f) create affirmative obligations for reasonable accommodation and reasonable modification for persons with disabilities, as well as design and construction to ensure accessible features for certain new housing. These disability provisions do not contain "because of" language, but rather prohibit the failure to carry out these obligations.

- **Administrative:** Section 3610 allows a person aggrieved by a discriminatory housing practice to file a complaint with HUD. HUD can investigate, issue a report, and attempt to conciliate these complaints. If HUD makes a determination that there is reasonable cause to believe a discriminatory housing practice has occurred, HUD can issue a charge of discrimination. Pursuant to §3612, this may lead to a hearing before an administrative law judge or, if either party elects, to a federal court action that is prosecuted by the Attorney General on behalf of the complainant. Section 3611 allows HUD to issue subpoenas and order discovery. HUD may refer such cases to a state agency if the state has a statute "substantially equivalent" to the FHA, with regard to substantive rights, procedures, remedies, and the availability of judicial review.
- **Private lawsuits:** Section 3613 allows private persons aggrieved by an unlawful housing practice to file a complaint directly in federal or state court, without exhausting administrative remedies by filing a prior HUD complaint.
- **Department of Justice:** Section 3614 authorizes the Attorney General to bring suit when there has been a "pattern or practice" of violations of fair housing rights, or when the denial of these rights "raises an issue of general public importance." Note that, as described above, the Attorney General must also file suit on behalf of aggrieved persons when a party to an administrative proceeding under §3612 elects to have the matter heard in federal court.

The FHA provides for extensive relief upon a determination that a discriminatory housing practice has occurred: compensatory and punitive damages with no statutory caps, permanent or temporary injunctions, temporary restraining orders, and reasonable attorney's fees and costs. Typically, fair housing complaints also request "such additional relief as the interests of justice may require." This nonmonetary relief can be designed not only to enjoin future violations but also to prevent them: revised policies and procedures to ensure compliance with the FHA; training protocols for supervisors and employees; ongoing monitoring and reporting; and affirmative advertising to groups previously excluded. The Department of Justice, suing on behalf of the United States, may seek a civil penalty to vindicate the public interest; such awards are paid to the U.S. Treasury.

The remaining FHA provisions cover a variety of matters such as the authority of HUD to engage in education and conciliation activities to promote fair housing and to contract with "substantially equivalent" state and local agencies to enforce the FHA; the authority of HUD to issue rules pursuant to the FHA; requirements that HUD collect data on the race and ethnicity of those benefiting from its programs; the appropriations necessary to administer the law; the preservation of state and local fair housing laws; and the severability of the individual provisions of the FHA.

C. INTERPRETIVE TOOLS FOR THE FHA

There are three principal tools for interpreting Title VIII: HUD regulations and "guidance," interpretations of Title VII of the 1964 Civil Rights Act, and—for disability provisions—the Americans with Disabilities Act (ADA) and the Rehabilitation Act. This section discusses the first two. The use of the ADA and Rehabilitation Act are discussed in Chapter 17.

1. HUD Regulations and Guidance

Congress has authorized HUD to promulgate regulations or rules (the two words have the same meaning). This authority appears in two provisions of the FHA and one provision of the Department of Housing and Urban Development Act. The FHA provisions are §3608(a), which states: "The authority and responsibility for administering this Act shall be in the Secretary of Housing and Urban Development," and §3614a, which states: "The Secretary may make rules . . . to carry out this title. The Secretary shall give public notice and opportunity for comment with respect to all rules made under this section." The HUD Act's provision is 42 U.S.C. §3535(d), which provides general rulemaking authority for HUD to carry out its functions, powers, and duties.

Agency promulgation of rules is governed by the Administrative Procedure Act (APA), 5 U.S.C. §551 *et seq.*, as well as the agency's authorizing statutes. The APA prescribes standards for both formal and "informal" (notice-and-comment) rulemaking. Most rulemaking, and all of HUD's rulemaking, is "informal." In general, rules that set enforceable standards, go through notice-and-comment rulemaking, and are published in the Code of Federal Regulations (CFR) are called "substantive" or "legislative" rules and have the "force of law."

The APA also authorizes agencies to promulgate material that does not satisfy these standards. Such material may be designated "interpretative" (or interpretive) rules, policy statements, memoranda, guidelines, handbooks, manuals, circulars, letters, or similar titles.[6] All such material usually is called "guidance."

The Supreme Court has developed principles governing judicial review of agency regulations interpreting statutes the agency is authorized to administer. Between 1984 and 2024, the governing principle was the *Chevron* doctrine, which provided in general that when Congress authorized an agency to promulgate substantive regulations regarding such a statute and the agency did so, the courts would give such regulations binding deference if they determined that Congress had not directly spoken to the precise question at issue

---

6. It is a bit confusing that an agency may promulgate either a "substantive" or an "interpretive" rule interpreting a statute, but confusion often is the fate of those who serve the law.

and the agency determination was reasonable.[7] The courts also gave such deference to agency adjudicatory decisions that reflected similarly thorough and serious consideration.[8]

On June 28, 2024, the Supreme Court overruled *Chevron* in Loper Bright Enterprises v. Raimondo, 603 U.S. __ (2024). It said that agency interpretations still would be entitled to some degree of "respect," but that judges should decide independently what statutes mean. As this casebook goes to press almost immediately after this decision, it would be premature to try now to predict how the details of this new regime will work in practice.

Some cases in this book show courts considering the *Chevron* doctrine with respect to agency interpretations embodied in regulations or in adjudication.[9] The Court said in *Loper Bright* that its ruling would not call into question prior decisions based on *Chevron*: They "are still subject to statutory *stare decisis*. . . ." We shall see how that is interpreted. Similarly, we shall see how the Court deals with principles it had established in Skidmore v. Swift & Co., 323 U.S. 134 (1944), a pre-APA decision that the Court cited several times in *Loper Bright*. Dealing with an interpretive bulletin and informal rulings issued by the Administrator of the Wage and Hour Division of the Department of Labor, the *Skidmore* Court said that:

> The rulings, interpretations and opinions of the Administrator . . ., while not controlling upon the courts by reason of their authority, do constitute a body of experience and informed judgment to which courts and litigants may properly resort for guidance. The weight of such a judgment in a particular case will depend upon the thoroughness evident in its consideration, the validity of its reasoning, its consistency with earlier and later pronouncements, and all those factors which give it power to persuade, if lacking power to control.

Id. at 140. However, the Court referred even in *Loper Bright* to the principle that *consistent* administrative interpretations of a statute are entitled to considerable deference. The *Loper Bright* Court also emphasized the significance of agency interpretations that are contemporaneous with the enactment of a statute.

The Supreme Court has taken HUD regulations into account, although not always consistently with respect to *Chevron*. For example, in Meyer v. Holley, 537 U.S. 280, 287 (2003), the Court offered as additional support for its holding: "For another thing, . . . HUD, the federal agency primarily charged with the implementation and administration of the statute . . ., has specified that

---

7. Chevron, U.S.A., Inc. v. Natural Resources Defense Council, Inc., 467 U.S. 837 (1984). In general, *Chevron* deference applied only to "substantive" or "legislative" regulations using the notice-and-comment provisions of the APA and published in the Federal Register (FR) and then Code of Federal Regulations (CFR).

8. *See* NLRB v. Bell Aerospace Co., 416 U.S. 267 (1974).

9. See, for example, *DiCenso v. Cisneros* (Chapter 15), where the Seventh Circuit divides over the question whether to give *Chevron* deference to a HUD adjudication interpreting the ban on sexual harassment differently than the court had interpreted sexual harassment under Title VII of the 1964 Civil Rights Act.

ordinary vicarious liability rules apply in this area. And we ordinarily defer to an administering agency's reasonable interpretation of a statute." (citing *Chevron* and *Skidmore*).

In contrast, in Texas Department of Housing & Community Affairs (TDHCA) v. Inclusive Communities Project, 576 U.S. 519 (2015), the Court noted that HUD had promulgated a regulation "interpreting the FHA to encompass disparate impact liability" and that the Fifth Circuit had relied on that regulation for its holding. Nonetheless, the Court did not rely on HUD's regulation for its holding that the FHA encompasses disparate impact liability, specifically grounding its ruling on other bases, including textual analysis, statutory purpose, and ratification through the 1988 amendments. Tellingly, the Court did not cite *Chevron* at all.

A court can, of course, invalidate a HUD regulation (or adjudicatory ruling or guidance); if that happens, the court ruling is binding at least within that court's jurisdiction. Because HUD regulations or adjudicatory rulings or guidance may be principles of decision in lower federal courts, in state courts, or before HUD and state fair housing agencies, absent Supreme Court determinations the legal standard might be different depending on where a case is resolved.

2. Title VII of the Civil Rights Act of 1964

From the earliest days of litigation under the 1968 FHA, courts have linked interpretation of the FHA to interpretations of Title VII of the 1964 Civil Rights Act, which governs equal employment opportunity. This makes sense for a number of reasons: Both statutes are remedial civil rights laws passed within a few years of each other; they follow a similar structure; they prohibit similar conduct (albeit in different contexts); and, in a number of places, they contain identical or very similar language. Because Title VII came first and has generated more litigation than has the FHA, courts hearing housing cases generally have looked to Title VII for guidance, rather than the other way around.

For example, in Trafficante v. Metropolitan Life Insurance Co., 409 U.S. 205, 209 (1972), the Court cited a Title VII ruling conferring broad standing to sue as a basis for interpreting Title VIII. As the Second Circuit later stated, both statutes should be given similar interpretation because both "are part of a coordinated scheme of federal civil rights laws enacted to end discrimination [and] the Supreme Court has held that both statutes must be construed expansively to implement that goal." Huntington Branch, NAACP v. Town of Huntington, 844 F.2d 926, 935 (2d Cir.), *aff'd per curiam*, 488 U.S. 15 (1988).

Many lower courts followed this lead, construing Title VIII by using Title VII decisions. For example, courts used the framework that the Supreme Court developed to analyze sexual harassment claims under Title VII, and applied it to cases involving sexual harassment in housing. Lower courts hearing housing cases similarly have adopted analysis that the Court developed in the Title VII context to recognize disparate impact claims. The Supreme Court validated this practice in *TDHCA v. Inclusive Communities Project*, in which the Court upheld the availability of disparate impact theory under Title VIII. The Court based its holding, in part, on "the Court's interpretation of similar language in Title VII and the [Age Discrimination in Employment Act (ADEA)]." The Court said that "[t]he cases interpreting Title VII and the ADEA provide essential background and instruction in the case now before the Court."

There are situations in which the textual provisions of Title VIII differ from those of Title VII, and thus comparison is not helpful. For example, Title VII applies only to specifically defined plaintiffs and defendants. Plaintiffs can be only prospective, current, or former employees. Defendants must be employers with 15 or more employees, or labor organizations or employment agencies that serve covered employers. There is no individual liability under the statute. In contrast, a plaintiff in an FHA case can be any person who is aggrieved by a discriminatory housing practice (and is found to have standing). Instead of defining who is a covered defendant, the FHA describes prohibited activity. Anyone capable of engaging in that activity, whether individuals or entities, can be a proper defendant under the statute.

Sections 3604(c) and 3617 also contain important differences in coverage from their Title VII counterparts:

- Section 3604(c)'s Title VII counterpart is 42 U.S.C. §2000e-3(b), which prohibits the "printing or publication of notices or advertisements" that indicate unlawful discrimination. Section 3604(c) goes further, however, by prohibiting "statements," which can include verbal communications, rules and bylaws, deeds and covenants, and many other types of expression. In addition, §3604(c) can apply to newspapers or other entities that publish discriminatory statements, whereas §2000e-3(b) is limited to employers, employment agencies, and labor unions.

- Section 3617 has a counterpart in 42 U.S.C. §2000e-3(a) of Title VII. This provision prohibits an employer from retaliating against an employee who has "made a charge, testified, assisted or participated in" any charge of unlawful discrimination under the statute. Section 3617 also prohibits retaliation, but it goes further by prohibiting intimidation or coercion against people for simply exercising their rights to fair housing, or assisting others in doing so.

There are also situations in which housing is factually and legally different from employment, so that comparing the two statutes is less helpful, even where Title VII provides the overall framework for analysis of the FHA claim. For example, although language prohibiting discrimination "based on sex" in Title VII and the FHA is identical, and the same "severe or pervasive" standard applies to hostile environment sexual harassment under both statutes, many courts have recognized that the differences in context between the workplace and the home justify applying the "severe or pervasive" standard differently. Conduct that is merely annoying in an office setting might take on a much more frightening character when it is carried out inside a person's home, by a perpetrator who literally holds the keys.

Similarly, in *TDHCA v. Inclusive Communities Project*, even as the Court validated a disparate impact cause of action based on Title VII precedents, it recognized that differences between the employment and housing contexts might affect how the affirmative defense to disparate impact claims would operate. Specifically, the "business necessity" defense available to employers faced with disparate impact claims does not translate neatly to the housing context. Although an employer's business needs are fairly straightforward, developers and municipalities might have multiple legitimate and competing factors to consider when making decisions about the siting and zoning of housing.

In addition, courts must be careful about using Title VII to interpret an FHA case when there are relevant differences between the underlying legal doctrines of the two statutes. For example, in Wetzel v. Glen St. Andrew Living Community, LLC, 901 F.3d 856, 863 (7th Cir. 2018), a woman sued her housing provider, alleging that she had been severely harassed by fellow residents of a senior living community because she was a lesbian. The court recognized that well-established Title VII and FHA precedents allowed the plaintiff to bring such a claim, but the more difficult question was how to define the standard of landlord liability for resident-on-resident harassment. The plaintiff asked the court to apply the Title VII standard of employer liability for employee-on-employee harassment, but the court declined:

> We recognize, however, that there are some potentially important differences between the relationship that exists between an employer and an employee, in which one is the agent of the other, and that between a landlord and a tenant, in which the tenant is largely independent of the landlord. We thus refrain from reflexively adopting the Title VII standard and continue our search for comparable situations.

There are other significant procedural differences between the two statutes:

- Compensatory and punitive damages were not available under Title VII until 1991, and thus jury trials historically were not available in Title VII cases. Damages always have been available under the FHA. Even today, damages are capped under Title VII but not in the FHA.
- Although both statutes provide for an administrative process (Title VII with the EEOC and the FHA with HUD or a state or local agency), under the FHA, an aggrieved person need not exhaust administrative remedies before filing a claim in federal court. Exhaustion of administrative remedies is required under Title VII.

Finally, the utility of Title VII law in interpreting FHA cases has been complicated in multiple ways by the Supreme Court and Congress. Congress enacted the Civil Rights Act of 1991 in part to overrule and in part to modify and codify the results in several Supreme Court decisions in Title VII cases. The 1991 Act applied only to Title VII. Congress has not amended the FHA since 1988, and so has not weighed in on how these developments affect Title VIII cases. Courts have disagreed about how persuasive the Supreme Court decisions "overruled" by the 1991 Act for Title VII might be for FHA cases.

MONDALE AND BROOKE: CO-SPONSORS OF THE FHA

Senator Walter Mondale
By Bradley Wilson

Senator Edward Brooke
Library of Congress

Chapter Summmary

- The Fair Housing Act took two years and a great deal of grassroots advocacy and legislative maneuvering to become law. It was finally passed in 1968 after the assassination of Dr. Martin Luther King, Jr. and much national turmoil.
- The FHA, as originally passed, prohibited discrimination based on race, color, national origin, and religion. Sex was added as a protected characteristic in 1974, and familial status and disability (handicap) were added with the Fair Housing Amendments Act of 1988.
- The FHA is codified at 42 U.S.C. §§3601-3619 and §3631. The primary substantive provisions, which outline prohibited conduct, are §§3604, 3605, 3608, and 3617. Additional sections set forth enforcement mechanisms and relief and outline HUD's responsibilities and authority.
- Courts previously gave binding deference to agency regulations and adjudications that met certain standards according to the 1984 decision in

Chevron, U.S.A. v. Natural Resources Defense Council. In 2024, the Supreme Court overruled *Chevron* in *Loper Bright Enterprises v. Raimondo.* It said that judges should decide independently what statutes mean. The Court also said that its ruling would not call into question prior decisions based on *Chevron*: They "are still subject to statutory *stare decisis. . . .*" In addition, the Court said that agency determinations still would be entitled to "respect" in accordance with the decision in *Skidmore v. Swift & Co.*

• Courts often use decisions under Title VII of the 1964 Civil Rights Act (employment) to interpret provisions of the FHA. There are, however, significant differences in language in some sections of the two statutes, and there are differences in how workplaces and homes should be treated. These considerations have led to distinctions in interpretations of the two statutes. In addition, in the 1991 Civil Rights Act, Congress modified or rejected some Supreme Court decisions regarding Title VII, and opinion is divided about what effect, if any, that statute has on interpretations of the FHA.

CHAPTER 4

PROPER PARTIES

The Fair Housing Act is somewhat unique among civil rights statutes in that it grants considerable latitude both on who can be a proper plaintiff and who can be liable as a defendant. This breadth appropriately reflects the myriad harms that housing discrimination can inflict, as well as the fact that many types of actors are capable of inflicting them.

According to the statute, a proper plaintiff under the FHA can be any person "aggrieved" by a fair housing violation. This broad and inclusive definition allows a variety of injured individuals and entities to bring claims, even those who were not themselves the direct targets of the discriminatory behavior. Thus, most of the early FHA cases focus less on whether a plaintiff is proper under the statute, and more on whether the plaintiff has alleged sufficient Article III injury to establish standing to sue as a constitutional matter. More recently, however, the Court has focused greater attention on the rights and interests Congress intended to protect through the statute and other common-law (judicial) limitations on civil liability like proximate cause.

This chapter begins by examining Article III and the FHA's provisions. It then reviews the early trilogy of Article III standing decisions on which litigants have relied for decades and that have provided standards for subsequent courts applying the FHA: *Trafficante*, *Gladstone*, and *Havens*. The chapter then looks at a more recent decision, *City of Miami*, which addresses common-law pleading and cause of action requirements that continue to unfold as the Supreme Court takes a new view of standing and other threshold litigation requirements. Until the Court further clarifies the law in this area, students should focus on what types of injuries the Court has recognized as sufficient to satisfy Article III standing in fair housing cases and what types of plaintiffs Congress has recognized as having a right to sue under the FHA.

Unlike its approach in other statutes such as Title VII, Congress did not create limited categories of permissible defendants under the FHA. Apart from some narrowly crafted exemptions, the FHA extends liability to a varied constellation of individuals and entities. Principles of vicarious liability apply to the FHA, as with other torts, so that owners, employers, and other individuals may be responsible for the discriminatory conduct of those who act on their behalf.

A. PROPER PLAINTIFFS: WHO HAS STANDING?

If a fellow student or coworker informs you they believe they were denied an apartment because of their race, ethnicity, sex, or disability, but they have no intention of taking any action, are you permitted to file a complaint on their behalf? What about discriminatory housing practices you have read about in the newspaper or seen online? Even though the FHA grants wide latitude with respect to who has a right to sue to enforce its provisions, Article III of the Constitution imposes jurisdictional limits on the ability to litigate in the federal courts.

Standing to sue under Article III is jurisdictional in that no one can waive it and a court should consider it even if no party raises it. Constitutional  standing, then, addresses who may access the power of a federal court. A different question, sometimes labeled as a prudential or statutory standing inquiry, is what kinds of "arguments or legal principles" may the litigant assert?[1] This includes whether the plaintiff comes "within the zone of interests" Congress protected when it passed the statute, that is, whether the statute "encompasses a particular plaintiff's claim." In Lexmark International, Inc. v. Static Control Components, Inc., 572 U.S. 118, 127-28 & n.4 (2014), the Court clarified that it did not consider this "zone of interests" question to be jurisdictional, or to be appropriately labeled as a "standing" question at all; it might be a statutory "cause of action" issue. Whatever we call it, the question whether a plaintiff falls within the class of persons Congress has granted a right to sue under a particular statute "always applies." *Id.* at 129.

This is a very complicated area, and the Supreme Court continues to shape it. We know that plaintiffs must establish Article III standing and come within the FHA's zone of interests. Let's begin with the Article III requirements. Under our system of separation of powers, Article III provides that "the judicial power" extends only to "cases" and "controversies" of various kinds. The doctrine of standing derives from these terms, as explained in TransUnion LLC v. Ramirez, 594 U.S. 413, 423 (2021):

> For there to be a case or controversy under Article III, the plaintiff must have a "personal stake" in the case—in other words, standing. . . . [T]o establish standing, a plaintiff must show (i) that he suffered an injury in fact that is concrete, particularized, and actual or imminent; (ii) that the injury was likely

---

1. *See* Curtis A. Bradley & Ernest A. Young, *Unpacking Third-Party Standing*, 131 Yale L.J. 1, 26 (2021).

caused by the defendant; and (iii) that the injury would likely be redressed by judicial relief.

The FHA constitutional standing decisions discussed in this chapter, and indeed most FHA Article III standing cases, focus on the Article III injury-in-fact requirement. But causation[2] and redressability[3] are also compulsory. The Supreme Court in FDA v. Alliance for Hippocratic Medicine, 602 U.S. 367 (2024) described causation, in particular, as "central." "Like the injury in fact requirement, the causation requirement screens out plaintiffs who were not injured by the defendant's action," by ensuring that the "links in the chain of causation" between the illegal conduct and injury are not "too speculative or too attenuated." Id. at 383. The FDA Court also noted that the second and third prongs of causation and redressability "are often 'flip sides of the same coin.' . . . If a defendant's action causes an injury, enjoining the action or awarding damages for the action will typically redress that injury." Id. at 380.

What about the FHA's zone of interests? Congress may define a statutory cause of action more narrowly than Article III would allow,[4] or it may permit parties to sue all the way to the limits of Article III, but Congress may not exceed the outer bounds of Article III standing. Congress does not delineate the categories of individuals it deems to have the right to sue to enforce the FHA. Instead, it simply defines unlawful conduct in the substantive provisions addressing what constitutes a "discriminatory housing practice." Sections 3604, 3605, 3606, and 3617 begin with "It shall be unlawful" without specifying who may sue or who may be liable for a violation. For example, recall that 42 U.S.C. §3604(a) does not tell us who may sue to challenge actions that "otherwise make unavailable, or deny, a dwelling." Elsewhere, the enforcement provisions provide the answer; they permit the filing of complaints by any "aggrieved person." See 42 U.S.C. §3610(a)(1)(A)

---

2. See El Dorado Ests. v. City of Fillmore, 765 F.3d 1118, 1122 (9th Cir. 2014) ("[Plaintiff's] delays and additional expenses . . . were a direct result of the City's alleged interference with the subdivision application [to prevent the conversion from a senior mobile home park to a family park]. El Dorado's allegations therefore demonstrate that its injury is fairly traceable to the City's conduct.").

3. See United States v. Texas, 599 U.S. 670, 676 (2023); see also Steel Co. v. Citizens for a Better Env't, 523 U.S. 83, 107 (1998) ("Relief that does not remedy the injury suffered cannot bootstrap a plaintiff into federal court; that is the very essence of the redressability requirement.").

4. The FHA standing trilogy found the so-called judge-imposed "prudential" limits on standing to be inapplicable to the FHA, although the modern Court has moved away from this construct of standing to focus on Congress's enactments. For background, the concept of prudential standing refers to judicially imposed limits beyond those required by Article III that the Court might impose out of "concern about the proper—and properly limited—role of the courts in a democratic society." Warth v. Seldin, 422 U.S. 490, 498 (1975). These limits (which have plenty of exceptions and are open to varying degrees of interpretation) generally include (1) the prohibition on a litigant's raising another person's legal rights, (2) the rule barring adjudication of generalized grievances more appropriately addressed in the representative branches, and (3) the requirement that a plaintiff's complaint fall within the zone of interests protected by the law invoked. As noted above, the Court in Lexmark characterized the zone of interests analysis as outside of the standing inquiry altogether.

(i) (administrative enforcement) and 42 U.S.C. §3613(a)(1)(A) (enforcement in state or federal court). Who is an aggrieved person?

The FHA defines "aggrieved person" in §3602:

> (i) "Aggrieved person" includes any person who—
> (1) claims to have been injured by a discriminatory housing practice; or
> (2) believes that such person will be injured by a discriminatory housing practice that is about to occur.[5]

The definition section also defines "person":

> (d) "Person" includes one or more individuals, corporations, partnerships, associations, labor organizations, legal representatives, mutual companies, joint-stock companies, trusts, unincorporated organizations, trustees, trustees in cases under title 11, receivers, and fiduciaries.

The touchstone, then, is the ability to demonstrate some concrete *injury*, whether it has already occurred or is about to occur. The Act's text and structure thus reveal that Congress did little to cabin the right to sue under the FHA short of the Article III "injury" requirement. Therefore, the FHA's zone of interests effectively extends to the outer boundaries of Article III. Indeed, "a plaintiff need not be among the class discriminated against in order to have standing." El Dorado Estates v. City of Fillmore, 765 F.3d 1118, 1121 (9th Cir. 2014).[6]

The three cases that follow, the "standing trilogy," provide a foundational understanding of the breadth of FHA standing doctrine; they demonstrate varying types of injuries in fact enforceable through the FHA and types of litigants understood to suffer these requisite injuries. Three important categories of harm the Court recognized in this trilogy are injuries to both white and Black people who seek integrated living environments, injuries to neighborhoods whose housing markets have been manipulated through racial steering, and injuries to fair housing organizations and "testers" who investigate possible violations of the FHA. As the Fifth Circuit stated in McCardell v. HUD, 794 F.3d 510, 517 (5th Cir. 2015):

> After Congress passed the Fair Housing Act, the Supreme Court handed down a trilogy of cases in which it recognized that deprivation of "the benefits that result from living in an integrated community" is sufficient injury. This theory of standing—deemed "neighborhood standing"—stems from

---

5. LeBlanc-Sternberg v. Fletcher, 67 F.3d 412, 425 (2d Cir. 1995) ("[T]he explicit grant of standing to anyone who believes he 'will be injured by a discriminatory housing practice that is about to occur,' . . . means that a person who is likely to suffer such an injury need not wait until a discriminatory effect has been felt before bringing suit.").

6. For example, chapters throughout this text illustrate that housing providers unable to rent, sell, purchase, develop, or operate housing because of the protected status of those they serve would be "aggrieved persons" able to show injury under the FHA.

the Court's conclusion that the harm caused by a racially discriminatory housing practice can, in some circumstances, extend beyond its immediate victim. Rather than a claim of direct discrimination against oneself, neighborhood standing finds the requisite injury, albeit indirect and immediately visited upon a third-party, in "an adverse impact on the neighborhood in which the plaintiff resides."[7]

1. Article III Standing Under the FHA: Neighborhood (and Neighbor) Standing

As you read the first of these cases, consider the nature of the injuries alleged by both the Black and the white plaintiffs. Observe how the Court reaches the conclusion that "a generous construction" of the FHA is required in the standing context. Notice the central role of the statutory analysis in the Court's determination on standing. Finally, you should be aware that Congress overhauled the FHA's enforcement provisions in 1988, thus this opinion's references to HUD having little enforcement power are no longer accurate.

Trafficante v. Metropolitan Life Ins. Co.
409 U.S. 205 (1972)

Before Chief Justice Burger and Justices Douglas, Brennan, Stewart, White, Marshall, Blackmun, Powell, and Rehnquist.

Justice DOUGLAS delivered the opinion of the Court. Justices White, Blackmun, and Powell concurred.

Two tenants of Parkmerced, an apartment complex in San Francisco housing about 8,200 residents, filed separate complaints with the Secretary of HUD pursuant to §3610(a) of the [FHA]. One tenant is black, one white. Each alleged that the owner of Parkmerced had discriminated against nonwhites on the basis of race in the rental of apartments within the complex in violation of §3604 of the Act.

---

7. In FHA cases, the distinctions between first-party standing and third-party standing have not been particularly salient because of the broad construction of the Act's zone of interests. Professors Bradley and Young offer this explanation for the difference between the two: "If litigants fall within the zone of interests of the substantive right they invoke and they have an injury in fact, they may rely on their own first-party rights for standing. If they fall outside the zone of interests, they must rely on the rights of third parties." Bradley & Young, 131 YALE L.J. at 5 (citing 1 Laurence H. Tribe, AMERICAN CONSTITUTIONAL LAW §3-19, at 446 (3d ed. 2000)). There are some exceptions to the general prohibition on "third-party standing." *See id.* Courts have described the limits on third-party standing as "prudential," although that label is in some doubt after *Lexmark.* 572 U.S. at 128 n.4.

Since HUD [EDS.—in accordance with the enforcement regime at the time] failed to secure voluntary compliance within 30 days, petitioners brought this action in [federal district court].

The complaint alleged that the owner had discriminated against nonwhite rental applicants in numerous ways, *e.g.*, making it known to them that they would not be welcome at Parkmerced, manipulating the waiting list for apartments, delaying action on their applications, using discriminatory acceptance standards, and the like.

They—the two tenants—claimed they had been injured in that (1) they had lost the social benefits of living in an integrated community; (2) they had missed business and professional advantages which would have accrued if they had lived with members of minority groups; (3) they had suffered embarrassment and economic damage in social, business, and professional activities from being "stigmatized" as residents of a "white ghetto."[8]

The District Court did not reach the merits but only held that petitioners were not within the class of persons entitled to sue under the Act. The Court of Appeals affirmed, construing §3610(a) narrowly to permit complaints only by persons who are the objects of discriminatory housing practices. We reverse the judgment below.

The definition of "person aggrieved" contained in §3610(a) is in terms broad, as it is defined as "any person who claims to have been injured by a discriminatory housing practice."

The Act gives the Secretary of HUD power to receive and investigate complaints regarding discriminatory housing practices. . . .

It is apparent, as the Solicitor General says, that complaints by private persons are the primary method of obtaining compliance with the Act. Hackett v. McGuire Bros., Inc., 445 F.2d 442, 446 (CA3) [1971], which dealt with the phrase that allowed a suit to be started "by a person claiming to be aggrieved" under [Title VII], concluded that the words used showed "a congressional intention to define standing as broadly as is permitted by Article III of the Constitution." With respect to suits brought under [Title VIII of] the 1968 Act [FHA], we reach the same conclusion, insofar as tenants of the same housing unit that is charged with discrimination are concerned.

The language of the Act is broad and inclusive. Individual injury or injury in fact to petitioners . . . is alleged here. What the proof may be is one thing; the alleged injury to existing tenants by exclusion of minority persons from the apartment complex is the loss of important benefits from interracial associations.

The legislative history of the Act is not too helpful. The key section now before us, *i.e.*, §3610 [with its reference to "person aggrieved"], was derived from an amendment offered by Senator Mondale and incorporated in the bill offered by Senator Dirksen. While members of minority groups

---

8. [Fn. 5 in original] Less than 1% of the tenants in this apartment complex are black.

were damaged the most from discrimination in housing practices, the proponents of the legislation emphasized that those who were not the direct objects of discrimination had an interest in ensuring fair housing, as they too suffered.

The Assistant Regional Administrator for HUD wrote petitioners' counsel that "it is the determination of this office that the complainants are aggrieved persons and as such are within the jurisdiction" of the Act. We are told that that is the consistent administrative construction of the Act. Such construction is entitled to great weight.

The design of the Act confirms this construction. . . . Since HUD has no enforcement powers and since the enormity of the task of assuring fair housing makes the role of the Attorney General in the matter minimal, the main generating force must be private suits in which, the Solicitor General says, the complainants act not only on their own behalf but also "as private attorneys general in vindicating a policy that Congress considered to be of the highest priority." The role of "private attorneys general" is not uncommon in modern legislative programs.[9] It serves an important role in this part of the FHA in protecting not only those against whom a discrimination is directed but also those whose complaint is that the manner of managing a housing project affects "the very quality of their daily lives." Shannon v. United States Dept. of Housing & Urban Dev., 436 F.2d 809, 818 (CA3) [1970].

The dispute tendered by this complaint is presented in an adversary context. Injury is alleged with particularity, so there is not present the abstract question raising problems under Art. III of the Constitution. The person on the landlord's blacklist is not the only victim of discriminatory housing practices; it is, as Senator Javits said in supporting the bill, "the whole community," and as Senator Mondale who drafted §3610(a) said, the reach of the proposed law was to replace the ghettos "by truly integrated and balanced living patterns."

We can give vitality to §3610(a) only by a generous construction which gives standing to sue to all in the same housing unit who are injured by racial discrimination in the management of those facilities within the coverage of the statute.

As you read the next case, consider how the Court extends its holding in *Trafficante* beyond apartment residents to address the harm racial residential segregation causes the entire neighborhood.

---

9. [Eds.—The Court is less inclined to use this analysis in the current era.]

Gladstone, Realtors v. Village of Bellwood
441 U.S. 91 (1979)

Before Chief Justice Burger and Justices Brennan, Stewart, White, Marshall, Blackmun, Powell, Rehnquist, and Stevens.

Justice POWELL delivered the opinion of the Court. Justice Rehnquist dissented and filed opinion in which Justice Stewart joined.

I

Petitioners in this case are two real estate brokerage firms, Gladstone, Realtors (Gladstone), and Robert A. Hintze, Realtors (Hintze), and nine of their employees. Respondents are the village of Bellwood, a municipal corporation and suburb of Chicago, one Negro and four white residents of Bellwood, and one Negro resident of neighboring Maywood. During the fall of 1975, the individual respondents and other persons consulted petitioners, stating that they were interested in purchasing homes in the general suburban area of which Bellwood is a part. The individual respondents were not in fact seeking to purchase homes, but were acting as "testers" in an attempt to determine whether petitioners were engaging in racial "steering," i.e., directing prospective home buyers interested in equivalent properties to different areas according to their race.

In October 1975, respondents commenced an action . . . against Gladstone and its employees . . . alleging that they had violated §3604 [of the FHA]. Simultaneously, respondents filed a virtually identical complaint against Hintze and its salespeople. The complaints, as illuminated by subsequent discovery, charged that petitioners had steered prospective Negro home buyers toward an integrated area of Bellwood approximately 12 by 13 blocks in dimension and away from other, predominately white areas. White customers, by contrast, allegedly were steered away from the integrated area of Bellwood. Four of the six individual respondents reside in this "target" area of Bellwood described in the complaint.[10] The complaints further alleged that the "Village of Bellwood . . . has been injured by having [its] housing market . . . wrongfully and illegally manipulated to the economic and social detriment of the citizens of [the] village," and that the individual respondents "have been denied their right to select housing without regard to race and have been deprived of the social and professional benefits of living in an integrated society."

The [district courts] decided that respondents were not within the class of persons to whom Congress had extended the right to sue under §3612. The

---

10. [Fn. 3 in original] Respondent Perry is a resident of Bellwood, but lives outside the area allegedly affected by petitioners' steering practices. Respondent Sharp lives in Maywood. These respondents are Negroes.

courts expressly adopted the reasoning of TOPIC v. Circle Realty, 532 F.2d 1273 (CA9 1976). In TOPIC the Ninth Circuit decided that Congress intended to limit actions under §3612 of the Act to "direct victims" of Title VIII violations, even though under Trafficante v. Metropolitan Life Ins. Co., standing under §3610 of the Act [authorizing administrative complaints with HUD] extends to the broadest class of plaintiffs permitted by Art. III. Since the individual respondents had been acting only as testers and thus admittedly had not been steered away from any homes they might have wished to purchase, the courts concluded that they were, at most, only indirect victims of Gladstone's alleged violations of the Act. The courts did not discuss Gladstone's contention that respondents lacked standing under Art. III and the prudential limitations on federal jurisdiction.

The Court of Appeals for the Seventh Circuit . . . first considered the significance of the fact that the individual respondents were merely testers not genuinely interested in purchasing homes. The court noted that while this precluded respondents from arguing that they had been denied their right to select housing without regard to race, "the testers did . . . generate evidence suggesting the perfectly permissible inference that [petitioners] have been engaging, as the complaints allege, in the practice of racial steering with all of the buyer prospects who come through their doors." Thus, although the individual respondents lacked standing in their capacity as testers, they were entitled to prove that the discriminatory practices documented by their testing deprived them, as residents of the adversely affected area, "of the social and professional benefits of living in an integrated society."

The Court of Appeals then turned to the question whether the Art. III minima for standing had been satisfied. Observing the similarity between the allegations of injury here and those accepted as constitutionally sufficient in *Trafficante*, it concluded that the individual respondents had presented a case or controversy within the meaning of Art. III. The court also read the complaints as alleging economic injury to the village itself as a consequence of the claimed racial segregation of a portion of Bellwood. Although this aspect of the case was not directly controlled by *Trafficante*, the court found that the requirements of Art. III had been satisfied.

The Court of Appeals reversed the judgments of the [district courts]. We granted certiorari to . . . consider the important questions of standing raised under Title VIII of the Civil Rights Act of 1968 [FHA]. With the limitation noted in n. 25, infra, we now affirm.

II

In recent decisions, we have considered in some detail the doctrine of standing in the federal courts. "In essence the question of standing is whether the litigant is entitled to have the court decide the merits of the dispute or of particular issues. This inquiry involves both constitutional limitations on federal-court jurisdiction and prudential limitations on its exercise. . . . In both dimensions it is founded in concern about the proper—and properly limited—role of the courts in a democratic society." Warth v. Seldin, 422 U.S. 490, 498 (1975). [Eds.—Note that the modern Court has moved away from the construct of "prudential limits" and considers standing primarily under Article III, with other restrictions focused on the rights granted under the particular statute at issue.]

The constitutional limits on standing eliminate claims in which the plaintiff has failed to make out a case or controversy between himself and the defendant. In order to satisfy Art. III, the plaintiff must show that he personally has suffered some actual or threatened injury as a result of the putatively illegal conduct of the defendant. Otherwise, the exercise of federal jurisdiction "would be gratuitous and thus inconsistent with the Art. III limitation."

Even when a case falls within these constitutional boundaries, a plaintiff may still lack standing under the prudential principles by which the judiciary seeks to avoid deciding questions of broad social import where no individual rights would be vindicated and to limit access to the federal courts to those litigants best suited to assert a particular claim. For example, a litigant normally must assert an injury that is peculiar to himself or to a distinct group of which he is a part, rather than one "shared in substantially equal measure by all or a large class of citizens." He also must assert his own legal interests rather than those of third parties.[11]

Congress may, by legislation, expand standing to the full extent permitted by Art. III, thus permitting litigation by one "who otherwise would be barred by prudential standing rules." In no event, however, may Congress abrogate the Art. III minima: A plaintiff must always have suffered "a distinct and palpable injury to himself" that is likely to be redressed if the requested relief is granted.

III

[Eds.—The Court rejected Defendant-Petitioners' assertion that, under the enforcement provision in place at the time, standing for litigants filing civil court actions under §3612 was limited to "direct victims," compared with standing for those filing administrative complaints under §3610, which extended to the fullest extent permitted by Art. III. The language omitted

---

11. [Fn. 6 in original] There are other nonconstitutional limitations on standing to be applied in appropriate circumstances. *See, e.g.,* Simon v. Eastern Kentucky Welfare Rights Org., 426 U.S. 26, 39 n. 19 (1976) ("the interest of the plaintiff, regardless of its nature in the absolute, [must] at least be 'arguably within the zone of interests to be protected or regulated' by the statutory framework within which his claim arises").

from this previous version of §3612, "person aggrieved," is included in the 1988 amendments to the FHA.][12]

IV

We now consider the standing of the village of Bellwood and the individual respondents in light of Art. III.

A

The gist of Bellwood's complaint is that petitioners' racial steering effectively manipulates the housing market in the described area of the village: Some whites who otherwise would purchase homes there do not do so simply because petitioners refrain from showing them what is available; conversely, some Negroes purchase homes in the affected area solely because petitioners falsely lead them to believe that no suitable homes within the desired price range are available elsewhere in the general area. Although the complaints are more conclusory and abbreviated than good pleading would suggest, construed favorably to Bellwood they allege that this conduct is affecting the village's racial composition, replacing what is presently an integrated neighborhood with a segregated one.

The adverse consequences attendant upon a "changing" neighborhood can be profound. If petitioners' steering practices significantly reduce the total number of buyers in the Bellwood housing market, prices may be deflected downward. This phenomenon would be exacerbated if perceptible increases in the minority population directly attributable to racial steering precipitate an exodus of white residents.[13] A significant reduction in property values directly injures a municipality by diminishing its tax base, thus threatening its ability to bear the costs of local government and to provide services. Other harms flowing from the realities of a racially segregated community

---

12. [Fn. 9 in original] Both petitioners and the dissenting opinion emphasize the language of §3612 that "[t]he rights granted by sectio[n] 3604 . . . may be enforced by civil actions. . . ." They argue that since §3604 on its face grants no right to have one's community protected from the harms of racial segregation, respondents have no substantive rights to enforce under §3612. That respondents themselves are not granted substantive rights by §3604, however, hardly determines whether they may sue to enforce the §3604 rights of others. If, as is demonstrated in the text, Congress intended standing under §3612 to extend to the full limits of Art. III, the normal prudential rules do not apply; as long as the plaintiff suffers actual injury as a result of the defendant's conduct, he is permitted to prove that the rights of another were infringed. The central issue at this stage of the proceedings is not who possesses the legal rights protected by §3604, but whether respondents were genuinely injured by conduct that violates *someone's* §3604 rights, and thus are entitled to seek redress of that harm under §3612.

13. [Fn. 23 in original] [In two cited cases,] real estate brokers were accused of "blockbusting," *i.e.*, exploiting fears of racial change by directly perpetuating rumors and soliciting sales in target neighborhoods. Respondents have not alleged that petitioners engaged in such unprincipled conduct, but the description in those cases of the reaction of some whites to a perceived influx of minority residents underscores the import of Bellwood's allegation that petitioners' sales practices threaten serious economic dislocation to the village.

are not unlikely.[14] As we have said before, "[t]here can be no question about the importance" to a community of "promoting stable, racially integrated housing." Linmark Associates, Inc. v. Willingboro, 431 U.S. 85, 94 (1977). If, as alleged, petitioners' sales practices actually have begun to rob Bellwood of its racial balance and stability, the village has standing to challenge the legality of that conduct.

B

The individual respondents appeared before the District Court in two capacities. First, they and other individuals had acted as testers of petitioners' sales practices. In this Court, however, respondents have not pressed the claim that they have standing to sue as testers, and we therefore do not reach this question. Second, the individual respondents claimed to be injured as homeowners in the community against which petitioners' alleged steering has been directed. It is in this capacity that they claim standing to pursue this litigation.

Four of the individual respondents actually reside within the target area of Bellwood. They claim that the transformation of their neighborhood from an integrated to a predominantly Negro community is depriving them of "the social and professional benefits of living in an integrated society." This allegation is similar to that presented in *Trafficante*. . . . Noting the importance of the "benefits from interracial associations," and in keeping with the Court's recent statement that noneconomic injuries may suffice to provide standing, we concluded that this injury was sufficient to satisfy the constitutional standing requirement of actual or threatened harm.

Petitioners argue that *Trafficante* is distinguishable because the complainants in that case alleged harm to the racial character of their "community," whereas respondents refer only to their "society." Reading the complaints as a whole, and remembering that we encounter these allegations at the pleading stage, we attach no particular significance to this difference in word choice. Although an injury to one's "society" arguably would be an exceptionally generalized harm or, more important for Art. III purposes, one that could not conceivably be the result of these petitioners' conduct, we are obliged to construe the complaint favorably to respondents, against whom the motions for summary judgment were made in the District Court. So construed, and read in context, the allegations of injury to the individual respondents' "society" refer to the harm done to the residents of the carefully described neighborhood in Bellwood in which four of the individual respondents reside.[15] The

---

14. [Fn. 24 in original] It has been widely recognized, for example, that school segregation is linked closely to housing segregation. See, e.g., . . . National Advisory Commission on Civil Disorders, Report 237 (1968); 114 Cong. Rec. 2276 (1968) (remarks of Sen. Mondale).

15. [Fn. 25 in original] As previously indicated, neither respondent Perry nor respondent Sharp resides within the target neighborhood of Bellwood. We read the complaints as claiming

question before us, therefore, is whether an allegation that this particular area is losing its integrated character because of petitioners' conduct is sufficient to satisfy Art. III.[16]

Petitioners suggest that there is a critical distinction between an apartment complex, even one as large as that in *Trafficante*,[17] and a 12- by 13-block residential neighborhood. Although there are factual differences, we do not view them as controlling in this case. We note first that these differences arguably may run in favor of standing for the individual respondents, according to how one views his living environment. Apartment dwellers often are more mobile, with less attachment to a community as such, and thus are able to react more quickly to perceived social or economic changes. The homeowner in a suburban neighborhood such as Bellwood may well have deeper community attachments and be less mobile. Various inferences may be drawn from these and other differences, but for the purpose of standing analysis, we perceive no categorical distinction between injury from racial steering suffered by occupants of a large apartment complex and that imposed upon residents of a relatively compact neighborhood such as Bellwood.[18]

The constitutional limits of respondents' standing to protest the intentional segregation of their community do not vary simply because that community is defined in terms of city blocks rather than apartment buildings. Rather, they are determined by the presence or absence of a "distinct and palpable injury," to respondents resulting from petitioners' conduct. A "neighborhood" whose racial composition allegedly is being manipulated may be so extensive in area, so heavily or even so sparsely populated, or so lacking in shared social and commercial intercourse that there would be no actual injury to a particular

---

injury only to that area and its residents, and we are unable to find any allegations of harm to individuals residing elsewhere. On the record before us, we therefore conclude that summary judgment [as] to these two respondents was appropriate. . . . Although we intimate no view as to whether persons residing outside of the target neighborhood have standing to sue under §812 of Title VIII, we do not foreclose consideration of this question if, on remand, the District Court permits respondents Perry and Sharp to amend their complaints to include allegations of actual harm.

16. [Fn. 26 in original] Apart from the use of "community" rather than "society," the complaint in *Trafficante* differed from those here in that it alleged that a segregated community was prevented from becoming integrated because of the defendant's conduct. Here, by contrast, respondents claim that an integrated neighborhood is becoming a segregated community because of petitioners' conduct. We find this difference unimportant to our analysis of standing. In both situations, the deprivation of the benefits of interracial associations constitutes the alleged injury.

17. [Fn. 27 in original] The apartment complex in *Trafficante* housed 8,200 tenants. The population of Bellwood, of which the target neighborhood is only a part, was estimated at 20,969 in 1975.

18. [Fn. 28 in original] *See* Shannon v. HUD, 305 F. Supp. 205, 208, 211 (E.D. Pa. 1969), *aff'd in part*, 436 F.2d 809, 817-818 (CA3 1970) (residents in a neighborhood affected by urban renewal project have standing to challenge the project's impact on the neighborhood's racial balance).

resident. The presence of a genuine injury should be ascertainable on the basis of discrete facts presented at trial.[19]

In addition to claiming the loss of social and professional benefits to the individual respondents, the complaints fairly can be read as alleging economic injury to them as well. The most obvious source of such harm would be an absolute or relative diminution in value of the individual respondents' homes. This is a fact subject to proof before the District Court, but convincing evidence that the economic value of one's own home has declined as a result of the conduct of another certainly is sufficient under Art. III to allow standing to contest the legality of that conduct.

NOTES AND QUESTIONS

1. **Deprivation of Benefits of Interracial Associations: Injury in Fact.** Consider whether the individual plaintiffs in *Trafficante* and *Gladstone* were claiming that housing was made unavailable to them. If not, were they seeking recovery for injuries suffered by others who were denied housing? No, neither is true. They claimed direct harm—that they personally suffered an actual injury—in the form of the "loss of important benefits from interracial associations." This claim satisfied the Article III injury-in-fact requirement even though it was a noneconomic injury and even though it rested in discriminatory conduct directed at others. In recognizing this type of "neighborhood standing," the Court took notice of the fact that housing discrimination causes damage not only to the "person on the landlord's blacklist" but also to "the whole community."

2. **Municipalities as Plaintiffs?** Unlike many other fair housing cases where the government is on the defendant side of the "v," the Village of Bellwood, "a municipal corporation and suburb of Chicago," was a plaintiff alongside its residents. It, too, claimed direct harm from defendants' steering practices, which "affect[ed] the village's racial composition, replacing what is presently an integrated neighborhood with a segregated one." The Court recognized that even a suburb could suffer noneconomic injury sufficient to establish neighborhood standing: "If, as alleged, petitioners' sales practices actually have begun to rob Bellwood of its racial balance and stability, the village has standing to challenge the legality of that conduct." How common are claims by cities and suburbs that private actors are manipulating the

---

19. [Fn. 29 in original] In addition to evidence about the community, it will be relevant at trial to consider the nature and extent of the business of the petitioner real estate brokers. This should include an inquiry into the extent of their participation in the purchase, sale, and rental of residences in the target area, the number and race of their customers, and the type of housing desired by customers. Evidence of this kind may be relevant to the establishment of the necessary causal connection between the alleged conduct and the asserted injury.

racial composition of their housing markets and causing them direct harm? In Chapter 11, we discuss claims by cities against banks alleging that predatory lending practices caused the cities injury in the aftermath of the foreclosure crisis.

3. **Economic and Noneconomic Harms.** Although "noneconomic injuries suffice to provide standing," *Gladstone*, 441 U.S. at 112, neighborhood standing also has an economic component. What were the economic harms the plaintiffs alleged as flowing from the discriminatory manipulation of housing markets and neighborhood racial composition? The plaintiffs in *Trafficante* alleged "embarrassment and economic damage in social, business, and professional activities from being 'stigmatized' as residents of a 'white ghetto.'" In *Gladstone*, the Court discussed the unique economic consequences to a municipality in the aftermath of racial steering: reduction in total buyers, housing prices trending downward, exodus of white residents, reduction in property values, diminishing tax base, and threatened ability to bear the cost of government services. The individual residents of Bellwood also alleged economic harm in the "absolute or relative diminution in value" of their homes. The Court almost treats the economic basis for neighborhood standing as a secondary concern. Why do you think this might have been the case during the era in which these cases were decided? Do you think the economic consequences of discrimination are more or less salient today? *See City of Miami, infra.* For analysis of contemporary claims of discrimination in property valuations in neighborhoods of color, *see* Chapter 11.

4. **The Limits of Neighborhood Standing.** How far does the ripple effect of neighborhood discrimination extend? Despite the central purpose of the FHA "to replace the ghettos 'by truly integrated and balanced living patterns,'"[20] racial residential segregation has endured. The persistence of segregation raises the question whether the injury alleged in *Trafficante* and *Gladstone* is a type of injury suffered almost universally. What guides the Court in determining who is responsible for the "deprivation of the benefits of interracial associations" and whether it creates the kind of "distinct and palpable" injury sufficient to satisfy Article III?

Recall that in *Trafficante* and *Gladstone* the plaintiffs alleged specific conduct by defendants that affected a discrete neighborhood's racial composition: exclusion of Black persons from an 8,200-resident apartment complex and manipulation of a "relatively compact" housing market of 12 by 13 blocks. Even though the *Gladstone* plaintiffs expanded the allegation made in the *Trafficante* case to allege deprivation of "the social and professional benefits of living in an integrated society," rather than integrated "community," the Court construed the complaint narrowly to "refer to the harm done to the residents of the carefully described neighborhood in Bellwood in which four of the individual respondents reside." The Court continued: "The question

---

20. 114 Cong. Rec. 3422; *Trafficante*, 409 U.S. at 211.

before us . . . is whether an allegation that this particular area is losing its integrated character because of petitioners' conduct is sufficient to satisfy Art. III." The *Gladstone* Court concluded it was. At the same time, the Court recognized the limits of neighborhood standing and the inherently factbound nature of the inquiry. Recall that the Court affirmed summary judgment dismissing two plaintiffs who lived outside the target neighborhood because they failed to allege actual harm under the neighborhood standing theory. The Court further held:

> A "neighborhood" whose racial composition allegedly is being manipulated may be so extensive an area, so heavily or even so sparsely populated, or so lacking in shared social and commercial intercourse that there would be no actual injury to a particular resident. The presence of a genuine injury should be ascertainable on the basis of discrete facts presented at trial.

The Court revisited this question in the third of its trilogy, *Havens Realty Corp. v. Coleman*.

5. **Standing to Sue on What Claim?** The focus in these standing cases is whether the plaintiffs have satisfied Article III's requirement that they demonstrate an actual injury. But, assuming plaintiffs establish that they have standing to sue, what claims will they be able to litigate? In *Trafficante*, the plaintiffs alleged discrimination against non-white rental applicants in numerous ways, including informing them they would not be welcome, manipulating the apartment waiting list, delaying action on their applications, and using discriminatory rental criteria. The claim, therefore, asserted concrete harm to plaintiffs resulting from discrimination against other people. Under *Gladstone*, the plaintiffs in the target area of Bellwood had standing to sue based on their ownership of homes in the area, but their claim alleged defendants' steering of prospective home buyers toward or away from the neighborhood based on race. The Court addressed this posture as follows:

> If . . . Congress intended standing under [the FHA] to extend to the full limits of Art. III, the normal prudential rules do not apply; . . . The central issue at this stage of the proceedings is not who possesses the legal rights protected by [§3604], but whether respondents were genuinely injured by conduct that violates *someone's* [§3604] rights, and thus are entitled to seek redress of that harm under [the FHA].

Gladstone, 441 U.S. at 103 n.9. Even the dissenting opinion in *Gladstone*, authored by Justice Rehnquist, agreed that "Congress . . . may grant to any person satisfying Art. III's minimum standing requirements a right "to seek relief on the basis of the legal rights and interests of others, [and] Congress did just that in enacting [the broad language in the FHA]" authorizing suit by "[a]ny person who claims to have been injured by a discriminatory housing practice."[21]

---

21. The dissenting opinion took issue with the failure of Congress to include "persons aggrieved" in the alternative enforcement provision under which the *Gladstone* plaintiffs filed

6. Is Article III the Limit? Both *Trafficante* and *Gladstone* concluded: "Standing under [the FHA's enforcement provisions] is 'as broa[d] as is permitted by Article III of the Constitution,'" with the Court discerning no intent by Congress to impose further limits. The holdings in *Trafficante* and *Gladstone* rested principally on interpretations of Article III.

7. Deference to HUD. Notice that the Court in *Trafficante* gave "great weight" to HUD's consistent construction of the FHA that considered complainants like those in *Trafficante* to be "aggrieved persons" even when they were not the direct victims of discrimination.

8. Pleading and Proving Standing. The Court's decisions in *Trafficante* and *Gladstone* do not resolve the cases on the merits. The Court reversed a dismissal of the complaint in *Trafficante* and affirmed a reversal of summary judgment in *Gladstone* that allowed plaintiffs' case to proceed. Note the limited scope of the *Gladstone* Court's holding: "the facts alleged in the complaints and revealed by initial discovery are sufficient to provide standing under Art. III. . . . The adequacy of proof of respondents' standing is not before us, and we express no views on it."

Indeed, the standing inquiry remains relevant because it is jurisdictional; a case or controversy must exist throughout all stages of the case. Virginia House of Delegates v. Bethune-Hill, 587 U.S. 658, 662 (2019). A court may examine standing at any time even if a defendant has not pressed the issue. *Id.* Further, "the standard used to establish standing is not constant but becomes gradually stricter in its demanded showing as the parties proceed through 'the successive stages of [a] litigation.'" McCardell, 794 F.3d at 516 (citing Lujan v. Defenders of Wildlife, 504 U.S. 555, 560-61 (1992)). Plaintiffs ignore standing at their peril.

2. Article III Standing Under the FHA: Tester and Organizational Standing

In the previous cases, the Court recognized that housing discrimination can cause concrete injuries to Black and white residents of apartment communities and neighborhoods as well as to municipal governments. But how would renters, homeowners, or governmental entities discover that their housing markets were being racially manipulated by steering and other discriminatory practices? The next case considers the Article III standing of fair housing organizations and "testers" who do the investigative work necessary to determine whether discrimination is occurring in a particular housing market. Testers are individuals who might not have an intent to rent or purchase housing but are deployed as putative homeseekers to gather information in the housing

---

a direct action in federal court. Congress resolved the *Gladstone* dissent's key objection in 1988 by adding the pivotal language, "aggrieved person," to the private enforcement provision of the FHA. *See* 42 U.S.C. §3613.

market. Testers with and without protected characteristics are assigned comparable profiles and housing searches except that the tester with the protected characteristic is made more qualified. Consider the types of injuries asserted by organizations and testers and whether it matters for standing purposes that they are not pursuing a sale or rental housing opportunity.

WHAT IS A FAIR HOUSING ORGANIZATION?

Fair housing organizations (FHOs) are nonprofit organizations that serve the public by promoting fair housing choice and opportunity in their local communities or regions. They provide a wide variety of services "to make equal opportunity in housing a reality."[22]

Housing and Complaint Counseling: FHOs provide counseling to individuals and families to help them identify housing opportunities that will enable them to thrive. FHO staff also process discrimination complaints across all housing sectors and on behalf of federally, state, and locally protected classes. FHO staff interview consumers regarding possible instances of discrimination and inform them of their rights and options. FHOs counsel the complainant on the results of any investigation, provide support and assistance on enforcement if appropriate, and participate in enforcement actions if warranted. According to an annual report published since the 1980s by the National Fair Housing Alliance (NFHA), 85 private, nonprofit organizations processed 73 percent of all such complaints in 2019 when compared with government enforcement agencies.[23]

Testing, Investigation, and Enforcement: FHOs have special expertise in operating fair housing testing and investigation programs. FHO staff members analyze complaints, interview witnesses, and conduct research of publicly available information. Investigative staff members train and deploy testers as neutral factfinders to gather evidence of housing market practices. If testing is appropriate, staff design and conduct tests that help determine if a protected characteristic is causing different treatment of testers, which can provide evidence of discrimination to support a homeseeker facing barriers in the housing market. If warranted, FHOs pursue enforcement actions to seek remedies for policies and actions that would otherwise go unchecked and that frustrate their services designed to promote an equal housing market and reverse patterns of segregation.

Education, Training, and Advocacy: Another way FHOs fulfill their mission is educating members of the public about fair housing law to encourage compliance and to deter potential violations. For example, public and individual education must ensure that individual housing consumers are able to recognize warning signs of discrimination, and know how to obtain information about their fair housing rights and file a complaint if necessary. Educating and

---

22. Havens Realty Corp. v. Coleman, 455 U.S. 363, 368 (1982).
23. National Fair Housing Alliance, 2020 Fair Housing Trends Report, 31-32 (2020).

counseling the public more broadly about the right to fair housing and the benefits of open and integrated neighborhoods is also paramount to remove barriers to a healthy democracy in which everyone has an opportunity to strive and thrive.

FHOs also educate planning and zoning departments, housing authorities, and other government officials about their affirmative fair housing duties under federal law to ensure their housing and neighborhood development programs do not isolate residents or perpetuate segregation.

FHOs also train housing industry members to avoid discriminatory practices and refrain from encouraging, even subtly, discriminatory consumer housing decisions. FHO education of real estate industry members can ensure that members use their positions to do everything possible to reverse past practices and support housing opportunity and choice.

Havens Realty Corporation v. Coleman
455 U.S. 363 (1982)

Before Chief Justice Burger and Justices Brennan, White, Marshall, Blackmun, Powell, Rehnquist, Stevens, and O'Connor.

Justice BRENNAN delivered the opinion of the Court. Powell, J., filed a concurring opinion.

I.

The case began as a class action against Havens Realty Corp. (Havens) and one of its employees, Rose Jones. Defendants were alleged to have engaged in "racial steering" violative of §3604 of the FHA. The complaint, seeking declaratory, injunctive, and monetary relief, was filed . . . by three individuals—Paul Coles, Sylvia Coleman, and R. Kent Willis—and an organization—Housing Opportunities Made Equal (HOME).

At the time suit was brought, defendant Havens owned and operated two apartment complexes, Camelot Townhouses and Colonial Court Apartments, in Henrico County, Va., a suburb of Richmond. The complaint identified Paul Coles as a black "renter plaintiff" who, attempting to rent an apartment from Havens, inquired on July 13, 1978, about the availability of an apartment at the Camelot complex, and was falsely told that no apartments were available. The other two individual plaintiffs, Coleman and Willis, were described in the complaint as "tester plaintiffs" who were employed by HOME to determine whether Havens practiced racial steering. Coleman, who is black, and Willis, who is white, each assertedly made inquiries of Havens on March 14, March 21, and March 23, 1978, regarding the availability of apartments.

On each occasion, Coleman was told that no apartments were available; Willis was told that there were vacancies. On July 6, 1978, Coleman made a further inquiry and was told that there were no vacancies in the Camelot

Townhouses; a white tester for HOME, who was not a party to the complaint, was given contrary information that same day.

The complaint identified HOME as "a nonprofit corporation organized under the laws of the State of Virginia" whose purpose was "to make equal opportunity in housing a reality in the Richmond Metropolitan Area." According to the complaint, HOME's membership was "multi-racial and include[d] approximately 600 individuals." Its activities included the operation of a housing counseling service, and the investigation and referral of complaints concerning housing discrimination.

The three individual plaintiffs, who at the time the complaint was filed were all residents of the city of Richmond or the adjacent Henrico County averred that they had been injured by the discriminatory acts of petitioners. Coles, the black renter, claimed that he had been "denied the right to rent real property in Henrico County." Further, he and the two tester plaintiffs alleged that Havens' practices deprived them of the "important social, professional, business and economic, political and aesthetic benefits of interracial associations that arise from living in integrated communities free from discriminatory housing practices." And Coleman, the black tester, alleged that the misinformation given her by Havens concerning the availability of apartments in the Colonial Court and Camelot Townhouse complexes had caused her "specific injury."

HOME also alleged injury. It asserted that the steering practices of Havens had frustrated the organization's counseling and referral services, with a consequent drain on resources. Additionally, HOME asserted that its members had been deprived of the benefits of interracial association arising from living in an integrated community free of housing discrimination.

[The district court dismissed the claims of the two testers and HOME on standing and other grounds. The Fourth Circuit Court of Appeals reversed and remanded, and the Court granted certiorari.]

III.

Our inquiry with respect to the standing issues raised in this case is guided by our decision in Gladstone, Realtors v. Village of Bellwood. . . .

A.

The Court of Appeals held that Coleman and Willis have standing to sue in two capacities: as "testers" and as individuals deprived of the benefits of interracial association. We first address the question of "tester" standing.

In the present context, "testers" are individuals who, without an intent to rent or purchase a home or apartment, pose as renters or purchasers for the purpose of collecting evidence of unlawful steering practices. Section 3604(d) states that it is unlawful for an individual or firm covered by the Act "[t]o represent to *any person* because of [a protected category] that any dwelling is not available for inspection, sale, or rental when such dwelling is in fact so available" (emphasis added), a prohibition made enforceable through the creation of an explicit cause of action in §3612(a) of the Act. Congress has thus conferred on all "persons" a legal right to truthful information about available housing.

This congressional intention cannot be overlooked in determining whether testers have standing to sue. As we have previously recognized, "[t]he actual or threatened injury required by Art. III may exist solely by virtue of 'statutes creating legal rights, the invasion of which creates standing. . . .'" Warth v. Seldin. Section 3604(d), which, in terms, establishes an enforceable right to truthful information concerning the availability of housing, is such an enactment. A tester who has been the object of a misrepresentation made unlawful under §3604(d) has suffered injury in precisely the form the statute was intended to guard against, and therefore has standing to maintain a claim for damages under the Act's provisions. That the tester may have approached the real estate agent fully expecting that he would receive false information, and without any intention of buying or renting a home, does not negate the simple fact of injury within the meaning of §3604(d). Whereas Congress, in prohibiting discriminatory refusals to sell or rent in §3604(a) of the Act, required that there be a "bona fide offer" to rent or purchase, Congress plainly omitted any such requirement insofar as it banned discriminatory representations in §3604(d). In the instant case, respondent Coleman—the black tester—alleged injury to her statutorily created right to truthful housing information.

As part of the complaint, she averred that petitioners told her on four different occasions that apartments were not available in the Henrico County complexes while informing white testers that apartments were available. If the facts are as alleged, then respondent has suffered "specific injury" from the challenged acts of petitioners, and the Art. III requirement of injury in fact is satisfied.

Respondent Willis' situation is different. He made no allegation that petitioners misrepresented to him that apartments were unavailable in the two apartment complexes. To the contrary, Willis alleged that on each occasion that he inquired he was informed that apartments *were* available. As such, Willis has alleged no injury to his statutory right to accurate information concerning the availability of housing. We thus discern no support for the Court of Appeals' holding that Willis has standing to sue in his capacity as a tester. More to the point, because Willis does not allege that he was a victim of a discriminatory misrepresentation, he has not pleaded a cause of action under §3604(d). We must therefore reverse the Court of Appeals' judgment insofar as it reversed the District Court's dismissal of Willis' "tester" claims.

B.

Coleman and Willis argue in this Court, and the Court of Appeals held, that irrespective of their status as testers, they should have been allowed to proceed beyond the pleading stage inasmuch as they have alleged that petitioners' steering practices deprived them of the benefits that result from living in an integrated community. This concept of "neighborhood" standing differs from that of "tester" standing in that the injury asserted is an indirect one: an adverse impact on the neighborhood in which the plaintiff resides resulting from the steering of persons other than the plaintiff. By contrast, the injury underlying tester standing — the denial of the tester's own statutory right to truthful housing information caused by misrepresentations to the tester — is a direct one. The distinction is between "third-party" and "first-party" standing.[24]

This distinction is, however, of little significance in deciding whether a plaintiff has standing to sue under §3612 of the FHA. Bellwood, as we have already noted, held that the only requirement for standing to sue under §3612 is the Art. III requirement of injury in fact. As long as respondents have alleged distinct and palpable injuries that are "fairly traceable" to petitioners' actions, the Art. III requirement of injury in fact is satisfied. The question before us, then, is whether injury in fact has been sufficiently alleged.

The two individual respondents, who according to the complaint were "residents of the City of Richmond or Henrico County," alleged that the racial steering practices of petitioners have deprived them of "the right to the important social, professional, business and economic, political and aesthetic benefits of interracial associations that arise from living in integrated communities free from discriminatory housing practices." The type of injury alleged thus clearly resembles that which we found palpable in *Bellwood*.

Petitioners do not dispute that the loss of social, professional, and economic benefits resulting from steering practices constitutes palpable injury. Instead, they contend that Coleman and Willis, by pleading simply that they were residents of the Richmond metropolitan area, have failed to demonstrate how the asserted steering practices of petitioners in Henrico County may have affected the *particular* neighborhoods in which the individual respondents resided.

It is indeed implausible to argue that petitioners' alleged acts of discrimination could have palpable effects throughout the *entire* Richmond metropolitan area. At the time relevant to this action the city of Richmond contained a population of nearly 220,000 persons, dispersed over 37 square miles. Henrico County occupied more than 232 square miles, in which roughly 170,000 people made their homes. Our cases have upheld standing based on the effects of discrimination only within a "relatively compact neighborhood," Bellwood, 441 U.S., at 114. We have not suggested that discrimination within a single housing complex might give rise to "distinct and palpable injury" throughout a metropolitan area.

---

24. [EDS.—Some scholars suggest that a plaintiff arguably coming within a statute's zone of interests (as were these plaintiffs under Court precedent) can claim first-party standing. *See* Bradley & Young, 131 YALE L.J. at 5.]

Nonetheless, in the absence of further factual development, we cannot say as a matter of law that no injury could be proved. Respondents have not identified the particular neighborhoods in which they lived, nor established the proximity of their homes to the site of petitioners' alleged steering practices. Further pleading and proof might establish that they lived in areas where petitioners' practices had an appreciable effect. Accordingly, on remand, the District Court should afford the plaintiffs an opportunity to make more definite the allegations of the complaint. If after that opportunity the pleadings fail to make averments that meet the standing requirements established by the decisions of this Court, the claims should be dismissed. . . .

C.

HOME brought suit against petitioners both as a representative of its members and on its own behalf. . . . While we . . . will not decide the question involving HOME's representative standing [because it abandoned the claim], we do proceed to decide the question whether HOME has standing in its own right; the organization continues to press a right to claim damages in that latter capacity.

In determining whether HOME has standing under the FHA, we conduct the same inquiry as in the case of an individual: Has the plaintiff "'alleged such a personal stake in the outcome of the controversy' as to warrant his invocation of federal-court jurisdiction"? In the instant case, HOME's complaint contained the following claims of injury to the organization:

> Plaintiff HOME has been frustrated by defendants' racial steering practices in its efforts to assist equal access to housing through counseling and other referral services. Plaintiff HOME has had to devote significant resources to identify and counteract the defendant's racially discriminatory steering practices.

If, as broadly alleged, petitioners' steering practices have perceptibly impaired HOME's ability to provide counseling and referral services for low- and moderate-income homeseekers, there can be no question that the organization has suffered injury in fact. Such concrete and demonstrable injury to the organization's activities—with the consequent drain on the organization's resources—constitutes far more than simply a setback to the organization's abstract social interests. We therefore conclude, as did the Court of Appeals, that in view of HOME's allegations of injury it was improper for the District Court to dismiss for lack of standing the claims of the organization in its own right.

V

In sum, we affirm the judgment of the Court of Appeals insofar as the judgment reversed the District Court's dismissal of the claims of Coleman and Willis as individuals allegedly deprived of the benefits of interracial association, and the claims of HOME as an organization allegedly injured by the racial steering practices of petitioners; we reverse the judgment insofar as it directed that [both] Coleman and Willis may proceed to trial on their tester claims. Further proceedings on the remand directed by the Court of Appeals shall be consistent with this opinion.

NOTES AND QUESTIONS

1. The Trilogy Is Complete. The Court for the third time held that "the sole requirement for standing to sue under [the FHA] is the Art. III minima of injury in fact. . . ." The *Havens* Court leaves little room to ponder whether its prior pronouncements were incidental musings: "In reaching [our conclusion that certain plaintiffs had standing in *Gladstone*], we held that 'Congress intended standing under [the FHA] to extend to the full limits of Art. III' and that the courts accordingly lack the authority to create prudential barriers to standing in suits brought under [the Act]."

2. Bona Fide Plaintiffs. Notice that the bona fide homeseeker in *Havens*, Paul Coles, had an additional claim beyond misrepresentation under §3604(d). He alleged he was steered away from the "unavailable" apartment in the predominantly white complex toward the "available" unit in the adjoining complex that happened to be integrated, that is, already occupied by Black people. Steering makes housing unavailable based on race, in violation of 42 U.S.C. §3604(a). *See* 455 U.S. 366, 368 n.4. Bona fide plaintiffs like Coles should have no difficulty demonstrating injury and establishing standing for their claims.

3. Tester Standing. In *Havens*, the Court considered the question whether fair housing testers have standing to sue in their own right. Fair housing organizations, researchers, and governmental agencies use the information testers collect to determine whether practices comply with fair housing laws and, if appropriate, to provide evidence of discrimination in enforcement actions. Testing may demonstrate that illegal discrimination is unlikely, or it may provide evidence of disparate treatment that would otherwise be elusive. In most instances, testers do not pursue claims on their own behalf.

As discussed in Chapter 8, section §3604(d) is particularly pertinent for testers. This provision prohibits a very narrow and specific type of conduct: misrepresenting to a person that housing is unavailable (when it *is* available) based on protected class status. Not all types of misrepresentations are illegal under this provision, only lies about housing availability. Matched-pair testing is a particularly effective means of uncovering this form of discrimination because housing availability is a threshold inquiry for a tester; when testers make inquiries in close proximity, any contradictions in the information they collect can provide probative evidence of a §3604(d) violation. And enforcement of this provision based on tester evidence can prevent future discrimination against other people.

Getting back to standing, what type of "distinct and palpable injury" have testers suffered when a housing provider lies to them about whether a home is still on the market and does so based on protected status? This simple provision packs a considerable punch where standing is concerned. *Havens* makes clear that Congress conferred a legal right to nondiscriminatory, truthful information about housing availability on not a particular subset of homeseekers, but "all 'persons.'" A tester who alleges a discriminatory violation of the right to truthful information under §3604(d), then, "has suffered injury in precisely the form the statute was intended to guard against, and therefore has standing to maintain a claim for damages under the Act's provisions." *Havens*, 455 U.S. at 373-74.

So all persons, even those not seeking to rent or buy housing, have a "statutorily created" right to be free from discrimination in representations about housing availability.[25] But does *Havens* imply a type of automatic standing for any tester engaged in the collection of this information? No. The Court distinguishes between the white tester, who obtained truthful information, and the Black tester, who (on four separate occasions) did not. The white tester alleged no injury and lacked standing; the Black tester alleged an injury to her own rights created by §3604(d), satisfying the requirements of Article III. In this way, the tester must allege injury in the same manner as any other person; a tester is neither removed from coverage under the FHA nor assumed to establish standing merely based on tester status.

4. The Limits of "Tester Standing." In TransUnion LLC v. Ramirez, 594 U.S. 413, 426-27 (2021), the Court dispelled the notion that a violation of a statutory legal right by itself can create actual injury under Article III.

> For standing purposes, therefore, an important difference exists between (i) a plaintiff's statutory cause of action to sue a defendant over the defendant's violation of federal law, and (ii) a plaintiff's suffering concrete harm because of the defendant's violation of federal law. Congress may enact legal prohibitions and obligations. And Congress may create causes of action for plaintiffs to sue defendants who violate those legal prohibitions or obligations. But under Article III, an injury in law is not an injury in fact. Only those plaintiffs who have been concretely harmed by a defendant's statutory violation may sue that private defendant over that violation in federal court.

In the particular context of the right granted under §3604(d), however, "all persons" may enforce it, and it seems clear that lying to persons about housing availability, based on their protected status, is a form of discrimination sufficient to cause concrete harm for standing purposes.[26] What about

---

25. *See Havens*, 455 U.S. at 374 ("Congress plainly omitted" any requirement of a "'bona fide offer' to rent or purchase" "insofar as it banned discriminatory representations . . .").

26. As discussed in Chapter 8, available relief for a proven violation of this right may be limited. For example, plaintiffs enforcing §3604(d) would not have standing to enjoin a housing provider to rent them a particular unit because they are not alleging a violation of a right, such as under §3604(a), to obtain housing free from discrimination. Testers may obtain monetary damages (and injunctive relief) under §3604(d), but, depending on the facts, the amount likely would be less than that awarded to a plaintiff enforcing rights under §3604(a).

contexts similar to tester standing where individuals who are not homeseekers sue to enforce provisions of the FHA? Viewers of discriminatory housing advertisements and those subject to discriminatory statements under
§3604(c) are examples, discussed in Chapter 9. Those observing violations of
the design and construction requirements under §3604(f)(3)(C), regardless of
their disability or homeseeker status, may be another example, discussed in
Chapter 17. *See* Fair Housing Justice Center, Inc. v. 203 Jay St. Associates, LLC,
No. 21-CV-1192, 2022 WL 3100557, at *7 (E.D.N.Y. Aug. 4, 2022) (a plaintiff
need not allege an individual act of discrimination against a disabled person
to state a violation of the FHA's design and construction provision). Even
if the FHA is interpreted to grant a cause of action in these circumstances,
under *TransUnion* plaintiffs will need to allege "concrete harm" and "adverse
effects," not a mere statutory violation, to establish injury in fact.[27]

In 2023, the Supreme Court resolved Acheson Hotels, LLC v. Laufer, 601
U.S. 1, 11-12 (2023), which posed a question of standing for testers in ADA
cases. While the Court dismissed the case as moot, Justice Thomas wrote a
concurrence in which he specifically recognized the standing of testers in
cases brought pursuant to the FHA:

> Laufer's ADA claim is thus different from the tester's claim under the FHA
> that the Court addressed in Havens Realty Corp. v. Coleman. In contrast to the
> ADA, the FHA explicitly prohibits "represent[ing] to any person because of
> race . . . that any dwelling is not available for inspection, sale, or rental when
> such dwelling is in fact so available." §3604(d). Accordingly, when Havens
> Realty told a black tester that no apartments were available but told a white
> tester that it had vacancies, the Court found that the black tester had standing
> to sue. The Court explained that the statute created "a legal right to truthful
> information about available housing." The black tester had been personally
> denied that truthful information, so she had standing to bring her claim.
> Havens Realty thus has no bearing on Laufer's standing as a tester of compli-
> ance with the ADA, which provides no such statutory right to information.

5. **Testers and Neighborhood Standing.** The Court had little trouble recognizing standing for testers based on the statutory right to truthful

---

27. *Compare* Ragin v. Harry Macklowe Real Estate Co., 6 F.3d 898, 904 (2d. Cir. 1993) ("There
is no significant difference between the statutorily recognized injury suffered by the tester in
Havens Realty and the injury suffered by the Ragins and the Cuylers, who were confronted
by advertisements indicating a preference based on race.") *and* Smith v. Pacific Properties &
Development Corp., 358 F.3d 1097, 1104, 1107 (9th Cir. 2004) (holding in a design and construction case that "[t]he history and language of the FHA and the FHAA make clear that testers fall
within the protected group of 'any person[s]' that may enforce rights created by §3604(f)(2) when
they are violated by discriminatory housing conditions, and recognizing "the dignitary harm to
a disabled person of observing such overtly discriminatory conditions") *with* DeBoard v. Ventry
Apartments, LLC, 1:22-CV-396-HAB, 2023 WL 4123310, at *7 (N.D. Ind. June 22, 2023) (citing
TransUnion, denying standing when the only alleged injury to a "serial tester" was the violation
of the FHA's design and construction requirements), *reaff'd*, 2024 WL 1528630 (N.D. Ind. Apr. 9,
2024) (holding that in the Seventh Circuit "intangible, emotional injuries [alleged in amended
complaint] are not concrete injuries that confer Article III standing").

information on housing availability, but what about the standing of neighbors or neighborhoods? Remember, neighborhood standing entails claims of "adverse impact on the neighborhood in which the plaintiff resides resulting from [discrimination against] persons other than the plaintiff." The injuries can be economic, noneconomic, or both.

What facts will a "neighbor plaintiff" need to assert to show injury in fact, other than that defendants' practices deprived them of the "social, professional, business and economic, political and aesthetic benefits" of living in an integrated community? In their attempts to assert "neighbor standing," the individual plaintiffs in *Havens* pleaded only that they were residents of the Richmond metropolitan area without demonstrating how the alleged steering practices affected their particular neighborhoods. This fell far short: "It is indeed implausible to argue that petitioners' alleged acts of discrimination could have palpable effects throughout the *entire* Richmond metropolitan area." This was not the "relatively compact neighborhood" the Court considered in *Gladstone*. The Court noted the "extreme generality" of the complaint but remanded to "afford the plaintiffs an opportunity to make more definite the allegations" because further pleading "might establish that they lived in areas where petitioners' practices had an appreciable effect." Although *Havens* did not revisit the question addressed in *Gladstone* of what facts a neighborhood or municipal entity itself must allege to establish standing, the Court reaffirmed its holding that the "only requirement" for FHA standing "is the Article III requirement of injury in fact."

6. **Organizational Standing.** In 2024, the Court upheld *Havens* even as it described it as "an unusual case," which it "has been careful not to extend . . . beyond its context."[28] The *Havens* Court held that an FHO can establish standing under Article III by alleging actual injury, which the Court described as "the same inquiry as in the case of an individual."[29] The FHO in *Havens*, Housing Opportunities Made Equal (HOME), could not demonstrate that it was the direct victim of the misrepresentations alleged in the case, but it did allege actual injury: Defendants' steering practices had "perceptibly impaired"

---

28. In FDA v. Alliance for Hippocratic Medicine, 602 U.S. 367 (2024), the Court considered a *Havens*-style argument to support medical associations' standing in the context of "legal, moral, ideological, and policy objections to elective abortion and to FDA's relaxed regulation of mifepristone" (a drug prescribed to achieve an early termination of pregnancy). The Court held that merely "incurring costs to oppose FDA's actions" was "an expansive theory of standing" that *Havens* did not support. The Court noted in contrast that the defendant in *Havens* "directly affected and interfered with HOME's core business activities."

29. The Supreme Court has not yet ruled and the lower courts are divided about tester and organizational standing under the 1866 Civil Rights Act (discussed in Chapter 2). *See* Schwemm, HDLL §27:17. The viability of steering claims under §1982 has not been resolved by the Supreme Court, but lower courts have upheld standing in such cases. In *Gladstone* and *Havens*, the Court did not reach the issue of standing under §1982. *See* Schwemm, HDLL §27:7.

its services in promoting open housing with a "consequent drain" on its resources. More specifically, HOME alleged it had been

> frustrated by defendants' racial steering practices in its efforts to achieve or encourage equal access to housing through counseling and other referral services. Plaintiff HOME has had to devote significant resources to identify and counteract the defendant's racially discriminatory steering practices.

Therefore, the formulation for organizational standing for an FHO, indeed any organization, litigating on its own behalf[30] has developed into two components, one noneconomic and one economic: frustration of mission and diversion of resources.

The "frustration of mission" prong addresses perceptible impairment to "the organization's noneconomic interest in encouraging open housing," which the Court recognized as a "concrete and demonstrable injury to the organization's activities." *Havens*, 455 U.S. at 379 & n.20. This noneconomic prong thus requires some description of the fair housing activities that are impaired; HOME alleged impairment of its ability to provide counseling and referral services for low- and moderate-income homeseekers. If an FHO can allege perceptible impairment to its mission-related services, (or, as under *FDA*, its "core business activities,") the Court was unequivocal: "[T]here can be no question that the organization has suffered injury in fact."

The "diversion of resources" prong addresses the economic injury to an FHO resulting from the need to "identify and counteract" the defendant's discrimination. Diversion of resources can be documented like other economic injury; the FHO can describe the number of hours its staff dedicated to investigations, educational outreach, counseling, or other activities traceable to the defendant. The FHO can also describe the out-of-pocket expenses it undertook in mounting these activities. The FHO can retain proof of these damages, for example, through staff time sheets and receipts.

Here are some examples of diversion of resource allegations that courts have found sufficiently tangible to satisfy Article III's injury-in-fact requirement.

- "[C]oncrete drains on . . . time and resources [included] [e]xpenditures to reach out to potential home buyers or renters who are steered away from housing opportunities by discriminatory advertising, or to monitor and counteract on an ongoing basis public impressions created by defendants' use of print media." Spann v. Colonial Village, Inc., 899 F.2d 24, 29 (D.C. Cir. 1990).
- "[Fair Housing of Marin] alleges that, as a result of the defendant's discriminatory practices, it has 'suffered injury to its ability to carry out its

---

30. The Court noted that HOME had initially brought suit on its own behalf *and* as a representative of its members; it subsequently abandoned its representative standing theory. 455 U.S. at 378.

purposes . . . [and] economic losses in staff pay, in funds expended in support of volunteer services, and in the inability to undertake other efforts to end unlawful housing practices.' Thus, fairly construed, [Fair Housing of Marin] complains that defendant's discrimination against African Americans has caused it to suffer injury to its ability to provide outreach and education (i.e., counseling)." Fair Housing of Marin v. Combs, 285 F.3d 899, 905 (9th Cir. 2002).

- The FHO deputy director testified at trial "that the services offered by the [FHO] included providing information at community seminars about how to fight housing discrimination. . . . [The deputy] also testified that the time she and her coworkers spent on matters related to this case prevented them from devoting their time and energies to other [FHO] matters. . . ." Ragin v. Harry Macklowe Real Estate Co., 6 F.3d 898, 905 (2d. Cir. 1993).

- "Plaintiff alleges an economic loss and drain on its resources specifically resulting from its inability to place the Twenty Clients in the Sand Castle [due to defendants' policies about criminal records]. . . . Specifically, Plaintiff demonstrates that, in addition to its employee, Mr. Carter, expending substantial time trying to find alternative housing . . . , Plaintiff hired a new employee . . . specifically to assist with placing the Twenty Clients. [This] required additional expenditures for brokers' fees and higher rents. . . ." Fortune Society v. Sandcastle Towers Housing Development Fund Corp., 388 F. Supp. 3d 145, 164 (E.D.N.Y. 2019).

Of course, as in all standing cases, the organizational plaintiff must offer sufficient proof to establish injury (and damages) as the litigation proceeds. And it must "demonstrate at trial that it has indeed suffered impairment in its role of facilitating open housing." *Havens*, 455 U.S. at 379 n.21.

7. **The Limits of Organizational Standing.** There is heft to the Article III standard. Abstract concern, psychic injury from witnessing noncompliance with the FHA, or an alleged setback to an organization's abstract social interests, will not do. *See Havens*, 455 U.S. at 379 (citing Sierra Club v. Morton, 405 U.S. 727, 739 (1972)); Spann v. Colonial Village, Inc., 899 F.2d 24, 27, 29 (D.C. Cir. 1990). And, to be sure, an FHO like any other plaintiff must allege specific facts demonstrating "distinct and palpable injury" that is "fairly traceable" to the defendant. In Arkansas ACORN Fair Housing, Inc. v. Greystone Development Co., 160 F.3d 433, 434-35 (8th Cir. 1998), the court found the plaintiff's summary judgment evidence insufficient to establish standing.

> Although ACORN provides general information concerning the resources spent each month monitoring advertisements of a broad base of housing providers and working to counteract the effects of discriminatory advertising, ACORN presents no facts to quantify the resources, if any, that were expended to counteract the effects of a single, allegedly discriminatory advertisement. ACORN has not shown, for example, what resources were used in identifying Greystone in particular as an alleged violator of the FHA,

in monitoring or otherwise investigating Greystone once identified, in determining the discriminatory effects specifically attributable to Greystone's advertisements, or in counteracting those discriminatory effects. While the deflection of an organization's monetary and human resources from counseling or educational programs to legal efforts aimed at combating discrimination, such as monitoring and investigation, is itself sufficient to constitute an actual injury, the injury must also be traceable to some act of the defendant. Absent specific facts establishing distinct and palpable injuries *fairly traceable* to Greystone's advertisements, ACORN cannot satisfy its burden at the summary judgment stage to establish the injury in fact requirement for standing under the FHA.

See also Louisiana ACORN Fair Housing v. Leblanc, 211 F.3d 298, 305 (5th Cir. 2000) ("[The FHO trial witness] neither mentioned any specific projects ACORN had to put on hold while working on [the] case nor did he describe in any detail [or demonstrate through time sheets] how ACORN had to redouble efforts in the community to combat discrimination.").

The circuits are split on the issue of whether FHOs may use the "legal efforts" they have undertaken to counteract a defendant's discriminatory practices to satisfy the diversion of resources prong of the *Havens* injury standard. A majority of circuits allow FHOs to use their litigation-related expenses to establish injury, including the Eighth Circuit as revealed in *Arkansas ACORN*. The D.C. Circuit, as well as the Third and Fifth Circuits, do not. *See Spann*, 899 F.2d at 27 ("An organization cannot, of course, manufacture the injury necessary to maintain a suit from its expenditure of resources on that very suit. Were the rule otherwise, any litigant could create injury in fact by bringing a case, and Article III would present no real limitation."); Equal Rights Center v. Post Properties, Inc., 633 F.3d 1136, 1140 (D.C. Cir. 2011) (rejecting the lower court's focus on voluntariness of diversion expenditures, emphasizing instead "first, whether Post's alleged discriminatory conduct injured the ERC's interest in promoting fair housing and, second, whether the ERC used its resources to counteract the harm [other than through testing or litigation].").

3. Statutory Right to Sue Under the FHA: Zone of Interests and Proximate Cause

In the next case, decided 35 years after *Havens*, the Court approached the issue of neighborhood standing with a greater focus on the rights created under the FHA than on the outer bounds of Article III. In *City of Miami*, the context was the post-2008 foreclosure crisis and widespread harms allegedly resulting from claimed predatory lending practices targeting consumers of color. Varied plaintiffs filed FHA suits in several cities seeking to recover these damages. Like the Village of Bellwood in *Gladstone*, a key plaintiff in these cases was the city itself.

Bank of America Corp. v. City of Miami, Fla.
581 U.S. 189 (2017)

BREYER, J., delivered the opinion of the Court, in which Roberts, C.J., and Ginsburg, Sotomayor, and Kagan, JJ., joined. Thomas, J., filed an opinion concurring in part and dissenting in part, in which Kennedy and Alito, JJ., joined. Gorsuch, J., took no part in the consideration or decision of the cases.

The Fair Housing Act (FHA or Act) forbids:

> discriminat[ing] against any person in the terms, conditions, or privileges of sale or rental of a dwelling, or in the provision of services or facilities in connection therewith, because of race. . . ." 42 U.S.C. §3604(b).

It further makes it unlawful for

> any person or other entity whose business includes engaging in residential real estate-related transactions to discriminate against any person in making available such a transaction, or in the terms or conditions of such a transaction, because of race. . . ." §3605(a).

The statute allows any "aggrieved person" to file a civil action seeking damages for a violation of the statute. §§3613(a)(1)(A), 3613(c)(1). And it defines an "aggrieved person" to include "any person who . . . claims to have been injured by a discriminatory housing practice." §3602(i).

The City of Miami claims that two banks, Bank of America and Wells Fargo, intentionally issued riskier mortgages on less favorable terms to African-American and Latino customers than they issued to similarly situated white, non-Latino customers, in violation of §§3604(b) and 3605(a). The City alleges that these discriminatory practices have (1) "adversely impacted the racial composition of the City"; (2) "impaired the City's goals to assure racial integration and desegregation"; (3) "frustrate[d] the City's longstanding and active interest in promoting fair housing and securing the benefits of an integrated community"; and (4) disproportionately "cause[d] foreclosures and vacancies in minority communities in Miami." Those foreclosures and vacancies have harmed the City by decreasing "the property value of the foreclosed home as well as the values of other homes in the neighborhood," thereby (a) "reduc[ing] property tax revenues to the City," and (b) forcing the City to spend more on "municipal services that it provided and still must provide to remedy blight and unsafe and dangerous conditions which exist at properties that were foreclosed as a result of [the Banks'] illegal lending practices." The City claims that those practices violate the FHA and that it is entitled to damages for the listed injuries.

The Banks respond that the complaints do not set forth a cause of action for two basic reasons. First, they contend that the City's claimed harms do not "arguably" fall within the "zone of interests" that the statute seeks to protect, Association of Data Processing Service Organizations, Inc. v. Camp, 397 U.S. 150, 153 (1970); hence, the City is not an "aggrieved person" entitled to sue under the Act, §3602(i). Second, they say that the complaint fails to draw a "proximate-cause" connection between the violation claimed and the harm allegedly suffered. In their view, even if the City proves the violations it charges, the distance between those violations and the harms the City claims to have suffered is simply too great to entitle the City to collect damages.

We hold that the City's claimed injuries fall within the zone of interests that the FHA arguably protects. Hence, the City is an "aggrieved person" able to bring suit under the statute. We also hold that, to establish proximate cause under the FHA, a plaintiff must do more than show that its injuries foreseeably flowed from the alleged statutory violation. The lower court decided these cases on the theory that foreseeability is all that the statute requires, so we vacate and remand for further proceedings.

I

In 2013, the City of Miami brought lawsuits in federal court against two banks, Bank of America and Wells Fargo. The City's complaints charge that the Banks discriminatorily imposed more onerous, and indeed "predatory," conditions on loans made to minority borrowers than to similarly situated nonminority borrowers. Those "predatory" practices included, among others, excessively high interest rates, unjustified fees, teaser low-rate loans that overstated refinancing opportunities, large prepayment penalties, and—when default loomed—unjustified refusals to refinance or modify the loans. Due to the discriminatory nature of the Banks' practices, default and foreclosure rates among minority borrowers were higher than among otherwise similar white borrowers and were concentrated in minority neighborhoods. Higher foreclosure rates lowered property values and diminished property-tax revenue. Higher foreclosure rates—especially when accompanied by vacancies—also increased demand for municipal services, such as police, fire, and building and code enforcement services, all needed "to remedy blight and unsafe and dangerous conditions" that the foreclosures and vacancies generate. The complaints describe statistical analyses that trace the City's financial losses to the Banks' discriminatory practices.

The District Court dismissed the complaints on the grounds that (1) the harms alleged, being economic and not discriminatory, fell outside the zone of interests the FHA protects; (2) the complaints fail to show a sufficient causal connection between the City's injuries and the Banks' discriminatory conduct; and (3) the complaints fail to allege unlawful activity occurring within the Act's 2-year statute of limitations. The City then filed amended complaints (the complaints now before us) and sought reconsideration. The District Court held that the amended complaints could solve only the statute of limitations problem. It consequently declined to reconsider the dismissals.

The Court of Appeals reversed the District Court. It held that the City's injuries fall within the "zone of interests," Lexmark Int'l, Inc. v. Static Control

Components, Inc., 134 S. Ct. 1377, 1388 (2014), that the FHA protects (relying on *Trafficante v. Metropolitan Life Ins. Co.*; *Gladstone, Realtors v. Village of Bellwood*; and *Havens Realty Corp. v. Coleman*). It added that the complaints adequately allege proximate cause. And it remanded the cases while ordering the District Court to accept the City's complaints as amended.

The Banks filed petitions for certiorari, asking us to decide whether, as the Court of Appeals had in effect held, the amended complaints satisfied the FHA's zone-of-interests and proximate-cause requirements. We agreed to do so.

II

To satisfy the Constitution's restriction of this Court's jurisdiction to "Cases" and "Controversies," Art. III, §2, a plaintiff must demonstrate constitutional standing. To do so, the plaintiff must show an "injury in fact" that is "fairly traceable" to the defendant's conduct and "that is likely to be redressed by a favorable judicial decision." This Court has also referred to a plaintiff's need to satisfy "prudential" or "statutory" standing requirements. *See* Lexmark, 134 S. Ct., at 1387, and n.4. In *Lexmark*, we said that the label "prudential standing" was misleading, for the requirement at issue is in reality tied to a particular statute. The question is whether the statute grants the plaintiff the cause of action that he asserts. In answering that question, we presume that a statute ordinarily provides a cause of action "only to plaintiffs whose interests fall within the zone of interests protected by the law invoked." We have added that "[w]hether a plaintiff comes within 'the zone of interests' is an issue that requires us to determine, using traditional tools of statutory interpretation, whether a legislatively conferred cause of action encompasses a particular plaintiff's claim."

Here, we conclude that the City's claims of financial injury in their amended complaints — specifically, lost tax revenue and extra municipal expenses — satisfy the "cause of-action" (or "prudential standing") requirement. To use the language of *Data Processing*, the City's claims of injury it suffered as a result of the statutory violations are, at the least, "*arguably* within the zone of interests" that the FHA protects. 397 U.S. at 153 (emphasis added).

The FHA permits any "aggrieved person" to bring a housing-discrimination lawsuit. 42 U.S.C. §3613(a). The statute defines "aggrieved person" as "any person who" either "claims to have been injured by a discriminatory housing practice" or believes that such an injury "is about to occur." §3602(i).

This Court has repeatedly written that the FHA's definition of person "aggrieved" reflects a congressional intent to confer standing broadly. We have said that the definition of "person aggrieved" in the original version of the FHA, §3610(a), "showed 'a congressional intention to define standing as broadly as is permitted by Article III of the Constitution.'" [citing *Trafficante, Gladstone,* and *Havens*]; *see also* Thompson v. North American Stainless, LP, 562 U.S. 170, 176 (2011) ("Later opinions, we must acknowledge, reiterate that the term 'aggrieved' [in the FHA] reaches as far as Article III permits"); Bennett v. Spear, 520 U.S. 154, 165-166 (1997) ("[Trafficante] held that standing was expanded to the full extent permitted under Article III by §3610(a) of the FHA").

Thus, we have held that the Act allows suits by white tenants claiming that they were deprived [of] benefits from interracial associations when discriminatory rental practices kept minorities out of their apartment complex, *Trafficante*; a village alleging that it lost tax revenue and had the racial balance of its community undermined by racial-steering practices, *Gladstone*; and a nonprofit organization that spent money to combat housing discrimination, *Havens Realty*. Contrary to the dissent's view, those cases did more than "sugges[t]" that plaintiffs similarly situated to the City have a cause of action under the FHA. They held as much. And the dissent is wrong to say that we characterized those cases as resting on "ill-considered dictum." The "dictum" we cast doubt on in *Thompson* addressed who may sue under Title VII, the employment discrimination statute, not under the FHA.

Finally, in 1988, when Congress amended the FHA, it retained without significant change the definition of "person aggrieved" that this Court had broadly construed. Indeed, Congress "was aware of" our precedent and "made a considered judgment to retain the relevant statutory text," Texas Dept. of Housing and Community Affairs v. Inclusive Communities Project, Inc., 135 S. Ct. 2507, 2519 (2015). See H.R. Rep. No. 100-711, p. 23 (1988) (stating that the "bill adopts as its definition language similar to that contained in Section 3610 of existing law, as modified to reaffirm the broad holdings of these cases" and discussing *Gladstone* and *Havens Realty*); *cf.* Lorillard v. Pons, 434 U.S. 575, 580 (1978) (Congress normally adopts our interpretations of statutes when it reenacts those statute[s] without change).

The Banks do not deny the broad reach of the words "aggrieved person" as defined in the FHA. But they do contend that those words nonetheless set boundaries that fall short of those the Constitution sets. The Court's language in *Trafficante*, *Gladstone*, and *Havens Realty*, they argue, was exaggerated and unnecessary to decide the cases then before the Court. Moreover, they warn that taking the Court's words literally — providing everyone with constitutional standing a cause of action under the FHA — would produce a legal anomaly. After all, in *Thompson*, we held that the words "person claiming to be aggrieved" in Title VII of the CRA of 1964, did not stretch that statute's zone of interest to the limits of Article III. We reasoned that such an interpretation would produce farfetched results, for example, a shareholder in a company could bring a Title VII suit against the company for discriminatorily firing an employee. The Banks say it would be similarly farfetched if restaurants, plumbers, utility companies, or any other participant in the local economy could sue the Banks to recover business they lost when people had to give up their homes and leave the neighborhood as a result of the Banks' discriminatory lending practices. That, they believe, cannot have been the intent of the Congress that enacted or amended the FHA.

We need not discuss the Banks' argument at length, for even if we assume for argument's sake that some form of it is valid, we nonetheless conclude that the City's financial injuries fall within the zone of interests that the FHA protects. Our case law with respect to the FHA drives that conclusion. The City's complaints allege that the Banks "intentionally targeted predatory practices at African-American and Latino neighborhoods and residents." That unlawful conduct led to a "concentration" of "foreclosures and vacancies" in those neighborhoods. Those concentrated "foreclosures and vacancies" caused "stagnation and decline in African-American and Latino neighborhoods." They hindered the City's efforts to create integrated, stable neighborhoods. And, highly relevant here, they reduced property values, diminishing the City's property-tax revenue and increasing demand for municipal services.

Those claims are similar in kind to the claims the Village of Bellwood raised in *Gladstone*. There, the plaintiff village had alleged that it was "'injured by having [its] housing market . . . wrongfully and illegally manipulated to the economic and social detriment of the citizens of [the] village.'" We held that the village could bring suit. We wrote that the complaint in effect alleged that the defendant-realtors' racial steering "affect[ed] the village's racial composition," "reduce[d] the total number of buyers in the Bellwood housing market," "precipitate[d] an exodus of white residents," and caused "prices [to] be deflected downward." Those circumstances adversely affected the village by, among other things, *producing* a "significant reduction in property values [that] directly injures a municipality by diminishing its tax base, thus threatening its ability to bear the costs of local government and to provide services."

The upshot is that the City alleges economic injuries that arguably fall within the FHA's zone of interests, as we have previously interpreted that statute. Principles of *stare decisis* compel our adherence to those precedents in this context. And principles of statutory interpretation require us to respect Congress' decision to ratify those precedents when it reenacted the relevant statutory text.

III

The remaining question is one of causation: Did the Banks' allegedly discriminatory lending practices proximately cause the City to lose property-tax revenue and spend more on municipal services? The Eleventh Circuit concluded that the answer is "yes" because the City plausibly alleged that its financial injuries were foreseeable results of the Banks' misconduct. We conclude that foreseeability alone is not sufficient to establish proximate cause under the FHA, and therefore vacate the judgment below.

It is a "'well established principle of [the common] law that in all cases of loss, we are to attribute it to the proximate cause, and not to any remote cause.'" *Lexmark*, 134 S. Ct., at 1390. We assume Congress "is familiar with the common-law rule and does not mean to displace it *sub silentio*" in federal causes of action. *Ibid.* A claim for damages under the FHA—which is akin to a "tort action," Meyer v. Holley, 537 U.S. 280, 285 (2003) [Eds.—featured below]—is no exception to this traditional requirement. "Proximate-cause analysis is controlled by the nature of the statutory cause of action. The question it presents is whether the harm alleged has a sufficiently close connection to the conduct the statute prohibits." *Lexmark*, 134 S. Ct. at 1390.

In these cases, the "conduct the statute prohibits" consists of intentionally lending to minority borrowers on worse terms than equally creditworthy non-minority borrowers and inducing defaults by failing to extend refinancing and loan modifications to minority borrowers on fair terms. The City alleges that the Banks' misconduct led to a disproportionate number of foreclosures and vacancies in specific Miami neighborhoods. These foreclosures and vacancies purportedly harmed the City, which lost property-tax revenue when the value of the properties in those neighborhoods fell and was forced to spend more on municipal services in the affected areas.

The Eleventh Circuit concluded that the City adequately pleaded that the Banks' misconduct proximately caused these financial injuries. The court held that in the context of the FHA "the proper standard" for proximate cause "is based on foreseeability." The City, it continued, satisfied that element: Although there are "several links in the causal chain" between the charged discriminatory lending practices and the claimed losses, the City plausibly alleged that "none are unforeseeable."

We conclude that the Eleventh Circuit erred in holding that foreseeability is sufficient to establish proximate cause under the FHA. As we have explained, proximate cause "generally bars suits for alleged harm that is 'too remote' from the defendant's unlawful conduct." *Lexmark*, 134 S. Ct., at 1390. In the context of the FHA, foreseeability alone does not ensure the close connection that proximate cause requires. The housing market is interconnected with economic and social life. A violation of the FHA may, therefore, "be expected to cause ripples of harm to flow" far beyond the defendant's misconduct. Nothing in the statute suggests that Congress intended to provide a remedy wherever those ripples travel. And entertaining suits to recover damages for any foreseeable result of an FHA violation would risk "massive and complex damages litigation."

Rather, proximate cause under the FHA requires "some direct relation between the injury asserted and the injurious conduct alleged." A damages claim under the statute "is analogous to a number of tort actions recognized at common law," and we have repeatedly applied directness principles to statutes with "common-law foundations." "The general tendency" in these cases, "in regard to damages at least, is not to go beyond the first step." What falls within that "first step" depends in part on the "nature of the statutory cause of action," and an assessment "of what is administratively possible and convenient."

The parties have asked us to draw the precise boundaries of proximate cause under the FHA and to determine on which side of the line the City's financial injuries fall. We decline to do so. The Eleventh Circuit grounded its decision on the theory that proximate cause under the FHA is "based on fore-seeability" alone. We therefore lack the benefit of its judgment on how the contrary principles we have just stated apply to the FHA. Nor has any other court of appeals weighed in on the issue. The lower courts should define, in the first instance, the contours of proximate cause under the FHA and decide how that standard applies to the City's claims for lost property-tax revenue and increased municipal expenses.

Justice THOMAS, with whom Justice Kennedy and Justice Alito join, concurring in part and dissenting in part.

Miami's complaints do not allege that any defendant discriminated against it within the meaning of the FHA. Neither is Miami attempting to bring a lawsuit on behalf of its residents against whom petitioners allegedly discriminated. Rather, Miami's theory is that, between 2004 and 2012, petitioners' allegedly discriminatory mortgage-lending practices led to defaulted loans, which led to foreclosures, which led to vacant houses, which led to decreased property values, which led to reduced property taxes and urban blight. Miami seeks damages from the lenders for reduced property tax revenues and for the cost of increased municipal services — "police, firefighters, building inspectors, debris collectors, and others" — deployed to attend to the blighted areas.

For the reasons explained below, I would hold that Miami's injuries fall outside the FHA's zone of interests. I would also hold that, in any event, Miami's alleged injuries are too remote to satisfy the FHA's proximate-cause requirement.

. . . Miami's asserted injuries are not arguably related to the interests the statute protects. . . . [N]othing in the text of the FHA suggests that Congress was concerned about decreased property values, foreclosures, and urban blight, much less about strains on municipal budgets that might follow.

Miami's interests are markedly distinct from the interests this Court confronted in *Trafficante*, *Gladstone*, and *Havens*. . . . In all three of these cases, the plaintiffs claimed injuries based on racial steering and segregation — interests that, under this Court's precedents, at least arguably fall within the zone of interests that the FHA protects.

Miami's asserted injuries implicate none of those interests. Rather, Miami asserts injuries allegedly resulting from foreclosed-upon and then vacant homes. The FHA's zone of interests is not so expansive as to include those kinds of injuries.

The Court today reaches the opposite conclusion, resting entirely on the brief mention in *Gladstone* of the village's asserted injury of reduced tax revenues, and on principles of *stare decisis*. I do not think *Gladstone* compels the conclusion the majority reaches. Unlike these cases, *Gladstone* involved injuries to interests in "racial balance and stability," which, our cases have suggested, arguably fall within the zone of interests protected by the FHA. The fact that the village plaintiff asserted a budget-related injury *in addition to* its racial-steering injury does not mean that a city alleging *only* a budget-related injury is authorized to sue. A budget-related injury might be necessary to establish a sufficiently concrete and particularized injury for purposes of Article III, but it is not sufficient to satisfy the FHA's zone-of-interests limitation.

Although the Court's reliance on Gladstone is misplaced, its opinion today is notable primarily for what it does not say. [T]he Court conspicuously does not reaffirm the broad language from *Trafficante*, *Gladstone*, and *Havens* suggesting that Congress intended to permit any person with Article III standing to sue under the FHA. The Court of Appeals felt bound by that language, and we granted review, despite the absence of a circuit conflict, to decide whether the language survived *Thompson* and *Lexmark*. Today's opinion avoids those questions presented and thus cannot be read as retreating from our more recent precedents on the zone-of-interests limitation.

NOTES AND QUESTIONS

1. Predatory Lending: The Ripple Effects. Plaintiff's theory of standing (and damages) rested on the following allegations. The banks "intentionally issued riskier mortgages on unfavorable terms" to customers of color compared to similarly situated white, non-Latino customers. The targeting of borrowers of color for predatory home mortgage loans "and inducing defaults by failing to extend refinancing and loan modifications to minority borrowers on fair terms," caused vacancies and foreclosures to be concentrated in Black and Latino neighborhoods, creating a cascading set of injuries to the City. The Court described the alleged injuries:

> Higher foreclosure rates lowered property values and diminished property-tax revenue. Higher foreclosure rates — especially when accompanied by vacancies — also increased demand for municipal services, such as police, fire, and building and code enforcement services, all needed "to remedy blight and unsafe and dangerous conditions" that the foreclosures and vacancies generate.

Like steering claims, predatory lending claims, discussed in more depth in Chapter 11, illustrate the potential for housing discrimination to cause widespread harm. Yet, not all of this can be addressed by the FHA. "The housing market is interconnected with economic and social life. A violation of the FHA may, therefore, 'be expected to cause ripples of harm to flow' far beyond the defendant's misconduct. . . . Nothing in the statute suggests that Congress intended to provide a remedy wherever those ripples travel." *City of Miami*, 581 U.S. at 202. How do courts determine which "ripples" are actionable and which are not? Do you think *City of Miami* answered this question? Is the answer consistent with the Court's prior standing precedents? What do you think the answer should be?

2. Zone of Interests. Notably, the Court in *City of Miami* spent considerably less time discussing the Article III injury-in-fact element than it did in its prior trilogy on FHA standing (*Trafficante, Gladstone,* and *Havens*). We do not see the same unequivocal pronouncement that Congress intended "distinct and palpable injury" under Article III to present "the sole requirement" for FHA standing.

Why would the Court dedicate so little ink to analyzing Article III? It seemed difficult for the banks to argue that the city lacked an injury in fact because Miami's claimed injuries were, as the Court observed, "similar in kind" to those found to satisfy Article III in *Gladstone;* both entities alleged economic injury in the form of a diminished tax base and increased demand for municipal services. Instead, the banks argued for a more stringent interpretation of "aggrieved person" under the FHA than the one endorsed by the trilogy. They likely were emboldened by the Court's 2011 Title VII precedent rejecting the view (originally expressed in *Trafficante*) that Title VII provided a cause of action to anyone claiming an Article III injury in fact.[31] Extending this precedent to the FHA, the banks argued that a "literal" reading of the Court's trilogy would lead to far-fetched results,[32] granting standing to every business owner who, like the city, could show financial injury resulting from the banks' lending discrimination and ensuing foreclosures and property vacancies. Remember that Congress in the FHA defined "aggrieved person" as *any* person who claims injury from a discriminatory housing practice, 42 U.S.C. §3602(i), in contrast to Title VII, which specifically delineates categories of permissible plaintiffs.

So if not a "literal reading," then what? Earlier, in *Gladstone,* the Court acknowledged that so-called "prudential" barriers, were they to apply, might limit plaintiffs from claiming injury from violations of rights held by third parties (in the instant case, victims of predatory loans). But *Gladstone* held prudential barriers did *not* apply: "courts . . . lack the authority to create prudential barriers to standing in suits brought under the [Act]." The *City of Miami* Court updated that labeling in light of intervening precedent in *Lexmark,*[33] framing the issue in terms of "whether the statute grants the plaintiff the

---

31. In a decision interpreting the scope of standing under Title VII, Thompson v. North Am. Stainless, L.P., 562 U.S. 170, 176-77 (2011), the Court described as "ill-considered" certain "dictum [in *Trafficante*] that the Title VII aggrievement requirement conferred a right to sue on all who satisfied Article III standing." The *Thompson* Court declined to follow the *Trafficante* pronouncement ("dictum") on Title VII because *Trafficante's* holding was limited to Title VIII and "it is Title VII rather than Title VIII that is before us here." Note that the *City of Miami* Court rejected the dissent's suggestion that *Thompson's* Title VII holding cast doubt on who may sue under Title VIII; even *Thompson* acknowledged that in cases subsequent to *Trafficante,* the Court reiterated its holding that standing under the FHA extends to the limits of Article III.

32. *Thompson* imposed a zone of interests requirement under Title VII (which unlike the FHA specifies categories of proper plaintiffs and defendants) and suggested "absurd consequences" would follow without it, which the banks posited in the Title VIII predatory lending context of *City of Miami. Thompson,* 562 U.S. at 177; *City of Miami,* 581 U.S. at 199.

33. *See* Lexmark Int'l, Inc. v. Static Control Components, Inc., 572 U.S. 118, 125, 129 (2014) (describing the label "prudential standing" as "misleading" and holding that the common-law zone of interests limitation applied "to all statutorily created causes of action . . . unless it is expressly negated").

cause of action he asserts" such that the plaintiff's interests "fall within the zone of interests protected by the law invoked."[34] This "zone of interests" inquiry requires the Court to use "traditional tools of statutory interpretation" to determine "whether a legislatively conferred cause of action encompasses a particular plaintiff's claim." In other words, did Congress grant cities a right to sue to recover economic damages flowing from discriminatory lending activity against others?

In answering this question, we must ask another: Do all aspects of the trilogy survive *City of Miami*? Even though the Court in *City of Miami* stopped short of reaffirming that Article III was the sole limit on who can sue under the FHA, it did lean heavily on its trilogy to answer the zone of interests argument, holding that the FHA granted the City a cause of action to seek recovery for financial injuries. The Court cited the trilogy to confirm that the Court had "repeatedly written" of a congressional intent to confer standing broadly, and with respect to an earlier version of the statute "an intention to define standing as broadly as is permitted by Article III." It cited the trilogy to demonstrate that its holdings allowed suits under the FHA in contexts involving similarly situated plaintiffs. It beat back the dissent's argument that its prior holdings were mere suggestions on what kind of injuries fell within the FHA's zone of interests. It stated that Congress was aware of the Court's trilogy when it amended the FHA's aggrieved person definition in 1988, "making a considered judgment to retain the relevant statutory text." And in holding that the City had a right to sue, it emphasized that "caselaw with respect to the FHA ["the trilogy"] drives that conclusion." The *City of Miami* Court's final homage to the trilogy ended as follows (emphasis added):

> The upshot is that the City alleges economic injuries that arguably fall within the FHA's zone of interests, *as we have previously interpreted* that statute. Principles of *stare decisis* compel our adherence to *those precedents* in this context. And principles of statutory interpretation require us to respect Congress' decision to ratify *those precedents* when it reenacted the relevant statutory text.

The Court's emphasis on establishing a right to sue under the FHA made clear that plaintiffs now must satisfy the zone of interests requirement in addition to Article III. As stated in the opening pages of this chapter, the Court in *Lexmark* held that the zone of interests limit "always applies." Do you anticipate this will be an onerous requirement?

> As in *Miami*, determining who is within the statute's "zone of interests" may be informed by the Court's prior standing decisions (i.e., the types of plaintiffs and injuries recognized in *Trafficante*, *Gladstone*, and *Havens* will continue to satisfy this "zone" test). . . . [T]he result is that—as both the Court and the dissent in *Miami* recognized—having statutory standing is essentially the same as having a cause of action on the merits under the FHA.

---

34. What do you make of the fact that the *Gladstone* Court, in a footnote, pointed to the "zone of interests" requirement as an example of "other nonconstitutional limitations on standing to be applied in appropriate circumstances"? 441 U.S. at 100 n.6.

Schwemm, HDLL §12A:2 (text accompanying notes 30 and 32). The dissent described the interests asserted in the trilogy as related to racial steering and segregation and as "at least arguably fall[ing] within the zone of interests that the FHA protects." It distinguished Miami's "budget-related injury" resulting from the foreclosure crisis as divorced from the "racial balance and stability" interests implicated in *Gladstone* and protected under the FHA. Do you think that Miami could have asserted injuries related to the racial manipulation of its housing market?

3. Proximate Cause. The FHA standing trilogy discussed the Article III injury-in-fact requirement at considerable length, but what did the cases say about proximate cause? You will not find any mention of it. This is because "[p]roximate cause is not a requirement of Article III standing," it is a pleading requirement. *Lexmark*, 527 U.S. at 134 n.6. As you will recall from Torts, proximate causation is an element of the cause of action, derived from common law, that limits allegations of injury to those directly caused by the defendant. And "like any other element of a cause of action, it must be adequately alleged at the pleading stage in order for the case to proceed." *Id.* The Court assumed this background common-law rule of proximate cause is incorporated into federal statutes unless Congress says otherwise. The Court will look at the nature of the statutory cause of action to determine "whether the harm alleged has a sufficiently close connection to the conduct the statute prohibits." In *City of Miami*, the Court held that the City did allege sufficient injury to fall within the zone of interests the FHA arguably protects, but that the lower court applied the wrong test on proximate cause: "To establish proximate cause under the FHA, a plaintiff must do more than show that its injuries foreseeably flowed from the alleged statutory violation." What proximate-cause test must litigants satisfy? The Court declined "to draw the precise boundaries of proximate cause" under the FHA, leaving the "contours" to the lower courts to define, "in the first instance."

The Court did provide a guidepost. It described an FHA damages claim as "akin to a tort action," citing Meyer v. Holley, 537 U.S. 280, 285 (2003), requiring a proximate-cause analysis: "proximate cause under the FHA requires 'some direct relation between the injury asserted and the injurious conduct alleged.'" These directness principles "generally bar suits for alleged harm that is 'too remote' . . . [or goes] beyond the first step" in the chain of causation.

Do you think the City of Miami's claims for lost property-tax revenue and increased municipal expenses have a sufficiently direct relationship with the lending discrimination claims? The Eleventh Circuit on remand held that the City's tax-revenue losses satisfied the Court's directness principles; but while a petition for certiorari was pending, the City voluntarily dismissed its lawsuits. The Court subsequently granted the petition and vacated the Eleventh Circuit's opinion as moot.[35]

---

35. 140 S. Ct. 1259 (2020); *see also* City of Oakland v. Wells Fargo & Company, 14 F.4th 1030, 1035 (2021) (describing procedural history). For an argument that Congress understood

4. Proximate Cause Aftermath. Courts in other circuits have applied the *City of Miami* "direct relation" principles for determining proximate cause in cases with similar fact patterns and have refused to hold that the FHA supports proximate cause beyond the first step. (Although the Court advised that "[w]hat falls within that 'first step' depends in part on the 'nature of the statutory cause of action.'") In City of Oakland v. Wells Fargo & Co., 14 F.4th 1030, 1032, 1036, 1039-42 (9th Cir. 2021), the Ninth Circuit, sitting en banc, considered the city's claims of lost property tax revenue and increased municipal expenditures and held that "these downstream 'ripples of harm' are too attenuated and travel too 'far beyond' Wells Fargo's alleged misconduct to establish proximate cause." The court also considered under *City of Miami* what was "administratively possible and convenient," finding too many independent factors at play in the city's chain of causation. It also noted the existence of "more direct plaintiffs" who could vindicate the FHA claims. What type of plaintiff do you think would be more direct? Do you think a municipality could ever be a "direct" plaintiff?

In County of Cook v. Bank of America Corp., No. 14 C 2280, 2018 WL 1561725, at *6-*7 (N.D. Ill. March 30, 2018), the court similarly rejected claimed tax losses and downstream social service expenses as too remote and insufficiently direct, but did hold that the out-of-pocket costs incurred by the sheriff and county court in processing the alleged discriminatory foreclosures satisfied the first-step directness requirement. Ultimately, the court granted summary judgment, holding that the county's evidence was insufficient to prove these damages.[36]

In City of Philadelphia v. Wells Fargo & Co., No. CV 17-2203, 2018 WL 424451, at *5-*6 (E.D. Pa. January 16, 2018), the court focused its proximate cause analysis on *noneconomic* harms: "The City has plausibly pled that discriminatory lending causes a higher rate of foreclosures against minority borrowers, which harms the City by reducing diversity in homeownership and by hindering fair housing and the furtherance of stable, integrated communities." *But see* County of Cook, Ill. v. Wells Fargo & Co., 314 F. Supp. 3d 975, 990 (N.D. Ill. 2018) (holding that insufficient proximate cause existed between Wells Fargo's alleged equity stripping practices and the alleged loss of racial balance and stability).

---

discrimination in the housing market to cause residential segregation *and* urban decay and passed the FHA to address the social and economic "ripples" related to these harms, see Nicole Summers, Setting the Standard for Proximate Cause in the Wake of Bank of America Corp. v. City of Miami, 97 *N.C. L. Rev.* 529, 599-600 (2019).

36. 584 F. Supp. 3d 562, 586 (N.D. Ill. 2022), *aff'd*, 78 F.4th 970 (7th Cir. 2023); *see also* County of Cook, Ill. v. Wells Fargo & Co., 314 F. Supp. 3d 975, 985 (N.D. Ill. 2018) ("The financial harms arising from the County's administering and managing mortgage foreclosures flow inexorably from Wells Fargo's alleged conduct, and thus are sufficiently "direct" for purposes of the proximate cause inquiry.").

5. FHA Violations as Torts? Similar to the expanded showing required on whether the plaintiff's claim comes within the FHA's zone of interests, plaintiffs must be prepared to plead and prove the injuries they claim to flow *directly* from defendants' FHA violations to satisfy the Court's proximate cause requirement. In this sense, the hurdles for FHA plaintiffs have shifted from showing injury under Article III, which the Court has interpreted to encompass a wide range of plaintiffs and harms, to the common-law limits on civil liability, which the Court has only recently begun to apply to FHA cases. Commentators have described this as a "substantial change . . . which hews to antiquated 'direct causation' approaches to proximate cause [in the *federal* common law developed in antitrust and racketeering cases] long rejected by states and scholars . . ." Daniel Yablon, *Proximate Cause in Statutory Standing and the Genesis of Federal Common* Law, 107 CAL. L. REV. 1609, 1634 (2019). For a critique of the Court's treatment of statutory regimes as the functional equivalent of tort actions, see Professor Sandra F. Sperino, *Statutory Proximate Cause*, 88 NOTRE DAME L. REV. 1199, 1200 (2013), making the following observation:

> While statutes are often torts in the broad sense that they are civil actions that do not arise from a contract, this definition is not helpful to understanding whether proximate cause should be applied to a particular statute, [such as one in which Congress has already incorporated complex systems limiting liability]. . . . Proximate cause is a notoriously flexible and theoretically inconsistent concept, [and] the term is often an empty vessel, into which the courts can pour multiple meanings.

6. Back to Steering. In City of Chicago v. Matchmaker Real Estate Sales Center, Inc., 982 F.2d 1086, 1095 (7th Cir. 1992), the Seventh Circuit held that the City of Chicago (along with an FHO and testers), had standing in a steering case, relying on *Gladstone*: "Noting the importance to a community of promoting stable, integrated housing, the Court indicated that if a party's sales practices begin to rob a city or town 'of its racial balance and stability, the [city or town] has standing to challenge the legality of that conduct.'" This theory of harm likely requires a pattern of conduct; a single instance of steering usually would not be sufficient to cause neighborhood segregation and certainly would fall short of causing segregation citywide. Whether a pattern of steering causes measurable injuries to a municipality will depend on the number of instances and the size and population of the affected area. *See, e.g., Havens Realty Corp. v. Coleman* (1982) (questioning whether the effects of steering in one particular neighborhood can be felt throughout a large metropolitan area). Ultimately, this will be a case-by-case and fact-dependent determination. After *City of Miami*, what factual showing and proof must a city offer to satisfy both the zone of interests and proximate cause requirements under the FHA?

7. Standing Under Section 1982. Standing under the 1866 Civil Rights Act (discussed in Chapter 2) is more limited than is standing under Title VIII. Consider Warth v. Seldin, 422 U.S. 490, 512-14 (1975), decided after *Trafficante* but before *Gladstone*, in which the Court rejected a *Trafficante*-style claim brought by a membership organization under the Civil Rights Act of 1866 (including section 1982) and the Constitution. The claim challenged exclusionary zoning practices rather than steering, but the Court held the "critical distinction" was that Congress created statutory rights under the FHA that are absent from the Civil Rights Act of 1866, namely, that the FHA's broad definition of "aggrieved persons" granted an "actionable right to be free from the adverse consequences to them of racially discriminatory practices directed at and immediately harmful to others." Without any FHA claim, the Court further found that the plaintiffs were inappropriately raising the rights of third parties, traditionally understood to be barred by "prudential standing" limitations. Could the organization simply have brought an identical claim under Title VIII and invoked *Trafficante* to establish an injury in fact?

8. Standing in State Court. Plaintiffs usually have the option of filing under comparable state fair housing and consumer protection laws in state court. State court standing doctrines will vary across the 50 states, but they might provide for broader standing than Article III depending on the facts and claims.[37]

B. COVERED DEFENDANTS: WHO MAY BE LIABLE?

Does the FHA specify categories of persons who may be liable under the Act? No. The same passive language that permits an open-ended array of potential plaintiffs to enforce the FHA's provisions (within the boundaries of Article III) also authorizes claims against an undefined group of potential defendants. Consider the prefatory text of §3604: "[E]xcept as exempted by [42 U.S.C. §3603(b) and §3607], *it shall be unlawful*" to engage in any of the forms of housing discrimination prohibited under §3604.[38] "Thus, anyone who commits one of the acts proscribed by the statute's substantive provisions is liable. . . ." Schwemm, HDLL §12B:1 (citing NAACP v. American Family Mutual Insurance Co., 978 F.2d 287, 298 (7th Cir. 1992) ("Congress wrote §3604 of the FHA in the passive voice—banning an outcome while not saying who the actor is, or how such actors bring about the forbidden consequence")).

At the same time, claims under §§3604(a), (b), and (c) generally only can be made against housing providers or housing professionals, because

---

37. *See* National Consumer Law Center, Consumer Class Actions, Appendix D: State-by-State Analysis of State Court Standing Requirements (11th ed. 2024), updated at www.nclc.org/library.

38. (Emphasis added.) 42 U.S.C. §3605 uses the same passive "it shall be unlawful" language and then proceeds to proscribe discrimination by "any person or other entity whose business includes engaging in residential real estate-related transactions." "Person" is defined in §3602(d) as "one or more individuals, corporations, partnerships, associations, labor organizations, legal representatives, mutual companies, joint-stock companies, trusts, unincorporated organizations, trustees, [bankruptcy] trustees, receivers, and fiduciaries."

those are the only parties who can discriminate with respect to "the sale or rental of housing." Section 3617 contains no such limiting language, and thus claims under this section can be brought against neighbors, community members, and others who do not have direct control over the plaintiff's housing, but nonetheless are capable of interfering with it.

Both individuals and entities may be potential defendants. As HUD has explained in guidance:

> Courts have applied the FHA to individuals, corporations, partnerships, associations, property owners, housing managers, homeowners and condominium associations, cooperatives, lenders, insurers, real estate agents, brokerage services, state and local governments, colleges and universities, as well as others involved in the provision of housing, residential lending, and other real estate-related services.[39]

The issue of whether a plaintiff has challenged a proper defendant under the FHA is not litigated very often. When it is, the parties typically disagree over whether an owner or employer who was not directly involved is responsible for the acts of another person allegedly acting under their control. This might arise in a rental management context where a property management company becomes legally responsible for the actions of rental agents or maintenance personnel; it might also arise where a mortgage lender is liable for the actions of its loan officers or brokers, or a property owner is liable for the statements of a real estate agent. In fair housing cases, federal courts ordinarily have applied traditional agency principles to hold principals liable for the acts of their agents operating within the scope of the agents' authority.[40] This doctrine of respondeat superior applies even when a property owner instructs an employee or agent *not* to discriminate. "A principal cannot free itself of liability by delegating to an agent the duty not to discriminate." City of Chicago v. Matchmaker Real Estate Sales Center, Inc., 982 F.2d 1086, 1096 (7th Cir. 1992). Why would a property owner's instruction to its agents to comply with fair housing law not operate as a shield against liability? The concept of vicarious liability means that principals need not authorize or know about the unlawful conduct, as long as the agent or employee is acting within the scope of their authority. *See* Meyer v. Holley, 537 U.S. 280, 285-86 (2003) (below); Schwemm, HDLL §12B:2 at n.24.

Of course, not all owners and principals are in the dark about how their businesses are being managed. Indeed, according to census data, of the

---

39. HUD Notice FHEO-2020-1: Assessing a Request to Have an Animal as a Reasonable Accommodation, at 3 n.3 (also broadly describing its reference to "housing provider" as "any person or entity engaging in conduct covered by the FHA").

40. An exception to this vicarious liability principle applies in the recovery of punitive damages, where some showing of intentional or reckless conduct on the part of the principal is required. *See* Kolstad v. American Dental Ass'n, 527 U.S. 526, 544 (1999) (it is "improper ordinarily to award punitive damages against one who is personally innocent and therefore liable only vicariously.") (quoting Restatement (Second) of Torts, §909, at 468, Comment b).

approximately 19.3 million rental properties in the United States, 13.3 million (nearly 70 percent) are managed directly by the owner or by the owner's unpaid agent (who is likely to be a family member or close friend).[41] An owner personally engaged in unlawful discriminatory acts will be directly, not vicariously, liable; direct liability will attach whether an owner acted alone, directed employees to discriminate, or approved of employees' discrimination. This is the straightforward case. But direct liability may extend to less obvious situations where an owner knows *or should have known* of discriminatory conduct of an agent/employee and fails to take prompt action to correct it. In the absence of applicable statutory text, HUD in 2016[42] opined on how direct and vicarious liability principles apply under the FHA.

§100.7 LIABILITY FOR DISCRIMINATORY HOUSING PRACTICES.

(a) *Direct liability.*

    (1) A person is directly liable for:

        (i) The person's own conduct that results in a discriminatory housing practice.

        (ii) Failing to take prompt action to correct and end a discriminatory housing practice by that person's employee or agent, where the person knew or should have known of the discriminatory conduct.

        (iii) Failing to take prompt action to correct and end a discriminatory housing practice by a third-party, where the person knew or should have known of the discriminatory conduct and had the power to correct it. The power to take prompt action to correct and end a discriminatory housing practice by a third-party depends upon the extent of the person's control or any other legal responsibility the person may have with respect to the conduct of such third-party.

(b) *Vicarious liability.* A person is vicariously liable for a discriminatory housing practice by the person's agent or employee, regardless of whether the person knew or should have known of the conduct that resulted in a discriminatory housing practice, consistent with agency law.[43]

Beyond the straightforward case, HUD's rule makes several distinctions between direct and vicarious liability that are worth noting. First, vicarious liability applies to situations where the principal has no reason to know of the

---

41. *See* https://www.census.gov/data-tools/demo/rhfs/#/?s_tableName=TABLE2&s_byGroup1=3 (2021). The picture looks somewhat different when the data are broken down by individual unit rather than property, but the numbers are still striking: Of the 49.5 million rental units in the United States, 19 million units (38 percent) are managed by the owner or the owner's unpaid agent. *Id.*

42. Liability for Discriminatory Housing Practices Under the Fair Housing Act, 81 Fed. Reg. 63054, 63074 (Sept. 14, 2016) (codified at 24 C.F.R. §100.7).

43. 24 C.F.R. §100.7 (2024).

agent's discriminatory conduct, whereas direct liability under (a)(1)(ii) covers situations where the principal's duty to correct is triggered because they are presumed to know of the agent's unlawful conduct despite claims of ignorance. Consider *Richards v. Bono*,[44] a sexual harassment case filed against both the perpetrator and his spouse (who co-owned the property). After refusing to dismiss the claim against Mrs. Bono based on an agency theory, the court considered the theory of direct liability:

> [T]he complaint contains allegations that Mrs. Bono may be liable directly. According to the complaint, Mrs. Bono knew or should have known of Mr. Bono's conduct towards the Plaintiff and other female tenants but failed to take any action to stop it. The complaint also alleges that both Defendants raised the Plaintiff's rent in retaliation for the Plaintiff having involved the police.

Thus, even in the context of a wife's liability for her husband's alleged sexual harassment of their tenants, the court was willing to impose direct liability under a "knew or should have known" standard.

Second, HUD extends this principle of direct liability in (a)(1)(iii) beyond agents to third parties, where the defendant can be presumed to know about a third party's discriminatory conduct and the defendant's degree of control or legal responsibility gives them the power to correct the conduct. Chapter 8 explores this latter, more challenging, theory of direct liability under §3604(b) in the context of neighbor-on-neighbor harassment.

Questions of vicarious liability may become more complicated when entities such as corporations, limited partnerships, professional management companies, and real estate brokerage firms are involved. An entity may own, manage, or assist in the sale of residential property; yet, entities are composed of individuals with various fiduciary obligations and ownership interests in the entity. How do agency principles deal with the question of who among these individuals may be held personally liable for the unlawful discrimination of an entity employee? The following case establishes the limits of a corporate officer's vicarious liability under the FHA.

Meyer v. Holley
537 U.S. 280 (2003)

Before Chief Justice Rehnquist and Justices Stevens, O'Connor, Scalia, Kennedy, Souter, Thomas, Ginsburg, and Breyer.

---

44. No. 5:04CV484-OC-10GRJ, 2005 WL 1065141, at *7 (M.D. Fla. May 2, 2005).

Justice BREYER delivered the opinion of the Court.[45]

The Fair Housing Act forbids racial discrimination in respect to the sale or rental of a dwelling. 42 U.S.C. §§3604(b), 3605(a). The question before us is whether the Act imposes personal liability without fault upon an officer or owner of a residential real estate corporation for the unlawful activity of the *corporation's* employee or agent. We conclude that the Act imposes liability without fault upon the employer in accordance with traditional agency principles, i.e., it normally imposes vicarious liability upon the corporation but not upon its officers or owners.

I

For purposes of this decision we simplify the background facts as follows: Respondents Emma Mary Ellen Holley and David Holley, an interracial couple, tried to buy a house in Twenty-Nine Palms, California. A real estate corporation, Triad, Inc., had listed the house for sale. Grove Crank, a Triad salesman, is alleged to have prevented the Holleys from obtaining the house—and for racially discriminatory reasons.[46]

The Holleys brought a lawsuit in federal court against Crank and Triad. They claimed, among other things, that both were responsible for a fair housing law violation. The Holleys later filed a separate suit against David Meyer, the petitioner here. Meyer, they said, was Triad's president, Triad's sole shareholder, and Triad's licensed "officer/broker." They claimed that Meyer was vicariously liable in one or more of these capacities for Crank's unlawful actions.

The District Court consolidated the two lawsuits. It dismissed all claims other than the FHA claim on statute of limitations grounds. It dismissed the claims

---

45. [EDS.—Robert G. Schwemm argued the case on behalf of the Plaintiffs-Respondents in the Supreme Court. The law firm of Brancart and Brancart litigated the Plaintiffs' case below; it litigates many fair housing cases. All italicized words in the opinion are italicized in the original.]

46. [EDS.—The Holleys alleged that they met with Triad agent Grove Crank and inquired about listings for new houses in the Twenty-Nine Palms area of California, in the range of $100,000 to $150,000. Crank showed them four houses in the area, all above $150,000. The Holleys located a home on their own that happened to be listed by Triad. In response to the Holleys' inquiry about the home, Triad agent Terry Stump informed them that the asking price for the house was $145,000. The Holleys offered to pay the asking price and to put $5,000 in escrow for the builder to hold the house for six months until they closed on their existing home. Stump told the Holleys that their offer seemed fair, as did the builder, Brooks Bauer, when Mrs. Holley called him with the same offer. Bauer did say, however, that the offer would have to go through Triad. Later, Stump called Mrs. Holley to tell her that more experienced agents in the office, one of whom was later identified as Grove Crank, felt that $5,000 would be insufficient to get the builder to hold the house for six months. The Holleys decided not to raise their offer and Triad never presented the original offer to Bauer. One week later, Bauer inquired at Triad about the status of the Holleys' offer. Crank then allegedly used racial invectives in referring to the Holleys, telling Bauer that he did not want to deal with those "n's" and called them a "salt and pepper team." The Holleys eventually hired a builder to construct a house for them and Bauer later sold his house for approximately $20,000 less than the Holleys had offered. Holley v. Crank, 258 F.3d 1127 (9th Cir. 2001).]

against Meyer in his capacity as officer of Triad because (1) it considered those claims as assertions of vicarious liability, and (2) it believed that the FHA did not impose personal vicarious liability upon a corporate *officer*. The District Court stated that "any liability against Meyer as an officer of Triad would only attach to Triad," the corporation. The court added that the Holleys had "not urged theories that could justify reaching Meyer individually." It later went on to dismiss for similar reasons claims of vicarious liability against Meyer in his capacity as the "designated officer/broker" in respect to Triad's real estate license.

The District Court certified its judgment as final to permit the Holleys to appeal its vicarious liability determinations. The Ninth Circuit reversed those determinations.

Meyer sought certiorari. We granted his petition, to review the Ninth Circuit's holding that the FHA imposes principles of strict liability beyond those traditionally associated with agent/principal or employee/employer relationships. We agreed to decide whether "the criteria under the FHA . . . are different, so that owners and officers of corporations" are automatically and "absolutely liable for an employee's or agent's violation of the Act [based on their authority to direct or control]"—even if they did not direct or authorize, and were otherwise not involved in, the unlawful discriminatory acts.

II

The FHA itself focuses on prohibited acts. In relevant part the Act forbids "any person or other entity whose business includes engaging in residential real estate-related transactions to discriminate," for example, because of "race." 42 U.S.C. §3605(a). It adds that "[p]erson" includes, for example, individuals, corporations, partnerships, associations, labor unions, and other organizations. §3602(d). It says nothing about vicarious liability.

Nonetheless, it is well established that the Act provides for vicarious liability. This Court has noted that an action brought for compensation by a victim of housing discrimination is, in effect, a tort action. And the Court has assumed that, when Congress creates a tort action, it legislates against a legal background of ordinary tort-related vicarious liability rules and consequently intends its legislation to incorporate those rules.

It is well established that traditional vicarious liability rules ordinarily make principals or employers vicariously liable for acts of their agents or employees in the scope of their authority or employment. And in the absence of special circumstances it is the corporation, not its owner or officer, who is the principal or employer, and thus subject to vicarious liability for torts committed by its employees or agents. The Restatement §1 specifies that the relevant principal/agency relationship demands not only control (or the right to direct or control) but also "the manifestation of consent by one person to another that the other shall act *on his behalf* and consent by the other so to act." A corporate employee typically acts on behalf of the corporation, not its owner or officer.

The Ninth Circuit held that the FHA imposed more extensive vicarious liability—that the Act went well beyond traditional principles. The Court of Appeals held that the Act made corporate owners and officers liable for the unlawful acts of a corporate employee simply on the basis that the owner or officer controlled (or had the right to control) the actions of that employee. We do not agree with the Ninth Circuit that the Act extended traditional vicarious liability rules in this way.

For one thing, Congress said nothing in the statute or in the legislative history about extending vicarious liability in this manner. And Congress' silence, while permitting an inference that Congress intended to apply *ordinary* background tort principles, cannot show that it intended to apply an unusual modification of those rules. Where Congress, in other civil rights statutes, has not expressed a contrary intent, the Court has drawn the inference that it intended ordinary rules to apply.

For another thing, the Department of Housing and Urban Development (HUD), the federal agency primarily charged with the implementation and administration of the statute, 42 U.S.C. §3608, has specified that ordinary vicarious liability rules apply in this area. And we ordinarily defer to an administering agency's reasonable interpretation of a statute. Chevron U.S.A. Inc. v. Natural Resources Defense Council, Inc. (1984); Skidmore v. Swift & Co. (1944).[47]

Finally, we have found no convincing argument in support of the Ninth Circuit's decision to apply nontraditional vicarious liability principles—a decision that respondents do not defend and in fact concede is incorrect. The Ninth Circuit referred to several cases decided in other Circuits. The actual holdings in those cases, however, do not support the kind of nontraditional vicarious liability that the Ninth Circuit applied. Nor does the language of these cases provide a convincing rationale for the Ninth Circuit's conclusions. The Ninth Circuit further referred to an owner's or officer's "non delegable duty" not to discriminate in light of the Act's "overriding societal priority." And it added that "[w]hen one of two innocent people must suffer, the one whose acts permitted the wrong to occur is the one to bear the burden."

"[A] nondelegable duty is an affirmative obligation to ensure the protection of the person to whom the duty runs." The Ninth Circuit identifies nothing in the language or legislative history of the Act to support the existence of this special kind of liability. In the absence of legal support, we cannot conclude that Congress intended, through silence, to impose this kind of special duty of protection upon individual officers or owners of corporations—who are not

---

47. [EDS.—*Chevron* is overruled. *See* Chapter 3. Note that in *Meyer*, however, the Court did not rely principally on *Chevron* deference. Regardless, the Court's prior holdings relying on the *Chevron* framework "are still subject to statutory *stare decisis.* . . ." *See* Loper Bright Enters v. Raimondo, 603 U.S. __ (2024).]

principals (or contracting parties) in respect to the corporation's unlawfully acting employee.

Neither does it help to characterize the statute's objective as an "overriding societal priority." We agree with the characterization. But we do not agree that the characterization carries with it a legal rule that would hold every corporate supervisor personally liable without fault for the unlawful act of every corporate employee whom he or she has the right to supervise. Rather, which "of two innocent people must suffer," and just when, is a complex matter. We believe that courts ordinarily should determine that matter in accordance with traditional principles of vicarious liability—unless, of course, Congress, better able than courts to weigh the relevant policy considerations, has instructed the courts differently. We have found no different instruction here.

III

Respondents, conceding that traditional vicarious liability rules apply, argue that those principles themselves warrant liability here. California law itself creates what amounts, under ordinary common-law principles, to an employer/employee or principal/agent relationship between (a) a corporate officer designated as the broker under a real estate license issued to the corporation, and (b) a corporate employee/salesperson.

The Ninth Circuit did not decide whether . . . the California broker relationship, when added to the "right to control," would, under traditional legal principles and consistent with "the general common law of agency," establish the necessary [principal/agent] relationship. But in the absence of consideration of that matter by the Court of Appeals, we shall not consider it.

Respondents also point out that, when traditional vicarious liability principles impose liability upon a corporation, the corporation's liability may be imputed to the corporation's owner in an appropriate case through a "'piercing of the corporate veil.'" The Court of Appeals, however, did not decide the application of "veil piercing" in this matter either. It falls outside the scope of the question presented on certiorari. And we shall not here consider it.

The Ninth Circuit nonetheless remains free on remand to determine whether these questions were properly raised and, if so, to consider them. The judgment of the Court of Appeals is vacated, and the case is remanded for further proceedings consistent with this opinion.

NOTES AND QUESTIONS

1. **Background Tort-Related Rules on Vicarious Liability.** Does the FHA explicitly address the question presented to the Court? The FHA is silent on vicarious liability but, as in other contexts, the Supreme Court in *Meyer* presumed that Congress legislates against a legal background of default rules, in this case, ordinary tort-related rules on vicarious liability. Federal courts

have avoided "the vagaries of state law" by deeming the determination of an agency relationship under the FHA to be a question of federal law. *See* Cleveland v. Caplaw Enterprises, 448 F.3d 518, 522 (2d Cir. 2006); Harris v. Itzhaki, 183 F.3d 1043, 1054 (9th Cir. 1999). "Nevertheless, because housing discrimination is considered a tort, the agency principles that govern tort cases are generally applicable in fair housing litigation." Schwemm, HDLL §12B:2, notes 11-12 and accompanying text.

Agency relationships can be based on "actual" or "apparent" agency. Actual agency requires more than the right to control; it assumes some agreement between the agent and the principal "to have the former act on the latter's behalf and subject to the latter's control." Schwemm, HDLL §12B:2, note 14 and accompanying text. HUD's FHA regulation defines "Agent" to include:

> Any person authorized to perform an action on behalf of another person regarding any matter related to the sale or rental of dwellings, including offers, solicitations or contracts and the administration of matters regarding [same] or any residential real estate-related transactions.

24 C.F.R. §100.20 (2024).

In addition, vicarious liability may apply in situations of "apparent" agency, that is, where a principal "has acted in a way that would make it reasonable for a third party dealing with the agent to believe" the principal has authorized the agent to conduct certain activities on the principal's behalf. *See* Schwemm, HDLL §12B:2, text accompanying note 17. For example, in United States v. SSM Properties, LLC, 598 F. Supp. 3d 478, 481-82, 485 (S.D. Miss. 2022), the government and four Black testers alleged an "extensive pattern" of racial discrimination at Oak Manor Apartments in Pearl, Mississippi. The defendant property owners claimed no agency relationship existed authorizing their co-defendant to act on their behalf; the district court denied summary judgment, deeming the issue of actual or apparent agency to be a jury question. With respect to apparent agency, the court held:

> It is undisputed that the Mauldings referred to Roe as their property manager, provided Roe with the master key to all their properties, gave him office space at SSM Properties, allowed Roe to hand out rental applications, and let him show properties. A reasonable jury could find that the Mauldings placed Roe in "a position to commit violations of the FHA[.]"

Additional vicarious liability principles include:

- The principal must have the ability to direct and control the agent's activities. An agent's unlawful conduct will not be imputed to a principal with "absent or weak" control.[48]

---

48. Schwemm, HDLL §12B:2, text accompanying notes 25-28.

- An employee's unlawful acts will be imputed up the chain of command to the employer, but not generally to other supervisory personnel along the way. *See* Holley v. Crank, 400 F.3d 667, 671 (9th Cir. 2005) ("liability in the typical employment relationship runs between the corporation and the salesperson and between the corporation and the supervisor, but not between the salesperson and the supervisor.").
- Vicarious liability "flows upward, not downward." Agents may be directly liable for their own unlawful acts, even if following orders, but they will not be vicariously liable for the acts of a principal.[49]

2. **Who Is the Principal?** In *Meyer*, the plaintiffs sought to impute personal liability from the employee up the chain of command not only to the corporate employer, but also to its president and sole shareholder. At first blush, it may not be apparent whether the corporate *officer*, an individual, is subject to vicarious liability to the same extent as the corporate *entity*. Does it matter that the corporate officer has the power to direct or control the actions of the employee perpetrating the unlawful discrimination? Is the mere power to direct or control sufficient to render the officer vicariously liable? What if the corporation has no assets to pay a judgment? For example, should an interracial couple denied a homeownership opportunity based on their race be permitted to pursue claims against any individuals who could have prevented the discrimination (and who can pay a judgment)?

Previous FHA cases had held: "A principal cannot free itself of liability by delegating to an agent the duty not to discriminate." City of Chicago v. Matchmaker Real Estate Sales Center, Inc., 982 F.2d 1086, 1096 (7th Cir. 1992). This is generally true where principals and agents are concerned. Should this concept of FHA compliance being a "non-delegable duty" subject an individual corporate officer and shareholder to vicarious liability in the same manner as the entity? Below, the Ninth Circuit reasoned that among innocent parties "the one whose acts permitted the wrong to occur" must be held to account. *See also Matchmaker*, 982 F.2d at 1097.

The *Meyer* Court, however, refused to impose any special duty of protection for FHA cases in the absence of an explicit instruction by Congress, holding that traditional agency principles applied instead. It cited the Restatement (Second) of Agency for the proposition that "the relevant principal/agency relationship demands not only control (or the right to direct or control) but also 'the manifestation of consent by one person to another that the other shall act on his behalf, and consent by the other so to act.'" The Court made clear that "it is the corporation, not its owner or officer, who is the principal or employer, and thus subject to vicarious liability for torts committed by its

---

49. Schwemm, HDLL §12B:2, text accompanying notes 29-31 & 33. *See* Chapter 10 for discussion of FHA protections under §3617 for employees suffering retaliatory termination for *refusing* to follow orders that would result in their own liability under the FHA.

employees or agents." The Court refused to adopt a more expansive rule "that would hold every corporate supervisor personally liable without fault for the unlawful act of every corporate employee whom he or she has the right to supervise." In other words, the "right to control is insufficient by itself, under traditional agency principles, to establish a principal/agent or employer/ employee relationship." Further, "[a] corporate employee typically acts on behalf of the corporation, not its [shareholder] or officer."

3. *Meyer,* **the Aftermath.** Its previous opinion vacated, the Ninth Circuit on remand addressed questions that the Supreme Court had declined to consider in the first instance but which ultimately provided the Holleys a path forward to recovery. The appellate court held that California law placed unique responsibilities on officers/brokers of real estate corporations beyond ordinary tort principles, reversing the district court's summary judgment for Meyer. It held specifically that state law "makes the designated real estate broker of a real estate corporation [Meyer] personally responsible for the supervision of the corporation's salespersons. . . . When Meyer delegated this responsibility to Crank, he created an agency relationship between himself and Crank, which made Meyer vicariously liable as the principal for the discriminatory actions of Crank as his agent." Holley v. Crank, 400 F.3d 667, 671 (9th Cir. 2005). The Ninth Circuit also held that plaintiffs preserved a corporate veil-piercing claim and remanded to allow them to amend to pursue this theory in the district court. There was evidence to suggest that Meyer should share liability with the corporation because that entity was Meyer's "alter ego": Meyer was Triad's sole shareholder at the time of the alleged discrimination, he failed to treat the corporation as a separate entity on his tax return, he failed to follow other corporate formalities, and the corporation was thinly capitalized (leaving it no assets to pay a judgment). *Id.* at 674-75. This veil-piercing theory would be another way to impute the corporation's liability to Meyer as owner and officer.

4. **Spouses and Family Members as Agents.** Consider the situation of being held vicariously liable for a spouse's discriminatory conduct:

> Although Beverly did not herself engage in overtly discriminatory conduct but merely deferred to George's [her husband's] decisions, she is nonetheless liable. Because they owned the 1461 Balmoral property as joint tenants, George acted as Beverly's agent in renting the apartment. As Coates v. Bechtel, 811 F.2d 1045, 1051 (7th Cir. 1987) has explained: ". . . In cases of racial discrimination in housing under both 42 U.S.C. §1982 and 42 U.S.C. §3604, the courts have imputed the wrongful acts of a real estate sales or rental agent to the property owner he is representing regardless of whether the owner specifically authorized the agent to engage in racial discrimination. The principal owner's liability is unaffected by the fact that the person committing the discriminatory acts in the course of disposing of the property is a relative or a neighbor rather than a professional real estate agent." Consequently both spouses are liable when one spouse engages in discriminatory conduct while renting jointly owned property.

Cato v. Jilek, 779 F. Supp. 937, 946 n.21 (N.D. Ill. 1991). The situation is particularly awkward for spouses who co-own property, where one spouse is accused of sexually harassing tenants at the property. This was the case in *Richards v. Bono*, discussed above, and occurs in many other housing sexual harassment cases. *See* Rigel C. Oliveri, *Housing Sexual Harassment: A Department of Justice Case Study*, JOURNAL OF AFFORDABLE HOUSING AND COMMUNITY DEVELOPMENT LAW (forthcoming 2024) (finding that in 20 of the 76 cases analyzed, the perpetrator of alleged sexual harassment jointly owned the property—either directly or through a closely held business entity—with his wife). In some cases, close family members "knew or should have known" of the alleged discrimination and failed to correct it, which could subject them to direct liability. *See* note 5, below. But even if they did not know, did not authorize, and did not approve, spouses or family members would be vicariously liable for unlawful discrimination carried out by their familial agents acting within the scope of their duties.

5. **Back to Direct Liability.** Remember that HUD's regulation makes clear at §100.7(a)(1)(i) that "A person is directly liable for [t]he person's own conduct that results in a discriminatory housing practice." Thus, none of the constraints on vicarious liability applies when a corporate officer, manager, superior, director, or shareholder *personally* participates in, directs, approves, authorizes, or ratifies unlawful housing discrimination. *See* Schwemm, HDLL §12B:3, notes 10-15 and accompanying text. This is because direct, not vicarious, liability would attach. *See* Fielder v. Sterling Park Homeowners Ass'n, 914 F. Supp. 2d 1222, 1227 (W.D. Wash. 2012) (upholding FHA race claims against homeowners association directors for their own discriminatory enforcement of rules); Housing Opportunities Project for Excellence, Inc. v. Key Colony No. 4 Condo. Assoc., 510 F. Supp. 2d 1003, 1013-14 (S.D. Fla. 2007) (holding that condo "board members can be held liable for their own unlawful conduct [on the basis of familial status] under the FHA" where plaintiffs alleged that each member "was personally involved in each and every discriminatory act").

Chapter Summary

- A proper plaintiff under the FHA can be any person "aggrieved" by a fair housing violation. This broad and inclusive definition allows a variety of injured individuals and entities to bring claims, even those who were not themselves the direct targets of the discriminatory behavior.
- The Supreme Court has given the FHA a broad construction and in early cases held that standing to sue under the FHA extends to the limits of what the Constitution allows. Article III of the Constitution provides that the federal judicial power extends to "cases and controversies," and this requires the plaintiff to demonstrate an actual injury, caused by the defendant, that can be remedied by the relief requested.

- Three early FHA cases, referred to as "the trilogy," interpreted FHA standing to extend to three important categories of plaintiff harm: injuries to both white and Black people who seek integrated living environments (*Trafficante*), injuries to neighborhoods whose housing markets have been manipulated through racial steering (*Gladstone*), and injuries to fair housing organizations and "testers" who are engaged in investigating possible violations of the FHA (*Havens*).
- In a more recent FHA case (*City of Miami*), the Court applied common law civil liability limits to the plaintiff's claim, including both a "zone of interests" and a proximate cause requirement. The zone of interests requirement is a statutory analysis that asks whether the plaintiff falls within the class of persons Congress granted a right to sue under the statute. The proximate cause requirement is a pleading standard requiring the plaintiff to allege injuries that are directly caused by the defendant. The Court held the city did fall within the FHA's zone of interests when it alleged economic injury from widespread predatory lending practices (likening these injuries to those recognized in *Gladstone*). The Court rejected the standard applied on proximate cause and remanded for the lower courts to establish the contours of this requirement.
- The same passive language that permits an open-ended array of potential plaintiffs to enforce the FHA's provisions (within the boundaries of Article III) also authorizes claims against an undefined group of potential defendants.
- In fair housing cases, federal courts apply traditional agency principles to hold principals liable for the acts of their agents operating within the scope of the agents' authority. In *Meyer v. Holley*, the Court declined to hold a corporate *officer*, sued as an individual, vicariously liable for the acts of the corporation's agent, reasoning that an employee typically acts on behalf of the corporation, not its owner or officer.
- An owner personally engaged in unlawful discriminatory acts will be directly, not vicariously, liable; direct liability will attach whether an owner acted alone, directed employees to discriminate, or approved of employees' discrimination. Direct liability also may extend to less obvious situations where an owner knows *or should have known* of discriminatory conduct of an agent/employee and fails to take prompt action to correct it.

CHAPTER 5

COVERAGE: "DWELLINGS" AND EXEMPTIONS

The FHA, like most statutes, contains provisions defining and limiting its application. In particular, much of its coverage is limited to "dwellings" (as opposed to temporary places of respite or commercial properties not meant for occupancy). In addition, there are a number of narrow exemptions that remove dwellings that would otherwise be covered from some or all of the Act's requirements.

A. DWELLINGS

Most of the substantive provisions of the FHA apply to a "dwelling," which is defined in §3602(b) as

> any building, structure, or portion thereof which is occupied as, or designed or intended for occupancy as, a residence by one or more families, and any vacant land which is offered for sale or lease for the construction or location thereon of any such building, structure, or portion thereof.

"Family" is defined in §3602(c) to include a single individual, but §3602(b)'s central word, "residence," is not defined in the statute. HUD's regulations and explanations as well as caselaw establish that "dwellings" include houses and apartments, mobile homes, trailers, manufactured housing, and time sharing arrangements, regardless of whether the financing arrangements are ownership or rental, cooperatives, or condominiums. *See* 54 *Fed. Reg.* 3238 (Jan. 23, 1989). Cases as well as HUD interpretations address the meaning of "residence" and apply the term to all these categories. Defendants most often challenge FHA dwelling status for housing that is less easily described as a

long-term, full-time place of abode, such as temporary shelters, transitional housing, nursing homes, and vacation properties. Consider the following case, in which the court addressed whether a residential drug and alcohol treatment facility should be deemed a dwelling.

Lakeside Resort Enterprises, LP v. Board of Supervisors of Palmyra Township
455 F.3d 154 (3d. Cir. 2006)

Ambro and Stapleton, Circuit Judges, and Stagg, District Judge.

AMBRO, Circuit Judge.

We consider whether a proposed drug and alcohol-treatment facility, under the facts of this case, qualifies as a dwelling under the FHA. Due to funding restrictions, residents of the facility would stay there for slightly more than two weeks on average. But the facility is intended for longer stays, and many stay longer. Moreover, while they are there, the residents would treat the facility like a home. We therefore deem it a dwelling under the Act.

I. FACTUAL BACKGROUND AND PROCEDURAL HISTORY

In late summer 2000, Lakeside was negotiating to sell a resort property to Greenway, Inc., which intended to use the property as a drug- and alcohol-treatment center. That September, they set a price of $1.75 million. The Lakeside property—zoned as Community Commercial—sits on Lake Wallenpaupack in Palmyra Township and includes a hotel-restaurant complex.

In October 2000, Palmyra's Board of Supervisors started working on (and in January 2001 passed) a zoning ordinance amendment that prohibited, among other things, drug- and alcohol-treatment centers in the Community Commercial district. The Board then denied Lakeside's application for a conditional use of the property as a drug- and alcohol-treatment center. As a result, the sale to Greenway fell through.

After losing the sale, Lakeside sued the Board, challenging the validity of the ordinance under, *inter alia*, the FHAA. [After various procedural steps], the Court entered judgment as a matter of law [for the Board of Supervisors] on the FHAA claim.

III. DISCUSSION

A.

The FHA proscribes discrimination in the sale of a dwelling due to a handicap of those who are to reside in the dwelling after the sale. 42 U.S.C. §3604(f)(1). We must decide whether the proposed drug- and alcohol-treatment facility is a dwelling under the FHA. In making this decision, we are to give a "generous construction" to the statute's "broad and inclusive" language. Trafficante v. Metro. Life Ins. Co. (1972). Our Court has dealt with similar issues twice before. In United States v. Columbus Country Club, we decided that a summer bungalow was a dwelling. 915 F.2d 877, 881 (3d Cir. 1990). Then, in Hovsons, Inc. v. Township of Brick, we held that a nursing home was a dwelling. 89 F.3d 1096, 1102 (3d Cir. 1996). We note that at least two other courts have held that recovering alcoholics and drug addicts are handicapped, so long as they are not currently using illegal drugs.

As "family" in the statute "includes a single individual," 42 U.S.C. §3602(c), *Columbus Country Club* held that "residence" is the key word in the dwelling definition. Because "residence" is not defined in the statute, we looked instead to the dictionary definition applied by another court 15 years earlier. *Id.* (citing United States v. Hughes Mem'l Home, 396 F. Supp. 544, 549 (W.D. Va. 1975)). Under that definition, a residence is "a temporary or permanent dwelling place, abode or habitation to which one intends to return as distinguished from the place of temporary sojourn or transient visit." *Id.*

Moving to the "dwelling" analysis, we then held that "the central inquiry [was] whether the [country club's] members intend to remain in the bungalows for any significant period of time and whether they view their bungalows as a place to return to." Accordingly, we concluded that the Act "would presumably cover . . . facilities whose occupants remain for more than a brief period of time and who view their rooms as a residence 'to return to.'" We also noted that there was "no indication in the statutory language that Congress intended to limit coverage of the Act to year-round places of abode and exempt seasonal dwellings." Because the country club's members returned nearly every summer to the bungalows and spent up to five months in them, we held that the bungalows were residences.

We also wrote approvingly of three cases from other courts, cases holding that a motel was not a dwelling, Patel v. Holley House Motels, 483 F. Supp. 374, 381 (S.D. Ala. 1979), that a children's home with a four-year average stay was a dwelling, United States v. Hughes Mem'l Home, 396 F. Supp. 544, 549 (W.D. Va. 1975), and that a hospice for terminally ill AIDS patients was a dwelling, Baxter v. City of Belleville, 720 F. Supp. 720, 731 (S.D. Ill. 1989).

In our 1996 *Hovsons* case, we had to decide whether a nursing home was a dwelling. After reviewing *Columbus Country Club*'s analysis, we stated simply: "To the handicapped elderly persons who would reside there, [the facility] would be their home, very often for the rest of their lives. We therefore hold that the proposed nursing home is a 'dwelling' within the meaning of §3602(b)."

The District Court [initially] decided that the record was not clear on how long the residents were going to stay at the Lakeside treatment facility, so it held that there was a genuine issue of material fact and denied summary judgment on the FHAA claim. But in its Rule 50(a) judgment as a matter of law—after trial testimony on the average length of stay—the Court held that the facility would not be a dwelling. First, it determined that 14.8 days (the average resident stay) was not a significant period of time. Second, it determined that the residents would not view the facility as a place to return to because they would live there solely for treatment. Third, it determined that the residents would be like mere transients because they would not view the facility as a permanent residence and, as pointed out, they would be there solely for treatment.

Before we begin the analysis in this case, we note that other courts have also addressed similar issues. Some have applied the FHA to various facilities without explicitly addressing the "dwelling" question.[1] *See, e.g.,* Turning Point, Inc. v. City of Caldwell, 74 F.3d 941, 945 (9th Cir. 1996) (homeless shelters); United States v. S. Mgmt. Corp., 955 F.2d 914, 923 (4th Cir. 1992) (drug- and alcohol-treatment facility). Several other courts have addressed the issue, coming out on both sides. *See, e.g.,* Schneider v. County of Will, 190 F. Supp. 2d 1082, 1087 (N.D. Ill. 2002) (a bed and breakfast is not a dwelling); Cohen v. Twp. of Cheltenham, 174 F. Supp. 2d 307, 323 (E.D. Pa. 2001) (a children's group home with an anticipated stay of nine or ten months is a dwelling); Conn. Hosp. v. City of New London, 129 F. Supp. 2d 123, 135 (D. Conn. 2001) (group homes for alcohol and drug treatment, in which residents stayed on average six weeks, are dwellings); Garcia v. Condarco, 114 F. Supp. 2d 1158, 1163 (D.N.M. 2000) (a city jail is not a dwelling); Project Life, Inc. v. Glendening, No. WMN-98-2163, 1998 WL 1119864, at *2 & n.4 (D. Md. Nov. 30, 1998) (suggesting that a decommissioned Navy hospital ship offering one-month stays to women recovering from substance abuse would be a dwelling); Villegas v. Sandy Farms, Inc., 929 F. Supp. 1324, 1328 (D. Or. 1996) (cabins occupied by migrant farm workers during the five-month harvest season are dwellings); Hernandez v. Ever Fresh Co., 923 F. Supp. 1305, 1308-09 (D. Or. 1996) (same).

B.

To repeat what we quoted above from *Columbus Country Club*, two factors determine whether a specific facility is a dwelling under the FHA. First, we must decide whether the facility is intended or designed for occupants who "intend to remain in the [facility] for any significant period of time." Second, we must determine whether those occupants would "view [the facility] as a place to return to" during that period.

---

1. [Fn. 6 in original] And both the Sixth Circuit and (perhaps) Congress suggest that group homes are presumably dwellings. *See, e.g.,* Larkin v. Mich. Dep't of Soc. Servs., 89 F.3d 285, 289 (6th Cir. 1996) ("It is well-settled that the FHAA applies to the regulation of group homes."); H.R.Rep. No. 100-711, at 24 (1988), as reprinted in 1988 U.S.C.C.A.N. 2173, 2185 (discussing the kinds of discrimination the Committee intended to prohibit under the FHAA, and noting in particular "the enactment or imposition of health, safety or land-use requirements on congregate living arrangements among non-related persons with disabilities").

1. Is the facility intended or designed for occupants who would intend to remain for a significant period of time?

We have not defined what is a "significant period of time" other than to say that (1) five months is significant, and (2) "for the rest of [the occupants'] lives" is significant, *Hovsons*, 89 F.3d at 1102. Cases from other courts, cited above, have found sufficient stays ranging from one month to four years.

Trial testimony here put the likely average stay at the proposed facility at 14.8 days. In Greenway's "early days," the average stay was 30 days. (In fact, at least one Greenway resident stayed more than a year.) The 14.8-day stay appears to result chiefly from caps on health-insurance funding, because people — those on "scholarship" — who stay at Greenway's expense often stay longer than that.

But the short, funding-limited, average stay is not dispositive here. Congress considered a dwelling to be a facility "which is occupied as, or designed or *intended[2] for occupancy as, a residence* by one or more families." 42 U.S.C §3602(b) (emphasis added). The facility (as we infer from the experience of Greenway's other facilities) is intended to accommodate 30-day stays as a matter of course and even longer stays on occasion. Congress did not, by its words, require only that a facility be "occupied as" a residence. Thus, that health-insurance funding limits some residents to 14.8 days or less does not itself deprive the proposed Lakeside facility of its residential status.

Moreover, the 14.8-day stay is an average. This suggests that some people — possibly half, depending on how the average was calculated — stay longer than 14.8 days. The residents on "scholarship," for example, stay longer because they are not limited by funding. In any event, the statute refers to "any building, structure, *or portion thereof*." 42 U.S.C. §3602(b) (emphasis added). Some rooms in the facility — *i.e.*, a "portion thereof" — would house residents staying for extended periods, thereby satisfying with ease the significant-stay factor.

While 14.8 days is much shorter than the five months we have previously held to have been a "significant period of time," it is certainly longer than the typical stay in a motel[3] or a bed and breakfast, which have been held not to be

---

2. [Fn. 7 in original] The Board argues that, because the Lakeside facility was built as a hotel, it cannot meet §3602(b)'s requirement that a dwelling be "designed or intended for occupancy as . . . a residence." We disagree. Though the facility was built as a hotel, Greenway was planning to turn it into a drug- and alcohol-treatment center. Somewhat analogously, Baxter (which we approved of in *Columbus Country Club*) involved an office building that was intended to be converted into an AIDS hospice. As in Baxter, we look here to Greenway's intent to make the Lakeside property a residential treatment center.

3. [Fn. 8 in original] In 2004, 63% of business travelers, and 73% of leisure travelers, spent only one or two nights per hotel stay. Am. Hotel & Lodging Ass'n, 2005 Lodging Industry Profile 4 (2005) [Eps. — These data are consistent with more recent industry trends. In 2015, 66 percent of business travelers and 76 percent of leisure travelers spent only one or two nights per hotel stay. Am. Hotel & Lodging Ass'n, *Lodging Industry Trends 2015*, https://www.ahla.com/sites /default/files/Lodging_Industry_Trends_2015.pdf.]

dwellings under the FHA. In this context, we conclude that the 14.8-day average stay at the proposed facility is more nuanced than perceived at first blush, and qualifies that facility under the first factor of *Columbus Country Club*.

2. Do occupants view the facility as a place to return to?

Columbus Country Club's second factor ("place to return to") was significant in that case, as club members returned to their bungalows every summer. What we meant by viewing a bungalow as a "place to return to" is that the country club's members saw their individual bungalows as homes. The members repeatedly returned to the same bungalow because they felt at home there.[4] Similarly, we noted in *Hovsons* that, "[t]o the handicapped elderly persons who would reside there, [the nursing facility] would be their home, very often for the rest of their lives." 89 F.3d at 1102; *see also* Villegas, 929 F. Supp. at 1328 ("Like the occupants of a homeless shelter, during the farmworkers' employment . . . , the cabins are their *homes*." (emphasis added)).[5]

Trial testimony about the experience at other Greenway facilities showed that the Lakeside residents would eat meals together (separated by gender), return to their rooms in the evening, receive mail at the facility, and make it their "residence" while they were there. Lakeside's counsel at oral argument added that Greenway residents hung pictures on their walls and had visitors in their rooms. Although residents in treatment were apparently not allowed off the grounds of the facility unsupervised, testimony showed that they treated it like a home for the duration of their stays. This satisfies (though barely) the second factor of *Columbus Country Club*.

IV. CONCLUSION

We hold that the facility intended by Greenway as a drug- and alcohol-treatment facility is a dwelling under the FHA. Therefore, we reverse the District Court's order and remand the case for further proceedings.

NOTES AND QUESTIONS

1. **Temporary Shelters as "Dwellings."** Although using "dwelling place" to define "residence" so as to define "dwelling" is circular, many courts, as in *Lakeside Resort*, have relied on this formulation within *United States v. Hughes Memorial Home* to define "dwelling" under the FHA. This has been particularly useful for cases involving temporary shelters for people who otherwise

---

4. [Fn. 9 in original] The members did not actually own particular bungalows. They owned the land collectively and leased the bungalows from the club.

5. [Fn. 10 in original] On the other hand, visitors to motels and bed and breakfasts do not see those places as their homes. *See Schneider*, 190 F. Supp. 2d at 1087; *Patel*, 483 F. Supp. at 381.

might be experiencing homelessness. For example, in Hunter v. District of Columbia, 64 F. Supp. 3d 158 (D.D.C. 2014), a father sued the District of Columbia on behalf of his minor daughter, who had severe disabilities and used a wheelchair. The two were in danger of becoming homeless and sought a placement, but the District's social services staff placed them in a third-story unit with no elevator. In denying the District's motion to dismiss, Judge Gladys Kessler rejected arguments that its shelters were not dwellings under the FHA, citing to a range of decisions:

> Applying the definition used in *Hughes*, several courts have concluded that temporary homeless shelters are "dwellings" under the FHA. Defiore [v. City Rescue Mission of New Castle], 995 F. Supp. 2d [413,] 417-20 [W.D. Pa. 2013)]; Boykin v. Gray, 895 F. Supp. 2d 199, 207 (D.D.C. 2012); Jenkins [v. New York City Dept. of Homeless Svcs.], 643 F. Supp. 2d [507,] 517-18; Woods [v. Foster], 884 F. Supp. [1169,] 1173–74 [(N.D. Ill. 1995)]. Other courts have noted without deciding that it is likely that at least some temporary shelters are "dwellings." Cmty. House, Inc. v. City of Boise, 490 F.3d 1041, 1044 n.2 (9th Cir. 2007) (en banc). Intermountain Fair Hous. Council v. Boise Rescue Mission Ministries, 717 F. Supp. 2d 1101 (D. Idaho 2010), *aff'd on other grounds,* 657 F.3d 988 (9th Cir. 2011), concluded that a particular homeless shelter did not qualify as a "dwelling," relying on specific factors regarding the terms of residence at the shelter: "[G]uests of the shelter are not charged a fee for staying in the shelter; are assigned a bed in a dormitory-style room, a hallway, or the day room; generally are allowed to stay for a maximum of seventeen consecutive nights (except during the winter months when the maximum stay is more flexible due to the danger that cold weather presents to homeless individuals during the night); are not guaranteed the same bed each night they return; with limited exceptions, are not allowed to stay at the shelter during the day, are required to leave the shelter every morning by 8:00 a.m., and may not return, except for lunch, until 4:00 p.m.; are not allowed to leave the shelter once they arrive in the evening; generally are not allowed to stay at the shelter on a particular evening if they do not check in during the designated hours; are not allowed to personalize the bed area assigned to them or leave belongings in their bed area; and, with extremely limited exceptions, are not allowed to receive phone calls, mail, or have visitors at the shelter."

Hunter, 64 F. Supp. 3d at 174-75 (also deferring to a HUD regulation). Noting that the shelters imposed no time limit on length of stay, provided families with their own rooms that were accessible at all times of day, and for some units provided an apartment-style room with a key, the court held that the Hunters alleged sufficient facts to establish that the District's shelters were "a temporary . . . dwelling place, abode or habitation to which one intends to return as distinguished from [a] place of temporary sojourn or transient visit."

2. **A Multifactor Test.** HUD has provided a "multi-factor" test to determine "whether a facility that includes short-term-residencies" is a "dwelling" within the FHA. How do these factors compare to the analysis in *Lakeside Resort*?

> (1) Length of stay; (2) whether the rental rate for the unit will be calculated on a daily, weekly, monthly or yearly basis; (3) whether the terms and lengths

of occupancy will be established through a lease or other written agreement; (4) what amenities will be included inside the unit, including kitchen facilities; (5) how the purpose of the property will be marketed to the public; (6) whether the resident possesses the right to return to the property; and (7) whether the resident has anywhere else to which to return.[6]

3. **Home Sweet Home?** Some courts have framed the analysis slightly differently but focused on the same types of facts, adding qualitative and quantitative measures to the test of *Hughes Memorial Home*. In Schwarz v. City of Treasure Island, 544 F.3d 1201 (11th Cir. 2008), for example, the Eleventh Circuit said "(1) the more occupants treat a building like their home—e.g., cook their own meals, clean their own rooms and maintain the premises, do their own laundry, and spend free time together in common areas—the more likely it is a 'dwelling'; and (2) the longer the typical occupant lives in a building, the more likely it is that the building is a 'dwelling.'" 544 F.3d at 1215. The court stated that "the patients' lifestyles while living at the treatment center satisfied [this] principle—treating the building like a home. The patients ate meals together, returned to their rooms in the evening, received mail at the facility, hung pictures on their walls, and had visitors in their rooms. In short, 'they treated it like a home for the duration of their stays.'" The Eleventh Circuit looked to Connecticut Hospital v. City of New London, 129 F. Supp. 2d 123, 125-26 (D. Conn. 2001), where patients lived in the houses for one to three months, with an average stay of six weeks. The homes were "generally self-governing, with house members setting their own rules and working out most problems." Moreover, "[h]ouse members often [ate] dinner together and attend[ed] a nightly Alcoholics Anonymous or Narcotics Anonymous meeting . . . as a group." On these facts, the district court concluded that the group homes were "dwellings." The Eleventh Circuit in *Schwarz* reasoned that:

> The six halfway houses in this case are even more like homes than the facilities examined in *Lakeside Resort* and *Connecticut Hospital*. In the first place, residents stay on average six to ten weeks—much longer than the one to two day stays of most hotel guests. Moreover, their stays far exceed the 14.8 day average stay of the residents in *Lakeside Resort*. And unlike the group homes in *Connecticut Hospital*, residents are not required to leave the halfway houses after completing their treatment with Gulf Coast. Indeed, they may remain indefinitely, and some residents have lived in them for as long as five months.

———————————

Another issue that has divided commentators is whether "dwellings" can include rooms inside a residence (although §3602(b)'s definition of "dwelling" includes "any building, structure, or *portion* thereof . . .") (emphasis added). In

———————————

6. HUD, *Equal Access in Accordance With an Individual's Gender Identify in Community Planning and Development Programs*, 81 FED. REG. 64763, 64771 (Sept. 21, 2016).

particular, this question will determine whether roommates are covered by the FHA, as discussed in the next case.

Fair Housing Council of San Fernando Valley
v. Roommate.com, LLC
666 F.3d 1216 (9th Cir. 2012)

Kozinski, Chief Judge; Reinhardt and Ikuta, Circuit Judges; Partial Dissent by Judge Ikuta.

KOZINSKI, Chief Judge:

There's no place like home. In the privacy of your own home, you can take off your coat, kick off your shoes, let your guard down and be completely yourself. While we usually share our homes only with friends and family, sometimes we need to take in a stranger to help pay the rent. When that happens, can the government limit whom we choose? Specifically, do the anti-discrimination provisions of the FHA extend to the selection of roommates?

FACTS

Roommate.com, LLC ("Roommate") operates an internet-based business that helps roommates find each other. Roommate's website receives over 40,000 visits a day and roughly a million new postings for roommates are created each year. When users sign up, they must create a profile by answering a series of questions about their sex, sexual orientation and whether children will be living with them. An open-ended "Additional Comments" section lets users include information not prompted by the questionnaire. Users are asked to list their preferences for roommate characteristics, including sex, sexual orientation and familial status. Based on the profiles and preferences, Roommate matches users and provides them a list of housing-seekers or available rooms meeting their criteria. Users can also search available listings based on roommate characteristics, including sex, sexual orientation and familial status. The Fair Housing Councils of San Fernando Valley and San Diego ("FHCs") sued Roommate, alleging that the website's questions requiring disclosure of sex, sexual orientation and familial status, and its sorting, steering and matching of users based on those characteristics, violate the FHA and the California Fair Employment and Housing Act.

The district court initially dismissed the claims, holding that Roommate was immune under section 230 of the Communications Decency Act ("CDA"). We reversed, holding that Roommate was protected by the CDA for publishing the "Additional Comments" section, but not for (1) posting questionnaires that required disclosure of sex, sexual orientation and familial status; (2) limiting the scope of searches by users' preferences on a roommate's sex, sexual orientation and familial status; and (3) a matching system that paired users based on those preferences.[7]

Our opinion was limited to CDA immunity and didn't reach whether the activities, in fact, violated the FHA. On remand, the district court held that Roommate's prompting of discriminatory preferences from users, matching users based on that information and publishing these preferences violated the FHA and FEHA, and enjoined Roommate from those activities. Roommate appeals the grant of summary judgment and permanent injunction, and also the district court's order awarding the FHCs $494,714.40 in attorney's fees. The FHCs cross-appeal the amount of the attorney's fees.

ANALYSIS

If the FHA extends to shared living situations, it's quite clear that what Roommate does amounts to a violation. The pivotal question is whether the FHA applies to roommates.

I

The FHA prohibits discrimination on the basis of [protected characteristics] in the "sale or rental *of a dwelling*" (emphasis added). The FHA also makes it illegal to make, print, or publish, or cause to be made, printed, or published any notice, statement, or advertisement, with respect to the sale or rental *of a dwelling* that indicates any preference, limitation, or discrimination based on [protected characteristics]. §3604(c) (emphasis added). The reach of the statute turns on the meaning of "dwelling."

The FHA defines "dwelling" as "any building, structure, or portion thereof which is occupied as, or designed or intended for occupancy as, a residence by one or more families." A dwelling is thus a living unit designed or intended for occupancy by a family, meaning that it ordinarily has the elements generally associated with a family residence: sleeping spaces, bathroom and kitchen facilities, and common areas, such as living rooms, dens and hallways.

It would be difficult, though not impossible, to divide a single-family house or apartment into separate "dwellings" for purposes of the statute. Is a "dwelling" a bedroom plus a right to access common areas? What if roommates share a bedroom? Could a "dwelling" be a bottom bunk and half an armoire? It makes practical sense to interpret "dwelling" as an independent living unit and stop the FHA at the front door.

There's no indication that Congress intended to interfere with personal relationships *inside* the home. Congress wanted to address the problem of landlords discriminating in the sale and rental of housing, which deprived

---

7. [EDS.—Section 230 provides that "no provider . . . of an interactive computer service shall be treated as the publisher or speaker of any information provided by another information content provider."]

protected classes of housing opportunities. But a business transaction between a tenant and landlord is quite different from an arrangement between two people sharing the same living space. We seriously doubt Congress meant the FHA to apply to the latter. Consider, for example, the FHA's prohibition against sex discrimination. Could Congress, in the 1960s, really have meant that women must accept men as roommates? Telling women they may not lawfully exclude men from the list of acceptable roommates would be controversial today; it would have been scandalous in the 1960s.

While it's possible to read dwelling to mean sub-parts of a home or an apartment, doing so leads to awkward results. And applying the FHA to the selection of roommates almost certainly leads to results that defy mores prevalent when the statute was passed. Nonetheless, this interpretation is not wholly implausible and we would normally consider adopting it, given that the FHA is a remedial statute that we construe broadly. Therefore, we turn to constitutional concerns, which provide strong countervailing considerations.

II

The Supreme Court has recognized that "the freedom to enter into and carry on certain intimate or private relationships is a fundamental element of liberty protected by the Bill of Rights." Bd. of Dirs. of Rotary Int'l v. Rotary Club of Duarte, 481 U.S. 537, 545 (1987). "[C]hoices to enter into and maintain certain intimate human relationships must be secured against undue intrusion by the State because of the role of such relationships in safeguarding the individual freedom that is central to our constitutional scheme." Roberts v. U.S. Jaycees, 468 U.S. 609, 617-18 (1984). Courts have extended the right of intimate association to marriage, child bearing, child rearing and cohabitation with relatives. While the right protects only "highly personal relationships," IDK, Inc. v. Clark Cnty., 836 F.2d 1185, 1193 (9th Cir. 1988) (quoting Roberts, 468 U.S. at 618), the right isn't restricted exclusively to family, Bd. of Dirs. of Rotary Int'l, 481 U.S. at 545. The right to association also implies a right *not* to associate.

To determine whether a particular relationship is protected by the right to intimate association we look to "size, purpose, selectivity, and whether others are excluded from critical aspects of the relationship." Bd. of Dirs. of Rotary Int'l, 481 U.S. at 546. The roommate relationship easily qualifies: People generally have very few roommates; they are selective in choosing roommates; and non-roommates are excluded from the critical aspects of the relationship, such as using the living spaces. Aside from immediate family or a romantic partner, it's hard to imagine a relationship more intimate than that between roommates, who share living rooms, dining rooms, kitchens, bathrooms, even bedrooms.

Because of a roommate's unfettered access to the home, choosing a roommate implicates significant privacy and safety considerations. The home is the center of our private lives. Roommates note our comings and goings, observe whom we bring back at night, hear what songs we sing in the shower, see us in various stages of undress and learn intimate details most of us prefer to keep private. Roommates also have access to our physical belongings and to our person. As the Supreme Court recognized, "[w]e are at our most vulnerable when we are asleep because we cannot monitor our own safety or the security of our belongings." Minnesota v. Olson, 495 U.S. 91, 99 (1990). Taking on a roommate means giving him full access to the space where we are most vulnerable.

Equally important, we are fully exposed to a roommate's belongings, activities, habits, proclivities and way of life. This could include matter we find offensive (pornography, religious materials, political propaganda); dangerous (tobacco, drugs, firearms); annoying (jazz, perfume, frequent overnight visitors, furry pets); habits that are incompatible with our lifestyle (early risers, messy cooks, bathroom hogs, clothing borrowers). When you invite others to share your living quarters, you risk becoming a suspect in whatever illegal activities they engage in.

Government regulation of an individual's ability to pick a roommate thus intrudes into the home, which "is entitled to special protection as the center of the private lives of our people." Minnesota v. Carter, 525 U.S. 83, 99 (1998) (Kennedy, J., concurring). "Liberty protects the person from unwarranted government intrusions into a dwelling or other private places. In our tradition the State is not omnipresent in the home." Lawrence v. Texas, 539 U.S. 558, 562 (2003). Holding that the FHA applies inside a home or apartment would allow the government to restrict our ability to choose roommates compatible with our lifestyles. This would be a serious invasion of privacy, autonomy and security.

For example, women will often look for female roommates because of modesty or security concerns. As roommates often share bathrooms and common areas, a girl may not want to walk around in her towel in front of a boy. She might also worry about unwanted sexual advances or becoming romantically involved with someone she must count on to pay the rent.

An orthodox Jew may want a roommate with similar beliefs and dietary restrictions, so he won't have to worry about finding honey-baked ham in the refrigerator next to the potato latkes. Non-Jewish roommates may not understand or faithfully follow all of the culinary rules, like the use of different silverware for dairy and meat products, or the prohibition against warming non-kosher food in a kosher microwave. Taking away the ability to choose roommates with similar dietary restrictions and religious convictions will substantially burden the observant Jew's ability to live his life and practice his religion faithfully. The same is true of individuals of other faiths that call for dietary restrictions or rituals inside the home.

HUD recently dismissed a complaint against a young woman for advertising, "I am looking for a female christian roommate," on her church bulletin board. In its Determination of No Reasonable Cause, HUD explained that "in

light of the facts provided and after assessing the unique context of the advertisement and the roommate relationship involved . . . the Department defers
to Constitutional considerations in reaching its conclusions." Fair Hous. Ctr.
of W. Mich. v. Tricia, No. 051017388 (Oct. 28, 2010) (Determination of No
Reasonable Cause). It's a "well-established principle that statutes will be
interpreted to avoid constitutional difficulties." "[W]here an otherwise acceptable construction of a statute would raise serious constitutional problems, the
Court will construe the statute to avoid such problems unless such construction is plainly contrary to the intent of Congress." Because the FHA can reasonably be read either to include or exclude shared living arrangements, we
can and must choose the construction that avoids raising constitutional concerns. *See* INS v. St. Cyr, 533 U.S. 289, 299-300 (2001) ("[I]f an otherwise acceptable construction of a statute would raise serious constitutional problems, and
where an alternative interpretation of the statute is fairly possible, we are obligated to construe the statute to avoid such problems."). Reading "dwelling"
to mean an independent housing unit is a fair interpretation of the text and
consistent with congressional intent. Because the construction of "dwelling"
to include shared living units raises substantial constitutional concerns, we
adopt the narrower construction that excludes roommate selection from the
reach of the FHA.

III

Because we find that the FHA doesn't apply to the sharing of living units, it
follows that it's not unlawful to discriminate in selecting a roommate. As the
underlying conduct is not unlawful, Roommate's facilitation of discriminatory roommate searches does not violate the FHA. While Roommate itself has
no intimate association right, it is entitled to raise the constitutional claims of
its users. The injunction entered by the district court precludes Roommate's
members from selecting roommates unfettered by government regulation.
Roommate may therefore raise these claims on their behalf.

IV

Because precluding individuals from selecting roommates based on their sex,
sexual orientation and familial status raises substantial constitutional concerns, we interpret the FHA and FEHA as not applying to the sharing of living
units. Therefore, we hold that Roommate's prompting, sorting and publishing
of information to facilitate roommate selection is not forbidden by the FHA or
FEHA. Accordingly, we vacate the district court's judgment and remand for
entry of judgment for defendant. Because the FHCs are no longer prevailing,
we vacate the district court's order for attorney's fees and dismiss the cross-
appeals on attorney's fees as moot.

NOTES AND QUESTIONS

1. Dormitories. Did the Ninth Circuit give due consideration to the question whether those who share living facilities inhabit a "portion" of a "structure . . . which is occupied as, or designed or intended for occupancy as, a residence" — that is, a "dwelling"?[8] HUD regulations provide that dormitories are covered dwellings, at least for some purposes. When HUD amended its regulations to interpret the FHAA's prohibition of disability-based discrimination, it added a statement that dormitories, as well as other facilities that offer shared sleeping and toileting facilities, may be "dwelling units":

> Dwelling unit means a single unit of *residence* for a family or one or more persons. Examples of dwelling units include: a single family home; an apartment unit within an apartment building; and [units] in other types of dwellings in which sleeping accommodations are provided but toileting or cooking facilities are shared by occupants of more than one room or portion of the dwelling rooms in which people sleep. Examples of the latter include dormitory rooms and sleeping accommodations in shelters intended for occupancy as a *residence* for homeless persons.

24 C.F.R. §100.201 (emphasis added). It is true that this regulation was promulgated to effectuate the FHAA's affirmative obligations for accessible housing, that the title of the subpart in which it appears is "Prohibition Against Discrimination *Because of Handicap*" (emphasis added), and that the introduction to §100.201 says that its definitions are "[a]s used in this subpart. . . ." However, courts generally have considered dormitories to be "dwellings" under the FHA, even in cases that do not involve disability discrimination.[9]

In United States v. University of Nebraska at Kearney, 940 F. Supp. 2d 974, 977-83 (D. Neb. 2013), the court relied on this regulation and the "principle that the FHA implements a policy to which Congress has accorded the highest

---

8. For a careful analysis of the issues in *Roommate.com*, see Tim Iglesias, *Does Fair Housing Law Apply to "Shared Living Situations"? or The Trouble with Roommates*, 32 J. Affordable Hous. & Community Dev. L. 111 (2014). For an argument that associational and privacy rights should prevent the FHA from being applied to people who share intimate living space, see Rigel C. Oliveri, *Discriminatory Housing Advertisements On-Line: Lessons from Craigslist*, 43 Ind. L. Rev. 1125 (2010), and for an argument that people generally should be free to choose their household companions free of government interference, see Rigel C. Oliveri, *Single-Family Zoning, Intimate Association, and the Right to Choose Household Companions*, 67 Fla. L. Rev. 1401 (2015).

9. *See* Schwemm, HDLL §9.2 n.23 (citing cases); *see also* Whitaker v. New York University, 531 Fed. App'x 89 (2d Cir. 2013) (without discussion, assuming in dicta that the FHA applies to a familial status complaint involving dormitories); Hack v. President and Fellows of Yale College, 237 F.3d 81 (2d Cir. 2000) (assuming in dicta and dissent that FHA applies to religious discrimination complaint involving dormitories); Congregation Rabbinical College of Tartikov, Inc. v. Village of Pomano, NY, 280 F. Supp. 3d 426, 491 n.37 (S.D.N.Y. 2017) (rabbinical college's student housing is covered by the FHA in a case involving religious discrimination), *aff'd in part and rev'd in part on other grounds*, 945 F.3d 83 (2019).

national priority" to hold a dormitory room a "dwelling" in an FHA case involving disability discrimination. The court recognized that many students had "permanent" addresses different from their temporary campus addresses, citing cases involving migrant farm workers; it recognized also that students were "assigned rooms and perhaps roommates." The court also noted that the students engaged in activities like those in which one would engage at home: "students living in those facilities eat their meals, wash their laundry, do their schoolwork, socialize, and sleep there, just as people ordinarily do in the place they call home." The court relied on HUD's regulation and its use of the word "dormitory":

> [T]he specific use of the word "dormitory" makes it useful here. If a "dwelling unit" is a unit of residence, then a building containing a "dwelling unit" must be a building designed or intended, at least in part, for occupancy as a residence. And if a dormitory room is an example of a dwelling unit, then the syllogism is complete: a building containing dormitory rooms, *i.e.*, a dormitory, must be a dwelling within the meaning of the FHA. . . .
>
> The HUD definition . . . describes the paradigmatical university dormitory, and it is consistent with the definition of "dormitory" that is more appropriate in this context: "a residence hall providing rooms for individuals or for groups usually without private baths." Merriam-Webster Dictionary. It suffices to conclude that HUD's definition of a "dwelling unit" as including a dormitory is compelling authority supporting the conclusion that UNK's housing facilities are "dwellings" within the meaning of the FHA.

In the Nebraska case, the University made the point Judge Kozinski did, that "dwelling" should not be interpreted to include roommates because "segregating housing on the basis of gender might be affected." The district court responded:

> If colleges and universities need to be exempted from the scope of the statutory language, they are free to ask Congress to amend the statute, or petition HUD to promulgate new regulations. In the meantime, the Court must apply the statute as it is written and has been authoritatively construed by HUD. And based on the statute, UNK's student housing facilities are clearly "dwellings" within the meaning of the FHA.

Who do you think has the better of the disagreement—the Ninth Circuit or the Nebraska district court? Why? If to any extent you agree with the Ninth Circuit that the First Amendment warrants caution in applying the FHA to premises that are shared by "roommates," should it matter how extensive a space is being shared—whether it is a large house or a small apartment? Whether sleeping quarters or only cooking or living quarters are shared? Should it matter if the issue is a difference in sex or religion or race or ability or familial status?

Should students at a university that insists upon nondiscrimination be able to reject—and to say, post, and publicize that they reject—roommates because of their race, color, religion, national origin, or disability status? Should universities or private developers be able to limit particular housing units to "students without children"?[10] Should universities be able to designate certain residences as available only to persons of a particular sex, race, or religion?[11] Why or why not?

2. **Domestic Violence Shelters and Sex.** Those who manage shelters for victims of domestic violence and shelters for transitional housing often insist that they must have single-sex accommodations to be successful. May they lawfully restrict the sex of their occupants? How are they to serve people who are nonbinary or transgender?

B. EXEMPTIONS

The FHA contains a number of statutory exemptions to its coverage of certain discriminatory acts or actors. This chapter discusses the exemptions contained in §3603(b) for particular single-family homes and small-scale landlords and in §3607(a) for private clubs and religious organizations. Other exemptions are discussed in the following chapters:

- Section 3607(b)(2)-(3) exempts specific Housing for Older People from the statute's familial status requirements. It is discussed in Chapter 16.
- Section 3607(b)(1) allows landlords to apply reasonable numerical occupancy limits. It is discussed in Chapter 16.
- Exemptions related to disability, including the exclusion of current users of illegal drugs from being considered disabled, and permitting denial of housing for those whose tenancy constitutes a direct threat to others, are discussed in Chapter 17.

1. Section 3603(b) Exemptions for Certain Single-Family Homes and Small-Scale ("Mrs. Murphy") Landlords

Section 3603(b)(1) states that nothing in §3604, other than subsection (c), shall apply to any single-family house sold or rented by an owner, so long as a number of conditions are met:

- That such private individual owner does not own more than three such single-family houses at any one time;
- That the exemption shall apply only with respect to one such sale by a private owner (not the most recent resident of the house) within any 24-month period;

---

10. *See* Alison Tanner, Note, *Live and Learn: Using the Fair Housing Act to Advance Educational Opportunity for Parenting Students*, 105 Geo. L.J. 1453 (2017).

11. *See* Tess Fortune, *Segregated Housing: Celebratory or Discriminatory?*, 46 J.L. & Educ. 599 (2017).

- That such bona fide private individual owner does not own any interest in or have a right to proceeds from the sale or rental of more than three such single-family houses at any one time;
- That any such single-family house is sold or rented without the use of any real estate broker, agent, or salesperson, or of such facilities or services of any person in the business of selling or renting dwellings,[12] and
- That any such single-family house is sold or rented without the publication, posting, or mailing, after notice, of any advertisement or written notice in violation of section §3604(c).

Note that under the single-family homeowner exemption, publication violations of §3604(c) not only subject the owner to liability under §3604(c), which always applies, but also results in the loss of the exemption.

Section 3603(b)(2), which is to be read independently of the single-family owner provision, exempts "rooms or units in dwellings containing living quarters occupied or intended to be occupied by no more than four families living independently of each other, if the owner actually maintains and occupies one of such living quarters as his residence." This commonly is called the "Mrs. Murphy" exemption. The origin of this term is discussed in the Notes below. As with §3603(b)(1), the Mrs. Murphy exemption under (b)(2) exempts owner-occupied properties of four or fewer units from all of §3604 *except* §3604(c).

Courts consider exemptions to the FHA to be affirmative defenses. This means that a defendant claiming an exemption bears the burden of proof, and also that the potential application of an exemption is not a jurisdictional fact issue that would deprive a federal court of subject matter jurisdiction. *See, e.g.,* United States v. Space Hunters, Inc., 429 F.3d 416 (2d Cir. 2005) ("Mrs. Murphy" exemption is an affirmative defense and not a jurisdictional fact issue); Massaro v. Mainlands Section 1 & 2 Civic Ass'n, 3 F.3d 1472, 1474, 1476 n.6 (11th Cir. 1993) (characterizing the "housing for older persons" exemption as an affirmative defense); United States v. Columbus Country Club, 915 F.2d 877, 882-85 (3d Cir. 1990) (treating the "religious organization" and "private club" exemptions as affirmative defenses); Singleton v. Gendason, 545 F.2d 1224, 1226 (9th Cir. 1976) (burden on defendants to show entitlement to Title VIII single-family exemption).

These requirements are relatively straightforward, although they have given rise to litigation. The following case provides an example of a court carefully analyzing the provisos of the §3603(b)(1) exemption.

---

12. The statute goes on, in §3603(c), to specify that a person will be deemed to be "in the business of selling or renting dwellings" if the person: (1) has, within the preceding 12 months, participated as principal in three or more transactions involving the sale or rental of any dwelling or any interest therein, (2) has, within the preceding 12 months, participated as agent (other than in the sale of his own personal residence) in providing sales or rental facilities or services in two or more sale or rental transactions involving dwellings, or (3) is the owner of any dwelling designed or intended for occupancy by, or occupied by, five or more families.

Hogar Agua y Vida en El Desierto, Inc. v. Suarez-Medina
36 F.3d 177 (1st Cir. 1994)

In September 1992, appellant HAVED entered into an oral agreement with Suarez to rent, with option to buy, two houses located on an undivided lot in the Los Llanos section of Corozal, Puerto Rico. Upon learning that HAVED intended to use the site as a group home for persons infected with HIV, defendants Milton Dolittle and Antonio Padilla organized neighborhood opposition and threatened and coerced Suarez into reneging on the rental-sale agreement. HAVED, along with its directors and a prospective resident of the proposed group home, initiated the present action. Suarez moved to dismiss the complaint for lack of subject matter jurisdiction, citing FHA §3603(b)(1).

A. The Suarez Properties

At the time of the September 1992 rental-sale agreement with HAVED, Suarez owned four separate parcels of land on which were located five structures. First, the "Los Llanos Property," the subject of the abortive rental-sale agreement, consists of one undivided lot containing two unattached residences. Suarez holds undisputed title to the entire lot and one residence (House A) where the Suarezes once resided. Their son built the second house on the lot (House B) as a residence for his own family. However, Mr. Suarez, Sr., was robbed while residing in House A, and the Suarezes and their son moved away from Los Llanos. Houses A and B remained unoccupied at the time of the HAVED–Suarez rental-sale agreement.

Second, the "Guarico Residence," located in the Guarico section of Corozal, was designed as a two-story house with a separately equipped, single-family apartment on each floor. Suarez held title to the lot and the house. At the time of the rental-sale agreement, the Suarezes resided primarily in the second-floor apartment, and the son and his family resided in the first-floor apartment. Due to his physical impairments, however, Mr. Suarez, Sr., sometimes lived "interchangeably" with his son's family in the first-floor apartment. The district court ruled that the Guarico Residence constituted one single-family house.

Third, the "Guarico Rental" is a two-story, single-family structure located near the Guarico Residence but on a separate lot. At the time of the rental-sale agreement, Suarez held title to the house and the lot, and the house was being rented to a single family.

The fourth real estate parcel, the "La Aldea Rental," is a single lot in the La Aldea section containing a one-story structure which Suarez purchased in April 1991, and rented to a single family (Apartment 1). Prior to the rental-sale agreement, however, Suarez renovated the basement of the building into a separate apartment (Apartment 2), and it was rented to another tenant.

II

We employ traditional tools of statutory interpretation, particularly the presumption that ambiguous language in a remedial statute is entitled to a generous construction consistent with its reformative mission. This presumption has been relied on consistently by the courts in interpreting the omnibus remedial provisions of the FHA. An important corollary for present purposes is that ambiguous exemptions from FHA liability are to be narrowly construed.

From this appellate perspective we consider which Suarez properties were "single-family houses" [SFH] within the meaning of Provisos 1 and 3 of FHA §3603(b)(1). The parties agree that two properties—the Guarico Rental and the La Aldea Rental—qualify as "single-family houses" within the meaning of the exemption. Thus, given the four-SFH limen established in §3603(b)(1), the FHA exemption cannot stand if the Suarezes were bona fide "owners" of two SFHs in addition to the Guarico Rental and the La Aldea Rental.

A. Los Llanos Property, House A

First, HAVED argues that the district court exceeded its authority by fashioning an "equitable" exception which resulted in the exclusion of Los Llanos, House A, from the four-SFH calculus on the ground that the Suarezes had been forced to vacate the Los Llanos area due to neighborhood crime.

Although courts have on occasion engrafted equitable exceptions where rigid adherence to literal legislative language clearly would disserve legislative intent, generally courts are loath "to announce equitable exceptions to legislative requirements or prohibitions that are unqualified by the statutory text." Guidry v. Sheet Metal Workers Nat'l Pension Fund, 493 U.S. 365, 376 (1990). Moreover, "[w]here Congress explicitly enumerates certain exceptions to a general prohibition, additional exceptions are not to be implied, in the absence of contrary legislative intent." Andrus v. Glover Constr. Co., 446 U.S. 608, 616-17 (1980). Further, exemptions from the requirements of a remedial statute—like the FHA—are to be construed narrowly to limit exemption eligibility.

For the foregoing reasons, we decline to endorse the equitable exception adopted by the district court, especially since Congress elected not to do so when it undertook to narrow FHA liability in 42 U.S.C. §3603(b). Nothing in §3603(b), nor in its legislative history, manifests a congressional intent to temper either the inflexible four-SFH formula or the categorical "ownership" standard.

B. The Guarico Residence

HAVED next contends that the district court committed reversible error in not treating the Guarico Residence as a SFH under Provisos 1 and 3 of FHA §3603(b)(1). Thus, the present dispute prompts two inquiries. The first is whether a defendant's current residence is excluded from the threshold four-SFH calculus under Provisos 1 and 3 simply because it is his primary or current residence, even though all other SFHs owned but not occupied by the defendant are included without regard to whether they were concurrently "on the market." The second inquiry is whether Congress meant to exclude from the threshold four-SFH calculus all SFHs owned by the defendant (including the primary residence) not on the market at the time the defendant—for discriminatory reasons—refused to sell or rent a different SFH to the plaintiff. We turn to these questions.

1. Exclusion for Residence Qua Residence

As its prefatory clause makes clear, the FHA §3603(b)(1) exemption—assuming its four provisos are satisfied—applies to any "single-family house sold or rented by the owner" in a discriminatory manner. For §3603(b)(1) purposes, therefore, the relevant SFHs in this case are Houses A and B, located on the Los Llanos Property Suarez refused to rent or sell to HAVED. Section 3603(b)(1) neither defines the term "SFH," nor does its prefatory clause expressly limit the term "SFH" to structures in which the defendant does not reside. Conversely, as Suarez acknowledges, if the Suarezes had refused to rent or sell their Guarico Residence to HAVED, the prefatory clause would not have debarred the Suarezes from a §3603(b)(1) exemption merely because the property being rented or sold was their residence.

The statutory context in which the prefatory clause appears undermines the Suarez contention as well. The four FHA §3603(b)(1) provisos do not give rise to four independent exemptions, as Suarez suggests, but represent four cumulative preconditions to the single exemption set out in the prefatory clause. If any of the four provisos is not satisfied, no §3603(b)(1) exemption is appropriate.

Proviso 2 refers specifically to a discrete subset of the "discriminatory" SFH sales focused upon in the §3603(b)(1) prefatory clause, namely, sales of SFHs in which the defendant is not residing. If the unqualified term "SFH" in the prefatory clause were intended to embrace only SFHs in which the defendant is not residing, no such further qualification would be needed in Proviso 2. Thus, if the term "SFH," as used in the prefatory clause, applies to residences and nonresidences, the pendent references to "such [SFHs]" in Provisos 1 and 3 also necessarily encompass the Suarezes's Guarico Residence qua residence.

Finally, the legislative history discloses no basis for second-guessing the "plain language" of §3603(b)(1). As initially introduced in Congress, the FHA contained few significant exemptions from liability, and the breadth of the FHA's coverage caused vigorous Senate opposition. Senator Everett M. Dirksen proposed to assuage opposition by exempting sales and rentals of "any single-family house sold or rented by an owner residing in such house at the time of such sale or rental, or who was the most recent resident of such house prior to such sale or rental." Yet even the "Dirksen substitute," later modified and enacted as Proviso 2, failed to gain enough Senate support. To break the deadlock, Senator Robert C. Byrd proposed the expanded four-part exemption, later codified as present §3603(b)(1).

Asked why "it was necessary to raise the number of houses owned by one party to three," Senator Byrd referred to two hypotheticals [that assumed] the houses in which the seller currently resided would be counted toward the four-SFH threshold in Provisos 1 and 3. Other senators likewise recognized that the "more than three" threshold would include houses in which the seller resided. Since this legislative history, at the very least, precludes our finding "a clearly expressed legislative intention to the contrary," we must conclude that a defendant's residence, qua residence, is not to be excluded under Provisos 1 and 3 of §3603(b)(1).

2. Exemption for "Off Market" SFHs

Suarez proposes to exclude the Guarico Residence under Provisos 1 and 3 because it was neither for rent nor sale at the time he refused to sell the Los Llanos Property to HAVED. The theory is that the term "such [SFHs]" in Provisos 1 and 3 unambiguously relates back to the complete phrase—"single-family house sold or rented by an owner"—in the §3603(b)(1) prefatory clause. The language of the statute is not dispositive on this issue, and the interpretation proposed by Suarez is at least plausible.

Although it is conceivable that Congress's choice of the indeterminate modifier "such" was intended only to require the counting of residences qua residences under Provisos 1 and 3—in direct contrast to the more constricted scope of the term "SFH" under Proviso 2—Provisos 1 and 3 reasonably might be read to impose the additional, distinct requirement that any SFH, regardless whether it is the defendant's "residence," be counted under Provisos 1 and 3 only if it is a "single-family house sold or rented by an owner." Indeed, Congress's choice of words—"sold or rented"—in the §3603(b)(1) prefatory clause is a most curious usage. In order for liability to attach under FHA §3604, a defendant need never have consummated the discriminatory rental or sale of the SFH to which the §3603(b)(1) prefatory clause adverts. Rather, FHA liability attaches as soon as the defendant "refuses to sell or rent after [the plaintiff makes] a bona fide offer," without regard to whether the SFH is ever "sold" or "rented" to anyone. With these linguistic difficulties in mind, it seems arguable at least, in keeping with the structure and language of the statute, that the term "such," as used in Provisos 1 and 3, imports the same "on the market" qualification necessarily implicit in the §3603(b)(1) prefatory clause.

As noted earlier, however, normally latent ambiguity in a statutory modifier like "such" should be construed in furtherance of the statute's remedial goals. Not only does the authoritative legislative history not contravene the HAVED interpretation, it contradicts the Suarez contention. Most importantly, neither hypothetical advanced by Senator Byrd assumed or intimated that the seller's residence was "on the market" at the time the discriminatory sale of the second house took place, yet Senator Byrd included both these SFHs under Provisos 1 and 3. Notwithstanding a conceivable vestige of literal ambiguity, therefore, we are persuaded to the view that the Guarico Residence must be included in the four-SFH calculus under §3603(b)(1) consistent with the FHA's legislative history and its broad remedial design.

III

At the time HAVED was denied the opportunity to acquire the Los Llanos Property, allegedly on discriminatory grounds, Suarez held an undisputed ownership interest in "more than three" "single-family houses": the Guarico Rental, the La Aldea Rental, the Los Llanos Property, House A, and the Guarico Residence. Since Suarez cannot satisfy either Proviso 1 or Proviso 3, the alleged discriminatory refusal to proceed with the HAVED rental-sale agreement relating to the Los Llanos Property did not qualify for exemption under FHA §3603(b)(1).

NOTES AND QUESTIONS

1. **Legislative Purpose of the Exemptions.** Why did Congress create these exemptions? The short answer is that they were the product of legislative compromise: Proponents hoped to use limits to the bill's coverage as a bargaining chip to help ensure its passage. The longer answer is that opponents of the FHA probably were concerned about its application to private individuals, particularly individual homeowners and small-scale landlords who might be less able to defend against lawsuits and administrative actions. Recall that for decades before *Jones v. Mayer* (1968), the Court had indicated that the 1866 Civil Rights Act was limited to state action and did not apply to private conduct. The FHA, like Title VII before it, was authorized by the Interstate Commerce Clause as well as the Thirteenth and Fourteenth Amendments. This allowed Congress to bypass concerns about state action and regulate private activity that previously had been considered outside the federal government's purview.

Although the legislative history of the FHA is sparse, bill opponents voiced concerns about the property, privacy, and associational rights of people who might be forced to reside near or sell their homes to people with whom they did not want to associate. As discussed in Chapter 3, early versions of the bills exempted private homes completely, or included private homes only in a later phase of implementation (with the assumption that such coverage might be traded away entirely to ensure passage of the broader bill). In the end, all manner of private dwellings were covered by the FHA, with only a few narrow exemptions.

There is a specific origin story for the so-called Mrs. Murphy exemption, as Professor Oliveri describes:

> Named for a fictitious elderly Irish widow who is forced to rent out rooms in her home to make ends meet, [the Mrs. Murphy exemption] first appeared in the debates over Title II of the Civil Rights Act of 1964, which addressed public accommodations, including hotels and other places of temporary lodging. Senator George D. Aiken of Vermont came up with the concept of Mrs. Murphy in order to argue that small boarding house operators should not be treated the same as big commercial hotels under the Act. He suggested that Congress "integrate the Waldorf and other large hotels, but permit the 'Mrs. Murphys,' who run small rooming houses all over the country, to rent rooms to those they choose."

During the debates over Title II, Senator Hubert Humphrey stressed that:

> There is no desire to regulate truly personal or private relationships. The so-called Mrs. Murphy provision results from a recognition of the fact that a number of people open their homes to transient guests, often not as a regular business, but as a supplement to their income. The relationships involved in such situations are clearly and unmistakably of a much closer and more personal nature than in the case of major commercial establishments.[13]

Congress ultimately defined Title II's coverage as "any inn, hotel, motel, or other establishment which provides lodging to transient guests, other than an establishment located within a building which contains not more than five rooms for rent or hire and which is actually occupied by the proprietor of such establishment as his residence." In 1968, Mrs. Murphy returned in the FHA, this time as the owner of rental property instead of an innkeeper.

What do you think of the rationales advanced for these exemptions? Are some more persuasive than others? Do they have the same force today? Is there a difference between the Mrs. Murphy who shares a boarding house with transient guests and the Mrs. Murphy who owns a four-unit building and lives in one of those units? Many of the scenarios put forth by exemption proponents assume that the individuals covered by these exemptions (e.g., Mrs. Murphy) have modest means and rely on their properties to make ends meet. Is this necessarily true? Should it matter to the application of the FHA?

2. **Narrow Construction.** What approach did the HAVED court take when engaging in statutory interpretation? Courts usually proceed from the position that, because the FHA is given a generous construction, exceptions to the statute must be construed narrowly. *See* City of Edmonds v. Oxford House, Inc., 514 U.S. 725, 731-32 (1995) (Chapter 17); *see also* Lamb v. Sallee, 417 F. Supp. 282 (E.D. Ky. 1976) (holding that a duplex is not a single-family home). As the HAVED court noted, this also mitigates against using equitable principles to expand exemptions or apply them in situations where the text has not explicitly warranted it.

---

13. Oliveri, 43 Ind. L. Rev. at 1136-37.

This is not to say that a defendant who claims the exemption will always lose in close cases. For example, in Michigan Protection and Advocacy Service, Inc. v. Babin, 18 F.3d 337, 342-43 (6th Cir. 1994), a real estate agent named Beverly Hammonds purchased a home and planned to lease it to a group home for disabled adults. Neighbors who opposed the lease offered to purchase the home from her, and she sold it to them, making a profit on the sale. A state agency and several persons with disabilities sued, challenging interference with the proposed lease. Hammonds claimed the §3603(b)(1) exemption, which the plaintiffs disputed, arguing that because she had participated in many home sales over the prior two years, she could not meet the requirement that she had not "made a similar sale within the past twenty-four months." The court disagreed, holding that this requirement referred to sales in which the defendant had an ownership interest in the property and was not merely earning a commission for brokering the sale. The plaintiffs also argued that Hammonds failed to meet the requirement that the sale be accomplished without the use "in any manner" of the sales or rental services or facilities of a real estate broker, because she had used closing documents featuring the logo of the company for which she worked (Century 21) and the preprinted signature of another agent (Kersten). The court held:

> Even though the statutory language, "in any manner," is very broad, Hammonds did not use the "facilities" or "services" of a real estate service or broker within the meaning of the FHAA. Although Hammonds used the Century 21 forms, she acquired the documents directly from Transamerica Title Company. Transamerica had these pre-printed forms in its possession because Century 21 frequently used the services of the title company. Transamerica, however, provided and assumed responsibility for the pre-printed forms. Finally, at the time of the sale, the 24 Mile Road property was not listed with Century 21, the Transamerica employees did not think that Kersten was involved in the sale, and Century 21 did not receive any commission from the sale. Consequently, the closing documents appear to be nothing more than form papers necessary to perfect title. As such, Hammonds's use of these documents does not vitiate the exemption provided by §3603(b).

3. **The §3604(c) Exception to the §3603(b) Exemptions.** Note that even properties and people that are exempted by §3603(b) from most of the FHA's provisions are *not* exempt from §3604(c). In this way, we can consider §3604(c) an "exception to the exemption." In essence, this means that a Mrs. Murphy landlord might lawfully discriminate against people with protected characteristics, but may not state or advertise the fact that she is doing so. In fact, an otherwise exempt single-family property owner loses the exemption entirely for certain violations of §3604(c). *See* §3604(b)(1) (exemption conditioned on rental or sale "without the publication, posting or mailing, after notice, of any advertisement or written notice in violation of section 3604(c)"). Why should the FHA's prohibition against discriminatory statements, notices, and advertisements remain applicable to otherwise exempt properties?

Professor Schwemm argues that this exemption exception can be explained by looking to the purposes of both §3604(c) and the broader FHA:

> The three main purposes of §3604(c) — avoiding market narrowing, protecting against psychic injury, and public education — directly bear on the FHA's ultimate goals of eliminating housing discrimination and achieving residential integration. These goals can only be achieved if the entrenched discriminatory system that pervaded America's housing markets in 1968 is eliminated and, in addition, if people come to believe this system is in fact being eliminated. Discriminatory statements in violation of §3604(c) discourage minority home seekers and other relevant participants from believing housing markets are indeed open to all. Thus, §3604(c), including its applicability to otherwise exempt housing . . . must be seen as a consciously devised and important part of the overall arsenal provided by Congress to battle housing discrimination.[14]

2. Private Clubs and Religious Organizations

Section 3607(a) provides two exemptions. The first is for religious organizations, specifying that:

> Nothing in this subchapter shall prohibit a religious organization, association, or society, or any nonprofit institution or organization operated, supervised or controlled by or in conjunction with a religious organization, association, or society, from limiting the sale, rental or occupancy of dwellings which it owns or operates for other than a commercial purpose to persons of the same religion, or from giving preference to such persons, unless membership in such religion is restricted on account of race, color, or national origin.

The second is for private clubs. It says:

> Nor shall anything in this subchapter prohibit a private club not in fact open to the public, which as an incident to its primary purpose or purposes provides lodgings which it owns or operates for other than a commercial purpose, from limiting the rental or occupancy of such lodgings to its members or from giving preference to its members.

The following case provides an example of a defendant that sought to claim both exemptions.

United States v. Columbus Country Club
915 F.2d 877 (3d Cir. 1990), *cert. denied*, 501 U.S. 1205 (1991)

Before Mansmann, Greenberg and Seitz, Circuit Judges.

---

14. Robert G. Schwemm, *Discriminatory Housing Statements and Section 3604(c): A New Look at the Fair Housing Act's Most Intriguing Provision*, 29 FORDHAM URB. L.J. 187, 250-51 (2001).

SEITZ, Circuit Judge.

The facts material to our disposition are not in dispute. The Columbus Country Club (defendant) was formed in 1920 by the Knights of Columbus, a Roman Catholic men's organization, and incorporated in 1922 as the Tri-Council Country Club. It changed its name to the Columbus Country Club in 1924. In 1936, defendant eliminated the requirement that members belong to the Knights of Columbus but retained the requirement that members be Catholic males. There is no legal relationship with the Knights of Columbus.

Defendant presently maintains a community of 46 summer homes (called "bungalows") located on a 23-acre tract of land along the Delaware River north of Philadelphia. Defendant's by-laws prohibit members from occupying their bungalows from October through April. Even if a family wanted to live in a bungalow year round, the lack of running water and heating facilities would make it impracticable.

Defendant is organized as a non-profit organization, and its membership is comprised of annual, associate and social members. Annual members are those members who own bungalows and vote on all matters affecting the organization. The annual members own the land collectively. Pursuant to a leasehold agreement, defendant leases bungalow lots to the annual members for an annual fee. Annual members must be members in good standing of the Roman Catholic Church. Associate members are adults over age 21 who live in the bungalows throughout the summer, but are not annual members. These individuals are generally the immediate family of annual members. Social members are close friends and relatives of annual members who do not occupy bungalows throughout the summer. Neither associate members nor social members are required to be Roman Catholic. Until amendment of the by-laws in 1987, the club restricted annual membership to men.

Defendant is not formally affiliated with the Roman Catholic Church, nor with any Catholic organization. Prior to 1987, the "purpose" section of defendant's by-laws did not mention Catholicism or affiliation with the Roman Catholic Church. As laid out in the original charter:

> The purpose for which the corporation is formed is the maintenance of a Club for social enjoyments, in order to cultivate cordial relations and sentiments of friendship among its members and provide accommodations for social intercourse, outdoor sport, and healthful recreation for them.

Notwithstanding the lack of formal ties between the Church and defendant, many of its members are practicing Catholics. In 1922, the Archbishop of Philadelphia granted the club special permission for the celebration of mass on the club grounds each Sunday and provided a priest from a nearby town for such services. Some members conduct the rosary each night in the chapel. A statue of the Virgin Mary stands in the grotto near the entrance to the club.

Defendant follows a formal procedure in admitting new members to the community. Since the 1987 amendments to the by-laws, the membership applications must be accompanied by a written recommendation from the applicant's parish priest stating that the applicant is a practicing Roman Catholic in good standing. The full Board, by majority vote, makes the final decision on the admission of new members.

This lawsuit stems from the efforts of associate member Anita Gualtieri to become an annual member. Mrs. Gualtieri first applied for membership in 1986 so that she could purchase from her mother the leasehold on the bungalow that her family had held since the 1950's. She was informed that she was not eligible for annual membership because she was a woman. Her husband was also ineligible for annual membership because he was not a member of the Roman Catholic Church. Failing to have the eligibility requirements amended, Mrs. Gualtieri wrote to the Cardinal's Commission on Human Relations and Urban Ministry to complain of defendant's discriminatory practices. After an investigation, the Archdiocese informed defendant that the allegations were not unwarranted and threatened to withdraw permission to hold mass at the club. Subsequently, defendant revised its by-laws to make them gender-neutral, but did not alter the requirement that annual members be Roman Catholic. Rather, language was added to the purpose section emphasizing the religious aspects of the community's life and adding the requirement of a written statement from the parish priest attesting to an applicant's status as a member of the Roman Catholic Church.

Mrs. Gualtieri's mother inherited her deceased husband's leasehold and quasi-proprietary interest in their bungalow. As a widow, she was given all the rights under the leasehold except annual membership in the club since at that time annual membership was restricted to males. Mrs. Gualtieri reapplied for annual membership in 1987. The Board of Governors considered and voted against her application based allegedly on the family's prior demonstrated lack of ability to get along with the community and lack of interest in the religious aspects of the community.

Mrs. Gualtieri notified the Civil Rights Division of the DOJ of defendant's policies, and it subsequently filed suit, alleging a pattern and practice of discrimination in the sale of dwellings, on account of religion and sex, in violation of the FHA. After a hearing on the parties' cross-motions for summary judgment, the district court held that defendant was exempt from the Act under both the religious organization and private club exemptions. [The court ultimately dismissed the action in its entirety with prejudice.] The government filed a timely notice of appeal.

III. FAIR HOUSING ACT

The government alleges that defendant's policy and practice of prohibiting the sale of bungalows to non-Catholics violates the FHA. Defendant does not deny that it discriminates on the basis of religion; rather, it contends that the bungalows are not "dwellings" because they are not capable of being occupied as year-round residences. [The court determined that the bungalows at issue were "dwellings" under the FHA.]

IV. STATUTORY EXEMPTIONS

Defendant asserts that even if the bungalows fall within the statutory definition of "dwelling," it is exempt from the FHA under the exemptions provided
by 42 U.S.C. §3607(a) for religious organizations and private clubs. "Under
general principles of statutory construction, '[o]ne who claims the benefit of
an exception from the prohibition of a statute has the burden of proving that
his claim comes within the exception.'" Thus, defendant has the burden of
proving that it falls within the statutory exemption provided for religious
organizations or private clubs as a matter of law.

Religious Organization Exemption

Defendant's first affirmative defense is that it is exempt from the FHA under
§3607(a)'s exemption for religious organizations. To fit into this exemption,
defendant must prove that it is either: (1) a religious organization, or (2) a
non-profit organization "operated, supervised or controlled by or in conjunction with" a religious organization.

The district court concluded and defendant does not dispute that it is not
itself a "religious organization." The dispute centers instead upon whether
defendant is "operated, supervised or controlled by or in conjunction with" a
religious organization.

The government argues that the quoted language implies a hierarchical relationship in which the non-profit entity is subordinate to the religious
organization. At the very least, the government contends, there must be some
direct affiliation between the religious organization and the other organization, as would be the case with a religious school, for example. This interpretation finds some support in the limited legislative history. Senator Mondale,
whose amendment to the 1968 Civil Rights Act was adopted by Congress to
create Title VIII, stated: "There is an exemption to permit religious institutions
or schools, etc., affiliated with them, to give preference in housing to persons
of their own religion despite the Act."

As the government argues, the Catholic Church does not operate, supervise or control defendant. There is no formal or legal relationship between
them. At the most, the Church approves of and supports defendant by permitting religious services to be conducted on the premises.

Defendant responds that it is "operated in conjunction with a religious
organization" and is directly affiliated with the Catholic Archdiocese. In support of its response, defendant argues that the exemption for religious organizations should be read broadly, and that the undisputed facts demonstrate
that defendant is entitled to the exemption as a matter of law.

Defendant contends that the broad language of the exemption and the
common dictionary meaning of the words used indicate that the relationship
between the religious organization and the non-profit organization may consist of anything ranging from a formal, highly structured, hierarchical relationship to an informal, loosely-structured relationship. Additionally, defendant

asserts, the religious exemption reflects Congress's sensitivity to first amendment rights. Consequently, defendant argues, the exemption should be broadly construed to cover activity that is permitted, but not required, by the Church.

We cannot agree with defendant's contention that the exemption is to be read broadly. A unanimous Supreme Court mandated in *Trafficante v. Metropolitan Life Ins.*, a "generous construction" of the FHA, in order to carry out a "policy that Congress considered to be of the highest priority." The logical corollary to such a construction, as well as the general rule of statutory interpretation, is to construe narrowly any exemptions to the Act. Such a narrow reading is also supported by the only case interpreting Title VIII's religious exemption that we have found. *See* United States v. Hughes Memorial Home, 396 F. Supp. 544, 550 (W.D. Va. 1975) ("In view of the Supreme Court's holding that the FHA must be accorded a generous construction, the general principle requiring the strict reading of exemptions from the Act applies here with even greater force.").

In holding that defendant fell within the exemption for religious organizations, the district court relied upon the defendant's affiliation with the Church as evidenced by the Church's grant of the privilege of having weekly mass celebrated on the grounds and its tacit approval of the recital of the rosary. In reaching its conclusion, the district court found that the Catholic Church does not actually "control" the club or its operations. The district court did state, however, that "the persons who, over the years, have operated and controlled the club, have done so 'in conjunction with' their continuing obligations as members of the Roman Catholic faith," and went on to conclude that "[a]s a practical matter, by virtue of its ability to grant or withhold the privilege of holding religious services in the club chapel . . . the Archdiocese does possess a very significant degree of control over the club itself."

We do not think that these undisputed facts are sufficient to hold that defendant carried its burden. The critical words of the exemption are "in conjunction with," and so there must be a mutual relationship between the non-profit society and a religious organization. The existence of this relationship cannot depend solely on the activities of the non-profit organization nor be viewed only from its perspective. Indeed, evidence of the club's unilateral activities would go to whether it is itself a religious organization not to whether it is operated "in conjunction with" a religious organization. Furthermore, the Church's ability to withdraw permission to hold mass and the fact that on one occasion it may have indirectly influenced the club's Board of Governors by threatening to do so are not enough. Without further evidence of interaction or involvement by the Church, we cannot conclude that as a matter of law the Church controlled the defendant or that the defendant was operated "in conjunction with" the Church. Consequently, on this record and in light of our unwillingness to read the statutory exemption broadly, we hold that the defendant failed to carry its burden of proving its entitlement to the religious organization exemption.

Private Club Exemption

Defendant's second affirmative defense is that it falls within the exemption for private clubs, as the district court held. Again, the defendant has the burden of proving its entitlement to this statutory exemption.

We believe that to fall within this statutory exemption five conditions must be met. The defendant must: (1) be a "private club not in fact open to the public;" (2) provide "lodgings;" and (3) only limit the "rental or occupancy of such lodgings." Furthermore, if a defendant provides "lodgings," those lodgings must be: (4) provided "as an incident to its [defendant's] primary purpose or purposes;" and (5) owned or operated "for other than a commercial purpose." We do not address the district court's determination that the defendant was a private club satisfying condition (1) because we are content that our conclusions with respect to conditions (2) and (3) are fully dispositive.

To determine whether defendant's bungalows satisfy condition (2), we begin, as we must, by examining the statutory text. Since the private club exemption is part of the same section that provides the exemption for religious organizations, it is instructive to note the differences. In the first place, the word "lodgings" has replaced the word "dwellings," and the word "sale" has been deleted. Furthermore, the private club exemption requires that the club provide lodgings only "as an incident to its primary purpose or purposes." Thus, the overall effect of these changes is to carefully limit the exemption.

Congress' intention to limit the exemption is borne out by the legislative history. Senator Kuchel, the sponsor of the amendment that modified the wording of the exemption, explained that the purpose of the changes was: "to tighten the exemption now provided in the substitute referring to bona fide private clubs."

The private club exemption was introduced in Senator Dirksen's amendment to his own substitute bill. The original wording was:

> Nor shall anything in this title prohibit a bona fide private club from limiting the sale, rental, or occupancy of dwellings which it owns or operates for other than a commercial purpose to members of the club or from giving preference to such members.

Senator Kuchel subsequently introduced an amendment that substituted the word "lodgings" for "dwellings," deleted the word "sale," and added the language "as an incident to its primary purpose or purposes."

Defendant argues that it provides "lodgings," because according to the dictionary, a lodging is a "dwelling," and Congress drew no durational distinction between the two terms, as it did in Title II when it modified "lodging" with the words "to transient guests." This indicates, defendant contends, that the word lodging by itself does not connote occupancy of limited duration and therefore the terms "lodging" and "dwelling" should be considered interchangeable.

Section 201 et seq. of Title II prohibits discrimination in places of public accommodation. A place of public accommodation is defined in part as: "any inn, hotel, motel, or other establishment which provides lodging to transient guests. . . ." The government responds that defendant does not provide "lodgings" because its bungalows are "dwellings" in the sense of summer residences, not temporary accommodations as Congress intended.

Although the district court recognized that a distinction might be drawn between "dwelling" and "lodging" on the basis of the duration of contemplated occupancy, it did not agree that Congress intended this distinction to have any significance. We do not think that this conclusion comports with Congress' deliberate substitution of the word "lodging" for "dwelling" and the plain statement of intent repeatedly expressed by Senator Kuchel, the amendment's sponsor, that the language modifications were designed "to tighten [Senator Dirksen's] amendment as much as possible to avoid possible abuse." Therefore, we conclude that defendant has not shown that it provides "lodgings" as required by condition (2) of the private club exemption.

The government also argues that the defendant fails to satisfy condition (3) because the private club exemption, by its express terms, applies only to the "rental or occupancy" of lodgings, not to their sale. Thus, the government claims that even if defendant were found to meet all the other conditions of the private club exemption, it cannot protect the discriminatory sale of dwellings by its annual members. Again, the government asserts that this interpretation is borne out by the legislative history which indicates that the word "sale" was deleted at the same time that the word "lodging" was substituted for "dwelling."

At oral argument, defendant responded to the government's argument, contending that it meets the "rental or occupancy" requirement. Defendant's argument is that by limiting the sale of the bungalows to Catholics, the club is limiting the occupancy of the bungalows and the rental of the ground on which the bungalows sit. So, defendant argues, the club is "in effect" limiting the occupancy and rental of lodgings.

Although the district court noted the government's argument, it did not address the government's position. We believe that the plain language of the exemption and the legislative history of the Act exempt only the "rental or occupancy" of lodgings, not their sale. So, even though limiting the sale of bungalows to Catholics might have the effect of limiting the rental or occupancy of lodgings, we conclude that defendant's policy and practice of discriminating against persons in the sale of bungalows falls outside the plain language of the private club exemption.

We conclude that defendant has failed to show that the bungalows are lodgings and that its restrictions upon the sale of bungalows are merely limits on "rental or occupancy." Therefore, we conclude that as a matter of law defendant has not met its burden of proving that it falls within Title VIII's limited statutory exemption for private clubs.

Defendant also argues that application of the FHA violates the free exercise and establishment clauses of the first amendment as well as the defendant's first amendment right to free association. Because the district court did not address those arguments, we will not do so either, preferring to have the district court consider them in the first instance.

V.

We are satisfied that the record does not, as a matter of law, support summary judgment for defendant on either of its affirmative defenses. We will, therefore, reverse the orders of the district court ruling that defendant meets the religious organization and private club exemptions of the FHA and dismissing the government's claim against the Columbus Country Club and remand for further proceedings.

NOTES AND QUESTIONS

1. **First Amendment Concerns.** Note that both the religious organization and the private club exemptions are rooted in First Amendment concerns about freedom of religion and associational rights. Similar concerns are reflected in the Civil Rights Act of 1964. Title II of this statute prohibits discrimination in public accommodations, but exempts private clubs from this definition. Title VII prohibits discrimination in employment, but specifically permits religious organizations to discriminate in favor of co-religionists.

2. **Limits to the Religious Exemption.** Note that the religious exemption is quite limited. To claim it, the defendant must be a bona fide religious organization, or be operating in direct conjunction with one. Why did the defendant in *Columbus Country Club* (CCC), which unquestionably was affiliated with the Catholic Church, fail to satisfy this requirement? Even if the CCC had satisfied this requirement, the exemption would permit it only to discriminate in favor of other Catholics (or against non-Catholics). In this case, the defendant was also accused of discriminating on the basis of sex, and had a clear record of sex-based discriminatory policy. What if a bona fide religious organization has, as a core religious tenet, the belief that women should not own property? Or that same-sex or interracial couples should not be permitted to live together?

3. **A Dissenting View.** Judge Mansmann wrote a lengthy dissent, in which he argued that the majority's narrow interpretation of the religious organization exemption went further than the text required:

> According to the majority, the words "in conjunction with" imply a "mutual relationship between a non-profit society and a religious organization. The existence of this relationship cannot depend solely on the activities of the non-profit organization nor be viewed only from its perspective." The majority concludes that "[w]ithout further evidence of interaction or involvement by the Church, we cannot conclude that as a matter of law the Church controlled the defendant or that the defendant was operated 'in conjunction with' the Church."

This result is not compelled by the text of the exemption itself. The language of the exemption does not focus solely upon "control" or "mutuality" but describes a number of different types of relationships which serve to bring an organization within the terms of the exemption. The majority's reliance on equivocal legislative history notwithstanding, I think it clear that the Columbus Country Club, under the terms of the statute itself, qualifies for the religious organization exemption. If Congress had meant to make control or mutuality the determinative evaluative criterion, it certainly would have expressed this intention more clearly. The exemption here must be interpreted at least as broadly as the common meaning of its text, rather than restricted to circumstances far more narrow than the meaning conveys. The majority approach simply is not supported by the plain language of the exemption.

What do you think of this argument? Is the majority's reasoning, that "in conjunction with" implies a requirement of mutuality, supported by the language of the exemption? You may be interested to know that a request for rehearing en banc garnered several votes, including that of then-Judge Samuel Alito and then Chief Judge A. Leon Higginbotham, Jr. Rehearing en banc was denied, however, as was a petition for certiorari.

4. **Exemptions and Other Statutes.** The 1866 Civil Rights Act contains no exemptions; the *Sullivan* and *Tillman* cases in Chapter 2 include unaddressed claims that the private club exemptions of the 1964 and 1968 statutes apply to the 1866 Act. These issues await resolution.

Chapter Summary

- In general, courts define a "dwelling" under the FHA by considering two factors: whether the facility is intended or designed for occupants who intend to remain for any significant period of time and whether those occupants view the facility "as a place to return to" during that period. Some courts also consider the extent to which those who occupy the facility treat it as people would treat their home.
- HUD has produced a multifactor test to determine whether a facility that includes short-term residencies is a "dwelling" within the FHA.
- Shared living facilities and roommates have presented FHA coverage issues. HUD has indicated that dormitories, as well as other facilities that offer shared sleeping and toileting facilities, may be "dwelling units." Several cases have held that dormitory rooms are "dwellings" within the meaning of the FHA, which defines "dwelling" to include a portion of a building or structure that is used or designed for use as a residence. The Ninth Circuit has held, however, that because precluding individuals from selecting roommates based on their sex, sexual orientation, and familial status raises substantial privacy-related constitutional concerns, it would not apply the FHA to the sharing of living units.
- The FHA contains a number of statutory exemptions to its coverage of certain discriminatory acts or actors. This includes exemptions

contained in §3603(b) for some single-family homes and small-scale ("Mrs. Murphy) landlords and in §3607(a) for private clubs and religious organizations.

- In general, courts have narrowly construed the reach of statutory exemptions in part because the FHA is intended to have broad coverage and application.

PART III

PROVING DISCRIMINATION: EVIDENTIARY FRAMEWORKS

The central provisions of the Fair Housing Act[1] require not only that the dwelling and the transaction at issue be covered under the Act, but also that the challenged practice be undertaken "because of" protected class status.[2] That is, the statute does not require a mere showing that the plaintiff is a member of a protected group and that the defendant took some adverse action; rather, the plaintiff also must establish by a preponderance of the evidence that the defendant took the action *because of* a protected category. Similarly, a housing practice that causes injury is not illegal under civil rights law merely because it is injurious; it is illegal only if it discriminates on the basis of protected class status.[3]

This part addresses two methods of proving that discrimination has occurred because of a protected characteristic: disparate treatment (or intentional discrimination) and disparate impact (or discriminatory effects). These theories of proof initially developed under the more frequently litigated

---

1. Housing discrimination may be actionable under a number of constitutional standards and statutes. This part deals with proving discrimination under the FHA unless otherwise indicated.
2. The FHA protected characteristics are race, color, national origin, religion, sex, familial status, and disability. This section focuses on the most typical proof frameworks relevant to 42 U.S.C. §§3604 and 3605. The provisions of the FHA requiring different proof methods are addressed in other chapters. *See, e.g.*, 42 U.S.C. §§3604(c); 3604(f)(3); 3608; 3617.
3. In some cases, the defendant may act on more than one basis. State and local governments may protect against additional bases for discrimination, such as source of income or marital status.

provisions of Title VII of the Civil Rights Act of 1964 addressing discrimination in employment and under the Constitution.[4] Subsequent case law interpreting the FHA adapted and expanded these theories to address the particular context of housing transactions and neighborhood segregation. Disparate treatment focuses on the motivation or intent behind a housing practice or, sometimes, the state of mind of the actor(s) making a particular housing decision.[5] Disparate impact focuses on the effects of a facially neutral policy or practice regardless of the intent behind it; disparate impact also may focus on the extent to which a facially neutral policy perpetuates residential segregation. Plaintiffs may pursue these theories in the alternative; they are not mutually exclusive, and "[a] single piece of evidence can support multiple theories of liability." Pacific Shores Properties, LLC v. City of Newport Beach, 730 F.3d 1142, 1166 (9th Cir. 2013).[6] Some lawyers believe that intent cases are harder to prove than are effects cases but, as the caselaw in this text demonstrates, no theory requires more or less evidence. Each theory imposes distinct evidentiary burdens to establish liability.

Chapter 6 explores the evidentiary frameworks for proving intentional discrimination. Both direct and circumstantial evidence are permissible to prove intent, with different types of circumstantial evidence being probative depending on the nature of the case.

Chapter 7 distinguishes FHA discriminatory effects claims from intent claims; features and analyzes the seminal Supreme Court opinion holding disparate impact claims cognizable under the FHA, Texas Department of Housing and Community Affairs v. Inclusive Communities Project, Inc., 576 U.S. 519 (2015); analyzes perpetuation of segregation claims; and describes the burden-shifting approaches currently applicable to FHA disparate impact claims, with some discussion of differences among the circuit courts of appeals.

---

4. Cases brought under the Fifth and Fourteenth Amendments and under the 1866 CRA require a showing of intentional discrimination. The standard for proving intent under the Constitution is discussed in Chapter 6.

5. However, intent is not relevant if a plaintiff can show "more than an isolated or accidental instance of conduct," such as a "regular, or repeated violation" of a right under the FHA. United States v. Quality Built Construction, Inc. 309 F. Supp. 2d 756, 760 (E.D.N.C. 2003) ("Defendants' intent is not relevant to the Court's determination of whether a pattern or practice of discrimination exists.").

6. Plaintiffs are not required to elect the theory of liability upon which they rely. Reyes v. Waples Mobile Home Park Ltd. P'ship, 903 F.3d 415, 421 (4th Cir. 2018). However, practically speaking, the theories have evolved to impose distinct pleading requirements and evidentiary showings; this counsels early identification of one or both theories.

CHAPTER 6

DISCRIMINATORY INTENT, DISPARATE TREATMENT

A disparate treatment claim is, as the name suggests, an allegation that a defendant treated someone differently *because of* a protected characteristic. Actions such as a refusal to rent or an eviction can be lawful when taken for legitimate reasons, such as the applicant's having insufficient income,[1] but can violate the FHA if taken for prohibited reasons. Disparate treatment need not be malicious to be unlawful;[2] nevertheless, the focus is on the intent, or motivation, behind the defendant's actions. This means that in this type of claim, the plaintiff is in the position of having to persuade a factfinder as to the state of mind of the defendant, who might not even be fully cognizant of all the motives underlying their decisions.

What if the defendant is motivated by more than one reason? An important issue in disparate treatment cases is one of causation, that is, how dominant a discriminatory motive must be to make the resulting action unlawful. It is well settled that a discriminatory motive need not be the *sole* cause of an adverse housing decision.[3] But evolving rules in other areas of civil rights law have created uncertainties about what standard of causation applies under the FHA. For example, consider a Black rental applicant with an average credit score alleging discriminatory refusal to rent. If the landlord rents to white applicants with similar or worse credit profiles but uses "bad credit" as the reason for the rejection, the Black applicant may allege that this reason is false and is a pretext for racial discrimination. But what if the landlord strictly applies credit standards across the board *and* avoids renting to Black tenants? Under the traditional FHA rule, as long as the plaintiff could establish that

---

1. *See* Akbar v. Interstate Realty Mgmt. Co., No. 22-1598, 2022 WL 4286498, at *2 (7th Cir. Sept. 16, 2022) (affirming summary judgment against rental applicant whose disability income was $15 short of minimum rental amount, holding "the Fair Housing Act does not bar discrimination based on income.").

2. *See, e.g.*, Cmty. Servs., Inc. v. Wind Gap Mun. Auth., 421 F.3d 170, 177 (3d Cir. 2005) (a plaintiff "need not prove the malice or discriminatory animus of a defendant" when challenging a facially discriminatory classification).

3. *See id.* ("The discriminatory purpose [under the FHA] need not . . . figure [] 'solely, primarily, or even predominantly' into the motivation behind the challenged action.").

race played some role and was a "motivating factor" for the refusal to rent, then the landlord's conduct could be held to have occurred "because of" race notwithstanding the credit requirements. However, a recent Supreme Court decision about a different antidiscrimination statute (§1981) applied a more stringent "but-for" causation requirement.[4] This has created some doubt about whether the traditional FHA rule applies. But-for causation means that the plaintiff must show that race made a difference to the outcome; in the above example, the plaintiff would have to show that if the applicant had not been Black, the landlord would have approved the application or applied more lenient standards. A neutral factor can be another but-for cause (there may be more than one), but the protected characteristic must make a difference to the outcome. These causation standards are further explored in §B, below.

Aside from causation, another central issue in disparate treatment cases is what kind of evidence the parties must offer and at what stage. Fair housing plaintiffs in civil litigation must prove FHA violations "by a preponderance of the evidence." Direct evidence is one type. For example, a landlord may verbalize a policy of excluding certain ethnic groups[5] or reveal a preference to avoid tenants with disabilities. Similarly, an apartment complex might adopt facially discriminatory rules restricting parts of the complex on the basis of sex or familial status. "Where a regulation or policy facially discriminates on the basis of the protected trait, in certain circumstances it may constitute per se or explicit discrimination because the protected trait by definition plays a role in the decision-making process."[6] These oral and written examples are considered direct evidence because there is no need to infer the motivation: It is explicitly stated by an individual with decisionmaking authority.[7] Thus, if valid direct evidence is presented, "very little else is required to prove a violation."[8]

In most cases, direct evidence of a housing provider's motivation is unavailable. As one court trenchantly observed: "Discriminatory intent does not always wear a top hat, twirl its mustache and cane, and laugh maniacally like an out-in-the open super villain."[9] The lack of such "smoking gun" evidence

---

4. *See* Comcast Corp. v. Nat'l Ass'n of African American-Owned Media, 589 U.S. 327 (2020).

5. *See* Watters v. The Homeowners' Ass'n at the Pres. at Bridgewater, 48 F.4th 779, 786 (7th Cir. 2022) ("[R]acial slurs are direct evidence of intentional discrimination.").

6. Curto v. A Country Place Condominium Ass'n, Inc., 921 F.3d 405, 411 (3d Cir. 2019) (holding sex-segregated swimming schedule unlawful under the FHA because its "specific inequitable features" reflected "particular assumptions about the roles of men and women" despite providing "roughly equal aggregate swimming time to each gender."). For additional analysis of the legality of facially discriminatory policies under the FHA, see Chapter 17.

7. *Cf.* Gallagher v. Magner, 619 F.3d 823, 831-32 (8th Cir. 2010), *cert. dismissed*, 565 U.S. 1187 (2012) (rejecting as direct evidence "statements by nondecisionmakers, or statements by decisionmakers unrelated to the decisional process itself").

8. Schwemm, HDLL §10:2 (text accompanying notes 6-8). Note that courts may differ in their interpretation of whether particular language constitutes direct evidence of discrimination. *See id.* (discussing cases reaching different conclusions on the use of the phrase "you people").

9. West v. DJ Mortgage, L.L.C., 164 F. Supp. 3d 1393, 1401 (N.D. Ga. 2016).

is not fatal to proving intentional discrimination, however. Plaintiffs may
establish intent by using circumstantial evidence to create an inference
that a defendant acted "because of"
protected class status.[10] The remainder of this chapter addresses the proof
frameworks available when using circumstantial evidence to prove intent.

Plaintiffs often use an inferen-
tial burden-shifting method when
no direct evidence is available, but
another approach (usually involving
groups of decisionmakers like governmental defendants) is a multifactor
inquiry, in which plaintiffs offer evidence demonstrating "'that a discriminatory reason more likely than not
motivated' the defendant and that the
defendant's actions adversely affected
the plaintiff in some way." Pacific

Shores Properties, L.L.C. v. City of Newport Beach, 730 F.3d 1142, 1158 (9th
Cir. 2013). We first turn to the more prevalent burden-shifting framework.

A. TRADITIONAL BURDEN-SHIFTING PROOF FRAMEWORK

Courts analyzing circumstantial evidence in FHA cases typically have relied
on a three-part burden-shifting standard developed by the Supreme Court for
employment cases, referred to as the *McDonnell Douglas*[11] framework:

- The plaintiff must first make an initial, multipart showing referred to
  as the **prima facie case**. The prima facie case creates a presumption of
  illegal discrimination. It is designed to raise the inference that a discriminatory motivation was behind a defendant's adverse conduct by eliminating the most likely nondiscriminatory reasons for it.

---

10. *See* Desert Palace, Inc. v. Costa, 539 U.S. 90, 100 (2003) (noting in an employment case
that "[t]he reason for treating circumstantial and direct evidence alike is both clear and deep
rooted: 'Circumstantial evidence is not only sufficient, but may also be more certain, satisfying
and persuasive than direct evidence'"). Discovery is a crucial tool for gathering additional evidence, direct and circumstantial, to prove discriminatory motivation.

11. McDonnell Douglas Corp. v. Green, 411 U.S. 792 (1973); *see also* St. Mary's Honor Center
v. Hicks, 509 U.S. 502 (1993); Texas Dept. of Community Affairs v. Burdine, 450 U.S. 248 (1981).
Note that if a plaintiff presents direct evidence of discrimination, the *McDonnell Douglas* framework is inapplicable.

- If the plaintiff is successful in making the prima facie showing, the **burden shifts** to the defendant, but only to provide one or more legitimate, nondiscriminatory reasons for the challenged action. Defendants' reasons must be "reasonably specific" and contemporaneous, not conjured after the fact, with subjective excuses inviting greater scrutiny.[12] This is not a difficult hurdle for the defendant because it requires simply offering admissible evidence of a **nondiscriminatory explanation**.[13] Moreover, this merely is a **burden of production**, not a burden of persuasion.
- The plaintiff bears the ultimate burden of persuading the factfinder that the protected characteristic motivated the defendant's decision. If the defendant succeeds in meeting its relatively low burden of production, the **burden shifts** back to the plaintiff to prove that each of the defendant's reasons is a **pretext** for some discriminatory motivation. This is a **burden of persuasion**.[14] A plaintiff may demonstrate pretext in one of two ways.[15] First, a plaintiff may show that the defendant's nondiscriminatory reason lacks credibility, which will permit (but not require) a factfinder to infer a discriminatory motive. Or a plaintiff may offer additional circumstantial evidence that a discriminatory reason more likely than not explains the outcome. For example, the plaintiff may point to the defendant's more favorable treatment of similarly situated individuals who are not members of the plaintiff's protected group.

Although parties tend to focus on the plaintiff's ability to satisfy the last step of showing pretext, defendants do occasionally challenge plaintiff's prima facie case. Here is an example of a prima facie case for a §3604(a) housing denial claim:

1. The plaintiff is a member of a protected class.
2. The plaintiff applied for and was qualified for the housing opportunity.
3. The plaintiff was rejected by the defendant.
4. The housing remained available thereafter (or was offered to a nonprotected class member).

Note that the specific allegations required to establish a prima facie case will vary according to the claims and facts for each case (for example, different facts would need to be alleged for a §3604(b) discriminatory terms and conditions claim).

---

12. *See* Schwemm, HDLL §10:2 (notes 47-52 and accompanying text).

13. *See* Crain v. City of Selma, 952 F.3d 634, 642 (5th Cir. 2020) ("[Antidiscrimination] laws 'do not require [defendants] to make proper decisions, only non-[discriminatory] ones.'").

14. Confusingly, the term "burden of proof" often is used to refer to both the burden of production and the burden of persuasion.

15. Reeves v. Sanderson Plumbing Prods., Inc., 530 U.S. 133, 146-48 (2000).

In the next case, the court considered both the form and function of the prima facie case and the degree of flexibility the court would permit the plaintiffs in satisfying this burden.

Lindsay v. Yates
578 F.3d 407 (6th Cir. 2009)

Before: Keith, Moore, and Cole, Circuit Judges.

Damon J. Keith, Circuit Judge.[16]

I.

This case arises from JoAnn Yates' refusal to sell her family home at 2268 Eckert Road in Mansfield, Ohio to qualified African American buyers Douglas and Tina Lindsay based on her alleged desire to keep the property "in the family." The property was acquired by JoAnn and her husband Gene Yates during the 1970s, and [their] children, Brent Yates and Deborah Yates, both grew up in the home. The house has remained vacant [in recent years]. At the time of trial, the properties surrounding 2268 Eckert were either owned directly by members of the Yates family or by Mid Ohio Pipeline, a business entity owned by Brent.

The district court summarized the time-line of relevant events:

> Around May 2004, with the house vacant, Gene suggested to JoAnn that they sell the home. JoAnn [allegedly][17] resisted, wanting to "keep it in the family." Ultimately, Gene prevailed, and he and JoAnn contacted defendant Carol Eicher to list the property for sale. Eicher is a licensed realtor associated with defendant Sluss Realty Company, a real estate brokerage. The house was put on the market, with the listing to expire on February 8, 2005.

> Towards the end of September 2004, Gene Yates was diagnosed with lung cancer. On January 12, 2005, Gene Yates passed away. [Joann alleges] that [a]bout two weeks before his death, [Gene] and JoAnn had agreed to take the house off the market. However, in the subsequent weeks before his death, Gene did not take the house off the market. Brent Yates took over responsibility for the sale of the home. . . .

> On February 8, 2005, Eicher called Brent Yates to tell him that the listing on his parents' property was about to expire and asked if she should speak with JoAnn. Brent indicated that would not be necessary because he had the authority to handle the paperwork; he subsequently signed a listing extension.

> During April 2005, plaintiffs Douglas and Tina Lindsay visited the Yates' property with their real estate agent. The Lindsays subsequently submitted a written offer through their agent to Eicher, the Yates' agent. Eicher conveyed the offer to Brent, who rejected it. However, after some negotiation, the parties arrived at a purchase price of $175,000. On May 12, 2005, the Lindsays signed a purchase agreement, and Brent signed the next day.

---

16. [Eds.—Notice that Judge Keith also authored the decision in *Zuch v. Hussey* (see Chapter 7 for a biographical note on his extraordinary life and career)].

17. [Eds.—All brackets in original unless otherwise indicated.]

On May 24, 2005, Sluss and Eicher informed the Lindsays that the sales contract would be terminated because JoAnn Yates could not bear to part with the property "for sentimental reasons." Based upon certain events that occurred between May 13, when Brent signed, and May 24, when JoAnn terminated the purchase agreement, the Lindsays believe that JoAnn's reason for terminating was pretext; they believe that JoAnn Yates did not want to sell them the property because they are African American. The exact timing of these intervening events is highly disputed. [EDS.—The district court noted that both parties offered inconsistent evidence.]

The parties agree that the purchase agreement was terminated on May 24th. Since [then, JoAnn] has not filed an extension of the real estate listing or otherwise made any effort to sell the home. After the commencement of the instant lawsuit in June 2005, JoAnn offered to sell the house to the Lindsays on the same terms as the original purchase agreement, but the Lindsays declined the offer.

II.

[EDS.—The Lindsays sued in federal court, which dismissed all the discrimination claims for failure to plead sufficient facts establishing each element of a prima facie case. On appeal, the court reversed and remanded, holding under Swierkiewicz v. Sorema N.A., 534 U.S. 506 (2002), that a discrimination plaintiff need not plead facts establishing a prima facie case to survive a motion to dismiss. On remand, the district court granted summary judgment to defendants based on the Lindsays' failure to offer evidence establishing the fourth element of the prima facie case, that the property remained on the market after termination of the purchase agreement.]

IV.

Before this Court on appeal are the Lindsays' claims of housing discrimination filed pursuant to the FHA, the 1866 CRA, and state law, which turn on the three-part evidentiary standard first developed in *McDonnell Douglas Corp. v. Green*.

A. *Prima Facie* Case

In this appeal, the Lindsays challenge the district court's award of summary judgment in favor of the defendants based on the court's ruling that the Lindsays could not demonstrate a *prima facie* case of housing discrimination. The Lindsays have not offered any direct evidence of intentional discrimination, thus we focus only on the requirements for establishing a *prima facie* case through circumstantial evidence.

This Court has employed a slightly different formulation [of the *McDonnell Douglas* test] in the context of housing discrimination. Specifically, we have held that a *prima facie* case arises when: (1) the plaintiff is a member of a racial minority; (2) he or she applied for and was qualified to purchase certain property or housing; (3) he or she was rejected; and (4) the housing remained available thereafter. The Yateses concede that the Lindsays can prove the first three elements of this test. However, the Yateses argue the district court correctly found the Lindsays were not able meet the fourth element ("remained available") in establishing a *prima facie* case. The Lindsays counter that the district court erred by requiring them to offer evidence that 2268 Eckert "remained available" after the Yateses terminated the purchase agreement. They contend that the evidence creates a genuine issue of material fact as to the *prima facie* case of discrimination under the *McDonnell Douglas* framework, as modified for housing claims, notwithstanding their inability to satisfy the "remained available" prong. For the reasons below, we rule in favor of the plaintiffs.

The Supreme Court has emphasized that the *prima facie* standard offered in *McDonnell Douglas* was not "inflexible" and that the specific proof required of the plaintiff in that particular case was "not necessarily applicable in every respect in differing factual situations." Texas Dep't of Comm. Affairs v. Burdine, 450 U.S. 248, 254 n.6 (1981) (quoting *McDonnell Douglas*). Satisfaction of the *McDonnell Douglas* four-element test creates an inference of discrimination "only because we presume these acts, if otherwise unexplained, are more likely than not based on the consideration of impermissible factors." Thus, the key question this Court must answer is whether the plaintiffs have "presented sufficient evidence to permit a reasonable jury to conclude [they] suffered" an adverse housing action "under circumstances giving rise to an inference of unlawful discrimination," not whether the *prima facie* elements specifically articulated in *McDonnell Douglas*—as reinterpreted for housing cases—could be established. We remain mindful that the burden of establishing, much less creating a genuine issue of material fact over, a *prima facie* case "is not onerous."

In *Shah v. General Elec. Co.*, this Court considered a summary judgment order to deny the plaintiff's employment discrimination claim stemming from his termination. Although ultimately affirming the district court's decision, we emphasized the plaintiff need not offer evidence that his "employer continued to solicit applications" to prove a *prima facie* case of discrimination. Embracing the flexibility characterizing *McDonnell Douglas*, we indicated that "some additional evidence tend[ing] to establish the inference of discrimination" could also satisfy the *prima facie* burden. "Continuing to solicit applications" is simply the employment analog to the housing discrimination element that a property "remain available" after the plaintiffs were rejected. Accordingly, a plaintiff's inability to create a genuine issue of material fact over the "remained available" element is not necessarily fatal to a *prima facie* housing discrimination claim on summary judgment so long as there exists "additional evidence" from which a reasonable juror could find an inference of discrimination. Thus, we rule the district court erred in granting the Yateses' motion for summary judgment on the ground that there was no evidence in the record that 2268 Eckert "remained available."

Nevertheless, a plaintiff cannot carry the *prima facie* burden for showing housing discrimination merely by offering evidence that he was a qualified minority purchaser whose competitive offer for a property was rejected. This Circuit has long held that satisfaction of the first three elements of the *McDonnell Douglas prima facie* case "without more" cannot give rise to an inference of unlawful discrimination.[18] The something "more" or "additional evidence" [to satisfy the fourth prima facie element] typically consists of favorable treatment for similarly-situated individuals not within the plaintiff's protected group.

But while a discriminatory inference is *usually*, and perhaps most readily, generated through evidence of unfavorable treatment of the minority plaintiff vis-a-vis similarly-situated individuals, *McDonnell Douglas* and its progeny do not require this always be the case as the Yateses contend. As this Court has recognized, the *prima facie* inquiry "was never intended to be rigid, mechanized, or ritualistic. Rather, it is merely a sensible, orderly way to evaluate the evidence in light of common experience as it bears on the critical question of discrimination." A *prima facie* case is established whenever the actions taken by the property owner lead one to reasonably "infer, if such actions remain unexplained, that it is more likely than not that such actions were based on discriminatory criterion" such as race. Keeping this ultimate inquiry in mind, we find that so long as "additional evidence" exists—beyond showing the first three elements of the *McDonnell Douglas* test—that indicates discriminatory intent in "light of common experience," the required "inference of discrimination" can be made in satisfaction of the *prima facie* case. This holds true even if the plaintiff is not necessarily able to identify similarly-situated individuals outside of the relevant protected group who were treated more favorably.

The "additional evidence" which can be relied upon to establish a *prima facie* claim depends on the attendant facts and circumstances. In this case, the suspicious timing of the termination of the purchasing agreement provides the evidentiary basis for inferring the Yateses acted with discriminatory motives.

[EDs. — The court discussed the significance of timing in the analogous context of Title VII retaliation claims.] To establish a *prima facie* case of unlawful retaliation, the plaintiff must demonstrate, *inter alia*, a causal connection between the protected activity (like filing a complaint for unlawful

---

18. [Fn. 9 in original] The Lindsays weakly suggest that it is in "dispute" whether the *prima facie* case can be established through demonstration of the first three elements alone. While this may be true of other circuits, the Sixth Circuit has clearly held that mere satisfaction of the first three elements of the *prima facie* discrimination case, "without more," cannot give rise to an inference of unlawful discrimination. [Plaintiffs' cited case] held that the African American plaintiffs could demonstrate a *prima facie* case of housing discrimination when the defendant refused to sell his home to the qualified plaintiffs and took it off the market but subsequently gave it to his daughter who rented it out to other persons. [Thus], the respective courts relied on "something more" than the first three elements of *McDonnell Douglas* to find the possibility of a *prima facie* case of discrimination.

discrimination) and the employer's materially adverse action (such as termination). Causation is found where the plaintiff "proffer[s] evidence sufficient to raise the inference that [the] protected activity was the likely reason for the adverse action." This Title VII retaliation analysis bears close resemblance to the *prima facie* inquiry required for racial discrimination claims analyzed under *McDonnell Douglas*. In both instances, the court is seeking to determine whether the circumstances create an inference that the defendant acted with impermissible motives. Just as a reasonable juror may infer a plaintiff's undertaking of a protected activity was the likely reason for the defendant's adverse action when the temporal proximity is "very close" in retaliation cases, so too could the juror infer discriminatory motives when the defendant refuses to consummate a purchase agreement for real property soon after discovering the racial identity of the prospective buyers.

In this case, Brent accepted in writing the Lindsays' purchase offer for 2268 Eckert on May 13, 2005. The Yateses cancelled the purchase agreement on May 24, 2005—just two days after the Lindsays allege that Brent met Douglas Lindsay and discovered the prospective buyers were African American. Prior to this face-to-face meeting, the Yateses had not given any indication that they intended to back out of the deal. Rather, Brent had agreed to modifications in the agreement on May 18, 2005. The two-day lapse alleged by the plaintiffs falls well within the range that constitutes "very close" temporal proximity. *See* Singfield v. Akron Metro. Hous. Auth., 389 F.3d 555, 563 (6th Cir. 2004) (finding that temporal proximity of three months was "significant enough to constitute sufficient evidence of a causal connection" in satisfaction of a *prima facie* case). Thus, we find that the very close temporal proximity between Brent and Douglas Lindsay's face-to-face meeting and the cancellation of the purchase agreement creates an inference of unlawful discrimination for the purposes of summary judgment.[19] In other words, it would permit a reasonable juror to find it more likely than not that racial animus motivated the Yateses' decision.

The Yateses contend that the termination of the purchase agreement on May 24, 2005, occurred several days after Douglas and Brent met, not just two days later as alleged by the Lindsays. As a result, they essentially argue the nexus of events is not as close as the Lindsays claim and is, therefore, inadequate to create an inference of discrimination. But even if the relevant time lapse was ten days, it would still fall within the very close temporal range, which a reasonable juror could consider suspicious. *See* DiCarlo [v. Potter, 358 F.3d 408, 421-22 (6th Cir. 2004)] (twenty-one day lapse between protected

---

19. [Fn. 13 in original] Although not nearly as significant as temporal proximity, the identity of the land owners surrounding 2268 Eckert also contributes to our inference of discrimination at the summary judgment stage. Specifically, the adjacent properties to the east and west, as well as the properties located to the rear of 2268 Eckert and directly across the street, were owned by either members of the Yates family or by a business owned and operated by Brent. The fact that the Yateses lived and worked in the surrounding area renders it more likely that they would act against their financial interests to the extent they harbored racial animus.

activity and adverse employer action was grounds for inferring an improper motive in Title VII retaliation context). Moreover, whether the alleged time line proffered by the Yateses is actually correct is not relevant at this stage of the proceedings. On summary judgment, we must accept the non-moving party's evidence as true. The Yateses' proposed time-line is simply beyond our purview in the instant appeal.

For these reasons, we conclude the Lindsays carried their *prima facie* burden on summary judgment and could establish an inference of discrimination based on the evidence. In doing so, we emphasize that this Court takes no position on the credibility of either side—as that is the province of the finder of fact. Our holding is limited to the recognition of a genuine issue of material fact concerning the *prima facie* case, as well as the issue of pretext as discussed *infra*, that renders judgment as a matter of law unsuitable. Accordingly, we find the district court erred in granting the Yateses' motion for summary judgment.

B. Pretext

The Yateses argue they are entitled to summary judgment, even if the Lindsays could create a genuine issue of material over the *prima facie* claim of housing discrimination, because the Lindsays have failed to offer evidence that the Yateses' articulated reason for terminating the purchase agreement was a pretext for discrimination. We disagree.

The non-discriminatory reason proffered by the Yateses for cancelling the purchase agreement was that JoAnn wanted to keep the 2268 Eckert property "in the family" and that she was unaware it was on the market when the Lindsays contracted to buy it. In support of this contention, the Yateses presented sworn testimony from JoAnn and Brent that JoAnn did not wish to sell the 2268 Eckert property—the residence in which her children were raised—and that the house was left on the market after the death of her husband as a result of a lack of communication between JoAnn and Brent. We find this explanation is non-discriminatory and satisfies the Yateses' burden of production under *McDonnell Douglas*. Accordingly, the "mandatory presumption of discrimination" created by the *prima facie* test "drops from the case."

The burden of production of evidence shifts back to the Lindsays to point to evidence that the Yateses' proffered justification is a pretext for unlawful discrimination. We have previously explained the applicable pretext analysis:

> Pretext can be established by (1) a direct evidentiary showing that a discriminatory reason more likely motivated the employer or by (2) an indirect evidentiary showing that the employer's explanation is not credible. However, mere conjecture that the employer's explanation is a pretext for intentional discrimination is an insufficient basis for denial of summary judgment. To avoid summary judgment, the plaintiff is required to produce evidence that the employer's proffered reasons were factually untrue. Despite the shifting burdens of production, the ultimate burden of persuasion remains at all times with the plaintiff.

The Lindsays seek to prove pretext by showing the Yateses' explanation for cancelling the purchase agreement is not credible. Although the Yateses claim the record does not include any evidence that could establish that the proffered reason for terminating the purchase agreement was factually untrue, the timing of the termination of the purchase agreement itself casts doubt on the veracity of the Yateses' explanation. *See* Asmo [v. Keane, Inc., 471 F.3d 588, 593 (6th Cir. 2006) (while temporal proximity "cannot alone prove pretext . . . [it] can be used as 'indirect evidence' to support an employee's claim of pretext"). Moreover, notable inconsistencies in the record further raise suspicion as to the validity of the Yateses' non-discriminatory reason. Specifically, Carol Eicher, the Yateses' realtor, testified that Brent explained to her that his mother's motivation for not selling the property was that "the closer we got to closing the more emotional [JoAnn] became." A reasonable juror could infer from this testimony that JoAnn gradually arrived at a decision not to sell the home for sentimental reasons after learning of the agreement with the Lindsays. But this notion is at odds with Brent's separate allegation that JoAnn instructed him to terminate the purchasing agreement as soon as she found out that he had contracted to sell the property. The possibility that JoAnn was aware of the contract on the house for several days prior to cancelling the deal, with Brent and Douglas Lindsay's meeting occurring in the intervening period, undermines the Yateses' fundamental allegation that JoAnn had already made up her mind not to sell the property before the Lindsays' offer and that she ordered Brent to cancel the deal when she first learned of it.

In addition, despite JoAnn's expressed desire to keep the home "in the family," she acknowledged that nobody in the family actually wanted the residence. She also maintained that she was emotionally attached to the property. Yet she admitted that she had agreed, even if reluctantly, to list 2268 Eckert before her husband's death and that she never took the property off the market nor did she advise her realtor not to sell the property before the Lindsays contracted to buy the property. These disconnects between motivation and conduct also cast doubt on the proffered explanation.

Finally, Brent claimed he first learned that his mother did not want to sell 2268 Eckert over the phone, three to five days after the purchase agreement was signed on May 13, 2005. He stated that he informed Eicher of JoAnn's decision that same day over the phone. But Eicher testified that Brent first notified her of JoAnn's decision in person at Brent's office, not over the phone. Eicher also indicated that this meeting did not occur on May 18th but rather on May 24th — the date the agreement was cancelled. A reasonable juror could find that the conflicts in the record over when and how Brent actually communicated the cancellation to Eicher provide a reason to disbelieve the Yateses' version of the events as they suggest a fabrication of the facts.

A discrimination case is submittable to a jury on the credibility of the defendants' explanation if the plaintiff offers evidence that could establish by a preponderance of the evidence that the proffered reasons had no basis in fact or did not actually motivate the adverse housing decision. We find the evidence discussed above could permit a fact-finder to reasonably conclude that the non-discriminatory explanation of seeking to keep the home "in the family" did not actually motivate the cancellation of the purchasing agreement. Therefore, a genuine issue of material fact exists as to whether the Yateses' proffered reason is a pretext for unlawful discrimination.

The Supreme Court has held that a *prima facie* case of discrimination combined with a showing that the proffered non-discriminatory reason is false is sufficient for a plaintiff to prevail on the ultimate issue of discrimination. *See* Reeves v. Sanderson Plumbing Prods., Inc., 530 U.S. 133, 148 (2000).[20] In other words, a plaintiff need not necessarily "introduce independent evidence of discrimination in addition to establishing the falsity of" the proffered motivation for the seller's action. Because sufficient evidence in the record exists for the Lindsays to establish a genuine issue of material fact regarding each element of their *prima facie* case and to show the Yateses' stated reasons for rescinding the purchasing agreement could be found to amount to pretext, we conclude that the Lindsays can prevail on their housing discrimination claims. Accordingly, we rule that the defendants are not entitled to summary judgment.

NOTES AND QUESTIONS

1. Flexible Application of Prima Facie Elements. Note that the key factual disputes in *Lindsay* occurred between May 13, when the owner's son (Brent) signed the purchase agreement with the Lindsays, and May 24, when the owner (JoAnn) terminated the purchase agreement. The plaintiffs argued that sufficient circumstantial evidence existed to support a claim of racial discrimination, while the defendants contended that they changed their mind about the sale because of a desire to keep the property in the family. The fact that the Yates family took the house off the market made it difficult for the Lindsays to establish the fourth element of the prima facie case—that the property remained available following defendants' refusal to sell to them.

Did the court dispense with plaintiffs' prima facie showing? If not, then how much leeway did the court grant to plaintiffs in satisfying this requirement?

---

20. [Fn. 14 in original] The Supreme Court specifically stated in Reeves, 530 U.S. at 148: Proof that the defendant's explanation is unworthy of credence is simply one form of circumstantial evidence that is probative of intentional discrimination, and it may be quite persuasive. . . . In appropriate circumstances, the trier of fact can reasonably infer from the falsity of the explanation that the employer is dissembling to cover up a discriminatory purpose. . . . Moreover, once the employer's justification has been eliminated, discrimination may well be the most likely alternative explanation, especially since the employer is in the best position to put forth the actual reason for its decision. . . . Thus, a plaintiff's *prima facie* case, combined with sufficient evidence to find that the employer's asserted justification is false, may permit the trier of fact to conclude that the employer unlawfully discriminated.

What is the primary function of the prima facie case, and does it provide a clue to the court's reasoning?

Consider another example of a plaintiff who may prove intentional discrimination without meeting every element of the prima facie case. Some landlords screen out prospective tenants illegally before they are able to reach the application stage. If a would-be applicant can show through testing or other evidence that a housing unit was available to others outside of plaintiff's protected class despite a landlord's refusal to make the unit available to plaintiff for inspection and application, then the second element of the prima facie case requiring application may be unnecessary.[21] *See* United States v. Badgett, 976 F.2d 1176, 1178 (8th Cir. 1992) ("The elements of a prima facie case of discrimination will vary from case to case, depending on the allegations and the circumstances.").

2. Something More? The court looked to employment discrimination precedent to determine what "additional evidence" would be appropriate to make up for the gap in the fourth element of the prima facie case. Even though courts usually look for comparative evidence,[22] such as that of "similarly situated individuals outside of [plaintiffs' group] who were treated more favorably," the Sixth Circuit disavowed a "rigid, mechanized, or ritualistic" approach to the prima facie inquiry. Do you think evidence of a comparator should be required on the facts and circumstances of this case? How would the Lindsays have obtained comparative evidence? What key "additional evidence" did the Lindsays offer, and was this the only additional evidence the court considered?

Other courts have recognized that comparative evidence will not be available in all cases, and sometimes other proof frameworks work better in this context. "*McDonnell Douglas* simply *permits* a plaintiff to raise an inference of discrimination by identifying a similarly situated entity who was treated more favorably. It is not a straitjacket *requiring* the plaintiff to demonstrate that such similarly situated entities exist." Pacific Shores Properties, L.L.C. v. City of Newport Beach, 730 F.3d 1142, 1158-59 (9th Cir. 2013) (using a multifactor totality of the circumstances proof framework showing a discriminatory reason "more likely than not motivated the defendant").

3. Suspicious Timing: Prima Facie or Pretext? The Lindsays alleged that the Yates family backed out of the parties' sales contract two days after their

---

21. A formal application also may be unnecessary if it would constitute a "futile gesture." In other words, if an applicant is interested in and well qualified for the housing opportunity but is informed of a discriminatory policy of the defendant, the plaintiff is not required to go through the motions of applying and subjecting themselves to discrimination to establish a violation of fair housing law. *See* Pinchback v. Armistead Homes Corp., 907 F.2d 1447, 1452 (4th Cir. 1990) (importing futile gesture theory from Title VII into §§1981 and 1982). Would the evidence in such a case be direct or circumstantial?

22. *See, e.g.*, Simms v. First Gibraltar Bank, 83 F.3d 1546, 1558 (5th Cir. 1996) (describing evidence of poor treatment as offered "in a vacuum" where no comparative evidence of other mortgage applicants was presented).

first face-to-face meeting. How does such evidence help support the Lindsays' claim? Is this "additional evidence" of suspicious timing being offered to satisfy the prima facie case or the ultimate burden of persuasion—or both? Remember that in addition to the burden of presenting evidence of a prima facie case, the plaintiff carries the ultimate burden of proving that the nondiscriminatory reason offered by the defendant is pretext for unlawful discrimination. Here, plaintiffs used evidence of suspicious timing to satisfy both the prima facie and pretext requirements.

The *Lindsay* court cited Reeves v. Sanderson Plumbing Products, Inc., 530 U.S. 133, 147-49 (2000), an employment case in which the Supreme Court considered whether a plaintiff's showing on pretext needed to include additional, independent evidence that defendant took some action because of a protected characteristic or whether it was sufficient for plaintiff to show that the defendant's nondiscriminatory reason was false. The *Reeves* Court held that such independent evidence was unnecessary; a jury could find unlawful discrimination based on the prima facie case combined with evidence that the defendant's nondiscriminatory reason was "unworthy of credence." After all, the Court said, the defendant "is in the best position to put forth the actual reason for its decision," and therefore if its proffered explanation is shown to be false, a factfinder is entitled to draw the conclusion that the defendant was concealing a discriminatory motive.

In addition to the suspicious timing of the cancellation of the purchase agreement, the Lindsays offered evidence to show the Yateses' explanation for cancelling was not credible. The court pointed to "disconnects" between the stated motivation for cancelling and the actual conduct leading up to it, as well as other conflicts in the record. Under *Reeves*, therefore, all the Lindsays' evidence showing the Yateses' explanations were false, coupled with the prima facie evidence, would be sufficient to support a jury finding of discrimination.

But what about the fact that the parties' evidence conflicted on the number of days between the face-to-face meeting and the cancellation of the contract? Remember that on summary judgment, the issue is whether there is sufficient evidence for a reasonable juror to find it more likely than not that the defendants' reason is false and that race actually motivated the Yates family to cancel the sale. The dispute of fact with respect to a material issue makes summary judgment for defendants inappropriate. How do you think a juror might vote on the evidence in the record?

4. Independent Evidence of Pretext: The Role of Discovery. Although independent evidence of discrimination is not required if the plaintiff can show the defendant's explanation lacks credibility, it certainly can bolster the plaintiff's case. What kind of independent evidence would be probative of intentional discrimination in the *Lindsay* case? How might the plaintiffs gather such independent evidence? Will this evidence likely be available before the plaintiffs file their complaint or afterwards?

5. Pleading Versus Proving the Prima Facie Case. Notice that the Sixth Circuit in an earlier decision had rejected the defendants' argument that the Yateses must plead facts establishing each element of the prima facie case to survive dismissal, citing Swierkiewicz v. Sorema N.A., 534 U.S. 506 (2002). Then the district court granted summary judgment on a similar issue. Are these rulings inconsistent? To avoid summary judgment plaintiffs are required to come forward with admissible evidence to support each element of the claim. Therefore, a court could grant summary judgment for a plaintiff's failure to prove each element of the prima facie case even if pleading such elements were not required.

FEDERAL PLEADING STANDARDS AND THE FHA

In 2009, the Supreme Court decided Ashcroft v. Iqbal, 556 U.S. 662 (2009), extending to all civil cases its earlier holding in Bell Atlantic Corp. v. Twombly, 550 U.S. 544 (2007), that a court would not be required to assume an allegation was true at the pleading stage if it amounted to a mere "formulaic recitation" of an element of a claim. After setting aside any "conclusory" allegations, under *Iqbal* a court must consider whether the remaining allegations have "nudged [the] claims" of purposeful discrimination "across the line from conceivable to plausible." In determining whether a claim is plausible at the motion to dismiss stage, a court may not consider whether the plaintiff is likely to be able to prove the facts in the pleading. But mere consistency with a theory of discrimination is insufficient; the court may rely on experience and "common sense" and consider other obvious alternative explanations for the defendant's conduct. Do you think a judge's perceptions about the prevalence of discrimination might influence the plausibility analysis? In Woods v. City of Greensboro, 855 F.3d 639, 652 (4th Cir. 2017), the Fourth Circuit reversed a dismissal of a claim under §1981 and offered these observations:

> [D]iscrimination claims are particularly vulnerable to premature dismissal because civil rights plaintiffs often plead facts that are consistent with both legal and illegal behavior, and civil rights cases are more likely to suffer from information-asymmetry, pre-discovery. *See, e.g.,* Suzette M. Malveaux, *The Jury (or More Accurately the Judge) Is Still Out for Civil Rights and Employment Cases Post*-Iqbal, 57 N.Y.L. Sch. L. Rev. 719, 722-23 (2012-2013). There is thus a real risk that legitimate discrimination claims, particularly claims based on more subtle theories of stereotyping or implicit bias, will be dismissed should a judge [without a developed record] substitute his or her view of the likely reason for a particular action in place of the controlling plausibility standard.

The idea that a court might dismiss a discrimination claim merely because another theory appears more plausible is particularly problematic given that the court is not even permitted to perform this kind of weighing at the summary judgment stage. *See* Thomas v. Eastman Kodak Co., 183 F.3d 38, 61 (1st Cir. 1999) ("the question at summary judgment is not which of the possible explanations is most convincing; it is whether the plaintiff has produced enough evidence to raise a genuine issue of fact regarding *her* explanation.").

> Where does this leave FHA litigants? We know that allegations regarding the prima facie elements are not required. Pleading sufficient factual detail to provide context for a plausible discrimination claim is essential. How much detail will cross that threshold? Does the *Lindsay* court's discussion of pretext assist you in answering this question?

6. Is Conscious Animus a Requirement? Was it necessary in *Lindsay* for plaintiff at the third step of the burden-shifting framework to show defendant harbored special animus toward Black persons? *See* Community Services, Inc. v. Wind Gap Municipal Authority, 421 F.3d 170, 177 (3d Cir. 2005) ("The discriminatory purpose need not be malicious or invidious. . . ."); Williams v. Matthews Co., 499 F.2d 819, 827 (8th Cir. 1974) ("subjective good intentions" are not sufficient to overcome disparate treatment). What if Mrs. Yates refused to sell to Black purchasers because of fears of alienating the neighbors or of threatening property values or subjecting the Black purchasers to a hostile reception, even violence? *See* Cato v. Jilek, 779 F. Supp. 937, 942 n.16 (N.D. Ill. 1991) ("Fear of . . . the reaction of other tenants does not, of course, excuse the racially motivated rejection of tenants."); United States v. City of Birmingham, Mich., 538 F. Supp. 819, 830 (E.D. Mich. 1982), *aff'd as modified*, 727 F.2d 560 (6th Cir. 1984) ("A person who attempts to prevent a black family from buying the house next door because [of beliefs about] decrease[d] property values violates the FHA. . . ."); *see also* Gautreaux v. Chicago Housing Authority, 296 F. Supp. 907 (N.D. Ill. 1969) (rejecting threat of violence as a justification for policy of segregation, discussed in Chapter 12). Treating housing consumers differently based on their race, even if fueled by economic or social concerns, constitutes intentional discrimination. Similarly, treating families with children differently, such as by refusing rental of a unit with a balcony, may be motivated by safety concerns for young children, but still makes housing unavailable "because of" familial status.

What if the defendant is not fully aware of his or her motivation? "The Supreme Court has long recognized that unlawful discrimination can stem from stereotypes and other types of cognitive biases, as well as from conscious animus." Thomas v. Eastman Kodak Co., 183 F.3d 38, 59 (1st Cir. 1999).[23] Some commentators have made textual arguments demonstrating that antidiscrimination law is capable of addressing bias that operates through less conscious, neuro-cognitive processes like implicit, rather than explicit, stereotyping.[24]

---

23. *See also* Linda Hamilton Krieger & Susan T. Fiske, *Behavioral Realism in Employment Discrimination Law: Implicit Bias and Disparate Treatment*, 94 CAL. L. REV. 997, 1034 (2006). ("The science of implicit bias demonstrates that disparate treatment can result not only from the deliberate application of consciously endorsed prejudiced beliefs, but also from the unwitting and uncorrected influence of implicit attitudes and associations [including stereotypes] in the social-perception process.").

24. *See id.* at 1054 (noting there is nothing in the statutory text of Title VII requiring conscious intentionality). *But see* Michael Selmi, *The Paradox of Implicit Bias and a Plea for a New Narrative*, 50 ARIZ. ST. L.J. 193, 199 (2018) ("[S]hifting the focus away from implicit bias and [toward general] stereotyping will align the social psychology research with existing legal standards of proof.").

Other scholars argue against a "misguided preoccupation with mental state" because entrenched disparities "are not primarily a consequence of contemporary racial bias. Thus, the goal of racial justice efforts should be the alleviation of substantive inequalities, not the eradication of unconscious bias." Ralph Richard Banks & Richard Thompson Ford, *(How) Does Unconscious Bias Matter?: Law, Politics, and Racial Inequality*, 58 EMORY L.J. 1053, 1054 (2009). A comprehensive discussion of the empirical research on implicit social cognition; how it might be used in civil rights litigation (perhaps as a form of "social framework evidence"); the ongoing debates about its significance; and what it portends for private and public policymaking is beyond the scope of this text. But several decades of research and scholarship on this subject have spawned a "behavioral realism" approach, which "insists that the law account for the most accurate model of human thought, decisionmaking, and action provided by the sciences," and asserts that "[w]e are not perceptually, cognitively, or behaviorally colorblind." Jerry Kang & Kristin Lane, *Seeing Through Colorblindness: Implicit Bias and the Law*, 58 UCLA L. REV. 465, 468 (2010).

Do you think the FHA as enacted addresses implicit bias? What kind of evidence would a plaintiff need to introduce to prove an allegation of implicit bias? The Supreme Court has partially answered these questions; in upholding a discriminatory effects method of proof under the FHA, it acknowledged the role of disparate impact evidence in "counteract[ing] unconscious prejudices and disguised animus that escape easy classification as disparate treatment." *See* TDHCA v. Inclusive Communities Project, Inc, 576 U.S. 519, 540 (2015).[25]

Consider a different example. Landlord screening of telephone voices or names can be explicit or implicit. Housing providers may or may not be aware that they harbor bias against certain accents or dialects, or in favor of names corresponding to their own culture and ethnicity. A consistent pattern of disparate treatment on the basis of race may be enough to create an inference of discrimination, regardless. *See* Wilson v. Souchet, 168 F. Supp. 2d. 860, 864 (N.D. Ill. 2001) (holding under §§1981 and 1982 that plaintiff created a fact issue on whether the defendant was able to discern race over the phone through three paired tests showing consistently different representations to the Black testers regarding housing availability). Nevertheless, expert testimony may be crucial in any case involving screening by phone voice or name. *See* Greater New Orleans Fair Housing Action Center, Inc. v. Hotard, 275 F. Supp. 3d 776, 786-89 (E.D. La. 2017) ("Plaintiff provides no expert testimony [at trial] to support its contention [that the defendant knew the testers'

---

25. For analysis of the way implicit racial stereotypes operate at the neighborhood level, see Michelle Wilde Anderson & Victoria Plaut, *Property Law: Implicit Bias and the Resilience of Spatial Colorlines*, *in* IMPLICIT RACIAL BIAS ACROSS THE LAW (Justin D. Levinson & Robert J. Smith eds., Cambridge U. Press 2012).

races based on their names and voices], even though expert testimony is typically used to prove linguistic profiling or that race is identifiable by a person's name.").

B. EVIDENTIARY FRAMEWORK IN MIXED MOTIVE CASES

The *McDonnell Douglas* framework is predicated on a binary distinction: The defendant's action was based either on a legitimate purpose or on an unlawfully discriminatory one, with the inquiry focused on whether the defendant's stated reason, although legitimate, is pretextual. However, the possibility exists that both the legitimate and the discriminatory purpose played some role, and that the defendant made a decision with "mixed motives." For example, in *Lindsay* the defendant stated she changed her mind about selling the family home "for sentimental reasons," whereas plaintiffs alleged the defendant changed her mind upon learning the plaintiffs were Black. Could both reasons have contributed to the outcome if the defendant were ambivalent about selling her house? If so, how does the FHA treat adverse housing decisions motivated only in part by discrimination? Rather than arguing under the *McDonnell Douglas* framework that the defendant's nondiscriminatory reason is a lie (providing sufficient evidence for the jury to infer discriminatory purpose), a plaintiff may argue that regardless of any legitimate motivations, a prohibited reason was *a motivating factor* in the defendant's decision, rendering the decision unlawful. "[T]his standard can produce liability if an illegal motive prompted the defendant's action in any way or, as some model jury instructions express the concept, 'contributed' to the defendant's decision."[26]

The motivating factor approach is to be contrasted with but-for causation, applied under §1981 (and likely §1982), which requires the plaintiff to prove that the prohibited motive "made a difference to the outcome," which "would not have occurred" in the absence of the improper motivation.[27] The Supreme Court has not addressed what standard of causation should govern mixed motive cases under the FHA, and the uncertainty is compounded by evolving legislative and judicial standards under Title VII and other civil rights statutes,[28] but the following case provides a starting point for understanding the traditional FHA approach to mixed motive analysis.

---

26. Robert G. Schwemm, *Fair Housing and the Causation Standard After* Comcast, 66 Villanova L. Rev. 63, 75 2021).
27. *See id.* at 71-72 (citing Univ. of Tex. Sw. Med. Ctr. v. Nassar, 570 U.S. 338, 347 (2013)).
28. *See* Schwemm, HDLL §10:3 "Mixed Motive" cases.

Marable v. H. Walker Associates
644 F.2d 390 (5th Cir. 1981)

Before Morgan, Fay and Frank M. Johnson, Jr., Circuit Judges.

Frank M. JOHNSON, JR., Circuit Judge:

Sylvester Marable brought this suit alleging that defendants Harold and Francis Walker refused to rent an available apartment to him because he is black, in violation of the FHA. After defendants answered that their policy was to rent only to married couples and that Marable was denied tenancy because he applied as a single male, Marable amended his complaint to add a claim of sex discrimination. The district court rendered judgment for defendants after a non-jury trial, concluding that the defendants did not discriminate against Marable on the basis of either race or sex. The district court found that the apartment was denied to Marable because he had a credit report that showed him to be an unacceptable tenant, he was single and the apartment complex had a policy of renting to families and married persons only, and he "constantly harassed" defendants about his application after it was submitted. Marable appeals.

Defendants Harold and Francis Walker own the Traces Apartments, a 56-unit apartment complex located in a predominantly white suburb of Birmingham, Alabama. Each of the apartments has either two or three bedrooms. When these apartments were first being rented, beginning in April 1974, defendants rented to at least eight single males and also to tenants with poor or no credit histories,[29] with poor or unverified employment records,[30] and with poor or no rental histories.[31] Thereafter, defendants adopted a policy of renting to married couples and families,[32] in part, Mrs. Walker stated, because they had some trouble with single male tenants.

---

29. [Fn. 3 in original] Defendants rented to at least two tenants who had gone into personal bankruptcy and who had had accounts turned over to collection agencies, and rented to at least seven other tenants who had been sued for collection of debts. One tenant had no credit references whatsoever and another had a history of late payments on his credit accounts. The evidence at trial showing the poor credit histories of these tenants was undisputed. Francis Walker testified at trial that credit reports were not required of all applicants. She even admitted that she would not have been surprised to learn that 73 of the 209 tenants who had rented at the Traces had not had their credit histories evaluated by independent credit reports.

30. [Fn. 4 in original] Defendants rented to numerous tenants whose employment was not verified and to others who were unemployed at the time they were accepted as tenants. Marable introduced evidence showing that 172 out of 213 white applicants did not have their incomes verified in their credit reports. Mrs. Walker testified at trial that credit reports are not required of all prospective tenants, only a "majority."

31. [Fn. 5 in original] Defendants rented to at least one tenant who had been evicted from another apartment for non-payment of rent. Several applicants who had never previously rented were accepted as tenants.

32. [Fn. 6 in original] Mark Hammond, the resident manager of the Traces Apartments at the time Marable applied, testified at trial that he was not aware of the policy of not renting to singles until Marable applied. However, Hammond also stated that Marable was the first single male to apply since he had been working as resident manager.

Francis Walker became the managing partner of the Traces Apartments on February 3, 1976. She testified at trial that since that time no single males had rented apartments and that only three single females and one widow had rented at the Traces. However, she stated that applications were taken from singles on a case by case basis. Mrs. Walker testified that from 1974 until 1978, the time of trial, out of 209 tenancy turnovers, defendants had rented to 22 non-married tenants, including ten single white males.[33] She testified that the Traces Apartments had never had a black tenant.

Sylvester Marable submitted his application for tenancy in the Traces Apartments in November 1976. The resident manager, Mark Hammond, showed Marable a vacant apartment and told him that he would be contacted in a few days about his application. [EDS.—Marable completed a credit application. Following an interview, the credit reporting company, Equifax, prepared a report detailing stable employment, salary, and payment history revealing no past due amounts on any accounts and no bankruptcies, suits, or judgments arising from debts. "The report concluded that there were no factors that might affect doing business with Marable on a credit basis." Marable made three phone calls to Mrs. Walker inquiring about his application: first, after his Equifax interview (Walker claimed Marable accused her of stalling because he was Black); second, after Walker received the credit report (Marable claimed she asked why he wanted to live on that side of town and then said she did not rent to unmarried applicants); and third, later that same day when he asked for an explanation of his denial (Walker claimed Marable "got a little smart" when she told him he had insufficient credit and rental history and unverifiable employment and income).]

The apartment for which Marable had applied remained vacant for three months, until it was rented to a white single female with no children. After being refused as a tenant, Marable then went to HUD and filed a charge against defendants alleging that they discriminated against him on the basis of his race. HUD concluded from its investigation that defendants denied Marable an apartment because of his race. This suit was filed after efforts at conciliation failed. [The district court rendered judgment for defendants.]

A plaintiff bringing a claim under the FHA charging defendants with refusal to provide housing on the basis of racial discrimination is not required to establish that his denial of housing was motivated solely by racial discrimination. It is sufficient that race was one significant factor considered by the defendants in dealing with the plaintiff. The race of an applicant for tenancy is not to be considered and the presence of other factors also motivating the refusal to rent cannot justify racial discrimination.

The district court's determination that the defendants did not discriminate against Marable is a finding of ultimate fact with respect to which this Court is

---

33. [Fn. 7 in original] Marable introduced evidence that defendants rented to 28 single white males and 25 single white females.

not bound by the clearly erroneous standard of review. However, the trial court's credibility determinations and findings of subsidiary fact are reviewed under the clearly erroneous standard. "A finding is 'clearly erroneous' when although there is evidence to support it, the reviewing court on the entire evidence is left with the definite and firm conviction that a mistake has been committed."

Several of the district court's findings of subsidiary facts are not supported by the record and are clearly erroneous. The finding that Marable claimed an estimated annual salary of $14,000 "with what proved to be a nonexistent corporate employer" was refuted by defendants' own exhibit which consisted of a copy of the article of incorporation of the Feather Corporation. The finding that Marable had "no significant employment history" is belied by Marable's credit report itself, which informed the defendants that he had been working full time for 8 1/2 months and had previously worked as a parole officer for the State of Alabama for 1 1/2 years, and which described his prospects for continued employment as good.

The finding that Marable was denied the apartment because he was single and the Traces had a policy of renting only to families and marrieds is contradicted by Mrs. Walker's own testimony that applications were accepted from singles on a case by case basis and that 22 of the total 209 tenants at the Traces had been singles. It is manifest from the documentary evidence and the testimony of Mrs. Walker that apartments were in fact rented to singles, and the exceptions made by defendants constitute over 10% of all the tenants who had ever rented at the Traces.

The finding that one of defendants' reasons for refusing to rent to Marable was because he "constantly harassed" the defendants is without support in the record. Even the testimony of Mark Hammond, the resident manager of the Traces, and that of Mrs. Walker does not warrant a finding that three phone calls to Mrs. Walker and two to Hammond constituted constant harassment. Neither Mrs. Walker nor Hammond claimed that they were "harassed" by Marable. Mrs. Walker testified merely that Marable got "a little smart" during one phone call but her perception that Marable, a young black man, was uppity toward her does not support the court's finding.[34]

The findings of fact mandated by Fed. R. Civ. P. 52(a) [EDS. — following trial on the merits] "must be sufficient in detail and exactness to indicate the factual basis for the ultimate conclusion reached by the court." The district court in this case failed to consider in its findings the evidence indicating that the defendants' credit and employment requirements and their single male

---

34. [Fn. 17 in original] This alleged "smartness" occurred after Marable was informed that he was not an acceptable tenant and after he suggested that his race was the reason for his rejection. The smartness was first mentioned as a reason for rejection at trial; it was not mentioned in defendants' statement to HUD, their answer to the complaint, their depositions, or their answers to interrogatories. Marable's so-called smartness, as alleged by Mrs. Walker at trial, has been described in defendants' appellate brief as Marable's "very belligerent," "abusive," and "obnoxious" phone conversation.

exclusionary policy were unequally applied as between Marable and white applicants. The court also failed to consider whether defendants' rejection of Marable's application for tenancy was a pretext for racial discrimination. [EDS. — Note, pretext analysis is more common in cases using the burden-shifting method under *McDonnell Douglas*; here the pretext analysis provides additional justification for reversing the lower court.]

Marable introduced documentary evidence consisting of applications for tenancy listing credit references and credit reports prepared by a credit agency, which demonstrated that defendants rented to numerous white persons with significant credit problems far greater than any deficiencies indicated by Marable's credit report.[35] Similarly, the undisputed evidence indicated that defendants had rented to (1) numerous tenants with unverified incomes, (2) several who were unemployed or who worked for companies with which the defendants were unfamiliar when they were accepted as tenants, and (3) several others for whom defendants ordered no independent credit report to be prepared. Also, by defendants' own admission in the testimony of Mrs. Walker, at least 10 single white males had rented at the Traces. The defendants' disparate treatment of white applicants and Marable, as reflected by their patterns of accepting white applicants who were credit risks or who were single, is clearly reflected by the evidence.

The district court erred in failing to consider the comparative evidence of the unequal application of defendants' rental criteria as between Marable and white applicants, which demonstrated that defendants' reasons for rejecting Marable were a pretext. The district court never considered the qualifications of Marable in relation to the qualifications of white applicants; rather, it considered Marable's qualifications only against the defendants' alleged absolute standards. However, even Mrs. Walker testified that the defendants' rental standards were not absolute and that tenants' applications were considered on a case by case basis.[36] The defendants' tenant selection process and criteria were shown by the testimony of Mrs. Walker and Mark Hammond to be subjective. Finally, the defendants admitted that no black applicants had ever been accepted as tenants at the Traces Apartments.[37]

The district court discounted the testimony of Marable on the ground that it lacked credibility because of contradiction and Marable's demeanor at trial. The court also discounted the testimony of two of Marable's witnesses on

35. [Fn. 18 in original] Even though many of the tenants whose credit histories were far worse than Marable's had been allowed to rent apartments prior to the time Francis Walker became personally involved in management of the Traces Apartments, Mrs. Walker has had an ownership interest in the Traces complex since its inception.

36. [Fn. 19 in original] Mrs. Walker testified that she gave potential tenants the benefit of the doubt in considering their applications. Also defendants' appellate brief states that they were "selective and discreet" in making exceptions to their policy of not renting to singles.

37. [Fn. 20 in original] Other housing discrimination cases have found this to be a significant evidentiary factor. *E.g.*, United States v. Reddoch, 467 F.2d 897, 899 (5th Cir. 1972); United States v. West Peachtree Tenth Corporation, 437 F.2d 221 (5th Cir. 1971).

the ground that they were biased.[38] Even if it is accepted as true that Marable and two of his witnesses lacked credibility—a district court finding that is binding on this Court unless it is clearly erroneous—documentary evidence in the record clearly indicates that Marable's race was a significant factor in his rejection as a tenant. A district court may not "bootstrap" its findings and conclusions by stating that they are based upon credibility when the documentary evidence and undisputed testimony reflected in the record show the findings and conclusions to be clearly erroneous.

We conclude, after careful examination of the record, that the unequal application of defendants' rental criteria, including marital status and employment and credit histories, as between Marable and white applicants demonstrates disparate treatment on the basis of race violating the FHA. For this reason we do not discuss Marable's contention that defendants' single male exclusionary policy violates the FHA on the basis of sex discrimination.

Accordingly, the judgment of the district court is REVERSED and the case is REMANDED for consideration of damages, attorney's fees, and injunctive relief.

HONORABLE FRANK JOHNSON

Office of Judge Frank M. Johnson, Jr.

The author of the *Marable* opinion, Judge Frank M. Johnson, Jr., was one of the great heroes of the Civil Rights Movement. "He probably adjudicated more high-profile civil rights cases during the civil rights movement than any other federal district judge," displaying "unflagging moral courage and legal brilliance. . . ."

He issued or participated in rulings connected to major events in the Civil Rights Movement, starting with the Montgomery Bus Boycott, when he was part of the majority of a divided three-judge district court that issued the "breathtaking" decision holding unconstitutional both the Montgomery city ordinance and the Alabama statute compelling racial segregation in intrastate

---

38. [Fn. 21 in original] One of the witnesses, Jean Sharp, a former resident manager at the Traces Apartments, testified that she was instructed by Mrs. Walker to refer all applications from black applicants to her if Ms. Sharp could not "handle it." Ms. Sharp also testified that Mrs. Walker told her that Mr. Walker "would just die" if she rented to a black applicant at the Traces Apartments.

transportation; the U.S. Supreme Court's per curiam affirmance was the effective overruling of *Plessy v. Ferguson*. He ordered the Ku Klux Klan to stop the beating and harassment of Freedom Riders and enjoined local police to protect the Riders, events that some attribute to the judge's increased vigor in providing and defending equal justice. After marchers from Selma to Montgomery, led by John Lewis and Hosea Williams, were beaten and tear-gassed on the Edmund Pettus Bridge in Selma on "Bloody Sunday" in 1965, Judge Johnson first enjoined further marching but then allowed the march and ordered state and local officials to protect the marchers. He was part of a three-judge district court that enjoined Selma Sheriff Jim Clark and his deputies and posse from interfering with Black people's rights to register to vote and to use public accommodations. Before the Selma-to-Montgomery March, Judge Johnson had vindicated the voting rights of Black people in the Middle District of Alabama. Judge Johnson also was on the three-judge panel in *White v. Crook*, which held unconstitutional Alabama's exclusion of women from jury service. He invalidated the Alabama poll tax. He ordered desegregation of public schools, bus and bus terminal facilities and rail terminals, the Montgomery YMCAs, all of state government, Montgomery's parks and zoo, the Montgomery airport, and the public library and museum of fine arts. Enforcing human rights, he "ordered that barbaric conditions in Alabama's mental institutions and prisons be reformed" and "in a decision overturned by the Supreme Court, . . . attempted to apply to gays and lesbians the fundamental right . . . to privacy in sexual acts."[39]

NOTES AND QUESTIONS

1. Evolving Reasons. Determining defendants' nondiscriminatory reasons for an adverse housing decision at the earliest time is an important agenda item for plaintiffs. Evolving reasons can undermine defendants' credibility and provide probative evidence of pretext. *Marable* illustrates the winding path of litigation and the numerous instances when defendants will be asked to state their nondiscriminatory reasons:

> Defendants have asserted different reasons at different times for rejecting Marable as a tenant. . . . they told a HUD investigator that Marable's inadequate credit and rental history were the reasons he was rejected. In their answer to

---

39. This material is taken from Raymond Arsenault, FREEDOM RIDERS: 1961 AND THE STRUGGLE FOR RACIAL JUSTICE 227, 299, 307, 315, 458 (Oxford U. Press 2006); Jack Bass, TAMING THE STORM: THE LIFE AND TIMES OF JUDGE FRANK M. JOHNSON, JR. AND THE SOUTH'S FIGHT OVER CIVIL RIGHTS 9, 46-49, 145-49, 151-55 (Doubleday 1993); Taylor Branch, AT CANAAN'S EDGE: AMERICA IN THE KING YEARS 1965-68, at 49-55, 68-71, 92, 122, 312-13, 438 (Simon and Schuster 2006); Randall Kennedy, *Martin Luther King's Constitution: A Legal History of the Montgomery Bus Boycott*, 98 YALE L.J. 999, 1050 n.314 (1989); Howell Raines, *Judge Frank Johnson Goes Home to the Hills*, N.Y. TIMES, July 26, 1999, A18, https://www.nytimes.com/1999/07/26 /opinion/editorial-observer-judge-frank-johnson-goes-home-to-the-hills.html?searchResultP osition=1; Myron H. Thompson, *Measuring a Life: Frank Minis Johnson, Jr.*, 109 YALE L.J. 1257, 1258 (2000); J. Mills Thornton III, DIVIDING LINES: MUNICIPAL POLITICS AND THE STRUGGLE FOR CIVIL RIGHTS IN MONTGOMERY, BIRMINGHAM, AND SELMA 102, 119-22, 128-32, 136-38, 441, 489, 617 n.150 (U. Ala. Press 2002); and Frank Sikora, THE JUDGE: THE LIFE & OPINIONS OF ALABAMA'S FRANK M. JOHNSON, JR. xi, 84-94, 100 (Black Belt Press 1992).

the complaint the only asserted reason was Marable's single marital status. In their answers to Marable's first interrogatories, Marable's alleged credit deficiencies were listed as the reason. At trial, two more reasons were stated: Marable was "a little smart" with Mrs. Walker during one phone call, and he was employed with a "new" company.

2. One Significant Factor v. But-For Causation. The *Marable* court found disparate treatment where race was "one significant factor" in the defendant's decision. Other courts applying this traditional FHA approach have found unlawful discrimination where the protected class status was a "motivating factor." *See* Smith & Lee Associates, Inc. v. City of Taylor, Mich., 102 F.3d 781, 790 (6th Cir. 1996) (citing Village of Arlington Heights v. Metropolitan Housing Dev. Corp., 429 U.S. 252, 270 (1977)). These approaches are functionally the same. The motivating factor test does not require the illegal motive to make a difference to the outcome, as is required for but-for causation. It is thus an easier test for plaintiffs to satisfy. As long as the prohibited reason contributes in any way, even if to a minor extent, plaintiffs can satisfy the motivating factor test.[40] Under but-for causation, however, if the housing provider would have made the same decision regardless of the protected characteristic, then the protected trait would not be a but-for cause. (Note that there can be more than one but-for cause.)

The Supreme Court has not yet spoken on the issue, but evolving legislative and judicial standards governing other civil rights statutes have called the traditional FHA approach into question. In Comcast Corporation v. National Ass'n of African American-Owned Media, 589 U.S. 327, 332 (2020), the Supreme Court held that the "but-for" causation test "supplies the 'default' or 'background' rule against which Congress is normally presumed to have legislated," including when enacting "federal antidiscrimination laws like §1981."[41] *See also* Schwemm, HDLL §10:3 (discussing the Court's increasing application of a but-for standard of causation under civil rights statutes other than the FHA). Professor Schwemm has articulated a strong counterargument to applying the but-for causation rule in FHA cases despite recent[42] pronouncements suggesting otherwise:

> For decades, the lower courts have rejected but-for causation in Fair Housing Act cases in favor of a more lenient standard. Moreover, this view was well-established by 1988 when Congress amended the Fair Housing Act without

---

40. *See* Schwemm, 66 Villanova L. Rev. at 75.

41. The Court also held that but-for causation is an essential element of the claim that "applies in all phases . . . from pleading through trial." *Id.* at 102 (citing *Comcast*, 589 U.S. at 332).

42. *See* Schwemm, 66 Villanova L. Rev. at 90 n.180 ("The Court's earliest suggestion that but-for causation should be the default standard for civil rights statutes was in 2009 in the *Gross* case."); Gross v. FBL Fin. Servs., Inc., 557 U.S. 167 (2009) (holding that a but-for causation standard was applicable to disparate treatment claims under the Age Discrimination in Employment Act).

changing its crucial "because of" language, a fact that the Supreme Court has held may indicate Congress's endorsement of prior established standards.[43]

At the time Congress passed the Fair Housing Amendments Act of 1988, all five circuits that had considered the question had adopted the motivating factor standard in some form, with four additional circuits following suit since 1988.[44] Thus, "most circuits will be bound by their precedents establishing a less-than-but-for standard, at least until an en banc decision makes a change. A circuit split on the issue seems likely. . . ."[45] Unless or until the Supreme Court rules, this is likely to be an issue that divides the courts of appeals.

What evidence did the plaintiff in *Marable* offer to satisfy the "one significant factor" test applied in the Fifth Circuit? Does this evidence differ from the type litigants use under the *McDonnell Douglas* pretext framework? Would Mr. Marable's evidence have been sufficient to satisfy the higher threshold of but-for causation? In Bostock v. Clayton County, Ga., 590 U.S. 644, 656 (2020), the Supreme Court explained: "a but-for test directs us to change one thing at a time and see if the outcome changes. If it does, we have found a but-for cause." Given the record evidence, do you think Marable's race changed the outcome?

Finally, note well a scenario that does *not* present a mixed motive problem: where a defendant uses a screening test that involves two linked factors, only one of which is prohibited under federal law. An example is a landlord who refuses to rent to unmarried men, but is willing to rent to married couples and single women. Marital status is not a prohibited basis for discrimination under federal law, but sex is. By treating individuals differently on the basis of sex, the landlord is engaging in unlawful discrimination regardless of the presence of the additional factor of marital status.

3. Sole Causation Unnecessary. Sole-factor causation requiring an unlawfully discriminatory motive to be the sole reason for the defendant's decision

---

43. Schwemm, 66 VILLANOVA L. REV. at 63-64.

44. *Id.* at 89-90.

45. *Id.* at 64. There is a standard in between "motivating-factor" and "but-for" causation that a handful of circuits and HUD administrative law judges have imported from Title VII into FHA cases. *See* Schwemm, HDLL §10:3 (notes 12-32 and accompanying text). This is essentially a motivating factor standard that shifts the burden of persuasion to the defendant to prove that they would have made the same decision even without consideration of the prohibited factor. Price Waterhouse v. Hopkins, 490 U.S. 228 (1989). The *Price Waterhouse* standard is more stringent than "motivating factor" because it recognizes an affirmative defense to liability, that is, the "same decision" defense. It is less stringent than but-for causation because it places the burden on the defendant to establish the absence of causation, rather than requiring the burden of proof on causation to remain with the plaintiff. This standard is similar to that used in Equal Protection cases, described below. It governed Title VII claims before Congress amended that statute in the 1991 Civil Rights Act to provide only a partial defense to mixed motive liability. It has continued to be applied in some FHA cases because the 1991 Act applied only to Title VII, not to Title VIII. Schwemm, HDLL §10:3 (notes 25-26 and accompanying text) (citing Pub. L. No. 102-166, 105 Stat. 1071 (1991)). The FHA is operating in an uncertain causation landscape, but the *Price Waterhouse* standard seems to be waning in influence as but-for causation gains traction as the default standard governing federal antidiscrimination claims.

does not apply to the FHA, and "is rarely used in federal civil rights statutes."[46] Even if the but-for causation standard ultimately is held to apply to FHA cases, it is not as demanding as a sole factor standard because there can be multiple but-for causes. *Bostock*, 590 U.S. at 656. Do you think the plaintiff in *Marable* could have prevailed if required to prove that discrimination was the "sole cause" of the refusal to rent?

4. Other Civil Rights Statutes. Congress has vast discretion in setting the causation standard, and statutes providing analogous protections can diverge on causation. This can lead to much complexity, as fair housing plaintiffs may bring multiple claims operating under different causation standards. Section 1981 requires but-for causation under *Comcast* (and presumably §1982 does, too). The FHA may allow a motivating factor standard, depending on the circuit.[47] Equal Protection claims (discussed below) are analyzed using motivating factor causation, state and local fair housing laws may apply more lenient causation standards, and none is governed by the federal statutory presumption announced in *Comcast*. Section 504 of the Rehabilitation Act protecting people with disabilities requires sole causation, but Title II of the Americans with Disabilities Act providing comparable rights and remedies does not. Professor Schwemm observes that "in multiclaim fair housing cases, courts will have to analyze the causation issue for each law separately, likely producing different results"[48] for different claims.

5. Coded Language? Recall the defense's (belated) explanation, rejected by the court, that Marable got "smart" on the phone and behaved in a "belligerent" and "harassing" manner. Do these characterizations strike you as problematic? They could be considered racially coded terms, reflecting a very limited tolerance for behavior by Black people outside of a narrow range of acceptability. It is possible that defendants perceived Marable in this way without recognizing the racial stereotypes underlying this perception. Marable was able to counter this explanation using circumstantial evidence. Plaintiffs also may counter such arguments through the use of expert testimony on the role of stereotypes in decisionmaking, as discussed in the note in section A, above.

---

46. Schwemm, 66 VILLANOVA L. REV. at 80. It does apply in the Rehabilitation Act, discussed below.

47. To make matters even more complicated, §3617 retaliation claims might mirror such claims under Title VII, which follow a but-for causation standard, resulting in different standards applying to different sections of the FHA. *See* Schwemm, 66 VILLANOVA L. REV. at 94 (citing Univ. of Tex. Sw. Med. Ctr. v. Nassar, 570 U.S. 338 (2013)).

48. *Id.*

C. EVIDENTIARY FRAMEWORK FOR DEMONSTRATING THE INTENT OF A MULTIMEMBER GOVERNMENT BODY

If individuals frequently make decisions based on more than one factor, it certainly follows that organizations comprising multiple decisionmakers can do so. The following is a landmark case establishing the types of circumstantial evidence considered probative in demonstrating intent on the part of a group or, in this case, a governmental entity. The *Arlington Heights* Court issued its standards while interpreting claims arising under the Equal Protection Clause of the U.S. Constitution, and, as illustrated in the case that follows it, subsequent courts have imported these standards when analyzing intent claims under the FHA.

Village of Arlington Heights v. Metropolitan Housing Development Corporation
429 U.S. 252 (1977)

POWELL, J., delivered the opinion of the Court, in which Burger, C.J., and Stewart, Blackmun, and Rehnquist, J.J., joined. Marshall, J., filed an opinion concurring in part and dissenting in part, in which Brennan, J., joined. White, J., filed a dissenting opinion. Stevens, J., took no part in the consideration or decision of the case.

In 1971 respondent Metropolitan Housing Development Corporation (MHDC) applied to petitioner, the Village of Arlington Heights, Ill., for the rezoning of a 15-acre parcel from single-family to multiple-family classification. Using federal financial assistance, MHDC planned to build 190 clustered townhouse units for low- and moderate-income tenants. The Village denied the rezoning request. MHDC alleged that the denial was racially discriminatory and that it violated the Fourteenth Amendment and the FHA.

I

Arlington Heights is a suburb of Chicago, located about 26 miles northwest of the downtown Loop area. Most of the land in Arlington Heights is zoned for detached single-family homes, and this is in fact the prevailing land use. The Village experienced substantial growth during the 1960s, but, like other communities in northwest Cook County, its population of racial minority groups remained quite low. According to the 1970 census, only 27 of the Village's 64,000 residents were black.

The Clerics of St. Viator, a religious order (Order), own an 80-acre parcel just east of the center of Arlington Heights. Part of the site is occupied by the Viatorian high school. . . . Much of the site, however, remains vacant. Since 1959, when the Village first adopted a zoning ordinance, all the land

surrounding the Viatorian property has been zoned R-3, a single-family speci-
fication with relatively small minimum lot-size requirements.

The Order decided in 1970 to devote some of its land to low- and moderate-
income housing. Investigation revealed that the most expeditious way to
build such housing was to work through a nonprofit developer experienced
in the use of federal housing subsidies.[49] MHDC is such a developer. It was
organized in 1968 by several prominent Chicago citizens for the purpose of
building low- and moderate-income housing throughout the Chicago area.

After some negotiation, MHDC and the Order entered into a 99-year
lease and an accompanying agreement of sale covering a 15-acre site in the
southeast corner of the Viatorian property. MHDC became the lessee immediately, but the sale agreement was contingent upon MHDC's securing zoning clearances from the Village and §236 housing assistance from the Federal
Government. If MHDC proved unsuccessful in securing either, both the lease
and the contract of sale would lapse.

MHDC engaged an architect and proceeded with the project, to be known
as Lincoln Green. The plans called for 20 two-story buildings with a total of
190 units, each unit having its own private entrance from outside. One hundred of the units would have a single bedroom, thought likely to attract
elderly citizens. The remainder would have two, three, or four bedrooms.
A large portion of the site would remain open, with shrubs and trees to screen
the homes abutting the property to the east.

The planned development did not conform to the Village's zoning ordinance and could not be built unless Arlington Heights rezoned the parcel to
R-5, its multiple-family housing classification. Accordingly, MHDC filed with
the Village Plan Commission a petition for rezoning, accompanied by supporting materials describing the development and specifying that it would be
subsidized under §236. The materials made clear that one requirement under
§236 is an affirmative marketing plan designed to assure that a subsidized
development is racially integrated. MHDC also submitted studies demonstrating the need for housing of this type and analyzing the probable impact
of the development. MHDC consulted with the Village staff for preliminary
review of the development. The parties have stipulated that every change recommended during such consultations was incorporated into the plans.

During the spring of 1971, the Plan Commission considered the proposal
at a series of three public meetings, which drew large crowds. Although
many of those attending were quite vocal and demonstrative in opposition
to Lincoln Green, a number of individuals and representatives of community
groups spoke in support of rezoning. Some of the comments, both from opponents and supporters, addressed what was referred to as the "social issue,"

---

49. [Fn. 2 in original] Section 236 [Eds.—suspended in 1973] provides for "interest reduction payments" to owners of [qualifying] rental housing projects if the savings are passed on to
the tenants in accordance with a rather complex formula.

the desirability or undesirability of introducing at this location in Arlington Heights low- and moderate-income housing, housing that would probably be racially integrated.

Many of the opponents, however, focused on the zoning aspects of the petition, stressing two arguments. First, the area always had been zoned single-family, and the neighboring citizens had built or purchased there in reliance on that classification. Rezoning threatened to cause a measurable drop in property value for neighboring sites. Second, the Village's apartment policy, adopted by the Village Board in 1962 and amended in 1970, called for R-5 zoning primarily to serve as a buffer between single-family development and land uses thought incompatible, such as commercial or manufacturing districts. Lincoln Green did not meet this requirement, as it adjoined no commercial or manufacturing district.

At the close of the third meeting, the Plan Commission adopted a motion to recommend to the Village's Board of Trustees that it deny the request. Two members voted against the motion and submitted a minority report, stressing that in their view the change to accommodate Lincoln Green represented "good zoning." After a public hearing, the Board denied the rezoning by a 6-1 vote.

The following June MHDC and three Negro individuals filed this lawsuit. A second nonprofit corporation and an individual of Mexican-American descent intervened as plaintiffs. The trial resulted in a judgment for petitioners. [Neither the district nor the appellate court held the Village was motivated by racial discrimination. The appellate court held that the discriminatory effect of the Village's denial of the Lincoln Green proposal violated the Equal Protection Clause of the Fourteenth Amendment.] . . .

III

Our decision last Term in *Washington v. Davis* made it clear that official action will not be held unconstitutional solely because it results in a racially disproportionate impact. "Disproportionate impact is not irrelevant, but it is not the sole touchstone of an invidious racial discrimination." Proof of racially discriminatory intent or purpose is required to show a violation of the Equal Protection Clause.

Davis does not require a plaintiff to prove that the challenged action rested solely on racially discriminatory purposes. Rarely can it be said that a legislature or administrative body operating under a broad mandate made a decision motivated solely by a single concern, or even that a particular purpose was the "dominant" or "primary" one. In fact, it is because legislators and administrators are properly concerned with balancing numerous competing considerations that courts refrain from reviewing the merits of their decisions, absent a showing of arbitrariness or irrationality. But racial discrimination is not just another competing consideration. When there is a proof that a discriminatory purpose has been a motivating factor in the decision, this judicial deference is no longer justified.

Determining whether invidious discriminatory purpose was a motivating factor demands a sensitive inquiry into such circumstantial and direct evidence of intent as may be available. The impact of the official action, whether it "bears more heavily on one race than another," may provide an important starting point. Sometimes a clear pattern, unexplainable on grounds other than race, emerges from the effect of the state action even when the governing legislation appears neutral on its face. Yick Wo v. Hopkins, 118 U.S. 356 (1886);[50] Gomillion v. Lightfoot, 364 U.S. 339 (1960).[51] The evidentiary inquiry is then relatively easy. But such cases are rare. Absent a pattern as stark as that in *Gomillion* or *Yick Wo*, impact alone is not determinative,[52] and the Court must look to other evidence.

The historical background of the decision is one evidentiary source, particularly if it reveals a series of official actions taken for invidious purposes. The specific sequence of events leading up to the challenged decision also may shed some light on the decisionmaker's purposes. For example, if the property involved here always had been zoned R-5 but suddenly was changed to R-3 when the town learned of MHDC's plans to erect integrated housing,[53] we would have a far different case. Departures from the normal procedural sequence also might afford evidence that improper purposes are playing a role. Substantive departures too may be relevant, particularly if the factors usually considered important by the decisionmaker strongly favor a decision contrary to the one reached.

The legislative or administrative history may be highly relevant, especially where there are contemporary statements by members of the decisionmaking body, minutes of its meetings, or reports. In some extraordinary instances the

---

50. [EDS.—In *Yick Wo*, the Supreme Court held that it could infer discriminatory intent in the application of a facially neutral ordinance, where the ordinance was administered in a clearly prejudicial manner. San Francisco imposed a permitting requirement for wooden laundries: Two hundred laundry owners of Chinese descent applied for permits, but only one was granted; 80 white owners applied, and all but one were successful.]

51. [EDS.—In *Gomillion*, the Supreme Court held that it could infer improper racial motivation from the fact that the Alabama legislature redrew the boundaries of the City of Tuskegee, creating a 28-sided boundary that excluded nearly all Black voters from the city and left all white voters in place. No other explanation for redrawing in this manner was offered.]

52. [Fn. 14 in original] This is not to say that a consistent pattern of official racial discrimination is a necessary predicate to a violation of the Equal Protection Clause. A single invidiously discriminatory governmental act—in the exercise of the zoning power as elsewhere—would not necessarily be immunized by the absence of such discrimination in the making of other comparable decisions.

53. [Fn. 16 in original] *See, e.g.*, Progress Development Corp. v. Mitchell, 286 F.2d 222 (C.A.7 1961) (park board allegedly condemned plaintiffs' land for a park upon learning that the homes plaintiffs were erecting there would be sold under a marketing plan designed to assure integration).

members might be called to the stand at trial to testify concerning the purpose of the official action, although even then such testimony frequently will be barred by privilege.[54]

The foregoing summary identifies, without purporting to be exhaustive, subjects of proper inquiry in determining whether racially discriminatory intent existed. With these in mind, we now address the case before us.

IV

This case was tried in the District Court and reviewed in the Court of Appeals before our decision in *Washington v. Davis*. The respondents proceeded on the erroneous theory that the Village's refusal to rezone carried a racially discriminatory effect and was, without more, unconstitutional. But both courts below understood that at least part of their function was to examine the purpose underlying the decision.

We also have reviewed the evidence. The impact of the Village's decision does arguably bear more heavily on racial minorities. Minorities constitute 18% of the Chicago area population, and 40% of the income groups said to be eligible for Lincoln Green. But there is little about the sequence of events leading up to the decision that would spark suspicion. The area around the Viatorian property has been zoned R-3 since 1959, the year when Arlington Heights first adopted a zoning map. Single-family homes surround the 80-acre site, and the Village is undeniably committed to single-family homes as its dominant residential land use. The rezoning request progressed according to the usual procedures.[55] The Plan Commission even scheduled two additional hearings, at least in part to accommodate MHDC and permit it to supplement its presentation with answers to questions generated at the first hearing.

The statements by the Plan Commission and Village Board members, as reflected in the official minutes, focused almost exclusively on the zoning aspects of the MHDC petition, and the zoning factors on which they relied are not novel criteria in the Village's rezoning decisions. There is no reason to doubt that there has been reliance by some neighboring property owners on the maintenance of single-family zoning in the vicinity. The Village originally

---

54. [Fn. 18 in original] This Court has recognized, ever since Fletcher v. Peck (1810), that judicial inquiries into legislative or executive motivation represent a substantial intrusion into the workings of other branches of government. Placing a decisionmaker on the stand is therefore "usually to be avoided." Citizens to Preserve Overton Park v. Volpe, 401 U.S. 402, 420 (1971).

55. [Fn. 19 in original] Respondents have made much of one apparent procedural departure. The parties stipulated that the Village Planner, the staff member whose primary responsibility covered zoning and planning matters, was never asked for his written or oral opinion of the rezoning request. The omission does seem curious, but respondents failed to prove at trial what role the Planner customarily played in rezoning decisions.

adopted its buffer policy long before MHDC entered the picture and has applied the policy too consistently for us to infer discriminatory purpose from its application in this case. Finally, MHDC called one member of the Village Board to the stand at trial. Nothing in her testimony supports an inference of invidious purpose.[56]

In sum, the evidence does not warrant overturning the concurrent findings of both courts below. Respondents simply failed to carry their burden of proving that discriminatory purpose was a motivating factor in the Village's decision.[57] This conclusion ends the constitutional inquiry. The [C]ourt of Appeals' further finding that the Village's decision carried a discriminatory "ultimate effect" is without independent constitutional significance.

V

Respondents' complaint also alleged that the refusal to rezone violated the FHA. The Court of Appeals, however, proceeding in a somewhat unorthodox fashion, did not decide the statutory question. We remand the case for further consideration of respondents' statutory claims.

Reversed and remanded.

The next case illustrates that, following *Arlington Heights*, "the FHA would become the preferred legal basis for challenging exclusionary zoning in the future."[58]

---

56. [Fn. 20 in original] Respondents complain that the District Court unduly limited their efforts to prove that the Village Board acted for discriminatory purposes, since it forbade questioning Board members about their motivation at the time they cast their votes. Respondents were allowed, both during the discovery phase and at trial, to question Board members fully about materials and information available to them at the time of decision. In light of respondents' repeated insistence that it was effect and not motivation which would make out a constitutional violation, the District Court's action was not improper.

57. [Fn. 21 in original] Proof that the decision by the Village was motivated in part by a racially discriminatory purpose would not necessarily have required invalidation of the challenged decision. Such proof would, however, have shifted to the Village the burden of establishing that the same decision would have resulted even had the impermissible purpose not been considered. If this were established, the complaining party in a case of this kind no longer fairly could attribute the injury complained of to improper consideration of a discriminatory purpose.

58. Robert G. Schwemm, *Reflections on* Arlington Heights: *Fifty Years of Exclusionary Zoning Litigation and Beyond*, 57 UIC L. Rev. 389, 444 (2024).

Hurricane Katrina aftermath
Credit: The U.S. National Archives

Greater New Orleans Fair Housing Action Center
v. Saint Bernard Parish
641 F. Supp. 2d 563 (E.D. La. 2009)

Helen G. Berrigan, District Judge.[59]

In the wake of the devastation wrought by Hurricane Katrina, St. Bernard Parish officials have had to rebuild their parish and community from near total ruin. [Eds.—On August 29, 2005, Hurricane Katrina made landfall as a Category 3 hurricane in Southeast Louisiana (and later in Mississippi), displacing more than a million people and damaging more than a million housing units in the Gulf Coast region. The New Orleans levee system failure flooded the metro area, leaving up to 80 percent of the city under water. It was at the time one of the deadliest hurricanes to hit the United States. The high poverty rate (28 percent in the city of New Orleans) and lack of access to vehicles disproportionately prevented Black and elderly residents from evacuating. This case features some of the fair housing challenges that emerged in the rebuilding effort.][60]

---

59. Counsel of record reported in this decision include M. Lucia Blacksher of GNOFHAC; John P. Relman and Katherine A. Gillespie, Relman Dane PLLC; and Jonathan P. Hooks, Joseph D. Rich, and Nicole Birch, Lawyers Committee for Civil Rights. These lawyers and firms litigate many fair housing cases, including others reported in this book.

60. [Eds.—This background is derived from Jeffrey Medlin et al., Extremely Powerful Hurricane Katrina Leaves a Historic Mark on the Northern Gulf Coast, Nat'l Weather Serv.,

The question presented to this Court is what limits [apply] to their efforts to shape the housing stock available, and thus the population, in the parish. Before the Court is plaintiff Greater New Orleans Fair Housing Action Center's ("GNO") and intervenor Provident Realty Advisors, Inc.'s ("Provident") Motion to Enforce Consent Order. Plaintiff and intervenor claim that in September 2008, defendants enacted a moratorium that violates the terms of a previous consent order governing this case [described below]. Defendants oppose. This Court held an evidentiary hearing [and] grants [the] Motion to Enforce the Consent Order for the following reasons.

I. BACKGROUND

The parties to this matter entered into a Consent Order, which was approved by this Court on February 27, 2008. The consent order settled plaintiffs' allegations that defendants violated the FHA and 1866 CRA in enacting several housing ordinances. The plaintiffs alleged that the ordinances were enacted with the intent and effect of discriminating against minorities, and plaintiffs sought in particular a preliminary injunction to stay the operation of the so-called "blood relative ordinance."[61] Pursuant to the Consent Order, St. Bernard Parish was enjoined from violating the terms of the FHA and 1866 CRA. GNO and St. Bernard Parish specifically agreed to the continuing jurisdiction of this Court for a period of three years from February 27, 2008 to resolve disputes regarding interpretation or compliance with the Consent Order.

. . . GNO and Provident filed a motion to enforce the . . . Consent Order [and] claimed that an ordinance passed by the Council in September 2008 violated the [order]. The challenged ordinance placed a moratorium on the construction of all multi-family housing (i.e. buildings with more than 5 units) for a period of twelve months or until the Council enacted certain zoning updates. At the time of the introduction and passage of the contested moratorium, and with the knowledge of certain St. Bernard Parish officials, Provident, a real estate development corporation, had initiated the process of constructing four affordable housing developments in St. Bernard Parish. GNO and Provident allege that the moratorium violated the FHA by making housing unavailable on the basis of race. Plaintiff and intervenor claim the moratorium was enacted with discriminatory intent and/or has a discriminatory effect in

---

https://www.weather.gov/mob/katrina (last updated Sept. 2022); Arloc Sherman & Isaac Shapiro, Essential Facts about the Victims of Hurricane Katrina, Ctr. on Budget & Pol'y Priorities 2 (Sept. 19, 2005), https://www.cbpp.org/sites/default/files/archive/9-19-05pov.pdf; Allison Plyler, Facts for Features: Katrina Impact, The Data Ctr. (Aug. 26, 2016), https://www.datacen terresearch.org/data-resources/katrina/facts-for-impact/.]

61. [Fn. 1 in original] The parties refer to the "blood relative" ordinance as shorthand for a housing ordinance passed by the St. Bernard Parish Council on September 19, 2006, that stated: "No person . . . shall rent, lease, loan, or otherwise allow occupancy or use of any single-family residence located in an R-1 zone by any person or group of persons, other than a family member(s) related by blood within the first, second or third direct ascending or descending generation(s), without first obtaining a Permissive Use Permit from the St. Bernard Parish Council."

violation of the FHA and the Consent Order. GNO and Provident request the Court "direct St. Bernard Parish to rescind the moratorium and enjoin the Parish from enforcing the moratorium until it is repealed."

The following facts were undisputed at the evidentiary hearing. The proposed Provident developments consist of four mixed-income rental apartment complexes with 72 units each. Thirty percent of these units will be rented at fair market rates. Fifty percent will be at 60% of Area Median Income ("AMI").[62] Twenty percent will be at 30% of AMI. The estimated cost of the developments is $60 million dollars. The majority of funding for these complexes was specifically geared towards providing affordable housing, thus the income restrictions and lowered rent on 70% of the units. $20 million of the funding would come from Community Development Block Grant funds, administered by the Louisiana Recovery Development Program. $30 million would be provided in Low Income Housing Tax Credits. The final $10 million required to fund the developments was expected to come from a permanent loan from Freddie Mac.

II. LAW AND ANALYSIS

[EDS.—The Court first found that the challenged moratorium had a disparate racial impact.]

B. Discriminatory Intent

To assess whether or not discriminatory intent exists, the Fifth Circuit, citing the Supreme Court, has held the following circumstantial evidence factors to be both pertinent and non-exhaustive: "(1) the historical background of the decision, (2) the specific sequence of events leading up to the decision, (3) departures from the normal procedural sequence, (4) substantive departures, and (5) legislative history, especially where there are contemporary statements by members of the decision-making body." Overton v. City of Austin, 871 F.2d 529, 540 (5th Cir.1989) (citing *Vill. of Arlington Heights v. Metro. Hous. Dev. Corp.*). In short, plaintiff and intervenor must establish "that race was a consideration and played some role in the real estate transaction." Hanson v. Veterans Admin., 800 F.2d 1381, 1386 (5th Cir.1986).

(1) The historical background of the decision

The moratorium at issue today is strikingly similar to one of the ordinances challenged in the 2006 litigation that resulted in the voluntary consent decree. On November 1, 2005, the Council enacted a twelve-month moratorium on the "re-establishment and development of any multi-family dwellings in St. Bernard Parish." Plaintiffs' claims regarding the legality of this, as well as

---

62. [EDS.—The household AMI for St. Bernard Parish in fiscal year 2008 was $59,800. National Low Income Housing Coalition, *Out of Reach 2007-2008*, at 84 (2008), https://nlihc .org/sites/default/files/oor/2007-2008-OOR.pdf.]

other, ordinances were settled by virtue of the Consent Order. . . . This [2008] moratorium prohibited the construction of all "multi-family residential and/ or any housing developments with five or more units for up to twelve (12) months or until such time as the Council approves these structures in the zoning updates to the St. Bernard Parish Code of Ordinances." Both ordinances prohibited the development of multi-family housing; both were applicable parish-wide.

In a similar vein, the Court finds the so-called "blood relative" ordinance relevant to the history of the challenged ordinance. St. Bernard Parish is an overwhelmingly Caucasian parish, particularly in comparison to its neighbors. Based on 2000 census data, Dr. Bradford[63] found that the racial composition for the entire New Orleans MSA was 57.4% Caucasian and 37.4% African American. However, the African American population was highly concentrated in sections of Orleans, Plaquemines, and Jefferson Parish. For example, the city of New Orleans included 66.3% of the African American population of the entire metropolitan area, even though it accounted for only 36.8% of the area's total population. Comparing neighboring parishes Orleans to St. Bernard further demonstrates the stark racial contrast. 67.3% of the Orleans Parish population was African American and 28.1% was Caucasian. St. Bernard Parish, however, was 88.3% Caucasian and 7.6% African American.

Within this racial context, the "blood relative" ordinance was introduced. In September 2006, the St. Bernard Parish Council enacted an ordinance, introduced by then Councilperson Craig Taffaro, to prohibit the rental or occupancy of a single family residence to someone other than a blood relative without first obtaining a permissive use permit. Mr. Taffaro later stated that the purpose of the "blood relative" ordinance was to "maintain the demographics of St. Bernard Parish." Given that St. Bernard Parish is overwhelmingly Caucasian, plaintiff claimed the ordinance was racially discriminatory since African Americans de facto became ineligible for rental housing in the Parish. Indeed, Council Chairperson Lynn Dean, who voted against the ordinance, said the ordinance was racially motivated and was clearly intended to preserve the nearly all-Caucasian demographic of the parish. Mr. Taffaro acknowledged that the Council even considered censoring Mr. Dean for his allegations.

To be clear, the settlement of the prior claims does not result in an inference of liability on behalf of the defendants, any more than it results in an inference of a frivolous claim by plaintiffs. Rather, the similarity between the 2005 multi-family ordinance, the 2008 ordinance, and the history of the "blood relative" ordinance is striking, independent of the settlement. They evidence

---

63. [EDS.—Dr. Calvin Bradford served as an expert witness in other cases featured in this book, including *Hargraves* and *American Family*, Chapter 11. Dr. Bradford assisted in research for and drafting of the Home Mortgage Disclosure Act of 1975 (HMDA) and the Community Reinvestment Act of 1977 (CRA). https://woodstockinst.org/about/staff/cal-bradford/ (CV on file with editors).]

repeated attempts to restrict certain types of housing in a parish whose housing stock, along with other structures, was largely obliterated. As was shown
by Dr. Bradford, *supra*, the type of housing restricted or forbidden is disproportionately utilized by African Americans. Noteworthy too is the involvement of some of the same public officials in the ordinances.

(2) The specific sequence of events leading up to the decision

The Court is also particularly troubled by the sequence of events preceding the Council's enactment of this moratorium. On July 14, 2008, Provident
developer Matt Harris met with several St. Bernard Parish officials to discuss
Provident's proposed developments. Harris and another Provident representative discussed the quality of the apartments, the mixed-income guidelines, the financial incentives for maintaining the property, and showed the
St. Bernard officials sketches of the proposed development. While some
questions arose as to who would actually occupy the units, it was not a big
focus of the meeting. St. Bernard Parish officials discussed how the developments would not cost the parish any money; in fact, the developments were
expected to create $40,000 in tax revenue each year for the parish. Ray Lauga,
the Councilperson for the district of three of the planned developments, testified that he told Harris he would "work with them" and was "very interested
in having a multi-family development be developed with the higher codes,
higher standards in place." Ray Lauga was personally impressed with Matt
Harris and knew the project would bring in $60 million dollars of investment
to the parish. The Court surmises the meeting went well—on July 23, 2008,
Jerry Graves, the Director of Community Development for St. Bernard Parish
certified in writing that the properties were properly zoned for each of the
four proposed developments.

On August 7, 8, 9, 2008, Provident ran a "Notice to the Public" for each of
the four developments announcing its application for housing tax credits and
Community Block Development Grants in the Times-Picayune newspaper.
The notice described the developments as "a new construction garden style
apartment community for families" and providing "supportive services." The
developments were clearly identified as "mixed income" and consisting of a
maximum of 72 units per development.

On Saturday, August 16, 2008, an editorial appeared on the front-page of
The St. Bernard Voice, the official newspaper of St. Bernard Parish, that read
in part:

> Should St. Bernard residents be concerned? Ours was a crime free community
> of homeowners with a deep appreciation for shared values . . . Is that now
> threatened?
>   The local newspaper had three entries in its legal notices this past week. All
> three relate to the use of private and public money to construct a total of 216
> apartments in three selected sites in the parish. . . . The fact that each develop-
> ment mentions that it will provide "supportive services in a community facility
> including . . . after school programs on a voluntary basis, adult basic education,

and personal finance" may provide some insights into the background of the intended occupants. . . .

Less we forget, Village Square started out as a middle class housing development that catered to teachers, other professionals, and their families. It was a wonderful place to live . . . when first opened. After a number of years, ownership changed, maintenance diminished, and the quality of renter fell to a much lower social/economic class. Result: Village Square became what can only be described as a ghetto with drugs, crime, vandalism, and violence.

That is generally the case with high density housing. It was just because such problems persist in that type of environment that HUD demolished the concentrated lifestyles of the "New Orleans Projects." Is St. Bernard about to buck the trend and construct them here in St. Bernard? What guarantees have the residents of St. Bernard that their tax money is not going to be used to create the kind of blight New Orleans recently destroyed?

But the fact remains that residents know little about what is going on, [and] are not impressed when they hear the term "mixed income development" mentioned in the project description. . . .

The references to "ghetto," "crime," "blight," and "shared values" are similar to the types of expressions that courts in similar situations have found to be nothing more than "camouflaged racial expressions." Smith v. Town of Clarkton, 682 F.2d 1055, 1066 (4th Cir. 1982) (affirming that statements about "undesirables," and concerns about personal safety due to "new" people are "camouflaged racial expressions"); Atkins v. Robinson, 545 F. Supp. 852, 871-72 (E.D. Va. 1982) (finding statement that she "feared the projects 'would degenerate to slum-like conditions, with an abundance of crime'" to be a veiled reference to race). In the Title VII hostile work environment context, "ghetto" is repeatedly associated with race. *See, e.g.*, Harrington v. Disney Regional Entm't, Inc., 276 Fed. App'x 863, 876-877 (11th Cir. 2007) (indicates "ghetto" was a racial slur); *see also* Clark ex rel. T.M.J. v. Pielert, 2009 WL 35337 (D. Minn. 2009) (noting "ghetto" was a "racially-charged term" in the §1983 context preventing summary judgment on qualified immunity). Furthermore, the Village Square complex cited in the article is a multi-unit housing complex in St. Bernard with a significant African American population. St. Bernard Parish, in general, is overwhelmingly Caucasian. Given the racial demographics of the parish in general and that Village Square has a significantly higher African American population than the parish at large, the Court finds that the references to Village Square in this context are racially-loaded.

The Court is also not persuaded by the disavowals of President Craig Taffaro and Councilperson Ray Lauga that the editorial did not refer indirectly to race. First, the Court is just as able as either witness to give a lay impression and interpretation to the written editorial. The references to ghetto, crime, drugs, violence, the Village Square, and to the Housing and Urban Development New Orleans Projects juxtaposed against their "threat" to the "shared values" of overwhelmingly Caucasian St. Bernard Parish clearly is an appeal to racial as well as class prejudice. Additionally, even Mr. Taffaro seemed at pains to evade a straight answer to plaintiffs' questioning on the subject, although he did eventually testify that he did not think the various terms constituted camouflaged racial expression.

Not surprisingly, a public outcry followed publication of the editorial. Ray Lauga testified that he had constituents calling his office expressing concern over the developments. Two business days later, on Tuesday, August 19, 2008, Ray Lauga introduced to the Council the moratorium at issue in this case, Ordinance SBPC # 905-09-08. Councilman Lauga admitted that public opposition to the Provident developments was a factor in the introduction of the multi-family moratorium.

On August 26, 2008, the foundation that owned the land for the proposed developments organized an informational meeting for the leadership of the St. Bernard community and Provident. Attendees included the author of the editorial, the school superintendent, Mr. Taffaro, Mr. Lauga, and the sheriff, among others. At the meeting, Provident developer Matt Harris answered questions regarding the lower-income units of the development, the screening policies, including for criminal history of the applicants, and the possibility of pre-leasing to elderly and government employees from St. Bernard parish. Mr. Harris was asked to step out of the room while the attendees discussed the project. When he was invited to return, he was informed that the attendees had agreed to support the development. After speaking with Councilperson Lauga, [Mr. Harris] was reassured that the moratorium was a temporary and necessary measure to address the public outcry and address improved design standards.

On September 9, 2008, Provident provided proposed design standards to Councilperson Lauga. Mr. Lauga did not contact anyone at Provident to discuss the proposed standards.

On September 18, 2008, the Council unanimously adopted Ordinance # 905-09-08, placing a moratorium on all housing developments with five or more units "for up to twelve months or until such time as the Council approves these structures in the zoning updates to the St. Bernard Parish Code of Ordinances."

Taken as a whole, the Court is disturbed by this relatively undisputed timeline of events. The initial positive reaction, including letters noting the developments were properly zoned, immediately eroded following the publication of the editorial. Although Mr. Lauga first claimed the timeline was "convenient," he later admitted that the outcry over Provident was a factor in the introduction and eventual passage of the moratorium.

(3) Departures from the normal procedural sequence

Kalima Rose, plaintiff's expert on affordable housing, testified about the normal process for enacting a moratorium in relation to a proposed construction project. Ms. Rose testified that "when communities are in the middle of zoning changes, they sometimes call moratoria if somebody's asking for a variance of use," to ensure the most up-to-date code governs the developer. But when, as here, land is zoned for a particular use and a developer seeks a permit to build for that use, a moratorium is not a normal occurrence. Ms. Rose's testimony on the irregularity of this moratorium is in fact supported by testimony from Dr. Wade Ragas, an expert for the defense. Dr. Ragas gave several examples of other moratoria in Orleans and Jefferson parishes. However, all of those examples concerned moratoria that were limited in geographic scope to a particular area instead of a blanket moratorium on all construction of certain structures.[64] Taken together, this Court finds that the moratorium at issue in this case—because it did not involve a variance and was not limited in geographic scope—departs from the normal procedure regarding local zoning moratoria.

(4) Substantive departures

"Substantive departures" are usually indicated when "factors usually considered important by the decisionmaker strongly favor a decision contrary to the one reached." *Vill. of Arlington Heights.*

As previously discussed, St. Bernard Parish officials recognized significant beneficial aspects of the proposed development, including the economic investment of $60 million dollars in their parish and the estimated annual $40,000 tax revenues. Since Hurricane Katrina, St. Bernard had been aggressively pursuing funding and infrastructure projects to get St. Bernard back on its feet, and indeed, appeared to support the Provident developments until the publication of the editorial decrying the developments in August 2008. Many of the justifications now cited by defendants to legitimate their opposition to the developments appear contrived, particularly in light of the substantial benefits of Provident's plan.

Justification # 1—Lack of infrastructure

On November 12, 2008, Councilmembers Wayne Landry and George Cavignac sent a letter to the Louisiana Housing Finance Agency claim[ing] that St. Bernard Parish does not have the required infrastructure, including medical care, to support the developments. This stands in stark contrast to an October 9, 2008 letter by Parish President Craig Taffaro to the same agency noting that the required infrastructure was in place to support the project. . . . Moreover, in June 2008, a deal was announced for the creation of a 40-bed hospital in the parish.

Justification # 2—Affordable housing not needed

Defendants also dispute that St. Bernard Parish needs additional affordable housing. In the same objection letter, Councilmembers Landry and Cavignac claimed that St. Bernard Parish was "flush" with rental properties. Faced with the conflicting testimony of Kalima Rose, plaintiff's expert in affordable

---

64. [Fn. 7 in original] The Court also notes that text of the ordinance indicates that the moratorium could be indefinite. The text states the moratorium lasts "for up to 12 months *or until such time* as the Council approves these structures in zoning updates."

housing, and Dr. Wade Ragas, defendants' expert in the local housing market, the Court finds the methodology of Ms. Rose more reliable and thus more persuasive. Dr. Ragas based his analysis solely on a snapshot of the parish's current condition ["with scant attention to future trends in the region"]. Ms. Rose took a more comprehensive and regional approach in her analysis, assessing not only the current but also projected trends in employment and housing which correlated with when the new housing would actually come online. . . . For example, in Ms. Rose's opinion, even if St. Bernard Parish proceeded with all of the currently allocated federal resources and projects (including Provident), it would only replace twenty percent of its lost rental stock. In addition, 25% of workers in St. Bernard Parish cannot afford a two-bedroom apartment at current market prices. . . . The Court finds these conclusions well-supported by both the methodology and facts. . . .

Justification # 3—Possibility of abandonment

At the hearing, defense witnesses expressed the fear that Provident will fail to maintain, and/or ultimately abandon the properties. . . . Defendants have offered no specific basis for their asserted fear that Provident will abandon the buildings as soon as the fifteen years are up, the debt service completed and therefore at the very moment that they would yield a greater return.

Justification # 4—Moratorium had another target: Village Square

At the evidentiary hearing, Mr. Lauga claimed that possible redevelopment of a housing development called Village Square prompted the moratorium. . . . First, as noted previously, Mr. Lauga also conceded that the Provident development was a factor in the moratorium. Second, the focus of the moratorium could have been more narrowly tailored to the specific Village Square area.

Justification # 6 [sic]—Codification of design standards/Zoning update

Finally, as noted previously, defendants have claimed the moratorium was justified by the need to update the zoning code, including codifying design standards prior to the Provident developments going forward. Defendants have failed to demonstrate any evidence of substantive action on the design standards [and had previously] indicated that each development's property was properly zoned.

None of the six justifications, individually or collectively, are persuasive as legitimate reasons for the St. Bernard parish government's abrupt change of heart, particularly given the financial benefits to the parish from the proposed developments. Accordingly, the Court concludes that the opposition to the Provident project is a "substantive departure" from normal decision-making. The Court also concurs with Ms. Rose's opinion that it is mystifying why "anybody would be hampering resources that can move quickly, because there are so many resources that have not moved quickly through FEMA [Federal Emergency Management Agency] and other channels" and risk "jeopardiz[ing] [a] project that's needed so greatly."

(5) Legislative history

While little comment was made publicly regarding the motive behind the moratorium, Councilperson Lauga admitted at trial that the public outcry regarding the Provident developments played a role. Moreover, the historical backdrop to the consent decree and the prior ordinances and the swift introduction of this ordinance only three days after the editorial is also indicative of the racial and class animus underlying the ordinance.

Based on all of the evidence discussed above, the Court concludes that the Parish and Council's intent in enacting and continuing the moratorium is and was racially discriminatory, and as such defendants have violated the FHA, 1866 CRA, and the terms of the February 2008 Consent Order.

[EDS.—The Court also held that the evidence supported a finding of discriminatory effect in violation of the FHA and the Consent Order. Therefore the court enjoined enforcement of the moratorium ordinance and ordered defendants to rescind it.]

NOTES AND QUESTIONS

1. Discerning the Intent Behind Local Government Zoning Decisions. The two previous cases illustrate the prominence of zoning decisions among those government actions challenged for unlawful motive. The challenged zoning decisions in both cases relate to restrictions on development of rent-subsidized, multifamily rental housing. In *Arlington Heights*, the plaintiffs challenged a refusal to "rezone" or remove long-standing restrictions on developing apartments outside "buffer zones." In *St. Bernard*, the plaintiffs challenged a recently enacted, total ban on multifamily housing development throughout the entire parish following a natural disaster.

The *Arlington Heights* Court developed its circumstantial evidence framework under the Equal Protection Clause, with subsequent courts importing that framework into their analysis of the FHA. The nonexhaustive, multifactor test includes: (1) the impact of the official action; (2) the historical background of the decision; (3) the specific sequence of events leading up to the challenged decision; (4) departures from the normal procedural sequence; (5) substantive departures, particularly if the factors usually considered important by the decisionmaker strongly favor a decision contrary to the one reached; and (6) the legislative or administrative history, especially where there are contemporary statements by members of the decisionmaking body, minutes of its meetings, or reports.

2. *Arlington Heights* Multifactor Test v. *McDonnell Douglas* Burden-Shifting Analysis Notice that *Arlington Heights* and *St. Bernard* do not use the *McDonnell Douglas* burden-shifting framework. *Arlington Heights* sets forth a test considering a mosaic of factors, with the burden of proof shifting only after the plaintiff uses the test to prove "that discriminatory purpose was a motivating factor" in the decision. The traditional *McDonnell Douglas* evidentiary framework, by contrast, requires the plaintiff to establish a prima facie case, then shifts the burden to defendant simply to offer admissible evidence of any legitimate, nondiscriminatory explanation, after which the burden shifts back to the plaintiff to prove that defendant's explanation is pretextual.

What are the practical differences between the two frameworks? Which is easier for a plaintiff to use? Why should the plaintiff not be required to use the *McDonnell Douglas* prima facie standard when challenging the government decisions in *Arlington Heights* and *St. Bernard*? Notice that the conduct under challenge is different from a rental or sales decision made by an individual landlord or property owner. The challenge instead is to a local law (zoning ordinance) or decision made by a group about whether to waive or amend the local law. Why might this make a difference in the analysis?

3. Back to Motivating Factor, But-For Causation, and Sole Causation. What kind of causation does the Supreme Court require in *Arlington Heights*? It obviously rejected a sole causation standard in reviewing government decisions for alleged racial motivation:

> [*Washington v.] Davis* does not require a plaintiff to prove that the challenged action rested solely on racially discriminatory purposes. Rarely can it be said that a legislature or administrative body operating under a broad mandate made a decision motivated solely by a single concern, or even that a particular purpose was the "dominant" or "primary" one. In fact, it is because legislators and administrators are properly concerned with balancing numerous competing considerations that courts refrain from reviewing the merits of their decisions, absent a showing of arbitrariness or irrationality. But racial discrimination is not just another competing consideration. When there is a proof that a discriminatory purpose has been a motivating factor in the decision, this judicial deference is no longer justified.

In rejecting a sole causation requirement, the Court embraced a motivating factor standard for the plaintiff, imposing no required showing of but-for causation. In a footnote, the Court recognized it to be the defendant's burden to prove the absence of causation: that it would have made the same decision notwithstanding the impermissible purpose.

> Proof that the decision by the Village was motivated in part by a racially discriminatory purpose would not necessarily have required invalidation of the challenged decision. Such proof would, however, have shifted to the Village the burden of establishing that the same decision would have resulted even had the impermissible purpose not been considered. If this were established, the complaining party . . . no longer fairly could attribute the injury [to] a discriminatory purpose.

The Court's "same decision" dictum in *Arlington Heights* "essentially takes 'the burden of proving but-for causation from the plaintiff and hand[s] it to the defendant as an affirmative defense.'"[65] Thus, the defendant would have to prove that a discriminatory reason would not have "ma[de] a difference to the outcome."[66] This is very different from the defendant's minimal burden of stating a nondiscriminatory motive under the *McDonnell Douglas* framework. Compare *Saint Bernard*, where the court examined the Parish's justifications for its moratorium within the multi-factor evidentiary framework. The court found the Parish's nondiscriminatory explanations, such as the contention that it had no need for affordable housing (with its accompanying tax revenue) anywhere in the storm-ravaged parish, to be substantive departures from its normal decisionmaking, thus contrived and unpersuasive. With no nondiscriminatory explanation remaining, there was no need for further consideration of the defendant's absence-of-causation burden.

Thus, under the *Arlington Heights* framework, an impermissible motive need not be the sole cause of the adverse action. The plaintiff must prove through the mosaic of permitted circumstantial evidence that discrimination was a motivating factor; if the plaintiff is successful in making this showing, the defendant has the opportunity to prove that the discriminatory reason did not contribute to the outcome.

4. Building the Record. Other than the fact that the courts reached opposite conclusions on whether the plaintiffs had proved discriminatory purpose, what differences do you perceive in the evidentiary records under review in the two cases? The Court in *Arlington Heights*, after summarizing the lower courts' assessments, conducted its own review of the evidence in two paragraphs. In *St. Bernard*, the court's review of the factual record spanned three dozen paragraphs. Obviously, the Supreme Court was exercising considerable deference to the lower court's factual findings, whereas the district court in *St. Bernard* was reviewing the record in the first instance. Nevertheless, these cases do underscore that plaintiffs need to develop a substantial factual record to carry their burden of proving that discriminatory purpose motivated the defendant's decisions. Considering the types of evidence that the plaintiffs assembled in the featured cases, where, when, and how might such information be obtained?

5. Sequence of Events. Notice the *Arlington Heights* Court's focus on the longstanding nature of single-family zoning in concluding that there was no discriminatory motive in the case:

> [T]he Village is undeniably committed to single-family homes as its dominant residential land use. . . . The Village originally adopted its buffer policy [using apartments primarily as a buffer between single family and commercial or manufacturing land uses] long before MHDC entered the picture and has applied the policy too consistently for us to infer discriminatory purpose. . . .

---

65. Schwemm, 66 VILLANOVA L. REV. at 78 (citing *Comcast*, 589 U.S. at 337).

66. *Id.* at 72 (citing Price Waterhouse v. Hopkins, 490 U.S. 228, 281 (1989) (Kennedy, J., dissenting)).

The Court elsewhere noted that "if the property involved here always had been zoned R-5 but suddenly was changed to R-3 when the town learned of MHDC's plans to erect integrated housing, we would have a far different case." In other words, there was nothing novel about the Village's conduct to warrant closer scrutiny.

Do you think a zoning (or any) decision must be novel to find that it is racially biased? Note that it was 1970, only two years after passage of the FHA, when the Clerics of St. Viator sought to build the Lincoln Green apartments on property it owned and occupied. Consider also the larger context in which the Village earlier adopted its single-family zoning scheme in 1959. How accessible were single-family homes (or the suburbs in general) to people of color from 1959 to the early 1970s when this case was litigated and when the zoning's consistent application was under review? *See* Chapter 1.

Despite its rejection of the Seventh Circuit's use of discriminatory effects to find a violation of the Equal Protection Clause, the Court highlighted the lower court's reasoning "that the denial of rezoning must be examined in light of its 'historical context and ultimate effect.'"

> Northwest Cook County was enjoying rapid growth in employment opportunities and population, but it continued to exhibit a high degree of residential segregation. The court held that Arlington Heights could not simply ignore this problem. Indeed, it found that the Village had been "exploiting" the situation by allowing itself to become a nearly all white community. The Village had no other current plans for building low- and moderate-income housing, and no other R-5 parcels in the Village were available to MHDC at an economically feasible price.

This "historical context" might have played a role in the Court's remand to the Seventh Circuit with instructions to consider the FHA claims (which included a disparate impact claim that ultimately was upheld by the court of appeals). Nevertheless, the *Arlington Heights* Court accepted the argument on the record before it that "concern for the integrity of the zoning plan" was incompatible with the racial motivation required to prove a constitutional violation. In other words, the Court considered a homebuyer's reliance in the 1960s on the maintenance of single-family zoning to be unrelated to maintaining the racial demographics of an all-white neighborhood. What about that same reliance of a property owner in the current era? Note the court's observation in *St. Bernard* that the parish was using its zoning power to engage in "repeated attempts to restrict certain types of housing . . . disproportionately utilized by African Americans." For further discussion of FHA's application to zoning, disparate impact, and perpetuation of residential racial segregation see Chapter 7.

6. Public Opposition as Evidence. Can public opposition serve as circumstantial evidence that government decisionmaking is motivated by a discriminatory purpose? If so, how? In *Arlington Heights*, the proposal to rezone land to allow development of affordable rental housing "drew large crowds" at three public meetings of the Plan Commission. Many members of the public "were quite vocal and demonstrative in opposition to Lincoln Green." Some of the comments addressed "the 'social issue'" of siting low-income, integrated apartment housing at the proposed site. Many others addressed the "zoning aspects," including reliance on the fact that "the area always had been zoned single-family," and rezoning "threatened to cause a measurable drop in property value." The Plan Commission recommended denial of the request to rezone, and the Village Board denied the rezoning request by a 6-1 vote. The district court acknowledged that some of those speaking at public hearings in opposition to Lincoln Green "might have been motivated by opposition to minority groups," but the court was unwilling to impute that motive to the government decision makers. The Supreme Court, in affirming the lower courts' findings on the issue, did not even mention the evidence of public opposition, but focused strictly on statements by the government decision makers "as reflected in the official minutes," which "focused almost exclusively on the zoning aspects," which were "not novel criteria in the Village's rezoning decisions."

Contrast the role of public opposition in the *St. Bernard* case. Following notice of a plan to seek funding for four mixed-income, 72-unit developments, a front-page editorial ran in the St. Bernard Parish newspaper that included references to "ghetto," "crime," "drugs," "violence" and neighboring New Orleans housing projects. A public outcry against the development ensued, and two business days later a parish council member introduced an indefinite, parish-wide multifamily moratorium. The court used the following analysis to impute racially motivated public opposition to the government decisionmakers:

> The initial positive reaction, including letters noting the developments were properly zoned, immediately eroded following the publication of the editorial. Although [the authoring council member] first claimed the timeline was "convenient," he later admitted that the outcry over Provident was a factor in the introduction and eventual passage of the moratorium.

If the public official in this case had denied that public outcry was a factor, do you think there was nevertheless sufficient evidence in the record to attribute publicly expressed racial motivation to the moratorium decision? Not every case will, like this one, involve such a sweeping multifamily housing ban in a community where the "housing stock, along with other structures, was largely obliterated."[67] The Court in *Arlington Heights*, by contrast, discussed the reluctance of courts to decipher and attribute discriminatory motives to government actors. Do you think that the lower courts in *Arlington Heights* gave proper weight to the public opposition evidence in the record?

---

67. Of course, in attributing racial motivation to the governing body, the court relied on the totality of the evidence; this included the historical background of several zoning decisions St. Bernard Parish made two years earlier, particularly the "blood relative" ordinance that the council chairperson at the time publicly described as "racially motivated." *St. Bernard*, 641 F. Supp. 2d at 569-70.

Biased opposition to group homes also may influence local land use ordinances restricting where group housing for people with disabilities may be located:

> Every public meeting leading up to the City Council's ultimate enactment of the Ordinance was marked by angry comment from citizens who referred to the disabled residents of the group homes as "criminals," "gang members," "druggies," "not true handicapped" and other derogatory terms. The record suggests that City Council members were responsive to the public views. . . . A jury could certainly infer from this record that private citizens' "hostility motivated the City in initiating and continuing its enforcement efforts."[68]

Consider also this guidance offered by HUD and the Department of Justice:

> When enacting or applying zoning or land use laws, state and local governments may not act because of the fears, prejudices, stereotypes, or unsubstantiated assumptions that community members may have about current or prospective residents because of the residents' protected characteristics. Doing so violates the Act, even if the officials themselves do not personally share such bias. . . . Of course, a city council or zoning board is not bound by everything that is said by every person who speaks at a public hearing. It is the record as a whole that will be determinative.[69]

7. Using Impact to Prove Intent. As discussed in the next chapter, the Supreme Court has recognized disparate impact claims to be cognizable under the FHA with no required showing of discriminatory purpose. But the *Arlington Heights* Court made clear, citing *Washington v. Davis*, that "official action will not be held unconstitutional solely because it results in a racially disproportionate impact. . . . Proof of racially discriminatory intent or purpose is required to show a violation of the Equal Protection Clause." Unless the impact creates a pattern so stark that it is "unexplainable on grounds other than race," the impact will not be determinative. Yet, the Court instructed that "the impact of the official action . . . may provide an important starting point" in uncovering discriminatory intent. *Arlington Heights* illustrates this point. The Court did consider impact evidence, finding that the impact of the Village's decision bore more heavily on people of color, who constituted only 18 percent of the population in Chicago but 40 percent of those eligible for the proposed housing. Yet, it ultimately held that the totality of evidence was insufficient to establish discriminatory motive under the Equal Protection Clause. The Court then remanded to the Seventh Circuit to consider the FHA claims. On remand, the Seventh Circuit held that the FHA did not require a showing of discriminatory intent; the court set forth and analyzed four factors

68. Pacific Shores Props., L.L.C. v. City of Newport Beach, 730 F.3d 1142, 1163 n.26 (2013) (citing Tsombanidis v. West Haven Fire Dep't, 352 F.3d 565, 580 (2d Cir. 2003)).
69. Joint Statement of the Department of Housing and Urban Development and the Department of Justice, State and Local Land Use Laws and Practices and the Application of the Fair Housing Act 5 (Nov. 10, 2016), https://www.justice.gov/opa/file/912366/download.

to guide the determination of whether conduct producing discriminatory effects (including perpetuating racial segregation) would violate the FHA. In remanding to the district court for further factual findings on effects, the Seventh Circuit held that the Village's denial of the zoning change violated the FHA if there were no other properly zoned and suitable sites within Arlington Heights where the housing could be built. The court advised that "if we are to liberally construe the FHA, we must decide close cases in favor of integrated housing." Metropolitan Housing Development Corp. v. Village of Arlington Heights, 558 F.2d 1283, 1290, 1294 (7th Cir. 1977) (*Arlington Heights II*).

In *St. Bernard*, the court noted that an assessment under the FHA of a law's disparate impact is "[c]entral to determining both discriminatory intent and discriminatory effect." The court found that African American households were 85 percent more likely than white ones in the New Orleans metropolitan area to live in the type of housing subject to the ban (5 or more units) and twice as likely to be renters. African American families were three times more likely than white ones to have incomes in the lowest range served by the subsidized units in the proposed developments. After holding that St. Bernard's moratorium was motivated by racially discriminatory purpose, the court also held that it had an unlawful racially discriminatory effect.

8. *Arlington Heights* **Aftermath.** Following remand to a new district judge, the parties settled by consent decree requiring Arlington Heights to annex land on its southeast border and zone it to allow for the construction of low-income housing. The bordering suburb, Mt. Prospect, intervened with some of its homeowners to challenge the decree; the district court held hearings and ultimately approved and entered the decree. "Construction of the MHDC project at the Golf Road site [along a major highway] was completed in 1983. With 190 units in a single four-story building and named "Linden Place," it was subsidized [for elderly and family tenants] under the federal Section 8 project-based programs and continues to operate today. . . ."[70]

"The first residents of Linden Place were approximately 60% white and the other residents were members of minority groups."[71] In 2022, Arlington Heights was 74.8 percent white non-Hispanic, 11.1 percent Asian, 8.9 percent Hispanic, 6.2 percent two or more races, and 2.8 percent Black.[72]

---

70. Robert G. Schwemm, *Reflections on Arlington Heights: Fifty Years of Exclusionary Zoning Litigation and Beyond*, 57 UIC L. Rev. 389, 450-51 (2024).

71. Henry Rose, *Arlington Heights Won in the Supreme Court but the Fair Housing Act's Goal of Promoting Racial Integration Saved the Low-Income Housing*, 35 Touro L. Rev. 791, 798-99 (2019).

72. U.S. Census Bureau, *QuickFacts*, Arlington Heights Village, Illinois, Population Estimates, July 1, 2023, https://www.census.gov/quickfacts/fact/table/arlingtonheightsvillageillinois/SEX255223#SEX255223.

Chapter Summary

- For the most typical FHA claims brought under §3604 and §3605, litigants must establish by a preponderance of the evidence that the defendant took some action *because of* a protected characteristic.
- To satisfy this proof, FHA litigants may use either or both of the following methods: disparate treatment (intentional discrimination) and disparate impact (discriminatory effects). Disparate treatment focuses on the motivation behind a housing practice. Disparate impact focuses on the effects of a facially neutral policy or the extent to which a practice perpetuates racial residential segregation.
- In most disparate treatment claims, direct evidence that explicitly demonstrates a housing provider's motivation will not be available. Regardless, plaintiffs may use other frameworks relying on circumstantial evidence.
- A common evidentiary method in disparate treatment cases is the *McDonnell Douglas* burden-shifting framework, which allows the plaintiff to create an inference of discrimination using circumstantial evidence. The plaintiff sets forth a prima facie case designed to eliminate the most likely explanations for the adverse decision; the burden shifts to the defendant to produce a legitimate, nondiscriminatory explanation; the ultimate burden of persuasion then shifts back to the plaintiff to demonstrate that the defendant's explanation is a pretext, that it lacks credibility. The plaintiff alternatively may offer other independent evidence, such as that comparing the defendant's treatment of the plaintiff to other nonprotected groups.
- Another method of proof is available in "mixed motive" cases. Where more than one reason might have motivated the defendant, the plaintiff under the traditional FHA approach may establish liability by proving that a protected characteristic was *a motivating factor* in the decision. A prohibited motive need not be the sole cause of an adverse housing decision to violate the FHA. A different standard exists in 1866 Civil Rights Act cases, that of "but-for" causation, which requires proof that a prohibited reason not only motivated, but made a difference to the outcome.
- Another evidentiary method is available in cases involving groups of decisionmakers, such as governmental entities. A plaintiff may use a multifactor test to prove that discrimination motivated the decision; if the plaintiff is successful in making this showing, the defendant has the opportunity to prove that the discriminatory reason did not contribute to the outcome.
- Providing sufficient evidence for a jury to infer discriminatory motive through any of the above frameworks does not require the plaintiff to demonstrate that the motive was malicious, or arguably, even conscious.

CHAPTER 7

DISCRIMINATORY EFFECTS: DISPARATE IMPACT AND PERPETUATION OF SEGREGATION

Disparate impact is a theory of liability for discrimination based on the effects of the defendant's action, rather than the defendant's intention in taking the action. Consider that some housing practices may be facially neutral but operate to exclude a disproportionate share of individuals with protected characteristics. For example, a rental application requiring that income be earned from a job might exclude a greater proportion of people with disabilities compared to people outside that definition. A mortgage lender's refusal to consider timely payment of rent and utilities in their assessment of creditworthiness may arbitrarily exclude members of certain ethnic groups or people with disabilities. A zoning ban on multifamily or government-subsidized housing might disproportionately exclude households of color. Disparate impact theory is a tool to ensure that policies are fine-tuned to achieve legitimate business or governmental objectives without posing unnecessary barriers. In this chapter we address how disparate impact liability is analyzed under the FHA.

The Supreme Court first recognized the disparate impact theory of liability in a unanimous 1971 employment case brought under Title VII, *Griggs v. Duke Power Co.*[1] In the ensuing decades, every appellate court to consider the question interpreted the FHA to permit claims based on discriminatory effects. One feature of discriminatory effects liability unique to fair housing cases is that, in addition to showing "adverse impact" on a protected group, plaintiffs also may make a prima facie case by showing "harm to the community generally by the perpetuation of segregation." Huntington Branch, NAACP v. Town of Huntington, 844 F.2d 926, 937 (2d. Cir. 1988), *aff'd in part per curiam,*

---

1. 401 U.S. 424 (1971).

488 U.S. 15 (1988). This "perpetuation of segregation" claim lends force to the understanding of disparate impact theory as fulfilling the purpose of the FHA to address racially segregated housing patterns.

In 2015, the Supreme Court in a 5-4 decision upheld disparate impact as a cognizable theory of liability under the FHA in *Texas Department of Housing and Community Affairs v. Inclusive Communities Project, Inc.*[2] Despite this controlling Supreme Court precedent and long-standing circuit court endorsement, disparate impact theory remains contested under the FHA and across the civil rights landscape.[3]

Why is the theory contested? Disparate impact, unlike disparate treatment, addresses *consequences* of practices, not the motivation of the decisionmaker. As the court reasoned in United States v. City of Black Jack, Missouri, 508 F.2d 1179, 1185 (8th Cir. 1974):

> Effect, and not motivation, is the touchstone, in part because clever men may easily conceal their motivations, but more importantly, because . . . we now firmly recognize that the arbitrary quality of thoughtlessness can be as disastrous and unfair to private rights and the public interest as the perversity of a willful scheme.

A theory based on discriminatory effects may be used to address racial inequities and segregation in housing programs and land use practices that were established in earlier decades. Supporters of disparate impact theory argue that policies excluding protected groups from resource-rich neighborhoods and wealth-building mortgage products, for example, are precisely the kinds of conditions that motivated Congress to pass the FHA, especially given the pervasive de jure policies discussed in Chapter 1. Opponents of the theory argue that the text of the FHA only protects individuals from intentional discrimination, thus placing attempts to address pervasive structural inequities beyond the scope of the statute. Moreover, they argue that these structural disparities are not entirely attributable to any particular defendant, given that many disparities will have multiple causes, and many practices will disproportionately affect some protected group or other. Proponents would counter that if the defendant's policy can be fine-tuned to remove unnecessary housing barriers while still serving legitimate business or governmental objectives,

---

2. 576 U.S. 519 (2015). Two editors of this text were members of the board of directors of ICP at the time this case was litigated.

3. Although the Supreme Court recognized disparate impact in 1971 for Title VII cases, it rejected disparate impact as a basis for liability for claims brought under the Fifth and Fourteenth Amendments. *See* Washington v. Davis, 426 U.S. 229 (1976) (involving a race discrimination claim under the Fifth Amendment) and Vill. of Arlington Heights v. Metro. Hous. Dev. Corp., 429 U.S. 252 (1977) (involving a race discrimination claim under the Fourteenth Amendment) (Chapter 6). The Court also has rejected disparate impact as a basis for liability for claims brought under the 1866 Civil Rights Act, Title VI of the 1964 Civil Rights Act, and other standards.

the FHA requires this fine-tuning. We discuss the historical and contemporary iterations of these perspectives throughout this chapter.

Another conceptual way to understand disparate impact theory is the Supreme Court's framing in the employment setting, describing the theory as addressing practices that are "functionally equivalent to intentional discrimination."[4] In fact, *Griggs* involved facts suggesting that the employer replaced its explicitly discriminatory and segregative policies (upon passage of Title VII) with neutral ones[5] that achieved the same result. Although the trial court found that there was no intentional racial discrimination, the employer's policies served to freeze in place the existing segregation it had created. As we studied in Chapter 1, racial zoning laws authorizing the maintenance of all white communities gave way to "use" zoning that, in combination with other practices, helped create and maintain the same racially segregated result throughout the 20th century and into the current era. It is important to keep in mind that disparate treatment and disparate impact are not mutually exclusive theories of liability. A neutral policy adopted with discriminatory intent is subject to challenge under both theories; the zoning barrier cases discussed below (and in Chapter 6) help illustrate this principle.

Demonstrating the discriminatory consequences of practices might seem to be simpler than persuading a jury to find the discriminatory motive behind them. This is not necessarily the case, because of the statistical showing needed to demonstrate that a practice is having a disproportionately adverse effect on a protected group. Experts usually are needed to assist plaintiffs in making the prima facie showing of disparate impact.[6] This suggests that disparate impact theory is not accessible to all fair housing plaintiffs, especially those without access to a lawyer or the resources necessary to engage experts. Consequently, it would be a mistake to assume that disparate impact theory requires *less* evidence because it does not require proof of discriminatory intent. Rather, disparate impact requires *different* evidence.

This chapter addresses HUD's interpretation of discriminatory effects liability in its rulemaking and adjudicatory decisions; the Supreme Court's

---

4. Watson v. Fort Worth Bank and Trust, 487 U.S. 977, 987 (1988).

5. The employer required new employees engaged in certain positions to have a high school diploma and pass two aptitude tests that were not job-related. Before the enactment of the 1964 Civil Rights Act, the employer had explicitly restricted those jobs to white employees. When the employer adopted its "race-neutral" requirements, it exempted incumbent employees (all of whom were white) who did not meet those requirements and required Black incumbent employees previously excluded from the positions to meet one of the two requirements.

6. For example, in a case discussed below, the plaintiffs' expert (Dr. Calvin Bradford) offered analysis on the disparate racial impact of a moratorium on the construction of multifamily housing (buildings with more than five units) and its reduction in the supply of rental units. The expert performed a statistical regression analysis showing, among other findings, that "51.7% of African-American households in the New Orleans metropolitan area live in rental units, compared to just over 25% of Caucasian households," such that "African-American households are twice as likely as Caucasians to live in rental housing." Greater New Orleans Fair Hous. Action Ctr. v. St. Bernard Parish, 641 F. Supp. 2d 563, 567 (E.D. La. 2009).

decision in *Inclusive Communities* recognizing disparate impact liability under the FHA, the grounds for the Court's holding, the unique role of segregative effects claims in FHA cases, the safeguards the Court announced but left to the lower courts to refine, the pronounced role of robust causality in the prima facie showing, and some of the mechanics of mounting the statistical evidence necessary to bring a disparate impact claim.

A. EARLY DISPARATE IMPACT REASONING

Courts frequently have looked to Title VII precedents to apply disparate impact theory in fair housing cases. The following case provides an example of a relatively straightforward claim that the defendant's policy of evicting families with children had a clear disparate impact on Black tenants. (Note that at the time this case occurred, Congress had not yet amended the FHA to prohibit discrimination based on familial status.)

Betsey v. Turtle Creek Associates
736 F.2d 983 (4th Cir. 1984)

Before Winter, Chief Judge, and Phillips and Ervin, Circuit Judges

WINTER, Chief Judge:

I.

The Point consists of three high-rise buildings constructed in the 1960's. In late 1979, Turtle Creek acquired all three buildings and began a systematic effort to upgrade the properties. At the time Turtle Creek acquired The Point, Building Three was generally considered to be more desirable than its counterparts.

Shortly after their acquisition of the complex, Turtle Creek instituted a series of new policies including: substantial rent increases, eviction notices based on alleged incidents of vandalism, and a change in the security staff. In May 1980, eviction notices were sent to all families with children residing in Building Three. Turtle Creek attempts to justify these evictions by contending that an "all-adult" conversion was necessary to reduce the vacancy rates in the complex.

In July 1980, this action was instituted. Plaintiffs alleged a pattern of harassment against the black tenants at The Point, and they asserted a "deliberate and systematic effort to alter the racial character" of the property. The "all-adult" conversion policy resulting in eviction notices to families with children in Building Three was described as one part of a broad systematic effort to alter the racial composition of the complex. [EDS. — The plaintiffs brought their claims using both disparate treatment theory and disparate impact theory.]

II.

The district court's judgment [dismissing the intent claim] is not before us. Rather, the central issue on appeal is the discriminatory impact issue. This claim was dismissed with the following explanation:

> The statistics in this case do show that the immediate effect of the conversion will have a disproportionate impact on the black tenants. However, there is no evidence that the conversion will have a continuing disproportionate impact on blacks. In fact, the percentage of blacks at The Point continues to exceed by a substantial margin both the percentage of black renters in the election district in which The Point is located as well as in Montgomery County as a whole. Absent statistics which indicate that the conversion of Building Three would perpetuate or tend to cause segregated housing patterns at The Point, the court would be reluctant to find that plaintiffs had made a prima facie case of discriminatory impact. There is no evidence that the conversion of Building Three will have a greater impact on blacks in the local community nor is there evidence that the conversion will perpetuate segregation at The Point.

The district court's rejection of clear proof of discriminatory impact thus rests on three factors: the absence of a continuing disproportionate impact, the high percentage of blacks in the entire complex, and the insignificant impact of the policy on blacks in the local community. We think that each of these factors is irrelevant to a prima facie showing of racially discriminatory impact.

In order to prevail in a discriminatory impact case under Title VIII, plaintiffs, members of a discrete minority, are required to prove only that a given policy had a discriminatory impact on them as individuals. The plain language of the statute makes it unlawful "[t]o discriminate against any person." Title VII cases construing almost identical language have resolved this question beyond serious dispute. The Supreme Court has recently reaffirmed its position on this issue in Connecticut v. Teal, 457 U.S. 440 (1982). There, it acknowledged that "[t]he principal focus of the statute [Title VII] is the protection of the individual employee, rather than the protection of the minority group as a whole." We and other courts of appeals have recognized the parallel objectives of Title VII and Title VIII. Accordingly, we conclude that plaintiffs are not required to show a discriminatory impact on anyone but the existing minority residents of Building Three. This simple verity renders consideration of the rest of the "local community," the rest of The Point, or even prospective applicants for space in Building Three irrelevant.

The correct inquiry is whether the policy in question had a disproportionate impact on the minorities in the total group to which the policy was applied. In this case, the all-adult conversion policy was applied to the residents in Building Three. "Bottom line" considerations of the number and percentage of minorities in the rest of the complex or the community are "of little comfort" to those minority families evicted from Building Three. Connecticut v. Teal, *supra*, 457 U.S. at 454-455.

Defendants argue that plaintiffs have in some way arbitrarily designated the tenants of Building Three as the relevant group on which to assess the impact of the conversion policy. We disagree. The conversion policy affects only the occupants of Building Three. Thus, we see no merit in the argument that the effects of the conversion should be judged with reference to The Point as a whole.

III.

From this record we think that there is little question that the all-adult conversion policy for Building Three had a substantially greater adverse impact on minority tenants. At the time when Turtle Creek began issuing eviction notices under the conversion policy, 62.9% of the tenants with children in the building were black and an additional 5.4% were other non-whites or Hispanic. In total, 54.3% of the non-white tenants in the building received termination notices as opposed to only 14.1% of the white tenants.

When the statistics are converted to reflect the total number of individuals affected, the results are even more striking. Of the total number of men, women and children living in Building Three, 74.9% of the non-whites were given eviction notices while only 26.4% of the whites received such notices. Under these circumstances, we believe a disparate impact is self-evident.

The findings of the district court are not to the contrary. Indeed, the district judge acknowledged that "the immediate effect of the conversion will have a disproportionate impact on the black tenants." The district court erroneously concluded, however, that this alone was insufficient to establish a prima facie case of discriminatory impact. Because the law clearly provides that such an immediate and substantial impact is sufficient, we reverse the judgment below and remand the case for further proceedings [on the question of whether the defendants met their burden of proving a compelling business necessity sufficient to justify the eviction policy].

NOTES AND QUESTIONS

1. Intentional Disparate Treatment and Disparate Impact. Note that there was evidence of both intentional discrimination against minority tenants and disparate impact of the adults-only conversion of Building Three. Even though the plaintiffs did not prevail on the first claim, the court leaves open the possibility that they might on the latter. Why might one fail and the other succeed? The difference lies both in the proof necessary for a plaintiff to make each type of claim, and the defenses available to the defendant. The precise contours of these showings have changed over time and are discussed later in this chapter.

2. Bottom Line Reasoning. How does the court address the defendant's argument that, even if the conversion of Building Three led to the eviction of a disproportionate number of Black tenants, the overall minority tenant population of Turtle Creek was still larger than in the surrounding areas, and therefore there was no disparate impact violation? This is often referred to as "bottom line" reasoning: the notion that specific practices have no disparate impact so long as the affected group as a whole is still treated favorably. The Supreme Court rejected such logic in the Title VII context in *Connecticut v. Teal*. In that case, a defendant employer used a written test to determine workers' eligibility for a promotion. The test screened out a disproportionately large percentage of Black employees. The defendant then sought to compensate for this by promoting a disproportionately large number of Black employees out of the eligibility pool, so that the ultimate percentage of employees promoted roughly matched their numbers in the original applicant group. A majority of the Court rejected the argument that this somehow cured the disparate impact created by the screening test, reasoning that the workers kept out of the eligibility pool were individually harmed, no matter what overall effect the defendant's actions ultimately had on the larger group of Black workers. The dissent focused on the group-based nature of the plaintiff's prima facie case, arguing that there could be no harm without disparate impact on the protected category members in the aggregate.

B. HUD DISPARATE IMPACT REGULATION

In 2013, HUD for the first time issued a final regulation that interpreted the FHA to recognize disparate impact claims (consistent with case precedent and HUD's formal adjudications); it also set out prima facie and burden-shifting requirements. Until then, the appellate courts had differed in their approaches to proving an FHA disparate impact violation. Various presidential administrations since 2013 have promulgated competing regulatory interpretations of the appropriate prima facie and burden-shifting frameworks. We set forth below the HUD disparate impact regulation effective at the time of this publication.

BRIEF HISTORY OF THE HUD DISPARATE IMPACT RULE[7]

2013: Under the Obama administration, HUD published its first final Discriminatory Effects Rule formalizing its long-held recognition[8] of discriminatory effects liability and adopting a uniform burden-shifting test for determining whether a given practice has an unjustified discriminatory effect.

---

7. This timeline is drawn from Department of Housing and Urban Development, Reinstatement of HUD's Discriminatory Effects Standard, 24 CFR Part 100, Docket No. FR-6251-F-02 (May 1, 2023).

8. In the previous 20 years, HUD adjudications had recognized that violations of the FHA may be premised on a theory of disparate impact. *Implementation of the Fair Housing Act's*

2015: The U.S. Supreme Court in *TDHCA v. Inclusive Communities* confirmed that the FHA provides for discriminatory effects liability.

2020: Under the Trump administration, HUD published its 2020 Rule making significant substantive changes to the 2013 Rule, including removing the definition of discriminatory effect, adding pleading elements, altering the burden-shifting framework, and creating new defenses.

2020: Prior to the effective date of the 2020 Rule, the U.S. District Court for the District of Massachusetts issued a preliminary injunction in Massachusetts Fair Housing Center v. HUD, 496 F. Supp. 3d 600 (D. Mass. 2020), staying HUD's implementation and enforcement of the Rule, describing it as a "massive overhaul" that probably was arbitrary and capricious. Consequently, the 2020 Rule never took effect, and the 2013 Rule remained in effect.

2021: Under the Biden administration, HUD reconsidered the 2020 Rule and published a proposed rule recodifying the 2013 Rule.

2023: After considering public comments, HUD issued a final rule reinstating and maintaining the 2013 Rule.

As of this writing, the Rule reads as follows (emphasis added):

24 CFR § 100.500 DISCRIMINATORY EFFECT PROHIBITED.

Liability may be established under the Fair Housing Act based on a practice's discriminatory effect, as defined in paragraph (a) of this section, even if the practice was not motivated by a discriminatory intent. The practice may still be lawful if supported by a legally sufficient justification, as defined in paragraph (b) of this section. The burdens of proof for establishing a violation under this subpart are set forth in paragraph (c) of this section.

(a) Discriminatory effect. A practice has a discriminatory effect where it actually or predictably results in a **disparate impact** on a group of persons or **creates, increases, reinforces, or perpetuates segregated housing patterns** because of race, color, religion, sex, handicap, familial status, or national origin.

(b) Legally sufficient justification.

(1) A legally sufficient justification exists where the challenged practice:

(i) is **necessary** to achieve one or more **substantial, legitimate, nondiscriminatory interests** of the . . . defendant . . .; and

(ii) Those interests **could not be served** by **another practice** that has a **less discriminatory effect**.

(2) A legally sufficient justification must be supported by evidence and may not be hypothetical or speculative. . . .

Discriminatory Effects Standard, 78 FED. REG. 11460, 11461 (Feb. 15, 2013) (citing HUD v. Twinbrook Village Apts., No. 02-00025600-0256-8, 2001 WL 1632533, at *17 (HUD ALJ Nov. 9, 2001)).

(c) ***Burdens of proof in discriminatory effects cases.***

(1) The charging party . . . or the plaintiff . . . has the burden of proving that a challenged practice caused or predictably will cause a discriminatory effect.

(2) [Once the plaintiff satisfies this burden], the respondent or defendant has the burden of proving that the challenged practice is necessary to achieve one or more substantial, legitimate, nondiscriminatory interests of the respondent or defendant.

(3) [If the defendant satisfies this burden], the charging party or plaintiff may still prevail upon proving that the substantial, legitimate, nondiscriminatory interests supporting the challenged practice could be served by another practice that has a less discriminatory effect.

NOTES AND QUESTIONS

1. Intent Showing Not Required. One of the common sources of confusion under disparate impact theory is the notion that some intent showing is still needed to nudge a disparate impact claim over the line; or, alternatively, that a discriminatory effects claim is advantageous for plaintiffs because it requires less evidence of intent than does a disparate treatment claim.[9] As stated earlier, a plaintiff certainly can bring both an intent and an effects claim, but these are distinct claims. HUD has clarified in the very first sentence of its disparate impact regulation that discriminatory effects liability does not hinge on evidence of motivation. Of course, in reality, litigants may offer some evidence suggesting discriminatory intent even if not required, in an effort to persuade the factfinder that the defendant's facially neutral practices are not actually neutral, warrant closer scrutiny, and serve no legitimate interest. Do you think this real-world approach contributes to the erroneous view that some intent evidence is necessary to prevail on a disparate impact claim?

2. HUD Recognizes Two Types of Discriminatory Effects. HUD defines discriminatory effect in paragraph (a) to include two types. Drawing on the analyses in the court decisions that preceded *Inclusive Communities*, it recognizes the traditional type involving a practice that "actually or predictably results in a disparate impact on a group of persons," that is, bears more heavily on one group than another. It also explicitly includes a second type of

---

9. In fact, the Seventh Circuit in Metropolitan Hous. Dev. Corp. v. Vill. of Arlington Heights, 558 F.2d 1283, 1290, 1292 (7th Cir. 1977) (*Arlington Heights II*) did provide for some showing of intent in its suggested framework for FHA disparate impact claims, even if it was considered less important than the other factors.

discriminatory effect that "creates, increases, reinforces, or perpetuates seg-regated housing patterns." The second type is unique to FHA claims and is illustrated in the case excerpts below. It originated in the first case to recog-nize disparate impact liability under the FHA.[10]

3. All Protected Groups Are Covered. Note that all seven federally pro-tected classes are covered in HUD's disparate impact regulation. Therefore, the analytical approaches and proof requirements are the same regardless of the basis of discrimination.

4. Practice, Effect, Causation. The first step for the plaintiff requires the identification of a specific *practice* that has a discriminatory effect. Pointing to an effect or disparity by itself is insufficient; the plaintiff must identify both practice and effect. And, what would have great import in the post-*Inclusive Communities* era, the plaintiff must prove causation: that the practice caused (or predictably will cause) a discriminatory effect.

5. Discriminatory Effects Do Not Create Liability Per Se. As HUD's reg-ulation reveals, liability is not established the instant the plaintiff identifies a discriminatory effect. After the plaintiff satisfies the burden of proof at the first step, the defendant has the opportunity to offer proof of a "legally suf-ficient justification" for the challenged practice. *Inclusive Communities* below reinforced the concept that defendants are given leeway to justify the dispro-portionate effects of their practices.

6. Both Parties Bear Some Burden of Persuasion. Before HUD issued its rule, there was some variation in the circuits regarding placement of eviden-tiary burdens. HUD's rule clarifies that the defendant's burden on justifica-tion is a burden of persuasion, not simply a burden of production. Therefore, the burden at the second step for defendants is more substantial than in the disparate treatment context under the *McDonnell Douglas* framework. As para-graph (b)(2) elaborates, it is not sufficient for the defendant merely to articu-late a justification that is "hypothetical or speculative"; the defendant must offer persuasive evidence that the challenged practice is *necessary* to achieve one or more substantial, legitimate, nondiscriminatory interests. For example, defendants often assert that prohibiting multifamily housing is necessary to avoid traffic congestion or school overcrowding.

Similarly, after a defendant's successful proof of justification, the plaintiff at the third step may still prevail by proving that the defendant's interests could be served by another practice that has a less discriminatory effect. Some courts previously had placed this final burden on the defendant whereas HUD shifts this burden back to the plaintiff.

---

10. United States v. City of Black Jack, Mo., 508 F.2d 1179 (8th Cir. 1974).

C. SUPREME COURT RECOGNITION OF DISPARATE IMPACT CLAIMS IN *INCLUSIVE COMMUNITIES*

The Supreme Court's 2015 decision in *Inclusive Communities* certainly resolved the threshold question on which it granted certiorari: Is disparate impact theory an available proof method under the FHA? Yes, was the majority's unequivocal answer. What remains contested, notwithstanding a HUD regulation on point, is how courts should analyze these claims. We will address the rationale for the Court's threshold decision recognizing FHA disparate impact claims, some of the Court's significant pronouncements related to its holding, and several uncertainties surfacing in the lower courts after *Inclusive Communities*.

Texas Department of Housing and Community Affairs v. Inclusive Communities Project, Inc.
576 U.S. 519 (2015)

KENNEDY, J., delivered the opinion of the Court, in which Ginsburg, Breyer, Sotomayor, and Kagan, JJ., joined.

Thomas, J., filed a dissenting opinion.

Alito, J., filed a dissenting opinion in which Roberts, C.J., and Scalia and Thomas, JJ, joined.

The underlying dispute in this case concerns where housing for low income persons should be constructed in Dallas, Texas—that is, whether the housing should be built in the inner city or in the suburbs. This dispute comes to the Court on a disparate impact theory of liability. In contrast to a disparate treatment case, where a "plaintiff must establish that the defendant had a discriminatory intent or motive," a plaintiff bringing a disparate impact claim challenges practices that have a "disproportionately adverse effect on minorities" and are otherwise unjustified by a legitimate rationale. Ricci v. DeStefano (2009). The question presented for the Court's determination is whether disparate impact claims are cognizable under the FHA.

I

A

Before turning to the question presented, it is necessary to discuss a different federal statute that gives rise to this dispute. The Federal Government provides low income housing tax credits that are distributed to developers through designated state agencies. 26 U.S.C. §42. Congress has directed States to develop plans identifying selection criteria for distributing the credits. Those plans must include certain criteria, such as public housing waiting lists, as well as certain preferences, including that low income housing units "contribut[e] to a concerted community revitalization plan" and be built in census tracts populated predominantly by low income residents. Federal law thus favors the distribution of these tax credits for the development of housing units in low income areas.

In the State of Texas these federal credits are distributed by the Texas Department of Housing and Community Affairs (Department). Under Texas law, a developer's application for the tax credits is scored under a point system that gives priority to statutory criteria, such as the financial feasibility of the development project and the income level of tenants. The Texas Attorney General has interpreted state law to permit the consideration of additional criteria, such as whether the housing units will be built in a neighborhood with good schools.[11] Those criteria cannot be awarded more points than statutorily mandated criteria.

The Inclusive Communities Project, Inc. (ICP) is a Texas-based nonprofit corporation that assists low income families in obtaining affordable housing. In 2008, the ICP brought this suit. As relevant here, it brought a disparate impact claim under §§364(a) and 3605(a) of the FHA.[12] The ICP alleged the Department has caused continued segregated housing patterns by its disproportionate allocation of the tax credits, granting too many credits for housing in predominantly black inner city areas and too few in predominantly white suburban neighborhoods. The ICP contended that the Department must modify its selection criteria in order to encourage the construction of [family] low income housing in suburban communities.

The District Court concluded that the ICP had established a prima facie case of disparate impact. It relied on two pieces of statistical evidence. First, it found "from 1999–2008, [the Department] approved tax credits for 49.7% of proposed non-elderly units in 0% to 9.9% Caucasian areas, but only approved 37.4% of proposed non-elderly units in 90% to 100% Caucasian areas." Second, it found "92.29% of [family low-income housing tax credit] units in the city of Dallas were located in census tracts with less than 50% Caucasian residents."

The District Court then placed the burden on the Department to rebut the ICP's prima facie showing of disparate impact. After assuming the Department's proffered interests were legitimate, the District Court held that a defendant—here the Department—must prove "that there are no other less discriminatory alternatives to advancing their proffered interests." Because, in its view, the Department "failed to meet [its] burden of proving that there are no less discriminatory alternatives," the District Court ruled for the ICP.

The District Court's remedial order required the addition of new selection criteria for the tax credits. For instance, it awarded points for units built in neighborhoods with good schools and disqualified sites that are located

---

11. [EDS.—This criterion was added as a result of this litigation.]
12. [EDS.—The district court dismissed the plaintiff's disparate treatment claims.]

adjacent to or near hazardous conditions, such as high crime areas or land-fills. The remedial order contained no explicit racial targets or quotas.

While the Department's appeal was pending, HUD issued a regulation interpreting the FHA to encompass disparate impact liability. *See Implementation of the Fair Housing Act's Discriminatory Effects Standard,* 78 Fed. Reg. 11460 (2013). The regulation also established a burden-shifting framework for adjudicating disparate impact claims. Under the regulation, a plaintiff first must make a prima facie showing of disparate impact. That is, the plaintiff "has the burden of proving that a challenged practice caused or predictably will cause a discriminatory effect." If a statistical discrepancy is caused by factors other than the defendant's policy, a plaintiff cannot establish a prima facie case, and there is no liability. After a plaintiff does establish a prima facie showing of disparate impact, the burden shifts to the defendant to "prov[e] that the challenged practice is necessary to achieve one or more substantial, legitimate, nondiscriminatory interests." HUD has clarified that this step of the analysis "is analogous to the Title VII requirement that an employer's interest in an employment practice with a disparate impact be job related." Once a defendant has satisfied its burden at step two, a plaintiff may "prevail upon proving that the substantial, legitimate, non-discriminatory interests supporting the challenged practice could be served by another practice that has a less discriminatory effect."

The Fifth Circuit held, consistent with its precedent, that disparate impact claims are cognizable under the FHA. On the merits, however, the Court of Appeals reversed and remanded. Relying on HUD's regulation, the Court of Appeals held that it was improper for the District Court to have placed the burden on the Department to prove there were no less discriminatory alternatives for allocating low income housing tax credits. In a concurring opinion, Judge Jones stated that on remand the District Court should reexamine whether the ICP had made out a prima facie case of disparate impact. She suggested the District Court incorrectly relied on bare statistical evidence without engaging in any analysis about causation. She further observed that, if the federal law providing for the distribution of low income housing tax credits ties the Department's hands to such an extent that it lacks a meaningful choice, then there is no disparate impact liability. . . .

B

De jure residential segregation by race was declared unconstitutional almost a century ago, *Buchanan v. Warley* (1917), but its vestiges remain today, inter-twined with the country's economic and social life. Some segregated housing patterns can be traced to conditions that arose in the mid–20th century. Rapid urbanization, concomitant with the rise of suburban developments accessible by car, led many white families to leave the inner cities. This often left minority families concentrated in the center of the Nation's cities. During this time, various practices were followed, sometimes with governmental support, to encourage and maintain the separation of the races: Racially restrictive covenants prevented the conveyance of property to minorities, *see Shelley v. Kraemer* (1948); steering by real-estate agents led potential buyers to consider homes in racially homogenous areas; and discriminatory lending practices, often referred to as redlining, precluded minority families from purchasing homes in affluent areas. *See, e.g.,* M. Klarman, Unfinished Business: Racial Equality in American History 140-141 (2007); Brief for Housing Scholars as *Amici Curiae* 22-23. By the 1960's, these policies, practices, and prejudices had created many predominantly black inner cities surrounded by mostly white suburbs.

The mid-1960's was a period of considerable social unrest; and, in response, President Lyndon Johnson established the National Advisory Commission on Civil Disorders, commonly known as the Kerner Commission. After extensive fact finding the Commission identified residential segregation and unequal housing and economic conditions in the inner cities as significant, underlying causes of the social unrest. The Commission found that "[n]early two thirds of all nonwhite families living in the central cities today live in neighborhoods marked by substandard housing and general urban blight." The Commission further found that both open and covert racial discrimination prevented black families from obtaining better housing and moving to integrated communities. The Commission concluded that "[o]ur Nation is moving toward two societies, one black, one white — separate and unequal." To reverse "[t]his deepening racial division," it recommended enactment of "a comprehensive and enforceable open-occupancy law making it an offense to discriminate in the sale or rental of any housing . . . on the basis of race, creed, color, or national origin."

In April 1968, Dr. Martin Luther King, Jr. was assassinated in Memphis, Tennessee, and the Nation faced a new urgency to resolve the social unrest in the inner cities. Congress responded by adopting the Kerner Commission's recommendation and passing the Fair Housing Act.

II

The issue here is whether, under a proper interpretation of the FHA, housing decisions with a disparate impact are prohibited. Before turning to the FHA, however, it is necessary to consider two other antidiscrimination statutes that preceded it.

The first relevant statute is §703(a) of Title VII of the CRA of 1964. The Court addressed the concept of disparate impact under this statute in *Griggs v. Duke Power Co.* (1971). There, the employer had a policy requiring its manual laborers to possess a high school diploma and to obtain satisfactory scores on two intelligence tests. The Court of Appeals held the employer had not adopted these job requirements for a racially discriminatory purpose, and the plaintiffs did not challenge that holding in this Court. Instead, the plaintiffs argued §703(a)(2) covers the discriminatory effect of a practice as well as the motivation behind the practice.

Section 703(a), as amended, provides as follows:

> "It shall be an unlawful employer practice for an employer—
>
> "(1) to fail or refuse to hire or to discharge any individual, or otherwise to discriminate against any individual with respect to his compensation, terms, conditions, or privileges of employment, because of such individual's race, color, religion, sex, or national origin; or
>
> "(2) to limit, segregate, or classify his employees or applicants for employment in any way which would deprive or tend to deprive any individual of employment opportunities or otherwise adversely affect his status as an employee, because of such individual's race, color, religion, sex, or national origin." 42 U.S.C. §2000e-2(a).

In interpreting §703(a)(2), the Court reasoned that disparate impact liability furthered the purpose and design of the statute. The Court explained that, in §703(a)(2), Congress "proscribe[d] not only overt discrimination but also practices that are fair in form, but discriminatory in operation." For that reason, as the Court noted, "Congress directed the thrust of [§703(a)(2)] to the consequences of employment practices, not simply the motivation." In light of the statute's goal of achieving "equality of employment opportunities and remov[ing] barriers that have operated in the past" to favor some races over others, the Court held §703(a)(2) of Title VII must be interpreted to allow disparate impact claims.

The Court held . . . that "business necessity" constitutes a defense to disparate impact claims. [T]he Court in *Griggs* found a violation of Title VII because the employer could not establish that high school diplomas and general intelligence tests were related to the job performance of its manual laborers.

The second relevant statute that bears on the proper interpretation of the FHA is the Age Discrimination in Employment Act of 1967 (ADEA). Section 4(a) of the ADEA provides:

> It shall be unlawful for an employer—
>
> (1) to fail or refuse to hire or to discharge any individual or otherwise discriminate against any individual with respect to his compensation, terms, conditions, or privileges of employment, because of such individual's age;
>
> (2) to limit, segregate, or classify his employees in any way which would deprive or tend to deprive any individual of employment opportunities or otherwise adversely affect his status as an employee, because of such individual's age; or
>
> (3) to reduce the wage rate of any employee in order to comply with this chapter. 29 U.S.C. §623(a).

The Court first addressed whether this provision allows disparate impact claims in Smith v. City of Jackson, 544 U.S. 228 (2005). There, a group of older employees challenged their employer's decision to give proportionately greater raises to employees with less than five years of experience.

Explaining that *Griggs* "represented the better reading of [Title VII's] statutory text," a plurality of the Court concluded that the same reasoning pertained to §4(a)(2) of the ADEA. The *Smith* plurality emphasized that both §703(a)(2) of Title VII and §4(a)(2) of the ADEA contain language "prohibit[ing] such actions that 'deprive any individual of employment opportunities or *otherwise adversely affect* his status as an employee, because of such individual's' race or age." As the plurality observed, the text of these provisions "focuses on the *effects* of the action on the employee rather than the motivation for the action of the employer" and therefore compels recognition of disparate impact liability. In a separate opinion, Justice Scalia found the ADEA's text ambiguous and thus deferred under *Chevron, U.S.A. Inc. v. Natural Resources Defense Council, Inc.* (1984), to an Equal Employment Opportunity Commission regulation interpreting the ADEA to impose disparate impact liability.

Together, *Griggs* holds and the plurality in *Smith* instructs that antidiscrimination laws must be construed to encompass disparate impact claims when their text refers to the consequences of actions and not just to the mindset of actors, and where that interpretation is consistent with statutory purpose. These cases also teach that disparate impact liability must be limited so employers and other regulated entities are able to make the practical business choices and profit related decisions that sustain a vibrant and dynamic free-enterprise system. And before rejecting a business justification — or, in the case of a governmental entity, an analogous public interest — a court must determine that a plaintiff has shown that there is "an available alternative . . . practice that has less disparate impact and serves the [entity's] legitimate needs." The cases interpreting Title VII and the ADEA provide essential background and instruction in the case now before the Court.

Turning to the FHA, the ICP relies on two provisions. Section 3604(a) provides that it shall be unlawful:

> To refuse to sell or rent after the making of a bona fide offer, or to refuse to negotiate for the sale or rental of, or otherwise make unavailable or deny, a dwelling to any person because of race, color, religion, sex, familial status, or national origin. 42 U.S.C. §3604(a).

Here, the phrase "otherwise make unavailable" is of central importance to the analysis that follows.

Section 3605(a), in turn, provides:

> It shall be unlawful for any person or other entity whose business includes engaging in real estate-related transactions to discriminate against any person in making available such a transaction, or in the terms or conditions of such a transaction, because of race, color, religion, sex, handicap, familial status, or national origin. §3605(a).

Applied here, the logic of *Griggs* and *Smith* provides strong support for the conclusion that the FHA encompasses disparate impact claims. Congress' use of the phrase "otherwise make unavailable" refers to the consequences of an action rather than the actor's intent. This results-oriented language counsels in favor of recognizing disparate impact liability. The Court has construed §3605(a) to include disparate impact liability. *See, e.g.,* Board of Ed. of City School Dist. of New York v. Harris, 444 U.S. 130 (1979) (holding the term "discriminat[e]" encompassed disparate impact liability in the context of a statute's text, history, purpose, and structure).

A comparison to the antidiscrimination statutes examined in *Griggs* and *Smith* is useful. Title VII's and the ADEA's "otherwise adversely affect" language is equivalent in function and purpose to the FHA's "otherwise make unavailable" language. In these three statutes the operative text looks to results. The relevant statutory phrases, moreover, play an identical role in the structure common to all three statutes: Located at the end of lengthy sentences that begin with prohibitions on disparate treatment, they serve as catchall phrases looking to consequences, not intent. And all three statutes use the word "otherwise" to introduce the results-oriented phrase. "Otherwise" means "in a different way or manner," thus signaling a shift in emphasis from an actor's intent to the consequences of his actions. Webster's Third New International Dictionary 1598 (1971). This similarity in text and structure is all the more compelling given that Congress passed the FHA in 1968—only four years after passing Title VII and only four months after enacting the ADEA.

It is true that Congress did not reiterate Title VII's exact language in the FHA, but that is because to do so would have made the relevant sentence awkward and unclear. A provision making it unlawful to "refuse to sell [,] . . . or otherwise [adversely affect], a dwelling to any person" because of a protected trait would be grammatically obtuse, difficult to interpret, and far more expansive in scope than Congress likely intended. Congress thus chose words that serve the same purpose and bear the same basic meaning but are consistent with the structure and objectives of the FHA.

Emphasizing that the FHA uses the phrase "because of race," the Department argues this language forecloses disparate impact liability since "[a]n action is not taken 'because of race' unless race is a *reason* for the action." *Griggs* and *Smith*, however, dispose of this argument. Both Title VII and the ADEA contain identical "because of" language, and the Court nonetheless held those statutes impose disparate impact liability.

In addition, it is of crucial importance that the existence of disparate impact liability is supported by amendments to the FHA that Congress enacted in 1988. By that time, all nine Courts of Appeals to have addressed the question had concluded the FHA encompassed disparate impact claims.

When it amended the FHA, Congress was aware of this unanimous precedent. And with that understanding, it made a considered judgment to retain the relevant statutory text. *See* H.R. Rep. No. 100-711, p. 21, n. 52 (1988) (H.R. Rep.) (discussing suits premised on disparate impact claims and related judicial precedent); 134 Cong. Rec. 23711 (1988) (statement of Sen. Kennedy) (noting unanimity of Federal Courts of Appeals concerning disparate impact); Fair Housing Amendments Act of 1987: Hearings on S. 558 before the

Subcommittee on the Constitution of the Senate Committee on the Judiciary, 100th Cong., 1st Sess., 529 (1987) (testimony of Professor Robert Schwemm) (describing consensus judicial view that the FHA imposed disparate impact liability). Indeed, Congress rejected a proposed amendment that would have eliminated disparate impact liability for certain zoning decisions.

Against this background understanding in the legal and regulatory system, Congress' decision in 1988 to amend the FHA while still adhering to the operative language in §§3604(a) and 3605(a) is convincing support for the conclusion that Congress accepted and ratified the unanimous holdings of the Courts of Appeals finding disparate impact liability. "If a word or phrase has been . . . given a uniform interpretation by inferior courts . . ., a later version of that act perpetuating the wording is presumed to carry forward that interpretation." A. Scalia & B. Garner, Reading Law: The Interpretation of Legal Texts 322 (2012).

Further and convincing confirmation of Congress' understanding that disparate impact liability exists under the FHA is revealed by the substance of the 1988 amendments. The amendments included three exemptions from liability that assume the existence of disparate impact claims. The most logical conclusion is that the three amendments were deemed necessary because Congress presupposed disparate impact under the FHA as it had been enacted in 1968.

The relevant 1988 amendments were as follows. First, Congress added a clarifying provision: "Nothing in [the FHA] prohibits a person engaged in the business of furnishing appraisals of real property to take into consideration factors other than race, color, religion, national origin, sex, handicap, or familial status." 42 U.S.C. §3605(c). Second, Congress provided: "Nothing in [the FHA] prohibits conduct against a person because such person has been convicted by any court of competent jurisdiction of the illegal manufacture or distribution of a controlled substance." §3607(b)(4). And finally, Congress specified: "Nothing in [the FHA] limits the applicability of any reasonable . . . restrictions regarding the maximum number of occupants permitted to occupy a dwelling." §3607(b)(1).

The exemptions embodied in these amendments would be superfluous if Congress had assumed that disparate impact liability did not exist under the FHA. Indeed, none of these amendments would make sense if the FHA encompassed only disparate treatment claims. If that were the sole ground for liability, the amendments merely restate black letter law. If an actor makes a decision based on reasons other than a protected category, there is no disparate treatment liability. But the amendments do constrain disparate impact liability. For instance, certain criminal convictions are correlated with sex and race. *See, e.g.,* Kimbrough v. United States, 552 U.S. 85, 98 (2007) (discussing the racial disparity in convictions for crack cocaine offenses). By adding an exemption from liability for exclusionary practices aimed at individuals with drug convictions, Congress ensured disparate impact liability would not lie if a landlord excluded tenants with such convictions. The same is true of the provision allowing for reasonable restrictions on occupancy. And the exemption from liability for real estate appraisers is in the same section as §3605(a)'s pro-hibition of discriminatory practices in real estate transactions, thus indicating Congress' recognition that disparate impact liability arose under §3605(a). In short, the 1988 amendments signal that Congress ratified disparate impact liability.

If a real estate appraiser took into account a neighborhood's schools, one could not say the appraiser acted because of race. And by embedding 42 U.S.C. §3605(c)'s exemption in the statutory text, Congress ensured that dis-parate impact liability would not be allowed either. Indeed, the inference of disparate impact liability is even stronger here than it was in *Smith* [where the ADEA included an analogous exemption at the outset.] [H]ere Congress added the relevant exemptions in the 1988 amendments against the backdrop of the uniform view of the Courts of Appeals that the FHA imposed disparate impact liability.

Recognition of disparate impact claims is consistent with the FHA's central purpose. The FHA, like Title VII and the ADEA, was enacted to eradicate dis-criminatory practices within a sector of our Nation's economy. *See* 42 U.S.C. §3601 ("It is the policy of the United States to provide, within constitutional limitations, for fair housing throughout the United States"); H.R. Rep., at 15 (explaining the FHA "provides a clear national policy against discrimination in housing").

These unlawful practices include zoning laws and other housing restric-tions that function unfairly to exclude minorities from certain neighborhoods without any sufficient justification. Suits targeting such practices reside at the heartland of disparate impact liability. *See, e.g., Huntington*, 488 U.S., at 16-18 (invalidating zoning law preventing construction of multifamily rental units); *Black Jack*, 508 F.2d, at 1182-1188 (invalidating ordinance prohibiting con-struction of new multifamily dwellings); Greater New Orleans Fair Housing Action Center v. St. Bernard Parish, 641 F. Supp. 2d 563, 569, 577-578 (E.D. La. 2009) (invalidating post Hurricane Katrina ordinance restricting the rental of housing units to only "'blood relative[s]'" in an area of the city that was 88.3% white and 7.6% black). The availability of disparate impact liability, further-more, has allowed private developers to vindicate the FHA's objectives and to protect their property rights by stopping municipalities from enforcing arbi-trary and, in practice, discriminatory ordinances barring the construction of certain types of housing units. Recognition of disparate impact liability under the FHA also plays a role in uncovering discriminatory intent: It permits plaintiffs to counteract unconscious prejudices and disguised animus that escape easy classification as disparate treatment. In this way disparate impact liability may prevent segregated housing patterns that might otherwise result from covert and illicit stereotyping.

But disparate impact liability has always been properly limited in key respects that avoid the serious constitutional questions that might arise under the FHA, for instance, if such liability were imposed based solely on a show-ing of a statistical disparity. Disparate impact liability mandates the "removal of artificial, arbitrary, and unnecessary barriers," not the displacement of valid governmental policies. *Griggs v. Duke Power Co.* (1971). The FHA is not an instrument to force housing authorities to reorder their priorities. Rather, the FHA aims to ensure that those priorities can be achieved without arbitrarily creating discriminatory effects or perpetuating segregation.

Unlike the heartland of disparate impact suits targeting artificial barriers to housing, the underlying dispute in this case involves a novel theory of liability. *See* Seicshnaydre, *Is Disparate Impact Having Any Impact? An Appellate Analysis of Forty Years of Disparate Impact Claims Under the Fair Housing Act*, 63 Am. U. L. Rev. 357, 360-363 (2013) (noting the rarity of this type of claim). This case, on remand, may be seen simply as an attempt to second guess which of two reasonable approaches a housing authority should follow in the sound exercise of its discretion in allocating tax credits for low income housing.

An important and appropriate means of ensuring that disparate impact liability is properly limited is to give housing authorities and private developers leeway to state and explain the valid interest served by their policies. This step of the analysis is analogous to the business necessity standard under Title VII and provides a defense against disparate impact liability. Just as an employer may maintain a workplace requirement that causes a disparate impact if that requirement is a "reasonable measure[ment] of job performance," so too must housing authorities and private developers be allowed to maintain a policy if they can prove it is necessary to achieve a valid interest. To be sure, the Title VII framework may not transfer exactly to the fair housing context, but the comparison suffices for present purposes.

It would be paradoxical to construe the FHA to impose onerous costs on actors who encourage revitalizing dilapidated housing in our Nation's cities merely because some other priority might seem preferable. Entrepreneurs must be given latitude to consider market factors. Zoning officials, moreover, must often make decisions based on a mix of factors, both objective (such as cost and traffic patterns) and, at least to some extent, subjective (such as preserving historic architecture). These factors contribute to a community's quality of life and are legitimate concerns for housing authorities. The FHA does not decree a particular vision of urban development; and it does not put housing authorities and private developers in a double bind of liability, subject to suit whether they choose to rejuvenate a city core or to promote new low income housing in suburban communities. As HUD itself recognized in its recent rulemaking, disparate impact liability "does not mandate that affordable housing be located in neighborhoods with any particular characteristic."

In a similar vein, a disparate impact claim that relies on a statistical disparity must fail if the plaintiff cannot point to a defendant's policy or policies causing that disparity. A robust causality requirement ensures that "[r]acial imbalance . . . does not, without more, establish a prima facie case of disparate impact" and thus protects defendants from being held liable for racial disparities they did not create. Wards Cove Packing Co. v. Atonio, 490 U.S. 642, 653 (1989). Without adequate safeguards at the prima facie stage, disparate impact liability might cause race to be used and considered in a pervasive way and "would almost inexorably lead" governmental or private entities to use "numerical quotas," and serious constitutional questions then could arise. Id.

The litigation at issue here provides an example. From the standpoint of determining advantage or disadvantage to racial minorities, it seems difficult to say as a general matter that a decision to build low income housing in a blighted inner city neighborhood instead of a suburb is discriminatory, or vice versa. If those sorts of judgments are subject to challenge without adequate safeguards, then there is a danger that potential defendants may adopt racial quotas—a circumstance that itself raises serious constitutional concerns.

Courts must therefore examine with care whether a plaintiff has made out a prima facie case of disparate impact and prompt resolution of these cases is important. A plaintiff who fails to allege facts at the pleading stage or produce statistical evidence demonstrating a causal connection cannot make out a prima facie case of disparate impact. For instance, a plaintiff challenging the decision of a private developer to construct a new building in one location rather than another will not easily be able to show this is a policy causing a disparate impact because such a one time decision may not be a policy at all. It may also be difficult to establish causation because of the multiple factors that go into investment decisions about where to construct or renovate housing units. And as Judge Jones observed below, if the ICP cannot show a causal connection between the Department's policy and a disparate impact—for instance, because federal law substantially limits the Department's discretion—that should result in dismissal of this case.

The FHA imposes a command with respect to disparate impact liability. Here, that command goes to a state entity. In other cases, the command will go to a private person or entity. Governmental or private policies are not contrary to the disparate impact requirement unless they are "artificial, arbitrary, and unnecessary barriers." *Griggs*, 401 U.S., at 431. Difficult questions might arise if disparate impact liability under the FHA caused race to be used and considered in a pervasive and explicit manner to justify governmental or private actions that, in fact, tend to perpetuate race based considerations rather than move beyond them. Courts should avoid interpreting disparate impact liability to be so expansive as to inject racial considerations into every housing decision.

The limitations on disparate impact liability discussed here are also necessary to protect potential defendants against abusive disparate impact claims. If the specter of disparate impact litigation causes private developers to no longer construct or renovate housing units for low income individuals, then the FHA would have undermined its own purpose as well as the free market system. And as to governmental entities, they must not be prevented from achieving legitimate objectives, such as ensuring compliance with health and safety codes.

Were standards for proceeding with disparate impact suits not to incorporate at least the safeguards discussed here, then disparate impact liability might displace valid governmental and private priorities, rather than solely "remov[ing] . . . artificial, arbitrary, and unnecessary barriers." And that, in turn, would set our Nation back in its quest to reduce the salience of race in our social and economic system.

It must be noted further that, even when courts do find liability under a disparate impact theory, their remedial orders must be consistent with the Constitution. Remedial orders in disparate impact cases should concentrate on the elimination of the offending practice that "arbitrar[ily] . . . operate[s] invidiously to discriminate on the basis of rac[e]." If additional measures are adopted, courts should strive to design them to eliminate racial disparities through race-neutral means. . . . Remedial orders that impose racial targets or quotas might raise more difficult constitutional questions.

While the automatic or pervasive injection of race into public and private transactions covered by the FHA has special dangers, it is also true that race may be considered in certain circumstances and in a proper fashion. Just as this Court has not "question[ed] an employer's affirmative efforts to ensure that all groups have a fair opportunity to apply for promotions and to participate in the [promotion] process," Ricci [v. DeStefano, 557 U.S. 557, 585 (2009)], it likewise does not impugn housing authorities' race neutral efforts to encourage revitalization of communities that have long suffered the harsh consequences of segregated housing patterns. When setting their larger goals, local housing authorities may choose to foster diversity and combat racial isolation with race-neutral tools, and mere awareness of race in attempting to solve the problems facing inner cities does not doom that endeavor at the outset.

The Court holds that disparate impact claims are cognizable under the FHA upon considering its results oriented language, the Court's interpretation of similar language in Title VII and the ADEA, Congress' ratification of disparate impact claims in 1988 against the backdrop of the unanimous view of nine Courts of Appeals, and the statutory purpose.

III

In light of the longstanding judicial interpretation of the FHA to encompass disparate impact claims and congressional reaffirmation of that result, residents and policymakers have come to rely on the availability of disparate impact claims. Indeed, many of our Nation's largest cities—entities that are potential defendants in disparate impact suits—have submitted an *amicus* brief in this case supporting disparate impact liability under the FHA. The existence of disparate impact liability in the substantial majority of the Courts of Appeals for the last several decades "has not given rise to . . . dire consequences."

Much progress remains to be made in our Nation's continuing struggle against racial isolation. In striving to achieve our "historic commitment to creating an integrated society," we must remain wary of policies that reduce homeowners to nothing more than their race. But since the passage of the FHA in 1968 and against the backdrop of disparate impact liability in nearly every jurisdiction, many cities have become more diverse. The FHA must play an important part in avoiding the Kerner Commission's grim prophecy that "[o]ur Nation is moving toward two societies, one black, one white—separate and unequal." Kerner Commission Report 1. The Court acknowledges the Fair Housing Act's continuing role in moving the Nation toward a more integrated society.

The judgment of the Court of Appeals for the Fifth Circuit is affirmed, and the case is remanded for further proceedings consistent with this opinion.

Justice ALITO, with whom The Chief Justice, Justice Scalia, and Justice Thomas join, dissenting.

No one wants to live in a rat's nest. Yet in *Gallagher v. Magner* (2010), a case that we agreed to review several Terms ago [which settled before argument], the Eighth Circuit held that the FHA could be used to attack St. Paul, Minnesota's efforts to combat "rodent infestation" and other violations of the city's housing code. The court agreed that there was no basis to "infer discriminatory intent" on the part of St. Paul. Even so, it concluded that the city's "aggressive enforcement of the Housing Code" was actionable because making landlords respond to "rodent infestation, missing dead-bolt locks, inadequate sanitation facilities, inadequate heat, inoperable smoke detectors, broken or missing doors," and the like increased the price of rent. Since minorities were statistically more likely to fall into "the bottom bracket for household adjusted median family income," they were disproportionately affected by those rent increases, *i.e.,* there was a "disparate impact." The upshot was that even St. Paul's good faith attempt to ensure minimally acceptable housing for its poorest residents could not ward off a disparate impact lawsuit.

Today, the Court embraces the same theory that drove the decision in *Magner*. This is a serious mistake. The FHA does not create disparate impact liability, nor do this Court's precedents. And today's decision will have unfortunate consequences for local government, private enterprise, and those living in poverty. Something has gone badly awry when a city can't even make slumlords kill rats without fear of a lawsuit. Because Congress did not authorize any of this, I respectfully dissent.

I

I begin with the text [discussing 42 U.S.C. §§3604(a) and 3605(a)]. In both sections, the key phrase is "because of." These provisions list covered actions and protected characteristics. The link between the actions and the protected characteristics is "because of." What "because of" means is no mystery. Two Terms ago, we held that "the ordinary meaning of 'because of' is 'by reason of' or 'on account of.'" A person acts "because of" something else, we explained, if that something else "was the 'reason' that the [person] decided to act." Univ. of Tex. Sw. Med. Ctr. v. Nassar, 570 U.S. 338 (2013).

Without torturing the English language, the meaning of these provisions of the FHA cannot be denied. They make it unlawful to engage in any of the covered actions "because of" — meaning "by reason of" or "on account of," — race, religion, etc. Put another way, "the terms [after] the 'because of' clauses in the FHA supply the prohibited motivations for the intentional acts . . . that the Act makes unlawful." Congress accordingly outlawed the covered actions only when they are motivated by race or one of the other protected characteristics.

It follows that the FHA does not authorize disparate impact suits. Under a statute like the FHA that prohibits actions taken "because of" protected characteristics, intent makes all the difference. Disparate impact, however, does not turn on "subjective intent." Instead, "'treat[ing] [a] particular person less favorably than others *because of* a protected trait" is "disparate treatment," *not disparate impact*.

This is precisely how Congress used the phrase "because of" elsewhere in the FHA [referring to 42 U.S.C. §3631]. "One ordinarily assumes" Congress means the same words in the same statute to mean the same thing. There is no reason to doubt that ordinary assumption here.

In an effort to find at least a sliver of support for disparate impact liability in the text of the FHA, the principal respondent, the Solicitor General, and the Court pounce on the phrase "make unavailable" [in §3604(a)]. The Solicitor General argues that "[t]he plain meaning of the phrase 'make unavailable' includes actions that *have the result* of making housing or transactions unavailable, regardless of whether the actions were intended to have that result." This argument is not consistent with ordinary English usage [arguing that "otherwise make unavailable" should be read restrictively to be like the previously listed terms describing intentional conduct]. The result of these ordinary rules of interpretation is that even without "because of," the phrase "make unavailable" likely would require intentionality.

The FHA's inclusion of "because of," however, removes any doubt. Sections 804(a) and 805(a) apply only when a party makes a dwelling or transaction unavailable "because of" race or another protected characteristic. In ordinary English usage, when a person makes something unavailable "because of" some factor, that factor must be a reason for the act.

Here is an example. . . . Of the 32 college players selected by National Football League (NFL) teams in the first round of the 2015 draft, it appears that the overwhelming majority were members of racial minorities. Teams presumably chose the players they think are most likely to help them win games. Would anyone say the NFL teams made draft slots unavailable to white players "because of" their race?

The text of the FHA simply cannot be twisted to authorize disparate impact claims. It is hard to imagine how Congress could have more clearly stated that the FHA prohibits only intentional discrimination than by forbidding acts done "because of race, color, religion, sex, familial status, or national origin". . . .

III

Congress has done nothing since 1968 to change the meaning of the FHA prohibitions at issue in this case. Rather than confronting the plain text of §§804(a) and 805(a), the Solicitor General and the Court place heavy reliance on certain amendments enacted in 1988, but those amendments did not modify the meaning of the provisions now before us.

The 1988 safe-harbor provisions have all the hallmarks of a compromise among factions. These provisions neither authorize nor bar disparate impact claims . . .

[Eds. — The majority did not defer to HUD in upholding FHA disparate impact claims, but the principal dissent argued that *Chevron* deference would have been inappropriate in any event. The dissent maintained that the FHA is unambiguous in foreclosing disparate impact claims, and it was troubled about the timing of HUD's rule: HUD issued its proposed disparate impact rule 43 years after the FHA's enactment and nine days after the Court granted certiorari on the issue in *Magner*; *Magner* settled before oral argument, and HUD issued a final rule after the Court had called for the views of the Solicitor General in a second case, Township of Mount Holly v. Mt. Holly Gardens Citizens in Action, Inc., 571 U.S. 1020 (2013). The Court also dismissed that case upon settlement after certiorari was granted, but before oral argument. (*See* Chapter 3 for a discussion of the Court's overruling of *Chevron* deference.)]

IV

[Eds. — The principal dissent reasoned that the operative provisions of the FHA that it found insufficient to support a disparate impact theory of liability were distinguishable from those found sufficient under *Griggs* and *Smith*.] The Court's decision today reads far too much into *Griggs v. Duke Power Co.*, and far too little into *Smith v. City of Jackson*. In *Smith*, the Court explained that the statutory justification for the decision in *Griggs* depends on language that [we believe] has no parallel in the FHA. And when the *Smith* Court addressed a provision that [we believe] does have such a parallel in the FHA, the Court concluded — *unanimously* — that it does not authorize disparate impact liability. The same result should apply here.

V

Not only is the decision of the Court inconsistent with what the FHA says and our precedents, it will have unfortunate consequences.

This case illustrates the point. The Department has only so many tax credits to distribute. If it gives credits for housing in lower income areas, many families — including many minority families — will obtain better housing. That is a good thing. But if the Department gives credits for housing in higher income areas, some of those families will be able to afford to move into more desirable neighborhoods. That is also a good thing. Either path, however, might trigger a disparate impact suit.

This is not mere speculation. Here, one respondent has sued the Department for not allocating enough credits to higher income areas. But *another* respondent [Frazier Revitalization Inc., a Dallas-based entity engaged in housing and economic development activities] argues that giving credits to wealthy neighborhoods violates "the moral imperative to improve the substandard and inadequate affordable housing in many of our inner cities." This latter argument has special force because a city can build more housing where property is least expensive, thus benefiting more people. In fact, federal law often favors projects that revitalize low income communities.

Because HUD's regulations and the Court's pronouncements are so "hazy," courts — lacking expertise in the field of housing policy — may inadvertently harm the very people that the FHA is meant to help. Local governments make countless decisions that may have some disparate impact related to housing. Certainly Congress did not intend to "engage the federal courts in an endless exercise of second-guessing" local programs. Canton v. Harris, 489 U.S. 378, 392 (1989).

VI

At last I come to the "purpose" driving the Court's analysis: The desire to eliminate the "vestiges" of "residential segregation by race."

When interpreting statutes, "'[w]hat the legislative intention was, can be derived only from the words . . . used; and we cannot speculate beyond the reasonable import of these words.'" "[I]t frustrates rather than effectuates legislative intent simplistically to assume that *whatever* furthers the statute's primary objective must be the law."

Here, privileging purpose over text also creates constitutional uncertainty. The Court acknowledges the risk that disparate impact may be used to "perpetuate race-based considerations rather than move beyond them." And it agrees that "racial quotas . . . rais[e] serious constitutional concerns." Yet it still reads the FHA to authorize disparate impact claims. We should avoid, rather than invite, such "difficult constitutional questions."

Justice THOMAS, dissenting.

I join Justice Alito's dissent in full. I write separately to point out that the foundation on which the Court builds its latest disparate impact regime — *Griggs v. Duke Power Co.* — is made of sand. That decision, which concluded that Title VII of the CRA of 1964 authorizes plaintiffs to bring disparate impact claims, represents the triumph of an agency's preferences[13] over Congress' enactment and of assumption over fact. Whatever respect *Griggs* merits as a matter of *stare decisis,* I would not amplify its error by importing its disparate impact scheme into yet another statute.

We should drop the pretense that *Griggs'* interpretation of Title VII was legitimate. The author of disparate impact liability under Title VII was not Congress, but the Equal Employment Opportunity Commission (EEOC). . . . The Court embraced EEOC's theory of disparate impact, concluding that the agency's position was "entitled to great deference." With only a brief nod to the text of §2000e-2(a)(2) in a footnote, the Court tied this novel theory of discrimination to "the statute's perceived *purpose*" and EEOC's view of the best way of effectuating it. But statutory provisions — not purposes — go through the process of bicameralism and presentment mandated by our Constitution. We should not replace the former with the latter, nor should we transfer our responsibility for interpreting those provisions to administrative agencies. . . . [Eds. — Congress codified disparate impact liability under Title VII in the Civil Rights Act of 1991.]

NOTES AND QUESTIONS: INCLUSIVE COMMUNITIES

1. Grounds for the Supreme Court's Holding. At the end of section II of the opinion, the Court summarized: "The Court holds that disparate impact claims are cognizable under the Fair Housing Act upon considering its result-oriented language, the Court's interpretation of similar language in Title VII and the ADEA, Congress' ratification of disparate impact claims in 1988 against the backdrop of the unanimous view of nine Courts of Appeals, and the statutory purpose." Is something missing from the list? We will examine each of these bases (and other factors) below.

a. **Were the Facts Relevant to the Court's Holding?** On the surface, the facts of the case were not particularly relevant because the Court granted certiorari on a very narrow question: "whether disparate impact claims are cognizable under the Fair Housing Act." Closer examination suggests, however, that the facts were very important because they galvanized both sides of the disparate impact issue. The case addressed an important housing equity and civil rights issue: whether the disparate impact theory could be used to challenge the mechanism by which a state housing agency located low-income

---

13. [Eds. — Before Justice Thomas's appointment to the federal bench (the U.S. Court of Appeals for the District of Columbia Circuit), he served as Chairman of the Equal Employment Opportunity Commission (EEOC), from 1982 to 1990.]

housing for families, when the mechanism resulted in the disproportionate allocation of the tax credit housing away from white neighborhoods and into neighborhoods of color. The case's use of disparate
impact theory to address the fundamental issue of residential racial
segregation linked the case to the core purpose of the FHA. The trial
court's remedial order illustrated this link, incorporating new selection criteria awarding additional points for "neighborhoods with good
schools and disqualif[ying] sites . . . located adjacent to or near hazardous conditions. . . ." At the same time, the facts of the case presented
an opportunity for opponents of disparate impact to ask whether disparate impact claims would be used to "second-guess which of two
reasonable approaches a housing authority should follow in the sound
exercise of its discretion." Critics pointed to the "double bind of liability" that government entities would face were disparate impact claims
permitted, because they would be "subject to suit whether they chose
to rejuvenate a city core or to promote new low income housing in
suburban communities." In upholding disparate impact theory, the
Court set out a number of "safeguards," discussed below, to address
the concerns of the theory's opponents.

b. **The History of Residential Segregation, the Purposes of the Fair
Housing Act, and Disparate Impact.** How prominently do the history
of residential segregation and statutory purpose figure in the Court's
holding? The integrative purpose of the FHA bookends the decision. The
Court began its legal analysis thus: "De jure residential segregation by
race was declared unconstitutional almost a century ago, . . . but its vestiges remain today. . . ." The Court then summarized many of the "policies, practices, and prejudices," discussed in Chapter 1 of this text, which
"[b]y the 1960's, . . . had created many predominantly black inner cities
surrounded by mostly white suburbs." The Court recited some of the
findings and recommendations of the National Advisory Commission
on Civil Disorders (the Kerner Commission), which Congress heeded in
enacting the FHA to combat residential racial segregation.

After a lengthy analysis, the Court in its last lines returned to the
FHA's integrative purpose.

> Much progress remains to be made in our Nation's continuing struggle
> against racial isolation. . . . Since the passage of the Fair Housing Act
> in 1968 and against the backdrop of disparate impact liability in nearly
> every jurisdiction, many cities have become more diverse. The FHA
> must play an important part in avoiding the Kerner Commission's grim
> prophecy. . . . The Court acknowledges the Fair Housing Act's continu-
> ing role in moving the Nation toward a more integrated society.

And, if there were any doubt, the Court midway through the opinion followed its textual analysis with an explicit discussion of purpose: "Recognition of disparate impact claims is consistent with the
FHA's central purpose." The Court then quoted the explicit purpose of

the FHA: "It is the policy of the United States to provide, within constitutional limitations, for fair housing throughout the United States."[14] These points had been strongly urged by counsel and *amici*, including in the Housing Scholars' amicus brief cited by the Court. What role do you think legislative purpose should play in interpreting the meaning of statutes and how do you think legislative purpose should be discerned?

c. **Title VII Precedent and FHA Text.** In holding that the text of the FHA supports disparate impact claims, the Court relied heavily on two employment precedents: *Griggs v. Duke Power Co.*, a unanimous holding adopting disparate impact liability under Title VII, and *Smith v. City of Jackson*,[15] in which a plurality of the Court recognized disparate impact liability under a similar provision of the Age Discrimination in Employment Act (ADEA). The Court described its employment cases as "provid[ing] essential background and instruction," noting that:

> *Griggs* holds and the plurality in *Smith* instructs that antidiscrimination laws must be construed to encompass disparate impact claims when their text refers to the consequences of actions and not just to the mindset of actors, and where that interpretation is consistent with statutory purpose.

A comparison of the text of Title VII and Title VIII appears below.

Title VII	Fair Housing Act, as amended.
42 U.S.C. § 2000e-2(a)	42 U.S.C. §§ 3604(a)
(a) It shall be an unlawful employment practice for an employer—...	[I]t shall be unlawful—
(2) to limit, segregate, or classify his employees in any way which would deprive or tend to deprive any individual of employment opportunities or otherwise adversely affect his status as an employee, because of such individual's race, color, religion, sex, or national origin.	(a) To refuse to sell or rent after the making of a bona fide offer, or to refuse to negotiate for the sale or rental of, or otherwise make unavailable or deny, a dwelling to any person because of race, color, religion, sex, familial status, or national origin.
	3605(a) (a) ... It shall be unlawful for any person or other entity whose business includes engaging in residential real estate-related transactions to discriminate against any person in making available such a transaction, or in the terms or conditions of such a transaction, because of race, color, religion, sex, handicap, familial status, or national origin.

---

14. 42 U.S.C. §3601.
15. 544 U.S. 228 (2005).

The Court in *Inclusive Communities* compared §(a)(2) of Title VII and similar language under the ADEA with §3604(a) of the FHA; it concluded that "Title VII's and the ADEA's 'otherwise adversely affect' language is equivalent in function and purpose to the FHA's 'otherwise make unavailable' language. In these three statutes the operative text looks to results." The Court also pointed to the common structure of the statutes, noting that the "otherwise" phrases follow prohibitions on disparate treatment and are "catchall phrases looking to consequences, not intent." The Court continued:

> And all three statutes use the word "otherwise" to introduce the results-oriented phrase. "Otherwise" means "in a different way or manner," thus signaling a shift in emphasis from an actor's intent to the consequences of his actions.

As to §3605(a), the Court found it had previously construed similar language to encompass disparate impact liability.

The principal dissenting opinion seized on the FHA's use of "because of" as "remov[ing] any doubt," arguing further that: "In ordinary English usage, when a person makes something unavailable 'because of' some factor, that factor must be a reason for the act." The majority opinion was not persuaded that Congress's use of "because of" foreclosed disparate impact liability, given that *Griggs* and *Smith* interpreted identical language to permit disparate impact claims.[16]

Which aspect of the Court's textual analysis do you find most persuasive? Least persuasive?

d. **Ratification.** The Court considered "of crucial importance" the fact that Congress amended the FHA in 1988 with awareness that all nine courts of appeals that had reached the question had held that the FHA permitted disparate impact claims: "with that understanding, it made a considered judgment to retain the relevant statutory text." In other words, the Court used a principle of statutory construction to conclude that Congress "accepted and ratified" the nine uniform holdings when it decided in its 1988 amendments to adhere to the same operative language of §3604(a) and §3605(a) that those courts had uniformly interpreted. The Court cited A. Scalia & B. Garner, *Reading Law: The Interpretation of Legal Texts* 322 (2012) for the statutory construction principle it applied: "If a word or phrase has been . . . given a uniform interpretation by inferior courts . . ., a later version of that act perpetuating the wording is presumed to carry forward that interpretation."

---

16. *See* Lee Anne Fennell, *Because and Effect: Another Take on* Inclusive Communities, 68 STAN. L. REV. ONLINE 85, 91 (2016) ("Requiring those regulable parties to refrain from acts and omissions that are the functional equivalent of decisions motivated by race—ones that make opportunities unavailable because of race—helps to chip away at the causal connection between status and opportunity."); Noah D. Zatz, *The Many Meanings of "Because Of": A Comment on* Inclusive Communities Project, 68 STAN. L. REV. ONLINE 68, 72 (2015) ("The phrase 'because of' refers directly to causal concepts, not mental ones.").

The Court also pointed to three exemptions incorporated into the 1988 amendments that provide "convincing confirmation" that Congress "assume[d] the existence of disparate impact claims." They relate to appraisals (nothing prohibits consideration of factors other than those the FHA protects); convictions based on illegal drug manufacture or distribution (nothing in the FHA prohibits conduct based on these convictions); and reasonable numerical occupancy restrictions (nothing in the FHA limits applicability of these restrictions). Would the amendments make sense without disparate impact theory? The Court concluded that these amendments "would be superfluous" if only a disparate treatment proof method were available.

For example, it would be unnecessary to enact an exemption for appraisal decisions based on factors other than those protected under the FHA in an intent-only proof world. But such an exemption would make sense where impact claims were permitted. This is because a facially neutral practice regarding appraisals would be "based on factors other than those protected under the FHA." If these neutral factors had a disproportionate impact on a protected class, they could result in liability if the defendant were unable to justify them. Similar logic applies to the exemptions for certain drug convictions: Conviction history is not a protected category under the FHA; therefore, exclusions based on certain types of convictions would fall outside the FHA unless a plaintiff could argue the policies had a disproportionate impact on, for example, persons of color. Finally, occupancy restrictions would not fall within the ambit of the FHA unless a plaintiff could argue that such restrictions disproportionately excluded families with children. "Indeed, none of these amendments would make sense if the FHA encompassed only disparate treatment claims. . . . If an actor makes a decision based on reasons other than a protected category, there is no disparate-treatment liability." The Court concluded: "In short, the 1988 amendments signal that Congress ratified disparate impact liability."

2. *Inclusive Communities* and the HUD Rule. How did *Inclusive Communities* navigate the HUD regulation? The Court never stated that it was adopting HUD's framework. HUD's disparate impact rule is noticeably absent from the Court's enumerated reasons for supporting FHA disparate impact liability. Why might the Court have refrained from relying on the view of the agency charged with interpreting the FHA? Note that the Court declined to grant cert. on the appropriate burden-shifting standard for FHA disparate impact claims.

The Court did cite HUD's rule in the procedural history of the case because the Fifth Circuit below had adopted HUD's burden shifting approach. After quoting HUD's pronouncement of the plaintiff's prima facie burden early in the opinion, the Court stated: "If a statistical discrepancy is caused by factors other than the defendant's policy, a plaintiff cannot establish a prima facie case, and there is no liability." The Court's emphasis on causation in its explanation of HUD's prima facie requirement previews its "robust causality" safeguard that comes much later.

3. Dual Role of "Smoking Out" Intent? Despite its holding that disparate impact claims are cognizable as distinct claims under the FHA, the Court stated that disparate impact liability "plays a role in uncovering discriminatory intent." Here, the Court acknowledged the type of case where a whiff of intentional discrimination appears to lie just beneath the surface of a defendant's practices but may "escape easy classification as disparate treatment." The Court effectively conceded the outmoded nature of a proof regime that requires evidence of a state of mind far less socially acceptable and discernable than in earlier decades. Some commentators and courts describe this function of disparate impact as "smoking out" discriminatory intent; Professor Primus refers to this approach as "evidentiary dragnet."[17] This is definitely a valuable function of disparate impact but it certainly keeps it tethered to state of mind. *See* Stacy Seicshnaydre, *Is the Road to Disparate Impact Paved with Good Intentions? Stuck on State of Mind in Antidiscrimination Law*, 42 WAKE FOREST L. REV. 1141, 1143 (2007) ("What goes on in the hearts and minds of those who exclude, or who can prevent exclusion but choose not to, is less important than how the benefits and burdens get distributed, how they build on past exclusion, and whether the exclusion is justified.").

The Court went further than suggesting that disparate impact theory is merely a tool for smoking out "disguised animus." It acknowledged also that disparate impact liability may "counteract unconscious prejudices." Thus, whether a stereotype is "covert and illicit" or "unconscious," disparate impact theory can be used to "prevent segregated housing patterns" that result. Of course, the upshot of *Inclusive Communities* is that disparate impact is an available method of proof regardless of whether a practice is motivated by discriminatory intent, and regardless of whether any intent is conscious or unconscious.

4. The Hallowed Heartland. The Court provided a quintessential example of disparate impact cases it considered to fall within the FHA's core purpose: claims challenging housing barriers. Legal actions targeting "zoning laws and other housing restrictions that function unfairly to exclude minorities from certain neighborhoods without any sufficient justification . . . reside at the heartland of disparate impact liability." The Court cited three decisions to illustrate "the heartland," all of them exclusionary zoning cases. Perhaps it was no accident that these cases spanned over three decades during which the appellate courts uniformly recognized disparate impact claims, forming the backdrop for Congress in enacting its 1988 amendments.

A few years before *Inclusive Communities* reached the Supreme Court, Professor Seicshnaydre conducted an analysis of four decades of FHA

---

17. *See* Richard A. Primus, *Equal Protection and Disparate Impact: Round Three*, 117 HARV. L. REV. 493, 520 (2003).

disparate impact claims; her inquiry was prompted by the Supreme Court's indication of its willingness to consider the cognizability of the theory in *Magner* (the code enforcement case Justice Alito discussed that settled before oral argument). The published results of the study, cited by the Supreme Court in *Inclusive Communities*, revealed that "the predominant type of FHA disparate impact claim . . . on which plaintiffs are receiving positive outcomes at the appellate level is the housing barrier claim," defined as "challenges to regulations that perpetuate segregation by preventing housing opportunities for [persons of color] outside of neighborhoods where they already live." *See* Stacy E. Seicshnaydre, *Is Disparate Impact Having Any Impact? An Appellate Analysis of Forty Years of Disparate Impact Claims Under the Fair Housing Act*, 63 Am. U. L. Rev. 357, 402, 420 (2013).

Essentially, the earliest FHA disparate impact claims, and the most successful "barrier" claims discussed in the article, are the "heartland" claims Justice Kennedy highlighted in his citations to *Black Jack, Huntington*, and *St. Bernard*. *Black Jack* is the first case in which an appellate court recognized FHA disparate impact theory, and it involved invalidation of a zoning ordinance barring the construction of new multifamily housing units in a hastily incorporated, predominantly white area of St. Louis. *Huntington* involved invalidation of "an overwhelmingly white [Long Island] suburb's zoning regulation . . . restrict[ing] private multi-family housing projects to a largely minority urban renewal area," which "significantly perpetuated segregation in the Town." The court also ordered the town to rezone the site to allow construction of subsidized housing in a white area. *St. Bernard*, discussed in Chapter 6, involved invalidation of a 12-month moratorium on the construction of all multifamily housing in a New Orleans suburb following a "post-Hurricane Katrina ordinance restricting the rental of housing units to only 'blood relative[s]' in an area of the city that was 88.3% white and 7.6% [B]lack."

Pertinent to the heartland, the Court supplemented its soaring language on statutory purpose with a more pragmatic nod to property rights: "The availability of disparate impact liability . . . has allowed private developers to vindicate the FHA's objectives and to protect their property rights by stopping municipalities from enforcing arbitrary and, in practice, discriminatory ordinances barring the construction of certain types of housing units."

5. Segregative Effect Claims. Remember that case precedent defines FHA discriminatory effects to include two types of claims: Those challenging practices that result in a disparate impact on persons because of a protected characteristic or that perpetuate segregated housing patterns, usually on the basis of race. The second type, commonly described as a segregative effect claim, is unique to the FHA and addresses harm to the community as a whole. For example, the court in Metropolitan Housing Development Corp. v. Village of Arlington Heights (*Arlington Heights II*), 558 F.2d 1283, 1290 (7th Cir. 1977), *cert. denied*, 434 U.S. 1025 (1978), held that if a facially neutral housing decision "perpetuates segregation and thereby prevents interracial association it . . . [is] invidious under the [FHA] independently of the extent to which it produces a disparate effect on different racial groups."

Inclusive Communities recognized this second type of claim when it explained: "the FHA aims to ensure that [defendants'] priorities can be achieved without arbitrarily creating discriminatory effects or perpetuating segregation." The Court makes six references to segregation, three references to integration, and two references to racial isolation, highlighting its view of the role of disparate impact in addressing racial segregation. Two of the "heartland" cases the Court cited, *Black Jack* and *Huntington*, recognized or relied on the perpetuation of segregation theory.

Courts since *Inclusive Communities* have applied or recognized segregative effect claims. For example, the court in Mhany Management, Inc. v. County of Nassau, 819 F.3d 581, 620 (2d Cir. 2016) agreed with the district court's assessment that the plaintiff established a prima facie case on perpetuation of segregation:

> Here, the district court concluded that "the R–T zone's restriction on the development of multi-family housing perpetuates segregation generally because it decreases the availability of housing to minorities in a municipality where minorities constitute approximately only 4.1% of the overall population . . . and only 2.6% of the population living in households."

Professor Schwemm, in *Segregative-Effect Claims under the Fair Housing Act*, 20 N.Y.U. J. Legis. & Pub. Pol'y 709, 712-13, 771 (2017), notes that the theory is used primarily in "heartland" cases "challenging municipal land-use restrictions on affordable housing projects." He described the prima facie showing as requiring three elements: "(1) identifying a particular practice of the defendant to challenge; (2) showing through statistical evidence that this practice exacerbates segregation in the relevant community to a sufficiently large degree; and (3) proving that the defendant's challenged practice actually caused this segregative effect." For an exploration of how the segregative effect doctrine may be used as a legal strategy to address algorithmic redlining, see Nadiyah J. Humber, *A Home for Digital Equity: Algorithmic Redlining and Property Technology*, 111 Cal. L. Rev. 1421 (2023).

The caselaw has not limited the claim to situations where the defendant itself created segregated housing patterns, but instead contemplates challenges to practices helping to maintain or intensify pre-existing residential segregation. *See* Inclusive Communities Project, Inc. v. Lincoln Property, 930 F.3d 660, 665 (2019) (Haynes, J., *dissenting from the denial of the petition for rehearing en banc*) ("No one suggests that Defendants began the ugly path to segregated housing, something that has been going on for decades [centuries, even]. Instead they are perpetuating and furthering it."). Professor Seicshnaydre has noted that modern-day decisionmakers can perpetuate segregation, "with or without discriminatory purpose, by simply engaging in practices that help maintain the residential status quo."[18]

D. SAFEGUARDS IN *INCLUSIVE COMMUNITIES*

A review of the principal dissent in *Inclusive Communities* provides important insight into the contested nature of disparate impact theory. In fact, the majority opinion dedicated considerable attention to addressing and aiming to resolve, or at least mitigate, the concerns raised in the dissent. The Court began its effort to tamp down the possibility of negative consequences flowing from its holding by asserting that "disparate impact liability has always been properly limited in key respects." It then pointed to these limits, characterizing them as "safeguards" and surmising how they might apply to the facts of the case before it. The Court's enumerated safeguards include:

- the defendant's long-standing ability to avoid disparate impact liability by proving that any disproportionate impacts are justified;
- restrictions against challenges to one-time decisions;
- protection against "abusive" claims by hearkening back to *Griggs* and its emphasis on mandating the "removal of artificial, arbitrary, and unnecessary barriers," in contrast to the "displacement of valid governmental [and private] policies"; and
- requiring a showing of robust causality at the prima facie stage, which ensures that the plaintiff identify a defendant's practice that causes a statistical disparity, rather than just pointing to the naked disparity itself.

We will address these safeguards in turn, but the Court's discussion reveals that they are interconnected.

1. Justification

One way that disparate impact theory "has always been properly limited" is the leeway given to government housing agencies and private market actors "to state and explain the valid interest served by their policies." This squares with the HUD rule and decades of circuit precedent on FHA disparate impact: Plaintiffs cannot establish disparate impact liability merely by making a prima facie showing. The prima facie showing shifts the burden of persuasion to the defendant to justify the impact. Observing this shift in burdens, Justice Kennedy stated that the defendant must "prove" the policy "is necessary to serve a valid interest." The Court analogized to the Title VII "business necessity" defense but acknowledged that this "framework may not transfer exactly to the fair housing context," given the range of public and private sector individuals and organizations whose practices may be subject to challenge.

---

18. 63 Am. U. L. Rev. at 416.

If this leeway to justify disparate impact is incorporated into the HUD rule and decades of precedent, why was it necessary for the *Inclusive Communities* majority to emphasize it? The principal dissent takes issue with the difficulty in predicting how much protection the defense may provide in particular cases. Consider also this portion of Justice Thomas's dissent: "Standing alone, the fact that a practice has a disparate impact is not conclusive evidence, as the *Griggs* Court appeared to believe, that a practice is 'discriminatory.' We should not automatically presume that any institution with a neutral practice that happens to produce a racial disparity is guilty of discrimination until proved innocent." There is a persistent concern, discussed further with respect to robust causality, that liability for bare racial disparities inexorably leads to racial balancing and quotas. Both dissenting opinions point outside the housing setting to professional sports leagues to signal the absurdity of a theory of discrimination based solely on racial disparities.

However, as *Inclusive Communities* and the HUD rule instruct, disparate impact liability does not result from racial disparities alone. If the plaintiff can jump through all the hoops required for a prima facie case, discussed in more detail in the robust causality section, then the defendant still has the opportunity to prove that any statistical disparities are justified.

2. Restrictions Against Challenges to One-Time Decisions

The Court clarified that a single decision of a housing provider, such as that of where to construct a new building, "may not be a policy at all." A single decision to deny a mortgage lending application or refuse an offer on a home might not be traceable to any facially neutral policy or practice and probably is better analyzed under a discriminatory intent theory of liability. This limit on use of disparate impact theory to challenge single acts or decisions is not new, but it is one of the guardrails the Court enumerates to counter the idea that the theory is too expansive.

In some heartland cases the plaintiff may challenge a particular zoning decision that obstructs the development of affordable housing, which is shown to be used disproportionately by people of color. It would be odd if FHA disparate impact theory were not available to challenge such a decision. In *Mhany Management*, 819 F.3d at 619, the court permitted a disparate impact challenge to an exclusionary zoning decision:

> Garden City argues that disparate impact liability does not exist when a plaintiff challenges a defendant's one-off decision. Rather than challenging the Village's zoning ordinances in general, the Plaintiffs complain about a decision affecting one piece of property. We decline Defendants' invitation to draw a line defining what constitutes a "one-off" zoning "decision" as opposed to a zoning "policy." Even assuming this distinction is relevant, given the many months of hearings and meetings, with charges that R–M zoning [EDs. — permitting multifamily housing] would harm traffic conditions and increase school overcrowding, and that the change required passage of a local law, we are confident this case falls well within a classification of a "general policy."

3. Removing Barriers, Not Second-Guessing Policy Priorities

The *Inclusive Communities* Court warned against what it considered to be an abuse of disparate impact claims in the form of second-guessing defensible policy choices, rather than removing "artificial, arbitrary, and unnecessary barriers." This safeguard addresses the concern that disparate impact theory potentially puts public and private defendants in a "double bind of liability" regardless of their chosen course of action. The Court admonished: "The FHA is not an instrument to force housing authorities to reorder their priorities. Rather the FHA aims to ensure that those priorities can be achieved without arbitrarily creating discriminatory effects or perpetuating segregation."

For example, on the facts of the case before it, the plaintiff had challenged the disproportionate allocation of low-income tax credit family housing subsidies to predominantly Black neighborhoods, with the result being to perpetuate racial segregation. The Court explained: "The FHA does not decree a particular vision of urban development; and it does not put housing authorities and private developers in a double bind of liability, subject to suit whether they choose to rejuvenate a city core or to promote new low income housing in suburban communities." The Court invoked multiple safeguards in this particular context of real estate siting and revitalization decisions and referred back to robust causality: "It may also be difficult to establish causation because of the multiple factors that go into investment decisions about where to construct or renovate housing units." In response to the criticized use of disparate impact claims to second-guess enforcement of health and safety codes, the Court rejoined: "*Magner* was decided without the cautionary standards announced in this opinion."

The Court thus expressed willingness to grant considerable deference to the policy choices of both public and private actors. However, given the Court's sweeping pronouncements on the FHA's role in removing the vestiges of segregation, this deference must have some limits. Professor Seicshnaydre, in *Disparate Impact and the Limits of Local Discretion After* Inclusive Communities, 24 GEO. MASON L. REV. 663, 664-65 (2017), offers this assessment:

> In *Inclusive Communities*, the Court upheld disparate impact liability as a targeted "barrier removal" mechanism rather than a blunt instrument "displac[ing] valid governmental and private priorities"; the Court cited its decision in *Griggs v. Duke Power Co.* three times for the proposition that FHA disparate impact theory mandates the removal of "artificial, arbitrary, and unnecessary barriers." . . . [T]his is the vision that the lower courts have largely implemented for forty years. . . .
>
> The only principled reading of Justice Kennedy's opinion is that the exercise of local policy discretion to overcome housing barriers and "mov[e] the Nation toward a more integrated society" is legitimate and entitled to deference. Local policy discretion that operates to maintain housing barriers and perpetuate the status quo of racial isolation, even under the auspices of "community revitalization," is not legitimate and is subject to challenge.

4. Robust Causality

Robust causality is a prominent disparate impact safeguard announced by the Court to "avoid the serious constitutional questions that might arise under the FHA . . . if such liability were imposed based solely on a showing of a racial disparity." Under a robust causality requirement at the prima facie stage, a plaintiff must point to a defendant's policy or practice causing the statistical disparity. Pleading racial imbalance alone is insufficient. *See* 24 CFR §100.500(c)(1) (imposing a burden on the plaintiff "of proving that *a challenged practice caused* or predictably will cause a discriminatory effect") (emphasis added).

What is the potential constitutional violation if such naked challenges to disparities were to be permitted? As reflected in the dissenting opinions, critics of disparate impact argue generally that disparate impact theory incentivizes defendants to adopt quotas to avoid liability for racial imbalances. The Court answers the quota critique as follows:

> [A] disparate impact claim that relies on a statistical disparity must fail if the plaintiff cannot point to a defendant's policy or policies causing that disparity. A robust causality requirement ensures that "[r]acial imbalance . . . does not, without more, establish a prima facie case of disparate impact" and thus protects defendants from being held liable for racial disparities they did not create. *Wards Cove Packing Co. v. Atonio*, 490 U.S. 642, 653 (1989). Without adequate safeguards at the prima facie stage, disparate impact liability might cause race to be used and considered in a pervasive way and "would almost inexorably lead" governmental or private entities to use "numerical quotas," and serious constitutional questions then could arise. *Id.*

In the opinion's next paragraph, the Court repeated its warning that "potential defendants may adopt racial quotas" without "adequate safeguards." Immediately following its second reference to quotas and safeguards, the Court continued: "Courts must therefore examine with care whether a plaintiff has made out a prima facie case of disparate impact [which requires a plaintiff] to allege facts at the pleading stage or produce statistical evidence demonstrating a causal connection." Thus, the robust causality requirement is inextricably tied to the Court's reassurance that disparate impact need not drive defendants toward a constitutional quota conundrum: "[C]ourts should avoid interpreting disparate impact liability to be so expansive as to inject racial considerations into every housing decision."

To be sure, the racial balancing and quota concerns that arise in the employment and school settings do not apply with the same force in the housing setting. Professor Seicshnaydre contends that "inclusion" is not a zero-sum game:

> [A] local government's consideration of its zoning ordinances to ensure that they do not disproportionately exclude certain groups should not implicate what Helen Norton has described as zero-sum notions of equality. Inclusive neighborhoods do not "make identifiable third parties worse off in tangible ways."[19]

---

19. *Is Disparate Impact Having Any Impact?*, 63 Am. U. L. Rev. at 417.

We examine several aspects of robust causality below.

a. Is Robust Causality New?

Is the Court's robust causality safeguard a new limitation on disparate impact? Causality certainly is not new. The Court cited a 25-year-old employment case, *Wards Cove*, in its description of robust causality. (The *Wards Cove* case represented a significant, and more restrictive, change in the Supreme Court's approach to disparate impact that had existed prior to that point. Congress amended Title VII in 1991 in part to repudiate the opinion.) This reinforces the Court's earlier statement that disparate impact "has always been properly limited." *See* Rigel C. Oliveri, *Disparate Impact and Integration: With* TDHCA v. Inclusive Communities *the Supreme Court Retains an Uneasy Status Quo*, 24 J. Affordable Hous. & Community Dev. L. 267, 276 (2015) (noting that *Inclusive Communities* "is not particularly remarkable in the sense that it merely leaves existing law and precedent undisturbed."). Courts since *Inclusive Community* have divided on whether use of the word "robust" ushered in a more onerous standard of causation or whether the Court was merely bringing special emphasis to the existing requirement codified by the HUD rule.

b. Robust Causality: Application

On remand, the district court in *Inclusive Communities* dismissed the disparate impact claim for failure to satisfy robust causality. Explaining that it had not had the benefit of the Supreme Court's opinion, but purporting to apply the HUD rule, the court found the plaintiff had failed to identify a specific practice that caused the disparity in the location of low-income housing.[20] The following cases apply different interpretations of the "robust causality" requirement discussed in *Inclusive Communities*. As you review their analyses, consider what it means for a defendant to "create" a statistical disparity.

In Southwest Fair Housing Council, Inc. v. Maricopa Domestic Water Improvement District, 17 F.4th 950, 965-66 (9th Cir. 2021), the court held that the plaintiff had established its prima facie case and satisfied robust causality (but affirmed summary judgment for the defendant on other grounds).

> Here, because the District explicitly applied the adverse effects of the policy—increasing the security deposit to $180—only to a subset of its customer base, the causation analysis is not all that complicated. The adverse impact complained about by Appellants derives wholly from the innerworkings of the policy. For no reason other than the District's decision to create two different security deposit amounts for its public housing customers and for its private housing customers did the disparate impact arise. After the implementation

---

20. No. 3:08-CV-0546-D, 2016 WL 4494322 (N.D. Tex. Aug. 26, 2016).

of the policy and as a direct result of it, a disproportionate percentage of protected-group members were subject to an increased security deposit.

Importantly, the adverse effect here is not some broad social condition. Appellants are not complaining that the Security Deposit Policy contributed to an overrepresentation of protected-group members in public housing. Rather, Appellants complain that the District's tying security deposit prices to public housing status directly caused the discrete adverse effect of an increased security deposit to apply disproportionately to members of protected groups. As such, it is not the case that we are left wondering whether members of a protected class are subject to the increased fee because of this policy or because of some other factor. The sole cause of the disproportionate impact of the increased security deposit was the District's decision to apply the policy only to a subset of its customers. . . .

This is a simple case where the policy explicitly bifurcated a population based on a non-protected characteristic: public housing. That bifurcation generated a disproportionate effect that would not have existed in its absence and ensured the adverse effects of the policy applied only to the population subset that was overrepresented (in comparison to the overall District customer population) by certain members of a protected group. The clarity of that causal relationship sets it apart from other cases.

In Reyes v. Waples Mobile Home Park Ltd. Partnership, 903 F.3d 415, 428-30 (4th Cir. 2018), the court held that the plaintiff satisfied robust causality, reversing the "grievous error" in the district court's analysis.

Plaintiffs satisfied step one of the *Inclusive Communities* framework by demonstrating that Waples' Policy of evicting occupants that are unable to provide documentation of legal status in the United States caused a disproportionate number of Latinos to face eviction from the Park compared to the number of non-Latinos who faced eviction based on the Policy. Notably, the evidence did not merely allege that Latinos would face eviction in higher numbers than non-Latinos. Instead, Plaintiffs satisfied the robust causality requirement by asserting that the specific Policy requiring all adult Park tenants to provide certain documents proving legal status was likely to cause Latino tenants at the Park to be disproportionately subject to eviction compared to non-Latino tenants at the Park. [The Court noted that "Latinos are ten times more likely than non-Latinos to be adversely affected by the Policy, as undocumented immigrants constitute 36.4% of the Latino population compared with only 3.6% of the non-Latino population."] Accordingly, we now hold that Plaintiffs have made a prima facie case that Waples' Policy disparately impacted Latinos in violation of the FHA, satisfying step one of the disparate impact analysis, and that the district court therefore erred in concluding otherwise. . . .

The district court's view threatens to eviscerate disparate impact claims altogether, as this view could permit any facially neutral rationale to be considered the primary *cause* for the disparate impact on the protected class and break the robust link required between the challenged policy and the disparate impact.

In Inclusive Communities Project, Inc. v. Lincoln Property Co., 920 F.3d 890, 906-07 (5th Cir. 2019), the Fifth Circuit held that the plaintiff failed to meet its prima facie burden on robust causality. Plaintiff ICP (the same plaintiff as in the featured case before the Supreme Court) alleged that the defendants' policy of not negotiating with or renting to households with vouchers in predominantly white "high opportunity" areas had a greater adverse impact on the Black renter population than the white renter population. ICP also claimed that the "no vouchers" policy perpetuated racial segregation in the Dallas area by excluding predominantly Black voucher households from predominantly white census tracts.

> Considering the instant record, we find no error in the district court's determination that the allegations of ICP's complaint fail to allege facts sufficient to provide the robust causation necessary for an actionable disparate impact claim. Moreover, we find this conclusion to be warranted under any of the analyses of robust causation discussed above, *i.e.* that of the Eighth Circuit in *Ellis*, the Fourth Circuit majority in *Reyes*, Judge Keenan's dissent in *Reyes*, or the Eleventh Circuit's per curiam in *Oviedo*. . . .
>
> The logic of both the majority and dissenting opinions in *Reyes*, as well as the Eleventh Circuit's per curiam in *Oviedo* [*Town Center v. City of Oviedo, Florida*, Fed. App'x 828 (11th Cir. 2018)], likewise applies here. Neither the aforementioned "city-level data" nor the "census-level data" cited by ICP supports an inference that the implementation of Defendants-Appellees' blanket "no vouchers" policy, or any change therein, caused black persons to be the dominant group of voucher holders in the Dallas metro area (or any of the other census areas discussed by ICP). Similarly, ICP alleges no facts supporting a reasonable inference that Defendants-Appellees bear any responsibility for the geographic distribution of minorities throughout the Dallas area prior to the implementation of the "no vouchers" policy. Indeed, ICP pleads no facts showing Dallas's racial composition before the Defendants-Appellees implemented their "no vouchers" policy or how that composition has changed, if at all, since the policy was implemented.
>
> Thus, as the district court noted, none of these factual allegations "show or infer that Defendants-Appellees' policy *diminished* the amount of rental opportunities for African American or Black prospective tenants previously available before Defendants' policy was implemented." (Emphasis added.) Accordingly, it is entirely speculative whether the "no vouchers" policy, as opposed to some other factor, *not* attributable to Defendants-Appellees, caused there to be less minority habitation in individual census tracts after the policy was implemented. Without that information, any landlord who did not accept vouchers would be vulnerable to a disparate impact challenge any time a less than statistically proportionate minority population lived in that landlord's census tract. Because "disparate impact liability has always been properly limited," *see ICP*, 135 S.Ct. at 2522, that cannot be the correct result.
>
> Finally, in the Eighth Circuit's view, the "no vouchers" policy, even if causing a "problematic disparity," does not state an actionable FHA disparate [impact] claim unless the policy is "artificial, arbitrary, and unnecessary." *Ellis* [*v. City of Minneapolis*, 860 F.3d 1106, 1112-1114 (8th Cir. 2017)]. A private entity's choice to opt out of participation in a government program that is *voluntary* under both federal and Texas law cannot be artificial, arbitrary, and unnecessary absent the existence of pertinent, contrary factual allegations sufficiently rendering a plaintiff's claimed entitlement to disparate impact relief plausible, rather than merely conceivable or speculative. As we have explained, on the record before us, we find none.

These varying circuit approaches reveal the fault lines that have emerged as the courts grapple with what it means to establish robust causality in FHA disparate impact claims. Thus, unless and until the Supreme Court intervenes, litigants will face uneven hurdles depending on their jurisdictions.

c. Robust Causality and Preexisting Market Conditions

Note that the majority in *Lincoln Property* appears to require the plaintiffs to show that the defendant is responsible, not just for practices that perpetuate segregation, but for the preexisting conditions in the housing market that caused segregation in the first place, or that cause defendant's practices to have the effect of retrenching this segregation. The dissenting opinion in *Lincoln Property* strenuously objected, arguing that this required an impossible showing. Judge Davis wrote:

> The majority . . . interprets "robust causation" to require the plaintiff in a disparate impact claim under the FHA to establish that the challenged policy was previously unenforced or that the challenged policy caused a "pre-existing condition." There is no precedent requiring such elements as part of the plaintiff's prima facie case. . . .
>
> Such a requirement turns disparate impact liability on its head because it would compel the plaintiff to establish that the offending policy not only had a disparate impact on a protected group, but that somehow the policy also created the characteristics making the protected group susceptible to the disparate impact. . . .
>
> [T]he majority concludes that robust causation is not alleged because ICP failed to state that Defendants were responsible for the fact that Black renters in Dallas hold a disproportionate number of vouchers for low income housing. Since obtaining a voucher requires a showing of limited financial resources, presumably the majority would require ICP to show why a disproportionate number of Black renters in Dallas had more limited financial resources than White renters and that defendants were responsible for this fact. . . .
>
> To require such proof for a plaintiff to establish causation would render disparate impact liability under the FHA a dead letter. This was certainly not the model of a disparate impact case adopted by the Supreme Court in *Griggs* under Title VII. The Court in that case held that the employer's policy of requiring an applicant for employment to have a high school education and to pass a standardized general intelligence test had an adverse impact on Black applicants. The Court did not require proof that the employer was responsible for the disproportionately lower educational levels and test scores for Blacks as compared to Whites.

920 F.3d at 921-22; 924-25. In an opinion dissenting from denial of rehearing en banc, Judge Haynes noted that "the panel majority opinion now renders [*Inclusive Communities*] almost meaningless by crafting an impossible pleading standard." *See* Inclusive Communities Project, Inc. v. Lincoln Property, 930 F.3d 660, 661, 667 (2019) ("The majority opinion takes the Supreme Court's robust causality requirement much further than it actually went, thus hampering enforcement of the FHA in three states that have numerous large cities, including three of the top ten most populous cities in the country.").

Would the heartland cases cited by *Inclusive Communities* with approval, including the *St. Bernard* case featured in Chapter 6, satisfy the robust causality standard as applied in *Lincoln Property*? In other words, could the plaintiff in *St. Bernard* have shown that the parish government caused Black households to be in the dominant group of renters excluded by the parish-wide ban on new multifamily housing? Does this resemble the argument defendants made in the Contract Buyers League litigation, Chapter 2, that they could not be held liable for exploiting a dual credit market that existed before they engaged in alleged exploitative transactions with plaintiffs? Professor Samuel Bagenstos, in *Disparate Impact and the Role of Classification and Motivation in Equal Protection Law After* Inclusive Communities, 101 Cornell L. Rev. 1115, 1133 (2016) opines:

> Nothing in the Court's analysis suggests that . . . disparate impact law is driven by a desire to respond only to the defendant's own past intentional discrimination. Rather, the goal is to combat "racial isolation" and "segregated housing patterns"—results that exist in the world, independent of whose actions caused them in the first place.

E. FHA DISPARATE IMPACT: OTHER ISSUES

1. Disparate Impact and Exemptions

Some courts have limited the reach of disparate impact theory when they believe it is being used to create a new protected characteristic not covered by the FHA. In *Lincoln Property*, the Fifth Circuit rejected a disparate impact challenge to a "no vouchers" policy applied at 43 apartment complexes in majority white census tracts in Dallas.

> To adopt the dissent's position [permitting the disparate impact claim to proceed] would effectively mandate a landlord's participation in the voucher program any time the racial makeup of a multi-family rental complex does not match the demographics of a nearby metropolitan area. . . . [I]f such a burdensome and extreme mandate were to be attempted, it should be expressly legislated by Congress, not this court.

920 F.3d at 909. Recall that the basic function of disparate impact claims is to identify *neutral* practices not explicitly prohibited under law that will have a disproportionate impact on individuals with protected characteristics. The panel dissent in *Lincoln Property* argued that unless Congress has exempted a particular practice or use of disparate impact theory, the claim should proceed.

> Congress has had the opportunity to exempt landlords from disparate impact liability under the FHA for discriminating against potential tenants based on their status as voucher holders, but Congress has not done so. . . . Therefore, under *ICP*, if such a policy results in a disparate impact on a protected group, then the policy may be subject to challenge under the FHA. The majority cannot carve out this exemption on Congress' behalf.

920 F.3d at 924. Consider another example. In *Reyes*, the Fourth Circuit upheld a disparate impact challenge to a policy targeting "illegal immigrants" in a mobile home park in Fairfax, Virginia.

> [I]n the absence of a specific exemption from liability for exclusionary practices aimed at illegal immigrants, we must infer that Congress intended to permit disparate impact liability for policies aimed at illegal immigrants when the policy disparately impacts a protected class, regardless of any correlation between the two.

903 F.3d at 431-32. Thus, characteristics that are *not* protected by the statute—such as using a voucher or being undocumented—will be implicated when they disproportionately affect protected groups. The dissent in *Reyes* took the opposite view:

> [A]ccepting the plaintiffs' theory of disparate impact liability would expand the FHA beyond its stated terms to protect undocumented aliens as a class, based solely on an allegation of disparate impact within that class. . . . [I]t is the role of Congress to consider whether, as a matter of public policy, the FHA should be amended to prohibit discrimination based on citizenship or immigration status.

903 F.3d at 434-35. Which of the two approaches do you find more persuasive? Is it satisfying to argue that if Congress had intended to protect these "neutral" characteristics it should have included them in the statute? Conversely, is it satisfying to argue that if Congress had intended to permit housing providers to exclude tenants with certain characteristics regardless of any resulting disparate impact, it should have exempted those factors from disparate impact liability? Does the text of the FHA aid in this analysis?

2. Statistical Showing

Of course, a threshold requirement in traditional discriminatory effects cases is the proper showing of disparate impact. How must a plaintiff make this showing? Statistics are crucial, and this usually requires an expert. In *Southwest Fair Housing Council*, 17 F.4th at 963, the court explained:

> Before any statistical disparate impact analysis can proceed, the correct comparative populations must be identified. There are multiple valid methods of analysis involving different comparative populations. *See* Robert G. Schwemm & Calvin Bradford, *Proving Disparate Impact in Fair Housing Cases After* Inclusive Communities, 19 N.Y.U. J. Legis. & Pub. Pol'y 685, 698-99, 703-06 (2016). One method that we have identified as a valid "basis for a successful disparate impact claim involves a comparison between two groups—those affected and those unaffected by the facially neutral policy."

The failure to identify the appropriate comparative populations for statistical analysis can result in a plaintiff's failure to establish the statistical disparity needed for the prima facie case. In Oviedo Town Center. v. City of Oviedo, Fla., 759 F. App'x 828, 835-36 (11th Cir. 2018) (per curiam), the developers and managers of an affordable housing complex challenged a change in the application of city policy resulting in an increase in the base rate the city billed plaintiffs for water and sewerage services. The court held that their failure to establish a statistical disparity made an analysis of causation unnecessary.

> The only statistical evidence presented in this case was a survey conducted by the plaintiffs. . . . The Survey showed that 75.73% of heads of [Oviedo Town Center (OTC)] households are members of racial minorities and that 24.27% of heads of OTC households are white. By way of comparison, the Survey cited census data indicating that only 32.7% of households in Oviedo are racial minority households while 65.8% of households are not. As the district court recognized, this data revealed only that more racial minorities live in Oviedo Town Center than lived in the rest of the City of Oviedo. It does not establish a disparate impact, let alone any causal connection between the 2012 Policy and the disparate impact. . . .
>
> As the district court observed, in order to establish a prima facie case of disparate impact, the appellants would have needed to draw a comparison between (a) the percentage of racial minorities occupying multifamily proper-ties impacted by the 2012 Policy throughout the City of Oviedo and (b) the per-centage of non-minorities living in such properties, again throughout the City of Oviedo. If this citywide comparison demonstrated that a disproportionate percentage of racial minorities in multifamily properties were impacted across the city, a prima facie case of disparate impact might have been presented, and we would then proceed to consider the causal relation. This kind of citywide comparative analysis would be necessary because, since the policy impacts the whole city, the whole city would need to be evaluated before we could deter-mine that the claimed impact might have disparately fallen on certain insular groups.

The vast majority of disparate impact cases allege racial or national origin impacts, but the claim is available based on any FHA protected characteristic. For example, disabled residents of a group home might use an effects the-ory to challenge neutral rules limiting the number of unrelated people who may live in single family zones. Chapter 17 focuses primarily on reasonable accommodation claims in these instances. Why?

> For plaintiffs in disability discrimination cases, disparate impact is typically the most difficult type of FHAA claim to prevail on, for several reasons [includ-ing] a general lack of available, localized, statistical data [to show that a neutral policy disproportionately burdens people with disabilities]. Unlike in racial discrimination cases, where United States Census Bureau data provide highly localized data, disability information is more limited. Moreover, while there is much statistical support to establish that there is high demand for housing for people with disabilities, that fact alone is insufficient to establish [that a particular policy is causing a] disparate impact. [In any event], it is almost uni-versally the case that FHAA claims by people with disabilities join disparate impact claims with other claims, including discriminatory intent and reason-able accommodation claims.[21]

---

21. Brian J. Connolly & Dwight H. Merriam, *Planning and Zoning for Group Homes: Local Government Obligations and Liability under the Fair Housing Amendments Act*, 47 Urban Lawyer 225, 272 (2015).

The requirement that a plaintiff retain an expert to make the necessary statistical showing of disparate impact, not to mention the need to establish that a defendant's practice is responsible for causing the impact, helps illustrate the complexity and elusiveness of this method of proof for many plaintiffs.

Chapter Summary

- Disparate impact is a theory of liability for discrimination based on the effects of the defendant's action, rather than on the defendant's intention in taking the action. It is a tool to ensure that policies do not sweep more broadly than necessary to achieve legitimate business or governmental objectives.
- Disparate impact claims do not require *less* evidence than disparate treatment claims; they require *different* evidence.
- One feature of discriminatory effects liability unique to fair housing cases is that in addition to showing "adverse impact" on a protected group, plaintiffs also may make a prima facie case by showing "harm to the community generally by the perpetuation of segregation."
- In 2015, the Supreme Court in a 5-4 decision upheld disparate impact as a cognizable theory of liability under the FHA in *Texas Department of Housing and Community Affairs v. Inclusive Communities Project*. The Court based its holding on the FHA's result-oriented language, the Court's interpretation of similar language in Title VII and the ADEA, Congress' ratification of disparate impact claims in 1988 against the backdrop of the unanimous view of nine courts of appeals, and the statutory purpose.
- The *Inclusive Communities* Court provided a quintessential, "heartland" example of disparate impact cases it considered to fall within the FHA's core purpose: claims targeting "zoning laws and other housing restrictions that function unfairly to exclude minorities from certain neighborhoods without any sufficient justification . . . reside at the heartland of disparate impact liability."
- The *Inclusive Communities* Court enumerated a number of safeguards to demonstrate that disparate impact theory "has always been properly limited." These include the defendant's long-standing ability to avoid disparate impact liability by proving a justification for their policies; restrictions against challenges to one-time decisions; protection from abusive claims by mandating removal of artificial, arbitrary, and unnecessary barriers, not displacement of valid policies; and requiring plaintiffs to plead robust causality, which guards against quotas and ensures that defendants are not held liable for disparities they did not create. The latter safeguard has imposed varying hurdles for plaintiffs depending on their jurisdiction.

- HUD in 2013 issued its first regulation interpreting the FHA to recognize disparate impact claims. This regulation also set forth a uniform burden-shifting proof framework. Different presidential administrations have taken varied approaches to disparate impact since then.
- The HUD approach in effect at the time of publication is as follows: (1) Plaintiff has the initial burden of proving that a challenged practice caused (or predictably will cause) a discriminatory effect. (2) The burden then shifts to the defendant to prove that the challenged practice is necessary to achieve one or more substantial, legitimate, nondiscriminatory interests. (3) The burden then shifts back to plaintiff, who still may prevail by proving that the interests supporting the challenged practice could be served by another practice that has a less discriminatory effect.

PART IV

THE FAIR HOUSING ACT: SUBSTANTIVE PROVISIONS

The Fair Housing Act is structured broadly to prohibit certain housing-related conduct when such conduct is carried out because of a person's protected characteristics, without specifying who must engage in the conduct. The substantive parts of the statute—§§3604, 3605, 3606, 3617, and 3631—describe the prohibited conduct. Many of the statute's most significant prohibitions are contained in Section 3604. Whereas some of these were modeled after employment-related prohibitions in Title VII of the 1964 Civil Rights Act, others are unique to the housing context.

Section 3604 is multifaceted, prohibiting discrimination in making housing unavailable, terms and conditions, advertising and statements, misrepresentations about housing availability, and inducement of panic selling (blockbusting). Section 3605 prohibits discrimination in residential real estate-related transactions, spanning mortgage lending, appraisals, homeowners insurance, and other related services. Any financing that is secured by residential real estate is covered, which means loans for improving and repairing (as well as purchasing) property come under the FHA's ambit. Section 3617 prohibits intimidation, threats, coercion, and interference with rights granted under other provisions of the FHA and also protects against retaliation for asserting these rights or assisting others in doing so; section 3631 is the companion criminal statute addressing violent obstruction of fair housing rights. We discuss these provisions in Chapters 8 to 11, with a separate substantive section, 3608, the focus of Chapter 13.

CHAPTER 8

PROHIBITED CONDUCT UNDER §§3604(a), (b), (d), AND (e)

This chapter explores examples of, and questions presented by, four subsections of §3604. Bear in mind as you read these materials that a single case could (and often does) involve violations of multiple provisions of the FHA and that prohibitions often overlap. Consider the limitations that some courts place on the reach of these prohibitions, even though there are few restrictions in the language of the statute itself.

A. SECTION 3604(a): REFUSAL TO SELL, RENT, OR NEGOTIATE OR OTHERWISE MAKE HOUSING UNAVAILABLE

A significant substantive provision of the FHA is 42 U.S.C §3604(a), which makes it unlawful:

> To refuse to sell or rent after the making of a bona fide offer, or to refuse to negotiate for the sale or rental of, or otherwise make unavailable or deny, a dwelling to any person because of race, color, religion, sex, familial status, or national origin.

Similar language is used in §3604(f)(1), which prohibits such discrimination on the basis of disability.[1]

---

1. Section 3604(f)(1), the FHA's ban on making housing unavailable because of disability, is set forth separately because it covers additional protected parties with disabilities (persons residing in the dwelling and associated with a buyer or renter) that apply only in the disability context. The FHA provisions covering disability discrimination are discussed in detail in Chapter 17. It is, however, generally true that the FHA's strictures apply to all protected classes in the same way, so that propositions relevant to, for example, "making housing unavailable" because of race usually would apply in a similar way to making housing unavailable because of another protected category.

This includes the relatively straightforward conduct of refusing to sell, rent, or negotiate for the sale or rental of housing. At the time the FHA was passed, outright refusals to deal were commonplace and this was clearly a primary evil that Congress sought to address. In the 21st century, such overt conduct is less prevalent, although it does still occur. There are many more subtle ways in which housing can be made unavailable because of protected characteristics. Congress addressed this by including the more expansive final clause of §3604(a), which broadens the provision's reach considerably, including a variety of other practices that might deny housing or make housing unavailable to a person. *See* Williams v. Matthews Co., 499 F.2d 819, 826 (8th Cir. 1974) (the statute "prohibit[s] all forms of discrimination, sophisticated as well as simpleminded, and thus disparity of treatment between whites and blacks, burdensome application procedures, and tactics of delay, hindrance, and special treatment must receive short shrift from the courts."). The "make unavailable or deny" provision also is used in litigation against government action, like zoning, which is discussed below.

A HUD regulation outlines some of the types of conduct that §3604(a) can cover; notice that the regulation encompasses "handicap," thus implementing §3604(f)(1) as well as §3604(a):

> **24 C.F.R. §100.60(b)** Prohibited actions under this section include, but are not limited to:
>
> (1) Failing to accept or consider a *bona fide* offer because of [protected characteristics].
>
> (2) Refusing to sell or rent a dwelling to, or to negotiate for the sale or rental of a dwelling with, any person because of [protected characteristics].
>
> (3) Imposing different sales prices or rental charges for the sale or rental of a dwelling upon any person because of [protected characteristics].
>
> (4) Using different qualification criteria or applications, or sale or rental standards or procedures, such as income standards, application requirements, application fees, credit analysis or sale or rental approval procedures or other requirements, because of [protected characteristics].
>
> (5) Evicting tenants because of their [protected characteristics] or because of the [protected characteristics] of a tenant's guest.
>
> (6) Conditioning the availability of a dwelling, including the price, qualification criteria, or standards or procedures for securing the dwelling, on a person's response to harassment because of [protected characteristics].
>
> (7) Subjecting a person to harassment because of [protected characteristics] that causes the person to vacate a dwelling or abandon efforts to secure the dwelling.

Note the potential for overlap: Many of the discriminatory practices that make housing unavailable violate other provisions of the statute discussed in this chapter and others that follow. Despite the broad scope of §3604(a), the provision's reach is not unlimited. As you read the material in this section, consider where the boundary lies between conduct that makes housing slightly less desirable or more inconvenient to obtain, and that which constitutes an actual or attempted deprivation of housing.

1. Discouraging Conduct

There are many ways in which a seller, landlord, or agent might prevent a homeseeker from renting or buying a property. One common tactic is for a housing professional simply not to show units or fail to inform the home seeker about available units or houses. A nationwide study published by HUD in 2012 found that Black renters who contacted agents about recently advertised housing units were told about fewer available units and shown fewer units than were equally qualified whites. The same study found that Black homebuyers who contacted agents about recently advertised homes for sale were told about fewer available homes and shown fewer homes than were equally qualified whites.[2] Obviously, a prospective renter or buyer who does not know about a property will not be in a position to rent or buy it.

There are many other ways in which home seekers might be discouraged from obtaining housing. In *United States v. Youritan Construction Company*, the court observed: "The imposition of more burdensome application procedures, of delaying tactics, and of various forms of discouragement by resident managers and rental agents constitutes a violation of Section 3604(a). . . ." 370 F. Supp. 643, 648 (N.D. Cal. 1973), *aff'd in part per curiam*, 509 F.2d 623 (9th Cir. 1975). In that case, the evidence showed that these tactics indeed worked to exclude Black applicants: Most of the apartment complexes at issue had never had a single Black resident. Consider the following case, in which a seller resorted to a variety of tactics to prevent Black would-be buyers from purchasing his home. This case also provides a good introduction to the enforcement options available under the FHA, requirements for proving FHA claims, and available relief.

United States Department of Housing and Urban Development v. Blackwell
908 F.2d 864 (11th Cir. 1990)

Before Hatchett, Circuit Judge, and Roney and Fairchild, Senior Circuit Judges.

HATCHETT, Circuit Judge:

---

2. HUD Office of Policy Development and Research, *Housing Discrimination Against Racial and Ethnic Minorities 2012*, https://www.huduser.gov/portal/publications/fairhsg/hsg_disc rimination_2012.html.

In this case of first impression under the FHAA of 1988, we are asked to enforce a decision and order of HUD. Concluding that the decision and order are supported by substantial evidence, we enforce.

FACTS

Gordon G. Blackwell, a white male, is the sole owner of the property located at 4010 Indian Lakes Circle, Stone Mountain, GA (the house). Since 1970, Blackwell has been a licensed real estate broker in Georgia. In August, 1988, the house became vacant. In April, 1989, Blackwell entered into a ninety-day exclusive listing of the house with real estate agent Don Wainwright.

In early May, 1989, Terryl and Janella Herron, an African-American couple, viewed the house accompanied by their agent, Kay Newbern. On May 10, 1989, the Herrons offered to buy the house for $80,000. Blackwell rejected the Herrons' offer.

Because the Herrons "really liked the house," on June 8, 1989, they offered to buy the house for $90,000. The following day, Wainwright brought the Herrons' offer to Blackwell. Blackwell also rejected this offer, but agreed to make a counteroffer of $92,000. According to Wainwright, at some point during their meeting, Blackwell asked whether the Herrons were black or white persons. Wainwright answered that he did not know because he was dealing directly with Newbern.

On June 10, 1989, Newbern presented Blackwell's counteroffer to the Herrons. Terryl Herron accepted the $92,000 purchase price by initialing and dating the counteroffer. Terryl Herron also made some changes to the terms, including a requirement that the "[s]eller [was] to pay total 5% towards closing & points."

A day later, Wainwright telephoned Blackwell and told him that the Herrons had accepted the $92,000 purchase price. According to Wainwright, he also described the changes that Terryl Herron had made to the counteroffer. Blackwell responded that they had an agreement, and instructed Wainwright to initial the changes on Blackwell's behalf and complete the acceptance block on the contract, indicating that all parties had agreed.

On June 13, 1989, the Herrons tendered their earnest money deposit and applied for a mortgage with Commonwealth Mortgage Company. At some time between June 13 and June 16, 1989, Blackwell telephoned Newbern and told her that the Herrons "got a great deal." According to Newbern, Blackwell also asked: "I know it's quite unusual for me to ask this question, I should not ask it, but are the purchasers black?" Newbern refused to answer the question, responding, "You're right, you're not supposed to ask that question."

On June 20, 1989, Wainwright brought a copy of the contract and a repair addendum to Blackwell's apartment. Blackwell reviewed the documents, initialed them, and dated the contract June 11, 1988 (the date on which he had agreed orally to the contract terms). Later that day, however, Blackwell left a message with Wainwright indicating that he wished to change the terms of the contract, to require the Herrons to pay the closing costs. Wainwright subsequently returned Blackwell's telephone call and informed him that they already had a completed contract. On June 22, 1989, Wainwright received a copy of the contract on which Blackwell had changed the terms to show that the buyer (the Herrons) would pay closing costs.

Thereafter, whenever Wainwright attempted to communicate with Blackwell about the matter, Blackwell would hang up the telephone. On July 9, 1989, Blackwell changed the locks on the front door of the house, and removed Wainwright's lock box. Three days later, Blackwell told Wainwright that he would not attend the scheduled closing with the Herrons.

On or before July 12, 1989, Blackwell posted "open for inspection" signs in front of the house. On July 16, 1989, Blackwell met with Brett and Audrey Cooper, who are white persons, and who were moving from Dallas, Texas, to Atlanta. On the same day, the Coopers signed a lease (starting July 25, 1989) with an option to purchase. Blackwell did not ask the Coopers about their rent or credit history, and did not ask them to complete an information sheet. Further, Blackwell did not inform the Coopers about his contract with the Herrons.

On July 18, 1989, Wainwright spoke with Brett Cooper, at the house, and told him that the house was under contract and that a closing had been scheduled. Brett Cooper then called Blackwell who said that they (the Coopers and Blackwell) had a good contract.

The next day, Wainwright telephoned Blackwell to explain that the appraiser from the Herrons' mortgage company needed access to the house on July 20, 1989. Blackwell hung up the telephone, after telling Wainwright that he would not be at the closing. On July 20, 1989, Wainwright and the appraiser went to the house but it was locked and no one was present. Subsequently, in a telephone conversation, Blackwell told Newbern that she should never go into the house, and that he would not be going to a closing with the Herrons. Further, according to Newbern, Blackwell stated that he had leased/purchased the house to "some really good white tenants."

PROCEDURAL HISTORY

On July 24, 1989, the Herrons filed a housing discrimination complaint with HUD[, which] commenced an investigation of the complaint, and attempted to conciliate the matter.

In late July, 1989, HUD's general counsel authorized the Attorney General of the United States to seek prompt judicial action in federal district court to prevent Blackwell from selling or renting the property to anyone other than the Herrons. On August 2, 1989, the district court entered a preliminary injunction restraining Blackwell from, among other things, selling or leasing the property except to the Herrons, and requiring Blackwell to notify the Coopers (who, on the advice of counsel, intervened and attended the hearing) that they would have to vacate the property before the Herrons closed on their contract. [Eds.—Note that an order providing relief for a discriminatory housing practice shall not affect any contract "consummated before the issuance of such order and involving a bona fide purchaser . . . or tenant without actual notice" of an FHA charge or complaint. 42 USC §3612(g)(4); 42 USC §3613(d).]

On August 15, 1989, Wainwright's office called Blackwell to inform him that the closing with the Herrons had been rescheduled for August 16, 1989. All of the necessary parties, with the exception of Blackwell, met for the closing. On August 17, 1989, the Coopers moved out of the house.

On August 30, 1989, the district court held Blackwell in civil contempt for, among other things, taking steps to sell or rent the property to someone other than the Herrons. The district court ordered Blackwell to pay a fine of $500 per day if he did not remove all "for sale" or "for rent" signs. Blackwell removed the signs the following day.

The Secretary issued a determination of reasonable cause and charge of discrimination against Blackwell on August 30, 1989, and filed it with the Office of Administrative Law Judges for HUD. After a three-day hearing, HUD's chief administrative law judge (ALJ) issued an initial decision and order in favor of the Secretary, the Herrons, and the Coopers. On February 14, 1990, this court granted the Secretary's motion for a restraining order prohibiting Blackwell from taking any actions in violation of the ALJ's order pending this court's final resolution of the Secretary's application for enforcement.

This court subsequently (a) granted the Coopers' motion to intervene. . . . [Ultimately, the Herrons decided not to purchase the house.]

ISSUE: The sole issue in this case is whether the ALJ's decision and order are supported by substantial evidence on the record taken as a whole.

DISCUSSION

A. The Fair Housing Act's Prohibitions

As amended by the FHAA of 1988, the FHA makes it unlawful, among other things:

(a) to refuse to sell . . . after the making of a bona fide offer, or to refuse to negotiate for the sale . . . of, or otherwise make unavailable or deny, a dwelling to any person because of race. . . .

(c) to make, print, or publish . . . any . . . statement . . . with respect to the sale . . . of a dwelling that indicates any preference, limitation, or discrimination based on race . . . or an intention to make any such preference, limitation, or discrimination.

(d) to represent to any person because of race . . . that any dwelling is not available for inspection [or] sale . . . when such dwelling is in fact so available.

42 U.S.C.A. §3604(a), (c) & (d). Further, the FHA makes it unlawful:

> to coerce, intimidate, threaten, or interfere with any person in the exercise or enjoyment of . . . any right guaranteed or protected by section 3603, 3604, 3605 or 3606 of this title.

41 U.S.C.A. §3617.

B. The FHAA's Administrative Enforcement Mechanism

Congress enacted the FHA to eliminate housing practices which discriminate on the basis of race, color, national origin, religion and sex. Inadequate enforcement provisions, however, frustrated achievement of the FHA's objectives.

Twenty years after the passage of the FHA, discrimination and segregation in housing continue to be pervasive. HUD estimates that 2 million instances of housing discrimination occur each year. In the most recent national study of housing discrimination, HUD concluded that a black person who visits 4 agents can expect to encounter at least one instance of discrimination 72 percent of the time for rentals and 48 percent of the time for sales.

Following is a brief overview of key provisions of the 1988 Act's administrative enforcement scheme. Under the 1988 Act, an "aggrieved person" may, not later than one year after an alleged discriminatory housing practice has occurred or terminated, file a complaint with the Secretary. 42 U.S.C.A. §3610(a)(1)(A)(i). An "aggrieved person" is defined as "any person who — (1) claims to have been injured by a discriminatory housing practice; or (2) believes that such person will be injured by a discriminatory housing practice that is about to occur." 42 U.S.C.A. §3602(i).

If the Secretary concludes, at any time following the filing of a complaint, that prompt judicial action is necessary to carry out the aims of the FHA, the Secretary may authorize the Attorney General to commence a civil action for appropriate temporary or preliminary relief pending final disposition of the complaint. 42 U.S.C.A. §3610(e).

If the Secretary determines that reasonable cause exists to believe that a discriminatory housing practice has occurred or is about to occur, the Secretary is required, with one exception, to immediately issue a charge on behalf of the "aggrieved person." 42 U.S.C.A. §3610(g)(2)(A).

Unless an election is made to have the claims decided in a civil action, the Secretary is required to provide an opportunity for a hearing before an administrative law judge.

After an administrative hearing, the ALJ is required to make findings of fact and conclusions of law. If the ALJ finds that a violation of the FHA has occurred or is about to occur, the ALJ is required to issue promptly an order for such relief as may be appropriate, including actual damages the aggrieved person suffered, as well as injunctive or other equitable relief. Further, in order to vindicate the public interest, the ALJ may assess a civil monetary penalty. . . .

E. The ALJ's Decision

[In this case, the Secretary establishes a prima facie case by proving: (1) that the Herrons are members of a racial minority; (2) that the Herrons applied for and were qualified to purchase Blackwell's house; (3) that Blackwell rejected the Herrons; and (4) that the house remained available thereafter.]

Applying this legal framework, the ALJ found that the Secretary established a prima facie case of racial discrimination. We hold that this determination is supported by substantial evidence on the record as a whole.[3] First, the Herrons are African-American persons. Second, the Herrons offered to buy the house and were qualified to buy the property. Specifically, the ALJ found (a) that the Herrons tendered their earnest money deposit, (b) that they made a timely application for a mortgage and (c) that they obtained a mortgage commitment. Third, Blackwell rejected the Herrons' offer when he repudiated the contract. Fourth, by posting "for sale" or "for rent" signs and attempting to rent the house to the Coopers, Blackwell made the property available to others after he had repudiated his contract with the Herrons. Having established a prima facie case, the Secretary created a rebuttable presumption that Blackwell unlawfully discriminated against the Herrons.

The burden then shifted to Blackwell to articulate a legitimate, nondiscriminatory reason for his actions. Blackwell argues that he refused to sell the house to the Herrons because he had not realized that the contract required him to pay closing costs and discount points. The ALJ correctly ruled that Blackwell "articulated a nondiscriminatory reason for rejecting the Herrons which, if taken in the light most favorable to him, would be legitimate."

Blackwell's articulation of a nondiscriminatory reason for his actions rebutted the presumption created by the prima facie case and shifted to the Secretary the burden of proving, by a preponderance of the evidence, that the reasons were merely a pretext for discrimination. The ALJ found that the Secretary demonstrated that Blackwell's proffered "reason for rejecting the Herrons was pretextual and that the motivation for his actions was discriminatory animus."

We conclude that the ALJ's finding is supported by substantial evidence. First, Blackwell is an experienced real estate broker who has studied commercial law at the college level. It is unlikely, therefore, that he signed a contract without realizing that it required him to pay closing costs and points. Second, numerous inconsistencies and contradictions in Blackwell's testimony

---

3. [EDS.—Under the Administrative Procedure Act (APA), when a court reviews an administrative agency's factual findings, it should uphold them if the court determines that they are supported by substantial evidence on the record as a whole. Universal Camera Corp. v. NLRB, 340 U.S. 474 (1951); Biestek v. Berryhill, 587 U.S. 97 (2019). This is a deferential standard that asks whether the evidence is adequate to support a conclusion.]

supported the ALJ's conclusion that Blackwell's proffered rationale for his actions was merely a pretext.

Third, the Secretary and the Herrons introduced evidence that race motivated Blackwell in this transaction. For example, Blackwell asked both real estate agents whether the Herrons were black persons. When questioned as to why he asked about the Herrons' race, Blackwell explained that "[i]t's just standard procedure, I like to know with whom I'm dealing . . . [j]ust as I asked of Ms. Judge Evans [the federal district judge who ruled on the government's prompt judicial action request], is she black or white." Further, in his deposition, Blackwell described his reaction when he learned the Herrons were black: "I'm not objectionable to them but I'm going to raise the price. I raised the price two thousand dollars. I figured that wouldn't be enough to run them off. I was glad to have them."

Fourth, other evidence demonstrated that Blackwell is obsessed with race. For example, he wrote a note to the last tenant who occupied the house at 4010 Indian Lake Circle, who was a white person, explaining that he would not evict him because "negros [sic] will be the next lessee [sic] . . . I do not want to see this area go black for the sake of the other residents of the area." In addition, after entering the lease with the Coopers, respondent Blackwell described them to Newbern as "really good white tenants" and to a newspaper reporter as "very fine white people." Further, in an interview with an investigator for the Georgia Real Estate Commission regarding charges filed against him because of his dealings with the Herrons, Blackwell stated that "he belonged to a club . . . he could take anybody to lunch that he wanted to as long as you weren't a n*****."

Finally, Blackwell's conduct following his inquiries about the Herrons' race supports the ALJ's determination that discriminatory animus motivated Blackwell's actions. For instance, despite his contract with the Herrons, Blackwell actively looked for other buyers, leaving up signs indicating the house was open for inspection. Further, Blackwell's treatment of the Coopers, who are white persons, supports the conclusion that he was eager to do business with white people.

On appeal, Blackwell contends that the ALJ erred for three reasons: (1) Newbern lied when she testified that she never received a "corrected contract" Blackwell claims he mailed her on June 11, showing that the Herrons would have to pay the closing costs; (2) Wainwright lied when he testified that he gave Blackwell a copy of the final contract and that Blackwell authorized him to initial the contract on his behalf; and (3) no contract existed between the Herrons and Blackwell and that, in any event, Blackwell "voided" the contract.

We are not persuaded by Blackwell's appellate contentions. As the Secretary correctly points out, this is not a contract law case; it is a race discrimination case. The FHA's prohibitions against, for instance, discriminatory refusals to sell or negotiate, apply regardless of whether a valid contract existed. Additionally, the ALJ found the testimony of the government's witnesses, including Newbern and Wainwright, to be credible. The ALJ's credibility determinations are entitled to special deference, and the record is replete with evidence supporting the ALJ's finding that Blackwell lacks credibility. Finally, substantial evidence supports the ALJ's conclusion that the Herrons and Blackwell entered into a valid contract and, further, that the contract was not legally voided by Blackwell's subsequent actions.

The evidence before the ALJ supports the finding that discriminatory animus motivated Blackwell in his dealings with the Herrons. Further, the ALJ's ultimate conclusions are supported by substantial evidence: (1) by refusing to sell the house to the Herrons, Blackwell violated 42 U.S.C.A. §3604(a); (2) by asking Wainwright and Newbern the race of the Herrons as potential buyers, Blackwell violated 42 U.S.C.A.§3604(c); (3) by Blackwell's statements that, among other things, he would not sell the house to the Herrons, by his actions attempting to lease or sell the house after contracting with the Herrons, and by his refusal to allow the Herrons' appraiser access to the house, Blackwell violated 42 U.S.C.A. §3604(d); and (4) by interfering with the Herrons' exercise and enjoyment of their rights under 42 U.S.C.A. §3604, Blackwell violated 42 U.S.C.A. §3617.

F. The ALJ's Remedies and Order

1. The Herrons

The ALJ awarded the Herrons $44,591.60, including damages for economic losses ($4,591.60) and embarrassment, humiliation and emotional distress ($40,000.00).

We find that the ALJ's award of damages to the Herrons is rational and fully supported by the record. Beyond the economic losses incurred by the Herrons including lost wages and profits, the ALJ found that the most significant damage suffered by the Herrons, as a result of Blackwell's actions, was "embarrassment, humiliation, and emotional distress." "[D]amages for emotional distress . . . 'may be inferred from the circumstances as well as proved by the testimony.'" Marable v. Walker, 704 F.2d 1219, 1220 (11th Cir. 1983).

In explaining the award of damages for "embarrassment, humiliation, and emotional distress," the ALJ relied upon the Herrons' testimony concerning their disappointment in being unable to move, and the humiliation caused by the knowledge that someone would deny them the right to buy a house because of their race. As Janella Herron testified, "I feel that everything that has been fought for over the last 30 years . . . was a waste of lives, a waste of time on the part of all those people who worked so hard for equal justice. . . . Our lives have been put on hold because we are not allowed to live where we can afford and choose to live." Further, the Herrons testified about the invasion of privacy caused by the publicity, and their physical symptoms which included loss of sleep and headaches.

2. The Coopers

The ALJ held that the Coopers are "aggrieved persons" under the FHA and awarded them $20,594.21 in damages. This award includes damages to compensate the Coopers for economic losses ($594.21) and embarrassment, humiliation and emotional distress ($20,000). We agree with the ALJ that the Coopers come within the definition of "aggrieved persons." The 1988 Act broadly defines an "aggrieved person" to include any person who has "been injured by a discriminatory housing practice." 42 U.S.C.A. §3602(i). The Coopers, like the Herrons, have been injured by Blackwell's discriminatory acts.

First, the Coopers suffered economic loss because they were forced to repack and relocate. Second, the Coopers endured embarrassment, humiliation and emotional distress as a direct consequence of Blackwell's actions. The Coopers testified that they felt "emotionally torn" and in "the middle of a tug-of-war." Although they were guilty of no wrongdoing, having unwittingly leased the house from Blackwell, they felt the need to defend themselves by hiring a lawyer. Because of the media attention the case received, the Coopers testified that they feared for the safety of their children and changed the locks on the house. Further, Audrey Cooper, who had recently started teaching at a racially mixed elementary school, testified that she felt she was "treated with suspicion." The forced move from the house not only placed a strain on "family unity," but it also deprived them of the home which they had hoped to purchase. We hold that the ALJ's award of damages to the Coopers is reasonable and supported by substantial evidence.

3. Civil Penalty

In addition to awarding compensatory damages to the Herrons and the Coopers, the ALJ imposed upon Blackwell the maximum civil penalty of $10,000. The 1988 Act provides that an ALJ may, "to vindicate the public interest, assess a civil penalty against the respondent — (A) in an amount not exceeding $10,000 if the respondent has not been adjudged to have committed any prior discriminatory housing practices." 42 U.S.C.A. §3612(g)(3).

The ALJ found the maximum civil penalty to be appropriate: (1) because of the egregious nature of Blackwell's actions; (2) because Blackwell "bears the full weight of responsibility for his actions and their effects on both the Herrons and the Coopers, since as a . . . licensed real estate broker with nearly 20 years experience, he knew or should have known that his actions were not only wrongful, but also, were unlawful"; (3) because Blackwell introduced no evidence concerning his financial circumstances that would militate against the maximum civil penalty; and (4) because the "goal of deterrence, as well as the interests of justice, will be served by the . . . maximum civil penalty." We hold that the ALJ's reasons for imposing the maximum civil penalty are rational, well supported by the record and consistent with the objectives of the FHA.

4. Injunctive Relief

The ALJ also enjoined Blackwell from discriminating against the Herrons, or anyone else, with respect to housing because of race, color, religion, sex, familial status, national origin, or handicap. "Injunctive relief should be structured to achieve the twin goals of insuring that the Act is not violated in the future and removing any lingering effects of past discrimination." *Marable*, 704 F.2d at 1221. Blackwell's past conduct amply supports the ALJ's conclusion that, without specific injunctions, Blackwell will continue his discriminatory conduct.

NOTES AND QUESTIONS

1. The Factual Record. Consider the numerous discriminatory hurdles that Blackwell placed in the path of the Herrons. The factual allegations present a damning portrait of an owner going to great lengths to deny housing on the basis of race. Cases like this illustrate the importance for plaintiffs of compiling as detailed a factual record as possible. Here, the plaintiffs encountered an exceptionally indiscreet defendant, whose attempts to deny them housing were quite blatant. What if the conduct had been more subtle? Consider that most people will have little way of knowing what steps an owner is taking, or what discussions are being had, to thwart a potential rental or sale. How should a plaintiff go about discovering this information?

2. Successful Purchase Not a Barrier to Claim. Recall Blackwell's (incriminating) statement about selling to the Herrons: "I'm not objectionable to them but I'm going to raise the price. I raised the price two thousand dollars. I figured that wouldn't be enough to run them off. I was glad to have them." What if, despite all the things Blackwell did to thwart the sale of the home, the Herrons had managed to purchase it anyway? Should a successful sale or lease negate a §3604(a) claim? See, for example, McDonald v. Verble, 622 F.2d 1227, 1233 (6th Cir. 1980), in which defendants attempted to thwart a Black couple's purchase of their house by repeatedly lying to them about its availability, rejecting their purchase offers, and instructing real estate brokers to discriminate against them. The sale took place only after the Black couple filed suit in court and obtained a temporary restraining order preventing the defendants from selling the house to anyone but them. Surprisingly, the district court denied the couple's §3604(a) claim, on the grounds that the sale had gone forward, albeit with the "reluctance" of the defendants. The court of appeals overturned this decision, noting: "The fact that subsequent to the filing of a lawsuit, the sale of the property was consummated with the McDonalds, does not alter the prior discriminatory conduct."

What about other obstructive conduct that falls short of an actual deprivation of housing? Even without the §3604(a) claims, how might the plaintiffs have prevailed? Claims based on §§3604(b) (discriminatory terms and conditions) and (d) (failure to provide truthful information about housing availability) are covered later in this chapter. Claims under §3604(c) (discriminatory statements) are discussed in Chapter 9.

At what point does discouraging conduct constitute a denial of housing? Consider the allegations of Smith v. Anchor Building Corp., 536 F.2d 231 (8th Cir. 1976), in which a Black woman applied for an apartment and subsequently contacted the complex 15 times over the course of three months to check on the status of her application. Each time the complex falsely told her there were no units available. (Note that discriminatory misrepresentations of availability also violate §3604(d)). She filed a complaint with a local civil rights organization and shortly afterward was offered a unit, which she declined. The Eighth Circuit reversed the district court's post-trial judgment in favor of the defendant as clearly erroneous. The court determined that even if the offer had not been made with knowledge of pending litigation (a fact that was in dispute), the plaintiff had "established an unrebutted case of racial discrimination in housing," although her refusal of the offer might affect the calculation of her damages.

Similarly, in Darby v. Heather Ridge, 806 F. Supp. 170, 175 (E.D. Mich. 1992), a Black couple alleged that rental agents made them wait for an hour and a half for assistance, treated them rudely, and told them that children were prohibited from using the complex pool (even as the couple saw a white child playing in the pool). The court denied the defendants' motion for summary judgment on the plaintiffs' §3604(a) claim, observing that:

> The subtle or discrete discrimination allegedly practiced by defendants' agents consisted of dilatory tactics, slight misrepresentations of fact, and subtle behavior intended to frustrate plaintiffs' attempts to secure housing at Heather Ridge. They cite in support of their argument the defendants' agents' requests that plaintiffs wait an hour, then an additional thirty minutes in their car before being assisted. Plaintiffs also cite the misstatement of defendants' agent regarding the use of the swimming pool by children. Finally, plaintiffs allege that there existed an overall unfriendly and unwelcoming attitude towards plaintiffs.
>
> Plaintiffs' assertions are sufficient to preclude a motion for summary judgment because the jury could reasonably draw different conclusions from these allegations. When subtle or discrete discrimination is alleged, a fine line separates discrimination from lawful behavior. For example, the jury might conclude that defendants' agents' request that plaintiffs wait in their car before being assisted was simply rude and not discriminatory. The jury could reasonably conclude that defendants' agents were merely preoccupied with work unrelated to customer assistance, or that such behavior constituted subtle attempts to steer plaintiffs away. Similarly, the unfriendly and unwelcoming atmosphere that plaintiffs claim existed might reasonably be construed as the product of plaintiffs' imagination or an accurate depiction of defendants' complex. Questions of interpretation are best resolved by the trier of fact when a fine line separates subtle discrimination from lawful behavior.

A home seeker who is so discouraged by off-putting conduct or remarks that she does not even apply for housing can almost certainly state a §3604(a) claim, as the discouragement has effectively made housing unavailable. *Cf.* Pinchback v. Armistead Homes Corp., 907 F.2d 1447 (4th Cir. 1990) (applying the "futile gesture" doctrine to Black plaintiff's §1982 claim, where she did not apply to residential co-op after being told by real estate agent that the co-op did not allow Black residents). What if the plaintiff is living in a unit owned by the defendant and alleges discriminatory denial of the opportunity to transfer to a more desirable unit? *See* Webb v. United States Veterans Initiative, 993 F.3d 970, 973 (D.C. Cir. 2021):

> U.S. Vets argues that even if Webb's factual allegations were adequate, his discrimination claim fails as a matter of law because he was never "deprived of a place to live." . . . Section 3604, however, contains no textual limitation making an otherwise discriminatory housing practice lawful simply because the aggrieved person is not yet homeless. Rather, alleging that someone made "*a* dwelling"—whether or not the plaintiff's current dwelling—unavailable based on a protected characteristic is sufficient. . . . Put differently, nothing in the statute required Webb to be kicked out of his multiple-occupancy unit to sue U.S. Vets for refusing to offer him a one-bedroom unit on the basis of his sex.

3. The Bona Fide Offer Requirement. The initial text of §3604(a) limits the prohibition on discriminatory refusals to sell or rent to situations where there has been a "bona fide offer." Thus, a plaintiff with no intention to purchase a property would not be able to state a claim under that portion of §3604(a). Note, however, that the bona fide offer requirement applies only to refusals to sell or rent, and not to the other conduct described by the provision, including refusals to negotiate and conduct that otherwise makes housing unavailable. *See* Grant v. Smith, 574 F.2d 252, 255 (5th Cir. 1978) ("Both negotiation and inspection involve aspects of real estate dealing which often precede the formation of any intent to buy or rent on the part of a prospective customer. To require a bona fide offer in such circumstances could render these protective provisions of §3604 meaningless."). Why would the statute contain the bona fide offer requirement at all? Why would the requirement be limited to refusals to sell or rent and not apply to other conduct prohibited by §3604(a)?

Fair housing testers by definition are *not* bona fide home seekers. They pose as home seekers to assist in determining whether discrimination is occurring. Significantly, they can bring claims under §3604(d), which prohibits false information about the availability of housing. Section 3604(d) and testers are discussed later in this chapter.

4. HUD and Appellate Review. Note the procedural posture of this case. As discussed in Chapter 3, there are multiple ways that housing discrimination claims can be brought. One path is for an aggrieved party to file a complaint with HUD. As *Blackwell* describes, if HUD investigates and determines that there is reasonable cause to believe a violation has occurred, under most circumstances HUD must issue a charge of discrimination and provide an opportunity for a hearing before an ALJ. The parties to the proceeding are HUD, acting on behalf of the aggrieved persons, and the respondent, as well as any intervenors. In *Blackwell*, the Coopers intervened because their interests had also been harmed by Blackwell's conduct. The Herrons, as aggrieved persons, also could have intervened. A complainant, other aggrieved persons, or respondent may elect to have the matter litigated in a federal district court rather than before an ALJ; in this event, the Department of Justice would file suit on behalf of the aggrieved persons.

The ALJ's findings of fact and conclusions of law are considered the "initial decision." This initial decision is then reviewed by the HUD Secretary (or designee), who may either affirm it as a "final order" or send it back to the ALJ on remand. If the Secretary takes no action, after 30 days the ALJ's decision becomes final. Any party to the administrative proceeding can seek judicial review of a HUD final order, with review taking place in the federal judicial circuit where the violation occurred. The HUD Secretary can also petition the court of appeals for enforcement of the ALJ's order. The *Blackwell* case is an example of the latter situation. *DiCenso v. HUD*, featured in Chapter 15, is an example of the former.

5. Relief Available in an FHA Case: Monetary Damages. The FHA provides for a range of monetary and nonmonetary relief, including compensatory and punitive damages, declaratory and injunctive relief, attorneys' fees, and other affirmative relief designed to prevent the violations from recurring. (In ALJ cases, civil penalties payable to the U.S. Treasury are available rather than punitive damages.) Compensatory damages are designed to reimburse plaintiffs for their injuries; that is, to make them "whole." Punitive damages are designed to "punish" for past conduct and deter future violations.

As to compensatory damages, there are two types: economic (or special) damages and general damages for mental anguish or emotional harm. Economic damages refer to the financial value of expenditures incurred as a result of the discrimination. These "out of pocket" damages are the easiest type to calculate because there are either receipts or other quantifiable ways of measuring the loss. In *Blackwell*, the Herrons sought "lost wages and profits," and the Coopers sought reimbursement for being "forced to pack and relocate." Other examples could include additional mileage traveled because a substitute apartment was farther from a plaintiff's job; higher sales amounts, rents, deposits, or fees for substitute housing of lower quality; or forfeited real estate commissions. This usually will be a smaller number than the other type of damages compensating plaintiffs for emotional harm. Regarding this latter category, the Herrons obtained a five-figure award for "embarrassment, humiliation and emotional distress." They were the targets of Blackwell's discrimination, were denied the right to buy a home because of their race, and suffered physical symptoms from the ordeal including loss of sleep and headaches. The Coopers also obtained a (smaller) five-figure emotional damages award based on media attention they received, fear for the safety of their children, and other stress and strain.

How do plaintiffs prove emotional damages given that these are less susceptible to measurement? The *Blackwell* court's focus on appeal was to ensure that there was sufficient evidence in the record to support the damages awarded by the ALJ, holding that the plaintiffs' testimony was sufficient on the facts to sustain the amounts. However, some courts require corroborative evidence on damages, particularly as the size of the award increases. This may come in the form of testimony of friends, family members, and coworkers who can describe the effect of the discrimination on the plaintiffs and any change in behavior following the alleged incidents. Plaintiffs also may offer testimony from medical or mental health providers on any symptoms reported, treatment provided, or expected severity or duration of conditions that are alleged to have resulted from or been exacerbated by the discrimination. Where damages are concerned, the more evidence the better, but advocates will want to consult with their clients about the ramifications of disclosing medical or mental health information in discovery and seek a protective order governing such information. Obtaining a sizable jury award on damages is of little benefit if an appellate court decides there is insufficient evidence to support it. Similarly, convincing a jury that defendants are liable under the law but failing to persuade them that the plaintiffs have suffered any harm (e.g., the $1 verdict) could be devastating for a plaintiff. Furthermore, the size of the compensatory award will be relevant to sustaining a large punitive damages award. For practitioners, a thorough interview of the client on the economic and emotional impacts of discrimination, at the earliest time, is essential.

With respect to punitive damages, the FHA provides no cap on the amount that is recoverable (unlike in Title VII cases), but the Supreme Court as a matter of due process requires the punitive damages figure not to be wildly out of proportion to the compensatory award, which it has suggested would be no more than a single-digit multiplier of the award.[4] For example, if a plaintiff recovers $10,000 in compensatory damages, a court will be unlikely to sustain a punitive damages award that is $1,000,000. A defendant's net worth also is relevant to punitive damages. An amount sufficient to deter a mom-and-pop landlord from discriminating in the rental of apartments will be much lower than an amount sufficient to deter a multinational mortgage lender. Also, punitive damages will not be recoverable for merely negligent conduct; a plaintiff seeking punitive damages must plead and prove that the defendant's conduct was intentional, often alleged as willful, malicious, or undertaken with reckless disregard for the plaintiff's rights and "in the face of a perceived risk that its actions will violate federal law."[5]

---

4. State Farm Mut. Auto Ins. Co. v. Campbell, 538 U.S. 408, 410 (2003) (citing BMW v. Gore, 517 U.S. 559, 581 (1996)).
5. Kolstad v. American Dental Ass'n, 527 U.S. 526, 536 (1999).

The FHA, like most other civil rights statutes, makes attorneys' fees available to prevailing plaintiffs. There is a substantial body of law relating to fee litigation that is beyond the scope of this text, but it is important for both litigants and law students to know that enforcement of the civil rights laws is not designed to depend primarily on government agencies and the good will and pro bono commitments of the private bar. Because of statutory attorneys' fees, lawyers can make a respectable living and a career assisting clients to obtain fair and equitable outcomes in the housing market. A number of cases in this text were brought by firms that specialize in litigation to enforce fair housing rights.

6. History. The setting of this case carries deep significance. Stone Mountain, Georgia, is the site of the world's largest monument to the Confederacy.[6] Stone Mountain is a large granite outcropping on which the likenesses of Jefferson Davis, Robert E. Lee, and Thomas Jonathan "Stonewall" Jackson are carved. The monument was begun during the ascendance of the "Lost Cause" movement in the early 1910s and completed in 1972. It long has served as a symbol of the Confederacy and racial oppression. In 1915, the Ku Klux Klan burned a cross at the base of the mountain to announce its refounding, and it continued holding rituals there over the decades. Segregationist gubernatorial candidate (later Governor) Marvin Griffin held a campaign rally there in 1954, just after *Brown v. Board of Education*, vowing to preserve segregation. Privately owned at first, it was made into a state park under Governor Griffin and its preservation was enshrined in state law, as it remains today. In 1963, Rev. Martin Luther King, Jr. referred to it in his "I Have a Dream" speech: "Let freedom ring from Stone Mountain of Georgia!"

The judge who wrote the opinion in this case was noteworthy as well. The Hon. Joseph Woodrow Hatchett was the first Black judge on the Florida Supreme Court and the first Black judge to serve on a federal court of appeals in the Deep South.[7] He graduated from Howard Law School, served in the Marine Corps Reserve, and was affiliated with the NAACP Legal Defense Fund before becoming an Assistant U.S. Attorney in 1966. In 1979 he was nominated by President Jimmy Carter to the 5th Circuit Court of Appeals (and later reassigned to the 11th Circuit). The United States Courthouse in Tallahassee, Florida, was named after him in 2022, after some political opposition.

---

6. Details about Stone Mountain are taken from Claire Haley, *Stone Mountain: Carving Fact from Fiction*, Atlanta History Center (Nov. 18, 2022), https://www.atlantahistorycenter.com/blog/stone-mountain-a-brief-history/.

7. Details about Judge Hatchett are taken from Jack Bass, *Black Judge Marks New Era*, Wash. Post (Aug. 5, 1979), https://www.washingtonpost.com/archive/politics/1979/08/05/black-judge-marks-new-era/08f2d18f-64c1-4017-93dd-9c9154698792/. The article quotes a leader in the business community as saying of Hatchett's nomination, "I'm sorry to see that damn n***** appointed." *See also Florida Courthouse Named for Judge Who Broke Racial Barriers*, https://www.gsa.gov/blog/2023/06/27/florida-courthouse-named-for-judge-who-broke-racial-barriers.

2. Steering

Most homebuyers rely on real estate brokers and agents to inform them about and show them homes that are for sale. If the buyer is relocating to a new city, the broker or agent might also be a primary source of information about the area and particular neighborhoods. Prospective tenants often rely on apartment brokers, landlords, or property managers for information about available units in a building, complex, or neighborhood. These housing professionals can wield significant influence over a person's housing choices just by controlling the amount and type of information they provide. When housing professionals guide a home seeker toward or away from a particular area, neighborhood, or complex because of the racial or ethnic composition of the area relative to the home seeker, they are engaging in steering. In Havens Realty Corp. v. Coleman, 455 U.S. 363, 366 n.1 (1982) (Chapter 4), the Supreme Court defined "steering" as:

> [A] practice by which real estate brokers and agents preserve and encourage patterns of racial segregation in available housing by steering members of racial and ethnic groups to buildings occupied primarily by members of such racial and ethnic groups and away from buildings and neighborhoods inhabited primarily by members of other races or groups.

In another case, the Court described steering as "directing prospective home buyers interested in equivalent properties to different areas according to their race." Gladstone Realtors v. Village of Bellwood, 441 U.S. 91, 94 (1979) (Chapter 4). And in Village of Bellwood v. Dwivedi, 895 F.2d 1521, 1529 (7th Cir. 1990), the Seventh Circuit set forth examples of different sorts of steering and the sections of the FHA that they would violate:

> Suppose a real estate broker falsely states to a black customer that no homes are for sale in Village X, which is primarily white, and he does so because the customer is black, so that the statement is a deliberate, racially motivated falsity. By doing this he denies a dwelling to a person because of the person's race (§3604(a)), discriminates on racial grounds against the person in the provision of real estate services (§3604(b)), and misrepresents to the person on racial grounds that a dwelling is not for sale (§3604(d)). He is acting intentionally to prevent a black from buying a house in a white neighborhood. He is treating a black customer differently from a white one because the customer is black. He knows they are of different races and treats them differently because of that knowledge. This is deliberate conduct, and unquestionably it is racial steering.
>
> Misrepresentation is not the only species of racial steering. If a broker simply refuses a customer's point-blank request to show him a house in a neighborhood that the broker wants to reserve for persons of a different race, this is steering even though there is no misrepresentation. The broker would be violating §§3604(a) and (b), but not (d)—that is all. A point-blank refusal is not necessary; any effort to discourage will do.

Havens Realty, Gladstone Realtors, and Dwivedi dealt with racial steering, but steering can be done based on any protected characteristic (e.g., families with children being steered away from particular buildings in an apartment complex).

A HUD regulation lists specific examples of conduct that constitutes steering:

24 C.F.R. §100.70(C)

(1) Discouraging any person from inspecting, purchasing or renting a dwelling because of [a protected characteristic of the person or the person's associates] or because of the [protected characteristics] of persons in a community, neighborhood or development.

(2) Discouraging the purchase or rental of a dwelling because of [protected characteristics], by exaggerating drawbacks or failing to inform any person of desirable features of a dwelling or of a community, neighborhood or development.

(3) Communicating to any prospective purchaser that he or she would not be comfortable or compatible with existing residents of a community, neighborhood or development because of [protected characteristics].

(4) Assigning any person to a particular section of a community, neighborhood or development, or to a particular floor of a building, because of [protected characteristics].

See also 24 C.F.R. §100.70(a) (stating that it is a violation of the Fair Housing Act "to restrict or attempt to restrict the choices of a person by word or conduct in connection with seeking, negotiating for, buying or renting a dwelling so as to perpetuate, or tend to perpetuate, segregated housing patterns, or to discourage or obstruct choices in a community, neighborhood or development.").

NOTES AND QUESTIONS

1. Steering Claims as Cognizable Under §3604(a). Note that steering does not entirely deprive a home seeker of access to housing; rather, it limits their choices, depriving them of access to *particular* homes or units and channeling them toward others.

Havens Realty and *Gladstone Realtors* involved steering allegations, but both cases turned on issues of standing. Neither case directly addressed the issue of whether steering claims are cognizable under §3604(a), but in both cases the Court appeared to assume that they are. Several lower courts have considered the issue and held that steering violates §3604(a).[8] To the extent that steering claims involve an agent misrepresenting available housing to inquiring home seekers, they are also likely to violate §3604(d), which prohibits the making of false statements regarding housing availability.

---

8. *See, e.g.*, Cabrera v. Jakabovitz, 24 F.3d 372, 390 (2d Cir. 1994); City of Chicago v. Matchmaker Real Estate Sales Ctr., Inc., 982 F.2d 1086, 1096 (7th Cir. 1992); Sanders v. Dorris, 873 F.2d 938, 943-44 (6th Cir. 1989); United States v. Mitchell, 580 F.2d 789, 791-92 (5th Cir. 1978).

2. Customer Preference. Many steering cases involve real estate agents or landlords who take it upon themselves to limit home seekers' choices, either by showing them housing only in particular areas or seeking to dissuade them from looking in particular areas. But what if the home seeker is the one to request the limitation? Put another way, what if a white home seeker asks a real estate agent to show him houses only in predominantly white neighborhoods? What if a Black home seeker asks for listings only in Black neighborhoods? To what extent can a housing professional cater to the preferences of their customers, even if those preferences are based on protected characteristics?

An influential early steering case suggested that an agent's steering would violate §3604(a) regardless of whether it was undertaken "on his own initiative or in response to the buyer's initiative." Zuch v. Hussey, 394 F. Supp. 1028, 1048 (E.D. Mich. 1975), *aff'd without opinion*, 547 F.2d 1168 (6th Cir. 1977). This was dicta, however, because in that case the evidence was clear that the agents were acting on their own initiative. A later case, Village of Bellwood v. Dwivedi, 895 F.2d 1521, 1530-31 (7th Cir. 1990), offered a differing view, also dicta, in an opinion by Judge Posner:

> The statute prohibits real estate agents from refusing to show properties because of the race of the customer, or misleading the customer about the availability of properties because of his race, or cajoling or coercing the customer because of his race to buy this property or that or look in this community rather than that. It does not place on individual brokers the duty to solve the collective-action problem that results when brokers serving (but not encouraging) the preferences of individual customers cumulatively affect the overall racial pattern in housing. . . .
>
> [T]he broker who responds to the customer's desires [] is not discriminating against the *customer*, or denying the *customer* a dwelling, or misrepresenting to the *customer* the unavailability of a dwelling. The statute does not require a broker to endeavor to make his customers better people by withholding information that they request about the racial composition of the communities in which the broker sells houses. It does not impose liability for failing to promote integration, or for failing to coordinate individual integrative acts that have an aggregate [d]esegregative effect. If the broker treats all his customers the same, regardless of race, he is not liable.

Judge Posner posited that when a real estate agent caters to a client's race-based preferences, the agent is acting not "because of race" but rather in response to the customer's request. Thus, he concluded, the agent is not discriminating. Is "client preference" a neutral factor, even when the preference itself is based on prohibited characteristics? Must a real estate agent force clients to consider homes in neighborhoods in which they do not think they want to live? The issue remains a legal "gray area." *See* Brian Patrick Larkin, *The Forty-Year "First Step": The Fair Housing Act as an Incomplete Tool for Suburban Integration*, 107 COLUMBIA L. REV. 1617, 1646 (2007) ("[B]oth HUD and the courts are in agreement that real estate agents may not limit consumer choice in the homebuying process. There is also agreement that consumer preferences to live in certain communities based on race are acceptable under the Fair Housing Act. Yet in between these two legal poles lies an ambiguous zone where geographic steering and consumer choice can be somewhat indistinguishable."). What if a client asks only to see homes in racially integrated neighborhoods?

3. Type of Statements. What *type* of statements can constitute impermissible steering? Blatantly discriminatory statements such as "You don't want to look in that neighborhood because it is the Hispanic part of town," obviously would qualify. (Such a remark probably also would violate §3604(c)'s prohibition against discriminatory housing statements; see Chapter 9.) For example, in Central Alabama Fair Housing Center v. Lowder Realty Co., 236 F.3d 629, 633 (11th Cir. 2000), plaintiffs' evidence included testimony that a real estate agent told a white tester couple who had asked to see homes in a predominantly Black area that it was "not a good idea," and that the testers would not want to live there because there were "too many of the other kind." Testers recounted that the agent did show the testers a home in the neighborhood, but stated, "I would hate to see you buy here, I'll be honest with you. It's just not a good idea. This used to be the nicest area 40 years ago. That's nothing but blacks over there in all those apartments."

But what about truthful information about neighborhood characteristics, such as school quality, crime rates, or trends in home values? Such information is obviously of interest to buyers and technically is neutral. On the other hand, these factors are heavily influenced by inequalities of race and class (and are themselves a product of segregated residential patterns). As such, they may serve as a proxy or "code" for race or other protected characteristics. A 2006 report on a series of tests by the National Fair Housing Alliance noted a "striking pattern":

> Instead of making blatant comments about the racial composition of neighborhoods, many real estate agents told whites to avoid certain areas because of the schools. It is evident from the investigation that schools have become a proxy for the racial or ethnic composition of neighborhoods.[9]

For example, white testers reported that agents told them to avoid the Tarrytown, New York, schools, which are predominately Hispanic. In several cases, the report says, agents there told whites that the schools were "bad," but agents told Latinos that the same schools were "good." *See also* Larkin, 107 Columbia L. Rev. at 1646 ("[A] consumer's preference for areas with good schools, low crime, or even diversity can open up opportunities for an agent to guide that buyer to neighborhoods that would perpetuate segregated living patterns."). Courts generally have taken the position that truthful

---

9. National Fair Housing Alliance, *Unequal Opportunity–Perpetuating Housing Segregation in America, 2006 Fair Housing Trends Report* at 11-12, https://nationalfairhousing.org/wp-content/uploads/2021/12/trends2006.pdf.

information, expressed in a nondiscriminatory manner, does not constitute unlawful steering.

The National Association of Realtors recognizes the dilemma that agents may be placed in by clients who want information about schools, particularly where there is a correlation between school quality and neighborhood racial composition.[10] It has developed an Equal Professional Service Model "to help real estate agents adopt practices that enable them to anticipate and to address housing search issues fairly and equitably." This model emphasizes consistency and systematic procedures to ensure equality of treatment. If clients have questions about schools, agents are instructed to provide objective, third-party sources of information, such as community-based websites that compare schools, rather than offering their own opinions.

4. Steering and Standing. Steering cases often present complex issues of standing. Clearly a home seeker who is steered is a proper plaintiff, and testers who are steered may have a claim under §3604(d). But some high-profile steering cases have included plaintiffs who were not home seekers or testers, including residents of neighborhoods that people were steered into or away from, and even municipalities in which steering has occurred. Why might such people and entities claim to have been injured by widespread steering practices? Standing for steering and other types of claims is addressed in Chapter 4.

5. The Continued Prevalence of Steering. Steering has continued to be pervasive in the housing market. The National Fair Housing Alliance's 2006 report, referenced above in note 3, described its multiyear, 12-city testing study. The findings were stark:

> The tests revealed a rate of steering of 87 percent, when testers were given an opportunity to see homes. [Eds. — In 51 cases the Black or Latino tester was offered very limited service or shown no homes at all. While this indicates discrimination, it also interfered with the paired test analysis, so those instances were removed from the total.] In 209 instances, testers were steered to neighborhoods on the basis of race and/or national origin. [T]esters were also steered based on religion and family status. . . .
>
> Patterns of steering were consistent. In most cases, Whites were shown homes in primarily White neighborhoods, African-Americans were shown homes in primarily African-American neighborhoods and Latinos were shown homes in primarily Latino neighborhoods. In many cases, an analysis of census data shows the dramatic difference in the racial and ethnic composition of neighborhoods shown to Whites as opposed to the composition of neighborhoods shown to African-Americans and Latinos.[11]

---

10. The information in this paragraph is derived from National Association of Realtors, *Steering, Schools, and Equal Professional Service* (June 9, 2014), https://www.nar.realtor/articles/steering-schools-and-equal-professional-service.

11. National Fair Housing Alliance, *Unequal Opportunity–Perpetuating Housing Segregation in America, 2006 Fair Housing Trends Report,* at 9, https://nationalfairhousing.org/wp-content/uploads/2017/04/trends2006.pdf.

A smaller but more recent testing study conducted in 2019 by *Newsday* on Long Island, New York, found steering by real estate agents in 24 percent of tests (with Black testers experiencing some kind of disparate treatment 49 percent of the time).[12] This report is particularly compelling because it features footage and quotations from the testers' encounters with the agents. Note that steering that is unaccompanied by discriminatory statements might be difficult to detect; therefore, this is an area in which testing is a particularly useful tool. A discussion of testing appears later in this chapter.

3. Zoning and Other Land-Use Controls

Zoning and other land-use controls involve the development of real estate and purposes to which it may be put. As discussed in Chapter 1, *Buchanan v. Warley* (1917) declared overtly discriminatory zoning ordinances unconstitutional more than a century ago. Today (most) zoning and land-use laws are facially neutral, which is to say that they do not explicitly reference protected characteristics. However, they still can make housing unavailable in a manner that continues the exclusion of persons with protected characteristics from a community, thus perpetuating segregated housing patterns. For example, zoning laws may prevent the development of affordable housing that likely would be occupied disproportionately by members of a particular racial or ethnic group, or other protected classes, or may limit the siting of such housing to areas that already have large numbers of lower income residents of color.

Zoning ordinances typically divide a municipality into residential, commercial, and industrial districts. These districts usually are kept separate from one another, with the use of property within each district being mostly uniform. Within these three main types of districts there can be other restrictions, such as those relating to number of dwelling units, minimum lot area, frontage of lots, building setbacks from the streets, size and height of buildings, and construction materials. Regulations of residences may restrict areas to detached, single-family homes, townhouses, or multifamily dwellings (apartment buildings or condominiums). Statutes, ordinances, or regulations also might limit the number of unrelated people who can live together in a single dwelling unit, in an effort to maintain the "single-family" nature of a neighborhood. Land-use regulation is designed to guide future development. Municipalities commonly follow a planning process that ultimately results in a comprehensive plan, addressing residential, commercial, and industrial development, roadways, and public amenities.

---

12. Ann Choi, Keith Herbert & Olivia Winslow, *Long Island Divided*, NEWSDAY (Nov. 7, 2019), https://projects.newsday.com/long-island/real-estate-agents-investigation/#nd-promo.

WHAT IS SINGLE-FAMILY ZONING?

Note that "single-family" can refer both to the kind of structure and to the relationships among the residents of the structure. Single-family zoning operates to restrict development to detached homes (often on a large lot), as opposed to townhomes, duplexes, and multifamily housing (apartments). Such zoning both increases the cost of housing units and decreases the supply. As a result, single-family zoning requirements are a way to keep property values high and to keep density low. They are also understood to be exclusionary in many cases because they prevent lower income people (disproportionately Black people and other people of color) from moving into neighborhoods by eliminating lower cost alternatives for housing.

In the wake of *Euclid*, virtually every municipality in the country developed zoning ordinances and implemented some form of land-use planning that designated residential areas for single families and defined "family" in terms of a "single, nonprofit housekeeping unit." Toward the middle of the twentieth century, as the baby boom went into full swing and the notion of the nuclear family was glorified in the popular imagination, the suburbs were developed as the ideal place for young (white) families to live. Zoning authorities moved away from the more neutral term "single housekeeping unit" and started defining "family" in terms of the relationships among the household members, requiring that they be related by "blood, marriage, or adoption." Most ordinances permitted families to include one or two unrelated individuals or allowed a small number of unrelated people to live together as a family.

Zoning laws have existed since the early 20th century in the United States. As discussed in Chapter 1, in *Village of Euclid v. Ambler Realty Co.*, 272 U.S. 365 (1926), the Supreme Court established that zoning was within the police power of the states to regulate in the interests of public health, safety, morals, and general welfare. In particular, the Court endorsed the view that individual municipalities were in the best position to address the needs of their residents, and that they must be given leeway to make site-specific and flexible determinations (i.e., that a "one-size fits all" approach is inappropriate). The court singled out and endorsed restrictions on apartment buildings, noting that:

> With particular reference to apartment houses, it is pointed out that the development of detached house sections is greatly retarded by the coming of apartment houses, which has sometimes resulted in destroying the entire section for private house purposes; that, in such sections, very often the apartment house is a mere parasite, constructed in order to take advantage of the open spaces and attractive surroundings created by the residential character of the district. Moreover, the coming of one apartment house is followed by others, interfering by their height and bulk with the free circulation of air and monopolizing the rays of the sun which otherwise would fall upon the smaller homes, and bringing, as their necessary accompaniments, the disturbing noises incident to increased traffic and business, and the occupation, by means of moving and parked automobiles, of larger portions of the streets, thus detracting from their safety and depriving children of the privilege of quiet and open spaces for play, enjoyed by those in more favored localities—until, finally, the residential character of the neighborhood and its desirability as a place of detached residences

are utterly destroyed. Under these circumstances, apartment houses, which in a different environment would be not only entirely unobjectionable but highly desirable, come very near to being nuisances.

Id. at 394. The Court's language describing certain land uses as nuisances is striking and oft-cited: "A nuisance may be merely a right thing in the wrong place, like a pig in the parlor instead of the barnyard." *Id.* at 388. Thus, from the earliest days of zoning, the Court expressed a concern that apartment buildings might create challenges for residential development, including traffic, parking, noise, blockage of sunlight, loss of open space, and loss of "neighborhood character." These same concerns surface in nearly every exclusionary zoning case, although whether they are rooted in reality or are pretextual remains for the court to determine. Apartment buildings and other higher-density housing often are assumed in the United States to be inhabited generally by people with lower incomes, and this group dispro-portionately will include racial and ethnic minority group members and people with disabilities. *See* Jade A. Craig, *"Pigs in the Parlor": The Legacy of Racial Zoning and the Challenge of Affirmatively Furthering Fair Housing in the South,* 40 Miss. C. L. Rev. 5, 8 (2022). Thus, attempts to block multifam-ily housing can easily serve as a smokescreen for discrimination against the potential occupants.

Determining whether there is discriminatory intent behind any particular zoning law or decision may be challenging, because these are actions taken by government bodies (such as legislatures and zoning commissions) with mul-tiple decisionmakers who may be motivated by a number of different con-cerns. The Supreme Court has set forth a framework for analyzing situations like this in *Village of Arlington Heights v. Metropolitan Housing Development Corporation* (1977) (Chapter 6). The opinion instructs courts to weigh factors such as the historical background of the action, legislative or administrative history (particularly where there are departures from regular procedure), and the impact of the action on groups with protected characteristics (especially where the pattern is stark).

Even if there is little evidence of discriminatory intent, the fact that zoning invariably has disproportionate effects means that many zoning decisions can be challenged under the FHA using disparate impact theory. The use of dispa-rate impact theory in zoning and land use cases is discussed in Chapter 7. In those cases, if the plaintiff is able to plead a practice that causes a dispropor-tionate adverse impact or perpetuates segregation, the municipality will have the opportunity to prove that its policies and practices are justified. There are many legitimate and nondiscriminatory government interests that could drive zoning actions, including environmental concerns, parking and traffic control, overcrowding, watershed protection, and resource management. If the defen-dant can justify its zoning practices with concrete evidence, the plaintiff still might be able to prevail by demonstrating that defendants' interests may be satisfied by a policy with less discriminatory effect.

Consider, for example, United States v. Black Jack, Missouri, 508 F.2d 1179, 1186-88 (8th Cir. 1974), an early case in which the all-white area of Black Jack incorporated so that it could adopt a land-use and zoning plan. The plan would prevent the proposed construction of a multifamily housing complex that was likely to attract Black residents from nearby St. Louis. The city asserted primarily three reasons to justify the ban on further apartments: (1) road and traffic control, (2) prevention of overcrowding of schools, and (3) prevention of devaluation of adjacent single-family homes. The court found that none of these reasons stood up to scrutiny. The evidence showed that multifamily construction would lead to *fewer* traffic hazards compared with single-family construction; that "apartments produced approximately one schoolchild for every five families, while single-family houses produced almost three schoolchildren, or fifteen times as many," that there was a "strong demand" for apartments in St. Louis County, and that "apartment complexes in the St. Louis metropolitan area had not had such an effect on property value."

NOTES AND QUESTIONS

1. Expulsive Zoning. There are other ways in which zoning and land-use planning might implicate the FHA. In particular, industrial or other harmful uses like hazardous waste sites (commonly referred to as LULUs for locally undesirable land uses) are located disproportionately in or near low-income neighborhoods of color.[13] Similarly, as discussed in Chapter 1, there is a history of highways being sited through predominantly Black and ethnic minority neighborhoods. One scholar coined the term "expulsive zoning" for these practices, arguing that the resulting increase in air, water, and ground pollution diminishes the quality of life and health for residents, ultimately destroying and depopulating neighborhoods over time.[14]

As discussed elsewhere in this chapter, the extent to which expulsive zoning practices are covered by the FHA typically hinges on two questions: (1) whether they actually drive residents out or prevent people from living in a particular area such that they "make housing unavailable" under §3604(a), or (2) whether they are considered sufficiently housing related to constitute a term or condition of housing under §3604(b).

---

13. *See, e.g.,* Vicki Been, *Locally Undesirable Land Uses in Minority Neighborhoods: Disproportionate Siting or Market Dynamics?*, 103 YALE L. J. 1383, 1406 (1994); *see also* Shriver Center on Poverty Law & Earthjustice, *Poisonous Homes: The Fight for Environmental Justice in Federally Assisted Housing* (June 2020), https://www.povertylaw.org/report/poisonoushomes (noting that 70 percent of the most hazardous, polluted sites in the United States are located within one mile of federally assisted housing).

14. *See* Yale Rabin, *Expulsive Zoning: The Inequitable Legacy of* Euclid, *in* ZONING AND THE AMERICAN DREAM: PROMISES STILL TO KEEP (Charles M. Haar and Jerold S. Kayden eds., Routledge 1990).

2. Ending Single-Family Zoning? At the time of this writing, the United States is experiencing a crisis in housing affordability. Both the cost of rent and home purchase prices are now more than many households can reasonably afford, and experts estimate that the U.S. housing market is short many millions of homes. Some of this undersupply is due to the decline in new home construction after the housing market crash of 2008. However, much of the problem also is caused by single-family zoning laws, which mandate only detached, single-family homes, often with large lot sizes and height restrictions.[15] A 2019 study found that nearly 75 percent of land zoned for housing in cities in the United States is reserved for single-family homes.[16] In many suburbs and growing Sun Belt cities this number is even higher. This makes it challenging for the market to meet the need for lower cost housing through higher density options (such as apartment buildings or townhouses) or low-density options (such as allowing Accessory Dwelling Units).

As governments respond to the crisis in housing affordability, some are reconsidering single-family zoning. A number of states and municipalities have passed or are considering legislation that would end or limit single-family zoning, such as through low-density alternatives like accessory units. In 2019 Minneapolis became the first large municipality to abolish single-family zoning. California passed such a law in 2021, SB 9, which a state court judge later enjoined. It remains to be seen whether other locations will follow suit and how successful they will be. For an up-to-date web resource on single-family zoning reforms across the country, see Joshua Cantong, Stephen Menendian & Samir Gambhir, Zoning Reform Tracker, https://belonging.berkeley.edu/zoning-reform-tracker (updated November 13, 2023).

3. Inclusionary Zoning. Many municipalities and some states across the country have sought to counteract the damage done by exclusionary zoning through "inclusionary zoning" policies. This usually involves providing incentives to for-profit developers to ensure that they offer a certain number or percentage of units in any new development at prices that are affordable for people with low to moderate incomes. In practice, this often involves placing deed restrictions on some amount of the housing to make it affordable to lower income households and to create a mix of "affordable housing" and "market-rate" housing.

---

15. *See* Richard D. Kahlenberg, EXCLUDED: HOW SNOB ZONING, NIMBYISM, AND CLASS BIAS BUILD THE WALLS WE DON'T SEE (Hachette 2023).

16. This study used interactive mapping tools to generate detailed portraits of many municipalities across the country. Emily Badger & Quoctrung Bui, *Cities Start to Question an American Ideal: A House with a Yard on Every Lot*, N.Y. TIMES (June 18, 2019), https://www.nytimes.com/interactive/2019/06/18/upshot/cities-across-america-question-single-family-zoning.html.

4. Other Conduct

As noted above, there are many ways in which housing can be made unavailable. A few of the more common of these "miscellaneous practices" are discussed below.

a. Discrimination in Mortgage Financing and Related Transactions

Discrimination in financial transactions such as mortgage lending, property insurance, and appraisals can make housing unavailable and thus may fall under §3604(a)'s coverage. With the exception of property insurance, these are also explicitly covered by §3605, which prohibits discrimination in "residential real estate-related transactions." Chapter 11 discusses discrimination in financing and related transactions under §3605 and other statutes.

b. Discriminatory Eviction

Eviction—the removal of a tenant from property they were occupying—is another way in which housing can be made unavailable. 2922 Sherman Ave. Tenants' Ass'n v. Dist. of Columbia, 444 F.3d 673, 685 (D.C. Cir. 2006) ("Telling the tenants either that their 'occupancy . . . is . . . prohibited' or that they must 'seek alternative housing' certainly qualifies as making the buildings 'unavailable' under the FHA."). HUD made this clear in 24 C.F.R. §100.60(b)(5) (evicting tenants because of their protected characteristics or those of their guests constitutes a violation of §3604(a)).

Section 3604(a) also may reach discriminatory conduct that results in something analogous to "constructive eviction," a common law property concept. A constructive eviction occurs when a landlord effectively deprives a tenant of the right to occupy the premises in habitable condition. To sustain a constructive eviction claim at common law, the tenant usually must show that (1) the landlord's actions have made the dwelling truly unavailable or resulted in a situation where continued occupancy is objectively unreasonable, and (2) the tenant abandoned the premises within a reasonable time after the landlord's wrongful act. Because the concept of constructive eviction derives from state common law, state property or landlord-tenant law usually is the source of guidance for federal courts seeking to determine whether it applies in an FHA case.

NOTES AND QUESTIONS

1. Availability of §3604(a) for Constructive Eviction and Post-Acquisition Conduct. As the above discussion notes, constructive eviction is a common law property concept. As such, it is not mentioned in the FHA but is often used by courts hearing FHA cases. Some defendants have argued that constructive eviction claims cannot lie under §3604(a). In Treece v. Perrier Condominium

Owners Association, Inc., 593 F. Supp. 3d 422, 437-39, 441 (E.D. La. 2022), a family claimed that the defendant condominium association had taken a number of actions to force them out because they had children. The Treeces never were evicted formally, and instead moved out of their own accord. They made a claim under §3604(a), to which the defendant argued that "because availability under §3604(a) refers only to acts that prevent the acquisition of housing, and because the acts Plaintiffs complain of occurred *after* Plaintiffs acquired housing, §3604(a) is inapplicable." The court rejected this argument, citing holdings of various circuit courts, that conduct resulting in a constructive eviction might constitute a violation of §3604(a), because it effectively makes housing unavailable to the plaintiff even if the plaintiff originally was able to occupy the housing.

Note that the type of conduct that might lead to a constructive eviction-type claim is also likely to be covered by other parts of the statute. For example, shoddy maintenance or lack of services might also fall under §3604(b). Harassing conduct could fall under §3604(b) or §3617. The question about whether §§3604(b) and 3617 can apply to post-acquisition conduct has proven more difficult for courts and is addressed below.

2. How Bad Must Conditions Be? The standard for constructive eviction is that the conduct must be so bad as to render the dwelling unfit for occupancy or continued residence objectively unreasonable. This would appear to be a high threshold. As one court observed: "As a purely semantic matter the [FHA] might be stretched far enough to reach a case of 'constructive eviction,' which is one way to describe the present case. . . . If you burn down someone's house you make it 'unavailable' to him. . . ." Halprin v. Prairie Single Family Homes of Dearborn Park Ass'n, 388 F.3d 327, 329 (7th Cir. 2004). The *Halprin* court went on to hold that the defendants' actions, which included spraying harmful chemicals on plaintiffs' yard and defacing their property with antisemitic graffiti, were not enough to constitute constructive eviction.

Are such dramatic conditions required? Consider the en banc Seventh Circuit's analysis subsequent to *Halprin* in Bloch v. Frischholz, 587 F.3d 771, 777 (7th Cir. 2009). The case involved a claim by a Jewish family who owned three condominium units. Their faith required them to affix a mezuzah (a small decorative case containing parchment inscribed with verses from the Torah) to the exterior doorframes of their units. The condo complex instituted a new rule that forbade any objects in the hallways of the building, including on doorframes. The Blochs argued that Jewish law requires mezuzot to be displayed on the exterior doorpost, rather than indoors, and that observant Jews could not live in a place that prohibited them from affixing mezuzot to their doorposts. Regarding their §3604(a) claim, the court reasoned:

> The question here is whether the defendants have made the Blochs' units "unavailable" because of their religion (or their race). Proving constructive eviction is a tall order, but it's the best analogy the Blochs give to support their argument. Ordinarily, the plaintiff in such a case must show her residence is

"unfit for occupancy," often to the point that she is "compelled to leave." Plaintiffs must show more than a mere diminution in property values, more than just that their properties would be less desirable to a certain group. Even in *Halprin,* the allegations of the defendants' blatantly discriminatory acts, including spraying the plaintiff's yard with harmful chemicals, were insufficient to give rise to a §3604(a) claim. Availability, not simply habitability, is the right that §3604(a) protects.

Still, despite the analogy to constructive eviction, nothing in §3604(a) suggests that "unavailability" refers only to the physical condition of the premises. "[C]ourts have construed the phrase 'otherwise make unavailable or deny' in subsection (a) to encompass mortgage 'redlining,' insurance redlining, racial steering, exclusionary zoning decisions, and other actions by individuals or governmental units which directly affect the availability of housing to minorities." In other words, the defendant need not burn the plaintiff's house down for the plaintiff to have an FHA claim. A defendant can engage in post-sale practices tantamount to "redlining" that make a plaintiff's dwelling "unavailable."

The Blochs argue that the defendants' reinterpretation of Hallway Rule 1 rendered Shoreline Towers unavailable to them and other observant Jews because their religion requires that they be able to affix mezuzot to their doorposts. Letters from the Mezuzah Division of Chicago Mitzvah Campaigns, the Rabbinical Council of Chicago, and the Decalogue Society of Lawyers state that Jewish law requires observant Jews to place mezuzot on the exterior of their entrance doorposts. One went so far as to explain that, "A Jew who is not permitted to affix mezuzohs as aforesaid to all of the doorposts of his dwelling would therefore be required by Jewish Law not to live there." We think this evidence is sufficient to establish a dispute about whether Shoreline Towers was unavailable to observant Jews.

3. (When) Must a Tenant Abandon the Property? A related question is whether or when the plaintiff must abandon the property to assert a claim of constructive eviction. Obviously, a plaintiff who alleges that conditions are objectively unreasonable or the dwelling is uninhabitable would be expected to vacate the premises. But how long do they have to vacate? The court in *Bloch,* 587 F.3d at 777-78 ultimately dismissed the §3604(a) claim on this ground:

> The defendants argue that the Blochs were never evicted, actually or constructively, because they never vacated the premises. The defendants' point is well-taken. To establish a claim for constructive eviction, a tenant need not move out the minute the landlord's conduct begins to render the dwelling uninhabitable — in this case, when the defendants began enforcing the Hallway Rule to take down the Blochs' mezuzot. Tenants have a reasonable time to vacate the premises. Nonetheless, it is well-understood that constructive eviction requires surrender of possession by the tenant. If the tenant fails to vacate within a reasonable time, she waives her claim for constructive eviction.
>
> We recognize that the analogy to constructive eviction is imperfect. Section 3604(a) concerns making a dwelling "unavailable," not constructive eviction *per se.* Still, the Blochs never moved out. Though the Blochs compare their plight to constructive eviction, they give no reason why they failed to vacate. Instead, they stayed put and resisted (by repeatedly replacing their mezuzot) the defendants' allegedly discriminatory enforcement of Hallway Rule 1 for over a year

before a court enjoined the Rule's enforcement and the Association amended the Rules. Whether "unavailability" means that a plaintiff must, in every case, vacate the premises to have a §3604(a) claim is an issue we refrain from reaching. But based on these facts, we see no possibility that a reasonable jury could conclude that the defendants' conduct rendered Shoreline Towers "unavailable" to the Blochs, which is what §3604(a) requires. *See* Infinity Broad. [Corp. of Ill. v. Prudential Ins. Co. of Am., 869 F.2d 1073 (7th Cir. 1989)] (holding that district court "correctly declined to render an advisory opinion" where plaintiff sued for constructive eviction but had not yet vacated premises); Shaker & Assocs., 733 N.E.2d [865, 873 (Ill. App. Ct. 2000)] (ten-month delay to find new location deemed unreasonable); Auto. Supply Co. [v. Scene-in-Action Corp.,] 172 N.E. 35 (Ill. 1930) (two-month delay after loss of heat deemed unreasonable); Sigsbee [v. Swathwood, 419 N.E.2d 789 (Ill. Ct. App. 1981)] (eight-month delay deemed unreasonable). Section 3604(a) does not contemplate attempted constructive eviction.

For another example, see Stevens v. Hollywood Towers and Condominium Ass'n, 836 F. Supp. 2d 800, 814 (N.D. Ill. 2011), in which the court rejected a constructive eviction theory because the plaintiffs remained in their condo for more than a year after "it was clear that the Condo Board did not plan to reconsider its policies and grant the requested accommodations" in the form of a service animal.

Consider the reasons why a plaintiff experiencing discriminatory treatment might remain in their housing. Should the burden be on a plaintiff to give up their home—including, like the Blochs and the Stevenses, a unit that they own—to state a claim? What impact should housing scarcity have on the requirement to vacate within a reasonable time? *Bloch* states that §3604(a) does not permit a claim for "attempted constructive eviction," but not all courts agree. Consider *Treece* again; in that case the plaintiffs ultimately moved out following alleged harassment based on familial status, although the reason they moved was disputed (the defendants argued that the family moved so the father could study for the bar exam). The court held that plaintiffs could maintain a claim under §3604(a), regardless of whether the alleged threats of eviction were carried through:

> Courts have extended [constructive eviction theory] to threats of eviction that, for various reasons, are not carried through. In Whyte v. Alston Management, Inc., the court held that a landlord's demands that various tenants "must move because of their children" were actionable under §3604(a) as "threat[s] of eviction" that made housing unavailable. Similarly, in Carlson v. Sunshine Villas HOA, Inc., an analogous case under 42 U.S.C. §3604(f)(1), which contains identical "otherwise make unavailable" language to §3604(a), the court held the defendant landlord's attempts to evict a disabled tenant halfway through her monthly lease due to her request for a service dog "attempted to make housing unavailable." The landlord served the tenant with multiple notices to vacate, harassed her, and attempted to evict her, but, ultimately, the day before she was to vacate, the landlord allowed the tenant to remain. The court held the threat of eviction sufficed, and "the fact that [the tenant] was allowed to stay in the apartment [was] not dispositive of her claim." Thus, Plaintiffs' claims that

the Defendants attempted to evict the Treeces using the occupancy limits and subsequent harassment fall within the protections of §3604(a).

593 F. Supp. 3d at 438-39. Note that *Treece* and the cases it cites focus on the severity of the defendants' conduct, and whether it is the sort of behavior that would drive a resident out of their housing. This contrasts with the other constructive eviction cases cited, which focus on whether the residents ultimately vacated because of the behavior. Is the requirement of vacating the premises necessary if the analogy to constructive eviction is to work? Does there need to be an analogy to constructive eviction at all for this type of conduct to fall under the FHA prohibition against making housing "unavailable"? Should the difficulty of finding alternative housing be taken into account? What approach is preferable, and why?

c. Neighborhood Conditions

Plaintiffs have brought FHA cases alleging that government or corporate defendants have discriminated by causing harmful, dangerous, or value-degrading conditions to persist in their neighborhoods. As an initial matter, for the claims to be cognizable under the FHA, the plaintiffs must plead that these conditions were caused or allowed to continue "because of" a protected characteristic of area residents. Such claims can rely on a theory of intentional discrimination or on "disparate impact" theory. Disparate impact claims allege that a defendant's facially neutral policies or actions nevertheless discriminate because they cause a disproportionate impact on members of a particular protected group, or because they perpetuate segregation. Theories of discrimination are discussed in greater detail in Chapters 6 and 7.

Even where such initial allegations can be made, plaintiffs have an uphill battle. In particular, plaintiffs might find it difficult to convince courts that the offensive conditions actually constitute a denial of housing sufficient to violate §3604(a). Such arguments typically hinge on whether the plaintiff can sufficiently show that the defendant's actions are (1) severe enough, and (2) sufficiently related to housing, such that they amount to a denial of housing. The following cases provide examples:

- In Southend Neighborhood Improvement Ass'n v. County of St. Clair, 743 F.2d 1207 (7th Cir. 1984), the County had obtained the deeds for more than 5,000 tax-delinquent properties. The plaintiffs alleged that the County failed to maintain the properties in predominantly Black neighborhoods, and neither boarded up nor demolished the dilapidated homes. The plaintiffs alleged that this diminished the value of their own properties in these neighborhoods and prevented them from securing loans and making other contracts related to their properties. The court held that the claim did not implicate §3604(a).
- In Cox v. City of Dallas, Texas, 430 F.3d 734, 740 (5th Cir. 2005), the plaintiffs challenged a city's persistent failure to police the operation of an

illegal dump near their homes in a majority-Black neighborhood. The site caught fire and burned on more than one occasion. The plaintiffs argued that the dump lowered the values of their homes. The court held: "The failure of the City to police the Deepwood landfill may have harmed the housing market, decreased home values, or adversely impacted homeowners' 'intangible interests,' but such results do not make dwellings 'unavailable' within the meaning of the Act."

• In Jersey Heights Neighborhood Ass'n v. Glendening, 174 F.3d 180, 192 (4th Cir. 1999), residents of a predominantly Black community challenged the siting of a new federal highway adjacent to their neighborhood. The highway would serve as the northern boundary to their community, closing off expansion in that direction and locking residents into what was allegedly the only neighborhood open to them. The court affirmed dismissal of their claims, stating:

> The Neighborhood Association does not allege that anyone has for discriminatory reasons been evicted from his home or denied the right to purchase or rent housing. Instead, the Association claims that appellees violated these statutory provisions simply by selecting the current corridor for the Route 50 Bypass. Because this challenge to the highway site selection process is too remotely related to the housing interests that are protected by the FHA, we affirm the district court's dismissal of this count of the complaint for failure to state a claim under the statute.
>
> With regard to §3604(a), the agencies did not "make unavailable or deny a dwelling to any person" within the meaning of the FHA. Although the Neighborhood Association claims that this provision reaches every practice having the effect of making housing more difficult to obtain, the text of the statute does not extend so far. This court has previously noted that §3604(a) does not reach every event "that might conceivably affect the availability of housing." Countless private and official decisions may affect housing in some remote and indirect manner, but the FHA requires a closer causal link between housing and the disputed action. To draw every outlying official decision into the orbit of §3604(a) would be to warp that statute into a charter of plenary review.

Compare these examples to National Fair Housing Alliance (NFHA) v. Bank of America, 401 F. Supp. 3d 619, 624, 638-39 (D. Md. 2019), in which plaintiff FHOs brought suit against Bank of America and its property management firm alleging their failure to maintain and market on an equal basis Real Estate Owned (REO) residential properties acquired after the properties had gone into foreclosure but failed to sell at auction. Specifically, the complaint alleged the results of a seven-year investigation: "Bank of America-owned homes located in predominantly white census block groups were better-maintained and exhibited fewer objective routine maintenance and marketing deficiencies than Bank of America-owned homes located in neighborhoods comprised primarily of African Americans and/or Latinos." As a result, plaintiffs alleged, among other claims, that defendants' actions made housing unavailable and perpetuated segregation in communities of color. The court upheld the plaintiffs' assertion of a claim under §3604(a):

> The defendants argue that the statute is inapplicable to the facts at hand because not all the REOs in question are for sale or rental, and because the plaintiffs have insufficiently alleged that the defendants' actions have rendered unavailable the REOs that are on the market. The first contention can be dealt with quickly. REOs by their nature are properties that the bank has attempted to sell, but that it failed to sell at the foreclosure sale. The houses in question remain empty, and it is fair to presume that, even if they are not actively listed for sale, the bank's maintenance responsibilities are conducted while the property awaits a permanent owner or tenant. Moreover, even if the property is not for sale or available for rental under the meaning of the statute, the statute applies where a defendant has allegedly "otherwise [made housing] unavailable." 42 U.S.C. §3604(a). . . .
>
> The allegedly discriminatory policies in this case are "housing-related," like racial steering and discriminatory rental practices, and are distinguishable from the more remote causal link posed by the placement of a highway [in *Jersey Heights*]. The practice of delegating REO maintenance has neither a remote nor an indirect relationship to housing availability; its effect is far more immediate. The plaintiffs have alleged that the policy in question renders REOs uninhabitable. While some home purchasers and real estate investors might consider a home's disrepair an advantage toward obtaining a cut-rate acquisition, it is fair to conclude that, on the whole, the kind of systemic neglect pled dissuades prospective purchasers from buying REOs. This is the link that was missing in *Jersey Heights*. But it is present here. . . . Here, while buyers may be of any race, the defendants' maintenance practices allegedly act upon housing availability to a degree decided by the racial demographics of the neighborhood in which an REO stands. The plain text of the statute forbids them to do so. The plaintiffs have sufficiently pled unavailability under §3604(a).

NOTES AND QUESTIONS

1. Distinguishing Discrimination in Service Cases. Can you distinguish *NFHA v. Bank of America* from the other cases cited above? What factors are likely to be necessary for a holding that discriminatory provision of services, by either a private entity or a municipality, makes housing unavailable in violation of §3604(a)?

2. Service Discrimination and §3604(b). Discrimination in services claims also can be, and often are, brought under §3604(b), which specifically covers discrimination in the provision of services or facilities and does not contain the requirement that a plaintiff be deprived of housing. *See, e.g.*, Cooke v. Town of Colorado City, Ariz., 934 F. Supp. 2d 1097, 1112 (D. Ariz. 2013) ("[W]here, as here, there is no evidence that the . . . [p]roperty was unavailable to Plaintiffs, but rather, evidence that the home was made less habitable and/ or that Defendants otherwise interfered with Plaintiffs' enjoyment of the residence because of discrimination in the provision of services, Plaintiffs can state a claim under [sections of the FHA other than §3604(a)] such as section §3604(b)"). These are discussed in the next section.

B. SECTION 3604(b): DISCRIMINATORY TERMS, CONDITIONS, PRIVILEGES, SERVICES, OR FACILITIES

Section §3604(b) of the FHA prohibits "discriminat[ion] against any person in the terms, conditions, or privileges of sale or rental of a dwelling, or in the provision of services or facilities in connection therewith" because of a protected characteristic. A similar provision, §3604(f)(2), prohibits such discrimination because of disability.[17]

Just as there are many ways to make housing unavailable, there are many types of "terms, conditions or privileges" that might relate to the sale or rental of a dwelling, and many housing-related "services or facilities" that might be provided. As a result, there are several different discrimination contexts in which §3604(b) might apply. HUD has promulgated regulations listing some of the more common types of behavior that violate §3604(b):

24 C.F.R. §100.65(b) Prohibited actions under this section include, but are not limited to:

(1) Using different provisions in leases or contracts of sale, such as those relating to rental charges, security deposits and the terms of a lease and those relating to down payment and closing requirements, because of [protected characteristics].

(2) Failing or delaying maintenance or repairs of sale or rental dwellings because of [protected characteristics].

(3) Failing to process an offer for the sale or rental of a dwelling or to communicate an offer accurately because of [protected characteristics].

(4) Limiting the use of privileges, services or facilities associated with a dwelling because of [the protected characteristics] of an owner, tenant or a person associated with him or her.

(5) Denying or limiting services or facilities in connection with the sale or rental of a dwelling, because a person failed or refused to provide sexual favors.

(6) Conditioning the terms, conditions, or privileges relating to the sale or rental of a dwelling, or denying or limiting the services or facilities in connection therewith, on a person's response to harassment because of [protected characteristics].

---

17. Section 3604(f)(2), the FHA's ban on discrimination in terms, conditions, privileges, services, and facilities because of disability, is discussed in detail in Chapter 17.

(7) Subjecting a person to harassment because of [protected characteristics] that has the effect of imposing different terms, conditions, or privileges relating to the sale or rental of a dwelling or denying or limiting services or facilities in connection with the sale or rental of a dwelling.

1. Discrimination in Terms, Conditions, or Privileges of Sale or Rental

Discriminatory differences in lease provisions or sale contracts violate §3604(b), as does the imposition of different conditions for application or sale. The following cases involve allegations that provide representative examples:

- In United States v. Balistrieri, 981 F.2d 916 (7th Cir. 1992), a rental agent quoted higher rents to Black apartment seekers. She also told Black testers later dates of availability for units.
- In Harris v. Itzhaki, 183 F.3d 1043 (9th Cir. 1999), the landlord told a Black tester there would be an additional rental charge that he had not cited to the white tester.
- In United States v. Hylton, 944 F. Supp. 2d 176 (D. Conn. 2013), a tenant's lease specified that he could sublet his unit with permission from the landlord. The landlord refused to give permission when he learned the proposed sublessee was Black. Both the tenant and the proposed sublessee were held to have claims under §3604(b). The tenant's claim was based on the discriminatory denial of the lease privilege to sublet; the proposed sublessee's claim was based on the landlord's "prevent[ing] her from assuming residency and enjoying the privilege of renting" the property. (The court also held that the landlord's refusal of the sublet constituted a denial of housing to the proposed sublessee in violation of §3604(a).)
- In Greater New Orleans Fair Housing Action Center v. Kelly, 364 F. Supp. 3d 635 (E.D. La. 2019) a property owner told a female tester she could apply for a unit simply by filling out an application, without undergoing a credit check, whereas the male tester was told that to apply he would have to undergo a credit check and present his driver's license, proof of employment, a copy of his current lease, and a deposit check.

Recall the defendant's statement in *HUD v. Blackwell*, above, that he would have been willing to sell his house to the Herrons for $2,000 more than the price he would charge to white buyers ("I'm not objectionable to them but I'm going to raise the price. I raised the price two thousand dollars. I figured that wouldn't be enough to run them off. I was glad to have them."). Had he actually sold the house to them at a price inflated due to their race, this would have constituted a clear violation of §3604(b).

2. Discrimination in the Services or Facilities of Housing

HUD's regulation makes clear that §3604(b) can be violated by discrimination in the provision of services, facilities, or privileges throughout the housing occupancy, not only at the point of sale or rental. This broader interpretation is significant, as it provides protection for current tenants and homeowners from discriminatory conditions and treatment that might arise after they have taken possession of their dwellings. (Indeed, such claims are the most common sort for renters, particularly those who experience harassment based on protected characteristics.) Not every court has agreed with this approach. The controversy surrounding such "post-acquisition" claims has been considerable, and is addressed below. This section discusses both pre- and post-acquisition claims.

a. Discrimination in Services or Restrictions on Access to Facilities

A housing provider might be obligated by law to provide certain types of services to tenants or could choose to offer services as privileges of the housing. In either event, the provider may not discriminate with respect to protected characteristics in the provision of these services. Similarly, a provider may not restrict access to particular facilities or amenities of housing or apply rules differently on the basis of protected characteristics. The following cases provide representative examples:

- In Schroeder v. DeBertolo, 879 F. Supp. 173 (D.P.R. 1995), survivors of a deceased plaintiff successfully stated a claim on her behalf that she had been denied access to the common areas of her condominium due to her mental disability.
- In United States v. Sea Winds of San Marco, Inc., 893 F. Supp. 1051 (M.D. Fla. 1995), a condominium complex allegedly enforced an ID requirement against Hispanic residents and monitored them in a way that it did not monitor other residents.
- In Fair Housing Congress v. Weber, 993 F. Supp. 1286 (C.D. Cal. 1997), the court ruled on summary judgment that an apartment complex's rule restricting play and other uses of the facilities by residents' children violated §3604(b).
- In Belcher v. Grand Reserve MGM, LLC, 269 F. Supp. 3d 1219 (M.D. Ala. 2017), the court denied the defendants summary judgment on plaintiffs' claims that their apartment complex created and enforced rules to discriminate against them on the basis of race and familial status, including preventing their teenage children from using the playground, pool, and gym; requiring adult supervision at all times; and imposing a curfew of 8:30 p.m.
- In 273 Lee Avenue Tenants Association v. Steinmetz, 330 F. Supp. 3d 778 (E.D.N.Y. 2018), the court denied summary judgment for defendants

against plaintiff's claims that their landlord refused to perform maintenance and repairs on the basis of tenants' religion and national origin, which caused their units to become dilapidated and dangerous.

- In United States v. Matusoff Rental Co., 494 F. Supp. 2d 740 (S.D. Ohio 2007), the court held that tenants were denied needed repairs because of their race.
- In Curto v. A Country Place Condominium Association, Inc., 921 F.3d 405 (3d Cir. 2019), the court held that defendants violated §3604(b) in setting sex-segregated hours for their communal swimming pool.

b. Discrimination in Municipal Services

Section 3604(b) also has been applied to the discriminatory provision of municipal or other services, such as water, trash collection, road maintenance, and snow clearing. Whereas discriminatory service claims brought under §3604(a) often turn on the question whether the discriminatory provision of services actually makes housing unavailable, claims brought under §3604(b) often turn on the *type* of service at issue, with courts requiring that the service be sufficiently housing-related to fall under the FHA. Other courts have denied relief due to a narrow reading of *when* §3604(b) can apply. As discussed below, some courts require that a discriminatory service must affect the point of sale or rental of housing, thus holding §3604(b) does not apply to discrimination that occurs after a person has acquired housing.

In many cases denying relief, the challenged municipal action involved a zoning or land-use decision alleged to cause harm to a community, such as siting a highway or granting permits for industrial uses. Some courts are reluctant to broaden the definition of a municipal service in the FHA context to encompass decisions about nonresidential property. To do so, they fear, would unduly limit the ability of local governments to address local priorities within resource constraints and also turn the FHA into a "civil rights statute of general applicability rather than one dealing with the specific problems of fair housing opportunities." *See* Clifton Terrace Assocs. v. United Technologies Corp., 929 F.2d 714, 720 (D.C. Cir. 1991) (refusing to apply §3604(b) to third-party provider of elevator maintenance services for privately operated federally subsidized housing complex).[18]

Professor Schwemm encapsulated the various court approaches to discriminatory municipal service claims in the 15 years after the FHA amendments and the 1989 HUD regulations:

---

18. Note that *Clifton Terrace* is *not* a municipal services case. The language cited above frequently is quoted in municipal services cases, hence its inclusion here. There is no question that elevator service is covered by §3604(b) when it is offered by a housing provider in connection with a dwelling. The issue for the *Clifton Terrace* court appeared to be that the claim was against a third party, not the operator of the housing complex.

-First, the FHA through §3604(a) provides a remedy for discriminatory municipal services, but only where such discrimination has the effect of making housing unavailable (e.g., where a municipality totally blocks development of new housing or renders current housing virtually uninhabitable);

-Second, §3604(b) outlaws the discriminatory provision of basic, housing-related municipal services, such as police and fire protection and garbage collection; and,

-Third, determining whether certain other government acts qualify as "services" or negatively impact the "privileges" covered by §3604(b) requires a case-by-case analysis, with the answer probably being "No" if the challenged act involves such one-time decisions as the siting of a highway, factory, or other residentially-disruptive use in or near the plaintiffs' neighborhood.[19]

The following case summarizes the approaches that courts have taken to different types of services.

Georgia State Conference of the NAACP
v. City of LaGrange, Georgia
940 F.3d 627 (11th Cir. 2019)

Before Wilson and Branch, Circuit Judges, and Vinson, District Judge.

Branch, Circuit Judge:

The municipal government of the City of LaGrange, Ga. ("the City"), is the sole provider of electricity, gas, and water utility services in LaGrange. The City requires that utility customers comply with two policies in order to initiate and maintain those basic utility services. First, both applicants and current utility customers must pay any debts they owe to the City, including court judgments and fines ("the court debt policy"). Thus, an applicant may not obtain utility services without first satisfying outstanding municipal debts, and current utility customers who owe an unpaid debt to the City may have their utility services terminated without advance notice. Second, the City requires an applicant seeking to open a new utility account to present valid state- or federally-issued photo identification, and at the time relevant to this litigation, required the applicant to provide a valid Social Security number ("the identification policy").

In 2017, . . . plaintiffs . . . filed the underlying complaint against the City. Specifically, the plaintiffs argued that the court debt policy disproportionately harms black residents because they are more likely to have outstanding municipal court debt. They asserted that the identification policy disproportionately harms Hispanic residents, as they are more likely to lack the required identification documents for opening a utility account.

---

19. Robert G. Schwemm, Cox, Halprin, *and Discriminatory Municipal Services Under the Fair Housing Act*, 41 Ind. Law Rev. 717, 755 (2008).

B. WHAT SERVICES FALL WITHIN THE SCOPE OF §3604(b)

Having concluded that some post-acquisition conduct falls within the scope of §3604(b), we must decide whether §3604(b) applies to the specific post-acquisition services at issue here: municipally provided electricity, gas, and water services.

To be clear, not all housing-related services necessarily fall within the scope of §3604(b). Rather, as noted by the D.C. Circuit, to extend the FHA to any and every municipal policy or service that touches the lives of residents "would be to expand that Act into a civil rights statute of general applicability rather than one dealing with the specific problems of fair housing opportunities." *See Clifton Terrace Assocs., Ltd. v. United Tech. Corp.* (D.C. Cir. 1991).

Other circuits that have considered §3604(b) challenges involving services provided by local governments have focused on whether said services have a sufficient nexus to housing. For example, while recognizing that §3604(b) may encompass certain post-acquisition conduct related to housing, the Fifth Circuit held that §3604(b) did not apply to claims that a city discriminated in the enforcement of zoning laws to prevent unlawful dumping near the plaintiffs' residences "because the service was not 'connected' to the sale or rental of a dwelling as the statute requires." [*Cox v. City of Dallas* (5th Cir. 2005).] Similarly, the Fourth Circuit held that a group of residents could not challenge the city's decision to locate a highway near their property under §3604(b), because such a decision did not "implicate 'the terms, conditions, or privileges of sale or rental of a dwelling, or . . . the provision of services or facilities in connection therewith.'" *Jersey Heights Neighborhood Ass'n v. Glendening* (4th Cir. 1999). By contrast, in [*Committee Concerning Cmty. Improvement ("CCCI") v. City of Modesto* (9th Cir. 2009)] the Ninth Circuit took a more expansive view of the meaning of "services" under §3604(b), holding that the "timely provision of law-enforcement personnel," fell within the scope of §3604(b).

Because the text of §3604(b) makes clear that the conduct at issue must relate to services provided in connection with the sale or rental of a dwelling, we find the Ninth Circuit's expansive view of services covered by §3604(b) unpersuasive. Law enforcement services are not provided in connection with the "sale or rental of a dwelling." Indeed, those services are provided regardless of whether an individual has housing and are not required in order to obtain housing. Rather, we find the narrower view of "services" articulated by the Fifth and Fourth Circuit persuasive and consistent with the plain language of §3604(b). Accordingly, we hold that a service within the meaning of §3604(b) must be a housing-related service that is directly connected to the sale or rental of a dwelling.

C. WHETHER THE PARTICULAR MUNICIPAL SERVICES IN THIS CASE FALL WITHIN THE SCOPE OF §3604(b)

The basic utility services at issue here — water, gas, and electricity — are distinct from other municipal services in two critical ways, both of which demonstrate their direct connection to the sale or rental of a dwelling: (1) they are services closely tied to the sale or rental of a dwelling, and (2) they are essential to the habitability of a dwelling. As explained further, these two distinctions support our conclusion that the water, gas, and electricity services at issue here fall within the scope of §3604(b).

First, basic utility services have an undeniably closer connection to the sale or rental of a dwelling than the generally provided municipal services at issue in *Cox* and *Jersey Heights*. Specifically, it is common knowledge that in connection with buying or leasing a dwelling, a resident must obtain basic utility services, such as water, gas, and electricity for the home. Moreover, in the context of housing, a person cannot obtain such services without first obtaining a dwelling. In other words, these basic utility services are inextricably intertwined with the dwelling itself. Indeed, it is practically impossible when considering housing to separate the "sale or rental of a dwelling" from the concept of obtaining basic utility services. Thus, the provision of these attendant services is clearly, directly connected to the sale or rental of a dwelling.

Second, these basic utility services are connected to the sale or rental of a dwelling because they are fundamental to the ability to inhabit a dwelling. In this case, the City is the sole provider of the basic utility services of water, gas, and electricity. And, accepting the complaint's allegations as true, as we must at this stage, some of the plaintiffs are unable to open utility accounts because they lack the required identification or have outstanding municipal court debt. Similarly, other plaintiffs who have utility services but have acquired municipal debt are at risk of having those services terminated without notice. As a result, even if the plaintiffs are able to purchase or rent a dwelling, they are unable to live in it due to being unable to obtain or maintain basic utility services. Therefore, we conclude that because the water, gas, and electricity services at issue in this case are essential to the habitability of a dwelling and closely connected with the sale or rental of housing, they unambiguously fall within the scope of §3604(b).

NOTES AND QUESTIONS

1. Covered Services. The cases discussed above wrestle with the issue of whether particular municipal services are sufficiently related to the sale or rental of housing to fall under §3604(b). As the court in *LaGrange* recognized, services such as utilities clearly meet this requirement, as they are both (1) directly tied to a home and (2) necessary for habitability. *LaGrange* held that these qualities make utilities distinguishable from other types of municipal services such as timely emergency services response (*Modesto*), cleaning up hazardous waste dumps in residential neighborhoods (*Cox*), and location of highways (*Jersey Heights*). Do you agree with the court's reasoning?

Consider the cases that *LaGrange* discusses, some of which are discussed also under §3604(a), above.

In *Modesto*, the plaintiffs based their FHA claim on the allegation that dispatch times for emergency services were between one and two minutes longer for predominantly Latino areas than for non-Latino areas. The court spent most of its discussion of the §3604(b) claim on whether it could apply to post-acquisition conduct (deciding that it could). After recognizing the importance that a difference of one or two minutes could make with respect to dispatch times for emergency services (and noting that there was no explanation for these differences in the record), the court apparently assumed without discussion that emergency services are sufficiently housing-related to be covered by §3604(b). *See also* Campbell v. City of Berwyn, 815 F. Supp. 1138 (N.D. Ill. 1993) (holding that plaintiffs stated a claim under §3604(b) when they alleged that the city terminated police service to their home on a racially motivated basis).

In *Cox*, the plaintiffs, residents of the majority-Black Deepwood neighborhood in Dallas, alleged that the city allowed an illegal hazardous waste dump to operate in their neighborhood, decreasing the value or habitability of their houses. On two occasions the dump had caught fire and burned for months. Despite repeated complaints, the city took almost no action to prevent dumping at the site for decades. (Eventually the dump's operators were convicted of criminal offenses related to their operation of the dump.) The court denied the plaintiffs' §3604(b) claims, holding that the city's failure to enforce its zoning laws against a hazardous waste dump in a residential area was not sufficiently housing-related to fall under the FHA:

> Even assuming that the enforcement of zoning laws alleged here is a "service," we hold that §3604(b) is inapplicable here because the service was not "connected" to the sale or rental of a dwelling as the statute requires. The district court observed that "it is necessary to decide whether the language 'in connection with' refers to the 'sale or rental of a dwelling' or merely the 'dwelling' in general." And as the district court correctly concluded, it is the former. This reading is grammatically superior and supported by the decisions of many courts. There is more.
>
> Although the FHA is meant to have a broad reach, unmooring the "services" language from the "sale or rental" language pushes the FHA into a general anti-discrimination pose, creating rights for any discriminatory act which impacts property values—say, for generally inadequate police protection in a certain area. . . . While sweeping widely, the FHA does so in the housing field and remains a housing statute—the focus of congressional concern. That the corrosive bite of racial discrimination may soak into all facets of black lives cannot be gainsaid, but this statute targets only housing. And the "services" subject to the alleged discrimination must be "in connection" with the "sale or rental of a dwelling. . . ."[20]

---

20. *Cox*, 430 F.3d at 745-46.

In *Jersey Heights*, the plaintiffs challenged the city's decision to site a highway bypass proximate to a majority-Black residential neighborhood. The court rejected their argument that the decision could constitute a housing-related service under the statute:

> The Bypass siting decision does not implicate "the terms, conditions, or privileges of sale or rental of a dwelling, or . . . the provision of services or facilities in connection therewith." This provision by its terms extends only to housing and housing-related services. Although the Neighborhood Association contends that the Bypass is a housing "service," and complains that it will disproportionately suffer its burdens, "that is a strained interpretation of the word."
>
> The FHA's services provision simply requires that "such things as garbage collection and other services of the kind usually provided by municipalities" not be denied on a discriminatory basis. *Id.* It does not extend to every activity having any conceivable effect on neighborhood residents. *See id.* (hazard insurance is not a "service"); Clifton Terrace Assocs., Ltd. v. United Techs. Corp., 929 F.2d 714, 720 (D.C. Cir. 1991) (elevator manufacturer is not a provider of "services"); Southend Neighborhood Improvement Ass'n, 743 F.2d at 1210 (maintenance of county-owned neighborhood property is not a "service"); Laramore v. Illinois Sports Facilities Auth., 722 F. Supp. 443, 452 (N.D. Ill. 1989) (stadium site selection is not the provision of a "service"). . . . In selecting a site for the Route 50 Bypass around the City of Salisbury, defendants did not become providers of housing services within the meaning of section 3604(b).[21]

Can you think of an argument for extending coverage of municipal services while still ensuring they are sufficiently housing-related to fall under §3604(b)? What additional services might be covered under a broader reading of the FHA?

2. "Water Racism."[22] Access to water is a core municipal service historically provided (or not) on a discriminatory basis in communities of color. There are recent examples of this phenomenon. Consider the case of Kennedy v. City of Zanesville, Ohio, 505 F. Supp. 2d 456, 463-64 (S.D. Ohio 2007). In denying the defendants' motion for summary judgment on plaintiffs' discrimination claims, the court summarized the plaintiffs' allegations:

> The individual Plaintiffs lived, at various times, in the Coal Run neighborhood located within the County and Township, and just outside the Zanesville city limits. The neighborhood includes approximately twenty-five homes, and historically the residents of Coal Run have been African-American. Currently, approximately eighty-five percent of the Coal Run neighborhood residents are African-American, while the County and Township both are over ninety-five percent white. Contaminated by years of mining in the area, the ground water in the Coal Run neighborhood is not safe for residential purposes. Prior to receiving public water service in 2004, Plaintiffs, therefore, used wells, hauled

---

21. *Jersey Heights*, 174 F.3d at 193.

22. This term was coined by Dr. Christopher Rhodes to refer to dramatic racial disparities in access to clean drinking water and swimming facilities, as well as in vulnerability to flooding. *See* Christopher Rhodes, *In America, Racism Is in the Water*, AL JAZEERA (Dec. 2022), https://www.aljazeera.com/opinions/2022/12/1/in-america-racism-is-in-the-water.

water, had water delivered to their homes, and even collected rain water and melted snow in order to have safe, usable water for drinking, cooking, and bathing. . . .

According to Plaintiffs, the residents of Coal Run suffered under a decades-long discriminatory government policy of refusing to provide clean water to their neighborhood due to its racial makeup. Plaintiffs claim that Coal Run was surrounded by waterlines going to predominately white areas and Plaintiffs, despite repeated requests, were not permitted to connect to the adjacent lines. Plaintiffs contend that the City, County, and Township are all responsible for the waterlines that run through the County, and even though Defendants had the power and ability to bring water to Coal Run, they engaged in three broad forms of discrimination to deny the neighborhood water. First, Plaintiffs claim that Defendants regularly passed over the Coal Run neighborhood in favor of funding and constructing waterlines for, often more distant, white areas. Second, Plaintiffs state that Defendants rejected or disregarded the numerous requests for waterlines to be extended into Coal Run, while at the same time pursuing projects in response to requests from white areas. Third, Plaintiffs claim that Defendants denied individual requests from Coal Run residents to connect to an existing line — the Old Adamsville Road line — while letting white homes connect.

On July 10, 2008, a jury returned a verdict against the city, county, and Water Authority for nearly $11 million.[23] Water quality (potability) is also a serious issue for communities of color. A report from the Natural Resources Defense Council, citing statistics from the U.S. Environmental Protection Agency, shows that these communities are more likely to have unsafe drinking water and less likely to receive federal funding to improve water safety.[24] Water crises in majority-Black cities such as Flint, Michigan, and Jackson, Mississippi, are dramatic examples of this problem,[25] as is the persistent lack of clean water for thousands of *colonias*, communities with an estimated 500,000 Latino residents on the Texas-Mexico border.[26]

3. Equal Protection. By definition, complaints about denials of or discrimination in municipal services involve a government actor. Thus, plaintiffs may pursue these claims under the Fourteenth Amendment's Equal Protection Clause and 42 U.S.C. §1983. Plaintiffs raised constitutional claims in the cases discussed in *LaGrange*, above.

---

23. An announcement of the award can be found at Relman Colfax, https://www.relman law.com/cases-zanesville (last viewed October 6, 2024).

24. Kristi Pullen Fedinick, Steve Taylor, & Michele Roberts, *Watered Down Justice*, NRDC (Mar. 27, 2020), https://www.nrdc.org/resources/watered-down-justice.

25. *See, e.g.*, Mona Hanna-Attisha, WHAT THE EYES DON'T SEE: A STORY OF CRISIS, RESISTANCE, AND HOPE IN AN AMERICAN CITY (2018); Rick Rojas, *Mississippi's Capital Loses Water as a Troubled System Faces a Fresh Crisis*, N.Y. TIMES, Aug. 30, 2022.

26. *See* HUD Exchange, Colonias History, https://www.hudexchange.info/cdbg-colonias /colonias-history (last visited July 30, 2024); Alejandra Martinez, *Texas Likely Will Spend Billions Fixing Its Water Systems. Will It Reach These Forgotten Colonias?*, TEXAS TRIBUNE (May 5, 2023), https://www.texastribune.org/2023/05/05/texas-water-infrastructure-colonias/.

Proceeding under a constitutional theory has both benefits and drawbacks compared to §3604(b). One benefit of a §1983 claim is that it can allow for broader coverage of discrimination claims regarding services that are not strictly housing-related or that do not affect the acquisition of housing. For example, in Drayton v. McIntosh County, Georgia, No. CV 216-053, 2017 WL 11717727, at *9 (S.D. Ga. Oct. 30, 2017), Black members of the Gullah-Geechee community (descendants of West Africans who were brought to the United States as enslaved persons) living on Sapelo Island, Georgia, alleged a variety of forms of discriminatory treatment by the state and county:

> Plaintiffs allege that Defendants intentionally discriminated by maintaining the roads for white residents while ignoring the needs of Plaintiffs. In particular, Defendant DNR provided a culvert for the driveway of a white property owner on Sapelo Island but Defendants have failed to replace or repair several culverts on the Island that have fallen into disrepair or have collapsed. Thus, while a white family can access their vacation home on Sapelo Island, Plaintiffs cannot access the cemetery in which their ancestors are buried. Further, Plaintiffs complain that McIntosh County adequately maintains the roads throughout the rest of the County. Specifically in the context of the mainland, Plaintiffs allege that McIntosh County has paved the roads of the predominantly white mainland communities of Poppell Farms (80% white) and Sapelo Circle (100% white), which are similarly sized to Hog Hammock, while Sapelo Island has mostly dirt roads that are "bumpy and pothole-ridden" and virtually impassable in inclement weather.
>
> Plaintiffs' complaint about the inequitable treatment of Sapelo Island residents as opposed to the predominantly white mainland goes beyond road maintenance and extends to the provision of other areas including water, sewage and trash services, fire and police protection, emergency medical services, and adequate transportation. Plaintiffs allege that the State and County Defendants have expended nearly all of their resources on the predominantly white mainland pursuant to a longstanding and ongoing policy or custom to discriminate against the predominantly African-American Gullah-Geechee residents on Sapelo Island.

The court dismissed the plaintiffs' §3604(b) claim, holding that the services at issue were not related to the acquisition, sale, or rental of dwellings. However, it allowed them to bring a §1983 claim regarding these services, and later denied the defendant's motion for summary judgment on this count. Banks v. McIntosh County, Georgia, 530 F. Supp. 3d 1335 (S.D. Ga. 2021).

One drawback for plaintiffs pursuing constitutional claims is that they cannot rely on discriminatory effects alone to establish liability. However, discriminatory intent can be inferred if the disparity is stark and otherwise unexplainable, if there has been a history of discrimination, or if there are other indicia that discrimination is at play. The facts of an early case, Hawkins v. Town of Shaw, Mississippi, 437 F.2d 1286, 1288 (5th Cir. 1971), provide an example:

> The Town of Shaw, Mississippi, was incorporated in 1886 and is located in the Mississippi Delta. Its population, which has undergone little change since 1930, consists of about 2,500 people — 1,500 black and 1,000 white residents.

Residential racial segregation is almost total. There are 451 dwelling units occupied by blacks in town, and, of these, 97% (439) are located in neighborhoods in which no whites reside. That the town's policies in administering various municipal services have led to substantially less attention being paid to the black portion of town is clear.

Nearly 98% of all homes that front on unpaved streets in Shaw are occupied by blacks. Ninety-seven percent of the homes not served by sanitary sewers are in black neighborhoods. Further, while the town has acquired a significant number of medium and high intensity mercury vapor street lighting fixtures, every one of them has been installed in white neighborhoods. The record further discloses that similar statistical evidence of grave disparities in both the level and kinds of services offered regarding surface water drainage, water mains, fire hydrants, and traffic control apparatus was also brought forth and not disputed. Finally, it was alleged that this disparity was the result of a long history of racial discrimination.

On rehearing en banc, 461 F.2d 1171, 1173 (5th Cir. 1972), the court reaffirmed the panel's judgment that the plaintiffs had stated a claim under §1983, observing:

> [T]he facts before us squarely and certainly support the reasonable and logical inference that there was here neglect involving clear overtones of racial discrimination in the administration of governmental affairs of the town of Shaw resulting in the same evils which characterize an intentional and purposeful disregard of the principle of equal protection of the laws.
>
> Federal Courts are reluctant to enter the field of local government operations. The conduct of municipal affairs is "an extremely awkward vehicle to manage." It is apparent from our original opinion, and we repeat here, that we do not imply or suggest that every disparity of services between citizens of a town or city creates a right of access to the federal courts for redress. We deal only with the town of Shaw, Mississippi, and the facts as developed in this record.

4. Segregation, Annexation, and "Underbounding." A persistent problem arises with the drawing of municipal borders, which typically define the areas to which services are provided. In some parts of the United States, municipal boundaries, set by white-controlled municipal governments, exclude neighborhoods of color. Annexation, the process by which a municipality expands its jurisdictional territory by acquiring adjacent land, in some areas is less likely when the "fringe" population is majority Black.[27] Municipalities might refuse to annex Black areas while annexing white areas. They might "de-annex" territory and withdraw services. *See, e.g.,* Franklin v. City of Marks, 439 F.2d 665 (5th Cir. 1971) (in decision determining proper statute of limitations, plaintiffs could state a constitutional claim under the Fourteenth Amendment

---

27. Daniel T. Lichter et al., *Municipal Underbounding: Annexation and Racial Exclusion in Small Southern Towns*, 72 RURAL SOC. 47, 52 (2007) ("Annexation—or the lack of annexation—can be a political tool used by municipal leaders to exclude disadvantaged or low-income populations, including minorities, from voting in local elections and from receiving access to public utilities and other community services.").

by demonstrating that a de-annexation order was an attempt to escape the obligation to provide equal municipal services to a minority neighborhood). Or white areas might "secede" and incorporate as separate municipalities to create their own school districts, enact exclusionary zoning ordinances, and consolidate a higher tax base.[28] As a result, neighboring areas of color may be deprived of services and basic infrastructure. This phenomenon has been described as "municipal underbounding," and can occur in rural, suburban, and urban areas.[29] Professor Michelle Wilde Anderson describes the situation this way:

> On the outskirts of small cities and incorporated suburbs across the country, hundreds of high-poverty neighborhoods of color lack rudimentary services like sewage systems, drainage, and streetlights. Integrated economically with city populations but excluded from participatory rights in city government, these unincorporated urban areas bear disproportionate numbers of landfills, municipal utility plants, and freeways that benefit urban populations but threaten local health and depress land values.[30]

Advocates generally have not used the Fair Housing Act to challenge municipal boundary exclusion,[31] and only one court has weighed in on the issue. *See* LeBlanc-Sternberg v. Fletcher, 781 F. Supp. 261, 270 (S.D.N.Y. 1991) (holding that plaintiffs could state an FHA claim for religious discrimination based on their contention that town's incorporation was done intentionally to limit the concentration of Jewish residents and enact zoning laws that would impede their religious observance of the Sabbath).

3. Harassment

Harassment against housing residents based on protected characteristics can constitute another type of discrimination in the terms and conditions of housing. The theory is that how people are treated and the sort of conduct to which they are exposed can be significant enough to affect a "term or condition" of housing even if not in a formal contract sense. The Supreme Court first developed this doctrine in the context of Title VII, which has identical

---

28. Jenna Raden, *Fragmenting Local Governance and Fracturing America's Suburbs: An Analysis of Municipal Incorporations and Segregative Effect Liability Under the Fair Housing Act*, 94 TULANE L. REV. 365, 376-82 (2020) (describing the successful secession efforts of St. George, Louisiana, in which a neighborhood in East Baton Rouge incorporated into a majority white and relatively affluent city, excluding poorer, majority Black areas).

29. Charles S. Aiken, *Race as a Factor in Municipal Underbounding*, 77 ANNALS OF THE ASS'N OF AMERICAN GEOGRAPHERS 564 (1987).

30. Michelle Wilde Anderson, *Mapped Out of Local Democracy*, 62 STANFORD L. REV. 931, 931 (2010).

31. Raden, *supra* note 28, at 393-96 (arguing that discriminatory municipal incorporation violates the FHA, but acknowledging that a new city defending its incorporation may contend that "the act of incorporation is not a 'housing practice' under the FHA but rather is a mechanism to recognize the political will for self-governance").

language prohibiting discrimination "because of sex" in employment. As the court noted in a sexual harassment case, Fox v. Gaines, 4 F.4th 1293, 1296-97 (11th Cir. 2021):

> The FHA makes it unlawful to "discriminate against any person in the terms, conditions, or privileges of sale or rental of a dwelling, or in the provision of services or facilities in connection therewith, because of . . . sex." 42 U.S.C. §3604(b). . . . When interpreting the FHA, we—like our sister circuits—look to cases interpreting Title VII, which uses language virtually identical to the FHA's. . . . Turning to cases interpreting Title VII confirms our conclusion that the FHA prohibits sexual harassment.
>
> Interpreting Title VII, the Supreme Court ruled that "[w]ithout question" sexual harassment is a form of sex discrimination within the meaning of Title VII's nearly identical prohibition on "discriminat[ion] . . . because of . . . sex." Meritor Savs. Bank, FSB v. Vinson (1986). In *Meritor* the Court relied on the reasoning of our decision in *Henson v. City of Dundee*, where we held that "a hostile or offensive atmosphere created by sexual harassment can, standing alone, constitute a violation of Title VII," explaining that a "pattern of sexual harassment inflicted upon an employee because of her sex is a pattern of behavior that inflicts disparate treatment upon a member of one sex with respect to terms, conditions, or privileges of employment."

Harassment claims can be based on any protected characteristic, although the law is the most developed for claims of housing sexual harassment. Sexual harassment cases are discussed in Chapter 15.

Housing harassment, as in *Fox*, can be carried out by a landlord or other person associated with the provision of housing, such as a property manager or neighborhood association official. Harassment also can be carried out by neighbors or other residents of a property. When such resident-on-resident harassment is based on protected characteristics, aggrieved persons may pursue fair housing claims against two categories of defendants. One claim lies against the individual who is engaging in the harassment. Claims of this sort typically are brought pursuant to a different section of the FHA, §3617 (discussed in Chapter 10), which makes it illegal to "coerce, intimidate, threaten, or interfere with any person in the exercise or enjoyment" of fair housing rights. Section 3617 more directly speaks to housing harassment and, significantly, is not limited to situations where the harassment is carried out in connection with the "sale or rental of a dwelling." An aggrieved person also may pursue a neighbor-harassment claim against a landlord, homeowners' association, or other housing provider who is aware of the harassment but takes no action to address it. HUD explicitly has acknowledged this type of claim, stating that a person can be liable for "[f]ailing to take prompt action to correct and end a discriminatory housing practice by a third-party, where the person knew or should have known of the discriminatory conduct and had the power to correct it." 24 C.F.R §100.7(a)(1)(iii).

Plaintiffs can pursue claims under §3604(b) against their housing providers for third-party housing harassment, but it could be difficult. To succeed, a plaintiff would have to demonstrate that the defendant provider knew about the harassment, was in a position to take action in response, and chose not to act. HUD recognized that whether or not a provider has power to take action against a harasser in a particular situation "depends upon the extent of the person's control or any other legal responsibility the person may have with respect to the conduct of such third-party." 24 C.F.R §100.7(a)(1)(iii). Moreover, as the majority in the following case holds, the plaintiff may also have to prove that this refusal to act was itself motivated by discriminatory intent.

Francis v. Kings Park Manor, Inc.
992 F.3d 67 (2d Cir. 2021)

EN BANC

CABRANES, Circuit Judge:

I. BACKGROUND

According to the Complaint, at all relevant times, Francis, a Black man, rented and lived in an apartment at Kings Park Manor, a residential complex in Suffolk County, N.Y., owned and operated by KPM. On approximately eight occasions between February and September of 2012, Endres, Francis's neighbor and fellow tenant, verbally attacked and otherwise attempted to intimidate Francis, including by racist insults and at least one death threat. On March 11, 2012, Francis reported Endres to the Suffolk County police, who in turn informed KPM of the reported events. Francis himself did not mention Endres to the KPM Defendants at this time, however, and several months later, on May 1, 2012, Francis renewed his lease without comment. In total, Francis wrote three certified letters to KPM, in which he recounted Endres's behavior, the police's involvement, and Endres's arrest for aggravated harassment in August 2012. Francis does not allege, nor do any of the exhibits to his Complaint show, that he ever requested any action by KPM. Francis alleges that KPM did not at any point investigate or intervene; in fact, Francis claims that KPM's owners expressly directed Downing, their property manager, "not to get involved." When Endres's lease expired in January 2013, five months after he was arrested, Endres vacated his apartment. He pleaded guilty to a charge of harassment in April 2013.

[Frances filed claims of racial discrimination against all defendants under the FHA, other state and federal statutes, and common-law causes of action. The district court granted the KPM defendants' motion to dismiss all Francis's claims pursuant to Fed. R. Civ. P. 12(b)(6). A divided Second Circuit panel reversed; rehearing en banc was ordered.]

II. DISCUSSION

I. Housing Discrimination Under the FHA

When, as here, a plaintiff brings a claim under the FHA that does not rest on direct evidence of landlord discrimination, we analyze the claim under the familiar *McDonnell Douglas* burden-shifting framework first developed in Title VII cases. Plaintiffs have specific, "reduced" pleading burdens in cases subject to the *McDonnell Douglas* analysis. For a plaintiff's claim to survive a motion to dismiss in a *McDonnell Douglas* case, he must plausibly allege that he "[1] is a member of a protected class, . . . [2] suffered an adverse . . . action, and [3] has at least minimal support for the proposition that the [housing provider] was motivated by discriminatory intent."

We conclude that the factual allegations in Francis's Complaint do not suffice to carry his modest burden. Although Francis has claimed that he is a member of a protected class, his Complaint lacks even "minimal support for the proposition" that the KPM Defendants were motivated by discriminatory intent. The Complaint alleges, in a conclusory fashion, only that the "KPM Defendants have intervened against other tenants at Kings Park Manor regarding non-race-related violations of their leases or of the law." But because the Complaint does not provide enough information to compare the events of which Francis complains to the KPM Defendants' responses to other violations, there is no factual basis to plausibly infer that the KPM Defendants' conduct with regard to Francis was motivated by racial animus.

This case raises questions of exceptional importance because the panel's ruling, if undisturbed, would significantly expand landlord liability, with the probable result of fundamentally restructuring the landlord-tenant relationship.

To hold that Francis has plausibly pleaded discriminatory intent on these facts would be to indulge the speculative inference that "because the KPM Defendants did something with regard to some incident involving some tenant at some past point," racial animus explains the failure to intervene here. Francis does not allege that the KPM Defendants regularly intervened in other disputes among tenants, much less that it had a practice of addressing tenant-on-tenant harassment when the matter did not involve an African American victim and a white harasser. Francis's vague allegation that the "KPM Defendants have intervened against other tenants . . . regarding non-race-related violations of their leases" could refer to efforts to collect rent, stop unauthorized subletting, or remedy improper alterations to the rental premises. Only untethered speculation supports an inference of racial animus on the part of the KPM Defendants. We decline to engage in such speculation.

In an apparent attempt to avoid the obligation to plead facts that plausibly support an inference that the KPM Defendants were motivated by racial animus, Francis asserts that his allegations establish that the KPM Defendants intentionally discriminated against him under a deliberate indifference theory of liability. This theory of liability has been applied almost exclusively in custodial environments such as public schools and prisons, where it is clear that the defendant has both "substantial control over the context in which harassment occurs" and "a custodial [power over the harasser] . . . permitting a degree of supervision and control that could not be exercised over free adults." Francis argues that a landlord may be held liable for intentional discrimination if the landlord "ignore[d] the known discriminatory harassment of a third party." We assume, for purposes of this appeal, that deliberate indifference may be used to establish liability under the FHA when a plaintiff plausibly alleges that the defendant exercised substantial control over the context in which the harassment occurs and over the harasser. Nevertheless, we hold that Francis has failed to state a claim because his Complaint provides no factual basis to infer that the KPM Defendants had "substantial control over [Endres] and the context in which the known harassment occur[red]." Nor can such control be reasonably presumed to exist in the typically arms-length relationship between landlord and tenant, unlike the custodial environments of schools and prisons. The typical powers of a landlord over a tenant — such as the power to evict — do not establish the substantial control necessary to state a deliberate indifference claim under the FHA. Francis's appeal to the employment context to support his theory of liability for landlords under the FHA is also unavailing. He argues that since employers are responsible for employee-on-employee harassment under Title VII, landlords must be responsible for tenant-on-tenant harassment under similarly worded provisions of the FHA. But the employer-employee relationship differs from the landlord-tenant relationship in important ways. Employees are considered agents of their employer. And a landlord's control over tenants and their premises is typically far less than an employer's control over "free adult[]" employees and their workspaces. We are hard-pressed to presume that an employer's manner and degree of control over its agent-employees is equivalent to that of a landlord over its tenants.

Contrary to the views of the dissenters, we draw no inferences against Francis, nor do we hold his Complaint to a "probability" standard or otherwise heighten his pleading burden. Rather, we conclude as a matter of law that the ordinary powers of a landlord do not establish the substantial control over tenants necessary to impose liability on landlords under the FHA for tenant-on-tenant conduct. Here, Francis simply fails to allege — either plausibly or implausibly — that the KPM Defendants had extraordinary power over tenants. Francis therefore fails to allege a necessary element of his FHA claim.

As the panel dissenter explained, "an employee is considered an agent of the employer while the tenant is not considered an agent of the landlord" and "employers . . . exert far more control over not only their employees, but also the entire workplace environment than do landlords over their tenants and the residences those tenants quite literally call their own." The Supreme Court has observed that the workplace is generally characterized by "[p]roximity and regular contact" among employers, supervisors, and employees.

Most employers have ready access to, effective control over, and the ability to move within, the physical workplace and can freely dismiss at-will employees. Employers typically can, and generally do, "monitor employees" as well as use a wide range of tools to adequately "investigate . . . misconduct" (including mandatory interviews and other means of gathering information) and "remediate . . . misconduct" (including suspension, compensation reduction, demotion, transfer, training, and dismissal), all of which gives employers extensive and reliable control over employee behavior. Accordingly, this Court has recognized employer liability for the actions of non-employees under Title VII only where "(1) the employer exercises a high degree of control over the behavior of the non-employee, and (2) the employer's own negligence permits or facilitates that non-employee's discrimination."

A landlord may well have contractual liabilities to tenants resulting from the acts of third parties, but these are typically satisfied by appropriate contractual remedies like rent abatement.

To hold the KPM Defendants liable for Endres's conduct on the facts alleged would also be inconsistent with the background tort principles against which the FHA was enacted. The Supreme Court has been clear that when Congress creates "a species of tort liability," as it did in enacting the FHA, Congress "legislates against a legal background of ordinary tort-related . . . liability rules" which it presumptively "intends its legislation to incorporate." Under New York law, landlords have a duty "to take reasonable precautionary measures to protect members of the public from the reasonably foreseeable criminal acts of third persons . . . on the premises." But New York tort law has long been clear that a landlord has no general duty to protect tenants even from "the criminal acts of yet another tenant, since it cannot be said that [a] landlord ha[s] the ability or a reasonable opportunity to control [the offending tenant]" and the "power to evict cannot be said to . . . furnish" such control.

[L]andlords cannot be presumed to have substantial control over tenants without allegations of unusual circumstances. Francis alleges no facts suggesting that KPM's relationship with its tenants was in any way atypical. The lease terms identified by the dissent to support an inference of substantial control (terms forbidding tenants from impairing the "rights, comforts or conveniences" of other tenants) are unremarkable, and do not suggest the existence of a special "arsenal of incentives and sanctions" reasonably attributable to KPM.

It is true that the Seventh Circuit, in Wetzel v. Glen St. Andrew Living Cmty., LLC (7th Cir. 2018), has recognized a deliberate indifference theory of liability for a claim of discrimination under the FHA. But, unlike in this case, the plaintiff's allegations in *Wetzel* gave rise to the plausible inference that the defendant-landlord had unusual supervisory control over both the premises and the harassing tenants.[32] Moreover, as the panel dissenter observed, the landlord in *Wetzel*, unlike the KPM Defendants, was alleged to have

---

32. [Fn. 40 in original] *See Wetzel* (defendant landlord ran a "living community" for senior citizens with "a common living area, a common dining area, common laundry facilities, and

affirmatively acted against the plaintiff. In the absence of any factual allegations suggesting that the KPM Defendants had a similarly unusual degree of control over the premises and tenants, or actively facilitated or compounded harm to Francis, the Seventh Circuit's decision in *Wetzel* does not suggest, much less compel, a different outcome here.

As a final matter, we note that even if Francis had plausibly pleaded that the KPM Defendants had substantial control over Endres, he would still have failed to state an FHA claim for discrimination under a deliberate indifference theory. To state a deliberate indifference claim, a plaintiff must plausibly plead that the defendant's response to harassment by a third party was "clearly unreasonable in light of the known circumstances." It cannot be said that the KPM Defendants' inaction was "clearly unreasonable" in light of the circumstances described in Francis's Complaint. The KPM Defendants were aware that the police were involved, and indeed, the police conducted an investigation that ultimately led to Endres's arrest and prosecution.[33] We therefore have no factual basis to infer that the KPM Defendants clearly acted unreasonably.[34]

We think that our decision today coheres with the aims of those who are concerned about mounting housing costs for renters and increasing risks of housing loss for some of the most vulnerable among us. The alternative pleading standard proposed by Francis would generate considerable uncertainty about the scope of a landlord's responsibility for tenant behavior. The prophylactic measures by which landlords would manage the ensuing uncertainty would come at a cost, one that would almost certainly be borne, in one form or another, by current and prospective renters.[35]

---

hallways" and had a demonstrated capacity to restrict tenants' access to common spaces, suspend cleaning services, assign dining locations, and enter private apartments).

33. [Fn. 44 in original] Although "[l]andlords have a common-law duty to take minimal precautions to protect tenants from foreseeable harm, including foreseeable criminal conduct by a third person," courts have been careful to avoid imposing standards of conduct that would effectively make the landlord an arm of law enforcement. Scholars have also warned that broad liability regimes might place landlords in the role of "cops" who threaten their tenants with "unrestrained vigilantism." *See* B. A. Glesner, *Landlords as Cops: Tort, Nuisance & Forfeiture Standards Imposing Liability on Landlords for Crime on the Premises*, 42 Case W. L. Rev. 679, 791 (1992).

34. [Fn. 45 in original] To be clear, we both (1) decline to apply a deliberate indifference theory of liability under the FHA in the circumstances of this case because there were no factual allegations to suggest that the KPM Defendants exercised substantial control over Endres; and (2) decline to infer discriminatory intent from the KPM Defendants' alleged deliberate indifference to Francis's reports of harassment. Had Francis plausibly alleged that KPM's inaction occurred against a backdrop of consistently exercised control over tenants in roughly comparable circumstances, it might be reasonable to infer that the KPM Defendants intended Endres's race-based harassment of Francis to occur. Instead, Francis alleges only that KPM intervened, with unspecified frequency and forcefulness, to address other unspecified violations of leases or of the law. Such allegations are insufficient as a matter of law to give rise to the inference that the KPM Defendants intended discrimination to occur.

35. [Fn. 47 in original] Specifically, under the alternative proposed by Francis, tenants would conceivably bear rent increases (or suffer lower quality housing) that reflect the costs of enforcing antidiscrimination protocols, such as by hiring security staff. Further, prospective

We accordingly affirm the District Court's dismissal of Francis's intentional discrimination claim under the FHA pursuant to Rule 12(b)(6).

Raymond J. LOHIER, JR., Circuit Judge, joined by Rosemary S. Pooler, Robert A. Katzmann, Denny Chin, and Susan L. Carney, Circuit Judges, dissenting in part and concurring in part:

This appeal asks us principally to consider whether a tenant has plausibly alleged that his landlord is liable for intentional discrimination . . . for refusing to address what it knew was an extended campaign of racial terror carried out against the tenant by another tenant. Worse still, the landlord had acted against other tenants to redress prior, non-race-related issues in the past.

Given the clear text and broad legislative intent to stamp out racial discrimination that anchors the FHA and related federal and state statutes, the straightforward answer to the question before us should have favored the harassed tenant, Donahue Francis, the plaintiff in this case. In my view, Francis's complaint clearly satisfies the very minimal burden for pleading discriminatory intent that we have until today imposed. But the majority instead favors the landlord. It does so on the narrow ground that Francis failed to allege facts that might lead a reasonable juror to decide that the landlord's inaction was motivated by race. And it does so even though the majority opinion itself assumes a landlord may be liable for being deliberately indifferent to the general circumstances Francis alleges. With no change in law or circumstance, without reason or justification, the majority raises the pleading bar imposed on victims of racial discrimination in this Circuit. By requiring Francis at the very start of his case to plead more than he has, the Court closes the door to a legitimate claim of housing discrimination.

BACKGROUND

We accept as true the allegations of harassment in the complaint, together with the documents incorporated by reference therein. They tell a story that remains too common today.

In 2010 Francis signed a rental lease agreement with [KPM]. The lease provided that Francis "shall peaceably and quietly have, hold and enjoy the Premises during the term of this Lease," and required that "Tenant . . . not allow or commit any objectionable or disorderly conduct . . . that disturbs or interferes with the rights, comforts or conveniences of other residents." Francis then moved into an apartment unit of a complex owned by KPM and managed by Corrine Downing (together with KPM, the "KPM Defendants").

---

and current renters would confront more restrictive leases rife with in terrorem clauses, intensified tenant screening procedures, and intrusions into their dealings with neighbors, all of which could result in greater hostility and danger, even culminating in (or beginning with) unwarranted evictions. Our holding should also be of special interest to those concerned with the evolution of surveillance by state actors or by those purporting to act at their direction.

Starting in February 2012, Raymond Endres, Francis's next-door neighbor, began a relentless campaign of racial and religious harassment, abuse, and threats. Among other things, Endres repeatedly called Francis, who is African American, a "fucking n*****" and complained about "fucking Jews," including while Francis was in his apartment with his front door open and in the parking lot of the apartment complex. On March 10, Francis overheard Endres and another tenant discussing Francis "in derogatory terms." The next day, Endres approached Francis's open front door, repeatedly called him a "n*****," and then stated, "fucking n*****, close your god-darn door, fucking lazy, god-damn fucking n*****." On at least one occasion in May, Endres even told Francis, "I oughta kill you, you fucking n*****." On yet another occasion that month, Endres approached Francis, who was leaving his apartment, and said, "keep your door closed you fucking n*****." In August, Endres called Francis a "fucking n*****" and a "black bastard." And on September 2, Endres stood in Francis's open front door and photographed the interior of Francis's apartment.

Needless to say, Francis was terrified. He felt "unwelcome in his own home" and "uncomfortable walking in the common areas at Kings Park Manor." In response, Francis repeatedly contacted the KPM Defendants, as well as the police. His first call to the police on March 11 prompted Suffolk County Police Hate Crimes Unit officers to visit the KPM apartment complex, interview witnesses, and warn Endres to stop threatening Francis with racial epithets. That same day Francis also filed a police report, and a police officer told the KPM Defendants about Endres's conduct. The KPM Defendants did nothing.

In May 2012 Francis called the police again and filed another police report. This time, by certified letter dated May 23, 2012, Francis notified the KPM Defendants directly about Endres's racist conduct between March and May 2012. That letter reported Endres for "racial harassment," and for making "racial slurs to [Francis]," and provided contact information for the Suffolk County police officers responsible for investigating Endres. Again, the KPM Defendants failed to respond at all.

Endres's conduct persisted. His escalating racial threats to Francis finally prodded the Suffolk County Police Department to arrest Endres on August 10, 2012 for aggravated harassment in violation of New York Penal Law §240.30. That same day, Francis sent a second certified letter to the KPM Defendants. It informed the KPM Defendants that Endres continued to direct racial slurs at Francis and "anti-semitic, derogatory slurs against Jewish people." It also disclosed that Endres had recently been arrested for harassment.

After Endres attempted to photograph Francis's apartment on September 2, Francis contacted the police. The following day he sent the KPM Defendants a third and final certified letter complaining about Endres's continued racial harassment. When it received the letter, KPM advised Downing "not to get involved." So the KPM Defendants again declined to respond or follow up on Francis's complaints, even though they had previously "intervened against other tenants at Kings Park Manor regarding non-race-related violations of their leases or of the law." As a result, Endres lived at the apartment complex without any warning, reprimand, or so much as a word from the KPM Defendants until his lease expired in January 2013.

That month, Endres moved out of his apartment. A few months later, in April 2013, Endres pleaded guilty to harassment in violation of New York Penal Law §240.26(1). That same month, the State court entered an order of protection prohibiting him from contacting Francis.

DISCUSSION

I. The FHA

B. Pleading Standards: Intentional Discrimination

Francis's complaint plainly asserts that the KPM Defendants engaged in intentional racial discrimination. To start, the KPM Defendants are generally alleged to have "discriminat[ed] against [Francis] by tolerating and/or facilitating a hostile environment." As factual support for this proposition, the complaint specifically alleges that KPM had the authority to "counsel, discipline, or evict [Endres] due to his continued harassment of [Francis]." Indeed, the complaint alleges, the defendants had "intervened against other tenants at Kings Park Manor regarding non-race-related violations of their leases or of the law." This suggests not only a material level of control over their tenants, but also that the KPM Defendants decided whether to intervene in tenant-related disputes "based on race."

While contesting the adequacy of Francis's complaint, the majority opinion leaves largely unchallenged the allegation that the KPM Defendants were aware of the hostile housing environment created by Endres's criminal racial harassment. Relying on the *McDonnell Douglas* evidentiary framework, however, it holds that the complaint "lacks even minimal support for the proposition that the KPM Defendants were motivated by discriminatory intent." In particular, the majority labels as "conclusory" Francis's assertion that "[a]ccording to the New York State Division of Human Rights Investigator's File, the KPM Defendants have intervened against other tenants at Kings Park Manor regarding non-race-related violations of their leases or of the law" — the allegation that best suggests the defendants' racially selective enforcement of lease violations.

The majority's attack on Francis's pleading is flawed for at least two basic reasons. First, it overlooks the fact that a plaintiff's pleading (rather than evidentiary) burden in FHA cases is minimal. It confuses plausibility with probability. In the pre-acquisition context, we do not even require evidence that non-protected-class members were treated more favorably than members of the protected class to establish a prima facie case. Second, the majority misapplies the pleading standard set out in *Ashcroft v. Iqbal* and *Twombly* by demanding significantly more than the short and plain statement of the claim under Rule 8 of the Fed.R.Civ.P. The majority faults Francis for failing to "provide enough information"—thereby conceding that he provided some—"to compare the events of which Francis complains to the KPM Defendants' responses to other violations."

Under the correct application of these pleading standards, Francis has provided at least "minimal support for the proposition" that the KPM Defendants' refusal to intervene was motivated by race. The majority worries that this view and "the panel's ruling, if undisturbed, would significantly expand landlord liability" with "the probable result of fundamentally restructuring the landlord-tenant relationship." But if that is true, how to explain that not one landlord or landlord advocacy group submitted an amicus brief denouncing the panel majority opinion or supporting the KPM Defendants? Why was the only amicus brief from a landlord in this case filed in support of Francis? Ultimately, the majority disparages the congressionally determined balance between landlords and tenants on matters of racial equality as reflected in the FHA itself. In my view, our judicial role is to enforce that balance, whether we like it or not.

C. Pleading Standards: Deliberate Indifference

Francis argues that he separately alleged KPM's deliberate indifference to complaints of race-based harassment. I agree.

We have explained that a defendant's deliberate indifference to racial harassment serves as "proof of racially discriminatory intent." That is because deliberate indifference consists of "a deliberate choice among various alternatives, rather than negligence or bureaucratic inaction." Thus, "deliberate indifference to [known] harassment can be viewed as discrimination by [defendants] themselves." As with other civil rights statutes, deliberate indifference is a theory of liability for a discrimination claim under the FHA.

The elements of a claim of deliberate indifference to a third party's harassment are straightforward: (1) the defendant had substantial control over the harasser, (2) the harassment was severe and discriminatory, (3) the defendant had actual knowledge of the harassment, and (4) the defendant's response was clearly unreasonable.

Francis satisfied each of these elements on any fair reading of his complaint. First, Francis explicitly alleged that the KPM Defendants "exercise[d] substantial control over both the harasser and the context in which the known harassment occur[red]." Specifically, he alleged that Endres's lease with KPM authorized KPM to "counsel, discipline, or evict [Endres] due to his continued harassment of [Francis]." He also alleged that Endres's racial harassment was not just severe but criminal. Finally, the KPM Defendants knew that racial harassment had occurred, yet they deliberately declined to do anything about it.

The majority disputes only that Francis's pleading satisfies the first element, that KPM could exercise substantial control over Endres, or that it satisfies the final element, that KPM's response to the harassment in this case was inadequate. I address each of these elements in turn on the assumption that they involve New York law.

1. The Landlord's Substantial Control

As an initial matter, Francis satisfied the substantial control element by alleging that the KPM Defendants could have exercised substantial control over and even evicted Endres under its lease. [According to the New York State Division of Human Rights, the KPM Defendants previously had "intervened against other tenants at Kings Park Manor regarding non-race-related violations of their leases or of the law.] The KPM Defendants' prior interventions, if true, plausibly suggest that the KPM Defendants retained the power to discipline tenants for violating the terms of their leases.

Determining the actual degree of a landlord's control turns principally on the terms of the tenant's lease, the rights and obligations imposed by state law on landlords and tenants, and the landlord's prior history of remedial action, all with the understanding that the landlord need not have "[c]ontrol in the absolute sense." It depends, in other words, on facts and circumstances developed in discovery.

Here, even assuming that Francis's allegations themselves do not adequately support a plausible inference that the KPM Defendants could exercise control over Endres in the circumstances of this case, then the lease between KPM and both Endres and Francis "nudges" his claim of landlord control over the plausibility line. The lease provides, for example, that the "Tenant shall not allow or commit any objectionable or disorderly conduct . . . that disturbs or interferes with the rights, comforts or conveniences of other residents." The lease thus points to that "arsenal of incentives and sanctions that" the KPM Defendants could have applied to affect Endres's conduct but failed to use.

New York's warranty of habitability, under which landlords warrant that "tenants are not subjected to any conditions endangering or detrimental to their life, health or safety," also persuades me that KPM could have responded to Endres's criminal harassment—because it was affirmatively obligated to do so. Regardless of a lease's terms, New York law requires landlords to take "minimal precautions to protect tenants from foreseeable harm, including a third party's foreseeable criminal conduct."

For the reasons already explained, landlords in New York may be obligated to respond to complaints of severe or pervasive tenant-on-tenant harassment, regardless of whether that harassment is motivated by discrimination. "Depending on the particular circumstances, a landlord's appropriate remedial actions may include warning the offending tenant, involving agencies with expertise investigating charges of discrimination in housing . . . , or—if less drastic action proves ineffective—beginning formal eviction proceedings." "The mere reminder that eviction . . . [i]s a possibility might . . . deter[] some of the bad behavior" directed at fellow tenants. In the alternative, landlords can investigate tenant complaints and issue fines. Although the FHA provides important additional remedies where a landlord neglects those obligations with discriminatory impact, the fact remains that land-lords already bear responsibility to address severe or pervasive harassment. Explicitly recognizing FHA liability in this context places no additional administrative burden on landlords.

2. The Adequacy of the Landlord's Response

As noted, the majority also concludes that Francis failed to allege that KPM's response to Endres's harassment was inadequate, as our precedent on delib-erate indifference requires. The majority first says that the complaint alleged only that the "landlord failed to respond to reports of race-based harassment by a fellow tenant." To the contrary, the complaint alleged much more: a land-lord ignored repeated requests to take action against a tenant who engaged in criminal harassment. The majority then accepts that KPM instructed Downing "not to get involved" in response to Francis's repeated letters asking KPM to address Endres's criminal behavior. Nevertheless, the majority summar-ily asserts, because "[t]he KPM Defendants were aware that the police were involved" there is "no factual basis to infer that the KPM Defendants clearly acted unreasonably." This defense draws all relevant inferences in favor of the KPM Defendants, not Francis.

As New York City explains [in an amicus brief filed in support of the plain-tiff], landlords in fact enjoy significant "flexibility" to "respond to known [tenant-on-tenant] harassment in a manner that is not clearly unreasonable" in light of the known circumstances. Whether KPM's explicit instruction not to act was "clearly unreasonable," or whether KPM's awareness that Francis had reported Endres to the police absolved KPM of liability for its inaction, depends on the actual degree of control exercised by the landlord rather than a fixed rule. It is for a jury, not judges, to decide.

IV. Final Considerations

Offering a final justification for its flawed reading of Francis's complaint under the FHA and the remaining statutes at issue in this case, the majority suggests that its ruling will help "the most vulnerable among us." In reality, it will do no such thing, and not a single feature of the majority's interpreta-tion reflects such a concern. The experts—amici here—who so aptly describe what serves their clients' interests tell a far different story. If anything, they suggest, the consequences of the majority opinion's holding will harm those most in need. Tenant-on-tenant sexual harassment in housing, for example, is a widespread problem that "[p]rompt and appropriate responses by housing providers to tenant complaints of harassment are critical to preventing—or stopping." "Absent liability under the FHA," another amicus explains, "land-lords receiving complaints of harassment may ignore the discrimination . . . or even worse, they may further the discrimination by retaliating against the complainant," thereby causing "harmful escalations."

In contrast, the Seventh Circuit (in a case referenced in *Francis*) held that the facts supported holding a housing provider liable for the harassment of one tenant by another.

Wetzel v. Glen St. Andrew Living Community, LLC
901 F.3d 856 (7th Cir. 2018)

Before Wood, Chief Judge, and Kanne and Hamilton, Circuit Judges.

Wood, Chief Judge:

I

After her partner of 30 years died, Wetzel moved into St. Andrew, a residential community for older adults; she continues to live there today. Her tenancy, presumably like that of St. Andrew's other residents, is governed by a form Tenant's Agreement ("Agreement"). Beyond a private apartment, the Agreement guarantees three meals daily served in a central location, access to a community room, and use of laundry facilities. It conditions tenancy at St. Andrew on refraining from "activity that [St. Andrew] determines unreasonably interferes with the peaceful use and enjoyment of the community by other tenants" or that is "a direct threat to the health and safety of other individuals." It also requires compliance with the "Tenant Handbook," which may "be amended from time to time." The Agreement authorizes St. Andrew to institute eviction proceedings against a tenant in breach, and if St. Andrew prevails, the breaching tenant must also reimburse St. Andrew for its attorney's fees. (Indeed, the Agreement requires reimbursement of St. Andrew's fees related to an alleged violation or breach even if suit has not been instituted.)

After arriving at St. Andrew, Wetzel spoke openly to staff and other residents about her sexual orientation. She was met with intolerance from many of them. The following is just a sample of what Wetzel has alleged that she endured. At this early stage of the litigation, we accept her account as true, recognizing that St. Andrew will have the right to contest these assertions at a trial.

Beginning a few months after Wetzel moved to St. Andrew and continuing at least until she filed this suit (a 15-month period), residents repeatedly berated her for being a "fucking dyke," "fucking faggot," and "homosexual bitch." One resident, Robert Herr, told Wetzel that he reveled in the memory of the Orlando massacre at the Pulse nightclub, derided Wetzel's son for being a "homosexual-raised faggot," and threatened to "rip [Wetzel's] tits off." Herr was the primary, but not sole, culprit. Elizabeth Rivera told Wetzel that "homosexuals will burn in hell."

There was physical abuse too. Wetzel depends on a motorized scooter. Herr at one time rammed his walker into Wetzel's scooter forcefully enough to knock her off a ramp. Rivera bashed her wheelchair into a dining table that

Wetzel occupied, flipping the table on top of Wetzel. In yet another incident, Wetzel was struck in the back of the head while alone in the mailroom; the blow was hard enough to push her from her scooter, and she suffered a bump on her head and a black eye. She did not see the assailant, but the person said "homo" when attacking her. Following this mugging, Herr taunted Wetzel, rubbing his head and saying "ouch." Wetzel also had two abusive trips in the elevator. During the first, Rivera spat on her and hurled slurs. During the second, Wetzel, Herr, and another resident, Audrey Chase, were together in the elevator when Herr again hit Wetzel's scooter with his walker.

Wetzel routinely reported the verbal and physical abuse to St. Andrew's staff, including Carolyn Driscoll, Sandra Cubas, and Alyssa Flavin (the "management defendants"). Wetzel's initial complaints won her a brief respite, prompting her to draft a thank-you note. But the management defendants, among whom we need not distinguish for purposes of this appeal, otherwise were apathetic. They told Wetzel not to worry about the harassment, dismissed the conduct as accidental, denied Wetzel's accounts, and branded her a liar. Wetzel's social worker accompanied her to one meeting about the harassment; despite that, the managers denounced Wetzel as dishonest.

Had the management defendants done nothing but listen, we might have a more limited case. But they took affirmative steps to retaliate against Wetzel for her complaints. For example, they relegated Wetzel to a less desirable dining room location after she notified them about being trampled by Rivera. Following other complaints, they barred her from the lobby except to get coffee and they halted her cleaning services, thus depriving her of access to areas specifically protected in the Agreement. They falsely accused Wetzel of smoking in her room in violation of St. Andrew's policy. Early one morning, two staff members woke Wetzel up and again accused her of smoking in her room. When she said that she had been sleeping, one of them slapped her across the face. One month, Wetzel did not receive the customary rent-due notice, though other tenants did. She remembered to pay on time, but she had to pry a receipt from management.

In response, Wetzel changed her daily routine. She ate meals in her room, forgoing those included as part of the Agreement. She stopped visiting the third floor of St. Andrew, where Herr lived. She did not use the laundry room at hours when she might be alone. And she stayed away from the common spaces from which she had been barred by management.

Eventually Wetzel brought this action against the management defendants and the entities that own and operate St. Andrew (the "corporate defendants"). Unless the distinction matters, we refer to the group collectively as defendants or St. Andrew. She alleged that St. Andrew failed to ensure a nondiscriminatory living environment. . . . [The complaint also alleged retaliation and related state law claims.]

All of the defendants moved for dismissal, contending that the FHA does not make a landlord accountable for failing to stop tenant-on-tenant harassment unless the landlord's inaction was animated by discriminatory animus. [The district court agreed and dismissed Wetzel's suit. She appealed.]

II

A

Under 42 U.S.C. §3604(b), it is unlawful "[t]o discriminate against any person in the terms, conditions, or privileges of sale or rental of a dwelling, or in the provision of services or facilities in connection therewith, because of race, color, religion, sex, familial status, or national origin." In addition, the Act makes it unlawful "to coerce, intimidate, threaten, or interfere with any person in the exercise or enjoyment of . . . any right granted or protected by section . . . 3604 . . . of this title." 42 U.S.C. §3617. Among other things, these sections prohibit discriminatory harassment that unreasonably interferes with the use and enjoyment of a home—by another name, a hostile housing environment.

A hostile-housing-environment claim requires a plaintiff to show that: (1) she endured unwelcome harassment based on a protected characteristic; (2) the harassment was severe or pervasive enough to interfere with the terms, conditions, or privileges of her residency, or in the provision of services or facilities; and (3) that there is a basis for imputing liability to the defendant.

B

We [now move] to the second element of the case: whether the harassment from which Wetzel suffered was severe or pervasive enough to interfere with her enjoyment of her dwelling. Harassment is severe or pervasive if it objectively interferes with the enjoyment of the premises or inhibits the privileges of rental. That standard requires us to consider the totality of the circumstances, including the frequency of the discriminatory conduct, its severity, and whether it is physically threatening or humiliating rather than merely offensive. There is no "magic number of instances" that must be endured before an environment becomes so hostile that the occupant's right to enjoyment of her home has been violated. While isolated minor affronts are not enough, either a small number of "severe episode[s]" or a "relentless pattern of lesser harassment" may suffice.

Though it need be only one or the other, the harassment Wetzel describes plausibly can be viewed as both severe and pervasive. For 15 months, she was bombarded with threats, slurs, derisive comments about her family, taunts about a deadly massacre, physical violence, and spit. The defendants dismiss this litany of abuse as no more than ordinary "squabbles" and "bickering" between "irascible," "crotchety senior resident[s]." A jury would be entitled to see the story otherwise. (We confess to having trouble seeing the act of throwing an elderly person out of a motorized scooter as one of the ordinary problems of life in a senior facility.) Wetzel has presented far more than "a simple quarrel between two neighbors or [an] isolated act of harassment."

C

That takes us to the main event: Is there a basis to impute liability to St. Andrew for the hostile housing environment? This question is new to our circuit. Our response begins, as it must, with the text of the statute. Again, 42 U.S.C. §3604(b) makes it unlawful "[t]o discriminate . . . because of . . . sex," and 42 U.S.C. §3617 forbids a housing provider to "interfere with any person in the exercise or enjoyment of . . . any right granted or protected by section . . . 3604 . . . of this title." The focus on the actor rather than the benefitted class, St. Andrew deduces, confines the world of possible defendants under these sections to those accused of carrying discriminatory animus. But St. Andrew relies on language defining the substantive contours of an FHA action to ascertain a landlord's potential liability for actionable abuse—in other words, it is looking at what is prohibited, not who is subject to those prohibitions. As the Supreme Court's cases in analogous areas demonstrate, the questions are different. True, a sex-harassment claim under the FHA demands sex-based discrimination, but Wetzel has alleged such discrimination. On its face, the Act does not address who may be liable when sex-based discrimination occurs or under what circumstances.

Because the text of the FHA does not spell out a test for landlord liability, we look to analogous anti-discrimination statutes for guidance. One natural point of reference is Title VII, which governs discrimination in employment. It and the FHA have been described as "functional equivalent[s]" to be "given like construction and application." The Supreme Court's interpretation of Title VII's parallel section is illuminating. That section makes it unlawful "to discriminate against any individual . . . because of . . . sex." Under operative language in Title VII identical to that of the 42 U.S.C. §3604(b), an employer may be liable under some circumstances when its own negligence is a cause of prohibited harassment. Indeed, "when Congress uses the same language in two statutes having similar purposes, particularly when one is enacted shortly after the other, it is appropriate to presume that Congress intended that text to have the same meaning in both statutes." The FHA followed Title VII by four years. St. Andrew provides no reason why the FHA requires in all instances that the defendant acted with discriminatory animus when an identically worded statute has not been read in such a manner. As a textual matter, we see none.

We recognize, however, that there are some potentially important differences between the relationship that exists between an employer and an employee, in which one is the agent of the other, and that between a landlord and a tenant, in which the tenant is largely independent of the landlord. We thus refrain from reflexively adopting the Title VII standard and continue our search for comparable situations.

That takes us to Title IX of the Education Amendments of 1972. Like the FHA and Title VII, Title IX aims to eradicate sex-based discrimination from a sector of society—education. The Supreme Court has held that Title IX supports a private right of action on the part of a person who experiences sex discrimination in an education program or activity receiving federal financial aid. In *Davis v. Monroe County Board of Education*, the Court confronted the question whether a school district's "failure to respond to student-on-student harassment in its schools can support a private suit for money damages." Because Title IX was enacted pursuant to the Spending Clause, private damages were available against a funding recipient only if it had adequate notice of its potential liability. Applying that limiting principle, the Court held that the district could be held accountable only for its own misconduct. But that is just what the *Davis* plaintiff was trying to do. As the Court put it, "petitioner attempts to hold the Board liable for its own decision to remain idle in the face of known student-on-student harassment in its schools." Indeed, the district itself subjected the plaintiff to discrimination by remaining "deliberately indifferent to known acts of student-on-student sexual harassment [when] the harasser is under the school's disciplinary authority." It emphasized that the recipient of funds exercised substantial control over both the harasser and the premises on which the misconduct took place.

Much of what the Court said in *Davis* can be applied readily to the housing situation. In *Davis*, the fund recipient's own misconduct subjected the student to actionable sex-based harassment. Here, we need look only to the management defendants themselves, asking whether they had actual knowledge of the severe harassment Wetzel was enduring and whether they were deliberately indifferent to it. If so, they subjected Wetzel to conduct that the FHA forbids. (We say nothing about the situation in a setting that more closely resembles custodial care, such as a skilled nursing facility, or an assisted living environment, or a hospital. Any of those are different enough that they should be saved for another day.) Wetzel may be in unchartered territory, but the Supreme Court's interpretation of analogous anti-discrimination statutes satisfies us that her claim against St. Andrew is covered by the Act.

D

St. Andrew offers several reasons why, in its view, we should not adopt the analysis we have just laid out. We respond to the most important points. It argues that there is no agency or custodial relationship between a landlord and tenant, and from that it reasons that a landlord has no duty to protect its tenants from discriminatory harassment. But we have not gone that far: we have said only that the duty not to discriminate in housing conditions encompasses the duty not to permit known harassment on protected grounds. The landlord does have responsibility over the common areas of the building, which is where the majority of Wetzel's harassment took place. And the incidents within her apartment occurred precisely because the landlord was exercising a right to enter. More broadly, St. Andrew has a statutory duty not to discriminate. As the Supreme Court said [in *Curtis v. Loether* (1974)], the FHA "defines a new legal duty, and authorizes the courts to compensate a plaintiff for the injury caused by the defendant's wrongful breach." The same is true of an action under Title VII or Title IX.

We need not address St. Andrew's arguments about vicarious liability, because it is irrelevant here to the management defendants' possible liability. (The Supreme Court has held already that the Act imposes vicarious liability on a corporation, but not upon its officers or owners. See Meyer v. Holley (2003).) The management defendants' liability, if any after a full trial, would be direct—the result of standing pat as Wetzel reported the barrage of harassment. Because liability is direct, "it makes no difference whether the person whose acts are complained of is an employee, an independent contractor, or for that matter a customer. . . . The genesis of inequality matters not; what does matter is how the employer handles the problem." A school district's liability under Title IX is the same.

St. Andrew complains that it would be unfair to hold it liable for actions that it was incapable of addressing, but we are doing no such thing. We have no quarrel with the idea that direct liability for inaction makes sense only if defendants had, but failed to deploy, available remedial tools. St. Andrew protests that it can only minimally affect the conduct of its tenants because tenants expect to live free from a landlord's interference.

Control in the absolute sense, however, is not required for liability. Liability attaches because a party has "an arsenal of incentives and sanctions . . . that can be applied to affect conduct" but fails to use them. St. Andrew brushes aside the many tools for remedying harassment that it has pursuant to the Agreement. For example, the Agreement allows St. Andrew to evict any tenant who "engages in acts or omissions that constitute a direct threat to the health and safety of other individuals" or who "engage[s] in any activity that [St. Andrew] determines unreasonably interferes with the peaceful use and enjoyment of the community by other tenants." The mere reminder that eviction (along with liability for attorneys' fees) was a possibility might have deterred some of the bad behavior. St. Andrew also could have updated the Tenant Handbook to clarify the anti-harassment and anti-abuse provisions. With respect to the common areas, St. Andrew could have suspended privileges for tenants who failed to abide by the anti-harassment policies, instead of taking a blame-the-victim approach.

Seeking a broader ruling, Wetzel points to a rule interpreting the FHA that HUD published in 2016. The HUD rule interprets the FHA to make a landlord directly liable for failing to "take prompt action to correct and end a discriminatory housing practice by a third party" if the landlord "knew or should have known of the discriminatory conduct and had the power to correct it." HUD's rule mirrors the scope of employee liability under Title VII for employee-on-employee harassment. We have no need, however, to rely on this rule. As we noted earlier, there are salient differences between Title VII and the FHA. In the end, it is possible that they could be overcome, but more analysis than

HUD was able to offer is necessary before we can take that step. It is enough for present purposes to say that nothing in the HUD rule stands in the way of recognizing Wetzel's theory.

It is important, too, to recognize that the facts Wetzel has presented (which we must accept at this stage) go far beyond mere rudeness, all the way to direct physical violence. This case is thus not, as St. Andrew would have it, one about good manners. Courts around the country have policed that line for years in the context of Title VII, for which they have ensured that the standard is "sufficiently demanding to ensure that Title VII does not become a general civility code," and "filter[s] out complaints attacking the ordinary tribulations of the workplace, such as the sporadic use of abusive language, gender-related jokes, and occasional teasing." We have no reason not to expect the same discipline here.

The district court's judgment is REVERSED and the case is REMANDED for further proceedings consistent with this opinion.

NOTES AND QUESTIONS

1. Assessing the Cases. Which opinion in *Francis* do you find more persuasive? Why? Do you agree with the *Francis* majority that its opinion is distinguishable from *Wetzel*? Does the *Francis* majority or dissent draw the correct line in balancing the level of landlord control over tenants and the duty to respond to race- or sex-based tenant-on-tenant harassment complaints? Should a landlord's failure to act after gaining knowledge about tenant-on-tenant harassment be categorized as intentional conduct? Negligence? Why would housing providers use lease provisions requiring that tenants adhere to standards of conduct if they are not prepared to enforce them? Should providers be shielded from FHA liability when they have the power to enforce standards to protect tenants from harm? What do you think about the argument that such liability would inevitably raise the cost of housing and ultimately hurt consumers?

Francis, although significant, might also be an outlier. A number of courts have recognized that §3604(b) claims can lie against landlords for tenant-on-tenant harassment. *See* Neudecker v. Boisclair Corp., 351 F.3d 361 (8th Cir. 2003) (holding that plaintiff stated a claim against landlord for harassment by fellow tenants); Allen v. Virgin Islands Housing Authority, Case No. 3:22-cv-0048, 2023 WL 5528566 (D.V.I. Aug. 28, 2023) (holding that plaintiff could pursue a claim against landlord for harassment by fellow tenants, but that plaintiff had failed to plead sufficient facts to support such a claim); Harris v. Vanderburg, 584 F. Supp. 3d 82 (E.D. N.C. 2022) (denying summary judgment for property owner on §3604(b) claim (among others), finding that she exercised substantial control over allegedly harassing tenant, who was also her nephew); Fair Housing Center of Central Indiana, Inc. v. New, 577 F. Supp. 3d 908 (S.D. Ind. 2021) (denying defendants' motion for summary judgment on §3604(b) claim based on harassment of tenants by neighboring homeowner); *see also* Bradley v. Carydale Enterprises, 707 F. Supp. 217 (E.D. Va. 1989) (holding that plaintiff stated a claim against landlord for racial harassment by fellow tenant under 42 U.S.C. §§1981 and 1982).

2. Employment Analogy. Is the employment analogy helpful or harmful for plaintiffs here? Note that the court in *Francis* limited FHA liability of landlords for tenants' conduct based, in part, on distinguishing the employment context, arguing that employers (who can be vicariously liable for the actions of their agent employees) exercise much more control over their employees than do landlords over their tenants. In contrast, Professor Aric Short argues that reliance on Title VII opens the door to FHA liability because it boils down to a simple negligence theory, even though the parameters of landlord control over third parties will differ from the employment context:

> [L]andlords may not ordinarily have the same powers in these areas as employers do. But it is unclear, even if this is true, why that fact should absolve landlords of the duty to act reasonably. Recognizing this FHA cause of action is not a silver bullet, and it does not impose strict liability on landlords. It is easily conceivable that landlords in some cases may not have actual or constructive knowledge of particular tenant-on-tenant harassment. Or they may acquire such knowledge and then run out of effective tools to investigate or stop the harassment. But they do have a range of options available to them for fact-gathering, remediation, and general education of the community. And in pursuit of the FHA's broad purpose to eliminate unlawful discrimination in housing, they should be required to utilize them when they have notice of unlawful harassment. The alternative—allowing landlords to sit idly by in the face of severe or pervasive harassment under their watch—is contrary to the spirit and letter of the FHA and inconsistent with parallel expectations of employers under Title VII.[36]

See also Fahnbulleh v. GFZ Realty, LLC, 795 F. Supp. 2d 360, 364 (D. Md. 2011):

> Just as employers sometimes have the ability and the duty to control the work environment to protect employees from harassment, including harassment by non-employees, landlords may also be held liable for the harassment of tenants by other tenants under certain circumstances. To hold otherwise would be to introduce an unjustified discrepancy between Title VII and Title VIII theories of harassment and discrimination. . . . [T]here is no categorical rule that

---

36. Aric Short, *Not My Problem? Landlord Liability for Tenant-On-Tenant Harassment*, 72 HASTINGS LAW J. 1227, 1273 (2021).

prevents FHA recovery for hostile-housing-environment sexual harassment based on tenant-on-tenant harassment.

3. Landlords as Cops? Note the concern in *Francis* that landlord liability for tenant-on-tenant harassment will force landlords to intrude into their tenants' lives in a manner that could interfere with the expectation of privacy that tenants have. What are the dangers here? A landlord who is overly aggressive in policing tenant conduct might alienate tenants. Worse, aggressive policing to stem harassment could ironically expose the landlord to yet more claims of harassment or discrimination, particularly if the landlord's behavior is targeted at particular groups of tenants with protected characteristics. Is it better to leave conflicts and peace disturbances to law enforcement officers? These questions are particularly salient in cases of domestic violence, where one tenant in a unit assaults another. As discussed in Chapter 15, and in contrast to the duties prevailing in *Francis*, landlords might be required to take certain actions to address tenant-on tenant-violence among cotenants, such as removing the abusing tenant from the lease. At the very least, landlords may be prohibited from discriminating *against* tenants who are victims of domestic violence.

4. Section 3604(b) and Post-Acquisition Claims

For decades, courts assumed that claims brought under §3604(b) could be brought at any stage of the housing transaction or relationship. Put another way, current tenants complaining of discriminatory treatment or harassment by their landlords could bring §3604(b) claims in the same manner as prospective tenants complaining about discriminatory terms of a proposed lease. Indeed, some types of §3604(b) claims, such as harassment or discriminatory provision of maintenance, are likely to arise *only* after a rental or sale has occurred.

However, in 2004, the Seventh Circuit issued an influential opinion, Halprin v. Prairie Single Family Homes of Dearborn Park Ass'n, 388 F.3d 327, 328-30 (7th Cir. 2004). This decision, written by Judge Richard Posner, called into question whether *current* tenants or homeowners could use §3604(b) for post-acquisition claims of discrimination, that is, for discrimination in the terms and conditions of their housing (including harassment) that occurred after they acquired it:

> The plaintiffs are a couple who own a home in a suburban subdivision. The principal defendant is the homeowners' association that manages the subdivision and provides various services to the homeowners [and the president of the association]. . . .
>
> The complaint—our only source of facts, because the suit was dismissed for failure to state a claim—alleges the following: One of the plaintiffs is Jewish. The president of the association wrote "H-town property" on a wall of the plaintiffs' property, "H-town" being short for "Hymie Town," and he further vandalized the property by damaging trees and plants and cutting down

strings of holiday lights. When the plaintiffs posted flyers offering a reward for identifying the vandal, the president destroyed or removed the flyers. To further thwart the plaintiffs' efforts to investigate the vandalizing of their property, the association destroyed minutes of its board meetings and erased a tape recording of a meeting at which the president had threatened to "make an example" of the plaintiffs. The defendants applied chemicals to the plaintiffs' yard against the plaintiffs' wishes and with adverse effects on their health and peace of mind and adopted rules restricting the plaintiffs' lawful use of their property. The entire campaign of harassment was caused or at least influenced by the religion of the Jewish plaintiff. . . .

The only one of the enumerated sections [of the FHA] that is possibly relevant here is §3604. . . . The language indicates concern with activities, such as redlining, that prevent people from acquiring property. Our plaintiffs, however, are complaining not about being prevented from acquiring property but about being harassed by other property owners. . . .

None of the five cases [discussed and involving postsale discrimination] contains a *considered* holding on the scope of the FHA in general or its application to a case like the present one in particular. . . .

The FHA [unlike Title VII] contains no hint either in its language or its legislative history of a concern with anything but access to housing. Behind the Act lay the widespread practice of refusing to sell or rent homes in desirable residential areas to members of minority groups. Since the focus was on their exclusion, the problem of how they were treated when they were included, that is, when they were allowed to own or rent homes in such areas, was not at the forefront of congressional thinking. . . .

So the plaintiffs have no claim under §3604. [EDS. — The court reversed dismissal of the §3617 claim (which covers third parties) and remanded.]

Halprin had a significant and immediate impact. A number of federal courts struck down post-acquisition claims brought by plaintiffs who complained of harassment or discrimination by homeowners' associations, landlords, municipalities, and others.[37] At the same time, other courts disagreed with this interpretation. In United States v. Koch, 352 F. Supp. 2d 970, 978 (D. Neb. 2004), the court stated:

[I]t is the Seventh Circuit's view that Congress sought to allow members of minority groups to acquire housing without facing discrimination but was not concerned with allowing such people to live in that housing without facing discrimination. I do not believe that this interpretation of the scope of the FHA is mandated by the Act's language or its legislative history. On the contrary, a broad interpretation of the FHA that encompasses post-possession acts of discrimination is consistent with the Act's language, its legislative history, and the policy "to provide . . . for fair housing throughout the United States."

See also Richards v. Bono, No. 5:04CV484-OC-10GRJ, 2005 WL 1065141, at *3 (M.D. Fla. May 2, 2005) ("Because the plain meaning of 'rental' contemplates an ongoing relationship, the use of that term in §3604(b) means that the statute

---

37. *See, e.g.,* Lawrence v. Courtyards at Deerwood Ass'n, 318 F. Supp. 2d 1133 (S.D. Fla. 2004) (claim of racially hostile environment); Farrar v. Eldibany, No. 04 C 3371, 2004 WL 2392242 (N.D. Ill. Oct. 15, 2004) (claim of landlord discrimination in services).

prohibits discrimination at any time during the landlord/tenant relationship, including after the tenant takes possession of the property.").

Commentators criticized *Halprin* as incompatible with the specific regulations put forth by HUD and the broad spirit of the FHA. As Professor Oliveri noted:

> A detailed analysis of the flaws in the reasoning behind *Halprin* should not obscure one of the most problematic aspects of the opinion: it leads to extremely anomalous results. According to *Halprin*, it would not violate §3604(b) for a condominium owners' association to prevent a disabled person from using the laundry facilities or for a landlord to refuse to provide maintenance to his Hispanic tenants. Similarly, it would not violate §3604(b) for a landlord to sexually harass a tenant or to raise the rent of only Jewish tenants. . . . All of these behaviors would be beyond the law's purview solely because of when they occurred.
>
> Most practitioners and scholars—and certainly most laypeople—would likely be alarmed to discover that the nation's remedial and comprehensive fair housing legislation had such a limited reach. And with good reason: such a regime would eviscerate nearly forty years of fair housing jurisprudence, particularly in the landlord-tenant context and would invalidate the results of hundreds of cases.[38]

Eventually, the Seventh Circuit changed course in Bloch v. Frischholz, 587 F.3d 771, 779-80 (7th Cir. 2009) (en banc). Although *Bloch* did not formally overrule *Halprin*, it limited the opinion significantly, and disavowed much of its reasoning:

> [Section] 3604(b) makes it unlawful "[t]o discriminate against any person in the terms, conditions, or privileges of sale or rental of a dwelling, or in the provision of services or facilities in connection therewith, because of race, color, religion, sex, familial status, or national origin." Again, our task is to determine whether this provision proscribes the sort of post-acquisition discrimination alleged in this case. Subsection (b)'s language is broad, mirroring Title VII, which we have held reaches both pre- and post-hiring discrimination. Nonetheless, *Halprin* found the scope of this provision more limited than Title VII, and the defendants rely on *Halprin* to argue that the FHA does not reach any claims of post-acquisition discrimination. We read *Halprin* more narrowly, however, and see two possibilities for relief in this case, only the latter of which is viable for the Blochs.
>
> Like subsection (a), constructive eviction is an option under §3604(b) as well. As we recognized in *Halprin*, the right to inhabit the premises is a "privilege of sale." Deprivation of that right by making the premises uninhabitable violates §3604(b). However . . . the Blochs have no constructive eviction claim. So this §3604(b) avenue is closed to them.
>
> But the "privilege" to inhabit the condo is not the only aspect of §3604(b) that this case implicates. The Blochs alleged discrimination by their condo association, an entity by which the Blochs agreed to be governed when they bought their units. This agreement, though contemplating future, post-sale

---

38. Rigel C. Oliveri, *Is Acquisition Everything? Protecting the Rights of Occupants Under the Fair Housing Act*, 43 HARV. C. R.-C.L. L. REV. 1, 22, 29-31, 32-33 (2008).

governance by the Association, was nonetheless a term or condition of sale that brings this case within §3604(b).

Shoreline Towers operates under a common plan or "Declaration" that sets forth the rights, easements, privileges, and restrictions subject to which condo owners take their units upon purchase. Unit owners must, for instance, pay their share of the expenses of administration, maintenance, and repair of the building's common elements. The Declaration also establishes a Board of Managers, elected by the unit owners, to oversee the administration of the building; the Declaration vests the Board with the authority to carry out this duty. For example, the Board can cause certain repairs to the common elements to be performed at a unit owner's expense. The Board may also adopt and enforce rules and regulations that it "deem[s] advisable for the maintenance, administration, management, operation, use, conservation and beautification of the Property, and for the health, comfort, safety and general welfare of the Unit Owners and Occupants of the Property." So, upon purchasing their units, the Blochs agreed to be bound by the enactments of the Board of Managers, both present and future.

This contractual connection between the Blochs and the Board distinguishes this case from *Halprin*. *Halprin* made it clear that §3604(b) is not broad enough to provide a blanket "privilege" to be free from all discrimination from any source. Plaintiffs generally cannot sue under §3604 for isolated acts of discrimination by other private property owners. Neither the FHA's text nor its legislative history indicates an intent to make "quarrels between neighbors . . . a routine basis for federal litigation." As deplorable as it might have been, the defendants' alleged conduct in *Halprin* was not linked to any of the terms, conditions, or privileges that accompanied or were related to the plaintiffs' purchase of their property. But that's what §3604(b) requires.

Here, however, the Blochs' agreement to subject their rights to the restrictions imposed by the Board was a "condition" of the Blochs' purchase; the Board's power to restrict unit owners' rights flows from the terms of the sale. And the Blochs alleged that the Board discriminated against them in wielding that power. Consequently, because the Blochs purchased dwellings subject to the condition that the Condo Association can enact rules that restrict the buyer's rights in the future, §3604(b) prohibits the Association from discriminating against the Blochs through its enforcement of the rules, even facially neutral rules.

What is left of *Halprin* after *Bloch*? The continued significance of *Halprin's* post-acquisition reasoning, if any, remains to be seen. The dissent in *Francis*, 992 F.3d at 88-89, argued in favor of holding that §3604(b) applies to post-acquisition conduct (rather than the majority's merely assuming that it did), and summarized the law as follows:

> [T]here are four reasons why widespread agreement exists on this issue.
>
> First, the text of the FHA plainly provides for coverage of post-acquisition conduct. Section 3604(b) prohibits discrimination in the "terms, conditions, or privileges of sale or rental of a dwelling, or in the provision of services or facilities in connection therewith." The words "conditions," "privileges," and "provisions of services or facilities" refer not just to the sale or rental itself, but to benefits and protections following the sale or rental. As the United States asserted at oral argument in this case, "by definition, a rental creates an ongoing legal relationship between a landlord and a tenant for a term, [and] phrases

like 'terms, conditions, or privileges' need to be interpreted using the ordinary plain language."

Second, the plain language of §3617 creates a separate cause of action that more comprehensively prohibits post-acquisition discriminatory conduct barred by §3604(b). Section 3617 makes it "unlawful to coerce, intimidate, threaten, or interfere with any person in the exercise or enjoyment of, or on account of his having exercised or enjoyed, or on account of his having aided or encouraged any other person in the exercise or enjoyment of, any right granted or protected by section . . . 3604." As the Seventh Circuit observed, "[c]oercion, intimidation, threats, or interference with or on account of a person's exercise of his or her [§3604(b)] rights can be distinct from outright violations of [§3604(b)]."

Third, any contrary interpretations of §§3604(b) and 3617 would contravene Congress's central intent to use the FHA to root out discrimination in housing.

Finally, all seven sister circuits that have addressed the issue have acknowledged that §3604(b) prohibits at least some post-acquisition conduct.

C. SECTION 3604(d): FALSE REPRESENTATIONS OF NONAVAILABILITY

Section 3604(d) makes it unlawful to "represent to any person because of [protected characteristics] that any dwelling is not available for inspection, sale, or rental when such dwelling is, in fact, so available." Courts have described this provision as creating a "right to truthful housing information." *See* Acheson Hotels, L.L.C. v. Laufer, 601 U.S. 1, 12 (2023) (Thomas, J., concurring). This can apply when a person such as a rental agent, real estate broker, or homeowner falsely informs a home seeker that a house or apartment that was advertised is no longer available. It can also apply to steering situations, where an agent, broker, or owner withholds information from a home seeker about properties that are available within their search parameters.

The broad interpretation given to §3604(a)'s "otherwise make housing unavailable" provision would seem to render §3604(d) superfluous. After all, lying to a prospective home seeker about the availability of a house or apartment is a very effective mechanism to deny that person housing. What purpose does this provision serve? As a general matter, it reflects a congressional recognition that protected access to truthful information about housing is itself an important tool to combat discrimination and segregation. As the Supreme Court has noted:

> Congress' decision to confer a broad right of truthful information concerning housing availability was undoubtedly influenced by congressional awareness that the intentional provision of misinformation offered a means of maintaining segregated housing. Various witnesses testifying before Congress recounted incidents in which black persons who sought housing were falsely informed that housing was not available.

Havens Realty Corp. v. Coleman, 455 U.S. 363, 374 n.14 (1982).

Also, as a practical matter, by providing an independent information-based cause of action, §3604(d) facilitates the use of testing. Testing involves investigation by persons who, without intention to rent or purchase, pose as prospective housing applicants and document the treatment they receive from housing providers. Usually they are assigned a tester profile and are not aware of the underlying complaint or information prompting the investigation. By comparing the ways different testers are treated, FHOs determine whether a violation of fair housing law has occurred and provide evidence to substantiate a home seeker's claims. Testing can also be used by researchers to measure the nature and incidence of housing discrimination in different markets.

Housing discrimination can be difficult for ordinary home seekers to detect. If a friendly rental agent apologetically tells a prospective tenant that the unit she came to see just got rented, the would-be tenant is likely to walk away believing what she has been told, regardless of whether the statement was true. Indeed, housing discrimination has been described as often coming "with a smile and a handshake." As one testing expert noted:

> [D]iscriminatory housing practices can be concealed by common courtesies, disguised by good manners, and obscured by inauthentic gestures of kindness. The only way to ferret out more subtle housing discrimination and ensure that housing is available and accessible to all on a non-discriminatory basis is to continually test the housing market.[39]

As a result, fair housing advocates (including the Department of Justice) have turned to testing to investigate violations of fair housing law and gather litigation-quality evidence of discriminatory practices. *See, e.g.*, Harris v. Itzhaki, 183 F.3d 1043 (9th Cir. 1999); City of Chicago v. Matchmaker Real Estate Sales Center, Inc., 982 F.2d 1086 (7th Cir. 1992); United States v. Balistrieri, 981 F.2d 916 (7th Cir. 1992) (government testing program). For a discussion of tester standing to sue for injuries resulting from violations of §3604(d), see Chapter 4.

NOTES AND QUESTIONS

1. Testing Protocols for Litigation and Research. To provide evidence useful for litigation, a test must be properly designed. Testers usually are "matched" to isolate the characteristic being tested. Thus, a test to discern discrimination based on race would feature two testers who are equally qualified and similar in all respects *except* race; often, the protected tester is slightly more qualified than the control tester. The testers must visit or make inquiries as close in time as possible, to minimize the likelihood that some other factors might account for differences in treatment. Finally, the testers must carefully

---

39. Fred Freiberg, *A Test of Our Fairness*, 41 THE URBAN LAWYER 239, 243 (Spring 2009).

document their treatment. Often, the most effective way to do this is through making a surreptitious recording; however, some jurisdictions prohibit making audio recordings without the consent of both parties. Many fair housing tests are conducted by FHOs, such as HOME in the *Havens* case. As discussed in Chapter 4, these organizations may themselves join as plaintiffs and seek compensation on the right facts as part of a "diversion of resources" and "frustration of mission" theory of damages.

In addition to being used as an investigative tool to gather evidence, testing also is an important research tool that can allow policymakers and advocates to assess how frequently different sorts of discrimination occur in various markets. HUD conducts a large-scale nationwide testing project every ten years and publishes a report of the results. At the time of this writing, the most recent report is *Housing Discrimination Against Racial and Ethnic Minorities*, published in 2012.[40] Researchers have explained the differences and similarities among the different types of tests as follows:

> The principal goals of research testing are to quantify the incidence and forms of discrimination in order to promote public understanding and identify sectors in which enforcement might be targeted. Testing for research, then, must produce generalizable results regarding discrimination for a specified unit of analysis: an industry, a metropolitan area, or the nation as a whole. To achieve these generalizable results, the tests are randomized, using an accepted sampling frame such as newspaper advertisements. Typically, research requires large numbers of tests in order to support statistically significant comparisons. To generate reliable and objective comparisons of minority and white experiences across a large number of tests, researchers usually use highly structured recording forms, with closed-ended, "check the box"-type items.
>
> By contrast, the purpose of an enforcement test is to establish legal violations and to correct them either through settlement or litigation. Testing for enforcement is often complaint driven, and is typically targeted to a single firm or a narrowly targeted set of firms. The small number of firms tested, and the reliance on targeting, limits the generalizability of enforcement testing's results. Enforcement testing often requires multiple tests of a single employer or agent, but generally does not involve the large numbers of tests typical of research testing. As a consequence, enforcement testing report forms tend to be much more open-ended, requiring test partners to provide greater narrative detail, rather than checking boxes. These forms are generally analyzed pair-by-pair by a knowledgeable analyst who compares the treatment of test partners across all aspects of the encounter, including subjective as well as objective information.
>
> Although research and enforcement testing differ in significant ways, the distinctions between the two should not be overdrawn. Both are based on the same core methodology and protocols. They differ primarily in the way test results are recorded and analyzed. Randomized testing of large numbers of market transactions need not be limited to research—it can and should also be applied in targeting for enforcement. Moreover, research and enforcement

---

40. HUD, Office of Policy Development and Research, *Housing Discrimination Against Racial and Ethnic Minorities* (2012), https://www.huduser.gov/portal/publications/pdf/hud-514_hds2012.pdf.

testing can be effectively conducted in tandem, yielding both market-wide estimates of the incidence of discrimination and case-specific evidence of individual violations.[41]

2. Testing and Litigation. Cases that are based on or supported by testing evidence present interesting litigation issues. For example, defense counsel may seek in discovery complete records of all relevant testing materials. These may include any combination of tester profiles; test reports and narratives; test coordinator logs; debriefing forms; any materials a tester received from the tested housing provider; testing methodology (which includes site and respondent selection criteria, choice of type of test(s) to be conducted, tester training materials, and tester procedures); and any other documents related to the tests. Lawyers for plaintiffs and defendants reviewing these files must consider whether the tests conducted are more or less probative of discriminatory treatment. For example, different information about availability is more probative the closer in time it is provided to testers. Decisions about whether to pursue enforcement actions might depend on whether the testing provides other information that might help to explain differences in treatment. On the other hand, testing can demonstrate discriminatory differences in quantity and quality of information provided about housing opportunities; different levels of access to viewing available units; different terms and conditions of rentals, including differences in discounts and incentives; different statements of policy; and different levels of encouragement or discouragement based on protected class. Even one test on an available unit can provide probative evidence in support of a fair housing complaint.

D. SECTION 3604(e): BLOCKBUSTING

Section 3604(e) makes it illegal "to induce or attempt to induce any person to sell or rent any dwelling by representations regarding the entry or prospective entry into the neighborhood of a person or persons" of a particular protected characteristic, when this is done *for profit*. In other words, this provision prohibits real estate agents or others from trying to convince homeowners to sell their properties by stoking fears or prejudices about demographic changes in the neighborhood. This form of real estate profiteering is commonly referred to as "blockbusting." Richard Rothstein describes the practice this way:[42]

---

41. Michael Fix & Margery Austin Turner, *Measuring Racial and Ethnic Discrimination in America,* in A NATIONAL REPORT CARD ON DISCRIMINATION IN AMERICA: THE ROLE OF TESTING 11-12 (Urban Institute 1998), https://www.urban.org/sites/default/files/publication/66646/308024-National-Report-Card-on-Discrimination-in-America.pdf.

42. Richard Rothstein, THE COLOR OF LAW: A FORGOTTEN HISTORY OF HOW OUR GOVERNMENT SEGREGATED AMERICA 95-96 (Liveright 2017).

> [B]lockbusting was a scheme in which speculators bought properties in bor-
> derline black-white areas; rented or sold them to African American families at
> above-market prices; persuaded white families in these areas that their neigh-
> borhoods were turning into African American slums and that values would
> soon fall precipitously; and then purchased the panicked whites' homes for
> less than they were worth. . . .
>
> Real estate firms then sold their newly acquired properties at inflated
> prices to African Americans, expanding their residential boundaries. Because
> most black families could not qualify for mortgages under [Federal Housing
> Administration] and bank policies, the agents often sold these homes on
> installment plans . . . in which no equity accumulated from down or monthly
> payments. Known as contract sales, these agreements usually provided that
> ownership would transfer to purchasers after fifteen or twenty years, but if
> a single monthly payment was late, the speculator could evict the would-be
> owner, who had accumulated no equity. The inflated sales prices made it all
> the more likely that payments would not be on time. Owner-speculators could
> then resell these homes to new contract buyers.

To state a claim under §3604(e), a plaintiff would need to show "(1) that the
solicitations are made for profit, (2) that the solicitations are intended to induce
the sale of a dwelling, and (3) that the solicitations would convey to a reasonable [person], under the circumstances, the idea that members of a particular race are, or may be, entering the neighborhood." *See* Heights Community
Congress v. Hilltop Realty, Inc., 774 F.2d 135, 141-42 (6th Cir. 1985). In *Heights
Community Congress,* a real estate broker was accused of blockbusting after he
mailed solicitations to residents of a mostly white neighborhood in which a
Black-owned home had recently sold to a white buyer. His solicitations made
no mention of race, and, according to the court, there was no evidence that the
neighborhood was "in the grip of panic" about Black people moving in. The
court ruled: "In the absence of evidence of panic selling or other incidents of a
racially charged atmosphere that would impute to any real estate solicitation
a racial connotation, or evidence of an actual representation respecting race,
whether suggestive or direct, there simply has not been a prohibited representation within the meaning of §3604(e)." *Id.* at 143-44.

The blockbusting cause of action is predicated on a pattern that was commonly observed in the 1950s, 1960s, and 1970s, of extreme segregation, incremental moves of people of color into predominantly white neighborhoods,
panic-selling, and white flight.[43] The following case, in which the court
enjoined blockbusting activity in a racially transitioning neighborhood in
Detroit, describes this dynamic.

---

43. One study concluded: "[B]lockbusting appears to have been a very common practice
across American cities, with the potential to have significant impacts on the lives of past and
future residents of the neighborhoods where it occurred." *See* Katherine Bennett, Daniel Hartley
& Jonathan Rose, *How Common Was Blockbusting in the Postwar U.S.?*, Chicago Fed Letter, No.
468 (July 2022), https://www.chicagofed.org/publications/chicago-fed-letter/2022/468.

Zuch v. Hussey
394 F. Supp. 1028 (E.D. Mich. 1975)

KEITH, District Judge

It is a well known fact that racial tensions and anxieties are generated when blacks move into previously all-white neighborhoods. It is also well known that many real estate agencies attempt to exploit such a situation by making repeated, uninvited solicitations for the sale of homes. In most instances, this activity (commonly referred to as 'blockbusting') has proven to be an effective means of stimulating the sale of homes in racially transitional neighborhoods. It does so by capitalizing upon the racial fears of whites, reminding them that blacks are moving into the area. This Court is well aware of the racial fears which exist in a community into which black families are entering for the first time. The testimony in this action has underscored the instability which results from these fears, and it is this instability upon which the real estate industry preys.

In entering its Opinion and Order, the Court is mindful of the contention of some people that black and white people are incapable of living together in peace and harmony in close proximity to one another. But certainly it is conceivable that in a city of the size of Detroit, racially integrated neighborhoods can evolve and sustain themselves. For there are enough fair-minded people of both races, who have respect for diversity, to insure that there will indeed be integrated, or at least desegregated, neighborhoods — neighborhoods where people will live because they want to, not because they have to.

Such neighborhoods can only exist when the black and white inhabitants of those neighborhoods develop mutual respect and tolerance. Such respect and tolerance is more likely to thrive in an atmosphere where people who affirmatively desire to live in a community are not continually subjected to the pressures of doomsday prophets making repeated representations that their property values as well as the quality of education offered their children will decline. Even white people who would not have wanted to sell their homes frequently feel forced to sell and move to neighborhoods where blacks are not encouraged to become residents or homeowners.

The activities of the defendants as determined herein cannot be countenanced. These defendants cannot be permitted to decide where the citizens of Detroit can and cannot live. This Court cannot compel people of different races to live together in any neighborhood. However, this Court does have the responsibility under the law, when presented with the evidence that is of record in this case, to take appropriate measures to see that realtors who are predatory intruders in neighborhoods where they transact business are not free to propagandize residents of those neighborhoods with the idea that they should sell their homes and move because of the changing racial composition of the neighborhood.

NOTES AND QUESTIONS

1. The Assumption of Racial Hostility. The court in *Zuch v. Hussey* reluctantly assumed that a significant number of white people felt they were incapable of living in the same neighborhood as Black people. Indeed, the case was brought by white homeowners who did not want their neighborhoods blockbusted. The court noted that:

> Witnesses testified that if their communities became significantly black, they would move. There was testimony about the initial reaction of residents to the entry of the first black family into the Emerson Community. Frantic meetings were described in which racial hatred was vented and schemes were suggested to physically remove the black family from the community.

The events in *Zuch v. Hussey* occurred in the early 1970s, just after the passage of the FHA. Half a century later, have conditions and attitudes changed? While racial transition still occurs, and efforts to maintain racially homogeneous neighborhoods persist (as illustrated in the exclusionary zoning cases featured in Chapters 6 and 7), the transition less often has the same air of panic and open displays of bigotry fomented by the housing industry, as described in the opinion. Real estate practices have changed, and overt industry blockbusting is no longer practiced to any significant degree. As a result, there have been virtually no blockbusting cases in recent decades.

2. Judge Damon Keith. Judge Keith was a significant Black jurist and civil rights icon. He was the grandson of enslaved people and grew up in poverty. He graduated from all-Black West Virginia State College and then served in the segregated U.S. Army during World War II. He said that when he returned to the United States and saw "German soldiers ride in the front [of buses] and . . . go into restaurants in the South that I could not go into, I made up my mind I was going to become a lawyer." He received his J.D. in 1949 from Howard University Law School, and an LL.M. degree from Wayne State University in 1956. He was cochair of Michigan's first Civil Rights Commission. In 1967, President Lyndon Johnson appointed Judge Keith to the U.S. District Court for the Eastern District of Michigan; in 1977, President Carter elevated Judge Keith to the U.S. Court of Appeals for the Sixth Circuit. Judge Keith hired more people of color and female clerks than any other federal judge. The NAACP awarded Judge Keith its highest honor, the Spingarn Medal; he also received the Edward J. Devitt Distinguished Service for Justice Award, the greatest accolade bestowed on a member of the federal judiciary. Judge Keith served as a federal judge for more than 50 years, from 1967 until his death in 2019.[44]

---

44. The information in this note comes from Robert D. McFadden, *Damon Keith, Federal Judge Who Championed Civil Rights, Dies at 96*, N.Y. TIMES (Apr. 28, 2019), https://www.nytimes.com /2019/04/28/obituaries/damon-keith-dies-at-96.html; Trevor W. Coleman & Peter J. Hammer, CRUSADER FOR JUSTICE: FEDERAL JUDGE DAMON J. KEITH (Wayne State U. Press 2013).

Chapter Summary

- The FHA contains specific provisions that prohibit different types of discriminatory conduct. These may overlap, meaning that a single act may violate more than one provision.
- Section 3604(a) prohibits discriminatory denials of housing and conduct that otherwise makes housing unavailable. This can cover a wide range of actions, including discriminatory refusals to rent, evictions, constructive evictions, steering, and land use and zoning.
- Section 3604(b) prohibits discrimination in the terms and conditions of the sale or rental of housing, including in the privileges, services, or facilities connected to housing. This covers discrimination in explicit terms such as rental rates and security deposits. It can also cover access to facilities, discrimination in services (including municipal services that are tied to housing), and harassment.
- Some courts have restricted the applicability of §§3604(a) and (b) to conduct that occurs only at the time of sale or the initiation of the rental. In recent years, courts have rejected this restriction on "post-acquisition" conduct, but may still limit some claims brought under §3604(a) where the plaintiff is not evicted or constructively evicted.
- Section 3604(d) prohibits the provision of false information about the availability of housing. It is this section that allows "testers" to bring claims even if they are not bona fide home seekers.
- Section 3604(e) prohibits "blockbusting," which is the profit-driven industry practice of inducing people to sell homes by fomenting racial fears about changing demographics in a neighborhood. Although this practice was more common in the 1960s and 1970s, it does not appear to be so today, and there are virtually no contemporary cases on the subject.

CHAPTER 9

SECTION 3604(c): DISCRIMINATORY ADVERTISEMENTS, NOTICES, AND STATEMENTS

Section 3604(c) of the Fair Housing Act makes it unlawful "[t]o make, print, or publish, or cause to be made, printed, or published any notice, statement, or advertisement, with respect to the sale or rental of a dwelling that indicates any preference, limitation, or discrimination" based on a protected category, "or an intention to make any such preference, limitation, or discrimination." HUD has promulgated a regulation stating that §3604(c) applies to virtually every written or oral statement that a landlord, agent, housing provider, broker, or other person engaged in the sale or rental of housing might make:

24 C.F.R. §100.75(b) The prohibitions in this section shall apply to all written or oral notices or statements by a person engaged in the sale or rental of a dwelling. Written notices and statements include any applications, flyers, brochures, deeds, signs, banners, posters, billboards or any documents used with respect to the sale or rental of a dwelling.

The materials in this chapter address a few key questions: How should courts determine whether a particular statement or advertisement is discriminatory if it is not overtly so? What kind of language indicates a preference or limitation? What constitutes a statement—a property name? unenforceable language in a deed? In addition, we invite consideration of how the courts and HUD should apply this section in light of changes in technology that alter how people are likely to place and encounter advertisements for housing.

A. STATEMENTS, QUERIES, AND ADVERTISEMENTS

The simplest cases involve verbal and written statements by a person engaged in the sale or rental of housing. The following case involves both types of statements.

Jancik v. Department of Housing and Urban Development
44 F.3d 553 (7th Cir. 1995)

Before Eschbach, Ripple, and Rovner, Circuit Judges.

ROVNER, Circuit Judge:

Stanley Jancik petitions for review of a decision of HUD, which found that he discriminated in the rental of an apartment on the basis of both race and family status in violation of the FHA, 42 U.S.C. §3604(c).

I.

Stanley Jancik owns Building No. 44 in King Arthur's Court, a large housing complex in the Chicago suburb of Northlake. King Arthur's Court houses people of all ages, including children, and although all of the apartments in Jancik's building have only one bedroom, they are large enough to house more than one occupant under local codes. The claims in this case arise out of Jancik's conduct in the rental of an apartment in that building. On August 29, 1990, Jancik placed this ad in a local suburban newspaper:

> NORTHLAKE deluxe 1 BR apt, a/c, newer quiet bldg, pool, prkg, mature person preferred, credit checked. $395. . . .

Suspecting that the request for a "mature person" might reflect a violation of the Act, the Leadership Council [for Metropolitan Open Communities']¹ Investigations Manager Glenn Brewer decided to "test" the property. In that process, "testers" bearing fictitious identities pose as potential renters in order to check for discriminatory practices. In this instance, Brewer chose to use volunteer testers Cindy Gunderson, who is white, and Marsha Allen, who is African American, for the task.

Gunderson spoke with Jancik by telephone on the evening of September 7, 1990. She subsequently related that after asking Gunderson her age and learning that she was 36, Jancik told her "that was good—he doesn't want any teenagers in there." Jancik also asked Gunderson her name and, upon hearing it, inquired "what kind of name" it was. Learning that the name was Norwegian, Jancik asked whether "that's white Norwegian or black Norwegian" and repeated the question a second time after Gunderson failed to answer. Gunderson asked Jancik whether he was inquiring as to her race and, after he responded affirmatively, told him that she was white. Gunderson then asked to view the apartment and the two arranged for her to do so the following morning.

Marsha Allen spoke with Jancik two hours later the same evening. Jancik asked Allen her occupation, income, age, marital status, race and whether she had any children or pets. Allen did not reveal her race, but in response to

---

1. [EDS.—The Leadership Council was a fair housing advocacy organization founded as the result of Dr. Martin Luther King, Jr.'s Chicago Freedom Movement in 1966.]

that question asked Jancik why he needed this information. He responded, in her words, "that he had to screen the applicants because the tenants in the building were middle-aged and he did not want anyone moving in who was loud, made a lot of noise and had children or pets." When Allen told Jancik that she did not have any children or pets he said "wonderful," and the two arranged for Allen to see the apartment the next morning. Both testers arrived the next morning at approximately 10:00, and Jancik's rental manager separately informed each that the apartment had been rented earlier that morning.

Based on the reports filed by Gunderson and Allen, the Leadership Council filed an administrative complaint with HUD. The Leadership Council claimed that Jancik's print advertisement violated [§3604(c)] by indicating a preference based on family status and that his interviews with the testers violated the section by indicating a preference based on both race and family status. After HUD's General Counsel issued a "Determination of Reasonable Cause and Charge of Discrimination," the matter was set for hearing before [an] Administrative Law Judge ("ALJ"). . . . [With the Council and Marsha Allen as intervenors, the ALJ conducted a two-day hearing and issued an Initial Decision and Order which found that Jancik had violated §3604(c). The ALJ awarded damages to the Leadership Council ($21,386.14) and to Marsha Allen ($2,000), assessed a civil penalty of $10,000, and enjoined Jancik from engaging in further acts of discrimination. The ALJ subsequently granted the Council's petition requesting $23,842.50 in attorney's fees. Jancik appealed.]

II.

We will reverse the Secretary's decision only if it is "not in accordance with law," "without observance of procedure required by law," or "unsupported by substantial evidence." 5 U.S.C. §706(2)(A), (D) & (E) [of the Administrative Procedure Act]. Substantial evidence is "such relevant evidence as a reasonable mind might accept as adequate to support a conclusion." "Although we review the entire record, we may not decide the facts anew, reweigh the evidence, or substitute our own judgment for that of the Secretary." We accord considerable deference to the credibility determinations of the ALJ.

Section 3604(c) prohibits the making or publishing of any statement or advertisement that "indicates" any preference or limitation based on, among other factors, race or family status. Whether a given statement or advertisement "indicates" such a preference is therefore central to our analysis. Although we have not previously dealt with the "indicates" aspect of §3604(c), the circuit courts that have done so have employed a relatively straightforward approach, which we also find appropriate. First, every circuit that has considered a claim under §3604(c) has held that an objective "ordinary reader" standard should be applied in determining what is "indicated" by an ad. Thus, "the statute [is] violated if an ad for housing suggests to an ordinary reader that a particular [protected group] is preferred or dispreferred for the housing in question." In applying the "ordinary reader" test, courts have not required that ads jump out at the reader with their offending message, but have found instead that the statute is violated by "any ad that would discourage an ordinary reader of a particular [protected group] from answering it." Ragin [v. The New York Times Co., 923 F.2d 995, 999-1000 (2d Cir. 1991)].

Significantly, no showing of a subjective intent to discriminate is therefore necessary to establish a violation of the section. At the same time, however, evidence of such intent is not irrelevant. Evidence that the author or speaker intended his or her words to indicate a prohibited preference obviously bears on the question of whether the words in fact do so. Thus, if such proof exists, it may provide an alternative means of establishing a violation of the section.

In view of these guidelines, the ALJ's finding that Jancik's advertisement and statements expressed a preference based on family status in violation of §3604(c) was certainly supported by substantial evidence. First, Jancik told Allen that he did not want any families with children and told Gunderson that he did not want any teenagers in the building. In our view, both of these statements quite clearly would suggest to an "ordinary" listener that Jancik had a preference or limitation based on family status. The advertisement indicating his preference for a "mature person" was similarly problematic. Not only do we view that term as suggesting an unlawful preference to an ordinary reader, the term is noted in the implementing regulation as being among "those most often used in residential real estate advertising to convey either overt or tacit discriminatory preferences or limitations." 24 C.F.R. §109.20(b) (7). [EDS.—These guidelines were withdrawn by HUD in 1996; see note 2, below.] Of course, as Jancik points out, use of the listed terms does not violate the Act per se, but it does "indicate a possible violation of the act and establish a need for further proceedings on the complaint, if it is apparent from the context of the usage that discrimination within the meaning of the act is likely to result." Id. Here, the context of the usage, which included explicit verification of Jancik's preference to each of two prospective tenants who responded to the ad, makes clear that the usage was meant to convey an unlawful preference.[2]

And, although we have no doubt that the Act has been violated based solely on this objective analysis, the record was also replete with evidence of Jancik's subjective intent to discriminate against families with children. For example, Jancik admitted at the hearing that he had told prospective tenants with children that there was no school in the area, when there was in fact a high school located on adjacent property and an elementary school within one mile. Jancik also told the HUD investigator that he had previously turned away a single parent with a ten-year-old child.

---

2. [Fn. 6 in original] Jancik cites Soules [v. HUD, 967. F.2d 817 (2d Cir. 1992)] for the proposition that questions about children may sometimes be asked for legitimate reasons, such as local zoning ordinances that limit the number of permitted occupants or conditions in the neighborhood that are dangerous to children. Not only is the record here completely devoid of evidence suggesting that Jancik's questions were asked for any such permissible reasons, it makes clear that his reasons were impermissible.

Although the question of whether Jancik violated §3604(c) by asking Gunderson and Allen about their race is somewhat more difficult, the ALJ's determination in that regard is also supported by substantial evidence. Unlike his comments regarding family status, Jancik did not expressly indicate a preference based on race, but merely asked the testers about their race. In the only case that has commented on the issue, the Second Circuit has indicated by way of dicta in Soules [v. HUD, 967. F.2d 817 (2d Cir. 1992)] that questions about race standing alone are sufficient to violate the section because "[t]here is simply no legitimate reason for considering an applicant's race." We need not decide that question here, however, because the context of the questions makes clear they did indicate an intent to discriminate on the basis of race. First, each question came in the midst of conversations in which Jancik was expressing other impermissible preferences. Hearing an inquiry about race immediately after being asked about children and told that applicants with children were undesirable, would, in our view, suggest to an ordinary listener that the racial question was part of the same screening process. Indeed, when Allen asked Jancik the purpose of his question about her race, he admitted that he was, in her words, "screening the applicants." Jancik's unlawful purpose was similarly revealed in his conversation with Gunderson by the pointedness of his inquiry. After asking the origins of the Gunderson name and learning that it was Norwegian, he twice inquired whether Gunderson was "white Norwegian or black Norwegian" and subsequently admitted, in answer to her question, that he was inquiring as to her race. It is unlikely that if the inquiry had been merely conversational, as Jancik has contended, he would have pursued it with such determination. In addition, the fact that Jancik had never rented to an African American tenant before the Coun[ci]l filed its complaint in this case further bolsters the ALJ's conclusion that Jancik's question reflected an intent to exclude tenants on the basis of race.

NOTES AND QUESTIONS

1. The Ordinary Listener Standard. Who is the ordinary listener (or reader)? Is there a difference between an ordinary reader and an ordinary reader with particular protected characteristics? (The court uses both descriptions.) The standard is described as an objective one, but isn't it likely that different statements will carry different meanings for different listeners? This brings up a related question: How should a court determine whether a statement indicates a preference or limitation under the ordinary listener standard? In cases with obviously discriminatory language, there will be little doubt, but what about more subtle or nuanced words? HUD attempted to provide some guidance on this point, discussed in the following note.

Finally, what should even qualify as a statement? Housing Rights Center v. Donald Sterling Corp., 274 F. Supp. 2d 1129 (C.D. Cal. 2003), *aff'd*, 84 Fed.

App'x 801 (9th Cir. 2003), provides an interesting discussion of how §3604(c) might apply to different types of "statements." In that case, the purchaser of several apartment buildings in Los Angeles changed the building names to contain references to Korea and Asia (e.g., "Korean World Towers," "The Sterling Korean Plaza," "Hancock Park Asian Towers"). The defendant, doing business as the "American Korean Land Company," also took out advertisements in the business section of the Los Angeles Times announcing the sales. One ad featured an American flag touching a South Korean flag. The plaintiffs alleged that the flag advertisement and building names constituted violations of §3604(c), but the court only agreed that the building names did, writing:

> *Plaintiffs have not demonstrated that their claim regarding use of the South Korean flag is likely to succeed.*
>
> Defendants' use of the South Korean flag in an announcement . . . does not give rise to a valid FHA claim. An ordinary reader would likely view the flag . . . as a symbolic representation of the "American Korean Land Company" corporate name, not as a discriminatory message — particularly because the American flag also appears in the announcement. Use of the word "Korean" in a corporate name does not inherently violate the FHA, and this announcement [does not advertise apartments for rent or sale and does not invite tenant or purchaser applications. Moreover, at the hearing on this motion, counsel for plaintiffs acknowledged that the cited announcement appeared in the business section of the newspaper, not in the real estate or classified section.]
>
> *Plaintiffs have demonstrated that their claims based on Defendants' use of the word "Korean" in apartment building names is likely to succeed.*
>
> At issue in this case is the FHA's prohibition against national origin discrimination. The very word used by Defendants — "Korean" — is necessarily and commonly understood to signify a particular national origin. Given this ordinary understanding, use of the word "Korean" in the names of residential apartment buildings would indicate to the "ordinary reader" that the buildings' owner is not only receptive to but actually prefers tenants of Korean national origin. Perhaps if Defendants' apartments were built in a "Korean" architectural style, the natural and predictable inference might be different. But there is no indication that such is the case here.
>
> Defendants argue strenuously that their use of the word "Korean" in the names of these apartment buildings is acceptable because the buildings at issue are in the Los Angeles neighborhood known as "Koreatown." But there is an undeniable and important, although perhaps subtle, difference between "Koreatown" and "Korean." Because "Koreatown" denotes a neighborhood while "Korean" denotes a national origin, an ordinary reader would naturally conclude that the former word refers to a specific Los Angeles geographical area while the latter refers to a particular group of people. In this case, Defendants' use of the word "Korean" is particularly likely to suggest a national origin preference, not a geographic area, given that Defendants' buildings names include additional words that do signify location — e.g., "Wilshire Korean Ambassador" and "Wilshire Korean Towers." An ordinary reader would logically assume that "Korean" must have a meaning other than geography, given that the locations of the buildings already are reflected by the word "Wilshire."
>
> Los Angeles is, moreover, a remarkably polyglot city that, sadly, has been plagued by ethnic divisions for decades. Uneasy relations among different racial and immigrant groups still prevail in various sections of this city, and

many residents would understandably regard the decision to place the word "Korean" in the name of a building in a racially diverse neighborhood as a coded message: "Koreans and Korean-Americans are welcome and preferred; others are not."

Of course, the Court recognizes that use of the word "Korean" is not necessarily a guise to achieve invidious discrimination. The word may commonly and appropriately be used on commercial buildings to designate a particular type of service or product—e.g., a Korean restaurant, a Korean market or a Korean video store. But when used in the name of an apartment building the word "Korean" has no similarly obvious, nondiscriminatory meaning, and Defendants have failed to identify one.[3]

2. Advertising Guidelines. In 1972 HUD published a set of Advertising Guidelines for Fair Housing. HUD issued these as regulations in 1980 and in 1989 updated them to include standards for disability and familial status after these protected characteristics were added to the FHA in 1988:

24 C.F.R. §109.20 USE OF WORDS, PHRASES, SYMBOLS, AND VISUAL AIDS.

The following words, phrases, symbols, and forms typify those most often used in residential real estate advertising to convey either overt or tacit discriminatory preferences or limitations. In considering a complaint under the FHA, the Department will normally consider the use of these and comparable words, phrases, symbols, and forms to indicate a possible violation of the act and to establish a need for further proceedings on the complaint, if it is apparent from the context of the usage that discrimination within the meaning of the act is likely to result.

(a) *Words descriptive of dwelling, landlord, and tenants.* White private home, Colored home, Jewish home, Hispanic residence, adult building.

(b) *Words indicative of race, color, religion, sex, handicap, familial status, or national origin—*

---

3. The defendant in this case, Donald Sterling, has a controversial history. In addition to being a real estate mogul, he was the owner of the Los Angeles Clippers basketball team from 1981 until 2014, when private recordings of him making racist comments were made public. Protests by the National Basketball Association (NBA) players and sponsors followed, and Sterling was ultimately banned from the NBA for life, forced to sell the team, and fined $2.5 million by the league. *See* Ramona Shelburne, *When the Donald Sterling Saga Rocked the NBA—And Changed It Forever*, ESPN (Aug. 20, 2019), https://www.espn.com/nba/story/_/id/27414482/when-don ald-sterling-saga-rocked-nba-changed-forever; Ben Golliver, *Adam Silver Issues -Lifetime Ban, $2.5M Fine to Clippers Owner Donald Sterling*, Sports Illustrated (Apr. 29, 2014), https://www.si .com/nba/2014/04/29/adam-silver-issues-lifetime-ban-2-5m-fine-clippers-owner-donald-sterl ing. After the Housing Rights Center lawsuit discussed in text settled for an undisclosed amount (and a $4.9 million attorneys' fee award) the Department of Justice sued Sterling for housing discrimination and settled that case for more than $2.7 million. *See* Office of Public Affairs, US DOJ, *Justice Department Obtains Record $2.725 Million Settlement of Housing Discrimination Lawsuit* (Nov. 3, 2009), https://www.justice.gov/opa/pr/justice-department-obtains-record-2725-million-set tlement-housing-discrimination-lawsuit.

(1) Race—Negro, Black, Caucasian, Oriental, American Indian.

(2) *Color*—White, Black, Colored.

(3) *Religion*—Protestant, Christian, Catholic, Jew.

(4) *National origin* — Mexican American, Puerto Rican, Philippine, Polish, Hungarian, Irish, Italian, Chicano, African, Hispanic, Chinese, Indian, Latino.

(5) *Sex*—the exclusive use of words in advertisements, including those involving the rental of separate units in a single or multi-family dwelling, stating or tending to imply that the housing being advertised is available to persons of only one sex and not the other, except where the sharing of living areas is involved. Nothing in this part restricts advertisements of dwellings used exclusively for dormitory facilities by educational institutions.

(6) *Handicap*— crippled, blind, deaf, mentally ill, retarded, impaired, handicapped, physically fit. Nothing in this part restricts the inclusion of information about the availability of accessible housing in advertising of dwellings.

(7) *Familial status*—adults, children, singles, mature persons. Nothing in this part restricts advertisements of dwellings which are intended and operated for occupancy by older persons and which constitute "housing for older persons" as defined in Part 100 of this title.

(8) *Catch words*—Words and phrases used in a discriminatory context should be avoided, e.g., "restricted," "exclusive," "private," "integrated," "traditional," "board approval" or "membership approval."

(c) *Symbols or logotypes*. Symbols or logotypes which imply or suggest race, color, religion, sex, handicap, familial status, or national origin.

(d) *Colloquialisms*. Words or phrases used regionally or locally which imply or suggest race, color, religion, sex, handicap, familial status, or national origin.

(e) *Directions to real estate for sale or rent (use of maps or written instructions)*. Directions can imply a discriminatory preference, limitation, or exclusion. For example, references to real estate location made in terms of racial or national origin significant landmarks, such as an existing black development (signal to blacks) or an existing development known for its exclusion of minorities (signal to whites). Specific directions which make reference to a racial or national origin significant area may indicate a preference. References to a synagogue, congregation or parish may also indicate a religious preference.

(f) *Area (location) description*. Names of facilities which cater to a particular racial, national origin or religious group, such as country club or private school designations, or names of facilities which are used exclusively by one sex may indicate a preference.

HUD removed these Guidelines from the Code of Federal Regulations in 1996, after the agency determined that such nonbinding guidance was not a regulatory requirement that should be codified in the CFR. Nevertheless, the remaining HUD regulations continue to refer to the material in Part 109, as does a 1995 internal HUD memo released to the public.[4] The information contained in the Guidelines and Memo remains useful for practitioners and housing providers; however, it is important to note that such guidance does not "have the force and effect of law" or "otherwise . . . bind private parties," Kisor v. Wilkie, 588 U.S. 558, 583 (2019), and is merely persuasive authority for the courts (*see* Loper Bright Enterprises v. Raimondo, __ U.S. __ (2024)).

3. Subjective Intent. The cases make clear that the "ordinary reader/listener" standard is an objective one when it comes to the speaker. In other words, whether the speaker subjectively intended to convey a preference, limitation, or discrimination is irrelevant to liability. What matters is how the statement is interpreted by the ordinary listener. In this way, §3604(c) almost operates as a strict liability provision: If a housing provider makes an offensive or discriminatory statement related to housing, inadvertent or not, this constitutes a violation. Why should a speaker with no intent to discriminate still be held to have violated §3604(c)? What would be the result if this were not the case? On the other hand, note that the *Jancik* court did not completely disregard evidence of Stanley Jancik's subjective discriminatory intent. What role did that evidence play in the court's analysis?

4. Preferences and Shared Housing. What if the advertisement is for shared housing — that is, for a person to share living space, or even a bedroom? Significant social norms and personal concerns such as safety, modesty, and religious observance may be implicated by people of different sexes sharing intimate living space, and for that reason a person advertising for a roommate might wish to state a preference for the sex or gender of the person with whom the person would share such space. Nothing in the language of the statute indicates that there should be an exception for sex-specific ads for shared housing or dormitory-style living. Nonetheless, the now-rescinded HUD regulation, the Achtenberg Memo referred to in the previous note, and the *Roomate.com* opinion of the Ninth Circuit discussed in Chapter 5 provide that the FHA's coverage of sex-based preferences might be limited where the sharing of living areas is involved, or when the dwelling at issue is a dormitory facility used by an educational institution. This guides HUD's actions in enforcing the FHA. Courts may view it as persuasive. Is this a reasonable approach? Why do you think Congress didn't include this exception in the statute? For a discussion of the limits on First Amendment protections for

---

4. *See* Memorandum from Roberta Achtenberg, HUD Assistant Secretary for Fair Housing and Equal Opportunity, Guidance Regarding Advertisements under §804(c) of the FHA (Jan. 9, 1995), https://www.hud.gov/sites/documents/DOC_7784.pdf.

stated housing-related preferences regarding sexual orientation or gender identity, see Section B, below.

5. Questions About Protected Characteristics. The race discrimination claim against Stanley Jancik was based on inquiries he made about the race of the testers even though he did not make an explicitly discriminatory statement. Acknowledging that this issue was "somewhat more difficult" than the familial status issue, the court nevertheless held that the questions violated §3604(c). Consider the logic the court used in reaching this conclusion: There was no legitimate reason for a landlord to ask the race of tenants, and the questions came during the "screening process." In this context, an ordinary listener could conclude that the questions indicated an intent to discriminate on the basis of race. Consider also HUD v. Blackwell, 908 F.2d 864 (11th Cir. 1990), in which a defendant property owner repeatedly asked the real estate agents who were brokering the sale of his house whether the prospective buyers were Black. The court held that such questions were evidence of racial animus and themselves violated §3604(c).

Similarly, in Housing Rights Center v. Donald Sterling Corp., 274 F. Supp. 2d 1129 (C.D. Cal. 2003), aff'd, 84 Fed. App'x 801 (9th Cir. 2003), the defendant landlord sent a notice to tenants that the parking garage would be closed and that tenants who wanted a garage remote control would need to complete an "application." The application asked tenants to state their place of birth, citizenship, and date of naturalization. The court held that "there is no rational relationship between national origin and ability to safely operate a remote garage door opener." It went on to find that, because the questions appeared in a document entitled "Application" these questions were part of a screening process. In this context, the questions violated §3604(c).

Contrast this with the statements in Soules v. HUD, 967 F.2d 817, 824 (2d Cir. 1992). In that case, a landlord asked a prospective tenant how many children would live in the apartment and what their ages were. While the inquiry might have indicated an intent to discriminate against families with children, there was also a legitimate reason for it: An applicable state law required that children over the age of five have separate bedrooms if they were of different sexes. The court determined that:

> [W]hereas "[t]here is simply no legitimate reason for considering an applicant's race . . ., there are situations in which it is legitimate to inquire about the number of individuals interested in occupying an apartment and their ages." Local zoning regulations, for example, might constitute a valid reason for asking whether and how many children a prospective tenant has. Conditions in the neighborhood known to be either ideally suited to or inherently dangerous to occupancy by families with children might well permit an inquiry about the ages of the family members. We agree with the respondents that, standing alone, an inquiry into whether a prospective tenant has a child does not constitute an FHA violation.

Recall that the *Jancik* court distinguished *Soules*, noting that there was no evidence of any permissible reason for Jancik's questions and that the context made clear that his intentions were discriminatory. Does *Soules* provide an exception for questions about familial status? Must the questioner provide evidence that the question was posed to ensure compliance with a relevant law or regulation?

6. Deeds and Restrictive Covenants. Note that HUD's regulation lists "deeds" as statements covered by §3604(c). This is significant because racially restrictive covenants usually were written into property deeds (although they also might be inserted into other documents). Recall from Chapter 1 that such covenants were designed to prevent racial and ethnic minorities from purchasing or occupying property in "white" neighborhoods. In 1948, in *Shelley v. Kraemer* and *Hurd v. Hodge*, the Supreme Court held that racially restrictive covenants were not enforceable by courts. *Shelley* and *Hurd* did not actually outlaw such covenants, though. It was only in 1968 that racially restrictive covenants became unlawful.

Although the FHA and *Jones v. Mayer* made covenants unlawful, millions of existing deeds still contain racially restrictive language, which remains painful, exclusionary, and offensive. Property deeds are legal documents that record transfers of ownership of real property. They usually are original documents that date back to the first recorded ownership of a parcel, with each new transfer being added to supplement a chain of title. The oldest original provisions often are handwritten. The storage of property deeds is decentralized, in the county and municipal offices of the recorder of deeds or similar official. Most deeds are not digitized and can be found only in hard copy form. Thus, the removal of existing racially restrictive covenants from property deeds is no easy feat, and many states lack a ready legal process for doing so. Only a few states (including Washington, Missouri, Maryland, California, Illinois, Connecticut, and Virginia) have passed laws that provide a mechanism for removing racially restrictive covenants from property deeds or acknowledging their unenforceability. Some advocates point out, moreover, that removal of such provisions alters the historical record, which is valuable for understanding the history and impacts of racist policies on communities. Before covenants are removed, these advocates urge, it would be beneficial to map the communities in which the covenants were applied. (In fact, there are many proponents of mapping regardless of their position on removal.)

Richard Rothstein suggests a provision in deeds that says the covenant is "unenforceable, unlawful, and morally repugnant" and that the owners "repudiate this clause, are ashamed for our country that many once considered it acceptable, and state that we welcome with enthusiasm and without reservation neighbors of all races and ethnicities."[5] Professor Florence Roisman offers an additional approach:

> Rothstein's proposal is an improvement on elimination of the covenants because it recognizes and addresses the evil of the racial exclusion. But these

---

5. THE COLOR OF LAW: A FORGOTTEN HISTORY OF HOW OUR GOVERNMENT SEGREGATED AMERICA 221-22 (Liveright 2017).

additions to the deeds would be seen by relatively few persons—those who search and record the deeds, and the parties to the transactions that involve the deeds. Drawing on work by Michael Gorra and Susan Nieman, I propose an additional response, that each house that is the subject of such a covenant bear a plaque reporting the covenant's creation, purpose, and repudiation. This would be similar to the Stolpersteine—stumbling stones—in Europe that are hammered into sidewalks before the last homes in which victims of the Nazis lived in freedom.[6]

The few federal courts to deal with the issue have come out differently in terms of applying the law, although the cases ultimately led to similar factual outcomes:

- In Mayers v. Ridley, 465 F.2d 630 (D.C. Cir. 1972), the court, sitting en banc, reversed dismissal of plaintiffs' claims that the Recorder of Deeds office in the District of Columbia violated §3604(c) by accepting deeds with racially restrictive covenants for filing and maintaining them as public records. The plaintiffs had sought an order enjoining the Recorder from "accepting such covenants for filing in the future[, requiring] the Recorder to affix a sticker on each existing liber volume stating that restrictive covenants found therein are null and void [and] preventing the Recorder from providing copies of instruments on file unless a similar notice is attached to the copies."

- United States v. University Oaks Civic Club, 653 F. Supp. 1469 (S.D. Tex. 1987) involved a homeowners' association whose members voted twice (in 1966 and 1976) to extend the package of land-use restrictions, including a racially restrictive covenant, that had applied to their homes since 1939. The ballots were recorded in the Deed Records office. In 1980 the association president sent letters to all members alerting them to the existence of the covenant and stating that it was void and unenforceable and did not reflect the attitudes of the association. Removing the restrictive covenant would be expensive and difficult. After being contacted by the Department of Justice, the association prepared declarations and affidavits that would be filed with the next round of ballots, stating that the covenant was void and expressing the association's lack of agreement with it. Under these circumstances, the court held that the association had "no intent whatsoever" in voting to extend the restrictions. It further noted that the solution arrived at by the association—including disclaiming language to be filed with the deed—was the functional equivalent of the stickers sought by plaintiffs in *Mayers*.

---

6. *Stumbling Stones at Levittown: What to Do About Racial Covenants in the United States*, 30 J. AFFORDABLE HOUS. & COMMUNITY DEV. L. 461, 463 (2022).

The Washington state legislature devised a solution that would allow any property owner to have a restrictive covenant removed and a corrected document substituted in the deed. However, the original document with the restrictive covenant would be retained and preserved for historical and archival purposes. The Supreme Court of Washington, sitting en banc, endorsed this approach in In re. That Portion of Lots 1 & 2 v. Spokane County, 199 Wash. 2d 389, 506 P.3d 1230, 1237-38 (Wash. Sup. Ct. 2022):

> We believe that the legislature's intent is clear and that the [amended statute] provide[s] a remedy that strikes the balance between keeping a historical record of racism in covenants, while also allowing homeowners to remove the repugnant covenants from their chains of title. Removing all trace of these discriminatory covenants would *not* effectuate the legislature's intent to eradicate discrimination. It would destroy only the physical evidence that this discrimination ever existed. It would be all too easy for future generations to look back at these property records with no physical evidence of the discriminatory covenants and conclude that the covenants never existed at all. As the Court of Appeals recognized below,
>
>> A policy of whitewashing public records and erasing historical evidence of racism would be dangerous. It would risk forgetting and ultimately denying the ugly truths of racism and racist housing practices. Such an outcome cannot be squared with the antidiscrimination purposes of Washington's Law Against Discrimination.
>>
>> We must ensure that future generations have access to these documents because, although the covenants are morally repugnant, they are part of a documented history of disenfranchisement of a people. It is our history.

7. Application to Otherwise Exempt Properties. Section 3604(c) always applies to properties (and thus people) that are exempt from the other substantive portions of the FHA. Recall from Chapter 5 that the FHA exempts "Mrs. Murphy landlords" and small-inventory owners of certain single-family homes who do not regularly sell or rent property, or use agents or brokers. *See* §3603(b)(1) and (2). However, the introductory phrase of these provisions makes clear that they exempt such individuals from every portion of the FHA *except* §3604(c): "Nothing in §3604 of this title (other than subsection (c)) shall apply to" these types of dwellings. Thus, a landlord who is shielded from liability for a discriminatory refusal to rent may nonetheless be liable for making a discriminatory statement about this refusal.[7] Why should this be the case?

---

7. Note that some violations of §3604(c) will result in loss of the exemption entirely, but only for single-family homeowners. *See* 42 U.S.C. §3603(b)(1) ("the sale or rental of any such single-family house shall be excepted from the application of this subchapter only if such house is sold or rented . . . without the publication, posting or mailing, after notice, of any advertisement or written notice in violation of section 3604(c)"). Discriminatory statements other than ads or notices are not included in those §3604(c) violations that will forfeit the exemption.

Professor Robert Schwemm reviewed the legislative history and court opinions analyzing §3604(c) and concluded that Congress had three purposes behind its application to otherwise exempt housing:

> [First, is the "anti-market-limiting" goal. Section 3604(c)] reduces barriers that might deter minorities seeking homes in neighborhoods that must be open to them under the FHA but might appear restricted if discriminatory ads, notices, or statements [for exempt properties] are allowed. . . . Section 3604(c)'s second key purpose is protecting minority home seekers from suffering insult, emotional distress, and other intangible injuries resulting from discriminatory ads, notices, or statements. . . . Section 3604(c) also helps break down the notion that illegal discrimination continues to permeate America's housing markets by banning every ad, notice, and statement suggesting the FHA's promise of nondiscrimination is not a reality.[8]

B. PUBLISHER LIABILITY

The FHA clearly prohibits an individual such as a landlord or real estate agent from making discriminatory housing statements, but it also makes it illegal "[t]o make, print, or publish, or cause to be made, printed, or published" discriminatory statements and advertisements related to the sale or rental of housing. Thus, the statute can apply to newspapers and other print media, as established in an influential early case, United States v. Hunter, d/b/a The Courier, 459 F.2d 205, 210-11 (4th Cir. 1972). *Hunter* involved two classified ads placed by a man offering to rent an apartment in what he described as a "white home." The Department of Justice brought suit against Bill Hunter, the editor and publisher of the newspaper that ran the ads. Hunter argued that §3604(c) was not intended to apply to newspapers that simply published advertisements. The court disagreed, holding that:

> The section here under examination provides on its face no exemptions in favor of newspapers. Rather, it uses precisely the language which would lead the ordinary reader to conclude that newspapers are to be brought within its purview. The section provides it shall be unlawful "to make, print, publish, or cause to be made, printed, or published" any advertisement prohibited by the Act. In the context of classified real estate advertising, landlords and brokers "cause" advertisements to be printed or published and generally newspapers "print" and "publish" them. Since each phrase in a statute must, if possible, be given effect, both landlords and newspapers are within the section's reach.
>
> Congressional intent disclosed by the meager legislative history concerning §3604(c) does not contradict our view of the unambiguous language chosen by the [drafters] of the section. Indeed there is some evidence that the publication of discriminatory classified advertisements in newspapers was precisely one of the evils the Act was designed to correct. We therefore agree with the District

---

8. *Discriminatory Housing Statements and 3604(c): A New Look at the Fair Housing Act's Most Intriguing Provision*, 29 FORDHAM URBAN L. J. 187, 249-50 (2001).

Court that the congressional prohibition of discriminatory advertisements was intended to apply to newspapers as well as any other publishing medium.

The advertisement at issue in *Hunter* was a simple classified ad that used only words. More sophisticated advertising also uses photographs, models, and other visual imagery. HUD regulations make clear that §3604(c) covers more than words.

> **24 C.F.R. §100.75(c)** Discriminatory notices, statements and advertisements include, but are not limited to:
>
> (1) Using words, phrases, *photographs, illustrations, symbols or form*s [emphasis added] which convey that dwellings are available or not available to a particular group of persons because of [protected characteristics].
>
> (2) Expressing to agents, brokers, employees, prospective sellers or renters or any other persons a preference for or limitation on any purchaser or renter because of [the protected characteristics] of such persons.
>
> (3) Selecting media or locations for advertising the sale or rental of dwellings which deny particular segments of the housing market information about housing opportunities because of [protected characteristics].
>
> (4) Refusing to publish advertising for the sale or rental of dwellings or requiring different charges or terms for such advertising because of [protected characteristics].

This leads to a host of questions addressed in the following case.

Ragin v. The New York Times Company
923 F.2d 995 (2d Cir. 1991)

Before Oakes, Chief Judge, Lumbard, and Winter, Circuit Judges.

WINTER, Circuit Judge:

BACKGROUND

The Times is the publisher of The New York Times, a nationally known newspaper. The individual plaintiffs are black persons who have been looking for housing in the New York metropolitan area. Plaintiff Open Housing Center, Inc., is a not-for-profit New York corporation, one of the primary goals of which is to eliminate racially discriminatory housing practices.

[P]laintiffs commenced this action under the FHA[.] A pertinent excerpt from the complaint states:

> During the 20 year[s] since the Act was passed . . . advertisements appeared in the Sunday Times featuring thousands of human models of whom virtually none were black. . . . [W]hile many of the white human models depict

representative or potential homeowners or renters, the few blacks represented are usually depicted as building maintenance employees, doormen, entertainers, sports figures, small children or cartoon characters. . . .

[T]he Times has continued to . . . publish numerous advertisements that picture all-white models in advertisements for realty located in predominantly white buildings, developments, communities or neighborhoods. It has also . . . published a few advertisements that picture all black models in advertisements for realty located in predominantly black buildings, developments, communities or neighborhoods.

The use of human models in advertising personalizes the advertisements and encourages consumers to identify themselves in a positive way with the models and housing featured. In real estate advertisements, human models often represent actual or potential purchasers or renters, or the type of potential purchasers or renters that the real estate owner has targeted as desirable occupants.

Therefore, the repeated and continued depiction of white human models and the virtual absence of any black human models . . . indicates a preference on the basis of race. . . .

The real estate display advertisements featured by the Times indicate a preference based on race through the use of human models reflecting the predominant race of the advertised building, development or community.

The Times moved under Fed.R.Civ.P. 12(b)(6) to dismiss the complaint for failure to state a claim upon which relief may be granted. [The trial court judge denied the motion, concluding that the pattern of ads alleged in the complaint, if proven at trial, would be sufficient to support a holding that the Times had published ads that indicated a racial preference.]

DISCUSSION

A threshold question is whether §3604(c) reaches the use of models as a medium for the expression of a racial preference. We hold that it does. Congress prohibited all expressions of racial preferences in housing advertisements and did not limit the prohibition to racial messages conveyed through certain means. Neither the text of the statute nor its legislative history suggests that Congress intended to exempt from its proscriptions subtle methods of indicating racial preferences.

The next question is whether and in what circumstances the use of models may convey an illegal racial message. We begin with another proposition that seems to us fairly obvious: namely, that a trier of fact could find that in this age of mass communication and sophisticated modes of persuasion, advertisers target as potential consumers groups with certain racial as well as other characteristics. In some circumstances, such targeting conveys a racial preference, or so a trier might find. We live in a race-conscious society, and real estate advertisers seeking the attention of groups that are largely white may see greater profit in appealing to white consumers in a manner that consciously or unconsciously discourages non-whites. They may do so out of simple inertia or because of the fear that the use of black models will deter more white consumers than it attracts black consumers. In any event, a trier plausibly may conclude that in some circumstances ads with models of a particular race and not others will be read by the ordinary reader as indicating a racial preference.

The Times does not deny that advertisers target groups but rather vigorously presses the claim that if §3604(c) is applied to the Times, the specter of racially conscious decisions and of racial quotas in advertising will become a reality. We need not enter the public debate over the existence or merits of racial quotas in fields other than advertising, or look to the scope of Supreme Court decisions that permit race-conscious decisions. Nor do we by any means suggest that an order directing such quotas is the only appropriate or usual remedy should a publisher be found liable.

We do believe, however, that the Times's concerns are overblown. The quota controversy principally concerns selection of persons for competitive opportunities, such as employment or admission to college. These are circumstances in which opinions differ whether individual skills or purely academic qualifications should govern and whether a race-conscious decision is itself an act of racial discrimination. The use of models in advertising, however, involves wholly different considerations. Advertising is a make-up-your-own world in which one builds an image from scratch, selecting those portrayals that will attract targeted consumers and discarding those that will put them off. Locale, setting, actions portrayed, weather, height, weight, gender, hair color, dress, race and numerous other factors are varied as needed to convey the message intended. A soft-drink manufacturer seeking to envelop its product in an aura of good will and harmony may portray a group of persons of widely varying nationalities and races singing a cheerful tune on a mountaintop. A chain of fast-food retailers may use models of the principal races found in urban areas where its stores are located. Similarly, a housing complex may decide that the use of models of one race alone will maximize the number of potential consumers who respond, even though it may also discourage consumers of other races.

In advertising, a conscious racial decision regarding models thus seems almost inevitable. All the statute requires is that in this make-up-your-own world the creator of an ad not make choices among models that create a suggestion of a racial preference. The deliberate inclusion of a black model where necessary to avoid such a message seems to us a far cry from the alleged practices that are at the core of the debate over quotas. If race-conscious decisions are inevitable in the make-up-your-own world of advertising, a statutory interpretation that may lead to some race-conscious decisionmaking to avoid indicating a racial preference is hardly a danger to be averted at all costs.

Moreover, the Times's argument would prevent a trier of fact from scrutinizing the selection of models and inferring from that selection and from the surrounding circumstances a race-conscious decision. The creator of an ad may testify, "Gosh, I didn't notice until this trial that all the models for tenants were white and the model for a custodian was black." However, a trier may justifiably disbelieve such an assertion in light of all the circumstances, much as triers of fact are allowed to draw inferences of racial intent in other contexts, or may consider such an assertion an inadvertent or unconscious expression of racism.

Given this scope for fact-finding, the present complaint cannot be dismissed for failure to state a claim for relief. It alleges a long-standing pattern of publishing real estate ads in which models of potential consumers are always white while black models largely portray service employees, except for the exclusive use of black models for housing in predominantly black neighborhoods. Finally, it alleges that this pattern reflects a targeting of racial groups. Given the ordinary reader test, it can hardly be said that these allegations are insufficient to enable plaintiffs to prove that the Times has published, and continues to publish, some discriminatory ads.

In the proceedings to follow, the standard for liability will no doubt be sharpened in the context of the parties' evidentiary submissions. We believe it useful to make some preliminary observations on that standard, however. First, we agree with the Times that liability may not be based on an aggregation of advertisements by different advertisers. Although the twenty-year pattern alleged in the complaint may have been a powerful engine for housing segregation and, if proven, will almost certainly include violations of §3604(c), the statute provides a prohibition only with regard to individual advertisers.

Second, as stated, liability will follow only when an ordinary reader would understand the ad as suggesting a racial preference. The ordinary reader is neither the most suspicious nor the most insensitive of our citizenry. Such a reader does not apply a mechanical test to every use of a model of a particular race. An ad depicting a single model or couple of one race that is run only two or three times would seem, absent some other direct evidence of an intentional racial message, outside §3604(c)'s prohibitions as a matter of law. A housing complex that runs ads several times a week for a year depicting numerous white models as consumers and black models as doormen or custodial employees would have difficulty persuading a trier of fact that its ads did not facially indicate a racial preference. It thus seems inevitable that the close questions of liability will involve advertisers that either use a large number of models and/or advertise repetitively. In such cases, the advertiser's opportunities to include all groups are greater, and the message conveyed by the exclusion of a racial group is stronger.

NOTES AND QUESTIONS

1. Ordinary Reader Standard. How does the court apply the ordinary reader standard in *Ragin*? Note that the court contends with at least two complicating factors: what "message" the use of human models sends in any one particular advertisement, and how many such advertisements a publisher must feature to constitute a violation. In this case, the facts were strong on both points—over 20 years the paper published thousands of advertisements featuring exclusively white models as home seekers and featuring Black models only as door attendants or maintenance workers. *Compare* Housing Opportunities Made Equal, Inc. v. Cincinnati Enquirer, Inc., 943 F.2d 644, 648 (6th Cir. 1991) ("[A] complaint alleging a violation of §3604(c) based on the single publication of an advertisement which uses a small number of all-white models does not, without more, state a cognizable claim under §3604(c). . . ."). Is the *Ragin* court right in saying that liability should not be based on an aggregation of advertisements by different advertisers? How much difference would it make to the ordinary reader whether she sees multiple ads from a single company that indicate a racial preference versus single ads from multiple different companies that do the same? How should a publisher manage ads from multiple advertisers, each of which only has a few ads but where the ads taken together might indicate a racial preference?

2. Contrast With Title VII. There is an employment provision similar to §3604(c) in Title VII of the 1964 CRA, 42 U.S.C. §2000-e3(b):

> It shall be an unlawful employment practice for an employer, labor organization, employment agency, or joint labor–management committee . . . to print or publish or cause to be printed or published any notice or advertisement relating to [employment, employment referral, training, or apprenticeship opportunities offered by these entities] indicating any preference, limitation, specification, or discrimination, based on [protected characteristics].

Note the important differences between these provisions: First, Title VII only makes it unlawful to print, publish, or cause to be printed or published a discriminatory notice or advertisement. Thus, it does not cover discriminatory oral statements as §3604(c) does. Second, Title VII applies only to particular types of defendants (statutorily defined employers, employment agencies, and labor unions). As such, it does not create liability for the newspapers or other media that might publish the discriminatory statements. In both these ways, §3604(c) is significantly broader than its Title VII counterpart.

3. First Amendment. Any restriction on speech by a government actor necessarily raises a potential conflict with the First Amendment. Whether speech is protected by the First Amendment depends on the nature of the speech. For example, advertising is considered commercial speech and generally can be regulated so long as there is a substantial government interest in doing so. Central Hudson Gas & Electric Corp. v. Public Service Commission, 447 U.S. 557 (1980).

The issue was addressed in *Hunter*, 459 F.2d at 211, with the court recognizing that commercial speech such as advertisements can be regulated to a greater extent than "pure" speech:

> Noting that §3604(c) limits advertising an intent to discriminate in the sale or rental of a dwelling only in a commercial context and not in relation to the dissemination of ideas, the District Court held that the statute does not contravene

the First Amendment, and hence that a court might constitutionally enjoin a newspaper's printing of classified advertisements which violate the Act.

The court's conclusion is supported by an unbroken line of authority from the Supreme Court down which distinguishes between the expression of ideas protected by the First Amendment and commercial advertising in a business context. It is now well settled that, while "freedom of communicating information and disseminating opinion" enjoys the fullest protection of the First Amendment, "the Constitution imposes no such restraint on government as respects purely commercial advertising."

Statements other than advertisements also can be considered commercial speech entitled to diminished First Amendment protection, so long as they are made "with respect to the sale or rental of a dwelling." For example, in Campbell v. Robb, 162 Fed. App'x 460, 472 (6th Cir. 2006), a landlord used a racial slur in the presence of a woman seeking to rent a house from him. The woman was white but had a Black fiancé. When she informed the landlord of this, he made statements about not wanting Black people hanging around his property. He later made similar statements to a Housing Authority employee who was there to inspect the property because the woman was using a §8 voucher. After the landlord failed to rent the property to her, the woman filed a discrimination claim against him, alleging in part that his statements to her and to the inspector violated §3604(c). The district court held that the statement to the inspector was not commercial speech, "due to the lack of any actual or intended commercial activity between Mr. Robb and the inspector." As a result, the court held the statement "was entitled to full First Amendment protection," meaning that §3604(c) could not constitutionally be applied to it. The Sixth Circuit reversed, holding that:

> Here, the §8 inspection was an integral component of the proposed rental transaction between Mr. Robb and Campbell, since without a completed inspection Campbell would have been unable to rent the dwelling. Indeed, the whole purpose of the interaction between Mr. Robb and the §8 inspector was to facilitate a proposed commercial transaction. In this context, Mr. Robb's statement to the §8 inspector was "linked inextricably" to the underlying rental transaction, and therefore falls within the "somewhat larger category of commercial speech" the government may regulate pursuant to its inherent power to regulate the underlying commercial transaction. [EDS. — However, the court did not find a racial slur to be covered by the FHA where it was unconnected to the rental transaction and made before the landlord knew the race of Campbell's fiancé.]

In contrast, in Salisbury House, Inc. v. McDermott, No. 96-CV-6486, 1998 WL 195693, at *10 (E.D. Pa. Mar. 24, 1998), the defendants were neighbors who wrote letters and circulated flyers opposing a proposed group home for residents with mental illnesses. The neighbors were charged with violating §3604(c), but the court refused to apply it to them:

> If we were to assume that any publication which makes reference to the sale or rental of property may be subject to the prohibitions of the FHAA, this would imply that any malcontent who publishes material stating that no homes should be sold to people in wheelchairs would be in violation of federal law. It

is easy to see how such a legal standard could come into conflict with the First Amendment if the person publishing the statement were not actually involved in buying, selling, or renting any real property. The alternative interpretation, that subsection (c) only applies to those directly involved in a particular transaction, does not implicate the First Amendment in the same manner.

Although we find this analysis helpful, our holding should not be read to imply that the only persons subject to liability under §3604(c) are those with authority to buy, sell, or lease a given piece of property. Rather, we hold that application of this section to the Defendants in this case would present a serious conflict with the First Amendment, and therefore we decline to apply the broad interpretation suggested by the Plaintiff.[9]

The statements of housing providers with objections to same-sex couples and transgender individuals might raise FHA issues. As discussed in Chapter 15, discrimination against such individuals now almost surely constitutes prohibited discrimination on the basis of sex, under Bostock v. Clayton County, 590 U.S. 644 (2020). Thus, it seems clear that a housing provider would not be permitted to "put up signs saying 'no [apartments for rent] if they will be used for gay [couples.]'" *See* Masterpiece Cakeshop, Ltd. v. Colorado Civil Rights Commission 584 U.S. 617, 634 (2018) (describing this kind of sign as "impos[ing] a serious stigma on gay persons"). But what if a housing provider were to state a religious viewpoint opposing gay marriage? Would such a statement indicate a preference on the basis of sex? Religion? What if a housing provider makes clear that he supports a political candidate who opposes same-sex marriage or a ballot initiative prohibiting gender-affirming health care? The Supreme Court's decision in 303 Creative v. Elenis, 600 U.S. 570 (2023), deals with First Amendment protections for religious objections to same-sex marriage but does not directly answer this question. In that case, the speech at issue was considered "pure" (noncommercial) speech, and the issue was whether civil rights laws addressing public accommodations could compel a creative professional to engage in speech to which she objected (specifically, to create websites for same-sex weddings). When it comes to housing providers, the FHA's coverage may well turn on how connected the speech activity is to a sale or rental transaction, that is, how connected it is to the sale or rental of housing.

4. Harassment and Other Statutory Provisions. Section 3604(c)'s focus on speech means that it can apply in many situations and overlap with other statutory provisions, in particular those addressed to harassment. As discussed in Chapters 8 and 10, harassment claims usually are brought under §3604(b), which prohibits discriminatory terms and conditions in housing, and §3617, which makes it unlawful "to coerce, intimidate, threaten, or interfere with any person in the exercise or enjoyment of" housing rights. However, harassment

---

9. [EDs.—Similar First Amendment issues arise with respect to speech or expressive conduct that interferes with housing rights, in potential violation of §3617. These cases are discussed in Chapter 10.]

typically also involves a verbal component (threats, slurs, sexual language, etc.). Sometimes the speech component may be the exclusive basis for the harassment claim. This means that most harassment plaintiffs may also assert a claim under §3604(c). In fact, given the relatively simple nature of a §3604(c) claim, and the more complicated proof requirements under these other sections, it might be easier for a plaintiff in a speech-only harassment case to prevail under §3604(c). *See* Robert G. Schwemm & Rigel C. Oliveri, *A New Look at Sexual Harassment Under the Fair Housing Act: The Forgotten Role of §3604(c)*, 2002 Wis. L. Rev. 771, 856-57 (2002) ("Because housing harassment almost always involves and indeed often consists entirely of verbal statements, a good deal of such harassment should be held to violate §3604(c). Focused as it is on discriminatory statements and without a 'severe or pervasive' standard, §3604(c) would seem to be a potent weapon for combating sexual harassment in the housing context.").

5. Possible Plaintiffs, Harm, and Damages. Who is harmed by discriminatory housing statements and advertisements, and what is the nature of that harm? A homeseeker who is a member of the group being discriminated against is an obvious plaintiff. However, harm can occur even if the hearer is not a member of the group that is the object of the discrimination. For example, discriminatory statements and advertisements may perpetuate a message to the general public that certain neighborhoods or complexes are segregated, which is harmful to society. The court noted in *Hunter*, 459 F.2d at 214:

> Widespread appearance of discriminatory advertisements in public or private media may reasonably be thought to have a harmful effect on the general aims of the Act: seeing large numbers of "white only" advertisements in one part of a city may deter non-whites from venturing to seek homes there, even if other dwellings in the same area must be sold or rented on a non-discriminatory basis.

A discriminatory statement also may harm a person closely connected to a person derogated by the comment, as in *Campbell v. Robb*, above. If the statement or advertisement dissuades a home seeker from obtaining housing, then the harm is clear and the situation probably also is covered by §3604(a). But simply hearing a discriminatory statement may cause harm, particularly if the statement is an offensive one (as most will be). Importantly, §3604(c) does not require a showing that a plaintiff was deterred from obtaining housing, or even that the plaintiff was seeking housing at all. Consider the following cases:

- In Harris v. Itzhaki, 183 F.3d 1043 (9th Cir. 1999), the plaintiff was the only Black resident of an apartment complex. She overheard a fellow tenant who helped manage the apartments telling a maintenance employee that "the owners don't want to rent to blacks." Despite the fact that the plaintiff was already a resident of the complex and was not the obvious target of the statement, the plaintiffs' evidence was sufficient to survive summary judgment under §3604(c).

- In HUD v. Ro, HUDALJ No. 03-93-0313-8, 1995 WL 326736 (June 2, 1995), a Black social worker named Julie Obi was attempting to help a white client rent an apartment. The apartment's owner, apparently confused as to whom the apartment was for, pointed to the white client and told Ms. Obi, "She's okay for the apartment, you are not." The HUD ALJ found that this incident upset Ms. Obi and caused her substantial humiliation and embarrassment, and that she was entitled to relief under §3604(c) even though she herself was not seeking to rent the apartment.

In Spann v. Colonial Village, Inc., 899 F.2d 24, 27 (D.C. Cir. 1990), the plaintiffs included two FHOs dedicated to ensuring equality of housing opportunity through education and other efforts. They claimed that the defendants' repeated and continued practice of exclusively using white models in housing advertisements steered Black homebuyers and renters away from the advertised properties. The court held that the organizations had standing because the defendants' practices forced these plaintiffs "to devote resources to checking or neutralizing the ads' adverse impact [and] to devote more time, effort, and money to endeavors designed to educate not only black home buyers and renters, but the . . . area real estate industry and the public that racial preference in housing is indeed illegal."

Similarly, as in *Jancik*, testers may claim damages under §3604(c) if they are exposed to discriminatory statements while posing as home seekers, even though they do not wish to buy or rent housing themselves. As a related matter, recall that §3604(c) applies to landlords and units that are exempt from other substantive portions of the FHA, based in large part on an "anti-market-limiting" rationale and the need to protect home seekers and others from psychic injury. In those cases, the only violation will be the discriminatory statement itself.

Even though a variety of plaintiffs can bring independent claims for §3604(c) violations, the question remains as to how to compute damages based on the harm from hearing or seeing a discriminatory statement. This will depend on the nature of the statements and the circumstances. For example, the complainant in HUD v. Gruzdaitis, HUDALJ 02-96-0377-8, 1998 WL 482759, at *1-2, *5 (Aug. 14, 1998), was awarded $25,000 for "severe emotional distress" caused by a landlord's angry and profane statements when the complainant inquired about housing. (The ALJ found that the landlord had said, "Not for you, no blacks. Fuck you, they don't pay rent." He then asked the complainant to move closer to him. When she did, he spit at her and said, "Fuck you all, you don't pay your rent. Get off my porch, get off my property.") In *HUD v. Ro* (discussed above), the ALJ determined that Julie Obi was entitled to $10,000 in emotional distress damages, in part because she was humiliated in front of a client she was trying to serve. The tester in *Jancik v. HUD* (discussed above), who was asked about her race when she inquired about an apartment, was awarded $2,000.

For a plaintiff who might wish to claim emotional distress damages after viewing or hearing a discriminatory advertisement the calculus is even more difficult. Consider the following passage from *Ragin*, 923 F.2d at 1004-05 (above):

> The individual plaintiffs seek compensatory and punitive damages for emotional injury resulting from the ads in question, and the Times is fearful that such claims from a multitude of plaintiffs might lead to a large number of staggering, perhaps crushing, damage awards that might over time impair the press's role in society. The problem is that a claimant may establish a prima facie case for such damages simply by oral testimony that he or she is a newspaper reader of a race different from the models used and was substantially insulted and distressed by a certain ad. The potential for large numbers of truly baseless claims for emotional injury thus exists, and there appears to be no ready device, other than wholly speculative judgments as to credibility, to separate the genuine from the baseless. However, we do not regard this possibility as a reason to immunize publishers from any liability under §3604(c), including injunctive relief. Rather, it is [a] reason to assert judicial control over the size of damage awards for emotional injury in individual cases.

C. ADVERTISING AND THE INTERNET

In 1968, print was the primary medium for most housing-related advertisements. Today, a significant number of people instead see advertisements on the Internet. This new context has created various issues with respect to the FHA's prohibition against discriminatory housing advertisements.

1. User-Generated Advertisements

Today there are several websites devoted exclusively to listings for housing rental and sales. Other platforms such as Facebook (now Meta) and Google display housing and other advertisements to users of their services. Websites that feature advertisements for housing, like traditional print media, ordinarily would be covered by the FHA's advertising prohibitions were it not for an exception created by Congress. To encourage the growth of the Internet as a tool for commerce and the exchange of ideas, Congress passed the Telecommunications Act of 1996, Title V of which is called the Communications Decency Act (CDA), 47 U.S.C. §230. The CDA shields website operators from liability for the contents of user-generated material that appears on their sites by specifically defining the website operators as service providers, not content providers:

> (c)(1) Treatment of publisher or speaker
> No provider or user of an interactive computer service shall be treated as the publisher or speaker of any information provided by another information content provider.

This negates the publisher liability provision in §3604(c) with respect to many website operators. For example, in Chicago Lawyers' Committee for

Civil Rights Under Law (CLC) v. Craigslist, Inc., 461 F. Supp. 2d 681, 698 (N.D. Ill. 2006), *aff'd*, 519 F.3d 666 (7th Cir. 2008), the plaintiffs sued Craigslist, an operator of an "on-line bulletin board," alleging it allowed users to post obviously discriminatory housing ads. The court held that the CDA shielded Craigslist from liability.

> Craigslist is a "provider . . . of an interactive computer service" because, as alleged in the Complaint, Craigslist operates a website that multiple users have accessed to create allegedly discriminatory housing notices. These notices, in turn, are "information" that originates, not from Craigslist, but from "another information content provider," namely the users of Craigslist's website. As a "provider . . . of an interactive computer service" that serves as a conduit for "information provided by another information content provider," Craigslist "shall not be treated as a publisher." 47 U.S.C. §230(c)(1). Because to hold Craigslist liable under §3604(c) would be to treat Craigslist as if it were the publisher of third-party content, the plain language of §230(c)(1) forecloses CLC's cause of action.

A website operator can lose its immunity under the CDA, however, if the website also acts as a content provider by eliciting or prompting users to add particular information. In Fair Housing Council of San Fernando Valley v. Roommate.com, LLC, 521 F.3d 1157, 1166 (9th Cir. 2008) (en banc), an online roommate-matching service queried users about characteristics such as sex, sexual orientation, and whether they had children, and matched them accordingly. The court held that this active involvement in content development caused Rommmate.com to lose its protection under the CDA:

> Here, the part of the profile that is alleged to offend the FHA and state housing discrimination laws — the information about sex, family status and sexual orientation — is provided by subscribers in response to Roommate's questions, which they cannot refuse to answer if they want to use defendant's services. By requiring subscribers to provide the information as a condition of accessing its service, and by providing a limited set of pre-populated answers, Roommate becomes much more than a passive transmitter of information provided by others; it becomes the developer, at least in part, of that information. And §230 provides immunity only if the interactive computer service does not "creat[e] or develop[]" the information "in whole or in part." *See* 47 U.S.C. §230(f)(3).
>
> . . . The FHA makes it unlawful to ask certain discriminatory questions for a very good reason: Unlawful questions solicit (a.k.a. "develop") unlawful answers. Not only does Roommate ask these questions, Roommate makes answering the discriminatory questions a condition of doing business. This is no different from a real estate broker in real life saying, "Tell me whether you're Jewish or you can find yourself another broker." When a business enterprise extracts such information from potential customers as a condition of accepting them as clients, it is no stretch to say that the enterprise is responsible, at least in part, for developing that information.

The Ninth Circuit ultimately vacated a subsequent judgment in this case after concluding that the FHA does not apply to shared living at all because of constitutional concerns about the freedom of intimate association. 666 F.3d 1216 (9th Cir. 2012). This issue is discussed in greater detail in Chapter 5.

2. Targeted Advertising and Algorithmic "Discrimination"

An even thornier set of problems is presented by the mechanics of *how* social media, search engines, and other platforms operate to deliver housing advertisements to their users. These platforms may permit advertisers to target ads based on protected characteristics (although many now have specifically forbidden this practice for ads relating to housing, employment, and other subjects that are governed by civil rights protections). In addition, data-mining practices and the algorithms behind artificial intelligence and machine learning also might prevent users from seeing housing ads that the system believes would not be of interest to them. These algorithms may not explicitly use characteristics that are protected under the FHA, but still may rely on "proxy characteristics" that closely track protected characteristics, such as surname, zip code, and so on. Finally, machine learning can be used to target ads based on users' own cross-platform online activity (websites they visit, products they buy, social media they use).

Consider the following allegations, excerpted from a Charge of Discrimination (an administrative enforcement action)[10] filed by HUD against Facebook (now Meta) in 2019:

> 7. Respondent collects millions of data points about its users, draws inferences about each user based on this data, and then charges advertisers for the ability to microtarget ads to users based on Respondent's inferences about them. These ads are then shown to users across the web and in mobile applications. Respondent promotes and distinguishes its advertising platform by proclaiming that "most online advertising tools have limited targeting options . . . like location, age, gender, interests and potentially a few others. . . . But Facebook is different. People on Facebook share their true identities, interests, life events and more." As Respondent explains, its advertising platform enables advertisers to "[r]each people based on . . . zipcode . . . age and gender . . . specific languages . . . the interests they've shared, their activities, the Pages they've like[d] . . . [their] purchase behaviors or intents, device usage and more." Thus, Respondent "use[s] location-related information—such as your current location, where you live, the places you like to go, and the businesses and people you're near—to provide, personalize and improve our Products, including ads, for you and others."
>
> 8. Advertisers pay Respondent to show targeted ads to users on Facebook, Instagram, and Messenger, and on Respondent's Audience Network. Targeted ads are generally placed through a single advertising platform called Ads Manager regardless of where the ads will be shown to users.
>
> 9. Respondent holds out its advertising platform as a powerful resource for advertisers in many industries, including housing and housing-related services. For example, Respondent promotes its advertising platform with "success stories," including stories from a housing developer, a real estate agency, a mortgage lender, a real-estate-focused marketing agency, and a search tool for rental housing.

---

10. *See* HUDALJ Charge of Discrimination, 01-18-0323-8 (Mar. 28, 2019), https://archi ves.hud.gov/news/2019/HUD_v_Facebook.pdf.

10. Respondent's advertising platform is actively being used for housing-related ads. Such ads include ads for mortgages from large national lenders, ads for rental housing from large real estate listing services, and ads for specific houses for sale from real estate agents.

11. Because of the way Respondent designed its advertising platform, ads for housing and housing-related services are shown to large audiences that are severely biased based on characteristics protected by the Act, such as audiences of tens of thousands of users that are nearly all men or nearly all women.

12. Respondent sells advertisers the ability to target advertisements to people who, according to Respondent's assessment of the data it collects, share certain personal attributes and/or are likely to respond to a particular ad. Users may disclose some data about themselves when they set up their profiles, such as name and gender. However, users disclose most of this data unwittingly through the actions they, and those associated with them, take on and off of Respondent's platforms.

13. Respondent determines which users will see an ad through a two-phase process. First, in the ad targeting phase, Respondent provides the advertiser with a variety of tools for selecting an ad's "eligible audience." In other words, the advertiser can specify attributes that the users who will be shown the ad must have and attributes that users who will be shown the ad must not have. Second, in the ad delivery phase, Respondent selects the ad's "actual audience," meaning Respondent chooses which users will actually be shown the ad from among the pool of eligible users.

14. During the ad targeting phase, Respondent provides an advertiser with tools to define which users, or which types of users, the advertiser would like to see an ad. Respondent has provided a toggle button that enables advertisers to exclude men or women from seeing an ad, a search-box to exclude people who do not speak a specific language from seeing an ad, and a map tool to exclude people who live in a specified area from seeing an ad by drawing a red line around that area. Respondent also provides drop-down menus and search boxes to exclude or include (i.e., limit the audience of an ad exclusively to) people who share specified attributes. Respondent has offered advertisers hundreds of thousands of attributes from which to choose, for example to exclude "women in the workforce," "moms of grade school kids," "foreigners," "Puerto Rico Islanders," or people interested in "parenting," "accessibility," "service animal," "Hijab Fashion," or "Hispanic Culture." Respondent also has offered advertisers the ability to limit the audience of an ad by selecting to include only those classified as, for example, "Christian" or "Childfree."

15. During this first phase, Respondent also provides a tool called Custom Audiences, which enables an advertiser to use a list of specific people whom the advertiser wants included in or excluded from the eligible audience for an ad. The advertiser can do this by uploading the personal information of its customers, or by having Respondent generate a list of people who have engaged with the advertiser's content on Facebook or Instagram, on other websites, in a mobile application, or offline.

16. Facebook offers a variant of its Custom Audiences tool called Lookalike Audiences. If an advertiser selects this option, the platform directs the advertiser to pick a Custom Audience that represents the advertiser's "best existing customers." Respondent then identifies users who share "common qualities" with those customers, and these users become the ad's eligible audience. To generate a Lookalike Audience, Respondent considers sex and close proxies for the other protected classes. Such proxies can include which pages a user visits, which apps a user has, where a user goes during the day, and the purchases a

user makes on and offline. Respondent alone, not the advertiser, determines which users will be included in a Lookalike Audience.

17. During the second phase, the ad delivery phase, Respondent selects from among the users eligible to see an ad [and] which users will actually see it. Respondent bases this decision in large part on the inferences and predictions it draws about each user's likelihood to respond to an ad based on the data it has about that user, the data it has about other users whom it considers to resemble that user, and the data it has about "friends" and other associates of that user. To decide which users will see an ad, Respondent considers sex and close proxies for the other protected classes. Such proxies can include which pages a user visits, which apps a user has, where a user goes during the day, and the purchases a user makes on and offline. Respondent alone, not the advertiser, determines which users will constitute the "actual audience" for each ad.

18. Respondent charges advertisers different prices to show the same ad to different users. The price to show an ad to a given user is based, in large part, on how likely Respondent believes that user is to interact with the particular ad. To decide how an ad will be priced for each user, Respondent considers sex and close proxies for the other protected classes. Such proxies can include which pages a user visits, which apps a user has, where a user goes during the day, and the purchases a user makes on and offline. Respondent alone sets the price the advertiser will pay to have Respondent show each ad to each user. Furthermore, Respondent uses the pricing differentials it sets to determine which users will see which ads rather than allowing advertisers to make that decision. As Respondent explains, "If there are more and cheaper opportunities among men than women, then we'd automatically spend more of [an advertiser's] overall budget on the men."

19. Respondent's ad delivery system prevents advertisers who want to reach a broad audience of users from doing so. Even if an advertiser tries to target an audience that broadly spans protected class groups, Respondent's ad delivery system will not show the ad to a diverse audience if the system considers users with particular characteristics most likely to engage with the ad. If the advertiser tries to avoid this problem by specifically targeting an unrepresented group, the ad delivery system will still not deliver the ad to those users, and it may not deliver the ad at all. This is so because Respondent structured its ad delivery system such that it generally will not deliver an ad to users whom the system determines are unlikely to engage with the ad, even if the advertiser explicitly wants to reach those users regardless.

20. To group users by shared attributes, to create a Lookalike Audience, to determine an ad's "actual audience" during the ad delivery phase, and to price each ad for each user, Respondent combines the data it has about user attributes and behavior on its platforms with data it obtains about user behavior on other websites and in the non-digital world. Respondent then uses machine learning and other prediction techniques to classify and group users so as to project each user's likely response to a given ad. In doing so, Respondent inevitably recreates groupings defined by their protected class. For example, the top Facebook pages users "like" vary sharply by their protected class, according to Respondent's "Audience Insights" tool. Therefore, by grouping users who "like" similar pages (unrelated to housing) and presuming a shared interest or disinterest in housing-related advertisements, Respondent's mechanisms function just like an advertiser who intentionally targets or excludes users based on their protected class.

The Department of Justice ultimately handled the complaint, and the parties settled in 2022.[11] Facebook (Meta) agreed to limit its targeting options for housing advertisements, and not to make its Look-Alike Audience tool available for housing ads.

NOTES AND QUESTIONS

1. Roommates and User Liability. With the threat of publisher liability eliminated by §230 of the CDA, websites have little incentive to screen out discriminatory ads. At the same time, anyone with access to a computer can post housing advertisements online. Indeed, this appears to be the most common way that people advertise housing today. In particular, individuals who are searching for roommates in shared housing situations are likely to use online platforms in their search. Consider the following observations, made from a study of the content of thousands of housing advertisements posted to the website Craigslist:

> The vast majority of potentially discriminatory ads are those for shared housing. Virtually all of the ads that mention the protected categories of race, religion, and national origin are roommate ads. . . . Another reason why roommate ads are the primary culprits is that most roommate-seekers are renters as opposed to property owners or professional landlords. As such, they are less likely to know about the FHA and its requirements as they pertain to advertising.[12]

Although the websites that host the ads are immunized from liability, the individuals who post the ads might not be. What problems might this present from an enforcement standpoint? From a fairness standpoint?

2. Disparate Impact and Algorithms. Claims about artificial intelligence or algorithmic discrimination typically rely on a disparate impact theory. (Disparate impact theory is discussed in Chapter 7.) In other words, there is seldom an allegation in this setting that anyone has intentionally discriminated against users on the basis of a protected characteristic; rather, the claim is that the design and modeling of the algorithm incorporate elements or factors that have a discriminatory effect on members of different groups according to protected characteristics.

A disparate impact claim requires the plaintiff to identify a particular practice or policy of the defendant that is alleged to cause the discriminatory effect. The plaintiff then must prove the claim using statistics about

---

11. The agreement is available at United States v. Meta Platforms, Inc. f/k/a Facebook, Inc., Settlement Agreement (S.D.N.Y June 21, 2022), https://www.justice.gov/opa/press-release/file/1514031/download.

12. Rigel C. Oliveri, *Discriminatory Housing Advertisements On-Line: Lessons From Craigslist*, 43 IND. L. REV. 1125, 1151-52 (2010).

the disproportionate effect on protected groups. The defendant can rebut these arguments by showing that the defendant's actions have not actually caused the effect. The defendant can also raise a "business necessity" defense, in essence arguing that its policy or practice was necessary for the operation of its business. If a defendant can meet its burden of proof, then a plaintiff may still prevail by showing that there is an alternative practice that would have a less discriminatory effect while achieving the legitimate purpose. How do these arguments play out in a case like that of Facebook/ Meta? What kind of data is necessary to identify the particular algorithm and plead its discriminatory effects, and how will the plaintiff obtain this information? What might Facebook/Meta argue in support of a business necessity defense?

3. Advertiser Prerogatives and Algorithmic Accuracy. A core function of advertising is to target and reach people whom the advertiser believes are most likely to purchase the product or service. Advertisers conduct extensive market research and often design different ad campaigns for different audiences. The availability of extensive individual user information and the users' own interactions with the Internet allow for microtargeting on a level that was unimaginable in 1968.

Is the mining of user data to create a customizable audience for any housing provider enough to render a platform like Meta a content provider rather than a publisher, and thus subject to the FHA?[13] Is this targeting of ads a benefit for users? Facebook and other platforms have argued that it is the user's own choices and activities that guide which ads the user sees. Meta has said that users can change the ads they are shown by interacting with different content and can always affirmatively seek out information on their own using different search methods. (The complaint above disputes this.) By relying on a single platform for news, advertisements, and communication, are users implicitly agreeing to have their content filtered? The change in practices agreed to by Facebook/Meta in the settlement agreement above will help address the issues raised by HUD's Charge, but as technology develops, new problems and challenges are likely to arise. Professor Valerie Schneider raises the following concerns:

> Because algorithms are so complex and are "trained" to recognize and utilize patterns in ways that even their developers may not have anticipated, rooting out bias in algorithms is incredibly difficult. One might think that simply removing data that relates to a protected class would be enough to root out bias from algorithms. Studies show, however, that since the advent of artificial intelligence and machine learning, algorithms do not make predictions based on correlations between just a few pieces of data, but instead make predictions

---

13. *See* National Fair Housing Alliance v. Facebook, Inc., DOJ Statement of Interest (S.D.N.Y. Aug. 17, 2018), https://www.justice.gov/crt/case-document/file/1089231/download. This issue remains unresolved by U.S. courts.

based on relationships between tens of thousands of data points. Simply removing data related to protected classes does little to change biased results.[14]

Chapter Summary

- Section 3604(c) prohibits making, printing, or publishing housing-related statements, notices, or advertisements that indicate a preference, limitation, or discrimination based on a protected characteristic.
- HUD has promulgated a regulation interpreting this provision, at 24 C.F.R. §100.75.
- The question whether statements, notices, and advertisements indicate a discriminatory preference or limitation is judged by an "ordinary listener/reader" standard.
- Use of human models in advertising, questions about protected characteristics, and unenforceable deed restrictions can all fall under this section.
- This section applies to properties that are otherwise exempt under 42 U.S.C. §3603(b) from the substantive provisions of the FHA.
- This section includes liability for publishers; however, the Communications Decency Act exempts operators of websites and platforms from liability for purely user-generated content.

---

14. Valerie Schneider, *Locked out by Big Data: How Big Data, Algorithms and Machine Learning May Undermine Housing Justice*, 52 COLUM. HUM. RTS. L. REV. 251, 291-92 (2020).

CHAPTER 10

SECTION 3617: PROHIBITED INTERFERENCE, THREATS, COERCION, OR INTIMIDATION, AND SECTION 3631: CRIMINAL PROVISION

Section 3617 of the FHA makes it unlawful "to coerce, intimidate, threaten, or interfere with any person in the exercise or enjoyment of, or on account of his having exercised or enjoyed, or on account of his having aided or encouraged any other person in the exercise or enjoyment of, any right granted or protected by section 3603, 3604, 3605, or 3606 of this title."

HUD's regulation further clarifies the conduct covered by §3617:

§100.400 PROHIBITED INTERFERENCE, COERCION OR INTIMIDATION.

(c) Conduct made unlawful under this section includes, but is not limited to, the following:

(1) Coercing a person, either orally, in writing, or by other means, to deny or limit the benefits provided that person in connection with the sale or rental of a dwelling or in connection with a residential real estate-related transaction because of [protected characteristics].

(2) Threatening, intimidating or interfering with persons in their enjoyment of a dwelling because of the [protected characteristics] of such persons, or of visitors or associates of such persons.

(3) Threatening an employee or agent with dismissal or an adverse employment action, or taking such adverse employment action, for any effort to assist a person seeking access to the sale or rental of a dwelling or seeking access to any residential real estate-related transaction,

because of the [protected characteristics] of that person or of any person associated with that person.

(4) Intimidating or threatening any person because that person is engaging in activities designed to make other persons aware of, or encouraging such other persons to exercise, rights granted or protected by this part.

(5) Retaliating against any person because that person has made a complaint, testified, assisted, or participated in any manner in a proceeding under the FHA.

(6) Retaliating against any person because that person reported a discriminatory housing practice to a housing provider or other authority.

Thus, this section prohibits three types of conduct: (1) coercion, threats, intimidation, or other harassing conduct that interferes with a person's exercise or enjoyment of fair housing rights; (2) threats or retaliation against a person for assisting others in exercising or enjoying their rights to fair housing; and (3) retaliation against any person for reporting a fair housing violation or participating in proceedings under the FHA.

There are a few important points to note, which will be discussed in greater detail in this chapter:

- First, a plaintiff need not be interfered with while specifically asserting or enforcing housing rights for this section to apply. A plaintiff need only be enjoying their right to fair housing, for instance by moving into or living in the housing, when they experience interference, threats, and so on, to have an actionable claim.

- Second, to the extent that §3617 covers harassing conduct, there is significant overlap between it and §3604(b), which has been interpreted to prohibit harassment where it affects the "terms and conditions" of a person's housing. Many plaintiffs alleging harassment by housing providers bring claims under both provisions.

- Third, §3617 claims are somewhat unique, because they can be brought against anyone. Claims under §§3604(a), (b), and (c) generally can be made only against housing providers or housing professionals, because those are the only parties who can discriminate with respect to "the sale or rental of housing." Section 3617 contains no such limiting language, and thus claims under this section can be brought against neighbors, community members, and others who do not have direct control over the plaintiff's housing, but nonetheless are capable of interfering with it.

- Fourth, §3617 creates a separate cause of action for retaliation. This provision can be invoked by groups and individuals who are not themselves aggrieved by a discriminatory housing practice but have experienced harm because they assisted others in exercising fair housing rights.

- Finally, while the language of this section refers to the other substantive provisions of the Act, courts of appeals have agreed that claims under this section can stand alone. In other words, a plaintiff can bring claims only under §3617 or can prevail on §3617 claims even if claims under other portions of the statute are unsuccessful. It is necessary, however, that a §3617 claim have a "predicate" in the substantive provisions of the FHA.

A. INTERFERENCE, THREATS, COERCION, OR INTIMIDATION

One of the most important questions for §3617 is what sort of conduct can constitute "interference, threats, coercion, or intimidation" in violation of the provision. Violent actions involving physical force or property destruction clearly violate §3617. *See, e.g.,* Johnson v. Smith, 810 F. Supp. 235, 238-39 (N.D. Ill. 1992) (allegations that defendants participated in cross-burning on plaintiff's property sufficient to state §3617 claim); Stirgus v. Benoit, 720 F. Supp. 119 (N.D. Ill. 1989) (firebombing of plaintiff's house); Seaphus v. Lilly, 691 F. Supp. 127 (N.D. Ill. 1988) (physical assault and attempted arson of plaintiff's home); Waheed v. Kalafut, No. 86 C 6674, 1988 WL 9092 (N.D. Ill. Feb. 2, 1988) (firebombing house, banging garbage cans, and screaming racial epithets); Stackhouse v. DeSitter, 620 F. Supp. 208 (N.D. Ill. 1985) (firebombing of plaintiff's car). Such violent acts are also likely to violate the FHA's criminal provision, §3631, discussed at the end of this chapter.

It is also clear, however, that violence and force are not *required* to establish a violation of §3617. *See* Michigan Prot. & Advoc. Serv., Inc. v. Babin, 18 F.3d 337, 347 (6th Cir. 1994) ("Section 3617 is not limited to those who used some sort of 'potent force or duress,' but extends to other actors who are in a position directly to disrupt the exercise or enjoyment of a protected right and exercise their powers with a discriminatory animus."); *see also* United States v. American Institute of Real Estate Appraisers, 442 F. Supp. 1072, 1079 (N.D. Ill. 1977) (observing that §3617 has been "broadly applied to reach all practices which have the effect of interfering with the exercise of rights" under the FHA). The inclusion of the word "interference" thus signals that Congress meant the provision to cover more than intimidating or threatening conduct.

On the other hand, there is a great deal of conduct that could be considered "interference," and courts have been wary about expanding the definition of the term. This is especially true because, as discussed further below, §3617 can apply to anyone, including fellow tenants, neighbors, and community members. Courts have been reluctant to enforce the FHA in situations that appear to be "nothing more than a series of skirmishes" between neighbors. *See, e.g.,* United States v. Weisz, 914 F. Supp. 1050, 1054 (S.D.N.Y. 1996) (§3617, read literally, could "federalize any dispute involving residences and people who live in them. Nothing in the statute or its legislative history supports so startling a proposition.").

Consider the following cases that address the issue of whether particular nonviolent conduct falls under §3617.

People Helpers Foundation, Inc. v. The City of Richmond
781 F. Supp. 1132 (E.D. Va. 1992)

Richard L. WILLIAMS, District Judge:

Plaintiff People Helpers Foundation, Inc. is a nonprofit Virginia corporation whose mission includes finding decent and affordable housing within neighborhood communities for individuals with mental and physical handicaps. In many instances, these individuals are black. In February of 1991, People Helpers rented apartments in and eventually purchased the building at 1207–09 West 47th Street in the City of Richmond (the "Building"). Subsequently, People Helpers moved a number of handicapped individuals into the Building as tenants.

The defendants, Joyce Riddell and William T. Riddell (collectively, the "Riddells"), live directly across the street from the Building. The Riddells also own other rental property in the immediate area. The Complaint alleges that the Riddells have made statements and committed acts designed to frighten or intimidate the Plaintiffs and thereby stop them from continuing to house their clients in the neighborhood, especially their black clients. For instance, Mr. Riddell asked Robert Elam, the chief operating officer of People Helpers and one of the Plaintiffs in this action, why People Helpers could not find any "white people" to put in the Building. Mr. Riddell also allegedly made another derogatory and sarcastic statement about blacks to Rebecca Thomas, another Plaintiff and a People Helpers volunteer.

The Complaint further alleges that Mrs. Riddell also took actions designed to intimidate People Helpers and to cause them to look elsewhere for housing their clients. Specifically, in June of 1991, Rebecca Thomas and Gary Thomas delivered mattresses and other furnishings to the apartments leased by People Helpers in the Building. When Mrs. Riddell noticed the furniture being moved into the Building, she went to the front door of many of her neighbors and then summoned them outside. She then allegedly gathered these neighbors in an intimidating and threatening manner in her front yard, directly across the street from the Building, while the People Helpers volunteers unloaded the apartment furnishings. In addition, Mrs. Riddell has on numerous occasions throughout the summer and fall of 1991, stood in her yard taking pictures of People Helpers' clients and staff. All of these actions, claim the Plaintiffs, were intended to create an atmosphere of intimidation and fear and to cause People Helpers to locate its clients in a different neighborhood.

In addition, the Plaintiffs claim that on October 24, 1991, the Richmond Bureau of Police made a decision that they would not allow People Helpers to continue to use the Building despite the fact that there were no actual violations of the Building Code, Zoning Ordinance, or any other state or local law. The reason given by the Police for its decision was that the neighbors did not like the "type" of people living in the Building. The Bureau of Police further stated that the neighbors were "intolerant of the People Helpers' Clients living in the Building, would not condone them much longer, and that Plaintiff Robert Elam's only reasonable course of action would be to evict People Helpers' Clients from the Building, and refrain from leasing to any people with mental and physical disabilities."

Based upon these allegations, the Plaintiffs contend that the Riddells violated their right to provide housing to blacks and disabled people free from intimidation, interference, and coercion pursuant to 42 U.S.C. §3617. They seek damages, permanent injunctive relief, and a declaratory judgment against the Riddells and the City of Richmond.

THE MOTION TO DISMISS

The Riddells argue that the facts outlined above simply do not add up to anything illegal. The defendants maintain that the Complaint does not suggest any facts that show the Riddells' actions were motivated by animus towards disabled people. Furthermore, the Riddells make the unsupported assertion that Plaintiffs have no standing to raise a claim of racial animus. Rather, the Riddells maintain that the Complaint only shows that they had fears about possible drug use and building code violations occurring in their neighborhood. Mr. Riddell also communicated his legitimate concerns about possible parking problems, and Mrs. Riddell complained to their councilman that the Building had too many residents.

Even assuming that they disliked handicapped people, the Riddells argue that their actions fall far short of anything designed to intimidate or force people out of their neighborhood. They did not approach anyone with threats, they did not damage anyone's property, they did not send hate mail, and they did not make a display of force. In other words, the facts alleged in the Complaint, according to the Riddells, do not reach the level of intimidation or coercion contemplated by §3617. Instead, the Riddells state that all they did is observe and document all that had happened and discuss possible violations of the law with public officials.

It is clear that the Riddells did not roll out the welcome wagon when People Helpers started integrating black disabled tenants into their neighborhood. It is less certain, however, that the Riddells' conduct was such as would constitute a violation of 42 U.S.C. §3617. This, then, is the primary question before the Court, and it is an issue of first impression.

The FHA was established by Congress to insure that people who have historically suffered from discrimination in the housing markets would have an equal opportunity to housing. Although most of the legislation is designed to prevent illegal discrimination on the part of housing providers, one provision specifically prohibits unrelated third parties from interfering with anyone who is attempting to aid others protected under the Act from obtaining housing of their choice.

The FHA is "broad and inclusive" in protecting against conduct which interferes with fair housing rights and is subject to "generous construction." *Trafficante v. Metropolitan Life Insurance Co.* (1972). Although there have not been many cases addressing §3617, it is clear that this provision "protects persons who aid or encourage others in securing rights to equal housing opportunities and conditions by making it unlawful to coerce, intimidate, threaten or interfere with them because of their aid or encouragement." Meadows v. Edgewood Management Corp., 432 F. Supp. 334, 335 (W.D. Va.1977).

In order to make out a violation of §3617, Plaintiffs must satisfy four elements. First, they must show that the residents of the Building are protected classes under the FHA. Next, People Helpers must prove, by a preponderance of the evidence, that they actually aided or encouraged the protected individual or group in the exercise or enjoyment of rights under 42 U.S.C. §3604 to equal services and conditions of housing. The third factor necessary for Plaintiffs to succeed on their claim is that they must prove either intentional discrimination or discriminatory impact. This demands the Court to engage in a sensitive inquiry into such circumstantial and direct evidence of intent as may be available. Finally, under §3617, Plaintiffs must show coercion, intimidation, threat, or interference on account of their having aided or encouraged the exercise of the residents' right to live in the neighborhood of their choice.

The first and second factors of this test are not in dispute. The third factor, discriminatory intent, may also be able to be proven at trial. The Complaint alleges that Mr. Riddell asked Mr. Elam, the director of People Helpers, why he could not find any "white people" to put into the Building, and he also made a derogatory and threatening statement about blacks to Plaintiff Rebecca Thomas. The Riddells also apparently expressed dissatisfaction to Lieutenant Carlson of the Richmond Police with the "type" of people that were living in the Building. These comments indicate that discrimination or racial animus was a motivating factor in the Riddells' actions towards People Helpers. The legitimate motivations claimed by the defendants—fear of parking problems and drug activity—may prove to be a pretext for the underlying discrimination.

As stated above, the last factor, whether interference or intimidation sufficient to establish a violation of §3617 can be shown, is the primary issue before the Court. It is clear that most of the cases involving violations of §3617 entail conduct much more egregious than that which occurred in this case. For instance, in Sofarelli v. Pinellas County, 931 F.2d 718, 722 (11th Cir. 1991), the complaint alleged that the plaintiff's neighbors committed certain actions—leaving a note threatening "to break [plaintiff] in half" if he did not get out of the neighborhood and running up to one of the plaintiff's trucks, hitting it, shouting obscenities and spitting at plaintiff—which would constitute intimidation and coercion under §3617. *See also* Stackhouse v. DeSitter,

620 F. Supp. 208, 211 (N.D. Ill. 1985) (firebombing minority plaintiff's car in order to drive him away from the previously all-white neighborhood is conduct squarely within the range of actions prohibited by §3617).

However, not all violations of §3617 involve violence or threats of violent action. In the instant case, there have been no allegations that the Riddells used force or threat of force to intimidate the Plaintiffs. And certainly, the defendants' behavior does not rise up to the level of coercion such as that described in *Sofarelli* or *Stackhouse*. But even if the acts of the Riddells were not violent or illegal per se, they may still have constituted interference, intimidation, or coercion under §3617. In addition to the derogatory remarks about the black residents, the Riddells are alleged to have organized their neighbors in front of the Building in order to threaten and intimidate the People Helpers volunteers. Of course, more facts need to be developed in order to enable the trier of fact to characterize this gathering either as one resembling an outdoor tea party or as a congregation more akin to a lynch mob.

On many other occasions, the Riddells have photographed both the occupants of the Building and the volunteers in what is labeled an intimidating manner. Finally, the Complaint alleges that indirect threats were communicated to Plaintiffs through the Richmond Bureau of Police. The Riddells are alleged to have done all these things in order to send the clear message to People Helpers that their organization and their clients, especially the black residents of the Building, were not welcome in the neighborhood.

Whether the Riddells actually interfered with the Plaintiffs in some way is a question of fact. Neither the cases nor the legislative history of §3617 attempt to define the minimum level of intimidation or coercion necessary to violate this statute. Therefore, the Court assumes that the words of the statute — "coerce, intimidate, threaten or interfere" — mean exactly what they say. The fact that the Riddells' behavior is not as severe or egregious as some other cases under §3617 does not mean that, as a matter of law, what these defendants did was not violative of this provision. Moreover, if the trier of fact considers that the acts of the Riddells constituted slight or de minimis interference, such a conclusion can be adequately reflected in an appropriate award of damages.

Viewing the allegations in the Complaint in the light most favorable to the nonmoving party, the Plaintiffs have stated a proper claim under §3617 and, therefore, the Riddells' Motion to Dismiss is denied.

Egan v. Schmock
93 F. Supp. 2d 1090 (N. D. Cal. 2000)

FOGEL, District Judge:

Plaintiffs are Kulwant Egan, his wife Tara Egan, and their minor son Sachit Egan ("the Egans"). They allege that their neighbors, Mr. and Mrs. Schmock, have been harassing and intimidating them for more than nine years because of their national origin, which is East Indian. The complaint sets forth a number of acts by Mrs. Schmock, including: calling the Egans "dirty Indians" and telling them to go back where they came from; wrapping a towel around her head turban-style and putting a dot of lipstick on her forehead to mock Mrs. Egan's traditional style of dress; calling Sachit Egan a "monkey" and throwing a banana over the fence onto the Egans' property; giving the "finger" to the Egans and their guests; photographing and videotaping the Egans and their guests; throwing water and yard clippings on the cars of the Egans' guests; and following the Egans on her bicycle. The complaint does not allege any such conduct on the part of Mr. Schmock.

The Egans filed the present action, asserting two claims, one under the FHA and one under 42 U.S.C. §1982. Defendants move to dismiss the two federal claims.

III. DISCUSSION

The Egans assert that the Schmocks' behavior violated §3617 of the FHA. The Schmocks contend that the Egans have failed to state a claim under §3617 because the alleged conduct is unrelated to the Egans' exercise of a right guaranteed by §§3603-3606, that is, a right to be free from discrimination in the sale or rental of real property. The Egans contend that they are not required to allege a connection between the Schmocks' conduct and the sale or rental of real property, and that they can state a claim under §3617 based solely upon the Schmocks' interference with the Egans' enjoyment of their home.

There does not appear to be any controlling authority on this point. In fact, the Court has found little case law discussing application of §3617 when the allegedly discriminatory conduct is not directly related to the sale or rental of real property. However, a few courts have applied §3617 to violent or threatening conduct designed to drive individuals out of their homes. For example, in Ohana v. 180 Prospect Place Realty Corp., 996 F. Supp. 238 (E.D.N.Y. 1998), the plaintiffs were Jewish individuals who had moved into an apartment in Brooklyn. They alleged that two neighbors engaged in harassing and intimidating conduct, including stalking the plaintiffs, expressing unhappiness that "whites" had moved in, yelling loudly that "the motherf—ker Jews" had to go, pounding on apartment walls while yelling "Jews move," and threatening to kill the plaintiffs. The district court found these allegations sufficient to state a claim under §3617, holding that the FHA "not only protects individuals from discrimination in the acquisition of their residences because of race, color, religion, sex, familial status, or national origin, but also protects them from interference by their neighbors for such discriminatory reasons in the peaceful enjoyment of their homes." Similarly, in Stirgus v. Benoit, 720 F. Supp. 119, 123 (N.D. Ill. 1989), the district court found sufficient the plaintiff's allegations that her home had been firebombed in order to scare her out of the neighborhood.

This Court agrees with the reasoning set forth in *Ohana* and *Stirgus* and therefore holds that a §3617 claim may be based upon discriminatory conduct which is designed to drive the individual out of his or her home. Plaintiffs, however, request that the Court interpret §3617 more broadly to cover any discriminatory conduct which interferes with an individual's enjoyment of his or her home. The Court concludes that Congress did not intend that the FHA reach so far. If Plaintiffs' construction were adopted, any dispute between neighbors of different races or religions could result in a lawsuit in federal court under the FHA. The few reported cases applying the FHA to neighbor disputes involve violent or threatening conduct designed to drive the victim out of his or her home; the Court is unaware of any cases applying the FHA as broadly as is requested by Plaintiffs.

The Court concludes that the conduct alleged in the present case is sufficient to come within §3617 provided that the intent of the conduct was to drive the Egans out of their home. The Egans have not alleged such intent. Accordingly, the Court will dismiss the FHA claim with leave to amend.

Revock v. Cowpet Bay West Condominium Association
853 F.3d 96 (3d Cir. 2017)

Before Fuentes, Vanaskie, and Restrepo, Circuit Judges.

Restrepo, Circuit Judge:

Appellants Barbara Walters and Judith Kromenhoek filed these civil rights actions under the FHA. Walters and Kromenhoek sought accommodations for their disabilities in the form of emotional support animals, which were not permitted under the rules of their condominium association. They allege violations of their right to a reasonable accommodation of their disabilities, 42 U.S.C. §3604(f)(3)(B), and interference with the exercise of their fair housing rights, 42 U.S.C. §3617.

Appellants Walters and Kromenhoek suffered from disabilities, for which each was prescribed an emotional support animal. Each woman obtained a dog. This violated the "no dogs" rule of their condominium association, Cowpet Bay West. The rule had no exceptions and Cowpet had no policy regarding assistive animals, such as emotional support animals. The "no dogs" rule was enforced by the Cowpet Board of Directors, which has the authority to enforce the Cowpet "Rules and Regulations with monetary fines and other sanctions. . . ."

Walters and Kromenhoek each attempted to request an accommodation for an emotional support animal by filing paperwork with Cowpet's office manager, Louanne Schechter. The paperwork included a doctor's letter prescribing an emotional support animal, and a dog certification. Each certification stated that the dog was "prescribed and deemed necessary to assist . . .

the confirmed disabled handler" and that "property managers and landlords are required to make reasonable accommodation" under the FHA. Walters submitted her paperwork in February 2011 and Kromenhoek in July 2011. Cowpet took no action at the time.

The presence of dogs at Cowpet drew the ire of some residents. One resident, Appellee Lance Talkington, fanned the flames by writing about dogs at Cowpet on his blog about the community [and questioning whether Walters was in compliance with the "no dog" rule]. In response to this blog post, Appellee Alfred Felice posted the first of many inflammatory comments on Talkington's blog. Felice wrote that dog owners might be "happier in another community rather than ostracized at [Cowpet], which would be another fine recourse, besides a significant $ $ fine, with progressive amounts." Walters, having been named by Talkington, [defended herself as a person with a disability and] wrote that she was "mortified, that my personal business has been laid out over the internet without my permission or forewarning." Felice replied that someone who needed an emotional support dog "might go off his/her gourd without the pet at his/her side" in a "violent reaction. We don't even know we need protection![] Bad Law![]". Talkington also commented that Walters "has a pet and should be fined."

There followed a flurry of emails among the Cowpet Board, Walters and Kromenhoek. [Eds. — In October 2011, Walters emailed the board that her paperwork was on file in the office. The Board president (Harcourt) responded by email (copying Talkington) that Walters and Kromenhoek were in violation of the "no dogs" rule, confirming they had "papers" in the office but that they had ten days to submit a request directly to the Board for an exception to the rule or be fined. Talkington posted this email on his blog. Walters and Kromenhoek separately emailed the Board stating "I qualify to keep a service animal even when policy explicitly prohibits pets." They each expressed concerns about sharing private medical information on file in the office with the Board members, given the members' previous conduct; Kromenhoek offered to share her history and paperwork upon Harcourt's signing a confidentiality agreement. The parties disputed whether Harcourt or any other Cowpet official actually reviewed the accommodation requests.]

The Board did not grant an accommodation to Walters or Kromenhoek in the fall of 2011. To the contrary, at a January 2012 Board meeting, the Board voted to fine Walters and Kromenhoek [$50 per day] for violating the "no dogs" rule. On Talkington's blog, Felice and Talkington continued to denigrate dog owners at Cowpet.

Talkington subsequently wrote a blog post stating that Walters and Kromenhoek have "certified" emotional support dogs, but that such certifications are issued without "verify[ing] either the animal's credentials or the purported disability." Talkington later posted that "[t]hese r[i]diculous puppy dog diplomas from the paper mills are out of line." Talkington wrote that the "diploma mill" would accept "stress" as "a disability that qualifies for their certification" without any doctor confirmation. Felice echoed this sentiment in belligerent terms. He wrote: "PAY a few $'s on the internet and 'PRESTO' a service dog is born . . . I could 'certify' my ceramic toy with THAT process."

Later that winter, Talkington wrote on his blog that Cowpet should "go on the offensive and lawyer up to pursue an action against owners who are non-compliant with the policy on service dogs. . . ." Felice then posted a comment, describing Walters and Kromenhoek as "miscreants." Felice wrote that "failure to comply [with the no dogs rule] must lead to liens and even foreclosure, if needed, for compliance to be effective. These ungracious owners are totally selfish, spoiled, brats, willing to flaunt their illegality in every one[']s face. . . . Such gall and nerve require full responce [sic], with ostracizing the offenders in every manner at our disposal![] Isolate them completely to their little 'dog patch' on the beach and ignore them at every venue or occasion![]" Talkington followed up by writing that Walters and Kromenhoek are "playground bullie[s]" attempting to "hang onto their puppies." He wrote that "it is time for the association to go on the offensive and file suit in a court of law to force the issue. When these ladies have to start spending their own cash . . . the rubber will meet the road on how far everyone is willing to go on this issue."

The ferment finally came to a close after Harcourt completed his term as President of the Cowpet Board and was succeeded by a new President, Ed Wardwell. In March 2012, Walters and Kromenhoek submitted to Wardwell formal requests for accommodation. In April 2012, the Board granted the requests and waived the accrued fines.

Walters and Kromenhoek, nevertheless, filed these civil rights cases under the FHA. They raised two federal claims: (1) that Cowpet denied their reasonable requests for accommodation in violation of §3604(f)(3)(B) and (2) that Cowpet and three individual Appellees (Talkington, Felice and Harcourt) interfered with the exercise of their fair housing rights in violation of §3617.

Tragically, Walters committed suicide while her case was pending in the District Court. Appellees moved for summary judgment. . . . Walters and Kromenhoek now appeal the District Court's [grant of summary judgment to the defendants].[1]

VI

A §3617 interference claim requires proof of three elements: (1) that the plaintiff exercised or enjoyed "any right granted or protected by" §§3603-3606; (2) that the defendant's conduct constituted interference; and (3) a causal connection existed between the exercise or enjoyment of the right and the defendant's conduct.

The term "interference" is not defined by the FHA or the implementing regulation, 24 C.F.R. §100.400 (2016). Therefore, the word must be "understood by its ordinary meaning." United States v. Piekarsky, 687 F.3d 134, 145

---

1. [EDS.—Kromenhoek also died while the appeal was pending. The appeal was pursued by their estates.]

(3d Cir. 2012). The Ninth Circuit has construed "interference" for the purposes of §3617 according to a dictionary definition as, "the act of meddling in or hampering an activity or process." Walker v. City of Lakewood, 272 F.3d 1114, 1129 (9th Cir. 2001) (quoting Webster's Third New Int'l Dict. 1178 (14th ed. 1961)). Interference is "broadly applied to reach all practices which have the effect of interfering with the exercise of rights under the federal fair housing laws." *Id.* at 1129. Interference does not require force or threat of force. *Id.* at 1128 (citing 42 U.S.C. §3631). Yet the prohibition on interference "cannot be so broad as to prohibit 'any action whatsoever tha[t] in any way hinders a member of a protected class.'" Brown v. City of Tucson, 336 F.3d 1181, 1192 (9th Cir. 2003) (quoting Michigan Prot. & Advocacy Serv., Inc. v. Babin, 18 F.3d 337, 347 (6th Cir. 1994)).

Interference under §3617 may consist of harassment, provided that it is "sufficiently severe or pervasive" as to create a hostile environment. [Eds.— Citations to *DiCenso v. Cisneros* and other cases interpreting §3604(b) omitted.]

Walters and Kromenhoek raised §3617 claims against Cowpet, Felice, [and] Talkington. We address each Appellee in turn. As to Cowpet, there is a material dispute as to whether Walters and Kromenhoek barred it from reviewing their accommodation requests. We addressed this factual dispute in the context of §3604(f)(3)(B). We now address the same facts under an entirely different legal standard. We conclude that the factual dispute is material to the §3617 interference claim. If Walters and Kromenhoek barred Cowpet from reviewing their accommodation requests, then Cowpet did not "interfere" with their rights. But if there was not such a ban, then Cowpet did "interfere" with their rights by failing to review their requests for a reasonable accommodation of their disabilities. Thus, we will reverse the District Court's grant of summary judgment in favor of Cowpet on the §3617 claim.

Walters and Kromenhoek allege that Felice, their neighbor, violated §3617 by posting derogatory, harassing and, at times, threatening comments on Talkington's blog. Felice posted at least nine harassing messages, over a period of more than five months. All of these writings were made public on the Internet. Felice continued his postings even after Walters responded, on the blog, that she was "mortified, that my personal business has been laid out over the internet without my permission or forewarning."

We conclude that there are genuine disputes of material fact "over the inferences that can be reasonably drawn from" Felice's blog posts. A reasonable jury could find that Felice's harassment was sufficiently severe or pervasive as to "interfere" with Walters and Kromenhoek's fair housing rights under §3617. A reasonable jury could also infer that there was a causal connection—that Felice engaged in harassing conduct "on account of" Walters and Kromenhoek's exercise of their fair housing rights. Accordingly, we will reverse the grant of summary judgment for Felice.

Walters and Kromenhoek allege that Talkington, their neighbor, interfered with their fair housing rights by writing on his blog. Talkington named Walters and Kromenhoek and made public and derided their requests for accommodation of their disabilities. Overall, Talkington posted numerous harassing blog posts and comments over more than five months. He posted these comments publicly on the Internet. He continued to do so after Walters expressed her "mortifi[cation]" that her need for an emotional support animal was made public.

We hold that there are genuine disputes of fact over the inferences that can be drawn from Talkington's blog posts. A reasonable jury could find that his conduct constituted harassment that was sufficiently severe or pervasive as to "interfere" with Walters and Kromenhoek's fair housing rights. A reasonable jury could also find that there was a causal connection between Talkington's conduct and Walters and Kromenhoek's exercise of their fair housing rights. As such, we will reverse the grant of summary judgment for Talkington.

NOTES AND QUESTIONS

1. Actionable Interference. Consider the conduct alleged in each lawsuit. Is any "worse" or more threatening than the other? What logic does the *Egan* court use to limit §3617 to violent or threatening conduct that is intended to drive a person out of their home? Do you agree? Note that *Revock* and *People Helpers* did not decide that the alleged conduct violated §3617, but rather that the issue of whether the conduct constituted interference with housing rights could be litigated further. Should there be some threshold finding of the severity of "interference" before a case can proceed to a jury? Or should the jury be permitted to decide whether conduct is "interfering" as a matter of liability, and then use its damage award to reflect its view of the severity of the conduct? *Revock* settled before a jury could address the question of interference. In *People Helpers*, the jury found in favor of the plaintiffs but awarded only nominal damages. The judge awarded the plaintiffs injunctive relief and attorneys' fees. The Fourth Circuit, however, reversed the damage award and the attorneys' fees award on appeal. 12 F.3d 1321 (4th Cir. 1993).

Consider the defendants in the cases discussed above: With the exception of the condo association in *Revock*, the rest were neighbors who did not provide or control the plaintiffs' housing. Section 3617 is the section most used to address harassment by people who are not housing providers because, unlike §§3604(a), (b), and (c), the provision is not limited to actions taken "in connection with the sale or rental of housing." This broadens the section's reach considerably. As a result, however, courts have demonstrated the inclination to impose some other extratextual limits to prevent routine conflicts among neighbors from potentially violating the FHA. *Egan* provides such an example, with the court requiring that the conduct be violent or threatening or intended to drive a person from their home, despite the fact that §3617 contains no such requirement. Another example is Sporn v. Ocean Colony Condominium

Ass'n, 173 F. Supp. 2d 244, 251-52 (D. N.J. 2001), in which the court held that "shunning" of plaintiffs in response to their filing a HUD complaint was not actionable under §3617. Specifically, the court stated that:

> Section 3617 does not, however, purport to impose a code of civility on those dealing with individuals who have exercised their FHA rights. Simply put, §3617 does not require that neighbors smile, say hello or hold the door for each other. To hold otherwise would be to extend §3617 to conduct it was never intended to address and would have the effect of demeaning the aims of the Act and the legitimate claims of plaintiffs who have been subjected to invidious and hurtful discrimination and retaliation in the housing market.

Consider the facts of HUD v. Hope, HUDALJ 04-99-3509-8 (2002), which involved a Black couple and their three children (the Keys family) who tried to purchase a home in a white neighborhood:

> The walk-through went very well, things worked as they should, and the Keys were very happy to be buying the house. The only problem they noticed was that during their tour of the back yard two dogs were barking fiercely behind the next-door fence, in Respondent's back yard. The dogs were more than a little frightening to Ms. Keys, but the walk-through continued in a light vein with the Keys couple, Michelle Nesbitt [the Keys' agent] and the sellers' daughter, Angela Osborne, talking, laughing and smiling.
>
> As the outdoor tour continued and they reached the front driveway, Respondent drove up to his house and got out of his car. Seeing his arrival, Ms. Nesbitt went over to the Respondent and invited him to come "meet your new neighbors." He agreed to do so, came over to the group, and shook hands all around. The Keys introduced themselves to him.
>
> Initially, Respondent's demeanor was friendly. He held a smile on his face and spoke not unpleasantly. However, within a few moments his manner and voice had turned to indicate anger. He stated a number of times, "You're kidding me," and he stated with incredulity, "You just bought this house." He repeated these statements a few times. As his voice began to indicate anger, he asked Mr. Keys why he would want to live there.
>
> Upon Mr. Keys' stating that it is a quiet street in a quiet neighborhood and a nice place to raise children, Respondent Hope stated words to the effect of, "Yeah. It is. It's an all-white neighborhood." Hope then asked, "Why . . . man, why do you want to move here? This is an all white neighborhood. We don't want blacks here. That's why my wife had to go hold the dogs. They were going crazy, and they don't like blacks, either."
>
> Mrs. Keys stated that the Keys are Christian people and were going to have their children catching the school bus there. Respondent Hope stated that he was also Christian, but that "we don't want blacks here." He asked why the Keys did not go back to South Jackson, which is a black neighborhood, whereupon Ms. Keys responded, "Sir, we didn't come from South Jackson. We live less than three minutes from here."
>
> Respondent then continued to ask why they would want to live there, referring once to the neighborhood as a "redneck" neighborhood. He also turned around and pointed to his neighbor's house, stating that his neighbor "who owns a gun shop, feels the same way I do."
>
> At that time Respondent started backing away while continuing to make like statements. He waved his arms and pointed at the dogs. He pointed at

the neighbor's house and said that he was going over to tell the neighbor who owns the gun shop. The Keys were frightened and departed.

Katherine Beard [the seller's agent] had remained in the house while the Keys and Ms. Nesbitt left the house to tour the yard. She was not aware of the confrontation in the driveway until Ms. Nesbitt knocked at the door and told her she had better come out because "a neighbor has just threatened the Keys." As she came out of the house, Respondent Hope began shouting at her. He was "visibly angry," and he was waving his hands and yelling. Respondent said to Ms. Beard that he did not know why blacks wanted to move into the neighborhood, that he did not like blacks, that his dogs did not like blacks, that his neighbors did not like blacks, and that his next door neighbor, who owned a gun shop, did not like blacks. Respondent acted "shocked in disbelief" that the Keys intended to move into the house next to his. By that time Mrs. Keys was "shaking and crying."

The Respondent's next door neighbor at the time was Gray ("Grumpy") Graham, who as of the time of the hearing still owned the Brandon Gun and Pawn shop.

Fearing Respondent's intent when he started moving back towards the dogs and the neighbor's house, and not knowing what he might do next, the Keys got into their car and "got out of there as soon as [they] could." As they drove away from the house they were extremely upset, and they quickly decided that they and their children could not live next door to the Respondent.

The ALJ determined that the respondent violated §3617 and awarded significant compensatory and punitive damages to the Keys family. The ALJ also awarded damages to the agents, who lost commissions on the sale. Respondent's behavior, taken as a whole, clearly intimidated everyone involved. At what point did his actions cross the line from rudeness to a §3617 violation?

Professor Robert Schwemm has argued that courts have been too skeptical of §3617 claims for neighbor-on-neighbor harassment, which runs contrary both to the statutory text and congressional purpose behind the FHA:

> Courts throughout the country have expressed . . . misgivings about applying the FHA to neighbor harassment unless it involves systematic or highly abusive behavior. But why should this be so? The text of §3617 outlaws interference "with any person in the exercise or enjoyment of . . . any right granted or protected by" [several of] the FHA's substantive provisions. This means, according to the governing interpretive regulation, that §3617 bans "interfering with persons in their enjoyment of a dwelling" because of race or other FHA-prohibited factor. Certainly, hostile race-based comments would seem likely to interfere with any reasonable minority's enjoyment of his or her home. . . .
>
> Court opinions that have dismissed such behavior as merely a neighbors' quarrel not worthy of being made into a "federal case" are essentially imposing some sort of de minimus defense on §3617 cases, because they believe the FHA was not intended to impose a "civility code" on neighbors. But the text of §3617—surely the best indicator of congressional intent—contains no such defense. . . . Furthermore, there are good reasons to suppose that congressional concerns underlying the FHA might well be advanced by broadly interpreting §3617 to outlaw all forms of invidious harassment among neighbors.[2]

---

2. *Neighbor-on-Neighbor Harassment: Does the Fair Housing Act Make a Federal Case out of It?*, 61 Case W. Res. L. Rev. 865, 868-69 (2011).

Note that a tenant who is harassed by another tenant may also have a claim against the housing provider under §3604(b). Some courts have held that a tenant can state a cause of action under this provision if the housing provider is aware of the conduct and has the power to address it but fails to take action, although at least one court has required a finding that this failure itself was motivated by discriminatory intent. These cases are discussed in Chapter 8.

2. Motivation Required? Unlike §§3604(a) and (b), §3617 does not require that the prohibited conduct be taken "because of" a protected characteristic. Instead, it refers to conduct that interferes with a person "on account of" their enjoyment or exercise of fair housing rights. In practice, this seems to mean that plaintiffs must make some showing that the conduct was undertaken intentionally based on a protected characteristic. This can be difficult if this proof is lacking or there might be some other nondiscriminatory reason for the defendant's actions.

Consider the following cases:

- Sofarelli v. Pinellas County, 931 F.2d 718 (11th Cir. 1991).

On September 16, 1989, Sofarelli loaded a house onto a trailer and moved it down various streets, pursuant to proper permits, in Pinellas County and Clearwater, Florida. Quite close to his destination, Sofarelli's progress was blocked on John's Parkway, a public roadway, by a vehicle owned by Hibbing. The Pinellas County Sheriff refused to remove Hibbing's automobile and ordered Sofarelli to stop the move. The house currently remains on its trailer in the middle of John's Parkway.

Sofarelli alleges that Pinellas County (through its employee, the Pinellas County Sheriff), the Pinellas County Sheriff, Hibbing, Swetay, and other participating members of Hibbing's community to whom we will refer as the "neighbors," violated his civil rights under the FHA §§3604 and 3617. Sofarelli argues that his plan to move the house onto a lot abutting John's Parkway and potentially to sell the house and lot to a minority purchaser constitutes aiding or encouraging that prospective purchaser's exercise of the right to housing under §3604. Therefore, Sofarelli contends that appellees' efforts to prevent the move of the house violate §3617 as unlawful interferences with his aid and encouragement of the purchaser's right to obtain the housing to which he is entitled under §3604.

In order to prevail under the Act, Sofarelli has to establish that race played some role in the actions of Hibbing, Swetay and the neighbors. We find that Sofarelli may be able to prove a set of facts which would establish violations of the FHA. Sofarelli alleges that members of Hibbing's community committed certain actions—such as leaving a note threatening "to break [Sofarelli] in half" if he did not get out of the neighborhood and running up to one of Sofarelli's trucks, hitting it, shouting obscenities and spitting at Sofarelli—which would clearly constitute coercion and intimidation under §3617. In addition, Sofarelli presented evidence to the district court which suggests that Hibbing, Swetay, and their neighbors had racial motivations for these actions. An article in the September 21, 1989 issue of the St. Petersburg Times quotes Swetay as stating, "What's stopping him (Sofarelli) from selling it to coloreds? . . . Once that happens, the whole neighborhood is gone." Marie Tessier, Tug of War Over House Turns Racial, St. Petersburg Times, Sept. 12, 1989. The article states that both Hibbing and Swetay "said they don't want the house on their block partly because they're afraid black people might move in." If Sofarelli can prove, as the quotations in the newspaper article suggest, that Hibbing and Swetay interfered with the house move in order to prevent someone of a particular race from being able to move into their neighborhood, Sofarelli would be able to establish a colorable claim against them under the FHA. The dismissal was also improper as to the neighbors because they purportedly acted in concert with and for the same reasons as Hibbing and Swetay.

Sofarelli must establish that race played some role in the actions of the sheriff to recover under the FHA. Sofarelli concedes that there is absolutely no evidence of racial motivation on the part of the sheriff. Because Sofarelli concedes that he "is not aware of and does not allege" any claims that the Pinellas County Sheriff acted with racial animus, Sofarelli fails to state a claim under the FHA. Therefore, we affirm the dismissals of the FHA claims against both Pinellas County and the Pinellas County Sheriff in the original federal case.

- United States v. Weisz, 914 F. Supp. 1050 (S.D.N.Y. 1996).

   Defendant Pearl Weisz resides at 26 South Parker Drive in the Town of Ramapo, Rockland County. The residence across the street at 27 South Parker Drive is inhabited by John and Carol Cronin and their three children, Sean, Bruce, and Suzanne (hereinafter "the Cronins"). Following a complaint by the Cronins to HUD, the U.S. Attorney for this district brought suit on the Cronins' behalf against Weisz, alleging that Weisz's conduct toward the Cronins violates the FHA. Weisz now moves for judgment on the pleadings dismissing the complaint under Rule 12(c), Fed.R.Civ.P.

   The government alleges that "[s]ince approximately April 1991 through the present, defendant Pearl Weisz has coerced, intimidated, threatened and interfered with the Cronins' enjoyment of their dwelling because of the Cronins' religion" (Roman Catholic) by conducting herself in specific ways. The complaint there alleges:

   During the period April 1991 through November 1992, Weisz complained to the Town of Ramapo Police Department about the Cronins' behavior, and asked that the police surveil the Cronins' home on days when the defendant or her neighbors are not permitted to make telephone calls during the Jewish Sabbath.

Commencing in July 1992, Weisz contacted public officials of the Town of Ramapo to complain about a "basketball pole" located on the Cronins' property. In September 1992, Weisz commenced a series of complaints to the U.S. Postal Service about the basketball pole.

On July 13, 1992, Weisz wrote a letter to the Office of the Supervisor of the Town of Ramapo, complaining of the behavior of the Cronins' sons and their friends. On August 17, 1992 Weisz signed a Criminal Court Information charging Sean Cronin with trespass, alleging that on August 10, 1992, Sean Cronin entered Weisz's property to retrieve a basketball.

On or about September 8, 1992 Weisz called Carol Cronin's place of employment at Yeshiva University in New York, spoke to Carol Cronin's supervisor, complained of a "Mrs. C" who lived on Weisz's block in Rockland County, stated that Weisz's two young children were being harassed by "Mrs. C's older children," and stated further that she [Weisz] "was Orthodox and that she was surprised that Yeshiva University hired non-Jews, especially those of German descent and who are anti-Semitic."

On September 23, 1992, as a result of Weisz's complaints to the town officials, the Town of Ramapo removed the Cronins' basketball pole. In April 1993, Weisz initiated an action in Small Claims Court against Sean Cronin for breach of a mediation agreement which had arisen out of the August 1992 criminal court information that Weisz had signed against Sean Cronin. On April 15 and May 23, 1993, Weisz called the police and made further complaints about noise made by the Cronins.

In December 1993, defendant caused to be placed an advertisement in The Jewish Press listing the Cronins' home for sale and stating that it was "open for four days, including Christmas Eve and Christmas Day, December 24 and 25, 1993, with the result that the Cronins suffered unwelcomed intrusions into their home during the Christmas holiday period." On February 24, 1994, Weisz called the police and "falsely accused Sean Cronin of hitting the defendant's son with a snowball."

I will assume arguendo that conduct may violate §3617 without having directly violated any of the other sections. Nonetheless, it seems clear enough that to bring a claim within §3617, a plaintiff must allege conduct on the part of a defendant which in some way or other implicates the concerns expressed by Congress in the FHA. If it were otherwise, the FHA would federalize any dispute involving residences and people who live in them. Nothing in the statute or its legislative history supports so startling a proposition.

Defendant's specific conduct, as alleged [in the complaint, is] nothing more than a series of skirmishes in an unfortunate war between neighbors. There is no indication in any of these allegations that defendant

Weisz was feuding with the Cronins because Weisz was Jewish and the Cronins were Roman Catholic. For all that appears from the complaint's factual allegations, Weisz was offended by the Cronins' conduct, not by their faith. For all that appears, Weisz would have been just as offended by the Cronins' alleged offensive behavior, public intoxication, basketball pole, trespass upon Weisz's property and harassment of her children if the Cronins had also been Orthodox Jews; or for that matter, Episcopalians, Baptists, Mohammedans, Buddhists, agnostics, or atheists.

My conclusion that the government's allegations do not make out a claim for religious discrimination under the FHA is not affected by the particular allegations that Weisz expressed surprise to Yeshiva University, Carol Cronin's employer, that the University would hire non-Jews; or that Weisz placed an advertisement listing the Cronins' home for sale in The Jewish Press in order to harass them. While these allegations add Jewish elements into the narrative, they reflect nothing more than the defendant's methods of making life miserable for the Cronins. They do not support an inference that Weisz wished to make life miserable for the Cronins because they were Roman Catholics. Accordingly defendant's Rule 12(c) motion will be granted and the complaint dismissed.

Can you distinguish the allegations in these two cases? In both, the defendants were alleged to have made statements referring to protected characteristics. In *Sofarelli*, the defendant's alleged actions were physically threatening and forceful, whereas in *Weisz* the defendant's actions were not. But should this matter for a determination of whether the defendant's actions were motivated by discriminatory intent? Note that both these cases came to the court on motions to dismiss at the pleading stage. In *Sofarelli* the court allowed the case to proceed, although it settled before trial. In *Weisz* the case was dismissed and never had the chance to proceed toward discovery and a jury. Was the *Weisz* court too quick to conclude that the government failed to allege sufficient evidence of discriminatory intent? Would additional facts, such as neighborhood demographics, have made the claim plausible for the court? What do you think a jury would have found had it been able to decide the issue?

Note also that in *Sofarelli*, the court was unwilling to ascribe a racial motivation to the Sheriff's Department, which was responding to (allegedly racially motivated) calls from the other defendants to block the mobile home's passage. Contrast those facts with Hidden Village, L.L.C. v. City of Lakewood, Ohio, 734 F.3d 519, 526 (6th Cir. 2013), in which the plaintiff alleged a police department aggressively targeted the residents of a group home for youth, many of whom were Black, with tickets and fines for offenses such as jaywalking, walking near railroad tracks, and riding bicycles without license plates. The Sixth Circuit held that it was a jury question whether this consti-tuted racially motivated harassment:

> It is bad enough that Lakewood officials targeted a predominantly black orga-nization in general. But worse, a jury could conclude that the officials targeted the organization's black members in particular. The program director testified that, although the program had white clients, none of them reported police harassment to her; all complaints of police harassment came from black clients. Another official from the Lutheran Metropolitan Ministry testified to the same effect.

3. Should §3617 Be Congruent With §3604(b)? Although §3617 does not contain the word "harassment," it clearly encompasses harassing behavior, and thus it would be logical for any harassment plaintiff to use this provision. As discussed in Chapter 8, §3604(b), which prohibits discrimination in the terms and conditions of housing, also covers harassment. Specifically, courts have held that a plaintiff can assert a hostile environment harassment claim under §3604(b), but only when that harassment is sufficiently "severe or per-vasive" that it has created a hostile environment, which in turn has altered the terms and conditions of the plaintiff's housing. This semantic shuffle was nec-essary to include the harassment cause of action in the terms and conditions language of §3604(b).

The *Cowpet* court explicitly adopts this standard for §3617, as have many other courts. But why should this be so? The language of §3617 is plain and explicitly covers intimidation, coercion, and interference. In other words, there is no need to press the claim into a "terms and conditions" violation mold. By interpreting the two sections as congruent, have the courts made §3617 superfluous for claims of housing provider harassment? Does this requirement heighten the bar for harassment-based §3617 claims, even when the courts have recognized other forms of interference that do not require a "severe or pervasive" showing? Can you think of a situation in which a land-lord accused of harassment might be held liable for a §3617 violation but not liable for a §3604(b) violation based on the same conduct?

4. Zoning Restrictions as Interference. A number of exclusionary zon-ing cases have included claims under §3617 in addition to claims under §3604(a) for making housing unavailable. In many of these, courts have held that a municipality's refusal to permit a developer to build housing for people with protected characteristics unlawfully interferes with the devel-oper and his prospective tenants. *See, e.g.*, Samaritan Inns, Inc. v. District of Columbia, 114 F.3d 1227 (D.C. Cir. 1997); United States v. Birmingham, Mich., 727 F.2d 560 (6th Cir. 1984); Gibson v. Riverside, 181 F. Supp. 2d 1057 (C.D. Cal. 2002).

No court, however, has held that an exclusionary zoning decision vio-lates §3617 without also finding a violation of §3604(a). Should a finding under §3604(a) be necessary in such circumstances? Could not a municipal-ity "interfere" with a development, perhaps by causing it delay and expense, even if the development eventually gets built? Is the danger with this broader interpretation that the routine delays and expenses inherent in the zoning and permitting process might give rise to too many §3617 claims against municipalities?

5. Economic Competition as Interference. What if a neighbor who wishes to prevent a person with a protected characteristic from moving into the neighborhood buys the house that the person was hoping to purchase? Does this constitute interference under §3617? On the one hand, it is commonplace for more than one person to wish to buy a house and for the unsuccessful party to be disappointed. On the other hand, preemptive purchase is a very effective way to interfere with a person's attempt to acquire property. Should the motivations of the successful purchaser matter? What about the motivations of the seller? Consider the two cases below. Which has the better argument?

Michigan Protection and Advocacy Service, Inc. v. Babin
18 F.3d 337 (6th Cir. 1994)

Before: Boggs and Suhrheinrich, Circuit Judges, and Brown, Senior Circuit Judge.

Boggs, Circuit Judge:

The plaintiffs filed several civil rights claims against the defendants, alleging that the defendants had denied and/or interfered with the plaintiffs' right to equal access to housing. The plaintiffs claim that their right to housing was violated when a house owner, who was negotiating with a state agency to rent the house as a group home for mentally disabled adults, sold the house at a profit to neighbors of the property. The plaintiffs allege that the seller's motivation for selling and the neighbors' motivation for buying the house were discriminatory. The plaintiffs brought suit against the seller, a real estate agency, and the group of neighbors who helped raise the money to purchase the property.

On a motion for summary judgment, the district court ruled against the plaintiffs on three separate grounds. The court found that the defendants (1) did not discriminate or otherwise make unavailable a dwelling to the plaintiffs; (2) did not discriminate against the plaintiffs in the course of a real estate-related transaction; and (3) did not interfere with the exercise and enjoyment of plaintiffs' right to fair housing. We hold that a proper interpretation of the text of the FHA does not reach the actions of the defendants in this case and we therefore affirm the district court's grant of summary judgment for the defendants.

I

In May 1988, the defendant Florence Hammonds was working as a real estate agent for Century 21 Town and Country Realty ("Century 21"). At that time, a couple listed their house ("24 Mile Road property" or "the house") with

Century 21 and Hammonds marketed the property on their behalf. After eight months on the market, however, Hammonds had not sold the house.

In November 1988, while acting as the broker for the house, Hammonds contacted the Macomb-Oakland Regional Center ("MORC"), a state agency. Hammonds asked MORC if it would be interested in leasing the property as a group home for mentally disabled adults if she purchased it. MORC indicated that it was interested in leasing the property.

In early February 1989, Hammonds purchased the house for $95,000. She paid a broker's commission to Century 21 as the buyer, but recouped part of the commission as the real estate agent.

According to Hammonds, in March 1989 MORC indicated that it would execute a written lease and begin paying rent to Hammonds by the middle of May 1989. The leasing arrangements, however, did not progress as quickly as planned. In April 1989, MORC informed her that the lease could not be executed until July 15, 1989, because MORC was still waiting for various state agencies to approve the arrangement.

Meanwhile, on April 26, MORC officials sent out a letter to residents in the vicinity of the 24 Mile Road property to inform them that the house would be used as a group home. On April 28, 1989, Peggy Babin, a resident of the area, called Hammonds to arrange a meeting with her. On April 29, 1989, Babin and five other neighbors met with Hammonds at Hammonds's house to discuss the lease. At the meeting, Hammonds attempted to allay the neighbors' fears about having a group home in their neighborhood, but she also insisted on going through with her lease with MORC.

The neighbors then began a campaign to prevent the property from becoming a group home. Peggy Babin organized a petition drive to stop the group home, contacted several newspapers about the drive, and prepared a "mailing" about group homes. This mailing included 1) a newspaper article about a resident of a group home who had raped a nine-year old girl; 2) a list of addresses of people to write to express concern about the group home; 3) MORC's April 26 letter with a note indicating that MORC was talking about a group home such as the one discussed in the enclosed newspaper article; 4) a sheet entitled "Group Homes: Things You Should Know" that stated that the neighborhood would no longer be safe and property values would plummet if a group home was situated in the neighborhood; and 5) form letters to send to Century 21 and MORC to express concern about the group home.

After the neighbors began their petition drive, Hammonds initiated a conversation with John Kersten, the owner and sole shareholder of Century 21. Hammonds mentioned that she was concerned about the reaction of the neighbors to the proposed use of the 24 Mile Road property. Kersten indicated that Hammonds would have to handle the situation herself.

On the morning of May 12, Hammonds met with MORC representatives about hastening the leasing arrangement. According to Hammonds, the representatives promised to inquire about the delay in the approval of the lease and to call her that same day with an answer. They did not call her. Also, on May 12 a town meeting was held and approximately one hundred people showed up to express their concerns about the group home. Hammonds did not attend the meeting.

On May 13, Nosh Ivanovic offered Hammonds $100,000 for the house. On May 15, Hammonds made a counteroffer of $104,000. Ivanovic was unable to raise the additional cash, so Scott Babin provided the funds. Scott Babin, with the help of Paul Hebert, then solicited funds from the neighbors to offset his donation to Ivanovic. Thomas Fortin donated $500.

The closing for the 24 Mile Road property took place on May 19. No one from Century 21 was at the closing and Hammonds did not pay a commission to the agency. Hammonds, however, used closing documents bearing the Century 21 logo, and the forms were pre-printed with Kersten's signature as the broker for the sale.

Based on these facts, the plaintiffs filed this suit against Hammonds, Kersten, Century 21, and the neighbors.

III

[EDS. — Plaintiffs made claims under §3604(f)(1), the analogue to §3604(a) for disability-based discrimination, §3605, and §3617. The Court held that Hammonds's sale was exempt under §3603(b), and that Hammonds was not acting as an agent for Kersten and Century 21. Thus, it affirmed the district court's grant of summary judgment to them on the §3604(f)(1) claim. It also held that there was no evidence of discrimination in the sale transaction, and therefore summary judgment was proper under the §3605 claim.]

Real estate, of course, is the quintessential unique commodity. If we are able to purchase a house because we can offer more money, we have in one sense "denied" it to everyone else. But that is not generally the way the word is used. Only hyper-technical economists would normally say that we interfere with another person's rights when we purchase a house in fair economic competition, just as most people would not say that we "directly affect" a merchant's livelihood when we choose to patronize A, rather than B, no matter what the motive.

Given this general usage of the words, it would be a huge and unwarranted expansion of the act, with no hint of any congressional authority, to say that every purchaser or renter of property is liable under the act if his motives are found unworthy in such a purchase or rental transaction. The entire language of the act, as well as the evils the act is aimed at as described in hearings and debates, was designed to target those who owned or disposed of property, and those who, in practical effect, assisted in those transactions of ownership and disposition.

Consequently, however broad §3604(f) may be, the scope of the statute cannot encompass the acts of the neighbors in this case. Their action in collecting money to buy the house is not direct enough to fall within the terms of §3604(f)(1).

V

The plaintiffs argue that all of the defendants violated 42 U.S.C. §3617 by interfering with the exercise and enjoyment of the plaintiffs' right to fair housing. As the plaintiffs point out, the language "interfere with" has been broadly applied "to reach all practices which have the effect of interfering with the exercise of rights" under the federal fair housing laws. United States v. American Inst. of Real Estate Appraisers, 442 F. Supp. 1072, 1079 (N. D. Ill. 1977), *appeal dismissed*, 590 F.2d 242 (7th Cir. 1978). We agree with the plaintiffs that Congress intended the FHAA to be read with its remedial purpose in mind. Still, a court "cannot discover how far a statute goes by observing the direction in which it points." *NAACP v. American Family Mut. Ins. Co.*

The plaintiffs would have us hold that any action whatsoever that in any way hinders a member of a protected class under the fair housing law in obtaining housing is a per se violation of §3617, so long as there is some evidence of discriminatory effect or intent on the actor's part. On the other hand, the district court found that, in order to state a claim under §3617, an allegation that a defendant "interfered with" a plaintiff's rights must include an allegation that the action had "some component of potent force or duress."

We believe, however, that the scope of §3617 should at least be analogous to the scope of §3604(f). Section 3617 is not limited to those who used some sort of "potent force or duress," but extends to other actors who are in a position directly to disrupt the exercise or enjoyment of a protected right and exercise their powers with a discriminatory animus. Under this standard, the language "interfere with" encompasses such overt acts as racially-motivated firebombings, Stirgus v. Benoit, 720 F. Supp. 119 (N.D. Ill. 1989), sending threatening notes, Sofarelli v. Pinellas County, 931 F.2d 718 (11th Cir. 1991), and less obvious, but equally illegal, practices such as exclusionary zoning, United States v. City of Birmingham, 727 F.2d 560 (6th Cir.), cert. denied, 469 U.S. 821 (1984), deflating appraisals because of discriminatory animus, *United States v. American Inst. of Real Estate Appraisers*, supra, and insurance redlining, Laufman v. Oakley Bldg. & Loan Co., 408 F. Supp. 489 (S.D. Ohio 1976).

Hammonds is not liable under §3617 merely because she sold the house to the highest bidder. There is no evidence that the negotiations between Hammonds and MORC had given rise to a legally enforceable right in either party. In the absence of such a right, we do not believe that Congress intended to compel a seller to agree to a less favorable offer simply because a member of a protected class made that offer. Furthermore, even if Hammonds's involvement in the transaction is direct enough to bring her actions within §3617, the evidence indicates that Hammonds's motivation for selling the house to the Ivanovics was purely economic.

[W]e do not believe that the neighbors' act of purchasing the house constituted "interference" within the meaning of the FHAA. Although the neighbor's actions did "interfere" with MORC's negotiations for the 24 Mile Road property, this interference is not direct enough to warrant a finding of lia-bility in this case: the neighbors' actions did not prevent MORC from meet-ing Hammonds's timetable, or even from continuing to bid for the property. Although there is evidence of a discriminatory animus on the neighbors' part, we do not find that they were in a position directly to disrupt, other than by economic competition, the plaintiffs' enjoyments of their rights, especially given MORC's own dilatoriness in the transaction.

We conclude that the district court was correct in granting summary judg-ment to the defendants on the plaintiffs' §3617 claims.

United States v. Hughes
849 F. Supp. 685 (D. Neb. 1994)

KOPF, District Judge:

Defendants Hastings State Bank, its holding company, and bank directors (here referred to collectively as the Bank) have filed a motion to dismiss the government's complaint pursuant to Fed.R.Civ.P. 12(b)(6). The government claims that the Bank intentionally discriminated on the basis of handicap against some mentally ill adults by financing the purchase of a house by third persons when a social services organization, acting on behalf of the mentally handicapped group, was trying to purchase the same house for use as a group home. A violation of the FHA is claimed.

Among other things, the Act makes it unlawful to discriminate in the sale of a dwelling because of a handicap of the buyer, the persons intending to reside within the dwelling after it is sold, or any person associated with the buyer. §3604(f)(1). The Act also makes it "unlawful to . . . interfere with any person in the exercise [of] . . . any right granted or protected by [the Act]." §3617.

I shall deny the motion to dismiss. If the Bank intentionally acted to aid other persons in violating the Act, by "economic competition" or otherwise, I am persuaded that a cause of action has been stated under the Act. The gov-ernment agrees that it must prove that the Bank acted intentionally.

So long as the Bank's "intentions" are part of the prima facie case of the government, I see no reason to construe the word "interference" found in §3617 in the limited manner proposed by the defendants. Thus, I hold that a Bank may violate the Act if it finances a purchase of property with the inten-tion of aiding the purchasers in keeping the home from being purchased by other buyers because those other buyers are or are associated with mentally ill persons.

I decline to follow *Michigan Protection & Advocacy Service, Inc. v. Babin*. Respectfully, I believe that both the opinion of the district court and the cir-cuit court in Babin are plainly wrong in suggesting that there is some sort of "economic competition" exception to the Act. I have two reasons for this conclusion.

First, this is not a matter of what the statute might say, but what it does say. The word "interference" as used in section 3617 plainly encompasses all "interference," economic or otherwise.

Second, true "economic competition" does not exist when the purpose of the competition is to deny a protected person access to housing, as opposed to securing housing for oneself or for investment purposes. In fact, it is irrational to spend money for the purpose of prohibiting someone else from living next to you, if the reason you do not wish to live next to that person is because he or she has a handicap protected by the Act.

For example, the decision to buy a house at a particular price is not driven by whether the neighbors are physically attractive, plain, or ugly. This is true because these traits have nothing to do with how rational market values are established. The same is true of handicaps protected by the Act (or race, religion, gender, family status or national origin). And, to the extent that market forces act irrationally based upon invidious and nonsensical assumptions, Congress has declared that such irrationality shall not be rewarded, protected, or freed from regulation. Accordingly, IT IS ORDERED that the motion to dismiss is denied.

B. FIRST AMENDMENT RIGHTS TO SPEECH AND LITIGATION

In many cases, interference behavior will take the form of public advocacy, complaints to public officials, or even litigation. This raises the possibility of a conflict with the First Amendment: Under what circumstances can expressive activity constitute a violation of the law? Clearly, threats will not be considered protected speech. *See, e.g.*, LeBlanc-Sternberg v. Fletcher, 781 F. Supp. 261, 265-67 (S.D.N.Y. 1991) (holding that the First Amendment does not protect defendants against §3617 claim based on their efforts to harass and discourage Orthodox Jews from living in the town). Nor will symbolic speech acts of a threatening character, such as burning a cross or painting a swastika, be protected.

What about public advocacy, like speaking at a City Council meeting or writing a letter to the editor to oppose a housing development? Bigoted comments in such statements might provide evidence of motivation for other disruptive conduct, but are the statements themselves protected? Should they even be considered "interference"? Are they actionable under §3604(c)? What if the interference activity consists of filing a lawsuit? Litigation can tie up development projects, prevent sales, and cause targets to spend significant time and money. But individuals have the right under the First Amendment to "petition the Government for a redress of grievances." The need to balance the right to litigate against the potential for harassment has given rise to the *Noerr-Pennington* doctrine, which courts have developed in a different legal context (antitrust law) but have applied in fair housing cases.

The following case involves neighbors accused of §3617 interference for their speech and litigation, a lengthy HUD investigation of their conduct, and the application of the *Noerr-Pennington* doctrine. As you read it, consider the types of expressive activity at issue and the merits of the lawsuit that gave rise to the investigation, as well as the motivation behind the lawsuit.

White v. Lee
227 F.3d 1214 (9th Cir. 2000)

Before Canby, Reinhardt, and Fernandez, Circuit Judges.

REINHARDT, Circuit Judge:

On May 12, 1992, a local nonprofit housing developer, Resources for Community Development (RCD), applied for a use permit from Berkeley's Zoning Adjustment Board. RCD sought to convert the Bel Air Motel, a property on University Avenue, to a multi-family housing unit for homeless persons. The use permit required approval by both the Zoning Adjustment Board and the Berkeley City Council.

The plaintiffs lived close to the Bel Air Motel and were opposed to its proposed conversion. They expressed their opposition in a variety of ways. They wrote to the Berkeley City Council, spoke out before the Zoning Adjustment Board and at other public meetings, and published a newsletter with articles critical of the project. The front page of the February 1993 issue of the plaintiffs' newsletter, Flatland News, for example, contained an article titled "City Forcing Bel Air Project Down Our Throats." The plaintiffs discussed their opposition to the project with the local press and attempted to persuade merchants on University Avenue to oppose the Bel Air project also.

The Zoning Adjustment Board granted RCD its use permit on October 1, 1992. An appeal to the Berkeley City Council failed, by a 4-4 vote, in April 1993. That same month, a coalition in which plaintiffs were involved ("the Coalition of Neighborhood Groups Opposing the Bel Air Conversion") filed a lawsuit against Berkeley and RCD in state court. Plaintiff White verified the complaint. It alleged that one of the Zoning Adjustment Board's members, Linda Maio, was also a member of RCD's board and, because of this conflict of interest, improperly participated in the Zoning Adjustment Board's hearings. On April 19, the coalition moved for a preliminary injunction to prevent the issuance of an effective use permit. The Alameda County Superior Court denied the motion and set the case for trial. The Superior Court entered final judgment against the plaintiffs' coalition on February 3, 1994.

Marianne Lawless (now deceased) was the executive director of Housing Rights, Inc. ("HRI"), a Berkeley housing rights advocacy group. On October 15, 1993, Lawless wrote a letter to the San Francisco Office stating her intention to file a HUD administrative complaint against the plaintiffs. Lawless also attached several flyers and other documents which, she stated, "demonstrate the discriminatory scare tactics used by the opponents."[3]

A HUD complaint intake analyst . . . concluded that HUD had jurisdiction and should accept Lawless's complaint for processing, and a supervisor concurred. On October 26, the intake analyst drafted an administrative complaint against the plaintiffs. The complaint included the following statement written on HRI's behalf:

> We are a fair housing agency in the city of Berkeley. As such, one of our missions is to ensure equal opportunities for all persons. The above named respondents have impaired our ability to ensure equal housing by impeding the proposed conversion of the Bel Air Motel to permanently house low-income homeless persons. One of their principal arguments against this project is that it will benefit people that are diagnosed as mentally disabled or disabled through substance abuse. Although the respondents unsuccessfully attempted to obtain a preliminary injunction against the developer acquiring a use permit, they have been given a trial date for November 15, 1993. We believe the above named individuals are blocking the proposed project because they perceive the primary residents of the facility will be the mentally disabled or the disabled through substance abuse.

The San Francisco Office's Investigation

In early November 1993, the San Francisco Office sent letters to [three of the residents named in the complaint,] White, Deringer, and Graham. The office enclosed HRI's complaint and stated that the plaintiffs could file an answer within ten days. HUD, the letters stated, would "commence an investigation of this complaint, and simultaneously encourage all parties involved to conciliate the matter." If conciliation failed and HUD's investigation produced "evidence to substantiate a finding that there is reasonable cause to believe that you have engaged in an unlawful discriminatory housing practice," HUD would issue a charge against them, at which point they would be exposed to certain penalties—including damages as great as $100,000—and could elect

---

3. [Fn. 4 in original] The flyers made a variety of points about the project. One, titled "Who are the Homeless?", showed a pie chart dividing the homeless into three, presumably discrete categories—economic, mentally ill, and substance abusers—and complained about the "inequitable distribution" of Berkeley housing and services for the homeless in poor areas or commercial corridors "with high ethnic concentrations." Another listed projects planned for the area near the intersection of University and Shattuck Avenues, stated that these projects would provide beds for "90 mentally ill and 90 'stabilized' substance abusers," and concluded, "This is commercial suicide! Impacts MUST be assessed!" A third flyer contended that inadequate information had been provided about the Bel Air project for the Berkeley City Council to make a "fair, complete and proper evaluation"; regarding the project's tenant population, it stated, "At least 71% will be homeless, but no details as to mentally ill, substance abusers, dual diagnosis, etc."

to have their case heard by an administrative law judge or referred for trial in U.S. District Court.

Defendant Smith assigned the complaint to defendant Lee to investigate and defendant Zurowski to conciliate. On December 17, 1993, Lawless sent Zurowski a "Proposal for Conciliation" containing the following settlement terms:

> That the above named respondents [White, Deringer, and Graham], and the Neighborhood Groups Opposing the Bel Air Conversion, cease all litigation against Resources for Community Development and the City of Berkeley regarding the development of the Bel Air Motel; and
>
> That the above named respondents, and the Neighborhood Groups Opposing the Bel Air Conversion, cease publication of discriminatory statements (including articles in the CNA Newsletter) and fliers about the potential residents of the Bel Air project.

On January 12, 1994, Lee drafted and Smith reviewed and signed, on behalf of the San Francisco Office's compliance director, a letter to the three plaintiffs. It stated that the San Francisco Office was investigating HRI's complaint and that it was HUD policy "to secure the voluntary cooperation of all persons in the collection of information during the investigation." The letter continued:

> When access to premises, records, documents, individuals and other possible sources of information and evidence which may be necessary for the furtherance of the investigation is not provided, the Department may issue subpoenas to compel such access, production or testimony. Any person who willfully fails or neglects to attend and testify or to answer any lawful inquiry or to produce records, documents or other evidence in obedience to a subpoena "shall be fined not more than $100,000 or imprisoned not more than one year, or both."

Attached to the letter was an "Attachment of Request to Produce Written Responses" listing ten items. This request was extremely broad. It directed the plaintiffs to submit, inter alia, the name and contact information of any person "who was involved in or witnessed the act(s) alleged on the complaint form;" "a copy of any documents or the contents of any file in your control concerning the Bel Air Motel conversion"; all correspondence with or minutes or reports generated by the Council of Neighborhoods Association regarding the Bel Air project; and all literature, posters, newsletters, and flyers about the project.

[HUD also informed the plaintiffs that it would issue a subpoena to compel their testimony if they refused to be interviewed. One plaintiff was interviewed by phone. The San Francisco Field Office staff prepared a report, which was approved and sent along with the case file to HUD headquarters in Washington, DC.]

The report concluded that the plaintiffs had violated the FHA and that there was reasonable cause to take further enforcement action against them. On July 22, 1994, the San Francisco Examiner reported that HUD defendant

Phillips had said "that HUD's preliminary investigation had concluded the three residents [White, Deringer, and Graham] had broken the law, but that it would be up to HUD and Justice Department attorneys to decide whether to prosecute."

Disposition of HRI's Complaint

For approximately two weeks Sara Pratt, the director of HUD's Office of Investigations in Washington, reviewed HRI's complaint and the San Francisco Office's report and case file. Pratt determined that the Alameda County Superior Court had in fact found that Linda Maio's simultaneous service on the Zoning Adjustment Board and RCD's board constituted a conflict of interest that violated a Berkeley ordinance. The court, however, had "found no violation of state law requiring invalidation of the use permit, and considered the good faith of the zoning board member in doing so." Pratt concluded:

> [A]t the time the complaint was filed, on November 1, 1993, the lawsuit presented material questions of fact and/or of law and was not clearly frivolous. Moreover, the state court decision in the case, entered in February 1994, indicated that the lawsuit was premised on a reasonable basis in fact or in law (that is, that it stated a violation of a local ordinance) and, but for the "good faith" exception contained in state law, would have constituted a successful legal claim. The respondents' actions in instituting and prosecuting a lawsuit are thus protected by the First Amendment.

Pratt also concluded that the plaintiffs' distribution of flyers and newsletters and lobbying of public officials were activities protected by the First Amendment and did not constitute a violation of the FHA. HUD issued a "Determination of No Reasonable Cause" on August 16, 1994.

Proceedings Below

The plaintiffs filed their complaint in May 1995. They alleged that defendants Gillespie, Smith, Lee, Zurowski, and Phillips investigated and harassed them solely because of the exercise of their First Amendment rights to free speech and to petition the government for a redress of grievances.

After discovery, the parties filed cross-motions for summary judgment. All five officials sued in their individual capacities argued that they were entitled to qualified immunity. Defendant Lee also moved for summary judgment on the ground that the plaintiffs had failed to establish his liability for any violation of the First Amendment. For their part, the plaintiffs moved for partial summary judgment against Lee, Smith, Zurowski, and Gillespie on the issue of liability. The district court denied the defendants' motions and granted the motion of the plaintiffs.

The defendants filed timely notices of appeal. The plaintiffs then filed a timely cross-appeal.

ANALYSIS

A. Have the Plaintiffs Stated a First Amendment Claim?

1. The Plaintiffs' First Amendment Activity
and the Defendants' Chilling Conduct

In opposing their local government's approval of the Bel Air project, White, Deringer, and Graham engaged in activity paradigmatically protected by the First Amendment. The HUD officials' eight-month investigation into the plaintiffs' activities and beliefs chilled the exercise of their First Amendment rights. The plaintiffs are entitled to seek a remedy for this constitutional violation.

a. The Speech

Here, the plaintiffs wrote and distributed flyers and published a newsletter in the advocacy of a politically controversial viewpoint—"the essence of First Amendment expression." They organized and participated in a coalition of neighbors who shared their views, admirable or not. The right to expressive association includes the right to pursue, as a group, discriminatory policies that are antithetical to the concept of equality for all persons.

The First Amendment also guarantees the right "to petition the Government for a redress of grievances." The plaintiffs exercised this right by attending and speaking out at Zoning Adjustment Board hearings and by challenging in the courts the board's decision to grant a use permit for the Bel Air project. Regardless of what we might think of their objectives, the plaintiffs "were doing what citizens should be encouraged to do, taking an active role in the decisions of government." *Christian Gospel Church*, 896 F.2d at 1226.

It is important to emphasize that a person's speech or petitioning activity is not removed from the ambit of First Amendment protection simply because it advocates an unlawful act. The First Amendment does not permit government "to forbid or proscribe advocacy of the use of force or of law violation except where such advocacy is directed to inciting or producing imminent lawless action and is likely to incite or produce such action." Brandenburg v. Ohio, 395 U.S. 444, 447 (1969). Advocacy is unprotected only if it is "intended to produce, and likely to produce, imminent disorder"; "advocacy of illegal action at some indefinite future time" is not actionable. Hess v. Indiana, 414 U.S. 105, 108-09 (1973).

It is clear that the term "advocacy," as used in *Brandenburg*, encompasses not only freedom of speech, but the other rights of expression guaranteed by the First Amendment as well. *Brandenburg* specifically held that "[s]tatutes affecting the right of assembly, like those touching on freedom of speech, must observe the established distinctions between mere advocacy and incitement to imminent lawless action." The Supreme Court has also explained that the right to petition is "inseparable" from and "was inspired by the same ideals of liberty and democracy that gave us the freedoms to speak, publish, and assemble." McDonald v. Smith, 472 U.S. 479, 485 (1985).

We need not decide whether the plaintiffs' primary objective—the defeat of the proposed conversion of the Bel Air motel—would have involved an unlawful act. The mere fact that citizens urge their government to adopt measures that may be unlawful does not deprive the speech involved of its First Amendment protection. Here, it is clear that nothing that the plaintiffs said or did came close to meeting the *Brandenburg* test. "Imminent lawless action," as used in *Brandenburg*, means violence or physical disorder in the nature of a riot. Peaceful speech, even speech that urges civil disobedience, is fully protected by the First Amendment. Were this not the case, the right of Americans to speak out peacefully on issues and to petition their government would be sharply circumscribed. We therefore hold that the standard set forth in *Brandenburg* applies to all the First Amendment activity at issue in this case, including plaintiffs' petitioning activity, regardless of whether the denial of the permit on the grounds urged would have been contrary to the provisions of the FHA.

b. The Chill

The investigation by the HUD officials unquestionably chilled the plaintiffs' exercise of their First Amendment rights. It is true that the agency did not ban or seize the plaintiffs' materials, and officials in Washington ultimately decided not to pursue either criminal or civil sanctions against them. But in the First Amendment context, courts must "look through forms to the substance" of government conduct. Informal measures, such as "the threat of invoking legal sanctions and other means of coercion, persuasion, and intimidation," can violate the First Amendment also. The HUD officials carried out [a lengthy investigation]. During the investigation, defendant Zurowski conveyed a conciliation proposal requiring the plaintiffs to cease all litigation and publications regarding the Bel Air project and advised the plaintiffs to accept it because they had violated the FHA by distributing "discriminatory" flyers. Defendants Lee and Smith directed the plaintiffs under threat of subpoena to produce all their publications regarding the Bel Air project, minutes of relevant meetings, correspondence with other organizations, and the names, addresses, and telephone numbers of persons who were involved in or had witnessed the alleged discriminatory conduct. Smith interrogated the plaintiffs, again under threat of subpoena, about their views and public statements in opposition to the Bel Air project. In a letter drafted by Smith, defendant Gillespie asserted HUD's purported authority to investigate "allegations that individuals have engaged in speech advocating illegal acts, including discrimination against persons based on their physical or mental disabilities" and stated that the plaintiffs had violated the FHA by writing "news articles which referenced the mental disability of the intended residents of the proposed project as a reason for denial of the project." Defendant Phillips told a major metropolitan newspaper that the plaintiffs had "broken the law." We conclude that these actions would have chilled or silenced a person of ordinary firmness from engaging in future First Amendment activities.

2. The FHA as a Justification

We have applied §3617 broadly to cover a variety of practices that have the effect of interfering with the exercise of fair housing rights protected by the FHA. In theory, §3617 could be interpreted even more broadly, so that a wide range of speech regarding the housing rights of others could be investigated and sanctioned. One person's persuasive editorial on a zoning dispute, for instance, might well "interfere" with another person's ability to secure housing. So construed, however, §3617 would quickly run afoul of the First Amendment principles discussed above.

For this reason, other courts have recognized that a speaker's advocacy of his views, however "ill-advised, uninformed, and even distasteful," can amount to a violation of §3617 of the FHA only in the event that the advocacy is directed to inciting or producing imminent violence and is likely in fact to do so. We agree. Threats of violence and other forms of coercion and intimidation directed against individuals or groups are, however, not advocacy, and are subject to regulation or prohibition. In this case, no such acts were alleged.

Although the HUD officials now concede that the plaintiffs' "protest activities of writing newspaper articles, leafleting, etc., [were], of course, constitutionally protected forms of speech," they suggest parenthetically in their brief that their investigation was necessary to determine whether the flyers distributed by the plaintiffs involved an incitement to imminent lawless action. This suggestion is not supported by the record. HRI executive director Lawless sent a letter to the San Francisco Office that enclosed the relevant flyers two weeks before she signed the complaint. The officials did not need to gather additional information before determining whether these flyers incited imminent lawless action or not. That the First Amendment protected the authors and distributors of the flyers was plain.

3. The Plaintiffs' Lawsuit as a Justification

In attempting to justify their eight-month investigation, the HUD officials rely mainly on the lawsuit filed by the plaintiffs' neighborhood coalition in April 1993. An unsuccessful state-court lawsuit, the officials argue, can violate the FHA if it is filed with a discriminatory motive; their theory is essentially that the First Amendment does not protect litigants who lose. Because the state court denied the plaintiffs their requested relief in February 1994, the HUD officials maintain that, after HRI filed its complaint in November 1993, they were entitled to investigate the plaintiffs' speech in opposition to the Bel Air project to determine whether they had filed their suit with an unlawful discriminatory motive.

The Supreme Court has described the right to petition as "among the most precious of the liberties safeguarded by the Bill of Rights" and "intimately connected, both in origin and in purpose, with the other First Amendment rights of free speech and free press." United Mine Workers of America, Dist. 12 v. Illinois State Bar Ass'n, 389 U.S. 217, 222 (1967). It is "cut from the same cloth as the other guarantees of [the First] Amendment, and is an assurance of a particular freedom of expression." McDonald v. Smith, 472 U.S. at 482.

The Court has further established that the right to petition extends to all departments of the government, including the executive department, the legislature, agencies, and the courts. California Motor Transport Co. v. Trucking Unlimited, 404 U.S. 508, 510 (1972). *California Motor Transport* involved *Noerr-Pennington* immunity, a doctrine initially promulgated "to protect efforts to influence legislative or executive action from liability under the Sherman Act." While the *Noerr-Pennington* doctrine originally arose in the antitrust context, it is based on and implements the First Amendment right to petition and therefore, with one exception, applies equally in all contexts.

The *Noerr-Pennington* doctrine ensures that those who petition the government for redress of grievances remain immune from liability for statutory violations, notwithstanding the fact that their activity might otherwise be proscribed by the statute involved. *Noerr-Pennington* is a label for a form of First Amendment protection; to say that one does not have *Noerr-Pennington* immunity is to conclude that one's petitioning activity is unprotected by the First Amendment.

With respect to petitions brought in the courts, the Supreme Court has held that a lawsuit is unprotected only if it is a "sham," —i.e., "objectively baseless in the sense that no reasonable litigant could realistically expect success on the merits."

In *Professional Real Estate Investors*, the Supreme Court rejected the contention that regardless of a lawsuit's objective merit an antitrust defendant can be found liable if the plaintiff showed that it brought the suit for a "predatory motive." Both requirements must be met to establish antitrust liability: "an objectively reasonable effort to litigate cannot be sham regardless of subjective intent." Furthermore, proof of a lawsuit's objective baselessness is the "threshold prerequisite": a court may not even consider the defendant's allegedly illegal objective unless it first determines that his lawsuit was objectively baseless.

The fact that a litigant loses his case does not show that his lawsuit was objectively baseless for purposes of *Noerr-Pennington* immunity:

> A winning lawsuit is by definition a reasonable effort at petitioning for redress and therefore not a sham. On the other hand, [t]he court must remember that "[e]ven when the law or the facts appear questionable or unfavorable at the outset, a party may have an entirely reasonable ground for bringing suit."

We do not lightly conclude in any *Noerr-Pennington* case that the litigation in question is objectively baseless, as doing so would leave that action without the ordinary protections afforded by the First Amendment, a result we would reach only with great reluctance.

Applying these principles to the present case, it follows that the plaintiffs' state-court lawsuit could have amounted to a discriminatory housing practice only in the event that (1) no reasonable litigant could have realistically expected success on the merits, and (2) the plaintiffs filed the suit for the purpose of coercing, intimidating, threatening, or interfering with a person's exercise of rights protected by the FHA. Because, in the present case, the first requirement cannot be sustained, we need not even consider the second. Objective baselessness is the sine qua non of any claim that a particular lawsuit is not deserving of First Amendment protection. The lawsuit filed by the plaintiffs was unquestionably not objectively baseless. Far from it: it challenged a rather egregious conflict of interest by a person who was simultaneously a member of both the Zoning Adjustment Board and the board for the developer seeking the Bel Air use permit. As the director of HUD's Office of Investigations ultimately concluded, the plaintiffs' action "would have constituted a successful legal claim" but for the court's application of the "good faith" exception under California law.

NOTES AND QUESTIONS

1. Comparing Cases. Compare this outcome to that of United States v. Wagner, 940 F. Supp. 972, 980-83 (N.D. Tex. 1996). In that case a group of neighbors opposed the proposed sale of a house to an organization that planned to open a group home for children with developmental disabilities. Shortly before the sale was to go through, the neighbors filed a lawsuit in state court seeking a temporary restraining order (TRO) to block the sale. Although the TRO was dissolved after a week and the sale eventually went through, the Department of Justice brought a §3617 claim against the neighbors. The court denied their First Amendment defense, because it found the lawsuit was filed (1) for an illegal objective; (2) without a reasonable basis in law or fact; and (3) with an improper motive.

Similarly, in Tizes v. Curcio, No. 94 C 7657, 1995 WL 476675 (N.D. Ill. Aug. 9, 1995), a Jewish couple purchased two houses in an exclusive neighborhood and obtained approvals from various municipal entities to convert the houses into a single home. A neighborhood association repeatedly challenged the issuance of the building permit in state court. The neighbors allegedly harassed the Tizes with ethnic slurs and vandalism. The Tizes filed a §3617 claim against the association and neighbors:

> Defendants maintain that because the Complaint is premised upon the Defendants' attempts to stop or delay the Tizes' home renovations through various administrative and state court proceedings, and that because such conduct constitutes a lawful petition of the government, the Complaint fails to state a legally valid claim for relief. . . .

In the present matter, Defendants argue that the conduct which forms the basis of the Tizes' Complaint—namely, Defendants' participation in proceedings before the Zoning Board of Appeals and Defendants' institution of suit—is precisely the type of activity which is protected by the *Noerr-Pennington* doctrine. Defendants therefore maintain that they are immune from liability for the conduct alleged and that, consequently, the Tizes' Complaint must be dismissed.

Defendants' argument is fundamentally flawed in two major respects: (1) Defendants conveniently overlook the well-established exception to the *Noerr-Pennington* doctrine for governmental or judicial petition undertaken for fraudulent or unlawful purposes; and (2) Defendants ignore the totality of the harassing conduct alleged in the Tizes' Complaint. These two deficiencies are fatal to Defendants' First Amendment immunity claim. . . .

The allegations contained in the Tizes' Complaint are sufficient to suggest that the Defendants' petitioning activities were designed to harass and intimidate the Tizes, were motivated by ethnic animus, and were intended to achieve discriminatory goals. . . . Thus, taking the Tizes' allegations of Defendants' motive and goals as true, this Court is not prepared to conclude that Defendants' conduct is protected by the First Amendment.

How can you distinguish these cases from *White v. Lee*? One difference is the merit of the lawsuits at issue. Courts view a person who files a purely frivolous lawsuit with the discriminatory purpose of interfering with a person's housing rights differently from a person bringing a claim with some basis in law, even though it ultimately may not prevail. Is the merit of the lawsuit more important under the *Noerr-Pennington* doctrine than the purpose behind it? Put another way, what if a person who is clearly motivated by the racist desire to keep Black people from moving into a community files a lawsuit with a facially valid claim against a proposed development? If the case has some validity, does this immunize the proceedings against a §3617 claim? Supreme Court doctrine as discussed in *White* suggests a "yes" answer; both baselessness and ill intent are required for a lawsuit to lose First Amendment protection.

2. Guidance for Enforcement. *White* involved a particularly aggressive investigation by HUD of the plaintiffs' speech activities, wielding HUD's subpoena and investigatory powers and authority to negotiate conciliations (settlements). Are First Amendment concerns heightened when the government is the party enforcing a case, as opposed to a private litigant availing herself of the court system to enforce fair housing rights? After the events in *White*, HUD issued a memorandum to guide the investigation and enforcement of §3617 claims when potential First Amendment issues arise. The memo, referred to as the Achtenberg Memo, which has been updated since, now states that:[4]

---

4. HUD, *Substantive and Procedural Limitations on Filing and Investigating Fair Housing Act Complaints That May Implicate the First Amendment* (May 26, 2015), https://www.hud.gov/sites/documents/5-26-2015NOTICE.pdf. Roberta Achtenberg, who was HUD Assistant Secretary for Fair Housing and Equal Opportunity from 1991 to 1993, was the first openly lesbian or gay presidential appointee confirmed by the U.S. Senate. Her confirmation was contentious, with

Absent force, physical harm, or a clear threat of force or physical harm to one or more individuals, public activities directed toward achieving action by a governmental entity or official—even where hostile, distasteful, and/or bigoted—can be part of a robust discussion of public issues. Activities to urge governmental action are an essential part of a constitutional democracy. Thus, this Department will not accept for filing, and will not investigate, any complaint under §3617 that involves public activities:

- that are directed toward achieving action by a governmental entity or official; and
- that do not involve force, physical harm, or a clear threat of force or physical harm to one or more individuals.

Examples of the types of public activities that are "directed toward achieving action by a governmental entity or official" and are covered by these guidelines include:

- distributing fliers, pamphlets, brochures, posters, or other written materials to the public at large;
- holding open community or neighborhood meetings;
- writing articles or letters to the editor or making statements in a newspaper;
- conducting peaceful demonstrations;
- testifying at public hearings; and
- communicating directly with a governmental entity concerning official governmental matters.

3. Public Officials. Public officials also may invoke a First Amendment defense for their actions. In Tri-Corp Housing, Inc. v. Bauman, 826 F.3d 446 (7th Cir. 2016), a town alderman was accused of violating §3617 based on his attempts to close a group home for mentally disabled persons:

Tri-Corp contends that Bauman is liable to it . . . for issuing statements and press releases critical of its operations and for lobbying other officials to rule against it in administrative proceedings. . . . We will assume, for the purpose of this appeal, that Bauman persuaded the Economic Development Authority to bring the foreclosure action—though the Authority says that it had begun that process on its own. . . .

Tri-Corp does not allege that Bauman himself denied it any right under the Act, or even was a member of a public body that did so. Tri-Corp accuses Bauman of *speech*, not action. And that's all the difference.

Public officials such as aldermen enjoy the right of free speech under the First Amendment, applied to the states through the Fourteenth. Speech is a large part of any elected official's job, in addition to being the means by which the official gets elected (or re-elected). Teddy Roosevelt called the presidency a "bully pulpit," and all public officials urge their constituents and other public bodies to act in particular ways. . . .

---

some senators attacking her sexual orientation and family, using slurs. Although some senators refused to vote, she won the confirmation battle (51-34). *See First Out LGBTQ+ Senate-Confirmed Presidential Appointee,* LGBTQ+ VICTORY INST., https://www.prideandprogress.org/hall-of -fame/roberta-achtenberg.

The First Amendment prevents both state and federal governments from controlling political speech. It would be most surprising to find in the FHA an attempt to penalize political speech, and Tri-Corp does not contend that the statute has any language doing so.

C. RETALIATION

Although the word "retaliation" does not appear in the statute, §3617 explicitly protects people if they encourage or assist others in exercising their fair housing rights. Two questions generally are presented in retaliation cases: (1) whether the plaintiff's actions are protected (i.e., whether they actually were encouraging or assisting others in exercising fair housing rights), and (2) whether the defendant's conduct actually was retaliatory and serious enough to fall under the statute.

The following case presents an example of the first question: Was the plaintiff's act of signing a petition in support of a women's shelter "encouraging or assisting others" in enjoying their rights to fair housing?

Linkletter v. Western & Southern Financial Group, Inc.
851 F.3d 632 (6th Cir. 2017)

Before: Merritt, Clay, and Donald, Circuit Judges.

MERRITT, Circuit Judge:

I. BACKGROUND

Western & Southern Financial Group, Inc. is an insurance company located in the Lytle Park neighborhood of Cincinnati, Ohio. Between 1997 and 2006, Linkletter worked as an employee of Western & Southern. The parties ended the first employment relationship amicably. In May 2014, Linkletter's former colleague at Western & Southern contacted her about a job opportunity at the company as a Senior Corporate Communications specialist. After several interviews, Linkletter accepted the position.

On September 8, 2014, before Linkletter began working, Western & Southern's Senior Vice President of Human Resources, Kim Chiodi, called Linkletter to notify her that Western & Southern had rescinded the employment offer. Linkletter claims that Chiodi justified the rescission due to Linkletter having taken "a position that was contrary to Western & Southern." Specifically, Chiodi mentioned Linkletter's support for the Anna Louise Inn.

Western & Southern had been in a controversial real estate dispute with the Anna Louise Inn women's shelter since 2011. The shelter, whose mission is "to provide women with safe, decent, and affordable housing, without regard to their economic condition, race, or lack of employment," was located in Lytle Park, the same neighborhood as Western & Southern. The residents of the shelter accused Western & Southern of violating the FHA by attempting to illegally pressure them out of the neighborhood. The presence of the shelter interfered with Western & Southern's "master plan for [that] end of town," and the company was frustrated in attempting to buy the land where the shelter stood. In December 2010, the president of the company that controls Western & Southern's real estate holdings sent a letter to Cincinnati's mayor, arguing that the shelter was "not appropriate for the Lytle Park neighborhood" and objecting to "85 low-income permanent housing units for women" and "housing for up to 25 recovering prostitutes."

After the shelter refused to sell, Western & Southern engaged in a campaign to force a sale of the property and get the Anna Louise Inn out of the neighborhood, and the shelter's residents sued. [Eds.—The case was Cooper v. Western & Southern Financial Group, Inc., 847 F. Supp. 2d 1031 (S.D. Ohio 2012).] When Western & Southern filed a motion to dismiss the complaint pursuant to Fed. R. Civ. P. 12(b)(6), the district court denied the motion, stating that the residents had sufficiently pled the elements of a §3617 claim. In its decision, the district court cited allegations that Western & Southern pursued frivolous appeals of zoning decisions affecting the renovation of the Inn, photographed residents of the shelter without their permission, and falsely accused residents of engaging in criminal activity and other inappropriate behavior. The court found that "[t]hese actions could be construed as intimidating, harassing, and threatening to the residents of the Inn. . . . In addition, plaintiffs allege facts that, if accepted as true, are sufficient to support a finding that Western & Southern has exercised its powers with a discriminatory animus." The parties eventually reached a settlement in which Western & Southern bought the property and removed the shelter from the Lytle Park neighborhood, and the suit was dismissed.

On February 21, 2012, while the dispute between the shelter and Western & Southern was ongoing, Linkletter signed a petition expressing support for the shelter. The petition was titled, "The Anna Louise Inn has my Support!" and the text stated, "I support the mission of the Anna Louise Inn, which has provided safe and affordable housing for women for 102 years in its current location." As a signor, Linkletter also stated that she appreciated "that women in Cincinnati have an option for permanent supportive housing," and that "[the] Anna Louise Inn should remain where it is and continue its mission of providing safe and affordable housing for single women." The Inn posted the petition online with the names of the signors, including Linkletter.

After the termination of her employment contract in 2014, Linkletter sued Western & Southern and its employee, Kim Chiodi. At the district court, Linkletter claimed that the rescission of her contract in response to her supporting the housing rights of the Inn's female residents violated §3617 of the FHA. Linkletter argued that by rescinding the contract, the defendants interfered with her employment because she encouraged the women of the Anna Louise Inn in the exercise of their rights under §§3603-06. Specifically Linkletter claimed she encouraged the rights in §3604(a)-(e) pertaining to anti-discrimination in the rental or sale of housing. The provision Linkletter sued under, §3617, protects individuals who "aided or encouraged" the rights protected by §3604.

The defendants moved to dismiss the complaint pursuant to Fed. R. Civ. P. 12(b)(6). The district court granted the motion, finding that Linkletter did not state a claim for relief. Without engaging in a trial or a fact-finding process, the district court agreed with the defendants that Linkletter did not "aid or encourage" the women of the Anna Louise Inn as contemplated by the statute, that the housing rights protected by §3604 were not at issue, and that the defendants as "non-houser employers" did not fall within the scope of the statute. Linkletter now appeals.

III. FHA

The purpose of the FHA is "to provide, within constitutional limitations, for fair housing throughout the United States." In keeping with the law's overarching purpose, 42 U.S.C. §3617 protects plaintiffs who "aided or encouraged" the housing rights enumerated in the statute. Essentially, §3617 allows a plaintiff to step into the shoes of the victims of certain types of housing discrimination when the plaintiff faces retribution for providing encouragement to the victims. As part of a remedial statute, the language of §3617 should be broadly interpreted and applied with the FHA's purpose in mind.

Linkletter claims that by signing a petition she "encouraged" women to pursue their right to be free from sex discrimination in the rental or sale of housing under §3604, and that the defendants illegally retaliated by "interfering" with her employment. She does not accuse them of discriminating against her or illegally interfering with her housing rights. Rather, she claims that the defendants interfered with her employment because she aided or encouraged women in the exercise of their housing rights under §3604.

A. "Interfere with"

The rescission of an employment contract can qualify as "interference" within the meaning of the statute. The complaint states that Linkletter and Western & Southern reached an employment agreement. After Linkletter accepted the job, Western & Southern's employee Chiodi terminated that employment agreement. It would be an understatement to say that the defendants' actions "hampered" Linkletter's employment process. The defendants' interference left Linkletter with a distinct and palpable injury.

HUD has also interpreted the FHA in a manner consistent with the proposition that "interference" can refer to employment disputes. It is illegal to "[t]hreaten[] an employee or agent with dismissal or an adverse employment action, or [to] tak[e] such adverse employment action, for any effort to assist a person seeking access to the sale or rental of a dwelling or seeking access to any residential real estate-related transaction, because of the . . . sex . . . of that person. . . ." 24 C.F.R. §100.400(c)(3).

Moreover, the language "interfere with" should be broadly interpreted to reach all practices which have the effect of interfering with housing rights. Therefore the scope of the statute extends to employers who cancel contracts in retaliation for FHA advocacy. As the interference alleged in the present case fits this description, it appears to be covered by the statute.

B. "Aided or Encouraged"

To qualify for a §3617 claim, a defendant's "interference" must still be in retaliation for a plaintiff having "aided or encouraged" another's enjoyment of the housing rights protected by §§3603-06. Linkletter's action, signing a petition, is seemingly innocuous. However the language and timing of the petition demonstrate that it existed to encourage the women to remain in their residence in opposition to the alleged discrimination by Western & Southern. The defendants point out that the petition did not specifically mention Western & Southern. But while the petition did not explicitly mention the dispute with Western & Southern, the context suggests that the litigation with Western & Southern was the basis for the petition. The petition supported keeping the shelter at the "current location" in "Lytle Park," and that "[the] Anna Louise Inn should remain where it is and continue its mission of providing safe and affordable housing for single women." For purposes of analyzing the defendants' motion to dismiss, the court should assume that Linkletter signed the petition to "encourage" the women in their dispute with Western & Southern.

The district court noted that this act of encouragement by Linkletter is minor comparatively speaking. However, the defendants fail to explain why a petition-signing is not encouragement beyond vague assertions that the action lacks "concreteness" or "directness." The allegations in the complaint show that the action was concrete and important enough to alert Linkletter's future employer to her public support, and result in her termination. If the encouragement is sufficiently concrete to lead to an individual's firing, it is sufficiently concrete to state a plausible claim.

Looking to the "structure, history, and purpose" of the statute, §3617 was meant to protect assistance and advocacy for FHA rights. A plain-meaning understanding of the word "encouraged" clearly covers the act of signing a petition advocating support for a women's shelter. Therefore, interpreting "encouraged" to include Linkletter's action is in keeping with both the plain meaning of the word and the overall purpose of the FHA.

C. Nexus to 42 U.S.C. §3604

Section 3617 requires a nexus with the rights protected by §§3603-06, without requiring an actual violation of the underlying provisions. In the present case, Linkletter claims her signing the petition implicated the rights of women against discrimination in the rental or sale of housing under §3604. The litigation between the women's shelter and Western & Southern is well documented[.] Just as the female residents of the Anna Louise Inn in the *Cooper* case stated a plausible §3617 claim for relief based on their own §3604 rights, so too Linkletter states a plausible claim for relief in facing retaliation for encouraging those rights.

The defendants argue that even if they fired Linkletter because she signed the petition, Western & Southern's motivation in the underlying dispute with the women's shelter was motivated by economics rather than by sex discrimination.

Western & Southern's actions against the shelter as alleged in the complaint only affected one class of people—women. The defendants assert that the motivation for attempting to remove the shelter from the neighborhood was "economic," not "sex," and that financial motives exclude the case from the type of sex discrimination forbidden by the FHA. But a violation of the FHA can be shown either by proof of discriminatory animus or by proof of disparate impact or effect. The existence of economic (or religious or moral) motivations does not protect the defendants from housing discrimination claims when their actions had a clear discriminatory effect. Economic motivation does not cleanse discrimination. The facts alleged by Linkletter, and detailed in the underlying *Cooper* case, are sufficient to state a valid claim that Western & Southern discriminated against the women of the shelter.

There is also no requirement in §3617 that the defendant-employer here operate the housing facility at issue to violate the statute. Section 3617 requires only that the plaintiff "encourage" a housing right protected by §3604 and face retaliatory "interference" for the encouragement. According to the complaint in the present case, the defendants sought to remove housing designated for a protected class from the neighborhood. As a non-houser that has allegedly denied housing rights to women, Western & Southern falls within the scope of the FHA.

Taking the complaint in the light most favorable to the plaintiff, we do not agree with the district court that the petition-signing did not sufficiently implicate opposition to housing discrimination. A factfinder could conclude that through the campaign against the shelter, Western & Southern interfered with housing rights under §3604, and that Linkletter encouraged those same rights under §3617. Accordingly, Linkletter states a plausible claim for relief under the FHA, and her claim should not have been dismissed.

The judgment of the district court is REVERSED, and we REMAND the case for further proceedings.

NOTES AND QUESTIONS

1. Employees as Targets for Retaliation. Section 3617 allows employees like Linkletter to sue their employers if they are retaliated against for aiding others in enjoying their rights to fair housing. *See, e.g.,* Cass v. American Properties, Inc., No. 94 C 2977, 1995 WL 132166 (N.D. Ill. Feb.

27, 1995) (agent alleged retaliation for refusal to participate in discrimination); Meadows v. Edgewood Management Corp., 432 F. Supp. 334 (W.D.
Va. 1977) (resident manager and maintenance technician alleged termination for aiding and assisting others within the meaning of the statute);
Smith v. Stechel, 510 F.2d 1162 (9th Cir. 1975) (apartment complex managers
alleged they were fired for renting to Black and Mexican American tenants).
This can hold true even for employers who are not themselves providers of
housing, as in *Linkletter*.

Compare Title VII of the 1964 CRA, the employment discrimination statute, which contains a provision that protects covered employees against retaliation, but only when the employee is opposing an unlawful employment
practice or participating in an investigation or proceeding pursuant to Title
VII. 42 U.S.C. §§2000e-3.

2. "Reasonable Belief" and Rights Under the Statute. Note that the plaintiff in *Linkletter* must tie her actions to the fair housing rights of people with
characteristics protected by the FHA. Thus, she must show (1) that she aided or
encouraged people (2) in the exercise or enjoyment of their rights under the statute. How does the *Linkletter* court connect the two with respect to Linkletter's
signing the petition? Why did the court need to analyze the defendant's motivations in opposing the women's shelter? Does it matter whether Linkletter
thought that Western & Southern was discriminating against the shelter based
on the sex rather than the economic status of the shelter residents? Should it
matter whether such discrimination is actually proven? (Note that in the underlying litigation between the shelter and the defendant the court held that the
shelter had successfully stated a claim under the FHA, but the case settled
before the question of discrimination could be decided as a substantive matter.)

In Title VII retaliation cases, courts have developed a "reasonable belief"
requirement to determine whether an employee's activities should be protected by the statute. Essentially, this requires that the plaintiff employee's
opposition or participation conduct be based on a good faith, reasonable
belief that the defendant employer has engaged in an unlawful employment
practice. This does not mean that a substantive violation must be found for
the employee's actions to be protected against retaliation. Whether or not
this "reasonable belief" requirement will apply in an FHA case is not clear.
Consider the following two cases.

- Pelot v. Criterion 3, LLC, 157 F. Supp. 3d 618 (N.D. Miss. 2016).

  The plaintiff worked for the apartment complex at which he was also
  a tenant. After his unit was burglarized (likely by another tenant), he
  investigated the complex's policies. He discovered that the complex performed no background checks on tenants and that at least one complex
  resident was a registered sex offender. He wrote a letter to the complex
  management, stating that the failure to conduct background checks on
  tenants violated the FHA, in particular because allowing sex offenders
  to reside in the complex endangered female residents. Following this

letter, he was fired and evicted. He filed a §3617 claim against the complex; the defendants moved to dismiss:

> For purposes of their motion to dismiss, Defendants solely argue that Plaintiff has failed to allege a protected activity under the FHA. Plaintiff contends that he engaged in protected activity by protesting Criterion's failure to exclude sex offenders from its premises, and by explaining that Criterion's inaction endangered women. Plaintiff has not stated in his amended complaint, nor does he argue in response to this motion, that the failure to conduct background checks actually violated §3604(a) or (b) of the FHA. Rather, he urges that his "reasonable belief" of unlawful gender discrimination qualifies as protected activity under §3617.
>
> At least two federal district courts outside the Fifth Circuit have applied the "reasonable belief" standard from Title VII by analogy to FHA retaliation claims, even though the language of Title VII's anti-retaliation provision is different from that of §3617 of the FHA. Under Title VII, an employee who opposes an unlawful employment practice is protected so long as she possesses a "reasonable belief" that the employer was engaged in unlawful employment practices.
>
> In the Fifth Circuit, however, it is less clear whether a "reasonable belief" of unlawful conduct is sufficient to trigger §3617's protections. . . . Thus, within the Fifth Circuit, §3617 arguably does not protect one who advocates against practices that he reasonably but erroneously believes violate the FHA.
>
> Even if the "reasonable belief" standard were available for FHA retaliation claims, Plaintiff's complaint falls short. A belief of discrimination "is not reasonable if the law is settled that the . . . practice complained of is not unlawful. . . ." Kummerle v. EMJ Corp., 3:11-CV-2839, 2012 WL 2995065 (N.D. Tex. July 23, 2012) (granting motion for judgment on the pleadings and noting "[a] plaintiff's belief is not objectively reasonable if the law is settled that the . . . practice complained of is not unlawful. . . ."); Wilson v. Delta State Univ., 143 Fed. App'x 611, 613 (5th Cir. 2005) (holding that a belief of discrimination contrary to "settled law in this Circuit" was objectively unreasonable). . . . As previously discussed, Plaintiff orally claimed that Criterion's failure to conduct background checks endangered women, and even cited the FHA in his letter. But these charges, even if true, would not constitute FHA discrimination.

- Broome v. Biondi, 17 F. Supp. 2d 211 (S.D.N.Y. 1997).

Simone Demou owned a unit in a co-op building that she wished to sublease to an interracial family (the Broomes). The sublease required the approval of the co-op Board, but actions taken by the co-op President led Demou to believe that the family was being discriminated against. She called Board members to voice her concerns, noting other instances in which she believed the co-op President had been racially discriminatory. The Board denied the Broomes permission to enter into the sublease, and they in turn sued the Board and the President under the FHA. The defendants responded by counterclaiming against the Broomes for defamation, and asserting third-party defamation claims against Demou. Demou counterclaimed against the co-op, alleging that its defamation suit against her constituted unlawful retaliation under §3617. After a trial, the jury found in favor of the couple and in favor of Demou, and awarded significant damages:

> The Beekman defendants argue that they are entitled to judgment as a matter of law because Demou failed to establish a prima facie case of retaliation. Specifically, the Beekman defendants claim that Demou failed to demonstrate that she engaged in a protected activity. To prove that she engaged in protected activity, Demou had to show that she took action to affirmatively oppose discrimination against the plaintiffs by the Beekman defendants. Demou did not have to establish that the conduct she opposed was in fact a violation of the Federal FHA . . ., but only that she had a "good faith, reasonable belief that the underlying actions of the [Beekman defendants] violated the law." Abel v. Bonfanti, 625 F. Supp. 263, 267 (S.D.N.Y. 1985).
>
> Demou testified that she reasonably believed the Board's actions toward the Broomes were motivated by racial prejudice. Demou presented evidence showing that she developed this perception because Nicholas Biondi and the Board treated the Broomes differently from former sublet applicants. Demou first spoke with Biondi about the Broomes' application on May 31 or June 1, and told him about their financial qualifications. Demou testified that Biondi said he would meet with Gregory Broome and that no full Board meeting would be required because the Board would go along with his decision concerning the application. After meeting with Gregory Broome on June 5, however, the record shows that the Broomes were required to meet with the full Board on the following evening. Demou testified that she became concerned about the requirement of a second meeting because this was an unprecedented requirement for the approval process, and she reasonably believed that this change was made based on race because the Broomes were otherwise qualified applicants.
>
> The evidence also demonstrates that Demou took affirmative action to oppose what she believed to be the Beekman defendants' attempt to frustrate the Broomes' sublet application because of Gregory Broome's race. Demou testified that she encouraged the Broomes to follow through the Board's approval process; spoke with Eddie Vega, the superintendent, to facilitate the Broomes' move into the apartment; tried to call Biondi and visited Maria Capraro at American Landmark to find out why a second Board meeting was required; and called each Board [Member] to ask them to approve the Broomes' sublet application. Based on this evidence, the court finds that the jury could conclude that the "protected activity" requirement of her retaliation claims was satisfied and, therefore, that she made a prima facie case of retaliation.

How can these cases be distinguished? In *Pelot*, the problem was that the plaintiff was incorrect as a matter of law. No court has ever found that failure to screen tenants or renting to sex offenders violates the FHA. (In fact, overly aggressive tenant screening might violate the FHA under certain circumstances.) But should a nonlawyer acting in good faith be held to this standard of legal knowledge? It certainly helped Demou's case that the jury found the co-op liable for discriminating against the Broome family. But what if it had found the co-op not liable (e.g., that the decision to deny the Broomes' sublease was made for legitimate nondiscriminatory reasons)? Under that hypothetical, should the fact that Demou was wrong as a matter of fact prevent her from claiming protection for actions taken based on a good-faith belief that the co-op was engaged in illegal conduct?

Finally, consider Frazier v. Rominger, 27 F.3d 828 (2d Cir. 1994), in which an interracial couple was denied the ability to rent an apartment. The couple had perceived what they believed to be reluctance on the part of the landlord to rent to them and had asked whether this hesitancy was "a racial thing." The landlord then refused to rent to them, allegedly because "being accused of race discrimination made him feel very uncomfortable." The couple sued, alleging a discriminatory denial of housing. At trial, the judge refused to instruct the jury on a cause of action for retaliation under §3617 (based on the plaintiffs' theory that they were denied housing for questioning the defendant's motives), and the jury returned a verdict for the defendant. The Second Circuit rejected the plaintiffs' appeal:

> Plaintiffs claim that Mr. Frazier's questioning of Mr. Rominger's potential bias constituted the "exercise or enjoyment of" one of his rights under the FHA, and that Mr. Rominger's refusal to rent because of this questioning constituted "interference" under §3617. We are therefore faced with the somewhat peculiar argument by plaintiffs that the defendants' refusal to rent to plaintiffs is at the same time a §3604(a) discrimination and a §3617 interference, thus giving rise to two separate causes of action.
>
> The fallacy in plaintiffs' argument lies in their equating the "right" to question defendant's motivation as racial with a "right granted or protected by section 3603, 3604, 3605, or 3606" of the FHA. Section 3617 prohibits interference with the exercise of Fair Housing rights only as enumerated in these referenced sections, which define the substantive violations of the Act. These sections provide that prospective tenants have a right not to be discriminated against on account of their race in a wide variety of housing transactions. Nowhere in these sections, however, can be found a right to question the potential racial motivations of landlords.

3. Other Types of Aiding and Encouragement. There are many forms that "aiding or encouraging" can take. Consider Grieger v. Sheets, 689 F. Supp. 835 (N.D. Ill. 1988), in which a married couple alleged they were harassed, threatened with violence, denied repairs, and threatened with eviction after the wife refused their landlord's demands for sex in exchange for repairs and continued tenancy. The court allowed the husband to proceed on a §3617 claim, under the theory that the landlord was engaging in the retaliatory behavior on account of his having encouraged his wife not to exchange sex for housing and repairs. *See also* United States v. Koch, 352 F. Supp. 2d 970 (D. Neb. 2004) (landlord allegedly evicted tenant after he learned that she was cooperating with a Department of Justice investigation into his sexual harassment of tenants).

A second common question in retaliation cases beyond whether the plaintiff's actions are protected is whether the actions taken by the defendant constitute retaliation under the statute. The plaintiff must prove that the defendant's actions were taken "on account of" the plaintiff's aiding or encouraging the exercise of fair housing rights, and not for some other reason. In addition, the plaintiff must prove that the conduct qualifies as retaliation under the statute. Consider the following case, in which the defendant City of Lakewood argues its actions—failure to renew the plaintiff's contract—should not qualify as retaliation because the plaintiff had no right to a contract renewal.

Walker v. City of Lakewood
272 F.3d 1114 (9th Cir. 2001)

Before: Noonan, Silverman, and Paez, Circuit Judges.

Paez, Circuit Judge:

Pursuant to its contract with the City of Lakewood ("City"), the Fair Housing Foundation of Long Beach ("FHF") operated a fair housing counseling program for the City. On September 2, 1992, a group of tenants and former tenants of the Park Apartments complex in Lakewood (the "Park Tenants" or "Park Plaintiffs") contacted the FHF, alleging that the Park Apartments management company was engaged in racial discrimination and harassment. After being presented with their various options, the Park Tenants requested referral to a private attorney. The FHF contacted the law firm of Traber, Voorhees & Olgun within a matter of days after first meeting with the Park Tenants. On July 29, 1993, the FHF advised the City that the residents of the Park Apartments were going to file a lawsuit against the owners and managers of the complex and that a press conference was going to be held at the FHF's offices on the following day. The FHF provided the City with a copy of the press release and a "case narrative," outlining the history of the anticipated litigation. The press release included the following statement by the FHF Executive Director, Barbara (Mowery) Shull, about the alleged discrimination at the Park Apartments:

> This case illustrates why it is critical for apartment owners and managers to receive training in how to provide fair housing. While many of these families had lived for years in this complex without problem, it only took one ignorant and biased manager a few months to uproot and displace at least eight or nine such families and to send the message to yet another generation of young African-Americans that they are still not welcome in middle class cities like Lakewood.

The City contends that this statement accused it of racism.

The Park Tenants filed suit on July 30, 1993. In the meantime, on August 4, 1993, Scott Barker, Vice President of the Park Apartments' management company and a named defendant in the Park lawsuit, sent a letter to City officials complaining about the lawsuit and the FHF's investigation and aiding of the Tenants. Barker asked the City officials to "[p]lease review the policies of the Foundation and ask them to truly investigate claims prior to making statements in the newspaper." The top of the letter had a handwritten note saying, "We will be responding to this request!—Jack G." Jack Gonsalves is Assistant Director of Community Development for the City. On August 17, 1993, Charles K. Ebner, the City's Director of Community Development, sent a letter to the FHF requesting a meeting to discuss "possible contract violations." Ebner wrote the FHF a second letter, on September 23, 1993:

> We believe FHF exercised poor judgement concerning the press release and conference in The Park apartments case. . . . The handling of The Park apartments case, and in particular the press conference, leaves us with serious concerns for the future. . . . Quite frankly we are looking for some assurance on the part of FHF that a similar scenario will not occur in the future and that you will have more regard for the community of Lakewood.

The FHF replied with a letter dated September 26, 1993, in which it informed the City that it was considering joining the Park Tenants suit as a plaintiff and that it was common practice for fair housing organizations to participate in press conferences, and expressed concern because the City's Housing Specialist, Michelle (Mitchell) Ramirez, had told Barbara Shull that the FHF would not be paid until it apologized. In a November 4, 1993, letter Ebner disputed the nature of the conversation between Ramirez and Shull:

> Ms. [Ramirez], in fact, simply informed Ms. [Shull] that the City was waiting for a response from the FHF before releasing payment for those months. The City's interest is in resolving any problems with the FHF and receiving some assurance on the part of FHF that a similar scenario will not occur in the future and that you will have more regard for the community of Lakewood.

The November letter included the back payments that the City owed the FHF.

Although the City had renewed the FHF's contract from 1990 to 1993 without requiring the FHF to submit a new bid each year, the City sent out requests for proposals to various fair housing organizations to replace the FHF. The City did not ask the FHF for a bid. Only the Fair Housing Council of San Bernardino and the FHF, which submitted a bid despite not receiving a request, submitted proposals. The FHF alleges it was excluded from consideration, and the San Bernardino organization was chosen to receive the 1994-95 contract.

Then-District Judge Tashima denied the FHF's request to join the underlying action as a co-plaintiff, but granted the Park Tenants' request to join the City and the Los Angeles County Sheriff's Department as defendants.

The City filed a third-party complaint against the FHF and Shull for breach of contract and indemnity. In response, the FHF filed this counterclaim against the City, alleging interference and retaliation in violation of the FHA. Judge Tashima dismissed the complaint against Shull and the breach of contract claim against the FHF. On May 17, 1999, District Judge Tevrizian granted summary judgment for the FHF on the City's indemnity claim and for the City on the FHF's state and federal fair housing claims.

1. SCOPE OF §3617

The mere fact that the parties were subject to a contract that could be canceled by either party at any time does not bar this suit. District courts have repeatedly allowed employees to pursue §3617 retaliation claims against their employers after they were terminated. In those cases, presumably, the employees were working under employment-at-will contracts that could have been canceled at any time. But the FHA nevertheless prohibits employers from canceling those contracts in retaliation for fair housing advocacy.

The City responds that the contract in this case was not canceled but instead was merely not renewed. No court has yet addressed the question of whether the failure to renew an annual contract may be the basis of an FHA retaliation claim. We conclude that this situation is analogous to the more-familiar situation of a retaliatory failure-to-hire in the Title VII and First Amendment contexts. In Ruggles v. Cal. Polytechnic State Univ., 797 F.2d 782 (9th Cir. 1986), we held that a former part-time instructor could bring a Title VII retaliation claim if the tenure-track teaching "position for which she applied was eliminated or not available to her because of her protected activities." Similarly, here, the FHF has alleged that the City refused to consider it for the 1994-95 contract because of its protected activities. As we explain below, there is no reason that the principles established in our other cases should not also apply in the FHA retaliation context.

Next, the City contends that it merely engaged in "economic competition" when it hired a new fair housing services provider, action that cannot give rise to a retaliation claim. *See Michigan Protection & Advocacy Serv., Inc. v. Babin* (6th Cir. 1994) (holding that "economic competition" does not constitute "interference" under §3617). In *Babin*, defendant Hammonds was negotiating to lease a house she owned to an organization that runs group homes for the mentally disabled. The defendant neighbors objected and raised enough money to buy the home from Hammonds. The plaintiffs sued, claiming, inter alia, a violation of §3617.

The Sixth Circuit's "economic competition" holding is, however, factually distinguishable. That holding applies only to the suit against the neighbors, who were merely competing with the group home for control of the property. The FHF has not sued the party engaged in economic competition in this case, the City's new fair housing services provider. Furthermore, unlike defendant Hammonds, the City did more than seek other bids and award the contract to another party; according to declarations submitted by the FHF, the City actually excluded the FHF from the competition for the 1994-95 contract. The FHF has also presented evidence, which we discuss below, that the City's motivation was retaliatory and not "purely economic."

In sum, the City has not provided a persuasive reason that we should not apply our well-settled principles for retaliation claims to this case. Our straightforward review of the facts reveals that this case is extraordinarily similar to those other retaliation cases and falls within the purview of §3617.

The FHF has alleged that, in response to protected advocacy, the City engaged in a series of actions designed to coerce and intimidate the FHF into changing or ceasing their activities. Therefore, the FHF has stated a cognizable claim under the FHA, and we proceed to determine whether the FHF introduced sufficient evidence to survive summary judgment.

2. SUMMARY JUDGMENT

As with any retaliation claim, we apply the familiar burden-shifting analysis established by the Supreme Court in *McDonnell Douglas Corp. v. Green* (1973). To establish a prima facie case of retaliation, a plaintiff must show that (1) he engaged in a protected activity; (2) the defendant subjected him to an adverse action; and (3) a causal link exists between the protected activity and the adverse action. If a plaintiff has presented a prima facie retaliation claim, the burden shifts to the defendant to articulate a legitimate nondiscriminatory reason for its decision. If the defendant articulates such a reason, the plaintiff bears the ultimate burden of demonstrating that the reason was merely a pretext for a discriminatory motive.

The FHF has shown that it participated in a protected activity, "aid[ing] or encourag[ing]," 42 U.S.C. §3617, the Park Plaintiffs in the exercise of their fair housing rights. The FHF met with the Park Tenants, presented them with their options, and referred them to an attorney; served in a "paralegal capacity" for the attorney; continued to investigate the Park Apartments, using their usual techniques; issued a press release and conducted a press conference in conjunction with the filing of the lawsuit; and attempted to join the lawsuit as a plaintiff.

Viewing the facts in the light most favorable to the FHF, the organization has also shown that it suffered an adverse action. In the context of a §3617 claim, that adverse action must be in the form of "coerc[ion], intimidat[ion], threat[s], or interfere[nce]." FHF has not sought to distinguish among these statutory terms, nor does the statute provide any definition. In determining what those terms mean, "we look first to the plain language of the statute, construing the provisions of the entire law, including its object and policy, to ascertain the intent of Congress." Northwest Forest Res. Council v. Glickman, 82 F.3d 825, 830 (9th Cir. 1996). As an initial matter, we observe that §3617 does not require a showing of force or violence for coercion, interference, intimidation, or threats to give rise to liability. When Congress intended to require such a showing, such as in the FHA's criminal provision, it did so. Compare 42 U.S.C. §3631 (imposing criminal liability when one "by force or threat of force willfully injures, intimidates or interferes with, or attempts to injure intimidate or interfere with" fair housing rights) with 42 U.S.C. §3617 (making it "unlawful to coerce, intimidate, threaten, or interfere with any person" in retaliation for fair housing activity). *See also Babin*, 18 F.3d at 347 ("Section 3617 is not limited to those who used some sort of 'potent force or duress'. . . ."). Turning to the plain meaning of these terms, we see that the

City's alleged activities could be characterized as interference, coercion, or threats. "Interference" is "the act of meddling in or hampering an activity or process." Webster's Third New Int'l Dict. 1178 (14th ed. 1961). To "coerce" is "to compel to an act or choice by force, threat, or other pressure." *Id.* at 439. And, more relevant for this case, "coercion" includes "the application of sanctions or force by a government [usually] accompanied by the suppression of constitutional liberties in order to compel dissenters to conform." *Id.* Finally, a "threat" is "an expression to inflict evil, injury, or other damage on another." *Id.* at 2382.

The Supreme Court has instructed that we are to treat "[t]he language of the [FHA as] broad and inclusive." *Trafficante v. Metropolitan Life Ins. Co.* (1972). We have previously explained that "interference," in particular, "'has been broadly applied to reach all practices which have the effect of interfering with the exercise of rights under the federal fair housing laws.'" United States v. Hayward, 36 F.3d 832, 835 (9th Cir. 1994). Most of the evidence presented by the FHF demonstrates that the City "interfered," or meddled, with its ability to conduct its fair housing activities. The City supervised the organization more closely than it had before, by sending city officials to monthly meetings, and also asked the FHF to "curtail the amount of exposure" it gave discrimination complaints. Additionally, the City contacted other cities to complain about the FHF and also filed suit against the FHF for breach of contract, which required time and money to defend. Lastly, the City refused to renew the FHF's contract, which altogether prevented the organization from working in Lakewood.

The FHF has presented further evidence of the City's conduct that, while certainly interference, might also be considered coercion or threats. The City suggested it would not renew the contract if the FHF did not apologize when Ebner sent a letter stating that "[t]he handling of The Park apartments case, and in particular the press conference, leaves us with serious concerns for the future. . . ." Further evidence of coercion is the letter from Ebner stating that payments would be withheld until the organization apologized.

Finally, the FHF has demonstrated the requisite causal link. As detailed above, the City sent its first letter to the FHF less than two weeks after receiving a complaint from the Park Apartments management company. That letter suggested that the City would not renew the FHF's contract without an apology for the Park Apartments investigation and lawsuit. The City's second letter acknowledges that it withheld payment because it was waiting for that apology and "some assurance on the part of the FHF that a similar scenario will not occur in the future. . . ."

The City, in turn, has met its burden of articulating a nonretaliatory reason for its actions. It alleges that the FHF was not complying with its contract, by not providing promised outreach activities, making necessary reports to the City, or undertaking pre-litigation conciliation efforts, and by using its office for the press conference.

The FHF's approach to a showing of pretext is two-pronged. First, while admitting it was not providing the City with case narratives, the FHF contests the City's claim that it was in violation of its contract, contending that it always submitted its monthly reports; that it is common practice for fair housing organizations to participate in press conferences; that it was not contractually obligated to report to the City prior to taking action; and that the FHF and the Park Tenants' attorneys attempted to conciliate the claims prior to filing the lawsuit. There is, we conclude, a disputed issue of material fact regarding whether the FHF was in compliance with its contract.

Second, the FHF identifies evidence that it asserts shows its protected activities were the real reason for the City's actions. The City had never before complained about the services the FHF was providing and had always renewed the contract without requesting new bids. The City only began to investigate and interfere with the FHF after receiving a letter from Scott Barker, of the Park Apartments management company, complaining about the lawsuit. In her declaration, Barbara Shull alleges that the City's reaction was not prompted by the alleged accusation of racism but was an attempt to placate Barker and his company. She claims that City Administrator Howard Chambers told her, "You need to understand the relationship between the City of Lakewood and the owners of the Park Apartments. . . . [Barker] continue[s] to invest millions of dollars in the City of Lakewood. This is no way to reward him for all the help he has given the City." Chambers denies making these statements. But if Shull's account is true, this would support the FHF's position that the City's motives were retaliatory. We conclude that there is a disputed issue of material fact regarding the City's motivations.

Accordingly, we reverse the summary judgment on the FHA claim and remand for further proceedings[.]

NOTES AND QUESTIONS

1. Title VII and the Materially Adverse Standard. In Title VII cases, the Supreme Court has adopted the "materially adverse" standard for determining whether retaliatory conduct is serious enough to qualify as a violation under that statute. *See* Burlington Northern & Santa Fe Railway Co. v. White, 548 U.S. 53, 68 (2006). Under this standard, an action constitutes illegal retaliation if a reasonable employee would have found the action materially adverse, which means it might have dissuaded a reasonable worker from making or supporting a charge of discrimination. Thus, under Title VII, "serious" retaliation such as a demotion, placement on administrative leave, or loss of pay would constitute a materially adverse action, because a worker might not bring a complaint if she knew this would be a consequence. A "lesser" outcome (such as being criticized, or receiving a mediocre performance review) would not, because a reasonable employee would presumably not let such outcomes deter her from making a complaint. This standard has been characterized as unwieldy, as it requires a court to decide, in retrospect, what a "reasonable" employee would have done or been deterred from doing had the employee known in advance the actions the employer would take in response.

This standard has not been specifically embraced by courts in §3617 cases. Would such a standard, with its focus on whether the plaintiff would have been deterred from taking protected action, even work in a case like *Lakewood*, in which a plaintiff organization's purpose is to combat discrimination or to provide housing to groups protected by the statute?

2. Lawsuits as Retaliation. Just as a person can use a lawsuit to interfere with another's fair housing rights, litigation can be used as a retaliatory tool against people for asserting their fair housing rights or for assisting others in doing so. For example, in *Broome v. Biondi* (discussed above), Demou, a resident of an apartment co-op, was sued by the President and Board of Directors for defamation, based on statements she made in support of an interracial family's (the Broomes') application to sublet her unit. When she suspected that the Board members were treating the Broomes unfairly because of Mr. Broome's race, Demou contacted each Board member and articulated her concerns that the Board president was being discriminatory. The Broomes sued the president and the Board after their application was denied, and the defendants filed third-party claims against Demou, alleging that she had defamed them. Demou counterclaimed, arguing that the filing of two lawsuits against her constituted retaliation for her supporting the Broome family's application. Following a jury trial, the Broomes prevailed in their FHA claim against the co-op, and Demou prevailed in her §3617 claim.

Or consider Zhu v. Countrywide Realty, Co., 165 F. Supp. 2d 1181 (D. Kan. 2001). In that case, Zhu, an Asian female homeowner, had a contentious relationship with Bunting, the real estate agent who oversaw the sale of her house, culminating in her allegations that he had committed fraud, harassed her, and sexually assaulted her. She filed a HUD complaint against him, alleging national origin and sex discrimination. A few weeks later Bunting's attorney sent a threatening letter to Zhu telling her to leave him alone, and shortly thereafter applied for a restraining order against her on Bunting's behalf. Zhu argued that this constituted retaliation under §3617. In denying Bunting's motion for summary judgment on this claim, the court noted:

> Counsel sent the letter just two weeks after plaintiff filed the HUD complaint, . . . and it threatened criminal proceedings — arguably unjustified — if plaintiff did not leave Bunting alone. The threat of legal action can be a "powerful instrument of coercion," Bill Johnson's Rests., Inc. v. N.L.R.B., 461 U.S. 731 (1983), and the timing of this letter supports an inference of causation. Summary judgment is inappropriate as to this claim.
>
> Similarly, the fact Bunting filed his petition for a restraining order roughly three weeks after plaintiff filed her HUD complaint raises an inference of causation. Plaintiff has therefore established a prima facie case of retaliation: (1) she has shown that she is a member of a protected class; (2) for the purposes of summary judgment, defendants do not contest that she engaged in

protected activity under the FHA by filing her HUD claim; (3) the timing of the letter and the lawsuit raises an inference of retaliation; and (4) Bunting's letter and suit constitute adverse actions that could deter plaintiff from exercising her rights under the FHA.

Zhu also filed a §3617 claim against the law firm that Bunting hired, but this suit was not successful. *See* Zhu v. Fisher, Cavanaugh, Smith & Lemon, P.A., 151 F. Supp. 2d 1254, 1259 (D. Kan. 2001). The court dismissed the claim, concluding that: "Mere legal representation of a third party who allegedly violated plaintiff's fair housing rights, however, does not give rise to an actionable claim against defendants. An attorney is not liable for the actions of a client simply because the attorney provided legal advice to the client." But the attorney did more than just "provide advice." Shouldn't an attorney recognize that such legal actions, when taken after a complaint has been filed against a client, might be construed as retaliatory under the statute? Or is the attorney's conduct justified because of the obligation to vigorously represent a client?

There have been cases of testers sued by housing providers as a result of the investigative activity they had undertaken. In Izard v. Arndt, 483 F. Supp. 261 (E.D. Wis. 1980), landlords sued testers for "malicious prosecution," and the testers responded with a §3617 counterclaim. The court dismissed the malicious prosecution claim and dismissed the §3617 counterclaim without prejudice to the testers' refiling to allege the dismissal.

Consider also Northside Realty Associates, Inc. v. Chapman, 411 F. Supp. 1195, 1199-2000 (N.D. Ga. 1976), in which real estate companies sued a group of testers in state court over their investigative activity. The testers removed the case to federal court, using a procedure, 28 U.S.C. §1443, that applies when a litigant has a civil right that might not be protected in state court. Denying the companies' motion to remand, the federal court relied on precedent interpreting identical language under the Voting Rights Act to recognize that the mere bringing of the state court action would deny the testers their federally protected rights under §3617 if they could establish that "the state court action was brought against them for their having aided and encouraged others in the exercise and enjoyment of the right to equal housing opportunity without regard to race, and that the action has the effect of coercing, intimidating, threatening, and otherwise interfering with their rights under §3617."

3. Threats of Retaliation. What if a landlord threatens to evict anyone who complains about a fair housing violation? The language in §3617 prohibiting threats surely covers this situation, even if the landlord never has carried through on such a threat. For example, see Hunter v. WPD Management, LLC, 476 F. Supp. 3d 731 (N.D. Ill. 2020), which involved a broken elevator in an apartment building and a disabled tenant who resided on the sixth floor. The tenant had called 911 after being unable to get out of the building. Later, building operators posted flyers stating that anyone who called 911 for a nonemergency would be evicted. The court held that the plaintiff's allegation that the flyers articulated a "retaliatory intent" was sufficient to state a claim under §3617.

D. STAND-ALONE NATURE OF §3617 CLAIMS

By its text, §3617 refers to substantive parts of the FHA, making it illegal to interfere with the exercise or enjoyment of rights under those provisions, or aiding or encouraging others to do so. This raises the question of whether a plaintiff must prove a violation of one of these substantive provisions to prevail on a §3617 claim. In other words, can a §3617 claim stand alone? The answer, now, almost certainly is "yes," for many reasons.

To begin, there have always been §3617 claims that could not come attached to other substantive statutory provisions. This would include claims against neighbors or community members who are not housing providers and are thus incapable of violating the substantive provisions under §3604 (e.g., denying housing, altering the terms or conditions of housing, or making statements connected with the sale or rental of housing). As the Ninth Circuit explained, §3617 "does not necessarily deal with a discriminatory housing practice, or with the landlord, financer or brokerage service guilty of such practice." Smith v. Stechel, 510 F.2d 1162, 1164 (9th Cir. 1975). Numerous courts have agreed. *See, e.g.*, Stackhouse v. DeSitter, 620 F. Supp. 208 (N.D. Ill. 1985) (applying §3617 in a case of neighbor harassment, and reasoning that §3617 would be superfluous if it were read as dependent on a violation of §§3603-3606).

Retaliation claims present another example. The harm alleged by a plaintiff bringing such a claim — that they have been subject to an adverse action for aiding or encouraging others in exercising or enjoying substantive rights — is distinct from an underlying violation of those rights. Indeed, if a plaintiff has succeeded in assisting others, there may be no underlying violation.

But in other cases, the plaintiff may be alleging conduct that potentially violates both §3617 and another substantive provision, as for a plaintiff who claims a discriminatory denial of housing under §3604(a) and interference under §3617. The question then becomes whether the plaintiff can proceed with the §3617 claim even if the substantive claim fails. This issue took on particular significance during the period in which some courts were denying claims of post-acquisition housing discrimination brought under substantive provisions of the FHA. As discussed in Chapter 8, starting with the 2004 decision in Halprin v. Prairie Single Family Homes of Dearborn Park Ass'n, 388 F.3d 327 (7th Cir. 2004), a number of courts narrowly interpreted §3604(a), (b), and (c) to apply only to discriminatory conduct that prevented a plaintiff from acquiring housing or that occurred at the point of sale or rental. This interpretation, now generally rejected, was based on the specific language in those provisions, for example, §3604(a)'s reference to "making housing unavailable," §3604(b)'s reference to discriminatory terms and conditions in the "sale or rental" of housing, and §3604(c)'s reference to discriminatory statements made "in connection with the sale or rental of housing." Section 3617, however, does not contain language that even arguably limits it in any temporal way. In fact, "interference with enjoyment" clearly applies to people who have acquired their housing. HUD's regulations underscore this interpretation. *See* 24 C.F.R. §100.400(c)(2) ("Threatening, intimidating or interfering with persons in their enjoyment of a dwelling because of" protected characteristics violates §3617).

As a result, the substantive claims of some post-acquisition plaintiffs had been foreclosed, leaving only the §3617 claim as a possibility. This raised the further question of whether a §3617 claim should be able to proceed under these circumstances. In *Halprin* the court avoided answering this question because the defendants had waived the argument below, although it took a skeptical posture, questioning the validity of the HUD regulation.

Much of the *Halprin* court's postacquisition reasoning was repudiated by the full Seventh Circuit in Bloch v. Frischholz, 587 F.3d 771 (7th Cir. 2009) (en banc). Significantly, *Bloch* also endorsed the HUD regulation and made clear that §3617 claims can stand alone:

> Whether a violation of §3617 can exist without a violation of §3604 or any other FHA provision is a question we have routinely reserved. . . . We know that the Association's enforcement of the Hallway Rule did not constructively evict the Blochs in violation of §3604(a) or (b). But that does not foreclose the possibility that the defendants "interfered" with the Blochs' enjoyment of their §3604 rights or "coerced" or "intimidated" the Blochs on account of their having exercised those rights. To hold otherwise would make §3617 entirely duplicative of the other FHA provisions; though its language is unique in the FHA, §3617 would have no independent meaning. But "when the legislature uses certain language in one part of the statute and different language in another, the court assumes different meanings were intended." Sosa v. Alvarez-Machain, 542 U.S. 692, 711 n.9 (2004). Coercion, intimidation, threats, or interference with or on account of a person's exercise of his or her §§3603-3606 rights can be distinct from outright violations of §§3603-3606. For instance, if a landlord rents to a white tenant but then threatens to evict him upon learning that he is married to a black woman, the landlord has plainly violated §3617, whether he actually evicts the tenant or not. That §§3604 and 3617 might overlap in some circumstances is neither unusual nor unfortunate. . . .
>
> We agree with the Blochs (and the United States, appearing as amicus in this case) that §3617 reaches a broader range of post-acquisition conduct. A claim for coercion, intimidation, threats, and interference with or on account of plaintiff's §3604 rights does not require that the plaintiff actually vacate the premises.

Even if §3617 does not require the defendant to have actually violated a substantive right under the FHA, it still refers to these rights. Therefore, plaintiffs must establish the existence of a predicate right to which they can link their §3617 claim, even if a violation of that right cannot be established. So long as there is a nexus with a recognized right, the §3617 claim should be supported.[5]

Finally, if the "right" that the plaintiff is invoking does not exist under the FHA, the plaintiff will be unable to state a claim for interference with that right. For example, see *Pelot v. Criterion 3* (discussed above), in which the plaintiff argued that the defendant's failure to conduct sex offender screening of tenants put female tenants at risk in violation of the FHA. The court held that this failure by the defendants did not, in fact, implicate any right under the FHA, and thus there was no predicate for the plaintiff's retaliation claim. Another example is *Frazier v. Rominger*, discussed above (characterizing plaintiff's predicate claim as the "right to question defendant's racial motivations," and declaring that this is not a predicate right under the FHA).

———————

The following case addresses many of the issues discussed above, including the availability of postacquisition claims, the independence of §3617 claims, and whether offensive conduct should be considered interference with housing.

Watters v. Homeowners' Ass'n at the Preserve at Bridgewater
48 F.4th 779 (7th Cir. 2022)

Before Easterbrook, St. Eve, and Jackson-Akiwumi, Circuit Judges.

JACKSON-AKIWUMI, Circuit Judge.

Tonca and Terence Watters, a married black couple, chose to build their dream home in the Preserve at Bridgewater, a subdivision of Kokomo, Indiana. What they found were neighbors who made it clear from the beginning that they did not want the Watters to live there. When [the Watters] bought their lots in June 2013 and when they moved in after building their home in December 2015, they were the only black couple in the Preserve.

From the very beginning, the Watters had several run-ins with another married couple, Ed and Kate Mamaril. Kate was the president of the HOA when the Watters initially bought their property. She remained president until the summer of 2015, when her husband took over the presidency. Ed holds this position to this day. Kate has had no other role in the HOA.

Conflict with the Mamarils ignited as soon as the Watters began construction on their home: Ed told the Watters that they were not welcome, called them "assholes," asked why "you people" moved here, told them he had them investigated, and suggested they live "somewhere else."

———

5. *Cf.* Treece v. Perrier Condominium Owners Ass'n, Inc., 519 F. Supp. 3d 342, 364-65 (E.D. La. 2021) (the plaintiffs' §3617 claim failed because they did not state a claim under §3604(a) and had not pled a retaliation claim).

The Mamarils' cats also roamed the Watters' property without limit. Even though the HOA had covenants prohibiting pets from roaming free—and there was an applicable city ordinance too—the HOA refused to intervene when the Watters requested enforcement. In any event, given the cat problem, the Watters contacted the Humane Society. The Humane Society caught several cats on the Watters' property and fined the Mamarils for allowing their cats to roam freely. When someone from the Humane Society was speaking with Tonca on her own property, Kate approached Tonca and called her a "black bitch" and a "black n-----."

The final confrontation between the families occurred at the local Cracker Barrel, just outside of the Preserve's boundaries, in June 2017. When the Watters were at the restaurant with their daughter and two grandchildren, the Mamarils pushed them, and Kate referred to the grandchildren as "little monkey n------." The Mamarils then sought a protective order against Tonca, which prevented her from attending HOA meetings, but the Mamarils later withdrew the underlying petition.

Beyond the Mamarils, the Watters had a series of conflicts with the HOA. Although new homeowners should ordinarily receive copies of the HOA's restrictive covenants from their realtor or the seller, Kate, who was not on the HOA board at the time, offered to provide copies of the covenants to homeowners, neighbor-to-neighbor. But when the Watters asked for copies of the HOA's restrictive covenants, Ed as HOA president refused to provide copies, even after the Watters made requests through an attorney. [There were disputes about where the Watters' mailbox could be placed, the position of their porch posts, and the color they could paint their house.]

The Watters make other allegations including that a neighbor parked his trailer in front of his own property in violation of the HOA's covenants; when they emailed the HOA about a person urinating and defecating on their property, only one HOA member responded; and when they emailed the HOA about the indecent exposure and, separately, a burglary, the HOA did not send out a mass email even though it did send out mass emails about a lost puppy and a car break-in.

The Watters' largest dispute with the HOA centered around a privacy fence. The HOA has a rule against privacy fences; only pool safety fences and decorative landscaping fences are allowed. The privacy fence issue arose because Terence is a veteran who was diagnosed with PTSD after being trapped in a cave, with a dog, behind enemy lines. Seeing dogs causes him emotional and physical distress. He is also unable to work and perform certain manual tasks because of a terminal lung condition. The lung condition further exacerbates his reactivity to dogs. Terence states that his doctors advised him to get a privacy fence to mitigate his PTSD triggers.

Without mentioning his disability, Terence initially requested a six-foot tall vinyl privacy fence that obstructed the view of his backyard. The HOA denied the request. Terence then requested the privacy fence as a reasonable and necessary accommodation. Terence had previously told the HOA, Ed

Mamaril, a committee of the HOA called the Architectural Control Committee ("ACC"), and two ACC members, about his lung condition. In his accommodation request, however, he did not mention his lung condition or his PTSD; he stated only that the Fair Housing Act prohibits disability discrimination. Terence says that he would have provided more information to the HOA about his disability, but they did not ask.

In response to Terence's accommodation request, the HOA wrote: "The Fair Housing Act does not pertain to your request for a privacy fence due to disability." The HOA rejected the request and suggested alternatives, such as a wrought iron fence or landscaping to create a sense of privacy.

For its part, the ACC stated that the Watters needed to build a pool to have a fence. The Watters submitted plans for a pool. Ed and other members of the ACC testified that the plans were not approved before construction began. On the day of installation, the ACC members, including Ed, physically prevented ground-breaking on the pool construction because they claimed that the plans had not been approved. But they reviewed the plans onsite, approved them, and allowed construction to begin the same day.

The Watters sued the HOA and its members, including the Mamarils. The parties agreed to have a magistrate judge decide the case, and defendants moved for summary judgment. The magistrate judge granted summary judgment in favor of all defendants on all claims. The Watters appeal with respect to only the HOA and the Mamarils.

II

The Watters' first claim against the HOA and the Mamarils is for race discrimination under the Fair Housing Act. Two sections of the FHA are key to this claim. First, §3604(a) explicitly prohibits making housing "unavailable" based on the potential renter or buyer's race or color. Second, §3617 prohibits coercion, intimidation, threats, or interference with "any person in the exercise or enjoyment of, or on account of his having exercised or enjoyed, or on account of his having aided or encouraged any other person in the exercise or enjoyment of, any right granted or protected by section [3604] of this title." Both §3604(a) and §3617 reach post-acquisition conduct, not just the initial sale or rental of housing. Bloch v. Frischholz, 587 F.3d 771, 782 (7th Cir. 2009) (en banc). The rights under §3604(a) that §3617 protects from interference include post-sale activity "that makes a dwelling unavailable to the owner or tenant, somewhat like a constructive eviction." Such post-sale activity includes "attempted discriminatory evictions" by interfering with an individual's §3604(a) rights—even if the plaintiff does not actually vacate the premises.

Plaintiffs need not invoke a specific right under §3604 in order to bring a §3617 claim. This is *Bloch's* very holding. In holding that rights under §3604(a) can cover post-acquisition conduct, the en banc court stated that §3617 "reaches a broader range of post-acquisition conduct" than §3604(a). *Id.* After all, if §3617 were entirely circumscribed by §3604(a), there would be little, if any, conduct that would not simultaneously violate §3617 and the underlying statute. Such a narrow reading of §3617 would render the statute useless. The en banc court in *Bloch* recognized this and therefore understood the statute to reach conduct outside the specific confines of §3604(a). See *id.* at 781-82 (recognizing the Blochs had §3617 claim even though they did not have a constructive eviction claim under §3604(a) because "[t]o hold otherwise would make §3617 entirely duplicative of the other FHA provisions.").

The core of the parties' dispute . . . is . . . whether any of the Mamarils' or the HOA's conduct interfered with the Watters' housing rights. After all, isolated acts of racial animus are not enough; there must be "'some nexus' between [a stray] remark and the challenged" action. See Scaife v. Cook Cnty., 446 F.3d 735, 741 (7th Cir. 2006).

The HOA and the Mamarils first argue that the Watters cannot point to any specific right under §3604(a) that was violated by the Mamarils' conduct. But, as explained earlier, a claim under §3617 does not require a specific violation of a right under §3604. Instead, §3617 prohibits the coercion, intimidation, threats, or interference with those rights. The Mamarils' repeated use of racist language is the quintessential example of interference that establishes "a 'pattern of harassment, invidiously motivated.'" Such a pattern of racially based harassment can function as an attempted constructive eviction, even if the Watters remained at their property.

The HOA and the Mamarils make the incredible claim that the Watters' FHA race discrimination claim should fail because "they continue to reside in [t]he Preserve[] to this day." The fact that the Watters chose to remain on the property they purchased, in the home that they built, despite the Mamarils' conduct cannot vitiate the Watters' claim. In the HOA and the Mamarils' view, the only way plaintiffs can succeed on a discrimination claim under §3617 is when the treatment is so bad that they are physically dispossessed of their property and run out of town. Our case law logically does not condone such a rule.

Stated otherwise, a reasonable factfinder could conclude that the Mamarils' pattern of harassment interfered with the Watters' post-acquisition enjoyment of their property, even if the Mamarils could not or did not actually force the Watters to leave. After all, the Mamarils' harassment of the Watters went directly to the Watters' choice to live at the Preserve: the Mamarils told them that "you people" should live elsewhere and the mere prospect of their moving into the subdivision warranted an investigation into their background. The harassment reemerged when the Watters called the Humane Society after the Mamarils' cats repeatedly entered their property, in violation of the neighborhood covenants. Even when the Watters tried to enjoy a meal just outside their home with their family, the Mamarils continued their racialized harassment.

The HOA and the Mamarils next suggest that the incidents involving the Mamarils' insults and epithets are simply personal in nature and have no relationship to the Watters' housing. They point out, for example, that Kate was not a member of the HOA board at the time she made her comments. And they note that Kate's first use of the N-word was when Tonca called the Humane Society about the Mamarils' cats, which had nothing to do with the HOA. Lastly, they assert that the incident at Cracker Barrel did not occur in the neighborhood or at an HOA function.

The problem with this argument is that it ignores the forest for the trees. While it is true that isolated incidents of racial slurs may not be enough on their own, this case involves the same defendant making two separate uses of one of the most horrendous slurs in our language, and her husband adding his own racially hostile innuendo. Add to this that the Mamarils are the president and former president of the HOA. These titles clothe the Mamarils with a certain power at the Preserve—even if one can debate the depth of that power. To be sure, a defendant's title alone does not absolve plaintiffs from proving the elements of their claims. But as in Title VII cases where we consider a supervisor's harassing conduct more serious than that of a co-worker, it stands to reason that the behavior of a defendant who exercises authority over a plaintiff's housing rights would also bear more consideration in a fair housing case. A reasonable factfinder can infer that being treated with racial disdain and hostility by the head of the HOA and his wife, who herself held the same position only recently, can directly affect how safe a family feels in their own home. More importantly, as discussed above, a reasonable factfinder can infer that the Mamarils' repeated harassment undermined the Watters' ability to enjoy the basic living conditions one expects when they purchase a home.

To be sure, interference under §3617 does not cover "a 'quarrel among neighbors' or an 'isolated act of discrimination,' but rather [] a 'pattern of harassment, invidiously motivated.'" But this is no simple quarrel among neighbors, and the Watters are not trying to use federal law to police general decorum in the neighborhood. The record shows that Kate and Ed Mamaril used racial slurs and epithets against the Watters ever since they first stepped foot in the Preserve. One cannot avoid liability by taking a film reel exhibiting harassment, slicing the reel into individual frames, and presenting them as mere isolated acts. The evidence here is enough that the Watters may present their claim against the Mamarils to a jury.

E. CRIMINAL PROVISION: §3631

Intimidating and threatening behavior can cross the line into criminal conduct. The FHA's lone criminal provision, 42 U.S.C. §3631, addresses this. It specifies that:

> Whoever, whether or not acting under color of law, by force or threat of force willfully injures, intimidates or interferes with, or attempts to injure, intimidate or interfere with—

(a) any person because of [protected characteristics] and because he is or has been selling, purchasing, renting, financing, occupying, or contracting or negotiating for the sale, purchase, rental, financing or occupation of any dwelling, or applying for or participating in any service, organization, or facility relating to the business of selling or renting dwellings; or

(b) any person because he is or has been, or in order to intimidate such person or any other person or any class of persons from—

(1) participating, without discrimination on account of [protected characteristics], in any of the activities, services, organizations or facilities described in subsection (a); or

(2) affording another person or class of persons opportunity or protection so to participate; or

(c) any citizen because he is or has been, or in order to discourage such citizen or any other citizen from lawfully aiding or encouraging other persons to participate, without discrimination on account of [protected characteristics] in any of the activities, services, organizations or facilities described in subsection (a), or participating lawfully in speech or peaceful assembly opposing any denial of the opportunity to so participate

shall be fined under title 18 [Eds.—The criminal title of the U.S. Code] or imprisoned not more than one year, or both; and if bodily injury results from the acts committed in violation of this section or if such acts include the use, attempted use, or threatened use of a dangerous weapon, explosives, or fire shall be fined under title 18 or imprisoned not more than ten years, or both; and if death results from the acts committed in violation of this section or if such acts include kidnapping or an attempt to kidnap, aggravated sexual abuse or an attempt to commit aggravated sexual abuse, or an attempt to kill, shall be fined under title 18 or imprisoned for any term of years or for life, or both.

It is difficult to overstate the role that racist violence has played in enforcing racial segregation. As discussed in Chapter 1, Black families who tried to move outside strictly defined neighborhoods faced cross-burnings, vandalism, assault, firebombings, and physical violence designed to keep them in restricted areas. The threat of such violence operated as a warning to other families who might wish to make similar moves, and perpetrators seldom were punished.

This sordid history motivated Congress to include §3631 in the FHA. As tempting as it might be to believe that such violence is a thing of the past, students should know that it persists today, as the following case illustrates.

United States v. Porter
928 F.3d 947 (10th Cir. 2019)

Before Matheson, Ebel, and Phillips, Circuit Judges.

MATHESON, Circuit Judge:

Mark Olic Porter shouted racial epithets at Lucas Waldvogel, a seven-year-old African American who lived in Mr. Porter's apartment complex. After hearing Mr. Porter's language, the boy's father, Michael Waldvogel, confronted Mr. Porter, who then assaulted Mr. Waldvogel with a stun cane. Shortly thereafter, Mr. Waldvogel and his family moved out of the complex.

A jury convicted Mr. Porter of interfering with Mr. Waldvogel's housing because of Mr. Waldvogel's race, a violation of the FHA, 42 U.S.C. §3631. The district court sentenced Mr. Porter to nine months in prison. He appeals his conviction. The Government cross-appeals his sentence.

I. BACKGROUND

The assault occurred at the Adagio Apartments in Draper, Utah, where both men lived in 2016. Mr. Waldvogel and his neighbor, Kaitlin Adair, described the incident at trial.

On November 3, 2016, Ms. Adair returned home from work and saw Mr. Porter on his front patio. He spoke to her, first making small talk and then "talking about immigration." Ms. Adair testified: "I don't remember specifically everything that he said, but I remember him saying that we need to exterminate all of the motherfucking n--, but first we need to exterminate all the motherfucking n-- lovers."

During this conversation, seven-year-old Lucas Waldvogel, who is African American, was riding his scooter on the sidewalk within view of Mr. Porter's patio. Ms. Adair noticed that Mr. Porter's attitude changed when he saw Lucas: "He seemed to get more agitated. His volume seemed to increase. It seemed like he was getting louder because the boy was out there." Ms. Adair withdrew from the conversation and considered calling the police. She did not do so.

Lucas went inside and informed his father "that there was a man outside shouting at him." Mr. Waldvogel told Lucas to go back outside. When Lucas returned with the same complaint, Mr. Waldvogel went to the balcony of his apartment to see what was happening. He heard Mr. Porter say to Lucas, "[G]et out of here, n--."

Mr. Waldvogel ran outside toward Mr. Porter's apartment. As he approached, Ms. Adair summoned him. She warned him that Mr. Porter "ha[d] been saying some pretty crazy things out here while your boy has been out here." She urged Mr. Waldvogel to "be cautious, because it looked like [Mr. Porter] had been drinking." She recalled that during this interaction, Mr. Waldvogel "didn't seem threatening" and "didn't make [her] feel nervous."

Mr. Waldvogel retrieved Lucas, and they began walking toward their apartment. As they passed Mr. Porter's patio, Mr. Porter came outside. Mr. Waldvogel approached the patio and said "something to the effect of . . . I don't care what you're saying in your house, but, you know, don't yell that stuff at my son." Mr. Porter responded, "[Y]ou and your n-- son can get out of here."

During this interaction, Mr. Porter was holding a stun cane in his hand near his right leg. The cane included a flashlight and a small barbed part on the end that, when activated, would send an electric shock into anything it touched. Mr. Waldvogel testified, "[T]he next thing I remember was hearing the arcing of a device as it came over this side of my head and then it hit me on my neck." The cane "pretty much incapacitated" Mr. Waldvogel, who fell to the ground. Mr. Waldvogel then grabbed the stun cane and pulled it away from Mr. Porter. Mr. Waldvogel fell backward into the grass, and the stun cane broke. Ms. Adair testified that, during this encounter, Lucas "stayed away," and remained "far off on kind of the other side of the grassy area."

Mr. Porter announced he was going to call the police because Mr. Waldvogel had stolen his property. Mr. Waldvogel responded that he intended to call the police, and, after discarding the broken stun cane and walking back to his apartment, he did. Mr. Waldvogel next saw Mr. Porter leave the apartment complex in his car.

While Mr. Porter was away, three Draper Police Department officers responded to Mr. Waldvogel's call. They examined and photographed Mr. Waldvogel's neck, which had a small red mark, and asked whether Mr. Waldvogel needed medical attention. He declined. The Government introduced a picture of Mr. Waldvogel's neck at trial.

When Mr. Porter returned to the Adagio, the police arrested him. Mr. Waldvogel recounted that, during the arrest, Mr. Porter "was telling all the officers to F off. He called the officers n-- lovers and a lot of F bombs."

Mr. Waldvogel testified that the altercation deeply affected Lucas. In the ensuing weeks, Lucas slept in Mr. Waldvogel's bed and insisted that Mr. Waldvogel block the front door with a large elliptical exercise machine. Lucas also stopped playing outside and would no longer retrieve the mail with his father. As a result, Mr. Waldvogel asked for and received permission to terminate his lease and move away from the Adagio. He eventually moved away from Draper because he feared running into Mr. Porter.

Mr. Porter's Animosity Toward African Americans

As conceded in his brief and as the evidence confirmed, Mr. Porter holds racist views.

When Mr. Porter moved to the Adagio Apartments in 2016, he asked the leasing agent how many African Americans lived there. After he moved in, Mr. Porter told Adagio maintenance worker Tyler Young, who was working on a vacant apartment above Mr. Porter's apartment, "not to move any n-- in above him." On another occasion, while fixing Mr. Porter's water heater, Mr. Young overheard Mr. Porter deliver a parody of Dr. Martin Luther King's "I Have a Dream" speech, offering his own dream "that all n-- were dead."

Ms. Adair said that Mr. Porter told her he was "concerned" that the paperboy, who was African American, would break into his apartment. She also stated, "The way [Mr. Porter] spoke about immigration led me to believe that he didn't like Mexicans or South Americans maybe." She added, "He didn't like black people."

Mr. Porter also demonstrated his racial animus in his comments to Ms. Adair immediately before the assault, to the Draper Police shortly after the assault, and later to the FBI when he was arrested the second time.

The FBI's Arrest of Mr. Porter

Mr. Porter was released after his initial arrest. Shortly thereafter, the Adagio evicted him, and he moved to Arizona. In 2017, nearly a year after the incident, FBI agents arrested Mr. Porter at his new home in Arizona and recorded their interviews with him. In one of these recordings, Mr. Porter recounted his version of the incident and admitted that he had told Lucas, "Get out of here you little stinking n--."

In another recording, Mr. Porter stated: "I don't want nothing to do with [African Americans]. I even told 'em when I moved in, I said, I don't want to live next to any of 'em. I told 'em at the complex." Mr. Porter continued to make anti-African American statements while the FBI agents transported him to a magistrate judge for his arraignment. Special Agent Elliot White reported: "[Mr. Porter] also said that real white men should kill n-- and asked if that was a federal offense. Also, during [sic] multiple times during the transport Mr. Porter said that Hitler had it right, he just had the wrong people, and that he felt that n-- were not even human."

Procedural History

A federal grand jury charged Mr. Porter with one count of "Interference with Housing" in violation of 42 U.S.C. §3631. Mr. Porter pled not guilty. At his three-day jury trial, the Government called nine witnesses and Mr. Porter called one. The jury found Mr. Porter guilty as charged. On its special verdict form, the jury found "[Mr.] Porter used a dangerous weapon," but it did not find "[Mr.] Porter caused bodily injury to [Mr.] Waldvogel."

II. DISCUSSION

Mr. Porter argues the trial evidence was insufficient to support Mr. Porter's conviction under 42 U.S.C. §3631. Mr. Porter argues the evidence was insufficient because it showed that Mr. Waldvogel "does not appear to be and does not identify as African American." Accordingly, despite Mr. Porter's demonstrated racial animus towards African Americans, he contends the Government failed to prove he assaulted Mr. Waldvogel on account of Mr.

Waldvogel's race. Mr. Porter further argues that even if the jury found Mr. Waldvogel is African American, the evidence still fell short of showing that he acted based on Mr. Waldvogel's race. We disagree with Mr. Porter.

Under this statute, the Government must prove that Mr. Porter (1) used force or the threat of force; (2) to willfully injure, intimidate, or interfere with Mr. Waldvogel (or attempt to do so); (3) because of Mr. Waldvogel's race; and (4) because Mr. Waldvogel was occupying a dwelling. To prove the conduct amounted to a felony that qualifies for a 10-year maximum sentence, the Government must also show the offense (1) involved the use of a dangerous weapon, or (2) resulted in bodily injury to Mr. Waldvogel. *See* 42 U.S.C. §3631.

Mr. Porter focuses on the third element: that he acted because of Mr. Waldvogel's race. This "specific intent" element turns on the defendant's motivation for his actions. To sustain a conviction, "the Government must prove beyond a reasonable doubt that the defendant acted with the specific intent to injure, intimidate or interfere with the victim because of [his] race and because of the victim's occupation of [his] home." United States v. Whitney, 229 F.3d 1296, 1303 (10th Cir. 2000).

Cases addressing §3631 have held that this element is satisfied as long as the defendant is motivated, at least in part, by the victim's race and occupation of a dwelling. The jury instructions here required the Government to prove "the defendant would not have acted but for the victim's occupancy of his home and the victim's race or color." To sustain a conviction under §3631, Mr. Waldvogel's race must have been a necessary motivation but not the sole motivation for Mr. Porter's assault. Because motivation is difficult to discern, the jury "is permitted to draw inferences of subjective intent from a defendant's objective acts" and statements.

In United States v. Magleby, 241 F.3d 1306 (10th Cir. 2001), we upheld the defendant's §3631 conviction against a sufficiency-of-the-evidence challenge. Mr. Magleby had burned a cross on the lawn of an interracial couple. He disclaimed knowledge that the couple who lived in the house was interracial, but we held the circumstantial evidence was sufficient to prove he acted out of racial animus. We noted that (1) the defendant understood cross-burning symbolized racial hatred, (2) witnesses "clearly recalled [the defendant] indicating the family was black" after he returned from setting fire to the cross, and (3) the husband of the couple was the only African American on the block. In addition, the defendant had a history of "racial slurs, racist jokes, racist music, and racist internet sites." We concluded this evidence sufficiently established that the defendant acted "because of" the victim's race.

Courts have credited a defendant's expression of racial animus before and after the criminal act as probative of intent. In another cross-burning case, for example, the Eighth Circuit upheld the convictions of defendants who had expressed racial animus before burning crosses in neighborhoods where they knew African Americans lived. United States v. J.H.H., 22 F.3d 821, 826-28 (8th Cir. 1994). In *Craft*, the Seventh Circuit upheld the defendant's conviction for setting fire to the homes of Mexican and African American families. 484 F.3d at 924-25. Although the defendant argued his crimes were not racially motivated, his post-arson racist slurs were sufficient to satisfy the specific intent element of §3631.

Mr. Porter argues he did not act based on race because Mr. Waldvogel did not appear to be African American to him. He points to his arrest interview, when he said Mr. Waldvogel "looked like he was white," and to Mr. Waldvogel's testimony that "I have always said my ethnicity is Latin American and my race is mixed." Mr. Porter therefore contends the evidence was insufficient for the jury to conclude that Mr. Waldvogel looked African American and that Mr. Porter assaulted him because of his race.

Even if Mr. Porter's theory were plausible, after considering all the evidence, and drawing all reasonable inferences in the Government's favor, we hold a reasonable jury could conclude that Mr. Porter assaulted Mr. Waldvogel because of his race.

First, the evidence showed Mr. Porter believed Mr. Waldvogel was at least partially African American. Although Mr. Porter stated during his FBI interview that Mr. Waldvogel "looked like he was white," he also said that Mr. Waldvogel was "probably half Negro." Based on this evidence, a reasonable jury could have concluded that Mr. Waldvogel was, and Mr. Porter perceived him to be, at least half African American.

Second, Mr. Porter's racial animus toward Lucas combined with his knowledge that Mr. Waldvogel is Lucas's father showed that Mr. Porter acted based on Mr. Waldvogel's race. Although Mr. Porter argues the incident happened too quickly for him to form an opinion about Mr. Waldvogel's race, the evidence suggests otherwise. Mr. Porter admitted that he yelled at Lucas, "Get out of here you little stinking n--." After that and before the assault, (1) Mr. Waldvogel testified that he told Mr. Porter, "[D]on't yell that stuff at my son;" and (2) Mr. Porter retorted, "[Y]ou and your n-- son can get out of here." Irrespective of whether he may have thought Mr. Waldvogel was Lucas's biological, adoptive, or step parent, Mr. Porter told the FBI interviewer that Lucas appeared a "hundred percent" African American and his father therefore was "probably half Negro." These statements described Mr. Porter's perception of Mr. Waldvogel.

Third, Ms. Adair's interaction with Mr. Porter and her warning to Mr. Waldvogel reflected her perception that Mr. Porter might act based on Mr. Waldvogel's race. Before the assault, Ms. Adair had spoken to Mr. Porter, had heard his racial slurs, and was concerned about the possibility of violence because Mr. Porter had been drinking and because of Mr. Waldvogel's race. This evidence was relevant to Mr. Porter's intent because it showed that an eyewitness to the events immediately leading up to the incident recognized the danger that Mr. Porter might act violently toward Mr. Waldvogel based on race.

Fourth, when the Draper Police arrested Mr. Porter, he called them "n-- lovers." Because this statement came shortly after Mr. Porter assaulted Mr. Waldvogel with a stun cane, a reasonable jury could infer that Mr. Porter perceived Mr. Waldvogel as an African American and acted on that perception.

Finally, as noted above, cases addressing §3631 establish that we may consider Mr. Porter's racial animus as corroborating his intent to act. Before the incident, Mr. Porter told workers at the Adagio that he did not want any African Americans living near him. Based on her interactions with Mr. Porter, Ms. Adair testified that "[h]e didn't like black people." During his arrest, Mr. Porter declared that "real white men should kill n--" and that "he felt that n-- were not even human." This evidence of Mr. Porter's racist views lends support to the jury's finding that he acted with racial motives.

[Eds.—The United States appealed the nine-month sentence, arguing that the District Court had incorrectly computed the offense under the Sentencing Guidelines. The court agreed and remanded for resentencing using a higher baseline.]

NOTES AND QUESTIONS

1. Differences Between §§3631 and 3617. The language of the two provisions is similar, and some conduct that violates §3617 will also violate §3631. What characteristics must the conduct have to make it criminal under §3631? The operative term is "force or threat of force." As discussed above, many types of nonviolent conduct can constitute interference.

Another important difference is enforcement. Like other criminal statutes, §3631 is not a provision under which private individuals can sue (although it is not infrequent for *pro se* litigants to try). Section 3631 is enforced through criminal proceedings brought by the Department of Justice (by the Criminal Division, not the Civil Rights Division). Federal criminal enforcement is a particularly important tool, because of the disturbing historical pattern of some local and state prosecutors failing to enforce civil rights violations in an adequate manner (the case in the following note provides an example). Of course, in a criminal proceeding the prosecuting party is the government, and the actual victim of the offense is not entitled to compensation. Thus, a civil case will be necessary to make victims "whole" in terms of compensatory damages. Due to the differences in burdens of proof, a criminal conviction of a defendant may be used as a collateral estoppel (establishing certain issues and preventing their relitigation) in a civil case based on the same conduct.

2. Intent. As with §3617, to prevail in a prosecution under §3631 the government must prove that the defendant acted with discriminatory intent on the basis of a protected characteristic. The government also must prove a connection between the conduct and the victim's housing. For §3631, this proof must be beyond a reasonable doubt. As a result, advocates must be careful to connect the defendant's actions to these specific intentions. *Porter* illustrates this, especially with the lengthy discussion of the victim's race. As *Porter* demonstrates, racist language can help to prove discriminatory intent. A defendant's use of racially charged symbols, such as a burning cross, noose, or swastika, is also sufficient to establish racially discriminatory intent. *See, e.g.*, United States v. Magleby, 241 F.3d 1306 (10th Cir. 2001) (cross-burning).

Conduct that occurs at the victim's residence can be understood as connected to housing. Statements can also connect a defendant's violent behavior to housing, even if the conduct occurs in a different place. For example, in United States v. Piekarsky, 687 F.3d 134 (3d Cir. 2012), two men were convicted of a §3631 violation after brutally beating a Hispanic man in a public park. The victim died of his injuries two days later. The defendants challenged their conviction, arguing that there was insufficient proof that they knew the victim "occupied or intended to occupy" housing in the town of Shenandoah (where the beating took place). The court disagreed:

> [T]he nexus to housing issues or housing rights is less explicit here than it is in cases involving crosses burning in front yards or targeted acts of arson. However, such explicit evidence is not required to support a finding of specific intent. . . .
>
> At trial, the government presented evidence that, on the night of July 12, 2008, the Defendants and their friends hurled an array of racially charged comments at Ramirez, repeatedly calling him a "spic" and, alternately, a "fucking spic," and a "fucking Mexican." Prior to the physical beating of Ramirez and immediately after, Scully—a member of the group—was heard to say, "This is Shenandoah. This is America. Go back to Mexico." During the fight, Scully also turned and said, "Go home you Mexican mother fucker." The same individual told Ramirez that Shenandoah was "our town" and that Ramirez didn't "belong" there. Finally—and in light of the extensive amount of violence and racial epithets which preceded it—after the beating had ended, and Ramirez lay unconscious and convulsing on the ground, Piekarsky yelled, "Tell your fucking Mexican friends to get the fuck out of Shenandoah, or you're going to be fucking laying next to him."
>
> Viewing this evidence—coupled with the other testimony about the Defendants' general dislike of Hispanic or Latino individuals moving into Shenandoah—in the light most favorable to the government, we conclude that a reasonable juror could rationally conclude that the nature of the beating of Luis Ramirez, the extent of the violence involved in this case, and the gratuitous nature of the racial epithets flung about during the beating—both at Ramirez, and at his friend, Victor Garcia—were, taken together, indicative that Donchak and Piekarsky intended to injure Ramirez with the purpose of intimidating him, or other Hispanic or Latino individuals, from residing in Shenandoah.
>
> Piekarsky was afforded the opportunity, at trial, to present his defense and to show the jurors that this was merely a case—in the words of Piekarsky's attorney—of "a single racial epithet . . . uttered in the anger and intemperate speech of an entirely random street fight." In light of the other evidence before them, the jurors were not convinced. Instead, the jury found that the specific intent elements of §3631 were met and it issued a guilty verdict. We see no basis to upset that finding.[6]

---

6. [Eds.--This horrific violence is not the only disturbing aspect of the *Piekarsky* case. As detailed in the Third Circuit opinion, the nature of the assault was originally covered up by the defendants' families, who were friends with the three police officers who investigated the crime. In state court proceedings, the defendants were convicted only of simple assault and served only six months in jail. In the federal proceedings, both defendants were sentenced to 108 months in prison. One defendant was also convicted of conspiring with local police to obstruct the federal investigation.]

3. Cross-Burning. The reference to fire or explosives as an aggravating factor is an important one, as many §3631 cases involve offenders burning crosses on the lawns or porches of people of color. These cases include: United States v. Milbourn, 600 F.3d 808 (7th Cir. 2010) (upholding defendants' convictions for burning a cross in the yard of a couple with biracial children); United States v. Magleby, 420 F.3d 1136 (10th Cir. 2005) (upholding defendant's conviction for violating §3631 for burning a cross outside the house of an interracial couple); United States v. Flowers, 389 F.3d 737 (7th Cir. 2004) (refusing defendant's motion to expunge her criminal record of violating §3631 by participating in a cross-burning outside the house of a white woman who was associating with a Black man); United States v. Colvin, 353 F.3d 569 (7th Cir. 2003) (en banc) (defendant convicted of violating §3631 for burning a cross in front of a Latino person's home); United States v. Whitney, 229 F.3d 1296 (10th Cir. 2000) (defendant convicted of aiding and abetting a violation of §3631 for helping to burn a cross in front of a Black family's home); United States v. Pospisil, 186 F.3d 1023 (8th Cir. 1999) (defendants convicted of violating §3631 for burning a cross in front of home of family of Cape Verdean ancestry); United States v. Hartbarger, 148 F.3d 777 (7th Cir. 1998) (defendants convicted of violating §3631 for burning a cross in front of home of interracial couple); United States v. Stewart, 65 F.3d 918 (11th Cir. 1995) (defendants convicted of violating §3631 for burning cross and firing pistol outside home of new Black family in white community); United States v. Montgomery, 23 F.3d 1130 (7th Cir. 1994) (defendant convicted of violating §3631 for burning a cross in front of racially integrated homeless shelter for veterans in an all-white neighborhood); United States v. J.H.H., 22 F.3d 821 (8th Cir. 1994) (defendants convicted of violating §3631 for burning crosses near homes of minority families); United States v. Hayward, 6 F.3d 1241 (7th Cir. 1993) (defendants convicted of violating §3631 for burning cross in front of home owned by whites who were entertaining black guests); United States v. Gresser, 935 F.2d 96 (6th Cir. 1991) (defendants convicted of violating §3631 by burning cross near black family's house); United States v. Skillman, 922 F.2d 1370 (9th Cir. 1990) (defendant convicted of violating §3631 for burning cross on the lawn of a black family's home).

Cross-burning has been a uniquely potent form of racial intimidation, deeply linked to the Ku Klux Klan. Nonetheless, attempts to specifically ban cross-burning have run afoul of the First Amendment. In R.A.V. v. City of St. Paul, 505 U.S. 377 (1992), the Supreme Court struck down a St. Paul "bias crimes" ordinance which prohibited symbolic acts, such as burning a cross, where such acts would "arous[e] anger, alarm or resentment in others on the basis of race, . . . religion," or other protected characteristics. The Court reasoned that by singling out symbolic acts that were offensive because of particular characteristics, the ordinance constituted impermissible viewpoint discrimination. Twelve years later, in Virginia v. Black, 538 U.S. 343, 363 (2003), the Court upheld a Virginia statute that banned cross-burning with "an intent to intimidate a person or group of persons." The crucial distinction, according to the Court, was that the Virginia statute outlawed *all* cross-burning with the intent to intimidate, not just cross-burning that was racially or religiously intimidating:

> The First Amendment permits Virginia to outlaw cross burnings done with the intent to intimidate because burning a cross is a particularly virulent form of intimidation. Instead of prohibiting all intimidating messages, Virginia may choose to regulate this subset of intimidating messages in light of cross burning's long and pernicious history as a signal of impending violence. Thus, just as a State may regulate only that obscenity which is the most obscene due to its prurient content, so too may a State choose to prohibit only those forms of intimidation that are most likely to inspire fear of bodily harm. A ban on cross burning carried out with the intent to intimidate is fully consistent with our holding in R.A.V. and is proscribable under the First Amendment.

Is §3631 as applied to cross-burnings more like the St. Paul ordinance or more like the Virginia statute? (A more philosophical question is whether it makes sense to decouple the intimidating quality of cross-burning from the racial intimidation at its heart.) Consider the analysis in United States v. Hayward, 6 F.3d 1241 (7th Cir. 1993), a case involving a defendant who burned a cross on the lawn of a white couple who frequently had Black visitors:

> Because the cross-burnings involved expressive conduct, we need to consider whether the government's regulation of that conduct was related to the suppression of free expression. If so, we apply a heightened standard of review. If not, we apply the less stringent test announced in United States v. O'Brien, 391 U.S. 367, 377 (1968).
>
> The purpose of §3631(b) is to protect the right of an individual to associate freely in his home with anyone, regardless of race. To achieve that end, the statute prohibits acts of willful intimidation against people based on race. The statute, then, is aimed at curtailing wrongful conduct in the form of threats or intimidation, and not toward curtailing any particular form of speech. Consequently, because §3631(b) is content-neutral, it does not directly regulate speech. As such, rather than a heightened standard of review, we employ the lesser standard enunciated in *O'Brien*:
>
>> a government regulation is sufficiently justified if it is within the constitutional power of the Government; if it furthers an important or substantial governmental interest; if the governmental interest is unrelated to the suppression of free expression; and if the incidental restriction on alleged First Amendment freedoms is no greater than is essential to the furtherance of that interest.
>
> Under *O'Brien*, §3631(b) qualifies as a sufficiently justified regulation. Because §3631(b) is part of the FHA, its enactment was a proper exercise of the government's power under the Thirteenth Amendment to eradicate all incidents and badges of slavery. Also, §3631(b) advances an important and substantial governmental interest by protecting a person's right to occupy a dwelling without fearing threats or intimidation based on race. We conclude that the statute is narrowly tailored to achieve that result. In this case, the statute did not proscribe cross burning as a form of expressive conduct. *Cf. R.A.V.*, 505 U.S. (finding unconstitutional a statute that specifically proscribed cross burning, among other things). Section 3631(b) prohibited the defendants' cross burnings

because they willfully intended to threaten and intimidate those in the Jones household for entertaining black people in their home. *See* United States v. Gilbert, 813 F.2d 1523, 1529 (9th Cir.) (explaining that the requirement in §3631 "of intent to intimidate serves to insulate the statute from unconstitutional application to protected speech"), *cert. denied*, 484 U.S. 860 (1987). The government's interest, then, in this case is unrelated to the suppression of free expression.

Finally, even though expressive speech may be involved in the proscribed conduct, that is insufficient to make §3631(b) unconstitutional. As the Supreme Court stated in *R.A.V.,*

> since words can in some circumstances violate laws directed not against speech but agains conduct (a law against treason, for example, is violated by telling the enemy the nation's defense secrets), a particular content-based subcategory of a proscribable class of speech can be swept up incidentally within the reach of a statute directed at conduct rather than speech. Thus, for example, sexually derogatory "fighting words," among other words, may produce a violation of Title VII's general prohibition against sexual discrimination in employment practices. Where the government does not target conduct on the basis of its expressive content, acts are not shielded from regulation merely because they express a discriminatory idea or philosophy.

Accordingly, we determine that any incidental restrictions on the alleged First Amendment rights in this case are no greater than is necessary to further the government's valid interest of protecting the rights of those in the Jones household to associate freely with whomever they choose.

We hold that §3631(b) regulates the wrongful conduct of threats and intimidation based on race and is content neutral on its face. The application, therefore, of §3631(b) to this case did not violate the defendants' First Amendment rights.

4. Other Federal Criminal Statutes. Violent acts committed by defendants in violation of §3631 can violate other federal criminal statutes as well. For example:

- When multiple perpetrators are involved, the defendants may also be prosecuted under 18 U.S.C. §241, which makes it a crime to "conspire to injure, oppress, threaten, or intimidate any [person] in the free exercise and enjoyment of any right or privilege secured to him by the Constitution or laws of the United States, or because of his having exercised the same. . . ." *See, e.g.,* United States v. Weems, 517 F.3d 1027 (8th Cir. 2008) (defendants conspired to burn a cross on Black man's yard).
- When fire or explosives are used by the perpetrators in a §3631 case, the defendants also may be prosecuted under 18 U.S.C. §844(h)(1), which provides for enhanced sentences for anyone who "uses fire or an explosive to commit any [federal] felony." *See, e.g.,* United States v. Colvin, 353 F.3d 569 (7th Cir. 2003) (en banc).
- When a firearm is used by the perpetrator in a §3631 case, the defendant may also be prosecuted under 18 U.S.C. §924(c), which provides for an enhanced sentence for any person who uses a firearm "during and in relation to any crime of violence." *See, e.g.,* United States v. Pospisil, 186

F.3d 1023 (8th Cir. 1999) (defendant fired gunshots in the air after burning cross on Black couple's lawn).

Chapter Summary

- Section 3617 prohibits (1) coercion, threats, intimidation, or other harassing conduct that interferes with a person's exercise or enjoyment of fair housing rights; (2) threats or retaliation against a person for assisting others in exercising or enjoying their rights to fair housing; and (3) retaliation against any person for reporting a fair housing violation or participating in proceedings under the FHA.
- Many types of conduct can interfere with fair housing rights, and such conduct does not need to be violent to do so. Whether particular conduct constitutes actionable interference because of a protected characteristic is a fact-dependent issue for courts.
- There are First Amendment concerns where a plaintiff argues that a defendant's non-commercial speech, advocacy, or litigation interferes with fair housing rights.
- Section 3617 claims can be brought against anyone, including neighbors, community members, and others who do not have direct control over the plaintiff's housing, but nonetheless are capable of threatening or interfering with it.
- Section 3617 creates a separate cause of action for retaliation. This provision can be invoked by groups and individuals who are not themselves aggrieved by a discriminatory housing practice but have experienced harm because they assisted others in exercising fair housing rights.
- A plaintiff can bring a claim only under §3617 or can prevail on a §3617 claim even if claims under other portions of the statute are unsuccessful. It is necessary, however, that a §3617 claim have a "predicate" in a substantive provision of the FHA.
- Section 3631 makes it a criminal offense to use force or threat of force to injure, intimidate, or interfere with people who are exercising their rights to fair housing. It is often used to prosecute people who burn crosses, issue violent threats, or commit assaults.

CHAPTER 11

DISCRIMINATION IN REAL ESTATE-RELATED TRANSACTIONS

A constellation of federal and state statutes protects consumers in their use of real estate-related financial tools. These protections include equal access to credit and prohibitions on discrimination based on a range of protected characteristics. Despite this, a long history of discriminatory denials of wealth-building financial products to people and neighborhoods of color has led to a "dual credit market" that persists today.[1] Discriminatory *denials* of credit at the individual and neighborhood level continue to enable predatory practices that *exploit* the dual credit market, with devastating consequences for renters, homeowners, neighborhoods, cities, and rural areas.

HUD reports that in 2020, the Black/white homeownership gap (31 percentage points) was greater than in 1968, when the FHA was enacted.[2] The Treasury Department reports that the white/Black racial gap in average household home value (2.5:1) was the same in the early 2020s as in 1970.[3] Treasury also reports research showing that the racial wealth gap, which is rooted at least in part to the dual credit market, was 8 to 1 in 2019.

This chapter focuses on the FHA as a tool for dismantling the dual credit market by facilitating access to homeownership on fair terms. In particular, the chapter discusses the FHA's coverage of mortgage discrimination and

1. Keeanga-Yamahtta Taylor, RACE FOR PROFIT: HOW BANKS AND THE REAL ESTATE INDUSTRY UNDERMINED BLACK HOMEOWNERSHIP 2 (UNC 2019) ("Despite the insistence on the rights of property ownership as integral to citizenship," as expressed in the earliest protections enshrined in the Civil Rights Act of 1866, "African Americans faced numerous obstacles in their efforts to secure homeownership.").

2. HUD, *Bridging the Wealth Gap: An Agenda for Economic Justice and Asset Building for Renters* 11 (2021), https://www.hud.gov/sites/dfiles/PIH/documents/Bridging_Wealth_Gap.pdf.

3. Department of the Treasury, *Racial Differences in Economic Security: Housing* (Nov. 4, 2022), https://home.treasury.gov/news/featured-stories/racial-differences-in-economic-security-housing#_ftnref16.

redlining, reverse redlining and predatory lending, discriminatory appraisals, and discrimination in the homeowners insurance markets.

Enforcement actions brought by consumers, experienced advocates, and government agencies have helped to eliminate some barriers to equitable financing, appraisals, and insurance markets. The most applicable antidiscrimination provision of the FHA, 42 U.S.C. §3605, covers a broad range of transactions[4] involving the purchasing, improving, appraising, brokering, financing, and insuring of residential real estate.[5]

42 U.S.C. §3605 DISCRIMINATION IN RESIDENTIAL REAL ESTATE-RELATED TRANSACTIONS

(a) In General. — It shall be unlawful for any person or other entity whose business includes engaging in residential real estate-related transactions to discriminate against any person in making available such a transaction, or in the terms or conditions of such a transaction, because of race, color, religion, sex, handicap, familial status, or national origin.

(b) Definition. — As used in this section, the term "residential real estate-related transaction" means any of the following:

(1) The making or purchasing of loans or providing other financial assistance —

(A) for purchasing, constructing, improving, repairing, or maintaining a dwelling; or

(B) secured by residential real estate.

(2) The selling, brokering, or appraising of residential real property.

Mortgage credit has been vital to achieving upward economic mobility in the United States.[6] We begin with an analysis of key historical and contemporary barriers to accessing mortgage credit and the FHA's effectiveness as a tool for removing those barriers.

---

4. The 1988 amendments to §3605 expanded its coverage beyond lenders to any real estate-related business providing financial assistance or services for mortgage loans, "secondary market" entities purchasing such loans, and entities conducting appraisals of properties securing the loans. Courts have held that mortgage loan modifications, maintenance and marketing of bank-owned foreclosed properties, and some loan servicer contracts are covered, whereas lawyers, settlement agents, and building product suppliers are not. *See* Schwemm, HDLL §18:1.

5. Courts generally have interpreted the Civil Rights Act of 1866, §§1981 and 1982, to cover discrimination in financing and other real estate-related transactions, including homeowners insurance and appraisals. *See* Schwemm, HDLL §27:10 nn.3, 7, & 11.

6. Lisa Rice, *The Fair Housing Act: A Tool for Expanding Access to Quality Credit, in* THE FIGHT FOR FAIR HOUSING, CAUSES, CONSEQUENCES, AND FUTURE IMPLICATIONS OF THE 1968 FEDERAL FAIR HOUSING ACT 77 (Gregory D. Squires ed., 2018). *But see* Dorothy A. Brown, THE WHITENESS OF WEALTH 82 (Crown 2021) ("[H]omeownership is not a straightforward wealth builder for black families: because the only guaranteed return on their investment is to buy in a community where they will be a small and vulnerable minority.").

A. MORTGAGE DISCRIMINATION AND REDLINING

A mortgage loan (or similar instrument) usually is used to buy a home or borrow money against the value of a home the borrower already owns. A mortgage is an agreement between a borrower and lender that gives the lender the right to take control of the property if the borrower fails to repay the money borrowed plus interest and costs. Thus, the availability and terms of a mortgage loan can affect access to housing in many ways. Any consideration of the laws addressing contemporary forms of lending discrimination and the consequences of unequal access to mortgage credit would be incomplete without a thorough grounding in history. Stephen Dane describes in "A History of Mortgage Lending Discrimination in the United States" how the government helped to create a dual housing and credit market:

> The depression of the 1930s prompted the federal government to intervene in the financial industry on a massive scale. . . . The Federal Housing Administration (FHA) . . . standardiz[ed] mortgage loan policies and practices. Because it was insuring mortgages held on real estate located throughout the country, FHA needed a uniform and objective method of deciding whether or not a particular mortgage loan was insurable. FHA published an underwriting manual which attempted to cover all aspects of the lending decision, including the creditworthiness of the applicant and the adequacy of the real estate securing the mortgage. Appraisal techniques, property valuation, and credit underwriting all became standardized for FHA-insured loans.
>
> One would think that the participation of the federal government in the mortgage loan underwriting process would lead to the eradication of racially discriminatory lending practices. In fact, just the opposite occurred. . . . Indeed, FHA hired Homer Hoyt, one of the economists who assisted in the development of racially based appraisal theory, to develop its underwriting standards. FHA's 1938 underwriting manual provided:
>
>> Areas surrounding a location are investigated to determine whether incompatible racial and social groups are present, for the purpose of making a prediction regarding the probability of the locations being invaded by such groups. If a neighborhood is to retain stability, it is necessary that properties continue to be occupied by the same social and racial classes. A change in social or racial occupancy generally contributes to instability and a decline in values.
>
> Prior to 1947 FHA rules required racial segregation and [recommended] racially restrictive covenants. The federal government, therefore, actually reinforced the institutionalization of racist attitudes in the lending decision calculus. . . . [B]lacks and other minorities were generally excluded from participation in the government-backed financing programs. . . . Because they were unable to secure either conventional or government-backed financing, minorities were able to purchase homes only through private financial arrangements that were predatory and abusive. The pent-up demand for financing enabled speculators to offer less attractive options, such as land installment contracts, at exorbitant

interest rates. Minority neighborhoods were condemned to the "underworld of real estate finance."[7]

This chapter demonstrates the persistence in the modern era of some traditional forms of discrimination: unequal access to mortgage credit on fair terms for applicants with protected characteristics and denial of loans to those seeking to buy or refinance homes in neighborhoods of color. It also addresses contemporary forms of predatory home financing schemes enabled by a dual credit market. Nevertheless, there are some success stories of conventional lenders working more vigorously to expand services to traditionally underrepresented groups. There also are instances of enforcement actions resulting in powerful remedies to correct the market failure of lending discrimination.

1. FHA Coverage

The text of §3605 reveals its broad coverage of home financing and related transactions, building on §3604's prohibition of discrimination in the sale or rental of housing.[8] This provision of the FHA covers home loans whether they are used to buy, construct, improve, or refinance the home. Mortgage loans, such as home equity loans, are covered by the FHA if residential real estate is used as collateral. In other words, even if the loan is used for a vacation or to fund a college education, it is covered by §3605 as long as residential property is used to secure the loan. A borrower does not need to live in the home securing the loan to have protection under the FHA.

Section 3605, like §3604, prohibits discrimination both in making available a real estate-related transaction and in its terms and conditions. HUD in 24 CFR §100.20(b) provides several examples of discrimination in making available loans or other financial assistance, including the following:

> (1) Failing or refusing to provide to any person information regarding the availability of loans or other financial assistance, application requirements, procedures or standards for the review and approval of loans or financial assistance, or providing information which is inaccurate or different from that provided others.

Thus, the FHA requires the provision of equal information and assistance to consumers seeking mortgage credit or financial assistance. For example, providing a white couple with advice for improving their credit score for the purpose of making available an affordable loan while failing to provide the same assistance to a Black applicant could violate §3605. The same would be true of withholding information or assistance based on sex or any other protected characteristic.

---

7. Stephen M. Dane, A History of Mortgage Lending Discrimination in the United States, 20 J. INTERGROUP REL. 16 (1993) (on file with authors).

8. The single-family home and "Mrs. Murphy" exemptions found in §3603(b) apply to §3604 (other than subsection c), but not §3605.

HUD in its regulations and guidance[9] provides several examples of covered discriminatory loan terms and conditions, if based on a protected characteristic:

- Policies, practices or procedures in evaluating or in determining creditworthiness of any person, such as refusing or delaying applications, prematurely rejecting applications, imposing different credit or employment requirements, or providing different levels of assistance in meeting credit requirements;
- Types of loans or other financial assistance to be provided, such as steering borrowers to higher cost mortgages when they could have qualified for loans on better terms;
- Amounts, interest rates, costs, duration or other terms or conditions, such as unnecessary closing costs, inflated appraisal costs, inflated broker or lender fees, unnecessary recording fees, or excessive prepayment penalties; and
- Servicing[10] or lending with other discriminatory terms or conditions, such as changing mortgage loan terms at closing without the consent of the borrower; being more aggressive or harsh in foreclosure or collection practices.

These examples show that discriminatory conduct may occur at any stage of the financing transaction.

2. Proving Lending Discrimination: Disparate Treatment

Most circuits permit plaintiffs who do not have direct evidence to use a burden-shifting method of proof in credit discrimination cases. For example, in Noland v. Commerce Mortgage Corp., 122 F.3d 551, 553 (8th Cir. 1997), the court stated that a plaintiff can establish a prima facie case of discrimination by offering circumstantial evidence showing:

(1) that the plaintiff is a member of a protected class;
(2) that the plaintiff applied for and was qualified for a loan from the defendant;
(3) that the loan application was rejected; and
(4) that the defendant has approved loans for applicants (outside the plaintiff's protected class) with similar qualifications.

---

9. 24 C.F.R. §100.130(b); HUD, *Fair Lending: Learn the Facts*, https://www.hud.gov/sites/documents/FAIR_LENDING_GUIDE.pdf (last visited July 29, 2024).

10. Loan servicers manage day-to-day tasks for managing the loan, including processing loan payments, responding to borrower questions, and sending mortgage statements. CFPB, *What's the Difference Between a Mortgage Lender and a Servicer*, https://www.consumerfinance.gov/ask-cfpb/whats-the-difference-between-a-mortgage-lender-and-a-servicer-en-198/#:~:text=If%20you%20can't%20find,originally%20gave%20you%20your%20loan (last visited Sept. 4, 2020).

Courts are divided about whether comparative evidence (in the fourth element) is required. For those courts requiring it, comparative evidence often will be the most challenging hurdle for plaintiffs. This is because the plaintiff will need to compare her treatment to that of others who are similarly qualified in their ability to afford the loan, whose credit histories pose a similar level of risk to the lender, and who have collateral (the home itself) that can be shown through appraisal to justify the loan amount. In other words, plaintiff will need more evidence than her own experience. In Hood v. Midwest Savings Bank, 95 F. App'x 768, 779 (6th Cir. 2004), the court explained that while the plaintiff "does not have to show an exact match between his application and the applicants outside of the protected class who received a loan, the comparator loan files must be significantly parallel in every material respect."

Those courts not requiring comparative evidence allow the prima facie case to be "tailored to the nature of the claim." In Anderson v. Wachovia Mortgage Corp., 621 F.3d 261, 272 (3d Cir. 2010), the court held that "requiring plaintiffs to ferret out, and the bank to produce, evidence as to others with myriad different factual situations in order to find 'similar' borrowers, goes beyond what is required for a prima facie case." In that case, comparative evidence did "not get to the heart of the matter" because the Black plaintiffs alleged that the bank imposed conditions on their loans because they sought to move into a predominantly white neighborhood.

As in other burden-shifting contexts, the defendant merely must produce some evidence of a nondiscriminatory reason for the adverse lending decision. The plaintiff then bears the burden of persuading the factfinder that the defendant's stated reason is a pretext for unlawful discrimination. In this arena, a lender will have an even greater advantage than a typical landlord or management company because of the complexity involved in underwriting, credit-risk determinations, and analysis regarding adequacy of the appraised value of the home. A court is likely to show considerable deference to a bank's business judgment on all these matters. Individual plaintiffs will have difficulty running the gauntlet in a fair lending case, but some plaintiffs manage to prevail, or at least to survive summary judgment. Consider Watson v. Pathway Financial, 702 F. Supp. 186, 188-89 (N.D. Ill. 1988), in which a Black couple denied a loan offered comparative evidence that the lender made loans to six white couples with similar late payment history.

> The Watsons have presented evidence on each of the essential elements of their prima facie case. Elements 1 and 3 are undisputed — the Watsons are black and their application was rejected. Element 2 is disputed but the Watsons have presented evidence that they were qualified for the loan. The Watsons' Conventional Income/Expense Evaluation was within First Western's guidelines. Although the Watsons have a history of late payments on credit cards, the Watsons present evidence that other applicants with late payments did receive loans from First Western. This evidence is also applicable to Element 4 which requires plaintiffs to establish that others with similar qualifications received loans.

The defendant articulates a business reason for not funding the loan. Defendant has consistently stated that the Watsons' application was rejected because of the late payments and an inadequate explanation therefor. Defendant presents the affidavits of two of the loan consultants at First Western who testify that the decision to reject the application was in no way related to the Watsons' race.

Although the Watsons did provide evidence of all the elements of a prima facie case, they must also present some evidence that race was a factor in the decision to reject their application. . . .

Here, the only competent evidence the plaintiffs present that their race contributed to the defendant's decision to reject their applications is evidence that at least six applications of white couples for loans were approved by First Western even though their credit histories showed late payments to creditors. This evidence gives rise at least to an inference that the Watsons were treated differently on account of their race. As the court must view the facts in a light most favorable to the non-moving party and make all inferences in favor of the non-moving party, this is enough to deny summary judgment.

In addition to discovering evidence of more favorable treatment of similarly situated comparators, plaintiffs can point to publicly available data demonstrating a pattern of lending that is probative of discrimination, and, if available, testing evidence documenting a pattern of disparate treatment. In Paschal v. Flagstar Bank, 295 F.3d 565 (6th Cir. 2002), the court used all of these to affirm judgment after jury trial in favor of two sets of plaintiffs on their mortgage lending discrimination claims under §§3605 and 3617.

Flagstar contends that the district court erred in denying its motion for judgment as a matter of law, which it filed following the jury's verdict. According to the district court, the following evidence was particularly central to its decision: (1) "[Calvin] Bradford's conclusions that the only variable in [the plaintiffs'] treatment by Flagstar compared to white applicants was that they were treated less favorably because of their race," (2) "the [Home Mortgage Disclosure Data Act (HMDA)] data which generally proved that Flagstar acted with a discriminatory animus," and (3) "the testing data which displayed a discriminatory animus." . . .

We now will describe briefly the testimony of two of the plaintiffs' expert witnesses, Calvin Bradford, Ph.D., and Martin Wing, Ph.D. Bradford testified for the plaintiffs as a mortgage-lending discrimination expert. Although Bradford acknowledged that no two loan applications are ever exact matches, he compared the plaintiffs' applications with those of Caucasian applicants who had similar financial qualifications [but whose mortgage applications were approved by Flagstar]. . . . Bradford concluded that the differences in how Flagstar treated the [plaintiffs] could not be explained by any valid underwriting criterion.

Wing testified for the plaintiffs as an expert in econometrics. Wing provided a detailed statistical analysis of Flagstar's lending practices based on HMDA [data, which] "consists of a set of variables that financial institutions must record for all . . . home mortgage loan applications." Wing testified that between 1988 and 1996, Flagstar denied African-American applicants three times more often than it denied Caucasian applicants. . . . Wing concluded that "the denial rates depend on race. The denial rate and race are dependent, not independent" [such] that the disparity between the rate at which Flagstar denied applications of African-Americans and the rate at which it denied applications of Caucasians could not be fully explained by other factors such as income or credit history.

Contrary to Flagstar's arguments, we are of the opinion that there was sufficient evidence to support the jury's finding of racial discrimination. First, the Edwardses and the Paschals both experienced numerous, seemingly unnecessary delays in applying for loans. [The Edwardses made four attempts to obtain a loan; the Paschals received two preliminary approvals that were subsequently withdrawn.] According to Bradford, none of the Caucasian applicants whose files he compared with the plaintiffs' experienced such a multitude of "tactics of delay" and "hindrance." Second, although the testing focused on preapplication contacts with Flagstar [and not the underwriting stage], it is not unreasonable to draw the inference that the disparate treatment encountered by African-American testers during their initial interactions with Flagstar might be indicative of what applicants for mortgages would experience. [Cliff] Schrupp, who has been the executive director of the FHC for 22 years, testified that it has been his experience that this sort of testing can provide "quite a bit of information about how people are treated and may be treated differently by loan officers." Third, the methodological concerns that Flagstar raises regarding Wing's testimony [that he aggregated data across different loan programs with different underwriting standards] are generally insubstantial. As the Supreme Court has held, "it is clear that a regression analysis that includes less than all measurable variables may serve to prove a plaintiff's case." Bazemore v. Friday, 478 U.S. 385, 400 (1986) (Brennan, J., concurring) (internal quotation marks omitted). Wing's finding that, between 1988 and 1996, Flagstar denied African-American loan applicants three times more often than Caucasian applicants provides support for the jury's verdict. Finally, the district court found that the expert testimony provided by Bradford was compelling. The district court stated that "Mr. [Bradford] was one of the best-prepared experts that I have heard in 20 years." Later, the district court noted that, "[y]ou know, without hearing the cross-examination, Bradford painted a pretty bleak picture for [Flagstar]."

Accordingly, we conclude that the district court did not err in holding that the evidence "supports the jury's verdict that both [plaintiffs] proved by a preponderance of the evidence that race was a factor in the way in which Flagstar dealt with each of them."

NOTES AND QUESTIONS

1. War of Attrition? Originally, eight sets of Black plaintiffs filed mortgage-lending discrimination claims against Flagstar Bank. The district court granted summary judgment dismissing the claims of three; the jury returned a verdict against another three; and of the two sets of plaintiffs obtaining a jury verdict in their favor, the Sixth Circuit reversed judgment against one set on statute of limitations grounds. Of the eight sets of initial plaintiffs, therefore, only one survived through appeal. What lessons might be learned from this litigation saga?

2. The Role of Experts in Fair Lending Cases. Notice the substantial role of experts in supporting plaintiffs' claims. One expert, Dr. Calvin Bradford, persuaded the jury of the discriminatory pattern revealed in comparing the plaintiffs' loan files with those of similarly situated white applicants. The other expert, Martin Wing, performed a statistical analysis to help the jury interpret the HMDA data, noting differences in the defendant's loan denial rates that could not be explained by variables other than race. In this case, there were eight sets of plaintiffs initially, which created a certain economy of scale. How feasible would it be for the average fair lending plaintiff to hire multiple experts? What is the plaintiff's likelihood of success without them? One experienced litigator opines that given the economics of such cases, "it is virtually a certainty" that they must be brought as class actions (which come with their own set of challenges).[11]

3. Use of HMDA Data to Prove Discrimination. As the court noted, data demonstrating different loan approval rates across racial groups do not alone establish racially discriminatory denials, or terms and conditions, with respect to particular loan files. But disparities reflected in the data, which are publicly available, might get the attention of regulators and enforcement agencies, which can then conduct more intensive investigations and reviews. As *Paschal* demonstrates, expert testimony on the HMDA data may strengthen an overall presentation of evidence, making it sufficient to survive summary judgment and support a finding of discrimination at trial.

4. Direct Evidence. Litigants may find direct evidence hard to acquire. That does not mean it is never available. For example, in its investigation of BancorpSouth Bank serving Memphis, Tennessee, and parts of Mississippi and Arkansas, the Department of Justice obtained an audio recording of a bank meeting in which a manager told loan officers and processors to turn down applications from Black and other protected class members within 21 days without subjecting white applicants to this same time frame. Employees also made racially disparaging comments followed by laughter. The DOJ filed a complaint, also alleging that the bank granted loan officers substantial discretion with minimal standards for determining interest rates and whether to grant or deny loans. The DOJ alleged this level of discretion led to redlining as well as other racially discriminatory underwriting and pricing practices that could not be explained by objective factors related to creditworthiness.[12]

5. Disparate Impact. As more fully discussed in Chapter 7, litigants may use disparate impact theory under the FHA to challenge a facially neutral policy that disproportionately disadvantages or injures a protected group without sufficient justification. In the lending context, this could consist of

---

11. Email from Stuart Rossman to Stacy Seicshnaydre (July 17, 2024) (on file with Seicshnaydre).

12. Press Release, DOJ, Justice Department and Consumer Financial Protection Bureau Reach Settlement with BancorpSouth Bank to Resolve Allegations of Mortgage Lending Discrimination (June 29, 2016), https://www.justice.gov/opa/pr/justice-department-and-consumer-financial-protection-bureau-reach-settlement-bancorpsouth; Complaint, United States and CFPB v. Bancorpsouth Bank (N.D. Miss. June 29, 2016), https://www.justice.gov/opa/file/871931/dl?inline.

underwriting criteria that favor use of mainstream credit markets and disadvantage use of alternative credit (e.g., payday loans) that is used disproportionately by people of color. "Borrowers who use non-traditional credit are disproportionately credit invisible or have lower credit scores because their positive payment history is not seen by the financial system, or in some cases, when it is seen, the credit behavior is devalued."[13] In addition, credit scoring systems traditionally have not considered timely rent payments or insurance premium payments. If there is a relatively cost-neutral way for a lender to determine a borrower's likelihood of making timely payments other than the one it normally uses, and this alternative would exclude fewer applicants of color from the mainstream market, do you think federal law should require it?

OTHER FAIR LENDING PROTECTIONS: ECOA, CRA, HMDA

Equal Credit Opportunity Act (ECOA), 15 U.S.C. §1691 et seq.

ECOA was enacted in 1974 to address credit discrimination based on sex and marital status.[14] Today, ECOA prohibits creditors, including mortgage lenders, from discriminating against credit applicants[15] based on race, color, religion, national origin, sex, marital status, age, receipt of public assistance income, and exercising rights under certain consumer protection laws. Many of the cases in this chapter involve claims under both the FHA and ECOA. The Consumer Financial Protection Bureau (CFPB) promulgates rules to implement ECOA and shares enforcement and supervisory authority with other federal regulators, depending on the type of institution involved, including the Federal Trade Commission. The DOJ has enforcement authority for pattern and practice violations. Regulation B establishes the substantive and procedural framework for ECOA's requirements and may provide more expanded avenues of redress than the FHA. A distinctive requirement of ECOA is that creditors must provide a statement of specific reasons for any "adverse action" by the creditor. §1691(d). Adverse action includes denial of credit or refusal to grant credit for an amount

---

13. Rice, *supra* note 6, at 99.

14. *See* Donna Dunkelberger Geck, *Equal Credit: You Can Get There from Here*, 52 N. Dak. L. Rev. 381, 382 (1975) (describing ECOA as the "first federal guarantee that credit will be available on a fair and impartial basis without regard to sex or marital status" and detailing credit barriers for single, widowed, separated, and divorced women and the inability of married women to get credit in their own names).

15. Prospective credit applicants likely also are covered under ECOA. *See* Consumer Fin. Prot. Bureau v. Townstone Fin., Inc., No. 23-1654, 2024 WL 3370023 (7th Cir. July 11, 2024) (reversing dismissal of claims alleging that statements on financial radio show discouraged mortgage applications from Black persons, holding: "When the text of the ECOA is read as a whole, it is clear that Congress authorized the imposition of liability for the discouragement of prospective applicants. Regulation B's prohibition on [the same] is therefore consistent with the ECOA's text and purpose.").

or on terms substantially similar to those requested. Mortgage applicants also have a right to request and obtain copies of any appraisal reports used by the lender. §1691(e).[16]

Consumer Reinvestment Act (CRA), 12 U.S.C. §2901 et seq.

The CRA, enacted in 1977, requires banks to demonstrate that they are serving the convenience and needs of the communities in which they do business, with a special emphasis on low- and moderate-income neighborhoods. The idea is that when banks take deposits from a certain neighborhood's residents, the banks also should be extending credit to those customers and thereby investing in their neighborhoods. Depending on the type of bank, the appropriate supervisory agency conducts reviews to determine if the bank is meeting its CRA goals. Banks take CRA regulation seriously because regulators consider CRA ratings when banks seek to engage in mergers or acquisitions.[17] Some commentators recommend that similar requirements be imposed on insurers. Although much progress has been made, HUD reports that a disproportionate number of Black households are unbanked and credit invisible (having no connection to any depositary institution and no credit score at all).[18]

Home Mortgage Disclosure Act (HMDA), 12 U.S.C. §2801 et seq.

HMDA is "a data collection, reporting, and disclosure statute enacted in 1975. HMDA data are used to assist in determining whether financial institutions are serving the housing credit needs of their local communities; facilitate public entities' distribution of funds to local communities to attract private investment; and help [government agencies in particular] identify possible discriminatory lending patterns and enforce antidiscrimination statutes. Institutions covered by HMDA are required to collect and report specified information about each mortgage application acted upon and mortgage purchased. The data include the disposition of each application for mortgage credit; the type, purpose, and characteristics of each home mortgage application or purchased loan; the census-tract designations of the properties; loan pricing information; demographic and other information about loan applicants, such as their race, ethnicity, sex, age, and income; and information about loan sales."[19] Some commentators urge that similar disclosure requirements be imposed on insurers to enable tracking of their level of service in different neighborhoods and markets.

---

16. This material in part is taken from DOJ, Civil Rights Division, The Equal Credit Opportunity Act, https://www.justice.gov/crt/equal-credit-opportunity-act-3 (last visited June 22, 2024).

17. HUD, Office of Policy Development and Research, *Report to Congress on the Root Causes of the Foreclosure Crisis* 41 (Jan. 2010), https://www.huduser.gov/publications/pdf/foreclosure_09.pdf.

18. HUD, *Bridging the Wealth Gap*, *supra* note 2, at 3.

19. CFPB, *Data Point: 2022 Mortgage Market Activity and Trends* (Sept. 27, 2023), https://www.consumerfinance.gov/data-research/research-reports/data-point-2022-mortgage-market-activity-trends/.

> ## SECONDARY MORTGAGE MARKET: FANNIE AND FREDDIE
>
> Section 3605 explicitly prohibits discrimination in the purchase of mortgage loans, thus extending coverage to the secondary mortgage market. Major players in this market include the Federal National Mortgage Association (Fannie Mae) and the Federal Home Loan Mortgage Corporation (Freddie Mac), both government-sponsored enterprises (GSEs). Because of substantial losses related to the fore-closure and financial crisis in the late 2000s, the Federal Housing Finance Agency (FHFA) placed Fannie and Freddie into conservatorship. (They are federally char-tered and shareholder-owned.) A key aspect of their public mission is to increase the availability of mortgage credit to low- and moderate-income families and in underserved areas. They do this by purchasing mortgages to enable lenders to offer mortgage loans to more people on the long-term, fixed-rate model that has become standard. They also package loans on both single- and multifamily prop-erties into mortgage-backed securities and guarantee them, attracting investors to the U.S. secondary mortgage market. They send mortgage payments received from servicers to investors as a form of income. Fannie Mae also develops and maintains underwriting and eligibility standards for its loans, as well as loan ser-vicing standards, which often become the standard for the industry as a whole. Both GSEs have been regulated by HUD and the FHFA.[20]

3. Redlining and Reverse Redlining

This section explores discrimination based not on the characteristics of the borrower seeking residential real-estate financing, but on the characteristics of the neighborhood surrounding the home. Of course, a lender may discrim-inate based on both neighborhood characteristics and the characteristics of the borrower. Also, it is possible for consumers of any race or ethnicity to be injured by redlining practices that thwart their ability to purchase or refinance in integrated areas or neighborhoods of color.

As referenced earlier in this chapter and in Chapter 1, the federal govern-ment in its massive housing investment programs of the 20th century used race and ethnicity as a basis for determining which neighborhoods were worthy of credit and which were not. As Richard Rothstein writes in THE COLOR OF LAW:[21]

> During the 1930s the Roosevelt administration created maps of every metro-politan area, divided into zones of foreclosure risk based in part on the race of

---

20. *Who We Are*, Fannie Mae, https://www.fanniemae.com/about-us/who-we-are (last visited July 23, 2024); *How the Secondary Mortgage Market Works*, My Home: By Freddie Mac, https://myhome.freddiemac.com/blog/homeownership/20160125-secondary-mortgage (last reviewed Sept. 28, 2021); Jean Folger, *Fannie Mae and Freddie Mac: An Overview*, Investopedia, https://www.investopedia.com/articles/economics/08/fannie-mae-freddie-mac-credit-crisis.asp (last updated Mar. 18, 2024); *see also* Florence Wagman Roisman, *Protecting Homeowners from Non-Judicial Foreclosure of Mortgages Held by Fannie Mae and Freddie Mac*, 43 REAL ESTATE L. J. 125 (2014); Florence Wagman Roisman, *Securing Judicial Review Under the Administrative Procedure Act of Denials of Modifications of Mortgages Held by Fannie Mae and Freddie Mac*, 35 REV. BANKING & FIN. L. 162 (2016).

21. Richard Rothstein, THE COLOR OF LAW 75 (Liveright 2017).

their occupants. The administration then insured white homeowners['] mortgages if they lived in all-white neighborhoods into which there was little danger of African Americans moving. After World War II the federal government went further and spurred the suburbanization of every metropolitan area by guaranteeing bank loans to mass-production builders who would create the all-white subdivisions that came to ring American cities.

These redlining maps reflected the view embedded in appraisal standards of the era that "[t]he infiltration of inharmonious racial groups . . . tend to lower the levels of land values and to lessen the desirability of residential areas."[22] The modern-day impacts of racial redlining on neighborhood conditions and household opportunities have been the subject of significant study:

> Redlining thus directed both public and private capital to native-born white families and away from African American and, to a lesser extent, immigrant families. As homeownership was arguably the most significant means of intergenerational wealth building in the United States in the twentieth century, these redlining practices from eight decades ago had long-term effects in creating wealth inequalities that we still see today. . . . Using the spatial data from *Mapping Inequality*, researchers in a variety of fields have shown how tight [are] correlations between the redlining grades drawn nine decades ago and the patterns of inequality in American cities today. Environmental researchers have shown that redlined areas are hotter, are more polluted, [and] have fewer trees than those that received high grades. Health researchers have shown that people living in redlined areas are less healthy, more likely to have asthma, more likely to experience pre-term births, less likely to have easy access to nutritious food, and more likely to die early deaths.[23]

Redlining as an organizing principle for depriving investment and wealth-building opportunities to neighborhoods of color in this country may have peaked before the civil rights era, but the practice has continued in the 21st century. The DOJ has conducted significant investigations and litigation challenging such practices; its website features 12 cases in which it entered consent decrees between 2021 and 2024 with banks it alleged had engaged in unlawful redlining.[24] These practices are not peculiar to any particular region: The DOJ challenged redlining practices from coast to coast, including in Charlotte and Winston-Salem, North Carolina; Columbus, Ohio; Houston, Texas; Jacksonville, Florida; Los Angeles, California; Memphis, Tennessee;

---

22. Federal Housing Administration, Underwriting Manual 1360 (1938), available at https://www.huduser.gov/portal/sites/default/files/pdf/Federal-Housing-Administration -Underwriting-Manual.pdf.

23. Robert K. Nelson, *Introduction, Mapping Inequality: Redlining in New Deal America, in* American Panorama: An Atlas of United States History (Robert K. Nelson & Edward L. Ayers eds., 2023), https://dsl.richmond.edu/panorama/redlining/introduction (last visited Oct. 8, 2024).

24. DOJ, Civil Rights Division, *Housing and Civil Enforcement Cases*, https://www.justice .gov/crt/housing-and-civil-enforcement-cases (using keyword search "redlining") (last visited July 21, 2024).

Newark, New Jersey; Philadelphia, Pennsylvania; Rhode Island; and Tulsa, Oklahoma.

For example, the DOJ was party to a consent order resulting from its complaint against a bank in October 2023, alleging redlining violations of the FHA and ECOA in Jacksonville, Florida:

> [F]rom 2016 through 2021, Ameris Bank avoided providing mortgage services to majority-Black and Hispanic neighborhoods in Jacksonville and discouraged people seeking credit in those communities from obtaining home loans. Ameris' home mortgage lending was focused disproportionately on white areas of Jacksonville while other lenders generated applications in majority-Black and Hispanic neighborhoods at three times the rate of Ameris. Additionally, although Ameris operates 18 branches in Jacksonville, Ameris has never operated a branch in a majority-Black and Hispanic neighborhood in the city.[25]

In another example, the DOJ was party to a consent order stemming from a complaint filed against a mortgage company in September 2022, alleging redlining violations of the FHA, ECOA, and Consumer Financial Protection Act in Philadelphia, Pennsylvania. The allegations entailed "engaging in unlawful redlining in the Philadelphia metropolitan area by avoiding providing credit services to neighborhoods of color because of the race, color, and national origin of the people living in those neighborhoods." The complaint also alleged that the company's loan officers and other employees sent and received work emails containing racial slurs and referring to communities of color as "ghetto."[26]

The relief required in DOJ's redlining consent orders is sweeping. For example, in a 2024 case filed against a national bank operating in North Carolina, the consent order required the defendant to:

- invest at least $11.75 million in a loan subsidy fund to increase credit opportunities for residents of majority-Black and Hispanic neighborhoods in Charlotte and Winston-Salem;
- spend $1 million on community partnerships to provide services to residents of those neighborhoods;
- spend $750,000 for advertising, outreach, consumer financial education, and credit counseling focused on those neighborhoods;
- open two new branches in majority-Black and Hispanic neighborhoods in Charlotte and one such branch in Winston-Salem;
- ensure that at least two mortgage bankers and two community home-ownership specialists are assigned to solicit loan applications from majority-Black and Hispanic neighborhoods in Charlotte and Winston-Salem; and

---

25. *Id.* (reporting consent decree in *United States v. Ameris Bank*, 3:23-cv-01232 (M.D. Fla.)).

26. *Id.* (reporting consent decree in *CFPB and U.S. v. Trident Mortgage Company*, 2:22-cv-02936 (E.D. Pa.)).

- employ a Director of Community Lending who will oversee the continued development of lending in communities of color in North Carolina.[27]

a. Proving Redlining

Similar to the cases in which individuals allege that adverse lending decisions are made on the basis of a protected characteristic, allegations that a bank has engaged in unlawful redlining require proof beyond an individual applicant's loan denial unless the plaintiff has compelling evidence of discrimination.

For example, in Cartwright v. American Savings & Loan Ass'n, 880 F.2d 912, 922-24 (7th Cir. 1989), the court rejected the plaintiff's argument that neighborhood racial disparities in the defendant's residential lending patterns constituted sufficient evidence of redlining: "it is absurd to allege a discriminatory refusal to approve loan applications in a particular area without proof that qualified borrowers actually applied and were rejected." Further, the court found the evidence did not support the contention that the bank discouraged the plaintiff from pursuing her loan or that the bank "had a policy of discouraging mortgage loan applications for property located in substantially or predominantly black neighborhoods." The court made clear that the FHA "does not require that a lender disregard its legitimate business interests," assuming they are nondiscriminatory:

> The evidence demonstrates nothing more than that American Savings was concerned about financing a large, relatively expensive home in an area lacking other homes of comparable market value and sound economic judgment of this nature cannot be considered as a violation of the FHA. As the lending institution, American Savings certainly has a real and substantial, legitimate interest in recouping its investment in the event the Cartwrights defaulted on their loan. Moreover, there is nothing in the record which leads us to believe that American Savings would have been concerned about the location of the Cartwrights' property had they intended to build a home of comparable value to others in the area. We affirm the district court's conclusion that American Savings did not engage in redlining in violation of §3605 of the FHA.

This decision highlights the complicated barriers to investment in neighborhoods of color. A borrower of any race seeking to make upgrades to their home or build a home larger than others in the area can be rejected for "legitimate business reasons" that may be neutral on their face ("the likelihood that the property will retain an adequate value over the term of the loan") but reflect judgments about the capacity of the neighborhood to increase in value. How common is it for all-white neighborhoods to be judged incapable of increasing in value through real estate improvements and expansions? Disparate impact theory provides a tool for fine-tuning neutral policies so that they can serve

---

27. *Id.* (reporting consent decree in *United States v. First National Bank of Pennsylvania,* 1:24-CV-88 (M.D.N.C.)).

legitimate business interests without disproportionately burdening protected groups and neighborhoods.

b. Reverse Redlining and Predatory Lending

Although much of this chapter addresses *denial* of mortgage credit, this section addresses the aggressive targeting of neighborhoods or groups with protected characteristics for adverse credit terms (often referred to as "predatory loans"). These practices violate §3605, which is not limited as is §3604 to the "sale or rental" (as opposed to, e.g., refinancing) of housing. Predatory conduct also may violate state laws prohibiting deceptive practices, fraud, conspiracy, and breach of fiduciary duty, as discussed in Hargraves v. Capital City Mortgage Corp., 140 F. Supp. 2d 7, 20 (D.D.C. 2000), *on reconsideration in part*, 147 F. Supp. 2d 1 (D.D.C. 2001):

> Redlining is the practice of denying the extension of credit to specific geographic areas due to the income, race, or ethnicity of its residents. . . . Reverse redlining is the practice of extending credit on unfair terms to those same communities. Reverse redlining has been held to violate civil rights laws, including the FHA[, ECOA,] and §1982. In order to show a claim based on reverse redlining, the plaintiffs must show that the defendants' lending practices and loan terms were "unfair" and "predatory," and that the defendants either intentionally targeted on the basis of race, or that there is a disparate impact on the basis of race.

Recall the discussion in Chapter 1 describing exploitative real estate practices, such as installment land contracts, that flourished in the dual housing and credit markets of the 20th century. The Dane excerpt in this chapter describes Black communities as being subjected to an "underworld of real estate finance" because of limited access to mainstream credit on fair terms. Unfortunately, unscrupulous lending practices have persisted,[28] with global consequences in the case of the real estate market crash in the late 2000s. There are many types of predatory practices, and a single loan might involve several. Note the allegations in *Hargraves*:

> Plaintiffs have alleged several "predatory" lending practices, including exorbitant interest rates, lending based on the value of the asset securing the loan rather than a borrower's ability to repay ("equity-stripping," in other words issuing a loan "designed to fail" and profiting by acquiring the property through default, rather than by receiving loan payments), repeated foreclosures, and loan servicing procedures in which excessive fees are charged.

---

28. *See* Taylor, *supra* note 1, at 3, 6 (examining "the critical turn in U.S. housing policy when the FHA . . . ended its long practice of redlining, instead turning to new policies that encouraged low-income African Americans to become homeowners in the 1970s. . . . But the transition . . . was fraught with problems. . . . The continuation of residential segregation after the fall of federal redlining and the passage of federal fair housing created the conditions for predatory inclusion.").

One issue that arises in predatory lending cases, or indeed any FHA case based on financial exploitation, is whether a lender that exclusively targets neighborhoods or applicants of color for predatory loans may be subject to liability without evidence that it has served white applicants on better terms. Courts have rejected the argument that comparative evidence is necessary in predatory lending cases where there is direct evidence of targeting or where there is an allegation of disparate impact, as in *Hargraves*.

> Plaintiffs have sufficiently alleged that the terms of defendants' loans are unfair and predatory; it is not necessary that the defendants make loans on more favorable terms to anyone other than the targeted class. *See Contract Buyers League* [*v. F&F Investment*, 300 F. Supp. 210, 216 (N.D. Ill. 1969)] (rejecting a similar argument because it would mean injustice would be allowed "so long as it is visited exclusively on negroes").

RACIAL STEERING TO HIGH-COST LOANS

The data show that many borrowers of color during the foreclosure crisis of the late 2000s had met the requirements for obtaining a prime mortgage loan in the mainstream market but nevertheless borrowed from high-cost lenders on unfavorable terms. Researchers have found "[s]ubstantial market-wide racial and ethnic differences in the incidence of high-cost [purchase] lending," even after controlling for borrower and loan characteristics, and that "African American and Hispanic borrowers tend to be concentrated at these high-risk lenders, even when their own credit scores are relatively unblemished."[29] Not all high-cost lenders were obscure players; many were well-known banks with subprime portfolios or subsidiaries. For example, the DOJ announced a large-scale settlement with Wells Fargo Bank in 2012 to resolve allegations that, between 2004 and 2009, the lender steered approximately 4,000 qualified African-American and Hispanic borrowers into subprime mortgages based on race or national origin (with similar white borrowers receiving prime loans), and charged approximately 30,000 African-American or Hispanic borrowers higher fees and rates than comparable white borrowers (based in part on "unguided pricing discretion.") Wells Fargo agreed to pay $184.3 million in compensation to wholesale borrowers (plus additional amounts to any identified retail borrowers) and also "provide $50 million in direct down payment assistance to borrowers in communities around the country where the department identified large numbers of discrimination victims and which were hard hit by the housing crisis." In 2011 the DOJ announced a $335 million settlement with Countrywide Financial Corporation, one of the nation's largest mortgage originators during the period, resolving similar allegations of discriminatory fees and rates and compensating more than 200,000 Black and Hispanic borrowers.[30]

---

29. Patrick Bayer, Fernando Ferreira & Stephen L. Ross, *What Drives Racial and Ethnic Differences in High-Cost Mortgages? The Role of High-Risk Lenders*, 31 THE REV. OF FIN. STUDIES 175, 200-01 (2017), https://doi.org/10.1093/rfs/hhx035 (examining seven metropolitan areas from 2004-2007).

30. DOJ, Press Releases, Justice Department Reaches Settlement With Wells Fargo Resulting in More Than $175 Million in Relief for Homeowners to Resolve Fair Lending Claims (July 12,

SIGNS OF PREDATORY MORTGAGE LOANS[31]

Not all high-cost (subprime) loans are predatory, but many are. Here are the major signs of a predatory mortgage loan:

- **Big Fees:** Requiring payment of "points" or a percentage of the loan amount above what is typical for the local lending market
- **Inflated Interest Rates from Brokers:** Charging more than the lender's actual charge and being rewarded by a "yield-spread premium"
- **Steering and Targeting:** Marketing to seniors and people of color unnecessarily expensive loans often designed to fail, rushing them into damaging decisions
- **Adjustable Interest Rates That "Explode":** Increasing interest rates significantly and abruptly, sometimes without proper disclosure
- **Promises to Fix Problems With Future Refinances:** Selling an unaffordable loan with a promise to refinance later
- **Repeated Refinances:** Flipping the loan and charging additional fees with each transaction, thus "stripping" or reducing the equity in the home
- **Penalties for Paying Off Early**: Adding prepayment penalties for refinancing and thus further decreasing the equity in the home
- **Not Counting Taxes and Insurance**: Misleading the consumer about the total monthly payment by not including all necessary costs

Consider the following case in which vulnerable, elderly consumers with multiple protected characteristics under the FHA and other equal credit laws alleged they had been targeted for harmful home loans on "grossly unfavorable" terms.

Matthews v. New Century Mortgage Corp.
185 F. Supp. 2d 874 (S.D. Ohio 2002)

CHATIGNY, District Judge:

This matter is before the Court on the Defendant's Motion to Dismiss the Plaintiffs' Second Amended Complaint.

Plaintiff Ruth Morgan, then an 87-year-old single woman, was contacted in October 1997 by an employee of Century 21 Home Improvement and Incredible Exteriors, Inc. ("Century 21"). The Century 21 employee told Ms. Morgan that the siding on her home had to be replaced because it was dirty and not up to code. Approximately one week later, Ms. Morgan signed

---

2012), https://www.justice.gov/opa/pr/justice-department-reaches-settlement-wells-fargo-resulting-more-175-million-relief; Justice Department Reaches $335 Million Settlement to Resolve Allegations of Lending Discrimination by Countrywide Financial Corporation (Dec. 21, 2011), https://www.justice.gov/opa/pr/justice-department-reaches-335-million-settlement-resolve-allegations-lending-discrimination (last visited July 26, 2024).

31. This information is derived from Center for Responsible Lending, 8 Signs of Predatory Mortgage Lending, https://www.responsiblelending.org/issues/8-signs-predatory-mortgage (last visited July 29, 2024).

a contract with Century 21 for new siding costing $17,325 after assurances by a different Century 21 employee, Antonio Barrett, that Ms. Morgan could obtain a loan to finance her new siding. Mr. Barrett also indicated that the loan would finance other home repairs and a used car.

On November 7, 1997, Mike Lewis, an employee of Century Mortgage, Inc. ("Century Mortgage"), met with Ms. Morgan in her home regarding her loan, although Ms. Morgan had neither contacted Central Mortgage, nor sought Central Mortgage's services in any way. Mr. Lewis brought to the meeting papers for Ms. Morgan to sign regarding what she believed was an application for a home-improvement loan to cover the cost of her new siding. Ms. Morgan signed numerous papers, but did not receive copies of what she signed. At that meeting, Ms. Morgan was not informed of her right to cancel her loan application.

On November 24, 1997, Mr. Mark Hanna, then the manager of Southeast Equity Title Agency ("Southeast Equity"), met with Ms. Morgan and Mr. Barrett at Ms. Morgan's home so that she could sign closing papers for her loan. According to Ms. Morgan, she had no opportunity to review the loan documents before she signed them, nor did she receive copies of the loan documents for review either prior to or at closing. Nonetheless, she felt obligated to agree to the terms of the loan, as the siding had already been removed from her house. Ms. Morgan was not informed at this meeting of her three-day right to cancellation [under the Truth in Lending Act]. Ms. Morgan's closing statement listed the Defendant, New Century Mortgage Corp. ("New Century"), as the lender of a $49,000 loan.

In December 1997, Ms. Morgan received, at her request, copies of the paperwork that Mr. Hanna had brought to her house. The copies, however, were not signed by Ms. Morgan. The paperwork included a "Notice of Right to Cancel" that was neither filled out nor signed. The documents did not include a Truth-in-Lending statement, a Loan Agreement Contract with the lender, employment verification forms, or Final Uniform Residential Loan Application.

Along with the paperwork, Southeast Equity sent a check payable to Ms. Morgan in the amount of $2345.07. Ms. Morgan cashed the check, and then gave it to Mr. Barrett, who had informed her that he would use the money to take care of her home repairs, other than the siding, and to buy her a used car. Ms. Morgan, however, has not had contact with Mr. Barrett since she gave him that money, and she never received either the promised home repairs or the used car.

In January 1998, Ms. Morgan began making monthly payments on the loan in the amount of $459.97. Shortly thereafter, Ms. Morgan received notice that the amount of her monthly payments would increase. Then, in December 1998 and January 1999, New Century returned Ms. Morgan's payment checks, stating that $459.97 did not represent the total amount due. In March 1999, New Century, through its trustee, U.S. Bank Trust National Association, filed a complaint against Ms. Morgan for foreclosure of her home.

Despite her prior efforts, Ms. Morgan did not learn the actual terms of the loan she had obtained from New Century until it filed for foreclosure. Thus, she learned that the loan that she had believed was intended only to finance her home repairs for $17,325.00 was actually for the refinancing of her home for $49,000.00. It was also at this time that she learned for the first time that her occupation had been listed as "quilt-maker" on the loan application forms, and that a business card stating that Ms. Morgan was a quilt-maker with American Quilts was a part of her mortgage file. In actuality, Ms. Morgan was never involved in a quilt-making business, nor did she have business cards to that effect. Finally, Ms. Morgan learned that her monthly income had been stated as $1500.00 on the loan application form, with quilt-making as her source of income, when, in actuality, her total monthly income was $713.00 in social security benefits.

The Plaintiffs allege, based on the foregoing facts, that Ms. Morgan relied on the Defendant's representations that she was receiving a home improvement loan that would result in lower monthly bill payments when, in fact, she paid high rates and fees for a loan that depleted the equity she had in her home. They contend that, as a result of the foreclosure proceedings, Ms. Morgan suffered extreme emotional and physical distress.

[The Court described three additional plaintiffs alleging similar conduct.]

[T]he Plaintiffs allege that the Defendants knew or should have known that the Plaintiffs' monthly incomes were insufficient to take on the debt obligations that were effectively forced upon them by the Defendants' fraudulent conduct, and that New Century, specifically, made the loans to the Plaintiffs despite the fact that New Century knew or should have known that the Plaintiffs had no ability to repay the loans.

Based on the foregoing, the Plaintiffs asserted against New Century claims under or of: (1) the Federal FHA; (2) the Equal Credit Opportunity Act; (3) the Truth-in-Lending Act; [and state law claims of civil conspiracy, fraud, and unconscionability]. Defendant New Century has filed a Motion to Dismiss all of the Plaintiffs' claims against it pursuant to Fed.R.Civ.P. 12(b)(6), for failure to state a claim.

[The court denied the defendants' motion to dismiss on the grounds that the claims were time-barred. The court granted the defendants' motion to dismiss plaintiffs' FHA claims under 42 U.S.C. §3604(b) because the financial assistance at issue was for improving homes that plaintiffs had acquired previously.]

The Plaintiffs have also alleged that New Century violated [§3605]. The Plaintiffs' claim brought under this provision essentially amounts to a claim that New Century engaged in "reverse redlining." "Reverse redlining" is the situation in which a lender unlawfully discriminates by extending credit to a neighborhood or class of people (typically living in the same neighborhood) on terms less favorable than would have been extended to people outside the particular class at issue. In like fashion, the Plaintiffs in this case allege that New Century violated the FHA by granting them a loan on grossly unfavorable terms based on their age, sex, and marital status,[32] and that such terms would not have been extended to credit applicants who were not elderly, unmarried women.

Although the issue has not been directly addressed by the Sixth Circuit, other courts have held that reverse redlining claims are cognizable under the FHA. *See, e.g.,* . . . Hargraves v. Capital City Mortgage Corp., 140 F. Supp. 2d 7, 20 (D.D.C. 2000) (recognizing that predatory loan practices can make housing unavailable by putting borrowers at risk of losing the real property that secures their loans). The elements of a reverse redlining claim brought under §3605 are a variation of the elements that typically must be shown for a claim of discrimination under §3605.

To set forth a cognizable reverse redlining claim under §3605, essentially the same elements must be established, except that the plaintiff need not show that the lender refused to transact business, but only that the lender refused to transact business *on fair terms.* Specifically, to establish a *prima facie* case of discrimination in violation of §3605 based on reverse redlining, the plaintiff must show: (1) that she is a member of a protected class; (2) that she applied for and was qualified for loans; (3) that the loans were given on grossly unfavorable terms; and (4) that the lender continues to provide loans to other applicants with similar qualifications, but on significantly more favorable terms. In the alternative, if the plaintiff presents direct evidence that the lender intentionally targeted her for unfair loans on the basis of sex and marital status, the plaintiff need not also show that the lender makes loans on more favorable terms to others. *See Hargraves* (finding that such a requirement would allow an injustice to continue so long as it was visited exclusively on one class of people).

This Court finds that the Plaintiffs have alleged sufficient facts to survive the motion to dismiss their claim under §3605. First, the Plaintiffs clearly are members of a protected class. Second, they applied for and were qualified for loans. Third, the Plaintiffs have alleged that New Century gave them their loans on grossly unfavorable terms. Finally, while the Defendant is correct that the Plaintiffs have not alleged that other similarly situated people were given loans on more favorable terms, the Plaintiffs have nonetheless presented a cognizable claim, as they allege and may be able to show directly that New Century intentionally targeted them for unfair loans on the basis of their sex and marital status, thus eliminating the necessity of proving the fourth element of the *prima facie* case.

---

32. [EDS. — Age and marital status are protected categories under the Equal Credit Opportunity Act (ECOA) and some state and local fair housing laws.]

NOTES AND QUESTIONS

1. Intentional Targeting. The claims in *Matthews* survived a motion to dismiss the FHA allegations in part because the plaintiffs provided direct evidence of discriminatory targeting. Notice the detailed accounts of the lender's initiating conduct with the *Matthews* plaintiffs. Would it have been enough merely to show that multiple protected class plaintiffs obtained predatory loans from the defendants? Compare Steed v. EverHome Mortgage Co., 477 Fed. App'x 722, 726-27 (11th Cir. 2012), where the court affirmed summary judgment for defendants on the FHA claim for lack of evidence of a pattern of targeting based on race. The court considered affidavits that the plaintiff and three other Black homeowners faced predatory practices leading to foreclosure and held it was insufficient to prove that the defendant "applies the allegedly predatory or unfair practices more often to African Americans than to people of other races." For an example of a successful claim of racial and ethnic targeting of grossly unfavorable loan products that was litigated through trial, see Saint-Jean v. Emigrant Mortgage Co., 337 F. Supp. 3d 186, 197 (E.D.N.Y. 2018). In this case, plaintiffs obtained a favorable jury verdict on their FHA, ECOA, and state law claims challenging an alleged equity stripping, "no document" loan product that triggered an 18 percent interest rate after one late payment. (The plaintiffs also argued violations under a disparate impact theory, discussed in next note). Among other rulings, the court denied defendants a new trial on the merits and granted a new trial on damages.

2. Reverse Redlining and Disparate Impact. Some reverse redlining plaintiffs argue a discriminatory effects theory in addition to a disparate treatment theory of discriminatory targeting. For example, in Horne v. Harbour Portfolio VI, 304 F. Supp. 3d 1332 (N.D. Ga. 2018), the plaintiffs brought reverse redlining claims for abusive credit terms under contracts for deed (CFD).[33] Plaintiffs alleged violations of the FHA, ECOA, TILA, and state law on the following facts:

> These homes were often in poor or uninhabitable condition, but no repairs were made prior to selling them via the CFDs. The Harbour Defendants would mark up the sale price of the home to four or five times their purchase price. Under the terms of the CFDs, interest rates were 9.9% or 10% over a 30-year period. The CFDs also put the burden of home repairs, maintenance, property taxes, and homeowner's insurance on the buyer. Each CFD contained a forfeiture clause giving the Harbour Defendants the right, upon default, to elect to cancel the contract, keep all amounts paid, and evict the buyer.

The court denied a motion to dismiss both the intent and disparate impact claims. On the impact claim, the court held that the plaintiffs properly alleged neutral policies that had a disproportionate impact on African

---

33. Plaintiffs' counsel in this case included Kristen Tullos, Sarah Mancini, and Sarah Stein with the Atlanta Legal Aid Society and Stuart Rossman with the National Consumer Law Center.

Americans: Defendants only purchased foreclosure properties available from Fannie Mae and only advertised via yard signs and word of mouth, both of which resulted in a disproportionate concentration of transactions in African-American census tracts.

3. Cities as Plaintiffs. As discussed in Chapter 4, cities throughout the country sued banks after 2008 for a variety of harms flowing from the banks' alleged predatory lending practices during the foreclosure crisis. The cities alleged that lenders caused the concentration of home vacancies and foreclosures in neighborhoods of color, resulting in increased foreclosure expenses, lowered property values, diminished property tax revenue, and increased demand for municipal services. In Bank of America Corp. v. City of Miami, Fla. 581 U.S. 189 (2017), the Supreme Court upheld the city's right to sue under the FHA because the economic injuries it alleged resembled those the Court had held sufficient in *Gladstone* and arguably fell within the FHA's zone of interests. The Court remanded, however, on the question of whether the alleged predatory lending practices "proximately caused" the city's alleged injuries. Since *City of Miami*, cities have struggled to survive dismissal of their claims, largely because courts are holding, based on causation principles, that the alleged injuries are too remote from the alleged discriminatory conduct. *See, e.g.*, City of Oakland v. Wells Fargo & Co., 14 F.4th 1030 (9th Cir. 2021) (en banc).

THE FORECLOSURE CRISIS

Foreclosure involves a lender's taking control of a property after a homeowner has fallen behind on mortgage payments or otherwise defaulted.[34] The foreclosure crisis in the 2000s earned its name by generating levels of mortgage defaults and foreclosures "draw[ing] comparisons to the levels of distress experienced in the Great Depression" beginning in 1929. In a 2010 Report to Congress on the Root Causes of the Foreclosure Crisis,[35] HUD summarized:

> In pursuit of high profits, lenders and investors poured capital into ever riskier loans particularly after 2003. This flood of capital helped to spur rising home prices that masked the riskiness of the loans being made, leading to continued loosening of underwriting standards[, easy capital availability, and refinancing]. When house price growth finally slowed in late 2006, the true nature of these risky loans was revealed, bringing down the "house of cards."

High profits earned by participants at each stage of the process fueled a housing bubble and a "race to the bottom in making risky loans." In other words, there

---

34. CFPB, *How Does Foreclosure Work?*, https://www.consumerfinance.gov/ask-cfpb/how-does-foreclosure-work-en-287/ (last reviewed Apr. 3, 2024).

35. HUD, Office of Policy Development and Research, *Report to Congress on the Root Causes of the Foreclosure Crisis* (Jan. 2010), https://www.huduser.gov/publications/pdf/foreclosure_09.pdf.

was little incentive for lenders to ensure that borrowers would be able to repay the loans because the loans were packaged and sold on the securities market; there was little incentive for the securities market to ensure the quality of the underlying assets because of the profitability of the transactions. Where were the regulators?

HUD pointed to federal deregulation leading up to the crisis, including changes that loosened restrictions on risky loan products, enabled risk-based pricing and securitization, and limited effectiveness of consumer protection laws and lack of meaningful oversight by regulators.

A Congressional commission also investigated the causes of the crisis and pointed to a breakdown in regulation, specifically, "widespread failures in financial regulation and supervision by key federal agencies; failures of corporate governance and heightened risk-taking; . . . loosening of due diligence standards applied in the securitization process; the repackaging and sale of questionable mortgage-backed securities into collateralized debt obligations . . .; failures of the credit rating agencies; and an unprepared government that responded inconsistently to the crisis." Deregulation also included federal preemption of state laws that had imposed limits on risky mortgage products, interest rate caps, and other protections.[36]

In 2010, Congress passed the Dodd-Frank Wall Street Reform and Consumer Protection Act (Dodd-Frank Act), which created the CFPB and codified certain consumer protections including requiring lender assessment of consumer ability to repay as a condition to originating, requiring independent appraisals, and prohibiting the following for certain loans: steering into unfavorable financing, prepayment penalties, and mandatory arbitration clauses.[37]

Scholars and advocates called attention to the fact that some high-cost lenders, who injured consumers across income and demographic categories, engaged in pernicious practices that preyed particularly on people of color and elderly consumers. Researchers reported that "high-cost lending appears to have been concentrated in minority neighborhoods in the run up to the housing crisis, and during the crisis especially high foreclosure rates were observed in those same neighborhoods."[38] Some homeowners raised FHA defenses in foreclosure actions, with mixed success.[39] The consequences of the foreclosure crisis have been devastating. "[T]he greater financial burden associated with high-cost loans not only leads directly to slower wealth accumulation due to the higher mortgage payments, but is also associated with a higher risk of future delinquency and default, with serious long-term consequences for credit scores and home ownership rates. These effects can be expected to exacerbate existing wealth gaps."[40]

---

36. This information is drawn from National Consumer Law Center, MORTGAGE LENDING §1.4.1 (4th ed. 2024) (Market Deregulation and the Crisis), *updated at* www.nclc.org/library (citing Fin. Crisis Inquiry Comm'n, *The Financial Crisis Inquiry Report: Final Report of the National Commission on the Causes of the Financial and Economic Crisis in the United States* xvii–xxviii (2011), https://www.govinfo.gov/content/pkg/GPO-FCIC/pdf/GPO-FCIC.pdf).

37. *Id.* at §1.4.5 (Aftermath: the Dodd Frank Act and the Consumer Financial Protection Bureau).

38. Bayer et al., *supra* note 29, at 175, 176. This research found the race and ethnicity of the borrower to be a stronger predictor than neighborhood of placement in high-cost loans.

39. *See* Schwemm, HDLL §18:2. If a loan servicer or mortgage lender has applied collection or foreclosure practices more harshly because of a protected characteristic of the borrower or the neighborhood's residents, this may violate the FHA, although proof of discrimination may be difficult.

40. Bayer et al., *supra* note 29, at 202.

HUD acknowledged the role of fraud but found "little evidence" to support the contention that the Community Reinvestment Act (CRA) (a federal statute requiring lenders to meet the credit needs of communities including those of low and moderate income) played an outsized role in the crisis, in part "because CRA loans had much lower risk of foreclosure than subprime loans generally." In the words of one lender, "The market is paying me more to do a no-income verification loan than it is paying me to do the full documentation loans. What would you do?"

DISTINGUISHING FAIR LENDING FROM CONSUMER PROTECTION LAWS

Fair lending laws, like the FHA and ECOA, provide consumers with civil rights protections from disparate treatment and disparate impact based on protected characteristics. (The Civil Rights Act of 1866 also provides protection from disparate treatment in lending transactions.) There are a host of other federal and state laws that protect consumers in a variety of contexts relating to mortgage credit, products, and services. The Dodd-Frank Act strengthened federal consumer protections in 2010 following the foreclosure crisis, with the Consumer Financial Protection Bureau (CFPB) promulgating rules and exercising administration and enforcement. This body of law is quite technical; the principal statutes[41] governing mortgage lending include the following:

- **The Truth in Lending Act (TILA),** implemented by Regulation Z, requires a uniform system of disclosing credit terms to allow for legible comparisons, sets limits on home equity lines of credit and minimum standards on most dwelling-secured loans, and prohibits unfair or deceptive practices.
- **The Real Estate Settlement Procedures Act (RESPA),** implemented by Regulation X, requires lenders, brokers, and servicers to provide borrowers with certain disclosures on the nature and costs of the real estate settlement process, also setting prohibitions on kickbacks and other limitations.
- **The National Flood Insurance Program (NFIP)** seeks to reduce the impact of flooding by providing affordable flood insurance to certain property owners in special flood hazard areas, with these flood policies required under other federal law and regulations. The Federal Emergency Management Agency (FEMA) administers NFIP.
- **The Home Ownership and Equity Protection Act (HOEPA),** an amendment to TILA, requires certain disclosures and homeownership counseling in advance of high-cost mortgage transactions, and places limits on fees and penalties.
- **The Secure and Fair Enforcement for Mortgage Licensing Act (SAFE)** mandates nationwide licensing and registration for residential loan originators to enhance public access to disciplinary information, consumer protection, and antifraud measures.

---

41. This material is drawn from Federal Deposit Insurance Corporation (FDIC), *Banker Resource Center, Consumer Compliance,* https://www.fdic.gov/resources/bankers/consumer -compliance/ (last visited May 30, 2024).

B. DISCRIMINATORY APPRAISALS

An appraisal, or estimate of the value of a dwelling, is a crucial component of a real estate-related transaction—a mortgage lender relies on an appraisal to ensure its loan is backed by sufficient collateral, and the borrower relies on it to obtain the mortgage necessary to become a homeowner. The lender typically will approve only a percentage of the value established by the appraisal, known as the loan-to-value ratio. Devaluing homes based on the racial profile of the neighborhood or loan applicant can block equal access to purchase and improvement loans on fair terms, which can obstruct wealth building and neighborhood flourishing. Research and investigations that examine whether race is (still) influencing property valuations reveal that, in far too many cases, it is. This section examines the historical background of the use of race in estimating and even establishing property value and loan risk; the FHA's coverage of appraisals; and contemporary research into the persistence and acceleration of race-based inequality in home valuations.

1. History of Discrimination in the Appraisal of Real Estate

Contemporary appraisal practices are difficult to disentangle from historical assumptions and disinvestment policies of government and private actors. This text draws on the extensive literature summarizing the ways in which racial zoning, deed restrictions, and government-assisted FHA and VA mortgages, along with private real estate steering and discrimination, created and maintained racially segregated neighborhoods. Appraisal practices additionally played a critical role in creating and maintaining racial hierarchies across neighborhoods:

> During the 1920's and 1930's economic theorists and appraisers began espousing the view that economic value and loan risk were related to race. The theory of "homogeneity" held that real estate values would remain stable or would increase only if the characteristics of the residents, including income levels and race, remained homogeneous. The principle of "conformity" buttressed this concept, and held that maximum value was realized only when sociological and economic conformity were present. The "infiltration" theory espoused the view that as different groups of people "infiltrated" or "invaded" a particular neighborhood, property values would decline. Thus, appraisers were required to note whether the particular neighborhood involved was likely to be affected in the near future by the introduction of any disharmonious racial or ethnic groups. . . . Widely influential texts of the time [including the first edition of the American Institute of Real Estate Appraisers' Manual in 1935, *Real Estate Appraisal*] reflected these values. . . . Lenders, of course, relied heavily on appraisers to make assessments regarding present and prospective real estate value and loan risk. [The federal government then standardized these practices and] drew upon the prevailing expertise and wisdom of the private lending community.[42]

---

42. Dane, *supra* note 7 (citing Calvin Bradford, *An Analysis of Underwriting and Appraisal Practices and Their Impact on Credit Availability*, 3 REAL ESTATE ISSUES 1 (Summer 1978)).

In the 1950s and 1960s, researchers and civil rights advocates began to examine and challenge the myths underlying the associations among race, property value, and loan risk, noting these economic theories "were not based on any systematic studies," but rather were based on Darwinistic and plant biology "life cycle" theories of neighborhood decline. The major studies, by contrast, demonstrated "that race and racial change had no adverse effect on property values." Despite this growing backlash, appraisal texts, lenders, regulatory agencies, and even HUD continued to embrace racial theories of value and risk into the 1970s. A series of fair housing and fair lending laws, including the FHA, prohibited discrimination in sales and lending transactions, which was interpreted to reach most discriminatory appraisal practices that made housing unavailable. The DOJ filed suit in 1976 against the American Institute of Real Estate Appraisers (AIREA) and other lending trade organizations, resulting in a consent decree requiring revision of the pivotal industry text, *The Appraisal of Real Estate*, to eliminate "the discriminatory assumptions and theories . . . taught to generations of appraisers and lenders."[43]

2. Contemporary Real Estate Appraisal Practices

In the 1980s, the appraisal industry collaborated with federal agencies to create a uniform appraisal report and uniform standards to ensure a "uniform definition of market value." The appraisal typically begins with "an in-person visual inspection" consisting of "taking photos of and notes on the home's internal and external structure" and features. Then, the prevailing approach requires appraisers "to derive market value by comparing the home they are appraising . . . with previously sold homes with comparable features in similar communities." Thus, the selection of "comps" is "critical in determining the final appraised value of the home." But, as demonstrated in the research findings below, the appraisal industry lacks uniform standards for selecting comps in the modern era, which "can create opportunities for racialized perceptions of neighborhoods to influence appraiser evaluations." Evidence shows that some appraisers conceptualize comparable neighborhoods as those with similar racial demographics regardless of the objective criteria available.[44]

Thus, the sales comparison approach has allowed race and past appraisal practices (which have devalued neighborhoods of color) to influence contemporary home values. Researchers report that since 1980, racial inequality in

---

43. *Id.* at 5, 8-9 (discussing U.S. v. American Institute of Real Estate Appraisers of Nat. Ass'n of Realtors, 442 F. Supp. 1072 (N.D. Ill. 1977)).

44. This information is drawn and quoted from Junia Howell & Elizabeth Korver-Glenn, *Neighborhoods, Race, and the Twenty-First-Century Housing Appraisal Industry,* 4 Sociology of Race and Ethnicity 473, 474-76, 482 (2018), https://doi.org/10.1177/2332649218755178.

home values has increased, with the rate of increase tripling in the last decade. One recent nationwide study found that homes in white neighborhoods are appraised at twice the value of comparable homes in communities of color with similar amenities and socioeconomic status. Researchers recently have called for reforms that abandon the sales comparison approach and use tools to "decouple the value of land from the racial or socioeconomic characteristics of its inhabitants."[45]

3. FHA Coverage of Discrimination in Real Estate Appraisals

Litigants may use the FHA to challenge discriminatory appraisals, although they also may pursue these claims under the ECOA and the 1866 Civil Rights Act, as well as state law. (ECOA requires the lender to furnish a copy of the appraisal report, on the credit applicant's request.) Section 3605 of the FHA explicitly covers discrimination in the making of appraisals and in the terms and conditions of appraisals. In prohibiting discrimination in "real estate-related transactions," §3605 defines that term to include "[t]he selling, brokering, or appraising of residential real property." (Of course, a discriminatory appraisal in a sale or rental transaction that makes housing unavailable also can violate §3604(a).)

HUD in 24 CFR §100.135(b) defines the term "appraisal" to mean:

> an estimate or opinion of the value of a specified residential real property made in a business context in connection with the sale, rental, financing or refinancing of a dwelling or in connection with any activity that otherwise affects the availability of a residential real estate-related transaction, whether the appraisal is oral or written, or transmitted formally or informally. The appraisal includes all written comments and other documents submitted as support for the estimate or opinion of value.

After defining the term, HUD in §100.135(d) offers a fairly typical example of appraisal discrimination: "using an appraisal of residential real property in connection with the sale, rental, or financing of any dwelling where the person knows or reasonably should know that the appraisal improperly takes into consideration" a protected characteristic. In early appraisal cases under the FHA, plaintiffs struggled to persuade trial courts that low appraisals were infected with racial bias. For example, in Hanson v. Veterans Administration,

---

45. *See* Junia Howell & Elizabeth Korver-Glenn, *Appraised: The Persistent Evaluation of White Neighborhoods as More Valuable Than Communities of Color* 2, 12-13, 20-21 (Nov. 2022), https:// nationalfairhousing.org/wp-content/uploads/2022/11/2022-11-2_Howell-and-Korver-Glenn -Appraised.pdf. In 2021, the Biden administration created an Interagency Task Force on Property Appraisal and Valuation Equity (PAVE) to evaluate appraisal bias and establish recommendations. The Task Force issued an Action Plan making a series of recommendations. It also designated alternatives to the sales comparison approach as requiring further research and consideration. PAVE, *Action Plan to Advance Property Appraisal and Valuation Equity: Closing the Racial Wealth Gap by Addressing Mis-valuations for Families and Communities of Color* (March 2022), https://pave.hud.gov/sites/pave.hud.gov/files/documents/PAVEActionPlan.pdf.

800 F.2d 1381, 1383-84, 1387-88 (5th Cir. 1986), the court reviewed the trial court's dismissal of the claim, which plaintiffs had supported with evidence of statistical disparities and alleged adherence to traditional associations between race and value:

> Each appellant was party to a different agreement for the sale of property in which a VA guaranteed home loan was sought. The properties at issue in all of the agreements are located in the MacGregor subdivision, a predominantly black, middle class neighborhood, in Houston, Texas. In each instance, the VA's appraisal estimate [was] below the price prospective purchasers had agreed to pay for the property. These "underappraisals," as they are referred to in the industry, caused many of the prospective purchasers to reduce their offers or look elsewhere for a home where a 100% VA loan was available.
>
> Appellants filed suit against the VA seeking an injunction and damages on the ground that the value of their property was discriminatorily adjusted downward by the VA fee appraisers because MacGregor was a racially mixed neighborhood. As support, appellants offered statistical evidence comparing the percentage of VA underappraisals in MacGregor with that of South Hampton, a white neighborhood allegedly similar to MacGregor. The evidence purported to show that MacGregor had a significantly higher percentage of underappraisals than South Hampton; appellants argued that the underappraisals resulted from the application of racially discriminatory appraisal practices by the VA. . . .
>
> Appellants introduced proof [through expert testimony] that a widely used appraisal text, *The Appraisal of Real Estate*, instructed appraisers until 1977 that the value of the property being appraised should be adjusted downward if the ethnic composition of the neighborhood to which it belonged was not homogeneous. The "principle of conformity" categorized different ethnic groups according to their detrimental effect upon property values after their "infiltration" into the neighborhood.
>
> Although this principle was no longer taught after 1977, appellants produced evidence that the VA had never issued guidelines instructing its appraisers not to use this racially biased practice and argued that the VA's appraisers, who had learned the "principle of conformity," continued to apply it. They contend that this is borne out by evidence that several VA appraisal reports concerning MacGregor property referred to "economic depreciation," "changes in the neighborhood" and "lack of pride of ownership," all of which their experts testified indicated racial considerations.

The trial court ultimately rejected the plaintiffs' evidence and credited the VA's experts, concluding that the VA appraisals "conformed to the established 'market approach' method of appraisal without discriminatory intent." (The court also rejected the plaintiffs' discriminatory effects claim, in part because the plaintiffs' expert's statistical analysis did not control for nonracial variables such as crime rate and school quality.) The VA's experts were five Houston appraisers who opined that the reports' phrases "did not have racial connotations" and that VA's appraisals "appeared reasonable." The VA's experts also stated "they were not aware of any Houston appraiser who used racial consideration in their appraisals," and the VA appraisal forms required certifications that the appraiser did not take race into account.

The Fifth Circuit in *Hanson* upheld the district court's dismissal of plaintiffs' discriminatory appraisal claim as not clearly erroneous, given its need to defer to a lower court's crediting of one set of experts over another where each "has told a coherent and facially plausible story that is not contradicted by extrinsic evidence" and is not internally inconsistent.

In another case, Thomas v. First Federal Savings Bank of Indiana, 653 F. Supp. 1330, 1339-41 (N.D. Ind. 1987), the trial court rejected plaintiffs' discrimination claims challenging denial of a $7,100 refinancing loan based on a low appraisal of their Gary, Indiana home.

> Here, after plaintiffs presented all their evidence, they still had not shown that defendants' knowledge of the Thomases' race contributed in any degree to either defendants' decision not to make the loan or in appraising the Thomas home [at $22,000]. Plaintiffs did present the testimony of George Wilkes, a second appraiser, who conducted an independent appraisal of the Thomas home and estimated its 1984 value at $40,000.00. However, by Wilkes' own admission, his appraisal was merely another subjective evaluation of the Thomas home through the inexact appraisal process. Moreover, Wilkes established that Beckham, First Federal's appraiser, was consistent in his appraisal methods, [using] the same techniques regardless of the race or neighborhood of the homeowners. . . . In determining whether or not to grant a second mortgage to the Thomases, First Federal considered the loan-to-value ratio of their home [and required the total mortgage debt to be no more than 80 percent of the appraised home value]. Included in the loan-to-value ratio are considerations of the marketability, the salability and the neighborhood of the property offered as security for the loan. The loan-to-value ratio was the dispositive factor in First Federal's decision to deny the loan. Such a factor is a legitimate business criterion and its use is not a violation of §3605.

Compare Steptoe v. Savings of America, 800 F. Supp. 1542, 1546-47 (N.D. Ohio 1992), in which the court held that plaintiffs had produced sufficient evidence of appraisal discrimination to survive summary judgment; defendants did not follow their policies, an expert testified that the appraisal was defective, another appraisal supported the plaintiff's contractual sales amount, and statistical analysis demonstrated different treatment based on neighborhood racial composition.

NOTES AND QUESTIONS

1. The Art of the Appraisal. If a plaintiff offers evidence demonstrating that another appraiser set the home value higher than the defendant and at an amount sufficient to qualify for the loan, should this be sufficient to survive a motion to dismiss? What about summary judgment? Trial? Do you think that the "subjective" nature of appraisals, apparently uncontested in the *Thomas* case, should make it easier or harder for a plaintiff to prove race-based appraisal discrimination?

In Latimore v. Citibank Federal Savings Bank, 151 F.3d 712, 715 (7th Cir. 1998), the Seventh Circuit held on summary judgment: "Real estate appraisal is not an exact science, . . . so the fact that Citibank's appraisal was lower than someone else's does not create an inference of discrimination." Compare Swanson v. Citibank, N.A., 614 F.3d 400, 405 (7th Cir. 2010), in which the court reversed dismissal: "Swanson's complaint identifies the type of discrimination that she thinks occurs (racial), by whom (Citibank, through Skertich, the manager, and the outside appraisers it used), and when (in connection with her effort in early 2009 to obtain a home-equity loan). This is all that she needed to put in the complaint." Do you think the appraisal industry should aim for more objectivity or less? More science or more art?

2. Consistency in Application of Appraisal Methods. Does the fact that a lender is "consistent" in how it applies appraisal methods or techniques across white and Black areas, as in *Thomas*, determine whether a violation of §3605 has occurred? Would inconsistency in methods necessarily prove discrimination? Professor Schwemm reminds us that the FHA "does not require that appraisers be good at their jobs; it only requires that they not consider unlawful factors." HDLL §18:8.

Can you think of a fact pattern where consistency might still result in liability under the FHA? As the research reveals below, the sales comparison ("market") approach accepted in *Hanson* has come under some scrutiny given the lack of standards governing how appraisers select comps and the racialized way appraisers historically have been taught to think about, and value, "markets."

3. Overimprovements? Mr. Thomas testified at trial that the lender's appraiser stated, after reviewing many improvements plaintiffs had made to the house, that *if the Thomas's house were located anywhere else* it would be worth $100,000, nevertheless appraising the home at $22,000. The court disbelieved this evidence, while pointing to other testimony that the home was in an "overimproved" condition compared to other properties in the area. If the court had believed this evidence, what bearing do you think it would have had on the discrimination claims?

4. Proof. The *Hanson* and *Thomas* cases above suggest the difficulty for plaintiffs in proving that an appraiser impermissibly took race into account when giving an estimate on property value. Consider the ease with which a bevy of appraisers in *Hanson* was able to persuade the trial court that they "were not aware" of any racial discrimination in the appraisal industry. That said, in recent years, Black appraisal-seekers sometimes have taken matters into their own hands, to dramatic effect.

For example, in Tate-Austin v. Miller, No. 21-CV-09319, 2022 WL 1105072 (N.D. Cal. April 13, 2022), an African-American couple and an FHO alleged that the appraisal of the couple's property in Marin City, California (home to a relatively high concentration of the county's African-American population), was racially discriminatory in violation of the FHA, the 1866 Civil Rights Act, and state law. The court dismissed the §3604 claim because the Austins did not allege that the defendants made their housing unavailable but discriminated against them in connection with refinancing "for the purpose of maintaining a home [they] already own[]." The court, however, relied on the following facts to deny the defendants' motion to dismiss the FHA claims under §§3605 and 3617 and the 1866 Civil Rights Act claims under §§1981 and 1982:

> In December 2016, the month in which the Austins purchased and financed the Pacheco Street House, it was appraised at an estimated market value of $575,500. In May 2018, after "completely remodel[ing]" the house, the Austins refinanced their mortgage based on an appraisal that estimated the house's value to be $864,000, and in March 2019, after making further renovations, the Austins again refinanced their mortgage, this time based on an appraisal that valued the house at $1,450,000.
>
> In 2020, the Austins sought to refinance their mortgage for a third time, in order "to take advantage of historically low interest rates and obtain additional funding to complete [a] basement conversion" as well as construction of an "accessory dwelling unit." In connection therewith, they contacted their mortgage broker, who retained the services of an appraisal management company, AMC Links, which company then hired the Miller Defendants to conduct an appraisal of the Pacheco Street House.
>
> In January 2020, Miller conducted an inspection of the Pacheco Street House. During the inspection, plaintiff Paul Austin "was present" and "introduced himself by name"; additionally, "photos of the Austins and their minor children, all of whom are African American," as well as "African-themed" art, were "conspicuous[ly]" on display. On February 12, 2020, AMC Links issued an appraisal report, in which Miller concluded the market value of the house was $995,000.
>
> The Austins, "shocked" by Miller's appraisal report, were informed by their mortgage broker that they "could not obtain refinancing at favorable terms because of the . . . low value ascribed to the Pacheco Street House" and, in February 2020, the Austins requested AMC Links provide a second appraisal and by a different appraiser. Prior to the next appraisal inspection, the Austins asked "a friend, who is white, to be present" and to "greet the appraiser as if she [were] the homeowner." In addition, the Austins replaced their family photos and African-themed art with photos depicting their friend's "white family." On the day of the inspection, the friend "answered the door . . . and sat in the dining area"; neither of the Austins was present. On March 8, 2020, the appraiser issued a report in which the value of the Pacheco Street House was estimated at $1,482,500, and, based thereon, "the Austins refinanced their mortgage" on terms that were less "favorable" than the "terms that had been available one month before."

The court pointed to the following allegations of disparate treatment in holding that the plaintiffs made "a plausible showing of race as a motivating factor" in the appraisal:

> (1) Miller knew the Austins were African American when she conducted her appraisal of the Pacheco Street House, (2) three of the six comparable sales ("comps") selected by Miller were located in Marin City, two of which "were not comparable to the Pacheco Street House in any way except for their location in Marin City" [EDS. — The court noted plaintiffs' reliance on a study

indicating that appraisers tend to choose comps in locations "substantially closer" to appraised properties when the latter are located in Black or Latino census tracts[46]], (3) Miller made "downward adjustments" to the remaining three comps, one of which was located in Sausalito and the other two in Mill Valley, ultimately concluding that the Pacheco Street House "was worth nearly 28% less per square foot than the price per square foot of the allegedly comparable properties" located in surrounding areas that were predominantly white, (4) Miller stated in her report that Marin City had a "distinct marketability which differs from the surrounding areas," which comment plaintiffs describe as "coded in race," (5) Miller's estimated market value of the Pacheco Street House was nearly $500,000 less than the value of the house as estimated by two other appraisers less than one year prior to and approximately three weeks after Miller's appraisal, respectively, and (6) Miller's above-referenced appraisal methods "deviated from [the] recognized methods and techniques of real estate appraisal" provided for in the Uniform Standards of Professional Appraisal Practice ("USPAP").

In another example, a Black couple (Drs. Nathan Connolly and Shani Mott), scholars in history and Africana Studies whose research included housing discrimination, filed suit challenging a low appraisal of their home in a predominantly white neighborhood in Baltimore, Maryland, that was adjacent to an area with a more significant Black population. After they "whitewashed" their home, a different appraiser came back with an appraisal nearly $300,000 higher than the first.[47]

In *Appraisal Discrimination: Five Lessons for Litigators*, 76 SMU L. Rev. 205 (2023), Professor Heather Abraham has compiled examples and news reports of similar instances of Black lending applicants "whitewashing" their homes, as the practice has been described, yielding similar results in varied geographic locations and segments of the housing market. The article offers additional recommendations about proof, some derived from experienced litigators. Rather than relying on one comparative appraisal, litigants might consider two additional appraisals, followed by the removal of evidence of the family's race, before conducting a fourth, independent appraisal. Professor Abraham suggests overcoming skepticism through persuasive, specific, and thorough pleading. She also discusses cultivation of effective experts who understand the historical and contemporary dynamics of race-based property

---

46. *See* Freddie Mac, *Research Note, Racial and Ethnic Valuation Gaps in Home Purchase Appraisals* (Sept. 20, 2021), http://www.freddiemac.com/research/insight/20210920_home_appraisals.page.

47. The case settled with the lender defendant in March 2024, shortly after Dr. Mott died of cancer at age 47. Professor Connolly's prize-winning book is A World More Concrete: Real Estate and the Remaking of Jim Crow South Florida (U. Chicago Press 2014). *News & Updates, Mortgage Giant loanDepot.com Commits to Industry-Leading Best Practices for "Reconsideration of Value" in Settlement of Appraisal Discrimination Lawsuit Filed by Relman Colfax*, Relman Colfax (Mar. 25, 2024), https://www.relmanlaw.com/news-525; *History, People*, John Hopkins University, https://history.jhu.edu/directory/nathan-connolly/ (last visited July 29, 2024); Rachel Wallach, *Shani Mott, Esteemed Black Studies Scholar and Champion for Social Justice, Dies at 47*, John Hopkins University (March 14, 2024), https://hub.jhu.edu/2024/03/14/shani-mott-history-africana-studies-obituary/.

valuations, including the way that appraisers may unconsciously use race rather than objective criteria to select comps for valuations.

4. The FHA Appraisal Exemption and Disparate Impact Liability

Congress, when amending the FHA in 1988, incorporated an exemption from liability in the appraisal context. 42 U.S.C. §3605(c) states that "Nothing in this title prohibits a person engaged in the business of furnishing appraisals of real property to take into consideration factors other than" protected characteristics. In TDHCA v. Inclusive Communities Project, Inc., 576 U.S. 519, 537-38 (2015), discussed in Chapter 7, the Supreme Court discussed the textual support in the FHA for disparate impact liability and reasoned that the appraisal exemption (and two others) would not make sense without disparate impact liability. This is because if the FHA prohibited only disparate treatment and not disparate impact, it would be unnecessary to create an exemption for practices that did not take protected characteristics into account. Given the plain text of the FHA and the Court's interpretation of the appraisal exemption, litigants likely would be unable to challenge the race-neutral factors in an appraisal, such as neighborhood crime rates or school quality, based on the theory that such factors had a disproportionate adverse impact on neighborhoods of color.

5. Contemporary Research on the Role of Race in Residential Property Valuations

In an interesting postscript to Hanson, researchers Junia Howell and Elizabeth Korver-Glenn studied single-family tax-appraised residences in the Houston housing market more than 30 years later. They used 2015 data and employed both quantitative and qualitative methods, concluding that "neighborhood racial composition still has an enduring and substantial influence on housing values" after controlling for many of the market variables that might explain the disparities:

> Our quantitative data demonstrate that comparable Harris County houses zoned with comparable schools and located within neighborhoods with equitable housing stock, housing demand, distances to parks, commute times, and crime, homeownership, poverty, and unemployment rates were valued systematically lower in Black and Hispanic neighborhoods. . . . Our qualitative [interview-based] data . . . highlighted how the inconsistency in comp selection strategies enables appraisers to select comps on the basis of their racialized assumptions about the comparability of communities, which in turn devalues communities of color, irrespective of actual demand. . . . [In other words,] appraisers often perceive comparable houses as those in communities with similar racial demographics, even if these comparable communities were further away or had drastically different socioeconomic [or other] characteristics.[48]

---

48. Junia Howell & Elizabeth Korver-Glenn, *Neighborhoods, Race, and the Twenty-First-Century Housing Appraisal Industry*, 4 Sociology of Race and Ethnicity 473, 482-83, 485 (2018), https://doi.org/10.1177/2332649218755178.

The data showed that appraisers valued an average Houston home in an average white neighborhood at \$289,000 but valued the same home in comparable Black and Hispanic neighborhoods at \$127,000 and \$120,000, respectively.[49] These results are not unique. In 2022, Howell and Korver-Glenn studied a nationwide, uniform appraisal data set (more than 32 million appraisals between 2013 and 2021) from the Federal Housing Finance Agency and found that licensed appraisers assessed homes in white neighborhoods at *double the value* compared with those in communities of color *even when the property and neighborhood features were comparable.*[50]

Moreover, Andre M. Perry, Jonathan Rothwell, and David Harshbarger published research in 2018 finding that "[h]omes of similar quality in neighborhoods with similar amenities are worth 23 percent less in majority Black neighborhoods, compared to those with very few or no Black residents. . . . Across all majority Black neighborhoods, owner-occupied homes are undervalued by \$48,000 per home on average, amounting to \$156 billion in cumulative losses."[51] The Federal Home Loan Mortgage Corporation (Freddie Mac) conducted a similar study of 12 million home purchase appraisals between 2015 and 2020, controlling for property and neighborhood characteristics. They found "properties in Black and Latino [neighborhood census] tracts receive appraisal values lower than the contract price more often than those in White tracts [and that] as the concentration of Black or Latino [persons] in a census tract increases, the appraisal valuation gap increases."[52]

Finally, in a 2021 paper, Howell and Korver-Glenn reported finding, after running a series of models, that "neighborhood racial composition has a stronger influence on current appraisals than on appraisals in 1980," with white neighborhoods since 1980 appreciating \$194,000 more than similar homes in comparable neighborhoods of color. They explain this increasing racial inequality in home valuations as follows:

> First, the continued use of the sales comparison approach after fair housing legislation meant appraisers used previous sales, which explicitly relied on neighborhood racial composition, to determine appraisals. Since no steps

49. *Id.* at 481-82.

50. Junia Howell & Elizabeth Korver-Glenn, *Appraised: The Persistent Evaluation of White Neighborhoods as More Valuable Than Communities of Color* (Nov. 2022), https://nationalfairhous ing.org/wp-content/uploads/2022/11/2022-11-2_Howell-and-Korver-Glenn-Appraised.pdf.

51. The Devaluation of Assets in Black Neighborhoods: The Case of Residential Property, 3 (Nov. 2018), https://www.brookings.edu/wp-content/uploads/2018/11/2018.11_Brooki ngs-Metro_Devaluation-Assets-Black-Neighborhoods_final.pdf. In a later report, Perry and Rothwell found these results to be "robust to many alternative modeling strategies and theoretical concerns about omitted variables bias," stating, "we are confident that housing is valued differently in Black neighborhoods, and racial discrimination—in some form or forms—is the best explanation available given current information." Jonathan Rothwell & Andre M. Perry, *Biased Appraisals and the Devaluation of Housing in Black Neighborhoods*, Brookings (Nov. 17, 2021), https://www.brookings.edu/research/biased-appraisals-and-the-devaluation-of-housing-in -black-neighborhoods/.

52. Freddie Mac, *Research Note, Racial and Ethnic Valuation Gaps in Home Purchase Appraisals* (Sept. 20, 2021), https://www.freddiemac.com/research/insight/20210920-home-appraisals.

were taken to rectify the historic inequities, this approach has enabled such inequalities to persist. Second, appraisers continue to use neighborhood racial composition to help determine which homes are comparable. In this way, much like historical practices . . . contemporary appraisers are constructing a racialized housing market and exacerbating racial inequality. Addressing the inequality created by racialized home appraisals will require transforming the appraisal industry.[53]

NOTES AND QUESTIONS

1. **Systemic Devaluations and Appraiser Perception.** Does the FHA reach systemic devaluations of the kind revealed in the contemporary research summarized above? Recall in *Hanson* that appraiser experts testified they did not see any discrimination in their industry, and the trial court credited this testimony. Would the appraisers interviewed in the above studies have perceived that they were acting intentionally to devalue Black and Hispanic neighborhoods? Should the perception of appraisers that their selection of comps is color-blind insulate discriminatory devaluations of Black and Hispanic neighborhoods from challenge or reform? According to statistics published by the Appraisal Institute in 2023, over two-thirds of appraisers in the United States who were willing to answer identified as male, and 77.0 percent identified as white, 5.5 percent as Hispanic, 2.2 percent as Black, and 1.8 percent as Asian, with 8.2 percent preferring not to disclose race or ethnicity.[54] What do you think are the relationships (if any) among the race, ethnicity, and gender of the appraiser and the appraiser's valuations?

2. **Neighborhood-Based Challenges to Appraisal Discrimination.** Would a plaintiff today fare better than the plaintiffs in *Hanson*, above, in challenging the type of appraisal discrimination identified in this research? Given your study of the standing doctrine under the FHA, who can sue for appraisal discrimination operating at the neighborhood level? What kinds of injuries would support standing and what kinds of allegations could plaintiffs make? What about devaluations occurring at the metro level? At the time of this writing, Houston, Texas, was the fourth most populous city in the United States and researchers using 2020 census data described it as a city of "high segregation."[55]

3. **Economic and Noneconomic Injury from Appraisal Discrimination.** What investments could Black communities have made with the $156 billion in losses identified in the Perry et al. research? The devaluing of homes in

53. Junia Howell & Elizabeth Korver-Glenn, *The Increasing Effect of Neighborhood Racial Composition on Housing Values, 1980-2015*, 68 Soc. Probs. 1051, 1068-69 (2021).

54. Appraisal Institute, 2023 U.S Valuation Profession Fact Sheet, https://www.appraisal institute.org/getmedia/bf70e869-945f-4fab-851c-44204f971224/2023_ai_fact_sheet (last visited May 30, 2024).

55. Othering & Belonging Institute, *Most to Least Segregated Cities in 2020*, https://belonging.berkeley.edu/most-least-segregated-cities-in-2020 (last visited July 30, 2024).

Black neighborhoods that are objectively the same as those in white neighborhoods certainly has pernicious implications for "educational, vocational, and recreational opportunities for residents" and would seem, perversely, to degrade the long-term equality of neighborhood conditions and value over time:

> When societal biases lessen the value on homes in Black neighborhoods, residents and communities lose the wealth and revenue to develop themselves as well as the institutions that expand the number of options residents have. Home values drive property taxes, which generates the revenue that helps determine school quality, infrastructure improvements, public safety, and recreation. . . . This is a vicious cycle: Devaluation leads to divestment, which leads to people moving out of the community; social services decline and crime and unemployment rise.[56]

4. Multigenerational Effects. Since 1980, after civil rights laws prohibited explicit use of race in appraisal writing, the gap in valuations of neighborhoods has increased, and it is accelerating. Do Black neighborhoods that were "unequal" at the time of these research studies and excluded from the comparative analysis reflect race-based valuations from prior decades? Once the devaluing of "comparable" Black neighborhoods in the present day ripens into unequal conditions, what remedy do residents have? How do unequal neighborhood conditions contribute to consumer perceptions that race affects home quality and neighborhood amenities? Appraiser perceptions? Must we continue to use valuation methods that we know are correlated with and are exacerbating race-based inequality? Which public- and private-sector actors are in the best position to address these market failures?

5. Major Bumps on the Road Home. Racial inequities in home appraisals can have unexpected consequences. Consider Greater New Orleans Fair Housing Action Center v. HUD, 723 F. Supp. 2d 14 (D.C. 2010), which involved a challenge to a postdisaster rebuilding grant formula. The "Road Home" was a federally funded, state-administered program assisting homeowners following catastrophic damage from Hurricanes Katrina and Rita in 2005.

> Under a portion of the Program called Option 1, an individual whose house was damaged by the hurricanes may choose to receive a grant to repair or rebuild her home. Each beneficiary of an Option 1 grant receives an award in the amount of either the value of her home before the storms or the cost of repairing her home, whichever is less, but not in excess of $150,000. . . . Plaintiffs initiated this action in November 2008 [against HUD and the State of Louisiana, alleging] that the reliance on home values in calculating Option 1 awards "has a discriminatory disparate impact on African Americans living in historically segregated communities." Specifically, they argue that because "African American homeowners in New Orleans are more likely than white homeowners in New Orleans to own homes with lower values," African-American recipients of Option 1 grants are more likely than white recipients to

---

56. Andre M. Perry, Know Your Price: Valuing Black Lives and Property in America's Black Cities 43, 57 (Brookings 2020).

receive only the amount of the pre-storm value of their homes. Consequently, plaintiffs allege, African-American homeowners are likely to have a larger gap than white recipients between the amount of their awards and the cost of rebuilding.

The court denied the motion to dismiss the effects claim under §3604(a), holding that it was not based "on a reduction in property values or a limit on the growth of a residential area but on the inability of homeowners to inhabit their houses because of a Road Home Program formula." (The court dismissed the §3605(a) claim because the defendant did not engage in residential real estate transactions.) HUD agreed to a $62 million settlement in 2011, but by that time it appeared many Black homeowners had already made their decisions not to return based on the lower award amounts offered.[57]

C. DISCRIMINATION IN HOMEOWNERS INSURANCE

> Insurance is essential. . . . It is a cornerstone of credit. Without insurance, banks and other financial institutions will not — and cannot — make loans. New housing cannot be constructed, and existing housing cannot be repaired. New businesses cannot be opened, and existing businesses cannot expand, or even survive. . . . Communities without insurance are communities without hope.[58]

Insurers must determine a price for individual homeowners policies before knowing what any loss would actually cost the company. As Professor Squires explains, to address this challenge, the industry assigns applicants to groups based on a prediction of losses associated with the characteristics of the property (including location) and the people to be insured. However, he notes that "perceptions of race have long influenced the industry's methods for assessing and responding to the ambiguous liabilities it assumes when it issues a policy."[59] Insurers' historical use of racial stereotypes describing redlined neighborhoods has been documented in government and scholarly reports, litigation, and marketing materials; industry-designed research in the mid-1990s revealed that the racial demographics of a neighborhood still were "associated with the number and cost of policies even after controlling [for] loss experience and other demographic factors"; and matched-pair testing by

---

57. Seicshnaydre et al., *Rigging the Real Estate Market: Disaster, Inequality, and Disaster Risk*, The Data Center (Apr. 2018), https://s3.amazonaws.com/gnocdc/reports/TDC-prosperity -brief-stacy-seicshnaydre-et-al-FINAL.pdf.

58. *Meeting the Insurance Crisis of Our Cities: A Report by the President's National Advisory Panel on Insurance in Riot-Affected Areas* (1968).

59. Gregory Squires, *Racial Profiling, Insurance Style: Insurance Redlining and the Uneven Development of Metropolitan Areas*, 25 J. URB. AFFAIRS 391, 395, 401 (2003). Risk factors that might be greater in cities than suburbs include older homes with outdated electrical and plumbing systems, densely constructed homes with wood framing that is susceptible to fire, and neighborhoods with higher rates of theft. But Squires also notes that industry decisions disfavoring urban neighborhoods may be "rational, only given the larger irrationality of private practices and public policies that have nurtured uneven development." *Id.* at 392-93, 406.

private FHOs isolating the role of race in homeowners insurance transactions has documented racial differences in making policies available and the terms and conditions on which policies were offered. Using race to classify and price risk is unlawful when race is "demonstrably not predictive" of loss. But even "statistical discrimination," or "us[ing] average characteristics of a racial group to determine whether housing related services will be provided to any particular individual" is unlawful.[60]

This section begins with some history of insurance redlining and the dual insurance market, followed by a description of federal interventions in the market and discussion of the FHA's coverage of insurance discrimination.

1. History of Discrimination in Homeowners Insurance Markets

Ramzee Nwokolo, writing for the Federal Reserve Bank of Chicago, describes the failure of market competition to make property insurance consistently available and affordable in Black communities:

> [M]ortgage loan redlining and property insurance redlining have a close shared history. The Federal Housing Administration [(FHA)] [through its] post-World War II cheap mortgage arrangements[,] accelerated growth of suburban areas and the flight of the [white] middle class from urban areas, which continued into the 1950s and 1960s. The FHA's strict enforcement of racial covenants segregated African Americans and largely excluded them from this suburban expansion. In the 1940s insurers developed a comprehensive homeowners policy to attract these new suburban homeowners and began to abandon the traditional fire insurance business that had been the norm in urban areas.
>
> A 1978 congressional report on discrimination by property insurers described this process as follows: "With the flight of insurance to suburbia in pursuit of the affluent and white middle class risks, there was a tighter constriction of the inner-city insurance market. . . . Credit and mortgage financing hinged on the purchase of property insurance. . . . Many lending institutions began to follow the example of the insurance industry and refused to do business in certain neighborhoods or sections of the inner city." Furthermore, the National Commission on Urban Problems tied the FHA to redlining practices in both mortgage lending and property insurance underwriting; in its 1968 report, the commission noted the following: "There was evidence of a tacit agreement among all groups—lending institutions, fire insurance companies, and FHA—to block off certain areas of cities within 'red lines,' and not to loan or insure within them. The net result, of course, was that the slums and the areas surrounding them went downhill farther and faster than before." These facts support the argument that property insurance redlining occurred in parallel with mortgage redlining, whose origins trace back to the 1930s.

---

60. *Id.* at 391, 395-98, 401. For a rejoinder, see Todd C. Pittman (National Insurance Task Force), *Rejoinder to Racial Profiling, Insurance Style; A Spirited Defense of the Insurance Industry*, 25 J. URB. AFFAIRS 411, 422 (2003) ("Efforts by insurance companies to eliminate even the appearance of discrimination have been and will continue to be extremely successful and productive . . . the insurance industry has provided considerable leadership, money, and wisdom to expand coverage among low income, minority consumers and will continue to do so.").

By the 1960s unavailability and high cost (unaffordability) of property insurance in urban areas had reached crisis levels. The aptly named Meeting the Insurance Crisis of Our Cities — a 1968 report produced by the U.S. President's National Advisory Panel on Insurance in Riot-Affected Areas (also known as the Hughes Panel) — found that many property owners could not find insurers that would offer them policies, and those owners who could were often charged unaffordable premiums.

The market failure — redlining — was rooted in perception. In areas with more perceived high risks, insurers assessed an average risk potential that exceeded the actual risk potential for all properties in the area. . . . The market failure stemmed from the insurers' inability to assess properties based on their individual risks and their dismissing entire areas based on area demographics or the risk profiles ["environmental hazards"] of select properties in the area.[61]

NOTES AND QUESTIONS

1. Risk Discrimination or Race Discrimination? One court in a featured case below has observed that "[r]isk discrimination is not race discrimination." NAACP v. American Family Mutual Insurance Co., 978 F.2d 287, 290 (7th Cir. 1992). But what about the use of racial or ethnic stereotypes and assumptions about risk that are not backed by empirical evidence? What happens when insurers use tools that are opaque, reflect inaccurate information, or rely on proxies (like geographic rating territories) that disproportionately exclude or price out racial groups in ways that do not accurately measure risk at the individual level?[62] The case files in *American Family* claim a sales manager put it this way in 1988: "Very honestly, I think you write too many blacks. . . . you got to sell good, solid premium paying white people."[63]

An August 2020 joint report of the National Association of Insurance Commissioners and the Center for Insurance Policy and Research, *Milestones in Racial Discrimination within the Insurance Sector,* confirms the history of discriminatory practices, also noting: "While many forms of direct unfair

---

61. Ramzee Nwokolo, *How FAIR Plans Confronted Redlining in America*, 1-3 (Chicago Fed. Letter, No. 484, Sept. 2023), https://doi.org/10.21033/cfl-2023-484.

62. *See* Anya E.R. Prince & Daniel Schwarcz, *Proxy Discrimination in the Age of Artificial Intelligence and Big Data*, 105 Iowa L. Rev. 1257 n.40 (2020); Stephen M. Dane, *The Potential for Racial Discrimination by Homeowners Insurers Through the Use of Geographic Rating Territories*, 24 J. Ins. Regul. 21 (2006), available at https://tinyurl.com/mptfccze. The use of credit scores in the pricing of insurance products is a matter of some regulation and even greater debate. *See* Public Hearing, Prop. & Cas. Ins. (C) Comm. Mkt. Regul. & Consumer Affs. (D) Comm., The Use of Credit-Based Insurance Scores (June 15, 2009), https://content.naic.org/sites/default/files/inline-files/committees_c_090615_public_hearing_transcript.pdf.

63. Gregory D. Squires, *Race, Politics, and the Law: Recurring Themes in the Insurance Redlining Debate in* Insurance Redlining: Disinvestment, Reinvestment, and the Evolving Role of Financial Institutions 1 (Gregory D. Squires Ed., Urban Inst. 1997).

discrimination have been eliminated, subtle, less obvious forms of discrimination remain in access to insurance and risk classification."[64]

2. Fair Access to Insurance Requirements (FAIR) Plans. Given the longstanding unavailability and unaffordability of property insurance in neighborhoods of color, and against the backdrop of the spike in civil unrest during the 1960s, Congress passed the Urban Property Insurance Protection and Reinsurance Act of 1968, creating an incentive for states to create FAIR plans through state-run insurers funded by subsidized private market players. These plans would operate as public-private partnerships to fill gaps in homeowners coverage left by the private market. The federal government incentivized the early FAIR plans by offering "reinsurance" to protect private insurers from risks related to riots or civil disorders. These FAIR plans counteracted redlining (in existence long before the 1960s' civil unrest) by "assessing properties individually" for expected losses rather than making underwriting decisions on "area-based perception." FAIR plans by design have addressed unavailability of insurance more than unaffordability, as they tend to be more expensive while providing less coverage. Although FAIR plans began as a response to racial redlining, their function as plans of last resort has resulted in their filling coverage gaps in disaster-prone and other hard-to-insure markets.[65]

3. Moral Hazard. Many insurance companies will refuse to issue a replacement cost policy, which pays to repair or replace the property fully after a loss, if the market value of the property is significantly less than the replacement cost. The industry justifies this practice using a "moral hazard" rationale, which posits that an insured would be induced to commit fraud to "burn down the house" to obtain more in insurance proceeds than would be available on the sale of the home. The moral hazard theory is not supported by empirical evidence. Given the above research and investigations concerning persistent racial discrimination in home appraisals, what is the potential impact of the refusal to offer replacement cost homeowners insurance coverage in neighborhoods of color?[66]

2. Fair Housing Act Coverage of Homeowners Insurance Discrimination

Discrimination in the provision of homeowners insurance can be based on the neighborhood in which the home is located (a form of redlining), the protected characteristic of the insured, or both. Insurance discrimination not only can make housing unavailable but also can take the form of discriminatory

---

64. Eryn Campbell et al., *Milestones in Racial Discrimination Within the Insurance Sector*, NAIC (Aug. 2020), https://content.naic.org/sites/default/files/cipr-report-milestones-racial-discrimination.pdf.

65. This material is derived from Nwokolo, *FAIR Plans, supra* note 61, at 3-4, 6-7.

66. This material is derived from Squires, *Racial Profiling, supra* note 59, at 395-96, 400.

pricing or claims handling. Although the lower courts are in disagreement about which provisions of the FHA cover homeowners insurance discrimination, it is reasonably well settled that the FHA covers it, as does the 1866 Civil Rights Act.

Most courts have held that insurance redlining is covered by §3604(a) because homeowners insurance is necessary for homeownership.[67] Just as a mortgage loan typically is a prerequisite to the purchase of a home, lenders will not issue a mortgage unless the property is adequately insured. As one court noted: "It is elementary that without insurance, mortgage financing will be unavailable, because a mortgage lender simply will not lend money on the property. Without mortgage financing, homes cannot be purchased. Thus, the availability of insurance and the ability to purchase a home go hand in hand and vary, in direct proportion, to one another." McDiarmid v. Economy Fire & Casualty Co., 604 F. Supp. 105, 107 (S.D. Ohio 1984). HUD in 1989 published regulations supporting the view that discrimination in homeowners insurance constitutes a violation of §3604(a); courts have found HUD's interpretation persuasive, as demonstrated in NAACP v. American Family Mutual Insurance Co., 978 F.2d 287 (7th Cir. 1992):

> Plaintiffs . . . contend that by refusing to write policies (or setting a price too dear) an insurer "make[s a dwelling] unavailable" to the potential buyer. Lenders require their borrowers to secure property insurance. No insurance, no loan; no loan, no house; lack of insurance thus makes housing unavailable [under §3604(a). With respect to discrimination in the provision of services and facilities under §3604(b),] Plaintiffs also submit that property insurance is a "service" rendered "in connection" with the sale of the dwelling. If the world of commerce is divided between "goods" and "services," then insurers supply a "service." "[I]n connection" may be read broadly, and should be (plaintiffs contend) to carry out the national goal of removing obstacles to minorities' ownership of housing. There you have it.
>
> Nothing in the text of the statute permits us to reject these proposed readings. The FHA does not define key terms such as "service" and "make unavailable." By writing its statute in the passive voice—banning an outcome while not saying *who* the actor is, or *how* such actors bring about the forbidden consequence—Congress created ambiguity.
>
> Although §3604 could bear the reading plaintiffs propose, it need not. It does not mention insurers or forbidden devices. Plaintiffs would like us to embrace the "remedial purpose" of the statute. Title VIII indeed is designed to root out racial discrimination in the housing market. Whether it reaches insurers, however, is not something a general reference to purpose discloses. One can always do "more" in pursuit of a goal, but statutes have limits. You cannot discover how far a statute goes by observing the direction in which it points.
>
> . . . [C]lassification of risks is important to insurance, and assigning higher rates to greater risks differs from assigning rates by race. Nothing in the nature

---

67. Not all courts have agreed. *See* Mackey v. Nationwide Insurance Co., 724 F.2d 419 (4th Cir. 1984) (upholding dismissal of plaintiff's insurance redlining claim under the FHA and concluding that Congress could not have intended for §3604(a) to reach "every discriminatory act that might conceivably affect the availability of housing").

of insurance implies that hazard insurers need to engage in disparate treatment, to draw lines on the basis of race rather than risk.

Silence in the legislative history could imply that Members of Congress did not anticipate that the law would apply to insurers. Silence equally could imply that the debate was about the principle of non-discrimination, leaving details to the future. The backward phraseology of §3604 suggests the latter possibility. What was in the heads of the legislators is not, however, the measure of their enactment. Only the statute, and not the debates, is part of the United States Code.

. . . In 1988 [Congress] enacted amendments to the FHA, authorizing HUD to "make rules . . . to carry out this subchapter." 42 U.S.C. §3614a. . . . The Secretary deployed this new rulemaking power in the predictable way, issuing regulations that include, among the conduct prohibited by §3604: "Refusing to provide . . . property or hazard insurance for dwellings or providing such . . . insurance differently because of race." 24 C.F.R. §100.70(d)(4). The United States has filed a brief as *amicus curiae* to support the plaintiffs' position in this case.

Section 3604 is sufficiently pliable that its text can bear the Secretary's construction. Courts should respect a plausible construction by an agency to which Congress has delegated the power to make substantive rules. . . . [I]ndeed long before the Secretary had the power to issue regulations and adjudicate complaints under Title VIII, the Supreme Court [in *Trafficante*] declared that the Secretary's views about the meaning of that statute are entitled to "great weight." . . . Section 3604 applies to discriminatory denials of insurance, and discriminatory pricing, that effectively preclude ownership of housing because of the race of the applicant.

Since *American Family*, courts generally have held that the FHA, particularly §§3604(a) and (b), applies to insurance denials and discriminatory terms and conditions.[68] Courts have divided on whether §3605 reaches insurance discrimination. The Seventh Circuit in *American Family* held that it does not; however, other courts have held that it does. In National Fair Housing Alliance, Inc. v. Prudential Insurance Co., 208 F. Supp. 2d 46, 58 (D.D.C. 2002), the court held:

It is undisputed that individuals are often unable to purchase or to maintain financing for homes without homeowners insurance. Without property insurance, most homeowners are unable to repair their homes when and if disaster should strike. For these reasons, insurance provides the financial assistance necessary to maintain a dwelling. As such, it is reasonable to conclude the Congress intended that homeowners insurance fall within the scope of §3605's protections.

NOTES AND QUESTIONS

1. FHA Litigation and Insurance Markets. The relief in *American Family* included the payment of $14.5 million in damages, $5 million of which was

---

68. *See* Schwemm, HDLL §13:15 n.32.

used to compensate more than 1,600 households, with the remainder directed toward community-based relief such as loan subsidies for home purchase and improvement, homeownership counseling, and a fund for emergency home repairs. The company agreed to create new products and conduct outreach to provide quality coverage to a wider market, including consumers insured through the state-run plan. Further, it agreed to conduct random testing and no longer exclude homes solely on the basis of the home's age or sales price. It also agreed to expand its marketing efforts and open offices in predominantly African-American communities.[69] Do you think that litigation settlements such as this have the potential to increase profits for the industry or expose them to more risk?

2. Disparate Impact and Homeowners Insurance. In the 1990s, the National Fair Housing Alliance (NFHA), with the assistance of Dr. Calvin Bradford, analyzed the effects of certain neutral underwriting criteria widely used by the major homeowners insurers. Restricting homeowners insurance eligibility to properties meeting a minimum value or maximum age requirement were two criteria examined in particular. After NFHA's finding of disproportionate racial impacts resulting from these policies, and after the filing of administrative fair housing complaints, NFHA and several major insurance companies agreed on a less discriminatory alternative that excluded fewer properties from coverage and satisfied the legitimate business interests of the companies.[70] Can you think of what those less restrictive alternatives might be?

The insurance industry consistently has disputed that the FHA applies to it, as further discussed in the next note. Moreover, the industry has pressed the argument that disparate impact theory is antithetical to fundamental insurance concepts because the theory allows the FHA to displace traditional, risk-based underwriting and pricing. More recently, since the Supreme Court recognized FHA disparate impact claims in 2015, the industry has argued that the theory improperly requires insurance companies to consider race rather than risk in rating and underwriting decisions (to avoid liability). No court at the time of publication has agreed that FHA disparate impact claims are categorically unavailable in the insurance setting.[71]

---

69. DOJ, Civil Rights Division, *Housing and Civil Enforcement Cases Documents*, https://www.justice.gov/crt/housing-and-civil-enforcement-cases-documents-469 (last visited July 30, 2024).

70. Contemporaneous announcements of these insurance settlements are on file with the Editors.

71. *See, e.g.*, Prop. Cas. Insurers Ass'n of Am. v. Todman, No. 13 C 8564, 2024 WL 1283581, at *25 (N.D. Ill. Mar. 26, 2024) (on appeal); Nat'l Ass'n of Mut. Ins. Companies v. United States Dep't of Hous. & Urb. Dev., No. CV 13-966 (RJL), 2023 WL 6142257, at *9 (D.D.C. Sept. 19, 2023); *see also* Application of the Fair Housing Act's Discriminatory Effects Standard to Insurance, 81 FED. REG. 69012-02 (Oct. 5, 2016) (on court-ordered reconsideration of industry comments to its 2013 disparate impact rule, HUD determined that "categorical exemptions or safe harbors for insurance practices [under the discriminatory effects standard] are unworkable and inconsistent with the broad fair housing objectives and obligations" of the FHA, and that industry concerns "can and should be addressed on a case-by-case basis.").

3. Homeowners Insurance and Claims Handling. The FHA covers not only denials of insurance but also handling of claims after policies are written. In Huskey v. State Farm Fire & Casualty Company, No. 22 C 7014, 2023 WL 5848164 (N.D. Ill. Sept. 11, 2023), the court held that discrimination in claims handling was a denial of a service in connection with a dwelling, denying dismissal of plaintiffs' §3604(b) claim. (The court dismissed claims under §§3604(a) and 3605.) The plaintiffs alleged that the company's use of algorithmic decisionmaking tools (to predict the likelihood of fraud and determine whether to pay claims immediately) resulted in statistically significant racial disparities in how the insurer processed claims. The court found that the plaintiffs' "survey of around 800 State Farm policyholders plausibly suggests that when Black policyholders file claims, relative to white policyholders, State Farm imposes longer wait times, and it demands extra paperwork and additional interactions." *Id.* at *8.

4. The McCarran-Ferguson Act and Inverse Preemption. In 1945, in light of Supreme Court precedent subjecting national insurers to federal regulation, Congress sought to preserve the traditional role of the states in the taxation and regulation of the business of insurance by passing the McCarran-Ferguson Act, 15 U.S.C. §1011, et seq. This Act provides that "No Act of Congress shall be construed to invalidate, impair, or supersede any law enacted by any State for the purpose of regulating the business of insurance . . . unless such Act specifically relates to the business of insurance." Insurance company defendants often argue that the primacy of state insurance law creates an "inverse preemption" problem, contending specifically that plaintiffs should not be able to seek remedies under the FHA for insurance discrimination where such insurance is subject to a state regulatory regime.

No court, however, has accepted these arguments to exempt the insurance industry entirely from the FHA's coverage. Today virtually every state has enacted fair housing laws similar to the FHA; these substantially equivalent laws give states access to federal enforcement funding. It would be difficult to contend that the FHA conflicts or interferes with insurance law or policy of a state when the state has also adopted the same requirements as the FHA. As the *American Family* court concluded, "[d]uplication is not conflict." On the other hand, courts have viewed disparate treatment and disparate impact claims differently in the insurance context. In Saunders v. Farmers Insurance Exchange, 537 F.3d 961, 967 (8th Cir. 2008), the court held: "Federal civil rights statutes are drafted broadly, so a statute might "impair" state insurance laws when applied in some ways, but not in others. For example, a federal claim alleging that an insurer's coverage denial was the product of overt racial animus would doubtless be in harmony with state insurance regulation, while a suit challenging the racially disparate impact of industry-wide rate classifications may usurp core rate-making functions of the State's administrative regime." Thus, it seems that, outside certain rate-making decisions at the heart of a state's regulatory purview, the FHA and state law will more likely complement than conflict with one another.

5. Homeowners Insurance and Access to Rental Housing. Discrimination in the making and pricing of homeowners policies can also harm renters. NFHA brought a case against Travelers challenging an alleged policy of refusing to provide insurance to landlords who were renting to tenants using federal housing vouchers. The complaint alleged that in the investigation, a Travelers broker said that "subsidized housing is a problem," and the landlord would need to "pay[] more for less" on the secondary insurance market. NFHA argued that this form of exclusion had a disproportionate impact on Black tenants and women-headed households. The court upheld the claim on a motion to dismiss, and the parties eventually settled. National Fair Housing Alliance v. Travelers Indemnity Co., 261 F. Supp. 3d 20, 22-23 (D.D.C. 2017).

Professor Allyson Gold, in *Insuring Justice*, 101 N.C. L. Rev. 729, 768-70 (2023), describes the "downstream effects" of homeowners insurance discrimination on tenants. Barriers to acquiring insurance for rental property owners, particularly those in neighborhoods of color, affect the supply of rental housing units and the ability of landlords to maintain their properties. "[H]omes and occupants that are most in need of protection may be the most difficult to insure, leaving tenants vulnerable to harms from personal injury and property damage."

6. Homeowners Insurance and Disability. Some housing providers serving people with disabilities have used the FHA to challenge insurers' refusal to provide property insurance based on disability. In Nevels v. Western World Insurance Co., 359 F. Supp. 2d 1110 (W.D. Wash. 2004), the court denied a motion to dismiss FHA claims under §§3604, 3605, and 3617 alleging refusal to renew policies for adult family homes because they provided housing to persons with mental illnesses. The court held that "[w]ithout such insurance, Plaintiffs cannot ensure that non-segregated, community-based housing for people with mental disabilities will remain available." *Id.* at 1122.

Chapter Summary

- A long history of discriminatory policies and practices in the provision of wealth-building financial products has created a dual credit market that continues to this day. As discriminatory *denials* of credit persist at the individual and neighborhood level, predatory practices that *exploit* the dual credit market also have endured, with devastating consequences for renters, homeowners, neighborhoods, and communities.
- Discrimination is subject to challenge whether it is based on the characteristics of the borrower seeking residential real-estate financing, or on the characteristics of the neighborhood surrounding the home ("redlining").
- A constellation of federal and state statutes prohibits discrimination against consumers in their use of mortgage credit and other financial services such as insurance and appraisals. These include the FHA, ECOA, Community Reinvestment Act, and §§1981 and 1982. There also

are a number of statutes, including TILA, RESPA, and HOEPA, that provide additional consumer protections from practices that are unfair, deceptive, or abusive.

- This chapter primarily addresses the most applicable antidiscrimination provision under the FHA, 42 U.S.C. §3605, covering a broad range of transactions involving the purchasing, improving, appraising, brokering, financing, and insuring of residential real estate.

- Section 3605, like §3604, prohibits discrimination because of a protected characteristic both in making available a real estate-related transaction and in its terms and conditions.

- To make a claim of reverse redlining, a plaintiff must show that the defendants' lending practices and loan terms were "unfair" and "predatory," and either that the defendants intentionally targeted on the basis of race, or that their practices had a disparate impact on the basis of race.

- An appraisal, or estimate of the value of a dwelling, is a crucial component of a real estate-related transaction; a mortgage lender relies on an appraisal to ensure its loan is backed by sufficient collateral, and the borrower relies on it to obtain the mortgage necessary to become a homeowner. Research and investigations that examine whether race is (still) influencing property valuations reveal that, in far too many cases, it is. Section 3605 of the FHA explicitly covers discrimination in the making of appraisals and in the terms and conditions of appraisals.

- It is reasonably well settled that the FHA, as well as the 1866 Civil Rights Act, covers discrimination in the provision of homeowners insurance, which can be based on the neighborhood in which the home is located (a form of redlining), the protected characteristic of the insured, or both. Insurance discrimination not only can make housing unavailable but also can take the form of discriminatory pricing or claims handling.

PART V

GOVERNMENT HOUSING AND DEVELOPMENT PROGRAMS AND AFFIRMATIVE DUTIES

Chapter 12 provides an overview of federal housing and development programs. Knowledge of these programs is important both because they encompass a significant share of affordable housing in this country and because of their roles in exacerbating and potentially ameliorating residential discrimination and segregation. Chapter 13 addresses the statutory mandate for government agencies affirmatively to further the antidiscrimination and pro-integration purposes of the Fair Housing Act.

CHAPTER 12

FEDERAL HOUSING AND DEVELOPMENT PROGRAMS

One of the greatest obstacles to achieving housing equity has been holding the federal government to its own professed ideals and constitutional and statutory mandates. Racial and other forms of discrimination and segregation were built into federal housing and development programs. Other federally funded programs (such as interstate highways) and supported activities facilitated and fueled segregation. Formally, the federal government took steps purporting to end (although not to undo) such discrimination and segregation with the 1962 Executive Order 11063, Title VI of the 1964 Civil Rights Act, the 1968 FHA, and similar provisions. Indeed, the FHA has two sections that direct HUD and all other executive agencies to act "affirmatively to further" the FHA in administering housing and urban development programs. Other housing and community development statutes include similar requirements. Yet, this chapter demonstrates (as do Chapters 1 and 13) that housing segregation has been entrenched in federal housing and development programs and has persisted for decades following formal declarations of equality. Community resistance and private enforcement actions have been crucial in breaking down barriers to fair housing in federal programs.

A. OVERVIEW OF CURRENT MAJOR FEDERAL HOUSING AND DEVELOPMENT PROGRAMS

1. Housing Programs

The federal government has a variety of housing assistance programs. These address both homeownership and rentals, for single-family (usually defined as one- to four-family) and multifamily housing.

Tax subsidies for homeowners are the largest and most expensive of the programs, costing taxpayers more than $80.1 billion in FY 2022.[1] These tax

---

1. U.S. Dep't of Treas., *Tax Expenditures: Fiscal Year 2023*, Tbl. I (2021), https://home.treasury.gov/system/files/131/Tax-Expenditures-FY2023.pdf.

subsidies (or "tax expenditures") include (1) the ability to exclude up to $250,000 of the capital gain from the sale of a home and (2) the ability of a taxpayer who itemizes to deduct interest paid on a mortgage loan and real estate taxes, all subject to conditions and limitations.[2] These subsidies are regressive; that is, they provide the most assistance to the highest income, highest wealth households who need assistance the least. For FY 2022, 66.6 percent of the benefit went to households with incomes exceeding $200,000 per year.[3]

These subsidies favor white families far more than Black or Hispanic families, with white families securing *more* than the average tax benefit and Black and Hispanic families only 54 percent and 38 percent, respectively, of the average tax benefit, all in 2019.[4] All homeownership assistance disproportionately benefits white households more than Black households or others of color. As of 2022, there was a 30-point difference between white homeownership and Black homeownership—75 percent for white people and 45 percent for Black people.[5] The racial gap in homeownership is multidimensional; there are also significant differences in home and neighborhood values along racial lines. Thus, "[e]ven when African Americans do own their own homes, they experience the supposed benefits differently in comparison with white homeowners."[6]

The next most extensive assistance is a separate structure of support for homeownership. This starts with the Federal Reserve system, the Government-Sponsored Enterprises (GSEs)—FNMA (Fannie Mae, the Federal National Mortgage Association) and FHLMC (Freddie Mac, the Federal Home Loan Mortgage Corporation)—and a government agency named GNMA (Ginnie Mae, the Government National Mortgage Association). Ginnie Mae is a federal agency; the GSEs are federally chartered and shareholder owned, making mortgage credit available by purchasing loans (and freeing lenders to make more loans), packaging the loans into mortgage-backed securities, and

2. Internal Revenue Service, U.S. Dep't of Treas., *Pub. No. 530, Tax Information for Homeowners* (2022), https://www.irs.gov/publications/p530#en_US_2021_publink100011835.

3. Joint Comm. on Tax'n, *Estimates of Federal Tax Expenditures for Fiscal Years 2022-2026*, at 50 (2022), https://www.jct.gov/publications/2022/jcx-22-22/; Tax Policy Center, *What Are Itemized Deductions and Who Claims Them?*, *in* Tax Policy Center Briefing Book, https://www.taxpolicy center.org/briefing-book/what-are-itemized-deductions-and-who-claims-them (last visited Aug. 10, 2023).

4. Janet Holtzblatt et al., Racial and Ethnic Disparities in the Home Mortgage Interest Deduction 2 (Tax Policy Center 2024), https://www.taxpolicycenter.org/sites/default/files/publication/165817/racial_and_ethnic_disparities_in_the_home_mortgage_interest_deduct ion.pdf.

5. HUD, Off. of Pol'y Dev. & Rsch., *Closing the African American Homeownership Gap* (2021), https://www.huduser.gov/portal/pdredge/pdr-edge-featd-article-032221.html (quoting U.S. Census Bureau); U.S. Dep't of Treas., Off. of Econ. Pol., *Racial Differences in Economic Security: Housing* (2022), https://home.treasury.gov/news/featured-stories/racial-differences -in-economic-security-housing (75 percent homeownership for whites, 45 percent for Blacks, 48 percent for Hispanics, and 57 percent for non-Hispanic households of any other race).

6. Keeanga-Yamahtta Taylor, Race for Profit: How Banks and the Real Estate Industry Undermined Black Homeownership 259-62 (UNC Press 2019).

guaranteeing them. The GSEs have been fully controlled by the federal government, which holds them in conservatorship, since 2008.

This structural assistance also includes the homeownership programs of the Federal Housing Administration (part of HUD[7]), the Department of Veterans Affairs (VA), and the Rural Housing Service of the Department of Agriculture. Some of these purportedly are "unsubsidized," which means that they serve households that are not in low-income and low-wealth strata, but of course the aid — the facilitation of mortgage financing and related services — comes at a cost that all taxpayers pay.

These aside, there are programs, designated as "subsidized" or "affordable" housing, that assist people who do not have enough income or wealth to secure decent housing in the private market. This is about half the households in the United States, or approximately 65.5 million households. Five points about these programs are essential to understanding federal housing subsidies for low- and moderate-income people:

- Taken as a whole, they assist only about one in four households who need and are eligible for housing assistance.[8] Between 2018 and 2020, more than 21 million households in the United States were cost-burdened enough to qualify for housing assistance, but only 5.3 million received it.[9]

- They do not all provide the same level of assistance. Some are "deep subsidy" programs that offer the most help; others are "shallow subsidy" programs that offer some aid but not enough to make decent housing affordable to people with low incomes or wealth.

- Altogether, they cost substantially less than what the United States spends to subsidize higher wealth homeownership — more than $80 billion in FY 2022 for homeownership compared to $67 billion for housing assistance in FY 2023, although this does not take into account the fact that some of the subsidized housing also involves capital assets held by state or local government agencies.[10]

---

7. References to "HUD" include references to its predecessor agencies, principally the Housing and Home Finance Agency (HHFA). The Department of Housing and Urban Development was created in 1965; the Honorable Dr. Robert C. Weaver became the first Secretary of HUD. *See* Wendell Pritchett, Robert Clifton Weaver and the American City: The Life and Times of an Urban Reformer (U. Chicago Press 2008); Robert C. Weaver, The Negro Ghetto (Harcourt, Brace 1948).

8. Nat'l Low Income Hous. Coal., Advocates' Guide 2023: A Primer on Federal Affordable Housing & Community Development Programs & Policies 4-2 (2023) [hereinafter *Advocates' Guide 2023*], https://nlihc.org/sites/default/files/2023-03/2023_Advocates -Guide.pdf. The Advocates' Guide is updated annually.

9. Erik Gartland, Ctr. for Budget and Pol'y Priorities, *Funding Limitations Create Widespread Unmet Need for Rental Assistance* 3 (Feb. 15, 2022), available at https://www.cbpp.org/research /housing/funding-limitations-create-widespread-unmet-need-for-rental-assistance.

10. *The Federal Government's Support for Low-Income Housing Expanded During the Pandemic*, Peter G. Peterson Found. (Apr. 23, 2024), https://www.pgpf.org/blog/2024/04/how-does -the-federal-government-support-housing-for-low-income-households. A program like public housing produces a capital asset (the housing) owned by a governmental unit. Programs like

- Even the one in four households who receive federal housing subsidies — including the portion of that group who receive deep subsidies — are not necessarily enjoying unmitigated blessings. Much of that subsidized housing is substandard, with some posing serious threats to life and health: the presence of lead-based paint, lead dust, mold, vermin, and rodents; or inadequate HVAC systems and roofs. Often that subsidized housing is in areas of high crime and substandard public education, transportation, recreation, and safety. Most of it is in high-poverty, racially segregated, and underresourced neighborhoods. Much of it is located near SuperFund sites and other environmentally hazardous locations.[11]
- "Affordability" is a misleading concept. Housing advocates long have urged that affordability be calculated by determining how much a household of a given size and composition requires for necessities other than housing and calculating how much income (if any) remains. This is called the "residual income" approach.[12] It never has been accepted by the government. Rather, the federal government has established affordability as a percentage of income, regardless of household size or composition, and regardless of variables such as how many are children or elderly or people with disabilities. Originally, affordability was set at 20 percent for homeowners and 25 percent for renters; however, in 1981, to reduce the amount of subsidy Congress was asked to pay, affordability was redefined as 30 percent of income.[13] For people with very low incomes, 30 percent of their income is far too much to pay for housing.

This chapter focuses on the "subsidized" or "affordable" housing programs. There are three major categories of these programs:

- Public housing, federally financed, low-rent units, usually owned by public housing authorities.
- Vouchers of various kinds.
- Project-based rental assistance.

---

resident-based vouchers and aid to private developers do not produce capital assets. But this difference is not reflected in budgetary calculations because the United States does not have a capital budget.

11. Shriver Center on Poverty Law & Earthjustice, *Poisonous Homes: The Fight for Environmental Justice in Federally Assisted Housing* (June 2020), available at https://www.povertylaw.org/report/poisonoushomes/; Elizabeth K. Julian & Michael M. Daniel, *Separate and Unequal: The Root and Branch of Public Housing Segregation*, 23 Clearinghouse Rev. 666 (1989-90); *see also* Baez v. N.Y. City Hous. Auth., No. 13-cv-8916, 2018 WL 6242224 (S.D.N.Y. Nov. 29, 2018) (mold and other defects in New York City public housing and Section 8 units); U.S. Gov. Accountability Off., *The Danger of Lead Paint Hazards in Two HUD Programs* (Oct. 26, 2021), https://www.gao.gov/blog/danger-lead-paint-hazards-two-hud-programs.

12. Michael E. Stone, *What Is Housing Affordability? The Case for the Residual Income Approach*, 17 Hous. Pol'y Debate 151 (2006); Whitney Airgood-Obrycki et al., *"The Rent Eats First": Rental Housing Unaffordability in the United States*, 33 Hous. Pol'y Debate 1272, 1273 (2023); Michael E. Stone, Shelter Poverty: New Ideas on Housing Affordability (Temple U. Press 1993).

13. Stone, Shelter Poverty, *supra* note 12, at 34.

In considering these, one should distinguish between supply-side and demand-side, project-based or resident-based, and deep or shallow subsidies. "Supply-side approaches include building hard units of public housing" and "creating tax incentives for private developers to build affordable units."[14] Most vouchers are demand-side subsidies tied to the household seeking housing; therefore, they are mostly resident-based, although some are project-based. Public housing and vouchers are deep subsidies, with cost to the resident based on resident income; project-based rental assistance usually involves shallow subsidies, reducing resident cost somewhat but without regard to what the household can in any sense afford.[15] We provide here a brief description of the programs, their historical development, and how they relate to one another.

WHAT IS A PUBLIC HOUSING AUTHORITY?

A public housing authority (PHA) is a state or local entity created by state law that is authorized to engage or assist in the development or operation of affordable housing, or a consortium of such entities or bodies. PHAs receive most of their funding from Congress through HUD and are subject to HUD oversight and regulation.

a. Public Housing

As discussed in Chapter 1, public housing began in 1933 as an employment program operated by the Public Works Administration. This was replaced in 1937 by the U.S. Housing Act, which created the public housing structure we know today. Public housing was a project-based, (initially) shallow subsidy program for which the federal government paid the initial capital costs of the housing, which was owned by local (and, in a few cases, state) public housing authorities (PHAs). All the later costs of maintenance and capital repairs came from tenants' rents. A federal agency (first the U.S. Housing Authority, then the Public Housing Administration, now HUD) regulates the PHAs' decisions about what housing shall be built where and who shall live in it; much of the federal control is exercised through the Annual Contributions Contract between HUD and the PHA as well as by regulations and guidance.

Public housing was racially segregated from its origin, but by the 1960s, public housing for families — housing of last resort in a dual housing market — increasingly became identified as serving Black tenants and other tenants of color.[16] Buildings aged, maintenance costs and the need for capital

---

14. Stacy Seicshnaydre, *Missed Opportunity: Furthering Fair Housing in the Housing Choice Voucher Program*, 79 Law & Contemp. Probs. 173, 174 (2016).

15. A resource that describes these and other programs is the Advocates' Guide 2023, *supra* note 8.

16. "By the early 1960s, public housing in the nation's largest cities was overwhelmingly housing for minorities. . . . The racial transformation of many projects was largely responsible for the decline in support for the program." Pritchett, *supra* note 7, at 234.

repairs increased, and residents' incomes stagnated at far too little to pay the rents demanded, let alone the real costs of operation. Racial and antipoverty protests drove changes in the public housing system. Congress provided a series of small subsidies to help with operating expenses. Then, in 1969, Congress made a major change with the enactment of the Brooke Amendment, which limited resident contributions to 25 percent of household income, transforming public housing into a deep subsidy program. (In 1981, Congress increased the resident contribution to 30 percent of household income.) This was accompanied by a representation that Congress would provide an operating subsidy adequate to maintain the properties and "modernization" funds to enable the PHAs to make necessary capital improvements. Congress never has honored these expectations: It provides only a fraction of the operating subsidy required each year and a portion of the funding required for capital repairs. In 2010, a HUD-sponsored study concluded that PHAs had a $25 billion capital needs backlog, which was estimated to grow by $3.4 billion each year. PHA organizations estimated the FY 2020 capital needs backlog at $70 billion.[17]

In 1993, Congress created the Housing Opportunities for People Everywhere (HOPE VI) program, which demolished tens of thousands of public housing units, usually replacing them with fewer public housing units on the original sites along with other units for market rate residents. Many displaced residents who were unable to return or chose to leave received vouchers. "The [professed] goal of the program was to bring new investment and optimism to neighborhoods suffering from concentrated poverty." Yet, HOPE VI made "almost no reference to desegregation." Most assisted residents experienced improved living conditions but remained in racially and economically segregated areas.[18]

The stock of public housing has been dwindling for decades, with many developments either demolished or converted into site-based or project-based "affordable" housing. The latter units may still be operated by the PHA, but the "rent" is paid through a voucher (described below). As of 2022, the 2,738 PHAs had 924,377 units, housing 1.7 million residents, of whom 616,125 were children.[19] Fifty-two percent of public housing residents were elderly and 43 percent were nonelderly families with children; 48 percent of the households were Black, 10 percent were Hispanic, and 39 percent were non-Hispanic white.[20]

---

17. ADVOCATES' GUIDE 2023, *supra* note 8, at 4-36.

18. Pritchett, *supra* note 7, at 348; Florence Wagman Roisman, *Keeping the Promise: Ending Racial Discrimination and Segregation in Federally Financed Housing*, 48 How. L.J. 913, 922-23 (2005).

19. ADVOCATES' GUIDE 2023, *supra* note 8, at 4-32, 33.

20. HUD, Off. of Pol'y Dev. & Rsch., *Public Housing: Image Versus Facts*, U.S. HOUS. MKT. COND. 3, 4 (May 1995), https://www.huduser.gov/periodicals/ushmc/1stqtr95.pdf.

b. *Vouchers*

Demand-side, consumer-based housing subsidies operate by giving assistance to individuals to increase their purchasing power in the private market. These subsidies have a long history in the United States because they seem to be less expensive and are ideologically more acceptable generally than is housing produced by government.[21] "Real estate interests proposed [such subsidies] in the 1930s as an alternative to the public housing program." The 1965 Housing Act introduced the "rent supplement" program that "allowed" households to find their own housing in the private market, with Congress paying the difference between rental cost and 25 percent of household income.[22] Congress launched an Experimental Housing Allowance Program in 1970[23] and then enacted the 1974 Housing Act, which initiated several programs under its Section 8, including certificates, which could be resident-based or project-based. The certificates have since become vouchers; the primary variety is called Housing Choice Vouchers (HCVs).

"The HCV program is HUD's largest rental assistance program, assisting nearly 2.3 million households as of August 2022. . . ."[24] The vouchers are administered by PHAs and other state and local agencies. Since FY 2008, Congress has funded a small number of vouchers for particular populations: HUD-Veterans Affairs Supportive Housing (HUD-VASH), Family Unification (to avert or end foster care), Foster Youth to Independence (FYI), and Mainstream and Non-Elderly Disabled.[25] In addition, there are Tenant Protection Vouchers and Enhanced Vouchers to address particular kinds of housing situations. HUD allocates vouchers to PHAs. PHAs then distribute the vouchers to households on the waiting list, and the voucher holder has

---

21. Supply-side subsidies seem to be more expensive because the U.S. budget does not credit capital assets. Demand-side subsidies are more consistent with small government, individualistic philosophies. But with demand-side subsidies, the public "buil[ds] up no equity, and possesses nothing. After 40 years of paying out subsidies for traditional public housing, the public owns, free and clear, a development with useful remaining life and the land it occupies." Chester Hartman, *Rejoinder to "Another Look at Housing Allowances,"* 5 J. URB. AFFAIRS 159, 159, 160 (1983); *see also* Chester Hartman, *Housing Allowances: A Critical Look*, 5 J. URB. AFFAIRS 41, 53 (1983) ("housing allowances do not . . . produce housing. . . . Thus, the argument that it's a cheaper approach is comparing apples and oranges. They are programs that do different things.").

22. Pritchett, *supra* note 7, at 257. The 1965 Act also introduced the Section 23 Leased Public Housing Program, which allowed PHAs to use private market housing for the first time. *See also* Taylor, *supra* note 6, at 222-23, 240-41, 246-47, 250.

23. Hartman, *Housing Allowances: A Critical Look*, *supra* note 21, at 41, 42. The program was not effectuated immediately, at least in part because HUD had indicated that integration would be a focus of its implementation. Pritchett, *supra* note 7, at 265-66.

24. ADVOCATES' GUIDE 2023, *supra* note 8, at 4-1, citing HUD's PIH (Public and Indian Housing) Data Dashboard.

25. This last category is to compensate for policies allowing exclusion of nonelderly persons with disabilities from housing designated for elderly persons only. Note that "nonelderly" means people 18 and older; in general, housing programs for households that include people with disabilities do not include households where children are the people who have disabilities.

a limited time period in which to find a unit that meets HUD's rental rate requirements (discussed below) and can pass an inspection by the PHA. If the voucher holder can find such a unit, the landlord must then be willing to accept the voucher (as discussed below, in most situations landlords are free to refuse to accept vouchers).

HUD reports that in 2021, 32 percent of voucher households were elderly and 25 percent had a household member with a disability; 65 percent of voucher households were Black or Hispanic, as compared to 40 percent of U.S. renter households; 78 percent were female-headed households, including 32 percent with children.[26] The demand for vouchers far exceeds the supply: HUD data analyzed by the Center on Budget Priorities showed that due to inadequate funding, just one in four voucher-eligible families received any type of federal rental assistance,[27] and the average time spent on a voucher waiting list was two and a half years, with some waits as long as eight years.[28] Because eligibility is limited to families of very low income, those on the waiting list are at high risk of eviction and homelessness.[29]

AN ILLUSTRATION OF LIFE ON THE WAITING LIST FOR A VOUCHER: TRIMUEL V. CHICAGO HOUSING AUTHORITY, 695 F. SUPP. 3d 972 (N.D. ILL. 2023).

In 2008, Vinzella Trimuel and her sister applied for vouchers from the Chicago Housing Authority (CHA). CHA approved their applications and placed them on the waitlist. In 2010, Ms. Trimuel was evicted from her home. She contacted CHA and was told she was still on the waitlist. In that same year, Ms. Trimuel married and experienced domestic violence at the hands of her spouse. As a consequence of the domestic violence, "she suffers from multiple disabilities, including anxiety, depression, and post-traumatic stress disorder."

Ms. Trimuel's housing situation was "unstable; she stayed at various times with her spouse, friends, family, and charitable organizations, including her parents' church and domestic violence shelters." She and caseworkers contacted CHA multiple times and were told that she was still on the waitlist. However, "[u]nbeknownst to" Ms. Trimuel, CHA removed her from the waitlist in 2013,

---

26. Laurie Goodman et al., *Leveraging Financing to Encourage Landlords to Accept Housing Choice Vouchers* 1 (Urban Institute 2022), https://www.urban.org/research/publication/leveraging -financing-encourage-landlords-accept-housing-choice-vouchers.

27. Will Fischer et al., *More Housing Vouchers: Most Important Step to Help More People Afford Stable Homes*, Ctr. on Budget & Pol'y Priorities (May 13, 2021), https://www.cbpp.org/research /housing/more-housing-vouchers-most-important-step-to-help-more-people-afford-stable -homes.

28. Sonja Acosta & Erik Gartland, *Families Wait Years for Housing Vouchers Due to Inadequate Funding; Expanding Program Would Reduce Hardship, Improve Equity*, Ctr. on Budget & Pol'y Priorities (July 22, 2021), https://www.cbpp.org/research/housing/families-wait-years-for -housing-vouchers-due-to-inadequate-funding.

29. *Id.*

"purportedly for failing to complete [a] Wait List Update Survey" that she says she never received.

When her sister reached the top of the waiting list in 2017, Ms. Trimuel inquired about her status and was told that she had been removed from the waitlist. She asked to be reinstated, requesting a reasonable accommodation, "outlining the effects of her disabilities, and noting that" if she had failed to update her address, it would have been because of her disabilities and housing instability. CHA's "reasonable accommodation department approved this request, but its Voucher Program department declined to follow through. . . ."

Ms. Trimuel sued CHA, the state agency that administers the federal voucher program designed "to assist low-income families to obtain decent, safe, sanitary, and affordable housing." CHA moved to dismiss her suit, arguing that she had no property interest to defend, that she lacked standing (because she suffered no injury), and that the statute of limitations and laches barred her suit. In addition, CHA challenged her claims on the merits under the FHA, Americans with Disabilities Act (ADA), Rehab Act, and Illinois Human Rights Act (IHRA).

The court rejected the arguments based on property interest, standing, limitations, and laches, and held that Ms. Trimuel's reasonable accommodation claim survived the motion to dismiss under the FHA, ADA, Rehab Act, and IHRA. CHA argued that the request for reinstatement on the waitlist was "not only unreasonable but impossible because the 2008 waitlist has since been terminated and a 2014 waitlist has taken its place. CHA claimed that it cannot possibly place Plaintiff 'on a closed wait list' or 'on the current wait list' when she has not applied to that list." One might think that only Dickens or Kafka could do justice to CHA's position, but District Judge John Robert Blakey rises to the occasion by observing that CHA's "argument boggles the non-bureaucratic mind."

Voucher holders pay at least 30 percent of household income for rent including utilities and could pay up to 40 percent of income in the first year and an unlimited percentage thereafter, up to a payment standard set by the PHA. Using funds appropriated by Congress and allocated by HUD, the PHA pays to the landlord the difference between the resident's contribution and the payment standard. The payment standard "must be between 90% and 110% of HUD's Fair Market Rent (FMR), the rent in the metropolitan area for a modest apartment. HUD sets FMRs annually. Nationally, the average voucher household in 2021 paid $395 a month for rent and utilities."[30]

The payment standard often is too low to enable voucher holders to live in areas "that have better schools, lower crime, and greater access to employment opportunities—often called high opportunity areas."[31] PHAs may increase the payment standard generally and specifically can do so as a reasonable accommodation for a person with a disability. PHAs may, and in 24 designated large metropolitan areas must, set payment standards up to 110 percent of Small Area Fair Market Rents (SAFMR), which enables the use of vouchers in more expensive, high-opportunity neighborhoods.[32]

---

30. ADVOCATES' GUIDE 2023, *supra* note 8, at 4-3.

31. *Id.*

32. *Id.*

SMALL AREA FAIR MARKET RENTS (SAFMRS)

The history of SAFMRs is instructive for advocates. In 2007, the Inclusive Communities Project (ICP) of Dallas, Texas, sued HUD, alleging that HUD's setting a single FMR for the 12-county Dallas metropolitan area steered Black voucher holders into high-poverty, low-opportunity neighborhoods of color.[33] In 2010, HUD settled that suit, creating a demonstration project for several metropolitan areas, including Dallas, that would use SAFMRs to "provide Section 8 tenants with greater ability to move into opportunity areas where jobs, transportation, and educational opportunities exist, and prevent undue subsidy in lower-rent areas."[34] In 2014, "ICP challenged HUD's subsequent decision to decrease rents in white-area zip codes and to increase rents in zip codes with high poverty rates."[35] A study of the demonstration program concluded that a "ZIP code policy improves neighborhood quality for voucher recipients substantially."[36] In 2016, HUD issued a final rule employing SAFMRs for certain metropolitan areas and allowing their use more generally, writing: "The use of Small Area FMRs is expected to give HCV tenants access to areas of high opportunity and lower poverty . . . by providing a subsidy that is adequate to cover rents in those areas . . ., replacing a "formula [that] has not proven effective in addressing the problem of concentrated poverty and economic and racial segregation in neighborhoods."[37]

In addition to the payment standard, there are other problems that reduce the utility of vouchers, particularly for people of color, people with disabilities, and families with children.[38] One is the limit on the amount of time within which the family must use the voucher. Generally, this is 60 days, although the PHA can extend the time (as a reasonable accommodation for a disability or for other reasons). "HUD's most recent data indicate that 30% of voucher recipients return their unused vouchers because they cannot find a suitable unit, though this figure varies significantly across housing agencies and markets."[39] HUD and PHA management problems also impede voucher utilization.[40] A HUD Office of Inspector General Report in 2021 noted that

---

33. This history draws extensively on Seicshnaydre, *Missed Opportunity, supra* note 14, at 176-77. Two editors of this casebook served on ICP's Board when these actions were taken.

34. 75 FED. REG. at 27, 808, *quoted in* Seicshnaydre, *Missed Opportunity, supra* note 14, at 177.

35. Seicshnaydre, *Missed Opportunity, supra* note 14, at 177 n.22.

36. Robert A. Collinson & Peter Ganong, *The Incidence of Housing Voucher Generosity* (2015), http://papers.ssrn.com/sol3/papers.cfm?abstract_id=2255799, *quoted in* Seicshnaydre, *Missed Opportunity, supra* note 14, at 177; Goodman et al., *supra* note 26, at 2-4.

37. *Establishing a More Effective Fair Market Rent System; Using Small Area Fair Market Rents in the Housing Choice Voucher Program Instead of the Current 50th Percentile FMRs*, 81 FED. REG. 80567 (Nov. 16, 2016) (codified at 24 C.F.R. pts. 888, 982, 983, 985 (2022)).

38. It long has been understood that "vigorous attacks on racial discrimination" are essential to the success of demand-side subsidy programs. Hartman, *Housing Allowances, supra* note 21, at 47, 50; Hartman, *Rejoinder, supra* note 21 at 165 (quoting, *inter alia*, President Reagan's Commission on Housing, which urged the use of housing allowances, stating that "Discrimination clearly impedes the ability of minority households to make full use of the program, either in terms of access to adequate housing or of freedom of locational choice").

39. Goodman et al., *supra* note 26, at 2.

40. "[I]n the HCV program, PHA budgeting structures and administrative incentives impede agencies from focusing on residential mobility." Megan Haberle, *Furthering Fair Housing: Lessons*

more than 62 percent of PHAs had utilization rates considered unsatisfactory by HUD, and that 81,000 vouchers were available for use but were unused.[41] In addition, many voucher holders live in substandard units, underresourced neighborhoods, or both. "[Fifty]% of voucher holders end up living in areas of concentrated poverty, which affects the renters and the well-being of their children as adults."[42]

As a matter of federal law, the voucher program is voluntary, and housing providers are free to reject voucher holders on the basis of their voucher status, unless the providers are funded by the Low Income Housing Tax Credit (LIHTC), HOME, or the Housing Trust Fund.[43] Many states and some local jurisdictions, however, have legislation forbidding "source of income" discrimination, which usually includes discrimination against voucher holders.[44] Some have argued that a "no-voucher-holder" policy must be waived as a reasonable accommodation for persons with disabilities; the cases adjudicating these claims have had mixed results. Voucher holders also have challenged voucher discrimination for its disproportionate racial impact or intentional racial discrimination; "vouchers" and "Section 8" often are identified with people of color.

c. *Project-Based Rental Assistance*

From the 1960s to the mid-1980s, Congress provided rental assistance to developments, offering below-market interest rate loans, subsidized interest rates, and some other aid so that rent levels would be reduced for specific periods of time, often 20 years. These were shallow subsidy programs. These programs were administered by HUD and the Department of Agriculture. No new units are being produced by these programs, but many of the buildings still exist. (In 1987, Congress created a somewhat similar program that operated through the Department of the Treasury, the Low Income Housing Tax Credit (LIHTC) program. It is discussed below.) As the rent restrictions expire

---

for the Road Ahead, in Furthering Fair Housing: Prospects for Racial Justice in America's Neighborhoods 210, 220 (Justin P. Steil et al. eds., Temple U. Press 2021).

41. HUD, Off. of Inspector Gen., *HUD's Oversight of Voucher Utilization and Reallocation in the HCV Program*, 2021CH-0001, at 7 (Sept. 15, 2021), https://www.hudoig.gov/sites/default /files/2021-10/2021-CH-0001_0.pdf.

42. Goodman et al., *supra* note 26, at 4; *see also* Off. of Pub. & Indian Hous., *PHA Concentration of Voucher Holders in High Poverty Areas*, HUD (May 20, 2023), https://www.hud.gov/sites/dfiles /PIH/documents/Voucher%20Concentration%20Spreadsheet%20May%2030%202023.pdf (showing voucher holder households with children still highly concentrated in high-poverty neighborhoods).

43. Off. of Pub. & Indian Hous., *Source of Income Protections for Housing Choice Voucher Holders*, HUD, https://www.hud.gov/program_offices/public_indian_housing/programs /hcv/source-of-income-protections#:~:text=Low%2DIncome%20Housing%20Tax%20Cre dit,LIHTC%20property%20owners%20for%20compliance.

44. Brian Knudsen, *Expanded Protections for Families With Housing Choice Vouchers*, PRRAC (2022), https://www.prrac.org/pdf/soi-voucher-data-brief.pdf (estimating that as of 2022 voucher holders were protected against discrimination by 17 states, 21 counties, and 85 cities). *See* Chapter 18.

on the developments previously so funded, other subsidy programs (principally vouchers and the LIHTC) sometimes are used to keep those units in the affordable housing stock.

The original HUD program in this category was §221(d)(3), created in 1961. It had both market rate and Below Market Interest Rate (BMIR) variants, with the BMIR developments producing subsidized housing, albeit with a shallow subsidy (reducing only part of the interest rate). This was replaced by the §236 program in 1968, which also was a shallow subsidy program. These were enhanced, however, by the Rent Supplement and Section 236 Rental Assistance Programs, which provided deep, project-based subsidies.[45] New commitments under §236 were suspended in 1973 by President Nixon's "moratorium" on subsidized housing; §236 was replaced by §8 New Construction in 1974.[46] That program, too, later was suspended.

Congress created similar programs to be administered by the Department of Agriculture for rural areas. These were the §515 Rural Rental Program and a similar program for farmworker housing.

In 1987, Congress created the Low Income Housing Tax Credit (LIHTC or §42) program administered by the Treasury Department. This is the largest subsidized housing production and substantial rehabilitation program operating in the 21st century, having produced approximately 3.65 million units as of 2022.[47] On its own, it is a shallow subsidy program, unable to serve very low-income households without a voucher. Some states have their own state low-income housing tax credit programs that supplement the federal subsidy. All LIHTC developments must be open to voucher holders and can serve very low-income households in that way. The LIHTC is the key financing mechanism for several of the cases presented in this book, including *Greater New Orleans Fair Housing Action Center v. Saint Bernard Parish* (Chapter 6) and *TDHCA v. ICP* (Chapter 7).

2. Development Programs

There also are federal development programs that may either destroy or facilitate housing and sometimes are essential to the financing of housing discussed in these cases. The urban renewal program, addressed in Chapter 1, is a development program that destroyed much housing, especially housing for low-income people and people of color. The Community Development

---

45. ADVOCATES' GUIDE 2023, *supra* note 8, at 4-79.

46. *See Vill. of Arlington Heights v. Metro. Hous. Dev. Corp.*, 429 U.S. 252, 255 n.2 (1977) (Chapter 6). For the 1973 moratorium, see Comm. of Penna. v. Lynn, 501 F.2d 848 (D.C. Cir. 1974), Pealo v. Farmers Home Administration, 412 F. Supp. 561 (D.D.C. 1976), and Rocky Ford Hous. Auth. v. U.S.D.A., 427 F. Supp. 118 (D.D.C. 1977). For discussion of these programs, see U.S. Nat'l Comm'n on Urb. Probs., *Building the American City*, H.R Doc. No. 91-34, 91st Cong., 1st Sess., pt IV, ch. 1 (1969) [hereinafter Douglas Commission Report].

47. Off. of Pol'y Dev. & Rsch., *Low-Income Housing Tax Credit (LIHTC): Property Level Data*, HUD (Apr. 12, 2024), https://www.huduser.gov/portal/datasets/lihtc/property.html.

Block Grant (CDBG) program was created in the Housing and Community Development Act of 1974, which "formally ended the federal urban renewal program, along with Model Cities and five other federal grant programs."[48] The Department of Agriculture also has a variety of loan and grant programs, some of which can be used for rural rental housing and facilities, like water treatment, that serve rural housing.[49]

B. DE JURE RACIAL DISCRIMINATION AND SEGREGATION IN FEDERAL HOUSING PROGRAMS

Racial segregation characterized public housing from its creation and continued to be an "intransigent" problem even after Executive Order 11063 in 1962 and Title VI of the 1964 Civil Rights Act, which prohibited discrimination in programs and activities receiving federal financial assistance.[50] Although there were some efforts from within, government agencies rarely acted effectively to undo the existing discrimination and segregation and continued to plan new projects to impose separation.[51]

In the 1940s and 1950s, advocates used equal protection principles to challenge discrimination and segregation in public housing as in public education, and these efforts continued after the enactment of Title VI of the 1964 Civil Rights Act.[52] The seminal challenge to racial discrimination and segregation in public housing was the *Gautreaux* litigation, filed in 1966 in Chicago, site of "the largest black ghetto in the nation."[53]

The *Gautreaux* litigation started with two suits, one against the Chicago Housing Authority (CHA) and the other against HUD. Each pursued claims under Title VI of the 1964 Civil Rights Act; the suit against the CHA also relied on the Fourteenth Amendment and the 1866 Civil Rights Act; the suit against

---

48. Douglas R. Appler, *Introduction, in* THE MANY GEOGRAPHIES OF URBAN RENEWAL: NEW PERSPECTIVES ON THE HOUSING ACT OF 1949, at 9 (Douglas R. Appler ed., Temple U. Press 2023). The CDBG program also is involved in *St. Bernard Parish* (Chapter 6) and *NAACP, Boston Chapter* (Chapter 13).

49. Rural Development, All Programs, U.S.D.A, https://www.rd.usda.gov/programs-services /all-programs?page=1 (last visited Aug. 2, 2024); USDA Rural Housing Programs, National Housing Law Project, https://www.nhlp.org/resource-center/usda-rural-housing-programs/ (last visited Nov. 9, 2024).

50. Gail Radford, MODERN HOUSING FOR AMERICA: POLICY STRUGGLES IN THE NEW DEAL ERA 85-109 (U. Chicago Press 1996); Kenneth T. Jackson, CRABGRASS FRONTIER: THE SUBURBANIZATION OF THE UNITED STATES 225 (Oxford U. Press 1985) (stating that "Because municipalities had discretion on where and when to build public housing, the projects invariably reinforced racial segregation").

51. Pritchett, *supra* note 7, at 313 (stating also that after HUD was created in 1965 and its first Secretary, Dr. Robert Clifton Weaver, appointed, his "staff collected thirty-three complaints about new public housing projects that resulted in increased racial segregation in the first four years after the executive order took effect."); *see also* Schwemm, HDLL §21:1.

52. For a discussion of early challenges, see Florence Wagman Roisman, *Affirmatively Furthering Fair Housing in Regional Housing Markets: The Baltimore Public Housing Desegregation Litigation,* 42 WAKE FOREST L. REV. 333, 339-43 (2007).

53. Pritchett, *supra* note 7, at 234-35; *see* Arnold R. Hirsch, MAKING THE SECOND GHETTO: RACE & HOUSING IN CHICAGO, 1940-1960 (Cambridge U. Press 1983).

HUD relied on the Fifth Amendment. Plaintiffs claimed that defendants intentionally chose sites for family public housing and adopted tenant assignment procedures for the purpose of maintaining existing patterns of residential separation of races in Chicago.

Ms. Dorothy Gautreaux

The district court held CHA liable for the intentional racial discrimination and segregation; the agency did not appeal. The district court dismissed the suit against HUD, but the Seventh Circuit reversed. Here are excerpts from those two liability decisions.

Gautreaux v. Chicago Housing Authority
296 F. Supp. 907 (N.D. Ill. 1969)

AUSTIN, District Judge:

I. DISCRIMINATORY TENANT ASSIGNMENT PRACTICES

Plaintiffs charge that defendants have imposed quotas at four White family housing projects to keep the number of Negro families to a minimal level. The Trumbull, Lathrop, Lawndale and Bridgeport projects were built before 1944 in areas which were then and are now substantially all White. Until 1954 CHA refused to permit Negro families to reside in these projects. The Negro population in the four projects on December 31, 1967 represented respectively about 7%, 4%, 6% and 1% of the total. At present Negroes comprise about 90% of the tenants in CHA family housing projects and about 90% of the waiting list of 13,000 persons. [The non-white population of Chicago at that time was 34.4 percent.]

The disparity between the low number of Negro families in these projects and the high number of Negro applicants for all projects indicates that CHA has imposed a Negro quota. . . . Harry Schneider, Deputy Executive Director of CHA, testified that until May 22, 1968 these four projects were listed on CHA tenant selection forms as appropriate for "A families only," that is, Whites only. He states that in these projects there are "controls" on the number of Negro applicants accepted, that Negro population in these projects is now "fairly close" to the "appropriate maximum number," and that if, for example, Trumbull attained the level of 35 Negro families a "hold" would maintain the occupancy at that level. The "history of tension, threats of violence and violence" urged in justification by CHA cannot excuse a governmentally established policy of racial segregation. Cooper v. Aaron, 358 U.S. 1 (1958). In fact, the only violent incident mentioned by Mr. Schneider occurred in 1953, and Mr. Rose recalled that one incident indicating White hostility to Negroes occurred at Bridgeport in 1959. These remote incidents do not show a clear threat of violence which might justify quotas as a very temporary expedient. In any case, CHA's quotas clearly have maintained Negro occupancy at a permanently low level.

II. DISCRIMINATORY SITE SELECTION PROCEDURES

[The procedure primarily used by defendants to maintain existing patterns of racial residential separation involved a pre-clearance arrangement under which CHA informally submitted sites for family housing to the City Council alderman in whose ward the site was located. The aldermen to whom White sites were submitted allegedly vetoed these sites because the 90% Negro waiting list and occupancy rate would create a Negro population in the White area. Plaintiffs allege that the few White sites which escaped an alderman's informal veto were eventually rejected on racial grounds by the City Council when they were formally submitted by CHA for approval.]

A. Statistics on Sites Considered and Selected.

As of July, 1968, CHA had in operation or development 54 family projects at 64 sites in Chicago consisting of 30,848 units. Exclusive of the four segregated White projects, CHA's family housing tenants are 99% Negroes. Exclusive of the four projects, housing units now located in neighborhoods between 50% and 100% Negro represent 99 1/2% of the total units operated by CHA; units in neighborhoods between 75% and 100% Negro are 92% of the total; and units in areas over 95% Negro are two-thirds of the total. A glance at a map depicting Negro areas of residence in Chicago confirms that the 50% to 90% Negro areas are almost without exception contiguous with 90% to 100% Negro areas and that the relatively small numbers of Chicago Negroes not concentrated in the over 90% areas are almost entirely concentrated in the over 50% areas. Therefore, given the trend of Negro population movement, 99 1/2% of CHA family units are located in areas which are or soon will be substantially all Negro. It is incredible that this dismal prospect of an all Negro public housing system in all Negro areas came about without the persistent application of a deliberate policy to confine public housing to all Negro or immediately adjacent changing areas.

No criterion, other than race, can plausibly explain the veto of over 99 1/2% of the housing units located on the White sites which were initially selected on the basis of CHA's expert judgment and at the same time the rejection of only 10% or so of the units on Negro sites.

B. Testimony on Site Selection Criteria.

High CHA officials clearly understood the message of the statistics, and with commendable frankness some of them said so. While Executive

Director, Mr. Rose testified in 1959 before the U.S. Commission on Civil Rights:

Q: Because of the present location of the existing sites, then, the Council of Chicago is guilty of practicing to a certain degree segregated housing, is that true?

A: You are only agreeing with me.

Q: Well, somebody is guilty of contributing to the segregation of housing of people in the City of Chicago, because when you look at the present location of the housing projects, they are predominately within the Negro area.

A: That is true.

On July 16, 1966, Mr. Humphrey, who was then Deputy Executive Director, responded to a question from an Alderman in testimony before the City Council:

Q: And did he then ask you why the Housing Authority hadn't presented any sites outside the segregated Negro neighborhoods?

A: I think he asked that question, yes.

Q: And did you answer that the reason was you couldn't find any suitable sites outside the Negro neighborhoods?

A: I didn't answer it that way at all.

Q: What answer did you give?

A: I answered it to the effect that he knew as well as I as to why we didn't have other sites; that he knew that if the site was approved by the alderman that it was included in the package and if it wasn't approved it wasn't included, and I added to that, incidentally, there are none in the package from your ward.

Mrs. Kathryn Moore, General Counsel of CHA, stated that in her opinion land in White areas equally suitable for development and often cheaper than land in Negro areas was unavailable solely because of the requirement of City Council approval.

CHA follows an unvarying policy "based upon actual experience in submitting sites to the City Council for approval" of informally clearing each site with the Alderman in whose Ward the site is located and eliminating each site opposed by an Alderman. The statements of Mr. Humphrey and Mr. Rose quoted above indicate that they personally knew that this procedure would result in the veto on racial grounds of substantial numbers of White sites. Mr. Humphrey also stated on deposition:

Q: Was the reason actually that you knew the City Council would probably not approve public housing sites in white neighborhoods?

A: I said no doubt, there.

Q: You mean that was no doubt the case?

A: Well, I am assuming from what had been going on the last few years that you just couldn't go anywhere in the City of Chicago that you wanted to and acquire a site.

Q: Particularly in the white neighborhoods, I take it?

A: Right.

An uncontradicted affidavit claims that Mr. Charles Swibel, Chairman of the Board of Commissioners of CHA, stated in private conversations on numerous occasions that the City Council had CHA "over a barrel" and consequently CHA acquiesced in choosing sites in Negro neighborhoods. Since CHA directly denies none of these statements or numerous other statements to a similar effect cited in Plaintiffs' briefs, there is no genuine issue as to the truth of the fact that the pre-clearance procedure was known by CHA to result in the veto of substantial numbers of sites on racial grounds.

C. Legal Consequences of the Site Selection Policies.

On March 2, 1967 this court ruled that "plaintiffs, as present and future users of the system, have the right under the Fourteenth Amendment to have sites selected for public housing projects without regard to the racial composition of either the surrounding neighborhood or of the projects themselves." The statistics on the family housing sites considered during the five major programs show a very high probability, a near certainty, that many sites were vetoed on the basis of the racial composition of the site's neighborhood. In the face of these figures, CHA's failure to present a substantial or even a speculative indication that racial criteria were not used entitles plaintiffs to judgment as a matter of law.

Defendants urge that CHA officials never entertained racist attitudes and that "the racial character of the neighborhood has never been a factor in CHA's selection of a suitable site." In view of CHA's persistent selection of White sites at the initial stage before the pre-clearance procedure and the candor of its officials on deposition, these statements are undoubtedly true. It is also undenied that sites for the projects which have been constructed were chosen primarily to further the praiseworthy and urgent goals of low cost housing and urban renewal. Nevertheless, a deliberate policy to separate the races cannot be justified by the good intentions with which other laudable goals are pursued. *Brown v. Board*. It is also true that there is no evidence that the Aldermen who vetoed White sites were necessarily motivated by racial animus when they followed a policy of keeping Negroes out of White neighborhoods. Most Aldermen apparently talked to their constituents and received unfavorable reactions before exercising their informal vetoes. But even if the Aldermen's informal surveys were correct in their uniform assessment of public opinion, they cannot acquiesce in the sentiment of their constituents to keep their neighborhoods White and to deny admission to Negroes via the placement of public housing.

CHA finally contends that the impulse originating and sustaining the policy against choosing White sites came from the City Council. But by incorporating as an automatic step in its site selection procedure a practice which resulted in a racial veto before it performed its statutory function of formally presenting the sites to the City Council, CHA made those policies its own and deprived opponents of those policies of the opportunity for public debate. It is no defense that the City Council's power to approve sites may as a matter of practical politics have compelled CHA to adopt the pre-clearance procedure which was known by CHA to incorporate a racial veto. In fact, even if CHA had not participated in the elimination of White sites, its officials were bound by the Constitution not to exercise CHA's discretion to decide to build upon sites which were chosen by some other agency on the basis of race. Cooper v. Aaron, 358 U.S. 1 (1958); Orleans Parish School Board v. Bush, 268 F.2d 78 (5th Cir. 1959).

Two further results of CHA's participation in a policy of maintaining existing patterns of residential separation of the races must be mentioned. First, as Dr. Baron's Affidavit discloses, the 188,000 White families eligible for public housing have understandably chosen in the main to forego their opportunity to obtain low cost housing rather than to move into all Negro projects in all Negro neighborhoods. This is an ironic but predictable result of a segregationist policy of protecting Whites from less than half as many (76,000) eligible Negro families. Second, existing patterns of racial separation must be reversed if there is to be a chance of averting the desperately intensifying division of Whites and Negroes in Chicago. On the basis of present trends of Negro residential concentration and of Negro migration into and White migration out of the central city, the President's Commission on Civil Disorders estimates that Chicago will become 50% Negro by 1984. By 1984 it may be too late to heal racial divisions.

NOTES AND QUESTIONS

1. **Legal Analogies of Housing Segregation and School Segregation.** Courts swiftly applied the constitutional principles underlying public school segregation litigation to cases involving public housing segregation — as, for example, in an early case that involved Detroit public housing, Detroit Housing Commission v. Lewis, 226 F.2d 180 (6th Cir. 1955). Thus, we see in the district court opinion above reliance on *Brown v. Board of Education, Cooper v. Aaron* (Little Rock), and *Orleans Parish v. Bush* (New Orleans). Such references to school cases were common in these housing cases. Federal housing agencies, however, did not apply the logic of *Brown* to the housing programs.[54]

2. **What Relief Should Be Provided Under Title VI of the 1964 Civil Rights Act? When, if Ever, Is a Funding Cutoff Appropriate?** Relief is what this type of litigation has been about since the liability holdings in 1969 and 1971. One point about relief was made in this liability decision. The district court granted plaintiffs' motion for summary judgment on the constitutional and 1866 Civil Rights Act claims but denied both parties' motions for

---

54. *See* Arnold R. Hirsch, *Choosing Segregation: Federal Housing Policy Between* Shelley *and* Brown, *in* FROM TENEMENTS TO THE TAYLOR HOMES: IN SEARCH OF AN URBAN HOUSING POLICY IN TWENTIETH CENTURY AMERICA 206, 218 (John F. Bauman et al. eds., PA State U. Press 2000).

summary judgment on the claims under Title VI of the 1964 Civil Rights Act, writing:

> Although this court held that Count II states a claim upon which relief can be granted under [Title VI of the 1964 Civil Rights Act], judgment on Count II would, in the context of this case, determine the propriety of granting a narrow, drastic kind of relief—that of enjoining the use of federal funds. The Public Housing Administration has already taken a position against denying federal funds. . . . In addition to the uncertainty of whether PHA would hold it appropriate to deny funds under the facts as they are now known, it is not clear whether even a temporary denial of federal funds would not impede the development of public housing and thus damage the very persons this suit was brought to protect. The use of a threatened denial of funds to coerce compliance with the Constitution, if coercion is necessary, would seem to be a less efficient remedy than an injunction available under [the constitutional and Civil Rights Act claims of] Count I. Therefore, summary judgment is denied without precluding plaintiffs from showing on the basis of more facts that denial of federal funds is an appropriate form of relief.

As will be seen again in the history of this litigation and in much other litigation, withholding funds is a remedy that agencies and courts are reluctant to impose. Later in this litigation, the district court withheld Model Cities funding that supports community development, but the court of appeals overturned the injunction. Agencies and courts also are reluctant to withhold funding for failure to comply with the affirmatively furthering fair housing mandate discussed in Chapter 13. A variety of explanations have been offered for this reluctance, including concerns that withholding funds will hurt the people whom the litigation is designed to help, about federalism, about agency motivation and capacity, and about politics. For a sophisticated consideration of these arguments, see Eloise Pasahoff, *Agency Enforcement of Spending Clause Statutes: A Defense of the Funding Cut-Off*, 124 YALE L.J. 248 (2014).

3. "Interest Convergence." The late Professor Derrick A. Bell, a pioneer of Critical Race Theory scholarship, famously wrote that remedies for injuries to people of color are not likely to be provided unless they serve the interests of white people. Derrick A. Bell, Jr., Brown v. Board of Education *and the Interest-Convergence Dilemma*, 93 HARV. L. REV. 518 (1980). Note that the district court here considered that the discriminatory conduct challenged had injured a substantial number of white people eligible for public housing who had chosen "to forego their opportunity to obtain low cost housing rather than to move into all Negro projects in all Negro neighborhoods." Do you think Professor Bell's theory is correct? Do you think interest convergence played a role in the problems addressed in *Gautreaux*?

4. Contemporary Veto. Compare the public housing "veto" exercised by the aldermen and City Council in *Gautreaux* to the bans on multifamily housing discussed in other chapters, including Chapter 6 (*St. Bernard Parish*) and Chapter 8 (*City of Black Jack*). How are they alike? How do they differ?

5. Public Housing "Containment." *Gautreaux* helps illustrate the out-sized role of federally funded public housing in creating and intensifying racial segregation in neighborhoods that previously had been integrated, with impacts beyond the public housing. Historian Arnold Hirsch describes this phenomenon as a "containment" strategy operating within the urban renewal program: "Family public housing increasingly became a minority reloca-tion program locked in the urban core, while government subsidies brought homeownership and suburban mobility within the reach of the white middle class." Arnold R. Hirsch, *Searching for a "Sound Negro Policy": A Racial Agenda for the Housing Acts of 1949 and 1954*, 11 Hous. Pol'y Debate 393, 431 (2000). Chapter 1 describes the conditions Black renters faced in a dual housing mar-ket: limited housing supply and mortgage capital, high rents, overcrowding, and long public housing waiting lists.

———————————

Here is the Seventh Circuit's liability decision against HUD. Defendant Romney is George Romney, who was the first Secretary of HUD in the Nixon Administration. With this you might like to compare the much later use of race to "contain" non-whites in New York City in 1992, reflected in "the inter-mittent use of codes denoting housing projects to which only white families could be assigned . . ." and "the use of racial goals or targets" the Housing Authority conceded that it used to steer white applicants to predominantly white projects.[55]

Gautreaux v. Romney
448 F.2d 731 (7th Cir. 1971)

Before Swygert, Chief Judge, Duffy, Senior Circuit Judge, and Fairchild, Circuit Judge.

Duffy, Senior Circuit Judge:

Plaintiffs seek a declaration that the Secretary has "assisted in the carry-ing on . . . of a racially discriminatory public housing system, within the City of Chicago, Illinois" [and seek] to enjoin the Secretary from making available to the CHA any federal financial assets to be used in connection with or in support of the racially discriminatory aspects of the Chicago public housing system.

The complaint challenges the role played by HUD and its Secretary in the funding and construction of certain public housing in the City of Chicago. The District Court dismissed this complaint upon the finding that HUD's financial

---

55. Davis v. New York City Housing Authority, Nos. 90 CIV. 628, 92 CIV. 4873, 1997 WL 407250, at *3 (Jul. 18, 1997), *vacated in part on other grounds*, 166 F.3d 432 (2d. Cir. 1999).

assistance to CHA was insufficient to make it a "joint participant" in CHA's racially discriminatory conduct.

The Government admits that HUD approved and funded CHA-chosen regular family housing sites between 1950 and 1969, knowing that such sites were not "optimal" and that the reason for their exclusive location in black areas of Chicago was that "sites other than in the south or west side, if proposed for regular family housing, invariably encounter[ed] sufficient opposition in the [Chicago City] Council to preclude Council approval."

Nevertheless, the District Court found that HUD had followed this course only after having made "numerous and consistent efforts . . . to persuade the Chicago Housing Authority to locate low-rent housing projects in white neighborhoods." That finding is not directly challenged on appeal. Moreover, given the acknowledged desperate need for public housing in Chicago, HUD's decision was that it was better to fund a segregated housing system than to deny housing altogether to the thousands of needy Negro families of that city.

We shall treat all of the above facts as true. The question then becomes whether or not, even granting that "numerous and consistent efforts" were made, HUD's knowing acquiescence in CHA's admitted discriminatory housing program violated either the Due Process Clause of the Fifth Amendment or [Title VI of the 1964 Civil Rights Act]. Given a previous court finding of liability against CHA, the pertinent caselaw compels the conclusion that both of these provisions were violated.

HUD's approval and funding of segregated CHA housing sites cannot be excused as an attempted accommodation of an admittedly urgent need for housing with the reality of community and City Council resistance. This question was argued and settled in the companion case as to these exact housing sites and the same City Council. The District Judge there well stated the applicable rule:

> It is also undenied that sites for the projects which have been constructed were chosen primarily to further the praiseworthy and urgent goals of low cost housing and urban renewal. Nevertheless, a deliberate policy to separate the races cannot be justified by the good intentions with which other laudable goals are pursued.

This court applied much the same rule in [earlier decisions where] we pointed to several cases holding ". . . that 'abstention' is inappropriate in constitutional cases of this sort and that community hostility is no reason to delay enforcement of proven constitutional rights." Courts have held that alleged good faith is no more of a defense to segregation in public housing than it is to segregation in public schools. Moreover, the fact that it is a *federal* agency or officer charged with an act of racial discrimination does not alter the pertinent standards, since ". . . it would be unthinkable that the same Constitution would impose a lesser duty on the Federal Government." Bolling v. Sharpe, 347 U.S. 497 (1954). The reason for courts' near uniform refusal to examine purported good faith motives behind alleged discriminatory acts was, perhaps, most succinctly put by the Supreme Court in Burton v. Wilmington Parking Authority, 365 U.S. 715, 725: "It is of no consolation to an individual denied the equal protection of the laws that it was done in good faith."

The fact that a governmental agency might have made "numerous and consistent efforts" toward desegregation has not yet been held to negate liability for an otherwise segregated result. Thus, for example, in Cooper v. Aaron, 358 U.S. 1 (1958), the local school board admittedly had been "going forward with its preparation for desegregating the Little Rock [Arkansas] school system," but was still held liable when it abandoned those plans in the face of stiff community and state governmental resistance.

With the foregoing considerations in mind, then, it is apparent that the "dilemma" with which the Secretary no doubt was faced and with which we are fully sympathetic, nevertheless cannot bear upon the question before us. For example, we have been advised that any further HUD pressure on CHA would have meant cutting off funds and thus stopping the flow of new housing altogether. Taking this assertion as true, still the basis of the "dilemma" boils down to community and local governmental resistance to ". . . the only constitutionally permissible state policy. . . ." [This is] a factor which, as discussed above, has not yet been accepted as a viable excuse for a segregated result. So, even though we fully understand the Secretary's position and do not, in any way, wish to limit the exercise of his discretion in housing related matters, still we do not feel free to carve out a wholly new exception to a firmly established general rule which, for at least the last sixteen years, has governed the standards of assessing liability for discrimination on the basis of race.

Turning to the facts now before us, there can be no question that the role played by HUD in the construction of the public housing system in Chicago was significant. The great amount of funds for such construction came from HUD. Between 1950 and 1966 alone HUD spent nearly $350,000,000 on CHA projects. The Secretary's trial brief acknowledged that "in practical operation of the low-rent housing program, the existence of the program is entirely dependent upon continuing, year to year, Federal financial assistance." We find no basis in the record with which to disagree with that conclusion. Moreover, within the structure of the housing programs as funded, HUD retained a large amount of discretion to approve or reject both site selection and tenant assignment procedures of the local housing authority. HUD's "Annual Contributions Contract" contained detailed provisions concerning program operations and was accompanied by eight pages of regulations on the subject of site selection alone.

It also is not seriously disputed on appeal that the Secretary exercised the above described powers in a manner which perpetuated a racially discriminatory housing system in Chicago, and that the Secretary and other HUD officials were aware of that fact. On such facts, and given the inapplicability of HUD's "good faith" arguments, we are unable to avoid the conclusion that the Secretary's past actions constituted racially discriminatory conduct in their own right. The fact that the Secretary's exercise of his powers may have more often reflected CHA's own racially discriminatory choices than it did any ill will on HUD's part, does not alter the question now before us.

In holding the Secretary liable on nearly identical facts as are now before us, the [court in *Hicks v. Weaver*] reasoned as follows:

> As noted above, HUD was not only aware of the situation in Bogalusa [Louisiana] but it effectively directed and controlled each and every step in the program. . . . HUD thus sanctioned the violation of plaintiffs' rights and was an active participant since it could have halted the discrimination at any step in the program. Consequently, its own discriminatory conduct in this respect is violative of [Title VI.]

Likewise, in *Shannon* [*v. HUD*] the Third Circuit recently enjoined further action on a HUD decision to change a proposed housing project in Philadelphia from the originally contemplated owner occupied buildings to a 100% rent supplement assistance program (which was found to be the "functional equivalent of a low rent public housing project.") The *Shannon* court acknowledged that HUD was vested with broad discretion to supervise its various programs, but held, nevertheless, that ". . . that discretion must be exercised within the framework of the national policy against discrimination in federally assisted housing . . . and in favor of fair housing."

So, even while we are fully sympathetic to the arguments advanced by the Secretary on appeal, we must conclude that the great weight of the caselaw favors plaintiffs' position. [W]e conclude that summary judgment should be granted in plaintiffs' favor[;] HUD violated the Due Process Clause of the Fifth Amendment (*Bolling v. Sharpe; Hicks v. Weaver*) and also has violated [Title VI] of the [1964 Civil Rights Act] (*Shannon v. HUD; Hicks v. Weaver*).

In so holding we state *only* that the Secretary must be adjudged liable on these particular facts and again point out that our holding should not be construed as granting a broad license for interference with the programs and actions of an already beleaguered federal agency. It may well be that the District Judge, in his wise discretion, will conclude that little equitable relief above the entry of a declaratory judgment and a simple "best efforts" clause will be necessary to remedy the wrongs which have been found to have been committed.

NOTES AND QUESTIONS

1. Cases Cited in *Gautreaux v. Romney*. Several of the cases cited by the Seventh Circuit are part of the civil rights canon, highly influential in all cases involving desegregation and discrimination, particularly on the basis of race. They are essential legal history for every well-trained lawyer. Bolling v. Sharpe, 347 U.S. 497 (1954), is the D.C. companion case to *Brown v. Board* *of Education.* Burton v. Wilmington Parking Authority, 365 U.S. 715 (1961), expanded the reach of state action doctrine. Cooper v. Aaron, 358 U.S. 1 (1958), was the unanimous, landmark decision rejecting the effort to delay school segregation in Little Rock, Arkansas. Hicks v. Weaver, 302 F. Supp. 619 (E.D. La. 1969) enjoined the construction in all-Black neighborhoods of public housing intended for Black occupancy by a PHA whose housing was entirely segregated by race. Shannon v. HUD, 436 F.2d 809 (3d Cir. 1970), which addresses HUD's duties with respect to site selection, is discussed in Chapter 13.

2. Segregated Housing or No Housing at All. The "dilemma" faced by HUD (and, for that matter, by CHA), is a common one and hearkens back to the decision by Congress in 1949 to "save" public housing by rejecting a ban on racial segregation. Most white neighborhoods (and upper income, non-white neighborhoods) are strongly opposed to subsidized housing developments, particularly—in the case of white neighborhoods—if the housing is likely to be occupied by non-white people. At the same time, there is an overwhelming need for subsidized housing, and that need is felt disproportionately by people of color. When a government (or nonprofit or other) housing agency is stymied in efforts to site housing in predominantly white neighborhoods, what should it do? For a discussion of a "path of least resistance" dynamic that allows for the "continued creation of government-assisted housing in impoverished, isolated, or resegregating communities," see Stacy E. Seicshnaydre, *How Government Housing Perpetuates Racial Segregation: Lessons From Post-Katrina New Orleans,* 60 CATH. U. L. REV. 661 (2011).

3. Continuing the Saga of the *Gautreaux* Litigation. As we have seen, the courts held both the CHA and HUD liable for intentional racial discrimination in public housing site selection and tenant assignment in Chicago. (The city of Chicago also was held liable.) Then the question was whether the remedy had to be limited to the city of Chicago or could involve the Chicago suburbs. Here are the decisions on that issue by the Seventh Circuit and then by the U.S. Supreme Court.

Gautreaux v. Chicago Housing Authority
503 F.2d 930 (7th Cir. 1974), *aff'd sub nom.* Hills v. Gautreaux, 425 U.S. 284 (1976)

Before Clark, Associate Justice, Cummings and Tone, Circuit Judges. [The dissent of Judge Tone is omitted.]

Mr. Justice CLARK:

This appeal [by Black tenants of and applicants for public housing] grows out of the decision of the district court on remand for a determination of appropriate relief. After some four years of hearings, several judgment orders and four appeals, the District Court on the last remand called on the parties to propose a "comprehensive plan" to remedy past effects of the public housing segregation indulged in by CHA and HUD, including "alternatives which are not confined in their scope to the geographic boundary of the City of Chicago." HUD proposed, and the District Court, after an evidentiary hearing, ordered a plan under which HUD would "cooperate" with CHA in the latter's efforts to increase the supply of public housing units but eliminated any relief not confined to the geographic boundary of the City of Chicago and refused to impose any specific affirmative obligations upon HUD beyond its "best efforts." The appellants contend that a metropolitan area remedial plan including housing in suburban areas, as well as those within the limits of Chicago, is necessary to remedy the past effects of said unconstitutional public housing segregation policy and attain that racial balance required by the Fourteenth Amendment. Given the eight years tortuous course of these cases, together with the findings and judgment orders of the District Court and the opinions of this Court (now numbering five) we believe the relief granted is not only much too little but also much too late in the proceedings. In effect, appellants, having won the battle back in 1969, have now lost the war. We are fully aware of the many difficult and sensitive problems that the cases have presented to the able District Judge and we applaud the care, meticulous attention and the judicious manner in which he has approached them. With his orders being ignored and frustrated as they were, he kept his cool and courageously called the hand of the recalcitrant. Perhaps in the opinion on remand [our statement] that: "It may well be that the District Judge, in his wise discretion, will conclude that little equitable relief above the entry of a declaratory judgment and a simple 'best efforts' clause, will be necessary . . ." led the beleaguered District Judge to limit any plan to the boundaries of the City of Chicago and the "best efforts" of CHA and HUD. This is to be regretted and we trust that upon remand the matter will be expedited to the end that the segregated public housing system which has resulted from the action of CHA and HUD will be disestablished, and the deficiency in the supply of dwelling units will be corrected as rapidly as possible and in the manner indicated in this opinion.

We shall not burden this opinion with the details of the eight-year delay that has thus far deprived the appellants of the fruits of the District Court's judgment entered on July 1, 1969. In addition the unconstitutional action of CHA had stripped thousands of residents of the City of Chicago of their Fifth and Fourteenth Amendment rights for a score of years. Indeed, anyone reading the various opinions of the District Court and of this Court quickly discovers a callousness on the part of the appellees towards the rights of the black, underprivileged citizens of Chicago that is beyond comprehension. [EDS. — The court reviewed the district court's findings supporting the liability of the CHA and the court's order requiring CHA to disestablish the segregated public housing system, and to increase the supply of dwelling units as soon as possible.]

Appellants and the District Court waited patiently for a year and a half but CHA submitted no sites for family dwellings to the City Council. The appellants contacted CHA and were advised that CHA had no intention to submit sites prior to the Chicago mayoralty election of April, 1971. The parties then asked for and were given informal hearings, so as to prevent publicity, and finally the District Court modified its "best efforts" provision in the July 1, 1969 judgment order so as to affirmatively require CHA to submit sites for no fewer than 1500 units to the City Council for approval on or before September 20, 1970. This order was appealed by CHA and affirmed.

During the progress of this litigation, HUD was conferring with the City of Chicago concerning grants under the Model Cities Program. A $38 million grant was made for the calendar year 1970. However, for the 1971 calendar year HUD required a "letter of intention" signed by the Mayor of Chicago, the Chairman of CHA and the Regional Administrator of HUD, indicating how Chicago's large housing deficiency would be met. Under this letter CHA was to acquire sites for 1700 units within a specified timetable. HUD approved $26 million and had released $12 million when the [liability] opinion in *Romney* came down. Appellants then sought an injunction from the District Court restraining further payments by HUD under the Model Cities Program unless and until sites in predominantly white areas for 700 dwelling units had been certified to the City Council for approval (at the time only 288 had been approved). The District Court granted this relief but on appeal the order was reversed. On remand the District Court entered a summary judgment against HUD, consolidated the cases and entered an order calling for each of the parties to file suggestions for a "comprehensive plan" to remedy the past effects of the public housing segregation, including "alternatives which are not confined in their scope to the geographic boundary of the City of Chicago."

2. A Metropolitan Plan Is Necessary and Equitable

After careful consideration and reflection we are obliged to conclude that on the record here it is necessary and equitable that any remedial plan to be effective must be on a suburban or metropolitan area basis. Our decision in regard to the necessity and equity of suburban or metropolitan area action is predicated on the following:

The equitable factors which prevented metropolitan relief in *Milliken v. Bradley* are simply not present here. There is no deeply rooted tradition of local control of public housing; rather, public housing is a federally supervised program with early roots in federal statutes. There has been a federal statutory commitment to non-discrimination in housing for more than a century, 42 U.S.C. §1982, and the Secretary of HUD is directed to administer housing programs "in a manner affirmatively to further the policies" of non-discrimination, 42 U.S.C. §3608(d)(5). In short, federal involvement is pervasive.

Similarly, the administrative problems of building public housing outside Chicago are not remotely comparable to the problems of daily bussing thousands of children to schools in other districts run by other local governments. CHA and HUD can build housing much like any other landowner, and whatever problems arise would be insignificant compared to restructuring school systems as proposed in *Milliken v. Bradley*.

In *Milliken v. Bradley*, the Chief Justice emphasized that there was no evidence of discrimination by the suburban school districts affected. Here, although the record was not made with the Supreme Court's *Milliken* opinions in mind, there is evidence of suburban discrimination. Plaintiff's Exhibit 11 indicates that of twelve suburban public housing projects, ten were located in or adjacent to overwhelmingly black census tracts. And although the case was not limited to public housing, it is not irrelevant that we recently took judicial notice of widespread residential segregation "in Chicago and its environs." Clark v. Universal Builders, Inc., 501 F.2d 324[, 335] (7th. Cir. 1974). We went on to hold that a prima facie showing had been made that this segregation had discriminatory effects throughout the metropolitan area.

Finally, the possibility of metropolitan relief has been under consideration for a long time in this case. While they disagree as to what relief the District Court should order, the parties are in agreement that the metropolitan area is a single relevant locality for low rent housing purposes and that a city-only remedy will not work. . . .

In addition to CHA's and HUD's strong, positive statements as to the necessity for a metropolitan plan here, the appellants also offered the testimony of a recognized demographer who estimated that a continuance of present trends in black and white census tracts would lead to at least a 30% black occupancy in every census tract in Chicago by the year 2000.

If this prediction comes true it will mean that there will be no "general Public Housing Area" left in Chicago on which CHA could build desegregated public housing. In the ten-year period 1960–1970 the population of the City of Chicago declined by 183,000 people, a decrease of 505,000 whites and an increase of 322,000 blacks. The expert demographer further testified that by providing desegregated housing opportunities in the suburban areas, the rate of white exodus from the city would diminish. There was no testimony to the contrary. In fact "White flight" has brought on the same condition in most of our metropolitan cities, such as Indianapolis, Indiana. Like conditions—but aggravated—exist in Washington, D.C. and Cleveland, Ohio.

The realities of "White flight" to the suburbs and the inevitability of "resegregation" by rebuilding the ghettos as CHA and HUD were doing in Chicago must therefore be considered in drawing a comprehensive plan. The trial judge back in 1969 ordered scattered-site, low-rise housing—despite much criticism—but the experts now agree that such requirements are mandatory. His warning that "By 1984 it may be too late to heal racial divisions[,]" rather than a cliché, is a solemn warning as to the interaction of "White flight" and "black concentration." It is the most serious domestic problem facing America today. As Assistant Secretary Simmons further advises:

> As Whites have left the cities, jobs have left with them. After 1960, three-fifths of all new industrial plants constructed in this country were outside of central cities. In some cases as much as 85% of all new industrial plants located

outside central cities were inaccessible to Blacks and other minorities who swelled ghetto populations.

These words also convey a solemn warning, i.e., we must not sentence our poor, our underprivileged, our minorities to the jobless slums of the ghettos and thereby forever trap them in the vicious cycle of poverty which can only lead them to lives of crime and violence.

By way of concluding, we have carefully read the records in these cases and find no evidence that the suburban or metropolitan area should not be included in a comprehensive plan. All of the parties, the Government officials, the documentary evidence, the sole expert and the decided cases agree that a suburban or metropolitan area plan is the *sine qua non* of an effective remedy. In fact the Judge himself recognized its importance in his original judgment order by authorizing housing units to be provided in suburban Cook County on a voluntary basis.

In light of all these considerations we can but conclude that the District Court's finding as to not including in a comprehensive plan of relief areas outside the City of Chicago, i.e., the suburban or metropolitan area, was clearly erroneous.

3. Action on Remand

The judgment order of September 11, 1973, is reversed and the causes are remanded for further consideration in the light of this opinion, to wit: the adoption of a comprehensive metropolitan area plan that will not only disestablish the segregated public housing system in the City of Chicago which has resulted from CHA's and HUD's unconstitutional site selection and tenant assignment procedures but will increase the supply of dwelling units as rapidly as possible.

Hills v. Gautreaux
425 U.S. 284 (1976)

Mr. Justice Stewart delivered the opinion of the Court. Mr. Justice Stevens took no part in the consideration or decision of the case. Mr. Justice Marshall filed a concurring statement in which Mr. Justice Brennan and Mr. Justice White joined.

STEWART, Justice:

[In Part I, the Court recited the history of the cases. In Part II, after an analysis of *Milliken v. Bradley*, the Supreme Court concluded: The District Court's desegregation order in *Milliken* was held to be an impermissible remedy not because it envisioned relief against a wrongdoer extending beyond the city in which the violation occurred but because it contemplated a judicial decree restructuring the operation of local governmental entities that were not implicated in any constitutional violation.]

The question presented in this case concerns only the authority of the District Court to order HUD to take remedial action outside the city limits of Chicago. HUD does not dispute the Court of Appeals' determination that it violated the Fifth Amendment and [Title VI of the 1964 Civil Rights Act] by knowingly funding CHA's racially discriminatory family public housing program, nor does it question the appropriateness of a remedial order designed to alleviate the effects of past segregative practices by requiring that public housing be developed in areas that will afford respondents an opportunity to reside in desegregated neighborhoods. But HUD contends that the *Milliken* decision bars a remedy affecting its conduct beyond the boundaries of Chicago for two reasons. First, it asserts that such a remedial order would constitute the grant of relief incommensurate with the constitutional violation to be repaired. And, second, it claims that a decree regulating HUD's conduct beyond Chicago's boundaries would inevitably have the effect of "consolidat(ing) for remedial purposes" governmental units not implicated in HUD's and CHA's violations. We address each of these arguments in turn.

A

We reject the contention that, since HUD's constitutional and statutory violations were committed in Chicago, *Milliken* precludes an order against HUD that will affect its conduct in the greater metropolitan area. The critical distinction between HUD and the suburban school districts in *Milliken* is that HUD has been found to have violated the Constitution. That violation provided the necessary predicate for the entry of a remedial order against HUD and, indeed, imposed a duty on the District Court to grant appropriate relief. Our prior decisions counsel that in the event of a constitutional violation "all reasonable methods be available to formulate an effective remedy," and that every effort should be made by a federal court to employ those methods "to achieve the greatest possible degree of (relief), taking into account the practicalities of the situation." As the Court observed in *Swann v. Charlotte-Mecklenburg Board of Education*: "Once a right and a violation have been shown, the scope of a district court's equitable powers to remedy past wrongs is broad, for breadth and flexibility are inherent in equitable remedies."

Nothing in the *Milliken* decision suggests a per se rule that federal courts lack authority to order parties found to have violated the Constitution to undertake remedial efforts beyond the municipal boundaries of the city where the violation occurred. As we noted in Part II, the District Court's proposed remedy in *Milliken* was impermissible because of the limits on the federal judicial power to interfere with the operation of state political entities that were not implicated in unconstitutional conduct. Here, unlike the desegregation remedy found erroneous in *Milliken*, a judicial order directing relief beyond the boundary lines of Chicago will not necessarily entail coercion of uninvolved governmental units, because both CHA and HUD have the authority to operate outside the Chicago city limits.

In this case, it is entirely appropriate and consistent with *Milliken* to order CHA and HUD to attempt to create housing alternatives for the respondents in the Chicago suburbs. Here the wrong committed by HUD confined the respondents to segregated public housing. The relevant geographic area for purposes of the respondents' housing options is the Chicago housing market, not the Chicago city limits. That HUD recognizes this reality is evident in its administration of federal housing assistance programs through "housing market areas" encompassing "the geographic area 'within which all dwelling units . . .' are in competition with one another as alternatives for the users of housing" [citing HUD material]. The housing market area "usually extends beyond the city limits" and in the larger markets "may extend into several adjoining counties." An order against HUD and CHA regulating their conduct in the greater metropolitan area will do no more than take into account HUD's expert determination of the area relevant to the respondents' housing opportunities and will thus be wholly commensurate with the "nature and extent of the constitutional violation." To foreclose such relief solely because HUD's constitutional violation took place within the city limits of Chicago would transform *Milliken*'s principled limitation on the exercise of federal judicial authority into an arbitrary and mechanical shield for those found to have engaged in unconstitutional conduct.

B

The more substantial question under *Milliken* is whether an order against HUD affecting its conduct beyond Chicago's boundaries would impermissibly interfere with local governments and suburban housing authorities that have not been implicated in HUD's unconstitutional conduct. In examining this issue, it is important to note that the Court of Appeals' decision did not endorse or even discuss "any specific metropolitan plan" but instead left the formulation of the remedial plan to the District Court on remand. On rehearing, the Court of Appeals characterized its remand order as one calling "for additional evidence and for further consideration of the issue of metropolitan area relief in light of this opinion and that of the Supreme Court in *Milliken v. Bradley*." In the current posture of the case, HUD's contention that any remand for consideration of a metropolitan area order would be impermissible as a matter of law must necessarily be based on its claim at oral argument "that court-ordered metropolitan relief in this case, no matter how gently it's gone about, no matter how it's framed, is bound to require HUD to ignore the safeguards of local autonomy and local political processes" and therefore to violate the limitations on federal judicial power established in *Milliken*. In addressing this contention we are not called upon, in other words, to evaluate the validity of any specific order, since no such order has yet been formulated.

HUD's position, we think, underestimates the ability of a federal court to formulate a decree that will grant the respondents the constitutional relief to which they may be entitled without overstepping the limits of judicial power established in the *Milliken* case. HUD's discretion regarding the selection of

housing proposals [for] funding as well as its authority under a recent statute to contract for low-income housing directly with private owners and
developers can clearly be directed toward providing relief to the respondents
in the greater Chicago metropolitan area without preempting the power of
local governments by undercutting the role of those governments in the federal housing assistance scheme. An order directing HUD to use its discretion
under the various federal housing programs to foster projects located in white
areas of the Chicago housing market would be consistent with and supportive
of well-established federal housing policy.

Among the steps taken by HUD to discharge its statutory duty to promote
fair housing was the adoption of project-selection criteria for use in "eliminating clearly unacceptable proposals and assigning priorities in funding to
assure that the best proposals are funded first." In structuring the minority
housing opportunity component of the project-selection criteria, HUD
attempted "to assure that building in minority areas goes forward only after
there truly exist housing opportunities for minorities elsewhere" in the housing market and to avoid encouraging projects located in substantially racially
mixed areas. More recently, in the Housing and Community Development
Act of 1974, Congress emphasized the importance of locating housing so as to
promote greater choice of housing opportunities and to avoid undue concentrations of lower income persons.

A remedial plan designed to insure that HUD will utilize its funding and
administrative powers in a manner consistent with affording relief to the
respondents need not abrogate the role of local governmental units in the
federal housing-assistance programs. Under the major housing programs in
existence at the time the District Court entered its remedial order pertaining
to HUD, local housing authorities and municipal governments had to make
application for funds or approve the use of funds in the locality before HUD
could make housing assistance money available. An order directed solely to
HUD would not force unwilling localities to apply for assistance under these
programs but would merely reinforce the regulations guiding HUD's determination of which of the locally authorized projects to assist with federal funds.

The Housing and Community Development Act of 1974 significantly
enlarged HUD's role in the creation of housing opportunities. Under the §8
Lower-Income Housing Assistance program, which has largely replaced the
older federal low-income housing programs, HUD may contract directly
with private owners to make leased housing units available to eligible lower
income persons. As HUD has acknowledged in this case, "local governmental approval is no longer explicitly required as a condition of the program's
applicability to a locality." Regulations governing the §8 program permit
HUD to select "the geographic area or areas in which the housing is to be constructed," and direct that sites be chosen to "promote greater choice of housing opportunities and avoid undue concentration of assisted persons in areas
containing a high proportion of low-income persons. In most cases the Act
grants the unit of local government in which the assistance is to be provided

the right to comment on the application and, in certain specified circumstances, to preclude the Secretary of HUD from approving the application. Use of the §8 program to expand low-income housing opportunities outside areas of minority concentration would not have a coercive effect on suburban municipalities. For under the program, the local governmental units retain the right to comment on specific assistance proposals, to reject certain proposals that are inconsistent with their approved housing-assistance plans, and to require that zoning and other land-use restrictions be adhered to by builders.

In sum, there is no basis for the petitioner's claim that court-ordered metropolitan area relief in this case would be impermissible as a matter of law under the *Milliken* decision. In contrast to the desegregation order in that case, a metropolitan area relief order directed to HUD would not consolidate or in any way restructure local governmental units. The remedial decree would neither force suburban governments to submit public housing proposals to HUD nor displace the rights and powers accorded local government entities under federal or state housing statutes or existing land-use laws. The order would have the same effect on the suburban governments as a discretionary decision by HUD to use its statutory powers to provide the respondents with alternatives to the racially segregated Chicago public housing system created by CHA and HUD.

Since we conclude that a metropolitan area remedy in this case is not impermissible as a matter of law, we affirm the judgment of the Court of Appeals remanding the case to the District Court "for additional evidence and for further consideration of the issue of metropolitan area relief."

NOTES AND QUESTIONS

1. Counsel for the Parties. Lead counsel for the plaintiffs in the *Gautreaux* litigation, from the beginning, was Alexander Polikoff. He began the case as a partner in a Chicago law firm, acting as a volunteer attorney for the ACLU, then became executive director of a public interest law firm known as Businessmen (later Business and Professional People) for the Public Interest (BPI) and now Impact for Equity. *See* Alexander Polikoff, WAITING FOR GAUTREAUX: A STORY OF SEGREGATION, HOUSING, AND THE BLACK GHETTO (Northwestern U. Press 2006).

2. The Aftermath of *Gautreaux*: Housing Mobility. After the Supreme Court's decision in *Hills v. Gautreaux*, HUD agreed with the plaintiffs that, in addition to other forms of relief, it would provide some 7,100 Section 8 certificates and vouchers for Black public housing residents and applicants. With the counseling and support of the Leadership Council for Metropolitan Open Communities, 83 percent of these families were able to move to areas where the Black population was less than 30 percent. This *Gautreaux* Housing Mobility Program (GHMP), which lasted from 1976 until 1998, was the largest residential racial desegregation program in the United States. Researchers

studied the program extensively and documented major beneficent consequences for the families who made integrative moves. As John Goering concluded: "Changes not observed in any other domestic urban policy initiative
had occurred in the lives of poor children apparently because they had moved
to less economically and racially isolated neighborhoods."[56]

These results led to expanded use of mobility remedies in other lawsuits,
the creation of the Moving to Opportunity demonstration (discussed below),
and the initiation of mobility programs by HUD, PHAs, and other state, local,
and private agencies. Mobility has been an important tool for implementing
the mandate to affirmatively further fair housing, particularly on a regional
basis.[57]

3. Other Cases. The jurisprudential victory in *Gautreaux* and the practical significance of the GHMP encouraged other litigators to bring similar
suits to desegregate public housing. In addition to *Gautreaux*, three of those
cases created "legacy" housing mobility programs: *Walker v. HUD* in Dallas,
Young v. Pierce in East Texas (both discussed below), and *Thompson v. HUD* in
Baltimore (discussed in Chapter 13).

The Dallas mobility program was administered by the Inclusive
Communities Project (ICP). Between 2005 and 2022, it assisted some 5,000
Black families to move to opportunity areas using vouchers. In addition to
mobility, *Walker* produced a host of other remedies against HUD, the city
of Dallas, and the Dallas Housing Authority. The remedies against the city
involved equalization of neighborhood conditions around the public housing
projects and the creation of low-income housing. In addition, the city financed
the Walker Housing Fund, which was used for developing public housing
and LIHTC units, and for voucher desegregation.[58]

---

56. John Goering, *Expanding Housing Choice and Integrating Neighborhoods: The MTO
Experiment, in* THE GEOGRAPHY OF OPPORTUNITY: RACE AND HOUSING CHOICE IN METROPOLITAN
AMERICA 134 (Xavier de Souza Briggs ed., Brookings Institution Press 2005); Gautreaux
v. Landrieu, 523 F. Supp. 665, 668-69 (N.D. Ill. 1981) (text of consent decree at 672-82), *aff'd sub. nom.*
Gautreaux v. Pierce, 690 F.2d 616 (7th Cir. 1982); Leonard S. Rubinowitz & James E. Rosenbaum,
CROSSING THE CLASS AND COLOR LINES FROM PUBLIC HOUSING TO WHITE SUBURBIA 40-43, 58 (U.
Chicago Press 2000) (Dr. Rosenbaum was one of the most persistent researchers of the *Gautreaux*
mobility program); Eric Chyn et al., *The Long-Run Effects of Residential Racial Desegregation
Programs: Evidence from Gautreaux* (Mar. 29, 2023) (unpublished manuscript), https://robcollinson
.github.io/RobWebsite/CCS_Gautreaux.pdf; Robert G. Schwemm, *Reflections on* Arlington
Heights: *Fifty Years of Exclusionary Zoning Litigation and Beyond*, 57 UIC L. REV. 389, 392-93 (2024)
(describing the Leadership Council).

57. See Chapter 13, especially the discussion of the *Thompson* and *Westchester County* cases.

58. The mobility remedies in *Walker* included funding for counseling, security deposits, moving
expenses, application fees, and landlord bonuses. *See* Walker v. HUD - Dallas Public Housing
Desegregation, Daniel & Beshara, P.C., https://www.danielbesharalawfirm.com/walker
-v-hud-dallas-public-housing-desegregation (last visited Aug. 2, 2024); Darryn Mumphery et al.,
Housing Mobility Programs in the U.S. 2022, PRRAC & MOBILITYWORKS 26-27 (Philip Tegeler ed.,
December 2022), available at https://www.prrac.org/housing-mobility-programs-in-the-u-s
-2022-december-2022/.

The *Young* litigation in East Texas (discussed below) produced a mobility program that enabled thousands of Black households to choose improved subsidized living accommodations in neighborhoods with more resources; it also produced "equalization" remedies that bettered the conditions at and around housing developments in which people of color live. Many other such cases were brought. As in *Gautreaux*, liability was straightforward; the challenge was relief. In almost every case, plaintiffs sought and obtained mobility remedies.[59]

4. Moving to Opportunity (MTO). In 1992, Congress created the MTO demonstration program, which enabled and studied voucher-based moves to lower poverty (but still minority-concentrated) areas in Baltimore, Boston, Chicago, Los Angeles, and New York. Fifty-four percent of participants were African American; 39 percent were Hispanic; and 93 percent were women with two or three children. Long-term studies showed that MTO children younger than 13 when they moved advanced significantly with respect to college attendance and earnings as adults. Further research has confirmed "that moving to lower-poverty, higher-opportunity neighborhoods earlier in childhood improves children's outcomes significantly."[60]

5. Mobility Programs at HUD and PHAs. In the wake of *Gautreaux*, its progeny, and the MTO program, HUD took some steps to make vouchers a better vehicle for mobility and created a variety of programs that built mobility into HUD's operations; also, some PHAs "initiated mobility programs without litigation or special HUD funding."[61] In 2019-20, Congress created a $50 million Housing Mobility Demonstration, now called "Community

---

59. For a discussion of these cases, see Roisman, *Affirmatively Furthering, supra* note 52, at 343-46; for a list, see Florence Wagman Roisman, *Long Overdue: Desegregation Litigation and Next Steps to End Discrimination and Segregation in the Public Housing and Section 8 Existing Housing Programs*, 4 CITYSCAPE 171, 194-96 (1999).

60. Peter Bergman et al., *Creating Moves to Opportunity: Experimental Evidence on Barriers to Neighborhood Choice*, 114 AMER. ECON. REV. 1281, 1282 (2024); Eric Chyn & Lawrence F. Katz, *Neighborhoods Matter: Assessing the Evidence for Place Effects*, 35 J. OF ECON. PERSPS. 197 (2021); Raj Chetty & Nathaniel Hendren, *The Impacts of Neighborhoods on Intergenerational Mobility I: Childhood Exposure Effects*, 133 THE Q. J. OF ECON. 1107 (2018); Raj Chetty, Nathaniel Hendren, & Lawrence F. Katz, *The Effects of Exposure to Better Neighborhoods on Children: New Evidence From the Moving to Opportunity Experiment*, 106 AM. ECON. REV. 855 (2016); Stefanie DeLuca, Susan Clampet-Lundquist, & Kathryn Edin, COMING OF AGE IN THE OTHER AMERICA 28-30 (Russell Sage Fndn. 2016); Charles M. Lamb, HOUSING SEGREGATION IN SUBURBAN AMERICA SINCE 1960: PRESIDENTIAL AND JUDICIAL POLITICS 193-94 (Cambridge U. Press 2005). Interim evaluations of MTO had shown the greatest benefits for women and adolescent girls in physical and mental health and perceptions of safety. Xavier de Souza Briggs & Margery Austin Turner, *Assisted Housing Mobility and the Success of Low-Income Minority Families: Lessons for Policy, Practice, and Future Research*, 1 NW. J. L. & SOC. POL'Y 25, 45 (2006).

61. Rubinowitz & Rosenbaum, *supra* note 56, at 177 (stating that HUD incorporated mobility into Regional Opportunity Counseling and its Vacancy Consolidation Program and discussing PHA innovations in several places); HUD Mobility Toolkit, https://www.hud.gov/sites/dfiles /PIH/documents/Housing_Mobility_Toolkit_Updating_Program_Materials.pdf; Housing Mobility Programs, *supra* note 58, at 20-21.

Choice," and in 2022 Congress appropriated $25 million in housing mobility grants.[62] Despite some advances, advocates claim HUD has made "slow progress in expanding crucial regulatory reforms in the voucher program to remove barriers and incentivize mobility."[63] As of this writing, the Housing Choice Voucher program has not incorporated across the board all the most effective of the *Gautreaux*-style mobility program tools, including counseling and moving assistance.

6. *Young v. Pierce.* One post-*Gautreaux* case reached beyond public housing in a single urban jurisdiction: It challenged racial segregation in all HUD's housing programs in 36 counties in East Texas. This was *Young v. Pierce*, filed in 1980 in the Eastern District of Texas before Judge William Wayne Justice and continuing until 2004.

In 1982, Judge Justice upheld the plaintiffs' standing and right to sue HUD and certified the class.[64] With respect to Title VI, he wrote:

> To the extent a plaintiff asserts that the federal agency is violating the terms of the federal statute, by abdicating an affirmative duty to eliminate discrimination, then the action is properly brought against the agency. In such a circumstance, the agency is a partner in discrimination, and may be held responsible for this complicity [citing Garrett v. City of Hamtramck, 503 F.2d 1236 (6th Cir. 1974); Gautreaux v. Romney (7th Cir. 1971); Hicks v. Weaver (E.D. La. 1969)].

With respect to the FHA, he considered HUD's duty to affirmatively further fair housing (AFFH) (Chapter 13):

> The scope of the CRA of 1968 is majestic, and its enforcement provisions are commensurately broad. The Act was passed in recognition of the sordid story of which all Americans should be ashamed developed by this country in the immediate post World War II era, during which the FHA, the VA, and other Federal agencies encouraged, assisted, and made easy the flight of white people from the central cities of white America, leaving behind only the Negroes and others unable to take advantage of these liberalized extensions of credit and credit guarantees.
>
> Traditionally the American Government has been more than neutral on this issue. The record of the U.S. Government in that period is one, at best, of covert collaborator in policies which established the present outrageous and heartbreaking living patterns which lie at the core of the tragedy of the American city and the alienation of good people from good people because of the utter irrelevancy of color.
>
> The "purpose or 'end' of the Federal Fair Housing Act is to remove the walls of discrimination which enclose minority groups." As the Supreme Court noted "the reach of the proposed law was to replace the ghettos 'by truly integrated and balanced living patterns.'" *Trafficante.*

---

62. *Housing Mobility Programs, supra* note 58, at 1, 47-48.

63. *Id.* at 1; specific suggestions and background are in Philip Tegeler, *Housing Choice Voucher Reform: A Primer for 2021 and Beyond*, PRRAC (Aug. 2020), https://www.prrac.org/pdf/housing-choice-voucher-reform-agenda.pdf.

64. Young v. Pierce, 544 F. Supp. 1010 (E.D. Tex. 1982).

In view of the clarity of this duty [under §3608(d)(5)], it seems axiomatic that violations of [AFFH] through inaction or indolence must be actionable. Failure of HUD "affirmatively to further the policies of (Title VIII)" is illegal in a fundamental sense. An agent of the federal government is no more at liberty to flout federal law than is a state governmental unit, or a private citizen. A private person victimized by an illegal act of the federal government may seek redress, by means of legal action against the offending governmental unit.

Viewed another way, the failure of HUD to perform its legal duties mandated by §3608(d)(5) constitutes a discriminatory housing practice, in itself. . . . Title VIII is founded on the irrefutable premise that the prevailing structure of the housing market in this country bears the stamp of a long history of discrimination in all forms of social life. Present housing allocation is distorted, both by the after-effects of legally sanctioned racial discrimination, and by the enduring prevalence of discrimination, despite a "complete arsenal of federal authority" aimed at eradicating it. *Jones v. Alfred H. Mayer Co.* The Supreme Court has acknowledged the "enormity of the task of assuring fair housing," *Trafficante.* In view of the scope of the mission, the "main generating force must be private suits. . . .

After the 1982 decision, but before the broader issues were addressed, a related lawsuit sought immediate relief for the named plaintiff, Ms. Lucille Young.[65] Ms. Young, a Black mother of six, lived in Clarksville, Texas, and had applied for public housing in 1979. When the lawsuit was filed in 1980, Ms. Young was in desperate need of housing and was at the top of the list for a four-bedroom unit. In a preliminary injunction opinion and order, Judge Justice made findings and provided relief:

[At the time of Ms. Young's application and from its inception, the Housing Authority of Clarksville (HAC)] did not follow the HUD required Method of Administration for tenant selection and assignment. [Rather,] tenants were assigned on the basis of race, with all black applicants being offered vacancies in the Cheathem Heights and Dryden sites, located in black neighborhoods, and all white applicants being offered vacancies in College Heights, located in a white neighborhood. The white site has paved streets, concrete curbs and gutters, and sidewalks. The black sites have unpaved streets, no drainage, and no sidewalks.

In 1981, HUD did a Title VI review of HAC, which found that HAC was maintaining historically racially identifiable housing developments, and that race was a factor in assigning tenants to housing. HAC did not contest these findings, but, rather, entered into a compliance agreement that called for an end to the assignment of tenants on the basis of race, as well as affirmative efforts to desegregate the projects. Since the signing of the compliance agreement in 1981, there has been no black tenant assigned to the white College Heights site, and no white tenant has been placed in the apartments at the two black sites.

---

65. For a discussion of *Young v. Pierce* and this related suit, see Frank R. Kemerer, William Wayne Justice: A Judicial Biography 340-55 (U. Texas Press 1991). (The related suit, Young v. Whiteman, Civ. Action No. P-82-37-CA (E.D. Tex., Oct. 11, 1983), is discussed at 343-46.)

Since the HUD finding of apparent non-compliance, there have been twenty-four vacancies in HAC, ten at the Dryden and Cheatham sites and fourteen at the College Heights site. One result of the assignment of tenants by race is that a number of units, in both black and white sites, are occupied by inappropriately sized family units, thereby reducing the number of available larger (two to four-bedroom) units. But for the purpose of maintaining racially segregated projects and the manipulation of the tenant selection and assignment process to that end, an appropriately sized unit would be available to plaintiff.

Because of her exclusion from HAC plaintiff Young and her family have been forced to live in seriously dilapidated and unsafe housing. Her eviction from this shelter is imminent. She has been excluded by the de jure segregationist policies and practices of HAC. The wrongful exclusion from public housing is an irreparable injury. HAC's continued use of segregation is also an irreparable injury.

The requested relief—integrative transfers, use of a non-segregative tenant selection and assignment plan, and admission of Plaintiff Young into the projects—will impose no legally cognizable harm on defendants. They will have to perform the administrative tasks necessary to end the segregation, steps which should have been taken years ago.

From its inception, HAC has flouted the law of the land by purposefully selecting and assigning tenants by the purpose of segregating them by race. The public has no interest that will not be served by the requested relief.

The court issued a preliminary injunction requiring defendants to "submit to this court for approval a mandatory tenant transfer plan" that would transfer residents to appropriately sized units in projects in which their race does not presently predominate: "Enough tenants must be transferred to insure that the racial make up of each site is within 5% of 50% white and 50% black—the present racial composition of the entire HAC tenant population. Defendants will provide any necessary moving assistance to all transferring tenants." The court also ordered "immediate offer of a unit to plaintiff Young."

Defendants unsuccessfully sought a stay from the Fifth Circuit. National media focused negative attention on the order. The order "made the issue of public housing segregation a nationwide concern." In 1985, two Dallas Morning News reporters, Craig Flournoy and George Rodrigue, published "an eight-part Pulitzer Prize-winning series . . . document[ing] pervasive discrimination in the nation's sixty thousand federally subsidized developments. . . ." The series also sparked investigations by the House of Representatives and the U.S. Commission on Civil Rights. Judge Justice said that the series made his task easier because it "saturated the East Texas countryside with all the evils of the existing system and how it had to be dismantled. . . ."[66]

After this October 1983 preliminary injunction, the court proceeded to address cross motions for summary judgment on the question of liability.

---

66. Kemerer, *supra* note 65, at 344-47.

Young v. Pierce
628 F. Supp. 1037 (E.D. Texas 1985)

JUSTICE, Chief Judge:

Plaintiffs in this class action allege that defendant HUD has knowingly maintained, and continues to maintain, a system of racially segregated housing in violation of the Constitution and laws of the United States. Specifically, the plaintiff class asserts that HUD, in funding and overseeing this housing, has discriminated against blacks in violation of the Fifth Amendment; Title VI of the CRA of 1964; Title VIII of the CRA of 1968; as well as the CRA of 1866, 42 U.S.C. §§1981 and 1982. The plaintiff class consists of all black applicants for, and residents of, HUD-assisted housing in 36 East Texas counties ("the class action counties"). HUD does not construct, own, or operate any housing itself. Rather, its role is essentially promotional. Through a number of programs, HUD provides significant financial support, technical assistance, and regulatory oversight for the providers of public housing.

[EDS. — The court noted that three types of HUD programs were at issue: public housing funded by HUD and managed by PHAs; programs where HUD subsidized mortgage and insurance costs to encourage the construction of low income housing; and the Section 8 voucher program.] In the class action counties, the three major programs at issue in this litigation can best be understood as representing periods of HUD activity: until the mid-1960s, HUD created low rent projects almost exclusively; from the late 1960s until the mid-1970s, the chief form of subsidy was "Insured-Assisted Housing"; since the mid-1970s, HUD has mostly been engaged in §8 new housing. The Insured-Assisted and §8 programs, while administratively distinct, are in many cases mixed in fact. According to HUD, a number of projects have enjoyed both forms of assistance.

THE MOTIONS FOR SUMMARY JUDGMENT

The parties have included with their motions extensive administrative records, depositions, interrogatories, and affidavits. In particular, HUD has produced some 105 volumes of records from its Fort Worth and Dallas offices, containing administrative documents relating to PHAs in the class counties.

The information produced by HUD indicates that the public housing sites it funds are segregated by race. Blacks live in one set of public housing sites, whites in another. Of 219 sites, 121 — more than half — are completely segregated, one-race projects. An additional sixty-two project sites are 85% or more one-race. In many cases the percentage of non-predominate racial group members . . . comprise[s] . . . one or two units in an otherwise one-race project site.

In its standard compliance agreement, defendant defines a race-predominate site as one in which 75% or more of a site is occupied by one race. Using this yardstick, an additional sixteen sites would be added to the list of segregated projects. An additional five sites can be added to this number if black and hispanic residents are treated together. Thus, 199 of the project sites—more than 90%—are either predominately minority or predominately white, with the great majority of these being completely segregated.

The pattern of segregation is as striking if projects are grouped according to the form of support they receive from HUD. A measure of the extent of segregation in HUD-assisted housing is that it is simpler to summarize racial occupancy patterns by giving the percentage of *integrated* facilities. Only eleven, or 7%, of the low rent projects are *not* predominately one race. Of thirty-six insured-assisted projects, four, or 11%, are *not* predominately one-race. Of twenty-two §8 new construction projects, five, or 23%, are *not* predominately one race. A close analysis also reveals skewed patterns of participation in these programs. While the races occupy low-rent housing in roughly equal numbers, 77% of all insured-assisted units in the class counties are occupied by blacks. In contrast, 76% of §8 new construction units are occupied by whites. Defendants' data also indicates that, in regard to these last two programs, discrimination can be parsed along temporal lines: 84% of projects approved before 1972 are 85 to 100% black. Of those approved after 1972, 48% are 85 to 100% white, 12% are 85 to 100% black, and 39% are at least partially integrated.

The parties agree that there is a rough equivalency of demand for public housing between white and minority groups in the class action counties. According to the 1980 Census, blacks constitute 43% of the persons living below the poverty level in the class action counties, and 66% of those living in housing without plumbing.

In conclusion, then, a number of factual conclusions may be drawn from defendants' data: (1) the vast majority of projects are predominately one race; (2) the percentage of one-race sites is highest in the low rent projects; (3) blacks participate disproportionately in older insured-assisted projects; (4) whites participate disproportionately in §8 new construction projects; and (5) the races have roughly equivalent needs for public housing.

The extent of HUD's knowledge of and support for this system of segregated housing is sharply disputed by the parties. In the early stages of this litigation, HUD professed ignorance of segregation in public housing, and now alleges that it has learned of its existence only through this action. HUD also argues that segregation exists in public housing only in spite of its vigorous efforts to eradicate it. Plaintiffs allege that HUD has a duty to acquaint itself with its own functionings, has been in fact aware of the racially identifiable nature of the housing it operates, and has continued to fund and operate this housing while knowing it to be segregated. In order to resolve the disputed questions, it is necessary to look at the historical background of the present situation of public housing in East Texas. The court will first set out the facts of the development of the national public housing system, of which the class action counties are a part. Specific facts relevant to HUD's actions in East Texas will then be discussed.

Prior to 1964, public housing was *de jure* segregated. These projects were operated according to a Public Housing Administration ("federal PHA") policy of "separate but equal." Cohen v. Public Housing Administration, 257 F.2d 73, 74 (5th Cir. 1958) (federal PHA regulations required that public housing programs "reflect equitable provisions for eligible families of all races determined on the approximate volume of their respective needs for such housing."). As of 1962, there was only one public housing project in the Southern states having even token integration.

In 1962, a nationwide policy against discrimination in federally assisted housing was established by President John F. Kennedy's Executive Order No. 11063. The federal PHA—HUD's predecessor agency—responded to this order by issuing regulations requiring future contracts with local housing authorities to include an anti-discrimination covenant, but exempting all existing projects from any duty to desegregate. The federal PHA had no policy of tenant selection and assignment aimed at desegregation until 1964. In [response to] Title VI of the [1964 Civil Rights Act], the federal PHA permitted local housing authorities to follow a "Freedom of Choice" policy, allowing prospective tenants to choose a housing site in which they desired to live. The only activity engendered by this new policy seems to have been the distribution by the federal PHA of Form PHA-3037, requiring the local provider to acknowledge previous segregation and adopt the freedom of choice plan. This new policy had no significant impact nationwide. The record is bereft of any evidence of a single project being desegregated in response to federal PHA pressure before 1964.

The record contains no indication of HUD activity designed to end segregation between 1965 and 1967. In 1967, HUD promulgated regulations, pursuant to Title VI, instituting a new tenant selection and assignment policy. This policy, which is still in effect, specifies a racially neutral tenant assignment plan "providing for assignment on a community-wide basis in sequence based upon the date and time the application is received, the size or type of unit suitable, and [other] factors." According to the 1981 Assessment Report by the Office of HUD Program Compliance:

> There were some assumptions about race which underlay the adoption of the 1967 policy. It was assumed that in many cities the local housing authorities had black projects with long waiting lists and white projects with no waiting lists at all. It was assumed that offers of units in white projects would overcome the reluctance of blacks to move into such projects, resulting in the desegregation of the previously white projects. The policy was not designed to desegregate black projects. . . .

In 1967, HUD also issued site-approval rules which prevented HUD approval of "any proposal to locate housing only in areas of racial concentration." These HUD policies were ineffective in remedying past segregation or preventing segregated occupancy in new project sites. This failure was apparent, in regard to the tenant selection plans, as early as 1969. In November 1972, HUD's Office of General Counsel wrote that the existing tenant selection and assignment policy was "difficult to enforce and of dubious value" and proposed a new plan.

In 1972, HUD promulgated regulations implementing Title VIII of the Civil Rights Act of 1968, which prohibit[ed] construction of new public housing projects in areas of minority concentration, and to require developers in other areas to follow an Affirmative Fair Housing Marketing Plan ("Fair Housing Plan").

HUD's actions in consistently refusing to fund housing in minority areas is balanced, in principle, by efforts to market new public housing to minority group members. HUD's Fair Housing Plan Handbook states that

> [t]he program indicated by the Plan should include efforts to reach those persons who traditionally would not have been expected to apply for the housing. For housing located in predominately white areas, it will normally be necessary to make special efforts to make its availability known to minorities; similarly, for housing in areas of minority concentration, special efforts may be needed to make its availability known to whites.

The Handbook goes on to state that the Equal Opportunity Staff will conduct compliance reviews of the Fair Housing Plan throughout the life of the HUD mortgage. As the then General Counsel of HUD succinctly wrote at the time these regulations were promulgated, "Clearly, the availability of low — and moderate — income housing outside an area of minority concentration means nothing to residents of that area who never learn of it."

Data supplied by HUD indicates that it began to process applications for §8 New Construction projects in 1977. These projects are subject to site selection and marketing regulations which parallel those of 1972 (relating to rent supplement and insured-assisted projects). The site selection standards provide:

> (c) the site must not be located in:
> (1) An area of minority concentration unless (i) sufficient, comparable opportunities exist for housing for minority families, in the income range to be served by the proposed project, outside areas of minority concentration, or (ii) the project is necessary to meet overriding housing needs which cannot otherwise feasibly be met in that housing market area. . . .
> or
> (2) A racially mixed area if the project will cause a significant increase in the proportion of minority to non-minority residents in the area.

24 C.F.R. §880.206. The Fair Housing Plan standards for Section 8 New Construction are the same as for other HUD projects. While these regulations do not hold HUD to any percentage of minority occupation, they clearly charge the agency with, at the very least, *knowing* the proposed and actual racial mixture.

The 1977 Interagency Survey of HUD Title VI enforcement activities, conducted by the Civil Rights Division of the Department of Justice, pointed out numerous deficiencies in HUD's nationwide performance of its duties to prevent and remedy segregation in public housing. The report found that HUD had failed to develop an effective Title VI review program [EDS.—and had admitted this fact].

If a HUD-sponsored project is found to be in violation of Title VI, HUD's response is today what it was in 1975: the offending owner or PHA is required to enter into a compliance agreement, ostensibly designed to eliminate racial segregation. Under this plan, an applicant is first offered units in projects where their race does not predominate. If no units are available at these sites, then the applicant will be offered units at sites where his or her race does predominate. An applicant may choose to postpone making a unit choice without losing his or her place on the waiting list for public housing. However, if applicants refuse all units in projects where their race does not predominate, they are moved to the bottom of the waiting list. Adoption of such a compliance agreement serves to administratively clear HUD's finding of Title VI non-compliance.

PLAINTIFFS' FIFTH AMENDMENT CLAIM

HUD has intentionally and knowingly continued to promote purposefully segregated housing in the class action counties. It is beyond dispute that the Constitution prohibits the government from funding racial discrimination with the public dollar. Indeed, *any* tangible assistance to segregation is prohibited if it has a "significant tendency to facilitate, reinforce, and support private discrimination." *Norwood v. Harrison*, 413 U.S. 455, 466 (1973); . . . *Cooper v. Aaron*, 358 U.S. 1, 19 (1959); . . . *Gautreaux v. Romney*, 448 F.2d 731 (7th Cir. 1971). HUD's funding, regulation and assistance of local PHAs is clearly unconstitutional support of segregation within the meaning of these cases.

Defendants argue that plaintiffs must show, not only that HUD has supported racial discrimination, but that it has done so with discriminatory intent. While the record does establish HUD's intent to discriminate, this argument fundamentally misapprehends the law. Defendants rely principally on Supreme Court cases involving facially neutral government practices allegedly having a disparate impact. The actions complained of here are not in any sense facially neutral: HUD supports those authorities it knows to discriminate. HUD has received numerous indications that substantially all local PHA's in the class counties discriminate, and even that they intend to keep doing so, and in *no instance* has effective action to end or discourage discrimination been taken. HUD has also followed racially conscious policies which have furthered this discrimination. These policies include refusal to fund projects in areas of minority concentration, failure to enforce its own affirmative marketing regulations, and use of race-conscious remedial tenant assignment plans which appear to be utterly ineffectual in effecting desegregation.

Even if HUD's discriminatory intent had to be shown, the same finding of liability would obtain. *Washington v. Davis* holds, first, that discriminatory intent must be shown to establish liability when facially neutral government action is at issue and, second, that a mere showing of statistically disparate impact will often be insufficient to give rise to a tenable inference of discriminatory intent. "'Discriminatory purpose,' however, implies more than intent as violation or intent as awareness of consequences. It implies that the decisionmaker . . . selected or reaffirmed a particular course of action at least in part 'because of,' not merely 'in spite of,' its adverse effects upon an identifiable group." [Personnel Adm'r of Mass. v. Feeney, 442 U.S. 256, 279 (1979).] These cases do not, as defendants suggest, set out a substantive rule of law that a massively discriminatory outcome cannot be used to show intent to achieve this result. Rather, they discuss the circumstances under which intent may be inferred from statistics. In a footnote, the Court in *Feeney* explained further:

> [w]hen the adverse consequences of a law upon an identifiable group are inevitable . . . a strong inference that the adverse effects were desired can reasonably be drawn. But in this inquiry—made as it is under the Constitution—an inference is a working tool, not a synonym for proof. When, as here, the impact is essentially an unavoidable consequence of a legislative policy that has in itself always been deemed to be legitimate, and when, as here, the statutory history and all of the available evidence affirmatively demonstrate the opposite, the inference simply fails to ripen into proof.

Id. at 279 n.25. This footnote is highly relevant to HUD's arguments. First, it is evident that the adverse consequences of HUD's policies upon blacks *were* inevitable: HUD's policies of ineffectively enforcing Title VI, of failing to supervise racially prejudiced local PHAs, of vetoing construction in minority neighborhoods, and of ignoring regulations requiring HUD to monitor affirmative action in marketing were simply a blueprint for segregation. Nor has HUD suggested that segregation is an "unavoidable consequence" of a legitimate policy. In this action, at least, the court is satisfied that the inference which arises from the segregated housing in the class counties *does* ripen into proof.

HUD's discriminatory intent is, moreover, demonstrated by an "inquiry into such circumstantial and direct evidence of intent as may be available." *Arlington Heights.* HUD's chief defense to the claim of intentional discrimination is the contention that, until this action was instituted, HUD was ignorant of the uses to which the public funds it distributes were being put. HUD seems to argue that it can fulfill its duty to eradicate segregation through the ostrich-like tactic of maintaining this ignorance.

It has been clear at least since the passage of Title VIII—if not from the date of Executive Order 11063 and HUD's inception as a federal agency—that HUD has had an affirmative duty to eradicate segregation. A necessary prerequisite for fulfilling this duty is to obtain information about discrimination practiced under HUD's auspices. Even if its protestations of ignorance were to be accepted, HUD would have violated the Fifth

Amendment by willfully ignoring the facts necessary to fulfill its constitutional and statutory duties.[67]

HUD's duty to investigate aside, it is clear that HUD was actually aware of the segregated housing which gave rise to this action. The record contains a number of instances where HUD received such knowledge directly. These incidents constitute compelling evidence that housing in the class action counties was substantially segregated long before this action was filed. The court has listed twenty such instances. In each case, a local housing authority was found, before the institution of this action, to be in substantive violation of Title VI or of the regulations promulgated to implement its mandates. Such a mass of violations in representative PHA's should have led HUD to a realization that violations of Title VI were endemic in the class counties.

HUD actually realized the true situation. Knowledge of discrimination in the class counties is demonstrated by the September 20, 1974, memorandum, titled "TO ALL HOUSING AUTHORITIES," which stated that surveys conducted by the Dallas Area Office had "revealed numerous cases of noncompliance in implementing the Tenant Selection and Assignment Plan. . . ." The memorandum informs all PHA's that adoption of the plan is required under Title VI, and that Title VIII mandates that all citizens be given an equal right to apply for public housing. It concludes that "[t]he Dallas Area Office Management and Equal Opportunity staff [of HUD] will continue to review housing [authorities'] compliance with the above requirements." This memorandum shows, first, that HUD was conducting periodic reviews; second, that these reviews indicated widespread non-compliance with HUD's Title VI regulations; and, finally, that HUD was aware that instances of non-compliance were not limited to the actual abuses officially reported in reviews. HUD's own surveys, as evidenced by the reports themselves and by its memorandum, clearly show that HUD was aware of the segregated nature of the housing which it funds. . . .

In addition, it should be noted, HUD had received numerous indications that segregation was present in HUD housing everywhere, and therefore *a fortiori* widespread in the class action counties. Allegations identical to those here have been raised in many cases against HUD.

Auxiliary information about the generally segregated nature of public housing was available to HUD through a number of major public events, such as the issuance of President Kennedy's Executive Order 11063, banning racial discrimination in federally funded programs, and from the passage of Titles VI and VIII. In particular, the passage of Title VIII was a recognition by the Congress that problems of discrimination existed in public housing throughout the nation. Senator Brooke, speaking in support of the Act, accused HUD of having an attitude of "amiable apartheid" and stated:

---

67. [Fn. 9 in original] "O foolish people, and without understanding: which have eyes and see not; which have ears, and hear not." 5 *Jeremiah* 21.

Rarely does HUD withhold funds or defer action in the name of desegregation. In fact, if it were not for all the printed guidelines the housing agencies have issued since 1964, one would scarcely know a Civil Rights Act had been passed.

114 Cong. Rec. 2281 (1968). As the facts of this action demonstrate, the same could be said at the present.

Defendants argue that any allegation of discriminatory intent is refuted by the mass of HUD regulations which contain declarations of intent not to discriminate. HUD cites no support for the proposition that publishing anti-discriminatory regulations is dispositive of the issue of intent. Nor could HUD do so, given that its officers have testified that they see no inconsistency between following these regulations and maintaining segregated housing.

HUD's intent to discriminate is established by the combination of HUD's disingenuous assertions of ignorance, its actual knowledge of segregation, and its continuing financial support of each public housing site in the class counties. In those instances where HUD responded at all to its knowledge of discrimination, it has been only through the use of compliance agreements which have been shown by HUD's own data to be ineffective in dealing with discrimination. The picture which emerges from the undisputed facts in this action is nearly identical to that painted by the Court of Appeals for the Eighth Circuit in its examination of HUD's role in nurturing segregation in Texarkana, Arkansas:

> In our view, the only reasonable inference that can be drawn is that HUD's actions were motivated at least in part by a discriminatory purpose. It is inconceivable that HUD would have so frequently acted to approve the [Texarkana Housing Authority's] actions for so long unless its officials held that view that segregation and discrimination were acceptable. The possible neutral explanations for the agency's actions concerning changes in the [Authority's] operation—a lack of resources or a desire to supply funds for low income housing—do not sufficiently negate the strong inference of discriminatory purpose that arises from the objective evidence contained in the agency's own files.

Clients' Council v. Pierce, 711 F.2d at 1423.

The record in this case clearly makes out defendant's violation of the Fifth Amendment to the United States Constitution. HUD has consistently supported and funded each project instituted under its aegis. HUD's inactivity has been limited to those aspects of its affirmative action responsibilities which might have an actual impact in desegregating federally funded housing. It has actively employed race-conscious policies which result in segregation. In the area covered by this action, those who have administered these projects have done so in a way clearly animated by racial prejudice. HUD has a duty to know how its money is spent, and in fact has known that it is supporting segregated housing in East Texas. Notwithstanding, it has continued to actively support the system in perhaps the most effective possible way—by paying for it. HUD has thus played a crucial and continuing role in creating and maintaining a large system of publicly funded segregated housing.

[Eds. — The Court granted summary judgment to plaintiffs on the issue of liability under the constitutional claims, which it held to be dispositive in finding defendants liable under §§1981 and 1982 of the Civil Rights Act, the FHA, and Title VI. With respect to Title VIII, particularly the AFFH mandate, the court stated, "It is obvious that intentional discrimination also violates Title VIII, 42 U.S.C. §3608(e)." Rejecting HUD's claim that plaintiffs were required to exhaust their administrative remedies under Title VI, the court said:] There can be no exhaustion requirement here, because it is "clear beyond doubt that the relevant administrative agency [in this case] will not grant the relief in question." The relief sought in this action is the disestablishment of segregated public housing in the class counties. The record is replete with instances of violations of Title VI regulations having been brought to HUD's attention. HUD cannot point to a single occasion where such information furnished to it has resulted in integration. Defendant is disingenuous in asserting that plaintiffs should be forced to go through a proven "exercise of futility" in the hopes that it will, for the first time, prove effective. This is especially true when HUD's own officials in charge of the Title VI review process in East Texas have testified, in depositions submitted by the parties, that in their view Title VI's requirements are satisfied whenever federal funding recipients carry out HUD procedures properly, and that HUD has no power or authority to seek actual desegregation.

NOTES AND QUESTIONS

1. The Subsequent History of *Young v. Pierce*; Housing Mobility in East Texas. After much discovery, the district court entered an injunctive order and appointed a master to oversee relief. HUD appealed to the Fifth Circuit, and the parties agreed that the plaintiff class and the case would be limited to the Low Rent Public Housing program, excluding the rent supplement and Section 8 programs. The Fifth Circuit then remanded the case to the district court. The litigation "produced a substantial record of HUD's complicity in racial discrimination and segregation, and led to significant improvements in the national administration of the public housing program."[68]

In 1990, Judge Justice required HUD to file desegregation plans (or a declaration of unitary status) for each of the 70 PHAs in East Texas and to fund a nonprofit FHO that would help provide desegregated housing opportunities in the 36 counties. About a decade of recalcitrance and contempt proceedings led to compliance, with remedies for the gross inequities between the living conditions for Blacks and whites who relied on subsidized housing. The developments in which many Black people lived were rehabilitated, including

---

68. Roisman, *Affirmatively Furthering, supra* note 52, at 344.

the provision of air conditioning for the first time. Thirteen million dollars in State Community Development Block Grant funds was used to improve water, sewer, and drainage, pave roads, and provide in Black neighborhoods other facilities that were available in white neighborhoods. More than 5,000 desegregated housing opportunities were created by the construction of new public housing units and the use of vouchers. The FHO was funded, and HUD provided millions of dollars for security deposits, counseling, moving expenses, application fees, and landlord incentives. Fair Market Rent levels were increased dramatically to enable the use of vouchers in better resourced, predominantly white neighborhoods.[69]

Young was filed by "Elizabeth K. Julian and Michael M. Daniel, two lawyers in Dallas who started out with legal services and then went into private practice"; they filed similar suits "in Texarkana, Arkansas, . . . and in Dallas."[70] Daniel, later joined by Laura Beshara, filed other similar suits, including the *Inclusive Communities* suit central to the disparate impact chapter of this book.

2. Judge Justice. The aptly named judge William Wayne Justice (1920-2009) was appointed by President Lyndon Johnson to the U.S. District Court for the Eastern District of Texas in 1968 and served until his death in 2009.[71] He was Chief Judge from 1980 to 1990 and assumed senior status in 1998. Born in Athens, Texas, he earned an LL.B. from the University of Texas School of Law and was in the U.S. Army from 1942-1946. President Kennedy appointed him U.S. Attorney for the Eastern District of Texas in 1961. He

Hon. William Wayne Justice

---

69. *Public Housing Desegregation*, Daniel & Beshara, P.C., https://www.danielbesharalawf irm.com/public-housing-desegregation (last visited Aug. 2, 2024); HUD & Texas State Office of Public Housing, *Young v. Martinez* Litigation: Desegregated Housing Opportunity Guide, available at https://static1.squarespace.com/static/61af25763e561d7c6ac7f6be/t/61c022ed2 f70593e63fbffe2/1639981806311/2+DHO+Guide.pdf; Email from Laura Beshara to FW Roisman (July 15, 2024) (on file with FW Roisman).

70. Roisman, *Affirmatively Furthering, supra* note 52, at 343.

71. The Honorable William Wayne Justice 1920-2009, William Wayne Justice Center for Public Interest Law, https:// law.utexas.edu/publicinterest/about/william-wayne-justice/ (last accessed Aug. 2, 2024); Douglas Martin, *William Wayne Justice, Judge Who Remade Texas, Dies at 89*, N.Y. TIMES, Oct. 15, 2009, https://www.nytimes.com/2009/10/16/us/16justice.html.

"issued comprehensive reform orders on statewide school desegregation, incarceration of juvenile delinquents in state institutions, the teaching of bilingual education in public schools, the operation of state prisons, and the care of institutionalized persons with mental retardation. In addition, he had been involved in landmark voter discrimination litigation, had ordered a tuition-free public education for undocumented alien children [*Doe v. Plyer*], and adjudicated important First Amendment, employment, and criminal cases."[72] In 2004, the William Wayne Justice Center for Public Interest Law was established in his honor at the University of Texas at Austin School of Law.

3. Title VI of the 1964 Civil Rights Act. In *Gautreaux*, in *Young*, and in many other cases, Title VI of the 1964 Civil Rights Act plays a supporting role, along with Title VIII, the 1866 Civil Rights Act, and the Fifth and Fourteenth Amendments. In its earlier years, Title VI was especially useful because it was understood to bar actions that had the effect, as well as the intent, of discriminating, and its regulations expressly authorized disparate impact liability. However, in Alexander v. Sandoval, 532 U.S. 275 (2001), a 5-4 majority maintained that Title VI itself barred only intentional discrimination and held that there was no private right of action to enforce regulations that purported to impose liability for actions with disparate impact. This has made Title VI significantly less useful to civil rights plaintiffs.

4. The Aftermath of *Young*: Vidor. Eight years after the decision in *Young*, a 1993 related court order brought the first Black tenant to public housing in the all-white, East Texas town of Vidor. Harassment by the Ku Klux Klan drove out this first Black tenant and the few others who followed him. In response, "[i]n a unique display of federal power, [HUD] Secretary Cisneros quickly marched into Vidor, seized the Orange County Housing Authority there, demanded the resignation of housing authority members, and pledged to move several African American families into HUD-owned Vidor Village."[73] Ultimately, the public housing in Vidor was closed because of the resistance to integration there.

Honorable Henry Cisneros, Secretary of HUD, 1993-1997

72. Kemerer, *supra* note 65, at x, xii; for other details about Judge Justice, see *id.* at 4, 10, 12, 15, 47.

73. Lamb, *supra* note 60, at 196.

Chapter Summary

- Tax subsidies for homeowners are the largest and most expensive of the federal housing programs, costing taxpayers more than $80.1 billion in FY 2022. These subsidies are most useful to those with the most costly homes and disproportionately benefit white people.
- The three major categories of federal housing programs that assist low- and moderate-income people now are public housing, vouchers, and project-based rental assistance, principally the Low Income Housing Tax Credit Program.
- Public housing was intentionally segregated by race at its inception, and governmental stewards of the program failed to dismantle segregation on their own. Lawsuits prompted serious desegregation efforts, starting with the *Gautreaux* litigation in Chicago. Mobility remedies using vouchers were deployed in such suits and in subsequent policy initiatives, producing substantial, documented benefits to families who made integrative moves. Equalization remedies, investing comprehensively in neighborhoods and people most injured by segregation, also have been important in desegregation litigation.

CHAPTER 13

THE GOVERNMENT'S AFFIRMATIVE DUTY TO FURTHER FAIR HOUSING

Perhaps no provision of the FHA has greater potential to remedy the multifaceted and mutually reinforcing mechanisms of government-sponsored racial segregation than the mandate imposed on many federal, state, and local government agencies to affirmatively further fair housing (AFFH). Yet, despite its promise, the AFFH mandate has largely eluded attention, commitment, and enforcement.

One of the most important issues relating to AFFH is recognizing what it means. The statute provides no explicit definition, although the Supreme Court has generally given the FHA a broad and inclusive construction. HUD did not offer a comprehensive regulatory interpretation until 2015, and the regulatory landscape has fluctuated since then. Legislative history gives powerful clues, and courts have used it to interpret the meaning of the AFFH mandate. At the very least, AFFH means that public resources must be used to open more choice and opportunity for those most burdened by historical segregation, as opposed to allowing the status quo, shaped by preexisting de jure discriminatory housing policies, to determine priorities, plans, and investments.

To address the AFFH mandate, we must consider actions by each federal branch — Congress, the courts, and HUD and other executive agencies — as well as state and local government entities. This chapter summarizes some of the fundamental principles and issues that have emerged from public advocacy and judicial interpretation of the statute. We follow this with the principal cases explicating the statutory AFFH mandate and conclude with a description of pertinent agency activity, regulations, and guidance.

A. THE STATUTORY TEXT

The 1968 FHA has two provisions regarding AFFH:

- Section 3608(e)(5), describing the functions of the Secretary of HUD, states that the Secretary shall "administer the programs and activities relating to housing and urban development in a manner affirmatively to further the policies of this subchapter."
- In addition, §3608(d) states: "All executive departments and agencies shall administer their programs and activities relating to housing and urban development (including any Federal agency having regulatory or supervisory authority over financial institutions) in a manner affirmatively to further the purposes of this subchapter and shall cooperate with the Secretary [of HUD] to further such purposes."[1]

Congress also has imposed an AFFH mandate on HUD grantees in public housing and certain community development programs.[2] In addition to these requirements, which are created by statute and implemented by regulation, some courts have held that the AFFH mandate also binds other entities that receive federal housing funds.[3]

In 1988, Congress added to the FHA the requirement that HUD "make studies . . . of discriminatory housing practices" (§3608(e)(1)) and produce studies, reports, and recommendations, including annual "data on the race, color, religion, sex, national origin, age, handicap and family characteristics" of those who do or may benefit from HUD programs (§3608(e)(6)).

The enforcement provisions of the FHA permit administrative complaints or civil actions by "aggrieved persons" claiming injuries from a "discriminatory housing practice." The FHA at §3602(f) defines a discriminatory housing practice as "an act that is unlawful under [§§3604, 3605, 3606, or 3617]." Section 3608 is conspicuously absent from this list of provisions, which means that Congress did not grant an explicit private right of action to enforce the AFFH mandate. Some courts early on had recognized an implied private right of action, but most litigants now rely on the Administrative Procedure Act (APA), which provides a cause of action against federal defendants. The sections throughout this chapter discuss the means by which litigants and community stakeholders have sought to achieve compliance with the mandate.

---

1. Although §3608(e)(5) refers to "policies" and §3608(d) refers to "purposes," no one has suggested that these provisions have different meanings. *See* Schwemm, HDLL §21:1 n.12.
2. 42 U.S.C. §1437c-1(d)(16) (public housing); 42 U.S.C. §§5304(b)(2), 5306(d)(7)(B), 12705(b)(15) (state and local entities).
3. Schwemm, HDLL §21:1, text at n.7.

B. BASIC JUDICIAL INTERPRETATIONS OF AFFH

Although the FHA "does not define the content of the obligation to further fair housing," the meaning of the mandate "has been fleshed out episodically through judicial interpretation and on occasion systematized in agency regulations and guidance governing siting, tenant selection, and other policies."[4]

1. The Basic Elements of AFFH

*   At a minimum, HUD is liable for violating the AFFH mandate "in two types of situations: first, when [HUD] has taken discriminatory action itself, and second, when [HUD] is aware of a grantee's discriminatory practices but has made no effort to force it to comply with the Fair Housing Act by cutting off existing federal financial assistance."[5] Thus, AFFH requires more of HUD than merely to refrain from discrimination.
*   The mandate means that the federal government should "use its grant programs to assist in ending discrimination and segregation, to the point where the supply of genuinely open housing increases."[6]
*   The mandate is not a tool to require HUD to fund a particular project or reach a particular result.[7]
*   The mandate imposes an affirmative duty to redress past wrongs: "purposeful discrimination of a pervasive and chronic nature" by a federal agency or the agency's acquiescence in discrimination by a grantee imposes "upon government actors an affirmative duty to remedy past wrongs."[8]

2. Cases of the 1970s: *Trafficante, Gautreaux, Linmark, Shannon,* and *Otero*

Five decisions of the 1970s gave shape to the AFFH mandate. Three are Supreme Court decisions: *Trafficante v. Metropolitan Life Ins. Co., Hills v. Gautreaux,* and *Linmark Associates v. Township of Willingboro.* The other two are *Shannon v. HUD* (3d Cir.) and *Otero v. NYCHA* (2d Cir.).

Trafficante (more fully discussed in Chapter 4) emphasized that integration was a purpose of the FHA, quoting Senator Mondale's explanation

---

4. Megan Haberle, *Furthering Fair Housing: Lessons for the Road Ahead, in* Furthering Fair Housing: Prospects for Racial Justice in America's Neighborhoods 210, 214 (Justin P. Steil et al. eds., Temple U. Press 2021).

5. Anderson v. City of Alpharetta, 737 F.2d 1530, 1537 (11th Cir. 1984).

6. NAACP, Boston Chapter v. Sec'y of HUD, 817 F.2d 149, 155 (1st Cir. 1987) (Breyer, J.).

7. *Id.* at 160.

8. Thompson v. U.S. Dep't of HUD, 348 F. Supp. 2d 398, 413 (D. Md. 2005). *See generally* Robert G. Schwemm, *Overcoming Structural Barriers to Integrated Housing: A Back-to-the-Future Reflection on the Fair Housing Act's 'Affirmatively Further' Mandate,* 100 Ky. L.J. 125 (2012).

that "the reach of the proposed law was to replace the ghettos 'by truly integrated and balanced living patterns.'"[9] *Gautreaux* (more fully discussed in Chapter 12) upheld a metropolitan remedy for unconstitutional segregation, citing §3608(d)(5) as a basis for requiring HUD to expand housing choice by giving priority to housing opportunities for people of color in areas other than those in which they already live.[10] The mobility remedies that originated in that case have important potential for implementing the AFFH mandate.

In Linmark Associates v. Township of Willingboro, 431 U.S. 85 (1977), the Court invalidated under the First Amendment a ban on most "For Sale" and "Sold" signs, which the township had enacted to stem what it perceived as the flight of white homeowners from a racially integrated community. Levitt & Sons had developed Willingboro as a white, middle-income community beginning in the late 1950s. During the 1960s, Willingboro underwent rapid growth. In the 1970s, however, the population increase subsided; the white population declined while the non-white population grew by approximately 60 percent. By 1973, non-white people constituted 18.2 percent of the township's population.

Witnesses for the township agreed that a major cause of the decline in the white population was "panic selling," that is, selling by white people who feared that the township was becoming all Black and that property values would decline. In the witnesses' view, "For Sale" and "Sold" signs were a major catalyst of these fears. The township had contacted National Neighbors, an organization promoting integrated housing, and obtained the names of other communities that had prohibited "For Sale" signs. After reviewing favorable reports and holding public hearings, the Council adopted the ordinance.

The township sought to distinguish this case from earlier precedents by relying on the vital purpose this ordinance served: promoting stable, racially integrated housing. Citing *Trafficante*, the Court agreed that residential integration was a significant objective: "There can be no question about the importance of achieving this goal. This Court has expressly recognized that substantial benefits flow to both whites and blacks from interracial association and that Congress has made a strong national commitment to promote integrated housing." However, writing for a unanimous Court (Justice Rehnquist recused), Justice Thurgood Marshall held that the First Amendment prohibited the local government's restricting residents' access to truthful information about an issue important to their lives.

Shannon and *Otero* are oft-cited parts of the fair housing canon. In Shannon v. HUD, 436 F.2d 809 (3d Cir. 1970), residents challenged a change in an urban renewal plan in Philadelphia. The change substituted a rent supplement project—a deep subsidy project for very low-income residents—for what had been planned

---

9. Trafficante v. Metropolitan Life Ins. Co., 409 U.S. 205, 211 (1972).
10. Hills v. Gautreaux, 425 U.S. 284, 302 (1976).

as market rate homeownership. The challengers objected to HUD's making the change without a public hearing or a Report on Minority Group Considerations, "foreclos[ing] any inquiry into the effect of the change in type of housing on racial concentration in the East Poplar area or in Philadelphia as a whole." The court described an evolving statutory mandate for HUD:

> Read together, the Housing Act of 1949 and the Civil Rights Acts of 1964 and 1968 show a progression in the thinking of Congress as to what factors significantly contributed to urban blight and what steps must be taken to reverse the trend or to prevent the recurrence of such blight. In 1949 the Secretary . . . could not act unconstitutionally, but possibly could act neutrally on the issue of racial segregation. By 1964 he was directed . . . to look at the effects of local planning action and to prevent discrimination in housing resulting from such action. In 1968 he was directed to act affirmatively to achieve fair housing . . . [B]y 1964 . . . a program had to be nondiscriminatory in its effects, and by 1968 the Secretary had to affirmatively promote fair housing.

HUD's decision about the location of a rent supplement project, the court held, "could have the 'effect of subjecting persons to discrimination because of their race . . . or have the effect of defeating or substantially impairing accomplishment of the objectives of the program or activity as respect persons of a particular race'" in violation of HUD's Title VI regulations. As the court observed:

> That effect could arise by virtue of the undue concentration of persons of a given race, or socio-economic group, in a given neighborhood. That effect could be felt not only by occupants of rent supplement housing and low cost housing, but by occupants of owner occupied dwellings, merchants, and institutions in the neighborhood.

This might have been permissible before 1964, the *Shannon* court said, but added, strikingly: "Today, such color blindness is impermissible." HUD was required to "utilize some institutionalized method whereby . . . it has before it the relevant racial and socio-economic information necessary for compliance with its duties under the 1964 and 1968 Civil Rights Acts."

Otero v. New York City Housing Authority (NYCHA), 484 F.2d 1122 (2d Cir. 1973), arose because a NYCHA regulation required, and NYCHA had promised, that families displaced from an urban renewal area would be given priority in occupying newly built housing there. Belatedly, NYCHA determined that because so many of these families were nonwhite their occupancy would create a "tipping point" that would turn the area from integrated to predominantly nonwhite. The court of appeals recognized that the housing authority was "obligated to take affirmative steps to promote racial integration" notwithstanding a housing authority regulation that assured minority displacees priority to return to a site. Agreeing with the parties "that the Authority has a duty to integrate under the 1968 Act," the court held:

> [T]he affirmative duty placed on the Secretary of HUD by §3608(d)(5) and through him on other agencies administering federally-assisted housing programs also requires that consideration be given to the impact of . . . programs on the racial concentration in the area in which the proposed housing is to be built. Action must be taken to fulfill, as much as possible, the goal of open, integrated

residential housing patterns and to prevent the increase of segregation, in ghettos, of racial groups whose lack of opportunities the Act was designed to combat.

The court held that the authority's "obligation to act affirmatively to achieve integration in housing" was imposed by the Constitution as well as the statute and noted that "affirmative action to erase the effects of past discrimination and desegregate housing patterns may be ordered." (citing *Gautreaux* cases). Rejecting the district court's insistence that housing opportunities could not be denied to people of color, the Second Circuit held that "[s]uch a rule of thumb gives too little weight to Congress' desire to prevent segregated housing patterns and the ills which attend them."

C. *NAACP, BOSTON CHAPTER v. SECRETARY OF HUD*

In 1978, the NAACP's Boston Chapter sued HUD, alleging (among other things) that HUD had failed to carry out its AFFH mandate in funding the Community Development Block Grant (CDBG) and Urban Development Action Grant (UDAG) programs for the city of Boston. The claims with respect to the CDBG program were that HUD had failed to impose and enforce adequate conditions on funding to promote fair housing goals; the complaint as to the UDAG funds focused on HUD's failure to use its leverage to cause the city to increase the supply of affordable, desegregated housing.

The district court held that HUD had failed to satisfy §3608(e)(5) in two respects. First, the agency did not require the City to establish an effective fair housing enforcement program in the face of its knowledge of pervasive racial discrimination in the jurisdiction. Second, despite its knowledge that a housing emergency existed, which had a disproportionate impact on low-income Black families, HUD did not condition its provision of federal (UDAG) funds on construction of affordable, integrated public housing. The court held, however, that it lacked authority under the Administrative Procedure Act (APA) to enforce the AFFH mandate against HUD.[11] The First Circuit reversed in an influential decision written by then-Judge Stephen Breyer.

NAACP, Boston Chapter v. Secretary of HUD
817 F.2d 149 (1st Cir. 1987)

Bownes, Breyer, and Torruella, Circuit Judges

BREYER, Circuit Judge.
The FHA declares as its "policy" the provision of "fair housing throughout the United States." Its substantive provisions prohibit discrimination related

---

11. This description of the earlier proceedings is taken from the later decision on remand, NAACP, Boston Chapter v. Kemp, 721 F. Supp. 361 (D. Mass. 1989).

to the rental or sale of dwelling[s]. In addition, it instructs the Secretary of HUD to

> administer the programs and activities relating to housing and urban development in a manner affirmatively to further the policies of this [Act].

The specific question raised in this appeal is whether federal courts have the legal authority to review claims that the Secretary has failed to carry out this instruction. The district court believed that, at least where the Secretary has not acted with a discriminatory purpose, the Secretary's compliance with §3608(e)(5) is a matter that Congress has "committed to agency discretion by law." 5 U.S.C. §701(a)(2).[12] Accordingly, it held that it could not legally review the appellant's claims of violation and it dismissed the case. We believe, however, that the court has the power to review appellant's claim that the Secretary has not "administer[ed]" certain HUD programs "in a manner affirmatively to further" the Act's basic policy. Hence, we reverse the district court's dismissal and remand the case for further proceedings.

BACKGROUND

Nearly nine years ago, in April 1978, the NAACP sued claiming that HUD had failed "to enforce constitutional and statutory proscriptions against discrimination in Federally assisted programs." Its complaint listed various acts and omissions related to HUD's administration of its CDBG and UDAG programs in the City of Boston, which acts and omissions, it said, taken together, established violations of various civil rights statutes, including HUD's duty "affirmatively to further" the FHA's policies.

In 1983, the district court after trial found, as factual matters, that Boston has a history of racial discrimination in housing; that Boston suffers from a shortage of low-income family housing; that a higher proportion of black than white families are renters and a higher proportion of black than white renters are families with children (and thus that the housing shortage impacts more heavily on blacks than on whites); that Boston's neighborhoods are racially separate; and that "at least in part [as] the result of the lack of safe, desegregated housing in white neighborhoods" black families find it difficult to move out of black areas. The court also found that both city and federal officials were aware of these facts; that the city had not effectively enforced fair housing requirements; that neither the city nor HUD had sought to obtain or to provide UDAG funds for low-income housing; and that HUD had not obtained from the city the assessment of "any special needs of identifiable segments of the lower income population" that HUD regulations then required.

In the court's view, these facts added up . . . to a violation of HUD's Title VIII duty "affirmatively to further" the Act's policy. In particular, it wrote that

---

12. [Eds.—In general, the APA provides a cause of action for persons aggrieved by final action of federal administrative agencies but matters "committed to agency discretion by law" are excluded from this enforcement authorization.]

HUD's failure to use its "immense leverage under UDAG" to provide "deseg-regated housing so that the housing stock is sufficiently large to give minority families a true choice of location," in the context of Boston's history and practices, violated HUD's Title VIII obligations.

In late 1985, the district court determined that it could not grant relief from the Title VIII violation because it did not have the legal authority to review the Secretary's compliance with the "affirmative furtherance" mandate. It held that Congress had not created any "private right of action" to enforce Title VIII's legal obligation, and that it could not review the Secretary's actions under the APA because Congress had "committed" compliance with the obligation "to agency discretion," The court accordingly dismissed the NAACP's claims. The NAACP now appeals this dismissal. . . .

III. THE SUBSTANTIVE CLAIM

Before turning to the question of APA reviewability, we consider the government's argument that we should affirm the court's decision on an alternative ground. The government argues that §3608(e)(5) imposes upon HUD only an obligation not to discriminate. It says that HUD's actions violate its obligations under Title VIII *only* when HUD engages in discriminatory conduct or when it funds a grantee who is engaged in such discriminatory conduct with the purpose of furthering the grantee's discrimination. Since the district court found neither actual discrimination by HUD nor an effort purposely to further the discrimination of others, HUD, in the government's view, could not have violated §3608(e)(5).

We do not agree that HUD's Title VIII obligations are as limited as the government claims. Rather, a statute that instructs HUD to administer its grant programs so as "affirmatively to further" the Act's fair housing policy requires something more of HUD than simply to refrain from discriminating itself or purposely aiding the discrimination of others. For one thing, as the government states its Title VIII obligation, it sounds very much like (and perhaps even less than) the obligation that the Fifth Amendment would impose upon HUD even in the absence of Title VIII. See *Washington v. Davis*. Yet, the history of Title VIII suggests that its framers meant to do more than simply restate HUD's existing legal obligations. See 114 Cong. Rec. 2281 (1968) (statement of Sen. Brooke) (a purpose of Title VIII is to remedy the "weak intentions" that have led to the federal government's "sanctioning discrimination in housing throughout this Nation"); *id.* at 2526-28 (statement of Sen. Brooke) (reviewing history of federal fair housing efforts); *id.* at 9577 (statement of Rep. Cohelan) (decrying historical "neglect" of minorities); *id.* at 9595 (statement of Rep. Pepper) (lamenting government's slowness in establishing truly "equal" rights).

For another thing, as a matter of language and of logic, a statute that instructs an agency "affirmatively to further" a national policy of nondiscrimination would seem to impose an obligation to do more than simply not discriminate itself. If one assumes that many private persons and local governments have practiced discrimination for many years and that at least some of them might be tempted to continue to discriminate even though forbidden to do so by law, it is difficult to see how HUD's own nondiscrimination by itself could significantly "further" the ending of such discrimination by others.

Further, the legislative history does not support so constricted a reading of the statute. It is true that the sponsors of the law, including Senator Mondale, its chief sponsor, made absolutely clear that Title VIII's policy to "provide . . . for fair housing" means "the elimination of discrimination in the sale or rental of housing. That is all it could possibly mean." 114 Cong. Rec. 4975; *see also id.* at 2279 (statement of Sen. Brooke) (Title VIII "does not promise to end the ghetto . . . but it will make it possible for those who have the resources to escape"); *id.* at 9589 (statement of Rep. Halpern) (Title VIII guarantees blacks the right to live "where [they] wish [] . . . and where [they] can afford"); *id.* at 9597 (statement of Rep. Brown) ("sense" of Title VIII is "a rather nebulous support of civil rights and opposition to the last vestige of white supremacy or exclusivity as it has been exercised in housing"). But it is equally true that the law's supporters saw the ending of discrimination as a means toward truly opening the nation's housing stock to persons of every race and creed. See 114 Cong. Rec. 2274 (statement of Sen. Mondale) (Title VIII is "an absolutely essential first step" toward reversing the trend toward "two separate Americas constantly at war with one another"); *id.* at 2524 (statement of Sen. Brooke) ("Discrimination in the sale and rental of housing has been the root cause of the widespread patterns of de facto segregation which characterize America's residential neighborhoods."); *id.* at 2985 (statement of Sen. Proxmire) (Title VIII will establish "a policy of dispersal through open housing . . . look[ing] to the eventual dissolution of the ghetto and the construction of low and moderate income housing in the suburbs").

This broader goal suggests an intent that HUD do more than simply not discriminate itself; it reflects the desire to have HUD use its grant programs to assist in ending discrimination and segregation, to the point where the supply of genuinely open housing increases. This view of the effect that Congress intended is at odds with the government's very narrow view of its obligation.

Finally, every court that has considered the question has held or stated that Title VIII imposes upon HUD an obligation to do more than simply refrain from discriminating (and from purposely aiding discrimination by others) [discussing *Shannon* and *Otero*].

Furthermore, the Supreme Court itself has identified the goal of Title VIII as "replace[ment of] ghettos 'by truly integrated and balanced living patterns.'" *Trafficante v. Metropolitan Life Insurance Co.* (1972) (quoting 114 Cong. Rec. 3422 (statement of Sen. Mondale)); see also *Gladstone Realtors v. Village of Bellwood* (1979) (upholding standing under Title VIII where plaintiffs' only claim of injury was denial of the benefits of an integrated community);

Linmark Associates v. Township of Willingboro (1977) (characterizing Title VIII as "a strong national commitment to promote integrated housing").

The government relies upon a recent Eleventh Circuit case, *Anderson v. City of Alpharetta* (1984), as support for its narrow view of HUD's duties. In *Anderson*, a class of plaintiffs sued HUD, claiming that HUD had illegally failed to counteract "the deliberate foot dragging of local governments" in constructing low-income public housing, which local delay the plaintiffs said was racially motivated. The Eleventh Circuit, in affirming dismissal for failure to state a claim, wrote that HUD itself is liable under Title VIII only

> first, when HUD has taken discriminatory action itself, such as approving federal assistance for a public housing project without considering its effect on the racial and socio-economic composition of the surrounding area; and second, when HUD is aware of a grantee's discriminatory practices and has made no effort to force it into compliance with the FHA by cutting off existing federal financial assistance to the agency in question.

This formulation, even if overly narrow, still does not support the government's view of HUD's duties. It does not limit HUD's liability to *purposive* support of discrimination by others, nor does it limit HUD's "discriminatory action" to activity that itself forecloses housing opportunities on the basis of race. Rather, it includes within the scope of such action a failure to "consider [the] effect [of a HUD grant] on the racial and socio-economic composition of the surrounding area." And, the need for such consideration itself implies, at a minimum, an obligation to assess negatively those aspects of a proposed course of action that would further limit the supply of genuinely open housing and to assess positively those aspects of a proposed course of action that would increase that supply. If HUD is doing so in any meaningful way, one would expect to see, over time, if not in any individual case, HUD activity that tends to increase, or at least, that does not significantly diminish, the supply of open housing.

Having concluded that HUD's obligations under Title VIII extend beyond what the government claims, we must reject its request that we affirm the judgment below on the ground that HUD has not violated any legal obligation. The district court's opinions state a plausible case of a violation of HUD's obligations, even under the minimal standard set forth in the last paragraph. The district court stated, *inter alia*:

1) In the case of the City of Boston . . . [HUD's] efforts to ensure fair housing have been ineffective. It has accepted from the City cosmetic changes in the form of a Mayor's Office of Fair Housing and some public relations efforts instead of genuine enforcement.
2) [I]t had not required the City to establish an effective fair housing program in the face of knowledge of pervasive racial discrimination in the City.
3) The financing of desegregated housing so that the housing stock is sufficiently large to give minority families a true choice of location seems . . . to be a[n] . . . obligation of HUD under . . . Title VIII.

4) [HUD] has not used any of its immense leverage under UDAG to provide adequate desegregated housing, except for Mission Park, which was not a project sponsored by the City.

These, and other roughly similar statements in the court's opinions, read as if the court had more in mind than a crude legal standard requiring HUD to provide housing for all those in need. We agree that HUD has no such obligation. Rather, the court's statements read like an affirmative response to a claim that HUD's pattern of grant activity in Boston reflects a failure, over time, to take seriously its minimal Title VIII obligation to evaluate alternative courses of action in light of their effect upon open housing.

IV. REVIEWABILITY UNDER THE APA

[EDS. — The court then held that the AFFH claim was reviewable because it did not fall under the APA's exception for agency action "committed to agency discretion by law" in 5 U.S.C. §701(a).]

Clearly, HUD possesses broad discretionary powers to develop, award, and administer its grants and to decide the degree to which they can be shaped to help achieve Title VIII's goals. This fact, however, does not in itself mean that HUD is immune from review for "abuse of discretion" in exercising those powers.

We believe that preclusion is inappropriate here for the following reasons. First, the right at issue — the right to HUD's help in achieving open housing — is a significant one. The congressional debates leave no doubt that Congress thought it important. See 114 Cong. Rec. 2275 (statement of Sen. Mondale) ("fair housing is a key and indispensable part of any solution of the interracial problems of our country"); *id.* at 2703 (statement of Sen. Javits) (terming fair housing "more important than jobs, and even more important than equal treatment under the law"); *id.* at 2986-91 (statement of Sen. Brooke) (ghetto is a root cause of other social problems); *id.* at 9616 (statement of Rep. McCormack) ("We must turn our face away from a course of segregation and separation."). And, it seems reasonable to believe that plaintiffs wrongly deprived of that assistance over a course of time might require judicial intervention to obtain it. Under all the circumstances of this case, the facts found by the district court (if true) strongly suggest a political process that has failed to offer plaintiffs adequate alternative relief.

Second, we believe that the court can find adequate standards against which to judge the lawfulness of HUD's conduct. This is a case in which plaintiffs, in effect, claim that HUD's practice over time, its *pattern* of behavior, reveals a failure "affirmatively . . . to further" Title VIII's fair housing policy. The NAACP does not complain of individual instances so much as it *uses* individual instances to show a pattern of activity, which pattern constitutes the alleged violation. Thus, we need not decide how, or whether, a court can fashion standards governing when, or the extent to which, HUD should use an *individual* grant decision affirmatively to bring about desegregation. Nor need we consider how a court is to review whether HUD in an individual instance has given appropriate weight to its UDAG mission "to make . . . grants to cities . . . experiencing severe economic distress to help stimulate economic development activity," 42 U.S.C. §5318(a), to its Title VIII objectives, and to various other factors such as . . . the availability of resources.

Rather, here the court must decide whether, over time, HUD's pattern of activity reveals a failure to live up to its obligation. The standard for reviewing that pattern can be drawn directly from the statutory instruction to "administer" its programs "in a manner affirmatively to further the policies" of "fair housing." This standard, like many, may be difficult to apply to borderline instances, yet a court should be able to determine a clear failure to live up to the instruction over time. It should be able to determine whether the agency's practice, over time, in respect to this mandate has been "arbitrary, capricious, an abuse of discretion, or otherwise not in accordance with law." 5 U.S.C. §706(2)(A). Doing so, in the context of a claim of serious failure over time to try to further Title VIII's goals, need not involve the court in "superintend[ing] economic and managerial decisions," or in reweighing matters that Congress has asked HUD to balance. Rather, this case seems to call for a more straightforward evaluation of whether agency activity over time has furthered the statutory goal, and, if not, for an explanation of why not and a determination of whether a given explanation, in light of the statute, is satisfactory. Of course, we do not mean to say that individual grant decisions are not reviewable under this statute—in appropriate cases they may be reviewable—but even if some, many, or all of them are not, nonetheless in the kind of "pattern or practice" case before us there is "law to apply." [EDS.--The Supreme Court requires a showing of "law to apply" to overcome the exclusion from judicial review of agency action "committed to agency discretion by law." 5 U.S.C. §706.]

Third, and perhaps most important, we do not believe that judicial review of this kind of claim threatens unwarranted interference with HUD's ability to carry out its basic statutory missions. The legal claim before us is not that, in the case of any particular decision, HUD must promote desegregation. Rather, the NAACP asks for review of a series of decisions to determine whether, taken together, they violate the obligation to further the goals of Title VIII. To make this determination does not threaten a large number of legal challenges or otherwise impair HUD's ability to make grants. We do not see how a one-time review of HUD's practices under an "abuse of discretion" standard can pose a serious threat to the agency's effectiveness.

Fourth, it does not seem impossible here for the court to develop an appropriate remedy. Of course, the court faces the difficult task of avoiding both remedies that may be too intrusive, interfering with HUD's ability to carry out its basic grant-awarding mission, and those that may prove to be ineffective. This difficulty is not, however, unsolvable. We do not see any reason why the court cannot effectively ensure HUD's future responsible exercise of discretion while at the same time preserving for the agency its discretionary options. In formulating its remedy, of course, the district court may, as it has already done, seek the advice and participation of HUD.

AUTHORITY TO AWARD RELIEF

The government makes one final point. It says that HUD's actions here are unreviewable because they are "inaction." HUD correctly points out that §706(1) does not ordinarily empower a court to order an agency to fund particular projects or to reach particular results. Nonetheless, a court "can compel an official to exercise his discretion where he has obviously failed or refused to do so." [EDS. — The court also cited authority in a separate APA provision empowering it to set aside improper agency action.] The APA defines "agency action" to include "failure to act." On these facts, we are not sure what difference, if any, there may be between HUD's "failure to exercise" the discretion conferred upon it by §3608(e)(5) and its "abuse" of that discretion as revealed in a pattern of HUD activity. We conclude that the court is empowered to order a remedy either for an act or a related omission of the sort here present.

NOTES AND QUESTIONS

1. What Authorizes a Cause of Action Under §3608(e)(5)? Because the FHA does not contain an express private right of action to enforce §3608(e)(5), HUD and the DOJ (the Federal Programs division of which represented HUD) argued that the section could not be enforced by private litigation. In Part IV of the opinion, the court rejected this argument, holding HUD's actions reviewable under the APA for four reasons. Although several earlier cases treated §3608(e)(5) as creating an implied private cause of action, AFFH litigation since 1987 usually relies on the APA.

2. The Substantive Significance of *Boston Chapter, NAACP*: Integration as a Purpose of Title VIII. In Part III of the opinion the court addressed the substantive claim. Parts III and IV are important because they emphasize that a "basic policy" of the FHA is to promote integration. (In Part IV, the court emphasized that "the right at issue — the right to HUD's help in achieving open housing — is a significant one" and that HUD must use its grant programs, over time, to promote integration.) In Part III, the court said that "the law's supporters saw the ending of discrimination as a means toward truly opening the nation's housing stock to persons of every race and creed," quoting Senator Brooke on "discrimination . . . [as] the root cause of the widespread patterns of de facto segregation which characterize America's residential neighborhoods" and Senator Proxmire on "a policy of dispersal through open housing . . . look[ing] to the eventual dissolution of the ghetto and the construction of low and moderate income housing in the suburbs." The court concluded, in language that often is quoted:

> The broader goal suggests an intent that HUD do more than simply not discriminate itself; it reflects the desire to have HUD use its grant programs to assist in ending discrimination and segregation, to the point where the supply of genuinely open housing increases.

The court drew on *Shannon*, *Otero*, and *Linmark*, all discussed above, and cited *Trafficante* and *Gladstone Realtors* (Chapter 4). The First Circuit interpreted the district court's statements not as an overbroad mandate to provide housing for all but as "an affirmative response to a claim that HUD's pattern of grant activity in Boston reflects a failure, over time, to take seriously its minimal Title VIII obligation to evaluate alternative courses of action in light of their effect upon open housing." The court distinguished *Anderson v. City of Alpharetta, Ga.*, as offering too narrow a view of HUD's responsibilities even if it was more demanding than the view urged by the government. Which of the two circuit court positions do you think is more persuasive?[13]

3. The Subsequent Resolution of the Boston Litigation. On remand, the district court granted declaratory and injunctive relief, including regional relief. The court ruled:

> The plaintiff seeks injunctive relief compelling HUD to require private landlords of HUD-assisted housing throughout the metropolitan area to participate in an affirmative marketing program targeting low income minorities now living in Boston. Such a program would be administered under the auspices of the Boston Fair Housing Commission. In my opinion this form of remedy is warranted because of (a) HUD's failure to encourage the construction of integrated housing within the City and (b) because there is a lack of safe housing for persons of color in the white areas of the City. The remedy sought is in my opinion a reasonable response to the conditions which I found to exist, even though I made no specific findings concerning suburban housing opportunities. . . . In my opinion, an order requiring the defendant to condition the federal funding of private suburban housing projects is legal, feasible and an appropriate remedy for the defendant's default. *Hills v. Gautreaux*, 425 U.S. 284, 305-6 (1976).
>
> The plaintiff seeks an order that HUD impose a series of Fair Housing Conditions on the City and Commonwealth, under any grant programs wherein it has power to impose conditions on grantees. These conditions include promulgation of legislation eliminating the current exemption of five or fewer unit housing from the reach of The Fair Housing Ordinance, and granting the Fair Housing Commission enforcement powers; the participation of all managers and owners of state or City assisted housing in the metropolitan area in rental assistance and affirmative marketing programs; and the implementation of an enforcement program. . . . At least insofar as the conditions requested promote integrated fair housing, they are permissible.

---

13. *See* Schwemm, HDLL §21:5 for a discussion of the two views.

Why do you think a court order was necessary to motivate HUD to take steps toward implementing its affirmative fair housing mandate?

D. OTHER CASES INVOLVING AFFH

1. *Clients' Council v. Pierce*

In Clients' Council v. Pierce, 711 F.2d 1406, 1408 (8th Cir. 1983), the court of appeals determined:

> Public housing in Texarkana was totally segregated from the occupancy of the first project in 1952 until 1971, and remained virtually one hundred percent segregated until after the initiation of this lawsuit in 1979. The units that housed black persons were less well constructed and less well maintained than the units occupied by whites. Black employees were also subject to discriminatory working conditions. HUD officials abdicated their affirmative duty to eliminate the racially discriminatory practices of the Texarkana Housing Authority, and in fact participated in that discrimination in violation of the federal constitution and federal housing laws.

Specifically, the court held that HUD was "liable under §3601 and §3608(e)(5). The court said:

> As the district court in *Resident Advisory Board v. Rizzo*[14] noted, Congress enacted §3608(e)(5) to cure the widespread problem of segregation in public housing. This problem was aptly characterized by Senator Brooke:
>
>> Rarely does HUD withhold funds or defer action in the name of desegregation. . . . In other words, our Government, unfortunately, has been sanctioning discrimination in housing throughout this Nation.
>
> Even if HUD were not liable under the Fifth Amendment, the facts here demonstrate that HUD failed to carry out its affirmative duty to "institute action [directly resulting in] the implementation of the dual and mutual goals of fair housing and the elimination of discrimination in that housing."

2. *Starrett City*: The Conflict Between Nondiscrimination and Integration

All the cases previously discussed emphasized the FHA's goal of achieving integration, which was served by the statute's prohibition of discrimination. There are, however, situations in which these two goals conflict (as they did in *Otero*). This tension arose in the context of Starrett City, a large, privately owned rental housing development. Starrett City (and New York City and State) discriminated against some Black and Hispanic applicants to maintain the development as a racially integrated one. Civil rights groups had challenged the precise formula used originally to maintain integration and settled

---

14. Resident Advisory Board v. Rizzo, 425 F. Supp. 987, 1013-18 (E.D. Pa. 1976), *aff'd in part, rev'd in part on other grounds*, 564 F.2d 126 (3d Cir.), *cert. denied*, 435 U.S. 908 (1977).

their case (the *Arthur* case) in a way that made more units available to applicants of color. Then the Civil Rights Division of the Department of Justice sued
to end all the integration maintenance preferences. In United States v. Starrett
City Associates, 840 F.2d 1096 (2d Cir. 1988), the U.S. Court of Appeals held,
2-1, that seeking to maintain integration could not justify using certain race-
conscious measures.

Starrett City, comprising 46 high-rise buildings containing 5,881 apartments in Brooklyn, New York, initially had created fear that it would become
"an overwhelmingly minority development." It was approved only "upon the
assurance of Starrett City's developer that it was intended to create a racially
integrated community."

Starrett originally adopted a tenanting procedure that produced a racial
distribution by apartment unit of 64 percent white, 22 percent Black, and
8 percent Hispanic; the settlement of the *Arthur* case increased the percentages
for Black and Hispanic people. Although the DOJ had declined to intervene in
Arthur, it brought this suit after the settlement, arguing "that Starrett violated
the Act by making apartments unavailable to blacks solely because of race,
§3604(a); by forcing black applicants to wait significantly longer for apartments than whites solely because of race, §3604(b); by enforcing a policy that
prefers white applicants while limiting the numbers of minority applicants
accepted, §3604(c); and by representing in an acknowledgement letter that no
apartments are available for rental when in fact units are available, §3604(d)."

Starrett maintained that the tenanting procedures "were adopted at the
behest of the [s]tate solely to achieve and maintain integration and were not
motivated by racial animus." (Although the burden of Starrett City's rental
policy usually fell on non-whites, occasionally the burden fell on whites
applying for senior housing.) To support its position, Starrett submitted
the written testimony of three housing experts. They described the "white
flight" and "tipping" phenomena, in which white residents leave a community as the community becomes lower income and the population of color
increases, resulting in the transition to a predominantly minority community.
Acknowledging that "the tipping point for a particular housing development,
depending as it does on numerous factors and the uncertainties of human
behavior, is difficult to predict with precision," their opinions varied, with
one expert stating that the consensus was between 10 percent and 20 percent
generally, another estimating a tipping point of 40 percent Black for the complex, and the third finding that a 2:1 white-minority ratio produced successful
integration.

The district court granted summary judgment for the government. On
appeal, the Second Circuit held:

> Starrett's allocation of public housing facilities on the basis of racial quotas,
> by denying an applicant access to a unit otherwise available solely because
> of race, produces a "discriminatory effect . . . [that] could hardly be clearer."
> Appellants do not contend that the plain language of §3604 does not proscribe
> their practices. Rather, they claim to be "clothed with governmental authority"

and thus obligated, under *Otero*, to effectuate the purpose of the FHA by affirmatively promoting integration and preventing "the reghettoization of a model integrated community." Even if Starrett were a state actor with such a duty, the racial quotas and related practices employed at Starrett City to maintain integration violate the antidiscrimination provisions of the Act.

The court acknowledged that when Congress enacted Title VIII, it believed that antidiscrimination policy would lead to residential integration. However, the court said that "[w]hile quotas promote Title VIII's integration policy, they contravene its antidiscrimination policy, bringing the dual goals of the Act into conflict." It noted that the legislative history provides no further guidance for resolving this conflict.

The court said that a race-conscious affirmative action plan is not necessarily unlawful, but it must be temporary and have a defined goal. "Moreover," the court said, citing constitutional precedents from the contexts of higher education and government contracting:

> [S]ocietal discrimination alone seems "insufficient and over expansive" as the basis for adopting so-called "benign" practices with discriminatory effects "that work against innocent people" in the drastic and burdensome way that rigid racial quotas do. Furthermore, the use of quotas generally should be based on some history of racial discrimination, within the entity seeking to employ them. Finally, . . . programs designed to maintain integration by limiting minority participation, such as ceiling quotas, are of doubtful validity because they "single[] out those least well represented in the political process to bear the brunt of a benign program," Fullilove [v. Klutznick, 448 U.S. 448, at 519 (1980)] (Marshall, J., concurring).

Based on these standards, the majority invalidated the quotas used to maintain integration at Starrett City. The court made three points: First, the quotas were "far from temporary," because their goal of integration maintenance by avoiding white flight involved no definite termination date; second, there was no showing of past discrimination at Starrett City or appellants' other complexes; finally, these were ceiling quotas, not access quotas. The court observed that "the impact of appellants' practices falls squarely on minorities, for whom Title VIII was intended to open up housing opportunities."

The court rejected Starrett's claim that "white flight" justified its quotas and distinguished *Otero*, noting especially that the NYCHA action challenged there applied only to the initial leasing of the new complexes and did not operate as a continuous, strict racial quota. The majority concluded:

> We do not intend to imply that race is always an inappropriate consideration under Title VIII in efforts to promote integrated housing. We hold only that Title VIII does not allow appellants to use rigid racial quotas of indefinite duration to maintain a fixed level of integration at Starrett City by restricting minority access to scarce and desirable rental accommodations otherwise available to them.

Judge Jon O. Newman dissented, agreeing with Starrett that "the statute was never intended to apply to such actions. This statute was intended to bar perpetuation of segregation. To apply it to bar maintenance of integration is precisely contrary to the congressional policy 'to provide, within constitu-tional limitations, for fair housing throughout the United States.'" The dis-sent added:

> None of the legislators who enacted Title VIII ever expressed a view on whether they wished to prevent the maintenance of racially balanced housing. Most of those who passed this statute in 1968 probably could not even contemplate a private real estate owner who would deliberately set out to achieve a racially balanced tenant population. Had they thought of such an eventuality, there is not the slightest reason to believe that they would have raised their legislative hands against it.
>
> Our case is much easier than *Otero*. Starrett City is not seeking to be released from a commitment it has previously made to any of the applicants for hous-ing. To prevail it need not find in Title VIII some affirmative obligation compel-ling it to promote integration. It has freely chosen to promote integration and is entitled to prevail unless something in Title VIII forbids its voluntary policy. If anything in Title VIII prohibited race-conscious rental policies adopted to promote integration, *Otero* would have been summarily decided against the defendant.

The dissent concluded:

> [At the very least,] Starrett City is entitled to a trial so that it can prove its con-tention that its policy is still needed to maintain integration. In opposing sum-mary judgment, Starrett City presented detailed affidavits providing abundant evidence to show that abandonment of its rental policies would cause the com-plex to pass the "tipping point" and soon become a segregated development. This evidence was solidly based on relevant experience. Several housing devel-opments near Starrett City, operating without a policy of integration mainte-nance, have become racially segregated, including one across the street from Starrett City.
>
> Whether integration of private housing complexes should be maintained through the use of race-conscious rental policies that deny minorities an equal opportunity to rent is a highly controversial issue of social policy. That policy choice should be left to the individual decisions of private property owners unless and until Congress or the New York legislature decides for the Nation or for New York that it prefers to outlaw maintenance of integration. I do not believe Congress made that decision in 1968, and it is a substan-tial question whether it would make such a decision today. Until Congress acts, we should not lend our authority to the result this lawsuit will surely bring about. In the words of [noted psychologist and civil rights advocate Dr. Kenneth] Clark: "[I]t would be a tragedy of the highest magnitude if this litigation were to lead to the destruction of one of the model integrated com-munities in the United States."

Who do you think has the better of the arguments in *Starrett City* as a matter of law? As a matter of policy? Should the standards for Starrett City have been considered without regard to what neighboring developments did with respect to integration?

In the last decade the Supreme Court has taken an increasingly strong position against the use of race-conscious measures in the constitutional setting, even when the goal is to encourage racial balance and diversity. In

Parents Involved in Community Schools v. Seattle School Dist. No. 1, 551 U.S. 701 (2007), the Court held unconstitutional two school assignment plans that sought to achieve racial balance and stability in public schools by considering the race of pupils when allocating certain attendance slots. Chief Justice Roberts, writing for a five-Justice majority, stated:

> What do the racial classifications do in these cases, if not determine admission to a public school on a racial basis? Before *Brown*, schoolchildren were told where they could and could not go to school based on the color of their skin. The school districts in these cases have not carried the heavy burden of demonstrating that we should allow this once again—even for very different reasons. . . . The way to stop discrimination on the basis of race is to stop discriminating on the basis of race.

In 2023, a six-Justice majority of the Court further cemented this position by striking down the use of race-conscious admissions procedures in higher education in Students for Fair Admissions v. Harvard, 600 U.S. 181 (2023) (procedures violate Title VI) and Students for Fair Admissions v. University of North Carolina, 600 U.S. 181 (2023) (procedures violate the Fourteenth Amendment). Justice Ketanji Brown Jackson maintained in dissent: "With let-them-eat-cake obliviousness, today, the majority pulls the ripcord and announces 'colorblindness for all' by legal fiat. But deeming race irrelevant in law does not make it so in life."

E. AFFH AND REGIONALIZATION

1. *Thompson v. HUD*

Chapter 12, which addresses government housing and development programs, includes a discussion of cases brought to integrate—or at least desegregate—public housing. The seminal epic is the *Gautreaux* litigation, a high point of which was Hills v. Gautreaux, 425 U.S. 284 (1976), which authorized desegregative relief in the Chicago region.[15]

One of the last major public housing desegregation cases was *Thompson v. HUD*, in which a class of Black residents of public housing in Baltimore City pursued statutory and constitutional claims against HUD and local defendants in 1995. In 2005, after a bench trial and consideration of "a vast quantity of evidence spanning more than a half century of governmental action and/or inaction," the district court ordered HUD to provide regional relief for Baltimore city residents, Black people surrounded by counties occupied

---

15. Because the plaintiffs filed the *Gautreaux* cases before the FHA was enacted, they did not bring AFFH claims, although mention of AFFH occurred later in the litigation. Other public housing desegregation cases that embraced AFFH claims, including *Young v. Pierce* (Chapter 12), are discussed in Schwemm, HDLL §21:4 and in Florence Wagman Roisman, *Long Overdue: Desegregation Litigation and Next Steps to End Discrimination and Segregation in the Public Housing and Section 8 Existing Housing Programs*, 4 CITYSCAPE 171 (1999).

primarily by white people. The court reviewed the history of de jure racial segregation in Baltimore city, "the largest municipality in Maryland, a former slave state." It observed that "in 1954 there was, to a large extent, a recognizable 'ghetto' within which lived essentially no Whites and virtually all of the Black residents of Baltimore City," while, "to the limited extent that there were Black residents of the counties in the Baltimore Region, the racial segregation there was, if different at all, even more pronounced." Until 1954, Baltimore had two downtowns, one white and one black, and in the white downtown, Black people "were typically made less than welcome and were unable to utilize eating facilities or theaters." A public swimming pool bore a sign, prominently posted, reading: "NO JEWS, DOGS OR COLOREDS ALLOWED."

Despite the background of de jure discrimination, the district court dismissed the plaintiffs' constitutional claims against federal and local defendants. The district court also dismissed plaintiffs' statutory claims against local defendants, but issued the following opinion holding that plaintiffs had proved their AFFH claim against HUD because HUD had failed adequately to consider regional approaches to ameliorating racial segregation in public housing.

Thompson v. HUD
348 F. Supp. 2d 398 (D. Md. 2005)

GARBIS, District Judge:

The Plaintiff class was, and will in the future be, affected by more than just HUD's policies and actions with regard to the area within the city limits. Indeed, it is readily apparent that HUD's responsibility to promote fair housing extends beyond the city borders.

The Court finds that HUD must take an approach to its obligation to promote fair housing that adequately considers the entire Baltimore Region. The need for such consideration requires, at a minimum, that HUD "assess negatively those aspects of a proposed course of action that would further limit the supply of genuinely open housing and to assess positively those aspects of a proposed course of action that would increase the supply." [NAACP, 817 F.2d at 156.] Ultimately, the Court must draw a legal conclusion based on its examination as to whether HUD's activities were "an abuse of discretion or otherwise not in accordance with law," which, the Court reiterates, requires HUD to "administer the programs and activities relating to housing and urban development in a manner affirmatively to further the policies of [the FHA.]"

1. THE REGIONAL EFFECTS OF FEDERAL DEFENDANT'S ACTIVITIES

The FHA was enacted with the intent to further the dual goals of preventing the increase of segregation in housing and attaining open, integrated residential housing patterns. *Otero*. [T]he evidence establishes that HUD excessively has focused its desegregation efforts within Baltimore City rather than the Baltimore Region as a whole. The question thus becomes whether HUD's long-term practice of focusing its efforts on Baltimore City has furthered fair housing on a regional basis by moving away from segregation and towards open, integrated residential housing for all. A brief review of the history and statistical data presented at trial is relevant to this inquiry.

[O]ver the course of the past half-century, Local and Federal Defendants have taken some steps to ameliorate the vestiges of de jure segregation. In regard to public housing, to the extent that there have been desegregative steps, in the context of the numbers involved, these efforts have consisted overwhelmingly in placing African-American low-income housing residents in public housing units located in Baltimore City. Geographic considerations, economic limitations, population shifts, etc., have reduced, as a practical matter, Federal Defendants' capacity to ameliorate the effects of past segregation and fulfill its statutory obligation under §3608(e)(5). It is simply inadequate to try to solve the problem by redistributing the population of Baltimore City within the city limits. Nevertheless, except for the limited relief provided by the use of Section 8 vouchers outside of Baltimore City for those few who were able to locate affordable private housing in the counties, such desegregation and integration as has resulted from Federal Defendants' policies has taken place exclusively within the Baltimore City limits.

The Section 8 program provides vouchers/certificates to tenants who find their own housing in the private market. The Court notes that any increase in federally-assisted housing opportunities during the 1990s came as a result of the Section 8 voucher/certificate program. In 1989, 2,414 vouchers/certificates were allocated to Baltimore City. By 1999, that number reached 9,715. Funding for public housing units remained as a key program for HUD, with some 2,367 units sited during the 1990s and some 2,600 units demolished during the same period.

Although Section 8 voucher-holders ha[d] the opportunity to pursue housing wherever they chose, in 2002 about 56% of the MSA's [Metropolitan Statistical Area's] Section 8 voucher-holders resided in Baltimore City. The majority use within the city limits may be explained by noting that HUD considers the Baltimore metropolitan area to have a tight housing market that makes it very difficult, even for families with vouchers, to secure housing. Indeed, HUD itself recognized that . . . housing vouchers are "not viable replacement housing options" in tight housing markets like Baltimore's. In sum, it appears that the relative expense and lack of affordability of housing outside of Baltimore City may present a significant barrier to Section 8 voucher-holders who might wish to pursue private housing in the Baltimore Region but outside the city.

Just as rearranging the siting of public housing units within Baltimore City is insufficient to advance the cause of desegregation, Section 8 vouchers are inadequate to achieve this end. Given Baltimore City's demographic composition, it is not surprising that the majority—more than 67%—of the City's Section 8 voucher holders live in census tracts that are 70 to 100% Black.

Baltimore City contains only approximately 30% of the Baltimore Region's households. In 1940, 19% of the population of Baltimore City was African-American. During the fifty-year period ending in 2000, Baltimore City lost one-third of its population, while experiencing a significant increase in the African-American population. By 2000, the population of Baltimore City was 64% African-American, while the population of the rest of the Baltimore Region was 15% Black. Such was the racial composition that Federal Defendants faced during the Open Period when purporting to fulfill their statutory duty under §3608 to consider the effect of a HUD grant on the racial and socio-economic composition of the surrounding area.[16]

As the First Circuit pointed out in similar circumstances, if HUD had, in fact, fulfilled this duty, HUD's actions would have tended to increase, or at least not significantly decrease, the supply of open housing. The Court thus turns to relevant features of the Title VIII housing supply during the Open Period.

During the 1990s, 89% of public housing units developed with HUD's support in the Baltimore Region were in Baltimore City. In sharp contrast, none at all was sited in contiguous Baltimore County. During the same period, seven of Baltimore City's largest public housing developments and two smaller developments were demolished. The 4,869 units that were demolished were, by-and-large, replaced by lower density housing in virtually the same sites, although Fairfield and Hollander Ridge saw no replacement housing on their former sites. Several smaller public housing developments also were constructed during the 1990s. The largest of these (some 39 units) was located in a Census tract with below-average African-American percentages, while the other two (some 43 units combined) were sited in Census tracts with above-average percentages of African-Americans.

All told, some 86% of all hardscape public housing units sited in Baltimore City during the 1990s were sited in Census tracts with African-American percentages above the citywide average in 1990. Within the public housing units themselves, in 2002, 98% of Baltimore's family tenants in public housing developments were African-American, and each public housing development was at least 91% African-American. Moreover, 56% of the Baltimore Region's Section 8 voucher-holders resided in Baltimore City.

The statistical evidence demonstrates that during the Open Period, the majority of those who benefited from any of HUD's federally-assisted housing activity ended up living in Baltimore City; that the vast majority of the public housing units in the Baltimore Region were occupied by African-Americans; that these public housing units remained concentrated within Baltimore City

---

16. [EDS.—The court uses "Open Period" to denote the period justiciable under the statute of limitations, 3 years for the local defendants and 6 for the federal.]

(where a majority of residents are African-American); and that 85% of these units were sited in Census tracts within Baltimore City with above average percentages of African-American residents. In contrast, a relatively meager percentage of public housing was sited outside of Baltimore City, where a minority of the residential population is African-American, and only 44% of those holding Section 8 vouchers in the Baltimore Region resided outside of Baltimore City.

The statistical evidence demonstrates that HUD's various housing programs, as implemented, failed to achieve significant desegregation in Baltimore City. This is true during the Open Period as it had been in the preceding decades. HUD's pattern of grant activity in the Baltimore Region indicates "a failure, over time, to take seriously its minimal Title VIII obligation to consider alternative courses of action in light of their impact on open housing." *NAACP*, 817 F.2d at 157.

The Court finds an approach of regionalization to be integral to desegregation in the Baltimore Region and that regionalization was an important alternative course of action available to Federal Defendants. By the term "regionalization" the Court refers to policies whereby the effects of past segregation in Baltimore City public housing may be ameliorated by the provision of public housing opportunities beyond the boundaries of Baltimore City. Testimony by HUD officials at trial indicates that Baltimore City itself recognized the importance of regionalization. But, of course, it was HUD and not Local Defendants, that could have meaningfully acted upon a regional approach.

As Professor john a. powell, wrote: "[N]o single jurisdiction can solve the housing problems, and no single organization can halt the forces of segregation and concentration of poverty. . . . Instead we must work together on a regional level." john a. powell, *Opportunity-Based Housing*, 12 J. Affordable Housing & Community Develop. L. 188, 191 (2003). It was manifestly within the jurisdictional authority of HUD to site public housing—the residents of which in the Baltimore MSA are overwhelmingly African-American—outside the boundaries of Baltimore City—where African-Americans compose a smaller proportion of the residential population than in Baltimore City. Through regionalization, HUD had the practical power and leverage to accomplish desegregation through a course of action that Local Defendants could not implement on their own, given their own jurisdictional limitations.

The evidence establishes that before, throughout and after the Open Period, HUD has not affected such region-wide involvement. Rather, the statistics discussed above establish that HUD (except, to an extent, in regard to Section 8 vouchers) focused its desegregative public housing efforts within the Baltimore Region almost exclusively on building (and sometimes demolishing) brick-and-mortar housing within Baltimore City. HUD failed to consider regionally-oriented desegregation and integration policies, despite the fact that Baltimore City is virtually surrounded by Baltimore County and there is public transportation between the two. In effectively wearing blinders that limited their vision beyond Baltimore City, Federal Defendants, at best, abused their discretion and failed to meet their obligations under the Fair Housing Act to promote fair housing affirmatively.

It is high time that HUD live up to its statutory mandate to consider the effect of its policies on the racial and socio-economic composition of the surrounding area and thus consider regional approaches to promoting fair housing opportunities for African-American public housing residents in the Baltimore Region. This Court finds it no longer appropriate for HUD, as an institution with national jurisdiction, essentially to limit its consideration of desegregative programs for the Baltimore Region to methods of rearranging Baltimore's public housing residents within the Baltimore City limits.

2. HUD'S EXPLANATION FOR NOT PURSUING REGIONALIZATION

In accordance with the requirements of the APA, the Court has reviewed the record to ascertain HUD's decisionmaking process with regard to regionalization. Federal Defendants presented virtually no evidence to substantiate whether or not they considered regionalization options in deciding which Title VIII programs to pursue in the Baltimore Region. Likewise, there is a dearth of evidence on the record of what process, if any, Federal Defendants employed in ultimately rejecting the pursuit of regionalization. The Court finds that HUD's explanation for its failure to consider pursuing regionalization options, such as it was, does not satisfy its statutory obligation under Title VIII to consider alternative courses of action in light of their impact on open housing.

HUD had more policy options and leverage to provide Plaintiffs suburban housing opportunities than Local Defendants had, and the record does not reflect that HUD pursued these options. Accordingly, the Court finds that, during the Open Period, Federal Defendants failed to fulfill the duties imposed by §3608(e)(5), as enforced through the APA, to seriously and thoroughly consider the regional effects of its desegregation policies and integration efforts. Thus, Federal Defendants violated their statutory obligations under §3608(e)(5) of the FHA. Moreover, HUD has failed adequately to consider regionalization over the past half-century and, absent judicial compulsion, appears most unlikely to do so in the foreseeable future. . . .

The Court finds that it is here called on to set aside HUD's practice of ignoring regionalization actions because it constitutes an "abuse" of HUD's "discretion" to administer its housing programs affirmatively to further the goals of the FHA. Moreover, the APA's definition of "agency action" includes an agency's "failure to act." . . . In sum, the APA, by its terms, has as its purpose judicial review of agency action and inaction that falls outside the agency's statutory powers. Thus, the Court concludes that the APA is the appropriate enforcement mechanism to address HUD's failure to act to fulfill its statutory duty to consider the regional effects of its desegregation policies. . . .

The absence of a finding of discriminatory intent is not an impediment to the Court's finding of a statutory violation. Under §3608(e)(5) HUD has had, and continues to have, a duty to forward the goal of open, integrated residential housing, which can only be achieved by ameliorating the effects of past discriminatory segregation. Federal Defendants' abdication of their statutory responsibilities stems from their failure *to even consider*, in any adequate way, regionalization policies.

NOTES AND QUESTIONS

1. What Is the Authority for Requiring Regionalization as Part of the AFFH Mandate? Courts have been insistent that integration generally and regionalization in particular are part of AFFH. Regionalization was central to the Supreme Court's decision in *Hills v. Gautreaux* and cases following *Gautreaux* (discussed in Chapter 12). Regionalization was important to the remedy in *NAACP, Boston Chapter* and is the heart of the court's holding in *Thompson*. But HUD argued in its post-trial brief in *Thompson* that AFFH does not obligate it to address regionalization and, as Westchester County argued in the case below,[17] that it was not obliged to focus on racial as opposed to other forms of discrimination.[18]

The words "integration" and "regionalization" do not appear in the statute, but the legislative discussions are replete with references to both, as is the Kerner Commission report, which influenced the enactment of the legislation.[19] Integration also is referenced in a different statute, the Congressional Declaration of National Housing Policy, 42 U.S.C. §1441.[20] To what extent should expressions of legislative purpose influence judicial interpretations of statutory meaning?

2. Regional Remedies and the *Mount Laurel* Doctrine. The necessity of regional remedies for structural housing discrimination and segregation is crystallized in the *Mount Laurel* litigation and legislation in New Jersey and the inclusionary zoning activities that have followed it, in New Jersey and elsewhere. The heart of the *Mount Laurel* doctrine is that the state constitution requires developing communities to provide their fair share of the regional need for low- and moderate-income housing.[21] Although this large-scale

---

17. United States ex rel. Anti-Discrimination Center v. Westchester County, 668 F. Supp. 2d 548 (S.D.N.Y. 2009).

18. The Post-Trial Reply Brief of Federal Defendants is discussed in Florence Wagman Roisman, *Affirmatively Furthering Fair Housing in Regional Housing Markets: The Baltimore Public Housing Desegregation Litigation*, 42 Wake Forest L. Rev. 333, 359, 368 (2007).

19. In addition to the excerpts quoted in the court decisions, other such expressions of legislative purpose and the Kerner Commission report are discussed in Roisman, *supra* note 18, at 371-88.

20. 42 U.S.C. §1441 provides that HUD and other federal departments or agencies "having powers, functions, or duties with respect to housing, shall . . . encourage and assist . . . the development of . . . integrated . . . neighborhoods. . . ." *See also* 42 U.S.C. §1441a.

21. *See* David L. Kirp et al., Our Town: Race, Housing, and the Soul of Suburbia (Rutgers U. Press 1995); Peter A. Buchsbaum, *Affordable Housing and the Mount Laurel Doctrine: Enforcement Has Returned to the Courts*, 2022 N.J. Law 56 (2022); Douglas S. Massey et al., Climbing Mount Laurel: The Struggle for Affordable Housing and Social Mobility in an American Suburb (Princeton U. Press 2019).

enforcement effort began with race-related concerns, the case ultimately was decided under state law with respect to economic discrimination and segregation. This body of law is, therefore, beyond the scope of this casebook.

3. Consequences of the *Thompson* Decision. As partial settlement of the suit, HUD and the plaintiffs created the Baltimore Housing Mobility Program (BHMP), which is administered by the Baltimore Regional Housing Partnership (BRHP).[22] BHMP provides housing choice vouchers for families of color in Baltimore City to rent homes in opportunity areas in the five predominantly white counties surrounding the city. Between 2003 and 2022, BRHP had assisted more than 5,000 families with young children. BRHP also administers a Regional Project-Based Voucher Initiative, which, as of 2022, had produced 150 units in opportunity areas in the counties.[23]

White communities initially did not celebrate this exercise of choice by poor people of color to move into the counties surrounding Baltimore City—perhaps especially into Baltimore County.[24] Baltimore had been one of the sites of HUD's Moving to Opportunity mobility program (see Chapter 12), and Baltimore suburbs—especially Baltimore County—had fought against even that small demonstration program.[25]

2. *United States ex rel. Anti-Discrimination Center v. Westchester County*

Westchester County is a wealthy, predominantly white county just north of New York City. (It does include some cities, like Yonkers, that have significant numbers of residents of color.) In this False Claims Act (FCA) suit, the Anti-Discrimination Center (ADC) alleged that between 2000 and 2006, the county secured more than $52 million from HUD, certifying that it was "affirmatively furthering fair housing" in its housing and community development programs although it never considered or discussed racial impediments to housing choice. In 2007, the county moved to dismiss, in part on the ground that the FHA "does not impose upon it any obligation to identify racial

---

22. For a discussion of the litigation, the settlement, and other efforts to desegregate Baltimore's suburbs, see Lawrence Lanahan, THE LINES BETWEEN US: TWO FAMILIES AND A QUEST TO CROSS BALTIMORE'S RACIAL DIVIDE (The New Press 2019).

23. The description in this paragraph is based on Darryn Mumphrey et al., PRRAC & MobilityWorks, HOUSING MOBILITY PROGRAMS IN THE U.S. 2022, at 7-9 (Philip Tegeler ed., 2022), https://www.prrac.org/housing-mobility-programs-in-the-u-s-2022-december-2022/. BRHP defines opportunity areas with 22 variables in three categories: education, poverty rate and other aspects of community strength, and economic factors (unemployment, transportation, etc.). *Id*. at 8.

24. *See* Lanahan, *supra* note 22, at 135-36, 157, 167.

25. David Moberg, *No Vacancy! Moving to Opportunity in Baltimore's Suburbs*, SHELTERFORCE, Jan. 1, 1995, https://shelterforce.org/1995/01/01/no-vacancy-moving-to-opportunity-in-baltimores-suburbs/; Doug Donovan, *Baltimore County to Curb Segregation in Housing*, THE BALTIMORE SUN, Mar. 15, 2016, https://www.baltimoresun.com/2016/03/15/baltimore-county-to-curb-housing-segregation/.

discrimination and segregation as impediments to 'fair housing'" when it makes its AFFH certification.[26] The district court rejected this (and other) bases for the motion. The court emphasized that the FHA was "designed primarily to . . . remedy . . . discrimination so that members of minority races would not be condemned to remain in urban ghettos, . . . [that it] bans practices that are motivated by a racially discriminatory purpose as well as those that 'disproportionately affect minorities.' . . . [and] is designed to fulfill 'the goal of open, integrated residential housing patterns and to prevent the increase of segregation, in ghettos, of racial groups.'" The court concluded: "In the face of the clear legislative purpose of the FHA, enacted . . . to combat racial segregation and discrimination in housing, an interpretation of 'affirmatively further fair housing' that excludes consideration of race would be an absurd result."

In a later opinion, after discovery had been completed, the court granted partial summary judgment to ADC and denied Westchester's motion for summary judgment.

United States ex rel. Anti-Discrimination Center v. Westchester County
668 F. Supp. 2d 548 (S.D.N.Y. 2009)

DENISE COTE, District Judge:

ADC contends that to obtain the HUD funds at issue here the County had to analyze and record its analysis of the impediments to fair housing choice, and then take appropriate actions to overcome those impediments and also record those actions. ADC contends that the County did none of these things, ignoring the fact that its actions were increasing patterns of segregation.

The County has taken a variety of tacks in defending these charges. In addition to disputing that it was required to analyze race when analyzing impediments to fair housing choice, it contends principally that in any event it did analyze race, determined that racial segregation and discrimination were not significant barriers to fair housing choice, and concluded that the most pressing impediment to fair housing was the lack of affordable housing stock. It argues that it did an outstanding job in increasing the stock of affordable housing within the County, and that this litigation represents little more than a policy dispute over the most effective means for addressing local government resistance to integration and affordable housing. The County has adopted a policy of cooperation with municipalities, in light of what it terms "political reality" and due to its belief that cooperation is the most productive avenue for increasing the stock of affordable housing in the County.

---

26. United States *ex rel.* Anti-Discrimination Center of Metro New York v. Westchester County, 495 F. Supp. 2d 375, 383-84 (2007).

A. Statutory and Regulatory Framework

Westchester County [comprises] 45 municipal entities. All of the municipalities are part of the Westchester Urban County Consortium ("Consortium"), except for the municipalities of Mount Pleasant, Mount Vernon, New Rochelle, White Plains, and Yonkers. The County applied to HUD for federal funding, including Community Development Block Grants ("CDBG"), on behalf of itself and the Consortium each year from April 1, 2000 to April 1, 2006 ("the false claims period").

The United States grants housing and community development-related funding to state and local entities. In order to receive certain federal funding, including CDBG funds, the County was required to certify that, *inter alia*, "the grant will be conducted and administered in conformity with the CRA of 1964 and the FHA, and the grantee will affirmatively further fair housing." To AFFH [EDS.—as HUD defined the requirement during this time period], the County was required to undertake three tasks: to "conduct an analysis of impediments [AI] to fair housing choice within the area, take appropriate actions to overcome the effects of any impediments identified through that analysis, and maintain records reflecting the analysis and actions in this regard."

Westchester entered into Cooperation Agreements with municipalities participating in the Consortium. The agreements pertained to CDBG grants, and provided that "the County is prohibited from expending community development block grant funds for activities in or in support of any local government that does not affirmatively further fair housing within its jurisdiction or that impedes the County's action to comply with its fair housing certifications." These Cooperation Agreements were submitted to HUD every three years.

B. The Requirement to Consider Race

[T]he statutory and regulatory framework set forth above—in requiring the grantee of funds to certify that the grant will be "conducted and administered" in conformity with the CRA of 1964 and the FHA, and to certify that the grantee will AFFH—requires the grantee to analyze the impact of race on housing opportunities and choice in its jurisdiction. In identifying impediments to fair housing choice, it must analyze impediments erected by race discrimination or segregation, and if such impediments exist, it must take appropriate action to overcome the effects of those impediments.

C. The County's AFFH Certifications

[Between 2000 and 2006, as required by statute and HUD regulations, Westchester submitted to HUD annual AFFH certifications. The county did provide figures showing] population by race, and also by race and income level. [It] also identified communities in the County that had "areas of minority concentration," and identified which municipalities in the Consortium had the largest black population, as well as which ones had the largest gain in black population during the 1980s. It also noted that blacks made up between

.1% and 16% of all homeowners in the Consortium's municipalities, and between 1 and 30% of the renters in the Consortium's municipalities. [It] also reviewed the waiting list for Section 8 rental assistance, and broke down the waiting list by race. [It] noted that "[l]ow-income families and individuals and those with special housing needs (e.g., mentally ill, disabled and persons with AIDS) are frequently excluded from housing opportunities due to illegal discrimination," and that the non-profit housing counseling agency Westchester Residential Opportunities ("WRO") reported that they received approximately 120 housing discrimination complaints in 1999.

[The county also noted] that while 72% of households in the Consortium own their own homes, only 46% of black households and 35% of Hispanic households own their own homes. [It] noted that "[m]inorities are priced out of the expensive homeownership market." [It also provided] data tables from the 2000 census, including tables showing 1) population by race and Hispanic Origin, 2) the population by age, 3) cost-burdened owners and renters, 4) overcrowded housing units, and 5) housing deficiencies and tables showing housing problems for Hispanic households and black, non-Hispanic households.

The County had received a copy of the HUD Fair Housing Planning Guide ("HUD Guide") [which explained the AFFH duty to provide an AI (analysis of impediments) that will] "[a]nalyze and eliminate housing discrimination in the jurisdiction" and to "[p]rovide opportunities for inclusive patterns of housing occupancy regardless of race, color, religion, sex, familial status, disability and national origin." [The Guide explained that] [a]n AI involves an "assessment of conditions, both public and private, affecting fair housing choice for all protected classes." Such impediments are "actions, omissions or decisions" which "restrict housing choices or the availability of housing choices," or which have the effect of doing so, based on "race, color, religion, sex, disability, familial status, or national origin," including "[p]olicies, practices, or procedures that appear neutral on their face." HUD's suggested AI format includes a housing profile describing "the degree of segregation and restricted housing by race, ethnicity, disability status, and families with children; [and] how segregation and restricted housing supply occurred."

The Guide cautions that grantees should prepare AIs using a "Fair Housing Perspective," and that this means that while

> the explanation of barriers to *affordable housing* to be included in the *Consolidated Plan* may contain a good deal of relevant AI information[, it] may not go far or deep enough into factors that have made poor housing conditions more severe for certain groups in the lower-income population than for others. Jurisdictions should be aware of the extent to which discrimination or other causes that may have a discriminatory effect play a role in producing the more severe conditions for certain groups. (Emphasis supplied).

The distinction between AFFH actions and affordable housing activities is further explained in the HUD Guide:

> The two concepts are not equivalent but they are also not entirely separate. When a jurisdiction undertakes to build or rehabilitate housing for low- and

moderate-income families, for example, *this action is not in and of itself sufficient to affirmatively further fair housing.* It may be providing an extremely useful service by increasing the supply of decent, safe, and sanitary affordable housing. Providing adequate housing and improving existing neighborhoods are vital functions and should always be encouraged.

Additionally, the provision of affordable housing is often important to minority families and to persons with disabilities because they are disproportionately represented among those that would benefit from low-cost housing. *When steps are taken to assure that the housing is fully available to all residents of the community, regardless of race, color, national origin, gender, handicap, or familial status, those are the actions that affirmatively further fair housing.* (Emphasis supplied).

[In 1996, HUD had] informed the County that its AI

should contain a description of the degree of segregation and restricted housing by race, ethnicity, disability status and families with children; explain how segregation and restricted housing supply occurred; and relate this information by neighborhood and cost of housing. Minorities should be categorized as follows: Black, Hispanic, Asian, Pacific-Islander, and American Indian/Alaskan Native. In addition, the County should submit data on the housing needs of homeless individuals and families by race/ethnicity in subsequent Consolidated Plan submissions.

Additionally, the County had its own internal documents relating to its AFFH obligations and the preparation of AIs [and] the County's Fair Housing Plan ("FHP"). [One such document] contains the following reminder: "Remember: This [the FHP] is not a report on affordable housing, but FAIR HOUSING!!!" [Another states]

[w]hile *this document [the FHP] is required by HUD to analyze Fair Housing* throughout the Westchester Urban County Consortium, it will also be a useful tool for future planning and development of affordable housing. As you know, *the Planning department has prepared several reports that address affordable housing, which should not be confused with the Fair Housing Plan. The goals of the Fair Housing Plan are: 1) to analyze barriers to housing that are based on race,* religion, sex, disabilities, familial status, or national origin; 2) *to develop strategies to remove those barriers; and 3) to maintain records of Fair Housing efforts,* thus indicating the County's commitment to fair housing choice. (Emphasis supplied).

[Other HUD] materials noted that "[d]uring the past thirty-seven years, Congress has spent more than one trillion dollars in a failed attempt to remedy the effects of a dual housing market in America," and they traced the evolution of the dual market to, *inter alia,* African-Americans migrating to cities and encountering obstacles "designed to segregate them from the majority, and to maintain a dual society."

The [County's 2000 AI] provides:

The FHP provides an evaluation of the needs for *handicapped persons, larger/smaller families, extended families, and tenure opportunities* when planning for their future development.

> It is important to note that within Westchester County, *the greatest impediment to fair housing is the lack of affordable housing. While there are other restrictions to housing choice,* Westchester's housing stock is expensive relative to income and this significantly limits one's housing options. (Emphasis supplied).

In response to the impediments analyzed, the [AI] outlines four objectives as "[a]ctions to be taken." [They all relate to low- and moderate-income housing and to seniors, not to race, except for a report that some CDBG funds go to WRO and that WRO and other agencies provide help with discrimination cases.]

The County's 2004 AI states that "the Fair Housing Plan is an evaluation of the needs for handicapped persons, larger/smaller families, extended families, and tenure opportunities [EDs. — presumably, opportunities for homeownership] when planning for their future development." The AI section lists 13 "Impediments to *Affordable* Housing Identified." (Emphasis supplied). The identified impediments are 1) "Lack of Affordable Housing in the New York Region"; 2) "Lack of Vacant Land"; 3) "High Cost of Land"; 4) "Limited Availability of Funds"; 5) "Limited Number of Section 8 Vouchers & Other Rental Assistance" [and landlord reluctance to participate]; 6) "Local Opposition (NIMBY)"; 7) "Limited Non-Profit Capacity"; 8) "High Construction Costs"; 9) "Lengthy Review Process"; 10) "Few High Density Zones"; 11) "Limited Shelter Allowance for Public Assistance Recipients"; 12) "High Prevalence of Lead-Based Paint in Housing Units;" and 13) "Limited Interest by Landlords and Developers."

In the section of the chapter pertaining to actions to be taken to overcome these identified impediments, five objectives are listed[; none relates to race]. In the Maintenance of Records section of the chapter, in addition to listing the WRO reports and HMDA data, the County noted that a Human Rights Commission was established "to process and investigate discrimination complaints."

D. Race and the County

Westchester was aware of the racial makeup of its municipalities (as reflected in the relevant censuses) when it prepared its 2000 and 2004 analyses of impediments to fair housing. According to the 2000 census, over half of the municipalities in the Consortium had African-American populations of 3% or less. In 1999, the Westchester Board of Legislators made a legislative finding that "there is no greater danger to the health, morals, safety, and welfare of the County than the existence of prejudice, intolerance, and antagonism among its residents because of . . . race, color, religion, ethnicity [, and other protected classes]" and that "there ha[d] been repeated instances of intolerance and discrimination committed in Westchester County."

The County's expert witnesses acknowledge the existence of racial "concentration" in parts of the County. An expert witness for the County testified that racial concentration may decrease if affordable housing opportunities were available in predominantly white areas and African-Americans chose to live or move to those areas. The ADC contends that the County's focus on affordable housing in its AI, rather than fair housing, meant that the County did not analyze how its placement of affordable housing affected segregation and racial diversity, and in fact that the County's production and placement of affordable housing increased segregation in the jurisdiction. The County admits that it did not undertake an analysis of whether the production of affordable housing between January 1, 1992 and April 1, 2006, had the effect of increasing or decreasing racial diversity in the neighborhood in which the housing was built.

[A county official] testified that she told the ADC that the County "sees discrimination in terms of income, rather than in terms of race." She also testified that she informed the ADC that the County's AI "is seen through the lens of income and affordability, as opposed to race discrimination and segregation by race."

E. Actions Taken by the County to AFFH and to Provide Affordable Housing

The County has not deemed any municipalities to be failing to AFFH, nor has it deemed any municipalities to be impeding the County's ability to AFFH. As such, the County has not withheld any funds or imposed any sanctions on any participating municipalities for failure to AFFH. When the County considers where to acquire land for affordable housing, it seeks the concurrence of the municipality where the land is situated, and during the false claims period the County would not acquire any such land without the municipality's agreement. The County produced no documentation showing that during the false claims period it funded or assisted the production of affordable housing in any municipality where the municipality opposed such production. The County set a goal in 1993 to create 5000 affordable housing units; however, as of July 2005, at least 16 [of 45] municipal units in the County had not created a single affordable housing unit.

DISCUSSION

In order to impose liability under the FCA, the plaintiff must show that defendants "(1) made a claim, (2) to the United States government, (3) that is false or fraudulent, (4) knowing of its falsity, and (5) seeking payment from the federal treasury." [T]he only elements that are in dispute are the third and fourth, *i.e.*, whether there is no genuine issue of material fact that the County submitted false or fraudulent claims, knowing of their falsity. [The county also argued that the plaintiff should be required to prove two more elements—that the falsity was material, and that the United States suffered damages. The court rejected this argument.]

A. Were the County's Certifications False?

As discussed above, the statutes and regulations require not just any AI, but one that analyzes impediments to fair housing that are related to race. There is no genuine issue of material fact such that a reasonable jury could find that the County analyzed race in conducting its AIs.

A review of the 2000 and 2004 AIs demonstrates that they were conducted through the lens of affordable housing, rather than *fair* housing and its focus on protected classes such as race. Both AIs are devoted entirely to the lack of affordable housing in the County and related obstacles. While the AIs specify that lack of affordable housing is the "greatest" impediment to fair housing, a determination that affordable housing is the greatest impediment does not absolve the County from its requirement to analyze race-based impediments to fair housing. Despite the regulatory obligation to maintain records reflecting the AI, there is simply no evidence that either of the County's AIs during the false claims period analyzed race-based impediments to fair housing within its jurisdiction.

The County argues that the HUD Guide is not persuasive on the issue of what is required for an AI. It tries to recast the issues in this litigation as a quibble over whether the County was required to follow the specific tasks and format HUD lays out, which are not spelled out in the case law and statutory and regulatory framework. As already described, however, the County's AIs during the false claims period utterly failed to comply with the regulatory requirement that the County perform and maintain a record of its analysis of the impediments to fair housing choice in terms of race. This failure is only compounded by the County's failure to follow the guidance provided by HUD.

Since the HUD Guide is firmly rooted in the statutory and regulatory framework and consistent with the case law, it is persuasive on the issue of whether the County was required to analyze race-based impediments in conducting its AI. The HUD Guide's suggestion that the AI is to focus on acts, omissions, and decisions that restrict housing choice for protected classes, and that the grantee should analyze the degree of segregation within its jurisdiction, are firmly rooted in the statutory and regulatory framework and case law (. . . finding goal of HUD grant programs is "to assist in ending discrimination and segregation, to the point where the supply of genuinely open housing increases"). While the County was certainly not required to follow every specific suggestion or every recommendation in the HUD Guide, it also cannot be completely wide of the mark regarding the suggestions relating to the central goal of the obligation to AFFH—to end housing discrimination and segregation—and still be considered compliant with its AFFH obligations.

In sum, the County has put forth no evidence, despite the AFFH obligation to maintain records of its AI, that it conducted an analysis of race as it pertains to impediments to fair housing choice, and likewise no evidence that after conducting any such analysis, the analysis led it to conclude that race-based discrimination or segregation was not an impediment to housing choice and relieved it of the duty to take action to overcome the effects that any such discrimination or segregation posed to fair housing choice. The County also proffers a fallback argument that, while it may not have explicitly analyzed race-based impediments to housing choice, as required to AFFH, it concluded that it could conduct the required race-based analysis by using income as a proxy for race.

The HUD Guide explains that while it is often the case that minorities are disproportionately represented among the low-income population, simply providing affordable housing for the low-income population "is not in and of itself sufficient to affirmatively further fair housing." This unsurprising statement is grounded in the statutory and regulatory framework behind the obligation to AFFH, which as already discussed, is concerned with addressing whether there are independent barriers to protected classes exercising fair housing choice. As a matter of logic, providing more affordable housing for a low income racial minority will improve its housing stock but may do little to change any pattern of discrimination or segregation. Addressing that pattern would at a minimum necessitate an analysis of where the additional housing is placed.

Moreover, even if the County's analysis led it to conclude that income was an appropriate proxy for race, then it was required to report that analysis and demonstrate how it acted to overcome the effects of that race-based impediment to fair housing. Again, however, the County has not pointed to records reflecting either that analysis or the actions driven by that analysis. The County has simply not shown that it analyzed whether there were race-based impediments to housing choice independent of the problem of low income, and as such, it did not comply with the requirement to AFFH. Thus, the County has not demonstrated an issue of material fact as to whether it appropriately analyzed race in conducting its AI and recorded that analysis, and as such, its certifications to HUD that it would AFFH were false.

As discussed above in regard to the related question of legally false certifications, the grant funds at issue in this case were expressly conditioned on the AFFH certification requirement. The AFFH certification was not a mere boilerplate formality, but rather was a substantive requirement, rooted in the history and purpose of the fair housing laws and regulations, requiring the County to conduct an AI, take appropriate actions in response, and to document its analysis and actions. The County's motion for summary judgment is therefore denied.

NOTES AND QUESTIONS

1. **The History of the** *Westchester* **Case.** When the ADC originally filed this case, DOJ declined to intervene. DOJ subsequently did intervene, taking control and presenting a consent decree that the court approved in 2009.

Under the consent decree, Westchester was to appropriate nearly $52 million in county funds and create at least 750 units of affordable housing in communities with very small Black and Latino populations; this was to be done under the supervision of a Monitor, chosen by the government and appointed by the court, who would report regularly to the court. In 2014, the ADC objected strenuously to many aspects of the consent decree, including the persistence of the exclusionary zoning barriers in the jurisdictions that made up the county.[27] On July 31, 2021, the district judge terminated the consent decree and released the Monitor, accepting representations by the United States and Westchester County that the 750 "AFFH units" had been completed.

2. What About Other Recipients? In 2024 alone, HUD announced an award of $3.3 billion in CDBG grants alone to states, urban counties, insular areas, Washington, DC, Puerto Rico, and localities.[28] As discussed in Section F, below, enforcement of the AFFH mandate by HUD or other federal actors has been relatively rare. DOJ assumed control of the *Westchester* case, but a private organization had initiated the suit; most efforts to enforce AFFH are spearheaded by private entities. Few other HUD recipients have been threatened, by FCA litigation or otherwise, with loss of funding or other consequences for failure to AFFH.[29]

3. Socioeconomics as a Proxy for Race. Like Westchester County here, the Supreme Court, lower courts, and others have suggested that socioeconomic status is a more appropriate or relevant criterion for analysis and that discussion of race should be avoided. This is a situation where HUD rejects such reasoning, and the district court agrees. What do you think of the arguments on either side? Consider other contexts, such as in disparate impact claims challenging bans on affordable housing, where plaintiffs might argue that the economic status of a group served by a program is being used as a proxy for protected characteristics.

4. *United States v. Yonkers.* One of the municipalities in Westchester County is the City of Yonkers. In 1980, the United States sued the City of Yonkers and its Board of Education for intentionally segregating by race both housing and schools. This was the only suit brought by the United States that challenged—and challenged successfully—both housing and school segregation.[30]

27. Anti-Discrimination Center, CHEATING ON EVERY LEVEL: ANATOMY OF THE DEMISE OF A CIVIL RIGHTS CONSENT DECREE (May 6, 2014), https://www.antibiaslaw.com/sites/default/files/Cheating_On_Every_Level.pdf; Nikole Hannah-Jones, *Soft on Segregation: How the Feds Failed to Integrate Westchester County*, PROPUBLICA, Nov. 2, 2012, https://www.propublica.org/article/soft-on-segregation-how-the-feds-failed-to-integrate-westchester-county.

28. HUD, No. 24-103, *Biden-Harris Announces $5.5 Billion in Grants for Affordable Housing, Community Development, and Homeless Assistance to Drive Economic Growth* (May 7, 2024), https://www.hud.gov/press/press_releases_media_advisories/hud_no_24_103.

29. *See, e.g.*, Heather R. Abraham, *Fair Housing's Third Act: American Tragedy or Triumph?*, 39 YALE L. & POL'Y REV. 1, 25-28 (2021).

30. United States v. City of Yonkers, 624 F. Supp. 1276 (S.D.N.Y. 1985), *aff'd*, 837 F.2d 1181 (2d Cir. 1987), *cert. denied*, 486 U.S. 1055 (1988). Professor Schwemm refers to this as an "infamous" case. Schwemm, HDLL §21:4. Although this was the only case in which the United States challenged both housing and school segregation, both forms of segregation often were at issue

This description of the first two decades of the litigation is drawn from United States v. Secretary of HUD, 239 F.3d 211 (2d Cir. 2001), an opinion by Judge Calabresi:

> In 1985, following a lengthy bench trial, Leonard B. Sand, District Judge, found that the City of Yonkers had intentionally segregated its public housing and public schools on the basis of race by relegating virtually all of its subsidized housing to the predominantly minority-resident southwest part of the City, all in violation of the FHA and the Equal Protection Clause. In 1986, the District Court entered a Housing Remedy Order ("HRO"), which aimed to desegregate public and subsidized housing by requiring the City to develop additional such housing in overwhelmingly white East and Northwest Yonkers. The HRO required the City to build a specified number of subsidized housing units in specified areas by a specified date and also gave the plaintiffs and plaintiffs-intervenors in the case — the United States and the NAACP — the right to petition the District Court for further remedial orders in case these goals were not timely met. This Court affirmed the District Court's liability and remedy rulings [and the Supreme Court denied certiorari.] [T]he City resisted (and at times even stood in contempt of) the District Court's efforts to remedy the City's intentional racial discrimination.[31]
>
> In 1988 the parties negotiated a consent decree [but] the City refused to take the actions required by the decree, and [so] the District Court entered a Long Term Plan Order ("LTPO") which:
>
> 1. required the City to ensure that a certain percentage of low income housing units were included in any new multi-family housing development;
> 2. directed the City to disperse the assisted housing units in a manner that avoids the "undue concentration of both public and assisted units in any neighborhood of Yonkers;" and
> 3. created a system of priorities among those eligible for assisted housing as follows:
>   priority 1 — persons who had been residents of public or subsidized housing in the City of Yonkers between January 1, 1971 and the date at which assisted housing under the LTPO was made available;
>   priority 2 — residents of the City of Yonkers;
>   priority 3 — persons employed in the City of Yonkers.
>
> Once again, the City failed to implement the terms of the remedial order, and in 1993, the District Court entered a Supplemental Long Term Plan Order

---

in what presented as school segregation cases. Perhaps the most pertinent of these for the connection between housing segregation and school segregation was the Detroit case, Milliken v. Bradley, 418 U.S. 717 (1974) (*Milliken I*). For an engrossing description and analysis of that litigation, see Michelle Adams, THE CONTAINMENT (forthcoming Jan. 2025), https://us.macmillan.com/books/9780374250423/thecontainment.

31. [Fn. 2 in original] The District Court found both the City and several individual City Councilmembers in civil contempt of its earlier remedial orders. This Court subsequently affirmed the contempt sanctions, although it limited the fines levied against the City, which had previously been doubling on each consecutive day of non-compliance, to $1 million per day. The Supreme Court subsequently reversed the contempt sanction as applied to the individual council members. Spallone v. United States, 493 U.S. 265, 280 (1990).

("SLTPO") setting forth additional measures to remedy the City's ongoing housing segregation. Although this Court affirmed the SLTPO, the City continued to fail to provide the new subsidized housing the SLTPO contemplated. Accordingly, [in] 1996, the District Court entered a Second Supplemental Long Term Plan Order ("SSLTPO") to promote further the implementation of the HRO.

[In 1999, the District Court held hearings concerning the lack of attention to priority one households and the SSLTPO's inadequate effect on furthering integration in the City's housing.] The Court determined that the housing program's "accomplishments to date fall far short of what one hoped for," and it ordered the parties to prepare a new remedial order. On December 29, 1999, the District Court granted the City [credit for housing it had produced but] only "on the condition and understanding that no future credits will be granted unless" the City creates housing opportunities that "further the racially integrative goals which are the essence of all the Court's prior housing remedy orders intended to counter the effects of prior racial discrimination in housing in Yonkers." To this end, the District Court entered the Third Supplemental Long Term Plan Order ("TSLTPO"), [which] specified that future housing credits would be awarded to the City only for priority one households that [made integrative moves].

The city appealed that order, arguing that modification of the consent decree was improper and that the new order employed race-conscious remedial devices in an unconstitutional manner. The Second Circuit held "that the TSLTPO's use of race satisfies even the strict scrutiny to which legislative race-conscious remedies must be subjected."

The court of appeals emphasized that "the City's actions under the SSLTPO were clearly failing to reflect the priority scheme that had been established under the HRO." Few of the beneficiaries were priority one, and "the City's actions under the SSLTPO were similarly inadequate in achieving the 'integrative goals which underlie the entire remedy order.'" The court of appeals agreed with the district court that the SSLPTO "prove[d] to be unworkable because of unforeseen obstacles"—specifically the continued failure of the City to serve priority one households and to promote integrative housing moves—and that continued "enforcement of the [SSLTPO] without modification would be detrimental to the public interest"—the achievement of the goals of serving priority one households and desegregating Yonkers public housing.

With respect to the race consciousness of the district court's order, the court of appeals noted Supreme Court dictum that strict scrutiny does not apply to race-based remedies ordered by "a district judge who has found that the governmental unit before him is guilty of racially discriminatory conduct that violates the Constitution." United States v. Paradise, 480 U.S. 149, 193-94 (1987) (Stevens, J., concurring). The Second Circuit held, nonetheless, that the remedy embodied in the TSLTPO clearly survived even strict scrutiny. The court said there was no doubt that the order served a compelling government interest: "The district court expressly found that the City has engaged in intentional racial discrimination in its subsidized housing program, and "[t]he Government unquestionably has a compelling interest in remedying past and present discrimination by a state actor." *Paradise*, 480 U.S. at 167. The court held also that the remedy was narrowly tailored.

> In spite of fifteen years of remedial efforts encompassing four race-neutral remedial regimes . . ., and at least partly because of the active and passive resistance to integration displayed by the City (and documented in both this and in our earlier opinions), Yonkers public housing remains substantially segregated even today. Roughly half of the housing moves under the most recent race-neutral remedy were non-integrative, and the District Court concluded that "the experience [of race-neutral remedies] has not been satisfactory."

The Second Circuit concluded:

> The District Court has first-hand experience of the long and often difficult effort that remedying the City's intentional racial discrimination entails, in other words, of the "realities of day-to-day implementation of . . . constitutional commands." Swann v. Charlotte-Meklenburg Bd. of Educ., 402 U.S. 1, 6 (1971). After having carefully and patiently attempted to achieve this end by race-neutral means, after having expressly determined that such means were not succeeding, and after hearing from both sides to the dispute, the District Court adopted a race-conscious remedy that is both temperate and responsible. We therefore hold that the TSLTPO is narrowly tailored to the compelling state interest of remedying the City's past intentional racial discrimination, and we reject the City's constitutional challenge to the order.

Judge Sand had ordered that the city provide 200 units of public housing outside the southwest area, which were built between 1990 and 1993 and occupied between 1992 and 1994. In addition, a 1998 plan required that "the state [would] designate a total of 740 units of affordable housing," some existing, some to be built, some involving the use of vouchers. Also in 1998, Judge Sand ruled that New York State's Urban Development Corporation was partly responsible for the housing segregation and would have to pay half the cost of the remedial plan. In 2007, the parties entered into a settlement that marked the satisfaction of this obligation.[32]

5. The Consequences of the Westchester and Yonkers Housing Litigation. What do you think of the impact of the contentious litigation in Yonkers and Westchester County? In both, the opposition to the effort to further fair housing was strong, as indeed had been the case in Baltimore. In both, the ultimate relief was small in relation to the size of the need. No study has been made of those who occupied the units produced in Westchester

---

32. Fernanda Santos, *After 27 Years, Yonkers Housing Desegregation Battle Ends Quietly in Manhattan Court*, N.Y. Times, May 2, 2007, https://www.nytimes.com/2007/05/02/nyregion /02yonkers.html; U.S. Dep't of Jus., 07-316, *Justice Department Agreement Will Resolve Housing Desegregation Lawsuit in Yonkers, NY* (May 1, 2007), https://www.justice.gov/archive/opa/pr /2007/May/07-crt-316.html. Information in this paragraph is taken from Xavier de Souza Briggs et al., *In the Wake of Desegregation: Early Impacts of Scattered Site Public Housing on Neighborhoods in Yonkers, New York*, 65 J. Amer. Planning Ass'n 27, 32-33 (1999) and Lisa Belkin, Show Me a Hero: A Tale of Murder, Suicide, Race, and Redemption 323 (1998 Epilogue) (Little, Brown 1995, 2015). The book Show Me a Hero was made into an HBO miniseries in 2015.

County, but studies of those who made integrative moves in Yonkers show positive results. As Lisa Belkin reported, after 200 public housing households had moved into newly created units: "the lives of [those who moved] . . . changed for the better, and the worst fears of the east side homeowners have not come to pass." As to the overall result, asked if this were worth the financial cost and upheaval, Judge Sand said, according to Belkin, "[T]he point of all this was never *integration*. It was *desegregation* . . . "[33] What do you understand to be the difference?

F. INTERPRETATION AND APPLICATION OF AFFH BY HUD AND OTHER AGENCIES

1. HUD

Early administrations of HUD took seriously the obligation affirmatively to further fair housing. Dr. Robert Weaver, HUD's first Secretary, tried to implement the mandate and so did George Romney, President Nixon's first HUD Secretary.

HUD SECRETARIES ON AFFH

George Romney became President Nixon's Secretary of HUD in 1969, shortly after the FHA took effect. Long a supporter of civil rights, he was determined to enforce the AFFH mandate of the statute because he believed racial integration was morally and politically essential. He stated that "[t]o solve problems of the 'real city,' only metropolitan-wide solutions will do." Romney created a program called "Open Communities," which would condition HUD financial assistance on a community's acceptance of subsidized housing. Having implemented this in a few places, HUD then addressed funding for Warren, Michigan, a suburb of 180,000 with only 28 minority families, 22 of whom "lived on a military reservation, despite a labor force that was nearly one-third black." Here, "[w]hat happened, all told, was that the first Republican HUD secretary . . . informed a northern white suburb . . . that housing integration absolutely must accompany HUD funds." Warren resisted, and protested to the White House, which was sympathetic to the suburb. Although it has been said that HUD cut off the funding for Warren, in fact HUD ultimately imposed anodyne conditions but Warren's residents were still so enraged that they forced the city to end the urban renewal program.

Despite hostility from President Nixon, Romney was able to promote the introduction of subsidized housing for minorities into some exclusionary

---

33. The quotations in this paragraph are from Belkin, *supra* note 32, at 320-21 (1998 Epilogue); other sources for information in the paragraph are Briggs et al., *supra* note 32, and Rebecca C. Fauth et al., *Seven Years Later: Effects of a Neighborhood Mobility Program on Poor Black and Latino Adults' Well-being*, 49 J. OF HEALTH AND SOC. BEHAV. 119 (2008).

suburbs, including by successfully encouraging DOJ to file the lawsuit against Black Jack, Missouri, that is discussed in Chapter 7. Romney finally left HUD after the midyear elections in November 1972.[34]

Only a few subsequent administrations took effective action to promote residential integration. President Carter's HUD Secretary, Patricia Roberts Harris, "believed the receipt of federal funds should be tied to the acceptance of subsidized housing." Henry Cisneros, President Clinton's HUD Secretary, also pursued suburban integration.[35]

In a dramatic advance, on July 16, 2015, near the end of the second term of the Obama administration, under Secretary Julián Castro, HUD promulgated a final rule that was the first comprehensive regulation implementing AFFH.[36] The Trump administration paused implementation in 2018 and then, on August 7, 2020, issued a final rule that repealed the 2015 Obama-era final rule.[37]

Hon. Patricia Roberts Harris

Under President Biden's HUD Secretary, Marcia Fudge, on June 10, 2021, HUD issued an AFFH interim final rule that repealed the 2020 final rule and reinstated the definitions of the Obama rule and related certifications but did not reinstate a "mandatory AFFH process."[38] In February 2023, HUD published a proposed final rule, on which it has received comments. The interim final rule is in effect as of the time of this writing.

2. Other Departments and Agencies and the AFFH Mandate

Section 3608(d) imposes the AFFH mandate on the "programs relating to housing and urban development" of "[a]ll executive departments and agencies.

---

34. The material in this sidebar is based on the following sources: Christopher Bonastia, KNOCKING ON THE DOOR: THE FEDERAL GOVERNMENT'S ATTEMPTS TO DESEGREGATE THE SUBURBS 93, 98, 105-07 (Princeton U. Press 2006) (stating that although Romney was "a long-time supporter of civil rights," he was "a man of complex and sometimes conflicting convictions."); Charles M. Lamb, HOUSING SEGREGATION IN SUBURBAN AMERICA SINCE 1960: PRESIDENTIAL AND JUDICIAL POLITICS 56-107, 192 (Cambridge U. Press 2005); Dean J. Kotlowski, NIXON'S CIVIL RIGHTS: POLITICS, PRINCIPLE, AND POLICY 54-59 (Harv. U. Press 2002); Yarborough v. City of Warren, 383 F. Supp. 676 (E.D. Mich. 1974). The quotation from George Romney is from Gautreaux v. Chi. Hous. Auth., 503 F.2d 930, 937 (7th Cir. 1974). *See* Chapter 1 of this book for a description of racial violence in Warren in 1967.

35. Lamb, *supra* note 34, at 173-79, 190-98.

36. 80 FED. REG. 42272, *et seq.* For a discussion of this rulemaking, see Raphael W. Bostic et al., *Fair Housing from the Inside Out: A Behind-the-Scenes Look at the Creation of the Affirmatively Furthering Fair Housing Rule, in* FURTHERING FAIR HOUSING: PROSPECTS FOR RACIAL JUSTICE IN AMERICA'S NEIGHBORHOODS 74, *supra* note 4, at 74.

37. 86 FED. REG. 30782-83 (June 10, 2021) (describing the regulatory history). For an analysis of the rules, see Abraham, *Fair Housing's Third Act, supra* note 29.

38. Restoring Affirmatively Furthering Fair Housing Definitions and Certifications, 86 FED. REG. 30779, *et seq.*; Heather Abraham, *Segregation Autopilot: How the Government Perpetuates Segregation and How to Stop It,* 107 IOWA L. REV. 1963, 1969 (2022).

Many other departments and agencies operate housing and urban development programs, notably the departments of Treasury, Agriculture, Defense, Veterans Affairs, and Transportation and the General Services Administration; all such programs are subject to the AFFH mandate.[39]

The most important of these departments is Treasury, which operates the Low Income Housing Tax Credit (LIHTC) program, the largest subsidized housing development and rehabilitation program in the United States.[40] In a Revenue Ruling, Treasury's Internal Revenue Service (IRS) acknowledges that the LIHTC program is subject to the AFFH mandate. In addition, some state housing finance agencies have taken steps to apply AFFH best practices. A recent study of state practices reports:

> Whether because of increasingly powerful public health and social science evidence, growing awareness of fair housing obligations, or positive leadership within the industry, an increasing number of states have eliminated potentially discriminatory provisions in their QAPs [Qualified Allocation Plans], added incentives for development in high opportunity communities, strengthened affirmative marketing and tenant selection practices, and defined requirements for concerted community revitalization plans accompanying developments in low income neighborhoods.[41]

The Department of Defense used to be "the Nation's largest landlord," operating, according to a 1990 report, some 400,000 dwellings allegedly without racial discrimination or segregation.[42] A 2024 budget justification indicates, however, that almost all the Department's 200,000 units have been "privatized" and says nothing about satisfying fair housing obligations.[43]

Litigation has recognized the AFFH obligation of the Department of Veterans Affairs[44]; AFFH suits also have been brought against the Department

39. Schwemm, HDLL §21:1, 21:3; Abraham, *Segregation Autopilot, supra* note 38, at 1970.

40. *See* Chapter 12 and *Texas Dept. of Hous. & Cmty. Affs. v. Inclusive Communities Project,* Chapter 7; *see also* Florence Wagman Roisman, *Mandates Unsatisfied: The Low Income Housing Tax Credit Program and the Civil Rights Law,* 52 U. MIAMI L. REV. 1011 (1998); PRRAC & Lawyers Committee for Civil Rights, *Civil Rights Mandates in the Low Income Housing Tax Credit (LIHTC) Program,* PRRAC (Dec. 2004), https://www.prrac.org/pdf/crmandates.pdf.

41. IRS Revenue Ruling 2016-29, available at https://www.irs.gov/irb/2016-52_IRB#RR-2016-29; this material is from Taylor, Lindsay & Tegeler, *Building Opportunity III: Affirmatively Furthering Fair Housing in the Low Income Housing Tax Credit Program* at 1, 2, 5-6, PRRAC (Oct. 2023), https://www.prrac.org/building-opportunity-iii-affirmatively-furthering-fair-housing-in-the-low-income-housing-tax-credit-program-october-2023/ (stating that 29 states encourage siting developments in opportunity areas, variously defined).

42. Chester Hartman & Robin Drayer, *A Research Note: Military-Family Housing: The Other Public-Housing Program,* 17 HOUS. & SOC'Y 67 (1990), https://doi.org/10.1080/08882746.1990.11430083.

43. U.S. Dep't of Defense, Off. of the Under Sec. of Def., *PB24 Family Housing, Defense-Wide, in* DEFENSE WIDE BUDGET DOCUMENTATION - FY2024 (2024), https://comptroller.defense.gov/Portals/45/Documents/defbudget/fy2024/budget_justification/pdfs/04_Family_Housing/PB_24_DW_FH_FHIF.pdf.

44. Jorman v. VA, 579 F. Supp. 1407, 1416 (N.D. Ill. 1984). But see Jorman v. VA, 830 F.2d 1420 (7th Cir. 1987) (affirming dismissal for lack of standing).

of Agriculture and the Office of the Comptroller of the Currency but have foundered on the ground of standing.[45]

As this chapter illustrates, implementation of the AFFH mandate is controversial, particularly when it involves creating housing options for low-income people of color in neighborhoods where most of the residents are white people with relatively high wealth. Yet, the FHA was created to undo segregation and promote opportunity. Consider this 1968 floor statement: "where a family lives, where it is allowed to live, is inextricably bound up with better education, better jobs, economic motivation, and good living conditions."[46]

Advocates and stakeholders have engaged in their own internal debates about the extent to which the path forward to creating a more equitable housing market should be focused on providing more housing choice outside of communities in which persons of color already live or improving communities of color that have been most harmed by decades of discrimination and disinvestment. This has been, too often, a false choice.[47] In its 2021 Interim Final rule, HUD expressed a "both/and" position:

> Specifically, affirmatively furthering fair housing means taking meaningful actions that, taken together, address significant disparities in housing needs and in access to opportunity, replacing segregated living patterns with truly integrated and balanced living patterns, transforming racially or ethnically concentrated areas of poverty into areas of opportunity, and fostering and maintaining compliance with civil rights and fair housing laws.[48]

There are potential constitutional concerns with some methods that might be used to AFFH, particularly in light of the Supreme Court's recent rejection of certain race-conscious policies in other contexts. There also are political and rhetorical arguments that efforts to AFFH amount to "social engineering" and federal overreach into inherently local land use matters, although many scholars have shown that social engineering is what created and exacerbated residential segregation and that federal efforts nurtured the racial hostility.[49]

---

45. DeBolt v. Espy, 832 F. Supp. 209 (S.D. Ohio 1993), *aff'd*, 47 F.3d 777 (6th Cir. 1994); Jones v. Office of the Comptroller of the Currency, 983 F. Supp. 197, 204 (D.D.C. 1997), *aff'd*, No. 97-5341, 1998 WL 315581 (D.C. Cir. May 12, 1998).

46. Sen. Phil Hart, 114 CONG. REC. 2276–2707 (1968); *see* Affirmatively Furthering Fair Housing, Proposed Rule, 88 FED. REG. 8516, 8521-22 (Feb. 9, 2023).

47. *See* Elizabeth K. Julian, *Fair Housing and Community Development: Time to Come Together*, 41 IND. L. REV. 555, 558 (2008) ("Fair housing and community development are two sides of the same coin. They grew out of the need to address the twin evils of Jim Crow: separate and unequal. . . . [T]he two goals are best advanced together.").

48. HUD, *Restoring Affirmatively Furthering Fair Housing Definitions and Certifications*, 86 FED. REG. 30779 (June 10, 2021).

49. *See, e.g.*, Sheryll Cashin, WHITE SPACE BLACK HOOD: OPPORTUNITY HOARDING AND SEGREGATION IN THE AGE OF INEQUALITY (Penguin Random House 2022); Olatunde C.A. Johnson, *"Social Engineering": Notes on the Law and Political Economy of Integration*, 40 CARDOZO L. REV. 1149 (2019); Richard Rothstein, THE COLOR OF LAW: A FORGOTTEN HISTORY OF HOW OUR GOVERNMENT

Financial objections also are common. There is consensus that enabling low-income families to move into well-resourced neighborhoods produces significant economic benefits.[50] Homeowners in those neighborhoods, however, often fear lowered property values may result from introducing lower cost housing into high-cost neighborhoods, especially when the housing will be occupied disproportionately by people of color. Recent, careful studies have shown that the introduction of subsidized housing into higher income neighborhoods has not had the harmful financial consequences some people anticipated, but this has not been enough to eliminate the fervent opposition that AFFH actions often evoke.[51] The political and rhetorical battles continue to rage.

Chapter Summary

- Courts have interpreted the statutory AFFH mandate as requiring that "HUD use its grant programs to assist in ending discrimination and segregation, to the point where the supply of genuinely open housing increases." Courts have interpreted the statute to impose on HUD, "at a minimum, an obligation to assess negatively those aspects of a proposed course of action that would further limit the supply of genuinely open housing and to assess positively those aspects of a proposed course of action that would increase that supply" so that, "over time, . . . HUD activity . . . [would] increase, or at least, . . . not significantly diminish, the supply of open housing."
- The AFFH mandate requires regionalization, as held in *Thompson v. HUD* and illustrated by *Anti-Discrimination Center v. Westchester County* (which also confirmed that AFFH requires attention to race).
- These cases show that legal remedies promoting regional racial desegregation in housing have been hard-won and modest, a point underscored by the story of Yonkers, where partial municipal desegregation required decades.
- HUD's interpretations of the AFFH mandate have followed the courts' development of the doctrine.

SEGREGATED AMERICA (Liveright 2017); Charles Abrams, FORBIDDEN NEIGHBORS: A STUDY OF PREJUDICE IN HOUSING (Harper & Bros. 1955); Kenneth T. Jackson, CRABGRASS FRONTIER: THE SUBURBANIZATION OF THE UNITED STATES (Oxford U. 1987); *see also* Chapter 1 of this book.

50. *See, e.g.*, Peter Bergman et al., *Creating Moves to Opportunity: Experimental Evidence on Barriers to Neighborhood Choice,* 114 AMER. ECON. REV. 1281, 1282 (2024); Eric Chyn & Lawrence F. Katz, *Neighborhoods Matter: Assessing the Evidence for Place Effects,* 35 J. OF ECON. PERSPS. 197 (2021); Raj Chetty & Nathaniel Hendren, *The Impacts of Neighborhoods on Intergenerational Mobility I: Childhood Exposure Effects,* 133 Q. J. OF ECON. 1107 (2018); Raj Chetty, Nathaniel Hendren, & Lawrence F. Katz, *The Effects of Exposure to Better Neighborhoods on Children: New Evidence from the Moving to Opportunity Experiment,* 106 AM. ECON. REV. 855 (2016).

51. *See, e.g.*, Briggs et al., *supra* note 32, at 7 (reviewing past studies); Michael D. Ericksen & Guoyang Yang, *Does Affordability Status Matter in Who Wants Multifamily Housing in their Backyard?*, SSRN (2024), https://papers.ssrn.com/sol3/papers.cfm?abstract_id=4716411.

PART VI

PROTECTED
CHARACTERISTICS

Like most civil rights statutes, the Fair Housing Act identifies specific characteristics that are protected against discrimination. In other words, discrimination because of these traits, and only these traits, is prohibited by the statute. The FHA originally prohibited only discrimination based on race, color, national origin, and religion. Prohibitions against discrimination based on sex, familial status, and disability were added later.

The statute does not contain a definition of race, color, national origin, religion, or sex. Definitional challenges have arisen for these characteristics, which this part covers. It is important to keep in mind that these categories are universal. Put another way, the statute assumes everyone has a racial, ethnic, religious, national origin, and sexual identity, and protects accordingly. In contrast, disability and familial status do have specific definitions that must be satisfied in order to establish liability for discrimination on those bases.

This part discusses all these characteristics, as well as source of income. This attribute is not addressed in the FHA, but it intersects in important ways with characteristics that are protected. In addition, a significant number of state and local jurisdictions have enacted legislation that prohibits discrimination on the basis of source of income.

CHAPTER 14

RACE, COLOR, RELIGION, AND NATIONAL ORIGIN

As discussed in Chapter 3, the original and primary focus of the Fair Housing Act was the prohibition of housing discrimination on the basis of race. As the paradigmatic protected characteristic, race sets the standard in statutory civil rights and constitutional law. This significance means that there are fewer analytical issues that are particular to race that require specific attention in a text such as this. Nor are there necessary cases to help illuminate race as a characteristic. (Indeed, most of the cases throughout this text involve race discrimination.) Thus, the discussion of race in this chapter is brief.

The 1968 Act also prohibited discrimination based on color, national origin, and religion. This chapter begins with a basic definition of all these terms and then discusses particular issues that arise with the characteristics of national origin and religion.

A. DEFINING TERMS

"Race" as a concept has many meanings.[1] Physical racial classification was a prevalent pseudo-science in earlier times, driven by colonialism, imperialism, and white supremacy. Today race is widely understood to be a social construct and not a biological or scientific characteristic. Racial categorization is a shifting process that reflects and reinforces broad assumptions about power, rights, and belonging. As Professor john a. powell observes, "[t]he process of racial categorizing is a power struggle implicating structural, cultural, economic, and identity politics."[2] Of course, the socially constructed nature of

---

1. A thorough discussion of this complex issue is well beyond the scope of this casebook. There are several crucial works on the subject, including Cheryl I. Harris, *Whiteness as Property*, 106 HARV. L. REV. 1707 (1993); Ian Haney López, WHITE BY LAW: THE LEGAL CONSTRUCTION OF RACE (NYU Press 2006); Dorothy Roberts, FATAL INVENTION: HOW SCIENCE, POLITICS, AND BIG BUSINESS RE-CREATE RACE IN THE TWENTY-FIRST CENTURY (The New Press 2011); Isabel Wilkerson, CASTE: THE ORIGIN OF OUR DISCONTENTS (Random House 2020).

2. john a. powell, *The Colorblind Multiracial Dilemma: Racial Categories Reconsidered*, 31 U.S.F. L. REV. 789 (1997).

race does not mean that race as a concept is insignificant. Indeed, race and more importantly *racism* (particularly anti-Black racism) have a myriad of real-world consequences, as the material in this book demonstrates.

"Color" is the simplest of the terms. It is sometimes used as a generic substitute for race. For example, in the mid-20th century, "colored person" was a customary way to refer to Black people; today the term "person of color" may be used to refer to any person who is non-white. More precisely, color refers to skin tone and the relative lightness or darkness of a person's complexion. Thus, if a darker skinned person of a particular race is discriminated against in favor of a lighter skinned person of that same race, this would constitute discrimination on the basis of color.

"National origin" refers to the geographic area in which a person was born or from which their ancestors came. The term originally was defined by the Supreme Court in an employment discrimination case, Espinoza v. Farah Manufacturing Co., 414 U.S. 86, 88 (1973), but subsequent courts have adopted this definition in the housing context.[3]

Although national origin is considered a category separate from race, there is overlap between the two. This is clear from the definition of racial categories currently used by the U.S. Census Bureau (based on standards set by the Office of Management and Budget (OMB)), in which race is explicitly defined in terms of geographic origin:[4]

> **White**—A person having origins in any of the original peoples of Europe, the Middle East, or North Africa.
>
> **Black or African American**—A person having origins in any of the Black racial groups of Africa.
>
> **American Indian or Alaska Native**—A person having origins in any of the original peoples of North and South America (including Central America) and who maintains tribal affiliation or community attachment.
>
> **Asian**—A person having origins in any of the original peoples of the Far East, Southeast Asia, or the Indian subcontinent including, for example, Cambodia, China, India, Japan, Korea, Malaysia, Pakistan, the Philippine Islands, Thailand, and Vietnam.
>
> **Native Hawaiian or Other Pacific Islander**—A person having origins in any of the original peoples of Hawaii, Guam, Samoa, or other Pacific Islands.

---

3. *See, e.g.*, Hous. Rights Ctr. v. Donald Sterling Corp., 274 F. Supp. 2d 1129, 1138-39 (C.D. Cal. 2003) (applying the definition of national origin in *Espinoza* to the FHA).

4. About the Topic of Race, U.S. Census Bureau (last updated Mar. 1, 2022), https://www.census.gov/topics/population/race/about.html. As of March 2024, OMB has recommended the inclusion of an additional racial category, "Middle Eastern and North African," for people with origins in those regions. *See* What Updates to OMB's Race/Ethnicity Standards Mean for the Census Bureau (Apr. 8, 2024), https://www.census.gov/newsroom/blogs/random-sampli ngs/2024/04/updates-race-ethnicity-standards.html.

Thus, a person may be discriminated against because they have physical characteristics associated with people from Asia (which would constitute race discrimination) or because they or their ancestors are from a country in Asia (which would constitute national origin discrimination). As a result, it might be difficult in some cases to distinguish whether discrimination is occurring because of national origin, race, or both, as courts have recognized. *See* Salas v. Wisconsin Department of Corrections, 493 F.3d 913, 923 (7th Cir. 2007) ("[T]here is uncertainty about what constitutes race versus national origin discrimination. . . . "); Deravin v. Kerik, 335 F.3d 195, 201-02 (2d Cir. 2003) ("[R]ace and national origin discrimination claims may substantially overlap or even be indistinguishable depending on the specific facts of a case."). Significantly, national origin also refers to whether a person is Hispanic (from a primarily Spanish-speaking country) or Latino/a (from a country in South or Central America). This means that a person who identifies as Hispanic or Latino/a can be of any race.

"Religion" is a concept of which most people have an intuitive understanding, although its precise legal definition remains elusive. The FHA does not define the term. According to an EEOC guidance document and summary of existing law,[5] "[a] belief is 'religious' for Title VII purposes if it is 'religious' in the person's 'own scheme of things,' i.e., it is a 'sincere and meaningful' belief that 'occupies a place in the life of its possessor parallel to that filled by . . . God.'" This EEOC guidance further states that "[r]eligion includes not only traditional, organized religions . . . but also religious beliefs that are new, uncommon, not part of a formal church or sect, only subscribed to by a small number of people, or that seem illogical or unreasonable to others." Note that religion can also overlap with race and national origin, to the extent that it might be a shared characteristic of individuals of a particular national origin or racial group.

The following Supreme Court opinions, issued on the same day, arise under the Civil Rights Act of 1866, specifically 42 U.S.C. §§1981 (now §1981a) and 1982, and demonstrate the intersection of race with national origin and religion as it was understood in the 19th century.

Saint Francis College v. Al-Khazraji
481 U.S. 604 (1987)

Before Chief Justice Rehnquist and Justices White, Marshall, Blackmun, Powell, Stevens, O'Connor, Scalia, and Brennan.

WHITE, J. delivered the opinion for a unanimous Court. Brennan, J. filed a concurring opinion.

---

5. Office of Legal Counsel, *Religious Discrimination*, Doc. No. EEOC-CVG-2021-3, section 12 (Jan. 15, 2021) (citing cases), https://www.eeoc.gov/laws/guidance/section-12-religious-dis crimination#_ftnref18.

Respondent, a citizen of the United States born in Iraq, was an associate professor at St. Francis College. He applied for tenure; the Board of Trustees denied his request. He filed complaints with the Pennsylvania Human Relations Commission and the EEOC. The state agency dismissed his claim and the EEOC issued a right-to-sue letter.

Respondent filed a pro se complaint in the District Court. The District Court ruled that §1981 does not reach claims of discrimination based on Arabian ancestry. The Court of Appeals held that respondent had alleged discrimination based on race and that although under current racial classifications Arabs are Caucasians, respondent could maintain his §1981 claim.

Although §1981 does not itself use the word "race," the Court has construed the section to forbid all "racial" discrimination in the making of private as well as public contracts. Petitioner college, although a private institution, was therefore subject to this statutory command. There is no disagreement among the parties on these propositions. The issue is whether respondent has alleged racial discrimination within the meaning of §1981. Petitioners contend that respondent is a Caucasian and cannot allege the kind of discrimination §1981 forbids. Concededly, McDonald v. Santa Fe Trail Transportation Co., 427 U.S. 273 (1976), held that white persons could maintain a §1981 suit, but that suit involved alleged discrimination against a white person in favor of a black, and petitioner submits that the section does not encompass claims of discrimination by one Caucasian against another. We are quite sure that the Court of Appeals properly rejected this position.

Petitioner's submission rests on the assumption that all those who might be deemed Caucasians today were thought to be of the same race when §1981 became law in the 19th century; and it may be that a variety of ethnic groups, including Arabs, are now considered to be within the Caucasian race. The understanding of "race" in the 19th century, however, was different. Plainly, all those who might be deemed Caucasian today were not thought to be of the same race at the time §1981 became law.

In the middle years of the 19th century, dictionaries commonly referred to race as a "continued series of descendants from a parent who is called the stock," "the lineage of a family," or "descendants of a common ancestor." The 1887 edition of Webster's expanded the definition somewhat: "The descendants of a common ancestor; a family, tribe, people or nation, believed or presumed to belong to the same stock." It was not until the 20th century that dictionaries began referring to the Caucasian, Mongolian, and Negro races, or to race as involving divisions of mankind based upon different physical characteristics. Even so, modern dictionaries still include among the definitions of race "a family, tribe, people, or nation belonging to the same stock."

Encyclopedias of the 19th century also described race in terms of ethnic groups, which is a narrower concept of race than petitioners urge. Encyclopedia Americana in 1858, for example, referred to various races such as Finns, gypsies, Basques, and Hebrews. The 1863 version of the New American Cyclopaedia divided the Arabs into a number of subsidiary races, represented the Hebrews as of the Semitic race, and identified numerous other groups as constituting races, including Swedes, Norwegians, Germans, Greeks, Finns, Italians, Spanish, Mongolians, Russians, and the like. The Ninth edition of the Encyclopedia Britannica also referred to Arabs, Jews, and other ethnic groups such as Germans, Hungarians, and Greeks, as separate races.

These dictionary and encyclopedic sources are somewhat diverse, but it is clear that they do not support the claim that for the purposes of §1981, Arabs, Englishmen, Germans, and certain other ethnic groups are to be considered a single race. We would expect the legislative history of §1981, which the Court held in Runyon v. McCrary had its source in the Civil Rights Act of 1866, as well as the Voting Rights Act of 1870, to reflect this common understanding, which it surely does. The debates are replete with references to the Scandinavian races, as well as the Chinese, Latin, Spanish, and Anglo-Saxon races. Jews, Mexicans, blacks, and Mongolians were similarly categorized. Gypsies were referred to as a race. Likewise, the Germans. . . . There was a reference to the Caucasian race, but it appears to have been referring to people of European ancestry.

The history of the 1870 Act reflects similar understanding of what groups Congress intended to protect from intentional discrimination. It is clear, for example, that the civil rights sections of the 1870 Act provided protection for immigrant groups such as the Chinese. This view was expressed in the Senate. In the House, Representative Bingham described §16 of the Act, part of the authority for §1981, as declaring "that the States shall not hereafter discriminate against the immigrant from China and in favor of the immigrant from Prussia, nor against the immigrant from France and in favor of the immigrant from Ireland."

Based on the history of §1981, we have little trouble in concluding that Congress intended to protect from discrimination identifiable classes of persons who are subjected to intentional discrimination solely because of their ancestry or ethnic characteristics. Such discrimination is racial discrimination that Congress intended §1981 to forbid, whether or not it would be classified as racial in terms of modern scientific theory. The Court of Appeals was thus quite right in holding that §1981, "at a minimum," reaches discrimination against an individual "because he or she is genetically part of an ethnically and physiognomically distinctive sub-grouping of homo sapiens." It is clear from our holding, however, that a distinctive physiognomy is not essential to qualify for §1981 protection. If respondent on remand can prove that he was subjected to intentional discrimination based on the fact that he was born an Arab, rather than solely on the place or nation of his origin, or his religion, he will have made out a case under §1981.

Justice BRENNAN, concurring.

I write separately only to point out that the line between discrimination based on "ancestry or ethnic characteristics," and discrimination based on "place or nation of . . . origin," is not a bright one. It is true that one's ancestry — the ethnic group from which an individual and his or her ancestors are descended — is not necessarily the same as one's national origin — the country "where a person was born, or, more broadly, the country from which his or her ancestors came." Often, however, the two are identical as a factual matter: one was born in the nation whose primary stock is one's own ethnic group. Moreover, national origin claims have been treated as ancestry or ethnicity claims in some circumstances. For example, in the Title VII context, the terms overlap as a legal matter. I therefore read the Court's opinion to state only that discrimination based on birthplace alone is insufficient to state a claim under §1981.

Shaare Tefila Congregation v. Cobb
481 U.S. 615 (1987)

Before Chief Justice Rehnquist and Justices Brennan, White, Marshall, Blackmun, Powell, Stevens, O'Connor, and Scalia.

Justice WHITE delivered the opinion for a unanimous Court:

On November 2, 1982, the outside walls of the synagogue of the Shaare Tefila Congregation in Silver Spring, Maryland, were sprayed with red and black paint and with large anti-Semitic slogans, phrases, and symbols. The Congregation and some individual members brought this suit, alleging that defendants' desecration of the synagogue had violated[, among other laws,] 42 U.S.C. §§1981 [and] 1982. The District Court dismissed all the claims. The Court of Appeals affirmed.

Petitioners' allegation was that they were deprived of the right to hold property in violation of §1982 because the defendants were motivated by racial prejudice.

The Court of Appeals held that §1982 was not "intended to apply to situations in which a plaintiff is not a member of a racially distinct group but is merely perceived to be so by defendants." The Court of Appeals believed that "because discrimination against Jews is not racial discrimination," the District Court was correct in dismissing the §1982 claim.

We agree with the Court of Appeals that a charge of racial discrimination within the meaning of §1982 cannot be made out by alleging only that the defendants were motivated by racial animus; it is necessary as well to allege that defendants' animus was directed towards the kinds of group that Congress intended to protect when it passed the statute.

We agree with petitioners, however, that the Court of Appeals erred in holding that Jews cannot state a §1982 claim against other white defendants. That view rested on the notion that because Jews today are not thought to be members of a separate race, they cannot make out a claim of racial discrimination within the meaning of §1982. That construction of the section we have today rejected in Saint Francis College v. Al-Khazraji. Our opinion in that case observed that definitions of race when §1982 was passed were not the same as they are today and concluded that the section was "intended to protect from discrimination identifiable classes of persons who are subjected to intentional discrimination solely because of their ancestry or ethnic characteristics." As Saint Francis makes clear, the question before us is not whether Jews are considered to be a separate race by today's standards, but whether, at the time §1982 was adopted, Jews constituted a group of people that Congress intended to protect. It is evident from the legislative history of the section reviewed in Saint Francis College that Jews and Arabs were among the peoples then considered to be distinct races and hence within the protection of the statute. Jews are not foreclosed from stating a cause of action against other members of what today is considered to be part of the Caucasian race.

NOTES AND QUESTIONS

1. Congressional Intent for the FHA. *Al Khazraji* and *Shaare Tefila* both rely on the Court's determination of how Congress understood the term "race" in the mid-19th century, when it passed the Civil Rights Act of 1866. How do you think that question would be answered with respect to the Congress that passed the original FHA in 1968? The Fair Housing Amendments Act of 1988? What sources would a court look to in making this determination? In *Bostock v. Clayton County*, discussed in Chapter 15, the Court rejected consideration of what Congress understood the term "sex" to mean at the time of enactment of Title VII of the Civil Rights Act, focusing exclusively on the statutory text. Which approach to statutory interpretation do you think is more sound?

2. Proving Race? When the government compiles data about race, the preferred means is self-identification. Thus, for example, individuals decide for themselves which racial category or categories they identify with on census forms. (This was not always the case: From 1790 to 1950, census takers would determine the race of the people they counted.)

How should an advocate go about proving to a factfinder that a person is of a particular race, and that the defendant acted because of that person's race? What if the defendant claims not to perceive the plaintiff as a member of the racial category the plaintiff adopts? See, for example, United States v. Porter, 928 F.3d 947 (10th Cir. 2019), discussed in Chapter 10, where a defendant claimed that he did not assault the victim on the basis of race because the victim (who was a Latino person of mixed race) appeared white to him. In that case the court determined that the jury was entitled to find that the defendant did harass the victim because of his race, because the jury was presented with the victim's own testimony about his racial background, a witness's perception of the victim's race, and the defendant's later statement to law enforcement that the victim might have been "half Negro."

B. NATIONAL ORIGIN

Certain groups continue to face significant levels of discrimination based on national origin in the private rental market. The most comprehensive national testing project completed to date found that Hispanic testers posing as apartment-seekers were told about fewer units than were non-Hispanic, white testers, and shown fewer units than were non-Hispanic, white testers.[6] A more recent study of inquiries about online property listings found that response rates were lower when the inquiry came from a profile with an Hispanic identity than from a profile with a non-Hispanic, white identity.[7]

Although some of this disparity might be based on national origin per se (i.e., a landlord's dislike of people from a particular country or region), other discrimination might be based on traits that some people associate with national origin, but that are not themselves specifically protected by the FHA. As Professor Oliveri argues:

> Without access to a person's birth certificate or family tree, it is impossible to know with certainty what country she or her ancestors come from. Instead we rely on ethnic markers such as language, accent, surname, cultural and religious practices, and race or "ethnic appearance" (itself a difficult to define term) to identify a person with a particular region of the world. Thus, national origin discrimination is less likely to consist of discrimination motivated by the fact that a person or her ancestors came from a particular country, and it is much more likely to consist of discrimination based on ethnic characteristics with regional associations.[8]

If a housing provider discriminates on the basis of traits associated with national origin, this can open the provider to a disparate impact-based challenge, at the least. Immigration status is one such characteristic that has been particularly contentious in recent years. Neither alienage (whether or not a person is a citizen of the United States) nor legal status (whether or not a non-citizen is legally present in the United States, and, if legally present, under what type of status) is protected in the statute. Both are correlated with national origin to the extent that they are likely to be associated with recent immigrants to the United States.

The following case provides an example of a court's permitting such a challenge to go forward and pointedly *not* crediting the defendant's proffered immigration-related business justification defense.

---

6. HUD Office of Policy Development and Research, *Housing Discrimination Against Racial and Ethnic Minorities 2012*, https://www.huduser.gov/portal/Publications/pdf/HUD-514_H DS2012_execsumm.pdf. This disparity was greater than that experienced by Black testers.

7. Peter Christensen, Ignacio Sarmiento-Barbieri, & Christopher Timmins, *Racial Discrimination and Housing Outcomes in the United States Rental Market*, National Bureau of Economic Research (Nov. 2021), https://www.nber.org/system/files/working_papers/w29 516/w29516.pdf.

8. Rigel C. Oliveri, *Between a Rock and a Hard Place: Landlords, Latinos, and Anti-Illegal Immigrant Ordinances*, 62 VANDERBILT L. REV. 55, 73 (2009).

Reyes v. Waples Mobile Home Park Ltd. Partnership
91 F.4th 270 (4th Cir. 2024)

Before Wilkinson, King, and Heytens, Circuit Judges

WILKINSON, Circuit Judge:

Residents of Waples Mobile Home Park challenged the Park's policy that required all adult tenants to provide proof of their legal status in the U.S. in order to renew their leases. The residents argued that the policy violated the FHA because it disproportionately ousted Latinos from the Park. The district court granted summary judgment in favor of the Park after finding that the policy was reasonably necessary for the Park to avoid criminal liability under a federal statute prohibiting the harboring of undocumented immigrants. But the district court's ruling rested upon a basic misapprehension of the statute. Moreover, the record was insufficient to establish the Park's proposed defense. For these reasons, we reverse.

I.

Waples Mobile Home Park in Fairfax, Virginia, (the "Park") is owned and operated by Waples Mobile Home Park LP, Waples Project LP, and A.J. Dwoskin & Associates, Inc. (collectively, "Waples"). Waples leases land to mobile-home owners looking to domicile in the area and serves as landlord for the Park.

Between 2010 and 2015, four noncitizen Latino families from El Salvador and Bolivia (the "Families") moved into the Park. Each family consisted of a father with legal status in the U.S., a mother who was undocumented and illegally residing in the U.S., and children who were U.S. citizens. The fathers were the leaseholders. Each had provided a valid Social Security number and passed credit and criminal background checks as part of the routine application process. The Families had successfully renewed their leases without issue until 2015.

In 2015, Waples began enforcing a policy that required all adults living at the Park to present proof of legal status in the U.S. (the "Policy"). Specifically, the Policy required lease applicants and tenants seeking to renew their leases to identify all proposed adult occupants of the mobile home. It further required that every identified adult occupant provide proof of lawful status in the U.S. by presenting either (1) an original Social Security card, or (2) an original foreign Passport, original U.S. Visa, and original Arrival/Departure Form (I-94 or I-94W).

If an occupant did not comply with the Policy, Waples provided notice that the leaseholder had 21 days from receipt of the notice to cure the violation, or 30 days from receipt to vacate the Park. And if the household did not cure the violation or vacate the Park, Waples converted the lease from a year-long term to month-to-month and increased the rent by $100 per month. Waples threatened to increase the monthly rent by an additional $300 if the household did not comply with the Policy, but that additional surcharge was never imposed.

Of course, the Policy posed a problem for the Families because the mothers could not provide proof of their legal status. The Families sought to use the mothers' Individual Taxpayer Identification Numbers ("ITINs") as an alternative way to comply with the Policy. The IRS issues ITINs to income-earning U.S. taxpayers irrespective of immigration status. The Families alleged that the ITINs could be used to run the requisite background checks. Waples declined to accept any alternative forms of identification, converted the leases to month-to-month terms, and imposed the $100 surcharge. Eventually each of the Families chose to vacate their homes at the Park due to the rent increases and fear of eviction.

The Families initiated this lawsuit against Waples in 2016. The Families proceeded under a disparate-impact theory, alleging the Policy violated the FHA by "disproportionately ousting Hispanic or Latino ('Latino') families from their homes and denying them one of the only affordable housing options in Fairfax County, VA." Waples moved to dismiss several counts in the complaint, including the FHA claim.

The district court denied Waples's motion to dismiss as to the FHA claim. It held, however, that the Families could proceed only under a disparate-treatment theory of liability, instead of the disparate-impact theory they had proposed.

The district court granted Waples's motion for summary judgment on the Families' FHA claim, which, in accordance with its prior ruling, the court only considered under the disparate-treatment theory of liability. The Families appealed, arguing that the district court's prior dismissal of their FHA claim under a disparate-impact theory of liability was in error.

This court vacated the district court's judgment and held that the claim should have been allowed to proceed under a disparate-impact theory. The court proceeded under the three-part burden-shifting framework established for disparate-impact claims in *Texas Dept. of Hous. and Community Affairs v. Inclusive Communities Project, Inc.* Under the *Inclusive Communities* framework, the plaintiff bears the initial burden of establishing a prima facie case of disparate impact. If satisfied, the burden shifts to the defendant to show that the discriminatory policy was necessary to achieve a legitimate nondiscriminatory interest. If the defendant does so, the burden shifts back to the plaintiff to show that the interest could be served through less discriminatory means.

The court concluded that the Families had satisfied Step One by demonstrating that the challenged Policy "caused a disproportionate number of Latinos to face eviction from the Park compared to the number of non-Latinos who faced eviction based on the Policy." Because the Families had established a prima facie case of disparate impact, the court remanded for the district court to consider Steps Two and Three of the Inclusive Communities framework in the first instance.

On remand, the Families pursued only a disparate-impact theory for their FHA claim and Waples filed a renewed motion for summary judgment. [The district court denied summary judgment to Waples, but the case was subsequently reassigned; the new district judge granted summary judgment, finding the Policy served a valid and necessary interest and rejecting the Families' proposed alternative of allowing tenants to use ITINs.] The Families timely appealed.

II.

As discussed above, we analyze disparate-impact claims under a three-step burden-shifting framework. The first time this case came before the court, we determined that the Families had satisfied their burden at Step One to show a causal connection between the Policy and an attendant disparate impact on Latino residents. We start from that holding.

As for Step Two of the *Inclusive Communities* proof scheme, Waples argues that the Policy of verifying its tenants' legal status was justified by the risk of prosecution under the federal anti-harboring statute, which provides criminal penalties for "[a]ny person" who "knowing or in reckless disregard of the fact that an alien has come to, entered, or remains in the United States in violation of law, conceals, harbors, or shields from detection, or attempts to conceal, harbor, or shield from detection, such alien in any place, including any building or any means of transportation." Waples points to this court's decision in United States v. Aguilar (4th Cir. 2012) (per curiam), which upheld a landlord's conviction under the anti-harboring statute, as proof that entering into a lease agreement with an undocumented immigrant could put it at risk. Thus, it contends, the Policy of verifying legal status before renewing a lease was necessary to serve its valid interest of avoiding criminal liability.

Step Two of the *Inclusive Communities* framework requires defendants to "state and explain the valid interest served by their policies." The "touchstone" of Step Two is "business necessity," *Griggs v. Duke Power Co.*, and business necessity in the context of the FHA is "analogous to the business necessity standard under Title VII," *Inclusive Communities*. "Just as an employer may maintain a workplace requirement that causes a disparate impact if that requirement is a 'reasonable measure[ment] of job performance,' a housing policy can stand if the landlord can prove it is necessary to achieve a valid interest." *Id.*

A business necessity need not be a do-or-die matter. A necessitous policy can be, but need not be, one that spells the difference between solvency and bankruptcy. The Ninth Circuit has put it well: "Although the Supreme Court in *Inclusive Communities* used the phrase 'business necessity' to describe this step of the analysis, that term is somewhat of a misnomer . . . the defendant need not demonstrate that the challenged policy is 'essential or indispensable' to its business—only that the policy 'serves, in a significant way,' its legitimate interests." Sw. Fair Hous. Council, Inc. v. Maricopa Domestic Water Improvement Dist. (9th Cir. 2021).

Avoiding criminal liability can certainly serve as the basis for a business necessity defense. But it also cannot be the case that defendants can claim business necessity by rattling off inapplicable statutes as their justification for promulgating a challenged policy. A "legitimate" interest cannot be a phony. Otherwise defendants could manufacture business necessity based on speculative, or even imagined, liability. It seems then that the risk of prosecution or liability under a statute must at least be plausible. Here, the anti-harboring statute simply does not apply to landlords merely leasing to undocumented immigrants, and Waples's risk of prosecution is too attenuated to cross the threshold of a plausible concern.

The text of the anti-harboring statute requires something more than merely entering a lease agreement with an undocumented immigrant. To violate the statute, one must "knowing[ly]" or "reckless[ly]" "conceal, harbor, or shield from detection" such a person. Conceal, harbor, and shield are all active verbs. Thus, the statute only applies to those who intend in some way to aid an undocumented immigrant in hiding from the authorities. It involves an element of deceit that is not present in run-of-the mill leases made in the ordinary course of business.

Our decision in *Aguilar* does not suggest otherwise. There we upheld a conviction under the anti-harboring statute of a woman who rented nine of the ten rooms in her home to undocumented immigrants. We held that substantial evidence supported her conviction because each of her tenants were undocumented, and she had been "repeatedly . . . warned by officials that numerous of her tenants were not properly documented." Looking at the trial evidence, it was clear that the defendant in *Aguilar* was running a flophouse to help offset her mortgage payments. In other words, evidence of an intent to harbor undocumented immigrants was present.

But *Aguilar* did not hold that housing was a synonym for harboring under the statute, and the case cannot be read to extend the threat of prosecution under the statute to merely renting to an undocumented immigrant. Indeed, every precedential appellate decision to address whether renting to an undocumented person, without more, violates the statute has come to the same conclusion. In light of the consensus reading of the anti-harboring law, giving credence to Waples's understanding of the statute would make us a distinct outlier in an area of law which should ideally be national in character and uniform in the circuits' interpretation of it.

It is instructive to contrast the extensive regulation of immigration status in employment with the lack of such regulation in housing. Since 1986, the Immigration Act has required employers to vet the immigration status of their employees or face civil and criminal sanctions. The government requires employers to complete and maintain a Form I-9 Employment Eligibility Verification for each employee. It maintains an electronic database to allow employers to verify the immigration information that employees submit, and it provides extensive guidance to employers on complying with the statute.

In contrast, no similar verification requirement, regulatory regime, or elaborate penal structure exists in the context of housing. This makes good sense. A policy that discouraged or prohibited landlords from housing any undocumented individual would lead to homelessness on an even greater scale than we are presently experiencing. Congress can of course modify its approach to housing policy at any time it so desires. In the meantime, we shall not misread the anti-harboring statute to facilitate the gratuitous infliction of homelessness upon countless numbers of people residing in this country.

In sum, the anti-harboring statute does not plausibly put Waples at risk for prosecution simply for leasing to families with undocumented immigrants. Accordingly, we hold that Waples did not satisfy its burden at Step Two because its Policy did not serve in any realistic way to avoid liability under the anti-harboring statute. Because Waples did not meet its burden at Step Two, we need not reach Step Three to determine whether the Families could show that a less discriminatory alternative was available. For these reasons, the district court erred in granting summary judgment to Waples.

There is a further infirmity in Waples's position specific to this case. The record here is simply too thin to support a business necessity defense. To begin with, the circumstances surrounding Waples's enforcement of the Policy were dubious. The Policy seemed to come out of nowhere. The Families had lived at the Park for years before Waples began enforcing the long-dormant Policy provision. And the decision to begin enforcing the Policy stemmed, not from any immigration-related developments or discoveries at the Park, but from unrelated violations of other Waples policies at other Waples properties. Having a Policy on the books that required the verification of the legal status of all adult tenants in residence, but disregarding its enforcement for years, calls into question Waples's contention that it was concerned about avoiding harboring liability.

Even more puzzling is how Waples proceeded when it discovered that there were undocumented individuals living at the Park. If Waples was truly concerned about being prosecuted for housing undocumented immigrants, its expected course would be to remove such tenants from the Park as quickly as possible. But Waples did not evict a single person who failed to comply with the Policy from the Park. Instead, Waples increased the rent payments that noncompliant tenants were charged every month. That meant that while Waples was representing that it could not house undocumented immigrants without facing criminal penalties, it was knowingly housing such immigrants and charging them a premium to stay. If Waples were at risk for prosecution under the anti-harboring statute, it would have a difficult time explaining to a prosecutor why, instead of evicting known undocumented immigrants, it opted to implement a surcharge instead.

On a record this thin, Waples cannot have met its burden to establish that the Policy served a legitimate interest. Proof schemes depend on record evidence and the record here falls short of anything approaching business necessity. For this reason too, the district court erred in granting summary judgment to Waples.

NOTES AND QUESTIONS

1. Disparate Impact and Disparate Treatment. Note that the plaintiffs in *Reyes* were permitted to pursue their case only under disparate impact theory. Can you think of a scenario in which a disparate treatment theory might also have been appropriate? For example, what if there were evidence that the defendants had adopted their Proof of Legal Status policy as a deliberate attempt to force Hispanic residents out, or where they enforced the policy selectively against Hispanic households?

2. Anti-Illegal Immigrant Housing Ordinances. In *Reyes* the defendants claimed that their Proof of Legal Status policy was motivated by their desire to comply with a federal statute that prohibits the "harboring" of undocumented immigrants. The court refused to credit this explanation, in part because the definition of "harboring" requires more than unknowingly entering into a lease agreement with an undocumented person.

In the early 2000s a number of state and local governments enacted laws aimed at punishing landlords, employers, owners of public accommodations, and others for doing business with undocumented people. As Professor Oliveri notes, at one point 42 municipalities had passed ordinances imposing civil and criminal penalties against landlords if any undocumented person were found to be living in one of their units.[9] Such ordinances increase the likelihood that landlords, who are not immigration professionals, will "overcomply" and simply discriminate against people who appear to be from particular national origin groups, even if they are citizens or otherwise legally present in the United States. As Professor Oliveri argues: "[u]nconscious bias, confusion about the law's requirements, and fear of punishment will almost certainly cause what I call 'discrimination slippage,' which is discrimination against large numbers of individuals who are not [technically] the targets of anti-illegal immigrant ordinances." This is even more likely to be the case when such ordinances are passed in a climate of hostility against immigrants generally or animus toward particular national origin groups.

Enforcement of the ordinances came to a halt after a federal district court struck down Hazleton, Pennsylvania's ordinance in Lozano v. City of Hazleton, 496 F. Supp. 2d 477 (M.D. Pa. 2007), *aff'd in part, rev'd in part*, 724 F.3d 297 (3d Cir. 2013). Significantly, the court invalidated Hazleton's ordinance not because of its potential to lead to widespread discrimination, but because of conflict preemption with federal immigration law. The court

---

9. Oliveri, 62 Vand. L. Rev. at 60.

observed that there are a number of instances in which an undocumented person might be permitted to remain in the United States under federal law, but Hazleton's ordinance did not contain such exceptions.

3. Language. Language is another trait closely associated with national origin. As HUD guidance has noted:

> Nearly all [persons with limited English proficiency (LEP)] are LEP because either they or their family members are from non-English speaking countries. The link between national origin and LEP is fairly intuitive but is also supported by statistics. In the United States, 34% of Asians and 32% of Hispanics are LEP as compared with 6% of whites and 2% of non-Hispanic whites. Focusing on place of birth, in the United States 61% of persons born in Latin America and 46% of persons born in Asia are LEP as compared with 2% of persons born in the United States. Thus, housing decisions that are based on LEP generally relate to race or national origin.[10]

For example, in CNY Fair Housing, Inc. v. Swiss Village, LLC, No. 5:21-CV-1217, 2022 WL 2643573 (N.D.N.Y. July 8, 2022), a rental agent allegedly refused to deal with non-English-speaking prospective tenants, even though they were clients of a nonprofit organization that would provide translation services. Specifically, the agent allegedly refused to give caseworkers information about available units and stated that she would not rent to tenants unless they were proficient in English because the tenants would need to communicate about matters such as the lease, repairs, and work orders. The organization sued for intentional violations of §3604(a), (b), and (c). The defendant moved to dismiss for failure to state a claim upon which relief can be granted, arguing that LEP is not a protected characteristic, and that discrimination on the basis of LEP is not a proxy for national origin discrimination. The district court deferred to HUD's guidance, ruled that language-related criteria could be evidence of discrimination based on national origin, and denied the defense motion to dismiss.

The HUD guidance in fact recognizes that the close connection between national origin and LEP means that plaintiffs who are discriminated against due to their LEP may have claims under a theory of intentional discrimination: "A housing provider violates the Fair Housing Act if the provider uses a person's LEP to discriminate intentionally because of . . . national origin[.] Selectively enforcing a language-related restriction based on a person's protected class violates the Act, as does using LEP as a pretext for intentional discrimination."

A plaintiff may also have a claim under disparate impact theory: "[W]here a policy or practice that restricts access to housing on the basis of LEP has a discriminatory effect based on national origin . . . such policy or practice

---

10. HUD Office of General Counsel, *Guidance on Fair Housing Act Protections for Persons With Limited English Proficiency* 2 (Sept. 15, 2016) (footnotes omitted), https://www.hud.gov/sites/documents/LEPMEMO091516.pdf.

violates the Act if it is not necessary to serve a substantial, legitimate, non-discriminatory interest of the housing provider, or if such interest could be served by another practice that has a less discriminatory effect." Of course, plaintiffs may assert claims under both theories, and HUD recognizes that in many cases it will be difficult to discern the difference between the two on the facts.

For an example of a disparate treatment claim, see Cabrera v. Alvarez, 977 F. Supp. 2d 969 (N.D. Cal. 2013). In that case, the plaintiff was a Spanish-speaking tenant of a public housing project. She alleged that housing authority employees refused to provide her with translation services (contrary to their policy). The court found that she did not state a disparate impact claim, but did have an intentional discrimination claim, based on the alleged hostility she faced when requesting translation services, including statements by housing authority employees that she "should learn English now that she is in America," and falsely saying that she was an undocumented immigrant.

C. RELIGION

Cases in which discrimination based on religion is alleged are relatively few. According to a recent report issued by the National Fair Housing Alliance, religious discrimination formed the basis of just 1.1 percent of the complaints received by FHOs and government agencies in 2023 (for a total of 353 complaints nationwide).[11] Many of the most significant religion-based cases are notable for their analysis of various aspects of the FHA unrelated to religion. For example, *Halprin v. Prairie Single Family Homes* (holding that §3604(b) claims cannot lie for post-acquisition harassment) and *Bloch v. Frischholz* (holding, contrary to *Halprin*, that plaintiffs can state claims under §3604(b) for post-acquisition discrimination in many circumstances, and that §3617 claims can stand alone), discussed in Chapter 8, both involved Jewish plaintiffs who complained of discriminatory and harassing treatment by their homeowners association (*Halprin*) and condominium board (*Bloch*). United States v. Weisz, 914 F. Supp. 1050 (S.D.N.Y. 1996), discussed in Chapter 10, also involved claims of religious harassment, specifically that a Jewish woman harassed her Catholic neighbors. The court dismissed the plaintiffs' claims, holding that they failed sufficiently to allege that the harassment was because of religion.

Of course, this does not mean that housing discrimination based on religion does not happen,[12] nor does it mean that religion is not an important aspect of fair housing law. Indeed, religious discrimination, notably against

---

11. *2023 Fair Housing Trends Report: Advancing a Blueprint for Equity*, at 12, https://national fairhousing.org/wp-content/uploads/2023/08/2023-Trends-Report-Final.pdf.

12. In particular, there was an increase in violence directed against Muslims and people perceived to be Muslim in the wake of the September 11 terrorist attacks. *See Combating Post-9/11 Discriminatory Backlash*, DOJ Civil Rights Division, https://www.justice.gov/crt/combat ing-post-911-discriminatory-backlash-6 (last visited Aug. 9, 2024).

Jewish people, was a significant catalyst for enactment of the FHA. There have been increasing reports of anti-Muslim discrimination with respect to housing and land use, and there have been significant cases involving alleged anti-Jewish discrimination in land use matters. The FHA also contains a specific exemption for religious organizations serving as housing providers. (This was addressed, for example, in *Columbus Country Club*, discussed in Chapter 5.)

NOTES AND QUESTIONS

1. Plaintiff's Legal Theories. A person's religious belief may be known only to that person, but that person's religious affiliation might be apparent to others to the extent that it involves observing particular customs and practices. Thus, discrimination based on these customs and practices can form the basis for a disparate treatment claim, where there is evidence that the defendant treated these factors as a proxy for religion.

But does a housing provider have to accommodate a tenant's request for a change to policies or procedures to permit the tenant to observe or practice their religious faith? On this question, there is a difference between the employment and housing contexts. Title VII makes clear that the term "religion" includes "all aspects of religious observance and practice as well as belief, unless an employer demonstrates that he is unable to reasonably accommodate an employee's or prospective employee's religious observance or practice without undue hardship on the conduct of the employer's business." 42 U.S.C. §2000e(j). Thus, for employment purposes there is an affirmative requirement that an employer provide a reasonable accommodation for a religious employee's practice and observance needs. There is no such requirement, however, in the FHA. The FHA requires reasonable accommodation only for disability. In *Bloch v. Frischholz*, the plaintiffs were Jewish residents of a condominium complex that prohibited the placement of objects in the hallways and on exterior doors. In accordance with their faith, the plaintiffs were required to affix a mezuzah (a small Jewish symbol) on their door frame, which the complex considered a violation of the prohibition. The Seventh Circuit, en banc, held that the plaintiffs could not make a claim that the complex was required to grant them an exception to the prohibition, stating that "[T]he FHA requires accommodations only for handicaps, 42 U.S.C. §3604(f)(3)(B), not for religion." *See also* Savanna Club Worship v. Savanna Club Homeowners Ass'n, 456 F. Supp. 2d 1223 (S.D. Fla. 2005) (holding that the FHA did not require a homeowners association to permit a group of homeowners to hold religious services in the common areas of the property).[13] The *Bloch*

---

13. Interestingly, the defendant homeowners association enacted a rule that specifically prohibited the holding of religious services in common spaces. The court held this did not discriminate on the basis of religion because it applied equally to any religion: "It is undisputed that

court did hold that the plaintiffs had sufficiently alleged that the defendants had deliberately interpreted and enforced the prohibition to target Jewish residents; thus the plaintiffs stated a claim for intentional discrimination under §3604(b).

Could a plaintiff reframe a failure to accommodate religion claim as a disparate impact claim? Probably, with the caveat that they would have to meet all the requirements for alleging the disparate impact cause of action. In addition, the plaintiff would need to demonstrate that the defendant's action (refusal to make an exception to a policy or procedure) resulted in a violation of the FHA, such as a denial of housing or making housing unavailable under §3604(a) or discrimination in housing-related terms, conditions, or services under §3604(b). The *Savanna Club* court held that the plaintiff's claim failed because providing a space for religious worship is not a housing-related service. The *Bloch* court held that the plaintiffs could not assert a claim using disparate impact theory because they had waived this argument below.

2. Statutory Religious Exemption. Recall from Chapter 5 that the FHA contains a narrow exception for certain religious organizations to discriminate in favor of co-religionists. Section 3607(a) states that:

> Nothing in this subchapter shall prohibit a religious organization, association, or society, or any nonprofit institution or organization operated, supervised or controlled by or in conjunction with a religious organization, association, or society, from limiting the sale, rental or occupancy of dwellings which it owns or operates for other than a commercial purpose to persons of the same religion, or from giving preference to such persons, unless membership in such religion is restricted on account of race, color, or national origin.

It is important to remember that this exemption only permits a religious entity to discriminate on the basis of religion, and not any other protected characteristic. Moreover, as an exemption, §3607(a) is narrowly construed. For example, in United States v. Columbus Country Club, 915 F.2d 877 (3d Cir. 1990), *cert. denied*, 501 U.S. 1205 (1991) (discussed in Chapter 5), the court held that a Catholic-affiliated organization was not sufficiently "operated, supervised, or controlled" by the Catholic Church to fall under the exemption.

3. Constitutional and Other Religious Protections. The Supreme Court also has recognized that First Amendment protections may shield religious actors from some discrimination claims. In the Title VII case of *Bostock v. Clayton County*

---

the Rule bans any and all religious services regardless of denomination, and that the Rule is imposed equally among all religions. Therefore, the crux of the claim is that the Club's members, who are fully entitled to assemble in Savanna's common areas for any non-religious purposes, are illegally being treated differently than other members who choose to assemble for non-religious purpose, and that such disparate treatment is a religion-based discrimination in the provision of services under the FHA." 456 F. Supp. 2d at 1230. The court recognized that such singling out of religious services (other gatherings and secular uses of the common areas were permitted) would constitute a First Amendment violation if the defendant were a state actor, but rejected the suggestion that this analysis could apply to the association.

the Court ruled that sexual orientation and gender identity are aspects of sex, and therefore discrimination on these bases constitutes sex discrimination. Although there were no religious defenses raised, the Court specifically acknowledged that prohibitions against discrimination based on sexual orientation and gender identity might conflict with some people's sincerely held religious beliefs. *Bostock*, 590 U.S. 644, 682 (2020). The Court noted, in dicta, that in addition to the religious exemptions in statutory antidiscrimination laws

> Congress has gone a step further yet in the Religious Freedom Restoration Act of 1993 (RFRA). That statute prohibits the federal government from substantially burdening a person's exercise of religion unless it demonstrates that doing so both furthers a compelling governmental interest and represents the least restrictive means of furthering that interest. Because RFRA operates as a kind of super statute, displacing the normal operation of other federal laws, it might supersede Title VII's commands in appropriate cases.

The contours of any First Amendment or RFRA defense to discrimination claims under the FHA or similar statutes are still being determined, and this issue is likely to be a significant one going forward. Is it likely that commercial housing providers would be permitted to engage in blanket refusals to serve people based on sexual orientation and gender identity? *See* Masterpiece Cakeshop, Ltd. v. Colorado Civil Rights Commission, 584 U.S. 617, 634 (2018) ("Nevertheless, while . . . religious and philosophical objections [to gay marriage] are protected, it is a general rule that such objections do not allow business owners and other actors in the economy and in society to deny protected persons equal access to goods and services under a neutral and generally applicable public accommodations law.").

The situation is complicated because RFRA was a reaction to the decision in Employment Division v. Smith, 494 U.S. 872 (1990), and some members of the Court have indicated that they would overrule this decision. *See* Fulton v. City of Philadelphia, 593 U.S. 522, 545 (2021). To add to the complexity, many states have enacted their own versions of RFRA.

4. The Religious Land Use and Institutionalized Persons Act. The Religious Land Use and Institutionalized Persons Act of 2000 (RLUIPA), 42 U.S.C. §§2000cc, *et seq.*, protects individuals, houses of worship, and other religious institutions from discrimination in zoning and other land-use actions. This statute, which covers commercial as well as residential property, is intended to codify constitutional protections for religious exercise and to provide a mechanism for enforcement of these rights. RLUIPA is particularly concerned with zoning decisions that affect places of worship. The bill's lead sponsors, Senators Edward Kennedy and Orrin Hatch, noted in their joint statement upon the bill's passage:

> Zoning codes frequently exclude churches in places where they permit theaters, meeting halls, and other places where large groups of people assemble for secular purposes. . . . Churches have been denied the right to meet in rented storefronts, in abandoned schools, in converted funeral homes, theaters and

skating rinks—in all sorts of buildings that were permitted when they generated traffic for secular purposes.[14]

The land-use section of the statute contains five separate provisions:

- 42 U.S.C. §2000cc(a): Prohibits the implementation of any land-use regulation that imposes a "substantial burden" on the religious exercise of a person or religious assembly or institution except where justified by a "compelling governmental interest" that the government pursues in the least restrictive way possible.
- 42 U.S.C. §2000cc(b)(1): Provides that religious assemblies and institutions must be treated at least as well as nonreligious assemblies and institutions.
- 42 U.S.C. §2000(b)(2): Prohibits discrimination "against any assembly or institution on the basis of religion or religious denomination."
- 42 U.S.C. §2000cc(b)(3)(A): Provides that governments must not totally exclude religious assemblies from a jurisdiction.
- 42 U.S.C. §2000cc(b)(3)(B): Provides protection against unreasonable limitation of "religious assemblies, institutions, or structures within a jurisdiction."

Chapter Summary

- Race, color, national origin, and religion were the original characteristics protected by the FHA. Race and national origin can be difficult concepts to define, and there is a good deal of overlap between them. The Supreme Court has interpreted the Civil Rights Act of 1866 as applying to race, national origin, and religion, because in the 19th century these traits were viewed as intertwined.

- National origin is defined as the geographic area in which a person was born or from which their ancestors came. Characteristics that are closely associated with national origin, such as language and immigration status, are not protected by the FHA, but can form the basis for a disparate impact claim.

- The FHA contains an exemption for certain religious housing providers. In addition, the RLUIPA protects individuals, houses of worship, and other religious institutions from religion-based discrimination in zoning and other land-use actions.

---

14. 146 CONG. REC. 16698 (2000) (Joint Statement of Senators Hatch and Kennedy).

CHAPTER 15

SEX AS A PROTECTED CHARACTERISTIC

Sex was not part of the original 1968 Fair Housing Act. It was added as a protected characteristic in 1974, with little debate.[1] A few points about sex as a protected characteristic are important as an introductory matter. First, there is the issue of terminology. "Sex" and "gender" have distinct meanings, with sex referring to biological and physical characteristics, and gender referring to socially constructed norms and behaviors associated with sex. However, the terms frequently are conflated or used interchangeably in cases involving sex discrimination.[2] Similarly, sexual orientation and gender identity are characteristics distinct from sex, but presenting overlapping concerns.[3] Indeed, as the final portion of this chapter discusses, a 2020 U.S. Supreme Court decision

---

1. *See* Housing and Community Development Act of 1974, Pub. L. No. 93-383, §808, 88 Stat. 633. Sex was among the list of characteristics protected by Title VII of the 1964 Civil Rights Act, the FHA's precursor statute addressing employment discrimination. The inclusion of "sex" in Title VII occurred under unusual circumstances: It was offered as an amendment by Congressman Howard Smith of Virginia, a segregationist and opponent of Title VII. The amendment was received with laughter in the House of Representatives, and conventional wisdom holds that this amendment was some combination of a joke on Rep. Smith's part and an attempt to sink the bill. Deeper scholarship, however, reveals that Rep. Smith might also have been motivated by his ties to anti-union groups. Forces in favor of organized labor were pushing for protective legislation for women, and the inclusion of sex in the Civil Rights Act was seen as a way of stymieing this attempt. Meanwhile, the National Women's Party, a group formed to advocate for suffrage and later the Equal Rights Amendment (ERA), was growing frustrated with its lack of success moving the ERA forward. The group saw the inclusion of sex in the Civil Rights Act as one way to advance its goal and approached Rep. Smith about proposing the amendment. Thus, strange alliances were formed: A conservative member of Congress introduced an amendment proposed by women's rights activists, while liberal groups and labor both opposed the amendment even as they worked for the bill's passage. Against this unlikely backdrop, the amendment, and the bill, succeeded in becoming law. *See* Robert C. Bird, *More Than a Congressional Joke: A Fresh Look at the Legislative History of Sex Discrimination of the 1964 Civil Rights Act*, 3 WM. & MARY J. WOMEN & LAW 137 (1997).

2. *See generally* Katherine M. Franke, *The Central Mistake of Sex Discrimination Law: The Disaggregation of Sex from Gender*, 144 U. PA. L. REV. 1 (1995).

3. *See generally* Francisco Valdes, *Queers, Sissies, Dykes, and Tomboys: Deconstructing the Conflation of "Sex," "Gender," and "Sexual Orientation" in Euro-American Law and Society*, 83 CALIF. L. REV. 1 (Jan. 1995); Mary Anne C. Case, *Disaggregating Gender from Sex and Sexual Orientation: The Effeminate Man in the Law and Feminist Jurisprudence*, 105 YALE L.J. 1 (Oct. 1995).

interpreting Title VII of the 1964 Civil Rights Act, *Bostock v. Clayton County*, held that sexual orientation and gender identity are linked inextricably to sex, and thus these characteristics are protected against employment discrimination by the statute. Given identical language prohibiting discrimination "because of sex" in the FHA, as well as similar statutory purposes and construction, these presumptively are protected characteristics under the FHA, as discussed further in Section D, below.

Second, "basic" cases of sex discrimination—discriminatory refusals to deal on the basis of sex—are relatively rare. Instead, cases alleging sex discrimination in housing tend to be based on claims of sexual harassment or the discriminatory treatment of victims of domestic violence. This is not to say that sex plays an insignificant role in housing. Indeed, in many ways sex is more predictive of housing outcomes than are many other factors. As Professor Noah Kazis points out:

> In some cities, between sixty and seventy percent of evicted tenants are women. . . . Women are also disproportionately likely to receive housing assistance. Three-quarters of households living in public housing are female headed, as are 83% of households receiving federal housing vouchers. Men, meanwhile, are far more likely to be homeless.[4]

It is likely, however, that much of this disparity results from the fact that women are more likely to be custodial parents or guardians of children (itself a protected characteristic under the FHA, as discussed in Chapter 16), and of course there are intersectional factors such as race and poverty at play.[5] Nonetheless, sex as a characteristic interacts with housing in important and complex ways.

A. SEX DISCRIMINATION

Discrimination on the basis of sex in the sale or rental of housing is less commonly reported than are other forms of housing discrimination, and there are relatively few published opinions on the issue. Reported cases involve discrimination against men and women, and sex is often combined with other characteristics (e.g., a landlord might be willing to rent to a married heterosexual couple, but not to a single mother or a group of Black men). Professor Noah Kazis argues that "both men and women . . . suffer from housing discrimination on the basis of sex, per se. That discrimination will usually, if not

---

4. Noah Kazis, *Fair Housing for a Non-Sexist City*, 134 Harv. L. Rev. 1683, 1685-86 (2021).

5. The concept of intersectionality was coined by Professor Kimberlé Crenshaw in her pathbreaking article, *Demarginalizing the Intersection of Race and Sex: A Black Feminist Critique of Antidiscrimination Doctrine, Feminist Theory and Antiracist Politics*, 1989 U. Chi. Legal F. 139 (1989). Intersectionality describes how race, class, gender, and other individual characteristics can combine, overlap, and reinforce one another, in particular to affect marginalized individuals and groups.

always, be intersectional, based on a combination of multiple protected class statuses interacting in ways that are more than merely additive."[6]

For example, in Walker v. Crigler, 976 F.2d 900 (4th Cir. 1992), the jury returned a verdict for the plaintiff, where the defendant property manager refused to rent an apartment to a single mother "in any circumstances," telling the woman she "had experienced problems with the boyfriends of single women in the past." She ultimately rented the apartment to two men, who paid less in rent than the plaintiff was willing to pay. In contrast, in Baumgardner v. HUD, 960 F.2d 572 (6th Cir. 1992), the 6th Circuit affirmed an ALJ's determination that the defendant landlord refused to rent to a group of four men, claiming that he believed men to be "messy and unclean." The landlord subsequently refused to show the unit to a male tester, while offering to show it to multiple female testers. The landlord ultimately rented the unit to a woman with children.

B. SEXUAL HARASSMENT

The majority of sex-based housing discrimination complaints allege sexual harassment. This includes harassing language or behavior, usually by male landlords, rental managers, maintenance workers, or other housing providers, against tenants, usually female. The complaints most frequently are brought under §3604(b), which prohibits discrimination in the terms and conditions of housing, and §3617, which makes it unlawful "to coerce, intimidate, threaten, or interfere with any person in the exercise or enjoyment" of housing.

The law of sexual harassment was first developed in the context of employment discrimination, based on Title VII's analogous language prohibiting discrimination "because of sex" in the terms and conditions of employment. In an early case, Henson v. Dundee, 682 F.2d 897 (11th Cir. 1982), the Eleventh Circuit laid out the prima facie elements for a claim of sexual harassment in employment. As an initial matter, plaintiffs must show that the conduct was "based on sex." With respect to conduct of an obviously sexual nature directed only at members of one sex, this is not a difficult hurdle for plaintiffs to clear. More complicated scenarios are addressed in note 3, below.

Plaintiffs also must demonstrate that the conduct was "unwelcome." In *Henson,* the Eleventh Circuit noted that "[i]n order to constitute harassment, this conduct must be unwelcome in the sense that the employee did not solicit or incite it, and in the sense that the employee regarded the conduct as undesirable or offensive." *Id.* at 903. Specific concerns with this requirement are discussed in note 8, below.

The determination of what type of conduct constitutes a substantive violation has proven to be more complicated. Relying on guidance from the EEOC, the courts recognized two distinct types of sexual harassment claims: (1)

---

6. Kazis, *supra* note 4, at 1690.

"quid pro quo" claims, where sexual favors are sought in exchange for continued employment or other job benefits; and (2) "hostile environment" claims, where unwelcome sexual advances, epithets, or other offensive conduct occurs but does not lead to lost employment or other economic injuries. Hostile environment claims can be raised by plaintiffs claiming harassment based on any protected characteristic; however, quid pro quo claims, due to their specific nature (involving coerced sexual activity) only apply to claims of sexual harassment.

In Meritor Savings Bank v. Vinson, 477 U.S. 57 (1986), the Supreme Court set out the basic principles governing sexual harassment as sex discrimination. The plaintiff alleged that she had been sexually harassed by her supervisor at the bank where she worked. Specifically, she alleged that he physically groped her, exposed himself to her, and coerced her into sex for fear of losing her job. The Court adopted the prima facie case as set forth in *Henson* and held that a terms and conditions violation can result not only from quid pro quo discrimination (where continued employment is conditioned on sexual favors) but also from a hostile working environment—harassment that is "sufficiently severe or pervasive 'to alter the conditions of [the victim's] employment and create an abusive working environment.'"

There have been relatively few federal court of appeals decisions to rule on the issue of whether sexual harassment violates the FHA, but the few that have done so all agree that it does. Consider the following case, in which the plaintiff appealed the district court's dismissal of her complaint for failure to state a claim under the FHA. As you read the case, consider which sexual harassment theories are supported by the plaintiff's allegations.

Fox v. Gaines

4 F.4th 1293 (11th Cir. 2021)

Before Pryor, Newsom, and Marcus, Circuit Judges

Pryor, Circuit Judge:

This case presents the question of whether sexual harassment claims are actionable under the FHA. After being forced out of her rented apartment for ending a sexual relationship with the property manager, Rita Fox sued the property manager and the property's owner, asserting sexual harassment claims under the FHA[.] Finding no guidance from this Court on the question, the district court dismissed Ms. Fox's complaint on the ground that her sexual harassment claims were not actionable under the FHA. Today we provide that guidance and hold that sexual harassment can be a form of sex discrimination prohibited by the FHA, provided the plaintiff can demonstrate that she would not have been harassed but for her sex.

I. BACKGROUND

A. Factual Background

Ms. Fox, a single mother facing foreclosure eviction, visited the Rose Bush Apartments in Jupiter, Florida, to view an apartment available for rent. Lucille Gaines owned the Rose Bush Apartments and employed Dana Gaines as the property manager.

When Ms. Fox went to apply for the unit, Mr. Gaines "commented on [her] looks, which made [her] feel uncomfortable." Mr. Gaines told Ms. Fox that he had a list of people interested in the unit but would "keep [it] available for her if she would give him a kiss." Mr. Gaines's comment gave Ms. Fox "slight reservations" about renting the unit, but because the apartment met her needs, she signed a lease. When Ms. Fox met Mr. Gaines to receive the keys to the apartment, he "reminded her about the kiss," and Ms. Fox kissed him.

Upon moving into the apartment, Ms. Fox paid the first month's rent, last month's rent, and a security deposit, but she soon found it difficult to make her full monthly rent payment. Mr. Gaines offered to help Ms. Fox with her rent if she would "help him" by providing him sexual favors. Ms. Fox "eventually acquiesced," and for about three and a half years Mr. Gaines reduced her monthly rent in exchange for sexual favors. Ms. Fox alleges that this arrangement was part of a "pervasive and persistent pattern of sexual harassment and discrimination." On top of the sexual favors, Mr. Gaines would question Ms. Fox about her whereabouts and demand that she not invite male visitors to her apartment. He also installed surveillance cameras facing Ms. Fox's unit and "monitored [her] daily activity."

Hoping to stop Mr. Gaines's "controlling and harassing behavior," Ms. Fox ended her sexual relationship with him. In response, Mr. Gaines started serving Ms. Fox with "fraudulent violation notices" and threatened to evict her from her apartment. About a week after Ms. Fox ended the relationship, she paid a portion of her monthly rent, as she had for the past three and a half years, and made an oral agreement with Mr. Gaines that she would pay the remainder within eight days. Eight days later, Ms. Fox paid the remainder of her rent, but Mr. Gaines told her that because she had failed to pay within seven days, he had "no choice but to file an eviction on [her]." He served her with a three-day notice to vacate the apartment for failure to pay rent, even though she owed no rent.

When Ms. Fox failed to move out within three days, Mr. Gaines initiated formal eviction proceedings against her. The day after he filed the complaint for eviction, he and Ms. Fox agreed that she would move out by midnight on the last day of the month. On the last day of the month, he called the police and tried to have her arrested for trespassing. She had to explain to the officers that she retained possession of the unit until midnight. As promised, Ms. Fox moved out of her apartment that day.

B. Procedural Background

After being forced out of her apartment by Mr. Gaines, Ms. Fox sued him and Ms. Gaines, arguing that Mr. Gaines's sexual harassment of her violated the FHA's . . . prohibitions on sex discrimination. Mr. Gaines and Ms. Gaines filed separate motions to dismiss Ms. Fox's complaint, which the district court granted. Even though the district court agreed that Ms. Fox had "sufficiently pled 'severe, pervasive harassment'" that was "well beyond what [was] required to withstand a motion to dismiss," the court decided that Ms. Fox's sexual harassment claim was not actionable under the FHA. The court acknowledged that its holding was in direct contrast with "the overwhelming weight of federal authority" but nevertheless concluded that the plain language of the FHA did not provide a cause of action for sexual harassment. This is Ms. Fox's appeal.

III. DISCUSSION

Whether sexual harassment qualifies as sex discrimination under the FHA is a question of first impression in our circuit. Today we join our sister circuits in concluding that it does. See *United States v. Hurt* (8th Cir. 2012) ("Sexual harassment is actionable under the FHA when it creates a hostile housing environment or constitutes quid pro quo sexual harassment."); *DiCenso v. Cisneros* (7th Cir. 1996) (recognizing that sexual harassment is an actionable sex discrimination claim under the FHA); *Honce v. Vigil* (10th Cir. 1993) (same); see also *Hall v. Meadowood Ltd. P'ship* (9th Cir. 2001) (unpublished).

The FHA makes it unlawful to "discriminate against any person in the terms, conditions, or privileges of sale or rental of a dwelling, or in the provision of services or facilities in connection therewith, because of . . . sex." 42 U.S.C. §3604(b). The Supreme Court has held that the words "because of" and "based on" indicate "but-for causality." *Burrage v. United States* (2014). So, by its plain meaning, the FHA protects a tenant or prospective homebuyer from receiving differential or less favorable treatment in housing terms, conditions, or privileges if the but-for cause of that treatment is her sex.[7]

When interpreting the FHA, we—like our sister circuits—look to cases interpreting Title VII, which uses language virtually identical to the FHA's. Turning to cases interpreting Title VII confirms our conclusion that the FHA prohibits sexual harassment.

Interpreting Title VII, the Supreme Court ruled that "[w]ithout question" sexual harassment is a form of sex discrimination within the meaning of Title VII's nearly identical prohibition on "discriminat[ion] . . . because of . . . sex." *Meritor Savs. Bank, FSB v. Vinson* (1986) (quoting 42 U.S.C. §2000e-2(a)(1)). In

---

7. [EDS.—Note that this formulation appears to incorporate a "but-for" causation standard (while citing a criminal non-FHA case), whereas the courts have traditionally applied a less stringent "motivating factor" standard under the FHA. The causation standard for FHA claims is addressed in Chapter 6.]

Meritor the Court relied on the reasoning of our decision in *Henson v. City of Dundee*, where we held that "a hostile or offensive atmosphere created by sexual harassment can, standing alone, constitute a violation of Title VII," explaining that a "pattern of sexual harassment inflicted upon an employee because of her sex is a pattern of behavior that inflicts disparate treatment upon a member of one sex with respect to terms, conditions, or privileges of employment." Following *Meritor* and *Henson*, we have consistently held that sexual harassment constitutes impermissible sex discrimination under Title VII where, but for the fact of the claimant's sex, she would not have been the object of harassment. As these Title VII cases make clear, the plain text of "discriminat[ion] . . . because of . . . sex," 42 U.S.C. §3604(b), includes sexual harassment where the plaintiff proves that, but for her sex, she would not have been subjected to sexual harassment.

Thus, we hold that sexual harassment—both hostile housing environment and quid pro quo sexual harassment—is actionable under the FHA, provided the plaintiff demonstrates that she would not have been harassed but for her sex. Because the district court erroneously concluded otherwise, we vacate the district court's order granting the Gaineses' motions to dismiss and remand with instructions to the district court to consider, in light of our ruling, whether Ms. Fox's complaint adequately alleged violations of the FHA.

The allegations in *Fox* likely are sufficient for plaintiff to proceed under both the quid pro quo and hostile environment theories: quid pro quo because of the exchange of a rent break for sexual favors and the eviction when the sex stopped, and hostile environment because of the stalking and surveilling. Quid pro quo cases like *Fox*, in which a defendant causes or threatens tangible harm (eviction or other action) to a plaintiff who might refuse his sexual demands are relatively simple for courts. The only question is whether the defendant threatened or took the negative action (at least in part) because of the plaintiff's refusal. The more difficult question for courts hearing sexual harassment cases has been how to determine when, in a hostile environment case, the conduct alleged satisfies the "severe or pervasive" standard.

In the employment context, a number of post-*Meritor* cases sought to flesh out the severe or pervasive standard for hostile environment claims brought under Title VII. In Harris v. Forklift Systems, Inc., 510 U.S. 17, 21-23 (1993), the Court held that this standard is met by conduct that creates an "objectively hostile or abusive work environment—an environment that a reasonable person would find hostile or abusive." The Court further observed that the harassing conduct does not have to be so extreme as to cause the employee to suffer concrete psychological harm or injury:

> Title VII comes into play before the harassing conduct leads to a nervous breakdown. A discriminatorily abusive work environment, even one that does not seriously affect employees' psychological well-being, can and often will

detract from employees' job performance, discourage employees from remaining on the job, or keep them from advancing in their careers. Moreover, even without regard to these tangible effects, the very fact that the discriminatory conduct was so severe or pervasive that it created a work environment abusive to employees because of their race, gender, religion, or national origin offends Title VII's broad rule of workplace equality.

Beyond this, however, the Court left the standard somewhat vague, noting that:

> [W]hether an environment is "hostile" or "abusive" can be determined only by looking at all the circumstances. These may include the frequency of the discriminatory conduct; its severity; whether it is physically threatening or humiliating, or a mere offensive utterance; and whether it unreasonably interferes with an employee's work performance.

The following is one of the first appellate court decisions to grapple with this question in an FHA case.

DiCenso v. Cisneros

96 F.3d 1004 (7th Cir. 1996)

Before Bauer, Eschbach, and Flaum, Circuit Judges

Bauer, Circuit Judge:

This case raises the question of whether one incident of harassment was sufficiently egregious to create a hostile environment sex discrimination cause of action under the FHA. An Administrative Law Judge ("ALJ") thought it was not, but the HUD Secretary's Designee disagreed, and remanded the case to the ALJ for a determination of damages. The landlord who committed the harassment now seeks relief from the Secretary's Order. We reverse.

BACKGROUND

[Christina Brown was 18 years old, living in an apartment with her boyfriend, Thomas Andrews, and their infant daughter. Albert DiCenso owned and managed the building.] Sometime in mid-October or early November, DiCenso came to Brown's apartment to collect the rent. According to the ALJ's findings, the following exchange took place:

While [Brown] stood at the door, [DiCenso] asked about the rent and simultaneously began caressing her arm and back. He said to her words to the effect that if she could not pay the rent, she could take care of it in other ways. [Brown] slammed the door in his face. [DiCenso] stood outside calling her names—a "bitch" and "whore," and then left.

[The next month] DiCenso again went to the apartment to collect the monthly rent. While there, he became involved in a confrontation with Andrews and the police were called. DiCenso informed the police that the disagreement was over Andrews' refusal to pay the rent. Brown and Andrews told DiCenso that they would be leaving the apartment within the next ten days. According to the police report, the two parties "both came to the decision of settling the matter in court."

Brown and Andrews did not move out, however, and in late January, DiCenso served them with a five-day notice to quit the premises. On January 31, Brown filed a housing discrimination complaint alleging that DiCenso had harassed her and her boyfriend, and had made sexual advances toward her. . . .

The Department investigated Brown's complaint and determined that reasonable cause existed to believe that discrimination had occurred. [HUD issued a charge against DiCenso for violations of §§3604(b) and 3617 of the FHA.]

[After a hearing] the ALJ issued a thorough decision, in which she acknowledged that any finding that the alleged acts occurred rested solely on credibility determinations. In making these determinations, the ALJ relied on the witnesses' demeanor while testifying, their ability and opportunity to observe what happened, their memory, any interest or bias they might have, the consistency of their statements, and the reasonableness of their testimony in light of all of the evidence received. On the whole, the ALJ found Brown more credible than DiCenso. However, the ALJ also found that Brown's testimony established only one act of sexual harassment by DiCenso—the mid-October incident. On this set of facts, the ALJ concluded that DiCenso's conduct did not rise to the level of severity required to create a hostile housing environment. Consequently, the ALJ found that Brown had failed to establish a claim of sex discrimination and dismissed the complaint.

The Department, acting on Brown's behalf, sought review of the ALJ's order. . . . The HUD Secretary's Designee affirmed the ALJ's findings of fact, but reached a different conclusion on the issue of whether the single incident amounted to a hostile housing environment for purposes of the FHA. Finding for Brown on the issue of liability, the Secretary's Designee vacated the ALJ's decision and remanded the case for a determination of damages. The ALJ awarded Brown $5,000 in compensatory damages, assessed a $5,000 civil penalty against DiCenso and entered injunctive relief. [DiCenso petitioned for review.]

A. Standard of Review

Before addressing whether DiCenso's conduct constitutes unlawful discrimination, we first must address the applicable standard of review. Both parties correctly acknowledge that we defer to the ALJ's findings of fact where they are supported by substantial evidence on the record as a whole. The issue, then, is whether we also should defer to the Department's legal conclusions. DiCenso understandably argues that we should review the legal conclusions de novo.

Chevron [v. Natural Resources Defense Council, 467 U.S. 837 (1984)] requires us to defer to the decisions of executive agencies where the agency has a particular expertise in the conflicting policy considerations that underlie a statute, or where the agency previously has considered the matter at issue in a detailed and reasoned fashion.[8] Neither of these situations exist here. [EDS.—HUD at that time had not yet issued either guidelines or regulations.] Rather, as the HUD Secretary's Designee acknowledged, a determination of what constitutes a hostile environment in the housing context requires the same analysis courts have undertaken in the Title VII context. Such a determination does not require deference to an administrative agency.

Despite the concession in its initial brief, the Department now argues that we should subject determinations of whether an incident of harassment is sufficiently egregious to constitute sex discrimination to a clearly erroneous standard. In this case, the existence of harassment is not at issue. The sole question is whether the incident of harassment that occurred is sufficient to state a cause of action under the FHA. This is purely a question of law which we review de novo.

B. Hostile Environment Sex Discrimination

Title VII of the CRA of 1964 allows a cause of action for harassment that creates a hostile or offensive working environment. Claims of hostile environment sex discrimination in the housing context have been far less frequent. The first district court to apply the hostile environment cause of action to housing discrimination did so in Shellhammer v. Lewallen, Fair Hous.–Fair Lend. Rep. (P-H) para. 15,742 (W.D. Ohio Nov. 22, 1983), affirmed by 1985 WL 13505 (6th Cir. July 31, 1985). . . . Like *Shellhammer* and *Honce [v. Vigil* (10th Cir. 1993)], other courts that have found harassment to create an actionable form of housing discrimination also have incorporated Title VII doctrines into their analyses.

Like the Tenth Circuit, we recognize a hostile housing environment cause of action, and begin our analysis with the more familiar Title VII standard. For sexual harassment to be actionable in the Title VII context, it must be sufficiently severe or pervasive to alter the conditions of the victim's employment and create an abusive working environment. "Conduct that is not severe or pervasive enough to create an objectively hostile or abusive work environment—an environment that a reasonable person would find hostile or abusive—is beyond Title VII's purview." *Harris v. Forklift Systems, Inc.* (1993). Applied to the housing context, a claim is actionable "when the offensive behavior unreasonably interferes with use and enjoyment of the premises." *Honce*, 1 F.3d at 1090. Whether an environment is "hostile" or "abusive"

---

8. [EDS.—The Supreme Court's decision in Loper Bright Enterprises v. Raimondo, 603 U.S. ___ (2024) overruled *Chevron* with respect to the level of deference that federal courts should give to certain administrative agency actions. This issue is discussed in Chapter 3.]

can be determined only by looking at all the circumstances, and factors may include the frequency of the discriminatory conduct; its severity; whether it is physically threatening or humiliating, or a mere offensive utterance; and whether it unreasonably interferes with an employee's work performance.

We repeatedly have held that isolated and innocuous incidents do not support a finding of sexual harassment. For example, in *Saxton v. American Tel. Tel. Co.* (7th Cir. 1993), the defendant on one occasion put his hand on the plaintiff's leg and kissed her until she pushed him away. Three weeks later, the defendant lurched at the plaintiff from behind some bushes and unsuccessfully tried to grab her. While these incidents were subjectively unpleasant, the defendant's conduct was not frequent or severe enough to create a hostile environment. Similarly, in *Weiss v. Coca-Cola Bottling Co. of Chicago* (7th Cir. 1993), the defendant asked the plaintiff for dates on repeated occasions, placed signs which read "I love you" in her work area, and twice attempted to kiss her. These incidents also were too isolated and insufficiently severe to create a hostile work environment. Common to all of these examples is an emphasis on the frequency of the offensive behavior. "Though sporadic behavior, if sufficiently abusive, may support a [discrimination] claim, success often requires repetitive misconduct." *Chalmers v. Quaker Oats Co.* (7th Cir. 1995).

In this context, the problem with Brown's complaint is that although DiCenso may have harassed her, he did so only once. Moreover, DiCenso's conduct, while clearly unwelcome, was much less offensive than other incidents which have not violated Title VII. DiCenso's comment vaguely invited Brown to exchange sex for rent, and while DiCenso caressed Brown's arm and back, he did not touch an intimate body part, and did not threaten Brown with any physical harm. There is no question that Brown found DiCenso's remarks to be subjectively unpleasant, but this alone did not create an objectively hostile environment.

We stress in closing that our decision today should not be read as giving landlords one free chance to harass their tenants. We do not condone DiCenso's conduct, nor do we hold that a single incident of harassment never will support an actionable claim. Considering the totality of the circumstances in this case, we agree with the ALJ that DiCenso's conduct was not sufficiently egregious to create an objectively hostile housing environment.

[EDS.—Judge Flaum dissented based on his view that *Chevron* required the court to defer to the Secretary's reasonable interpretation of what constitutes a hostile housing environment. With respect to *Chevron*, see Chapter 3, Section C.]

NOTES AND QUESTIONS

1. HUD Regulation. HUD proposed a regulation governing sexual harassment in housing in November 2000. That proposed regulation never became final. In 2016, however, the Obama administration published a final rule governing Quid Pro Quo and Hostile Environment Harassment and Liability for Discriminatory Housing Practices Under the FHA. Interestingly, this rule applies to alleged harassment on the basis of any protected characteristic—race, color, religion, national origin, sex, familial status, or disability—while the 2000 proposed rule would have applied only to sexual harassment.

§100.600 Quid pro quo and hostile environment harassment.

(a) *General.* Quid pro quo and hostile environment harassment because of race, color, religion, sex, familial status, national origin or handicap may violate §§3604, 3605, 3606 or 3617 of the Act, depending on the conduct. The same conduct may violate one or more of these provisions.

(1) *Quid pro quo harassment.* Quid pro quo harassment refers to an unwelcome request or demand to engage in conduct where submission to the request or demand, either explicitly or implicitly, is made a condition related to: The sale, rental or availability of a dwelling; the terms, conditions, or privileges of the sale or rental, or the provision of services or facilities in connection therewith; or the availability, terms, or conditions of a residential real estate-related transaction. An unwelcome request or demand may constitute quid pro quo harassment even if a person acquiesces in the unwelcome request or demand.

(2) *Hostile environment harassment.* Hostile environment harassment refers to unwelcome conduct that is sufficiently severe or pervasive as to interfere with: The availability, sale, rental, or use or enjoyment of a dwelling; the terms, conditions, or privileges of the sale or rental, or the provision or enjoyment of services or facilities in connection therewith; or the availability, terms, or conditions of a residential real estate-related transaction. Hostile environment harassment does not require a change in the economic benefits, terms, or conditions of the dwelling or housing-related services or facilities, or of the residential real-estate transaction.

(i) *Totality of the circumstances.* Whether hostile environment harassment exists depends upon the totality of the circumstances.

(A) Factors to be considered to determine whether hostile environment harassment exists include, but are not limited to, the nature of the conduct, the context in which the incident(s) occurred, the severity, scope, frequency, duration, and location of the conduct, and the relationships of the persons involved.

(B) Neither psychological nor physical harm must be demonstrated to prove that a hostile environment exists. Evidence of psychological or physical harm may, however, be relevant in determining whether a hostile environment existed and, if so, the amount of damages to which an aggrieved person may be entitled.

(C) Whether unwelcome conduct is sufficiently severe or pervasive as to create a hostile environment is evaluated from the perspective of a reasonable person in the aggrieved person's position.

. . .

(b) *Type of conduct.* Harassment can be written, verbal, or other conduct, and does not require physical contact.

(c) *Number of incidents.* A single incident of harassment because of race, color, religion, sex, familial status, national origin, or handicap may constitute a discriminatory housing practice, where the incident is sufficiently severe to create a hostile environment, or evidences a quid pro quo.

2. Hostile Environment Harassment and the Severe or Pervasive Standard. The severe or pervasive standard is disjunctive: The more severe the conduct, the less frequently it needs to occur, and the more frequent the conduct, the less severe it needs to be to constitute discrimination in the terms and conditions of housing. Despite the majority's insistence, does *DiCenso* in fact give an alleged harasser "one free pass" for misconduct? How severe would a single instance of conduct need to be to satisfy this standard? Do you think a reasonable person in Ms. Brown's position would find DiCenso's actions offensive? Would it matter if the reasonable person were male or female? Note that in *DiCenso* five different adjudicators attempted to answer this question, with differing results: The HUD ALJ and two members of the Seventh Circuit panel held that Ms. Brown's complaint failed to describe severe or pervasive conduct; the HUD Secretary's Designee held that it did; and the dissenting judge on the panel held that the court should have deferred to the HUD Designee's conclusion under the *Chevron* doctrine because the HUD interpretation was reasonable.

The standard is supposed to be an objective one, but is the determination of this standard—coming as it is from members of the judiciary who are likely older, male, white, and not low income—likely to reflect the reality for housing harassment victims, who disproportionately are young, female, low income, and often people of color? (Note, however, that the ALJ in *DiCenso* was a woman.) The opinion was handed down in 1996, well before the #MeToo movement and other significant shifts in how sexual harassment and assaults are viewed in the popular and legal discourse. Do you think *DiCenso* would be decided the same way today? What do you think would or should be the impact of the HUD regulation, taking into account the Supreme Court's overruling of *Chevron*?

3. Quid Pro Quo. Note that in *DiCenso* the defendant attempted a quid pro quo by suggesting that Ms. Brown could "take care of" the rent in "other ways," but Ms. Brown refused. She subsequently was evicted. Why didn't the majority also treat this as a quid pro quo case? Had the majority done so, it would not have needed to focus on whether the conduct was severe or pervasive (at least for the quid pro quo claim), but instead on whether the eviction was "because of" Ms. Brown's refusal to engage in sexual activity. Perhaps the majority already had concluded that the eviction was because Ms. Brown had failed to pay rent. It is reasonable to assume, however, that if Ms. Brown had acquiesced to her landlord's demands he would have allowed her to avoid paying rent and not evicted her. In this sense, it is clear that the eviction resulted, at least in part, because of the tenant's sex. Consider, for example, Krueger v. Cuomo, 115 F.3d 487, 491-92 (7th Cir. 1997), in which a landlord rented to a woman whom he knew would not be able to pay her portion of the rent (she was using a voucher that paid the bulk of her rent, but she still owed an individual contribution). He suggested that they could "fool around" to make up the difference. She refused, and throughout her tenancy he repeatedly propositioned her for sex, grabbed her, and stalked her. After the landlord learned she had filed a complaint against him with HUD, he attempted to evict her, claiming that her rent payment had been inadequate. While this attempt was not successful (the Housing Authority that administered her voucher got involved and brokered a settlement), the tenant ultimately was so miserable in the tenancy that she moved out. The Seventh Circuit reviewed the findings of a HUD ALJ, noting:

> The ALJ also rejected Krueger's proffered explanations for his attempts to evict Maze (her hostility toward him, her failure to pay rent) and found that Krueger's actions were a direct response to her refusal to submit to his demands and to her filing of harassment charges. Because Maze's rejection of Krueger's advances resulted in an adverse consequence (i.e., being forced out of her apartment), the ALJ concluded that Krueger had engaged in quid pro quo sexual harassment. . . .
>
> Krueger's arguments ultimately rest on the assertion that he attempted to evict Maze for "legitimate business reasons" and that there was "no causal connection between Krueger's alleged sexual advances and her moving out of the apartment"—a view of the evidence directly in conflict with the ALJ's findings. . . . On this record, we have no basis for upsetting the agency's findings.

What theory should be used when a landlord propositions his tenant for sex and she refuses, but he takes no action against her? In other words, this would be an attempt to extort sexual activity upon threat of some negative consequence, where neither the sex nor the consequence occurs. The Supreme Court ruled in an employment case that such claims should be characterized as hostile environment claims and assessed according to the severe or pervasive standard. See Burlington Industries, Inc., v. Ellerth, 524 U.S. 742 (1998). Thus, the question for the court would be whether being propositioned for sex constitutes severe or pervasive harassment. A court might look to the number of times this happens and whether it is accompanied by other offensive behavior.

   4. The Employment Context vs. the Housing Context. Starting with *Shellhammer*, the first case to recognize a cause of action under the FHA for sexual harassment in housing, courts hearing housing harassment cases have borrowed heavily from the doctrinal framework set forth by courts in employment cases. (Note the extensive discussion of Title VII in *Fox* and *DiCenso*, above.) On the one hand, this comparison has been helpful to guide courts on an issue — sexual harassment — that the Supreme Court has not addressed in the housing context. The existence of a framework for analysis of sexual harassment claims under Title VII made it easier for housing plaintiffs to maintain those claims under the FHA.

What happens, however, when courts rely on specific factual scenarios from employment contexts to guide their opinions in housing cases? Do the employment-based examples that the *DiCenso* court cites translate easily to the housing context? For example, the court cited a Title VII case, *Weiss v. Coca-Cola*, in which the plaintiff alleged the defendant put notes in her work space that said "I love you," repeatedly asked her on dates, and twice tried to kiss her. The court characterized these as "isolated and innocuous incidents" in the workplace. In another Title VII case cited by the court, *Saxton v. American Tel. Tel. Co.*, the defendant put his hand on the plaintiff's leg and kissed her until she pushed him away, and later "lurched at the plaintiff from behind some bushes and unsuccessfully tried to grab her." The *DiCenso* majority described these as "subjectively unpleasant incidents" that were not frequent or severe enough to create a hostile workplace environment. Do you agree that these are accurate characterizations of conduct in a work setting? And even if they are, should the result be the same if these complainants were tenants, the defendants were their landlords, and the conduct occurred at the-complainants' homes?

Commentators have noted that the housing/employment analogy may create difficulties for plaintiffs in arguing that harassing conduct meets the severe or pervasive standard. Conduct that may not appear to be severe or pervasive in the workplace may seem more serious when it occurs at a person's home, which is supposed to be a place of privacy. As Professor Regina Cahan argues:

> When sexual harassment occurs at work, at that moment or at the end of the workday, the woman may remove herself from the offensive environment. She will choose whether to resign from her position based on economic and personal considerations. In contrast, when the harassment occurs in a woman's home, it is a complete invasion in her life. Ideally, home is the haven from the troubles of the day. When home is not a safe place, a woman may feel distressed and, often, immobile.[9]

---

9. Regina Cahan, *Home Is No Haven: An Analysis of Sexual Harassment in Housing*, 1987 Wis. L. Rev. 1061, 1073 (1987); *see also* Michelle Adams, *Knowing Your Place: Theorizing Sexual Harassment at Home*, 40 Ariz. L. Rev. 17, 18 (1998) ("We must develop a more sophisticated and nuanced understanding of sexual harassment at home by examining the context in which the harassment occurred. Furthermore, we must recognize the cultural history and continuing significance of that context by examining the culturally constructed meaning of 'home.'").

Other characteristics of the landlord-tenant relationship may also make housing harassment more severe. As noted by Professors Robert Schwemm and Rigel Oliveri:

> In addition, a harassing landlord is seen as more threatening than a job supervisor, both because a landlord has virtually unlimited access to his potential victims at any time and because the unequal power relationship that is inherent in harassment cases is generally more pronounced in a landlord-tenant situation than in an employment setting. This latter consideration is underscored by the fact that most reported cases of sexual harassment in housing have involved low-income women whose need for the housing controlled by their harasser is even more desperate than their counterparts' need for a job in most workplace harassment cases.[10]

Some courts have recognized the differences in context between the workplace and the home that might affect the way courts conduct the severe or pervasive analysis. For example, in Beliveau v. Caras, 873 F. Supp. 1393, 1398 (C.D. Cal. 1995), the court ruled that the plaintiff stated a claim for sexual harassment when she alleged that the resident manager had touched her in an offensive way in her bathroom. The court explained that the defendant's alleged conduct constituted sexual harassment because it "was committed (1) *in* plaintiff's own home, where she should feel (and be) less vulnerable, and (2) by one whose very role was to provide that safe environment." *See also* Quigley v. Winter, 598 F.3d 938, 947 (8th Cir. 2010) (emphasizing that defendant's harassing conduct was made "even more egregious" by the fact that it occurred in plaintiff's home, "a place where [she] was entitled to feel safe and secure and need not flee"); Salisbury v. Hickman, 974 F. Supp. 2d 1282, 1292 (E.D. Cal. 2013) ("[c]ourts have recognized that harassment in one's own home is particularly egregious and is a factor that must be considered in determining the seriousness of the alleged harassment"); Williams v. Poretsky Management, Inc., 955 F. Supp. 490, 498 (D. Md. 1996) (noting sexual harassment in the home was more severe than in workplace).

In the commentary on its 2016 regulation, HUD also articulated that harassment in the home should be viewed differently from workplace harassment:[11]

> [T]he home and the workplace are significantly different environments such that strict reliance on Title VII case law is not always appropriate. One's home is a place of privacy, security, and refuge (or should be), and harassment that occurs in or around one's home can be far more intrusive, violative and threatening than harassment in the more public environment of one's work place.

---

10. Robert G. Schwemm and Rigel C. Oliveri, *A New Look at Sexual Harassment Under the Fair Housing Act: The Forgotten Role of §3604(c)*, 2002 Wis. L. Rev. 771, 786 (2002).

11. *Quid Pro Quo and Hostile Environment Harassment and Liability*, 81 Fed. Reg. 63054, 63055 (Sept. 14, 2016) (codified at 24 C.F.R. §100).

5. When Is Harassment "Because of" Sex? This element of the prima facie case seldom has proved to be a problem in practice for plaintiffs in sexual harassment housing cases, whether the harassment is perpetrated in opposite-sex or same-sex contexts. However, there are some potentially complicated questions. For example, what about an "equal opportunity harasser" (i.e., a person who harasses members of both sexes equally)? In Holman v. Indiana, 211 F.3d 399, 403 (7th Cir. 2000), a Title VII case, the Seventh Circuit denied the claims of a married, heterosexual couple who both claimed to have been sexually harassed by their supervisor at work:

> [B]ecause Title VII is premised on eliminating discrimination, inappropriate conduct that is inflicted on both sexes, or is inflicted regardless of sex, is outside the statute's ambit. Title VII does not cover the "equal opportunity" . . . harasser, then, because such a person is not *discriminating* on the basis of sex. He is not treating one sex better (or worse) than the other; he is treating both sexes the same (albeit badly).

Note that this is different from a situation, as in *Shellhammer*, in which a landlord evicted a heterosexual married couple because the woman refused to accede to his sexual demands. In that case, the harassment was based on the woman's sex, even though the consequences were felt by members of both sexes.

The focus on relative equality of treatment shown in cases like *Holman* leads to another potential issue: What if the landlord offers women *favorable* terms, such as reducing rent or waiving security deposits, in an attempt to extort sex? What if a landlord deliberately seeks out women as tenants because he hopes to target them for sexual harassment? Indeed, anecdotal evidence suggests that some sexually harassing landlords may rent almost exclusively to women. Instead of negating a female tenant's claims of sexual harassment, this might actually compound the potential claims against the landlord: For example, in Greater New Orleans Fair Housing Action Center v. Kelly, 364 F. Supp. 3d 635 (E.D. La. 2019), an FHO alleged that Kelly, a property owner, sexually harassed several of his female tenants and treated female testers more favorably than male testers in a number of tests. A former leasing agent for Kelly's properties allegedly told investigators that Kelly prefers to rent to "young, skinny, white" girls. Kelly also allegedly told a newspaper reporter that for one of his properties, he "likes to keep it with just girls." The court in *Kelly* held that the plaintiff (a fair housing center) stated more than one claim: that the defendant had discriminated against male testers "because of sex" and also that the defendant had sexually harassed female tenants.

Academics have commented on the fact that, in this sense, housing harassment cases depart from the traditional narrative of discrimination. As Professor Rigel Oliveri notes:

> In the housing setting there is no male-dominated realm from which women are being excluded. There is no comparable group of low-income male renters gaining access to housing on more favorable terms. Rather, the sex-for-rent proposition is a landlord's way of taking advantage of the low-income woman's structurally vulnerable position in order to extort sex. In this way,

sexual harassment in housing is . . . different from other forms of housing discrimination.[12]

Sexual harassment differs from other types of harassment as well. The distinction is between what scholars refer to as "exclusion harassment" and "exploitation harassment." Professor Aric Short argues:

> A neighbor who burns a cross in the lone African [] American family's yard is presumably intending to force that family out of its home. The same result is likely intended when insults and religious epithets are scrawled outside a Jewish family's house. But the landlord who sexually harasses his tenant is not intending to drive her out; instead, he is attempting to draw her in . . . to satisfy his own desire to control and exploit.[13]

Should courts view a landlord's attempts to solicit sexual activity from a tenant (or actually engaging in sexual activity with a tenant) as conduct that occurred "because of" the tenant's sex per se? Is there any situation in which a woman who submits to a landlord's demands for sexual activity would fail to prove this aspect of her prima facie case? Note that the court in *Fox v. Gaines* recognized that the plaintiff who was evicted after refusing to continue submitting to her landlord's demands for sex could state claims for both quid quo pro and hostile environment harassment, "provided the plaintiff demonstrates that she would not have been harassed but for her sex." Is there any way she could fail to make this showing?

6. What Does Sexual Harassment in Housing Look Like? Sexual harassment in housing is not a well-researched phenomenon. Only a few studies have analyzed factors such as its frequency, characteristics of victims, and types of conduct. Those reports are summarized here.

- In 1987, Regina Cahan surveyed 150 public and private FHOs across the country to see whether they had received complaints of sexual harassment.[14] Of the 87 centers that provided usable responses, 65 percent reported receiving a collective total of 288 complaints of sexual harassment. A smaller number of centers provided Cahan with specific information about the income of the victims and the nature of the harassing conduct. The victims overwhelmingly were poor, with 75 percent earning less than $10,000 per year and 23 percent earning between $10,000 and $20,000 per year. More than two-thirds of the complaints involved landlord requests for sexual activity, almost 39 percent involved abusive remarks, and 34 percent involved unwanted touching.

---

12. Rigel C. Oliveri, *Sexual Harassment of Low-Income Women in Housing: Pilot Study Results*, 83 Mo. L. Rev. 597, 623 (2018).

13. Aric K. Short, *Slaves for Rent: Sexual Harassment in Housing as Involuntary Servitude*, 86 Neb. L. Rev. 838, 841-42 (2008).

14. Regina Cahan, *Home Is No Haven: An Analysis of Sexual Harassment in Housing*, 1987 Wis. L. Rev. 1061 (1987).

- In 1991, a doctoral student in sociology named Sylvia I. Novac mailed surveys to 1,000 rental households in Ontario.[15] She received 352 usable survey responses. Of these, 25 percent of the respondents reported experiencing sexual harassment in housing.
- In 2005, Drs. Louise Fitzgerald, Linda Collinsworth, and Maggie Reed reviewed deposition testimony given by 39 victim-witnesses in three cases prosecuted by the DOJ.[16] The authors then analyzed all published federal sexual harassment in housing cases that contained details about the sexually harassing conduct (a total of 18 cases). Between the reported cases and the depositions, the researchers identified 389 separate instances of misconduct. The authors classified the majority of the instances as "Unwanted Sexual Attention" (60.0 percent), followed by "Sexual Coercion" (18.0 percent) and "Gender Hostility" (13.9 percent).
- In 2008, Dr. Griff Tester analyzed 137 housing sexual harassment complaints made to the Ohio Civil Rights Commission (OCRC) between 1990 and 2003.[17] He was the first to obtain data on the race of the victims and perpetrators and found that 68 percent of the reported victims were Black or "other women of color" while virtually all the perpetrators were white men. The OCRC did not collect specific data about the complainants' socioeconomic status, although information in the files indicated that many women were poor and in need of housing assistance.
- In 2018, Professor Rigel Oliveri published an observational study of a group of 100 low-income women to determine their experiences with sexual harassment in housing.[18] Interviews with the women indicated that 10 percent had experienced actionable housing sexual harassment. The study revealed other notable findings about the women who experienced harassment, including:
  - The women disproportionately were members of minority racial groups, with 90 percent identifying as Black or multiracial (although some of this reflected the fact that 85 percent of the women in the interview pool identified as Black or multiracial). The perpetrators were evenly divided, with 50 percent white and 50 percent Black.
  - The women were much younger than their harassers. The median age of the women at the time they were harassed was 25, while the estimated median age of the perpetrators was 50.

---

15. Sylvia I. Novac, BOUNDARY DISPUTES: SEXUAL HARASSMENT AND THE GENDERED RELATIONS OF RESIDENTIAL TENANCY (Univ. Toronto 1994).

16. Maggie E. Reed, Linda L. Collinsworth & Louise F. Fitzgerald, *There's No Place Like Home: Sexual Harassment of Low Income Women in Housing*, 11 PSYCHOL. PUB. POL'Y & L. 439 (2005).

17. Griff Tester, *An Intersectional Analysis of Sexual Harassment in Housing*, 22 GENDER & SOC'Y 349 (2008).

18. Rigel C. Oliveri, *Sexual Harassment of Low-Income Women in Housing: Pilot Study Results*, 83 Mo. L. REV. 597 (2018).

- The women all were in tenuous financial situations at the time they were harassed. The few who were working had low-wage and/or part-time jobs. Most received no rental assistance and no public benefits.
- Most of the women were explicitly propositioned by their landlord/harassers to trade sex for rent and subjected to lewd sexual comments. Half of the women also experienced serious (probably criminal) conduct such as sexual battery, indecent exposure, and home invasion.

Thus, some common themes emerge in the limited research that is available: Victims are likely to be poor and disproportionately likely to be women of color. The landlord/perpetrators tend to be older, and may be more likely to be white. The harassment usually consists of various kinds of threatening conduct (hostile environment), as well as attempts to exploit the victims' lack of income and resources by trying to extort sex in lieu of rent (quid pro quo).

7. Sex of Victim and Perpetrator. It is important to note that, even though most reported cases of sexual harassment involve male perpetrators and female victims, a sexual harassment claim can be made by a male victim against a female perpetrator. Similarly, the law also recognizes same-sex sexual harassment. In Oncale v. Sundowner Offshore Services, Inc., 523 U.S. 75, 78-79 (1998), the Supreme Court unanimously held, in an opinion by Justice Scalia, that Title VII's prohibition against sex discrimination applied to a claim brought by a man who alleged he was sexually harassed by his male co-workers:

> Title VII's prohibition of discrimination "because of . . . sex" protects men as well as women, and in the related context of racial discrimination in the workplace we have rejected any conclusive presumption that an employer will not discriminate against members of his own race. . . . If our precedents leave any doubt on the question, we hold today that nothing in Title VII necessarily bars a claim of discrimination "because of . . . sex" merely because the plaintiff and the defendant (or the person charged with acting on behalf of the defendant) are of the same sex.
>
> We see no justification in the statutory language or our precedents for a categorical rule excluding same-sex harassment claims from the coverage of Title VII. As some courts have observed, male-on-male sexual harassment in the workplace was assuredly not the principal evil Congress was concerned with when it enacted Title VII. But statutory prohibitions often go beyond the principal evil to cover reasonably comparable evils, and it is ultimately the provisions of our laws rather than the principal concerns of our legislators by which we are governed.

Although the Supreme Court never has addressed this issue in an FHA case, it is reasonable to assume that it would reach the same conclusion.

8. When Is Conduct "Unwelcome"? The unwelcomeness element of the plaintiff's prima facie case, as set forth in *Henson*, contains both subjective and objective components. The plaintiff must demonstrate that she experienced the conduct as offensive or undesirable and also that she did not behave in a manner that would indicate she actually welcomed the behavior.

It is important to note that "welcome" should not be equated with "voluntary." Put another way, if the plaintiff submits to a defendant's demands for sexual activity, as did the plaintiff in *Fox* (above), she still can argue that the conduct was unwelcome. *Meritor*, 477 U.S. at 68-69, addressed this situation in the workplace, and the Court was clear that:

> [T]he fact that sex-related conduct was "voluntary," in the sense that the complainant was not forced to participate against her will, is not a defense to a sexual harassment suit brought under Title VII. The gravamen of any sexual harassment claim is that the alleged sexual advances were "unwelcome." . . . The correct inquiry is whether the respondent by her conduct indicated that the alleged sexual advances were unwelcome, not whether her participation in sexual conduct was voluntary.

Thus, a plaintiff who submits to unwelcome overtures can still maintain a cause of action for harassment. However, the *Meritor* Court added some additional considerations to its analysis:

> While "voluntariness" in the sense of consent is not a defense to such a claim, it does not follow that a complainant's sexually provocative speech or dress is irrelevant as a matter of law in determining whether he or she found particular sexual advances unwelcome. To the contrary, such evidence is obviously relevant.

What are the implications of the focus on the plaintiff's conduct and the determination that a plaintiff's speech and dress are "obviously relevant" to whether sexual harassment was welcome? A number of commentators have criticized this standard for implying that victims are responsible for harassing behavior. *See* Susan Estrich, *Sex at Work*, 43 STAN. L. REV. 813, 828 (1991) ("[M]ost pernicious of all, since the focus of the inquiry is on the plaintiff, and since the unwelcomeness test must be met by her conduct, should we be surprised if the trial focuses on what the plaintiff wears, how she talks, even who she sleeps with?"); *see also* Henry L. Chambers, Jr., *(Un)Welcome Conduct and the Sexually Hostile Environment*, 53 ALA. L. REV. 733, 763-65 (2002) ("[A]n unwelcomeness requirement will put the burden of proving unwelcomeness on the plaintiff and create the presumption that sex-related workplace conduct is not unwelcome until proven otherwise. . . . This is problematic because, although sexual advances can be welcome in some contexts, the suggestion that sex-based or gender-motivated conduct in the workplace should be considered welcome until the employee subjected to those advances objects may not be a reasonable one."). In practice, disputes about the relevance of such evidence often are handled according to Fed. R. Evid. 412(b)(2), which states that evidence about a victim's sexual behavior or predisposition is admissible only if its probative value "substantially outweighs" the danger of harm to the victim or unfair prejudice to any party.

9. Who May Be Liable for Sexual Harassment? These cases raise questions about who may be liable for harassment. The perpetrator clearly is liable. This is different from employment cases, because Title VII restricts liability to the "employer," which typically is the company itself and not an individual.[19] In many cases the perpetrator is also the property owner and primary manager, so liability is clear. But there are many situations in which vicarious liability is possible. What about the property owner's spouse who co-owns the property? What about a corporate owner? Will a property owner be liable for the harassing conduct of a property manager or maintenance worker? How should liability work with respect to harassment caused by another tenant? Chapters 4, 8, and 10 discuss these complex issues.

10. Statutory Provisions and Sexual Harassment. As discussed at the beginning of this section, most housing sexual harassment cases are brought under §3604(b) and §3617. However, causes of action also may arise under other sections of the statute, depending on the specific nature of the conduct. For example, an actual or constructive eviction could give rise to a claim under §3604(a) (which prohibits making housing unavailable) and offensive language or sexual propositions could give rise to a claim under §3604(c) (which prohibits discriminatory statements).

C. DOMESTIC VIOLENCE

It is common for lease provisions or homeowners association rules to prohibit criminal activity or disturbing the peace. Some landlords might reserve the right to evict tenants who call the police to their units. This can result in landlords evicting people — usually women — who are victims of domestic violence in their homes. Additionally, landlords may be reluctant to rent to women who are identified as domestic violence victims out of fear that the abuser will return and cause problems, out of concern for their own liability for harm the abuser might cause, or out of stereotyped beliefs about such women. For example, one testing study, performed by the Anti-Discrimination Center of Metro New York, Inc., found significant discrimination in this

---

19. Every court to consider the issue has concluded that Title VII's exemption of employers with fewer than 15 employees means that individual bad actors are not proper defendants under the statute. Miller v. Maxwell's Int'l, Inc., 991 F.2d 583, 587 (9th Cir. 1993) ("If Congress decided to protect small entities with limited resources from liability, it is inconceivable that Congress intended to allow civil liability to run against individual employees."), cert. denied, 510 U.S. 1109 (1994)); see also Williams v. Banning, 72 F.3d 552 (7th Cir. 1995); Smith v. Lomax, 45 F.3d 402 (11th Cir. 1995); Grant v. Lone Star Co., 21 F.3d 649 (5th Cir.), cert. denied, 513 U.S. 1015 (1994).

In the Title VII context, the Supreme Court has recognized an affirmative defense to an employer's vicarious liability for hostile environment harassment perpetrated by an employee. The employer must prove (1) that it exercised reasonable care to prevent and correct the harassment, and (2) that the plaintiff unreasonably failed to take advantage of any preventive or corrective opportunities offered by the employer, or failed otherwise to avoid the harm. See Burlington Industries, Inc. v. Ellerth, 524 U.S. 742 (1998) and Faragher v. Boca Raton, 524 U.S. 755 (1998). There is no such affirmative defense under the FHA, and the HUD regulation specifically rejects the concept. 24 C.F.R. §100.600(a)(2)(ii).

context.[20] A Center staff member posing as a housing coordinator for a fictitious survivor-assistance organization called 40 different housing providers to inquire about apartments that were advertised as being available, purportedly to help arrange housing for a domestic violence survivor. More than a quarter of respondents either flatly refused to rent or failed to follow up as promised. In another 20 percent of cases, the housing providers "voiced stereotypical . . . questions and comments such as to the potential renter's mental stability and concern for safety of the renter, other tenants, and the housing providers themselves."

The FHA does not explicitly address the rights of domestic violence victims. However, because victims of domestic violence are significantly more likely to be women, actions taken by landlords against women who are domestic violence victims raise the possibility of claims based on sex discrimination under a disparate impact theory. Disparate impact theory is discussed in Chapter 7. The following case provides an example.

Butler v. Sundo Capital, LLC
559 F. Supp. 3d 452 (W.D. Pa. 2021)

RANJAN, Judge:

Ms. Butler is a victim of domestic violence and stalking by her ex-husband. When she informed Defendants that her ex-husband's behavior had caused her to fear for her life at her residence, they refused to let her out of her lease without penalty. Ms. Butler still surrendered possession of the property to Mr. Sundo, which triggered an early termination clause in the lease that accelerated all remaining rental payments. When she didn't pay, Defendants filed a landlord-tenant action to recover this accelerated rent and other damages.

From these core allegations, Plaintiffs bring claims under the FHA and various Pennsylvania statutes. For their FHA claims, Plaintiffs allege that the early termination clause is discriminatory because it has a disparate impact on domestic violence victims[,] the majority of whom are women[.]

Defendants argue that all of Plaintiffs' FHA claims fail as a matter of law for [the following] reasons. First, the disparate impact claim fails because "domestic violence victim" is not a protected class that is recognized under the FHA. Second, Plaintiffs failed to meet the "robust causality" requirement for a disparate impact claim because they have not pled facts or statistics connecting Defendants' challenged policy to the alleged disparate impact.

---

20. *Adding Insult to Injury: Housing Discrimination Against Survivors of Domestic Violence* (Aug. 2005), http://www.antibiaslaw.com/sites/default/files/all/DVReport.pdf.

DISCUSSION & ANALYSIS

I. Plaintiffs Have Adequately Pled Their Sex Discrimination Claim Under a Disparate Impact Theory.

To establish a disparate impact claim under the FHA, the plaintiff must show (1) the occurrence of certain outwardly neutral practices, (2) which have a significantly adverse or disproportionate impact on members of the protected class. Disparate impact claims "do not require proof of discriminatory intent," and "permit federal law to reach conduct that has the necessary and foreseeable consequence" of causing discrimination by burdening a particular group.

Here, Plaintiffs allege that Defendants' facially neutral policy of "[r]efusing early lease termination in cases involving domestic violence has an inherent disparate impact on female tenants." Defendants agree that their policy is neutral on its face. Thus, this dispute comes down to the second element—whether the early termination clause, as applied to cases involving domestic violence, has a significantly adverse or disproportionate impact on a protected class.

On this score, Defendants make two core arguments. First, Ms. Butler is not a member of a recognized protected class under the FHA. Second, Plaintiffs have insufficiently pled that the challenged policy caused the alleged disparate impact. After careful consideration, the Court finds neither of these arguments persuasive at this early stage of the proceedings.

A. Ms. Butler Is a Member of a "Protected Class" Under the FHA.

Defendants argue that "domestic violence victims or survivors" are only treated as members of a "protected class" for purposes of the FHA under "certain eviction circumstances." Since this "is not an eviction situation," Defendants contend that Plaintiffs cannot bring their disparate impact claim. Defendants' view, however, conflicts with both the existing case law and the broad, remedial purpose of the FHA.

It is true that the "FHA does not expressly include domestic violence victims or survivors as protected classes." Wilson v. Guardian Mgmt., LLC, 383 F. Supp. 3d 1105, 1108 (D. Or. 2019). That said, there is "substantial case law and scholarship . . . suggesting that claims alleging discrimination based on status as a victim of domestic violence are not per se invalid." Id. at 1109. Moreover, in 2011, the then-HUD Deputy Assistant Secretary for Enforcement and Programs issued a report that explained that discrimination against victims of domestic violence "because of their history or the acts of their abusers" may be illegal under the FHA.[21] These claims are not per se invalid because domestic violence victims tend to overwhelmingly be women. The DOJ reports that 85% of victims of intimate partner violence nationwide are

---

21. HUD, *Assessing Claims of Housing Discrimination Against Victims of Domestic Violence Under the FHA (FHA) and the Violence Against Women Act (VAWA)*, https://www.hud.gov/sites/documents/fheodomesticviolguideng.pdf.

women. So, essentially, discrimination against domestic violence victims is likely to be discrimination against women, and therefore the effects of that discrimination are more acutely felt by women.

Although the Third Circuit has not weighed in on this issue, most district courts that have addressed it have held that domestic violence victims are members of a protected class and may bring a claim for housing discrimination under the FHA through a theory of sex discrimination. *See, e.g., Wilson* ("Summary judgment against Plaintiff's housing discrimination claims is not warranted simply because those claims are based on her status as a domestic violence victim"); *Dickinson v. Zanesville Metro. Hous. Auth.* (S.D. Ohio 2013) (holding that use of plaintiff's status as a domestic violence victim to evict could support a claim of sex discrimination under the FHA); *Meister v. Kansas City* (D. Kan. 2011) ("[E]vidence that defendant knew that domestic violence caused damage to plaintiff's housing unit would help support a claim that she was evicted under circumstances giving rise to an inference of sex discrimination").

Defendants argue that while these cases recognize domestic violence victims' membership in a protected class under the FHA, they limit that membership to eviction cases. That is not correct. While most of these cases were decided in the context of evictions, there is nothing in those decisions that specifies that domestic violence victims can only bring cases challenging evictions. Indeed, in *Dickinson*, the court held that plaintiff could bring a discrimination claim based on defendant's act of sending negative reference letters to other landlords.

Plaintiffs are therefore not barred from bringing their disparate impact claim based on Defendants' allegedly discriminatory enforcement of their early termination and rent acceleration provisions.

B. Plaintiffs Have Adequately Pled Causation.

To establish causation, Plaintiffs rely on an array of statistics and the "reasonable inferences" that can be drawn from them. While they admittedly do not plead any statistics that establish a direct link between enforcement of early termination and acceleration clauses and a disparate impact on victims of domestic violence, they have offered enough to support the inference. That is, Plaintiffs have pled that, statistically speaking, victims of domestic violence are overwhelmingly women, victims of domestic violence are more likely to suffer from physical violence or stalking, particularly at or near their home, and victims are often in a precarious economic situation. Those facts, taken as true, suggest the following causal chain:

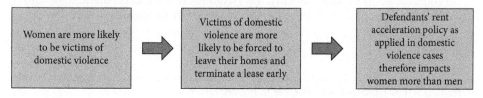

The type of statistical evidence offered here is analogous to what was pled in *Reyes*, which that court held was enough to survive a motion to dismiss. In *Reyes*, the plaintiffs alleged that the defendants' policy of requiring all occupants of a trailer park above the age of eighteen to provide documentation evidencing legal status or face eviction disproportionately impacted Latinos. In support, the plaintiffs pointed to statistics showing that Latinos constituted 64.6% of the total undocumented immigrant population in the relevant area, and were ten times more likely than non-Latinos to be harmed by the policy. The court held that, "accepting [those] statistics as true," the plaintiffs "sufficiently alleged a prima facie case of disparate impact." The court reached that decision because the statistical evidence suggested that "the specific Policy requiring all adult Park tenants to provide certain documents providing legal status was likely to cause Latino tenants at the Park to be disproportionately subject to eviction compared to non-Latino tenants at the Park."

As was the case in *Reyes*, the statistics Plaintiffs pled in the complaint are enough to satisfy the robust causality requirement set forth in *Inclusive Communities*, at least at the pleading stage. As a result, the Court will deny Defendants' motion to dismiss Plaintiffs' disparate impact claim.

NOTES AND QUESTIONS

1. Housing and Domestic Violence. Domestic violence harms women's ability to obtain and maintain housing in a number of ways. As described by Leonora Lapidus in an early and influential article:

> [A]s a result of mandatory arrest policies and courts issuing mutual orders of protection, battered women may actually show up on these record checks as the perpetrator of the violence. A second problem that battered women face at the admissions stage is that as a result of the domestic violence, they may not have solid work histories, credit, or references because the batterer has prevented them from holding a steady job, from maintaining a bank account, or from developing relationships with others, each of which may be a strike against them in the application process and may lead landlords to decline their applications.[22]

Women who, like the plaintiffs in the cases featured above, are living with their partners at the time of the abuse, may be evicted or prevented from terminating a lease so that they can move. As Lapidus further notes:

> [I]n many cases only the husband's name is listed on the lease, leading the housing authority to assert that it cannot evict the abuser and allow the victim to continue her occupancy. Finally, the victim is often held accountable for the acts of the abuser and is required to pay for property damage that he caused.

---

22. Leonora Lapidus, *Doubly Victimized: Housing Discrimination Against Victims of Domestic Violence*, 11 Am. U.J. Gender Soc. Pol'y & L. 377, 385 (2003).

Finally, even without discrimination, the financial disruptions caused by domestic violence — the need to find new housing, the loss of the abuser's income — can lead victims to become homeless. Indeed, numerous studies have found a strong correlation between domestic violence and homelessness.[23]

2. Federally Subsidized Housing Policy. *Butler* cited a 2011 HUD memo suggesting that discrimination against domestic violence victims may be illegal. However, for many years, federal housing policy contributed to the problem. In 1988, in reaction to concerns about violent crime and drug activity in public and subsidized housing, Congress passed the Anti-Drug Abuse Act, 42 U.S.C. §11901. The Act required managers of subsidized and public housing to take steps to rid their properties of drug use or other criminal activity. In 1996 Congress passed the Housing Opportunity Program Extensions (HOPE) Act, 42 U.S.C. §1437d(l)(6), which broadened the power of public housing authorities to evict entire households where any household member or guest "or other person under the tenant's control" engaged in drug-related criminal activity, on or off the premises.

Housing authorities around the country implemented so-called "One-Strike" policies. Such policies were upheld by the Supreme Court in HUD v. Rucker, 535 U.S. 125 (2002). *Rucker* involved four elderly public housing residents who were evicted after younger members of their households or guests were found with drugs (in one case, the resident's daughter was caught with drugs three blocks from her apartment; in another, a bedridden resident's caregiver used drugs in the resident's apartment). The plaintiffs challenged their evictions, arguing that the policy did not give housing authorities the discretion to evict residents for situations in which the residents "did not know, could not foresee, or could not control behavior by other occupants of the unit." The Court disagreed, holding that the plain language of the statute provided otherwise, and that, regardless, "a tenant who 'cannot control drug crime, or other criminal activities by a household member which threaten health or safety of other residents, is a threat to other residents and the project.'" *Id.* at 134 (citing HUD regulations).

Although the HOPE Act and *Rucker* were primarily concerned with drugs and related criminal activity, One-Strike policies led to domestic violence victims being evicted from public and voucher-based housing. Examples of claims based on such evictions include Dickinson v. Zanesville Metropolitan Housing Authority, 975 F. Supp. 2d 863 (S.D. Ohio 2013), and Meister v. Kansas City, Kansas Housing Authority, No. 09-2544-EFM, 2011 WL 765887 (D. Kan. Feb. 25, 2011).

---

23. Congress made findings to this effect at 34 U.S.C. §12471. The U.S. Department of Health and Human Services maintains a helpful compilation of research studies on this subject, which can be found at Office of Family Violence Prevention and Services, https://www.acf.hhs.gov /ofvps/fact-sheet/domestic-violence-and-homelessness-statistics-2016 (last visited October 19, 2024).

Eventually, Congress and HUD recognized that domestic violence victims were being evicted unjustly and that families experiencing domestic violence had needs that were not being addressed by those administering federal housing programs. In 2005 and 2013 Congress revised the Violence Against Women Act to provide certain housing rights for victims of domestic violence. 34 U.S.C. §12471-91. These rights apply to public housing or units subsidized with a Housing Choice Voucher (commonly referred to as "Section 8"), as well as other housing programs funded through HUD. The law provides a host of protections, including:

- Covered housing providers cannot discriminate against victims of domestic violence in admission to or eviction from housing if the victims otherwise meet the qualifications for housing.
- Being a victim of domestic violence cannot be considered a lease violation under a housing program or good cause for termination.
- Covered providers can bifurcate leases, allowing them to keep the victim on the lease while evicting the perpetrator of domestic violence.
- If the perpetrator is the only tenant receiving assistance under a housing program, the landlord must provide the remaining tenant/the survivor the opportunity to establish their eligibility to remain in the house.
- Covered housing providers must create an emergency transfer plan for victims of domestic violence, which allows them to transfer to another "available and safe dwelling unit" if requested.

On November 16, 2016, HUD published its "VAWA Final Rule," 81 Fed. Reg. 80724, implementing the requirements of the 2013 amendments to VAWA.[24]

3. Municipal Anti-Nuisance Laws. Many municipalities around the country have anti-nuisance ordinances that prescribe civil penalties against property owners who allow harmful, dangerous, or noxious conditions to exist on their property. If the conditions are not abated, or recur, the owner can be fined or suffer revocation of the occupancy permit for the property. While such ordinances initially focused on hazardous or offensive physical conditions, in recent decades these provisions also have operated to ensure that properties are not used as drug houses or sites for other criminal activity. Under such regimes, a "dangerous" or "noxious" condition may be defined as a peace disturbance or repeated calls to law enforcement. Anti-nuisance ordinances can also be used as a way of imposing costs for the use of municipal services.

Such ordinances are sometimes used against victims of domestic violence, and indeed some are explicitly written to make clear that they apply in this way. For example, the City of Maplewood, Missouri, had an ordinance that defined "nuisance" as "[m]ore than two instances within a 180-day period of

---

24. Implementing regulations can be found at 24 C.F.R. Part 5, Subpart L, Protection for Victims of Domestic Violence, Dating Violence, Sexual Assault, or Stalking, as well as various subparts of 24 C.F.R. Parts 905, 960, 966, 982, and 983.

incidents of peace disturbance or domestic violence resulting in calls to . . . the police." Watson v. City of Maplewood, Mo., No. 4:17CV1268 JCH, 2017 WL 4758960 (E.D. Mo. Oct. 10, 2017). The city invoked the ordinance to force a woman, Rosetta Watson, to vacate an apartment that she was renting because she called the police repeatedly after being assaulted by her former boyfriend. The city further ordered that Watson could not occupy any dwelling units in the city for six months, effectively banning her. As a result, she lost her housing voucher. Watson challenged the City's actions in federal court under a variety of constitutional arguments, with mixed success. Interestingly, she did not pursue a claim under the FHA. If she had, what do you think the outcome would have been? In a companion case, an FHO sought to challenge Maplewood's ordinance under the FHA, alleging that it had a disparate impact on Black people, women, and people with disabilities, and pointing to 43 instances of enforcement against members of those groups. The court granted the City's motion to dismiss, holding that "at best the statistical evidence merely shows an imbalance resulting from enforcement of the ordinance," and that the plaintiff had failed to allege that the ordinance *caused* the disparity. *See* Metropolitan St. Louis Equal Housing and Opportunity Council v. City of Maplewood, Mo., No. 4:17CV886 RLW, 2017 WL 6278882, at *5 (E.D. Mo. Dec. 8, 2017). (Chapter 7 discusses the standards for adjudicating disparate impact claims under the FHA.)

Municipalities may use their ordinances to exert pressure on landlords to evict tenants who have experienced domestic violence. Professors Matthew Desmond and Nicol Valdez reviewed every nuisance property citation issued by police in Milwaukee, Wisconsin, during a two-year period.[25] They found that 31 percent of all nuisance citations in Milwaukee were triggered by domestic violence and that in 83 percent of domestic-violence-related citations the landlords either evicted or threatened to evict the tenant if she continued to call 911. The majority of tenants threatened with eviction were victims rather than abusers. This led the professors to conclude that "[t]he nuisance property ordinance has the effect of forcing abused women to choose between calling the police on their abusers (only to risk eviction) or staying in their apartments (only to risk more abuse)."

Advocates have challenged these laws using a variety of legal claims, including procedural and substantive due process, denial of the right to petition the government for redress, Equal Protection, and state and federal fair housing law. As this text goes to press (2024), we are not aware that any of these challenges has resulted in a published legal opinion.

4. State Laws Protecting Domestic Violence Victims. A number of states have enacted laws prohibiting discrimination against tenants because they are victims of domestic violence. Many more states offer victims other protections,

---

25. Matthew Desmond & Nicol Valdez, *Unpolicing the Urban Poor: Consequences of Third-Party Policing for Inner-City Women*, 78 Am. Sociological Rev. 117 (2012).

which can include an eviction defense if the landlord tries to evict the victim because the abuser committed a crime or lease violation at the rental unit; barring landlords from limiting a tenant's right to call for police or emergency assistance; requiring landlords to change locks where tenants have provided documentation of domestic violence; permitting courts to exclude the abuser from housing and grant possession of property to the victim; and requiring that landlords permit early lease termination without further obligation to pay rent where tenants provide landlords with documentation of domestic violence. The National Housing Law Project maintains a compendium of such laws, by state and locality, that it updates regularly.[26]

5. Domestic Violence Shelters and Zoning. People fleeing domestic violence may need to leave their homes quickly. They might not have new housing lined up and could need to keep their whereabouts concealed from their abusers. Domestic violence shelters meet this need. Because such shelters are residential in nature and allow a number of unrelated people to live in a single home on a transitional basis, they are vulnerable to the argument that they do not comport with single-family zoning ordinances. If a municipality refuses to grant a variance or special use permit to allow a domestic violence shelter to operate, this could lead to a sex-based disparate impact challenge. If domestic violence shelters are treated differently from other types of shelters, this also may provide grounds for a challenge based on intentional discrimination.

For example, in Doe v. City of Butler, 892 F.2d 315, 323-24 (3d Cir. 1989), the issue was whether the city's six-person limit for transitional housing, which would impede the operation of domestic violence shelters, violated the FHA. The court denied the plaintiffs' sex discrimination claim, holding that "the fact that the ordinance will have an impact on group homes established for abused women does not alone establish discriminatory effect, because the resident limitation would have a comparable effect on males if the transitional dwelling was established for a different group, such as, for example, recovering male alcoholics." The court left open, however, the possibility that such a restriction could violate the FHA's prohibition against familial status discrimination:

> Plaintiffs argue that the across-the-board restriction on the number of residents who may occupy a transitional dwelling operates to limit or exclude women with children in violation of the familial status provision of Title VIII. Although the dissent argues that the legislative history indicates that the Act is designed to protect the individual family unit, we are not prepared to rule in the first instance that the Act is inapplicable to plaintiffs' situation. The dissent's statutory interpretation is plausible, but it fails to answer plaintiffs' argument, supported by the testimony, that it is not economically feasible to have a transitional dwelling for abused women limited to six residents. If children are counted for that purpose, it will, plaintiffs claim, violate amended Title VIII

---

26. Housing Rights of Domestic Violence and Sexual Assault Survivors: A State and Local Law Compendium (2024), https://www.nhlp.org/wp-content/uploads/2024-NHLP-Compendium-of-Housing-Rights-for-DVS.pdf.

by adversely affecting the ability of abused mothers to bring their children with them when seeking refuge. We cannot discount the possibility that the six-person limit may in fact have a general dampening effect on the ability of women with children to take advantage of transitional dwellings.

D. SEXUAL ORIENTATION AND GENDER IDENTITY

Housing discrimination is a barrier for LGBTQ+ individuals. In 2017, the Urban Institute conducted a multistate, in-person testing project, the most significant such project to date at the time of this writing.[27] The researchers found that gay men posing as homeseekers were told about fewer units and quoted higher rental fees than straight testers were. Transgender testers were less likely to be told about available units, or were told about fewer units, than cisgender testers were. Another nationwide study noted an intersectional effect: Same-sex couples generally were told about fewer units than heterosexual couples were, but Black same-sex couples were treated even worse than white same-sex couples were.[28]

The problem is particularly acute for older LGBTQ+ individuals seeking to live in facilities for seniors. In 2014, a national investigation found that 48 percent of older LGBTQ people inquiring about housing in a senior living facility experienced "adverse, differential treatment" and significant discrimination, including being given less information about available units, being charged higher fees, and being denied housing outright.[29] LGBTQ+ seniors might also experience harassment at the hands of fellow facility residents or management.[30]

Sexual orientation and gender identity are not explicitly stated in the list of protected characteristics in the FHA. They are not among the listed characteristics in Title VII, either. For years, housing and employment plaintiffs who wished to bring claims based on sexual orientation or gender identity discrimination would attempt to bring the claims as sex discrimination. Some courts allowed such claims if they could be described as discrimination based on impermissible sex stereotyping. Others allowed such claims under an

---

27. Diane K. Levy et al., *A Paired-Testing Pilot Study of Housing Discrimination Against Same-Sex Couples and Transgender Individuals*, viii, xiii (Urban Inst. 2017), https://www.urban.org/sites/default/files/publication/91486/2017.06.27_hds_lgt_final_report_report_finalized_0.pdf.

28. David Schwegman, *Rental Market Discrimination Against Same-Sex Couples: Evidence from a Pairwise-Matched Email Correspondence Test*, 29 Hous. Pol'y Debate 250, 251 (2019).

29. *Opening Doors: An Investigation of Barriers to Senior Housing for Same-Sex Couples*, Equal Rts. Ctr. 5 (2014), https://equalrightscenter.org/wp-content/uploads/senior_housing_report.pdf.

30. For example, in Wetzel v. Glen St. Andrew Living Community, LLC, 901 F.3d 856 (7th Cir. 2018), a lesbian woman alleged severe harassment by fellow residents of her senior living community, including threats, slurs, and physical violence. She also alleged that the community's managers were aware of the harassment and did nothing to stop it, and at times harassed her as well.

associational causation theory, specifically, that plaintiffs were discriminated against because of the sex of their partners. Others rejected these arguments entirely and dismissed such claims as not supported by statute.

Walsh v. Friendship Village of South County, 352 F. Supp. 3d 920, 924 (E.D. Mo. 2019), provides an example of a court refusing to credit either argument. In that case, Mary Walsh and Beverly Nance, a married, same-sex couple, were hoping to move to a senior living community called Friendship Village. After submitting a deposit and putting their names on the waitlist for a unit, they were contacted by the Village's Resident Coordinator and told that Friendship Village's Cohabitation Policy did not permit the couple to share a unit there. They filed a complaint alleging discrimination on the basis of sex in violation of the FHA. Each plaintiff alleged that that she was denied housing at Friendship Village

> because of her own sex (female) and because of the sex of her spouse (female), since if either Plaintiff had been a man married to a woman, they would not have been denied housing. Furthermore, Defendants denied Plaintiffs housing because they do not conform to traditional sex stereotypes, including that a married woman should be in a different-sex relationship; that a married woman's spouse should be a man; and that women should be attracted to and form relationships with men, not women.

The court rejected their first argument, holding that sexual orientation rather than sex was at the heart of their claims. The court recognized that gender stereotyping can violate civil rights laws but rejected attempts to use a sex-stereotyping theory to bring "what is in essence a claim for discrimination on the basis of sexual orientation."

Shortly after the decision in *Walsh*, the Supreme Court decided Bostock v. Clayton County, Georgia, 590 U.S. 644, 660-62 (2020). *Bostock* was actually a trio of cases that presented the question whether employment discrimination on the bases of sexual orientation and gender identity constituted sex discrimination in violation of Title VII. The Court held that it did, in an opinion written by Justice Neil Gorsuch:

> The statute's message for our cases is equally simple and momentous: An individual's homosexuality or transgender status is not relevant to employment decisions. That's because it is impossible to discriminate against a person for being homosexual or transgender without discriminating against that individual based on sex. Consider, for example, an employer with two employees, both of whom are attracted to men. The two individuals are, to the employer's mind, materially identical in all respects, except that one is a man and the other a woman. If the employer fires the male employee for no reason other than the fact he is attracted to men, the employer discriminates against him for traits or actions it tolerates in his female colleague. Put differently, the employer intentionally singles out an employee to fire based in part on the employee's sex, and the affected employee's sex is a but-for cause of his discharge. Or take an employer who fires a transgender person who was identified as a male at birth but who now identifies as a female. If the employer retains an otherwise identical employee who was identified as female at birth, the employer intentionally penalizes a person identified as male at birth for traits or actions that

it tolerates in an employee identified as female at birth. Again, the individual employee's sex plays an unmistakable and impermissible role in the discharge decision. . . . [H]omosexuality and transgender status are inextricably bound up with sex. Not because homosexuality or transgender status are related to sex in some vague sense or because discrimination on these bases has some disparate impact on one sex or another, but because to discriminate on these grounds requires an employer to intentionally treat individual employees differently because of their sex.

. . . For an employer to discriminate against employees for being homosexual or transgender, the employer must intentionally discriminate against individual men and women in part because of sex. That has always been prohibited by Title VII's plain terms—and that "should be the end of the analysis."

NOTES AND QUESTIONS

1. The Aftermath of *Bostock*. The *Walsh* plaintiffs were pursuing an appeal when *Bostock* was decided. Even though *Bostock* dealt with a different statute, the Eighth Circuit vacated the judgment of the district court and remanded the case for further proceedings in light of the opinion. No: 19-1395, 2020 WL 5361010 (8th Cir. July 2, 2020). The case eventually settled.

On January 20, 2021, President Biden issued an executive order addressing *Bostock* and directing federal agencies to enforce the law in a manner consistent with that opinion. Executive Order 13,988, 86 FED. REG. 7023 (Jan. 20, 2021). HUD was the first agency to do so. HUD's Office of Fair Housing and Equal Opportunity (FHEO) issued a memorandum stating that, in light of the executive order and *Bostock*, it would begin enforcing the FHA to combat discrimination on the basis of sexual orientation and gender identity as a form of sex discrimination.[31]

This memo applies only to HUD and does not bind courts, but it is still significant for a number of reasons. First, the Supreme Court and lower courts have said that since Congress has charged HUD with enforcement of the FHA, HUD's interpretation of the statute is entitled to some weight. Second, HUD itself processes a significant number of administrative housing discrimination complaints. Finally, the memo affects state and local agencies that enter into agreements with HUD under its Fair Housing Assistance Program (FHAP). Such agencies process the majority of administrative housing discrimination complaints filed in the United States. They can receive funding and technical support for processing state housing discrimination claims only so long as the law of their state is certified as "substantially equivalent" to the federal FHA. Thus, FHAP agencies may be risking their substantially equivalent status if

---

31. Implementation of Executive Order 13988 on the Enforcement of the Fair Housing Act (Feb. 11, 2021), https://www.hud.gov/sites/dfiles/PA/documents/HUD_Memo_EO13 988.pdf.

they do not operate in a manner consistent with the 2021 Executive Order, HUD's enforcement memorandum, and *Bostock*.

2. *Bostock*'s Reasoning. Justice Gorsuch's analysis in *Bostock* relied on a but-for causation argument: "a but-for-test directs us to change one thing at a time and see if the outcome changes. If it does, we have found a but-for cause." Thus, discrimination on the basis of sexual orientation is "because of" sex if by changing the sex of the plaintiff (that is, if a woman attracted to women were instead a man attracted to women), the discriminatory treatment would not occur. Labels and additional intentions based on sexual orientation and gender identity bias "cannot make a difference" because "but-for" causation does not require a showing of a "sole" cause. "Often, events have multiple but-for causes. . . . It doesn't matter if other factors besides the plaintiff's sex contributed to the decision."

The counterargument—accepted by the court in *Walsh*—is that discrimination based on sexual orientation is *not* sex discrimination, because it applies equally to men and women. The Court in *Bostock* firmly rejects this logic because "in *both* cases the employer fires an individual in part because of sex. Instead of avoiding Title VII exposure, this employer doubles it." In other words, an employer "cannot escape liability by demonstrating that it treats males and females comparably as groups." Of course, it is well-established that discrimination against interracial couples is unlawful, even though this would apply equally to people of all races.

Elsewhere in the opinion Justice Gorsuch dismissed the objection that Congress almost certainly did not intend for the word "sex" to include the concept of "sexual orientation" when it included the term in Title VII. It is difficult to know exactly what the 535 voting members of Congress were thinking when they adopted the amendment adding sex to the bill that would become Title VII (see footnote 1, above). However, in 1964 few people would have interpreted the word in this way. Congress itself has failed repeatedly to amend Title VII to add explicit protections based on sexual orientation or gender identity (although Congress's failure to take action is an uncertain basis for conclusions about Congressional intent). Nevertheless, Justice Gorsuch used textualist reasoning to conclude, in essence, that the word "sex" carries this inclusive meaning whether Congress intended for it to or not: "[W]hen the meaning of the statute's terms is plain, our job is at an end. The people are entitled to rely on the law as written, without fearing that courts might disregard its plain terms based on some extratextual consideration."[32] He also cited the Court's decision in *Oncale v. Sundowner Offshore Services*, discussed in Section B, above, which held that Title VII's prohibition against sex

---

32. 590 U.S. at 674. Justice Gorsuch added that "to refuse enforcement . . . because the parties before us happened to be unpopular at the time of the law's passage . . . would not only require us to abandon our role as interpreters of statutes; it would tilt the scales of justice in favor of the strong or popular and neglect the promise that all persons are entitled to the benefit of the law's terms." 590 U.S. at 677-78.

discrimination could include same-sex sexual harassment, even though this probably was not what Congress had intended when it included "sex" in Title VII.

3. Employment and Housing, Part II. Note that once again employment discrimination law serves as a guide for interpreting the FHA. An earlier note in this chapter discusses potential difficulties with courts reflexively using the same standards for determining "severe or pervasive" conduct in the housing context as in the employment context. Are there similar concerns with courts using *Bostock's* reasoning to interpret "because of sex" in the FHA? Professor Rigel Oliveri argues that there are not:

> [T]here is no reason why Bostock's interpretation of "because of sex" in Title VII to include claims of discrimination based on sexual orientation or gender identity should not apply equally to the FHA. There is no relevant contextual difference to support a distinction, either as a factual or a legal matter, nor is there any policy justification or historical reason to do so. The similarities in the language, structure, and purpose of Title VII and the FHA support the application of Bostock's reasoning to the housing context.[33]

4. Religious Defense? In *Walsh,* the defendant retirement community asserted a faith-based objection to allowing the plaintiffs to live together in a single unit. Religious objections have been a consistent issue with the expansion of rights and protections for LGBTQ+ individuals. The argument is that prohibitions against discrimination based on sexual orientation and gender identity might conflict with some people's sincerely held religious beliefs, and thus implicate a First Amendment free exercise right. Indeed, in *Bostock,* Justice Gorsuch explicitly left open the possibility that employers might be able to assert religious beliefs as a defense:

> [T]he Religious Freedom Restoration Act of 1993 (RFRA) . . . prohibits the federal government from substantially burdening a person's exercise of religion unless it demonstrates that doing so both furthers a compelling governmental interest and represents the least restrictive means of furthering that interest. Because RFRA operates as a kind of super statute, displacing the normal operation of other federal laws, it might supersede Title VII's commands in appropriate cases.[34]

Note that the FHA has its own exception for religious entities, which are permitted to favor co-religionists, but not to discriminate on the basis of other protected characteristics. 42 U.S.C. §3607. Additionally, as discussed in Chapter 5, the FHA contains other exceptions for small landlords who live in close proximity to their tenants. 42 U.S.C. §3603(b)(2). Are these protections enough to safeguard the free exercise rights of landlords? Under what circumstances should a corporate provider of housing like Friendship Village

---

33. Rigel C. Oliveri, *Sexual Orientation and Gender Identity Discrimination Claims Under the FHA After* Bostock v. Clayton County, 69 U. KAN. L. REV. 409, 435-36 (2021).
34. 590 U.S. at 682.

that wishes to deny housing to gay or transgender individuals on religious grounds be able to claim an exemption from the FHA? *See* Burwell v. Hobby Lobby Stores, Inc., 573 U.S. 682 (2014) (holding that RFRA exempts a for-profit closely held corporation from complying with the Affordable Care Act's mandate to cover contraception in employee health insurance plans). *But cf.* Masterpiece Cakeshop, Ltd. v. Colorado Civil Rights Commission, 584 U.S. 617, 631 (2018) ("Nevertheless, while . . . religious and philosophical objections [to gay marriage] are protected, it is a general rule that such objections do not allow business owners and other actors in the economy and in society to deny protected persons equal access to goods and services under a neutral and generally applicable public accommodations law."). A religious school that provides dormitories for students attempted to challenge the HUD Memorandum described in note 1 of this section, seeking to enjoin it on the grounds that it violates the school's rights under the Constitution's Free Exercise Clause and the RFRA. *See* School of the Ozarks, Inc. v. Biden, 41 F.4th 992 (8th Cir. 2022). The case was dismissed for lack of standing.

Chapter Summary

- Sex discrimination claims not involving harassment are rare.

- Claims based on sexual harassment are interpreted in HUD regulation 24 C.F.R. §100.600.

- The two types of harassment are described as quid pro quo (where a housing benefit or harm is conditioned on unwelcome sexual activity) and hostile environment (where unwelcome sexual activity alters the terms and conditions of housing).

- Harassment must be "severe or pervasive" to create a hostile environment.

- "Unwelcome" does not mean involuntary—voluntary sexual conduct by plaintiff can still be unwelcome.

- Discrimination against victims of domestic violence—either directly or through housing policies that disproportionately harm domestic violence victims—can constitute discrimination on the basis of sex due to the correlation between domestic violence and sex.

- Discrimination based on sexual orientation or gender identity most likely constitutes discrimination on the basis of sex, in accordance with the Supreme Court's opinion in *Bostock v. Clayton County*, a Title VII case.

CHAPTER 16

FAMILIAL STATUS

Congress added familial status to the list of characteristics protected by the Fair Housing Act in 1988, when it enacted the Fair Housing Amendments Act (FHAA). The statute defines "familial status" in 42 U.S.C. §3602(k) as:

> [O]ne or more individuals (who have not attained the age of 18 years) being domiciled with
>> (1) a parent or other person having legal custody of such individual or individuals; or
>> (2) the designee of such parent or other person having such custody, with the written permission of such parent or other person.

The statute goes on to specify that these protections apply to any person who is pregnant or is in the process of securing legal custody of a minor. This last category could include a family that is in the process of adopting a child or serving as foster parents.

This chapter discusses the background conditions of discrimination against families with children that led Congress to add familial status as a protected characteristic, and the most common applications of this aspect of the statute. It then addresses the statute's exemption of reasonable numerical occupancy limits; these limits are permitted (and even required) by many building and housing codes but can create disproportionate impacts for families with children if overly restrictive. In addition, Congress enacted a formal designation for Housing for Older Persons, which is exempt from the prohibition against familial status discrimination. The chapter ends with cases involving group homes for youth, which may present coverage difficulties under the familial status definition.

A. BACKGROUND AND PREVALENCE OF DISCRIMINATION AGAINST FAMILIES WITH CHILDREN

Familial status protections were groundbreaking when they were passed in 1988. No other federal civil rights statute included households with children as a protected class (nor does any at the time of this writing). Members of Congress thought it was necessary to include familial status protections in the FHAA because of pervasive and growing housing discrimination against families with children and the apparent use of such discrimination as a pretext for racial and sexual discrimination. Two reports, included in the legislative history of the FHAA, found that such discrimination was widespread and significant. A survey conducted for HUD[1] of 79,000 rental units found that 25 percent of rental units excluded children entirely, and an additional 50 percent restricted occupancy by children in some way (e.g., by imposing maximum or minimum age limits for children, assigning families with children to certain areas within a complex, or limiting the total number of children a unit could contain). Such policies were increasing during the 1970s and 1980s, with significant numbers of new developments (one in three built after 1970) covered by some type of restriction on children. The survey also found that low-income households, female-headed households, and people of color were more likely to be affected by such policies. Another HUD survey[2] of affected families found that this discrimination had serious consequences:

- 22.4 percent of respondents were forced to move, either because they were expecting a child in a no-child unit or because their complex changed its policy to prohibit children.
- 19.2 percent of respondents reported having to split up the family, sending children to live with relatives while the parents searched for housing (of these, more than a third were separated for more than three months).
- 39.1 percent of respondents had to live with other families or relatives in overcrowded conditions because they could not find housing that would accept children.

Survey respondents also reported being forced to live in substandard housing, to live farther away from jobs and schools, and to spend more on housing because they were prevented by discrimination from living in their preferred housing. This discrimination, when combined with a lack of affordable housing generally, led to a dire situation for low-income families with children. A 1986 nationwide study[3] found that 8 million low-income renters were competing for only 4 million affordable, vacant units. As a result, more than one-third of homeless households were families with children. In some cities, homeless families comprised almost 50 percent of the total population of homeless people.

The addition of familial status to the FHA theoretically protected millions of families in the United States from housing discrimination, but it has taken some time for these protections to emerge from obscurity. A study conducted

---

1. Robert W. Marans & Mary Ellen Colten, *A Report on Measuring Restrictive Rental Practices Affecting Families with Children: A National Survey*, Mich. Inst. for Soc. Research (July 1980).

2. Jane G. Greene & Glenda P. Blake, *A Study of How Restrictive Rental Practices Affect Families with Children*, HUD Office of Policy Development and Research (1980).

3. 134 CONG. REC. H4611 (daily ed. June 22, 1988) (statement of Rep. Miller).

When it comes to housing,
little things shouldn't make a difference.

If you have children or are pregnant and a landlord refuses to rent to you, requires a higher security deposit, limits the use of facilities, or says you can only live in certain areas of a housing complex... that could be discrimination. And housing discrimination because of familial status is against the law.

If you believe you may be a victim of housing discrimination, contact HUD or your local Fair Housing Center.

Visit www.hud.gov/fairhousing or call the HUD Hotline
1-800-669-9777 (voice) 1-800-927-9275 (TTY)

Your Choice. Your Right. Your Home.

in 2002 found that of all the protected categories of the FHA, familial status was least likely to be known by the general public.[4] Only 38 percent of survey respondents recognized that housing discrimination against families with children was illegal. Twenty years later, familial status was the fourth most frequent basis for housing discrimination complaints made to administrative agencies and fair housing organizations.[5] It is not clear, however, even in the third decade of the 21st century, how aware people are of the existence of these protections. In some situations, discrimination against families with children still is blatant, as the following case demonstrates.

United States v. Louis A. Rupp, II

68 F.4th 1075 (8th Cir. 2023)

Before Kelly, Erickson, and Stras, Circuit Judges

KELLY, Circuit Judge:

[Louis] Rupp has been a landlord in St. Louis, Missouri, since the 1970s. In 2016, Laura Erwin and Mack Teal sought to rent an apartment from Rupp to live in with their six-year-old son (collectively, the Erwin-Teals or the family). Because Erwin and Teal were not married at the time, Rupp required that they file separate rental applications. Both application forms stated that no children were permitted to reside in the apartment. Erwin and Teal told Rupp they had a son who would be living with them, and Rupp responded that he would allow them to rent on a "trial basis." Rupp gave Erwin and Teal a lease that contained a "no children" clause, but he included a handwritten amendment stating that the "lease contract is being entered on a trial basis in consideration of the 'no children' clause. . . ." Erwin and Teal signed their lease, which was to expire in one year. Later that year, Erwin became pregnant with her and Teal's second child.

4. Martin D. Abravanel & Mary K. Cunningham, *How Much Do We Know? Public Awareness of the Nation's Fair Housing Laws*, HUD Office of Policy Development and Research (Apr. 2002).

5. National Fair Housing Alliance, *2023 Fair Housing Trends Report: Advancing a Blueprint for Equity* 12 (2023).

After their lease ended in early 2017, Erwin and Teal continued to rent their apartment month-to-month. Then, in May 2017, Rupp sent Erwin and Teal a letter stating he wanted to renew their lease. Erwin and Teal agreed and signed a renewal contract. Erwin and Teal were relieved to renew the lease, as it gave them "peace of mind" to know they would have stable housing while caring for a newborn child.

Erwin gave birth on May 25, 2017. It was a difficult birth, and Erwin underwent an emergency C-section surgery. She spent a few days recovering in the hospital and was in severe pain for at least a month afterward. She struggled with basic tasks like getting out of bed and climbing the steps of the apartment. Erwin planned to take two-and-a-half months off from work to recover and spend time with her newborn daughter.

But on June 12, just two weeks after Erwin gave birth, Rupp delivered an eviction letter to Erwin and Teal. The letter demanded that the family vacate the apartment no later than July 31, 2017, because the Erwin-Teals had violated the no children clause in the lease: their son lived in the apartment with them, and Erwin had "given birth to a girl who is also now living at the apartment." The letter concluded, "In light of . . . your total disregard for the terms and conditions of your lease contract; we . . . [must] terminate your occupancy." It further warned the Erwin-Teals that their "failure to comply will result in legal action."

Erwin and Teal were distraught. They implored Rupp for "a little more time, some advance notice" to move out. Teal tried to reason with Rupp that it would be "inhumane" to put "a couple out in the street with a newborn baby." Rupp responded, "This conversation's not going to happen. You got to go." Erwin and Teal were "[c]ompletely blindsided" by the sudden eviction, and it was a "devastating" and "very physically demanding" task to move out by Rupp's deadline, especially while caring for a newborn and with Erwin still recovering from her surgery. They had trouble finding a suitable apartment by the move-out date, so they moved into Erwin's father's house, which was a challenging living situation for the Erwin-Teals. Because they needed a second income to pay for rental application fees and other expenses related to finding a new home, Erwin returned to work just five weeks after giving birth—over a month sooner than she had intended. Ultimately, it took six months for Erwin to fully recover from her surgery, which she attributed to the fact that she did not have enough time to rest and heal.

The government filed suit against Rupp on behalf of the Erwin-Teals under the FHA. Following discovery, the district court granted summary judgment for the government, determining that Rupp violated the FHA by terminating the Erwin-Teals' lease based on their familial status; imposing different lease conditions upon the Erwin-Teals based on their familial status; and using application and lease forms that expressed a preference based on familial status. The case then proceeded to a jury trial on the issue of damages.

The verdict form asked the jury to consider both compensatory damages and punitive damages for Erwin, Teal, their son, and their daughter. [I]n total, the jury awarded the family $14,400 in compensatory damages and $60,000 in punitive damages.

The district court then denied Rupp's post-trial motion to set aside or reduce the punitive damages award, in which he argued (1) that there was not a sufficient basis to submit punitive damages to the jury, and (2) that alternatively, the punitive damages award was excessive. Rupp appeals[.]

Victims of discriminatory housing practices can recover punitive damages under the FHA. Quigley [v. Winter, 598 F.3d 938, 952 (8th Cir. 2010)]. Punitive damages are warranted "when the defendant's conduct is shown to be motivated by evil motive or intent, or when it involves reckless or callous indifference to the federally protected rights of others." *Id.* at 952-53 (quoting Badami v. Flood, 214 F.3d 994, 997 (8th Cir. 2000)). "Evil motive" or "reckless indifference" pertains to whether a defendant knows he "may be acting in violation of federal law," not his awareness that he is "engaging in discrimination." To be liable for punitive damages, "it is sufficient that a defendant discriminate in the face of a perceived risk that his actions will violate federal law."

Upon reviewing the record, we conclude there was sufficient evidence for a reasonable jury to find that Rupp acted with at least reckless indifference. Although Rupp asserted at trial that he was unaware discrimination based on familial status was unlawful when he evicted the Erwin-Teals, Rupp had 50 years of experience as a landlord. He testified that he managed "everything" as to the eight rental properties he owned, that he read the news "profusely," and that he researched tenants' rights issues. He had detailed knowledge of various laws and regulations governing his obligations as a landlord, and he was sophisticated enough to navigate eviction proceedings against tenants in court without a lawyer. And when Rupp evicted the Erwin-Teals, he was aware that it was unlawful to discriminate against tenants on the basis of race, religion, and disability. Notably, the disability basis was added to the FHA in 1988—at the same time the familial status basis was added to the Act. A reasonable jury could conclude that if Rupp was aware of the contemporaneously added disability basis, he must have known about, or was recklessly indifferent to, the familial status basis as well.

Despite his extensive experience and knowledge as a landlord, Rupp proceeded to evict the family shortly after learning Erwin gave birth to a second child. The evidence was sufficient to support the conclusion that Rupp, at the very least, acted recklessly and discriminated against the Erwin-Teals "in the face of a perceived risk" that his actions would "violate federal law." Indeed, the government presented evidence that Rupp continued to use his unlawful lease forms even after the Erwin-Teals filed their complaint, which had put Rupp on notice that the FHA prohibits familial-status discrimination. The district court did not err by submitting punitive damages for the jury's consideration.

NOTES AND QUESTIONS

1. A Broad Definition. Note that the definition of familial status is broad and can encompass people who are pregnant or in the process of adopting or becoming foster parents. For example, in Gorski v. Troy, 929 F.2d 1183, 1189 (7th Cir. 1991), a couple in the process of becoming licensed as foster parents asked their landlord for permission to have children in their unit (the lease they signed in 1988 prohibited children). The landlord refused and evicted them when they protested. In response to their FHA claim, the landlord argued that the couple had not yet qualified to be licensed foster parents and thus were not entitled to familial status protections. The district court agreed, but the Seventh Circuit reversed, refusing to parse the familial status language and holding:

> Here, the alleged injuries are stark: the complaint alleges that the Gorskis were evicted from their apartment because of their attempt to qualify as foster parents. This allegation is sufficient to give the Gorskis standing because, in the words of the governing statute, they are persons who "claim[ ] to have been injured by a discriminating housing practice." Even if we assume, arguendo, that the Gorskis had not yet achieved "familial status" as that term is defined in the Act, the Troys' alleged actions, at the very least, still were discriminatory[.]

See also Andujar v. Hewitt, No. 02 CIV. 2223, 2002 WL 1792065 (S.D.N.Y. Aug. 2, 2002), in which the court held that a tenant who was in the process of adopting her goddaughter had standing to bring a familial status claim even though the adoption was not finalized. In that case, the tenant had physical custody of her goddaughter and had begun foster parent training. She alleged that her landlord threatened to evict her based on the presence of the goddaughter, and this threat was the only thing preventing her (the tenant) from becoming licensed as a foster parent.

2. Disparate Impact. What sort of impact will child-restrictive policies have on groups with other protected characteristics? Recall that one of the surveys discussed above found that child-restrictive policies were more likely to affect female-headed families and people of color. Indeed, women are more likely than men to be the custodial parents of minor children. And families with lower incomes, who are disproportionately people of color, are also more likely to be renters affected by child-restrictive policies. Prior to the addition of familial status protections in the FHAA, two federal courts of appeals upheld FHA challenges to such policies on the grounds that they had a disparate impact on Black and Hispanic families. *See* Betsey v. Turtle Creek Associates, 736 F.2d 983 (4th Cir. 1984); Halet v. Wend Inv. Co., 672 F.2d 1305 (9th Cir. 1982). Note also that some facially neutral policies, particularly the enforcement of numerical occupancy limits, will have a disparate impact on families with children, as discussed in Section C, below.

3. Stated Reasons for Child Exclusion Policies. Why would landlords refuse to rent to families with children? One of the surveys cited above found that landlords generally believed that children would damage property and disturb other tenants. Do you think these concerns are well-founded? Or are they based on stereotypical assumptions about households with children? The same survey found that one in four renters without children in their household preferred not to live near children, and one in five residents of child-free buildings moved there to live in a child-free environment. At the time the FHAA was passed, child-restrictive policies were increasing throughout the country, particularly in newly built housing. Discrimination against households with children was seen in many quarters as socially acceptable. Twenty years after the FHAA, a nationwide study of Internet ads for housing documented that familial status discrimination was the most commonly observed basis for discrimination.[6]

B. FAMILIAL STATUS DISCRIMINATION AND STATUTORY PROTECTIONS

Familial status discrimination can take many forms besides refusal to rent or eviction. Other types of discrimination could include the following.

- Designating certain floors or buildings for families with children, or steering families with children to reside in particular areas: Although this does not constitute a complete denial of housing, it does deny particular units to families with children and restricts their housing opportunities, thus violating §3604(a). *See* Hamad v. Woodcrest Condominium Ass'n, 328 F.3d 224 (6th Cir. 2003) (challenging condo rules requiring families with children to live in ground-floor units); Llanos v. Estate of Coehlo, 24 F. Supp. 2d 1052 (E.D. Cal. 1998) (366-unit apartment and townhome complex restricting occupancy by children to the 100 units in the "family" section violated the FHA).
- Charging additional rent, security deposit, or fees because a household has children under 18 years of age: Such conduct violates §3604(b). *See* QBE Insurance Corp. v. Witherington, No. 08-0364-M, 2008 WL 4627453 (S.D. Ala. Oct. 16, 2008) (plaintiff who alleged she was subject to a $15/month charge by her mobile home park operator for each child in her unit stated a claim under §3604(b)).
- Advertising a preference for households without children or otherwise making statements to discourage families: Such conduct violates §3604(c). *See, e.g.,* Jancik v. HUD, 44 F.3d 553 (7th Cir. 1995) (advertisement

---

6. National Fair Housing Alliance, *For Rent: No Kids! How Internet Housing Advertisements Perpetuate Discrimination* (Aug. 11, 2009); *see also* Rigel C. Oliveri, *Discriminatory Housing Advertisements On-Line: Lessons from Craigslist*, 43 IND. L. REV. 1125, 1147-48 (2010) (nationwide review of discriminatory housing ads found that "the most common basis for discrimination—by far—is familial status"). Many of these advertisements were for roommates or housemates, who did not want to share living space with children. *Id.*

stated a preference for a "mature person" and landlord later stated that he did not want "children or pets"); Guider v. Bauer, 865 F. Supp. 492 (N.D. Ill. 1994) (advertisement stated that apartment was "perfect for single or couple," and owner subsequently told plaintiff that the apartment was not suitable for children).

- Using procedures or requirements that have a disparate impact on families with children: *See, e.g.,* Gilligan v. Jamco Development Corp., 108 F.3d 246 (9th Cir. 1997) (couple who were denied apartment because they received Aid to Families With Dependent Children, a benefit available only to families with children, stated a disparate impact claim under the FHA).

One frequent sort of familial status complaint arises when an apartment or condo complex restricts children's access to common areas or amenities, requires that children be supervised or accompanied by an adult, or applies or enforces rules against children or equipment associated only with children. Such restrictions constitute discrimination in the terms and conditions of housing, in violation of §3604(b). The mere existence of facially discriminatory rules also violates §3604(c), whether the rules are enforced or not. *See., e.g.,* Blomgren v. Ogle, 850 F. Supp. 1427, 1440 (E.D. Wash. 1993) (child-restriction rule violated §3604(c), even though defendants testified the rule was never enforced). If a tenant is evicted for failing to comply with such rules, this can constitute a violation of §3604(a).

For example, in Iniestra v. Cliff Warren Investments, Inc., 886 F. Supp. 2d 1161 (C.D. Cal. 2012), an apartment complex distributed extensive child-related rules to new tenants:

> When Plaintiffs moved into the apartment complex, [defendant manager] gave them a copy of the "House Rules" and "Pool Rules" (together, the Rules) in effect at that time. The Rules included the following restrictions against children.
>
> - Children on the premises are to be supervised by a responsible adult at all times. Resident agrees that violation of any of the above covenants . . . shall be deemed sufficient cause of termination of this tenancy by the Owner. ("Adult Supervision Rule")
> - Children under the age of 18 are not allowed in the pool or pool area at any time unless accompanied by their parents or legal guardian. ("Pool Usage Rule")
>
> In addition to the House Rules, [the manager] gave them a memorandum entitled "Unsupervised Children" to remind tenants about the Rules ("Unsupervised Children Memo"). The Unsupervised Children Memo stated:
>
> - It has come to our attention that we are having problems with unsupervised children in the courtyard and walkways of the apartments. House Rules do not allow children to be unsupervised. Resident parents are responsible for the conduct of their children.
> - Children under the age of 7 years of age are to be accompanied by an adult at all times.

- When the building lights come on all children are to be in their apartments. This is for the protection of the children and respect of your neighbors. Knott Village Apartments is a quiet complex and we must insist the children play in a place more suitable for them. ("Curfew Rule")
- If you do not comply with the House Rules you will leave us no alternative but to give you a 30 Day Notice to vacate.

The court held that these rules violated §3604(b) and (c):

> Plaintiffs have provided evidence of four facially discriminatory policies. The Pool Use Rule ("Children under the age of 18 are not allowed in the pool or pool area at any time unless accompanied by their parents or legal guardian.") does not place the same pool-use restrictions on adults. Likewise, the Adult Supervision Rule ("Children on the premises are to be supervised by a responsible adult at all times."), the Unsupervised Children Memo (children under 7 cannot be unsupervised), and the subsequent June 2011 Memo (requiring adult supervision for children under 10), explicitly discriminate against children by requiring that they—unlike adults—be supervised by an adult at all times.
>
> The Court finds that all of these rules enforce some limitation on children's use of apartment facilities. They thus "indicate" discrimination based on familial status, and violate §3604(c). An ordinary reader of these rules could not interpret them otherwise.

See also Bischoff v. Brittain, 183 F. Supp. 3d 1080 (E.D. Cal. 2016) (apartment complex policy that allowed management to call social services or police and to evict tenants if they allowed "young children" to be outside unsupervised constituted a prima facie violation of the FHA); United States v. Plaza Mobile Estates, 273 F. Supp. 2d 1084 (C.D. Cal. 2003) (age restrictions on use of facilities and adult supervision requirements constituted prima facie violation of FHA); Llanos v. Estate of Coehlo, 24 F. Supp. 2d 1052 (E.D. Cal. 1998) (defendant's rule restricting children under 18 from using adult pools was "overly broad, 'paternalistic' and unduly restrictive"); Fair Housing Congress v. Weber, 993 F. Supp. 1286, 1292 (C.D. Cal. 1997) (rule prohibiting children from playing inside building violated FHA).

NOTES AND QUESTIONS

1. Permissible Rules. Not all rules against recreation and playing will violate the law. Only rules that either facially single out children or are selectively enforced against them will constitute familial status discrimination. *See* Khalil v. Farash Corp., 277 Fed. App'x 81 (2d Cir. 2008) (no violation where complex enforced congregation rules against families without children, as well as those with children); Pack v. Ft. Washington, 689 F. Supp. 2d 1237 (E.D. Cal. 2009) (prohibition against bicycle riding, skating, and skateboarding on apartment complex sidewalks applied equally to adults and to children); Fair Housing Congress v. Weber, 993 F. Supp. 1286 (C.D. Cal. 1997) (rule against leaving "bikes, carriages, strollers, tricycles, wagons, etc. . . ." outside was not facially discriminatory and referred to equipment like bicycles that could also be used by adults).

Similarly, generally applicable rules, such as anti-noise rules, can be applied against families with children without running afoul of the FHA, so long as such rules are applied consistently against all residents and are not a smokescreen for anti-child bias. Consider In re Council of Unit Owners of 100 Harbor Drive Condominium, 580 B.R. 135 (D. Md. 2018), in which the court held that a condo association did not discriminate in enforcing noise rules against the family of a five-year old, despite the fact that the noise complaints and association's internal communications consistently identified the source of the noise as a child (including references to "romper room" and a "children's playground"). According to the court, these references to the child "were of a descriptive nature, as a means of identifying the alleged source of the noise," and not a motivating factor.

2. Reasons Offered for Child-Restrictive Rules. The FHA contains no exemptions that would allow housing providers to impose these types of facially discriminatory policies against children. Nevertheless, courts in these cases often examine the reasons that defendants offer for why they enacted their policies. Housing providers typically cite concerns such as safety and noise prevention. These justifications almost always fail, because blanket policies that target minors, especially ones that exclude families with children entirely, are an overly restrictive way of accomplishing these goals. An age-specific curfew could penalize a quiet 16-year-old returning home from babysitting, but not a rowdy adult in the parking lot. A ban on "all children's play" could prohibit a "quiet, safe game of checkers." *See* Fair Housing Congress v. Weber, 993 F. Supp. 1286, 1293 (C.D. Cal. 1997). Similarly, a pool restriction against unaccompanied minors could exclude a 17-year-old certified lifeguard, while allowing adult nonswimmers. *See, e.g.*, Iniestra v. Cliff Warren Investments, Inc., 886 F. Supp. 2d 1161, 1167-68 (C.D. Cal. 2012) ("The Pool Use Rule — which uniformly prevents children under 18 from entering the pool without an adult — is not an efficient method of achieving pool safety. Indeed, it is entirely possible that younger children might be more adept swimmers than their older counterparts."); Pack v. Fort Washington II, 689 F. Supp. 2d 1237 (E.D. Cal. 2009) (making the point about teenagers certified as lifeguards).

Even where such concerns are legitimate, a restriction probably will fail if it is overly broad or if the housing provider could easily mitigate the safety risk. *See, e.g.*, Bischoff v. Brittain, 183 F. Supp. 3d 1080, 1092 (E.D. Cal. 2016) ("The city street, fenced swimming pool, and grilling equipment could . . . plausibly pose safety concerns for young children, but the adult supervision guidelines extend beyond these areas and extend to activities other than swimming or grilling. The guidelines broadly direct managers to take action if they 'have a young child not being supervised,' without mention of any of these purported dangers."); Fair Housing Congress v. Weber, 993 F. Supp. 1286, 1293 (C.D. Cal. 1997) ("Even if [the landlord's] preference [for not renting second-floor apartments to families with children] is based on legitimate safety concerns, this does not cure the violation . . . such judgments are to be left to parents, not landlords, especially when the landlord has failed to employ a less restrictive means of protecting health and safety, for example by modifying the balcony in some way.").

In addition, child-restrictive policies cannot be justified by stereotypes about minors. For example, in Fair Housing Center of the Greater Palm Beaches, Inc. v. Sonoma Bay Community Homeowners Assoc., 136 F. Supp. 3d 1364, 1373 (S.D. Fla. 2015), the court granted summary judgment on the plaintiffs' §3604(b) and (c) claims, rejecting a housing complex's policies prohibiting minors from being in the complex unsupervised or being outside at all after dark:

> The rules restricted all children to their homes at sunset without any exception whatsoever. Defendants' justifications [of safety and crime prevention] are not legitimate because Defendants' justifications are premised upon the assumption that the concept of "safety" may be invoked—not in response to a tangible dangerous condition, such as a pool—but for the intangible purpose of general crime prevention. While the Court can evaluate a tangible threat to safety for legitimacy, such as the conditions surrounding pool access, the Court cannot evaluate the legitimacy of an intangible goal of general crime prevention. Defendants provide no concrete evidence of statistics or arrest records showing that the children in their communities were so heavily predisposed to crime that mass confinement of those children was in response to a legitimate safety concern. Evidence of this sort is what the law requires because a legitimate justification cannot be based on mere stereotypes. Furthermore, Defendants' justifications are additionally not legitimate because Defendants fail to articulate how a seventeen-year-old needs to be confined in his or her home les[t] they be in danger of injuring themselves. Finally, Defendants' justifications are also discriminatory insofar as Defendants assume that the children affected by the rule had a propensity to commit criminal acts and that the children's parents were incapable of supervision of outside activities.
>
> Even if the justifications for the Loitering Rule and Curfew Rule—safety and crime prevention—were valid and non-discriminatory, these are not rules that use the least restrictive means to accomplish their goals. If the rules were to be read in the strictest fashion, a child would not be permitted to exit a burning apartment, attend night school, or go to work at night, nor could a child exit his or her home under the supervision and protection of parents or guardians. The plain text of the rules confines children to their home for the duration of the night. The discrimination inherent in these provisions is patently obvious.

Regardless of whether courts accept defendants' proffered reasons for facially discriminatory child restrictive policies, the question remains: Why do courts consider these reasons at all? What if these types of policies targeted people based on other protected characteristics—race, for example. Can you imagine a scenario in which a court would consider a landlord's reasons for enforcing a rule preventing Black tenants from using a complex's facilities? Why do you think courts are willing to examine these reasons when it comes to children?

C. NUMERICAL OCCUPANCY LIMITS

Most municipalities have occupancy codes that regulate the number of people who can live in an apartment or house. These codes usually are based on the minimum square footage of sleeping and living spaces required per occupant. The purpose of a numerical occupancy limit is to prevent overcrowding and the problems that might stem from it, including overuse of municipal services, noise, traffic, and unsafe and unsanitary conditions. Fire safety is a particular concern. Private housing providers might also wish to limit the number of people who can occupy their units, for a variety of reasons, as discussed below.

> Since the early twentieth century, experts in engineering, design, and construction have developed model building and property maintenance codes in an attempt to standardize best practices, protect public health and safety, minimize unnecessary costs, and avoid preferential treatment of specific materials or methods of construction. The codes are written for all manner of buildings (residential, commercial, industrial) and cover topics ranging from floor coverings to ventilation, roofing materials to plumbing. One of the most widely used standards for numerical residential occupancy limitations was developed by the Building Officials and Code Administrators (BOCA). In 1994 BOCA merged with two other code developers to form the International Code Council (ICC), so that it could unify standards for an international audience.
>
> As of this writing, numerical residential occupancy limitations are addressed by the International Code Council, Inc., 2018 International Property Maintenance Code (IMPC), Chapter 4, Section 404, https://codes.iccsafe.org/content/IPMC2018P2/chapter-4-light-ventilation-and-occupancy-limitations. This section uses a formula that includes minimum square footage requirements for bedrooms per occupant (70 square feet for one occupant, with an additional 50 square feet of floor area for each additional occupant). This is combined with minimum square footage requirements for other living areas to determine the maximum number of occupants a unit should have to not be considered overcrowded:
>
> - Units with one or two occupants must have 120 square feet (sf) of living space plus a compliant bedroom(s).
> - A unit can have three to five occupants if it has 120 sf of living space, 80 sf of dining space, and a compliant bedroom(s).
> - A unit can have six or more occupants if it has 150 sf of living space, 100 sf of dining space, and compliant bedrooms.
> - There are different rules for efficiency units, which are capped at three occupants regardless of size.

As important as these codes are, they are models only. They are not legal requirements unless adopted by a government. There is no single nationally mandated building or housing code. Federal entities such as HUD and the Department of Defense use their own standards, informed by the model code. Most adoption of building and property maintenance codes takes place at the state and local level. Some states have no statewide codes, leaving the process entirely to local governments. Others impose statewide codes but permit significant carve-outs and local flexibility. Thus, adoption of standard codes has been piecemeal and nonuniform, the very opposite of standard.

Because the presence of children in a household increases the number of people in that household, numerical occupancy limitations implicate familial status. In some cases, occupancy limits can prevent or severely restrict families with children from occupying dwellings. For example, if a complex imposes a one-person-per-bedroom limit and has only one-bedroom units, such a limitation would effectively bar children from occupancy entirely. Even if children are not excluded, strict occupancy limits can force families into larger, less affordable housing. A limit of one person per bedroom would force a couple with one child to rent a three-bedroom apartment. Larger apartments are less affordable, and for low-income renters they could be completely out of reach. Nationally, the average fair market rate for a two-bedroom apartment is $250 more than that for a one-bedroom apartment.[7] Even if tenants are able to pay, the supply of apartments with more than two bedrooms is very limited. In 2021, only 8 percent of apartments nationwide had more than two bedrooms, with a majority (52 percent) being either one-bedroom or efficiency units.[8]

Clearly some housing providers use strict occupancy limits intentionally to prevent families with children from residing at their properties. Indeed, the cases reflect a number of housing providers enacting such policies immediately after the FHA was amended to prohibit familial status discrimination. For example, in United States v. Lepore, 816 F. Supp. 1011 (M.D. Pa. 1991), a couple living in a two-bedroom trailer was told they had to vacate after they learned they were expecting a child, because the family would exceed the mobile home park's two-person-per-trailer policy. The government argued that although the two-person requirement was neutral on its face, it reflected

---

7. *See* National Low Income Housing Center, *Out of Reach: The High Cost of Housing*, https://nlihc.org/oor (last visited Aug. 11, 2024). Because of the affordability crisis, many low- and moderate-income households are severely cost-burdened by rent: Nearly 50 percent of wage earners cannot afford a modest one-bedroom rental home at the fair market rent while working one full-time job. At least 60 percent of wage earners cannot afford a modest two-bedroom rental home while working one full-time job.

8. *See* National Multifamily Housing Council, *Characteristics of Apartment Stock*, https://www.nmhc.org/research-insight/quick-facts-figures/quick-facts-apartment-stock/characteristics-of-apartment-stock/ (last visited Aug. 11, 2024).

a deliberate plan by the defendants to exclude families from living at the park, which had been an "adults-only" park until the statute was amended. In ruling for the government, the court stated that it was "confident that in changing [the park's] written policy to a two person per trailer limitation, the Lepores knew that the new restriction would essentially perform the same function as the adults only policy."

The FHA provides an express exemption for certain numerical occupancy limitations that a government might impose, 42 U.S.C. §3607(b)(1): "Nothing in this subchapter limits the applicability of any reasonable local, State, or Federal restrictions regarding the maximum number of occupants permitted to occupy a dwelling." HUD has a regulation tracking the language of the statutory exemption. 24 C.F.R. §100.10(a)(3). Compliance with such governmentally imposed restrictions can constitute a "safe harbor" defense for housing providers who are accused of discrimination in enforcing occupancy limits. (The alleged discrimination can be on any basis in order for the exemption to apply, not just familial status.)

Note that this exemption only refers to *government-mandated* occupancy limits. HUD opined in the Preamble to the regulations that it believed, in principle, private landlords could impose "reasonable" residential occupancy standards without incurring FHAA liability.[9] HUD did not, however, promulgate a corresponding regulation, and it is far from clear that courts would hold that HUD has the authority to expand the exemption beyond what Congress has prescribed.

The crucial requirement for a government occupancy standard is that it be "reasonable," a notoriously malleable term that usually requires further definition. As Professor Tim Iglesias points out:

> In applying the exemption to governmental entities, courts have struggled with the meaning of "reasonable" in the context of this exemption. "Reasonable" is not defined in the statute and is indisputably ambiguous. Thus, courts must look to relevant regulations, the rest of the statute, and legislative history to determine its meaning. As the federal agency charged with implementing the FHAA, HUD's guidance, if any, would be relevant and worthy of consideration. . . . Unfortunately, HUD's guidance on this issue has been minimal and unhelpful because it has not offered a meaning for "reasonable."[10]

HUD, through its General Counsel, attempted to clarify its position regarding occupancy standards in a March 20, 1991 memo (known as "the Keating Memo"),[11] which was published in the Federal Register in late 1998. Like

---

9. *See* Implementation of the Fair Housing Amendments Act of 1988, 54 Fed. Reg. 3232, 3237 (Jan. 23, 1989) (codified at 24 C.F.R. pts. 14, 100, 103, 104, 105, 106, 109, 110, 115, and 121) (HUD's responses to public comments in the Preamble to the final rule on the FHAA in 1989).

10. Tim Iglesias, *Clarifying the Federal Fair Housing Act's Exemption for Reasonable Occupancy Restrictions*, 31 Fordham Urb. L.J. 1211, 1244 (2004).

11. Memorandum from HUD General Counsel Frank Keating to all Regional Counsel regarding "Fair Housing Enforcement Policy: Occupancy Cases" (Mar. 20, 1991) (reprinted at 63 Fed. Reg. 70256-57 (Dec. 28, 1998)).

HUD's Preamble, this memo is not a regulation and does not have the force of law. The memo provides:

> Specifically, the Department believes that an occupancy policy of two persons in a bedroom, as a general rule, is reasonable under the FHA. . . . However, the reasonableness of any occupancy policy is rebuttable, and neither [an earlier] memorandum nor this memorandum implies that the Department will determine compliance with the FHA based *solely* on the number of people permitted in each bedroom.
>
> On the other hand, there is no basis to conclude that Congress intended that an owner or manager of dwellings would be unable to restrict the number of occupants who could reside in a dwelling. Thus, the Department believes that in appropriate circumstances, owners and managers may develop and implement reasonable occupancy requirements based on factors such as the number and size of sleeping areas or bedrooms, and the overall size of the dwelling unit. In this regard, it must be noted that, in connection with a complaint alleging discrimination on the basis of familial status, the Department will carefully examine any such nongovernmental restriction to determine whether it operates unreasonably to limit or exclude families with children.

The memo goes on to discuss additional relevant factors including: (1) size of bedrooms and unit (e.g., other living areas), (2) age of children, (3) configuration of unit (e.g., other possible sleeping spaces), (4) other physical limitations of the housing (e.g., capacity of septic, sewer, or other building systems), (5) applicable residential occupancy standard from state and local law, and (6) other relevant factors (including whether the housing provider has taken other steps to discriminate against families with children).

Significantly, the Keating Memo did not purport to establish a federal standard governing residential occupancy limits. It was intended to provide internal guidance and a rebuttable presumption for HUD's regional counsel to evaluate FHA claims for enforcement, after an earlier memorandum had caused some confusion. Nevertheless, as Professor Iglesias notes:

> [T]he two-person-per-bedroom standard has become a focal point for landlords and professional property management companies. . . . Even though the identification of the two-person-per-bedroom standard as "presumptively reasonable" was only intended by HUD as an internal enforcement guideline, it became widely used. With widespread practice comes broad expectations, a sense of legitimacy, a perception of normativity, and then a force of fairness behind the standard—a self-reinforcing process. This focal point in turn promotes what is experienced as justifiable reliance that is more self-reinforcing the longer it goes on. Now, landlords and professional property management companies reassure each other that, in the midst of uncertainty, this is a reliable legal safe harbor.[12]

Professor Iglesias goes on to observe that advocates "sometimes articulated the [two-person-per-bedroom] standard without reference to the numerous

---

12. Tim Iglesias, *Moving Beyond Two-Person-Per-Bedroom: Revitalizing Application of the Federal Fair Housing Act to Private Residential Occupancy Standards*, 28 Ga. St. U. L. Rev. 619, 680-81 (2012).

special circumstances or factors that the Keating Memo itself identified as qualifiers on its reasonableness," and "sometimes . . . failed to convey that a two-person-per-bedroom standard could be found to violate the FHAA."[13] In fact, when compared with typical government occupancy standards, a two-person-per-bedroom standard often is more restrictive. Moreover, courts themselves have had difficulty determining the proper analysis for occupancy limit cases. Some courts apply disparate impact analysis, treating occupancy limits as neutral rules that might have a disproportionate effect on families. Others view occupancy limits as a form of intentional discrimination, where housing providers institute them in an obvious attempt to keep families with children out. But how should either analysis interact with HUD's formulations? According to Professor Iglesias:

> [M]ost courts do apply some version of disparate treatment or disparate impact using the traditional burden-shifting tests. However, several courts discuss "reasonableness" based upon either HUD's Preamble to the FHAA regulations or the Keating Memo. And, while no case has treated the Keating Memo as a complete substitute for disparate treatment or disparate impact analysis, some courts appear to use "reasonableness" to modify the disparate treatment or disparate impact standards.[14]

Indeed, the cases below demonstrate that the courts muddle the analysis between disparate impact and disparate treatment. Further inconsistency results from the fact that over the years and across different circuits, courts have applied different versions of the analysis for disparate impact claims. In addition, the two-person-per-bedroom standard has likely caused the law to stagnate: Plaintiffs' lawyers may be unwilling to bring cases where the residents are arguing for a more generous standard; defense lawyers may be unwilling to defend cases where the housing provider is imposing a more restrictive standard. In both situations, lawyers are likely to recommend settlement rather than litigate the issue of whether a standard that deviates from the two-person-per-bedroom standard is reasonable. Thus, the law has been both confusing and underdeveloped in this area. The following subsections grapple with the complexities of the exemption both in cases where the occupancy limit is privately imposed and where it is mandated by a governmental entity.

1. Privately Imposed Occupancy Standards

As discussed above, the exemption for government-imposed occupancy standards makes no mention of privately imposed standards. Nonetheless, HUD has stated that such limitations are acceptable so long as they are "reasonable," and, as shown below, courts take the same position. Beyond this assumption, however, there is little consistency in the cases on this issue, particularly in

13. *Id.* at 671-72.
14. *Id.* at 674.

the theory of liability to be applied. As you read the following two influential cases, consider the different approaches each court used, and the different outcomes each reached:

Mountain Side Mobile Estates Partnership v. HUD
56 F.3d 1243 (10th Cir. 1995)

Before Kelly, Barrett, and Henry, Circuit Judges

BARRETT, Senior Circuit Judge:

FACTS

Mountain Side owns a mobile home park in Jefferson County, Colorado, which was built in the 1960's. Robert and Marilyn Dalke have been the park's resident managers since December, 1989. The park consists of 229 mobile home lots, each of which is available to be leased as real property for placement of one mobile home. The park provides utilities, including water, power, telephone, and sewer hookups, to each lot.

Prior to March, 1989, the park was an adults-only park; Mountain Side prohibited any person under 21 years of age from living in the park. After the 1988 amendments to the FHA, effective March 12, 1989, Mountain Side instituted a new occupancy policy of no more than three persons per mobile home.

In September, 1991, Jacqueline VanLoozenoord (VanLoozenoord), her three minor children, and her "roommate and companion," Michael Brace (Brace), moved into a [three-bedroom][15] mobile home in the park. Neither VanLoozenoord nor Brace contacted the park management or submitted an application for tenancy prior to their occupancy. They purchased the mobile home in place. The sellers did not advise them that the park had a three person occupancy limit.

Shortly after they moved in, Robert Dalke inquired of Brace as to the number of residents in the mobile home. When Brace informed him that five people were living there, Dalke informed him of the park's three person per lot occupancy limit and told him they would have to move. Subsequently, Mountain Side served VanLoozenoord and Brace with a notice demanding that they vacate the park.

[An eviction hearing was held at which the court ruled in favor of Mountain Side solely on the ground that VanLoozenoord and Brace had failed to apply for residency in the park, and ordered them to remove their mobile home from the park. VanLoozenoord and Brace filed complaints with HUD, which issued charges of discrimination. Mountain Side elected

---

15. [EDS.—This fact was omitted from the majority opinion in the case, although readers will note that it is mentioned by the dissent.]

to have a hearing of the charges before a HUD ALJ. After a full evidentiary hearing, the ALJ issued an Initial Decision and Order dismissing the charges. The Secretary of HUD remanded the case for reconsideration. The ALJ issued an Initial Decision on Remand and Order again rejecting HUD's claims. The Secretary again remanded the case to the ALJ who issued his Second Initial Decision on Remand and Order, again dismissing the charges. The Secretary overturned the ALJ's decision, entered judgment for HUD, and remanded the case for further proceedings consistent therewith. The ALJ issued his Third Decision on Remand and Order, granting injunctive relief and awarding damages to Complainants. The decision became final after the expiration of the Secretary's 30–day review period.]

V. THE MERITS

The three factors we will consider in determining whether a plaintiff's prima facie case of disparate impact makes out a violation of Title VIII are: (1) the strength of the plaintiff's showing of discriminatory effect; (2) the defendant's interest in taking the action complained of; and (3) whether the plaintiff seeks to compel the defendant affirmatively to provide housing for members of a protected class or merely to restrain the defendant from interfering with individual property owners who wish to provide such housing. [EDS. — Long after this decision, the Supreme Court in 2015 recognized disparate impact claims under the FHA in *TDHCA v. ICP*, and HUD has issued various regulations establishing a different framework than this one for pleading and proving FHA disparate impact claims. Both are addressed in Chapter 7. Relevant here, the defendant's justification for any prima facie showing of disparate impact remains an important part of the framework.]

1. Strength of Plaintiff's Showing of Discriminatory Effect

The Secretary relied on national statistics that "at least 71.2% of all U.S. households with four or more persons contain one or more children under the age of 18 years; that at least 50.5% of U.S. families with minor children have four or more individuals; and that at most 11.7% of households without minor children have four or more persons" to determine that the plaintiffs had proven discriminatory effect. Although discriminatory effect is generally shown by statistical evidence, any statistical analysis must involve the appropriate comparables. In some cases national statistics may be the appropriate comparable population. However, those cases are the rare exception and this case is not such an exception.

In this case, the appropriate comparables must focus on the local housing market and local family statistics. The farther removed from local statistics the plaintiffs venture, the weaker their evidence becomes. There is no dispute about the veracity of the Secretary's findings of discriminatory effect on the national level. However, this national level discriminatory effect, although substantially supported by the record, is so far removed from the local arena that it is of little weight in our analysis.

2. Interest of Defendant in Taking the Action Complained Of

The second factor which we consider is the interest of the defendant in taking the action which produces the discriminatory effect. Mountain Side presented two legitimate, non-pretextual reasons for its occupancy limit: (1) sewer systems limitations, and (2) concern over the quality of park life. These overcame plaintiffs' prima facie case, as more fully hereafter discussed.

A. Business Necessity

Here, a primary constraint on the application of the disparate impact theory lies in the nature of the "business necessity" or "job relatedness" defense.

Mountain Side contends that even assuming that disparate impact was proven, it was established that the three person per lot occupancy limit was required by a business necessity and that Complainants failed to demonstrate any feasible alternatives that would be less discriminatory.

HUD contends that Mountain Side failed to rebut the prima facie case of disparate impact on the grounds of business necessity. HUD argues that the Secretary applied the correct definition of business necessity when Mountain Side was required to show "compelling need or necessity" not merely "demonstrable relationship to . . . legitimate business interests," and that the Secretary's finding that Mountain Side failed to prove a business necessity is supported by substantial evidence in the record.

The Secretary correctly determined that the business necessity standard in Title VIII cases is imported from employment discrimination case law under Title VII. However, the Secretary went beyond the business necessity test that the Supreme Court has enunciated in Title VII cases and incorrectly required that Mountain Side demonstrate a "compelling need or necessity."

When Congress amended Title VII in 1991 one of the purposes of the act was "to codify the concepts of 'business necessity' and 'job related' enunciated by the Supreme Court in Griggs v. Duke Power Co. (1971) and in other Supreme Court decisions." Civil Rights Act of 1991 (hereinafter "the Act"). The Act placed the burden on the defendant to rebut a showing of disparate impact by demonstrating "that the challenged practice is job related for the position in question and consistent with business necessity." Therefore, we look to *Griggs* and its progeny for direction.

In *Griggs*, the Court concluded that in disparate impact cases "Congress has placed on the employer the burden of showing that any given requirement must have a manifest relationship to the employment in question." The Court stated that "[t]he touchstone is business necessity. If an employment practice which operates to exclude Negroes cannot be shown to be related to job performance, the practice is prohibited."

In accordance with *Griggs* and the Act, we hold that for the purposes of Title VIII FHA housing discrimination cases, the defendant must demonstrate that the discriminatory practice has a manifest relationship to the housing in question. A mere insubstantial justification in this regard will not suffice, because such a low standard would permit discrimination to be practiced through the use of spurious, seemingly neutral practices. At the same time, there is no requirement that the defendant establish a "compelling need or necessity" for the challenged practice to pass muster since this degree of scrutiny would be almost impossible to satisfy.

Mountain Side presented two reasons for the three person per lot occupancy limit: (1) sewer capacity limitations, and (2) concern over quality of park life. In support of the occupancy limit, Mountain Side presented extensive evidence before the ALJ. In his Findings of Fact, the Secretary found:

> By March of 1989, [Mountain Side] became aware of the addition of families with children to the classes protected by the [FHA], and that it must decide whether the Park should remain an adult park or whether residency should be thrown open to families with children. At the time, there were many Park vacancies because of the limited market for an adult mobile home community. Accordingly, [Mountain Side] decided that the option of becoming a family park was a more "viable opportunity."
>
> An October 15, 1988, survey of the Park population was used to establish the new policy. According to the study, 318 people resided on 213 lots. Each occupied unit had one or two residents. Mr. Brooks and Mr. Noakes [two Park managers] opined that the condition and age of the utilities, the density of homes, and the overall size of the Park would not support more than a three-person per lot limit without negatively affecting the quality of life at the Park. Accordingly, [Mountain Side] determined that a limit of three residents per unit, resulting in a total of 687 residents, was the maximum number that the Park could reasonably accommodate.
>
> Historically, the Park experienced periods of low water pressure and sewer blockages. With a density of almost ten homes per acre, the Park is almost twice as dense as new parks which average five to six homes per acre. Mr. Brooks and Mr. Noakes believed that a population greater than three residents per home would cause overcrowding resulting in a strain on the utilities and a negative effect on the quality of Park life.
>
> In early 1991, [Mountain Side] retained QCI Development Services Group, Inc. ("QCI") and its president and principal engineer, Roger Walker, to perform a study to assist [Mountain Side] in evaluating the three-person occupancy limit.
>
> In March 1991, QCI completed its study entitled "Community Guidelines Report, Mountainside Mobile Home Park" ("QCI Study"). It evaluates two sets of concerns which affect Park residents: 1) their health and safety based on an objective evaluation of the infrastructure of the Park (i.e., the adequacy of the Park's water and sewerage pipes), and 2) their comfort based on the size of homes and lots, recreational facilities, and the adequacy of parking.
>
> Mr. Walker estimated the adequacy of the Park's sewer system based on repair records and interviews with David Ramstetter, who performed maintenance for the Park. Based on these sources, the Study concluded that sewer pipes were adequate to support a maximum of 916 persons. Mr. Walker described his figure of 916 as a "brick wall," or an absolute maximum. If the

Park had 916 residents, he asserted that the sewer system would not be able to accommodate additional visitors.

Because the recommendation that the Park be limited to 916 individuals was based on interviews with Park personnel rather than actual excavation and examination of the sewerage system, the Study further recommended that the Park conduct a "survey of field conditions" which would cost approximately $4,000. [Mountain Side] did not perform this survey.

The QCI Study also made recommendations based on its evaluation of the Park in terms of human comfort. Mr. Walker opined that the Park has "very small lots . . . [and is] crowded." Based on the assumption that most of the homes currently in the Park have two bedrooms, the Study recommends a population limit of two people per bedroom in addition to the previously discussed absolute maximum population of 916.

Notwithstanding Mr. Walker's recommendation of a maximum of 916 residents, or four residents per home, [Mountain Side] has continued to maintain the limit of three, rather than four, residents per unit. Because of the parking problems, density of the homes, and overall size of the Park, [Mountain Side] decided that the quality of life at the Park would be severely diminished if the Park had a maximum of 916 residents. Furthermore, if the Park reached maximum capacity, it could not accommodate guests, including visiting children.

Based on the foregoing findings, Mountain Side demonstrated that the three person occupancy limit has a manifest relationship to housing in the Park.

Our analysis leads us to conclude that the Complainants failed to establish a violation of the FHA. Mountain Side overcame Complainants' prima facie case by evidence of legitimate, non-pretextual justifications for its occupancy limitations.

HENRY, Circuit Judge, dissenting.

The majority holds it arbitrary and capricious for the Secretary of HUD to conclude that Mountain Side's policy had a discriminatory effect upon families with children and that Mountain Side did not meet the "business necessity" exception to the FHA. I must respectfully dissent[.]

Before explaining my dissent, I note that the majority assumes in part IV of its opinion what I believe it should acknowledge: Policies that create a disparate impact upon families with children are prima facie discriminatory. However, whether one assumes, arguendo, or acknowledges that disparate impact is sufficient to state a prima facie case under the FHA, my view is the same. Five people will be evicted from a home they purchased based upon what I believe to be an erroneous application of the law to the facts of this case.

STATISTICAL ANALYSIS

The majority holds that the Secretary erred by relying upon national statistics. However, without strong evidence showing that the relevant market differs from the national average to such an extent that the three-person limit does not have a disparate impact on families with children, I cannot agree. In my view, the Secretary established a prima facie case of discrimination through the use of statistical evidence, and Mountain Side failed to rebut that case. Unless we suppose that Mountain Side's market is dramatically different from the national average, it seems clear that its rule limiting occupancy to three-people-per-unit has a disparate impact upon families with minor children.

However, the majority holds that the Secretary must provide a statistical analysis of Jefferson County, Colorado, in order to rely upon disparate impact. I can find no authority for the proposition that the Secretary must explicitly focus upon the county housing market and family statistics when evaluating a housing discrimination claim. Without convincing evidence defining Mountain Side's market and conclusively showing how that market differs materially from national statistics, I do not believe we are in a position to conclude that the Secretary erred by relying upon census data.

BUSINESS NECESSITY

[T]he majority holds that the Secretary erred by finding that Mountain Side did not have a business necessity to engage in activities that disparately impacted a protected class. I cannot agree.

Prior to 1988, Mountain Side prohibited children from living in its park. In 1988, however, Congress passed legislation preventing landlords from maintaining adults-only properties, except under limited and specific circumstances. During the week before the legislation went into effect, Mountain Side revoked its adults-only policy and instituted a three-person-per-unit limit. After adopting this new policy, and at the suggestion of legal counsel, Mountain Side retained a consultant and initiated its study. The study concluded that the existing sewage system could support 916 residents. In 1991, however, the park had only 341 residents. In addition to being well below the limit its expert concluded the infrastructure can support, Mountain Side failed to follow its own expert's advice. The expert suggested a policy that limited occupancy to two-people-per-bedroom in each unit. Under this policy, the family in this case would have been permitted to live in their three-bedroom unit. Given the timing of the policy change from adults-only to a three-person-per-unit limit, the timing and substance of the sewer study, Mountain Side's failure to accept its consultant's recommendation on limiting park population, the fact that the population was well below half of the maximum suggested by the consultant in the study upon which Mountain Side relies, and the lack of evidence of a population explosion, I cannot agree that the Secretary erred by rejecting Mountain Side's business necessity defense to the occupancy restriction.

Finally, I believe that the majority's consideration of quality of life at the park is misplaced. Some would argue that the FHA makes an explicit trade-off between the quality of life for children and other citizens. However, Congress chose to protect children and resolved this question in favor of nondiscrimination.

From the time of *Shelley v. Kraemer*, the courts have realized that public policy concerns are relevant in housing law. Congress's desire to prohibit discrimination against children is certainly appropriate in cases of multifamily housing developments that require significant and disproportionate outlays of public resources to provide police, fire, health, and other public services. Congress has recognized that multifamily housing providers who enjoy this public subsidy must meet certain standards in exchange for entering this potentially lucrative market. The FHA seeks to prohibit discrimination against families with children in multifamily housing, and I believe that is an appropriate exercise of congressional power. I would therefore affirm the decision of the Secretary.

United States v. Badgett
976 F.2d 1176 (8th Cir. 1992)

Before John R. Gibson, Circuit Judge, Floyd R. Gibson, Senior Circuit Judge and Beam, Circuit Judge

Beam, Circuit Judge:

This appeal comes to us from a FHA case filed in the district court for the Eastern District of Arkansas. The district court found a housing policy requiring single occupancy for one-bedroom apartments to be facially neutral and therefore not to be a violation of the FHA, as amended in 1989. We reverse and remand for further proceedings consistent with this opinion.

I. BACKGROUND

Georgetown Apartments is a 156-unit apartment complex located in Little Rock, Arkansas. J. Rogers Badgett, Sr., is the sole owner, and Jean Brittain was employed by Badgett as a Georgetown leasing agent. Until March of 1989, Georgetown was an all-adult complex that had an explicit policy which excluded families with children. Georgetown also has a long-standing policy of limiting occupancy of one-bedroom apartments to one person. Appellees admitted during discovery that they also have a policy limiting occupancy of two- and three-bedroom apartments to two people.

Total living space in a one-bedroom apartment at Georgetown is 636 square feet. It is undisputed that the living space in a one-bedroom apartment is well in excess of the legally required minimum for two persons under the Little Rock municipal code [Eds.—250 square feet].

On May 15, 1989, Ms. Donna Mayeaux and her five-year-old daughter, Lauren, went to Georgetown to inquire about renting a one-bedroom apartment. Brittain refused to show Mayeaux a one-bedroom apartment on the grounds that Georgetown did not rent one-bedroom apartments to more than one person. Brittain mentioned the two-bedroom apartments, but told Mayeaux the complex had no playground equipment, and no other children of the same age, so her daughter would have no playmates. Brittain admitted in court that such information would have discouraged her from renting at Georgetown, had she been in Mayeaux's position. Mayeaux and her daughter left without looking at an apartment.

II. DISCUSSION

The district court held that the occupancy standard at issue, which limited occupancy of one-bedroom apartments to one person, did not violate the FHA because the requirement was facially neutral. In doing so, the district court applied an incorrect analysis. HUD has adopted the three-part test set forth in *McDonnell Douglas Corp. v. Green* (1973) for evaluating claims of discrimination under the FHA. The district court failed to apply the *McDonnell Douglas* standard, and therefore erred as a matter of law. The elements of a prima facie case of discrimination will vary from case to case, depending on the allegations and the circumstances. HUD has a rule of thumb that an occupancy policy of two persons per bedroom is presumptively reasonable. HUD's general rule does not mean that a single occupancy requirement is always invalid, but it does render such a requirement suspect; particularly when the single occupancy requirement is accompanied by other factors enumerated in the HUD Memorandum.

Some of the factors identified in the HUD Memorandum are applicable to Georgetown. Georgetown previously marketed itself as an "adults only" complex. In addition, Georgetown has "taken other steps to discourage families with children from living in its housing," through Brittain's representations of the disadvantages of living in the complex. The mere fact that the one person/one bedroom requirement was "applied to everybody, whether they be married [sic] or whether they be couples [sic] seeking to live together without benefit of marriage or whether they be a child [sic]," Transcript of Court's Findings, is not sufficient to demonstrate compliance with the FHA. If the result of this policy is a disparate impact on a protected class, facial neutrality will not save the restriction from violating the Act.

The restrictions at issue in this case are not governmentally imposed, and are far in excess of restrictions imposed by the applicable municipal code. Rather than authorizing any facially neutral occupancy standard, the FHA requires that a court examine the totality of the circumstances to determine whether the facially neutral standard results in discrimination against a protected class.

The district court placed significant emphasis on the fact that Brittain did not refuse to rent Mayeaux a two-bedroom apartment. There are three problems with this reliance. First, the issue is not whether any housing was made available to Mayeaux, but whether she was denied the housing she desired on impermissible grounds. Second, there is a significant increase in cost between a one-bedroom and a two-bedroom apartment. Third, Brittain volunteered discouraging information which makes it understandable that Mayeaux did not wish to view a two-bedroom apartment. A prima facie case of discrimination was clearly presented, and thus the burden shifts to Appellees to provide a non-discriminatory explanation for the restriction.

The only explanation offered by Appellees is the limited availability of parking. We find, as a matter of law, that no reasonable fact-finder could accept this proffered justification as anything other than a pretext. Mayeaux's five year old daughter could not possibly affect the availability of parking spaces. While parking may indeed be at a premium at Georgetown, the occupancy restriction is not a reasonable means of dealing with the problem. There is nothing in the restriction to prevent a resident of a one-bedroom apartment from having more than one car, and the restriction does not take into account the fact that infants will not require parking spaces. Appellees have never attempted any alternative method of allocating parking.

We therefore find that the occupancy restrictions imposed by Georgetown violate §§3604(a)-(d) of the FHA. Based on this conclusion, we remand this matter to the district court and direct that the district court enjoin Georgetown from discriminating on the basis of familial status, and that it determine the affirmative steps that may be necessary to notify the public that Georgetown will be operated in a manner that comports with the FHA. On remand, the district court should also determine any other appropriate remedy to be awarded Mayeaux.

Furthermore, Appellees admitted that occupancy of the two-bedroom and three-bedroom apartments is restricted to two persons. As a result of this policy, no family which consisted of two parents and a child, or a single parent and two children could rent any apartment at Georgetown. While there is no allegation that these policies were adopted in response to the 1989 amendments to the FHA, these policies prevent the majority of families with children from living at Georgetown, and therefore violate the Act.

NOTES AND QUESTIONS

1. Comparing the Cases. What do these cases have in common, and what distinguishes them? Both involve a private housing provider who wished to impose an occupancy limit considerably stricter than what would be required by the state and local health and safety codes exempted by Congress, and stricter than HUD's presumptive "2 people-per-bedroom" standard. The housing providers in both cases previously had operated as "adults only" until the FHA was amended to include familial status. The courts took much different approaches, though. *Mountain Side* relied on disparate impact theory, based on the plaintiffs' showing, using national data, of a statistical disparity falling more heavily on families with children. It held that the defendant's occupancy limit was neutral and did not violate the FHA because the reasons offered for it (sewer system limitation and quality of life) had a "manifest relationship to housing in the park." In contrast, *Badgett* applied a disparate treatment analysis, considering other evidence of discrimination (the leasing agent's discouraging statements) and concluding that the occupancy policy was applied intentionally to discriminate against families with children in violation of the FHA. The defendant's proffered reason (limited parking) was dismissed as obviously pretextual.

What accounts for this difference in approach? It could be that once the *Badgett* court determined that disparate treatment analysis applied, it more closely scrutinized the defendant's policy and proffered reasons. The *Mountain Side* court, in contrast, seemed skeptical from the beginning about whether the plaintiffs could even state a claim under disparate impact theory, and was willing to approve the defendant's occupancy limit despite the fact that it was stricter than that recommended by the defendant's own expert. Do the additional facts described in the *Mountain Side* dissent—including that the park was at all times well below the maximum capacity identified by the defendant's expert—change the way you view the case? Note that parties may pursue both intent and effects theories of liability, and courts may analyze FHA claims pursuant to both theories.

Consider also the tortured procedural history of *Mountain Side*, in which the HUD secretary remanded the ALJ's decision dismissing the charges three times, only to be overruled by a divided panel on the court of appeals. Despite this background, and the fact that the disparate impact framework has evolved, the case has remained influential and is cited frequently on the issue of occupancy limitations.

2. Infrastructure as a Justification for Occupancy Limitations. Note that the primary reason offered for the occupancy limit in *Mountain Side* was the burden on the park's water and sewer systems, a justification commonly offered for limiting occupancy. Capacity limits on infrastructure are one of the "other considerations" that the Keating Memo states should be weighed in determining the reasonableness of an occupancy limitation. Should a property owner who imposes a highly restrictive occupancy policy, citing infrastructure capacity, be required to make improvements if doing so will allow the housing to accommodate more occupants, including families with children? Consider the following two cases, both of which occurred in housing that had been adults-only prior to the FHAA.

United States v. Lepore, 816 F. Supp. 1011 (M.D. Pa. 1991), involved a mobile home park that imposed a limit of two people per trailer and tried to evict a married couple occupying a two-bedroom trailer after they had a baby. The court addressed the defendants' reasons:

> Here, defendants assert that the occupancy limitation is necessary to prevent sewage overflow in an admittedly inadequate and outdated septic system.
> Defendants' expert, Tom Wallace, testified that the present system is adequate given the number of lots and people presently occupying them. An

increase in the number of residents, however, would overload the various tanks and result in frequent breakdowns. Mr. Wallace further testified that alternatives to the present set up of nine separate septic systems—an on lot disposal system, a private waste water treatment facility, or attachment to the York City sewer system—would be inordinately expensive or physically impossible.

The most important factor with regard to the volume of water consumed and waste generated is, in defendants' expert's opinion, the number of people residing in each unit. Given the state of affairs at the L & L park, he stated the two person per home limitation was reasonable.

The government presented its own expert, Bruce Willman, who testified that water usage could be cut to half or more of its present level through the use of several techniques. First, Mr. Willman suggested that water meters be installed on each unit to permit the monitoring of water use and the detection of any inordinate individual use. The meters would also provide a method for billing each individual for water according to the volume used as opposed to the present system where the park pays the water bills. An individual billing program would result in an automatic water savings, according to Mr. Willman.

Second, the park could require that trailer owners install water saving devices such as low flush toilets and low volume shower nozzles. These devices alone could save over 50% in water use, and are widely available for a reasonable cost. Additional savings could be realized by the installation of faucet aerators.

Third, Mr. Willman opined that more frequent pumping of the septic tanks would alleviate much of L & L's tank overflow problem . . . and found a low estimate of $6.95 per trailer per month to pump out the tanks on a monthly basis. Mr. Willman concluded that each unit could reasonably bear three to four persons if the water savings policies he outlined were instituted.

Defendants' expert disagreed with Mr. Willman's assessment [, because] the savings would not make up for the increased volume concomitant to the rise in the number of occupants. Mr. Willman's analysis, he pointed out, did not take into account the human factor—i.e. that it is difficult to change people's water use habits despite the use of savings devices and charges for water.

The court is inclined to believe that the real answer lies somewhere in between the answers of the two experts. The court is convinced that Mr. Willman's plan would result in significant water savings, certainly to the point where additional residents could be added to each trailer. However, the court has doubts as to whether the number could double, based on Mr. Wallace's testimony regarding the human factor.

At any rate, the court is satisfied that the two person limitation promulgated by L & L is not a reasonable restriction within the meaning of §3607(b)(1) of the Act. The two person figure was arrived at with no experimentation on the part of defendants. It was instead merely a guess on the part of Mr. Lepore's father 25 years ago. Defendants now attempt to bootstrap the requirement as reasonable. However, defendants have never attempted to implement any type of water saving program in lieu of the occupancy requirement. Given the court's previous finding that the two person limitation violates the amended FHA and that the Lepores' actions in enforcing that limitation violated the Meilers' rights, the court cannot say that the two person requirement is reasonable when defendants have never attempted any alternative. Accordingly, the court finds that defendants' two person restriction does not come within the exception provided by §3607(b)(1).

In United States v. Weiss, 847 F. Supp. 819 (D. Nev. 1994), a large apartment complex had a policy limiting occupancy to no more than three people in a two-bedroom unit and no more than four people in a three-bedroom unit. The court addressed the defendants' reasons:

> Defendants respond that they have established a neutral policy of housing occupancy based upon business necessity. The physical layout of the defendant's premises is essential to an understanding of the controversy. The defendants are co-owners of Grand Plaza Apartments ("Grand Plaza") along with the Weiss charitable trust. Grand Plaza is a 652 unit apartment complex located on Koval Lane in Las Vegas, Nevada. The apartments are located in 128 buildings; 93 of the buildings contain 4 apartments and are referred to as four-plexes; 35 of the buildings are eight-plexes which are two co-joined four-plexes. Each four-plex (including each of the two co-joined units in the eight-plexes) is heated by one hot water heater.
>
> Harvey H. Irby, P.E., a Registered Professional Engineer licensed in Nevada, California, Mississippi and Arizona, examined the hot water supply systems at Grand Plaza and submitted a declaration setting forth his professional opinion:
>
>> [T]he maximum number of persons each hot water system in each four-plex can serve is as follows: (i) the gas-fired hot water heaters—which serve most of the four-plexes—can serve 11 people; and (ii) the electric hot water heaters can serve 6 people. [T]he only way the hot water systems reasonably could serve more residents in each four-plex building is for Grand Plaza to purchase and install entirely new, larger hot water heaters and retrofit the entire hot water piping system.
>>
>> Specifically, I am advised that the Government's position is that Grand Plaza should permit 18 occupants in each four-plex. In other words, the Government asserts that 18 occupants, plus their guests, should be making demand on each hot water system. . . . In my professional opinion, in order to serve 18 occupants—without accounting for guests—Grand Plaza would have to install in each four-plex an 89 gallon, 154,000 BTU/hr gas-fired hot water heater. Each new 89 gallon heater cost approximately $3,600. . . . The total cost of upgrading the present system would be $1.63 million dollars.
>
> This Court finds that defendants have shown a compelling business necessity to limit the number of persons who may occupy an apartment in Grand Plaza. For a Court to order a 1.63 million dollar expenditure to upgrade the hot water capacity of the complex to accommodate families with children would be an unwarranted extension of Congressional intent in enacting the Familial [Status] Amendments to the FHA. This conclusion is especially compelled on this record where there has been no proof that defendants intentionally discriminated against families with children and is under no public duty to furnish such families with housing accommodations.

Note the difference between the *Weiss* court's opinion of the duty owed by large property owners to accommodate families with children and the dissent's view in *Mountain Side* ("Congress's desire to prohibit discrimination against children is certainly appropriate in cases of multifamily housing developments that require significant and disproportionate outlays of public resources to provide police, fire, health, and other public services. Congress has recognized that multifamily housing providers who enjoy this public subsidy must meet certain standards in exchange for entering this potentially lucrative market.") Which do you think has the better argument? Why?

3. Establishing a Prima Facie Case of Disparate Impact. Note the discussion in *Mountain Side* of the proper showing a plaintiff must make to establish the disparate impact of a numerical occupancy limitation on families with children. Should such policies be considered to have a presumptive disparate impact on families with children, because children automatically increase the size of a household? Is it enough for a family of a particular size and configuration to argue that a policy will exclude their family and every other family like theirs, or must they make some other showing, such as what percentage of excluded households include children compared to nonexcluded households, or what percentage of total families with children will be excluded by the occupancy limit compared to households that do not contain children?

If the plaintiff is required to make a more specific showing of a particular policy's impact, what should that showing include? The *Mountain Side* plaintiffs offered nationwide statistics about household sizes and composition to show disparate impact, yet the court gave those statistics little weight because they were not tailored to the specific geographical area at issue. Is there reason to believe that nationwide household statistics will differ significantly from statistics for any particular region? Moreover, does requiring a local analysis not turn the question on its head? In other words, if a large housing provider in a rural area is imposing strict occupancy standards, this could skew the local population statistics. Further, a more refined method might be to look at renter households rather than households generally, and to further consider households at the income range suggested by the rental rate of the property in question.

Consider Rhode Island Commission for Human Rights v. Graul, 120 F. Supp. 3d 110 (D.R.I. 2015), in which the court found the plaintiff's statistical analysis persuasive:

> In the instant case, the Commission submitted a report of its expert, Dr. Calvin P. Bradford. In this case Dr. Bradford used census data to compare the impact of the Briarwood policy on "households with children that is compared to households without children when controlling for household size." Drilling down, he limited the households counted specifically to rental households, calculating the "sub-population of household size that is subject to the occupancy policy at issue" in each group (households with children and households without). He further refined the calculation by limiting the inquiry by income range of families likeliest to be renting apartments at the Briarwood level (between $900 to $1,400 per month). His data came from the entire state, as he reasoned that because the complex is a large one, "roughly in the center of the State of Rhode Island," and close to major highways, the rental market would be statewide.

What about a policy of charging increased rent for each additional member of the household over a certain base number? Compare Meyer v. Bear Road Associates, 124 Fed. App'x 686 (2d Cir. 2005), which held that charging more for groups larger than four states a disparate impact claim, with Maki

v. Laakko, 88 F.3d 361 (6th Cir. 1996), which found no problem with a land-lord's policy of charging additional rent for each occupant. The *Maki* court reasoned: "The Act merely outlaws discrimination on the basis of familial sta-tus. Under a rental pricing system that charges additional rent for additional occupants, a mother, father, and one child would be charged the same amount of rent as three unrelated individuals."

2. Government-Imposed Occupancy Standards

Government-imposed occupancy standards are specifically mentioned in the statute and can provide a safe harbor for landlords who wish to comply with them. Thus, they usually become relevant to FHA cases when, as in the cases discussed above, a housing provider imposes an occupancy limit that is stricter than what the government would require. However, government-imposed occupancy standards must themselves be reasonable not to run afoul of the law. Challenges to such standards can be difficult because courts are likely to give considerable deference to a municipality when it is exercising its police powers to regulate for health, safety, and welfare. The following case illustrates this dynamic.

Fair Housing Advocates Ass'n, Inc. *v. City of Richmond Heights, Ohio*
209 F.3d 626 (6th Cir. 2000)

Before Jones, Cole, and Batchelder, Circuit Judges

JONES, Circuit Judge:

Plaintiff-appellant Fair Housing Advocates Association, Inc. ("Housing Advocates") filed a complaint against defendants-appellees the City of Warrensville Heights, Ohio; the City of Fairview Park, Ohio; and the City of Bedford Heights, Ohio (collectively "the Cities") asserting that each city's occu-pancy ordinance discriminated against certain individuals based on familial status, thereby violating the FHA. Conversely, the Cities argue that their ordi-nances are reasonable occupancy ordinances, enacted in full compliance with the FHA. The district court, after a bench trial, entered judgment on behalf of the Cities. For the reasons that follow, we AFFIRM the district court's judgment.

I.

In 1993, while investigating another fair housing matter, Housing Advocates discovered that each of the Cities' housing codes contained what it consid-ered to be unusually restrictive occupancy standards. Housing Advocates conducted further tests and investigations in each of the Cities, and deter-mined that the occupancy ordinances were unduly restrictive and discrim-inated against families. Defendants-appellees are suburban cities located in

Cuyahoga County, Ohio, adjacent to the City of Cleveland. None of the Cities own, operate or rent any apartments.

Housing Advocates filed a complaint against the Cities asserting that each city enacted an occupancy ordinance which impermissibly discriminates against individuals based on family status in violation of the FHA. [T]he parties presented testimony from various expert witnesses.

[All three cities enacted their occupancy ordinances in the wake of the FHAA's adding familial status to the FHA. All three required minimum square footage for the first occupant and additional square footage requirements for each additional occupant. Bedford Heights and Warrensville Heights required a minimum of 650 square feet for a dwelling with four occupants, and Fairview Heights required 750. Given the size and configuration of many apartment complexes in each city, no more than three people could reside in a typical two-bedroom unit. Landlords testified that they wished to observe a two-persons-per-bedroom occupancy standard but doing so would violate the municipal ordinances.]

Housing Advocates submitted evidence regarding model occupancy standards established by the Building Officials and Code Administrators ("BOCA"). All three Cities were members of BOCA at the time they enacted their respective occupancy ordinances. Housing Advocates further established that the Cities did not conduct any formal studies before enacting their respective ordinances.

Housing Advocates consulted several land planners and housing experts, each of whom testified at trial that the Cities' occupancy ordinances are unreasonable[,] more restrictive than BOCA standards[, and failed to analyze appropriate square footage requirements]. On cross-examination, however, [one] admitted that the issue of reasonableness was debatable.

[T]he district court concluded that Housing Advocates had the burden of proving that the Cities' occupancy ordinances were unreasonable, and that Housing Advocates failed to meet its burden. The district court also concluded that the ordinances were health, safety and welfare measures, and were thus entitled to a presumption of validity. [T]he district court granted judgment for the Cities.

III.

Based on the plain language of §3607(b)(1), and the standards articulated in the legislative history, the administrative regulations and [City of] Edmonds [v. Oxford House, 514 U.S. 725 (1995) (Chapter 17)], we find that in order to qualify for a §3607(b)(1) exemption, each city's ordinance must be a (1) reasonable; (2) "local, State, or Federal restrictio[n];" (3) regarding "the maximum number of occupants permitted to occupy a dwelling." The occupancy ordinances at issue here clearly meet prongs two and three because they are ordinances enacted by municipalities that set restrictions on the number of occupants permitted to occupy an apartment. Thus, we must determine

744 Part VI Protected Characteristics: Federal and State and Local

whether these occupancy ordinances are "reasonable," and whether Housing Advocates or the Cities bear the burden of proving that these ordinances are reasonable.

A. Allocation of Burdens of Proof

Federal courts have repeatedly concluded that the party claiming the exemption "carries the burden of proving its eligibility for the exemption," and that "[e]xemptions from the [FHA] are to be construed narrowly, in recognition of the important goal of preventing housing discrimination."

We further conclude that placing the burden on the defendants in this case comports with our caselaw discussing exemptions from other statutes, and holding that the party seeking to invoke the exemption bears the burden of proving that it is entitled to that exemption.

Based on the foregoing caselaw, we find that the district court erred in concluding that Housing Advocates was required to establish that the ordinances were unreasonable, as opposed to requiring the Cities to establish that the ordinances were reasonable.

B. Presumption of Validity

Citing Kutrom [Corp. v. City of Centerline, 979 F.2d 1171 (6th Cir. 1992)],[16] the district court also concluded that the Cities' occupancy ordinances are "an exercise of the local government's police power on social legislation enacted to protect the public health, safety and welfare and, [are] therefore, entitled to a presumption of validity." Housing Advocates also challenges the district court's conclusion in this regard, arguing that FHA exemptions are to be read narrowly, and thus, the district court erred in finding that the occupancy ordinances were presumptively valid. Housing Advocates' position on this point is also well-taken. We find the district court's reliance on Kutrom to be misplaced, for the Cities are not entitled to the presumption of validity where they attempt to invoke an exemption under the FHA.

C. Reasonableness Inquiry

As set forth above, the Cities bear the burden of proving that the ordinances are reasonable. However, at trial, the district court placed that burden on Housing Advocates. Despite the district court's improper allocation of the burden of proving reasonableness, we find that based on the ample evidence presented in the record, the Cities have presented evidence sufficient to establish that their ordinances fall within the exemption set forth in §3607(b)(1), thereby rendering a remand unnecessary.

---

16. [Eds.—Kutrom involved a city's attempts to regulate the operation of massage parlors, not an occupancy ordinance. Because no constitutionally or statutorily protected characteristic was at issue, the Sixth Circuit used an Equal Protection analysis and applied a deferential rational basis review standard.]

The exemption specifically requires that the ordinances be "reasonable," and in interpreting that exemption, we must give effect to this requirement. Thus, despite the Cities' suggestion to the contrary, the mere fact that the ordinances are municipal occupancy ordinances does not remove them from the reasonableness requirement set forth in the §3607(b)(1) exemption. Thus, in order to establish that the ordinances were valid measures entitled to the §3607(b)(1) exemption, the Cities were required to establish that the ordinances were "reasonable."

We find that the following evidence indicates that the Cities satisfied that burden. First, the Cities' occupancy ordinances "apply uniformly to all residents of all dwelling units." Second, the Cities have presented convincing evidence that the ordinances were enacted "to protect health and safety by preventing dwelling overcrowding," not to impermissibly limit the family composition of dwellings. Third, [the Cities were permitted to choose which occupancy standard] was the most appropriate for that particular city, particularly in light of the fact that Congress made clear that there is no national occupancy standard. Housing Advocates suggests that only the two-person-per-bedroom standard or a different minimum square foot per-person standard would be appropriate. However, the fact that the Cities used a square footage calculation, as opposed to a total number per apartment calculation, does not make the ordinances unreasonable. Similarly, the fact that the ordinances differed from the standards in the BOCA model code and the standards suggested by the apartment associations does not make the ordinances unreasonable. Finally, the Eighth Circuit considered the issue of whether the City of St. Louis violated the FHA by enforcing the city's zoning code to limit the number of residents in group homes to eight individuals, and concluded that the code did not violate the FHA. *See* Oxford House–C v. City of St. Louis, 77 F.3d 249 (8th Cir. 1996). The Eighth Circuit concluded that the rule was rational and noted that:

> Cities have a legitimate interest in decreasing congestion, traffic, and noise in residential areas, and ordinances restricting the number of unrelated individuals who may occupy a single family residence are reasonably related to these legitimate goals. The City does not need to assert a specific reason for choosing eight as the cut-off point, rather than ten or twelve. Every line drawn by a legislature leaves some out that might well have been included. That exercise of discretion, however, is a legislative, not a judicial, function.

Id. at 252. The rationale of *Oxford House–C* applies with equal force here. The "exercise of discretion" as to whether to require a minimum of 650 square feet for an apartment of four people, as opposed to a minimum of 500 square feet or 800 square feet, is a legislative, not a judicial function.

IV.

Finally, Housing Advocates contends that the Cities' occupancy ordinances were invalid because they (1) were enacted to discriminate against families of four; and (2) had a discriminatory impact on families of four. We have applied the discriminatory treatment and impact analyses to FHA claims. However, we conclude that based on the evidence presented, Housing Advocates has failed to satisfy either of these tests, and the district court thus properly denied Housing Advocates' claim on this ground.

In support of its discrimination argument, Housing Advocates notes that the population was decreasing in each city; the ordinances were passed shortly after enactment of the FHA amendments extending protections to families; the ordinances were more restrictive than BOCA's standards; and the ordinances would prohibit many families from finding housing. We find this evidence insufficient to establish that the Cities intended to discriminate against families. The ordinances are facially neutral and apply equally to families and unrelated individuals who occupy dwellings in the respective Cities. Further, Housing Advocates conceded in the parties' joint stipulations that "[n]one of the square footage restrictions in the occupancy ordinances of the defendant municipalities facially discriminate on a familial basis." Housing Advocates has also failed to establish that the occupancy ordinances had a discriminatory effect on families as required by the discriminatory impact analysis. Further, as the Cities point out, families of four, as opposed to families of three, are not protected classes.

NOTES AND QUESTIONS

1. **Burdens and Presumptions.** Note the various burdens and presumptions that the court worked through before it tackled the ultimate issue of whether the cities' ordinances were reasonable. The court held that, because a reasonable occupancy limit is an exemption to the statute, whether or not the exemption applies is an affirmative defense, meaning that it is the defendants' burden to prove.

The court also rejected the defendants' argument that, because they are municipalities exercising their police powers, their actions are presumptively valid and the burden on the issue of reasonableness lies with the challenger to the action. Defendants' argument is consistent with Supreme Court doctrine regarding standards for reviewing economic and social legislation that does not implicate a constitutionally protected characteristic under the Equal Protection Clause. The Court has applied a very lenient rational basis review standard in these cases, in which the defendant's action will survive so long as it has any relationship to a legitimate government objective, and it is the challenger's burden to prove otherwise. *See, e.g.,* Williamson v. Lee Optical, Inc., 348 U.S. 483, 487 (1955) ("[T]he law need not be in every respect logically consistent with its aims to be constitutional. It is enough that there is an evil at hand for correction, and that it might be thought that the particular legislative measure was a rational way to correct it."); *see also* Berman v. Parker, 348

U.S. 26 (1954) (Chapter 1). Thus, many "routine" matters such as zoning and building codes and regulations of businesses, are upheld. Such was the case in *Kutrom*, which the defense invoked in *Housing Advocates*, above. In *Kutrom*, the Sixth Circuit upheld against Equal Protection challenge a municipal ordinance restricting the hours that massage parlors could operate and requiring that masseuses be fully clothed. How did the court distinguish the occupancy standards at issue here from the regulation in *Kutrom*? Was the distinction important to the outcome?

Despite "wins" for the plaintiff on the burden of proof and presumption of reasonableness, the court had little difficulty concluding that the occupancy standards at issue satisfied the reasonableness requirement. What factors did the court find persuasive? How did the court address the fact that the cities' codes are more restrictive than what model building codes would require? How would you characterize the level of scrutiny that the Sixth Circuit applied here to "legislative" exercises of discretion? How much value does the reasonableness requirement have if the logic of this case is followed?

2. Occupancy Limits vs. Family Composition Ordinances. The Supreme Court never has addressed the issue of government-imposed numerical occupancy standards in a case alleging familial status discrimination. The Court did address a related issue in a case involving a group home for people with disabilities, City of Edmonds v. Oxford House, Inc., 514 U.S. 725 (1995), which is referenced in *Richmond Heights* and discussed in Chapter 17. In *Edmonds*, the Court determined whether a municipality's "family composition" rule should be considered a numerical limitation on occupancy that would fall under the FHA exemption. Family composition rules define who can constitute a legally recognized family for zoning purposes. For example, many such rules define a family as a group of people who are related by blood, genetics, marriage, or adoption. Typically, ordinances include some number of unrelated individuals who also can be considered a "family" for cohabitation purposes, but cap this at a maximum number. While numerical occupancy limits are intended to prevent overcrowding, family composition ordinances are meant, somewhat circularly, to preserve the "single-family" character of housing by preventing large groups of unrelated adults (e.g., college students) from living in neighborhoods designed for families. The *Edmonds* Court held that family composition rules are distinct from numerical occupancy rules, even though they may define family in part by imposing limits on the number of unrelated people who can reside together in a household. Thus, according to *Edmonds*, family composition rules are not covered by the FHA's exemption for reasonable occupancy limits.

D. THE "HOUSING FOR OLDER PERSONS" EXEMPTION

When it was considering amending the FHA, Congress recognized that many senior citizens wish to live in senior-oriented communities and that the prohibition against familial status discrimination would reduce the availability of senior housing. To address that concern, Congress created a narrow Housing for Older Persons (HOP) exemption to ensure that the familial status protections would not interfere with the ability of seniors to choose housing suited to their needs. The exemption operates as an affirmative defense to allegations of familial status discrimination, meaning the defendant has the burden of proving that it qualifies for the exemption. It is important to note that this exemption is from the familial status provisions *only*—the statute still prohibits HOP communities from discriminating based on any of the other protected characteristics (unless they satisfy some other exemption).

The statute exempts three types of HOP from the familial status provisions:

> §3607(b)(2) As used in this section, "housing for older persons" means housing—
>
> (A) provided under any State or Federal program that the [HUD] Secretary determines is specifically designed and operated to assist elderly persons (as defined in the State or Federal program); or
>
> (B) intended for, and solely occupied by, persons 62 years of age or older; or
>
> (C) intended and operated for occupancy by persons 55 years of age or older, and—
>
>> (i) at least 80 percent of the occupied units are occupied by at least one person who is 55 years of age or older;
>>
>> (ii) the housing facility or community publishes and adheres to policies and procedures that demonstrate the intent required under this subparagraph; and
>>
>> (iii) the housing facility or community complies with rules issued by the Secretary for verification of occupancy . . .

With respect to (A), the most significant federal program is HUD's Section 202 Supportive Housing for the Elderly program. This program addresses both affordability and the connection between housing and supportive services. Under the program, HUD provides interest-free capital advances to nonprofit organizations to develop housing that offers project-based rental assistance and supportive services for very low-income elderly residents. *See* 24 C.F.R. §891; 12 U.S.C. §1701q.

With respect to (B) and (C), HUD has published regulations regarding the different types of private, for-profit HOPs. *See* 24 C.F.R. §100.303 (62+ housing); 24 C.F.R. §100.304-307 (55+ housing). The age-related occupancy requirements for 62+ communities are stricter than those for 55+ communities. 55+ communities, however, have other requirements: They must publish policies and procedures demonstrating an intent to operate as a HOP, and they must conduct regular age verification of their occupants. *See* Hooker v. Weathers, 990 F.2d 913 (6th Cir. 1993) (community failed to qualify for 55+ HOP status because it did not publish or adhere to policies demonstrating an intent to operate as a HOP and the defendant's own affidavit stated that only 78 percent of the units were occupied by "older persons"). The regulation requires communities to conduct surveys of residents at least once every two years to verify that at least 80 percent of its occupied units are occupied by at least one person 55 years of age or older. The surveys must verify the ages of residents by using reliable documents or affidavits. And the surveys themselves must be maintained and produced in any administrative or judicial proceeding in which the community asserts the exemption as a defense to a charge of discrimination. *See* Balvage v. Ryderwood Improvement and Service Ass'n, Inc., 642 F.3d 765 (9th Cir. 2011) (community that operated as a 55+ HOP for many years but did not properly conduct age verification of residents may be liable for discrimination that occurred during the period when it was out of compliance).

These requirements are to prevent communities from operating merely as informal or de facto housing for older people and discriminating against families with children, then attempting to claim the HOP exemption. If a community wishes to exclude children, it must be deliberate and intentional about housing older people consistent with the terms of the FHA. The following case represents another example of a community with a no-child policy attempting, unsuccessfully, to demonstrate that it met the requirements for the 55+ HOP exemption.

Simovits v. Chanticleer Condominium Ass'n

933 F. Supp. 1394 (N.D. Ill. 1996)

KEYS, United States Magistrate Judge:

The Simovits[es] owned a condominium in the Chanticleer Condominium Complex ("Chanticleer"), an 84 unit housing facility located in Hinsdale, Illinois. Since 1985, the Association has had a restrictive covenant in its Declaration of Condominium Ownership, stating that "no minor children under the age of eighteen (18) years may reside in any unit purchased after the effective date of this amendment" without the prior written approval of the Board of Managers. Residents of Chanticleer who violate the Covenant are subject to injunctive relief and a $10,000 fine. This provision is construed as barring an owner from selling a unit to anyone with children under the age of eighteen.

A large number of Chanticleer's residents are 55 years of age or older. However, there is no requirement that residents must be 55 years old or older. According to the president of the Association, Jim Londos, Chanticleer is intended for people who are "any age over 18."

[The Simovitses purchased their condominium in June of 1993 for $130,000. After making a number of improvements, the Simovitses put the condo on the market in May of 1995, for $187,500. A prospective buyer expressed an interest, but the Simovitses decided not to enter into negotiations with that individual because she had a minor child, and they did not wish to cause any problems. After several weeks passed without any interested buyers, the Simovitses lowered their asking price to $169,900. Another prospective buyer expressed an interest, but had 3 children, all under the age of 18. When Mr. Simovits informed Mr. Londos that he had a potential buyer with minor children, Mr. Londos replied that the Covenant prohibited such a sale. Mr. Londos also told the prospective buyer's agent about the Covenant, at which point the prospect was no longer interested in making an offer.]

On the same day he informed Mr. Simovits that he could not sell to this prospective buyer, Mr. Londos contacted the Association's lawyer, who called the Simovits[es], warning them that the Covenant prohibited a sale to a person with minor children. On November 14, 1995, Mr. Londos received a letter from the Association's lawyer regarding the Simovits[es] and the questionable legality of the Covenant. The letter warned Mr. Londos that discriminating against families with children is illegal. The letter stated that the statutory exemptions to the FHA are "strictly construed" and that "[u]nless Chanticleer can produce hard evidence that the community meets these narrowly construed exemptions, the financial liability to Chanticleer could be substantial." Mr. Londos shared the contents of this letter with the Association's board members on the day he received it. Despite the warnings in the letter, the Association decided to continue to prevent the Simovits[es] from selling to a buyer with minor children.

Immediately after contacting the Association's lawyer in early November, Mr. Londos began to compile a list of all the Chanticleer residents' ages in order to determine the percentage of residents who were 55 years of age or older. This was the first time the Association had conducted a survey of this nature. In compiling the survey, Mr. Londos speculated as to the residents' ages. He testified that he "had a pretty good idea . . . in [his] head who was of what age." He did not take any steps to verify these presumptions. Consequently, the list contained inaccuracies.

In preparation for the hearing herein, Mr. Londos conducted another similar survey. In this May 21, 1996 survey, conducted 2 days prior to the hearing, Mr. Londos used signed affidavits to verify the residents' ages. However, he did not obtain affidavits from all of Chanticleer's residents. He resorted to guessing the ages of those residents who did not submit an affidavit.

On April 15, 1996, the Simovits[es] entered into a contract to sell their condominium to Brian Weigus and Ramona Caracheo, a couple without children, for $145,000. However, the buyers were young, and thus wanted the Covenant waived. The Association agreed to waive it, and the deal closed on April 30, 1996.

The Simovits[es] brought suit for the economic damages that they suffered as a result of the Covenant. They allege that the Covenant diminished the value of their condominium by $30,000. In addition to diminishing the value of their condominium, the Simovits[es] allege that the Covenant caused them to incur additional mortgage obligations. Because the Covenant delayed the sale of their condominium, the Simovits[es] allege that they paid an extra $3,560.15 in mortgage payments.

II. LIABILITY

The question of the Association's liability under the FHA for discrimination based on familial status turns on whether or not Chanticleer meets the exemption for "housing for older persons" in §3607(b)(2) of the FHA. One category of "housing for older persons" is "housing intended and operated for occupancy by persons 55 years and older."

The statute requires that the defendant meet [three] requirements to qualify for the exemption. In addition, the defendant has the burden of proving that it meets the . . . requirements.

A. Eighty Percent Test

The Association has failed to provide reliable evidence that, since 1985, 80% of the occupied dwellings at Chanticleer have had at least one person 55 years of age or older in residence. The Association relies on the results of the two surveys conducted by Mr. Londos to qualify for the exemption. Such reliance, however, is misplaced. Most significant, in the first survey, is the absence of corroborating source documentation. Mr. Londos merely estimated the ages of the Chanticleer residents, neglecting to verify them by using affidavits or other signed statements. A survey compiled in such an unscientific manner does not provide reliable evidence that 80% of the occupied dwellings had at least one person age 55 in residence. Moreover, the circumstances surrounding the taking of this survey—upon the advice of counsel in response to Mr. Simovits' threat to file a lawsuit—makes it clear that, even if the 80% requirement were met, it was merely fortuitous and is not indicative of any intent to provide housing for persons age 55 or older.

As to the second survey, the corroborating source documentation is incomplete. Mr. Londos did not obtain affidavits from every resident at Chanticleer, and he speculated as to the ages of those residents from whom he did not obtain an affidavit. Consequently, the survey's results are totally unreliable. Accordingly, the Court finds that the Association has failed to meet the 80% test.

B. Policies and Procedures Test

The Association freely admits that it does not publish and adhere to policies and procedures that demonstrate an intent to provide housing for persons aged 55 years or older.[17] Thus, the Association has, in fact, conceded its liability under the FHA, since qualification for the exemption requires

---

17. [Fn. 18 in original] The Association argues that it is in "effective compliance" with this prong of the statute because Chanticleer has a "longstanding reputation" in the community as a facility for older persons. However, the "[e]xemptions from the FHA are to be construed narrowly, in recognition of the important goal of preventing housing discrimination." The Association's argument for "effective compliance" directly conflicts with this principle of narrow construction.

that all three of its requirements be met. HUD provides a list of six nonexclusive factors for determining whether a facility is in compliance with this test. These factors are: (1) the housing facility's written rules and regulations; (2) the manner which the housing is described to prospective residents; (3) the nature of advertising; (4) age verification procedures; (5) lease provisions; and (6) the actual practices of the management in enforcing the relevant rules and regulations.

In the case at bar, neither the Association's written rules and regulations, nor its age verification procedures, demonstrate an intent to provide housing for persons age fifty-five and older.

1. Written Rules and Regulations

The Association's written rules and regulations fail to demonstrate an intent to provide housing to persons 55 years of age or older. To demonstrate this intent, the Association's rules and regulations must explicitly restrict residency to persons 55 years or older. There has never been [such] a rule at Chanticleer. Indeed, the Association has done nothing to actively pursue prospective residents age 55 or over, and all of its sales in 1995 and 1996 were to individuals under the age of 55. Rather, the only rule relating to age is the one prohibiting residency by children under 18. Therefore, the Association's "no children" policy does not adequately demonstrate an intent to provide housing to persons 55 years of age and older.

2. Age Verification Procedures

Insofar as the Association has belatedly implemented age verification procedures, the Record does not demonstrate that those procedures are consistent with an intent to maintain the 55 year and older exemption. In order to establish the requisite intent, the Association's age verification procedures must be reliable. For the reasons previously discussed, neither of Mr. Londos' surveys is reliable.

In addition, age verification procedures must be performed on a consistent basis. The Association, however, has not consistently verified the ages of the Chanticleer residents. The timing of the events in early November strongly suggests that Mr. Londos only began compiling his surveys once he was warned, by the Association's lawyer, of a potential legal conflict with the Simovits[es]. Moreover, the Record contains no evidence that the Association ever performed any age verification surveys of the residents prior to those completed by Mr. Londos. The age verification procedures used by the Association, therefore, fall short of demonstrating an intent to provide housing for persons age 55 and older.

C. Compliance with HUD Rules

The Association has not complied with the HUD rules for verification of occupancy. The statute requires that the HUD rules: (1) provide for verification by reliable surveys and affidavits; and (2) include examples of the types of policies and procedures relevant to a determination of intent to provide housing for persons 55 years and older. These requirements for the HUD rules duplicate the requirements under the 80% test and the policies and procedures test. As previously discussed, the Association does not meet either of these two prongs. Thus, the Association fails this third statutory prong as well.

In sum, the Court finds that the Association does not qualify for the exemption in §3607(b)(2)(C) of the FHA. The Association failed all three requirements of the "55 and older" exemption. Therefore, the Association is liable for familial status discrimination that occurred as a result of the Covenant.

NOTES AND QUESTIONS

1. A Shift from Adults-Only to HOP? Like *Simovits*, many cases involving the HOP exemption arose in the decade following the addition of familial status to the FHA. Communities that had maintained "adults only" policies to exclude children prior to 1988 scrambled to claim the HOP exemption. As *Simovits* demonstrates, just because these communities had large numbers of older residents does not mean they could meet the age, intent, and census requirements of the statute and regulations.

What if a nonexempt community decides it wants to become a HOP community? HUD guidance suggests that communities can obtain exempt status by achieving compliance with the statutory and regulatory requirements but must not evict or otherwise discriminate against families with children.[18] Conversion must happen naturally through population shifts, and only then can the community publish its statement of intent. Consider Massaro v. Mainlands Section 1 & 2 Civic Ass'n, Inc., 3 F.3d 1472 (11th Cir. 1993), which presents an example of a community that did not go about conversion properly. In that case, a community of 529 single-family homes was governed by bylaws that restricted occupancy to "permanent residents sixteen (16) years of age or older." The community association attempted to evict two families for having infants living in their homes. The families filed complaints with HUD, and the association eventually amended its bylaws to raise the age limit to 55. In its defense, the community argued that its bylaw prohibiting occupancy by anyone under 16 should qualify as a published statement of intent to operate as a 55+ HOP. The court refused to accept this argument, reasoning that "[t]he declaration's restriction on residency by children cannot show that the community intended its housing to be for older persons because then any policy

---

18. Memorandum from Bryan Greene, HUD Deputy Assistant Secretary for Enforcement and Programs, *Conversion to Housing for Older Persons Under the Fair Housing Act and the Housing for Older Persons Act of 1995* (Mar. 6, 2006), https://www.hud.gov/sites/dfiles/FHEO/docume nts/BBH%20CONVERSION%20TO%20HOPA.pdf.

against families would suffice for the exemption, swallowing the rule against such discrimination."

2. Constitutional Challenges. The addition of familial status protections and the HOP exemption gave rise to constitutional challenges from all sides. In Seniors Civil Liberties Ass'n, Inc. v. Kemp, 965 F.2d 1030 (11th Cir. 1992), senior citizens and a group representing them argued that, even with the HOP exceptions, the prohibition against familial status discrimination violated a number of their constitutional rights. The Eleventh Circuit handily dismissed these claims. With respect to plaintiffs' due process arguments, the court held they had "shown no arbitrary or irrational congressional action":

> After conducting extensive studies and hearings, Congress determined that families with children were being discriminated against in the housing market. Congress then enacted legislation to cure this perceived discrimination. If Congress had not also acted to protect the rights of persons situated similarly to the Riedels — that is, older, potentially more vulnerable home owners and renters — perhaps plaintiffs' argument that the 1988 amendments were arbitrary and irrational might have some strength. Congress, however, expressly exempted qualified housing for older persons from the reach of the familial status amendments. Because of the strong deference accorded legislation in the field of national economic policy and because Congress seems to have acted rationally by protecting persons similarly situated to plaintiffs, the Fifth Amendment due process claim fails.

The court also dismissed the plaintiffs' discrimination claims under the Fifth Amendment, as well as their claimed rights to privacy and freedom of association. With respect to the right to privacy, the court held that "the Act violates no privacy rights because it stops at the Riedels' front door. Whatever the penumbral right to privacy found in the Constitution might include, it excludes without question the right to dictate or to challenge whether families with children may move in next door to you." The court rejected the association argument, noting that "if plaintiffs followed the exemption guidelines, they would lawfully be able to restrict occupancy based on age to an even greater degree than is the case in the condominium complex now."

Similarly, in Park Place Home Brokers v. P-K Mobile Home Park, 773 F. Supp. 46 (N.D. Ohio 1991), operators of a mobile home park that wanted to limit housing to elderly residents but failed to qualify for the HOP exemption unsuccessfully argued that the familial status protections violated their constitutional right to Equal Protection. The court rejected the Equal Protection challenge under a deferential rational basis review: "the Court finds no Congressional intention to make elderly citizens of modest income a "sensitive" class." In contrast, in Taylor v. Rancho Santa Barbara, 206 F.3d 932 (2000), a nonelderly person who wished to move into a mobile home park that was limited to 55+ residents challenged the HOP exemption, arguing that it unconstitutionally sanctioned discrimination based on age (anyone younger than 55), in violation of the Equal Protection Clause. The Ninth Circuit rejected these arguments:

Congress intended the FHAA to protect families with children while still "fully protect[ing] the rights of senior citizens who live in retirement communities, and . . . allow[ing] those communities to exclude families with children if they so choose." The housing-for-older-persons exemption as amended bears a rational relationship to the government's legitimate interest in preserving and promoting housing for older persons. Congress reasonably determined that older persons have a particular need for an affordable "safe, supportive environment." Many live on fixed incomes, have particular health needs, and may no longer need a home big enough for a large family.

The housing-for-older-persons exemption permits exempted communities to reduce costs. The exemption permits communities to exist in areas less appropriate or desirable for younger people. Sites typically lack schools or day care facilities. Parks can thrive relatively far from employment centers. The land can be acquired at low cost, and often might otherwise go underused.

The exemption also allows exempted housing communities to offer facilities more appropriate for older persons than for children. Conversely, communities can devote more resources to facilities and services for older persons.

That Congress drew the line at age 55 — rather than at age 35 or 65 or 67 — does not violate equal protection. The selection of age 55 accommodates those who retire early and those who desire to relocate prior to reaching retirement or very old age, when moving might be more difficult. Furthermore, even though the selection of age 55 — or any age — might be over and underinclusive on the margin, legislatures are given leeway under rational-basis review to engage in such line drawing.

3. Short-Lived "Significant Facilities and Services" Requirement. Under the HOP exemption originally enacted in the FHAA, 55+ HOP communities had an additional requirement. Specifically, the statute required that such communities offer "significant facilities and services specifically designed to meet the physical or social needs of older persons." 42 U.S.C. §3607(b)(2)(C)(i). HUD issued regulations that proved problematic; after HUD issued several versions of revised rules in response to a Congressional mandate, Congress amended the FHA to eliminate the "significant facilities and services" requirement entirely. HUD subsequently revised its implementing regulations to reflect the amendment. Professor Mark Bauer critiques the elimination of the requirement for developers:

> The elimination of the requirement for significant facilities and services permitted 55-plus communities to discriminate against families without requiring the real estate developers to offer elders anything more than a child-free environment. Developers could build new elder communities offering services no greater than a "mobile home park." Even today, a race to the bottom continues in building many 55-plus communities that offer little beyond a restriction against children.[19]

---

19. Mark D. Bauer, *"Peter Pan" as Public Policy: Should Fifty-Five-Plus Age-Restricted Communities Continue to Be Exempt from Civil Rights Laws and Substantive Federal Regulation?*, 21 ELDER L.J. 33 (2013).

4. HOP and Bases for Discrimination Other Than Familial Status. Recall that the statute exempts HOP communities only from the familial status provisions of the FHA. Thus, HOP communities cannot discriminate on the basis of any other protected characteristic. Assisted living homes and skilled nursing facilities also are prohibited from discriminating on the basis of any protected characteristic (although, as discussed below, they may be required by regulation to transfer patients who have certain medical needs).

- Race: As this text goes to press (2024), there have not been any comprehensive studies of race discrimination in 55+ communities; however, it appears that many such communities are racially segregated, with the majority being overwhelmingly white. For example, a survey of independent living facilities in 2017 found that 95 percent of their residents were white, with 4 percent Black and 1 percent Asian residents.[20] What do you think accounts for this disparity? How do you think it could be ameliorated—if you think that should be done?

- Sexual orientation: Housing discrimination on the basis of sexual orientation has been a serious issue for seniors. In 2014, a national investigation found that 48 percent of older LGBTQ+ people inquiring about housing in a senior living facility experienced "adverse differential treatment" and significant discrimination, including being given less information about available units, being charged higher fees, and being denied housing outright.[21] Walsh v. Friendship Village, 352 F. Supp. 3d 920 (E.D. Mo. 2019), involved plaintiffs who originally were approved to move into a 55+ community (with an ironic name), but then had their application rejected after the facility's management became aware that they were a married, same-sex couple. Wetzel v. Glen St. Andrew Living Community, 901 F.3d 856 (7th Cir. 2018) (discussed in Chapter 10), involved a lesbian resident of a senior community who alleged severe harassment by other residents because of her sexual orientation. It is important to note that this research and these cases predate the Supreme Court's ruling in *Bostock v. Clayton County*, in which the Court held that sexual orientation discrimination is a form of sex discrimination prohibited by Title VII. As discussed in Chapter 15, this almost certainly applies to the FHA as well. It is possible, therefore, that the incidence of sexual orientation discrimination and harassment in senior living facilities will decrease in light of this ruling (although the persistence of racial discrimination, 60 years after the enactment of Title VIII, certainly

---

20. The Love & Company Report, *Diversity in Senior Living Communities: Insights into Creating a More Diverse Census* (June 2018), https://loveandcompany.com/wp-content/uploads/2020/08/Love-Report-Summer-2018-Diversity-in-Senior-Living-Communities.pdf. The survey also found that 96 percent of board members of such communities are white.

21. Equal Rights Center, *Opening Doors: An Investigation of Barriers to Senior Housing for Same-Sex Couples* (2014), https://equalrightscenter.org/wp-content/uploads/senior_housing_report.pdf.

tempers any such optimism). Do you think there might be a basis for optimism in either respect?

• Religion: The FHA contains another exemption, 42 U.S.C. §3607(a), which allows religious organizations and related institutions to limit dwellings they own or operate to people of the same religion, or to prefer co-religionists for such housing. This exemption is narrow, however, and applies only to specific types of housing and only to religious preferences. As Professor Schwemm and Michael Allen explain:

> First, the exemption by its terms extends only to those dwellings that are "owned or operated for other than a commercial purpose," which means that all religious-affiliated housing operated for a commercial purpose would fail to qualify for this exemption. Second, this exemption only authorizes a qualifying institution to discriminate in favor of its co-religionists and thus does not authorize racial or other non-religious types of discrimination. Third, the exemption only allows a religious organization to favor its co-religionists with respect to certain transactions—"limiting the sale, rental or occupancy" and "giving preference"—thereby implying that such organizations may not engage in the other types of discriminatory transactions condemned by the FHA, such as discriminating in the terms of rental in violation of §3604(b), publishing discriminatory advertisements in violation of §3604(c), or refusing to take certain mandated steps for persons with disabilities in violation of §3604(f)(3). Fourth, the FHA's religious exemption is not available unless the particular housing involved is owned or operated by either "a religious organization, association, or society" or a "nonprofit institution or organization operated, supervised or controlled by or in conjunction with" such a religious organization, association, or society. The former phrase would cover only a few religiously affiliated senior housing complexes, and even under the more generous second alternative, many such complexes would fail to qualify because they lack a sufficiently close involvement with their affiliated religious organization.[22]

For example, United States v. Lorantffy Care Ctr., 999 F. Supp. 1037 (N.D. Ohio 1998), involved an assisted living facility that was accused of discriminating against Black applicants. The facility was established by a minister of the Free Hungarian Reformed Church and maintained close ties with the church, despite being a separate legal entity. The court held that, regardless of whether the facility qualified as a religious entity, it would not be entitled to claim the exemption because it was accused of discriminating on the basis of race, not religion.

---

22. Robert G. Schwemm & Michael Allen, *For the Rest of Their Lives: Seniors and the Fair Housing Act*, 90 Iowa L. Rev. 121, 158-60 (2004). For an example of the kind of relationship one court required between the housing provider and the religious organization, see *Columbus Country Club*, discussed in Chapter 5.

The exemption for religious organizations is discussed in Chapter 5. It is important to note also that there is no religious exemption from liability under 42 U.S.C. §1982 and some state or local fair housing laws.

5. Zoning. HUD's regulation purports to extend the type of housing that can qualify for HOP exemption to "municipally zoned" senior housing. 24 C.F.R. §100.304(b)(4). This would allow municipalities to enact zoning ordinances that favor—or even require—senior housing. For example, in Putnam Family Partnership v. City of Yucaipa, 673 F.3d 920 (9th Cir. 2012), the Ninth Circuit upheld a municipal ordinance that prohibited any of the city's mobile home parks that were operating as 55+ housing from converting to all-ages housing. The owners of a mobile home park challenged the ordinance, arguing that they did not fit under the HOP exemption because they did not have the required intent to operate as senior housing. The Ninth Circuit disagreed, pointing to the fact that Congress had amended the FHA to remove the requirement that the intent to provide senior housing demonstrated in published policies and procedures must be that of the "owner or manager." The court also cited HUD guidance suggesting the owner or operator of housing did not need to have such intent so long as there was a municipal ordinance requiring it: "HUD has explained that a housing facility or community satisfies the senior exemption's intent requirement if, inter alia, '[z]oning requirements include the 55-or-older requirement' and '[z]oning maps containing the senior housing designation are available to the public.' 64 FED. REG. at 16332 ex. 2."

Why might municipalities want to specifically zone certain areas or complexes to operate as senior housing? One reason might be to meet the needs of an aging community. A more cynical reason might be to reduce the burden on (and costs associated with) public elementary and secondary schools. Given that exemptions to the FHA are to be narrowly construed, should the courts countenance HUD's effort to enlarge an exemption by regulation?

A NOTE ON SENIOR HOUSING AND DISABILITY

It is important to recognize that HOP communities, particularly 55+ HOPs, are not synonymous with other housing commonly associated with seniors, such as nursing homes or assisted living facilities. There are many types of housing that are appropriate for seniors, depending on their health and degree of independence. Professor Robert Schwemm and Michael Allen describe the various housing options for elderly people as follows:[23]

> [Independent Living] The first option for older persons is to remain in the home where they lived in their pre-senior life. . . . The second residential option available to older persons is to move to a different home, but one that is

---

23. *Id.* at 134-41 (emphasis added).

still characterized by "independent living;" that is, one that provides no special medical or other supportive services. Within this second category, the types of housing units available include all of those enjoyed by the general public. . . . One key difference, however, between this option and the staying-in-place option is that, *regardless of the type of unit involved, an individual who chooses to move might select a community that is restricted to older persons and therefore qualifies for the FHA's "housing for older persons" exemption.*

[Assisted Living] [M]ost assisted-living facilities have three common characteristics: (1) they provide a variety of on-site health-related and other personal-living services; (2) they are subject to some state licensing requirements; and (3) they offer only private—as opposed to shared—occupancy units. . . . ALFs are distinguished by the fact that the care they make available to residents is a major component of the services provided, albeit still secondary to the more traditional housing and housing-related services they also provide.

[Nursing Homes] Nursing homes provide skilled-nursing care or rehabilitation services for injured, disabled, or sick persons who require full-time medical and related services (e.g., administration of medication and prescribed treatments), "but who do not need the acute care provided by hospitals." Nursing homes are heavily regulated. . . . Historically, nursing homes focused primarily on older persons who needed "custodial care" (i.e., assistance mainly with the activities of daily living). *While modern nursing homes are generally not restricted to older people, the vast majority of residents are seniors*, with the over-65 age group accounting for some 2.0 million of the total nursing-home population of 2.3 million.

[Continuing Care Retirement Communities] Continuing care retirement communities ("CCRCs") offer in a single-campus setting a variety of residential options designed exclusively for senior citizens, including those here described as "independent living," "assisted living," and "nursing home." The housing units available include cottages, townhouses, apartments, and nursing-infirmary rooms. In addition to offering dining and recreational facilities to all, a range of health and personal-care services is provided, from independent living with perhaps minor services to full-time care in nursing home-type units. Assuring convenient access to higher levels of care through transfer arrangements is one of the advantages of residing in a CCRC.

Thus, while 55+ and 62+ HOP communities might provide some amenities that are appealing to seniors, most describe themselves as independent living facilities that do not provide skilled nursing, memory care, or assistive services for their residents. Assisted living and nursing home facilities primarily serve elderly populations because disabling conditions such as dementia, frailty, and mobility impairments are associated with older age, but these facilities typically do not impose the sort of minimum age requirements necessary for 55+ and 62+ HOP communities to qualify for the familial status exemption under the FHA. (Of course, given the nature of the housing and the care provided, such living arrangements typically are available only to an individual resident or couple, and not to other family members who might have shared a household with them previously.)

Indeed, many 55+ HOP communities seek to avoid looking too much like homes for the elderly, and instead market themselves to younger retirees as "active adult communities," offering golf, tennis, swimming, and other recreational activities. Such communities have become increasingly popular in recent years, particularly in the Sun Belt states of Arizona, California, and Florida. The Villages in central Florida is the largest, with more than 145,000 residents in 2023. Late singer Jimmy Buffet developed several "Latitude Margaritaville" 55+ communities, which focus on "food, fun, music and escapism." Recall that Congress created the HOP exemption to ensure that older people would be able to find housing specific to their needs. What "needs" do communities like this serve and why is excluding children necessary? Are the "needs" of the elderly changing as much of the population lives longer and is generally healthier than in decades past? Ironically, many active adult communities are not designed for the needs of the "older elderly." Professor Mark Bauer refers to such communities as "Peter Pan housing," that is, home construction that presumes its owners will never grow old.[24] Professor Bauer notes that "[i]t is challenging to meet the needs of the aging populations of these communities, which were never designed to offer services for extreme elders, while at the same time stabilizing (or even increasing) property values by maintaining some appeal for younger retirees."

The different types and target audiences of senior living options have implications for disability protections under the FHA. "Active adult" communities might view older people with disabilities, whether age-related or not, as incongruous with their fun and recreation-focused atmospheres (or as unwelcome reminders of the inevitable deterioration of the human body). Operators of such communities might not want to feel responsible or liable for a resident who has extra needs. Disability-based discrimination by providers of housing for older people is thus not uncommon but is still prohibited by the disability protections of §3604(f) (discussed in Chapter 17).

HOP providers are prohibited, for example, from imposing "independent living" requirements on residents or from evicting residents who become disabled.[25] If a disabled person wishes to live in a 55+ or 62+ HOP community that does not provide supportive services, he or she can still obtain those services privately. *See, e.g.*, Cason v. Rochester Housing Auth., 748 F. Supp. 1002 (W.D.N.Y. 1990) (upholding §3604(f)(1) claim by disabled tenants against public housing authority after it had rejected them for failing to meet its "ability to live independently" eligibility requirement); United States v. Forest Dale,

---

24. Bauer, *supra* note 19, at 33.

25. At the same time, however, assisted living facilities, nursing homes, and CCRCs may be required by state regulations to establish "level of care" protections for their residents. Such measures are designed to ensure that these facilities do not accept people whose care they are not licensed to provide or capable of providing. CCRCs also may have a financial incentive to transfer residents into facilities that provide a higher level of care. All of this creates tensions with fair housing law that may ultimately require legislative intervention. *See* D. Trey Jordan, *Continuing Care Retirement Communities Versus the Fair Housing Act*, 9 MARQUETTE ELDER'S ADVISOR 205 (Fall 2007) (noting that while there are legitimate medical circumstances that warrant the forced transfer of a resident into a skilled nursing facility, medically unnecessary transfers create a significant fair housing issue that likely can only be solved through legislation).

Inc., 818 F. Supp. 954 (N.D. Tex. 1993) (upholding §3604(f)(1) claim challenging apartment complex's policy of terminating a tenancy where "a prolonged illness of the Tenant shall require special care or treatment and such care or treatment shall tend to disrupt the general atmosphere and operation of [the complex]").

Similarly, providers cannot impose restrictions on the use of wheelchairs or other assistive devices in senior housing (other than to impose reasonable safety rules). *See, e.g.,* Weinstein v. Cherry Oaks Retirement Community, 917 P.2d 336 (Colo. Ct. App. 1996) (senior housing provider's policy of requiring wheelchair users to transfer to regular chairs to eat in the dining room was adopted so that the facility could "maintain a 'disability-free' atmosphere," which constituted discriminatory intent and a failure to reasonably accommodate under substantially similar state fair housing law); United States v. Hillhaven Corp., 960 F. Supp. 259 (D. Utah 1997) (retirement community's policy of restricting motorized carts to certain common areas at meal times did not violate the FHA because it was motivated solely by a desire to ensure "the safety of all . . . residents, many of whom have their own handicaps of vision, hearing, or balance," and the policy did not prevent the complainant from using her cart at other times and places, thereby allowing her to have "meaningful access to [the complex] as a whole"). Consider also a requirement that residents using motorized wheelchairs obtain liability insurance; a HUD ALJ concluded such a requirement violated the FHA, where the senior housing facility had no "empirical basis to conclude that operators of motorized wheelchairs pose a substantial risk of harm to themselves or others." HUD v. Country Manor Apartments, No. 05-98-1649-8, 2001 WL 1132715, *7–8 (HUD ALJ September 20, 2001).

E. GROUP HOMES FOR YOUTH

As discussed in Chapter 17, group homes in which unrelated people live together, sometimes receiving supportive services or treatment, are a residential model often used to serve people with disabilities. Such homes might be geared toward young people with substance use disorders or other disabilities. Group homes also could serve nondisabled youth who have been removed from their families and placed in state custody, who are homeless, or who have been involved with the criminal justice system. Most group home cases under the FHA involve adults with disabilities, but there is a small but significant set of cases involving groups homes for youth.

Municipal zoning ordinances may create hurdles for such housing. Although by definition these are residences, some municipal ordinances seek to limit the types of neighborhoods in which they may locate, impose spacing requirements, or limit the number of occupants in a way that makes the homes difficult, if not impossible, to operate.

NOTES AND QUESTIONS

1. Cases. There are not many reported group home cases that involve only familial status. Minors living in group homes might also have some type of disability (or be perceived as such), and therefore disability-based accommodation claims, which involve affirmative duties and are easier to bring, tend to dominate those cases. For example, in Children's Alliance v. Bellevue, 950 F. Supp. 1491 (W.D. Wash. 1997), the court addressed a municipal ordinance that first sought to ban, and then heavily regulated, group care facilities for children. The court noted that "[t]he children in these facilities usually are abandoned, abused, or neglected; have mental health problems or developmental disabilities; require treatment for drug or alcohol abuse; or are finishing their sentence for a juvenile offense." The court held that the regulations, which specifically targeted this type of land use, were facially discriminatory, on the bases of both familial status and disability.

> Analyzing the language of Ordinance No. 4861 demonstrates its facial invalidity. The Ordinance's definition of "Family" very clearly may include group homes: "One or more persons (but not more than six unrelated persons) living together as a single housekeeping unit." The Ordinance also defines a "Group Facility": "A staffed living facility for a group of persons, which may include both children and adults. . . ." The Ordinance thus distinguishes Group Facilities from Families in part based on the presence of "Staff," those who provide "care and supervision for and assistance with the daily living activities of the Residents in a Group Facility," and the Court finds that this use of "Staff" is a proxy for a classification based on the presence of individuals under eighteen and the handicapped as both groups require supervision and assistance. If a group home fits within the definitions of both "Family" and "Group Facility," the Ordinance specifies that the latter characterization controls, resulting in different treatment for groups, similarly situated in terms of the Ordinance's own definition of "Family," on account of their familial status or handicaps.

Diamond House v. Ammon, 381 F. Supp. 3d 1262 (D. Idaho 2019), involved a claim based solely on familial status, in a situation similar to *Bellevue* in which a city passed an ordinance restricting group foster homes for youth. The circumstances of the ordinance were suspicious: A group home operator purchased a large home in a residential neighborhood zoned R-1, with the goal of opening a state-licensed foster home and indicated an intent to buy three more houses for this purpose. There were no restrictions on this use in the city's zoning code, but the city denied the operator's application for a business license, stating, in part, that "[t]he numbers of children that could be housed in the four units you are suggesting would in our opinion change the dynamics of the neighborhood in regard to the number of children and the potential of integrating the children in your care into the neighborhood community." The city then amended its zoning code to prohibit group foster homes entirely in neighborhoods zoned R-1. The operator challenged the ordinance under the FHA and sought a preliminary injunction. The court agreed that the ordinance was facially discriminatory:

The Court concludes the classification drawn by Ordinance 598 and the burdens it places on certain Ammon residents renders it discriminatory on its face. Section 1 of Ordinance 598 defines "foster family care home" as "a location within the City where a minor or minors have been placed in a ward, group home, private home, or any other facility approved as an Idaho State-certified foster caregiver." The Ordinance therefore only affects households where children are domiciled. Section 6 of Ordinance 598 limits "foster family care homes" to an R2-A zone. Thus, the law places burdens on homes where minors are domiciled, while any number of unrelated adults are permitted to reside together in an R-1 zone under the City's zoning laws. Of course, Ordinance 598 does not burden all households with children, but it does not need to apply to all households with children to be facially discriminatory. In addition, even though most households with children are unaffected by Ordinance 598, the fact that the ordinance does not apply to any households that do not contain children renders it facially discriminatory.

In both cases, the municipalities justified their ordinances on the basis of public safety, and both of these were rejected by the court. The *Bellevue* court reasoned:

> Generalized interests in public safety, stability, and tranquility have been enough to redeem ordinances that drew distinctions between groups when subjected to rational basis review. But under the stricter level of scrutiny appropriate here, these interests are only sufficient if they are threatened by the individuals burdened by the Ordinance.
>
> As to the concern for public safety, that too must fail because the Court finds that defendant is operating under stereotyped notions about certain types of group home residents rather than specific concerns raised by individuals. For example, Bellevue's city attorney stated that the evidence of crime committed by individuals with a prior criminal history prompted Bellevue's concern for public safety. But Bellevue offers no evidence showing that residents of Class II facilities are more dangerous than if they lived with their relatives or than the residents of Class I facilities. Defendant's public safety rationale does not stand up under scrutiny and defendant cannot invoke the statutory exemption from the FHA found in §3604(f)(9) because it has not demonstrated how any specific individuals attempting to reside in a Class II facility constitute a "direct threat."

Similarly, the *Diamond House* court held that:

> Where a law is discriminatory against a protected class on its face, the law may only be justified if the restriction benefits the protected class, or if the restriction responds to legitimate safety concerns that are raised by the individuals affected, rather than being based on stereotypes. [The City does not suggest that] Ordinance 598 benefits foster children living in group homes or that Ordinance 598 responds to legitimate safety concerns.

2. The Need for Group Homes for Youth. Both these cases took place against the backdrop of a shortage of housing for children who were homeless or in the child welfare system. The restrictions in the ordinances would only exacerbate the situation.

The *Bellevue* court noted that "[a]s a result of Bellevue's recent ordinances regulating group-care facilities, there are only four beds for homeless youth in all of Bellevue. In 1994 Bellevue was able to house five of its forty-five home-less youths placed in group homes, and only fourteen of fifty-four in 1995. The record reflects that there are no Class II facilities in Bellevue, and that the Ordinance's restrictions deter placement of group homes for youths in the city." The *Diamond House* court found that in the years leading up to the law-suit, the state of Idaho had only 974 licensed foster homes to care for approxi-mately 1,351 foster children.

Such shortages are chronic and widespread. As this text goes to press, the COVID-19 pandemic and the opioid crisis have caused the number of children in the child welfare system to grow even as the number of families available to serve as foster parents drops.[26] Some states have been forced to provide shel-ter for children in casino hotels, emergency rooms, retirement homes, offices, and detention facilities. This suggests that group homes for youth will remain an important housing option for the foreseeable future.

3. Are Youth in Staffed Group Homes Covered by Familial Status Protections? As *Gorski v. Troy* (featured in note 1 in the Notes and Questions section at the beginning of this chapter) illustrates, there is little doubt that children who are in foster care and living with a foster parent are covered by the familial status protections of the FHA. However, some courts have held that certain staffed group homes do not qualify for protection under the defi-nition of familial status in the statute.

For example, in Keys Youth Services v. Olathe, 248 F.3d 1267 (10th Cir. 2001), the court held that the operator of a home for "troubled youth" could not sustain a claim under the FHA because, although the youth were residents of the shelter, the operator and staff were not. Instead, the staff worked shifts at the home (their workplace) and then returned to their own domiciles. This, the court reasoned, made the familial status protections inapplicable:

> "Familial status" requires that the minors be domiciled "with" their caretaker. This means that the youths and Keys' staff must be domiciled together, at the same dwelling. The question thus becomes whether any Keys' staff members would be "domiciled" at the proposed home with the youths. . . . Since the staff members clearly do not live at the group home, they must of necessity be residing someplace else, presumably at their actual homes/domiciles. The fact that some of Keys' employees work a night shift or a twenty-four or thirty-six hour shift does not alter our conclusion. The critical fact remains that the only proffered reason these employees occupy the home is for employment. As a matter of law under these circumstances, we cannot conclude that Keys' employees, collectively or individually, are domiciled at the group home. Thus, the youths cannot be "domiciled with" them, and Keys' proposed group home therefore cannot qualify for "familial status" under the FHA. Any other con-clusion stretches the meaning of "domiciled" and the scope of "familial status" protection beyond sensible bounds.

---

26. For a discussion of this problem, see Paige Sutherland, Meghna Chakrabarti & Tim Skoog, *Inside America's Critical Shortage of Foster Care Homes*, On Point (July 20, 2023), https://www.wbur.org/onpoint/2023/07/20/inside-americas-critical-shortage-of-foster-care-homes.

The court in Estvanko v. City of Perry, No. 5:09-CV-137, 2011 WL 1750232 (M.D. Ga. May 6, 2011) went even further, questioning whether group homes in any form fall under the statute's familial status protections:

> There is no evidence that Congress intended the FHA to provide protection for children living in staffed group homes—regardless of whether the staff resides on the premises. On the contrary, the principle statutory construction for this provision is that families with children must be provided the same protections as other classes of persons protected by the FHA. When enacting the familial status provision, Congress was not concerned about the zoning of group homes for children. Rather, Congress amended the FHA to include familial status protection because of the growing concern that "[i]n many parts of the country families with children [were being] refused housing despite their ability to pay for it."

Are these courts suggesting that staffed group homes for youth are not enough like traditional families to be covered by familial status protections? Consider this reasoning from a purposive framework. Should it matter whether Congress was concerned primarily with protecting individual families with children (as opposed to group homes for children) when it passed the FHAA? Now consider this reasoning from a textualist standpoint. Are these courts being overly technical in their reading of the statute? The court in *Diamond House* rejected such reasoning, determining that the statute's use of the term "designee" is broad enough to encompass caregivers in group home settings, even if they do not use the homes as their primary residence:

> Under Idaho law, children who reside at group foster homes are wards of the State in legal custody of the Department of Health and Welfare. The Department may place the children of whom it has been given custody in "foster care, shelter care, or other diagnostic, treatment, or care centers or facilities[.]" Under *Estvanko* and *Keys Youth*, children who are in the custody of the Department, but who have not yet been placed with foster parents, would only be protected from discrimination if they resided in the same building as agents for the Department. Nor would children be protected if placed in shelter care or other care centers without a custodial adult who also permanently resided in such facilities. However, the FHA provides familial status protection for individuals who are domiciled with "the *designee* of such parent or other person having such custody, with the written permission of such parent or other person." 42 U.S.C. §3602(k)(2) (emphasis added). The Department is a "person" having legal custody of the minors who would live at Diamond House, and Diamond House would be the designee of the Department. *See e.g., Gorski v. Troy* (7th Cir. 1991) (recognizing the Illinois Department of Child and Family Services was a "person" having custody of a minor, and potential foster parents were its "designees" under the FHA). Thus, it appears the potential residents of Diamond House are entitled to familial status protection under the FHA.

Who do you think was meant to be the focus of familial status protections: the child? the custodial adult? the family unit? all three? How might the answer affect the outcomes of the cases throughout this chapter?

Chapter Summary

- In 1988 Congress amended the FHA to include protection against discrimination based on familial status. "Familial status" is defined as one or more individuals who have not attained the age of 18 years being domiciled with (1) a parent or other person having legal custody of such individual or individuals; or (2) the designee of such parent or other person having such custody, with the written permission of such parent or other person.

- The FHA contains an exemption, 42 U.S.C. §3607(b)(1), allowing for certain reasonable numerical occupancy limitations that a government might impose. Such limits usually are imposed for health and safety reasons, such as fire safety. Because families with children are almost always larger than families without children, such standards are likely to affect families with children disproportionately.

  - Many courts, and HUD, have assumed this exemption also permits private landlords to set their own occupancy standards, although the statute is silent on this point.

- The Housing for Older Persons (HOP) exemption, 42 U.S.C. §3607(b)(2), provides for three types of HOP that are exempt from the familial status provisions:

  - state and federally funded housing designed to serve elderly people,

  - housing exclusively for people 62 years of age or older, and

  - housing intended and operated for occupancy by persons 55 years of age or older where at least 80 percent of the occupied units are occupied by at least one person who is 55 years of age or older and other statutory requirements are satisfied.

- Local governments sometimes discriminate against group homes for youth through zoning restrictions. Facially discriminatory ordinances often will fail when challenged.

CHAPTER 17

DISABILITY RIGHTS IN HOUSING

Estimates from 2023 indicate that people with disabilities make up 13.5 percent of the U.S. population.[1] In 1988, Congress on an overwhelmingly bipartisan vote passed the Fair Housing Amendments Act (FHAA),[2] adding protections for people with disabilities[3] (and families with children) and creating the most comprehensive federal disability rights statute covering dwellings. The Congressional purpose in expanding the FHA reflects the ideals of both nondiscrimination and integration, with an express emphasis on inclusion:

> The Fair Housing Amendments Act . . . is a clear pronouncement of a national commitment to end the unnecessary exclusion of persons with handicaps from the American mainstream. It repudiates the use of stereotypes and ignorance, and mandates that persons with handicaps be considered as individuals. Generalized perceptions about disabilities and unfounded speculations about threats to safety are specifically rejected as grounds to justify exclusion. . . . The right to be free from housing discrimination is essential to the goal of independent living.[4]

In addition to traditional intent and effects theories of liability, the FHA imposes affirmative duties to address disability discrimination that is "the product, not of invidious animus, but rather of thoughtlessness and

---

1. Rehabilitation Research and Training Center on Disability Statistics and Demographics, *Annual Report on People with Disabilities in America: 2023*, https://disabilitycompend ium.org/sites/default/files/user-uploads/Accessible-Annual%20Report%20---%202023%20 ---%20Accessible.pdf (derived from the American Community Survey conducted by the U.S. Census Bureau).

2. Pub. L. No. 100-430, 102 Stat. 1619 (1988). The FHA passed on a 94-3 vote in the Senate and a 376-23 vote in the House. Congress.gov, H.R.1158—Fair Housing Amendments Act of 1988, 100th Congress (1987-1988) (All Actions, Roll Call Votes), https://www.congr ess.gov/bill/100th-congress/house-bill/1158/all-actions?overview=closed&q=%7B%22roll-call -vote%22%3A%22all%22%7D.

3. *See* Samuel R. Bagenstos, Disability Rights Law: Cases and Materials, at 4 n.a (3d ed. 2021) ("Politically active Americans with disabilities are divided on whether to use people-first terminology [e.g., "people with disabilities"] or disability-first terminology [e.g., "disabled people"]."). Like Prof. Bagenstos, we alternate between these approaches.

4. H.R. Rep. No. 100-711, at 18 (1988); *see also id.* (noting that people with disabilities experience discrimination "because of prejudice and aversion—because they make non-handicapped people uncomfortable.").

indifference—of benign neglect."[5] As one advocate explains, disability rights consciousness and legislation did not "fall[ ] from the sky" but reflect the efforts of "many thousands of people":

> The disability rights movement, over the last couple of decades, has made the injustices faced by people with disabilities visible to the American public and to politicians. This required reversing the centuries long history of "out of sight, out of mind" that the segregation of disabled people served to promote. The disability rights movement adopted many of the strategies of the civil rights movements before it. . . .
>
> From a legal perspective, a profound and historic shift in disability public policy occurred in 1973 with the passage of Section 504 of the 1973 Rehabilitation Act. Section 504, which banned discrimination on the basis of disability by recipients of federal funds, was modelled after previous laws which banned race, ethnic origin and sex based discrimination by federal fund recipients. . . .
>
> Working in coalition again, in 1988, the civil rights community amended the Fair Housing Act (FHA) to improve enforcement mechanisms, and for the first time disability anti-discrimination provisions were included in a traditional civil rights statute banning race discrimination. During these years . . ., alliances were forged within the civil rights community that became critical in the fight for passage of the ADA [the Americans with Disabilities Act].[6]

Professor Samuel R. Bagenstos describes the "two big ideas" that drove the disability rights movement:

> The first big idea was antipaternalism—a challenge to the widespread societal view that people with disabilities should be "objects of pity or charity," or were "people who 'inspire' those without disabilities by 'overcoming' the hardships imposed by fate." . . . "At best . . . these attitudes placed people with disabilities on a pedestal that is in fact a cage." The second big idea has come to be known as the "social model" of disability. The social model posits that disability is not something that is inherent in the body of the person with a disability; instead, disability results from the interaction between an individual's physical or mental characteristics and the social choices and attitudes that attach disadvantage to those characteristics. . . . [In this view,] we are more likely to see the proper response as one that requires *society to* change its aspects that make some mental or physical conditions disabling.[7]

---

5. H.R. Rep. No. 100-711, at 25 (1988) (quoting Alexander v. Choate, 469 U.S. 287, 297 (1985)).

6. Arlene Mayerson, *The History of the Americans with Disabilities Act: A Movement Perspective*, Disability Rights Education & Defense Fund (DREDF) (1992), https://dredf.org/about-us/publications/the-history-of-the-ada/. In advance of the ADA's passage, Mayerson recounts: "A national campaign was initiated to write 'discrimination diaries.' People with disabilities were asked to document daily instances of inaccessibility and discrimination. The diaries served not only as testimonials of discrimination, but also to raise consciousness about the barriers to daily living which were simply tolerated as a part of life. Justin Dart, Chair of [a] Congressional Task Force . . ., traversed the country holding public hearings which were attended by thousands of people with disabilities, friends, and families. . . ."

7. Bagenstos, *supra* note 3, at 10.

As you read the FHA's prohibitions against disability-based discrimination, consider whether you think they particularly reflect the antipaternalism or social model of disability—or perhaps something else.

In expanding the FHA to include disability protections, Congress relied on the definition and concepts developed under §504 of the Rehabilitation Act of 1973, which applies only to programs and activities receiving federal financial assistance.[8] The Americans with Disabilities Act (ADA), enacted in 1990, also imposes some duties of nondiscrimination and accessibility on entities providing housing. Title II of the ADA applies to public entities, reaching state and local public housing agencies and housing made available by state educational institutions. Title III applies to public accommodations such as rental offices and shelters open to the public. Section H, below, describes the distinct protections available in the housing arena under §504 and the ADA. Although the FHA uses the word "handicap," Congress, courts, and commentators all agree that "disability" is what should be used today.[9]

This chapter begins with discussion of the basic structure of the FHA disability protections, then addresses the threshold question of how the FHA defines disability, followed by extensive treatment of the affirmative duty of reasonable accommodation in rules, policies, practices, or services. The chapter then analyzes the duty to permit reasonable modifications, or physical changes to dwellings, and the design and construction requirements imposed on certain multifamily dwellings first occupied after March 13, 1991. The text then describes an exemption for direct threats to health and safety; coverage of land use discrimination and group homes; and §504 and ADA rights governing residences.

A. PROTECTIONS UNDER THE FHA AND THE STRUCTURE OF §3604(f)

Congress created a unique structure of protection for disabled people compared to other characteristics protected under the FHA. The amendments added "handicap" to the list of protected characteristics specified in certain sections of the FHA, but not the core sections of §§3604(a) and (b).[10]

---

8. *See* H.R. Rep. No. 100-711, at 17 (1988) (noting the FHA "uses the same definitions and concepts" from §504; *see, e.g.,* Southeastern Cmty. Coll. v. Davis, 442 U.S. 397, 410, 412 (1979) (developing concepts used to determine reasonable accommodations under §504). For additional discussion of §504, see Section H, below.

9. This book uses the term "disability" unless quoting from the FHAA's statutory language or court decisions. *See* Bhogaita v. Altamonte Heights Condo. Ass'n, 765 F.3d 1277, 1285 n.2 (11th Cir. 2014) (describing "handicap" and "disability" as interchangeable and noting that Congress's subsequent use of "disability" in the ADA reflects its preference for that term).

10. Sections 3604(c), 3604(d), 3604(e), 3605, and 3606 of the FHA insert "handicap" in the list of protected groups without creating a unique structure of protection for people with disabilities.

Congress crafted a new §3604(f)(1) to address the wide-ranging conduct prohibited under §3604(a) relating to the refusal to sell or rent or otherwise making housing unavailable. It also crafted a new §3604(f)(2) to address conduct prohibited under §3604(b) relating to discriminatory terms and conditions or provision of discriminatory services or facilities in the sale or rental of housing. In these parallel provisions, Congress explicitly broadened coverage to co-residents and visitors, recognizing that disability-based protections would extend beyond the "primary purchaser or named lessee" to include "denials of housing opportunities to applicants because they have children, parents, friends, spouses, roommates, patients, subtenants or other associates who have disabilities."[11] This unique structure of protection follows:

> It shall be unlawful under §3604(f):
> (1) To discriminate[12] in the sale or rental, or to otherwise make unavailable or deny, a dwelling to any buyer or renter because of a handicap of —
>> (A) that buyer or renter,
>> (B) a person residing in or intending to reside in that dwelling after it is so sold, rented, or made available; or
>> (C) any person associated with that buyer or renter.
> (1) To discriminate against any person in the terms, conditions, or privileges of sale or rental of a dwelling, or in the provision of services or facilities in connection with such dwelling, because of a handicap of —
>> (A) that person; or
>> (B) a person residing in or intending to reside in that dwelling after it is so sold, rented, or made available; or
>> (C) any person associated with that person.

Section 3604(f)(3) creates what Professor Schwemm describes as the "three special provisions."[13] These provisions define discrimination to include refusals or failures to comply with distinct affirmative duties applying only to individuals with disabilities.

- The first, §3604(f)(3)(A), defines discrimination to include a refusal to permit reasonable physical modifications of existing premises at the expense of the disabled person if necessary to afford full enjoyment of the premises.

---

11. H.R. Rep. No. 100-711, at 24 (1988).
12. Note the variation in text from §3604(a), which prohibits the refusal "to sell or rent after the making of a bona fide offer" or the refusal "to negotiate for the sale or rental of" a dwelling. Both provisions include the catch-all phrase "otherwise make unavailable or deny," however, which renders such textual variation inconsequential.
13. *See* Schwemm, HDLL §11D:6.

- The second, §3604(f)(3)(B), which this text covers in great detail, defines discrimination to include the refusal to make reasonable accommodations in rules, policies, practices, or services, when such accommodations may be necessary to afford a person with a disability equal opportunity to use and enjoy a dwelling.
- The third, §3604(f)(3)(C), defines discrimination to include failure to comply with certain accessible design and construction requirements for multifamily dwellings first occupied after March 13, 1991.

Each of these "special provisions" is discussed below.

B. DEFINING DISABILITY

A threshold question under any disability rights statute is whether the person seeking protection can satisfy the statute's broad definition of "disability." The FHA, like the ADA and §504, uses a three-pronged definition.[14] The first prong at §3602(h)(1) is most salient and defines disability as:

- a physical or mental impairment
- which substantially limits
- one or more major life activities.

Plaintiffs commonly are able to establish that they suffer a physical or mental impairment under this definition. HUD provides this nonexhaustive list of impairments in its regulation at 24 CFR §100.201(a):

(1) Any physiological disorder or condition, cosmetic disfigurement, or anatomical loss affecting one or more of the following body systems: Neurological; musculoskeletal; special sense organs; respiratory, including speech organs; cardiovascular; reproductive; digestive; genitourinary; hemic and lymphatic; skin; and endocrine; or

(2) Any mental or psychological disorder, such as mental retardation, organic brain syndrome, emotional or mental illness, and specific learning disabilities. The term "physical or mental impairment" includes, but is not limited to, such diseases and conditions as orthopedic, visual, speech and hearing impairments, cerebral palsy, autism, epilepsy, muscular dystrophy, multiple sclerosis, cancer, heart disease, diabetes, Human Immunodeficiency Virus infection, mental retardation, emotional illness,

---

14. The provisions that defined disability in the ADA, 42 U.S.C. §12102(a); §504, 29 U.S.C. §705(9)(B); and the FHA were substantially the same until 2008, when Congress enacted the ADA Amendments Act (ADAAA) adding "rules of construction" and additional disability definitions to abrogate or modify certain restrictive Supreme Court interpretations. *See* 42 U.S.C. §12102. When Congress passed the ADAAA, it amended the definition of disability under §504 to conform to the new definition of disability for the ADA. Pub. L. No. 110-325, §7. Congress did not similarly amend the FHA, so courts interpret the FHA using pre-ADAAA caselaw. *See* Schwemm, HDLL §11D:2 (Note on terminology).

drug addiction (other than addiction caused by current, illegal use of a controlled substance) and alcoholism.

Of course, it is insufficient simply to point to an impairment. The definition of disability requires proof that the impairment *substantially limits* a *major life activity*. Major life activities as defined in HUD's regulation include this non-exhaustive list: "caring for one's self, performing manual tasks, walking, seeing, hearing, speaking, breathing, learning and working." 24 C.F.R. §100.201(b). Courts have recognized other major life activities, including living independently and obtaining housing.[15] HUD recognizes as major life activities the operation of major bodily activities, systems, and organs, as well as normal cell growth.[16]

Substantial limitations suggest those that are "considerable" or "to a large degree" and do not include those "interfer[ing] in only a minor way with activities."[17] Nature and severity, expected duration, and the likely long-term impact of the impairment all are pertinent to the disability determination.[18] Under ADA caselaw abrogated by amendment but still applied to the FHA, impairments may not be substantially limiting if they can be ameliorated through medicines or corrective devices, such as hearing aids, prostheses, and eyeglasses.[19]

The second and third prongs of the definition cover persons: (2) who have a record of having such an impairment, or (3) who are regarded as having such an impairment even if there is no current, substantially limiting impairment. 42 U.S.C. §3602(h). The FHA makes no distinction in protecting individuals whether they meet the first, second, or third prong of the definition.[20] The definition recognizes that perceptions about a person's impairment can result in harmful exclusion and discrimination regardless of whether the plaintiff can establish a substantially limiting impairment. The regulation at 24 C.F.R. §100.201 further defines these terms as follows:

---

15. *See* Schwemm, HDLL §11D:2 n.9 (citing cases); Harmony Haus Westlake, L.L.C. v. Parkstone Prop. Owners Ass'n, 851 Fed. App'x 461, 463-65 (5th Cir. 2021) (holding that residents recovering from addiction met the disability definition under the FHA based on the impairment of their ability to live independently). *Cf.* Eastwood v. Willow Bend Lake Homeowners Ass'n, No. 4:20-CV-00400, 2020 WL 3412409, at *2-3 (E.D. Tex. June 22, 2020) (holding resident could not establish that "staying away from strangers" was a major life activity where an immunocompromised cancer patient susceptible to COVID-19 wanted private use of an unfenced portion of his backyard for therapeutic sunlight and requested a reasonable accommodation to his HOA's restrictive covenants to build a second fence).

16. HUD, Disability Overview, https://www.hud.gov/program_offices/fair_housing_eq ual_opp/disability_overview#additional-resources (last visited June 21, 2023).

17. *See* Schwemm, HDLL §11D:2 (citing pre-ADAAA caselaw, Toyota Motor Mfg., Kentucky, Inc. v. Williams, 534 U.S. 184, 196 (2002), *abrogated with respect to the ADA and §504 by* U.S. Pub. L. 110-325, §§ 2, 7 (Jan. 1, 2009)).

18. *See id.*

19. *See* Schwemm, HDLL §11D:2 (citing pre-ADAAA caselaw, Sutton v. United Air Lines, 527 U.S. 471 (1999), *abrogated with respect to the ADA and §504 by* U.S. Pub. L. 110-325, §§ 2, 7 (Jan. 1, 2009)).

20. The ADA expands the definition of "regarded as" at §12102(3) but does not provide a right of accommodation to those qualifying under the "regarded as" prong. *See* 42 U.S.C. §12201(h).

(c) ***Has a record of such an impairment*** means has a history of, or has been misclassified as having, a mental or physical impairment that substantially limits one or more major life activities.

(d) ***Is regarded as having an impairment*** means:

(1) Has a physical or mental impairment that does not substantially limit one or more major life activities but that is treated by another person as constituting such a limitation;

(2) Has a physical or mental impairment that substantially limits one or more major life activities only as a result of the attitudes of other[s] toward such impairment; or

(3) Has none of the impairments defined in paragraph (a) of this definition but is treated by another person as having such an impairment.

Consider an example arising from a refusal to allow a condominium owner to rent to a nurse during the COVID-19 pandemic:

> Piraino, an ICU nurse, is "regarded as" a handicapped person within the meaning of 42 U.S.C. §3602(h)(3), because she was allegedly treated by Respondents in a discriminatory manner on account of her association with COVID-19 patients who have an impairment, COVID-19. . . . "Persons with COVID-19 and persons associated with persons with COVID-19 . . . including medical personnel, may be subjected to discrimination under the FHA because they are regarded as having an impairment that substantially limits [a] major life activity, even if they do not have one."

United States v. Boca View Condominium Ass'n, No. 22-80139-MC, 2023 WL 2534087, at *3 (S.D. Fla. Mar. 16, 2023).

ADA AMENDMENTS ACT

Congress enacted the ADA Amendments Act (ADAAA) in 2008 following several Supreme Court decisions issuing restrictive interpretations of the definition of disability. (As discussed in Section H, below, Title II of the ADAAA covers certain programs, activities, and services operated by state and local governments, and Title III covers places of public accommodation, such as rental offices.) The ADAAA abrogates the decisions in a number of ways. Significantly, it retains the traditional three-pronged definition and adds expansive rules of construction for both the ADA and §504 (covering federally assisted programs and activities), but does not address the FHA:

- It rejects the demanding standard under Toyota Motor Manufacturing, Ky., Inc. v. Williams, 534 U.S. 184 (2002), and requires the definition of disability to be "construed in favor of broad coverage." 42 U.S.C. §12102(4)(A). In *Toyota*, the Court had held that whether a plaintiff's carpal tunnel syndrome was substantially limiting required consideration of manual tasks that are of central importance to most people's daily lives, rather than a more limited class of manual tasks assigned for work on the auto assembly line. The ADAAA also rejects the Court's holding that an impairment's impact must be permanent or long-term.

- It rejects the consideration under Sutton v. United Airlines, Inc., 527 U.S. 471 (1999), of possible "ameliorative effects of mitigating measures" to determine if an impairment substantially limits a major life activity. 42 U.S.C. §12102(4)(E) (including exception for fully corrective eyeglasses or contact lenses). In *Sutton*, the Court had held that "the determination of whether an individual is disabled should be made with reference to measures that mitigate the individual's impairment, [such as, in the case of commercial airline pilots,] eyeglasses and contact lenses."
- It rejects *Toyota*'s interpretation of "substantially limits" to require a showing of a limitation that is "considerable" or "to a large degree" pursuant to a broader rule of construction requiring that "[t]he term 'substantially limits' shall be interpreted consistently with the findings and purposes of the ADA Amendments Act of 2008."
- It provides that an impairment need only limit one major life activity to meet the definition. 42 U.S.C. §12102(4)(C).
- It provides that "[a]n impairment that is episodic or in remission is a disability if it would substantially limit a major life activity when active." 42 U.S.C. §12102(4)(D).
- It incorporates a nonexhaustive list of "major life activities," including "working" (which was a question reserved in *Toyota and Sutton*); it also adds activities not included in HUD's regulation: eating, sleeping, standing, lifting, bending, reading, concentrating, thinking, and communicating. 42 U.S.C. §12102(2)(A).
- It rejects the suggestion in *Toyota* that a condition must affect activities of daily life by adding "major bodily functions" to the major life activity definition. 42 U.S.C. §12102(2)(B).
- It responds to the holding in *Sutton* that the "regarded as" prong requires an alleged perception that the person's impairment substantially limited them from working in a broad class of jobs rather than in a particular job. Instead, a showing of a prohibited action because of an actual or perceived impairment is sufficient. 42 U.S.C. §12102(3). (However, this "regarded as" prong does not trigger the right to an accommodation, 42 U.S.C. §12201(h), and does not apply to "impairments that are transitory [6 months or less] or minor.")

See Bagenstos, Disability Rights Law, at 35-41.

Current illegal[21] use of (or addiction to) a controlled substance is excluded from coverage under §3602(h);[22] the inverse proposition is also true and

---

21. At least one court has held that tenants were not entitled to use medical marijuana, still illegal at the time under federal law, in their rental units as a reasonable accommodation because the FHA excludes illegal drug use from coverage; also, such illegal use would fundamentally alter the nature of the federally assisted housing program. *See* Forest City Residential Mgmt., Inc. v. Beasley, 71 F. Supp. 3d 715, 728-31 (E.D. Mich. 2014); *see also* HUD, Memorandum on Use of Marijuana in Multifamily Assisted Properties (Dec. 29, 2014) ("owners must deny admission to assisted housing for any household with a member determined to be illegally using a controlled substance, e.g., marijuana. . . . [Federal law] affords owners the *discretion* to evict or not evict current tenants for their use of marijuana."). This landscape may change as federal law evolves on legality of marijuana use.

22. *See also* 29 U.S.C. §705(20)(C)(i) (under §504, the term "'individual with a disability' does not include an individual who is currently engaging in the illegal use of drugs, when a covered

discussed further in Section G on group homes: people recovering from addiction or using drugs legally may meet the FHA's definition of disability. Also, as discussed more fully in Section F below, the FHA does not protect a person whose tenancy would pose a direct threat to the health or safety of others or substantially damage another's property. 42 U.S.C. §3604(f)(9). However, housing providers cannot use stereotypes and generalizations to determine whether a disabled person's tenancy constitutes "a direct threat."

DISABILITY AND THE TRANS EXEMPTION

A stray note under the FHA's definitional section, 42 U.S.C. §3602(h), alerts the reader: "Neither the term 'individual with handicaps' nor the term 'handicap' shall apply to an individual solely because that individual is a transvestite." Professors Hillier and Benten provide much-needed context for this anti-trans exclusion:

> The year 1988 brought further changes to the Fair Housing Act. . . . It was within the debates about who warranted protection under the category of "persons with physical or mental disabilities" that discussion of gender identity was introduced—and with it the first explicit acknowledgment of trans people within fair housing legislation. As these additions were being debated, Jesse Helms [R-NC] [EDS.—one of three Senators to vote against the FHA amendments] was afraid. A 1986 court opinion had found that trans status represents a handicap and that trans people are protected under antidiscrimination employment law as written (*Blackwell v. United States Department of the Treasury* [D.D.C., aff'd D.C. Cir.] 1986). Helms . . . feared that trans people might sue for protection under the FHA and win. He therefore put forward an amendment that made explicit that "individual with handicaps" in no way meant a person who was transgender. "I have no doubt that sometime, somewhere, another Federal court will be asked to revisit that issue . . .," explained Helms. "When that happens, it should be clear to the courts that Congress does not intend for transvestites to receive the benefits and protections that is [sic] provided for handicapped individuals." Senator Alan Cranston (D-CA) rose in opposition to Helms's amendment: "As a principal author of section 504 [of the Rehabilitation Act of 1973], I see this amendment as a direct attack on the heart and soul of anti-discrimination laws, which protect individuals against discrimination based on stereotypes," he insisted. "It is an appeal to our worst instincts—saying that we shouldn't have to associate with individuals who are different from ourselves . . .," he argued further. "If we were to start excluding one category of individuals from coverage, we would be threatening to undermine the very essence of anti-discrimination laws." The amendment passed the Senate 89-2.

Amy Hillier & Devin Michelle Bunten, *A Queer and Intersectional Approach to Fair Housing*, in PERSPECTIVES ON FAIR HOUSING 154-55 (Vincent J. Reina et al.

---

entity acts on the basis of such use."); 28 C.F.R. §35.108 (g) (under Title II of the ADA governing public services, "[t]he term "disability" does not include—(3) Psychoactive substance use disorders resulting from current illegal use of drugs.").

eds., U. Penn. 2021). Now that the Court has defined "sex" in *Bostock* to include gender identity and sexual orientation, thus prohibiting discrimination based on trans status in employment (and probably in housing; *see* Chapter 15), what effect is the Helms amendment likely to have? Note that antidiscrimination provisions on the basis of sex lack the affirmative duties to provide reasonable accommodations.

Who has the burden of proof with respect to the threshold question of establishing disability? Unless the disability is obvious, plaintiffs must offer evidence that an impairment substantially limits a major life activity, because disability is "an individualized inquiry."[23] For example, while recovery from addiction generally is considered to be an impairment, courts usually will not decide disability status for recovering people "as a matter of law." *See* Oxford Investments, L.P. v. City of Philadelphia, 21 F. Supp. 3d 442, 454 (E.D. Pa 2014) ("With no direct or circumstantial evidence [on substantial limitation], Oxford's claim requires the Court to assume that all recovering addicts are handicapped. Such an analysis clearly conflicts with the Supreme Court's directive to conduct individualized disability assessments. . . ."). Similarly, alleging that a person is elderly does not by itself satisfy the definition of disability under the FHA. *See* Caron v. City of Pawtucket, 307 F. Supp. 2d 364, 368 (D.R.I. 2004). However, if a recovering drug addict or elderly person is perceived as having a substantially limiting impairment even if they do not, they would be covered by the FHA's disability definition.

INQUIRING ABOUT DISABILITY

The FHA prohibits housing providers from asking questions about the disabilities of tenants or buyers, or those residing or associated with them. Note that a provider may ask in some instances for supporting information in response to a request for reasonable accommodation or modification, as discussed in Sections C and D. In addition, the following inquiries are permitted as long as they are made of all applicants:

1. Inquiry into an applicant's ability to meet the requirements of ownership or tenancy;
2. Inquiry to determine whether an applicant is qualified for a dwelling available only to persons with disabilities or to persons with a particular type of disability;
3. Inquiry to determine whether an applicant for a dwelling is qualified for a priority available to persons with disabilities or to persons with a particular type of disability;

---

23. *See Sutton*, 527 U.S. at 483.

> 4. Inquiring whether an applicant for a dwelling is a current illegal abuser or addict of a controlled substance;
> 5. Inquiring whether an applicant has been convicted of the illegal manufacture or distribution of a controlled substance.
>
> 24 C.F.R. §100.202(c).

When a disability is not as obvious as, say, a mobility impairment requiring use of a wheelchair, the issue frequently litigated is whether a physical or mental impairment *substantially limits* an identified major life activity. The following case illustrates (in the context of reasonable accommodation) how one plaintiff demonstrated that his impairment of post-traumatic stress substantially limited his ability to work in a broad class of jobs.

Bhogaita v. Altamonte Heights Condominium Ass'ns, Inc.

765 F.3d 1277 (11th Cir. 2014)

Before Carnes, Chief Judge, Dubina, and Siler (by designation), Circuit Judges

DUBINA, Circuit Judge:

Appellee Ajit Bhogaita persuaded a jury that Appellant Altamonte Heights Condominium Association, Inc., ("the Association") violated the disability provisions of the Federal and Florida Fair Housing Acts when it enforced its pet weight policy and demanded Bhogaita remove his emotional support dog from his condominium. The jury awarded Bhogaita $5,000 in damages, and the district court awarded Bhogaita more than $100,000 in attorneys' fees.

I. BACKGROUND

A. Factual History

The Association is a non-profit homeowners association for a condominium complex located in Altamonte Springs, Florida. Bhogaita is a United States Air Force veteran who suffers from post-traumatic stress disorder ("PTSD") that developed after a sexual assault he endured during his military service.

In 2001, Bhogaita bought a condominium unit managed by the Association and subject to its rules. Among those rules, the Association prohibited occupants from keeping dogs weighing more than twenty-five pounds. In 2008, Bhogaita acquired a dog, Kane, that exceeded the weight limit. Though no medical professional prescribed the dog initially, Bhogaita's psychiatric symptoms improved with Kane's presence, so much so that Bhogaita began to rely on the dog to help him manage his condition. He kept the dog for the next two years.

The Association demanded that Bhogaita remove Kane from his unit, pursuant to the weight limit. Bhogaita responded by providing the first of three letters from his treating psychiatrist, explaining that the dog was an emotional support animal. The first letter read in relevant part:

> Due to mental illness, Mr. Bhogaita has certain limitations regarding social interaction and coping with stress and anxiety. In order to help alleviate these difficulties, and to enhance his ability to live independently and to fully use and enjoy the dwelling unit, I am prescribing an emotional support animal that will assist Mr. Bhogaita in coping with his disability.

In the second letter, sent days later, [the treating doctor provided more detail regarding Bhogaita's therapeutic relationship with his specific dog, Kane. Two months later, the Association requested additional information regarding Bhogaita's disability and his need for Kane. Later that month, Bhogaita provided a third letter from his doctor, who indicated the nature and cause of the disability: anxiety related to military trauma which limited his ability to work with other people. The treating doctor also stated that Kane enabled Bhogaita to work.

The Association sent Bhoghaita a second letter requesting additional documentation about Bhoghaita's disabilities and his need for an oversized support animal, treatment information, and details about Kane's training. Two and a half months later, with no response from Bhogaita, the Association sent a third request for information seeking a sworn doctor's statement on details regarding the disability, medications, diagnoses, specific treatments, and the need for an oversized dog. The Association also requested documentation regarding Kane's training. Absent a response by a given deadline, the Association issued a formal demand for removal of Kane, enforceable by arbitration.

Bhogaita filed a complaint with HUD and the Florida Human Relations Commission, which issued findings of reasonable cause to believe that discrimination occurred.] Accordingly, the Association agreed to allow Bhogaita to keep Kane.

B. Procedural History

Bhogaita brought suit [EDS. — rather than pursue an administrative enforcement proceeding]. A two-day jury trial followed. The jury returned a verdict in favor of Bhogaita: It found that Bhogaita was disabled and requested an accommodation for his disability, that the accommodation was necessary and reasonable, and that Bhogaita suffered damages because of the Association's refusal to accommodate. It awarded Bhogaita $5,000 in compensatory damages but declined to award punitive damages.

[The court denied post-trial motions, including] Bhogaita's motion for a permanent injunction, as the Association had already agreed to allow Kane to remain, [and] ordered the Association to pay $127,512 in attorneys' fees, almost $70,000 less than the sum Bhogaita's lawyers sought. [On appeal, the court considered, among other things, whether there was sufficient evidence for the jury to find that Bhogaita has a disability that substantially limits a major life activity.]

V. DISCUSSION

The FHA prohibits discriminating against a person on the basis of a "handi-cap," or a disability, by refusing to make reasonable accommodations when necessary to afford the person equal opportunity to use and enjoy a dwelling. §3604(f)(3)(B). A successful failure-to-accommodate claim has four elements. To prevail, one must prove that (1) he is disabled within the meaning of the FHA, (2) he requested a reasonable accommodation, (3) the requested accom-modation was necessary to afford him an opportunity to use and enjoy his dwelling, and (4) the defendants refused to make the accommodation [The court granted summary judgment for Bhogaita on this final element].

A. Bhogaita Was Entitled to Partial Summary Judgment on the Refusal-to-Accommodate Element.

Bhogaita requested an accommodation in May 2010. More than six months later, when he filed a complaint with HUD and the Commission, the Association had not responded to his request except to request additional information [through three letters] and to indicate that if Bhogaita failed to provide that information, the Association would file for arbitration. The Association insists that its deliberative process was ongoing and that its requests were only meant to help it discern whether Bhogaita had a disability requiring accommodation.

The Association produced no evidence at the summary judgment stage to support its contention that it had not constructively denied Bhogaita's request. Neither Bhogaita's silence in the face of requests for information the Association already had nor his failure to provide information irrelevant to the Association's determination can support an inference that the Association's delay reflected an attempt at meaningful review.

Dr. Li's three letters contained the information the Association needed to make a determination: They described the nature and cause of Bhogaita's PTSD diagnosis, stated that Bhogaita was substantially impaired in the major life activity of working, and explained that the dog alleviated Bhogaita's symp-toms. Though Dr. Li's letters identified a cognizable disability and explained the necessity of accommodation, the [Association's second] request sought the same information already provided. Bhogaita's failure to respond to that request cannot support the Association's position because the Association possessed all the information essential to its determination.

Likewise, Bhogaita's failure to respond to the [Association's third] request for information cannot support an inference that the Association was still undertaking meaningful review. That it is "incumbent upon" a skeptical defen-dant "to request documentation or open a dialogue" rather than immediately refusing a requested accommodation, Jankowski Lee & Associates v. Cisneros, 91 F.3d 891, 895 (7th Cir. 1996), does not entitle a defendant to extraneous information. Generally, housing providers need only the information neces-sary to apprise them of the disability and the desire and possible need for an accommodation. . . . Joint Statement [of HUD and DOJ on Accommodations] at 14 (counseling that, "[i]n most cases, an individual's medical records or detailed information about the nature of a person's disability is not necessary for" determining whether an accommodation is required).

The Association's critical inquiries were whether Bhogaita's PTSD amounted to a qualifying disability and whether Kane's presence alleviated the effects of the disorder. The [third] letter requested, in addition to the pertinent information it already had thanks to Dr. Li's letters: "additional information regarding Bhogaita's treatment, medications, and the number of counseling sessions he attended per week; details about how the diagnosis was made; whether the condition was permanent or temporary; and 'details of the prescribed treatment moving forward.'" The requested information exceeded that essential for the Association's critical inquiries. On the record before it, the district court was correct in declining to hold Bhogaita's silence in the face of the last two letters against him.

B. Bhogaita Offered Sufficient Evidence to Show He Has a Disability Within the Meaning of the FHA.

A person has a disability under the FHA if, among other things, he has "a physical or mental impairment which substantially limits one or more of such person's major life activities." 42 U.S.C. §3602(h). The parties agree that Bhogaita suffers from a physical or mental impairment, and they agree that working is a major life activity. They depart company, however, on whether Bhogaita's impairment substantially limited his ability to work. When considering what it means for an impairment to limit substantially one's ability to work, we find cases interpreting and applying the ADA relevant.

When interpreting the pre-ADAAA definition of "disability," a definition virtually identical to the FHA's definition of "handicap," the Supreme Court concluded that an impairment substantially limits one's ability to work only where it renders a person "unable to work in a broad class of jobs." Sutton v. United Air Lines, Inc., 527 U.S. 471, 491 (1999). We apply the same interpretation here because of the similarity between the preamendment ADA and the FHA.

Bhogaita presented ample evidence at trial to show that his PTSD left him unable to work in a broad class of jobs. Bhogaita's own testimony revealed his belief that colleagues persecuted him, a belief that made it practically impossible for him to work outside his home. Dr. Li's letters stated that Bhogaita's condition "limits his ability to work directly with other people" and that social interactions had the tendency to be so overwhelming for Bhogaita, they could possibly render him "unable to perform work of any kind." For one to gain remuneration of any sort one must engage, at a minimum, with either a superior or a customer, and most jobs require much more. To note that the cloistered laboratory scientist occasionally presents his research to others and that the warehouse stocker takes some direction from supply managers is to acknowledge that the sales clerk, the teacher, and the construction foreman, for example, interact significantly and almost constantly. Certainly jobs requiring significant social interaction amount to a broad class.

Viewing the evidence in the light most favorable to the jury's verdict and drawing all inferences in its favor, a reasonable jury could agree to the verdict reached. The district court did not err in denying judgment as a matter of law on the disability element.

C. Bhogaita Produced Evidence Supporting the Conclusion That the Requested Accommodation Was Necessary.

A successful FHA accommodation claim requires that the accommodation sought be "necessary to afford [the claimant] equal opportunity to use and enjoy" the relevant dwelling. §3604(f)(3)(B). "The word 'equal' is a relative term that requires a comparator to have meaning." Under the FHA, the comparator is a person without a disability, and an accommodation extends an equal opportunity when it addresses the needs the disability creates. Thus, a "necessary" accommodation is one that alleviates the effects of a disability. The jury was properly instructed to that effect.

[Dr. Li's letters] directly support the jury's verdict: The requested "accommodation was necessary to afford [Bhogaita] an opportunity to use and enjoy the dwelling."

NOTES AND QUESTIONS

1. Predominance of Disability Complaints. According to the HUD FHEO [Fair Housing and Equal Opportunity's] Annual Report for 2022, its most recent at the time of this writing: "For the past five years, complaints alleging disability discrimination have been the most common complaint filed with HUD and FHAP [Fair Housing Assistance Program] agencies, followed by race and sex."[24] What factors might explain the predominance of disability-based complaints among all protected categories?

2. Substantially Limiting Impairments. The *Bhogaita* court, like most courts, held that cases interpreting and applying the ADA (before its amendment)[25] are relevant to the question whether a physical or mental impairment "substantially limits" a major life activity, which in this case

---

24. *See* HUD, Office of Fair Housing & Equal Opportunity, STATE OF FAIR HOUSING, ANNUAL REPORT TO CONGRESS: FY 2022, at 66 (noting that disability complaints represented 59.5 percent of total complaints filed).

25. *See also* Rodriguez v. Vill. Green Realty, 788 F.3d 31, 40 n.10 (2d Cir. 2015) (noting that Congress did not amend the FHA when it amended the ADA in 2008 "so [the court's] FHA interpretation is still guided by pre-ADAAA cases"). This means that although the ADAAA was enacted specifically to repudiate the restrictive standard announced in *Sutton* and several other cases, courts are still citing these holdings in FHA cases.

was the ability to work. Citing Sutton v. United Air Lines, Inc., 527 U.S. 471, 491 (1999), the court focused its inquiry on whether the impairment substantially limited the ability to work not in any particular job, but in a broad class of jobs. (In *Sutton*, plaintiffs claimed they were disabled because their uncorrected eyesight left them unable to meet the employer's requirements for global airline pilots.) What evidence did the court find sufficient to support the jury's verdict that Bhogaita's PTSD "left him unable to work in a broad class of jobs"?

Plaintiffs have the burden of proving they have a substantially limiting impairment under the FHA. Consider the kinds of evidence used, with varying degrees of success, to meet this burden in the examples below.

- In Castillo Condominium Ass'n v. HUD, 821 F.3d 92, 99-100 (1st Cir. 2016), the court affirmed the HUD Secretary's rejection of the ALJ's holding of no disability, stating the complainant offered sufficient evidence of "a lifelong history of depression" that substantially limited his major life activities. The court agreed with the Secretary's crediting of the testimony of the complainant and the two doctors who had "treated [him] for years." First, the court agreed that the complainant *can* "supply key testimony verifying his own disability status." Second, the court agreed that the complainant's psychiatrist should not be discounted solely on the basis of his personal friendship with the complainant and provision of services pro bono, because "verification of a person's disability can come from any reliable third party who is in a position to know about the individual's disability." Finally, agreeing that the primary care physician also offered probative testimony, the court upheld the Secretary's conclusion on disability.
- In Thomas v. The Salvation Army Southern Territory, 841 F.3d 632, 639 (4th Cir. 2016), the court held plaintiff's allegation of mental disability to be deficient. "Thomas provides limited evidence in her complaint that she has some type of mental illness—she received care from a behavioral health organization, she had an appointment with a doctor, and she was on medication. . . . Thomas specifies her mental illness as a mood disorder. This evidence, though, does not suggest that her mental illness is a handicap covered by the FHA. Moreover, Thomas alleges that she was 'mentally stable' and that the mental evaluation requested by the Salvation Army was 'unnecessary.'"

C. REASONABLE ACCOMMODATIONS

The *Bhogaita* court determined whether the plaintiff had a disability for the purpose of deciding whether a reasonable accommodation was required. This chapter dedicates substantial coverage to this issue because failure to make reasonable accommodations comprised a whopping 44.2 percent of total housing discrimination complaints filed on any issue with federal, state, and local agencies in 2022.[26]

The FHA, like other disability rights statutes,[27] defines disability discrimination to include:

> a refusal to make **reasonable** accommodations in rules, policies, practices, or services, when such accommodations may be **necessary** to afford [protected persons] **equal opportunity to use and enjoy** a dwelling.

42 U.S.C. §3604(f)(3)(B) (emphasis added). This means the FHA imposes an affirmative obligation on housing providers to make reasonable accommodations. This brief definition raises a number of questions: What kinds of requests will be recognized as *accommodations*? How should a court determine whether an accommodation is "reasonable"? What constitutes a "necessary" accommodation? And what is the process for requesting such an accommodation and responding to such requests? As the definition suggests, these are largely fact-bound questions decided on a case-by-case basis.

DOJ and HUD, which are jointly responsible for enforcing the federal FHA, have developed technical assistance that some courts, including the Eleventh Circuit in *Bhogaita*, have found persuasive.[28] This type of agency guidance document is intended to provide a useful tool but not to expand or alter existing law or regulations.[29] *See* Chapter 3. An excerpt follows.

The Joint Statement of The Department of Housing and Urban Development and the Department of Justice, Reasonable Accommodations under the Fair Housing Act (May 17, 2004) (hereinafter, *Joint Statement on Accommodations*).[30]

REASONABLE ACCOMMODATION DEFINED

A "**reasonable accommodation**" is a change, exception, or adjustment to a rule, policy, practice, or service that may be **necessary** for a person with a

---

26. HUD, Office of Fair Housing & Equal Opportunity, STATE OF FAIR HOUSING, ANNUAL REPORT TO CONGRESS: FY 2022, at 67.

27. *See* Summers v. City of Fitchburg, 940 F.3d 133, 139 (1st Cir. 2019) ("For present purposes, the elements of reasonable accommodation claims under the FHAA and the ADA do not differ in any meaningful respect.").

28. *Bhogaita*, 765 F.3d at 1286 n.3 ("The Joint Statement is a policy statement [and] 'entitled to respect' to the extent it has the 'power to persuade.'"). This respect for agency statements is known as "Skidmore" deference. Skidmore v. Swift & Co., 323 U.S. 134, 140 (1944). This form of deference survives the Supreme Court's overruling of *Chevron*, which required binding deference to certain agency regulations. Loper Bright Enters. v. Raimondo, __ U.S. __ (2024).

29. *See* 2020 Assistance Animal Notice, *infra* note 33, at 5.

30. Paragraph numbers are not sequential and are included at the end of the paragraphs for reference. Emphasis is added by the editors.

disability to have an **equal opportunity to use and enjoy** a dwelling, including public and common use spaces.

Since rules, policies, practices, and services may have a different effect on persons with disabilities than on other persons, treating persons with disabilities exactly the same as others will sometimes deny them an equal opportunity to use and enjoy a dwelling. [6]

NECESSITY

To show that a requested accommodation may be necessary, there must be an identifiable relationship, or nexus, between the requested accommodation and the individual's disability.

A housing provider can deny a request for a reasonable accommodation if the request was not made by or on behalf of a person with a disability or if there is no disability-related need for the accommodation. [7]

REASONABLENESS

In addition, a request for a reasonable accommodation may be denied if providing the accommodation is **not reasonable** — i.e., if it would impose an **undue financial and administrative burden** on the housing provider or it would **fundamentally alter** the nature of the provider's operations.[31]

The determination of **undue financial and administrative burden** must be made on a case-by-case basis involving various factors, such as the cost of the requested accommodation [some costs may be required of the housing provider], the financial resources of the provider, the benefits that the accommodation would provide to the requester, and the availability of alternative accommodations that would effectively meet the requester's disability-related needs.

A **"fundamental alteration"** is a modification that alters the essential nature of a provider's operations. *An example would be providing transportation or medical assistance not generally offered to tenants.* [8]

INTERACTIVE PROCESS

When a housing provider refuses a requested accommodation because it is not reasonable, the provider should discuss with the requester whether there is an alternative accommodation that would effectively address the requester's disability-related needs without a fundamental alteration to the provider's operations and without imposing an undue financial and administrative burden. If an alternative accommodation would effectively meet the requester's disability-related needs and is reasonable, the provider must grant it. An interactive process in which the housing provider and the requester discuss

---

31. *See* Southeastern Cmty. Coll. v. Davis, 442 U.S. 397, 410, 412 (1979).

the requester's disability-related need for the requested accommodation and possible alternative accommodations is helpful to all concerned because it often results in an effective accommodation for the requester that does not pose an undue financial and administrative burden for the provider. [7]

There may be instances where a provider believes that, while the accommodation requested by an individual is reasonable, there is an alternative accommodation that would be equally effective in meeting the individual's disability-related needs. In such a circumstance, the provider should discuss with the individual if she is willing to accept the alternative accommodation. However, providers should be aware that persons with disabilities typically have the most accurate knowledge about the functional limitations posed by their disability, and an individual is not obligated to accept an alternative accommodation suggested by the provider if she believes it will not meet her needs and her preferred accommodation is reasonable [EDS.—and necessary]. [7]

A failure to reach an agreement on an accommodation request is in effect a decision by the provider not to grant the requested accommodation. [10]

CONDITIONS

Housing providers may not require persons with disabilities to pay extra fees or deposits as a condition of receiving a reasonable accommodation. [11]

PROCESS FOR MAKING THE ACCOMMODATION REQUEST

A housing provider is only obligated to provide a reasonable accommodation to a resident or applicant if a request for the accommodation has been made. [14]

Under the Act, a resident or an applicant for housing makes a reasonable accommodation request whenever she makes clear to the housing provider that she is requesting an exception, change, or adjustment to a rule, policy, practice, or service because of her disability. She should explain what type of accommodation she is requesting and, if the need for the accommodation is not readily apparent or not known to the provider, explain the relationship between the requested accommodation and her disability. [12]

However, the FHA does not require that a request be made in a particular manner or at a particular time. An individual making a reasonable accommodation request does not need to mention the Act or use the words "reasonable accommodation." Although a reasonable accommodation request can be made orally or in writing, it is usually helpful for both the resident and the housing provider if the request is made in writing.

The Act does not require that a housing provider adopt any formal procedures for reasonable accommodation requests. If a provider adopts formal procedures for processing reasonable accommodation requests, the provider should ensure that the procedures, including any forms used, do not seek information that is not necessary to evaluate if a reasonable accommodation may be needed. [13]

PROCESS FOR RESPONDING TO THE ACCOMMODATION REQUEST AND SEEKING VERIFICATION

A provider has an obligation to provide prompt responses to reasonable accommodation requests. An undue delay in responding to a reasonable accommodation request may be deemed to be a failure to provide a reasonable accommodation. [15]

If a person's disability is obvious, or otherwise known to the provider, and if the need for the requested accommodation is also readily apparent or known, then the provider may not request any additional information about the requester's disability or the disability-related need for the accommodation. [17]

If the requester's disability is known or readily apparent to the provider, but the need for the accommodation is not readily apparent or known, the provider may request only information that is necessary to evaluate the disability-related need for the accommodation.

[If a disability is not obvious, then] in response to a request for a reasonable accommodation, a housing provider may request reliable disability-related information that (1) is necessary to verify that the person meets the Act's definition of disability (i.e., has a physical or mental impairment that substantially limits one or more major life activities), (2) describes the needed accommodation, and (3) shows the relationship between the person's disability and the need for the requested accommodation. [18]

Depending on the individual's circumstances, information verifying that the person meets the Act's definition of disability can usually be provided by the individual himself or herself (e.g., proof that an individual under 65 years of age receives Supplemental Security Income or Social Security Disability Insurance benefits or a credible statement by the individual). A doctor or other medical professional, a peer support group, a non-medical service agency, or a reliable third party who is in a position to know about the individual's disability may also provide verification of a disability.

In most cases, an individual's medical records or detailed information about the nature of a person's disability is not necessary for this inquiry.

NOTES AND QUESTIONS

1. Requests and Denials. The *Bhogaita* court described the required showing for a claim of failure to provide a reasonable accommodation:

1) Plaintiff or a person associated with plaintiff is a person with a disability,
2) who requested a reasonable accommodation,

3) that is necessary to afford an equal opportunity to use and enjoy the dwelling,
4) which defendants refused to make.[32]

What must a plaintiff plead to establish that they made a proper request for accommodation? Consider that many of these requests may be verbal, and tenants may be unaware that a court may later examine the sufficiency of their request. In Hunt v. Aimco Properties, L.P., 814 F.3d 1213, 1225-26 (11th Cir. 2016), the court addressed this question in the context of a refusal to renew a family's lease after an allegedly threatening incident involving their adult child with Down Syndrome:

> The district court decided that the Hunts could not proceed with this claim because Dyan had failed to request from Aimco a reasonable accommodation for Karl's disability as required by §3604(f)(3). But the complaint alleged that Dyan asked Aimco staff to let her and her son remain in their apartment while she found "a place/organization that will have [Karl] for the day while she is at work to avoid any more situations." We conclude that the complaint presented a plausible set of facts from which we can infer that Dyan requested an accommodation and thus sufficiently pled this claim. . . .
>
> We have yet to determine "precisely what form the request [for a reasonable accommodation] must take." Several other circuits have addressed this issue in the context of Title I of the ADA, which includes a similar provision requiring employers to make reasonable accommodations for their employees with disabilities. The Third Circuit, for example, has stated that what matters is not "formalisms about the manner of the request," but that the employer has notice of the employee's disability and wish to be accommodated. Similarly, the Tenth Circuit has emphasized that a plaintiff "need not use magic words" to express a request for accommodation. However stated, a plaintiff can be said to have made a request for accommodation when the defendant has "enough information to know of both the disability and desire for an accommodation." We agree with the Third Circuit that "circumstances must at least be sufficient to cause a reasonable [housing provider] to make appropriate inquiries about the possible need for an accommodation."
>
> Here, the complaint contained allegations that, taken together, meet this standard. Dyan explained to Ms. Jackson, the community manager, that Karl was not making threats but rather describing scenes from a cartoon he watched regularly, and that he "was harmless and . . . has a speech impediment that causes him to speak without properly explaining himself," resulting in his words being misconstrued. After Ms. Jackson and Deputy Kushel left the Hunts' home, Dyan called Ms. Jackson crying and apologizing profusely. Dyan told her that she would look for a facility that would take care of Karl during the day while she was away at work to prevent any more incidents. It is clear from the context that Dyan communicated that she was attempting to make these arrangements for the express purpose of avoiding future conflict as a result of Karl's disability. We conclude that these factual allegations were sufficient to plead that Dyan sought an

---

32. Compare this formulation to the one used by the Ninth Circuit in Giebeler v. M & B Assoc., 343 F.3d 1143, 1147 (9th Cir. 2003), below, which has no formal element requiring the plaintiff to request the accommodation but rather a showing that defendant knew or should have known of plaintiff's disability.

accommodation in the form of an exception to Aimco's apparent policy or practice of not renewing the leases of tenants who make threats.

Assuming a plaintiff requests an accommodation, how long must they wait for an answer? The *Bhogaita* court explained: "The FHA does not demand that housing providers immediately grant all requests for accommodation." The housing provider is entitled to conduct a "meaningful review." But the court also stated: "The failure to make a timely determination after meaningful review amounts to constructive denial of a requested accommodation, 'as an indeterminate delay has the same effect as an outright denial.'" In *Bhogaita*, the plaintiff waited six months without receiving the requested accommodation; the court upheld partial summary judgment for plaintiff on the refusal to accommodate element.

In another case, Groome Resources Ltd., LLC v. Parish of Jefferson, 234 F.3d 192, 199-200 (5th Cir. 2000), the claim was ripe because "ninety-five days had elapsed between the time the application [for reasonable accommodation] was submitted and the filing of the lawsuit." The court further noted:

> [F]our months after the filing of the lawsuit, the Parish officials in charge of the application could not provide any timetable or plan for acting on the application. While never formally denying the request, the Parish's unjustified and indeterminate delay had the same effect of undermining the anti-discriminatory purpose of the FHAA.

The provider alleged it was forced to delay the closing on its group home for people with Alzheimer's, incur financial penalties, and suffer economic loss in the delayed operation of the home, resulting in "concrete hardships" making the issue ripe for review.

2. Animals as Reasonable Accommodations. One of the most common types of fair housing complaints filed with HUD involves requests for reasonable accommodations from "no pet" policies so that individuals are able to use assistance animals in housing and common use areas. In 2020, HUD updated its guidance on the issue in the form of an Assistance Animal Notice, excerpted below.[33] Recognizing that the FHA "requires housing providers to modify or make exceptions to policies governing animals when it may be necessary to permit persons with disabilities to utilize animals," HUD clarified that:

> **Assistance animals** are *not pets*. They are animals that do work, perform tasks, assist, and/or provide therapeutic emotional support for individuals with disabilities. There are two types of assistance animals: (1) **service animals**, and (2) other trained or untrained animals that do work, perform tasks, provide assistance, and/or provide therapeutic emotional support for individuals with disabilities (referred to in this guidance as a "**support animal**").

---

33. HUD FHEO Notice; FHEO-2020-01, *Assessing a Person's Request to Have an Animal as a Reasonable Accommodation Under the Fair Housing Act* (Jan. 28, 2020) (emphasis added), https://www.hud.gov/sites/dfiles/PA/documents/HUDAsstAnimalNC1-28-2020.pdf (hereinafter, *2020 Assistance Animal Notice*).

An animal that does not qualify as a service animal or other type of assistance animal is a pet for purposes of the FHA and may be treated as a pet for purposes of the lease and the housing provider's rules and policies. A housing provider may exclude or charge a fee or deposit for pets in its discretion and subject to local law but not for service animals or other assistance animals. . . .

[The FHA requires accommodation for individuals whose disabilities are ameliorated through the use of either service or support animals; in this way it is broader than the ADA, which does *not* require accommodation for those using support animals.]

[HUD recommends preliminary reference to DOJ ADA regulations[34] to determine whether an animal is a **service animal**.] Under the ADA, "service animal means any **dog that is individually trained** to do work or perform tasks for the benefit of an individual with a disability, including a physical, sensory, psychiatric, intellectual, or other mental disability. Other species of animals, whether wild or domestic, trained or untrained, are not service animals for the purposes of this definition. The work or tasks performed by a service animal must be directly related to the individual's disability."

[Further inquiries regarding whether a service dog is trained are unnecessary and inappropriate if] the dog is observed guiding an individual who is blind or has low vision, pulling a wheelchair, or providing assistance with stability or balance to an individual with an observable mobility disability.

[If the dog's training is not readily apparent,] the housing provider may ask in substance

(1) "Is the animal required because of a disability?" and
(2) "What work or task has the animal been trained to perform?"

---

34. *See* DOJ Civil Rights Division, Frequently Asked Questions About Service Animals and the ADA, https://www.ada.gov/regs2010/service_animal_qa.html; ADA Requirements: Service Animals, https://www.ada.gov/service_animals_2010.htm (last updated Feb. 28, 2020).

> Do not ask about the nature or extent of the person's disability, and do not ask for documentation.

If the answer to question (1) is "yes" and work or a task is identified in response to question (2), grant the requested accommodation, if otherwise reasonable, because the animal qualifies as a service animal.

If the answer to either question is "no" or "none," the animal does not qualify as a service animal under federal law but may be a support animal or other type of assistance animal that needs to be accommodated.

[For **assistance animals other than service animals**,] [a] resident may request a reasonable accommodation either before or after acquiring the assistance animal. [If the individual has requested a reasonable accommodation], housing providers may use the following questions to help them assess whether to grant the requested accommodation.

> Does the person have an observable disability or does the housing provider . . . already have information giving them reason to believe that the person has a disability? [IF not, has] the person requesting the accommodation provided information that reasonably supports that the person seeking the accommodation has a disability?[35]

[If the answer to any of the previous questions is yes,]

> Has the person requesting the accommodation provided information which reasonably supports that the animal does work, performs tasks, provides assistance, and/or provides therapeutic emotional support with respect to the individual's disability?[36]

If yes,

> Is the animal commonly kept in households? If the animal is a dog, cat, small bird, rabbit, hamster, gerbil, other rodent, fish, turtle, or other small, domesticated animal that is traditionally kept in the home for pleasure rather than for commercial purposes, then the reasonable accommodation should be granted. . . . If the individual is requesting to keep a unique type of animal that is not commonly kept in households as described above, then the requestor has the substantial burden of demonstrating a disability-related therapeutic need for the specific animal or the specific type of animal.[37]

---

35. *See 2020 Assistance Animal Notice, supra* note 33, at 16 *(Guidance on Documenting an Individual's Need for Assistance Animals in Housing)*. Supporting information could include a determination from a government agency, receipt of disability benefits or services, or confirmation from a health care professional.

36. *See id.* at 12 ("Reasonably supporting information often consists of information from a licensed health care professional — e.g., physician, optometrist, psychiatrist, psychologist, physician's assistant, nurse practitioner, or nurse — general to the condition but specific as to the individual with a disability and the assistance or therapeutic emotional support provided by the animal.").

37. *See also id.* ("For purposes of this assessment, reptiles (other than turtles), barnyard animals, monkeys, kangaroos, and other non-domesticated animals are not considered common household animals."). For an example of the type of documentation needed to demonstrate therapeutic need for a "unique" animal, *see* Whiteaker v. City of Southgate, 651 F. Supp. 3d 893 (E.D. Mich. 2023) (holding summary judgment improper where the plaintiff in support of the request for accommodation from a city ordinance provided documentation that all six of his chickens functioned as a unit and were emotional support animals necessary to address his disabilities,

> A housing provider may . . . refuse a reasonable accommodation for an assistance animal if the specific animal poses a **direct threat** that cannot be eliminated or reduced to an acceptable level through actions the individual takes to maintain or control the animal.
>
> **Pet rules do not apply** to service animals and support animals. Thus, housing providers may not limit the breed or size of a dog used as a service animal or support animal just because of the size or breed but can, as noted, limit based on specific issues with the animal's conduct because it poses a direct threat or a fundamental alteration.
>
> A housing provider may not charge a deposit, fee, or surcharge for an assistance animal. A housing provider, however, may charge a tenant for damage an assistance animal causes if it is the provider's usual practice to charge for damage caused by tenants (or deduct it from the standard security deposits imposed on all tenants).
>
> Before denying a reasonable accommodation request due to lack of information confirming an individual's disability or disability-related need for an animal, the housing provider is encouraged to engage in a good-faith dialogue with the requestor called the "interactive process."

HUD's Notice makes clear that "assistance animals are not pets." In HUD's view, therefore, Mr. Bhogaita would not have been subject to a size limit on his dog if he were otherwise entitled to an assistance animal as a reasonable accommodation. The Notice also does not allow blanket limitations on animal breeds, but also acknowledges that housing providers may refuse to accommodate an assistance animal that poses a "direct threat." We consider this issue further in Section F, below.

3. No Intent Showing Required for Reasonable Accommodation Claims. Notice that the court did not require Mr. Bhogaita to show that the housing provider intended to exclude him based on his disability. The FHA recognizes the failure to make a reasonable accommodation as a distinct type of discrimination against people with disabilities. If the accommodation is refused, no showing of intentional discrimination is required. *See* Good Shepherd Manor Foundation, Inc. v. City of Momence, 323 F.3d 557, 562 (7th Cir. 2003) ("reasonable accommodation is a theory of liability separate from intentional discrimination").

In contrast to *Bhogaita*, where the housing provider engaged in repeated requests for verifying information, some housing providers are tempted to summarily deny requested accommodations when the disability or need for accommodation is not obvious. The following case shows the risk to housing providers in such instances.

Major Depressive and General Anxiety Disorders; the city in support of its motion failed to produce evidence that the chickens posed a direct threat to public health and that "their burden outweigh[ed] plaintiff's therapeutic] benefit").

Jankowski Lee & Associates v. Cisneros

91 F.3d 891 (7th Cir. 1996)

Before Eschbach, Manion, and Evans, Circuit Judges

ESCHBACH, Circuit Judge:

On March 8, 1993, Andrew Rusinov filed a complaint against River Park Apartments (RPA), alleging that Petitioners Jankowski Lee & Associates and Sue Sellin discriminated against him based on his handicap in violation of the FHA by refusing to make a reasonable accommodation in their rules, policies, practices and services related to parking. On September 30, 1994, HUD issued a Determination of Reasonable Cause and Charge of Discrimination against Jankowski Lee and Associates [and others] (collectively, "Petitioners"), alleging that they had violated §§3604(f)(2) and 3604(f)(3)(B). Administrative Law Judge Robert Andretta (the "ALJ") held a two-day hearing and issued an "Initial Decision and Order" holding that Petitioners had violated the FHA by failing to accommodate Rusinov's need for a parking space as close as possible to his apartment building. The ALJ enjoined Petitioners from discriminating against Rusinov, required Petitioners to assign Rusinov his own parking spot as close as possible to the RPA building, assessed a civil penalty of $2,500 against Petitioners jointly and severally, and awarded Rusinov $2,500 in compensatory damages. The Initial Decision and Order became the final order of the Secretary of HUD.

Petitioners seek review in this court. For the following reasons, we deny the request and affirm the Secretary's order.

I.

Mr. Rusinov was diagnosed with multiple sclerosis ("MS") in 1982. For the first five years after the onset of the disease, Rusinov was severely disabled with paralysis from the waist down, loss of control of bodily functions, temporary blindness, slurred speech, and anxiety attacks. Since then, Rusinov's condition and the severity of MS's symptoms have varied with remissions, exacerbations, and relapse. Rusinov does everything in his power not to appear disabled because he feels that he is treated with less respect and credibility once other people see him as disabled. The documentation is, however, unequivocal that Rusinov's MS severely limits his activities.

In 1986, Rusinov moved into an apartment in the RPA complex. On his application for an apartment at RPA, Rusinov indicated that he was disabled and that he had MS. Petitioner Jankowski Lee & Associates is the managing agent for the owners of RPA. Petitioner Sellin is employed by RPA as the on-site manager.

The RPA complex consists of two apartment buildings. Most of RPA's residents are elderly and many use wheelchairs, walkers, or canes. The complex includes a total of 108 parking spaces. Before 1993, visitors were permitted to park in the RPA lot. In 1993, parking was limited to tenants only. Parking at RPA is permitted on a "first come, first served basis." As of December 1994, there were approximately 96 persons registered to park in the lot. In 1986, when Rusinov moved into RPA, there was one handicapped space at each of the two buildings. By March 1993, there were two handicapped spaces at each building.

Rusinov has had a car since he first moved into RPA. He has always had problems locating a space close to his building because the handicapped spaces and the nonhandicapped spaces close to the entrance are usually filled. Rusinov requires a large space that is close to the building for a number of reasons. Rusinov cannot get in and out of his car if it is parked in a narrow spot. Rusinov has trouble walking and he cannot walk great distances without resting. Rusinov does not have full, voluntary control of his bladder and carries a portable urinal for those times when he cannot find a space close enough to his apartment to use his bathroom.

In the fall of 1992, Rusinov and his father visited the RPA management office twice regarding parking. On the first visit, they asked the office secretary for an assigned space or a "sufficient" number of handicapped spaces to accommodate Rusinov's disability. The secretary, who had no authority to grant the request, told them she did not think it was possible and that they needed to speak to the manager, Petitioner Sellin. Rusinov and his father later returned to the office and told Sellin that Rusinov needed an assigned parking space because of his disability. Although this was the first time that Sellin spoke personally with Complainant, she had been informed by the office secretary that Rusinov had previously requested an assigned parking space. Without further inquiry, Ms. Sellin denied Rusinov's request and the office secretary told Rusinov and his father that Rusinov would have to take his chances in finding a spot close to the building.

Sellin testified that she knew Rusinov had MS, but that she did not know the degree to which the disease affected Rusinov's mobility. She denied the request because she did not consider it to be a reasonable request given that she had seen Rusinov walking to and from his car without any apparent difficulty.

In the complaint filed with HUD Rusinov states, "I have asked the management to either increase the number of handicap spots or assign me a parking spot." Shortly after Rusinov filed his complaint with HUD, Petitioners increased the number of handicapped parking spaces at each building from two to four and added a van-accessible handicapped parking space to the lot in front of Rusinov's building.

II.

Petitioners present two reasons why we should overturn the Agency's decision: First, Petitioners were not aware of the extent to which Rusinov's condition limited his mobility; and second, Petitioners argue that, as a matter of law, they did not violate the FHA because they granted Rusinov's request when they increased the number of handicapped parking spaces. We reverse the Secretary's decision only if it is "not in accordance with law," "without observance of procedure required by law," or "unsupported by substantial evidence." We review the entire record, but we do not decide the facts anew, reweigh the evidence, or substitute our judgment for that of the agency.

Petitioners' first argument is essentially that Rusinov bore the burden of producing documentation establishing the extent of his handicap and his need for the requested accommodation. Petitioners admit that they knew that Rusinov had MS, but they argue that they were unaware that Rusinov's MS affected his mobility such that he needed an assigned parking space. Petitioners' denial of Rusinov's request based on their lack of knowledge of the extent of his injury is simply a ruse to avoid the penalty for violating the FHA. It is telling that Petitioners denied his request without asking Rusinov for more information regarding his condition. Regardless of their motive for pursuing the issue, however, Petitioners' position is untenable.

The FHA prohibits discrimination "against any person in the terms, conditions, or privileges of sale or rental of a dwelling, or in the provision of services or facilities in connection with such dwelling, because of a handicap. . . ." §3604(f)(2). This prohibition on discrimination also makes it unlawful to refuse "to make reasonable accommodations in rules, policies, practices, or services, when such accommodations may be necessary to afford [a handicapped] person equal opportunity to use and enjoy a dwelling[.]" §3604(f)(3) (B). It is clear that Rusinov's MS is a handicap within the meaning of the FHA.

Petitioners were aware that Rusinov had MS, Rusinov's MS qualified as a handicap, Rusinov informed Petitioners that he required a parking space close to his building because of his handicap, and Rusinov requested an assigned parking space as a reasonable accommodation. At that point, Petitioners had a duty to make a reasonable accommodation. They did not make a reasonable accommodation, so they violated the FHA. It is irrelevant whether Rusinov's mobility did not "appear" to Petitioners to be limited by his MS. The existence of a handicap, as defined by Congress in §3602(h), does not depend on Rusinov's appearance, it depends upon his physical condition.[38] Petitioners denied Rusinov's request without asking for more information regarding the extent to which Rusinov's MS limited his activities. Had they asked, we presume that Rusinov would have provided them with the substantial

---

38. [Fn. 1 in original] As the district court in *Shapiro* stated:

[D]iscrimination against the handicapped often begins with the thought that she looks just like me — that she's normal — when in fact the handicapped person is in some significant respect different. Prejudice, it bears recalling, includes not just mistreating another because of the *difference* of her outward appearance but also assuming others are the *same* because of their appearance, when they are not.

Shapiro [v. Cadman Towers], 844 F. Supp. [116, 121 (E.D.N.Y. 1994)].

documentation that he provided to HUD and the ALJ. If a landlord is skeptical of a tenant's alleged disability or the landlord's ability to provide an accommodation, it is incumbent upon the landlord to request documentation or open a dialogue.

Petitioners' second argument is that they did all that the FHA requires when they increased the number of parking spaces in response to Rusinov's complaint. Rusinov's HUD complaint requested that Petitioners accommodate his disability by *either* increasing the number of handicap spaces or assigning a space to him. Petitioners increased the number of handicapped parking spots in front of Rusinov's building from two to four.

Petitioners cannot prevail on this issue because Petitioners' action still falls short of providing a "reasonable accommodation." Whether an accommodation is "reasonable" is a question of fact, determined by a close examination of the particular circumstances. The ALJ appropriately found that the two additional handicapped spaces were not a "reasonable accommodation." Petitioners do not challenge this finding as a factual matter and the ALJ's finding was not clearly erroneous. Even after the additional spots were added, there were only eight handicapped parking spaces and one van space for the 27 tenants registered to park at RPA with handicapped stickers or tags for their vehicles. At night, the handicapped spaces and all of the parking spaces close to the entrance to Rusinov's building were usually taken. During the day, the handicapped spaces were filled between 50% and 75% of the time.

For the foregoing reasons, the Petition for Review is denied and the ALJ's Initial Decision and Order and the Secretary's final order are, therefore, AFFIRMED.

NOTES AND QUESTIONS

1. Opening a Dialogue. The court in *Jankowski* stated, in the context of a case involving a physical impairment, that the existence of a disability under the FHA "does not depend on . . . appearance, it depends upon . . . physical condition." *Jankowski* illustrates the possible consequence to housing providers who allegedly "go with their gut" on whether an individual has a disability-related need for a reasonable accommodation. 2020 HUD guidance observes that most HUD findings or "charges" of housing discrimination following a full investigation involve refusals to accommodate disabilities "that the housing provider cannot readily observe." 2020 Animal Assistance Notice, at 4. As *Jankowski* admonishes: "If a landlord is skeptical of a tenant's alleged disability or the landlord's ability to provide an accommodation [after it has been requested], it is incumbent upon the landlord to request documentation or open a dialogue."

2. Housing Provider Access to Disability-Related Information. What information may a housing provider request? Some disabilities are obvious, such as a mobility impairment requiring use of a wheelchair, whereas others, such as Mr. Bhogaita's PTSD, are not. Similarly, some disability-related needs for accommodation are obvious and some, like Mr. Jankowski's need for a designated parking space, are not.

In general, a housing provider may not ask a tenant about the existence, nature, and severity of a disability unless the tenant invokes FHA protections; if the tenant does so, the provider may only seek verifying information when the disability or need for accommodation is *not* obvious or known to the provider.[39] If the disability or need for accommodation are not obvious, a housing provider is entitled only to "information that is necessary to evaluate the disability-related need for the accommodation. . . . In most cases, an individual's medical records [are] not necessary. . . ." *Joint Statement on Accommodations* at 13-14. In the context of assistance animals, HUD guidance answers the question this way: "Housing providers may not require a health care professional to use a specific form (including this document), to provide notarized statements, to make statements under penalty of perjury, or to provide an individual's diagnosis or other detailed information about a person's physical or mental impairments."[40]

Back to Mr. Bhogaita, was his disability-related need for an assistance animal obvious to his landlord? If not, what kind of verifying information did the landlord seek and what information did the court deem sufficient to support the jury's finding that "his dog alleviated the effects of his PTSD"?

3. Pleading vs. Proving Reasonableness. The reviewing court in *Jankowski* noted that "[w]hether an accommodation is 'reasonable' is a question of fact, determined by a close examination of the particular circumstances." The *Jankowski* court reviewed a final order by the HUD Secretary following an administrative hearing on the merits before an ALJ. The court in *Bhogaita* heard an appeal from a jury trial on the merits, and the next case, *Giebeler*, involved an appeal from a grant of summary judgment based on documentary evidence. In contrast, consider that motions to dismiss accommodation claims for lack of reasonableness may be unsuccessful at the pleading stage where there is no evidentiary record. For example, in Hunter v. WPD Management, LLC, 476 F. Supp. 3d 731, 733, 736 (N.D. Ill. 2020), the plaintiff alleged a mobility impairment stemming from a heart condition and that she lived in a sixth-floor apartment building without elevator service for ten weeks before filing her disability discrimination complaint. She further alleged that on one

---

39. *See* 24 CFR 100.202(c); *Joint Statement on Accommodations* at 12-14; *see also* H.R. Rep. No. 100-711, at 30 (1988) ("only an inquiry into a prospective tenant's ability to meet tenancy requirements would be justified. . . . [such as] questions that he or she asks of all other applicants that relate directly to the tenancy. . . . Nor may the landlord or owner ask . . . the applicant or tenant to waive his right to confidentiality concerning his medical condition or history. [A] landlord or owner may ask whether the individual is a current illegal abuser or addict of controlled substances.").

40. 2020 *Assistance Animal Notice, supra* note 33, at 16.

occasion, she required teams of paramedics to carry her up and down multiple flights of stairs for a disability-related hospitalization. The court held that whether the request to fix the elevator immediately was unreasonable was a question of fact inappropriate for dismissal at the pleading stage of a reasonable accommodation claim. Even with an evidentiary record, a court is not allowed to weigh evidence on summary judgment. *See* Anderson v. City of Blue Ash, 798 F.38 at 363 (regarding request for zoning waiver to allow a miniature horse at a residence: "Factual disputes pervade the question of the accommodation's reasonableness and the 'highly fact-specific' balancing of the City's interests against the plaintiffs' . . ., precluding summary judgment for the City.").

As discussed above, the reasonable accommodation requirement raises questions about:

- What kinds of requests will be recognized as *accommodations*?
- How does one determine the *reasonableness* of an accommodation?
- What does it mean for an accommodation to be *necessary* for one's equal use and enjoyment of a dwelling?

The following case assists in disentangling these concepts in the particularly thorny context of determining financial qualifications for rental.

Giebeler v. M & B Assoc.
343 F.3d 1143 (9th Cir. 2003)

Before: Thompson, Fletcher and Berzon, Circuit Judges.

Berzon, Circuit Judge:

John Giebeler has AIDS. Because he has AIDS, he is disabled and can no longer work, although he had worked and earned an adequate living until he became ill. Once he was no longer earning a salary, his former apartment became too expensive for him. In addition, he needed assistance with daily matters because of his illness and so wanted to live closer to his mother.

Giebeler's lack of an income stream meant that he could not meet the minimum financial qualifications of the apartment complex where he sought an apartment. Giebeler's mother, however, did meet those standards, and offered to rent the apartment so that her son could live in it. The owners of the apartment complex refused to rent either to Giebeler or to his mother, citing a management company policy against cosigners.

The question in this case is whether the FHAA required the apartment owners reasonably to accommodate Giebeler's disability by assessing individually the risk of nonpayment created by his specific proposed financial arrangement, rather than inflexibly applying a rental policy that forbids cosigners.

Concluding that the statute does so require, we reverse the district court's grant of summary judgment and remand the case for further proceedings.

BACKGROUND

John Giebeler had worked as a psychiatric technician for approximately five years before becoming disabled by AIDS. At the time Giebeler had to leave work because of his disability, he was earning approximately $36,000 per year. Since 1996, Giebeler has supported himself through monthly disability benefits under the Social Security Disability Insurance (SSDI) program and housing assistance from the Housing Opportunities for People with AIDS program (HOPWA).

[Giebeler sought to move from a two-bedroom apartment to a less expensive one-bedroom unit at the Park Branham Apartments (Branham), a rental property owned by defendants (M & B) that was closer to his mother's home. He had a record of consistent and prompt payment of rent during his previous six years of residency, and his credit record contained no negative notations.

Giebeler did not qualify for tenancy because he did not have a minimum gross monthly income equaling three times the monthly rent; he had earned the required minimum income at his job before he became ill. Giebeler's mother, Anne, attempted to assist her son by filling out an application with him and indicating he would be the only resident. Branham rejected the applications on the basis that it considered Anne Giebeler a co-signer, in violation of their policy. Anne Giebeler had a positive credit report, had owned the same home for 27 years and had completely paid off her mortgage. The home was located less than a mile from Branham. With the aid of a legal services lawyer, Giebeler requested a reasonable accommodation in the form of a cosigner or other alternative arrangements to meet the financial requirements for tenancy. Branham denied the request to waive the cosigner policy and did not otherwise check either applicant's financial qualifications or explore alternatives.

Giebeler filed suit under the FHA and other laws advancing theories of intentional discrimination, disparate impact, and failure to make a reasonable accommodation. Giebeler appealed the grant of summary judgment on his reasonable accommodation claim (but not the disparate impact claim) and settled the intent claim.]

DISCUSSION

. . . To make out a claim of discrimination based on failure to reasonably accommodate, a plaintiff must demonstrate that (1) he suffers from a handicap as defined by the FHAA; (2) defendants knew or reasonably should have known of the plaintiff's handicap; (3) accommodation of the handicap "may be necessary" to afford plaintiff an equal opportunity to use and enjoy the dwelling; and (4) defendants refused to make such accommodation.

A. Giebeler's Disability

The defendants do not dispute that Giebeler is disabled for the purposes of the FHAA and that they knew of his disability, nor do they deny that they refused to make the accommodation Giebeler requested. The defendants contend, rather, that the accommodation Giebeler requested is not one the FHAA requires them to accord.

Infection with HIV, the virus that causes AIDS, qualifies as a "physical or mental impairment" for the purposes of the FHAA. 24 C.F.R. §100.201(a) (2). FHAA regulations further define "major life activities" to include "functions such as caring for one's self, performing manual tasks, walking, seeing, hearing, speaking, breathing, learning, and *working*." 24 C.F.R. §100.201(b) (emphasis added).

Giebeler's AIDS-related impairments substantially — indeed, entirely — limited his ability to work. If Giebeler were still able to work in the position he held before becoming ill, he would have met Branham's financial requirements. A direct causal link therefore existed between Giebeler's impairment, his inability to work, and his inability to comply with defendants' minimum income requirement relying solely on his individual income.

Given these undisputed facts, we must determine whether relaxation of Branham's no-cosigner policy to allow Giebeler to live in an apartment rented for him by his mother constituted a reasonable accommodation required by the FHAA.

B. Accommodation under the FHAA

The central issue in dispute in this case is whether bending a landlord's usual *means* of testing a prospective tenant's likely ability to pay the rent over the course of the lease is an "accommodation" at all within the meaning of the FHAA, let alone a reasonable one. [EDS.—The court emphasized that this question was "only the first step in a multi-pronged statutory analysis."] Permitting Giebeler to live in an apartment rented for him by his qualified mother would have adjusted for his inability, because of his disability, to earn his own income, while providing M & B with substantial assurance that the full rent — not a discounted amount — would be paid monthly. Branham maintains, however, that an adjustment of this kind is not the type of alteration in housing policy that Congress had in mind in enacting the FHAA. Noting that Branham's no-cosigner rule adversely affects many prospective tenants who cannot meet the financial specifications without relying on the income or assets of a relative or friend, M & B would have us hold that altering that rule to aid a disabled potential tenant does not come within the FHAA's concept of accommodation because it would (1) prefer disabled over nondisabled impecunious individuals; (2) accommodate Giebeler's poverty rather than his disability; and (3) increase M & B's financial exposure, with potential cost to the landlord should its fears that it could not collect the rent prove true. We conclude that the FHAA's accommodation requirement does reach adjustments in the means of proving financial responsibility, and that each of Branham's arguments to the contrary runs afoul of binding caselaw elucidating the "accommodation" concept in the FHAA and related statutes.

1. The plain language of the FHAA provides scant guidance concerning the reach of the accommodation requirement. Similarly, the FHAA's legislative history and regulations provide us with little specific guidance as to the scope and limitations of "accommodation" under the FHAA. The House Committee Report on the FHAA does state, however, that the interpretations of "reasonable accommodation" in Rehabilitation Act ("RA") regulations and caselaw should be applied to the FHAA's reasonable accommodation provision. . . . Also, since the enactment of the ADA, we have relied on ADA cases in applying the RA. . . .

We therefore look to both RA and ADA interpretations of "accommodation" of disabled individuals as indicative of the scope of "accommodation" under the FHAA. In doing so, we interpret the FHAA's accommodation provisions with the specific goals of the FHAA in mind: "to protect the right of handicapped persons to live in the residence of their choice in the community," and "to end the unnecessary exclusion of persons with handicaps from the American mainstream."

2. The Supreme Court's most extensive discussion of the overall scope of the accommodation concept appears in a recent ADA case, *U.S. Airways v. Barnett*, 535 U.S. 391 (2002). *Barnett* guides our analysis concerning the reach of the accommodation obligation under the FHAA, in two respects: First, *Barnett* holds that an accommodation may indeed result in a preference for disabled individuals over otherwise similarly situated nondisabled individuals. And second, *Barnett* indicates that accommodations may adjust for the practical impact of a disability, not only for the immediate manifestations of the physical or mental impairment giving rise to the disability.

In *Barnett*, an airline cargo handler requested, as accommodation of his back injuries, an exception to the company's seniority system so that he could transfer to a less physically demanding position. The airline refused, contending that because the ADA ensures *equal* treatment of persons with disabilities, any sort of preferential exception to a disability-neutral policy was outside the scope of the "reasonable accommodations" mandated by the statute.

The objection that Branham need not permit Giebeler to live in an apartment rented by his financially-qualified mother because other prospective tenants unable to meet the financial qualifications on their own also cannot rent apartments therefore runs afoul of *Barnett*. Just as Barnett was not disqualified from an adjustment to his seniority rank simply because other, nondisabled employees desired the position he sought but were barred from obtaining it by the seniority policy, so Giebeler was not disqualified from an adjustment in Branham's financial qualification/no cosigner standard simply because there were other prospective tenants similarly unable—albeit for reasons other than disability—to earn enough money to meet the rental company's credit standards.

Additionally, *Barnett* indicates, inferentially if not expressly, that a required accommodation need not address "barriers that would not be barriers *but for* the [individual's] disability." Justice Scalia maintained vigorously in his dissent in *Barnett* that [the ADA] does not require adjustment of "rules and practices that bear no more heavily upon the disabled employee than upon others. . . ." Changes in seniority rules, maintained Justice Scalia, cannot be accommodations on this understanding of the accommodation concept, as "a seniority system . . . burdens the disabled and nondisabled alike . . .," and so is not "a disability-related obstacle."

The majority in *Barnett* did not accept this reasoning . . . *Barnett* therefore recognized that the obligation to "accommodate" a disability can include the obligation to alter policies that can be barriers to nondisabled persons as well.

It is worth noting that Giebeler's inability to pay the rent without drawing on his mother's financial resources was *not*, in Justice Scalia's words, the result of "obstacles that have nothing to do with the disability." Although Barnett's inability to meet the seniority requirement for the position he wanted was simply the result of his tenure in his job, not of his disability, the reason Giebeler could not pay the rent from his own income was that his disability prevented him from working and earning a monthly paycheck as he used to. So, applying Justice Scalia's understanding of the accommodation concept, Giebeler's request that he be permitted to assure his prospective landlord of payment through his mother's financial resources rather than his own would qualify as an accommodation. Yet, under *Barnett*, even if one disregards the fact that Giebeler had formerly held a qualifying job and was forced to leave it because of his disability, the accommodation he seeks might still qualify as an accommodation under the FHAA, as long as adjusting Branham's method of judging financial responsibility would aid him in obtaining an apartment he could otherwise not inhabit because of his disability.

Our cases involving FHAA challenges to generally applicable zoning policies [Eds.—such as those restricting the number of unrelated persons who can reside in a single-family neighborhood], confirm that reasonable accommodations can function to adjust for special needs that flow from the inability of disabled residents [living in group homes] to meet otherwise applicable financial requirements. In *City of Edmonds* we recognized [Eds.—before the case reached the Supreme Court] that even when a neutral policy's adverse effect on disabled persons is attributable to financial limitations faced by disabled persons in securing housing, the FHAA may require an exception to the policy as a reasonable accommodation.

3. There is one additional principle regarding the general nature of the concept of accommodations that is pertinent here as well: Accommodations need not be free of all possible cost to the landlord (although, again, a landlord need not incur a cost or risk of cost that is not "reasonable," a major qualification that we discuss later).

Mobile Home I establishes that financial considerations do not *automatically* disqualify a requested accommodation:

> We find the effort to distinguish accommodations that have a financial cost from other accommodations unconvincing. Besides the fact that §3604's reasonable accommodations requirement contains no exemption for financial costs to the landlord, the history of the FHAA clearly establishes that Congress anticipated that landlords would have to shoulder certain costs involved, so long as they are not unduly burdensome.

Thus, disability-neutral administrative policies like Branham's tenant income qualifications do not escape all scrutiny under the FHAA's reasonable accommodation mandate simply because they are based on financial considerations or may involve a *risk* of some financial cost to the landlord.[41]

4. Despite this solid line of Supreme Court and Ninth Circuit precedent, the district court and the defendants rely on two out-of-circuit cases that hold that however reasonable the requested accommodation, the FHAA does not require landlords or cities to accommodate needs generated by the inability of disabled individuals to generate income by working. *See* Salute v. Stratford Greens Garden Apartments, 136 F.3d 293 (2d Cir.1998); Hemisphere Building Co. v. Village of Richton Park, 171 F.3d 437 (7th Cir.1999). But *Salute* and *Hemisphere* held, inconsistently with *Barnett*, that courts should never *get* to the reasonableness inquiry where economic circumstances related to disability are at stake. Now that *Barnett* has been decided, that approach is foreclosed.

We conclude that Giebeler's request that he be permitted to reside in an apartment rented by his financially qualified mother is a request for an accommodation that, under the FHAA, he was entitled to receive *if* the adjustment both "may be necessary to afford [him] equal opportunity to use and enjoy a dwelling" and was "reasonable" within the meaning of that statute. It is to those questions that we now turn.

C. Causation and Reasonableness

1. Causation

To prove that an accommodation is necessary, "[p]laintiffs must show that, but for the accommodation, they likely will be denied an equal opportunity to enjoy the housing of their choice." Put another way, "[w]ithout a causal link between defendants' policy and the plaintiff's injury, there can be no obligation on the part of defendants to make a reasonable accommodation."

Imposition of burdensome policies, including financial policies, can interfere with disabled persons' right to use and enjoyment of their dwellings,

---

41. [Fn. 7 in original] It is quite possible—indeed, likely—that in fact there will be *no* financial loss to the defendants. Giebeler requested only a different way of proving that the same rent will be paid for the apartment he lives in as is paid for similar apartments in the complex. He did not seek to pay less rent or to provide evidence of a lower monthly income with which to pay the rent—he only asked that the income relied upon be his mother's instead of his own.

thus necessitating accommodation. While in some cases the plaintiff will not be able to show that alteration of a particular policy "may be necessary" to her use and enjoyment of the property, the causation requirement poses little hurdle in a case such as this one, where a landlord's policy entirely prevents a tenant from living in a dwelling.

Here, the causal link between Branham's failure to accommodate and Giebeler's disability is obvious. Giebeler was unemployed because of his disability and therefore had insufficient income to qualify for the apartment. Once Branham refused to allow Anne Giebeler to rent an apartment for her son to live in, Giebeler could not show financial ability to pay the rent and therefore could not live in the housing complex. Allowing Anne Giebeler to rent an apartment on her son's behalf, or in some other manner accommodating his inability to prove financial responsibility in the usual way, was necessary to enable Giebeler to live in an apartment at Branham.

In addition to causation, equal opportunity is a key component of the necessity analysis; an accommodation must be possibly necessary to afford the plaintiff equal opportunity to use and enjoy a dwelling. M & B's refusal to allow Anne Giebeler to rent an apartment for her son denies him an opportunity for which he would otherwise be qualified. With Anne Giebeler as renter, Giebeler could satisfy Branham's minimum income requirement and ensure that Branham receives its monthly rent. Giebeler is similarly situated to other tenants at Branham in terms of the financial resources he can bring to a tenancy at Branham. It is his way of demonstrating and deploying these resources that is different.[42] So defendants' relaxation of their no cosigner policy "may be necessary" to afford Giebeler equal opportunity to use and enjoy a dwelling at Branham.

2. Reasonableness

(a) *Burden of Proof:* We have not decided previously whether the plaintiff or the defendant in an FHAA case bears the burden of showing whether a proposed accommodation is reasonable. There is, however, both RA [*Vinson*] and ADA [*Barnett*] precedent on the question. . . . There is no need in this case, though, to decide whether *Vinson* and *Barnett* state essentially the same allocation of burdens or differ in a way likely to be outcome determinative in some instances. Either description of the burden allocation leads to the same result in this case: Giebeler's requested accommodation was reasonable.

---

42. [Fn. 9 in original] Unlike the ADA, the FHAA does not explicitly require that a disabled individual must be "qualified" except for his disability or able to meet the "essential" requirements of the housing he seeks to occupy. Even if similar requirements are implicit in the "reasonable accommodation" requirement, a question we do not decide, Giebeler meets them: He has been a model tenant in his other apartments; he has good credit; and relaxation of the no cosigner policy does not waive the essential financial requirement for tenancy, namely, access to sufficient financial resources to pay the monthly rent.

(b) *Merits of the Reasonableness Analysis:* Ordinarily, an accommodation is reasonable under the FHAA "when it imposes no 'fundamental alteration in the nature of the program' or 'undue financial or administrative burdens.'" In this case, Giebeler has met his burden of demonstrating that the particular accommodation he requests—allowing an eligible relative to rent an apartment for him—is "reasonable on its face, *i.e.,* ordinarily or in the run of cases." He has also met his burden, as articulated in *Vinson,* of producing evidence showing that the accommodation was reasonable and possible.

The record reveals that, as one would expect, the purpose of M & B's minimum income requirement is to ensure that tenants have sufficient income to pay rent consistently and promptly. This interest is, of course, considerable. However, allowing a financially eligible relative to rent an apartment for a disabled individual who, except for his current financial circumstances, is qualified to be a tenant does not unreasonably threaten this interest.

The rental arrangement requested by Giebeler would not require Branham to accept less rent, would not otherwise alter the essential obligations of tenancy at Branham (such as appropriate behavior and care of the premises), and would provide a lessee with the proper financial qualifications and credit history. As the official renter of the apartment, Anne Giebeler would be primarily responsible for the rent, thereby obviating the need for M & B to first go to her son to collect rent before pursuing her for unpaid rent. Rentals by parents for children are not unusual in most rental markets. Even if M & B does not ordinarily permit such rentals at the Branham complex, asking a landlord to accept an alternative way of proving financial responsibility acceptable to many other landlords is likely to be reasonable in the run of cases.

Indeed, the FHAA recognizes that nondisabled persons may choose to rent apartments for occupancy by disabled persons and protects these arrangements: "[I]t shall be unlawful . . . [t]o discriminate in the sale or rental, or to otherwise make unavailable or deny, a dwelling to any buyer or renter because of a handicap of . . . a person residing in or intending to reside in that dwelling after it is so sold, rented, or made available." §3604(f)(1). Thus, the FHAA appears to protect not just disabled people who buy or rent their own residences, but also disabled people who reside in a residence rented by a non-disabled person, the arrangement Giebeler sought in this case.

Giebeler made the necessary initial showing that the requested accommodation was reasonable on the particular facts of this case. Branham, however, failed to meet its burden of demonstrating that in the particular circumstances of this case the requested accommodation would cause it to suffer undue hardship. Branham also failed to carry its burden as articulated in *Vinson* of rebutting the showing made by Giebeler that the requested accommodation was in fact reasonable.

There is no evidence in the record demonstrating that M & B is in any way unusual among landlords in its need to insist that the resident alone rather than a relative sign the lease and take responsibility for paying the rent. The particular parent seeking to rent for her disabled child, Anne Giebeler, presented no unusual risks either. Although, like any other such parent, she would not have lived on-site, she was both a good credit risk and easy to track down; her income, based on monthly pension checks, was a reliable and ample source of rent funds; and she had an unblemished credit record. Anne Giebeler also had significant assets, including a home which she had owned and resided in for 27 years and for which she had paid off the mortgage in full. Her home is located less than a mile from the Branham complex. In short, by allowing Anne Giebeler to rent the apartment so that her disabled son could live in it, Branham would not assume any substantial financial or administrative risk or burden.

Even if one views the requested arrangement as the defendants did—i.e., as a cosignership, requiring waiver of the partnership's no-cosigner policy—the requested accommodation was still reasonable on the particular facts here. While Branham managers have identified some administrative burdens and expenses that could result from having to track down a cosigner when a tenant fails to pay rent, they have on occasion waived the minimum income requirement and allowed cosigners and other alternative arrangements.

We stress once more that Giebeler was in no way trying to avoid payment of the usual rent for the apartment he wanted to live in, nor was he proposing to leave M & B without a means of ascertaining that an individual with the means to pay that rent would be responsible for doing so. Giebeler's modest request that his financially qualified mother be allowed to rent an apartment for him to live in, affording him the opportunity to live in a suitable dwelling despite his disability, was a request for a reasonable accommodation within the intendment of the FHAA, and should have been honored.

CONCLUSION

The judgment of the district court is reversed, and the case remanded for further proceedings consistent with this opinion.

NOTES AND QUESTIONS

1. The Meaning of Accommodation. Note the *Giebeler* court's instruction that "the first step" is to determine whether a requested change to a policy fits within the meaning of "accommodation" before considering whether it is reasonable and necessary. What guideposts should be used when determining whether a particular accommodation request falls within the scope of the FHAA? Does the statutory language exempt certain kinds of accommodations from this mandate?

2. Broad Standing. The court in *Giebeler* found it significant that "the FHAA appears to protect not just disabled people who buy or rent their own residences, but also disabled people who reside in a residence rented by a non-disabled person, the arrangement Giebeler sought in this case." The plain

text of the FHA prohibits disability discrimination in the sale or rental of a
dwelling "to any buyer or renter because of a handicap of . . . a person residing in or intending to reside in that dwelling after it is . . . rented." §3604(f)(1)
(B). As illustrated throughout this chapter, discrimination is prohibited based
on the disabilities of buyers, renters, household members, and those associated with buyers and renters.

   **3. Necessary to Afford Equal Opportunity to Use and Enjoy the
Dwelling.** The court in *Giebeler* described the showing of necessity as one
of causation: "To prove that an accommodation is necessary, plaintiffs
must show that, but for the accommodation, they likely will be denied an
equal opportunity to enjoy the housing of their choice." The *Bhogaita* court
described a necessary accommodation as "one that alleviates the effects of
a disability" and affirmatively enhances quality of life: "Bhogaita produced
evidence from which a reasonable fact finder could conclude that his dog
alleviated the effects of his PTSD. Specifically, Dr. Li's letters said that Kane
assists Bhogaita 'in coping with his disability,' and 'ameliorate[s]' Bhogaita's
'psychiatric symptoms,' and that without the dog, Bhogaita's 'social interactions would be so overwhelming that he would be unable to perform work
of any kind.'"

   What does it mean for an accommodation to ameliorate the "effects" of a
disability and not merely the disability itself? The *Giebeler* court cited Supreme
Court ADA precedent in observing: "*Barnett* indicates that accommodations
may adjust for the practical impact of a disability, not only for the immediate
manifestations of the physical or mental impairment giving rise to the disability." Thus, *Giebeler* emphasized that the Supreme Court majority in *Barnett*
recognized an obligation to alter policies burdening disabled persons that
might also burden nondisabled persons.

   Does this adjustment for "practical impact" include economic effects of the
disability? Giebeler's disability "prevented him from working and earning a
monthly paycheck as he used to" before becoming disabled, rendering him
unable to demonstrate financial responsibility in the usual way. He needed his
well-qualified mother to rent the apartment for him to have an equal opportunity to use and enjoy the dwelling. The court in *Giebeler* held that the causal
link between the accommodation and Giebeler's disability was "obvious." It
also held that "[i]mposition of burdensome policies, including financial policies, can interfere with the disabled persons' right to use and enjoyment of
their dwellings, thus necessitating accommodation."

   In a similar case, the Eleventh Circuit reversed as "too simplistic" a summary judgment holding that a requested change in the manner of meeting
a minimum income requirement "went solely to [plaintiff's] financial condition—not [his] disability" of quadriplegia. *See* Schaw v. Habitat for Humanity
of Citrus County, 938 F.3d 1259, 1270-71, 1273 (11th Cir. 2019).

> Schaw asserts that the "effect[ ] of [his] disability" relevant to this case is his
> inability to work. Because of this limitation, Schaw says, his income consists
> largely of SSDI—a fixed monthly amount. Schaw contends that because he is

unable to work and therefore unable to supplement his SSDI [through wages], he should be granted an accommodation allowing him to demonstrate additional income in another form: either his food stamps or a notarized letter indicating familial support. . . .

[Even in the paradigmatic example of service animal accommodations for blind persons,] "it's not the handicap itself, but rather the effect of the handicap, that is being accommodated." [W]e think it significant that federal law lists "working" as a major life activity alongside "seeing, hearing, speaking, and walking." It would be odd, then, if the Act deemed "necessary" those accommodations that "alleviate[ ] the effects of" an inability to see, hear, speak, or walk, but not those that alleviate the effects of an inability to work. . . .

[T]he district court neglected to acknowledge an important nuance—that the "financial" aspect of the accommodation here concerns only the *form* of funding and not the *amount*. Schaw didn't request, for example, that Habitat lower its minimum-income standards or allow him to get away with doing or paying any less than other applicants. He stood ready to pay the monthly mortgage in full and to demonstrate a gross annual income exceeding the minimum required level. [Plaintiff's requested accommodation would put] him in the same position as an able-bodied person who could (theoretically) increase his income through W-2 wages. This request—to show an equal income from a different source—could be construed as an invitation to "dispense with formal equality of treatment in order to advance a more substantial equality of opportunity." . . .

The inquiry is whether the requested accommodation would provide a disabled person an opportunity to enjoy a dwelling that would otherwise—due to his disability—elude him.

Does the fact that "work" is listed as a major life activity mean that whenever a disability prevents someone from working, they should be entitled to an economic accommodation? Or will this depend on the nature of the economic accommodation requested? Compare *Giebeler* and *Schaw* with Salute v. Stratford Greens Garden Apartments, 136 F.3d 293, 301 (2d Cir. 1998), in which the divided court held that an accommodation requiring participation in the voluntary governmental housing voucher program (formerly, Section 8) would impose "unreasonable costs, an undue hardship, and a substantial burden."

At a more basic level, the court held that a policy of refusing vouchers was a form of economic discrimination not cognizable as a failure to make reasonable accommodation under the FHA.

We think it is fundamental that the law addresses the accommodation of handicaps, not the alleviation of economic disadvantages that may be correlated with having handicaps. . . . What stands between these plaintiffs and the apartments at Stratford Greens is a shortage of money, and nothing else. . . . Thus, the accommodation sought by plaintiffs is not "necessary" to afford handicapped persons *"equal opportunity"* to use and enjoy a dwelling.

Salute, 126 F.3d at 301; *accord* Klossner v. IADU Table Mound MHP, LLC, 65 F.4th 349, 351 (8th Cir. 2023). In dissent in *Salute*, Judge Calabresi reasoned that allowing tenants to qualify based not only on their own income but also on other resources available to them is like "allowing a blind tenant to keep a seeing eye dog despite a rule against pets, an accommodation of a need created by the disability."

Which argument do you find more persuasive? *See* Chapter 18 discussing state and local protections against discrimination based on sources of income. Note that the *Giebeler* court distinguished *Salute* as decided before the Supreme Court's ruling in *Barnett*. Consider these other discussions of the necessity showing:

- In Anderson v. City of Blue Ash, 798 F.3d 338, 361-63 (6th Cir. 2015), the court reversed summary judgment in a case involving a parent's request for waiver of a residential zoning restriction against horses to allow keeping a miniature horse as an assistance animal for a disabled child. The court held that the FHA "requires accommodations that are necessary to achieve housing equality, not just those accommodations that are absolutely necessary for the disabled individual's treatment or basic ability to function." Nor must the plaintiff show the accommodation is required to reside in a particular dwelling. The plaintiff "testified that Ellie [the miniature horse] allows C.A. to play independently and exercise in her backyard and that, without the horse, C.A. cannot do so for any significant length of time, and would effectively be denied the equal opportunity to play in her own backyard as non-disabled children can. This evidence, viewed in a light most favorable to the plaintiffs, is sufficient for a reasonable jury to find that the requested accommodation of keeping the miniature horse at her house is necessary for C.A.'s equal use and enjoyment of her dwelling."

- In Howard v. HMK Holdings, LLC, 988 F.3d 1185, 1190-91 (9th Cir. 2021), a landlord sought to increase a disabled tenant's rent. The tenant's wife informed the landlord that the tenant was medically fragile and requested that they be permitted to remain in the unit paying the original rent amount for an indefinite time until the tenant could be stabilized enough to relocate across the country. The court explained that the "plaintiff's disability must cause the need for an accommodation. . . . In other words, absent an accommodation, the plaintiff's disability must cause the plaintiffs to lose an equal opportunity to use and enjoy a dwelling." Plaintiffs failed to show their requested lease extension was necessary to accommodate an impairment rather than make it more convenient for them to move out of state.

- In Vorchheimer v. Philadelphian Owners Ass'n, 903 F.3d 100, 103-05, 113 (3rd Cir. 2018), the court affirmed the dismissal of a plaintiff's complaint on the basis that she did not plausibly plead that her requested accommodation, storing her rolling walker in the lobby of her building, was necessary or essential rather than preferable to the alternatives offered and rejected. The plaintiff's complaint attached doctors' letters verifying her medical need but describing her requested accommodation as "preferable" rather than "necessary." The court reasoned:

First, "necessary" means "required." It is a high standard. Second, we must consider what is necessary to satisfy the particular disabled person's need. This statute pegs necessity to affording this disabled person equal opportunity to use and enjoy her dwelling. And third, we must gauge necessity in light of proposed alternatives. . . . Plaintiff preferred to have access to her walker without having to wait for a staffer. But she did not plausibly plead that she needed to leave it in the lobby. To enjoy her home, she needed access to her walker without having to stand for minutes. She pleaded four alternatives on offer that, on their face, satisfied those needs. And she attached doctors' letters that distinguish her needs from her preferences. Because the Act guarantees her only a "reasonable accommodation" that satisfies her needs, not the particular accommodation that she wanted, we will affirm.

4. Equal Treatment vs. Equal Opportunity. The necessity element does not exist in a vacuum. It "requires the demonstration of a direct linkage between the proposed accommodation and the 'equal opportunity' to be provided" to the disabled person. Bryant Woods Inn, Inc. v. Howard County, Md., 124 F.3d 597, 604 (4th Cir. 1997). How can one reconcile the possible tension between an accommodation's aim of granting a person with a disability an "equal opportunity" to use and enjoy housing and the fact that only disabled people have the right of reasonable accommodation? Would treating people with disabilities exactly the same as those without disabilities usually provide them an equal opportunity to use and enjoy their housing?

In *Giebeler*, the court observed the Supreme Court's admonition that "preferences will sometimes prove necessary to achieve the [FHA's] basic equal opportunity goal" of granting those with disabilities "the same [housing] opportunities that those without disabilities enjoy. By definition any special 'accommodation' requires the employer to treat an employee with a disability differently, i.e., preferentially." And in *Schaw*, the court stated, "the fact that a theoretical non-disabled person also could potentially benefit from an accommodation [does not render] that accommodation improper." 938 F.3d at 1272-73. In close cases, courts must consider where to draw the line between guaranteeing equal opportunity and providing special privileges. Consider this analysis from then-Judge Gorsuch:

[T]he object of the statute's necessity requirement is a level playing field in housing for the disabled. . . . [U]nder the FHA it is sometimes necessary to dispense with formal equality of treatment in order to advance a more substantial equality of opportunity. And that is precisely the point of the reasonable accommodation mandate: to require changes in otherwise neutral policies that preclude the disabled from obtaining "the same . . . opportunities that those without disabilities automatically enjoy." But while the FHA requires accommodations necessary to ensure the disabled receive the same housing opportunities as everybody else, it does not require more or better opportunities. The law requires accommodations overcoming barriers, imposed by the disability, that prevent the disabled from obtaining a housing opportunity others can access. But when there is no comparable housing opportunity for non-disabled people, the failure to create an opportunity for disabled people cannot be called necessary to achieve equality of opportunity in any sense. . . . [T]he evidence shows that in seeking to occupy the top floor of a motel in a commercial zone [EDS.—for a residential treatment facility], Cinnamon Hills is seeking an opportunity that isn't available to others rather than one that is. And that's a result the statute does not compel.

Cinnamon Hills Youth Crisis Center, Inc. v. Saint George City, 685 F.3d 917, 919, 923-24 (10th Cir. 2012); *see also* Dayton Veterans Residences Limited Partnership v. Dayton Metropolitan Housing Authority, No. 21-3090, 2021 WL 5411220, at *9 (6th Cir. Nov. 19, 2021) ("A reasonable jury could find that amending the [housing authority's] plan [was necessary because it] would have afforded disabled veterans an opportunity to live near the VA campus and placed them on equal footing with non-disabled persons living in the Dayton community.").

5. Reasonableness. *Giebeler* observed that an accommodation is reasonable "when it imposes no 'fundamental alteration in the nature of the program' or 'undue financial or administrative burdens.'" In its reasonableness analysis, the *Giebeler* court noted: "The rental arrangement requested by Giebeler would not require [the housing provider] to accept less rent, would not otherwise alter the essential obligations of tenancy . . . (such as appropriate behavior and care of the premises), and would provide a lessee with the proper financial qualifications and credit history." The *Bhogaita* court noted that the reasonableness determination requires a "balancing of the parties' needs" and that the defendant failed to raise the issue of reasonableness. Compare *Bhogaita* and *Giebeler* with the following cases:

- In Davis v. Echo Valley Condominium Ass'n, 945 F.3d 483, 491-92 (6th Cir. 2019), the court engaged in a textual analysis of "accommodation" against the backdrop of §504 precedent and held that a total smoking ban was not a "moderate adjustment" as the term dictates, but a "fundamental change" to a condominium policy allowing smoking. "It is more rewrite than adjustment." The court also reasoned that the total ban would "intrude on the rights of third parties," noting that "an adjustment goes too far if the costs of implementing it exceed any expected benefits it will provide the person requesting it."
- In Schaw v. Habitat for Humanity of Citrus County, Inc., 938 F.3d 1259, 1269 (11th Cir. 2019), the court explained: "'[t]he difference between [an] accommodation that is required and [a] transformation that is not is the difference between saddling a camel and removing its hump.'" The court went on to hold in the context of a minimum-income requirement that a request for Habitat to accept documentation of food stamps or familial support (in lieu of ordinary wages) was sufficient to meet the facial reasonableness bar at the first step. The court remanded to allow the case to proceed to the second step: defendant's showing of any undue burden or fundamental alteration.

- In Summers v. City of Fitchburg, 940 F.3d 133, 140-41 (1st Cir. 2019), a nonprofit operator of sober-living homes sought a waiver of a sprinkler system requirement for boarding houses with six or more unrelated residents. After engaging in the necessary "factbound balancing," the court noted plaintiff's failure to rebut key evidence on unreasonableness: "On this record, there is no principled way for us to conclude that the sober house residents would accrue enough financial and/or therapeutic benefits from a Sprinkler Law exemption to outweigh the safety risks that they and the public would face if the plaintiffs were allowed to forgo sprinklers."
- In Groner v. Golden Gate Gardens Apartments, 250 F.3d 1039, 1041-43, 1047 (6th Cir. 2001), plaintiff suffered a serious mental illness, which resulted in complaints of his making noise ("yelling, screaming, and slamming" of doors) at all hours, leading to eviction. He otherwise "paid his rent in a timely manner and properly maintained the condition of his apartment." Affirming summary judgment for the apartment complex, the court held that the plaintiff did not meet his burden of demonstrating reasonableness of a request to renew his 12-month lease and contact his social worker each time a noise complaint was lodged against him (among other requests). The record showed that 10 to 12 complaints had been made over the course of his roughly 18-month tenancy, with the complex repeatedly informing plaintiff's social worker and even agreeing to extend tenancy by one month to facilitate treatment, but that "previous delays [in eviction] had not helped to resolve the problem and that it would be too burdensome for Golden Gate to continue apprising [the social worker] each time Groner caused a disturbance." The court concluded there was "no showing of a reasonable accommodation that would have enabled Groner to remain in his apartment without significantly disturbing another tenant."

6. Who Has the Burden on "Reasonableness"? Note that circuit courts differ on which party has the burden of showing a proposed accommodation is reasonable or not and on the nature of the showing required. The *Giebeler* court observed subtle differences between §504 and ADA precedent, explaining the ADA approach in detail:

> *Barnett* stresses . . . that the plaintiff need only show that an accommodation "seems reasonable on its face, i.e., ordinarily or in the run of cases." Once the plaintiff has made this showing, the burden shifts to the defendant to demonstrate that the accommodation would cause undue hardship in the particular circumstances. [If unable to make the initial showing, the plaintiff] "nonetheless remains free to show that special circumstances warrant a finding that . . . the requested accommodation is reasonable on the particular facts."

The *Giebeler* court ultimately held there was "no need . . . to decide" who had the burden because the requested accommodation was reasonable regardless.

See Schwemm, HDLL §11D:8 n.14 (noting the circuit split on this issue under the FHA). *Compare* Lapid-Laurel, LLC v. Zoning Board of Adjustment of Township of Scotch Plains, 284 F.3d 442, 446 (3d Cir. 2002) ("We think that under §3604(f)(3)(B) the plaintiff bears the initial burden of showing that the requested accommodation is necessary to afford handicapped persons an equal opportunity to use and enjoy a dwelling, at which point the burden shifts to the defendant to show that the requested accommodation is unreasonable.") *with* Hollis v. Chestnut Bend Homeowners Ass'n, 760 F.3d 531, 541 (6th Cir. 2014) ("The ultimate burden to prove both the reasonableness and the necessity of the requested accommodation or modification rests always with the plaintiff.").

Which party do you think should bear the burden of showing that an accommodation is reasonable on its face? The responsibility of demonstrating an "undue administrative or financial burden" or fundamental alteration? Why might each be different?

7. Interactive Process. The *Joint Statement on Accommodations* recommends an interactive process as "helpful to all concerned" in the event a housing provider wishes to refuse an accommodation request because it appears unreasonable. In that case, "the provider *should* discuss with the requester whether there is an alternative accommodation that would effectively address the requester's disability-related needs" without a fundamental alteration and without imposing an undue burden. Ultimately, "[i]f an alternative accommodation would effectively meet the requester's disability-related needs and is reasonable, the provider must grant it." *Joint Statement on Accommodations* at 7 (emphasis added). Recall that agency guidance provides technical assistance, but it does not create new or expanded rights and obligations. Thus, the pertinent question remains whether a landlord has discriminated by refusing to provide a reasonable accommodation, not whether a landlord has refused an interactive process. *See* Howard v. HMK Holdings, LLC, 988 F.3d 1185, 1194 (9th Cir. 2021) ("No other circuit has found that failing to engage in an interactive process provides an independent basis for liability under the FHAA . . ."); Lapid-Laurel, 284 F.3d at 455-56 (holding that the FHA does not impose an interactive process requirement on local land use authorities "because they already face detailed state and municipal requirements mandating formal procedures").

After requesting an accommodation that is reasonable and necessary, is a person with a disability bound to accept an alternative accommodation preferred by a housing provider? Probably not. "[W]hen it comes to reasonable accommodation of a disability, a court at the summary-judgment stage[43] must consider first whether the plaintiff's own requested accommodation 'seems reasonable on its face' before turning to consider a defendant's objections

---

43. The Eleventh Circuit also applies this standard at the motion to dismiss stage. *See* Unger v. Majorca at Via Verde Homeowners Ass'n, No. 21-13134, 2022 WL 4542348 (11th Cir. Sept. 29, 2022).

and counterproposals." Schaw v. Habitat for Humanity of Citrus County, Inc., 938 F.3d 1259, 1269 (11th Cir. 2019) (citing Supreme Court ADA precedent in *Barnett*). However, a plaintiff unable to demonstrate the necessity of a requested accommodation may be required to accept the alternatives on offer. Vorchheimer v. Philadelphian Owners Ass'n, 903 F.3d 100, 103-05, 113 (3d Cir. 2018).

What duties do plaintiffs have to interact? In Astralis Condominium Ass'n v. Secretary, HUD, 620 F.3d 62, 68-69 (1st Cir. 2010), the court rejected the argument that the complainant failed to participate in an interactive process where defendants "effectively short-circuited" the process: allegedly stonewalling by offering to grant the requested parking space but failing to follow through and requiring the "futile act" of a full vote of the condominium owners.

8. Who Pays for Accommodations? The *Joint Statement on Accommodations* notes at page 8, "Courts have ruled that the Act may require a housing provider to grant a reasonable accommodation that involves costs [for the provider]," as long as those costs do not pose an undue burden or fundamentally alter the provider's operations. As discussed in note 5, some cost-benefit analysis may be required. *See* Dadian v. Village of Wilmette, 269 F.3d 831, 839 (7th Cir. 2001) (upholding jury verdict finding village failed to reasonably accommodate in denying front driveway permit under hardship exception; jury weighed testimony on minor administrative costs against the plaintiff's disability-related need to avoid twisting and turning and walking long distances that would result from rear garage turnabout design).

Consider another case involving a generally applicable fee. In United States v. California Mobile Home Park Management Co., 29 F.3d 1413, 1414 (9th Cir. 1994), a mother whose daughter had a respiratory disease requiring a home health care aide sought a waiver of guest fees applicable to all residents. The mobile home park charged long-term guests $1.50 per day and $25 per month for guest parking. Guided by the "generous spirit" of construction afforded the FHA, as well as its legislative history and incorporation of §504 standards, the court reversed the dismissal of the claim at the pleading stage, holding that the generally applicable fees were "not immune from scrutiny for compliance with the . . . requirement of reasonable accommodation."

> We find the effort to distinguish accommodations that have a financial cost from other accommodations unconvincing. Besides the fact that §3604's reasonable accommodations requirement contains no exemption for financial costs to the landlord, the history of the FHAA clearly establishes that Congress anticipated that landlords would have to shoulder certain costs involved, so long as they are not unduly burdensome. [Congress based the FHA reasonable accommodation duty on §504 regulations and caselaw; the Supreme Court's holding in *Southeastern Community College v. Davis* that] a proposed accommodation should not impose "undue financial . . . burdens" upon the accommodator . . . clearly contemplates *some* financial burden resulting from the accommodation. . . .
>
> There are, of course, many types of residential fees that affect handicapped and non-handicapped residents equally; such fees are clearly proper. Fees that merit closer scrutiny are those with unequal impact, imposed in return for

permission to engage in conduct that, under the FHAA, a landlord is required to permit. Some generally applicable fees might be too small to have any exclusionary effect. Other fees might be sustained because to require their waiver would extend a preference to handicapped residents, as opposed to affording them equal opportunity. The waiver of others might impose an undue financial burden on the landlord. The reasonable accommodation inquiry is highly fact-specific, requiring case-by-case determination. In a case such as this one, a reviewing court should examine, among other things, the amount of fees imposed, the relationship between the amount of fees and the overall housing cost, the proportion of other tenants paying such fees, the importance of the fees to the landlord's overall revenues, and the importance of the fee waiver to the handicapped tenant. . . . [The plaintiff] must be afforded the opportunity to develop a full record in support of her claim.[44]

Housing providers may *not* charge a fee or extra deposit for either processing reasonable accommodation requests or granting them. Imposing a fee as a condition of granting an accommodation would not provide an "equal opportunity to use and enjoy a dwelling." Compare the duty of *making* reasonable accommodations with the duty of *permitting* reasonable structural modifications, at the tenant's expense. *See* Section D.

What about pet deposits? Recall that assistance animals are not considered "pets" and therefore would not be subject to a pet deposit or fee. *See* 2020 Assistance Animal Notice, at 3 ("A housing provider may exclude or charge a fee or deposit for pets in its discretion and subject to local law but not for service animals or other assistance animals.").

D. REASONABLE MODIFICATIONS

The duty to permit reasonable modification of physical aspects of a dwelling is another "special provision" in §3604(f) of the FHA that imposes an affirmative duty on housing providers.[45] A plaintiff "need not prove discriminatory intent to establish a viable reasonable-modification claim." Hollis v. Chestnut Bend Homeowners Ass'n, 760 F.3d 531, 541 (6th Cir. 2014). This provision defines discrimination to include:

a **refusal to permit, at the expense of the handicapped person, reasonable modifications** of existing premises occupied or to be occupied by such

---

44. Following remand and a bench trial, the Ninth Circuit affirmed judgment for defendant because the plaintiff failed to introduce evidence showing why waiver of the caregiver's parking fees was "necessary for [the plaintiff's] own use and enjoyment of her home," for example, because the parking fees "prevented a third party from being able to provide care services, or . . . diminished the care [plaintiff] could receive." United States v. California Mobile Home Park Mgmt. Co., 107 F.3d 1374, 1380-82 (9th Cir. 1997).

45. For a discussion of who may be liable under the FHA, and therefore, who must comply with the affirmative duties set forth in the FHA's special provisions for individuals with disabilities, see Chapter 4. See Section H, below, for discussion of the additional duties that §504 and the ADA impose on certain housing providers.

person if such modifications may be **necessary to afford such person full enjoyment** of the premises except that, in the case of a rental, the landlord may where it is reasonable to do so condition permission for a modification on the renter agreeing to restore the interior of the premises to the condition that existed before the modification, reasonable wear and tear excepted.

42 U.S.C. §3604(f)(3)(A) (emphasis added).

The following questions are designed to highlight the unique aspects of the FHA's affirmative duty to permit modifications.[46] Consider the case of Mr. Rusinov, discussed in the *Jankowski* decision, Section C, above:

1. If Mr. Rusinov's impairments worsened to the point where he needed to use a wheelchair to fully enjoy his apartment, would the FHA require his landlord to widen doorways into and throughout the unit to enable wheelchair access?

2. What options are available to Mr. Rusinov to address his emergent need for wheelchair access?

3. If Mr. Rusinov's father lived in a different apartment complex and requested permission there to widen the doorway into his dwelling unit to accommodate his son's wheelchair during visits, would the FHA require approval?

4. Does the FHA require a housing provider to permit any modification Mr. Rusinov wants, wherever he wants it?

---

46. For answers to these questions, see §3604(f); 24 C.F.R. §100.203; Joint Statement of HUD and DOJ, *Reasonable Modifications Under the Fair Housing Act* (Mar. 5, 2008).

5. Is the analysis for determining Mr. Rusinov's right to modify his doorway the same as his right to obtain an assigned parking space as a reasonable accommodation?

6. How would the analysis change if Mr. Rusinov's landlord received federal financial assistance or were a state or local entity?

7. How would the analysis change if Mr. Rusinov lived in a "covered multi-family dwelling" under §3604(f)(3)(C),[47] first occupied in 2020?

8. Whose obligation is it to perform maintenance on any modifications made to interiors and exteriors?

9. Does the modification of a rental unit become a permanent structural change once it is made?

10. Is Mr. Rusinov required to pay a fee or increased security deposit as a condition for receiving permission for a reasonable modification?

11. But how can the landlord ensure that funds will be available to restore the property to its original condition, if restoration is reasonable?

12. Can Mr. Rusinov's landlord propose that he move to a different unit that already has the structural features that he needs?

13. How much control may the landlord exercise over Mr. Rusinov's design and implementation of any structural modification?

E. DESIGN AND CONSTRUCTION REQUIREMENTS

As the previous section on reasonable modifications demonstrates, Congress did not require housing providers to make all existing dwelling units accessible to persons with disabilities at the time of the FHA's passage. Congress did require in its third "special provision" that, after a 30-month grace period, certain newly constructed units comply with seven basic "design and construction requirements." 42 U.S.C. §3604(f)(3)(C).

1. Design and Construction: Overview

Which units must comply with the affirmative duty under the FHA to make dwellings accessible? The FHA accessibility standards apply to "the design and construction of *covered multifamily dwellings* for first occupancy after" March 13, 1991. The FHA defines covered multifamily dwellings as *"buildings consisting of 4 or more units if such buildings have one or more elevators; and ground floor units in other buildings consisting of 4 or more units."* 42 U.S.C. §3604(f)(7). A ground floor requires a building entrance on an accessible route, and there may be more than one ground floor. This means that a townhouse building with two units, even if it were part of an apartment complex with dozens of

---

47. Note that Mr. Rusinov moved into his apartment complex in 1986, confirming that the FHA design and construction requirements were not yet in effect. *See Jankowski*, 91 F.3d at 894.

buildings, would not be covered. If a 12-unit building has an elevator, then all 12 units are covered. If a 12-unit building does not have an elevator, then only the units on the ground floor(s) must comply.

What does it mean to design and construct for *first occupancy* after March 13, 1991? HUD defines first occupancy as "a building that has never before been used for any purpose." A 2025 conversion of an early 20th-century warehouse into an apartment building, therefore, would not be covered under this interpretation. Also, state and local governments must issue or renew the last building permit after June 15, 1990, for a newly constructed dwelling to be covered, regardless of occupancy date.[48]

The FHA defines discrimination to include the failure to meet the seven accessibility standards detailed below.[49] Like the affirmative duties of accommodation and modification, the plain text of the FHA with respect to design and construction does not require any showing of animus or intent to make dwellings inaccessible because of disability. Nor does the statute include any exceptions for ignorance of the law, undue burden, good faith attempts at compliance, or perceived lack of need for the accessible units.[50]

As you review the seven standards, which are intended to be "modest,"[51] consider how they might differ from those required by the ADA and §504, discussed in Section H, below. As HUD explains, "A unit that meets the FHA's accessibility requirements will be one that does not have as great a degree of accessibility as a [publicly funded] unit, but is one that may be easily adapted to be fully accessible without significant costs and the need to do significant modifications."[52] On the other hand, the FHA standards apply to a wider range of dwelling units, such as those on upper floors served by an elevator or all ground floor units in a building with no elevator. We

---

48. *See* 24 C.F.R. §§100.201, 100.205(a); Schwemm, HDLL §11D:9 n.11 (explaining that HUD extended the permit cut-off date to coincide with publication of its guidelines).

49. 42 U.S.C. §3604(f)(3)(C); 24 C.F.R. §§100.201, 100.205; HUD, Fair Housing Accessibility First, https://www.hud.gov/program_offices/fair_housing_equal_opp/accessibility_first _requirements (last visited June 18, 2023) (HUD's Accessibility First website derives the seven design and construction requirements from the FHA and its regulations; the definitions of key terms are excerpted from §100.201 of HUD's regulations).

50. *See* Schwemm, HDLL §11D:9 at nn.3-5 & 20 and accompanying text. HUD in its regulation excuses the requirement of at least one accessible building entrance on an accessible route in instances of "site impracticality." 24 C.F.R. §100.205(a).

51. H.R. Rep. No. 100-711, at 18 (1988) ("These modest requirements will be incorporated into the design of new buildings, resulting in features which do not look unusual and will not add significant additional costs.").

52. HUD, Section 504, Frequently Asked Questions, https://www.hud.gov/program_offi ces/fair_housing_equal_opp/disabilities/sect504faq (last visited Aug. 6, 2024); *see also* H.R. Rep. No. 100-711, at 26 (1988) ("[T]he Committee intends to use a standard of "adaptable" design, a standard developed in recent years by the building industry and by advocates . . . to provide usable housing for handicapped persons without necessarily being significantly different from conventional housing.").

have included definitions of key terms from the HUD regulations where appropriate.[53]

Requirement 1: An accessible building entrance on an accessible route.[54]

Each covered multifamily dwelling must have *at least one* accessible building entrance on an accessible route unless it is impractical to do so because of the terrain or unusual characteristics of the site [such as hills or waterfronts requiring stairways or stilts].

> An *accessible route* means a continuous, unobstructed path connecting accessible elements and spaces within a building or site that can be negotiated by a person with a disability who uses a wheelchair, and that is also safe for and usable by people with other disabilities.
>
> An *accessible entrance* is a building entrance connected by an accessible route to public transit stops, accessible parking and passenger loading zones, or public streets and sidewalks.

Requirement 2: Accessible public use and common use areas.

Covered housing must have accessible and usable public and common-use areas. Public and common-use areas cover all parts of the housing *outside individual units*. They include—for example—building-wide fire alarms, parking lots, storage areas, indoor and outdoor recreational areas, lobbies, mailrooms and mailboxes, and laundry areas.

> *Accessible* when used with respect to the public and common use areas [connected with covered dwellings], means that they . . . can be approached, entered, and used by individuals with physical disabilities. . . .
>
> *Public use areas* means interior or exterior rooms or spaces of a building that are made available to the general public. Public use may be provided at a building that is privately or publicly owned.

---

53. In addition to its implementing regulations at 24 C.F.R. §100.205, HUD over the years has provided various forms of technical guidance on the FHA's design and construction requirements, which are beyond the scope of this text. These include Accessibility Guidelines; a Question-and-Answer Supplement to the Guidelines; a Design Manual, which is filled with detailed illustrations and sample room designs; and a designation of safe harbors. HUD, Accessibility Requirements for Buildings, https://www.hud.gov/program_offices/fair_housin g_equal_opp/disabilities/accessibilityR (last visited, June 19, 2023). For more information, see Fair Housing Accessibility, FIRST, https://www.hud.gov/program_offices/fair_housing_eq ual_opp/accessibility_first_home (last visited June 19, 2023); Joint Statement of HUD and DOJ, *Accessibility (Design and Construction) Requirements for Covered Multifamily Dwellings Under the Fair Housing Act* (Apr. 30, 2013), https://www.hud.gov/sites/documents/jointstatement.pdf.

54. The FHA does not make this requirement explicit, suggesting only six standards, but HUD guidelines set forth the additional requirement of an accessible entrance on an accessible route as "implicit in subparts (i) and (iii)(I)." See Schwemm, HDLL §11D:9, at n.12 (citing 56 Fed. Reg. 9472, 9503-15 (Mar. 6, 1991)).

Common use areas means rooms, spaces or elements inside or outside of a building that are made available for the use of residents of a building or the guests thereof. These areas include hallways, lounges, lobbies, laundry rooms, refuse rooms, mail rooms, recreational areas and passageways among and between buildings.

Requirement 3: Usable doors (usable by a person in a wheelchair).

All *doors that allow passage* into and within all premises must be wide enough to allow passage by persons using wheelchairs.

Requirement 4: Accessible route into and through the dwelling unit.[55]

There must be an accessible *route into and through* each covered unit.

Interior accessible routes may include corridors, floors, ramps, elevators, and lifts. Exterior accessible routes may include parking access aisles, curb ramps, walks, ramps, and lifts. . . .

Requirement 5: Light switches, electrical outlets, thermostats and other environmental controls in accessible locations.

Light switches, electrical outlets, thermostats and other environmental controls must be in *accessible locations*.

Requirement 6: Reinforced walls in bathrooms for later installation of grab bars.

Reinforcements in bathroom walls must be installed, so that grab bars can be added when needed. The law does not require installation of grab bars in bathrooms.

Requirement 7: Usable kitchens and bathrooms.

Kitchens and bathrooms must be usable—that is, designed and constructed so an individual in a wheelchair can *maneuver* in the space provided.

2. Design and Construction: Application

These requirements can become quite technical in application. Consider the following interpretation of the requirement to make public and common use areas accessible.

---

55. The FHA and HUD's implementing regulations state that compliance with the accessibility standard known as "ANSI A117.1" satisfies the last four of the design and construction requirements. See 42 U.S.C. §3604(f)(4); 24 C.F.R. §100.205(e).

United States v. Edward Rose & Sons

384 F.3d 258, 260-63 (6th Cir. 2004)

Before Siler, Moore, and Sutton, Circuit Judges

SILER, Circuit Judge:

This housing discrimination case turns on what [entrance] doors must be accessible to the handicapped [under the FHA]. At issue are two sets of apartment complexes, designed with an inaccessible front door, but an accessible back patio door. The district court granted the DOJ ("government") a preliminary injunction halting the construction and occupancy of the buildings. The main defendant, the builder and owner, Edward Rose & Sons ("Rose"), appeals. . . . We AFFIRM the district court's grant of the preliminary injunction. . . .

Defendant Rose constructed and owns the nineteen apartment buildings, located in Michigan and Ohio, at issue. These buildings are at various stages of construction, but all have the same basic design. [They have no elevator, thus only the ground floor units are "covered dwellings."] The ground floor apartments at issue have two exterior entrances—a front door and rear patio door. The "front" door is closer to the parking lot, but is handicapped inaccessible because it can only be reached by descending stairs. At the bottom of the stairs is a landing shared by two front doors leading into two different apartments. The rear patio entrance is accessible, but is located farther from the parking lot. . . .

The basic question of this litigation is whether the space outside the front door is a public or common use area that must be handicapped accessible. We are the first circuit to consider the issue. . . .

[The government argued that the stair landing was a primary entrance that most visitors will use, and thus was a public or common use area subject to the FHA's accessibility requirements. The defendant argued that the government's interpretation required almost every unit entrance to be accessible, thus making the separate requirement of "an accessible route" superfluous.]

We find that, in this particular case, the stair landing in front of the entrance is a common area that the statute mandates be accessible. The fact that two apartment units share the stair landing makes the space a common area. The plain meaning of "common use" unambiguously covers the entrance under dispute. At the time of the statute's enactment, dictionaries generally defined "common" as belonging to or shared by two or more individuals. Here, the stair landing belongs to, and is shared by, two apartments, and exists for their "common use."[56]

---

56. [Fn. 4 in original] While our finding that the plain meaning of "common use" unambiguously covers the stair landing at issue, even if we found the statute ambiguous, the space in front of the two entrances would fall under the HUD regulations defining "common use area." *See generally* Chevron U.S.A. v. Natural Resources Defense Council, 467 U.S. 837 (1984)

Our ruling is narrow; we simply hold in this case that because the two apartments share the stair landing, the stair landing qualifies as a "common area" that must be accessible. We express no opinion on what the FHA would require if the stairs only led to one apartment unit entrance and decline to delve into the parties' "primary entrance" arguments because we find them unnecessary for the resolution of this case. Assuming *arguendo* that, as Rose submits, not every entrance constitutes a "common area" because otherwise §3604(f)(3)(C)(iii)(I)'s mandate that all premises have "*an* accessible route" is superfluous, we still would find that the shared landing is a common area. Section §3604(f)(3)(C)(iii)(I) would not be superfluous because that section would ensure that apartment units that share no entrance with another apartment unit would still have "an accessible" entrance.

In sum, we find that the stair landing qualifies as a "common area" that the FHA mandates be accessible. Thus, the government's likelihood of success on the merits is strong. [Eds.—Likelihood of success on the merits is an important element that a party must establish to obtain a preliminary injunction, in this case, halting construction and occupancy until a trial on the merits could be held (or other resolution obtained).]

The next case involves allegations of widespread violations of the design and construction requirements. Note the summary judgment posture of the case, the types of documentary evidence the government offered to establish liability, and whether the defendants controverted the government's proof.

United States v. Quality Built Construction, Inc.
309 F. Supp. 2d 756, 758 (E.D. N.C. 2003)

Boyle, Chief Judge

Plaintiff, the United States, filed the underlying complaint against Defendants [a builder, its major shareholder, and its interior design architect] alleging violations of the FHA. . . . Plaintiff claims that Defendants failed to design and construct the Breezewood Condominiums and Hyde Park Apartments in Greenville, NC in compliance with the Act because the [ground floors of the] properties are not accessible to handicapped persons.

(finding regulatory interpretation of ambiguous statute controlling if not contrary to the statute) [Eds.—*Chevron* is overruled; *see* Chapter 3.]; Meyer v. Holley, 537 U.S. 280, 288 (2003) (Supreme Court using HUD regulations and commentary in Federal Register in interpreting the FHA). The regulation defines "common use areas" as "rooms, spaces or elements inside or outside of a building that are made available for the use of residents of a building or the guests thereof . . . includ[ing] hallways, lounges, lobbies, laundry rooms, refuse rooms, mail rooms, recreational areas and passageways among and between buildings." 24 C.F.R. §100.201. In the instant case, the shared landing is like a common "hallway" shared by the two apartments. Thus, even if we found "common area" ambiguous, Rose still would lose under the regulations.

DISCUSSION

A. Plaintiff's Motion for Partial Summary Judgment as to Liability

Plaintiff contends that it is entitled to summary judgment on the issue of liability. According to Plaintiff, the uncontested facts of this case demonstrate that Defendants failed to design and construct the Breezewood and Hyde Park units in accordance with the requirements of §3604(f)(3)(C). In response, Defendants contend that several material questions of fact exist with respect to the issue of liability. [The Court considered and rejected Defendants' arguments, including that the United States lacked standing, that any violations were unintentional, and that they were not all proper Defendants.] . . .

2. Plaintiff's Evidence in Support of Summary Judgment

Having rejected Defendants' arguments in opposition to summary judgment, the Court must now determine whether Plaintiff is entitled to judgment as a matter of law on the issue of liability. Defendants Quality Built and Dansey claim that whether the alleged violations were accidental or intentional is a question of fact that precludes summary judgment. However, intent is not a required element of a suit under [this provision of] the Act. . . . Therefore, the only question relevant to Defendants' liability is whether the properties were designed and constructed to be accessible to handicapped persons, as required by the Act.

a. *42 U.S.C. §3604(f)(3)(C)(i)*

Plaintiff first contends that Defendant [builders] violated §3604(f)(3)(C)(i) because the public and common use areas of the properties are inaccessible to handicapped persons. The inaccessible features of the Breezewood property include the following: (1) only one of the fifteen buildings has a curb ramp from the parking lot to the walkway; (2) there are no compliant accessible parking spaces; (3) the mailboxes are surrounded by a six-inch curb and no curb ramp exists; (4) the pool area is not served by a curb ramp and the gate entrance handle requires grasping and twisting; (5) the pool bathrooms are not accessible because of a 4 ½ inch step at the entrance and a lack of clear space in the doorway or interior; and (6) the primary entrances to the units have door knobs that require grasping and twisting. With respect to the Hyde Park property, the inaccessible features include the following: (1) each unit is on a breezeway which requires a six-inch step up; (2) only one of six buildings has a curb ramp from the parking lot to the walkway; (3) the designated handicapped parking space does not have a sufficiently wide access aisle to allow space to get from a car to the sidewalk; (4) the mailboxes are surrounded by a six-inch curb and no curb ramp exists; and (5) the primary entrances to the units have door knobs that require grasping and twisting.

The Fair Housing Accessibility Guidelines ("HUD Guidelines") provide specific characteristics and features required for accessible public and common areas.[57] Plaintiff has provided evidence, including [expert witness] measurements and photographs, showing violations of these specifications. In response, Defendants [offered a statement of their president that he] "believe[s] that the public use and common use portions of the subject properties are readily accessible and usable by handicapped persons." [They] have not come forward with alternative measurements or any other evidence to show that a triable issue of fact exists. The Court therefore grants Plaintiff's motion for summary judgment as to liability for violations of §3604(f)(3)(C)(i) as to Defendant [builders].

b. 42 U.S.C. §3604(f)(3)(C)(ii)

Plaintiff contends that the doors into and within the units are not sufficiently wide to comply with §3604(f)(3)(C)(ii) of the Act. The HUD Guidelines provide that, "[w]ithin individual dwelling units, doors intended for user passage through the unit which have a clear opening of at least 32 inches nominal width when the door is open 90 degrees, measured between the face of the door and the stop, would meet [the Act's] requirement."

Defendants admit that the bathroom doors, bedroom doors, patio doors, and doors to the closets and storage areas have a clear width of thirty inches or less. Defendants . . . argue that accessibility is a relative term and the present width of the doors is sufficient. However, the undisputed facts before the Court indicate that the widths of the unit doors are thirty inches or less, and in some cases are as narrow as twenty-two inches. Accordingly, the Court grants Plaintiff's motion for summary judgment as to liability for violations of §3604(f)(3)(C)(ii). . . .

c. 42 U.S.C. §3604(f)(3)(C)(iii)(I)

Plaintiff next argues that Defendants violated §3604(f)(3)(C)(iii)(I) of the Act by failing to provide an accessible route into and through the units at Breezewood and Hyde Park. Under the HUD Guidelines, accessible routes into and through dwelling units exist where: (1) a minimum clear width of 36 inches is provided; [and other technical specifications are met].

The evidence before the Court shows, and Defendants concede, that there is a four-inch step at the front door to each unit at Breezewood and Hyde Park. The Court also has before it the testimony of Plaintiff's expert, Phillip Zook, who examined the units and found that the inside thresholds of the patio doors [at certain units are too high and] are not beveled. [Other units have passages in bathrooms and utility rooms less than 36 inches and] a four-inch step up to the storage room door. Plaintiff's expert concluded that the inadequate door widths inside the units at both properties impede accessibility.

---

57. [Fn. 3 in case] The [March 6, 1991] HUD Guidelines were issued by HUD pursuant to §3604(f)(5)(C) of the Act, which directs HUD to provide technical assistance in implementing the requirements of the Act.

Defendants Quality Built and Dansey contend that the units are accessible and usable in their current form but fail to provide the Court with evidence to challenge Plaintiff's claims or to show that Zook's measurements are incorrect. As noted above, conclusory allegations are not sufficient to defeat a motion for summary judgment. Therefore, the Court finds that Defendants have failed to present evidence of a genuine factual dispute as to the existence of an accessible route into and through the units. The Court grants Plaintiff's motion for summary judgment as to liability for violations of §3604(f)(3)(C) (iii)(I) as to Quality Built, Dansey, and Hite.

d. 42 U.S.C. §3604(f)(3)(C)(iii)(II)

Similarly, Defendants fail to demonstrate any issues of material fact with respect to Plaintiff's claim that the placement of light switches, electrical outlets, and thermostats violates §3604(f)(3)(C)(iii)(II). In his declaration, Zook states that [various outlets, thermostats, and light switches are non-compliant.]

The HUD guidelines provide that switches, outlets, and thermostats should be located "no higher than 48 inches, and no lower than 15 inches, above the floor." Defendants do not submit evidence to challenge Zook's measurements, nor do they present evidence of alternative compliance. . . . The Court finds that the Defendants' mere conclusory assertions do not create an issue of material fact, and the Court grants Plaintiff's motion for summary judgment as to liability for violations of §3604(f)(3)(C)(iii)(II) as to [defendant builders].

Defendant Hite contends that, although it did provide general and structural drawings for the interior units at Breezewood and Hyde Park, it was not responsible for the specific positions of outlets, switches, and thermostats. . . . However, Hite placed its seal and certification on the design plan pages for the interior units at Breezewood and Hyde Park. As the party responsible for the design of the interior units, Hite's failure to specify compliant locations contributed to the inaccessible outlets, switches, and thermostats. As Hite does not dispute Plaintiff's factual allegation that the outlets, switches, and thermostats are in non-compliant locations, the Court also grants Plaintiff's motion for summary judgment as to liability for violations of §3604(f)(3)(C) (iii)(II) as to Hite.

e. 42 U.S.C. §3604(f)(3)(C)(iii)(III)

Plaintiff contends that the bathrooms walls are not reinforced to allow for later installation of grab bars, in violation of §3604(f)(3)(C)(iii)(III). Plaintiff offers expert testimony that the architectural plans . . . do not show reinforcements in the bathroom walls for the later installation of grab bars. . . . Defendant [builders] argue that there are factual disputes with respect to this matter. . . . However, [they] provide no substantive evidence to support this assertion. Moreover, because Hite concedes that the plans did not provide for reinforcements and because [the builders] claim to have relied on Hite's design, Defendants have not demonstrated that a triable issue of fact exists with respect to this matter. Accordingly, Plaintiff's motion for summary judgment as to liability for violation of §3604(f)(3)(C)(iii)(III) is granted. . . .

f. 42 U.S.C. §3604(f)(3)(C)(iii)(IV)

Finally, Plaintiff contends that the properties violate §3604(f)(3)(C)(iii)(IV) because Defendants failed to design and construct usable kitchens and bathrooms in the units. The HUD Guidelines clarify this requirement by providing specific minimum dimensions for clear space and approach space in kitchens and bathrooms. The Guidelines provide that usable kitchens and bathrooms require: (1) a clear floor space at least 30 inches by 48 inches that allows a parallel approach by a person in a wheelchair at the range or cooktop and kitchen sink; (2) sufficient maneuvering room outside the swing of the door so that a person using a wheelchair can enter the bathroom and have enough space to close the door; and (3) a clear floor area around bathroom fixtures of [various possible measurements].

In response [to proof of noncompliance, including Plaintiff's expert measurements and Defendants' admissions, Defendants] argue that "the plaintiff's experts' measurements are wrong; the bathrooms and kitchens are large enough so that an individual in a wheelchair can maneuver about the space." Plaintiff has provided specific measurements showing that the properties fail to provide at least one bathroom in each unit that is accessible and usable in accordance with the Act. While Defendant [Builders] state that they disagree with the measurements, they have not provided alternative measurements or other evidence to support their contention. Therefore, Defendants have failed to show that there is an issue of material fact with regard to this issue, and Plaintiff's motion for summary judgment as to liability for violations of §3604(f)(3)(C)(iii)(IV) is granted. . . .

NOTES AND QUESTIONS

1. Determinate Standards. There certainly are instances where fact-bound determinations must be made in design and construction cases, but there is no question that the violations addressed in *Quality Built*, many of which can be resolved with a measuring tape, are far more determinate than the issues at play in reasonable accommodation cases. This in part helps explain the greater number of complaints filed alleging reasonable accommodation violations, described above.

2. Broad Scope of Protection. As discussed in reference to §§3604(f)(1) and (f)(2), the disability rights incorporated into the FHA extend to entire households and associates of the buyer or renter. The design and construction requirements define discrimination simply as a failure to meet the standards, without further limiting who may enforce them. This raises interesting questions about who has standing to sue. As explored in Chapter 4, the FHA requires that the plaintiff be "aggrieved," with the Supreme Court requiring plaintiffs to demonstrate an injury in fact, not just in law,[58] but the structure of §3604(f)(3)(C) suggests that this is a very broad class of potential litigants:

> Inclusion of the "general public" within the FHAA right of barrier-free access ensures such access to any handicapped individual. Whether one is a wheelchair bound neighbor, friend, or family member, a political candidate, or a repairman — all are making "public use" as they approach a Brooklyn Park unit's sidewalk-adjoining front door. Not to let them get there unimpeded, and, in effect, to send them away as if unwelcome, is precisely the discrimination the FHAA forbids.

Ability Center of Greater Toledo v. James E. Moline Builders, Inc., 478 F. Supp. 3d 606, 608-09 (N.D. Ohio 2020). Where accessible entrances are concerned, how would you draw the line between injury in law and injury in fact? That is, at what point does technical noncompliance with accessibility standards create a concrete injury? Would an investigator or tester have standing to sue?

3. Statute of Limitations. An important question that remains unresolved in design and construction cases is when the two-year statute of limitations under the FHA begins to run. If an individual is injured by a defendant's failure to comply with the requirements, do they have two years from the time they discover or encounter the noncompliance? Or must an individual file suit within two years of the conclusion of the design and construction phase, such as upon issuance of the last unit's certificate of occupancy? Compare the holdings reached in the following two circuits.

In Garcia v. Brockway, 526 F.3d 456, 461-63 (9th Cir. 2008) (en banc), the Ninth Circuit adopted a more restrictive approach.

> Here, the [discriminatory housing] practice is "a failure to design and construct," which is not an indefinitely continuing practice, but a discrete instance of discrimination that terminates at the conclusion of the design-and-construction phase. This violation differs from the one Congress codified as "continuing" in light of *Havens*, where the claims were "based not solely on isolated incidents . . ., but a continuing violation manifested in *a number of incidents* — including at least one . . . that [wa]s asserted to have occurred within the [limitations] period."
>
> Put differently, "[a] continuing violation is occasioned by continual unlawful acts, not by continual ill effects from an original violation." . . . Although the ill effects of a failure to properly design and construct may continue to be felt decades after construction is complete, failing to design and construct is a single instance of unlawful conduct. Here, this occurred long before plaintiffs brought suit.

The Sixth Circuit in Fair Housing Council, Inc. v. Village of Olde St. Andrews, Inc., 210 Fed. App'x 469, 480-81 (6th Cir. 2006) noted in an unpublished

---

58. *See* TransUnion LLC v. Ramirez, 594 U.S. 413, 427 (2021).

opinion that "an overwhelming majority of the federal courts . . . [have] adopted a less restrictive interpretation." After considering the various alternatives, the court reached a more generous tolling standard.

> We therefore find that . . . the limitations period will depend on the specific circumstances of each case. For example, where a disabled individual seeks to buy a particular unit and discovers that the unit is inaccessible because it was not designed in conformity with the FHA, the limitations period for that individual's claim would begin to run from the date that the individual attempted to buy the unit and discovered the nonconforming conditions. However, in a case such as the instant case, where the plaintiff [housing organization] alleges that the owner or developer engaged in a policy or practice throughout the entire development of constructing housing units that fail to comply with the FHA, the continuing violations doctrine applies to toll the statute of limitations until the sale of the last unit in that development. Along those same lines, where the plaintiff can show that the owner of several housing developments engaged in a continuous policy or practice with regard to the noncompliant design and construction of each of the developments, the continuing violation doctrine may toll the running of the limitations period until the last unit of all of the implicated developments is sold.

Which approach do you think is more persuasive? Why?

4. United States as Plaintiff. The two principal cases above involved the United States as plaintiff. The court in *Garcia* highlighted the special role the government plays in design and construction cases and the ability of the DOJ to file suit outside the limitations period applicable to private litigants:

> This [ruling that plaintiffs' claims were untimely] does not leave plaintiffs without any recourse. They can still report the violation to the Attorney General, and—long after construction is complete—he can seek to enforce defendants' legal duty to design and construct if there's "a pattern or practice of resistance," or if "any group of persons has been denied any [FHA] rights . . . and such denial raises an issue of general public importance." §3614(a). They can also request [modifications], for which they bear the costs, to remedy an impediment.

Garcia, 526 F.3d at 461 n.2. Additional commentary by Prof. Schwemm illustrates the range of relief and corresponding limitations periods available in DOJ cases:

> It must also be noted that §3614, which is the FHA's third enforcement technique and which authorizes the Department of Justice to bring "pattern or practice" and "group denial of rights" actions, presents an additional set of its own statute-of-limitations issues. Such §3614 actions may seek three different types of relief (equitable orders, monetary damages to persons aggrieved, and civil penalties), and each of these types of relief is governed by a different limitations period.
>
> Section 3614 does not specifically provide for a statute of limitations for "pattern or practice" or "group denial of rights" actions. In these circumstances, courts have uniformly held—both in §3604(f)(3)(C) and in other types of FHA cases—that such actions seeking equitable relief are not subject to any time limit. On the other hand, §3614 claims for monetary damages for persons aggrieved are subject to the three-year limitations period provided in 28 U.S.C.

§2415(b), and those for civil penalties must be "commenced within five years from the date when the claim first accrued." To make matters even more complicated, the former contains an explicit discovery rule, while the latter does not and has generally been interpreted in §3604(f)(3)(C) cases not to be extendable by a discovery rule.[59] [EDS. — A discovery rule allows a plaintiff to bring suit within a time period commencing from discovery of a violation, which is more generous than a period commencing from the violation itself.]

5. Proper Defendants. In some cases, including *Quality Built Construction*, the builder of noncompliant buildings attempted to escape liability by pointing to the architect's failure to produce FHA-compliant designs. But this is unlikely to be a winning strategy. In Baltimore Neighborhoods, Inc. v. Rommel Builder, Inc., 3 F. Supp. 2d 661, 665 (D. Md. 1998), the court put it this way: "When a group of entities enters into the design and construction of a covered dwelling, all participants in *the process as a whole* are bound to follow the FHAA. To hold otherwise would defeat the purpose of the FHAA to create available housing for handicapped individuals and allow wrongful participants in the design and construction process to remain unaccountable. In essence, any entity who contributes to a violation of the FHAA would be liable." This includes a builder who follows an architect's plans.

6. Remedies. Consider the types of relief the parties might request in a design and construction case. After some or all of the dwelling units in a property have been constructed, is it possible for a plaintiff to obtain an order requiring any noncompliant units to be retrofitted? Which units? What about public or common use areas? In *Edward Rose and Sons*, one of the featured cases in this section, the Sixth Circuit affirmed the district court's grant of a preliminary injunction halting the construction of buildings in varying stages of completion and restraining occupancy of the covered dwellings not yet leased. The parties eventually settled in the form of a consent order, in which the developer and architectural firms agreed to retrofit 5,400 ground-floor apartments in 49 apartment complexes in seven states, pay up to $950,000 to compensate individuals harmed by the lack of accessible features, and pay a $110,000 civil penalty to the United States.[60] The settlement also resolved a lawsuit alleging violations of the ADA for failure to ensure accessibility in rental offices. In *Quality Built Construction*, the DOJ and the builder eventually reached a settlement in the form of a consent order in which the builder agreed to pay $700,000 to retrofit the nearly 200 noncompliant ground floor dwellings; pay $70,000 to six injured families; pay a $30,000 civil penalty; and adopt nondiscriminatory policies and an educational program for employees

---

59. Robert G. Schwemm, *Barriers to Accessible Housing: Enforcement Issues in "Design and Construction" Cases Under the Fair Housing Act*, 40 U. RICH. L. REV. 753, 834-35 (2006).

60. *See* Press Release, *Justice Department Obtains Over $1 Million Settlement in Major Disability Discrimination Suit Involving 49 Apartment Complexes in Seven States* (Sept. 30, 2005), https://www.justice.gov/archive/opa/pr/2005/September/05_crt_515.htm.

and agents. The DOJ reached a separate agreement with the architectural firm for retrofits, damages, and employee training, "making the combined settlement for the United States' lawsuit over $1.1 million."[61] In a more recent case against Mid-America Apartment Communities, Inc., the DOJ reached an $11.3 million settlement of a design and construction case involving 50 apartment complexes, requiring retrofits, victim compensation, training, future compliance, and periodic reports.[62]

7. State Standards. The FHA makes explicit that "[n]othing in this title shall be construed to invalidate or limit any law of a State or political subdivision of a State . . . that requires dwellings to be designed and constructed in a manner that affords handicapped persons greater access than is required by this title." 42 U.S.C. §3604(f)(8). Does your state of residence require a greater level of accessibility than that provided by the FHA?

F. DIRECT THREAT TO HEALTH AND SAFETY

When Congress amended the FHA to prohibit disability-based discrimination, it incorporated a defense available under existing case precedent interpreting §504.[63]

> Nothing in this subsection [§3604(f)] requires that a dwelling be made available to an individual whose tenancy would constitute a direct threat to the health or safety of other individuals or whose tenancy would result in substantial physical damage to the property of others.

42 U.S.C. §3604(f)(9). Therefore, the FHA disability protections do not require housing providers to assume responsibility for legitimate threats to health or safety or for substantial property damage. However, as the legislative history of the FHA suggests, generalized perceptions, subjective fears, and unfounded speculation may not be used to determine whether a person constitutes a direct threat.[64] Housing providers may not exclude or discriminate against individuals who use wheelchairs or scooters, for example, because of

---

61. *See* Press Release, *Justice Department Announced $800,000 Settlement with North Carolina Developer for Housing Discrimination Lawsuit* (Feb. 8, 2005), https://www.justice.gov/archive/opa/pr/2005/February/05_crt_052.htm; *see also*, Press Release, *Justice Department Announced Settlement with North Carolina Architectural Firm Regarding Alleged Violations of FHA* (Feb. 11, 2003), https://www.justice.gov/archive/opa/pr/2003/February/03_crt_088.htm.

62. *See* Press Release, *Justice Department Obtains $11.3 Million Settlement of Disability-Based Housing Discrimination Lawsuit in District of Columbia* (Nov. 21, 2018), https://www.justice.gov/opa/pr/justice-department-obtains-113-million-settlement-disability-based-housing-discrimination.

63. *See* School Bd. of Nassau County, Fla. v. Arline, 480 U.S. 273 (1987); *see also* H.R. Rep. No. 100-711, at 29 (1988) ("the direct threat requirement incorporates the *Arline* standard").

64. *See, e.g.,* H.R. Rep. No. 100-711, at 22 (1988) ("Just like any other person with a disability, . . . former drug-dependent persons do not pose a threat to a dwelling or its inhabitants simply on the basis of status. Depriving such individuals of housing, or evicting them, would constitute irrational discrimination that may seriously jeopardize their continued recovery.").

unfounded speculation that they pose a threat to property maintenance. Nor may providers generally assume that individuals with certain types of disabilities will be unable to live independently or will pose a health risk to others.[65] For example, in Support Ministries for Persons with AIDS, Inc. v. Village of Waterford, 808 F. Supp. 120, 137 (N.D.N.Y. 1992), the defendant village asserted the direct threat defense to justify its refusal to allow a group home for people with AIDS, arguing that the home posed an infection risk to village residents. The court rejected this argument, characterizing it as "uneducated, discriminatory [and] totally unsupported by the medical evidence." *See also* Corey v. Secretary, HUD, 719 F.3d 322, 328 (4th Cir. 2013) (holding that in a case where a sister and brother with severe autism sought a rental home, the defendant lacked objective evidence of any direct threat sufficient to support his imposed rental conditions, including $1 million in renter's insurance; the court found that all discriminatory terms were based on unsubstantiated stereotypes about autistic people in general).

The *Joint Statement on Accommodation* at 4-5 provides this guidance:

> A determination that an individual poses a direct threat must rely on an individualized assessment that is based on reliable objective evidence (e.g., current conduct, or a recent history of overt acts). The assessment must consider: (1) the nature, duration, and severity of the risk of injury; (2) the probability that injury will actually occur; and (3) whether there are any reasonable accommodations that will eliminate the direct threat.

1. Who Has the Burden of Proof on Direct Threat to Health or Safety or Substantial Physical Damage?

Courts generally have held that the party defending an FHA claim by asserting the tenancy of a person with a disability poses a "direct threat" to health or safety "bears the burden of proof on that defense at trial." *See, e.g.,* Dadian v. Village of Wilmette, 269 F.3d 831, 840-41 (7th Cir. 2001) (reaching this conclusion after review of FHA text, legislative history, and Supreme Court precedent interpreting §504). Thus, "direct threat" operates as an affirmative defense.

2. What Is the Scope of the Direct Threat Defense?

The "direct threat" defense by its terms may arise in response to a claimed violation of any of the various provisions of §3604(f), but presumably not those arising under other provisions protecting people with disabilities, including §§3604(c),(d), & (e), 3605, 3606, and 3617.[66] Consider Hunt v. Aimco Properties, L.P., 814 F.3d 1213, 1224-25 (11th Cir. 2016), an example of a defendant using

---

65. *See* H.R. Rep. No. 100-711, at 18 (1988).
66. *See* Schwemm, HDLL §11D:3 & n.16.

the defense to seek dismissal of a "terms and conditions" claim under §3604(f)(2). Remember that defendants must not only plead, but prove, affirmative defenses.

> We now address the Hunts' claim under §3604(f)(2) for disparate treatment in the terms, conditions, or privileges of their rental. The Hunts alleged that because of Karl's disability Aimco representatives mistreated him by yelling at him, making him do maintenance work around the complex, and barring him from the community rooms and the office.
>
> These alleged facts sufficiently pled that Aimco placed conditions on Karl that were not imposed on other residents and restricted his access to facilities in the complex that were open to other residents. The complaint therefore satisfies the pleading requirements for a §3604(f)(2) claim.
>
> Aimco argues that it cannot be liable under §3604(f)(2) because the police, not Aimco, instructed Karl to stay out of the community room. This is a distinction without a difference. A private entity may not use the police as a front for discrimination.
>
> [A]lthough it was Deputy Kushel who warned Karl that he would be arrested if he entered the community room, it was an Aimco employee who called the police and accompanied Deputy Kushel to the Hunts' apartment.
>
> Naturally, in some circumstances it may be legitimate or even necessary to protect public safety by calling the police. Indeed, the FHA contemplates such a situation [in its direct threat exception]. It may well be that Aimco took reasonable actions based on Karl's direct threat. But the direct threat exception described in §3604(f)(9) is an affirmative defense and thus does not aid Aimco at the motion to dismiss stage. Considering the alleged facts in the light most favorable to the Hunts, as we must at this stage, the threat of police involvement—regardless of who spoke the warning—restricted Karl's use of the complex's facilities.

3. How Might a Direct Threat Defense Arise in the Land Use Context?

In Oconomowoc Residential Programs, Inc. v. City of Milwaukee, 300 F.3d 775, 777, 786 (7th Cir. 2002), the court rejected the city's public safety defense where a community home for six unrelated adults impaired by traumatic brain injury or developmental disabilities sought an exception to a requirement that they operate at least 2,500 feet from similar homes. The court affirmed the lower court's holding that the requested "variance" was reasonable and necessary: "A denial of a variance due to public safety concerns or concerns for the safety of the residents themselves cannot be based on blanket stereotypes about disabled persons rather than particularized concerns about individual residents."

In another case, Bangerter v. Orem City Corp., 46 F.3d 1491, 1495-96, 1503-04 (10th Cir. 1995), the court reversed the dismissal of an FHA claim, holding that the city's restrictions of 24-hour supervision and a neighborhood advisory committee were not "tailored to particularized [public safety] concerns about individual residents" of a group home serving mentally disabled adults.

4. Are Certain Assistance Animal Breeds Inherently Dangerous?

For analysis of a direct threat defense in the context of an assistance animal, consider Chavez v. Aber, 122 F. Supp. 3d 581, 586, 596-97 (W.D. Tex. 2015). Plaintiff Yvonne Chavez requested that the owner and manager of her rented duplex accommodate her minor son's mental health disabilities by allowing a mixed-breed pit bull named Chato as an emotional support animal. Defendants argued unreasonableness, claiming a dog that is part pit bull would cause an undue burden because of the danger it presented to tenants and third parties, for which they would be held legally responsible, and that the assistance animal would fundamentally alter and reconfigure the common area used by all tenants. Defendants further argued "[a]s a matter of law, it is not a reasonable accommodation to keep [such] a dangerous dog on the premises." Plaintiffs responded that the defendant "cannot reject a support animal that is a pit bull based only on the dog's breed." In holding that plaintiffs' pleading was sufficient, the court noted: "Plaintiffs have pleaded that a veterinarian found that Chato 'did not show signs of aggression.'" Further, Plaintiffs claim that "a canine behaviorist" concluded that Chato exhibited a "calm manner that is indicative of a dog with no aggression, fear or . . . socialization issues." Ultimately the court held: "Plaintiffs have alleged sufficient facts that Chato did not pose a direct threat, and, therefore, allowing Chato to remain on the premises was a potentially reasonable accommodation."

5. What Is the Housing Provider's Obligation Following Recent Overt Acts That Pose Safety Threats?

Health and safety risks must be evaluated in the context of an individual's tenancy, and accommodations are required "[i]f a reasonable accommodation could eliminate the risk."[67] If a disabled person has a recent history of problematic overt acts, "a provider must take into account whether the individual has received intervening treatment or medication that has eliminated [or significantly reduced] the direct threat (i.e., a significant risk of substantial harm)." The housing provider may request documentation of changed circumstances and require satisfactory assurances that the disabled individual no longer poses a direct threat affecting their tenancy. This obligation also extends to local governments in the land use context. *See Joint Statement on Accommodations* at 4-5; *see also* Joint Statement of HUD and DOJ, *State and Local Land Use Laws and Practices and the Application of the Fair Housing Act*, at 9 (November 10, 2016), https://www.justice.gov/opa/file/912366/download (hereinafter *Joint Statement on Land Use*).

For example, in Sinisgallo v. Town of Islip Housing Authority, 865 F. Supp. 2d 307, 341-42 (E.D.N.Y. 2012), the court stated:

---

67. *See* H.R. Rep. No. 100-711, at 29 (1988).

Congress did not "intend [ ] accommodations to be attempted or implemented if there is no reasonable expectation that the accommodation will protect the other tenants. . . . However, in order to comply with the relevant statutes "if a handicapped tenant is a direct threat to the health and safety of other tenants, the landlord is obligated to either reasonably accommodate the tenant's handicap or show that no reasonable accommodation will eliminate or acceptably minimize the risk posed by the handicapped tenant. . . . When the landlord shows that no reasonable accommodation will curtail the risk, its duty to accommodate ceases."

In *Sinisgallo*, the court granted preliminary injunctive relief against eviction where the plaintiff argued that adjustments to medication and treatment made the day after an assault would prevent him from constituting a direct threat to the safety of neighbors, and the housing authority failed to show plaintiff's requested accommodation of a "second chance" probationary period was unreasonable. Compare *Sinisgallo* to a case in which the plaintiff challenged as discriminatory an offer of shelter conditioned on a mental health evaluation. In Thomas v. Salvation Army Southern Territory, 841 F.3d 632, 639-40 (4th Cir. 2016), shelter employees asked the plaintiff to leave after they claimed she "exhibited disrespect and hostility toward the staff." The plaintiff sought readmission to a sister shelter, the Salvation Army. After several refusals to readmit her, "the staff member suggested Thomas would be readmitted if she obtained a mental health evaluation" and certain stabilization services. The plaintiff sued on multiple claims and the court affirmed dismissal of her complaint for, among other reasons, failure to plead a plausible claim of disability discrimination.

> The Salvation Army was within its rights to require reasonable steps to ensure that Thomas was stable before admitting her to the shelter. The Salvation Army is charged with protecting all of those in its shelters, and it simply cannot run the serious risk of admitting a resident who will be disruptive and may inflict harm on others. . . . The district court was right not to put the shelter between a rock and a hard place by imposing liability for exercising prudence in the course of its admissions decisions.

In another case, Roe v. Sugar River Mills Associates, 820 F. Supp. 636, 637-40 (D.N.H. 1993), the court denied summary judgment for a federally subsidized housing complex, Sugar River Mills, holding that genuine factual disputes existed on the question of plaintiff's disability and "whether any 'reasonable accommodation' would in fact permit plaintiff to live, peaceably and safely, among the other tenants at Sugar River Mills." An 82-year-old resident reported that "plaintiff threatened him with physical violence, [accosting him] using obscene, offensive and threatening language." Other tenants corroborated these events. Plaintiff was convicted of disorderly conduct. Sugar River Mills threatened plaintiff with eviction, and plaintiff sued under the FHA for failure to provide a reasonable accommodation. Sugar River Mills asserted the direct threat defense, and the court considered whether the direct threat exception foreclosed the right to reasonable accommodation, or whether, as plaintiff argued, "defendants have a statutory duty to explore whether reasonable accommodations might be undertaken in order to eliminate or sufficiently minimize the impact of his handicap (and its physical manifestations) upon the other tenants at Sugar River Mills to allow him to remain as a tenant." The court concluded that "plaintiff's position is both better reasoned and more consistent with the express provisions and goals of the Act," citing Supreme Court precedent interpreting §504: "In *Arline* the Supreme Court held that an individual with tuberculosis may be 'handicapped' . . . and that an employer must, if possible, 'reasonably accommodate' that individual to minimize the risk her disease presents to those around her, provided that she is 'otherwise qualified' to retain her position."[68]

For an example of a court's determination that a proposed accommodation would not curtail the risk, consider Keys Youth Services, Inc. v. City of Olathe, KS, 248 F.3d 1267, 1273-75 (10th Cir. 2001), where a home for ten juveniles (some of whom had disabilities) was denied a special use permit. After a bench trial, the lower court had held that the city's asserted neighborhood safety concerns were not a pretext for disability-based discrimination. The reviewing court saw no clear error, observing that the "youths [at issue] are undisputedly dangerous and have caused problems of real concern in the past. It is not unreasonable to think that they are capable of causing similar problems in the future." The plaintiff also did not satisfy the court that the requested accommodation of increasing the number of residents from eight to ten was reasonable given the legitimate threat presented.

6. May a Housing Provider Address a Health or Safety Threat Through an Accommodation That a Person With Disability Does Not Want?

Probably not. *See* Blatch ex rel. Clay v. Hernandez, 360 F. Supp. 2d 596, 635 (S.D.N.Y. 2005) ("[T]he Court rejects . . . the notion that the [New York housing agency] has an obligation to impose financial management, guardianship or other ameliorative measures on mentally disabled tenants who do not seek or wish to accept such accommodations.").

G. LAND USE DISCRIMINATION AND GROUP HOMES

Persons with disabilities may, because of individualized circumstances, require a group living arrangement with people outside their families to have an equal opportunity to live in a residential neighborhood. "Group home" does not have a particular legal meaning. Whether the home provides supportive services, requires participation in a treatment program, houses people

---

68. *See* School Bd. of Nassau Cnty. v. Arline, 480 U.S. at 287-88 (1987). The *Roe* court further observed that the FHA's legislative history grounds the duty to make reasonable accommodations in §504 precedent. *See Roe*, 820 F. Supp. at 639.

who have a particular type of disability, or is operated by an individual or organization on a profit or nonprofit basis is irrelevant to FHA coverage of the group home. However, state and local health, safety, and land use rules, zoning decisions and practices, and private covenants[69] often restrict these communal or group homes and do so in a variety of ways. The restrictions might explicitly target congregate living arrangements (for disparate treatment) or they could take a "neutral" form. The FHA applies regardless.

> The Act is intended to prohibit the application of special requirements through land-use regulations, restrictive covenants, and conditional or special use permits that have the effect of limiting the ability of such individuals to live in the residence of their choice in the community. . . . [Similarly, discriminatory application of neutral rules and regulations] often results from false or overprotective assumptions about the needs of handicapped people, as well as unfounded fears of difficulties about the problems that their tenancies may pose. These and similar practices would be prohibited.[70]

Thus, even though "regulation of land use and zoning is traditionally reserved to state and local governments," as explained in Chapter 8, "the Supremacy Clause of the U.S. Constitution [may require that] federal laws such as the FHA take precedence over conflicting state and local laws."[71]

Challenges to zoning ordinances and decisions necessarily require suing a government entity or officials or both. When the challenge involves a claim that the government is discriminating against a particular group, the constitutional doctrine of Equal Protection is implicated. However, the FHA's clear statutory protection is much easier to navigate than are murky constitutional standards.[72] As a result, plaintiffs who wish to assert a cause of action for disability-based housing discrimination virtually always proceed under the FHA. Constitutional claims can still be asserted, but they rarely have any independent significance.

---

69. *See* United States v. Wagner, 940 F. Supp. 972, 979 (N.D. Tex. 1996) ("Since the FHA Amendments took effect, courts have made clear that single family deed restrictions cannot be used to exclude group homes for disabled persons from single family neighborhoods.").

70. H.R. Rep. No. 100-711, at 24 (1988).

71. *See* Joint Statement of HUD and DOJ, *State and Local Land Use Laws and Practices and the Application of the Fair Housing Act*, at 1-2 (November 10, 2016), https://www.justice.gov/opa/file/912366/download. The FHA provides that the Secretary of HUD shall refer matters involving "legality of any State or local zoning or other land use law or ordinance" to the Attorney General for appropriate enforcement. 42 U.S.C. §3610(g)(2)(C). State or local law enacted outside the traditional police power is afforded even less deference. *See* Astralis Condo. Ass'n v. Sec'y, U.S. Dep't of Hous. & Urb. Dev., 620 F.3d 62, 70 (1st Cir. 2010) ("To say that private agreements under a state's condominium statute are capable of trumping federal anti-discrimination law verges on the ridiculous. We disavow that proposition.").

72. For example, in the case of City of Cleburne v. Cleburne Living Center, Inc., 473 U.S. 432 (1985), the Court struck down on equal protection grounds the city's denial of a special use permit for a proposed group home housing people with intellectual disabilities, which the city had classified as a "hospital for the feebleminded." The Court refused to subject the disability-based denial to heightened scrutiny, but held there was no rational basis for a decision based on negative attitudes and unsubstantiated fears about disabled people.

1. Single-Family Restrictions: FHA Coverage

Two types of restrictions that may come within the ambit of the FHA are zoning laws or private covenants defining what kind of "family" is permitted to live in a single-family area. Although these might seem similar, there are important differences between them: Zoning laws, of course, are government actions, and covenants are private agreements. Their language might be similar, but their legal ramifications could differ.

Some local standards define "family" as any number of related persons but no more than a certain number of unrelated persons. Based on the financial necessity and therapeutic benefits of communal living for people with disabilities, housing providers often request a waiver of the legal limit to allow additional unrelated disabled persons to reside in a group home, nursing home, or other congregate living setting. They might alternatively request that the group home residents be considered the functional equivalent of a family regardless of their blood or legal relationship. The following case addresses a threshold question of whether the FHA applies in the single-family zoning context.

GROUP HOMES, SOBER-LIVING HOMES

In *Edmonds* and in other cases discussed in this chapter, plaintiffs sought FHA protection from discrimination in the context of "group homes" for disabled persons. "A household where two or more persons with disabilities choose to live together, as a matter of association, may not be subjected to requirements or conditions that are not imposed on households consisting of persons without disabilities." *Joint Statement on Land Use* at 7. Some cases discussed in this section involve sober-living homes, and Oxford House is an example of a national program that supports the operation of such homes: "Individual Oxford Houses are designed to create a supportive familial atmosphere to help their residents recover from alcohol and substance addiction. Each house is financially self-supporting, democratically run, and will evict any resident who returns to alcohol or substance abuse. The houses do not have state licenses or a permanent staff." Oxford House, Inc. v. City of Baton Rouge, La., 932 F. Supp. 2d 683, 686 (M.D. La. 2013).

Group home providers do not have to allege their own disability; they can allege they have suffered discrimination based on the disabilities of those they serve. SoCal Recovery, LLC v. City of Costa Mesa, 56 F.4th 802, 813 (9th Cir. 2023). As in any other context, the status of disability must be established on the facts to invoke FHA protections in the context of group or sober-living homes. "[T]here is no *per se* rule that categorizes recovering alcoholics and drug addicts as disabled or handicapped, and a case-by-case evaluation is necessary. . . ." *Oxford House, Inc.*, 932 F. Supp. 2d at 688. But "sober living home operators . . . need not provide individualized [medical] evidence of the 'actual disability' of their residents. Rather, they can [demonstrate actual disability on a collective basis by showing they have] policies and procedures to ensure that they serve or will serve those with actual disabilities and that they adhere or will adhere to such policies and procedures." *SoCal Recovery, LLC*, 56 F.4th at 814-15. Note that

> many group home discrimination cases involve parallel claims under the ADA, which Congress has amended to provide broader rules of construction for the definition of "disability."

In *City of Edmonds v. Oxford House*, a group home case, the Supreme Court considered the narrow question whether a family composition rule "designed to preserve the family character of the [single-family zoned] neighborhood" was a type of occupancy limit exempted by the FHA.

City of Edmonds v. Oxford House, Inc., et al.

514 U.S. 725 (1995)

Ginsburg, J., delivered the opinion of the Court, in which Rehnquist, C.J., and Stevens, O'Connor, Souter, and Breyer, JJ., joined. Thomas, J., filed a dissenting opinion, in which Scalia and Kennedy, JJ., joined.

Justice GINSBURG delivered the opinion of the Court:

The Fair Housing Act prohibits discrimination in housing against, *inter alios*, persons with handicaps. Section 3607(b)(1) of the Act entirely exempts from the FHA's compass "any reasonable local, State, or Federal restrictions regarding the maximum number of occupants permitted to occupy a dwelling." This case presents the question whether a provision in petitioner City of Edmonds' zoning code qualifies for §3607(b)(1)'s complete exemption from FHA scrutiny. The provision, governing areas zoned for single family dwelling units, defines "family" as "persons [without regard to number] related by genetics, adoption, or marriage, or a group of five or fewer [unrelated] persons."

The defining provision at issue describes who may compose a family unit; it does not prescribe "*the* maximum number of occupants" a dwelling unit may house. We hold that §3607(b)(1) does not exempt prescriptions of the family-defining kind, *i.e.,* provisions designed to foster the family character of a neighborhood. Instead, §3607(b)(1)'s absolute exemption removes from the FHA's scope only total occupancy limits, *i.e.,* numerical ceilings that serve to prevent overcrowding in living quarters.

I

In the summer of 1990, respondent Oxford House opened a group home in the City of Edmonds, Washington, for 10 to 12 adults recovering from alcoholism and drug addiction. The group home, called Oxford House–Edmonds, is located in a neighborhood zoned for single family residences. Upon learning that Oxford House had leased and was operating a home in Edmonds, the City issued criminal citations to the owner and a resident of the house. The citations charged violation of the zoning code rule that defines who may live in single family dwelling units. The occupants of such units must compose a "family," and family, under the City's defining rule, "means an individual or two or more persons related by genetics, adoption, or marriage, or a group of five or fewer persons who are not related by genetics, adoption, or marriage." Oxford House–Edmonds houses more than five unrelated persons, and therefore does not conform to the code.

Oxford House asserted reliance on the FHA, which declares it unlawful "[t]o discriminate in the sale or rental, or to otherwise make unavailable or deny, a dwelling to any buyer or renter because of a handicap of . . . that buyer or renter." §3604(f)(1)(A). The parties have stipulated that the residents of Oxford House–Edmonds "are recovering alcoholics and drug addicts and are handicapped persons within the meaning" of the Act.

Discrimination covered by the FHA includes "a refusal to make reasonable accommodations. . . ." §3604(f)(3)(B). Oxford House asked Edmonds to make a "reasonable accommodation" by allowing it to remain in the single family dwelling it had leased. Group homes for recovering substance abusers, Oxford urged, need 8 to 12 residents to be financially and therapeutically viable. Edmonds declined to permit Oxford House to stay in a single family residential zone, but passed an ordinance listing group homes as permitted uses in multifamily and general commercial zones.

Edmonds sued Oxford House . . . seeking a declaration that the FHA does not constrain the City's zoning code family definition rule. Oxford House counterclaimed under the FHA, charging the City with failure to make a "reasonable accommodation" permitting maintenance of the group home in a single family zone. The United States filed a separate action on the same FHA "reasonable accommodation" ground, and the two cases were consolidated. . . .

[T]he District Court held that [the Edmonds' rule] defining "family," is exempt from the FHA under §3607(b)(1) as a "reasonable . . . restrictio[n] regarding the maximum number of occupants permitted to occupy a dwelling." The . . . Ninth Circuit reversed; [and the] decision conflicts with an Eleventh Circuit decision. . . .

II

The sole question before the Court is whether Edmonds' family composition rule qualifies as a "restrictio[n] regarding the maximum number of occupants permitted to occupy a dwelling" within the meaning of the FHA's absolute exemption. §3607(b)(1).[73] In answering this question, we are mindful of the Act's stated policy "to provide, within constitutional limitations, for fair housing throughout the United States." §3601. We also note precedent recognizing

---

73. [Fn. 4 in original] Like the District Court and the Ninth Circuit, we do not decide whether Edmonds' zoning code provision defining "family," as the City would apply it against Oxford House, violates the FHA's prohibitions against discrimination set out in 42 U.S.C. §§3604(f)(1) (A) and (f)(3)(B).

the FHA's "broad and inclusive" compass, and therefore according a "generous construction" to the Act's complaint-filing provision. *Trafficante* (1972). Accordingly, we regard this case as an instance in which an exception to "a general statement of policy" is sensibly read "narrowly in order to preserve the primary operation of the [policy]." *Commissioner v. Clark*, 489 U.S. 726, 739 (1989).

A

Congress enacted §3607(b)(1) against the backdrop of an evident distinction between municipal land use restrictions and maximum occupancy restrictions. Land use restrictions designate "districts in which only compatible uses are allowed and incompatible uses are excluded." D. Mandelker, Land Use Law §4.16, pp. 113-114 (3d ed.1993). These restrictions typically categorize uses as single family residential, multiple-family residential, commercial, or industrial.

Land use restrictions aim to prevent problems caused by the "pig in the parlor instead of the barnyard." *Euclid v. Ambler Realty* (1926). In particular, reserving land for single family residences preserves the character of neighborhoods, securing "zones where family values, youth values, and the blessings of quiet seclusion and clean air make the area a sanctuary for people." *Belle Terre v. Boraas* (1974); *see also Moore v. East Cleveland* (1977) (Burger, C.J., dissenting) (purpose of East Cleveland's single family zoning ordinance "is the traditional one of preserving certain areas as family residential communities"). To limit land use to single family residences, a municipality must define the term "family"; thus family composition rules are an essential component of single family residential use restrictions.

Maximum occupancy restrictions, in contradistinction, cap the number of occupants per dwelling, typically in relation to available floor space or the number and type of rooms. *See, e.g.,* [citing four national building and housing codes]. These restrictions ordinarily apply uniformly to *all* residents of *all* dwelling units. Their purpose is to protect health and safety by preventing dwelling overcrowding.

We recognized this distinction between maximum occupancy restrictions and land use restrictions in *Moore v. East Cleveland*. In *Moore*, the Court held unconstitutional the constricted definition of "family" contained in East Cleveland's housing ordinance. East Cleveland's ordinance "select[ed] certain categories of relatives who may live together and declare[d] that others may not"; in particular, East Cleveland's definition of "family" made "a crime of a grandmother's choice to live with her grandson." In response to East Cleveland's argument that its aim was to prevent overcrowded dwellings, streets, and schools, we observed that the municipality's restrictive definition of family served the asserted, and undeniably legitimate, goals "marginally, at best." Another East Cleveland ordinance, we noted, "specifically addressed . . . the problem of overcrowding"; that ordinance tied "the maximum permissible occupancy of a dwelling to the habitable floor area." Justice Stewart, in dissent, also distinguished restrictions designed to "preserv[e] the character of a residential area," from prescription of "a minimum habitable floor area per person," in the interest of community health and safety.

Section 3607(b)(1)'s language — "restrictions regarding the maximum number of occupants permitted to occupy a dwelling"—surely encompasses maximum occupancy restrictions.[74] But the formulation does not fit family composition rules typically tied to land use restrictions. In sum, rules that cap the total number of occupants in order to prevent overcrowding of a dwelling "plainly and unmistakably," fall within §3607(b)(1)'s absolute exemption from the FHA's governance; rules designed to preserve the family character of a neighborhood, fastening on the composition of households rather than on the total number of occupants living quarters can contain, do not.[75]

B

Turning specifically to the City's Community Development Code, we note that the provisions Edmonds invoked against Oxford House are classic examples of a use restriction and complementing family composition rule. These provisions do not cap the number of people who may live in a dwelling. In plain terms, they direct that dwellings be used only to house families. Captioned "USES," ECDC §16.20.010 provides that the sole "Permitted Primary Us[e]" in a single family residential zone is "[s]ingle-family dwelling units." Edmonds itself recognizes that this provision simply "defines those uses permitted in a single family residential zone."

A separate provision caps the number of occupants a dwelling may house, based on floor area:

> "Floor Area. Every dwelling unit shall have at least one room which shall have not less than 120 square feet of floor area. Other habitable rooms, except kitchens, shall have an area of not less than 70 square feet. Where more than two persons occupy a room used for sleeping purposes, the required floor area

---

74. [Fn. 8 in original] The plain import of the statutory language is reinforced by the House Committee Report, which observes: "A number of jurisdictions limit the number of occupants per unit based on a minimum number of square feet in the unit or the sleeping areas of the unit. Reasonable limitations by governments would be allowed to continue, as long as they were applied to all occupants, and did not operate to discriminate on the basis of race, color, religion, sex, national origin, handicap or familial status." H.R. Rep. No. 100-711, p. 31 (1988).

75. [Fn. 9 in original] Tellingly, Congress added the §3607(b)(1) exemption for maximum occupancy restrictions at the same time it enlarged the FHA to include a ban on discrimination based on "familial status." The provision making it illegal to discriminate in housing against families with children under the age of 18 prompted fears that landlords would be forced to allow large families to crowd into small housing units. Section 3607(b)(1) makes it plain that, pursuant to local prescriptions on maximum occupancy, landlords legitimately may refuse to stuff large families into small quarters. Congress further assured in §3607(b)(1) that retirement communities would be exempt from the proscription of discrimination against families with minor children. In the sentence immediately following the maximum occupancy provision, §3607(b)(1) states: "Nor does any provision in this subchapter regarding familial status apply with respect to housing for older persons."

shall be increased at the rate of 50 square feet for each occupant in excess of two." ECDC §19.10.000 (adopting Uniform Housing Code §503(b) (1988)).

This space and occupancy standard is a prototypical maximum occupancy restriction.

Edmonds nevertheless argues that its family composition rule, ECDC §21.30.010, falls within §3607(b)(1), the FHA exemption for maximum occupancy restrictions, because the rule caps at five the number of unrelated persons allowed to occupy a single family dwelling. But Edmonds' family composition rule surely does not answer the question: "What is the maximum number of occupants permitted to occupy a house?" So long as they are related "by genetics, adoption, or marriage," any number of people can live in a house. Ten siblings, their parents and grandparents, for example, could dwell in a house in Edmonds' single family residential zone without offending Edmonds' family composition rule.

Family living, not living space per occupant, is what ECDC §21.30.010 describes. Defining family primarily by biological and legal relationships, the provision also accommodates another group association: Five or fewer unrelated people are allowed to live together as though they were family. This accommodation is the peg on which Edmonds rests its plea for §3607(b)(1) exemption. Had the City defined a family solely by biological and legal links, §3607(b)(1) would not have been the ground on which Edmonds staked its case. It is curious reasoning indeed that converts a family values preserver into a maximum occupancy restriction once a town adds to a related persons prescription "and also two unrelated persons."[76]

Edmonds additionally contends that subjecting single family zoning to FHA scrutiny will "overturn Euclidian zoning" and "destroy the effectiveness and purpose of single family zoning." This contention both ignores the limited scope of the issue before us and exaggerates the force of the FHA's antidiscrimination provisions. We address only whether Edmonds' family composition rule qualifies for §3607(b)(1) exemption. Moreover, the FHA antidiscrimination provisions, when applicable, require only "reasonable" accommodations to afford persons with handicaps "equal opportunity to use and enjoy" housing. §§3604(f)(1)(A) and (f)(3)(B).

The parties have presented, and we have decided, only a threshold question: Edmonds' zoning code provision describing who may compose a "family" is not a maximum occupancy restriction exempt from the FHA under §3607(b)(1). It remains for the lower courts to decide whether Edmonds'

---

76. [Fn. 11 in original] This curious reasoning drives the dissent. If Edmonds allowed only related persons (whatever their number) to dwell in a house in a single family zone, then the dissent, it appears, would agree that the §3607(b)(1) exemption is unavailable. But so long as the City introduces a specific number — *any* number (two will do) — the City can insulate its single family zone *entirely* from FHA coverage. The exception-takes-the-rule reading the dissent advances is hardly the "generous construction" warranted for antidiscrimination prescriptions. *See Trafficante* (1972).

actions against Oxford House violate the FHA's prohibitions against discrimination set out in §§3604(f)(1)(A) and (f)(3)(B).

Justice THOMAS, with whom Justice Scalia and Justice Kennedy join, dissenting.

... To my mind, the rule that "no house ... shall have more than five occupants" (a "five-occupant limit") readily qualifies as a "restrictio[n] regarding the maximum number of occupants permitted to occupy a dwelling." In plain fashion, it "restrict[s]" — to five — "the maximum number of occupants permitted to occupy a dwelling." To be sure, as the majority observes, the restriction imposed by petitioner's zoning code is not an absolute one, because it does not apply to related persons. But §3607(b)(1) does not set forth a narrow exemption only for "absolute" or "unqualified" restrictions regarding the maximum number of occupants. Instead, it sweeps broadly to exempt *any* restrictions *regarding* such maximum number. It is difficult to imagine what broader terms Congress could have used to signify the categories or kinds of relevant governmental restrictions that are exempt from the FHA. ...

The majority does not ask whether petitioner's zoning code imposes any restrictions regarding the maximum number of occupants permitted to occupy a dwelling. Instead, observing that pursuant to ECDC §21.30.010, "any number of people can live in a house," so long as they are "related 'by genetics, adoption, or marriage.'" The majority concludes that §21.30.010 does not qualify for §3607(b)(1)'s exemption because it "surely does not answer the question: 'What is the maximum number of occupants permitted to occupy a house?'" The majority's question, however, does not accord with the text of the statute. To take advantage of the exemption, a local, state, or federal law need not impose a restriction *establishing* an *absolute* maximum number of occupants; under §3607(b)(1), it is necessary only that such law impose a restriction "regarding" the maximum number of occupants. Surely, a restriction can "regar[d]" — or "concern," "relate to," or "bear on" — the maximum number occupants without establishing an absolute maximum number in all cases.

I would apply §3607(b)(1) as it is written. Because petitioner's zoning code imposes a qualified "restrictio[n] regarding the maximum number of occupants permitted to occupy a dwelling," and because the statute exempts from the FHA "any" such restrictions, I would reverse the Ninth Circuit's holding that the exemption does not apply in this case. ...

[W]e require that "'Congress should make its intention "clear and manifest" if it intends to pre-empt the historic powers of the States.'" It is obvious that land use — the subject of petitioner's zoning code — is an area traditionally regulated by the States rather than by Congress, and that land use regulation is one of the historic powers of the States. As we have stated, "zoning laws and their provisions ... are peculiarly within the province of state and local legislative authorities." *Warth v. Seldin* (1975); ... *Belle Terre v. Boraas* (1974) (Marshall, J., dissenting) ("I am in full agreement with the majority that zoning . . . may indeed be the most essential function performed by local government"). . . . Accordingly, even if it might be sensible in other contexts to construe exemptions narrowly, that principle has no application in this case. . . .

In sum, it does not matter that ECDC §21.30.010 describes "[f]amily living, not living space per occupant," because it is immaterial under §3607(b)(1) whether §21.30.010 constitutes a "family composition rule" but not a "maximum occupancy restriction." The sole relevant question is whether petitioner's zoning code imposes "any . . . restrictions regarding the maximum number of occupants permitted to occupy a dwelling." Because I believe it does, I respectfully dissent.

NOTES AND QUESTIONS

1. A Bit of Procedure. Notice the procedural posture of the FHA claim in *Edmonds*. After issuing criminal citations against the home, the city was the first to file suit by seeking a declaratory judgment that its land use regulation (capping the number of unrelated residents in a single-family zone) was a type of occupancy limit exempt from FHA coverage under §3607(b)(1). Oxford House counterclaimed that the city violated the FHA by failing to make a reasonable accommodation to its single-family composition rule. Which of these issues did the Court decide?

2. What Is the Zoning Rule at Issue in *Edmonds*? The City of Edmonds, like most local governments, had created a single-family residential zone and separated other land uses deemed incompatible. As the cases in this section demonstrate, definitions of "family" in these zones vary widely. In this case, the city's family composition rule defined a "family" as any number of related persons but only five or fewer persons "not related by genetics, adoption, or marriage." Thus, Oxford House's group home for 10 to 12 unrelated adults recovering from addiction was not a permitted use in a single-family zone, necessitating an accommodation, whereas a family of 10 or 12 related persons would be permitted.

As discussed in Chapter 8, "use" zoning, notably the single-family zone, emerged and was upheld in *Euclid* after the Supreme Court prohibited explicit racial zoning in *Buchanan v. Warley*. Justice Ginsburg, rather matter-of-factly, reminds us of the purpose of single-family zones: "preserv[ing] the *character* of neighborhoods, securing 'zones where family values, youth values, and the blessings of quiet *seclusion* and clean air make the area a *sanctuary* for people.'" (emphasis added). The city denied Oxford House's request for accommodation, but added group homes as a permitted use in multi-family and general commercial zones. Why would Oxford House locate in a single-family zone in the first place and expend scarce resources fighting to remain there?

Professor Oliveri has observed that

more recently some municipalities have liberalized their ordinances to permit
so-called "functional families" (unrelated people who live together as a family) or unmarried couples with children to live in single-family zoned areas.
A number of commentators similarly argue that the right of intimate association must also protect nontraditional yet clearly intimate family-like relationships, and a handful of state courts have relied on their state constitutions to
invalidate single-family ordinances as they applied to functional families. [But
these "functional family" reforms] do not go far enough and ultimately miss
the point. . . . [They] require courts and zoning boards to make value judgments about whether particular households are acceptable family substitutes
and to condition their ability to live together on how they measure up. While
this approach allows more groups to live together than a restrictive regime, it
still does violence to the concept of associational rights. If it means anything,
the right to choose household companions must protect all people who wish
to live together—or co-reside—regardless of their identities, relationship, or
reason for doing so.

Rigel C. Oliveri, *Single-Family Zoning, Intimate Association, and the Right
to Choose Household Companions*, 67 Fla. L. Rev. 1401, 1405 (2016). The FHA
provides people with disabilities living in group homes several tools to seek
"functional family" status. As you read the cases and notes below, consider
whether you think these tools are appropriate. Are they adequate? Are they
effective?

3. Is a Single-Family Zone an Occupancy Limit? The Court's answer to
this narrow question is "no." What is an occupancy limit? According to the
Court, it addresses "living space per occupant" not "family living." The FHA
provides a "complete exemption from FHA scrutiny" for reasonable government restrictions "regarding the maximum number of occupants permitted
to occupy a dwelling." §3607(b)(1). As discussed in Chapter 16, these provisions often take the form of a limit on the total number of occupants based
on the square footage or number of bedrooms in the dwelling. This type of
provision often is challenged as having a disproportionate effect on families
with children. The Court noted an "evident distinction" between a maximum
occupancy restriction and a municipal land use regulation defining families,
and said that Congress understood this distinction when crafting the exemption. Do you agree that a rule "fastening on the composition of households" is
distinct from a "numerical ceiling that serves to prevent overcrowding"? The
dissent rejected the labels as "immaterial" to the "sole relevant question," that
is, "whether petitioner's zoning code imposes 'any . . . restrictions regarding
the maximum number of occupants permitted to occupy a dwelling.'"

How much emphasis did the Court place on the apparent function ("family values preserver") of the single-family zoning rule compared with the
maximum occupancy limit? Do you agree with that analytical frame?

4. Recurring Rule of Construction. We see the FHA's recurring rule of
construction articulated again in *Edmonds*. The Court noted the FHA's ambi-
tious policy "to provide, within constitutional limitations, for fair housing

throughout the United States." §3601. The Court cited *Trafficante*, discussed in Chapter 4, as "precedent recognizing the FHA's 'broad and inclusive' compass, which accorded a "generous construction" to the FHA. An exception to FHA coverage, in the Court's view, was "sensibly read 'narrowly in order to preserve the primary operation of'" FHA policy. Was this rule of construction necessary to the outcome?

Note that the dissent rejects this "interpretive premise" in the particular context of land use regulation, stating that Congress must make clear its intention to preempt "an area traditionally regulated by the States rather than by Congress." Justice Thomas does not reject wholesale the "generous construction" premise: "even if it might be sensible in other contexts to construe exemptions narrowly, that principle has no application in this case" because land use is "one of the historic powers of the States." (Note that Justice Thomas bolsters his argument by quoting Justice Thurgood Marshall.) Was Congress silent about whether the FHA extends to state and local land use regulation? Would the duty to accommodate apply at all to local governments if this coverage were not clear? Consider that Congress designated the Attorney General as the appropriate governmental enforcement body to address "the legality of any State or local zoning or other land use law ordinance." §3610(g)(2)(C). The Third Circuit in *Hovsons, Inc. v. Township of Brick* addressed this fundamental question one year after *Edmonds*:

> The district court's statement that the FHAA "does not ask [municipalities] to disregard their own zoning requirements in order to provide sufficient accommodations for the disabled" runs counter to the entire thrust of the FHAA. . . . It is uncontroverted that the Township of Brick has a substantial interest in enforcing its zoning code and that, under appropriate circumstances, local zoning codes are entitled to a considerable amount of deference. We are also mindful of the fact that "[i]n requiring reasonable accommodation, . . . Congress surely did not mandate a blanket waiver of all facially neutral zoning policies and rules, regardless of the facts." Nor did Congress intend to "give handicapped persons carte blanche to determine where and how they would live regardless of zoning ordinances to [the] contrary." Nonetheless, the FHAA's promise that "reasonable accommodations" be provided to handicapped persons would be an empty one indeed if Brick Township were permitted to do nothing to accommodate the elderly disabled who are in need of nursing home care and desire to live in one of the Township's residential zones.

89 F.3d 1096, 1103, 1106 (3d Cir. 1996). Consider also the statutory duty of federal, state, and local governments to affirmatively further fair housing. *See* Chapter 13.

5. Dueling Interpretations. The Court held that the FHA's "absolute exemption removes from the FHA's scope only total occupancy limits." A numerical restriction that limited unrelated but not related occupants for purposes of a single-family composition rule did not answer the question: "What is the maximum number of occupants permitted to occupy a house?" Thus, the Court concluded it did not qualify for the exemption.

Justice Thomas, writing for the dissenters, noted in reply that the Court's conclusion "fails to give effect to the plain language of the statute," which "sweeps broadly to exempt *any* restrictions *regarding*" the maximum number of occupants (emphasis added). The fact that the zoning rule "is not an absolute one, because it does not apply to related persons" is irrelevant, he says, because "3607(b)(1) does not set forth a narrow exemption only for 'absolute' or 'unqualified' restrictions."

Justice Ginsburg, writing for the Court, pointed to the language in §3607(b)(1) immediately following the occupancy limit exemption: "Nor does any provision in this title regarding familial status apply with respect to housing for older persons." Congress created the occupancy exemption in the context of extending FHA protections to families with children under the age of 18, which, according to the majority, "makes plain that, pursuant to local prescriptions on maximum occupancy, landlords legitimately may refuse to stuff large families into small quarters." The occupancy limit exemption resting alongside another familial status exemption arguably suggests it is aiming at restrictions on large families rather than at restrictions on unrelated cohabiting adults.

Justice Thomas considered it sufficient pursuant to a plain reading that the city "establish[ed] a specific number—five—as the maximum number of unrelated persons permitted to occupy a dwelling in the single family neighborhoods of Edmonds, Washington." He noted that maximum occupancy restrictions, a category of zoning rules "invented by the majority," "does not exhaust the category of restrictions exempted from the FHA. . . ." Justice Ginsburg questioned as "curious reasoning" whether merely adding a number to any land use rule should qualify it for a complete exemption under the FHA: "so long as the City introduces a specific number—*any* number (two will do)—the City can insulate its single family zone *entirely* from FHA coverage." Which arguments do you find more persuasive? Why?

6. **Legislative History, Anyone?** The House Committee Report accompanying the 1988 FHAA adding familial status as a protected category describes the occupancy limit exemption as one "relating to the familial status provisions." The report further explains: "A number of jurisdictions limit the number of occupants per unit based on a minimum number of square feet in the unit or the sleeping areas of the unit. Reasonable limitations by governments would be allowed to continue, as long as they were applied to all occupants, and did not operate to discriminate. . . ." H.R. Rep. 100-711, at 31. The majority cites this history as reinforcing the "plain import" of the statutory exemption. The Report does not mention single family zones. Does this matter?

2. Single-Family Restrictions: Reasonable Accommodations

Edmonds did not reach the merits of Oxford House's FHA claim. The following cases demonstrate the FHA analysis governing whether, how, and in what circumstances a housing provider can obtain a reasonable accommodation to exceed the limit on the number of unrelated persons allowed under a "single-family" restriction. For example, in Groome Resources Ltd., LLC v. Parish of Jefferson, 234 F.3d 192, 197-98 (5th Cir. 2000), the court affirmed a permanent injunction prohibiting the parish from interfering with or withholding approval of a reasonable accommodation permitting a group home operator to house five unrelated residents with Alzheimer's rather than the four allowed by parish ordinance. The court rejected the parish's challenge to the constitutionality of the FHA's reasonable accommodation provision after detailing the basis for the court's injunction:

> In determining the merits of the reasonable accommodations application, the district court found that the addition of one person to the four person limit was reasonable and necessary to allow individuals with Alzheimer's disease an equal opportunity to live in a residential setting, and that "[t]he trial evidence convinces the Court that the artificial limit of four unrelated persons living in a single group home will make it economically unfeasible for [Groome Resources] to operate the proposed home." The district court concluded:
>
> > . . . There is absolutely no evidence that this proposed group home with five Alzheimer's patients would cause any problems or in any way impact the health, safety, welfare or character of the neighborhood. If the home was occupied by a family, there would be no limit on the number of persons who reside there, or the number of automobiles or visitors at the home. In fact, the same residential zoning permits small home businesses, schools, and day care centers, all of which cause more congestion and traffic problems than is expected from the group home. The requested accommodation is clearly reasonable and necessary to allow the handicapped to have equal opportunity to live in residential settings of their choice, as mandated by the FHAA of 1988.

NOTES AND QUESTIONS

1. Discrimination Based on Some Disabilities and Not Others. Would a zoning authority or homeowners association be permitted to restrict or refuse accommodations for, say, sober-living homes, if it waived restrictions for people with other types of disabilities? No. The fact that a defendant complies with the FHA for group homes serving a particular subset of disabled persons does not excuse discrimination against another subset of disabled persons.[77]

---

77. *See, e.g.,* SoCal Recovery, LLC v. City of Costa Mesa, 56 F.4th 802 (9th Cir. 2023) ("The City adopted the 650-foot separation restriction and other restrictions in an explicit effort to reduce the number of sober living homes operating within the City."); Oxford House v. City of Baton Rouge, La., 932 F. Supp. 683, 697 (M.D. La. 2013) (holding ordinance discriminatory where it limited zoning accommodations in a single-family zone to "Special Homes" that could confirm type of developmental disability, licensing, and 24-hour staffing; the single-family zone defined family, in part, as having no more than two unrelated persons).

   2. Family Composition Rules. Additional examples further illustrate the variety of family composition rules litigated under the FHA, with accommodation requests often centering on increasing the number of unrelated people permitted in a single-family zone.

- In Harmony Haus Westlake, LLC v. Parkstone Property Owners Ass'n, 851 Fed. App'x 461 (5th Cir. 2021), an operator of a sober-living home had obtained a reasonable accommodation from the City of Austin to operate a "rooming house" for up to 12 unrelated people in the Parkstone gated community. The homeowners association refused to allow 12 unrelated residents but did waive its deed restriction to permit up to six unrelated residents. The court reversed the grant of an injunction for plaintiff on the basis of failure to demonstrate necessity. "To prove a certain minimum size is essential, plaintiff may show that number of residents is necessary for a sober-living home to be 'therapeutically meaningful' or 'financially viable.'" The house was functioning at the time of trial with six residents, and, according to the court, the plaintiff did not otherwise show that, but for its chosen model involving 12 residents (phasing in new and maintaining some established residents), people with disabilities would be denied an equal opportunity to enjoy the housing of their choice. Nor did Harmony Haus show that 12 residents were necessary for financial viability; a showing that it could not operate with six residents was insufficient.
- In Lapid-Laurel, L.L.C. v. Zoning Bd. of Adjustment, 284 F.3d 442, 446-47, 460-61 (3d Cir. 2002), the court affirmed summary judgment for defendant on a denial of variance to build a 95-bed care facility for disabled elderly persons on two large lots totaling four acres in a single-family zone. "While we think it clear that the use variance that Lapid requested was necessary to provide the elderly handicapped an equal opportunity to live in a residential neighborhood, . . . [a] strict interpretation of the 'necessity' requirements of §3604(f)(3)(B) would require Lapid to show that a building of the size that it proposed is required . . . to make it financially viable or medically effective." The court held that plaintiff's evidence was insufficient to create a triable issue for the jury on both the necessity and reasonableness prongs; the plaintiff failed to rebut issues of traffic safety and emergency vehicle access that defendant argued created an undue burden and fundamental alteration of the zoning scheme.
- In Bryant Woods Inn, Inc. v. Howard County, Md., 124 F.3d 597, 605 (4th Cir. 1997), the court held: "The zoning variance that Bryant Woods Inn seeks is not aimed at permitting [persons with Alzheimer's] to live in group homes in residential communities — that, as we have noted, is already permitted — but at *expanding* its group home size from 8 to 15 persons. While 'some minimum size may be essential to the success' of group homes, the Inn has introduced no evidence that group homes are

not financially viable with eight residents. [Moreover,] Bryant Woods Inn has also presented no evidence in this case that expansion from 8 to 15 residents would be therapeutically meaningful [and thus necessary]. If Bryant Woods Inn's position were taken to its limit, it would be entitled to construct a 10–story building housing 75 residents, on the rationale that the residents had handicaps."

- In Smith & Lee Associates, Inc. v. City of Taylor, Mich., 102 F.3d 781, 795-96 (6th Cir. 1996), the court affirmed a district court holding after a bench trial that the requested accommodation to allow adult foster care (AFC) homes to house nine (rather than six) elderly disabled residents in single-family neighborhoods was reasonable and necessary: "[E]lderly disabled citizens have a right to live in Taylor's single family neighborhoods . . . [and they] need an accommodation. Because the elderly disabled can no longer live independently, AFC homes often provide the only means by which this population can continue to live in residential neighborhoods [and they are not economically feasible with less than nine residents]. . . . Michigan already permits AFC homes to operate with six or fewer residents in areas zoned for single family use. We are not convinced that an additional three residents will fundamentally alter the nature of single-family neighborhoods. The residents of AFC homes live like most of the other families in their neighborhoods. They eat together, and they rely on each other for social activities and succor. Moreover, as none of Mortenview's elderly disabled residents drive, traffic and parking problems should not significantly increase with three more residents. Weighing the benefits to the elderly disabled against the cost to Taylor, we conclude that permitting AFC homes for the elderly disabled to operate with nine residents in neighborhoods zoned for single family use is a reasonable accommodation."

Recall that in *Giebeler*, the court cited zoning accommodations as a type of case in which courts have recognized the connection between disability-related needs and "financial limitations . . . in securing housing." The above examples demonstrate the importance of plaintiff's evidence demonstrating therapeutic need or economic necessity for accommodations related to congregate living options.

3. Group Homes as Families. Another type of group home accommodation is a request to be treated, and regulated, like a family. In Oxford House, Inc. v. Browning, 266 F. Supp. 3d 896, 904, 915-18 (M.D. La. 2017), the court granted summary judgment in favor of a sober-living home against the state Fire Marshal, holding as reasonable and necessary their requested accommodation that the Fire Marshal treat their home for more than three unrelated persons as the "functional equivalent of a family . . . and the use of the property as a single family use." The Fire Marshal judged the group home as a lodging or rooming house requiring more extensive and costly fire safety features. The court held the requested accommodation was reasonable because it did not undermine the basic purpose of the state's fire safety code:

> [T]he residents of Oxford House West Hale exhibit informal and formal social structures that resemble the hierarchies traditionally displayed by families, and the residents share a close bond with each other that prompts them to aid each other in times of need, as families tend to do. Because of these social structures and tight-knit relationships among the residents, the residents would react in a manner similar to a family in the event of a fire.

Compare the result in *Oxford House* with Summers v. City of Fitchburg, 940 F.3d 133, 139-40 (1st Cir. 2019), where a sober-living home sought an accommodation from a law requiring installation of sprinklers on the basis of financial burden, rather than treatment comparable to single families. The court found the safety justification for the sprinkler law unrebutted where plaintiff failed to make a specific showing of financial burden or interference with therapeutic benefits of their homes: "the desire to alleviate those costs is, on its own, insufficient to render an accommodation reasonable."

Is the group home's request to be treated as a family necessary to obtain an equal opportunity to use and enjoy their particular dwelling? The *Browning* court held that it was:

> [R]esidency in an Oxford House directly ameliorates the effects of alcoholism and drug addiction, and at least six otherwise unrelated individuals who are recovering from alcoholism or drug addiction must reside together in a dwelling in order to achieve these ameliorative effects. . . . Without this accommodation, the residents of Oxford House West Hale could not live in their home due to the exorbitant costs [required to install a fire alarm system, an automatic sprinkler system, and single-station smoke alarms not required of other "single families" leasing the same house], and their recovery from alcoholism and drug addiction thus would be hampered.

4. Group Homes and Housing Choice. May a zoning authority evade liability simply by offering a group home an alternative location to the one it seeks? No. In Schwarz v. City of Treasure Island, 544 F.3d 1205, 1223-26 (11th Cir. 2008), the court considered whether a waiver of an occupancy-turnover restriction was necessary:

> [T]he essential question in reasonable accommodation cases is whether the handicapped have an equal opportunity to live in the dwellings *of their choice*, not simply an opportunity to live somewhere in the City. . . . We therefore conclude that the availability of another dwelling somewhere within the City's boundaries is irrelevant to whether local officials must accommodate recovering substance abusers in the halfway houses of their choice.[78]

---

78. The court in *Schwartz* held that waiver of an occupancy-turnover rule was unreasonable in a zone where low turnover was essential; but it held the waiver was reasonable in a different zone where high turnover was already permitted for other multifamily dwellings.

5. How to Request a Land Use Accommodation. In other contexts, requests for accommodation need not contain magic words or be made in a particular manner. However, "[w]here a local land use or zoning code contains specific procedures for seeking a departure from the general rule, courts have decided that these procedures should ordinarily be followed. If no procedure is specified, or if the procedure is unreasonably burdensome or intrusive or involves significant delays, a request for a reasonable accommodation may, nevertheless, be made in some other way. . . ."[79] *Joint Statement on Land Use* at 16. Local government procedures for requesting an accommodation may vary, the results may be "foredoomed,"[80] indefinite delays in processing requests may operate as denials, and some procedures like public hearings may do more to trigger widespread opposition than to make housing available in a residential neighborhood. How far must an applicant for a reasonable accommodation go in utilizing the procedures offered by a local government? In Bryant Woods Inn, Inc. v. Howard County, Md., 124 F.3d 597, 602 (4th Cir. 1997), the plaintiff applied for a variance from the county planning board but did not appeal the denial to the county board of appeals; the county argued the FHA required plaintiff to exhaust all local remedies. The Fourth Circuit disagreed: "Under the FHA, . . . a violation occurs when the disabled resident is first denied a reasonable accommodation, irrespective of the remedies granted in subsequent proceedings. Bryant Woods Inn has alleged a completed violation of the FHA, which is consequently ripe for review."

The court in Tsombanidis v. West Haven Fire Dept. summarized the key principles governing plaintiffs' obligation to make an accommodation request in the land use setting:

> To prevail on a reasonable accommodation claim, plaintiffs must first provide the governmental entity an opportunity to accommodate them through the entity's established procedures used to adjust the neutral policy in question. *Oxford House–C v. City of St. Louis,* 77 F.3d 249, 253 (8th Cir.1996); *see also United States v. Vill. of Palatine,* 37 F.3d 1230, 1234 (7th Cir.1994) (holding that an administrative procedure must be used unless plaintiff can show such an action would be futile). Furthermore, requiring OH–JH to utilize facially neutral procedures to request an accommodation from the fire code is not by itself a failure to reasonably accommodate plaintiffs' handicaps. A governmental entity must know what a plaintiff seeks prior to incurring liability for failing to affirmatively grant a reasonable accommodation. It may be that once the governmental entity denies such an accommodation, neither the FHAA nor the ADA require a plaintiff *to exhaust* the state or local administrative procedures [EDS.—for instance, through further appeals]. . . . But a plaintiff must first use the procedures available to notify the governmental entity that it seeks an

---

79. DOJ and HUD "strongly encourage local governments to adopt formal procedures for identifying and processing reasonable accommodation requests." *Joint Statement on Land Use, supra* note 71, at 17.

80. *See* Oxford House, Inc. v. City of Baton Rouge, 932 F. Supp. 2d at 691 (where city refused an accommodation request made through the city's required form, "it would have been futile" for Oxford House to use the form to make an identical request for a different group home).

exception or variance from the facially neutral laws when pursuing a reasonable accommodation claim.

3. Other Restrictions on Group Homes

In addition to single-family restrictions, another type of local land use rule limiting group homes is a requirement that the home not be located within a specific distance of another group home, referred to as a spacing or dispersal requirement. Such requirements often are justified as a way of preventing group homes from being clustered together and forming segregated pockets, rather than helping to provide integrated options for disabled people in different neighborhoods. However, as the next case illustrates, these limits also can prevent group homes from operating at all, thus deny housing opportunities to disabled people. Consider the way the court addresses this tension and analyzes how "protective" legislation could still be actionable.

Larkin v. State of Michigan Department of Social Services
89 F.3d 285 (6th Cir. 1996)

Before Suhrheinrich and Siler, Circuit Judges; Aldrich, District Judge

ALDRICH, District Judge:
[Geraldine Larkin requested a license to operate an adult foster care (AFC) facility that would provide care for up to four disabled adults in Westland, Michigan. State law required notice of the application to all residents within 1,500 feet of the proposed facility and prohibited issuance of the license because of an existing AFC facility within 1,500 feet of the proposed facility, although waiver was possible. Larkin sued the State of Michigan Department of Social Services (MDSS), challenging Michigan's statutory scheme under the FHA; the court granted summary judgment enjoining enforcement of the state law provisions. The state appealed.]

III.

. . . It is well-settled that the FHAA applies to the regulation of group homes. . . . Moreover, Congress explicitly intended for the FHAA to apply to zoning ordinances and other laws which would restrict the placement of group homes. . . .

This brings us to the crux of the case: whether the statutes at issue discriminate against the disabled in violation of the FHAA. The district court held that two different aspects of [state law] violate the FHAA: (1) the 1500-foot spacing requirement . . .; and (2) the notice requirements. . . .

[F]acially discriminatory actions are just a type of intentional discrimination or disparate treatment, and should be treated as such. . . . Here, the challenged portions of [state law] are facially discriminatory. The spacing requirement prohibits MDSS from licensing any new AFC facility if it is within 1500 feet of an existing AFC facility. The notice requirements require MDSS to notify the municipality of the proposed facility, and the local authorities to then notify all residents within 1500 feet of the proposed facility. By their very terms, these statutes apply only to AFC facilities which will house the disabled, and not to other living arrangements. As we have previously noted, statutes that single out for regulation group homes for the handicapped are facially discriminatory. Accordingly, this is a case of intentional discrimination or disparate treatment, rather than disparate impact.

MDSS argues that the statutes at issue cannot have a discriminatory intent because they are motivated by a benign desire to help the disabled. This is incorrect as a matter of law. The Supreme Court has held in the employment context that "the absence of a malevolent motive does not convert a facially discriminatory policy into a neutral policy with a discriminatory effect." [International Union, United Auto. Aerospace & Agricultural Implement Workers v. Johnson Controls, Inc., 499 U.S. 187, 199 (1991)]. Following *Johnson Controls*, all of the courts which have considered this issue under the FHAA have concluded the defendant's benign motive does not prevent the statute from being discriminatory on its face. . . .

Because the statutes at issue are facially discriminatory, the burden shifts to the defendant to justify the challenged statutes. However, it is not clear how much of a burden shifts. MDSS urges us to follow the Eighth Circuit and rule that discriminatory statutes are subject to a rational basis scrutiny, i.e., they will be upheld if they are rationally related to a legitimate government objective. *See* Oxford House–C v. City of St. Louis, 77 F.3d 249, 252 (8th Cir. 1996); Familystyle [of St. Paul, Inc. v. City of St. Paul, 923 F.2d 91, 94 (8th Cir. 1991)]. Plaintiffs urge us to reject the rational basis test and adopt the standard announced by the Tenth Circuit, which requires the defendant to show that the discriminatory statutes either (1) are justified by individualized safety concerns; or (2) really benefit, rather than discriminate against, the handicapped, and are not based on unsupported stereotypes. Bangerter [v. Orem City Corp., 46 F.3d 1491, 1503-04 (10th Cir. 1995)].

Although we have never explicitly decided the issue, we have held that in order for special safety restrictions on homes for the handicapped to pass muster under the FHAA, the safety requirements must be tailored to the particular needs of the disabled who will reside in the house. Therefore, in order for facially discriminatory statutes to survive a challenge under the FHAA, the defendant must demonstrate that they are "warranted by the unique and specific needs and abilities of those handicapped persons" to whom the regulations apply. [Eds.—The court thus rejects rational basis review of facially discriminatory statutes.] MDSS has not met that burden. MDSS claims that the 1500-foot spacing requirement integrates the disabled into the community and prevents "clustering" and "ghettoization." In addition, it argues that the spacing requirement also serves the goal of deinstitutionalization by preventing a cluster of AFC facilities from recreating an institutional environment in the community.

As an initial matter, integration is not a sufficient justification for maintaining permanent quotas under the FHA or the FHAA, especially where, as here, the burden of the quota falls on the disadvantaged minority. *See* United States v. Starrett City Associates, 840 F.2d 1096, 1102-03 (2nd Cir. 1988), cert. denied, 488 U.S. 946 (1988). . . . The FHAA protects the right of individuals to live in the residence of their choice in the community. If the state were allowed to impose quotas on the number of minorities who could move into a neighborhood in the name of integration, this right would be vitiated.

MDSS argues that the state is not imposing a quota because it is not limiting the number of disabled who can live in a neighborhood, it is merely limiting the number of AFC facilities within that neighborhood. However, as we have previously noted, disabled individuals who wish to live in a community often have no choice but to live in an AFC facility. Alternatively, if the disabled truly have the right to live anywhere they choose, then the limitations on AFC facilities do not prevent clustering and ghettoization in any meaningful way. Thus, MDSS's own argument suggests that integration is not the true reason for the spacing requirements.

Moreover, MDSS has not shown how the special needs of the disabled warrant intervention to ensure that they are integrated. MDSS has produced no evidence that AFC facilities will cluster absent the spacing statute. In fact, this statute was not enforced from 1990 to 1993, and MDSS has offered no evidence that AFC facilities tended to cluster during that period.

Instead, MDSS simply assumes that the disabled must be integrated, and does not recognize that the disabled may choose to live near other disabled individuals. The result might be different if some municipalities were forcing the disabled to segregate, or cluster, in a few small areas. However, Michigan already prohibits such behavior:

> a state licensed residential facility [serving] 6 or less persons shall be considered a residential use of property for purposes of zoning and a permitted use in all residential zones, including those zoned for single family dwellings, *and shall not be subject to a . . . procedure different from those required for other dwellings of similar density in the same zone.*[81]

The only clustering or segregation that will occur, then, is as the result of the free choice of the disabled. In other words, the state's policy of forced integration is not protecting the disabled from any forced segregation; rather, the state is forcing them to integrate based on the paternalistic idea that it knows best where the disabled should choose to live.

In contrast, deinstitutionalization is a legitimate goal for the state to pursue. However, MDSS does not explain how a rule prohibiting two AFC facilities

---

81. [EDS.—This statute has been repealed and reenacted in a different form without apparent substantive changes.]

from being within 1500 feet of each other fosters deinstitutionalization in any real way. Two AFC facilities 500 feet apart would violate the statute without remotely threatening to recreate an institutional setting in the community. In fact, the spacing requirement may actually inhibit the goal of deinstitutional-ization by limiting the number of AFC facilities which can be operated within any given community.

MDSS relies again on *Familystyle*, where both the district court and the Eighth Circuit found that the goal of deinstitutionalization justified facially discriminatory spacing requirements. However, *Familystyle* is distinguish-able from the present case. In *Familystyle*, the plaintiff already housed 119 dis-abled individuals within a few city blocks. The courts were concerned that the plaintiffs were simply recreating an institutionalized setting in the commu-nity, rather than deinstitutionalizing the disabled.

Here, however, Larkin seeks only to house four disabled individuals in a home which happens to be less than 1500 feet from another AFC facility. The proposed AFC facility, and many more like it that are prohibited by the spac-ing requirement, do not threaten Michigan's professed goal of deinstitutional-ization. Because it sweeps in the vast majority of AFC facilities which do not seek to recreate an institutional setting, the spacing requirement is too broad, and is not tailored to the specific needs of the handicapped.[82] . . . Therefore, the 1500-foot spacing requirement violates the FHAA and is preempted by it.

MDSS also has failed to provide an adequate justification for the notice requirements. MDSS merely offers the same justifications as it offers for the spacing requirements, i.e., integration and deinstitutionalization. Notifying the municipality or the neighbors of the proposed AFC facility seems to have little relationship to the advancement of these goals. In fact, such notice would more likely have quite the opposite effect, as it would facilitate the organized opposition to the home, and animosity towards its residents. Furthermore, MDSS has offered no evidence that the needs of the handicapped would war-rant such notice. We find that the notice requirements violate the FHAA and are preempted by it.

By this holding, we in no way mean to intimate that the FHA, as amended by the FHAA, prohibits reasonable regulation and licensing procedures for AFC facilities. As was stated in Marbrunak [v. City of Stow, Ohio, 974 F.2d 43, 47 (6th Cir. 1992)], "the FHAA does not prohibit the city from imposing *any* special safety standards for the protection of developmentally disabled persons." Rather, it merely prohibits those which are not "demonstrated to be warranted by the unique and specific needs and abilities of those handi-capped persons."

---

82. [Fn. 4 in original] We express no opinion on whether a more narrowly tailored law pro-hibiting such a concentration would pass muster under the FHAA.

NOTES AND QUESTIONS

1. Statutes and Theories. Because plaintiffs generally must sue governmental agencies to challenge public land use restrictions (as opposed to covenants or other private instruments), claims often are available under §504 (covering federally assisted entities) and Title II of the ADA (covering state and local entities) in addition to the FHA. These statutes operate in substantial symmetry in the group home context. In Valencia v. City of Springfield, Illinois, 883 F.3d 959, 967 (7th Cir. 2018), the court explained:

> Importantly, all three statutes apply to municipal zoning decisions. A plaintiff may prove a violation of the FHA, ADA, or Rehabilitation Act by showing: (1) disparate treatment; (2) disparate impact; or (3) a refusal to make a reasonable accommodation. For each respective theory, the same analysis generally applies under all three statutes.

Why might a plaintiff seek to sue a defendant under more than one statute if there is significant overlap in their coverage? Notice that the *Larkin* court, applying the FHA, rejected the rational basis review urged by the defendant, a deferential standard that governs disability-based constitutional claims. The defendant failed to justify its facially discriminatory spacing and notice requirement, as explored in the next note.

2. Group Homes and Intentional Discrimination. The *Larkin* court rejected as "incorrect as a matter of law" the argument that defendants could not "have a discriminatory intent because they are motivated by a benign desire to help the disabled." Regulations purporting to benefit people with disabilities must be tailored to their specific needs and abilities and not be based on stereotypes. Moreover, intentional discrimination does not require a showing of "personal animus or bias on the part of individual government officials." *Joint Statement on Land Use* at 3; Bangerter v. Orem City Corp., 46 F.3d 1491, 1501 (10th Cir. 1995). For challenges to spacing requirements under an intent theory, courts consider the effect of the requirement on housing for disabled persons; the intent behind it; the existence, size and location of other group homes; and whether there are other methods for achieving the jurisdiction's stated purpose. *Joint Statement on Land Use* at 12.

Consider the following discussion of intentional discrimination in an Oxford House group home case, Tsombanidis v. West Haven Fire Dept., 352 F.3d 575, 580 (2d Cir. 2003). Do you think the analysis in a disability case is like or different from intent claims involving other protected classes?

> The district court's finding of intentional discrimination was not clearly erroneous. . . . Among other things, the district court noted the history of hostility of neighborhood residents to OH-JH and their pressure on the Mayor and other city officials. Evidence supports the court's finding that this hostility motivated the City in initiating and continuing its enforcement efforts. There was also evidence the City rarely took enforcement action against boarding houses in residential neighborhoods. . . . The court also cited the reaction of [a property maintenance code official who] ordered Tsombanidis to evict the residents without any authority in the City Code. Finally, there was record support

for the court's finding of bias in the denial of OH-JH's request for a special use exception by the Zoning Board of Appeals. We therefore affirm the district court's conclusion that the city intentionally discriminated.

See also Pacific Shores Properties, LLC v. City of Newport Beach, 730 F.3d 1142, 1163 (9th Cir. 2013) ("a jury could find . . . that the primary purpose of the Ordinance was to shut down group homes and prevent new ones from opening in Newport Beach, but to do so in facially neutral terms to avoid invalidation by a court.").

Thus, intentional disability-based discrimination in the land use context might include:

- adopting neutral rules with discriminatory intent;
- enforcing neutral rules differently against disabled persons;
- governmental acquiescence to community hostility or bias based on fears, prejudice, or unsubstantiated assumptions;[83]
- different treatment and application of laws based on stereotypes regarding disabled persons' needs, abilities, or threats to safety; and
- imposing facially discriminatory standards such as requiring housing providers to obtain special permits, comply with dispersal requirements, receive services or supervision, or follow different procedures because they serve people with disabilities.[84]

3. Facial Challenges. Not all facial challenges succeed, underscoring that these claims will turn on the text and nature of the restriction. For example, in Community Services, Inc. v. Wind Gap Mun. Authority, 421 F.3d 170, 179, 184 (3d Cir. 2005), the court reversed summary judgment for plaintiff and granted it for defendant on the intent claim, holding that assessing fees to a "personal care home" did not involve a facial violation of the FHA because the term was not a proxy for disability; it could include housing for those without disabilities. Nor was the home singled out for disparate treatment based on disability status. The court remanded the case for further proceedings on the disparate impact and reasonable accommodation claims.

4. Spacing or Dispersal Requirements and Reasonable Accommodations. *Larkin* considered a facial challenge to the Michigan spacing requirement, which it analyzed as a form of intentional discrimination. The lower court had dismissed plaintiff's reasonable accommodation claim because it held the city

---

83. As demonstrated throughout this section, "[n]ot all community opposition to requests by group homes is necessarily discriminatory." *Joint Statement on Land Use, supra* note 71, at 14.

84. *See* Marbrunak, Inc. v. City of Stow, Ohio, 974 F.2d 43, 46-47 (6th Cir. 1992) (ordinance violated FHA where it imposed "onerous safety and permit requirements on single family residences occupied by developmentally disabled persons" that it did not impose on other single-family residences); *see also* Courage to Change Ranches Holding Co. v. El Paso Cnty., Colo., 73 F.4th 1175 (10th Cir. 2023) (reversing summary judgment, finding five-person occupancy cap against group homes for disabled persons facially discriminatory where eight-person cap allowed for other structured group-living arrangements; also finding sufficient evidence to support disparate treatment where group homes for the aged were allowed to engage in medical and mental-health therapies while prohibiting these activities in sober living home).

had no discretion under state law to waive the requirement. *See* Larkin v. State of Michigan, 883 F. Supp. 172, 179 (E.D. Mich. 1994).

Decisions addressing group home spacing requirements under a reasonable accommodation theory include Valencia v. City of Springfield, Illinois, 883 F.3d 959, 962, 968 (7th Cir. 2018). There, the court affirmed a preliminary injunction against the city's eviction of three people with substantial physical or mental disabilities from a single-family residence they leased within 600 feet of a "family care residence" for people with developmental disabilities.[85] The provider sought a "conditional permitted use" exception from the spacing requirement, which the city denied.

The *Valencia* court applied an analysis to the reasonable accommodation claim similar to that discussed in Section C, but tailored it to the group home setting. For example, "'[t]he equal opportunity element limits the accommodation duty so that not every rule that creates a general inconvenience or expense to the disabled needs to be modified.'" [However,] "'[o]ften, a community-based residential facility provides the only means by which disabled persons can live in a residential neighborhood, either because they need more supportive services, for financial reasons, or both.'" The court held the home was necessary to enable residential services in a community-based setting, as such homes were in short supply. The accommodation was reasonable because it "would further advance the integration" of individuals with disabilities into the community; its "benefits likely outweigh the costs;" "the financial and administrative burden on the City is negligible [as] . . . there [had] been 'no issues' with the home" over the three years it had operated.

5. Group Home Residents and Their Caregivers. As stated in many of the noted cases, the reason a group home provider might seek a zoning waiver is to secure for residents an equal opportunity to live in a residential neighborhood. The usual goal is to locate a dwelling "in family-like settings in typical residential communities," so that "there is nothing about the exterior" that suggests it is anything other than a family residence. *Valencia*, 883 F.3d at 963. If the purpose of use zoning is to separate incompatible land uses, and group homes seek to create "family-like" settings, why would group homes ever be considered "incompatible" with single-family zones? At the public hearing in *Valencia*, "certain residents . . . asked that the CPU be denied because caregivers 'rac[ed] up and down their block to get to work on time,' 'listen[ed] to . . . loud music in their vehicles,' 'park[ed] on the wrong side of the street,' and blocked driveways and sidewalks." 883 F.3d 964. Are group homes unique with respect to the presence of caregivers in residential neighborhoods? Are the complaints about caregiver behavior unique to caregivers? To what extent should a court credit this evidence?

---

85. The plaintiffs also made a facial challenge to the spacing requirement, but the court chose to affirm the injunction only on the reasonable accommodation ground. *Valencia*, 883 F.3d at 967.

6. The Supreme Court's Ruling in *Olmstead* and Spacing Requirements.
The *Joint Statement on Land Use* provides this guidance on the compatible goals
of the *Olmstead* decision and the FHA:

> In Olmstead v. L.C., [527 U.S. 581 (1999)], the Supreme Court ruled that the
> Americans with Disabilities Act (ADA) prohibits the unjustified segregation
> of persons with disabilities in institutional settings where necessary services
> could reasonably be provided in integrated, community-based settings. An
> integrated setting is one that enables individuals with disabilities to live and
> interact with individuals without disabilities to the fullest extent possible. By
> contrast, a segregated setting includes congregate settings populated exclu-
> sively or primarily by individuals with disabilities. Although *Olmstead* did not
> interpret the FHA, the objectives of the FHA and the ADA, as interpreted in
> *Olmstead*, are consistent. . . . The integration mandate of the ADA and *Olmstead*
> can be implemented without impairing the rights protected by the FHA. . . . [A]
> locality would violate the [FHA] and the integration mandate of the ADA and
> *Olmstead* if it required group homes to be concentrated in certain areas of the
> jurisdiction by, for example, restricting them from being located in other areas.
>   [Therefore,] the FHA does not prevent state or local governments [when
> reviewing requests for land use accommodations] from taking into account
> concerns about the over-concentration of group homes that are located in close
> proximity to each other. Sometimes compliance with the integration mandate
> of the ADA and *Olmstead* requires government agencies responsible for licens-
> ing or providing housing for persons with disabilities to consider the location
> of other group homes when determining what housing will best meet the needs
> of the persons being served. . . . Because an across-the-board spacing require-
> ment may discriminate against persons with disabilities in some residential
> areas, any standards that state or local governments adopt should evaluate the
> location of group homes for persons with disabilities on a case-by-case basis.[86]

Larkin, decided before *Olmstead*, recognized that "deinstitutionalization is
a legitimate goal for the state to pursue," but found "the [1,500 foot] spacing
requirement may actually inhibit the goal of deinstitutionalization by limiting
the number of AFC facilities which can be operated within any given community." Do you think the spacing requirement reviewed in *Larkin* enhanced
opportunities for disabled people to live and interact with individuals without disabilities? The court, in note 4 of the opinion, stated "[w]e express no
opinion on whether a more narrowly tailored law prohibiting such a concentration would pass muster under the FHAA." How would you tailor the law
to better promote the housing needs and choices of people with disabilities?

7. Affirmatively Furthering Fair Housing. There is another provision of
the FHA creating affirmative duties for state and local governments in the
context of housing rights of disabled persons. Sections 3608(d) and (e)(5)
require HUD, its grantees, and other federal agencies with housing and urban
development programs to affirmatively further fair housing. This means governmental entities must use their programs and activities to create accessible,

---

86. *Joint Statement on Land Use, supra* note 71, at 11-12.

open, and inclusive communities for all classes protected under the FHA, including people with disabilities. This duty is discussed in Chapter 13.

For example, state or local governments may use affirmative marketing strategies or incentives in the form of variances to integrate group homes and other housing options in particular neighborhoods where they are not currently located. *See Joint Statement on Land Use* at 14. Notice the balancing act in both *Olmstead* and *Larkin*: The goal of integration cannot justify group home quotas limiting the number of disabled persons in a neighborhood, but government agencies may engage in planning to avoid segregation by developing a range of housing choices for people with disabilities in a variety of locations.

H. OTHER DISABILITY RIGHTS STATUTES IN HOUSING: SECTION 504 AND THE ADA

Section 504 of the Rehabilitation Act of 1973 provides:

> No otherwise qualified individual with a disability in the United States . . . shall, solely by reason of her or his disability, be excluded from the participation in, be denied the benefits of, or be subjected to discrimination under any program or activity receiving Federal financial assistance. . . .[87]

This statute applies to a broad array of *recipients* or subrecipients but it does not reach the ultimate *beneficiary* of the federal financial assistance.[88] For example, §504 covers federally subsidized housing agencies and housing providers, but not private landlords paid rent through a tenant-based voucher program[89] or those developing affordable housing under the Low Income Housing Tax Credit (LIHTC) program.[90]

Although the FHA typically offers more protection from disability discrimination than do §504 and the ADA,[91] §504 imposes some additional duties on federally assisted housing providers,[92] and Title II of the ADA extends these

---

87. 29 U.S.C. §794(a).

88. 24 C.F.R. §8.3.

89. HUD, Section 504: Frequently Asked Questions, https://www.hud.gov/program_offices/fair_housing_equal_opp/disabilities/sect504faq (last visited Aug. 7, 2024).

90. Adam Cowing, *Section 504 Protections Apply to ARRA-funded LIHTC Projects*, 39 Nat'l Housing L. Proj. Bull., 182, 183 (July 2009) (referring to the American Recovery and Reinvestment Act of 2009), https://www.nhlp.org/wp-content/uploads/NHLP-Section-504-Protns-Apply-to-ARRA-funded-LIHTC-Projects-39-Hous.-L.-Bull-182-July-2009.pdf (last visited July 20, 2023).

91. *See* Schwemm, HDLL §29:3 (noting broad standing provisions, available relief, and recognition of disparate impact claims); *see also* Cummings v. Premier Rehab Keller, P.L.L.C., 596 U.S. 212 (2022) (holding that plaintiffs may not recover emotional distress damages under §504 and other "Spending Clause" antidiscrimination statutes); *id.* at 221-22 (noting punitive damages are not recoverable under Spending Clause statutes).

92. *See generally* HUD, Section 504: Frequently Asked Questions, https://www.hud.gov/program_offices/fair_housing_equal_opp/disabilities/sect504faq (last visited Aug. 7, 2024); *see also* Schwemm, HDLL §29:3 n.10 (describing the possibility that plaintiffs may have more time to file suit under §504 in some states and that some landlords exempt under the FHA may be subject to suit under §504).

duties to state and local government programs, activities, and services regardless of whether they receive federal funding.[93]

In 1988, HUD issued regulations[94] interpreting §504 to impose the following duties on publicly assisted housing providers:

- Pay for a needed structural change as a required accommodation, if reasonable.
- Provide a reasonable accommodation even if not requested if the need is obvious.
- Ensure that programs, when viewed in their entirety, are readily accessible and usable, meaning people with disabilities must have the same opportunity to participate in and benefit from programs and must have the same range of choices and amenities offered to others without disabilities.
- Regarding physical accessibility,[95] adopt suitable means to assure that information about available accessible units reaches qualified persons who need the features of those units. 24 C.F.R. §8.27.
- Offer an available mobility-accessible unit first to a qualified tenant who requires the features; if no such tenant exists, offer to a similarly qualified applicant on the waiting list who needs the features. 24 C.F.R. §8.27.
- Take steps to ensure accessible communication, such as through outreach to service organizations and furnishing auxiliary aids and services (interpreters, transcription and captioning, accessible electronic materials and websites, and materials in alternate formats). 24 C.F.R. §8.6.[96]
- In new construction or substantially altered[97] housing projects, make 5 percent of the dwelling units accessible for persons with mobility disabilities and make an additional 2 percent of units accessible for persons with hearing or visual disabilities. 24 C.F.R. §8.22.
- Provide housing opportunities in "the most integrated setting appropriate to the needs of the person with a disability" to "enable individuals with disabilities to live independently with individuals without disabilities."

---

93. 42 U.S.C. §12132. Section 504 and the ADA are the disability counterparts to Title VI, which prohibits discrimination in government-assisted programs and activities on the basis of race, color, and national origin. *See* Schwemm, HDLL §29:3 (text accompanying note 4 and n.4) (citing Alexander v. Choate, 469 U.S. 287, 295 n.11 (1985)).

94. In 2023, HUD issued notice of new rulemaking on Section 504. *Advanced Notice of Proposed Rulemaking, Nondiscrimination on the Basis of Disability: Updates to HUD's §504 Regulations*, 88 FED. REG. 79 (Apr. 25, 2023) (to be codified at 24 C.F.R. pts. 8 & 9).

95. Section 504 defines an accessible unit as one that is on an accessible route and can be approached, entered, and used by individuals with physical disabilities.

96. For additional information on effective communication requirements under the ADA, see ADA.gov.

97. Substantial alterations are defined as those made to a project having 15 or more units at a cost of 75 percent or more of the replacement cost of the completed facility. 24 C.F.R. §8.23(a). Alterations that do not meet this threshold may still trigger requirements to make accessible that particular unit or individual element being altered. *See* 24 C.F.R. §8.23 (b).

- Disperse accessible units throughout buildings and sites.
- Make nonhousing facilities readily accessible to and usable by people with disabilities. 24 C.F.R. §8.21.

In the ADA Amendments Act of 2008, Congress changed the definition of disability under §504 to conform with the new definition of disability for the ADA, without addressing the FHA.[98] "The Senate Statement of Managers noted the importance of maintaining uniform definitions in the two statutes so covered entities 'will generally operate under one consistent standard, and the civil rights of individuals with disabilities will be protected in all settings.'"[99]

Title III of the ADA applies to places of public accommodation at housing developments or other dwellings that are open to the general public, such as rental offices, shelters, and social service entities.[100] The private entities that own, lease (to and from), and operate these public accommodations must design, construct, and alter them in compliance with the applicable standard of accessibility under the ADA, currently the 2010 ADA Standards for Accessible Design.[101]

Many of the FHA land use and zoning claims in Section G filed against local government entities also included an ADA claim. *See, e.g.*, Valencia v. City of Springfield, Illinois, 883 F.3d 959 (7th Cir. 2018). Where coverage under the FHA is not available in land use matters, an ADA claim may be available. *See, e.g.*, Innovative Health Systems, Inc. v. City of White Plains, 117 F.3d 37, 44-46 (2d Cir. 1997) (holding that zoning was a "program, service, or activity" covered under Title II of the ADA [and §504] where outpatient addiction treatment center sought injunction following alleged discriminatory denial of building permit).

Most federally assisted units are covered by multiple federal accessibility standards and compliance with all is necessary; for purposes of physical accessibility the standard element that would provide the greatest accessibility must be met.[102]

- Compliance with the Uniform Federal Accessibility Standards (UFAS) satisfies the technical criteria for accessibility under Section 504.[103] 24 C.F.R. §8.32.

---

98. Pub. L. 110-325, §7.

99. Nancy Lee Jones, *Section 504 of the Rehabilitation Act of 1973: Prohibiting Discrimination Against Individuals with Disabilities in Programs or Activities Receiving Federal Assistance*, CRS Report RL34041 (citing 153 CONG. REC. S. 8347 (Sept. 11, 2008) (Statement of Managers to Accompany S. 3406, the Americans with Disabilities Act Amendments Act of 2008)).

100. 42 U.S.C. §12181-89.

101. HUD, Disability Overview, https://www.hud.gov/program_offices/fair_housing_eq ual_opp/disability_overview#reasonable-modifications (last visited June 21, 2023).

102. HUD, Section 504: Frequently Asked Questions, https://www.hud.gov/program_offi ces/fair_housing_equal_opp/disabilities/sect504faq.

103. HUD plans to revise its Section 504 regulation to adopt an updated accessibility standard. *See* Advanced Notice of Proposed Rulemaking, Nondiscrimination on the Basis of Disability: Updates to HUD's §504 Regulations, 88 FED. REG. 79 (Apr. 25, 2023) (to be codified at 24 C.F.R. pts. 8 & 9).

- State and local government programs covered under Title II of the ADA must meet the 2010 ADA Standards for Accessible Design.
- The Architectural Barriers Act requires that buildings or facilities designed, built, or altered with federal funds or leased by federal agencies after August 12, 1968, be accessible in compliance with UFAS.
- State and local laws may require greater protection.

Chapter Summary

- The FHA is the most comprehensive disability rights statute covering dwellings. It mandates that persons with disabilities be treated as individuals, repudiates the use of stereotypes and unfounded speculation as grounds for exclusion, and declares the right to be free from housing discrimination as essential to the goal of independent living.

- People with disabilities, people who reside with them, and anyone associated with them are all protected under the FHA.

- Establishing disability is a threshold showing required to gain FHA protection. This is defined as a physical or mental impairment that substantially limits a major life activity. Current illegal drug use is not covered, but recovering substance abusers or alcoholics can be considered persons with disabilities.

- Having a record of a disability or being regarded as (perceived as) disabled also qualifies for FHA protection.

- As with other protected categories under the FHA, housing providers may not make housing unavailable; discriminate in terms, conditions, facilities, or services; make discriminatory statements; or misrepresent availability of housing on the basis of disability.

- Unlike other protected groups, people with disabilities have a right of reasonable accommodation at the housing provider's expense. This means that housing providers must waive or adjust rules if it would be reasonable (not unduly burdensome) and necessary to give the disabled person an equal opportunity to use and enjoy a housing opportunity.

- People with disabilities also have a right to make structural modifications at their own expense to the interior or exterior of their homes if reasonable and necessary to give them an equal opportunity to use and enjoy their housing, and in some circumstances they will be required to restore the dwelling to its original condition.

- Housing providers who have designed and constructed certain dwellings for first occupancy after March 13, 1991, must comply with seven basic accessibility standards enabling people with disabilities to use or easily adapt the dwellings to meet their needs.

- The FHA does not apply when an individual's tenancy would constitute a direct threat to the health and safety of others or cause substantial property damage. Direct threats must be established by objective, concrete evidence.

- The FHA applies to zoning, covenants, and other land use restrictions that prevent people with disabilities from living in residential neighborhoods, whether in group homes or other settings.

- Other disability rights statutes, such as Section 504 of the Rehabilitation Act (applying to federally assisted housing) and ADA (applying to public entities and public accommodations like rental offices) might provide greater protection than the FHA in certain circumstances.

CHAPTER 18

SOURCE OF INCOME (PROTECTED BY STATE AND LOCAL LAW)

Source of income discrimination can be defined as discriminating against a person based on *where* their income originates. Thus, a landlord who refuses to rent to a prospective tenant because he receives the bulk of his income through veteran's benefits, or because she will pay for a portion of the rent using a Housing Choice Voucher ("HCV," commonly referred to as Section 8), is discriminating based on source of income.

Note that this is a different issue from *whether* the prospective tenant has enough income (from whatever legal source) to pay rent reliably. Housing providers are allowed to take a person's ability to pay into consideration when determining whether to enter into a housing transaction with them. But a landlord who insists on verifying income only through a W-2 tax form (reflecting income from employment) will exclude large numbers of people who receive income through different, legal channels. A person who receives government benefits or a housing subsidy typically receives such assistance on a monthly basis for as long as they qualify, which could be at least as reliable as income received from working at a job.

Source of income is not a characteristic protected by the federal FHA. Nonetheless, it merits treatment in this casebook for several reasons. Source of income (SOI) discrimination implicates many of the same populations the FHA protects. The categories of people who are disproportionately likely to receive certain types of government benefits overlap with protected characteristics, including race, sex, disability, and familial status. This is one reason why a number of state and local governments have enacted SOI protections as part of their civil rights statutes. This chapter addresses state and local laws as well as theories for bringing SOI claims under the federal statute.

SOI discrimination, particularly discrimination against HCV holders, is widespread and prevalent. According to the National Fair Housing Alliance, in

2022 private fair housing organizations received 2,395 complaints of SOI discrimination.[1] This is noteworthy because even though only a minority of states and localities have SOI protections, the number of complaints on this basis was greater than the number of complaints nationwide for many federally protected characteristics such as national origin, familial status, and religion.

As discussed more fully in Chapter 12, vouchers are one of the most significant forms of federal housing assistance to low-income families, with approximately 2.2 million families participating in the program. Although the program subsidizes a portion of the voucher holder's rent, it usually requires the voucher holder to locate a property within the required rental rate and a landlord who is willing to rent to her. Widespread SOI discrimination can mean that a person with a voucher could be unable to find a landlord willing to accept the voucher and might ultimately forfeit the voucher as a result. SOI discrimination also can entrench racial and economic segregation, where landlords in more affluent and whiter areas refuse to accept vouchers. (See, for example, the discussion of using disparate impact theory to challenge "no voucher" policies in *Lincoln Property*, Chapter 7.)

A. STATE AND LOCAL SOI PROTECTIONS

As this text goes to press (2024), at least 17 states, 21 counties, and 85 cities prohibit discrimination based on SOI.[2] The language of these provisions varies in its definition of what, exactly, is meant by SOI. For example, one ordinance might use general language to protect "any lawful source of income," whereas another ordinance might specify types of income, such as "receipt of government benefits." The next case involves a court considering the question of whether a housing voucher falls under the state's SOI protections.

Commission on Human Rights and Opportunities v. Sullivan Assocs.
739 A.2d 238 (Conn. 1999)

Before Callahan, Chief Justice, and Norcott, Palmer, McDonald and Peters, Justices.

---

1. National Fair Housing Alliance, *2023 Fair Housing Trends Report: Advancing Blueprint for Equity* 12-14, https://nationalfairhousing.org/wp-content/uploads/2023/08/2023-Trends-Report-Final.pdf.
2. The Poverty & Race Research Action Council maintains an updated list of SOI-protective statutes and ordinances around the country, as well as proposed legislation, existing protections in government programs, and other resources. It can be found at Appendix B: State, Local, and Federal Laws Barring Source-of-Income Discrimination, http://www.prrac.org/pdf/AppendixB.pdf (updated Sept. 2024).

PETERS, Justice:

Under General Statutes §46a-64c, a landlord may not refuse to rent to a prospective low income tenant because that tenant will pay the stipulated rent from a lawful source of income, such as rental assistance under §8 of the housing assistance program administered by HUD pursuant to §8 of the United States Housing Act of 1937, as amended in 1974 and codified at 42 U.S.C. §1437f (§8). There is no dispute that, unlike the federal rules regulating the §8 program, state law makes mandatory landlord participation in the program as administered by state agencies. The principal issues in this case are whether a landlord may avoid renting to otherwise qualified §8 tenants by requiring the use of a standard lease that deviates from §8 lease specifications or by insisting on tenant income requirements beyond those contemplated by the state statute. We conclude that, in enacting the antidiscrimination mandate of §46a-64c, the legislature did not intend to permit such deviations from the statutory scheme.

Patricia Hanson and Patricia Roper (the relators) filed separate complaints with the plaintiff in each case, the commission on human rights and opportunities (commission), alleging that the defendant in each case, Sullivan Associates, had violated §46a-64c by refusing rentals to the relators because they expected to pay for their housing using their lawful source of income, namely, housing assistance from the state §8 program. The commission filed petitions in the Housing Session of the Superior Court on behalf of the relators. The defendant, denying that it had discriminated against the relators, alleged that its refusal to rent was based on its uniform policy of insisting on the terms of its own standard lease and its own standard income requirements. In addition, by way of special defense, the defendant raised constitutional objections to §46a-64c if it were applied as construed by the commission. The trial court, Cocco, J., concluded that the defendant had not violated the statute and, accordingly, rendered judgments on its behalf. The commission appealed[.] We reverse the judgments of the trial court.

FACTUAL BACKGROUND

The commission is a state agency charged with the enforcement of a number of antidiscrimination statutes including §46a-64c. The defendant was, at the time of the incidents that gave rise to this action, a general partnership that owned 4 residential rental properties in the city of Bridgeport, 3 single-family houses and one 3-family house.

The defendant followed a standardized policy in renting its properties. Once a vacancy had been advertised, the defendant's employees responded to telephone inquiries by asking callers to identify themselves, their coresidents and their gross household income. Only if the caller's answers were deemed satisfactory, and the caller agreed to pay both the first month's rent and a security deposit of 2 additional months' rent would the potential rental property be identified specifically and shown to the caller. If the defendant and the prospective tenant agreed to the rental, the defendant required the tenant to sign its own standard form lease. The defendant had kept rental units vacant for as long as 6 months rather than rent those units to persons it considered unqualified. The defendant never has rented any of its properties to any recipient of §8 assistance, because prospective tenants receiving §8 assistance consistently have been excluded from consideration in the initial telephone screening process.

On March 2, 1994, the defendant advertised the rental of a house on Lindley Street in Bridgeport. That same day, Hanson, a single parent of 2 minor children residing in Bridgeport, inquired about the rental but was turned away when she identified herself as a person whose income was derived from §8 assistance and the federal aid to families with dependent children program (AFDC) [Eds. — This program has been replaced by Temporary Assistance to Needy Families, or TANF.]. She was told that "the landlord did not qualify for §8 because the landlord required 2 months' rent as security and §8 would not allow 2 months' security as the landlord understood the program." Shortly thereafter, an employee of a local fair housing office, posing as a prospective tenant relying on §8 rental assistance, received a similar reply. One month later, Roper, a single parent of 3 children, inquired about renting the same property. When she disclosed that she had no income other than §8 housing assistance, she was informed that she would need an annual income of $38,000 in order to qualify to rent the house.

On June 6, 1994, the defendant ran another newspaper advertisement offering to rent the same house in Bridgeport. That day, Roper again called the defendant. Although she stated that she had a §8 certificate sufficient to pay the rent, she again was informed that her income did not meet the defendant's $38,000 minimum income requirement. On that occasion, Roper also was told that the defendant's policy of requiring 2 months rent as security made the defendant ineligible to participate in the §8 housing program.

Both relators filed complaints with the commission alleging that the defendant's refusal to rent to them because of their reliance on financial assistance from the §8 program violated the antidiscrimination provisions of §46a-64c. The commission then brought the present actions on their behalf. The trial court rendered its judgments in favor of the defendant on the ground that the statute permitted the defendant to decline to rent to the relators as long as the defendant consistently conducted its rental business by use of its standard rental agreement and income requirements.

On appeal, the commission contends that the trial court improperly construed §46a-64c with respect to: (1) the statutory requirement of mandatory §8 lease terms; and (2) the income requirements of potential §8 tenants. We agree with the commission, and, accordingly, reverse the judgments of the trial court.

THE §8 PROGRAM

Analysis of the claims of the parties requires an understanding of the §8 housing program as it is administered in this state. The §8 program exists "[f]or the purpose of aiding low-income families in obtaining a decent place to live and of promoting economically mixed housing. . . ." 42 U.S.C. §1437f (a) (1994). Section 8 is a cooperative venture between HUD and state and local public housing agencies, which oversee the day-to-day operations of the program. While state and local housing agencies contract with landlords who own dwelling units to make assistance payments, HUD enters into annual contribution contracts with the agencies.

Although it is the local public housing authorities [PHAs] that actually run the §8 program, they must do so in accordance with applicable federal regulations. The §8 program in Connecticut also must comply with state law, including the antidiscrimination provisions of §46a-64c.

Section 8 rental assistance is available only to persons who are classified as very low income or as low income[.] The program permits otherwise qualified tenants to rent private units and to pay personally only a small portion of the total rent, commensurate with their income. The local PHA contracts separately with the landlord to pay the remainder of the rent directly to the landlord.

In 1994, federal regulations required a prospective tenant and landlord to use a standardized lease and addendum in order to participate in the §8 program. In the present case, the defendant has raised objections to the terms in the standardized §8 lease provisions that regulate lease termination by the landlord and prescribe maximum allowable security deposits. The maximum security deposit authorized by state law is the same as that authorized by federal law.

PREEMPTION

The defendant maintains that, if §46a-64c requires landlords to accept tenants whose income includes §8 assistance, then its provisions are preempted by the federal §8 statute itself, 42 U.S.C. §1437f, which makes participation in the program voluntary. The trial court concluded that nothing in the federal program prevents a state from mandating participation. We agree with the trial court.

"The question of preemption is one of federal law, arising under the supremacy clause of the United States constitution. . . . Determining whether Congress has exercised its power to preempt state law is a question of legislative intent. . . ."

On its face, 42 U.S.C. §1437f contains no express preemption clause. [With respect to implied preemption], the federal statute does not "occupy the field" so comprehensively that states implicitly are prohibited from acting in the arena of low income housing assistance. Indeed, 42 U.S.C. §1437f explicitly contemplates state and local participation in the §8 program.

Requiring landlords to extend rental opportunities to otherwise eligible §8 recipients, in accordance with the terms of §8 leases, is not an obstacle to the congressional agenda but serves instead to advance its remedial purpose. Finally, it is not impossible for landlords to obey both 42 U.S.C. §1437f and §46a-64c, because nothing in the text of 42 U.S.C. §1437f requires participation to be voluntary.

For all these reasons, the defendant's claim of federal preemption cannot be sustained.

LEASE TERMS REQUIRED BY SECTION 46A-64C

Although the trial court recognized that §46a-64c made landlord participation in "housing assistance" programs mandatory, the court concluded that the statute did not require landlords to agree to the terms of §8 leases. Construction of a statute raises an issue of law in which our review of the trial court's conclusion is plenary. The commission argues that the court misconstrued the statute. We agree with the commission.

Section 46a-64c (a)(1) forbids landlords from refusing "to sell or rent after the making of a bona fide offer, or to refuse to negotiate for the sale or rental of, or otherwise make unavailable or deny, a dwelling to any person because of race, creed, color, national origin, ancestry, sex, marital status, age, lawful source of income or familial status." Section 46a-64c (a)(2) forbids discrimination "in the terms, conditions, or privileges of sale or rental of a dwelling, or in the provision of services or facilities in connection therewith, because of race, creed, color, national origin, ancestry, sex, marital status, age, lawful source of income or familial status." General Statutes §46a-63 (3) provides, in addition, that "'lawful source of income' means income derived from social security, supplemental security income, housing assistance, child support, alimony or public or general assistance."

Three preliminary observations inform our construction of these provisions. First, as the trial court concluded, the lawful sources of income protected from discrimination by §46a-64c include "§8 rental subsidies as a form of housing assistance." Second, compliance with §8 requirements for the use of a §8 lease for those eligible for §8 assistance does not require a landlord to forbear from insisting on adequate security for its lease, including a 2 months' rental security deposit, and on reasonable provisions for its termination, including nonpayment of rent and changes in the economic use of the property. Third, nothing in the statutes forbidding discrimination against tenants receiving §8 rental subsidies requires landlords to accept tenants who may be unqualified to rent for nondiscriminatory reasons such as, for example, a poor rental history, poor references, or poor credit. The target of the statutes is, instead, the unspoken presumption that §8 assistance recipients, by virtue only of their source of income, are undesirable tenants for a landlord's rental properties.

The question before us in the present case is whether §46a-64c, while prohibiting landlords from discriminating on the basis of source of income, was intended to excuse landlords from participation in §8 programs if they did not wish to accept the terms of §8 leases. It is crucial to our consideration that, under the applicable federal regulations, at the relevant time, federal §8 reimbursement required the use of standardized §8 leases for all §8 participants. A landlord's refusal to substitute such a lease for its own, therefore, operated as a blanket rejection of all prospective tenants whose income included §8 assistance. We must decide whether that result is what the legislature contemplated in enacting this antidiscrimination statute.

[W]e consider first the words of §46a-64c. The statute does not speak directly either to whether the broad prohibition against discrimination based on source of income requires landlords to adhere to the requirements of the §8 program for prospective §8 tenants, or whether a landlord's insistence on using its own lease constitutes a defense to the antidiscrimination mandate.

The legislative history of §46a-64c demonstrates that the legislature intended to prohibit landlords from denying rental opportunities to people whose source of income included federal or state housing assistance. Interpreting §46a-64c as the trial court has, to allow an exception to its antidiscrimination provisions for those landlords who refuse to use the required §8 lease, would eviscerate the basic protection envisioned by the statute. It would lead to the unreasonable result that while the legislature mandated that landlords may not reject tenants because their income included §8 assistance, the legislature at the same time also intended that landlords might avoid the statutory mandate by refusing to accede to a condition essential to its fulfillment. Such a result is untenable.

[W]e conclude that the legislature, in requiring landlords to make rental housing available to potential tenants relying on §8 housing assistance, intended thereby to require landlords to use §8 leases. We reach this conclusion because, under the federal law applicable at the time in question, the failure to use such a lease would have resulted in the denial of §8 reimbursement as a matter of federal law. Any other construction of §46a-64c would be impossible to reconcile with the legislature's expressed purpose of affording to those protected by the statute "an equal chance in the rental housing market."

INSUFFICIENT INCOME EXCEPTION

The defendant argues, in the alternative, that even if §46a-64c does not permit it to insist on using its own lease form, its refusal to rent to the relators in this case was justified by the statutory exception for "insufficient income." The prohibition in §46a-64c against discrimination on the basis of lawful source of income contains an exception in §46a-64c (b)(5), which provides that "[t]he provisions of this section with respect to the prohibition of discrimination on the basis of lawful source of income shall not prohibit the denial of full and equal accommodations solely on the basis of insufficient income." As part of its standard practice, the defendant consistently required any potential tenant to have a minimum weekly income that approximated or equaled the amount of the total monthly rent. That minimum income requirement was authorized, according to the defendant, by the exception in §46a-64c (b)(5).

The trial court concluded that, because the relators' income did not meet the defendant's minimum income standard, their income was "insufficient" under §46a-64c (b)(5). It agreed with the defendant that, although the defendant's high minimum income standard resulted, in fact, in the disqualification of all low income tenants, the express terms of the statutory exception made this conduct legal. The court concluded that the statutory rule "is not to protect all low income groups, or a particular subset within the low income group, but to protect all groups from discrimination based on source of income." We disagree.

A proper assessment of the merits of the trial court's conclusion requires us to consider two questions. First, what is the meaning of the term "insufficient income" in §46a-64c (b)(5)? Second, how does that term, properly defined, apply under the circumstances of the present case? Because this case comes to us on the basis of stipulated facts, both issues present questions of law, subject to our plenary review.

A

The proper definition of "insufficient income" is a question of statutory construction[.] In the present case, however, there is a lamentable dearth of clues as to the legislature's intent. Section 46a-64c nowhere defines the term "insufficient income." There is no legislative history that illuminates the legislature's intent in enacting such an exception to its general mandate that landlords accept tenants regardless of the source of their income. No legislator addressed the facial inconsistency between making it mandatory for landlords to accept low income §8 tenants and making it permissible for landlords to reject tenants with an "insufficient income."

Confronted with the lack of a statutory definition, the trial court concluded that "the legislature appears to have left [the determination of insufficient income] to the business discretion of the property owners." The defendant, amplifying this view, emphasizes that the purpose of its own minimum income requirement is not to discriminate but to reflect economic judgments that it reached long before the enactment of §46a-64c and uniformly has implemented since then. The defendant notes, in addition, that the absence of statutory standards for what constitutes "insufficient income" does not authorize courts, or the commission arbitrarily to denominate some sum of money to fill the statutory gap.

The commission responds that the trial court's construction is untenable because it undercuts the fundamental mission of §46a-64c. We agree with the commission that, in light of the lack of a statutory or historical definition, we must construe §46a-64c (b)(5) in terms of the overall legislative purpose manifested by this remedial statute. We also agree with the defendant, however, that, in the absence of guidance from the legislature, we cannot simply designate an independent numeric requirement as the determinant of what constitutes "insufficient income."

The purpose of the relevant provisions of §46a-64c is to prevent low income families from being "rejected or denied a full and equal opportunity for . . . public accommodation based solely on the presence of" a particular source of income. 32 H.R. Proc., *supra*, p. 8776, remarks of Representative Taborsak. It would be inconsistent with the remedial mandate of §46a-64c for the legislature to have afforded to landlords carte blanche authority to define the term "insufficient income" so as to qualify for the exception in §46a-64c (b)(5). Such a construction would swallow the statute whole and render it meaningless. We have long held to the rule that statutory exceptions are to be strictly construed. In light of the remedial nature of the statute, we are not persuaded that the legislature contemplated such a hands-off approach.

A closer examination of the statute makes it clear that the exception is not as lacking in standards as would appear on first reading. We may obtain useful guidance by considering the common meaning of the statute's terms. The word "sufficient" is a relative term. Black's Law Dictionary (6th Ed. 1990) defines it as "[a]dequate, enough, as much as may be necessary, equal or fit for end proposed, and that which may be necessary to accomplish an object. Of such quality, number, force, or value as to serve a need or purpose."

In determining the contours of the exception afforded by §46a-64c (b)(5), we, therefore, must consider the meaning of "insufficient income" with respect to the need or purpose that the income is to serve. The reasonable need or purpose that the legislature would likely have considered, with respect to the statute, would be the sufficiency of the tenant's income to meeting his or her own financial obligations to the landlord, ordinarily the tenant's own periodic rental obligation.

Although the commission does not say so expressly, it seems to take the position that, because §8 rental assistance payments are calculated with the expectation that the prospective tenant will have sufficient remaining income to cover the tenant's personal share of the rent, that tenant's income never will fall within the "insufficient income" exception. Perhaps an argument could be made that the statutory exception covers housing assistance payments from sources other than §8, which may not include such an encompassing assessment of the potential tenant's overall assets and liabilities.

We are not persuaded, however, that §8 assistance recipients categorically are excluded from the class of potential tenants with "insufficient income" to sustain their tenancies. Such a construction of the exception would, in effect, read it out of the statute under the very circumstances in which the statute, ab initio, is most likely to apply. That cannot be what the legislature had in mind.

The more plausible construction of the statutory exception is to give it a narrow reading that comports with the policy of the statute overall. Under that narrow construction, the exception affords a landlord an opportunity to determine whether, presumably for reasons extrinsic to the §8 housing assistance calculations, a potential tenant lacks sufficient income to give the landlord reasonable assurance that the tenant's portion of the stipulated rental will be paid promptly and that the tenant will undertake to meet the other obligations implied in the tenancy. The statutory exception does not prescribe a single methodology for making such a determination, and in that respect, as the trial court held, leaves room for discretion to be exercised by the landlord. It does contemplate, however, that, in accordance with the statute's antidiscrimination mandate, that any method adopted by the landlord must be applied consistently with respect to all potential tenants.

B

The question remains whether the defendant's standard requirement that each potential tenant have a gross weekly income that approximates one month's rent bore a reasonable relationship to the defendant's ability to enforce the potential tenant's personal rental obligation. If the defendant's formula is applied to the raw numbers of the relators' incomes, its requirements are amply met. Hanson had an income of $581 a month (or $135 a week) to cover a personal rental obligation of $11; Roper had a monthly income of $776 (or $181 a week) to cover a monthly rental obligation of $64. As the defendant notes, however, these figures do not take into account those parts of the tenant's disposable income that must cover items such as the tenant's utility expenses, which, according to the defendant's estimates, would have amounted to roughly $227 a month. Furthermore, they do not address the tenant's ability to reimburse the defendant if, hypothetically, damages to the rented property were to exceed the amount of the stipulated two month rental deposit. These were not, however, the articulated bases for the defendant's decision not to rent to the relators in this case.

In short, on the stipulated factual record of the reasons given for turning down the relators, the defendant has failed to demonstrate that the relators in the present case have "insufficient income" to qualify them as tenants for the defendant's rental property. Although we could direct the entry of a judgment on liability on this basis, we are persuaded that the defendant should be afforded a fair opportunity to make such a showing if it can.

The present case is the first instance in which we have construed the text of §46a-64c. Our narrow construction of the statutory exception for "insufficient income" contemplates a specific fact-bound determination of a potential tenant's capacity to carry his or her part of the bargain. The construction that we have adopted departs significantly from that urged at trial, or in this court, by the commission. The defendant deserves the chance to make its case in accordance with our ground rules.

We emphasize that our order for a new trial is limited to the issue of whether the defendant can establish that the relators properly were denied access to his rental property because they had "insufficient income" within the exception contained in §46a-64c (b)(5). The burden of proving its eligibility for the exception must be assumed by the defendant. To determine whether the defendant has met its burden, a finder of fact on this issue properly may consider criteria that include, but are not limited to, the potential tenant's income, personal rental obligation, foreseeable utility expenses and foreseeable liability for other than ordinary wear and tear.

In light of the nondiscriminatory purpose for which §46a-64c was enacted, the defendant may not rely solely on §8 eligibility as a basis for turning potential tenants away nor may it apply more stringent income requirements to §8 rental applicants than to other rental applicants. Unless the defendant makes the requisite showing that the relators had "insufficient income" to meet the totality of their rental obligations, the commission is entitled to prevail on the issue of liability. In that event, there must be a hearing on what the proper remedy should be.

CALLAHAN, C.J., with whom McDonald, J., joins, dissenting:

Even if the majority is correct that §46a-64c does not permit a landlord to reject a prospective tenant on the basis of objections to the provisions of §8 leases, under the disparate treatment mixed-motive analysis, the defendant may avoid liability for its actions by establishing that it would have rejected Hanson and Roper even if they had not been §8 housing assistance recipients. In the present case, it is undisputed that the defendant had a long-standing policy of rejecting all applicants whose gross weekly income was less than one month's rent. It is also undisputed that neither Hanson's nor Roper's income met the defendant's minimum standard. In my view, the evidence does not permit a conclusion that the defendant would not have made the same decisions if the applicants had not been §8 housing assistance recipients. Because the evidence does not permit a conclusion that the defendant discriminated against Hanson and Roper because of the source of their income — as opposed to the amount of their income — I would conclude that the defendant's actions were not violative of §46a-64c. I therefore respectfully dissent.

McDONALD, J., dissenting:

The majority's holding obliges every landlord in this state to offer its property for rent with terms that meet the requirements of §8, other assistance programs, or any other lawful income providers. I conclude that §46a-64c does not require this. Instead, the statute simply means that, if all things are equal among the prospective tenants, a landlord may not disqualify a prospective tenant simply because of that tenant's status as a recipient of public assistance under the §8 program.

I would conclude that there is not a violation of §46a-64c every time a landlord declines to accept a lease dictated to the landlord by the tenant's income source, whether the source is a public assistance program, a spendthrift trust or some other benefactor of the tenant. If the legislature wished to impose on all landlords of this state a requirement that they accept all the lease terms required by a tenant's source of income, it simply could have said so. It did not. The legislature's addition of the language "lawful source of income" was not intended to turn every property in this state into a government regulated and "lease controlled" rental facility.

The very implementing of statewide lease control by court fiat fails to recognize the basic American rights to property and freedom. The freedom to own and control private property is fundamental to freedom.

The majority's opinion in this case requires landlords in this state either to lease on the terms dictated in a §8 lease, or not to lease their property at all. Such a result will have profound and adverse effects on all property owners in this state. Because the statute provides for no compensation to property owners, I also would conclude that the majority's holding, when applied, results in a taking of private property from landlords without just compensation.

The defendant in this case refused to lease to the relators, Patricia Hanson and Patricia Roper, because its established requirements for renting its property were in conflict with those of the §8 program. There is no basis, as the majority concludes, to find that the defendant crafted its rental policy in order to discriminate against §8 recipients. I would conclude that refusing to accept the terms of a §8 lease does not itself constitute unlawful discrimination as proscribed by §46a-64c. I, therefore, would affirm the trial court's judgment.

NOTES AND QUESTIONS

1. Other Perspectives. Not all courts agree with *Sullivan*, and in other jurisdictions that have enacted general SOI protections, courts have distinguished HCVs from other sources of income. See, for example, Knapp v. Eagle Property Management Corp., 54 F.3d 1272, 1282 (7th Cir. 1995), in which the federal court refused to interpret a state SOI statute to cover vouchers:

> That statute prohibits landlords from discriminating in housing on the basis of "lawful source of income," which the Wisconsin Administrative Code defines as:
>
>> includ[ing] but . . . not limited to lawful compensation or lawful remuneration in exchange for goods or services provided, profit from financial investments, any negotiable draft, coupon, or voucher representing monetary value such as food stamps, social security, public assistance or unemployment compensation benefits.
>
> The district court held that §8 vouchers are more analogous to subsidies than income. The court relied on a dictionary definition of income, however, and Wisconsin has enlarged the meaning of that term. . . . Even given the state's broader definition, we reach the same conclusion as the district court.

Knapp receives a §8 voucher, but that assistance does not clearly equate to the other forms of aid specified in the statute. Of the categories listed in [the state statute] the voucher is most analogous to food stamps. Unlike food stamps, however, §8 vouchers do not have a monetary value independent of the voucher holder and the apartment sought. In addition, unlike other forms of support, the local housing authority makes payments directly to the owner pursuant to a contract between those parties, rather than to the voucher holder. While this form of assistance could arguably be included within the Wisconsin Act, we decline to ascribe such an intent to the state legislature because of the potential problems in doing so.

Consider another example. The court in Apartment Association of Metropolitan Pittsburgh, Inc. v. City of Pittsburgh, 228 A.3d 960, 973-74 (Pa. 2020) examined a municipal ban on SOI discrimination that specifically covered vouchers:

[T]he addition of the "source-of-income" class does more than just ban housing discrimination based on source of income. By expressly defining "source of income" to include federal housing assistance, and specifically §8 Program vouchers, the Ordinance requires residential landlords to participate in the §8 Program, when previously their participation was wholly voluntary.
The Trial Court set forth the obligations imposed on landlords who participate in the §8 Program as follows:

[Under the Ordinance, l]andlords will be forced to comply with the numerous and often burdensome requirements of the §8 [P]rogram. For example, they will have to use the Housing Authority's model lease and/or submit a preferred lease to the Housing Authority for pre-approval. That lease must include word-for-word provisions of the HUD Tenancy Addendum. They will be prohibited from including notice of termination waivers in leases and must accept a mandatory "cure period" of five days in advance of issuing a Notice to Quit. Landlords will be required to accept "reasonable rent" obligations as established by the Housing Authority and provide at least 60 days' notice of any change in rent amounts. They will have to obtain approval from the Housing Authority to raise a tenant's rent. Finally, landlords will be forced to agree to month-to-month leases subsequent to an initial one[-]year lease term.

In addition, a landlord participating in the §8 Program is required to enter into a Housing Assistance Payment (HAP) Contract with the Housing Authority, which is separate from the lease agreement between the landlord and his or her tenant. The HAP Contract also contains a tenancy addendum that sets forth the duties and obligations of both the landlord and the tenant under the HAP Contract. Given the nature and extent of the §8 Program requirements, we cannot conclude that mandating landlords' participation in the §8 Program is merely an "incidental" burden, as the City suggests.

The Pennsylvania Supreme Court ultimately upheld this ruling, agreeing that the state's home-rule statute did not permit a municipality like Pittsburgh to enact an ordinance that would burden business in this way. 261 A.3d 1036 (2021).

Many of these state and local cases will come down to the specific circumstances of each ordinance or statute, including legislative history, state home-rule charters, and state-specific precedent. As a general matter however, the policy debate remains the same: Should SOI protections include a mandate that landlords accept vouchers? Can affordable housing programs like the HCV program, that depend on the participation of private market actors, function without such a mandate? For example, the Pittsburgh ordinance was passed after the Pittsburgh Housing Authority reported that over 40 percent of vouchers it issued were returned, unused, because the holders were unable to secure housing. Do you think it is reasonable for a federal program to have to rely on state and local mandates to be effective?

2. *Sullivan's* **Dissents.** What do you think of the arguments made by the dissenters in *Sullivan*? If, as one contends, a landlord should be able to avoid participating in the HCV program by imposing minimum income requirements, would this eviscerate the whole point of SOI protections? The other dissent takes issue with the notion that local and state governments might make participation in a voluntary federal program mandatory, an issue that could be obviated if Congress added SOI protections to the FHA. Why do you think it has not done so? Multiple bills adding SOI protections to the FHA have been proposed in both chambers in recent years, and none has made it out of committee.

3. **Other Sources of Income.** Vouchers are a common "alternate" source of income, but there are others with which courts grapple. For example, in Commission on Human Rights and Opportunities v. Forvil, 302 Conn. 263, 25 A.3d 632, 640-41 (2011), the question was whether a security deposit guarantee in lieu of cash should be considered "income" within the state's SOI law. The guarantee was a product of state law, which authorized the commissioner of social services to provide "a written agreement to pay the landlord for any damages suffered by the landlord due to the tenant's failure to comply with such tenant's obligations" "for use by [qualified persons] in lieu of a security deposit on a rental dwelling unit." General Statutes §17b-802 (a)-(b). The court reasoned:

> [T]he defendants claim that the trial court improperly concluded that a guarantee is a "lawful source of income" within the meaning of §§46a-64c and 46a-63 (3). The defendants acknowledge that a guarantee is a benefit, but contend that, insofar as a guarantee does not "involve money," it does not qualify as "income." The commission replies that a guarantee is "housing assistance," and accordingly is expressly included within the definition of a lawful source of income in §46a-63 (3). We agree with the commission.
>
> [W]e begin with the statute's legal meaning. "[I]ncome" is defined as "[t]he money or other form of payment that one receives, usu[ally] periodically, from employment, business, investments, royalties, gifts, and the like." Black's Law Dictionary (9th Ed. 2009). In turn, "payment" is defined as "[p]erformance of an obligation by the delivery of money or some other valuable thing accepted in partial or full discharge of the obligation. . . ." Accordingly, to constitute income, something does not need to be money; rather, it can be something else of value.

Insofar as the legal definition of payment contemplates the thing of value being satisfaction of some "obligation," we note the inclusion of "Social Security, . . . housing assistance . . . or public or state-administered general assistance" in the definitional list of lawful sources for income. This indicates that the legislature views income as including within its scope the obligation of the state to provide certain forms of assistance.

Although this analysis strongly indicates that a guarantee does constitute a lawful source of income, we nevertheless acknowledge that the defendants' position that income must "involve money" is a reasonable interpretation. Income commonly is used consistently with the defendants' narrower view. *See, e.g.,* The American Heritage New Dictionary of Cultural Literacy (3d Ed. 2005) (defining income as "[t]he amount of money received during a period of time in exchange for labor or services, from the sale of goods or property, or as a profit from financial investments"). Moreover, most benefits provided by the state come in the form of a money payment, rather than a guarantee. Accordingly, we conclude that the statute is susceptible to two competing interpretations, [thus] we consider the legislative history of §46a-64c. Our review of that legislative history has revealed unusually conclusive evidence that indisputably settles the question before us [in favor of the commission's view that a security deposit guarantee is income].

4. Preemption. In some cases, local SOI ordinances have provoked the state legislature to preempt and prohibit such protections. For example, Iowa, Texas, and Indiana passed preemption statutes to counter local SOI protections. Why might a state seek to override local SOI ordinances?

By contrast, courts consistently have held that state and local SOI protections are *not* preempted by federal law. In addition to *Sullivan,* above, consider Attorney General v. Brown, 400 Mass. 826, 511 N.E.2d 1103, 1106 (1987), *superseded on other grounds by statute,* DiLiddo v. Oxford St. Realty, Inc., 450 Mass. 66 (2007), which held that a state law banning housing discrimination on the basis of housing subsidies, essentially making the acceptance of HCV vouchers mandatory, was not preempted by 42 U.S.C. §1437f (which describes the HCV program as voluntary). As the *Brown* court noted, the state's SOI law and §1437f share a common goal of ensuring affordable, decent housing for low-income people. The court further observed:

It does not follow that, merely because Congress provided for voluntary participation, the States are precluded from mandating participation absent some valid nondiscriminatory reason for not participating. The Federal statute merely creates the scheme and sets out the guidelines for the funding and implementation of the program by HUD through local housing authorities. It does not preclude State regulation.

See also Franklin Tower One, LLC v. N.J., 157 N.J. 602, 725 A.2d 1104 (1999) (federal statute does not preempt state law requiring landlords to accept tenants with §8 assistance).

5. Enforcement and Results. Enforcement of fair housing law is challenging in general, and enforcement of SOI protections is especially so. A lack of awareness by landlords, rental agencies, and voucher holders themselves all might inhibit enforcement.[3] So might limited enforcement resources or priorities.

If SOI laws are enforced, the outcomes appear positive, in terms of both voucher utilization rates and locational outcomes. A 2012 study found that state and local SOI laws appear to increase voucher utilization among local public housing authorities covered by the laws.[4] A follow-up study found SOI laws were associated with recipients living in neighborhoods with lower poverty rates and less racial segregation, but had no apparent effect on concentration of voucher recipients.[5]

B. APPROACHES UNDER THE FHA

In jurisdictions without SOI protections, it is still possible for advocates to bring SOI discrimination claims under the FHA, but it is challenging. As Professor Oliveri observes:

> Discrimination against voucher-holders is difficult to combat using the FHA as it is currently written. Economic status and receipt of public assistance are not protected classes under the FHA. But voucher discrimination can mask discrimination that is really based on characteristics that the FHA *does* protect: in particular, race, ethnicity, gender, disability, and familial status. In order to establish disparate treatment or discriminatory intent in such cases, the plaintiff would need to prove that the prohibited basis for discrimination was the actual one and that the refusal to accept vouchers was merely pretext. But this may be difficult. For example, if the defendant adheres to a strict "no-voucher" policy (and many do), the plaintiff will be hard-pressed to demonstrate that the landlord is really using this policy as a cover for discrimination based on a protected characteristic in a particular instance.
>
> As an alternative, plaintiffs may challenge a no-voucher policy using a disparate impact claim. The FHA prohibits practices that may appear neutral, such as refusing to accept vouchers, but that result in "disparate impacts" for a protected class. The Section 8 program disproportionally serves members of protected classes — women, families with children, racial and ethnic minorities, and persons with disabilities. Thus, a landlord whose units would otherwise qualify for the program based on their rental price but who refuses to accept vouchers creates a disparate impact on those groups. This argument has had mixed success in the courts. Some courts have allowed

---

3. Robbie Sequeira, *Some States Protect Section 8 Renters, but Enforcement Is Elusive*, The Missouri Independent (July 21, 2023); *see also* Rigel C. Oliveri, *Source of Income Protections Are Only as Effective as Their Enforcement*, The Columbia Missourian (Nov. 9, 2023).

4. Lance Freeman, *The Impact of Source of Income Laws on Voucher Utilization*, 22 Housing Policy Debate 297 (2012).

5. Lance Freeman & Yunjing Li, *Do Source of Income Anti-Discrimination Laws Facilitate Access to Less Disadvantaged Neighborhoods?*, 29 Housing Studies 88 (2014); *see also* Alison Bell, Barbara Sard, & Becky Koepnick, Center on Budget and Policy Priorities, *Prohibiting Discrimination Against Renters Using Housing Vouchers Improves Results* (Dec. 20, 2018), https://www.cbpp.org/research/housing/prohibiting-discrimination-against-renters-using-housing-vouchers-improves-results.

plaintiffs to proceed under a disparate impact theory, but others, pointing to the voluntary nature of the program and the costs associated with it, have been skeptical.[6]

The following case presents an example of a plaintiff successfully clearing the first hurdle of an SOI claim based on disparate impact theory.

Housing Rights Initiative v. Compass, Inc.
21-cv-2221 (SHS), 2023 WL 1993696 (S.D.N.Y. Feb. 14, 2023)

STEIN, Judge:

Plaintiff Housing Rights Initiative ("HRI") has brought this action against 77 defendants that are landlords and brokers of housing accommodations, or have the right to approve rental accommodations. HRI alleges that each defendant refuses to rent its housing units to prospective tenants who hold a federal Housing Choice Voucher ("HCV"), even though the prospective tenants can afford to pay the advertised rent for the units.

Eleven defendants have moved to dismiss the action, one defendant has moved for judgment on the pleadings, and two defendants have moved for both. These defendants allege that even if HRI has standing to bring this action, its federal claims—both brought under the Fair Housing Act ("FHA")—must be dismissed for failure to state a claim upon which relief can be granted. For the reasons set forth below, the motions to dismiss and the motions for judgment on the pleadings are denied.

I. BACKGROUND

HRI is a "national nonprofit housing watchdog group" that is "dedicated to promoting fair and lawful housing practices." From its inception "a core part of HRI's mission has been preserving affordable housing in New York City and assisting tenants in securing and maintaining access to affordably priced housing."

Starting in 2017, HRI "began hearing from community partners and attorneys at legal services organizations about the struggles that many individuals and families face in being unable to locate rental properties that would accept their vouchers, and that this problem had become an insurmountable barrier to safe and affordable housing for many members of the New York City community."

At the time HRI began learning about tenants' inability to use HCVs, landlords of most buildings (and their representatives) were already barred from turning away HCV holders: since 2008, New York City law has prohibited property owners with buildings of six or more units from refusing to rent to

---

6. Rigel C. Oliveri, *Vouchers and Affordable Housing: The Limits of Choice in the Political Economy of Place*, 54 HARV. CR-CL LAW REV. 795, 799-800 (2019); *see also* Chapter 7 (citing cases).

HCV holders or otherwise make their units unavailable to HCV holders and since April 12, 2019, New York State has banned landlords and their representatives from refusing to rent to HCV holders.

Claims for Relief

Plaintiff's first claim, under a disparate-impact theory of liability, alleges that defendants' refusal to rent to HCV holders violates the FHA by having a discriminatory impact on disabled individuals. Plaintiff pleads that:

(i) "About 28% of New York City residents [who] live in Housing Choice Voucher households have a disability," while only "9.8% of New York City residents in non-Housing Choice Voucher households have a disability."

(ii) "A voucher-holder is 2.9 times more likely to be disabled than a non-voucher holder."

(iii) "A strong link exists between the Housing Choice Voucher population and the disabled population, such that a policy that adversely affects voucher holders will likewise have a significant disproportionate effect on New York City's disabled population."

(iv) "Defendants' policy of automatically denying housing to any person with a voucher . . . has a disparate impact on the basis of . . . disability."

(v) "By denying all New Yorkers with Housing Choice Vouchers the opportunity to apply for and obtain housing in their buildings, each Defendant's policy prevents 9.2% of New York City's disabled population from applying for or obtaining housing in Defendants' buildings, while preventing just 2.8% of New York City's non-disabled population from applying for or obtaining housing in their buildings."

(vi) "Disabled New York City residents are 3.3 times more likely than non-disabled New York City residents to be adversely affected by Defendants' policies."

(vii) "As a result of widespread voucher discrimination, voucher holders must frequently accept subpar housing in segregated neighborhoods, or risk losing their voucher altogether."

Plaintiff's second claim, also under a disparate-impact theory of liability, alleges that defendants' refusal to rent to HCV holders violates the FHA by having a discriminatory impact on African Americans and Hispanic Americans. In so arguing, Plaintiff pleads that:

(i) "[V]oucher-holders are much more likely to be Black or Hispanic than non-voucher holders in New York. Some 35% of New York City's voucher-holders are Black, and 47% are Hispanic, or a total of 82% of the City's voucher-holding population is Black or Hispanic. By comparison, just 21% of New York City's general, non-voucher population is Black, 29% of New York City's non-voucher population is Hispanic, for a total of 50% of the general population is Black or Hispanic."

(ii) "Voucher-holders are 1.6 times more likely to be Black or Hispanic than non-voucher holders."

(iii) "Because there is a strong link between the Housing Choice Voucher population and the Black and Hispanic population, a policy that adversely affects voucher holders will likewise have a significant disproportionate effect on New York City's Black and Hispanic population."

(iv) "Defendants' policy of automatically denying housing to any person with a voucher . . . has a disparate impact on the basis of . . . race."

(v) "Defendants' ban on Housing Choice Vouchers, by denying all New Yorkers with vouchers the opportunity to apply for and obtain housing in their buildings, prevents 5.5% of all Black New York City residents from securing housing in Defendants' buildings, and 5.5% of all Hispanic New York City residents from securing housing, while only preventing 1.7% of white New Yorkers from obtaining housing."

(vi) "Overall, Black and Hispanic New York City residents are 3.2 times more likely than white New York City residents to be adversely affected by Defendant's policy."

(vii) "As a result of widespread voucher discrimination, voucher holders must frequently accept subpar housing in segregated neighborhoods, or risk losing their voucher altogether."

II. DEFENDANTS' MOTIONS TO DISMISS AND DEFENDANTS' MOTIONS FOR JUDGMENT ON THE PLEADINGS

HRI only seeks relief under the FHA under a theory of disparate impact liability. Plaintiff makes no argument for disparate treatment. Thus, because HRI proceeds on a disparate impact theory, it has no burden—whether at the pleading stage or after discovery—to show that defendant intended to discriminate or even had knowledge that its actions would lead to a discriminatory outcome.

Analysis: The Policy Has a Disparate Impact on Protected Groups

HRI needs to allege sufficient factual support to make it plausible that the facially neutral practice outlined above—to prohibit HCV holders at the Subject Properties—has "a significantly adverse or disproportionate impact on persons of a particular type produced by the defendant's facially neutral acts or practices." MHANY Mgmt., [Inc. v. County of Nassau, 819 F.3d 581, 617 (2016)].

Because among New York City residents, HCV holders are far more likely to be disabled, Black, and Hispanic than the population as a whole, a landlord or broker's policy to refuse housing to HCV holders will have the impact of keeping that real estate actor's housing disproportionally less Black, disproportionally less Hispanic, and disproportionally less disabled than such housing would be if the landlord accepted tenants with HCVs.

Contrary to Coney Island's statement that "HRI asks this Court to simply assume that the person who was seeking housing must have been Black, Hispanic or a disabled person," HRI never makes such an argument. Rather, HRI's argument is that barring HCV holders from renting apartments will have the impact of tending to exclude far more disabled, Black, and Hispanic individuals than other individuals. Consequently, for instance, Coney Island's policy or practice of excluding HCV holders would—all else held constant—have the discriminatory impact of reducing the share of its housing lived in by disabled, Black, and Hispanic people.

i. Disabled Individuals

Contrary to Coney Island LLC's assertion that "HRI fails to allege the bare minimum of what is required to assert a disparate impact claim: the number of individuals, by protected category, who applied for, and were excluded from, housing," a plaintiff need not provide at the pleading stage the precise number of individuals or even an estimate of those who have been adversely affected or who are at risk of being adversely affected by challenged conduct. Second Circuit law makes clear that disparate impact claimants need not submit all conceivable quantitative evidence as an attachment to their complaint.

Further, HRI's proffered statistics support a claim that defendants' policies prohibiting HCV holder use will continue to disparately impact disabled New York City residents. At least at this pleading stage, HRI has adequately alleged facts that plausibly indicate that an HCV ban "predictably results" in discrimination.

Thus, HRI's Amended Complaint is adequate at the pleading stage to show that each of the defendants (i) has a practice of barring HCV holders from its housing units and (ii) that this practice has had, is having, and is predictably expected to have a disparate impact on disabled New York City residents—by disproportionately denying them access to housing relative to non-disabled New York City residents—in violation of 42 U.S.C. §3604(f).

ii. Black and Hispanic Individuals

For substantially the same reasons set forth in the immediately preceding discussion on disabled individuals, HRI's Amended Complaint is adequate at the pleading stage to show that each of the defendants (i) has a practice of barring HCV holders from its housing units and (ii) that this practice has had, is having, and is predictably expected to have a disparate impact on Black and Hispanic New York City residents—by disproportionately denying them access to housing relative to non-Black and non-Hispanic New York City residents—in violation of 42 U.S. §3604(a).

NOTES AND QUESTIONS

1. Disparate Impact and Vouchers. Contrast the result in *Compass* with that of Inclusive Communities Project, Inc. v. Lincoln Property Company, 920 F.3d 890, 896-97 (5th Cir. 2019). The plaintiff in that case presented evidence that roughly 90 percent of voucher holders in the Dallas area were non-white. The plaintiff further alleged that the defendant's policy of refusing to accept vouchers at any of its 43 properties in majority-white census tracts (while negotiating with and renting to voucher holders in communities of color) led to a concentration of Black and Hispanic families in areas that were already "racially concentrated areas [of color and] of high poverty that are marked by substantially unequal conditions."

> Although acknowledging that ICP had shown "a possible statistical imbalance with the amount of voucher households in the census tract," the district court concluded that ICP had not provided facts linking the "no vouchers" policy to the "possible statistical disparity." Further, the court found ICP's statistical information and arguments to be "conclusory rather than descriptive of how [the defendants'] policy actually caused a disparate impact." . . . [The ICP's data fails to support] an inference that the implementation of [the] blanket "no vouchers" policy . . . caused black persons to be the dominant group of voucher holders in the Dallas metro area[, and] ICP alleges no facts supporting a reasonable inference that [Defendants] bear any responsibility for the geographic distribution of minorities throughout the Dallas area prior to the implementation of the "no vouchers" policy.

Id. at 906-07. The Fifth Circuit, applying a novel interpretation of disparate impact theory, affirmed the district court's dismissal of the case. For additional discussion of the majority and dissenting opinions in *Lincoln Property*, see Chapter 7.

2. Disability, Reasonable Accommodation Requirements, and SOI. As discussed in Chapter 17, the FHA's disability provisions include the affirmative requirement that housing providers make accommodations to their policies where reasonable and necessary to afford the disabled person equal opportunity to use and enjoy a dwelling. Some courts have interpreted this requirement to mean that defendants must make exceptions to restrictive SOI policies. For example, in Giebeler v. M & B Assoc. 343 F.3d 1143 (9th Cir. 2003), the plaintiff had a disability that prevented him from working. His mother was prepared to cosign the lease for his apartment and accept full financial responsibility for paying his rent, but the complex refused to rent to him, citing its policy against cosigners. The Ninth Circuit held that the complex was required to make an exception to its policy as a reasonable accommodation. Another example is Schaw v. Habitat for Humanity of Citrus County, Inc., 938 F.3d 1259 (11th Cir. 2019), in which the Eleventh Circuit held that a request for the defendant to accept documentation of food stamps or familial support (in lieu of ordinary wages) in meeting its minimum-income requirement was a facially reasonable accommodation.

Other courts have refused to recognize changes to payment policies as a reasonable accommodation. These courts question whether the accommodation is necessary to ameliorate the plaintiff's *disability*, or whether the plaintiff's problem is in fact a *lack of income*. Additionally, they conclude that the supposed burdens of participating in a voucher program are too great to make the requested accommodation "reasonable." See, for example, Salute v. Stratford Greens Garden Apartments, 136 F.3d 293, 301 (2d Cir. 1998), in which the divided court held that an accommodation that would require the defendant landlord to participate in a voucher program would impose "unreasonable costs, an undue hardship, and a substantial burden[.]" A more recent example is Klossner v. IADU Table Mound MHP, LLC, 65 F.4th 349, 354 (8th Cir. 2023), which held that a landlord's duty to make reasonable accommodations extends to direct amelioration of disability-related impediments "but does not encompass an obligation to accommodate a tenant's 'shortage of money,' . . . and the far-reaching implications that such an obligation would entail."

3. Federal Programs. Federal affordable housing programs (discussed in Chapter 12) have SOI protections built in. For example, units funded under the Low Income Housing Tax Credit (LIHTC) program, HUD's HOME block grant, and the National Housing Trust Fund, are prohibited from discriminating against voucher holders.[7]

Chapter Summary

- Source of income is not a protected characteristic in the FHA, but a number of jurisdictions protect it in their state laws or local ordinances.

- Source of income refers to *where* a person's funds come from. This is a different issue from *whether* the prospective tenant has enough income (from whatever legal source) to reliably pay rent.

- Even in jurisdictions with SOI protections, whether specific sources of income fall under these protections could depend on the wording of the statute or ordinance. In particular, whether Housing Choice Vouchers should be considered income has been a recurring question for courts.

- Plaintiffs who wish to bring SOI discrimination claims under the federal FHA may use disparate impact theory, given the significant overlap between SOI and many of the characteristics protected by the statute.

- A housing provider might have to modify its payment policies or requirements with respect to SOI to accommodate a plaintiff's disability.

---

7. *See* Poverty & Race Research Action Council, *Expanding Choice: Practical Strategies for Building a Successful Housing Mobility Program*, Appendix B: State, Local, and Federal Laws Barring Source-of-Income Discrimination 253-56, http://www.prrac.org/pdf/AppendixB.pdf (updated Sept. 2024).

TABLE OF CASES

INDEX